Athletic Training
and
SPORTS
MEDICINE

American Academy of Orthopaedic Surgeons

Athletic Training
and
SPORTS
MEDICINE

Athletic Training and Sports Medicine, Third Edition
American Academy of Orthopaedic Surgeons®

Athletic Training and Sports Medicine, Third Edition
Edited by Robert C. Schenck, Jr, MD
Design by Studio Montage, St. Louis, Missouri
Cover Photograph: © Telegraph Colour Library, 1997, FPG International LLC
Chapter Openers: PhotoDisc, Inc.
Chapter 4 Opener: © Telegraph Colour Library, 1997, FPG International LLC
Chapter 30 Opener: © Shilo Sports, 1999, FPG International LLC

Published by the
American Academy of Orthopaedic Surgeons
6300 North River Road
Rosemont, IL 60018

Library of Congress Cataloging-in-Publication Data

Athletic training and sports medicine/edited by Robert C. Schenck—3rd ed.
p. ; cm.
At head of title: American Academy of Orthopaedic Surgeons, American Association of Orthopaedic Surgeons.
Includes bibliographical references and index.
ISBN 0-89203-172-7
1. Sports medicine. 2. Physical education and training. I. Schenck, Robert C. II. American Academy of Orthopaedic Surgeons. III. American Association of Orthopaedic Surgeons.
[DNLM: 1. Sports Medicine. 2. Athletic Injuries. 3. Physical Education and Training. QT 261 A8718 1999]
RC1210.A84 1999
617.1'027—dc21

99-048744

ACKNOWLEDGMENTS

EDITORIAL BOARD

Athletic Training and Sports Medicine,
Third Edition

Editor

Robert C. Schenck, Jr, MD
Associate Professor, Deputy Chairman
Department of Orthopaedics
University of Texas Health Science Center
  at San Antonio
San Antonio, Texas

Section Editors

Ronnie P. Barnes, MS, ATC
Head Athletic Trainer
New York Football Giants
East Rutherford, New Jersey

Robert S. Behnke, HSD, ATC
Sport First Aid Director
American Sport Education Program
Human Kinetics, Inc.
Champaign, Illinois

Kevin M. Guskiewicz, PhD, ATC
Assistant Professor, Athletic Trainer and Director
Sports Medicine Research Laboratory
Department of Physical Education, Exercise,
  and Sport Science
University of North Carolina
Chapel Hill, North Carolina

Clayton F. Holmes, EdD, PT, ATC
Assistant Professor
Physical Therapy Department
University of Central Arkansas
Conway, Arkansas

Robert J. Moore, PhD, PT, ATC
Professor
Exercise, Nutrition Science Department
San Diego State University
San Diego, California

Jack Ryan, MD, FACS
Staff Physician
St. John Macomb Hospital
Warren, Michigan

Chad Starkey, PhD, ATC
Athletic Training Program Director
Associate Professor
Northeastern University
Boston, Massachusetts

American Academy of Orthopaedic Surgeons
Board of Directors, 1999

Robert D. D'Ambrosia, MD
President

S. Terry Canale, MD
First Vice President

Richard H. Gelberman, MD
Second Vice President

William J. Robb III, MD
Secretary

Stuart A. Hirsch, MD
Treasurer

David A. Halsey, MD
James D. Heckman, MD
Joseph P. Iannotti, MD, PhD
Douglas W. Jackson, MD
Ramon L. Jimenez, MD
Thomas P. Schmalzried, MD
William A. Sims, MD
Vernon T. Tolo, MD
John R. Tongue, MD
Edward A. Toriello, MD
Richard B. Welch, MD
William W. Tipton, Jr, MD (Ex Officio)

STAFF

Marilyn L. Fox, PhD
  Director,
  Department of Publications
Lynne Roby Shindoll
  Managing Editor
Susan Morritz Baim
  Associate Senior Editor
Loraine Edwalds
  Production Manager
Sophie Tosta
  Assistant Production Manager
Pamela Hutton Erickson
  Graphic Design Coordinator
Gayle Ekblad
  Editor
Karen Danca
  Production Assistant
Vanessa Villarreal
  Production Assistant
Jackie Shadinger
  Publications Secretary

Studio Montage
  Book Design

CONTRIBUTORS

James R. Andrews, MD
Medical Director
American Sports Medicine Institute
Birmingham, Alabama

Bernard R. Bach, Jr, MD
Professor, Orthopaedic Surgery
Director, Sports Medicine Section
Department of Orthopaedic Surgery
Rush Medical College
Rush-Presbyterian-St. Luke's Medical Center
Chicago, Illinois

Ronnie P. Barnes, MS, ATC
Head Athletic Trainer
New York Football Giants
East Rutherford, New Jersey

Jeffrey T. Barth, PhD, ABPP
Director, Neuropsychology Assessment Laboratory
Department of Psychiatric Medicine and Neurosurgery
University of Virginia
Charlottesville, Virginia

Robert S. Behnke, HSD, ATC
Sport First Aid Director
American Sport Education Program
Human Kinetics Inc.
Champaign, Illinois

John Bergfeld, MD
Head Section Sports and Medicine
Department of Orthopaedics
The Cleveland Clinic
Cleveland, Ohio

Wilma F. Bergfeld, MD
Head, Dermatopathology and Clinical Dermatology
    Research
Dermatology and Pathology
The Cleveland Clinic
Cleveland, Ohio

Craig Bischoff, MD, MPH, FACSM
Head Sports Medicine
Sports Medicine
Marine Corps Combat Development Command
Naval Medical Clinic Quantico Virginia
Quantico, Virginia

Christine M. Bonci, MS, ATC
Assistant Athletics Director, Sports Medicine
    Head Athletic Trainer
Intercollegiate Athletics for Women
The University of Texas at Austin
Austin, Texas

Barry D. Brause, MD
Department of Infectious Diseases
Cornell Medical Center
New York Hospital
New York, New York

Bart Buxton, EdD, ATC
Department of Health and Kinesiology
College of Health and Professional Studies
Georgia Southern University
Statesboro, Georgia

Lisa Rowland Callahan, MD
Medical Director, Women's Sports Medicine Center
Sports Medicine
Hospital for Special Surgery
New York, New York

Walter L. Calmbach, MD
Director, Sports Medicine Fellowship
Department of Family Practice
University of Texas Health Science Center
San Antonio, Texas

John D. Campbell, MD
Team Physician, Montana State University
U.S. Mens Alpine Ski Team
Bridger Orthopaedic and Sports Medicine, P.C.
Bozeman, Montana

Colleen Capurro, MD
University of Nevada
Reno, Nevada

Dave Carrier, MA, ATC
Certified Athletic Trainer
Athletic Department, Michigan State University
East Lansing, Michigan

Cindy J. Chang, MD, FACSM
Head Team Physician
Department of Intercollegiate Athletics and Recreational
    Sports and University Health Services
The University of California at Berkeley
Berkeley, California

Thomas O. Clanton, MD
University of Texas Medical School
Department of Orthopaedic Surgery
Houston, Texas

Mark De Carlo, MHA, PT, SCS, ATC
Director, Physical Therapy
Methodist Sports Medicine Center
Indianapolis, Indiana

Daniel L. Dent, MD
Assistant Professor of Surgery
University of Texas Health Science Center
    at San Antonio
San Antonio, Texas

Nathaniel E.P. Ehrlich, Esq, ATC
Attorney/Partner
Anapol, Schwartz, Weiss, Cohan,
    Feldman & Smalley
Philadelphia, Pennsylvania

Michael S. Ferrara, PhD, ATC
Associate Professor
Department of Exercise Science
University of Georgia
Athens, Georgia

Dale A. Funk, MD
Orthopaedic Surgery and Sports Medicine
Orthopaedic Associates of Abilene
Abilene, Texas

Jaime R. Garza, MD, DDS
Associate Professor and Chief
Division of Plastic and Reconstructive Surgery
The University of Texas Health Science Center
    at San Antonio
San Antonio, Texas

Paul Grace, ATC
PMI
Upper Darby, Pennsylvania

Ann C. Grandjean, EdD
Director
The Center for Human Nutrition
Omaha, Nebraska

Kevin M. Guskiewicz, PhD, ATC
Assistant Professor, Athletic Trainer, and
    Director, Sports Medicine Research Laboratory
Department of Physical Education,
    Exercise & Sport Science
University of North Carolina
Chapel Hill, North Carolina

Jeffrey A. Guy, MD
Department of Orthopaedic Surgery
Massachusetts General Hospital
Boston, Massachusetts

Jo A. Hannafin, MD, PhD
Assistant Attending Orthopaedic Surgeon and
    Assistant Professor, Department of Orthopaedic Surgery
Sports Medicine and Shoulder Service
Hospital for Special Surgery
Cornell University Medical Center
New York, New York

Samer S. Hasan, MD, PhD
Chief Resident
Department of Orthopaedic Surgery
Rush-Presbyterian-St. Luke's Medical Center
Chicago, Illinois

Thomas N. Helm, MD
Assistant Clinical Professor of Dermatology
State University of New York at Buffalo
Director, Buffalo Medical Group
    Dermatopathology Laboratory
Williamsville, New York

Elliott B. Hershman, MD
Associate Director
Department of Orthopaedic Surgery
Lenox Hill Hospital
New York, New York

Rob Higgs, MS, ATC
Assistant Athletic Trainer
Montana State University
Bozeman, Montana

Clayton F. Holmes, EdD, PT, ATC
Assistant Professor
Physical Therapy Department
University of Central Arkansas
Conway, Arkansas

Shawn Hunt, MSPT, ATC
Assistant Athletic Trainer
New York Football Giants
Staff Physical Therapist
Health South—East Rutherford
East Rutherford, New Jersey

Wendy Hurd, PT
Staff Physical Therapist
Health South Sports Medicine
Birmingham, Alabama

Deidre Leaver-Dunn, PhD, ATC
Assistant Professor and Director
Athletic Training Education Program
Department of Health Science
The University of Alabama
Tuscaloosa, Alabama

Craig Levitz, MD
Orthopaedic Surgeon
New York, New York

Bert Mandelbaum, MD
Fellowship Director
Santa Monica Orthopaedics and Sports Medicine Group
Santa Monica, California

Malissa Martin, EdD, ATC, CSCS
Assistant Professor
Athletic Training Program Director
Department of Health, Physical Education,
    Recreation and Safety
Middle Tennessee State University
Murfreesboro, Tennessee

Sheri L. Martin, MSPT, ATC
Assistant Clinical Specialist in Athletic Training Program
Athletic Training Program
Northeastern University
Boston, Massachusetts

Jerry R. May, PhD
Associate Dean and Professor
School of Medicine
University of Nevada
Reno, Nevada

Sean E. McCance, MD
Attending Orthopaedic Spine Surgeon
Coordinator of Spine Education
Orthopaedic Surgery
Lenox Hill Hospital
New York, New York

Lyle J. Micheli, MD
Director
Division of Sports Medicine
Orthopaedic Surgery
Children's Hospital
Boston, Massachusetts

Robert J. Moore, PhD, PT, ATC
Professor
Exercise, Nutrition Science Department
San Diego State University
San Diego, California

Robert Murray, PhD
Director
Gatorade Exercise Physiology Laboratory
The Gatorade Company
Barrington, Illinois

Jeffrey D. Nelson, MD
Primary Care Sports Medicine Fellow
Department of Family and Community Medicine
University of California—Davis
Sacramento, California

Gregory R. Palutsis, MD
Senior Attending
Orthopaedic Surgery
Evanston Northwestern Healthcare
Evanston, Illinois

David H. Perrin, PhD, ATC
Professor
Curry School of Education
University of Virginia
Charlottesville, Virginia

James C. Puffer, MD
Professor and Chief
Division of Sports Medicine
Department of Family Medicine
UCLA School of Medicine
Los Angeles, California

Bart P. Rask, MD
Orthopaedic Fellow
Methodist Sports Medicine Center
Indianapolis, Indiana

Kristin J. Reimers, MS, RD
Associate Director
International Center for Sports Nutrition
Omaha, Nebraska

Arthur C. Rettig, MD
Orthopaedic Surgeon
Methodist Sports Medicine Center
Methodist Sports Medicine Center and
Associate Professor, Orthopaedic Surgeon, Department
    of Surgery, Indiana University School of Medicine
Indianapolis, Indiana

Jaime S. Ruud, MS, RD
Nutrition Consultant in Private Practice
Nutrition Link
Lincoln, Nebraska

Jack B. Ryan, MD, FACS
Staff Physician
St. John Macomb Hospital
Warren, Michigan

Robert C. Schenck, Jr, MD
Associate Professor, Deputy Chairman
Department of Orthopaedics
University of Texas Health Science Center
    at San Antonio
San Antonio, Texas

Judy L. Seto, MA, PT
Administrator
Department of Rehabilitation
HealthSouth Sports Medicine and Rehabilitation Center
Los Angeles, California

K. Donald Shelbourne, MD
Associate Clinical Professor
Indiana University School of Medicine
Methodist Sports Medicine Center
Indianapolis, Indiana

Donald Shell, MD
Assistant Clinical Professor
Team Physician
Division of Family Practice—Department of Health
    Care Sciences
George Washington University
Washington, D.C.

David L. Shepherd, MD
Assistant Professor of Urology
University of Texas Health Science Center
    at San Antonio
San Antonio, Texas

Chad Starkey, PhD, ATC
Athletic Training Program Director
Associate Professor
Northeastern University
Boston, Massachusetts

Ronald M. Stewart, MD
Director of Trauma and Emergency Surgery
Department of Surgery
University of Texas Health Science Center
    at San Antonio
San Antonio, Texas

Jennifer A. Stone, MS, ATC
Manager, Clinical Programs
Division of Sports Medicine
U.S. Olympic Committee
Colorado Springs, Colorado

Robyn M. Stuhr, MA
Administrative Director & Exercise Physiologist
Women's Sports Medicine Center
Hospital for Special Surgery
New York, New York

John M. Sullivan, MD
Resident, General Surgery
Department of General Surgery
University of Texas Health Science Center
    at San Antonio
San Antonio, Texas

Fred Tedeschi, MA, ATC
Head Athletic Trainer
Department of Intercollegiate Athletics/University
    Health Service
University of California, Berkeley
Berkeley, California

William O. Thompson, MD
Assistant Attending of Orthopaedic Surgery
Hospital for Special Surgery
New York, New York

Karen R. Toburen, EdD, ATC
Professor and Department Head
Sports Medicine and Athletic Training
Southwest Missouri State University
Springfield, Missouri

Katie Walsh, EdD, ATC
Director of Sports Medicine
East Carolina University
Greenville, North Carolina

Russell F. Warren, MD
Surgeon in Chief
Hospital for Special Surgery
Orthopaedics, Cornell Medical College
New York, New York

Diane Watanabe, PT
Santa Monica Orthopaedics and Sports Medicine Group
Santa Monica, California

Robert G. Watkins, MD
Associate Professor
Center for Orthopaedic Spinal Surgery
USC University Hospital
Los Angeles, California

Kevin E. Wilk, PT
National Director of Research and Clinical Education
HealthSouth Rehabilitation
Birmingham, Alabama

Kenneth E. Wright, DA
Professor and Chair, Athletic Training Education
The University of Alabama
Tuscaloosa, Alabama

PEER REVIEWERS

Marc Galloway, MD
Yale School of Medicine
New Haven, Connecticut

Douglas M. Kleiner, PhD, ATC, FACSM
University of North Florida
Jacksonville, Florida

Peter Koehneke, MS, ATC
Canisius College
Buffalo, New York

Thomas E. Koto Jr., ATC
Idaho Sports Medicine Institute
Boise, Idaho

Robert F. LaPrade, MD
University of Minnesota Health Center
Minneapolis, Minnesota

Brent C. Mangus, EdD, ATC
University of Nevada, Las Vegas
Las Vegas, Nevada

John W. McChesney, ATC, PhD
Boise State University
Boise, Idaho

Craig S. Roberts, MD
Louisville, Kentucky

Susan Foreman Saliba, PhD, ATC, PT
University of Virginia
Charlottesville, Virginia

Gretchen Schlabach, PhD, ATC
Northern Illinois University
DeKalb, Illinois

Rene Revis Shingles, MS, ATC
Central Michigan University
Mt. Pleasant, Michigan

D. Rod Walters II, DA, ATC
University of South Carolina
Columbia, South Carolina

TABLE OF CONTENTS

SECTION 3

REGIONAL PATHOLOGY— continued

SECTION 5

SPECIAL ATHLETE POPULATIONS 781

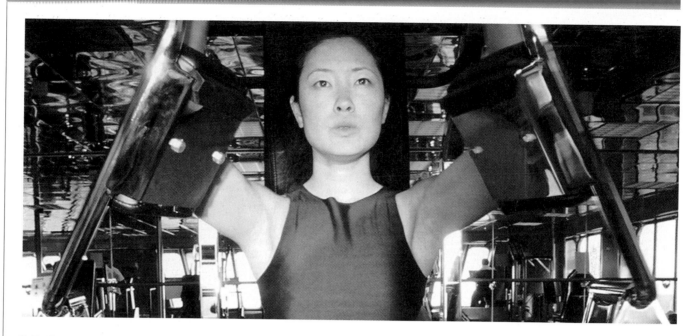

SECTION EDITORS
Clayton F. Holmes, EdD, PT, ATC
Robert J. Moore, PhD, PT, ATC

APPENDICES 853

PREFACE

Athletic Training and Sports Medicine, now in its third edition, has been a dynamic text for both the practicing athletic trainer and student athletic trainer for many years. This newest edition, which captures the essence of the two previous editions without narrowing their scope, focuses on current sports medicine issues and necessary updates.

Letha "Etty" Yurko-Griffin, MD, PhD, the editor of the second edition, provided excellent guidance and advice during "the hand off" of the project to me. The editorial board of the first edition of the book, Arthur E. Ellison, MD; Arthur L. Boland, Jr, MD; Kenneth E. DeHaven, MD; Paul Grace, ATC; George A. Snook, MD; and Heather Calehuff, ATC, PA-C, provided Dr. Yurko-Griffin with a strong foundation for the second edition of Athletic Training and Sports Medicine, and Dr. Yurko-Griffin continued that tradition of excellence in the second edition.

Our first goal for the third edition was to evaluate the first and second editions and attempt to improve on two already excellent texts. After much discussion and brainstorming, we decided to continue the wide breadth of topics covered in the first two editions and include areas other than musculoskeletal injuries. Furthermore, we wished to create and revise chapters using the expertise of authors with a certified athletic trainer's perspective as well as those with a physician's perspective. When possible, we asked an orthopaedic surgeon to contribute material to the book. Creating this edition has proved to be a prodigious task; however, with the assistance of my editorial board and the outstanding support staff at the AAOS, we were able to produce what I believe is an exceptional third edition of Athletic Training and Sports Medicine.

Athletic Training and Sports Medicine, third edition, is divided into the following five sections:

Section 1: The Athletic Healthcare System

Section 2: Basic Concepts

Section 3: Regional Pathology

Section 4: Other Medical Issues

Section 5: Special Athlete Populations

Information in the third edition of Athletic Training and Sports Medicine is organized differently from the first and second editions, and new areas of interest as well as updates of current information in sports medicine are covered. The great breadth and depth of information provided in this edition will be useful as a single resource for the practicing sports medicine specialist.

As with the first two editions of Athletic Training and Sports Medicine, the third edition is aimed at clinicians and caregivers who are generally or specifically involved in athletic training and sports medicine. This audience includes athletic trainers (who, for the purposes of this text, have been NATABOC certified and/or state licensed), sports physical therapists, primary care sports medicine physicians, and primary care physicians with an interest in sports medicine. Furthermore, material in this book is intended to provide the orthopaedic surgeon with a broader background in sports medicine problems, going beyond musculoskeletal injuries. We hope that this edition continues to be a valuable source of information for all certified athletic trainers, physical therapists, sports medicine physicians, and others who are involved in the care of the athlete.

Publication of this book would not have occurred without the valuable support of many individuals. I would like to thank James D. Heckman, MD, for recommending me as editor and providing his support throughout this project. In addition, the initial efforts by Robert Behnke, HSD, ATC, in recruiting editorial board members was instrumental to the success of this book. I am greatly indebted to Ronnie Barnes, MS, ATC, for his tremendous influence, enthusiasm, and diligence throughout the creation of this book and the countless hours of work he contributed to the project. Mr. Barnes' efforts were tireless, and without them, this book could not be a success. I would also like to thank my friend and mentor, Jack Ryan, MD, FACS, for his humor, steadfast support, and keen thought to this edition of the book. I especially would like to thank Clayton Holmes, EdD, ATC, PT, for his extraordinary efforts as well as his willingness to "pitch in" when a request was made for extra duty. Without the expertise and continued faith of the editorial board members, Robert S. Behnke, HSD, ATC; Ronnie P. Barnes, MS, ATC; Jack B. Ryan, MD, FACS; Clayton F. Holmes, EdD, ATC, PT; Chad Starkey, PhD, ATC; Kevin M. Guskiewicz, PhD, ATC; and Robert J. Moore, PhD, PT, ATC, this book could not have been completed.

On behalf of the editorial board, I would like to express our appreciation to all the authors who spent so much time meeting the demands of deadlines, revisions, and requests made by the Board, as well as making significant style changes to the chapter format of the first two editions. The authors contributed so much to the excellence of this book and gave their time and effort without complaint.

I would also like to thank the peer reviewers for the many hours spent reading the book and the comments they provided that ensure the accuracy and excellence of the book.

Special thanks goes to the American Academy of Orthopaedic Surgeons for providing support and staff of such excellence, without whom this book could not have been completed. I would like to thank Lynne Shindoll, Managing Editor, Department of Publications, whose advice and time spent crafting the blueprint for this edition proved to be essential to its evolution. Furthermore, I would like to thank Sophie Tosta, Assistant Production Manager, Department of Publications, whose desire for excellence and sense of humor were greatly appreciated.

I would also like to thank Susan Baim, Associate Senior Editor, Department of Publications, who continued to have high energy and tremendous devotion for countless revisions and efforts to bring the book into its final stages. All three, Ms. Shindoll, Ms. Tosta, and Ms. Baim deserve tremendous credit for the completion and excellence of this book. In addition, I would like to thank Pamela Erickson, Graphic Design Coordinator, Department of Publications, for working so well with the designer, typesetter, and printer to ensure that production of the book went as smoothly as possible. Finally, I would like to thank Marilyn Fox, PhD, Director, Department of Publications, and the AAOS Publications Committee for their support throughout the many months of production of the book.

I would also like to thank Jerry Greeson, ATC, and his assistant, Terry Gault, ATC, for their efforts in San Antonio and Chicago on behalf of the book. The many new images that were created for this book would not have occurred without their assistance and creativity.

I would like to thank my assistant, Sandy Mosher, for her endless support and hard work on behalf of the third edition. Lastly, but most importantly, I would like to thank my wife, Patricia Jane, whose constant support and devotion kept my life in balance while allowing me to continue with this project over the last 2 years.

On behalf of the editorial board and the American Academy of Orthopaedic Surgeons, we present this book with great pride in its content, and the devotion of all its participants. Much like the care we give to our athletes, this book was a team effort and will remain so through future editions.

Robert C. Schenck, Jr, MD
San Antonio, Texas

1

The Athletic Healthcare System

Section Editor
Robert S. Behnke, HSD, ATC

Roles, Relationships, and Organizations

Robert S. Behnke, HSD, ATC
John A. Bergfeld, MD

QUICK CONTENTS

- The evolution of the athletic training profession.

- The members of the sports medicine team and their responsibilities in caring for the athlete.

OVERVIEW

Sports medicine has assumed an increasingly important role in today's society. This chapter addresses the development of athletic training as a profession, describing the educational background and requirements for certification. The members of the sports medicine team are listed, along with their functions and responsibilities. These members include the physician, athletic trainer, coach, athlete, parents, athletic administrator, student athletic trainer, and other medical and allied health professionals.

DEFINITION

Sports medicine is a term that is universally used but difficult to define. Sports medicine encompasses the services of most medical, paramedical, and allied health professions as well as the individuals who provide those services.

History

In the 2nd century AD, Galen cared for the gladiators and is commonly recognized as the first team physician. Although he recognized the danger of some of the sporting events of his day, Galen taught and did an enormous

FOCUS ON . . .

History of Athletic Training

Sports medicine encompasses the services of most medical, paramedical, and allied health professions. The first team physician was Galen, who cared for gladiators in the 2nd century AD. Today, increasing sports participation has created the need for a healthcare profession devoted to injury prevention, immediate care, treatment, and rehabilitation of athletes. Certified athletic trainers have passed a national certification examination and hold baccalaureate degrees; more than 70% possess advanced degrees.

In the past, athletic programs have been conducted by schools and professional organizations. Today, organized programs are available from a variety of sources, as are recreational activities. All these activities carry the potential for injury, which many interscholastic and intercollegiate programs have addressed by hiring athletic trainers and developing private and hospital-based sports medicine clinics.

amount of research in anatomy, physiology, and sports injuries. He did not believe in excessive exercise; however, he did recommend moderate exercise to maintain health and to treat many diseases.

Today, growing participation in sports at both the professional and amateur levels (particularly through interscholastic and intercollegiate competition), has created the need for a profession that is devoted to the prevention, immediate care, treatment, and rehabilitation of athletes. The *athletic trainer* is a multiskilled individual who can provide these services on a day-to-day basis and work with physicians in various sports settings. During the latter half of the 20th century, this profession evolved to a point at which all of the country's certified athletic trainers hold baccalaureate degrees, and more than 70% possess advanced degrees. Many athletic trainers are also physical therapists, emergency medical technicians, physician assistants, and other allied health professionals. In addition, certified athletic trainers have passed a national certification examination (including a written knowledge test, a practical test, and a written simulation test) and must participate in a continuing education program to maintain certification.

The Need for Athletic Trainers

Historically, schools and professional organizations conducted athletic programs. Today, with increasing emphasis on health and the benefits of physical activity, more individuals are engaging in physical activity through organized programs and other recreational endeavors. Also, preinterscholastic activities available to youths have become an extremely large part of the elementary school student's after-school regimen, as well as on weekends and vacation periods.

No matter what the level of activity, the potential for trauma exists. In recent years, interscholastic and intercollegiate athletic programs have addressed this risk by employing athletic trainers and developing private and hospital-based sports medicine clinics to serve the growing number of athletes. In addition, interest in employing healthcare specialists in the industrial settings to address work-related injuries has grown.

SPORTS MEDICINE TEAM

The Physician

The American Medical Association (AMA) defines a physician as someone who is a medical doctor (MD) or a doctor of osteopathic medicine (DO). Typically, the physician functions as the leader of the sports medicine team and makes the final determination of an athlete's eligibility for participation in organized athletic activity. In

FOCUS ON . . .

The Role of the Physician

The sports medicine team is typically led by the physician (a doctor of medicine, MD, or osteopathy, DO), who decides whether the athlete can participate in the sport, oversees the sports medicine program, and determines the roles and responsibilities of all personnel. The physician supports and participates in the education of athletic trainers, coaches, athletes, athletic administrators, and parents with regard to the prevention, immediate care, treatment, and rehabilitation of common athletic injuries and illnesses.

addition, the *team physician* oversees all aspects of the sports medicine program, including conditioning to prevent injury, an emergency care protocol for injuries, illnesses, as well as the treatment and rehabilitation of those conditions. Regarding the emergency protocol, the team physician determines the roles and responsibilities of all personnel: the athletic trainer, the coach, and the athlete. Team physicians also support professional preparation programs for future athletic trainers, as follows:

The team physician should have a sincere interest in the professional preparation of the athletic training student and should be willing to share his or her knowledge through ongoing informal discussion, clinics, and other in-service educational sessions. Involvement of the team physician as a full-time or part-time classroom instructor or guest lecturer is encouraged. The athletic training room provides the clinical setting in which the student athletic trainer is exposed to the medical practices of the team physician. Thus, the team physician's presence in the athletic training room on a regular basis is an important aspect of the student's clinical experiences.[1]

In addition to helping educate future athletic trainers, the team physician is involved in the education of certified athletic trainers, coaches, athletes, athletic administrators, and, when appropriate, parents. Team physicians teach about prevention, immediate care, treatment, and rehabilitation of common athletic injuries and illnesses.

Therefore, the team physician is not only a healthcare provider, but also an administrator and educator. Although many physicians are trained to provide specialized medical care, team physicians should be aware of these other roles as well. Team physicians may work on a voluntary basis or for compensation, and the extent of their responsibilities will depend on the size of the athletic program or clinical setting.

The Athletic Trainer

Because athletes often have daily contact with athletic trainers, they are most likely to seek help from athletic trainers before any other members of the sports medicine team. As a result, the athletic trainer often becomes a coordinator through whom appropriate health care is obtained.

In 1990, the AMA recognized athletic training as an allied health profession. Today, the certified athletic trainer possesses, at minimum, a baccalaureate degree that includes demonstration of competencies in (1) risk management and injury prevention, (2) pathology of injuries and illnesses, (3) assessment and evaluation, (4) acute care of injury and illness, (5) pharmacology, (6) therapeutic modalities, (7) therapeutic exercise, (8) general medical conditions and disabilities, (9) nutritional aspects of injury and illness, (10) psychosocial intervention and referral, (11) health care administration, and (12) professional development and responsibilities. These competencies, developed by the *National Athletic Trainers' Association (NATA)*, serve as a basis for both the design of entry-level educational programs and the national certification examination. Through a combination of formal classroom instruction and clinical experiences, the student athletic trainer gains knowledge and learns to apply a wide variety of techniques.

The American Academy of Family Physicians, the American Academy of Pediatrics, the American Orthopaedic Society for Sports Medicine, the NATA, and the Joint Review Committee on Educational Programs in Athletic Training have developed the following definition of an athletic trainer:

An athletic trainer is a qualified allied health care professional educated and experienced in the management of health care problems associated with sports participation. In cooperation with physicians and other allied health care personnel, the athletic trainer functions as an integral member of the athletic health care team in secondary schools, colleges and universities, professional sports programs, sports medicine clinics, and other athletic health care settings. The athletic trainer functions in cooperation with medical personnel, athletic administrators, coaches, and parents in the development and coordination of efficient and responsive athletic health care delivery systems.[1, 2]

The term "athletic trainer" used throughout this text refers to an individual who has been NATABOC certified and/or state licensed. Like the team physician, the athletic trainer is also a healthcare provider, an educator, and an administrator.

Risk management and injury prevention

The athletic trainer is involved in all aspects of sports medicine from injury prevention to return to activity. In terms of prevention, the athletic trainer arranges the prepartici-

FOCUS ON . . .

Responsibilities of the Athletic Trainer

Risk management and injury prevention

The athletic trainer is heavily involved in preventive efforts. Athletic trainers arrange the preparticipation physical examination and work with coaches and athletes, equipment managers, and groundskeepers to ensure that preventive measures are in place that can help avert injuries and illnesses.

Recognition, evaluation, and immediate care

The athletic trainer uses his or her knowledge of anatomy, physiology, pathology, and athletic injuries to evaluate common athletic injuries and illnesses and provide immediate care. Once the problem is identified, appropriate care is initiated, which may include standard first aid of cold application, elevation, compression, and restriction of motion.

Treatment and disposition

Once immediate care has been administered, the athletic trainer must decide how to proceed, whether a physician should evaluate the athlete, whether the problem requires immediate transportation to a physician's office, hospital, or clinic, and whether to implement the program's emergency medical service plan. In consultation with the physician, the athletic trainer initiates a treatment and rehabilitation program.

Rehabilitation

Rehabilitation, which is necessary to most sports-related musculoskeletal injuries, relies on the athletic trainer's knowledge of kinesiology, biomechanics, and forms of exercise. Although the immediate goal is to return the athlete to activity as safely as possible, the athletic trainer must act responsibly to protect the athlete's long-term health and welfare.

pation examination and works with coaches and athletes. In addition, athletic trainers work with equipment managers to select, fit, and apply protective equipment that includes wraps, braces, tape, and pads. Furthermore, athletic trainers work with groundskeepers to inspect and maintain safe playing areas and surfaces. As a result, athletic trainers often direct most of their efforts to prevention because simple measures often prevent common illnesses and injuries that would otherwise require much more time and effort to treat.

Recognition, evaluation, and immediate care

If, after all reasonable efforts to prevent it, an athletic injury or illness occurs, the athletic trainer must be ready to recognize and evaluate it and initiate immediate care. The athletic trainer's knowledge of human anatomy, human physiology, pathology, and athletic injuries should enable him or her to evaluate common athletic injuries and illnesses. A history of injury or illness, observation, and palpation of the affected site, followed by appropriate physical examination, will help the athletic trainer evaluate the nature and severity of the problem.

The initial evaluation of an injury is the most critical. Without a physician available at all times, the responsibility for conducting this evaluation most often falls on the athletic trainer. Information gained from the initial evaluation by the athletic trainer is extremely valuable to the physician who later examines the athlete.

Once the problem is identified, appropriate care must be initiated (**Figure 1-1**). Depending on the circumstances, standard first aid procedures are performed. These may include the application of ice, elevation, compression, and restriction of motion using splints, slings, and crutches. First aid for sports-related illness and injury should be provided, whenever possible, by the athletic trainer. However, if an athletic trainer is not available, coaches, athletic administrators, game officials, or emergency medical services personnel should be prepared to administer initial first aid care. Others involved in the athletic program should be instructed about how to contact the program's athletic trainer.

Treatment and disposition

Once immediate care has been administered, the athletic trainer must rely on education and experience to decide how to proceed. He or she may ask the following questions:

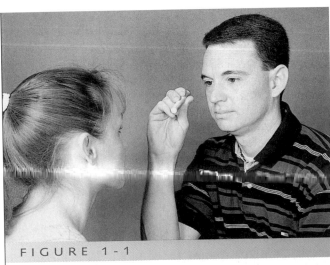

FIGURE 1-1

The initial evaluation of an injury is critical. Once the problem is identified, appropriate care must follow.

- Should a physician evaluate the problem?
- Is the problem severe enough to require immediate transportation to a physician's office, hospital, or clinic?
- Has an emergency medical service plan been developed, and how can it be accessed?

At this point, the athletic trainer, after consultation with the physician, initiates a program of treatment and rehabilitation. The athletic trainer must be familiar with the appropriate use of various forms of physical modalities and rehabilitation techniques to resolve the condition.

Rehabilitation

Rehabilitation, with an emphasis on full recovery, is essential to most sports-related musculoskeletal injuries. The athletic trainer must have a thorough knowledge of kinesiology, biomechanics, and forms of exercise, in particular, to successfully rehabilitate athletes.

Although the immediate goal may be to return the athlete to activity without risk of further injury, the athletic trainer must also remember long-term outcomes. The injured athlete should never be subjected to additional risk of injury just to continue playing. The athletic trainer must act responsibly, despite pressures from athletes, coaches, or parents. For the sports medicine team, the top priority is the participant's health and welfare.

Administration

The athletic trainer is the one member of the sports medicine program who has daily contact with the athletes, coaches, physicians, administrators, and parents/guardians. As a result, the athletic trainer is responsible for numerous administrative functions, including the coordination of communication among members of the sports medicine team. For example, communication between the athletic trainer and the physician is essential in determining the availability of injured or sick athletes to return to practice and competition. Because the athletic trainer has daily contact with the athlete, he or she becomes an invaluable asset to assessing the athlete's health status. The communication between the physician and the athletic trainer is essential to the success of any sports medicine program.

Athletic trainers must exercise the greatest degree of discretion when communicating with coaches and athletes because athletes will often reveal things to the athletic trainer that they would never share with a coach, and coaches may reveal things that they would never share with the athlete. Loss of this trusted position will create an environment that would make the work of the athletic trainer impossible.

Athletic trainers need to keep coaches informed about the status of their athletes so that coaches can plan practices and competitions. Also, coaches require information about their athletes because, in most athletic programs, they are responsible for media relations. A well-informed

Athletic Trainers as Administrators

The athletic trainer plays an important administrative role in the athletic program. The athletic trainer coordinates communication among the team members and works with the physician to determine the return-to-play status of injured or sick athletes. The athletic trainer and coach must communicate about the status of the athlete so that the coach can plan practices and competitions and release appropriate and accurate information to the media.

Record keeping is another important aspect of the athletic trainer's responsibilities. Accurate preparticipation physical examination, injury, and illness records are needed for medical and legal issues, research, and may be required by insurers. Records may reveal injury trends that can be corrected with changes in equipment, environment, or playing surface. In addition, records allow the athletic trainer to provide the program administrator with vital data that may help resolve current conditions and prevent similar occurrences in the future.

The athletic trainer is responsible for maintaining a clean, safe athletic training room, including equipment, supplies, and the facility itself. He or she must ensure that all staff members have the necessary training, equipment, and supplies to perform their assigned responsibilities and that all events are adequately staffed and equipped.

coach can decide what and how much information may be released. Therefore, both the physician and the athletic trainer must provide accurate information to the coach.

In addition, athletic trainers must be able to communicate effectively with physicians, coaches, athletes, and parents in order to facilitate understanding and avoid confusion. For example, athletic trainers may use visual aids to explain injuries to the coaches, athletes, and parents. Also, they should use appropriate anatomic and physiologic terminology when communicating with physicians. When everyone is properly informed, evaluation and rehabilitation can proceed without confusion to a positive conclusion.

Another important aspect of the athletic trainer's administrative function is record keeping. Accurate records of illness and injury are important for medical and legal issues, research, and insurance. Today, many health maintenance organizations, preferred provider organizations, and other healthcare organizations require accurate records of the preparticipation examination, immediate care and

TABLE 1-1

SPORTS MEDICINE RESOURCES

American Academy of Family Physicians
8880 Ward Parkway
Kansas City, Missouri 64114
(816) 333-9700

National Athletic Trainers' Association
2952 Stemmons Freeway
Dallas, Texas 75247
(214) 637-5282
Fax: (214) 637-2246

American Academy of Orthopaedic Surgeons
6300 North River Road
Rosemont, Illinois 60018
(847) 823-7186
Fax: (847) 823-8125
www.aaos.org

National Association for Intercollegiate Athletics
6120 South Yale Avenue, Suite 1450
Tulsa, Oklahoma 74136
(918) 494-8828
Fax: (918) 494-8841

American Academy of Pediatrics
P.O. Box 927
141 Northwest Point Boulevard
Elk Grove Village, Illinois 60009
(847) 228-5005
Fax: (847) 228-5097
www.aap.org

National Collegiate Athletic Association
700 W. Washington Ave.
Indianapolis, IN 46206
317-917-6222
www.ncaa.org

National Federation of State High School Athletic Associations
11/4 Plaza Circle
P.O. Box 20626
Kansas City, Missouri 64195

National Strength Coaches Association
1955 North Union Boulevard
Colorado Springs, Colorado 80909
(719) 632-6722
Fax: (719) 632-6367

American College of Sports Medicine
P.O. Box 1440
Indianapolis, Indiana 46206
(317) 637-9200
Fax: (317) 634-7817

Sports Physical Therapy Section of the American Physical Therapy Association
1111 North Fairfax Street
Alexandria, Virginia 22314
(703) 684-2782
Fax: (703) 684-7343

American Orthopaedic Society for Sports Medicine
6300 North River Road, Suite 200
Rosemont, Illinois 60018
(847) 292-4900
Fax: (847) 292-4905

United States Olympic Committee Sports Medicine Division
One Olympic Plaza
Colorado Springs, Colorado 80909
(719) 578-4618

American Sports Education Program
1607 North Market Street
Champaign, Illinois 61820
(800) 747-5698

American Red Cross
Call the local ARC chapter or access their web page at www.redcross.org

Program for Athletic Coaches Education Institute for the Study of Youth Sports
213 IM Sports Circle
Michigan State University
East Lansing, Michigan 48824
(517) 353-6689

Parents/Guardians

Other members of the sports medicine team should inform parents and guardians about the policies and procedures that govern the sports-related health care of their children. In addition, team members should instruct parents about providing nutrition and rest and about purchasing and fitting any equipment that is not provided by the program. Parents/guardians should be assured that the health and welfare of their children is the most important priority of the program and when members of the sports medicine team make decisions, they do so with this priority in mind. As always, communication between the parents/guardians and other members of the sports medicine team is essential for team members to administer the most appropriate care and for the parents to feel comfortable that their child is being properly treated. Parents and guardians should be encouraged to support their children in their sporting activities.

The Athletic Administrator

In the sports medicine program, the athletic administrator, or athletic director, is responsible for having appropriate personnel, equipment, supplies, and policies and procedures in place to ensure the best health care possible for the program's participants. The athletic director must establish a "chain of command" for the members of the sports medicine team and ensure that they have appropriate credentials, access to continuing education, and opportunities to contribute to the development of policies and procedures for quality care (**Figure 1-3**). The chain of command may vary depending on whether the organization is conducting an athletic program at the professional, intercollegiate, or interscholastic level. However, when the portion of the chain of command directly involves the health care of the participants, there should be no differences. In addition, athletic directors are required to adhere to national, state, local, and conference rules and regula-

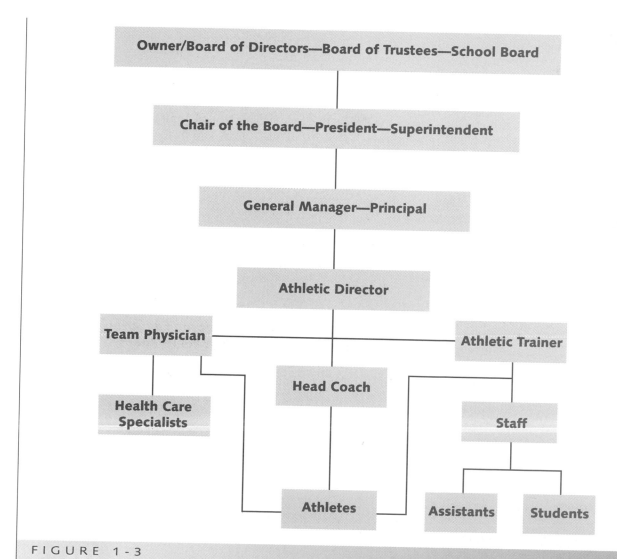

FIGURE 1-3

The athletic director establishes a chain of command to ensure that members of the sports medicine team are able to provide quality care.

tions. Furthermore, athletic directors also handle insurance coverage (including medical coverage), emergency medical service plans (with emergency equipment and personnel when appropriate), safety of the practice and competition facilities and equipment, and general safety of participants and spectators. The success of any interscholastic or intercollegiate sports medicine program relies heavily on the athletic director's ability to address the needs of each member of the sports medicine team.

Student Athletic Trainers

Student athletic trainers at the secondary or collegiate level should not be placed in positions of authority to make decisions about health care. Student athletic trainers work under the direct supervision of a certified athletic trainer. They typically are responsible for maintenance of facilities and equipment, preventive services, and, as experience is gained, possible first aid or emergency care similar to what coaches who have taken sports first-aid courses might provide. The physician, the certified athletic trainer, or, possibly, the coach must take responsibility for making healthcare decisions. Placing student athletic trainers in positions more appropriately assigned to other members of the sports medicine team is not only unfair to the student, but it may place the program in jeopardy. State laws may also prohibit students from performing certain acts. In the case of high school students, minors cannot be placed in positions of authority to perform healthcare procedures. Students who have not yet completed their educational and clinical experiences at the collegiate level may not be capable of performing certain healthcare procedures. Students should be encouraged to learn, observe, and assist as instructed. Every program that uses student athletic trainers should develop lists of "Dos and Don'ts" for student athletic trainers with strict instructions for them to never assume authority for healthcare decisions. Various states have legislation that will help establish what students may or may not be allowed t.o do. Moreover, every athletic trainer must consider what the students in his or her program can and cannot do and should put these "Dos and Don'ts" in writing.

Other Medical and Allied Health Personnel

Although the vast majority of team physicians today are family physicians, pediatricians, or orthopaedic surgeons, team physicians may be trained in other specialties as well. Whatever their specialty, team physicians have the responsibility of recruiting other medical and allied health professionals to provide specialized care and serve as members of the sports medicine team. Usually, the team physician determines the need for a consultation with a specialist. **Table 1-2** provides a list of medical specialists and other professionals who can assist the sports medicine team.

Rarely can a sports medicine program operate successfully without the appropriate medical and allied health personnel. Members of the sports medicine team, including team physicians, athletic trainers, coaches, and administrators should make efforts to establish and nurture positive relationships with a vast array of medical and allied health personnel. Again, communication among these medical and allied health professionals and the members of the sports medicine team is essential to provide high-quality health care.

TABLE 1-2
MEDICAL SPECIALISTS AND OTHER PROFESSIONALS WHO CAN ASSIST THE SPORTS MEDICINE TEAM

Medical specialists		Other professionals	
Allergists	Ophthalmologists	Conditioning coaches	Pharmacists
Cardiologists	Oral surgeons	Emergency	Physical therapists
Dentists	Orthopaedists	medical technicians	Physician assistants
Dermatologists	Otolaryngologists	Equipment managers	Podiatrists
Family physicians	Pediatricians	Hospital and clinic staff	Radiology
General surgeons	Plastic surgeons	Lawyers	technicians
Gynecologists	Radiologists	Nurses	Sport physiologists
Internists	Urologists	Nutritionists	Sport psychologists
Neurosurgeons		Optometrists	Substance abuse
		Orthotists	counselors

CHAPTER REVIEW

Sports medicine describes the services of most medical, paramedical, and allied health professions, as well as the individuals who provide these services. In the past century, as the number of sports participants at all levels has grown, athletic training has become the healthcare profession devoted to injury prevention and immediate care, treatment, and rehabilitation of these athletes. Certified athletic trainers hold baccalaureate degrees (more than 70% have advanced degrees) and are required to pass a national certification examination. Many athletic trainers also have credentials in other allied health professions.

The sports medicine team is led by the physician, who makes the final determination as to the athlete's ability to play and oversees all aspects of the sports medicine program. The athletic trainer is often the athlete's first point of contact with the sports medicine team and is the coordinator for appropriate health care. The athletic trainer's roles include prevention, immediate care, treatment and disposition, rehabilitation, administration, and education. The coach is an educator who must be familiar with the rules and regulations of the sport to teach appropriate techniques and strategies. The coach should also be able to provide first aid and immediate care in the absence of the athletic trainer.

The athlete's responsibilities include listening to, learning from, and cooperating with the other members of the sports medicine team and reporting all injuries and illnesses promptly. Parents and guardians must be informed about policies and procedures that govern the sports-related health care for their children,

providing nutrition and rest guidelines, and purchasing and fitting equipment that is not provided by the program. Above all, parents and guardians must be assured that their children's health and welfare is the top priority of the sports medicine program and will guide all decisions.

The athletic administrator is responsible for having appropriate personnel, equipment, supplies, and policies and procedures in place to ensure the best possible health care for the participants while adhering to national, state, local, and conferences rules and regulations. The athletic administrator establishes the chain of command for the sports medicine team and makes certain that each member has appropriate credentials, access to continuing education, and the opportunity to contribute to policy development. Insurance coverage, emergency medical plans, facilities and equipment safety, and participants' and spectators' safety are also the province of the administrator.

The student athletic trainer should be encouraged to learn, observe, and assist as instructed, but should not make decisions about health care. He or she is responsible for maintenance of facilities and equipment, preventive services, and as experience is gained, first aid and emergency care. Other medical and allied health professionals are recruited by the team physician to provide specialized care.

To operate successfully, a sports medicine program requires all of these medical and allied health professionals. To make certain that all athletes receive the best health care possible, communication among members of the sports medicine team, the athlete, and the parents and guardians is key.

SELF-TEST

1. What percentage of certified athletic trainers possess advanced degrees?
   A. 30%
   B. 50%
   C. 70%
   D. 90%

2. Which member of the sports medicine team is considered the leader of the team and makes the final determination about the athlete's ability to participate in sport?
   A. Coach
   B. Parent/guardian
   C. Physician
   D. Athletic trainer

3. The first person the athlete is likely to seek medical help from is the:
   A. coach.
   B. parent/guardian.
   C. physician.
   D. athletic trainer.

4. The sports medicine team's primary goal in treating an injured athlete is to:
   A. protect the athlete's health and welfare.
   B. allow the athletic team to remain competitive.
   C. transport the athlete to the hospital immediately.
   D. return the athlete to participation as soon as possible.

5. Who is usually responsible for the initial evaluation of an injured athlete?
   A. Coach
   B. Physician
   C. Athletic trainer
   D. Student athletic trainer

6. What should coaches focus on when teaching athletes sport techniques?
   A. Injury prevention
   B. Winning techniques
   C. Equipment modification
   D. Maximum practice time

7. Which member of the sports medicine team is responsible for ensuring appropriate staff, equipment, supplies, and policies and procedures to provide the best health care for program participants?
   A. Coach
   B. Physician
   C. Athletic trainer
   D. Athletic administrator

8. Which member of the sports medicine team is most responsible for determining the athlete's eligibility for sports participation?
   A. Coach
   B. Physician
   C. Athletic trainer
   D. Student athletic trainer

9. Which member of the sports medicine team is responsible for recruiting other medical and allied health professionals for the team?
   A. Coach
   B. Physician
   C. Athletic trainer
   D. Athletic administrator

10. Which of the following factors is essential for allowing the sports medicine team to provide proper health care?
    A. Skill
    B. Common sense
    C. Communication
    D. Chain of command

Answers on page 891

References

1. Education Council, *Competencies in Athletic Training*. Dallas, TX, National Athletic Trainers' Association, 1999.

2. Joint Review Committee for Educational Programs in Athletic Training (JRC-AT). *Standards and Guidelines for the Development and Implementation of Accredited Entry-level Athletic Training Education Programs*. Englewood, CO, Association of Surgical Technologists, 1999.

Legal Issues in Sports Medicine

Nathaniel E. P. Ehrlich, Esq, ATC
Paul Grace, ATC

QUICK CONTENTS

- Description of a tort.

- Explanation of negligence and defense to negligence.

- Discussion of liability for tortious acts.

- Liability issues in drug testing programs.

- Alternative theories of liability, disclosure of medical information, and protection against liability suits.

Litigation involving sports participants, schools, and medical providers has dramatically increased as more individuals begin to participate in sports and as sports become a more integral part of our everyday lives. In addition to the economic impact of increased participation in athletics, the activities of all employees involved in sports are being closely scrutinized, especially those employees on the front lines—the athletic trainer and the team physician. The legal issues facing the sports medicine professional include malpractice, breach of contract, and invasion of privacy.

This chapter begins with a brief definition of a tort, followed by an explanation of the doctrine of negligence and defenses to claims of negligence. Liability of the institution, athletic trainer, and team physician for tortious acts is discussed, and drug testing issues and the applicability of contract claims to sports medicine are briefly investigated. The chapter ends with some insight into how the sports medicine professional can reduce the likelihood of involvement in a lawsuit or reduce the liability if sued.

TORTS

There is no easy definition of a tort. William L. Prosser, one of the most renowned legal experts on the topic, has defined a tort as "a civil wrong, other than breach of contract, for which the court will provide a remedy in the form of an action for damages."[1] A *tort* is the principal form of litigation resulting in lawsuits that involve physical education and athletics. Negligence is the form of tort most frequently identified in claims against sports medicine professionals. A tort may be intentional or unintentional. *Battery,* which may involve unpermitted and unintentional contact with another person, as in the case of medical treatment that is provided without the consent of the patient, is an unintentional tort. Acts of libel or slander because of the release of information by a sports medicine professional would be considered intentional torts.

Consent must always be obtained before treatment is provided. The circumstances for providing treatment to minors may be less clear than for adults because the minor athlete is generally considered, by law, to be incapable of giving valid consent. The general rule is that consent for treatment of a minor must be obtained from the parent or guardian.[2] However, some states also have statutory provisions that allow a minor to give valid consent when an emergency exists, when the parent or guardian is not available, or when the patient is near or at majority age.[3-5] The team physician and athletic trainer should be concerned with the type and scope of consent that has been obtained. Consent should be in writing and the team athletic trainer should possess a copy of the consent in case the athlete needs to be transferred to a hospital where consent is necessary. A sample medical consent form is shown in **Figure 2-1.** However, because the forms shown in this chapter are fact and state specific, an attorney should be consulted before any form is used. The terms and scope of the consent should be clear and provide the physician and athletic trainer with the general and specific authority to perform necessary procedures in a particular case. However, in some states, if the consent appears to provide blanket authority to the physician to do whatever he or she deems appropriate, the consent may be invalid.[6]

NEGLIGENCE

Negligence is defined as the conduct of a person that falls below a hypothetical standard of care established by law. The standard of care varies from state to state and is generally defined by case law in a given state rather than by statute. Four elements provide the basic concept of negligence.

The first element of negligence is a duty recognized by law that requires one to conform one's conduct to a certain standard, generally called a *standard of care.* For a duty to exist, there must be a contractual, statutory, or common practice relationship between the parties.

The second element is a breach of the duty that the law has recognized. A breach of duty would be the failure to

Torts

A tort is the principal form of litigation resulting in lawsuits that involve physical education and athletics. Negligence is the tort most frequently identified in claims against sports medicine professionals. An intentional tort is libel or slander as a result of the release of information, and an unintentional tort is battery, such as medical treatment provided without the patient's consent.

Before treatment is provided, valid consent must be obtained. Such consent for a minor must usually be obtained from the parent or guardian, but some states allow a minor to give valid consent in an emergency. The consent should be in writing and a copy should be forwarded to the athletic trainer. Consent should provide the physician with the general and specific authority to perform necessary procedures in a particular case. Giving blanket treatment authority to the physician may invalidate the consent.

Medical Consent Form

I/we hereby grant permission to _____ (school) and its physicians and/or athletic trainers to render aid, treatment, medical, or surgical care deemed reasonably necessary to the health and well being of _____ (student).

I/we further authorize the athletic trainers at the above-named institution who are under the direction and guidance of _____, the team physician, to render any first aid or preventive, rehabilitative, or emergency treatment deemed reasonably necessary to protect the health and well being of _____ (student).

I/we additionally grant, when necessary for protecting the health and well being of _____ (student), permission for hospitalization, treatment, or surgery at a competent and/or accredited facility.

I/we further release _____ (school) and its athletic trainers, agents, servants, and employees from any liability for damage and injury to _____ (student) and hereby accept the full responsibility for any and all damages or injuries sustained as a result of participation in _____ (sport).

_____
Student

_____
Date

_____
Parent/Guardian(s)

The forms in this chapter are fact and state specific, and an attorney should be consulted before any form is used.

FIGURE 2-1

A medical consent form should be in writing and the athletic trainer should have a copy in case the athlete is sent to the hospital.

---

exercise reasonable care by acting in a manner that falls below the accepted standard of care, failing to act when one had a duty to act, or violating a statutory provision that created a duty. Malpractice, faulty teaching, inadequate supervision, the improper use of equipment, and the use of equipment that fails to meet its intended purpose are areas in which a sports medicine professional may be accused of breaching a duty. Malpractice might include the following:

- the failure to prevent injury by permitting an athlete to participate when he or she is not medically qualified to do so[7]
- failure to have an ambulance or qualified medical personnel present or to have a "plan of action" [8]
- permitting a patient to return to sports participation before he or she is medically ready
- failure to diagnose a condition[9,10]
- failure to examine an athlete properly following an injury[11,12]
- allowing an individual to participate in sports when he or she is not medically capable[13]

FOCUS ON . . .

Negligence

Negligence is conduct that falls below a standard of care typically established by state case law. The basic concept of negligence is composed of four elements. First is the duty recognized by law that requires one's conduct conform to the standard of care. For a duty to exist, a contractual, statutory, or common practice relationship must be in place between the parties. Second is a breach of duty recognized by law, such as acting in a manner that falls below the accepted standard of care, failing to act when one had a duty to act, or violating a statutory provision that created a duty. Third, the breach of duty must be the proximate cause of the resulting injury. Fourth, the injury must result from the breach of duty.

The third element of negligence requires that the breach of duty must be the proximate cause of the resulting injury. A substantial body of legal literature that defines the concept of proximate cause has been developed. The concept of proximate cause is often discussed in terms of whether the injury was foreseeable. The most frequently cited case for this concept is *Palsgraf v Long Island Railroad Company*.[14] In this case, a railroad employee attempted to assist a passenger running to catch a train onto the moving train. The employee knocked a package from the passenger's arms. The package, which contained fireworks, fell onto the railroad tracks and exploded, causing a scale on the train platform to fall. The falling scale injured the plaintiff. The court held that the defendant was not responsible for the plaintiff's injuries because negligence requires some relationship between the parties that is based on the foreseeability of harm to the person who was actually injured. Thus, usually no duty is owed to a plaintiff if the type of harm that occurred was unforeseeable. However, more recent cases have expanded the duty to injured parties when the injury did not necessarily appear foreseeable. As a practical matter, if the injury is serious enough, the courts will generally expand the definition of foreseeability to allow compensation to the injured party.

The fourth element that must be present for an action to be considered negligent is injury that results from the breach of duty.

Defense to Negligence

Although the law differs from state to state, most states have recognized some defenses that will not permit liability despite negligence on the part of the sports medicine professional. Some generally recognized defenses to a negligence action follow.

Contributory and/or comparative negligence

If a plaintiff commits an act that causes his or her own injury in a state that recognizes contributory negligence, there will be no liability. In states that recognize comparative negligence, the negligence of the plaintiff and defendant are compared. In some jurisdictions that recognize comparative negligence, if the plaintiff's negligence exceeds 50%, the plaintiff's claim may be barred. In other states, the award is reduced by the percentage of the plaintiff's negligence no matter how great, as long as the plaintiff is not 100% responsible.

For example, in a jurisdiction that recognizes contributory negligence, the plaintiff's claim would most likely be barred if the plaintiff was injured because he or she used his or her head as a battering ram to tackle an opponent while wearing a neck collar that was fitted improperly. In a jurisdiction that recognizes comparative negligence, the

relative negligence of the plaintiff and the defendant who fitted the plaintiff with the collar would be compared, potentially reducing or eliminating any verdict.

Assumption of the risk

The law recognizes that there are some risks inherent in all sports activities. *Assumption of risk* can be defined as the voluntary assumption (express or implied) of known and appreciated risks. An individual who participates in certain activities and is injured as the result of the ordinary risk associated with the activity will not succeed in an action for negligence. An individual who assumes a risk created by the conduct of another individual cannot recover damages if harm occurs. In sports injuries, the plaintiff (usually an athlete or spectator) will assume the ordinary risks of the game. However, participants and spectators do not assume the risk of injury from the violation of the duty owed to them by the promoter or stadium operator. Therefore, they are not precluded from recovery for injury resulting from the negligence of others under those circumstances.

The seminal case on the concept of assumption of risk in sports is *Nabozny v Barnhill*, in which recovery was allowed for injuries resulting from a violation of a rule in soccer.[15] In this case, the plaintiff caught the ball and held it to his chest. The defendant kicked the plaintiff in the head as he held the ball. The plaintiff asserted negligence on the part of the individual who kicked him. At the trial, the court directed a verdict for the defendant, finding that because the parties were participating in an athletic competition, they owed no duty toward each other. The plaintiff appealed the case, and the appellate court stated that a player would be liable for injury if the player's conduct displayed a deliberate, willful, or reckless disregard for the safety of another player if injury occurred.

In the case of *Bourque v Duplechin*, the plaintiff (a second baseman) was allowed to recover damages because of the intentional misconduct of a base runner who went 5' off of the base path to collide with him.[16] In most jurisdictions, if a spectator who attends a baseball game is struck by a batted ball, he or she has assumed a risk in attending a baseball game and, therefore, cannot collect damages for injuries.[17] In the case of *Rutter v Northeastern Beaver County School District*, a football player who was injured during a practice session while not wearing protective equipment was found to have assumed the risk of injury.[18]

Most states in which skiing is a prevalent sport have legislated that skiers assume the risk of injury when undertaking that sport.[19]

Assumption of the risk is unlikely to preclude a claim in a case involving a sports medicine professional's treatment of a patient because one does not assume the risk of negligent acts of another. However, if the injury occurred as the result of participation in the event itself rather than as the result of the healthcare professional's negligence, the sports medicine professional might conceivably escape liability.

Immunity

Two additional defenses to a negligence action may be applicable in the sports setting. The doctrine of *sovereign immunity* is based on the English doctrine that the "king can do no wrong." Therefore, this defense is generally available only to a governmental entity or government employees who are acting within the course and scope of their employment and performance of their duties. The defense of sovereign immunity is very specific to each state and has been falling into disfavor in many courts in recent years.

The doctrine of *charitable immunity* is based on the notion that a person who is carrying out a charitable function should not be held accountable for negligent acts. In many jurisdictions, this is called a Good Samaritan Act. This doctrine may be applicable to some schools and colleges because they are charitable institutions with an affiliation with a religious institution. The doctrine of charitable immunity has also fallen into disfavor in many courts in recent years as it relates to the liability of institutions affiliated with religious entities. However, the Good Samaritan Act may still apply in situations in which an individual is providing services in an emergency.

LIABILITY FOR TORTIOUS ACTS

Liability of the Institution

The law has long recognized the doctrine known as *vicarious liability* or *respondent superior,* in which an employer may be held accountable for the wrongful acts of an employee that were committed within the course and scope of employment. However, even when the doctrine applies, the individual is and may still be held accountable for his or her own acts.

Entities such as corporations, schools, and colleges cannot act except through the actions of their employees or agents. Therefore, for an institution to be found negligent, the employee or agent of that institution must have performed some negligent action. The negligence of the employee is then charged to the employer, making the employer responsible to the injured party as well. The liability of both the institution and the employee is sometimes known as joint liability, and the institution and employee are known as joint tortfeasors. In joint liability, both the employer and the individual who committed the tortious act may be found liable for damages for the same act.

Athletic trainers and team physicians often are employed by institutions. However, once a suit is instituted, many institutions will attempt to create an independent contractor relationship between the physician and the institution or the athletic trainer and the institution. If an independent contractor relationship is established, liability for the institution might be avoided because the tortious acts of an independent contractor are not imputed to the employer. However, under the corporate theory of liability, even if an institution establishes an independent contractor status, the institution might still be liable for injuries caused by the independent contractor if it is proven that the institution was negligent in selecting, monitoring, or supervising the sports medicine professional.

The institution's insurance would not cover either the defense of the claim or the judgment against a sports medicine professional who is acting as an independent contractor. Some attorneys suggest that a sports medicine professional may in effect make him- or herself "judgment proof" by not having insurance. By not having insurance, the sports medicine professional will be taking the risk that he or she will be left out of a suit rather than having a judgment placed against him or her and/or incurring the costs of defense and judgment. However, in most

FOCUS ON . . .

Liability for Tortious Acts

The institution

Liability for tortious acts affects the institution, the athletic trainer, and the team physician. Vicarious liability (respondent superior) is the doctrine by which an employer can be held accountable for the wrongful acts of an employee committed within the course and scope of employment. Because institutions can act only through their employees or agents, an institution can only be held negligent if the employee or agent was negligent. This is known as joint liability, and both the employer and the individual (joint tortfeasors) can be found liable for the same act. However, if the athletic trainer or team physician is an independent contractor, the institution might avoid liability unless the institution is proven negligent in selecting, monitoring, or supervising the athletic trainer or team physician. The independent contractor is not usually covered by the institution's insurance without a special agreement, and such an agreement may protect the independent contractor from suit.

The athletic trainer

Athletic trainers have begun to receive greater recognition for their work, but along with this comes an increased risk of liability. The standards of care are often based on the national standard of care set by the National Athletic Trainers' Association (NATA), but they can also be set by state law or state boards of licensure or certification. Athletic trainers who continue to practice after failing to meet minimum licensure or certification requirements may also face criminal sanctions. Athletic trainers are now being named individually or as the only defendant in some lawsuits resulting from injuries to athletes.

The team physician

The team physician must practice with a level of reasonable knowledge and skill common for members of the profession in which he or she is practicing. Therefore, a general practitioner who is functioning as a sports medicine specialist may well be held to the higher standard of care of a trained sports medicine physician. A physician should never guarantee a treatment or outcome and should always obtain appropriate consent for treatment after fully explaining the nature of the injury, possible consequences, and proposed treatments. However, neither consent nor lack of compensation for services protects the physician from a malpractice suit (unless there is an accident, in which case the Good Samaritan Act may offer protection).

The physician-patient relationship begins once the treating physician accepts the athlete as a patient by providing services, at which point liability may attach. The preparticipation physical examination may not, by itself, constitute the establishment of a physician-patient relationship, because the physical is performed for the benefit of the employer.

Team physicians can be held liable for injuries caused by the coaching staff or other personnel, for releasing confidential information about an individual, or for withholding information about the injury from the athlete. The physician employed by an institution to treat student athletes has responsibilities to both the institution and to the student athlete.

The team physician must adhere to the standard of care when performing preparticipation physical examinations and when administering medication that may cause injury. In addition, the physician who travels out of state with a team must understand his or her legal status outside the home state and act accordingly.

circumstances, the plaintiff's attorney will not know that the sports medicine professional has no insurance until suit is actually filed. The sports medicine professional might instead consider securing an agreement with the institution to ensure that any claims made against him or her while acting at the institution or on its behalf would be insured by the institution or be covered by the institution's budget agreement. In the case of *Hemphill v Sayers*, suit was brought against the team athletic trainer and others for injuries sustained by an athlete. The indemnification policy of the university held that the team athletic trainer "shall be indemnified by [the university] against all

costs and expenses...in connection with...an action, suit,...."[20]

It was argued that because any judgment would be paid by the state university that they should be exempt from suit. The court disagreed and further held that the sovereign immunity provided by the Eleventh Amendment of the United States Constitution (immunity for federal employees) would not protect the healthcare professional from suit unless the cost or expense of suit could not be paid from any other source. If the contractual language had been clearer, the athletic trainer might have been exempt from suit if the state were the primary source of payment of a judgment on the athletic trainer's behalf.

Instances in which institutions were held responsible for the actions of the sports medicine professional are far too numerous to present; however, some examples may be instructive. In one case, a freshman athlete was injured during a softball practice when a ball struck her in the right eye. The coach applied ice and told her to go to her room and rest. The coach did not suggest that she see a doctor although the school's medical clinic was across the street from the softball field. The next day, the student had trouble with her vision and sought medical treatment. The type of trauma she suffered required prompt immobilization of the eye and absolute bed rest. Because she did not receive this treatment, secondary hemorrhaging occurred and the softball player eventually lost the sight in her right eye. She filed suit against the institution and recovered an $800,000 verdict. The court held that the institution had a duty to ensure that medical assistance was available and the coaches had a duty to evaluate the severity of the injury.[21] This case reinforces the need for institutions to have qualified medical personnel at both practices and games and that these individuals must provide follow-up treatment once an injury occurs.

In the case of *O'Brien v Township High School District 214*, the court held that a school district could be liable for allowing an incompetent and untrained student to provide medical care to an injured athlete.[22] The injury resulted from an activity that took place away from the school; however, the injury was treated before football practice by a student assistant athletic trainer for the football team.

In the case of *Fox v Board of Supervisors of Louisiana University and Agricultural and Mechanical College*, a court in Louisiana, which is the only state that relies on the Napoleonic Code rather than the English common law, held that Louisiana State University did not have a duty to require club sports to have a "trainer/manager/coach" work with the rugby team to eliminate dangerous conditions created by the lack of rest or conditioning.[23] The decision was based on the fact that rugby was a club activity and therefore not controlled by the institution. However, the decision implies that a school may be found liable for failing to provide sufficient qualified supervisory personnel for sports that it controls and sponsors.

In a more recent case, *Kleinknecht v Gettysburg College*,[8] a student participating in fall lacrosse practice suffered a heart attack. The court held that the college owed a duty to the athlete based on the special relationship between the college and player in the player's capacity as an intercollegiate athlete engaged in a school-sponsored activity. The court further held that the college owed a duty to take reasonable precautions against risk of reasonably foreseeable life-threatening injury during participation in athletic events. In addition, the court held that the Good Samaritan Law did not apply to the college.

Liability of the Athletic Trainer

Athletic trainers have begun to receive the recognition deserved by long hours of work, training, and expertise and from enhanced education, certification, and licensure. However, with that increased exposure comes an increased risk for liability. Athletic trainers must now adhere to higher standards of care. These standards may be set by the National Athletic Trainers' Association (NATA), state law, or state boards of licensure or certification. The standards form a legal duty that may form the basis for a negligence action if the standards are breached. Furthermore, in jurisdictions with licensure or certification requirements, athletic trainers who still practice after failing to meet the minimum requirements set by those laws may face criminal sanctions. Even with a reduced state standard, the standard of care for an athletic trainer in a negligence action may well be based on the national standard of care set by NATA.

It is becoming more common for athletic trainers to be individually named or named as the only defendant in lawsuits resulting from injuries to an athlete. In the case of *Gillespie v Southern Utah State College*, a student athletic trainer for the college basketball team advised the team's physician that he had been "icing" a basketball player's sprained ankle.[24] The physician assumed that "icing" meant applying ice packs. Instead, the student athletic trainer had been treating the ankle with ice water immersion. The athlete slept overnight with the ankle immersed in a bucket of ice water and continued to immerse the foot for several days. After discovering that the basketball player was still immersing the foot in ice water 3 days later, the student athletic trainer immediately called the physician, who instructed the student athletic trainer to stop the ice water treatment. Six days after the injury, the athlete visited the physician again and was diagnosed with thrombophlebitis and frostbite of the fourth and fifth toes. Ultimately, muscle tissue in the foot had to be removed and a gangrenous toe amputated. The athlete sued both the college and the student athletic trainer. The jury returned a verdict in favor of the institution and its student athletic trainer because it believed that the athlete had been contributorily negligent in the situation and was responsible for his own injuries. However, in a jurisdiction that recognizes comparative negligence, it is likely that a finding would have been made against the institution and the sports medicine professional.

In the case of *Hemphill v Sayers*, a football player sued both the athletic trainer and the helmet manufacturer, alleging that the athletic trainer failed to warn the athlete of the dangers of wearing a football helmet when the player suffered a cervical spine injury.[20] Implicit in this decision is the possibility that an athletic trainer may have a duty to warn an athlete of inherent dangers of equipment that the athlete may use.

In a well-publicized case, Marc Buoniconti, a football player at the Citadel, fractured his neck. The athletic trainer, team physicians, and institution were sued because numerous acts of alleged negligence had occurred, including failure to properly diagnose the plaintiff's condition prior to injury and improperly altering equipment that allegedly lead to his injury.[25] The case involving the athletic trainer was ultimately settled before verdict. The team physician was found not to have been negligent in failing to warn of existing abnormalities in Buoniconti's neck that may have made it dangerous for him to continue playing football. The defense contended that Buoniconti caused his own injuries by spearing an opponent.

In the case of *Cramer v Hoffman*, athletic trainers for St. Lawrence University were sued based on the assertion of negligent lifting and carrying by the athletic trainer and assistant coach and for failure to stabilize and immobilize the cervical spine, which aggravated the plaintiff's condition.[26] The team physician was sued for permitting the student to play in a weakened condition after suffering from the flu and for failing to properly train the staff about immobilization. The jury found in favor of the defendants.

Liability of the Team Physician

Generally, a physician must practice with a level of reasonable knowledge and skill common for members of the medical profession in good standing. Before ours was such a mobile society, this standard was isolated to the geographic area in which the physician practiced. However, that standard has eroded and is now more of a nationwide standard for any given specialty. A physician who practices outside of his or her area of specialty is still required to perform with the same degree of reasonable skill and knowledge that would be used by members of the profession in which he or she is practicing. In other words, a general practitioner who is acting as a sports medicine specialist may well be held to the higher standard of care of a trained sports medicine physician despite the fact that he or she may have less specialized training. A specialist will be held to the standard of care measured in terms of the specialty rather than the standard of the general medical profession. Thus, a sports medicine practitioner will be required to perform to the same degree of reasonable skill and knowledge that would be used by sports medicine experts across the country.

Although, as a practical matter, a physician cannot guarantee a treatment or outcome, a bad outcome or poor relationship with a patient may cause the patient to doubt the physician's care and ultimately result in either informal inquiry or litigation. By no means should a physician guarantee an outcome or make anything other than a cautious prognosis. To obtain appropriate informed consent for treatment from the patient, the physician must provide a full explanation of the nature of the injuries, possible consequences associated with the specific injury, and proposed treatments, both good and bad. Generally, physicians obtain a written or videotaped consent for treatment to avoid a claim of battery if the patient asserts that an unauthorized procedure was performed or that an unauthorized physician performed a procedure. **Figure 2-2** shows a sample acknowledgement of injury form. An attorney should be consulted before any form is used to ensure that the necessary information for the jurisdiction is included in the form. Although the physician may have obtained consent for treatment, consent will in no way act to bar the physician from a malpractice suit. The fact that the physician is not being compensated for his or her services does not alter the general standard of care owed by a physician to a patient unless the physician is providing emergency care at the scene of an accident, in which case the Good Samaritan statutes may be in effect. It is unlikely that a team physician will be able to use a Good Samaritan statute to protect his or her actions in response to an emergency involving a player at a sporting event. The physician most likely will be operating in some official capacity according to an agreement, paid or unpaid, with the athletic department.[8]

The physician-patient relationship is established once the treating physician accepts the athlete as a patient by providing services. Once the relationship has been established, liability may attach for any number of reasons. Liability may attach for improper performance of a preseason physical as in the case of *Gambrell v Kansas City Chiefs Football Club*, in which a team physician was sued for improperly clearing a player.[13] In this case, the team physician performed a physical examination on the player. However, it was alleged that by clearing the player, the physician was declaring that the player was fit to play. In fact, the player had preexisting injuries to his neck and spine that made him unfit to play. Subsequently, the player suffered spinal injuries in training camp that ended his career.

An argument may be made that a physician-patient relationship is not yet established when a physical examination is performed on an individual prior to his or her being signed to a contract in professional sports. In this case, the physical is performed for the benefit of the employer, who is considering retaining the individual's services, rather than for the benefit of the potential employee. In these circumstances, it might be wise to obtain an acknowledgment or release from the athlete/patient stating that the

Acknowledgement of Injury

1. I have been informed by the team physician that I have the following physical condition(s):

    _____

    _____.

2. I have received a full explanation from the team physician that to continue to play _____
    (sport) may result in the deterioration or aggravation of such physical condition(s), rendering me physically unable to
    perform life's daily functions.

3. I fully understand the possible consequences of playing _____ (sport) with the physical condition(s) set
    forth in paragraph 1 above. Nevertheless, I desire to continue to play _____ (sport) and hereby
    assume all risks inherent in the sport of _____.

4. Because I desire to play _____ (sport) for _____ (institution), I hereby waive
    and release _____ (institution), its agents, employees, physicians, and athletic trainers from any
    and all liability or responsibility in the event I become physically disabled as a result of this or any other injuries
    sustained while participating in _____ (sport) or as a result of a deterioration or aggravation of the
    physical condition(s) set forth in paragraph 1 above.

_____   _____
             Student   Parent/Guardian(s)

_____   _____
             Witness   Date

The forms in this chapter are fact and state specific, and an attorney should be consulted before any form is used.

FIGURE 2-2

The physician may obtain a written consent for treatment from an athlete such as this sample acknowledgement of injury form.

physician-patient relationship has not been established and that the examination is being performed solely for the benefit of the employer.

In the case of *Betesh v United States*, a physician who missed the diagnosis of Hodgkin's disease during a physical examination was held to have a responsibility to the patient, even though the traditional physician-patient relationship had not yet been established.[10]

Allegations were made in the case of *Wilson v Vancouver Hockey Club* that the physician failed to diagnose cancer and thereby shortened the player's career.[9] Although the physician was found to have been negligent, no damages were awarded as the court determined that no damages occurred. In addition, the argument was made that the Vancouver Hockey Club was also responsible for the actions of the doctor. The team took the position that the

physician was an independent contractor; therefore, they were not responsible for his actions. The team's position was upheld.

In the case of *Robitaille v Vancouver Hockey Club*, a player suffered a minor spinal cord injury in two separate games.[11] The team athletic trainer's duties included determining the severity of each injury and who needed to see the team physicians. The physician did not examine the player and the team owner threatened the player with suspension if he did not play while injured. In this case, the physician and club were both held responsible because the club sent the player home with instructions to "take a few shots of Courvoisier®." The player suffered a third and more serious spinal injury that ended his career. The team physician and the team were both found liable for the malpractice committed by the team.

In the case of *Speed v State*, an athletic trainer gave cold pills to a player who apparently had had a cold for 1 month.[12] After the toothache and headache persisted, an oral surgeon extracted two infected teeth. The surgeon followed the patient for several days, treating the patient for an increasingly severe headache. The congestion and headache remained, and the player again took oral medication. After 2 more days of headaches, the player returned to the oral surgeon. No explanation for the symptoms was given and eventually the player was examined by the team physician who found headache, nausea, loss of appetite, dehydration, dizziness, lethargy, and inflamed eyelids. The team physician considered mononucleosis, a brain abscess, or septicemia but ordered no tests. Just after the team physician left, the patient began to experience projectile vomiting. The patient was then seen by another school physician who ordered tests. The patient continued to get worse and a fourth physician ultimately diagnosed the condition as cavernous sinus thrombosis; however, the patient was left blind. The team physician was found responsible even though he only "stopped in to look at the player."

Team physicians may also be responsible for injuries caused by coaching staff or other personnel. In the case of *Welch v Dunsmuir Joint Union High School District*, a high school quarterback was injured while participating in an interschool scrimmage.[27] After the play, he was unable to get to his feet. At the coach's direction, the athlete was able to move his hands. The athlete's teammates carried him to the sidelines but with no supervision as to how he was carried. At the sidelines, the athlete was unable to move his hands or feet. A doctor was present at the scrimmage but it was unclear as to whether he examined the player on the field or only on the sidelines. At the trial, testimony determined that because the player was able to move prior to being carried to the sidelines and because the team physician was in attendance, the team physician, along with other individuals, was found liable for negligence in not treating the injury immediately and in allowing the injured athlete to be carried from the field by his teammates rather than by stretcher.

A team physician who is treating an individual while being paid by the institution may face a dilemma about releasing information. In *Chuy v Philadelphia Eagles Football Club*, the team physician advised the news media that the employee who had just been released had a fatal condition.[28] When the player heard that information on the radio, he had a nervous breakdown. An award was made against the team physician.

In the case of *Krueger v San Francisco Forty-Niners*, the team physician injected the player's knee and told him that he had a "good repair" and was cleared to play.[29] A year later, the knee was drained and injected again.

Subsequent treatment was rendered during the player's 10-year career; however, the player was allegedly never advised of the nature or consequences of his injuries. Fifteen years after his career ended, the player was again treated by the team physician. Many years later, the player determined the true nature and extent of his injuries, which required a tibial osteotomy. Although the applicable statute of limitations for bringing suit had passed, the court found that the active and willful concealment by the team and physician would permit the case to proceed. A jury awarded the player $6.5 million, which was later reduced to $3.5 million.

A physician who is employed by an institution to treat student athletes may be in a somewhat awkward position. The physician may have a responsibility to the institution for which he or she works as well as to the athlete. The institution may have full access to the athlete's records if an appropriate consent form has been executed that authorizes the release of such information. A sample authorization for release of information is shown in **Figure 2-3**. A denial of consent form is shown in **Figure 2-4**. As with other forms, an attorney should be consulted before these forms are used to determine whether the forms are applicable for the jurisdiction in which they are to be used.

The physician may be faced with a dilemma if a player wishes to participate and the team or institution feels it is not safe, or, alternatively, the institution (or coach) wishes the player to participate when the student or physician has reservations about the athlete's ability to participate.

The team physician may be approached for information regarding the athlete's condition when a student athlete is being recruited by another school or by a professional team. **Figure 2-5** shows a sample of a request for confidential information that may be adapted for use based on the requirements of the jurisdiction in which it is to be used. The physician's greatest obligation must be to the patient, regardless of his or her source of compensation.

During contract negotiations with the institution, the physician should insist that decisions regarding participation in athletic competition or practice are left to the physician. Prior cases have shown that if the physician does not meet the accepted medical standards of care for releasing an injured athlete to continue participation, the physician might be liable for negligence if the athlete is injured. Furthermore, the physician might face liability if the injured athlete is released and not warned that he or she is either not ready for participation or may be at risk for additional injury.

The physician-patient relationship obligates the physician to maintain confidentiality regarding disclosures made by the patient during the course of treatment. This duty of confidentiality is part of the Hippocratic Oath and is provided statutorily in some states. A physician might be

Authorization for Release of Information

Name: _____   Sport(s): _____

Position(s): _____   Number (Jersey): _____

Height: _____   Weight: _____   Birthdate: _____

Grade: _____   School: _____

Junior college transfer? ____ Yes ____ No   If yes, what junior college? _____

High school: _____

Glasses? ____ Yes____ No   Contact lenses? ____ Yes____ No

Injuries and/or problems about which information will be released: _____

_____

I/we, _____ (parent/guardian(s)) give my/our consent for the team physician, athletic trainers, or other medical personnel at _____ (school) to release the above information regarding the medical history, record of injury or surgery, record of serious illness, and rehabilitation results of _____ (student) as may be requested by the scout or representative of any professional or amateur athletic organization seeking such information. Said information shall include, but is not limited to, any and all information within their knowledge or contained in any records of treatment, hospitalization, examinations, x-rays, or tests rendered to me, and allow them to furnish to such persons or organizations copies of all such reports, records, tests, and x-rays.

I/we understand that such scout or representative of the team has made representations to the team physician, athletic trainer, or other medical personnel of _____ (school) that the purpose of this request is to assist that organization in making a determination regarding future employment.

I/we understand that record will be kept of all individuals requesting such information and the date of each request. The information above may under normal circumstances be confidential and except as provided in this release will not be otherwise released by the parties in charge of this information.

The _____ (school), its officials, employees, and athletic trainers *shall not be liable* in any respect or under any theory whatsoever as a result of the information released pursuant to this authorization. I expressly waive any claim for any damages that may result as a result of the release of the above information.

This release remains valid until revoked by me in writing.

Name: _____

School address: _____   Phone number: _____

Permanent address: _____   Phone number: _____

_____   _____
            Student   Parent/Guardian(s)

_____
            Date

The forms in this chapter are fact and state specific, and an attorney should be consulted before any form is used.

FIGURE 2-3

An appropriate consent form should be on file before any information about an athlete is released.

Denial of Release of Information

Name: _____   Sport(s): _____

Position(s): _____   Number (Jersey): _____

Height:_____   Weight:_____   Birthdate: _____

Grade: _____   School:_____

Junior college transfer? ____ Yes ____ No   If yes, what junior college? _____

High school: _____

Glasses? ____ Yes____ No   Contact lenses? ____ Yes____ No

Injuries and/or problems about which information will be released: _____

_____

I/we _____ (parent/guardian(s)) do not give consent for the team physician, athletic trainers, or other medical personnel at _____ (school) to release the above information regarding the medical history, record of injury or surgery, record of serious illness, and rehabilitation results of _____ (student) as may be required by the scout or representative of any professional or amateur athletic organization seeking such information.

The _____ (school), its officials, employees, and athletic trainers *shall not be liable* in any respect or under any theory whatsoever as a result of the failure to release said information pursuant to this authorization. I expressly waive any claim for any damages that may result of the failure to release the above information.

This release remains valid until revoked by me in writing.

Name: _____

School address:_____   Phone number: _____

Permanent address: _____   Phone number: _____

_____   _____
                Student   Parent/Guardian(s)

_____
                Date

The forms in this chapter are fact and state specific, and an attorney should be consulted before any form is used.

FIGURE 2-4

A denial of release form should be on file so that information about the athlete is not released.

held liable for disclosure of confidential information relating to the patient.

Examination of athletes

A frequent team physician responsibility is performing preparticipation examinations.[30] **Figure 2-6** shows a sample preseason physical examination form that can be adapted by an attorney for the jurisdiction in which it is to be used.

A physician retained by the state examined a professional boxer who had suffered two knockouts in a 3-week period. The physician believed the boxer should not participate in a third fight because of the two previous technical knockouts. However, at that time, the custom was to defer to the judgment of the physician who examined the boxer after the most recent fight. Because the physician who examined the boxer after the second fight had found nothing wrong, the physician examining the boxer prior to the third fight cleared him. The boxer died shortly after being knocked out in the third fight. The physicians were held to the normal standard of care in the medical com-

Request for Confidential Information

I hereby state that I am a scout for and/or representative of _____ (employer) and hereby request the athletic department, team physician, and athletic trainers of _____ (school) to release medical information relating to the health and physical fitness of _____ (athlete) for the purpose of determining his or her suitability for possible competition in or employment by _____ (employer).

I will keep such information confidential and will not release it except as is necessary to ascertain the employability or fitness for competition of _____ (athlete). It is expressly understood that the information obtained will not be released to or published in any news media.

I hereby agree to indemnify, defend, and hold harmless _____ (school) in any action for damages or otherwise that may be brought as a result of the release and use of said information.

_____
Scout/Representative

Individually, as a representative of:

_____   _____
Employer   Date

The forms in this chapter are fact and state specific, and an attorney should be consulted before any form is used.

FIGURE 2-5

A request for confidential information should be on file in the event a team physician is approached by another school or a professional team wishing to recruit an athlete.

munity that a patient who has received a severe beating to the head should be kept inactive to avoid the further risk of injury. The failure of the physicians to follow this custom was introduced as evidence of negligence and, at the trial court, resulted in an award against the state because of the third physician's negligence. On appeal, the verdict was overturned because there was no proof that this physician worked for the state; there was no rule prohibiting the boxer from fighting; there was no proof that the blow, regardless of prior injury, would have resulted in death; and because the boxer was engaged in a dangerous activity.[30]

Finally, the physician may be found responsible for administering medication that causes injury. In the case of *Bayless v The Philadelphia National League Club*, a successful suit was made against the team physician for mental illness that resulted from the prescription of pain-killing medication.[31]

The physician's attorney should investigate whether a physician who is licensed in one state but travels with the team out of state is practicing medicine without a license prior to advising the physician to undertake any out-of-state responsibilities.

LIABILITY ISSUES IN DRUG TESTING PROGRAMS

The National Collegiate Athletic Association (NCAA) has mandated year-round drug testing in certain activities. As a result, a number of high schools, colleges, and universities have adopted drug testing and counseling programs for athletes to deal with the very real problem of drug abuse.

The role of the athletic trainer and physician in these drug testing programs may be critical. The physician may have prescribed medications to an athlete that could cause a positive result on a drug test. The physician needs to communicate with the athletic trainer and the institution about any medications an athlete may be taking. The physician also must be certain that the use of such medications will not endanger the athlete's health if the medications are used while in practice or in competition. In addition, the physician and athletic trainer will likely play a key role in the education and counseling of athletes who test positive for drugs.

Standard Minimum Preparticipation Physical Examination

Should there be the need for additional examination or testing in any specific area, such will be permitted.

Name of student: _____

General medical examination

History	❑ Player	❑ Family	
	❑ Thorough review of all team physicians and athletic trainers		
	❑ Reports from preceding seasons		
Examination	❑ Head	❑ Face	❑ Scalp
	❑ Ears (external and ear drums)	❑ Sinus	
	❑ Throat	❑ Eyes (pupils, reaction to movement and light)	
	❑ Lungs (palpation)	❑ Chest	❑ Heart
	❑ Visceral (hernia)	❑ Rectum (hemorrhoid, fistula)	
	❑ Gastric system	❑ Unusual marks on body (scars, birthmarks)	
	❑ Height	❑ Weight	❑ Temperature
	❑ Blood pressure	❑ Pulse	❑ Heart rate

Orthopaedic examination

Visual examination, including stress testing and range of motion, for all of the following:

❑ Neck and spine	❑ Shoulder	❑ Elbow
❑ Wrist	❑ Fingers	❑ Hips
❑ Knees (also check knee jerk)		
❑ Ankle (check Achilles' tendon for abnormalities; also use jerk test)		

Flexibility Test: ❑ Hamstrings   ❑ Neck

Electrocardiogram Test for heart abnormalities

Stress testing Test cardiovascular system (at physician's discretion) with treadmill or bicycle

Blood test Using standard grid, test for (including but not limited to):

❑ Chemistry	❑ Calcium	❑ Phosphorus
❑ Glucose	❑ Uric acid	❑ Cholesterol
❑ Iron	❑ Triglycerides	❑ Lipids
❑ Sodium	❑ Chlorides	❑ White blood count
❑ Red blood count	❑ Mono screen*	
❑ Tay Sachs*	❑ Sickle cell anemia*	❑ Venereal disease*

* Where applicable. If found, individual counseling may be necessary.

Urinalysis Test for (including but not limited to):

❑ Protein	❑ Glucose	❑ pH factor
❑ Diabetes	❑ Renal failure	❑ Gout

Vision testing ❑ Peripheral vision   ❑ Standard eye test

Hearing test

Dental examination

Chest x-ray Check for (at appropriate intervals and only as recommended by the American Medical Association standards):

❑ Tumor	❑ Tuberculosis	❑ Lesions

X-ray of all previously injured areas (at physician's discretion)

By: _____   _____
         Physician   Date

FIGURE 2-6

The team physician frequently must perform a preparticipation physical examination that includes, among others, a general medical exam, an orthopaedic exam, and a dental exam. (Continued on next page.)

Acknowledgement

I have reviewed the medical history report on the above form and affirm to the best of my ability that it is true and correct. The above-named student consents to participation in _____ (sport), which may include travel.

_____
Parent/Guardian(s)

_____
Student

We, the undersigned, grant permission for the school employees to secure medical services for _____ (student), if necessary.

It is understood that although the athlete wears protective equipment whenever needed, the possibility of an accident still remains. Neither _____ (school) nor its athletic trainers assume any responsibility in the event of an accident. In consideration of the above-named student being permitted to participate in _____ (sport), I/we hereby release the above-named institution and its employees and athletic trainers, together with all persons, both employees and volunteers, including parents, assisting with any phase of such activities, from all liability and responsibility in connection with such activity.

I/we further agree to indemnify and hold harmless said parties from all claims hereafter made and asserted by or on behalf of the above-named student, his or her parents, guardian(s), heirs, executors, or assigns.

I/we further authorize any physician to release confidential information to the athletic trainer involved concerning an athletic injury.

I/we further authorize the athletic trainer to release confidential information to the coaches or sports information director concerning the athletic injury.

By: _____
Parent/Guardian(s)

By: _____
Student

_____
Date

The forms in this chapter are fact and state specific, and an attorney should be consulted before any form is used.

FIGURE 2-6 (Continued)

FOCUS ON . . .

Liability Issues in Drug Testing Programs

The National Collegiate Athletic Association (NCAA) has mandated year-round drug testing in certain activities, which has resulted in many high schools, colleges, and universities adopting drug testing and counseling programs. The athletic trainer and physician play important roles in drug testing programs. A medication the physician prescribed may result in a positive test; therefore, the physician must inform the athletic trainer and institution about any medications the athlete is taking. Also, the physician must be certain that the athlete's health will not be endangered by any medications used during practice or competition. The athletic trainer and physician play key roles in the education and counseling of athletes who test positive for drugs. The athletic trainer, physician, and institution's attorney must work closely together when developing a program to clearly define the roles and expectations of all parties.

Drug testing programs can raise a number of legal issues and questions, such as invasion of privacy and the obligation of the physician who obtains information from a patient that drugs are being used. In developing drug testing programs, the athletic trainer, the physician, and the institution's attorney should work in concert to define clearly the roles and expectations of all parties.

ALTERNATIVE THEORIES OF LIABILITY

In addition to a tort action for claims of negligence because of principles of contributory negligence, charitable immunity, sovereign immunity, or other defenses, an institution, physician, or athletic trainer may still be faced with another type of legal action: worker compensation. A student athlete has made a successful claim against a university based on the fact that the university provided the student with a work-study job in exchange for participation on the football team.[32] That was held to be sufficient grounds to allow the athlete to obtain worker compensation benefits. In this case, a university student who worked at the tennis courts was allowed time off to play football and was injured while playing football.[32]

FOCUS ON . . .

Alternative Theories of Liability

An institution, physician, or athletic trainer can also be faced with another type of legal action: worker compensation on the basis of a work-study job in exchange for sport participation.

DISCLOSURE OF MEDICAL INFORMATION

A potential source of tort liability for physicians is disclosure of a patient's medical information. The unauthorized disclosure of a patient's medical information exposes the physician to tort liability for any resulting harm.[33] With today's high salaries in professional sports, a team may choose to not sign a player based on the release of information obtained from the physician-patient relationship or wrong information that the team physician released regarding a player's condition or release from a team.[28]

PROTECTING AGAINST LIABILITY SUITS

The sports medicine professional must be aware of the legal obligations to standards established by the medical profession in carrying out professional responsibilities.

FOCUS ON . . .

Disclosure of Medical Information

Disclosing a patient's medical information is a potential source of tort liability. A sports organization may choose not to sign an athlete based on information obtained from the physician-patient relationship or erroneous information released by the team physician regarding a player's condition.

Failure to adhere to the standards of care may result in individual liability for the practitioner and/or liability for the employing institution. The sports medicine professional should be aware of the current state of knowledge in the profession and should conform his or her conduct accordingly. The sports medicine professional must remain current with what is occurring in the profession by attending seminars, continuing education classes, and by subscribing to and reading appropriate journals. He or she should seek out the advice of colleagues and research available literature if there is any question about the treatment of a particular condition.

FOCUS ON . . .

Protecting Against Liability Suits

To protect against liability suits, the sports medicine professional must be familiar with the standards to be upheld when carrying out professional responsibilities. Failure to adhere to these standards can result in liability for the practitioner, the institution, or both. The practitioner must also remain current with the state of knowledge in the profession and should seek the advice of colleagues and research the available literature if a question arises about the treatment of a condition. The institution, physician, and athletic trainer should maintain precise written records pertaining to an athlete's condition.

The sports medicine professional must have and follow a written definition of his or her job responsibilities, ensuring that employees are adequately and properly trained and that they maintain and comply with protocol especially regarding prescribing medication, obtaining appropriate consent, and discussing the patient's treatment. Knowing one's legal and professional limitations is essential, as is carrying appropriate insurance that provides liability coverage and defense by a qualified attorney of the practitioner's choice.

The institution, physician, and athletic trainer must maintain precise written records of treatment, physical conditioning, and advice received from other professionals, as well as communication with the individual athlete or teammates.

A written definition of the sports medicine professional's job and responsibilities must be obtained and followed. He or she must ensure that employees are adequately and properly trained and that they maintain and comply with appropriate protocol. In addition, the sports medicine professional should avoid prescribing medication that masks injury or will subject the athlete to potential injury. Appropriate consents must be obtained, and the athlete's condition or treatment must not be discussed with anyone other than those to whom the athlete has authorized information to be released. The sports medicine professional must know his or her legal and professional limitations.

Finally, because the cost of defending even a frivolous lawsuit can be prohibitive, all sports medicine practitioners should carry insurance policies that provide not only liability coverage but a defense by a qualified attorney of the individual practitioner's own choice.

Sports medicine professionals must realize that their activities are subject to scrutiny because of the very visible nature of athletics in society. Furthermore, economic consequences to the participants as a result of lost careers or lost income can lead to litigation. By adhering to accepted norms of professional conduct, the sports medicine professional stands a better chance of defending such actions.

CHAPTER REVIEW

In recent years, litigation involving sports medicine professionals has increased as the number of sports participants has grown and as the activities of sports medicine professionals are scrutinized. Sports medicine professionals may face lawsuits involving negligence, battery, libel, slander, and malpractice, but by following the standards of care, they can reduce their vulnerability.

Torts are the usual form of litigation involving sports, with negligence the most frequently identified tort in claims against sports medicine professionals. Torts can be intentional (libel, slander) or unintentional (battery). Obtaining valid consent before providing treatment will help to reduce the risk of legal action for battery. Negligence requires four components: a duty recognized by law that one's conduct conform to the standard of care; a breach of the duty recognized by law; the breach of duty is the proximate cause of the resulting injury; and injury results from the breach of duty.

Defenses to negligence include contributory negligence (the plaintiff's act caused the injury) and comparative negligence (the plaintiff and defendant are both liable to different degrees). Assumption of risk is another defense. Here, the athlete or a spectator voluntarily assumes the known and appreciated risks of the sport activity. Sovereign immunity is available to governmental entities or employees who are acting within the course and scope of their employment and performance of duties. Charitable immunity prevents a person who is carrying out a charitable function from being held liable for negligence.

Liability for tortious acts can fall to the institution, the athletic trainer, or the team physician, or a combination of these. However, certain actions can reduce the possibility of lawsuits. All sports medicine professionals must abide by the established standard of care, remain current in their knowledge of the field, maintain precise written records, obtain and follow written descriptions of their responsibilities, and carry insurance to cover themselves in case of lawsuits. Following these suggestions can help sports medicine professionals lessen the threat of lawsuits and to defend themselves if lawsuits do occur.

SELF-TEST

1. Which form of tort is cited most frequently in claims against sports medicine professionals?
   A. Libel
   B. Battery
   C. Slander
   D. Negligence

2. Which of the following statements about the standard of care is true?
   A. State case law defines the standard of care
   B. The standard of care is defined by the federal government
   C. Failing to provide the standard of care is a form of battery
   D. The standard of care is described in the Good Samaritan Act

3. The voluntary acceptance of known hazards is called:
   A. immunity.
   B. assumption of risk.
   C. contributory negligence.
   D. comparative negligence.

4. Holding an employer accountable for the wrongful acts of an employee committed within the course and scope of employment is considered:
   A. malpractice.
   B. sovereign immunity.
   C. charitable immunity.
   D. respondent superior.

5. To whom does a team physician who treats a collegiate athlete have the greatest obligation?
   A. Coach
   B. School
   C. Athlete
   D. Parents/guardians

6. Providing medical treatment without the consent of the patient is considered:
   A. battery.
   B. negligence.
   C. breach of duty.
   D. defense to negligence.

7. Which of the following terms best describes permitting an athlete to return to participation before he or she is medically ready?
   A. Libel
   B. Malpractice
   C. Proximate cause
   D. Vicarious liability

8. What is the seminal case on the concept of assumption of risk in sports?
   A. *Hemphill v Sayers*
   B. *Nabozny v Barnhill*
   C. *Bourque v Duplechin*
   D. *Rutter v Northeastern Beaver County School District*

9. The standard of care for an athletic trainer in a negligence action is likely to be based on the standard of care set by the:
   A. college or university.
   B. state athletic trainers' association.
   C. National Athletic Trainers' Association.
   D. National Collegiate Athletic Association.

10. When is the physician-patient relationship first established?
    A. When the physician bills for services provided
    B. When the physician accepts the patient and provides services
    C. When the physician diagnoses the patient and prescribes treatment
    D. When the physician performs the preparticipation physical examination

Answers on page 891

References

1. Prosser WL (ed): *Handbook of the Law of Torts*, ed 4, St. Paul, MN, West Publishing Co, 1971, p. 2–4

2. See Harney: *Medical Malpractice* Section 2.1(B) (1973, ed 2)

3. *Bakker v Welsh*, 144 Mich 632, 108 NW 94 (Mich 1906)

4. *Lacey v Laird*, 166 Ohio St 12, 139 NE 2d 25 (Ohio 1956)

5. *Smith v Seibly*, 72 Wash 2d 16, 431 P2d 719 (1967)

6. *Rogers v Lumbermens Mutual Casualty Company*, 119 So2d 649 (1960)

7. *Gathers v Loyola Marymount University*, Superior Court of California, C759027

8. *Kleinknecht v Gettysburg College*, 989 F.2d 1360 (3rd Cir 1993)

9. *Wilson v Vancouver Hockey Club*, 5 DLR 4th 282 (1983)

10. *Betesh v United States*, 400 F Supp 238 (1974)

11. *Robitaille v Vancouver Hockey Club*, 124 DLR 3d, 228 (1981)

12. *Speed v State*, 240 NW2d 901 (Iowa 1976)

13. *Gambrell v Kansas City Chiefs Football Club*, 562 SW2d 163 (Mo 1978)

14. *Palsgraf v Long Island Railroad Company*, 248 NY 339, 162 NE 99, 59 ALR 1253 (NY 1928) rearg. den. 249 NY 511, 164 NE 564

15. *Nabozny v Barnhill*, 31 Ill App 3d 212, 334 NE2d 258, 77 ALR3d 1294 (1975)

16. *Bourque v Duplechin*, 331 So2d 40 (1976)

17. *Schentzel v Philadelphia National League Club*, 173 Pa Super 179, 96 A2d 181 (1953)

18. *Rutter v Northeastern Beaver County School District*, 283 Pa Super 155, 423 A2d 1035 (1980)

19. *Kotovsky v Ski Liberty Operating Corp*, (412 Pa Super 442, 603 A2d 663 (1992)

20. *Hemphill v Sayers*, 552 F Supp 685 (1982)

21. *Steinman v Fontbonne College*, 664 F'2d 1082 (8th Cir 1981)

22. *O'Brien v Township High School District 214*, 83 Ill 2d 462, 415 NE2d 1015 (1980)

23. *Fox v Board of Supervisors of Louisiana University and Agricultural and Mechanical College*, 559 So2d 850 (1990)

24. *Gillespie v Southern Utah State College*, 669 P2d 861 (Utah 1983)

25. Articles pertaining to Buoniconti: *New York Times*, July 15, 1988; *Chicago Tribune*, July 15, 1988; *Sports Illustrated*, July 25, 1988; *Chicago Tribune*, August 7, 1988, October 29, 1988

26. *Cramer v Hoffman*, 390 F2d 19 (2d Cir 1968)

27. *Welch v Dunsmuir Joint Union High School District*, 326 P2d 633 (1958)

28. *Chuy v Philadelphia Eagles Football Club*, 595 F2d 1265 (3d Cir 1979)

29. *Krueger v San Francisco Forty-Niners*, 189 Cal App 3d 823 (Cal 1987)

30. *Rosenweig v State*, S.A.D. 2d 293; 171 NYS. 2d 912 (1958) 146 NY2d 589 (1955)

31. *Bayless v Philadelphia National League Club* 472 F Supp 625 (1979)

32. *University of Denver v Nemeth*, 257 P2d 423 (1953); *Rensing v Indiana State University Board of Trustees*, 444 NE2d 1170 (1983), revg 437 NE78 (1982)

33. *Hammonds v Aetna Casualty & Surety Company*, 243 F Supp 793 (1965)

Injury Prevention

Craig Bischoff, MD, MPH, FACSM
David H. Perrin, PhD, ATC

QUICK CONTENTS

- Why injury prevention is so important.

- The various models of health care.

- The components and setup of the preparticipation physical examination.

- The environmental factors that can affect injury prevention in the athlete.

- The roles of equipment and facilities in injury prevention.

- How conditioning can promote injury prevention.

- Factors that are influential in the prevention of injuries in pediatric and female athletes.

Although injury prevention has proven to be an important part of health care today, many still access the medical system only when illness or injury occurs. This chapter begins with a brief discussion of injury prevention, followed by an explanation of two models of health care: the disease model and the prevention model. The preparticipation physical examination, which is usually conducted prior to participation in an organized sport, is discussed, and the setting of the exam is described.

The influence that environmental factors may have on athletes, including supervision, coaching, medical care, and rules of the sport, is explained. The use of equipment such as helmets, braces, and athletic taping is discussed in detail, and some of the advantages and disadvantages of each are explained. The facilities that an athlete participates in are an important factor in injury prevention, and measures to prevent injuries in different sports are described.

Conditioning programs to prevent injury are discussed in detail, including flexibility and stretching, endurance training, strengthening, and risk factors. A discussion of pediatric sports follows, and the chapter closes with a description of the opportunities for the female athlete today and how these opportunities evolved.

INJURY PREVENTION

Nearly everyone agrees that "an ounce of prevention is worth a pound of cure." Although this statement makes empirical sense, our medical system usually pays more attention to the pound of cure than to the ounce of prevention. As healthcare consumers, we access the medical system when illness or injury occurs. From childhood, we learn to visit the doctor when we are sick, not when we are well. The medical education system emphasizes the diagnosis and treatment of illness and injury. Discussions about prevention of illness and injuries usually serve as an introduction to what people perceive as the more relevant and interesting topics of the curriculum, such as assessment and treatment of injuries. Research dedicates few resources to prevention when compared to that spent on

treatment; funding for illness and injury prevention is pennies to the dollar of that dedicated to researching cures. Insurance companies stand to gain the most financially from successful prevention programs; however, they often do not pay for preventive services. Despite this, most of the improvement in our national healthcare morbidity and mortality statistics are attributable to prevention activities. Except for the development of antibiotics, nothing has had a more positive effect on improved longevity over the past half century than prevention. National cancer organizations concluded recently that improvements in cancer mortality are attributed almost solely to prevention activities and that the treatment protocols, which have received most of the funding, have done little to affect cancer survival rates.

Pillar programs in health promotion include quitting smoking, controlling hypertension and weight, reducing cholesterol, and preventing injury. Exercise is a common denominator in each of these health promotion initiatives and is the primary factor in health promotion of the healthy population.

Two significant developments that have occurred over the past few years may have great impact on the certified athletic trainer's future role in the healthcare system. The

Injury Prevention

Although our medical system emphasizes the diagnosis and treatment of illness and injury, greater efforts and funding would be better spent on prevention activities. Prevention is responsible for most of the improvements in our national healthcare morbidity and mortality statistics, improved longevity over the past 50 years, and reductions in cancer mortality rates. Health promotion programs share exercise as a common and primary factor in the healthy population.

The certified athletic trainer's role will likely expand in the future as a result of two developments. First is the emergence of managed care as a primary healthcare model. Qualified healthcare extenders and allied health professionals are more important in such a healthcare system, as are wellness programs. Second is the National Athletic Trainers' Association's (NATA) broadening of its target population to include the "healthy person" rather than just the "athlete."

first development is the emergence of managed care as a primary model of health care in our country. Skyrocketing healthcare costs have spawned an explosion in health maintenance organizations. Although the final chapter on managed care has yet to be written, it appears that qualified healthcare extenders and allied health professionals will have greater importance to the healthcare system as managed care evolves. Prevention, more specifically exercise, will have greater importance in such a system. Faced with mushrooming healthcare costs, the corporate world has already taken steps, independent of the healthcare system, to implement wellness programs using certified athletic trainers and other allied healthcare professionals to lower the high cost of health care.

The second development that may impact the future practice of the certified athletic trainer is the decision made by the National Athletic Trainers' Association (NATA) to broaden its defined target population to include the "healthy person" instead of the more limited traditional athlete. Certified athletic trainers already serve as "healthcare extenders" of sorts to the athletes with whom they work, practicing prevention as a matter of routine, such as with preparticipation screens, exercise prescription, taping, and care of minor injuries. The same concepts that apply to preventing injuries and improving performance in the athlete can be transferred to the healthy population. The athletic training profession has much to offer to the national healthcare system.

MODELS OF HEALTH CARE

The Disease Model

Any discussion of illness and injury prevention requires an evaluation of current healthcare management practices. For the most part, the current system operates under the *disease model of health care* or the "fix it when it breaks" approach. Healthcare consumers access the system only when symptoms occur. The healthcare provider's role is to diagnose and treat the patient based on the presenting symptoms. In the disease model, the endpoint of care occurs when the problem has healed. Absence of symptoms denotes a cure. The healthcare provider, most often a physician, is the primary and often the only medical practitioner involved. Third-party reimbursement through insurance companies supports this model. For the most part, medical research is geared toward discovering "new and improved" treatments for symptoms that exist, with little or no financial incentive for prevention. Under this system, which is responsive rather than proactive in its approach to health, the responsibility for maintaining good health lies mainly with the system, specifically the skill of

the provider involved. Healthcare consumers, whose responsibility is to "follow doctor's orders," can be seen as passive participants in their healthcare maintenance.

There is no question that the disease model is necessary as there will always be injuries or diseases that require treatment, despite prevention.

The Prevention Model

The *prevention model of health care* offers a more proactive, multidisciplinary approach to medicine. *Primary prevention* is the prevention of illness or injury prior to its occurrence. Preseason strength, flexibility, endurance programs, prophylactic taping, and aerobics and nutritional programs to lower high blood pressure or cholesterol are examples of primary prevention. Prevention of a major illness or injury through early and accurate detection of a minor illness or injury is referred to as *secondary prevention*. Treatment of tendinitis in the early stages before it develops into a major injury is an example of secondary prevention. *Tertiary prevention* is the prevention of a chronic or debilitating illness or injury through appropriate care and rehabilitation. The aggressive rehabilitation of an anterior cruciate ligament (ACL) reconstruction is an example of tertiary prevention.

The prevention model differs from the disease model in several key aspects. First, it is based on function and performance rather than on symptoms. Functional deficits are identified before symptoms develop and attempts are made to correct them. Unlike the disease model, end results are based on performance and function rather than on the absence of symptoms. In the prevention model, the absence of symptoms does not necessarily mean the patient has been cured. The occurrence of weak ankles is more often a result of inadequate rehabilitation of a sprained ankle rather than a truly weak ankle. The second key difference between the two models is the multidisciplinary approach to illness and injury that the prevention model takes. In addition to the athletic trainers, who serve as "gatekeepers" in the traditional training room, the healthcare team includes primary care sports medicine physicians, orthopaedic surgeons, podiatrists, physical therapists, exercise physiologists, sports psychologists, nutritionists, and others. Another difference is that the prevention model is proactive as opposed to the more reactive symptom-based disease model. Biomechanical and physiologic deficits are identified prior to the appearance of symptoms. Finally, the prevention model shifts primary responsibility for health to the individual healthcare consumer rather than to the healthcare provider.

Although athletic trainers have been involved in the traditional disease model, they have also approached the care

FOCUS ON . . .

Models of Health Care

The disease model

One of the two models of health care is the disease model, which takes the "fix it when it breaks" approach, in which consumers use the system only when they have symptoms, and the role of the healthcare provider is to diagnose and treat based on those symptoms. Care ends when the problem has healed. This responsive system is supported by third-party reimbursement through insurance companies and usually is the focus of medical research. Maintaining health is the responsibility of the clinician, and the patient frequently takes a passive role.

The prevention model

The second model of health care is the prevention model, which takes a proactive, multidisciplinary approach. Primary prevention averts illness or injury before it occurs when possible. Secondary prevention is the avoidance of a major illness or injury through early and accurate detection of a minor illness or injury. Tertiary prevention uses appropriate care and rehabilitation to deter a chronic or debilitating illness or injury. Unlike the disease model, the prevention model is based on function and performance and does not equate the absence of symptoms with a cure.

The healthcare team includes athletic trainers (training room "gatekeepers"), primary care sports medicine physicians, orthopaedic surgeons, podiatrists, physical therapists, exercise physiologists, sports psychologists, nutritionists, and others. This model gives the individual consumer the primary responsibility for health.

The American College of Sports Medicine has proposed a "negative feedback vicious cycle" to relate biomechanical and physiologic function to tissue overload and injury. Function is affected by five complexes: the Functional Biomechanical Deficit Complex, which is the individual's inflexibilities, muscle weaknesses, and strength deficits; a Subclinical Biomechanical Adaptation Complex, which comprises the physiologic and biomechanical responses to these deficits; a Tissue Overload Complex, which describes the tissues placed under increased tensile or compressive stress by these biomechanical adaptations; the Tissue Injury Complex, which is the group of tissues that suffer the resulting physiologic derangement; and the Clinical Symptoms Complex, which is the set of signs and symptoms that brings the patient to the healthcare provider. The Tissue Injury Complex introduces a return to the Functional Biomechanical Deficit, and the cycle begins again. The disease model often treats the injury without addressing potential preventive measures. Despite the best efforts of prevention, the disease model is still required as injury and illness continue.

of the athlete from a prevention perspective, employing concepts of injury prevention, flexibility, strength, power, and endurance. This approach has an even greater potential for positive outcomes in the healthy "nonathletic" population, particularly among the older population. The NATA recently expanded its target population to include the healthy, physically active individual who uses strength, power, endurance, speed, flexibility, range of motion, and agility during athletic, recreational, or occupational activities. This move, coupled with the growth of managed care, potentially places the athletic trainer in an expanded role as an initial evaluator for the healthy population as well as for the athlete. The concept of primary, secondary, and tertiary prevention is common in the athletic training room and has great potential in the healthy but nonathletic population.

The prevention model of health care is based on function and performance. The American College of Sports Medicine has proposed a "negative feedback vicious cycle" as a paradigm that relates biomechanical and phys-

iologic function to tissue overload and injury (**Figure 3-1**).[1,2] In this paradigm, five interrelated complexes affect function. The Functional Biomechanical Deficit Complex is the group of inflexibilities, muscle weaknesses, and strength deficits that may exist in an individual, such as a tight or weak posterior compartment of the leg (gastrocnemius-soleus complex, posterior tibialis, and long flexors). These deficits contribute to a Subclinical Biomechanical Adaptation Complex, the physiologic and biomechanical responses to these deficits. In a patient with a tight or weak posterior compartment of the leg, a shortened stance phase and flatter heel strike could be a biomechanical adaptation to this biomechanical functional deficit.

The biomechanical adaptation results in a Tissue Overload Complex in which tissues, such as the Achilles tendon or plantar fascia, are placed under increased tensile or compressive stress. The Tissue Injury Complex, the group of tissues that suffer the physiologic derangement, results from the Tissue Overload Complex. These tissues may or may not be the same tissues involved in the Tissue Over-

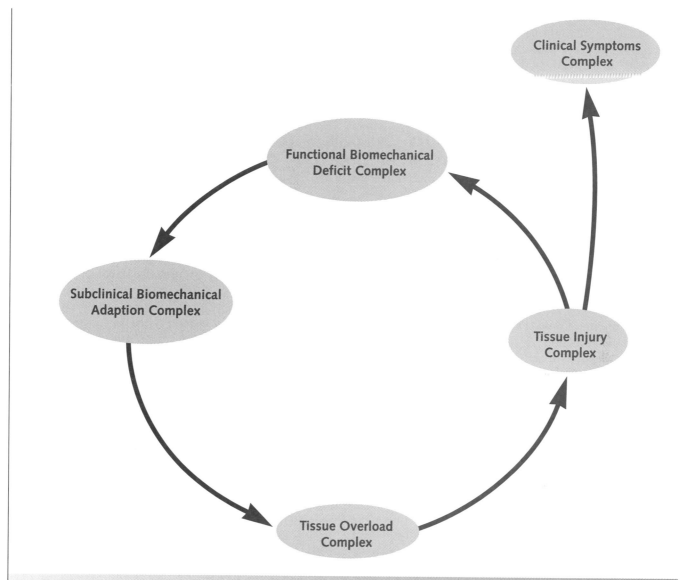

FIGURE 3-1

The prevention model of health care is based on function and performance as shown in the "negative feedback vicious cycle" that relates biomechanical and physiologic function to tissue overload and injury. (Adapted with permission from the American College of Sports Medicine Team Physician Videotapes: *Rehabilitation Injuries*, 1997.)

load Complex. The Tissue Injury Complex leads to the Clinical Symptoms Complex, the set of symptoms and signs, such as pain from plantar fasciitis or Achilles tendinitis, that brings a patient to the healthcare provider. The Tissue Injury Complex also introduces a return to the Functional Biomechanical Deficit and the vicious cycle begins again, this time perhaps with involvement of a different set of tissues. Often, in the disease model approach, the symptoms are treated without addressing the biomechanical deficits, and the problem returns. Unless the entire kinetic chain is evaluated, biomechanical and physiologic deficits will be missed, which may predispose the patient to injury. These deficits are easily evaluated in the preparticipation physical examination but require an exhaustive effort on the part of the athletic trainer.

THE PREPARTICIPATION PHYSICAL EXAMINATION

The *preparticipation physical examination* is traditionally conducted prior to participation in an organized sport and is often a legal requirement.[3] With more than 6 million youth examined and 1 million man hours used annually, some disagree as to the utility, usefulness, and cost effectiveness of the exam. In one study, 16 problems were identified in 763 adolescents, and two adolescents were ultimately disqualified from participation.[4] In another recent study, 5,615 high school athletes were screened using cardiac history, auscultation, blood pressure, and electrocardiogram in an effort to identify potentially life-threatening conditions. The results included 582 cardio-vascular variances that were referred for further work-up. Of these, 22 patients (0.4%) were not approved for athletic participation and required further testing.[5] The only cardiac event, a ventricular fibrillation that was successfully resuscitated, occurred in an individual who was not identified during the screening process. The ability of the preparticipation physical examination to identify life-threatening cardiac abnormalities has been severely questioned.

To fulfill legal or insurance requirements, many exams are conducted quickly, on the spur of the moment, and in substandard conditions. These exams rarely produce useful information and are generally a waste of time. However, there are compelling reasons to conduct a comprehensive, thorough exam. In many cases, the preparticipation exam may be the only contact with the medical system for the athlete. The exam can lay a valuable foundation for the team physician and athletic trainer in the future care of the athlete. Studies that document that injuries are indeed prevented by a preparticipation physical exam are generally lacking, and most exams performed are not standardized, focused, or directed.

Identification and rehabilitation of structural, biomechanical, or physiologic abnormalities are the foundation of therapy when an injury occurs. If these abnormalities can be identified and corrected before the season begins, injury can be prevented. The key is an organized, focused, and directed exam that includes assessment of anatomic as well as physiologic parameters for the specific sport involved. The preparticipation physical exam should be performed far enough in advance of the season, usually 6 to 12 weeks, to allow for the prehabilitation of deficiencies identified at the time of the exam.[6] **Table 3-1** outlines the objectives of the preparticipation physical exam.

The Preparticipation Physical Examination Setting

The preparticipation physical exam is usually performed in either the private office setting or the multiple-station setting. Familiarity with the athlete and an established patient-physician relationship are the advantages of an exam held in the private office setting, making this type of exam ideal for the athlete who is well known to his or her family physician. However, the examining physician must be familiar with the physical demands and the physiologic requirements of the sport involved.

TABLE 3-1

OBJECTIVES OF THE PREPARTICIPATION PHYSICAL EXAMINATION

1. Evaluate and review overall health

2. Identify conditions that may disqualify the athlete from competition

3. Assess physical maturity and its appropriateness to the sport

4. Develop a physiologic profile that includes the following:
   - Endurance and cardiovascular fitness
   - Flexibility
   - Strength and power

5. Develop a database

6. Identify deficits that may be corrected

Setup of the multiple-testing station exam

The multiple-testing station format, which requires more organization but is more time and effort efficient and can collect volumes of superior data, is useful for high-volume settings such as academic or club teams. The athlete rotates through serial examination testing stations staffed by experienced and competent personnel who complete their assigned portion of the preparticipation exam before the patient moves to the next station. The evaluation stations should be set up and equipped well in advance to provide easy and smooth access. At least one station should allow privacy to be maintained. Athletes should be advised to wear loose-fitting shorts and shirts. Staggered start times will ensure a smooth flow. Each athlete should carry duplicate medical examination forms to each station so that one can be kept on file and the other given to the athlete. Circumstances may dictate modifications of this format.[7] **Table 3-2** lists the equipment needed for the preparticipation physical exam.

Generally, in a multiple-testing station environment, the athlete's medical history is reviewed at the first station. This station is among the most important of the preparticipation exam because most disqualifying conditions are identified here. Information is often incomplete or inaccurate, so it is important that a knowledgeable person, often a parent, completes the medical history form well in advance of the exam. A staff member at this station reviews the medical history with the athlete, and areas of concern are explored in depth. The reviewer should take extra time to delineate previous injuries. Previous injury is the highest risk factor for future injury.

FOCUS ON . . .

The Preparticipation Physical Examination

The preparticipation physical examination usually takes place 6 to 12 weeks before participation in an organized sport. Some experts disagree about the utility of the examination, but exams should not be conducted quickly in substandard conditions to satisfy legal or insurance requirements. However, a thorough screening can provide a foundation for the athlete's future medical care. If abnormalities can be identified before the season, injury can often be prevented. The objectives of the preparticipation physical exam are to evaluate and review overall health; identify potentially disqualifying conditions; assess physical maturity and its appropriateness to the sport; develop a physiologic profile that includes endurance and cardiovascular fitness, flexibility, and strength and power; develop a database; and identify correctable deficits.

The preparticipation physical examination

The physical setting for the exam can be either a private office or multiple-testing stations. The athlete well known to the family physician benefits from an exam in the private setting, as long as the practitioner is familiar with the physical demands and physiologic requirements of the sport.

Setup of the multiple station exam

Multiple-testing stations are more efficient for higher volumes of athletes. Each athlete proceeds through a series of stations staffed by qualified personnel. Athletes should dress in loose-fitting shorts and shirts and have their start times staggered for a smooth flow. Each athlete carries duplicate medical exam forms to each station so that one can be kept on file and the other given to the athlete.

At the first station, the athlete's medical history is reviewed. A knowledgeable person, such as a parent, completes the history form before the exam, and then a staff member reviews it with the athlete, exploring any areas of concern and delineating previous injuries. General body habitus is noted to check for conditions such as Marfan's syndrome and obesity.

At the second station, vital signs are taken. Anxiety or a small-fitting blood pressure cuff can cause elevated systolic readings, which should be repeated with the proper size cuff. Readings greater than 130/75 mm Hg in athletes 6 to 11 years old and 140/85 mm Hg in athletes 12 to 18 years old require referral of the athlete for further testing.

At the third station, the head, ears, eyes, nose, throat, and visual acuity are screened.

At the fourth station, the cardiovascular, respiratory, and gastrointestinal systems are evaluated. Cardiac conditions that disqualify an athlete from their sport include obstructive hypertrophic cardiomyopathy, congenital coronary artery abnormalities, Marfan's syndrome, severe pulmonic stenosis, and aortic stenosis. The athlete should be asked about any history of passing out, feeling dizzy, or fainting during exercise and should be examined by an experienced professional. The heart should be auscultated with the patient upright as well as with the Valsalva's maneuver. Systolic murmurs that are grade 3 or greater or are accentuated with Valsalva's maneuver and all diastolic murmurs require that the athlete be referred for further evaluation.

The musculoskeletal exam occurs at the fifth station. Competitive team and individual athletes requiring greater physiologic and performance demands should undergo a more complete musculoskeletal exam that can be accomplished with the creation of a physiologic profile. The physiologic profile reflects the results of standardized tests and fitness parameters, including flexibility, endurance, strength, and power, and identifies biomechanical and physiologic deficits that can be corrected before the season. The physiologic profile can serve as a baseline if the athlete is later injured and can provide normative data for future reference.

While measuring all fitness parameters, physiologic profile testing should concentrate on those that are more sport specific: football requires greater power and strength while basketball requires more flexibility and endurance. Therefore, football's physiologic profile includes more strength and power than flexibility or endurance tests. The order of stations and testing can be arranged based on personal preference and experience.

At the first station, general body *habitus* (posture or physique) is recorded. A tall, lanky stature with excessive limb length may indicate Marfan's syndrome, which is an inherited disorder of collagen synthesis and is a leading cause of sudden death in young athletes, usually as a result of aortic or valvular rupture. All male patients taller than 6' and female patients taller than 5' 10" who have a family history of Marfan's syndrome or who manifest a marphanoid habitus should be screened with an ECG.[8] **Table 3-3** list the characteristics of Marfan's syndrome. Obesity has also been implicated in sudden death, and patients who are significantly obese may require additional

TABLE 3-2
EQUIPMENT FOR THE PREPARTICIPATION PHYSICAL EXAMINATION

Oto-ophthalmoscope with tongue depressors and speculums

Sphygmomanometers (blood pressure cuff)

Eye charts

Goniometers

Tape measures

Gloves

TABLE 3-3
CHARACTERISTICS OF MARFAN'S SYNDROME

Cardiac murmur or midsystolic click

Kyphoscoliosis

Pectus carinatum (pigeon chest)

Arm span that is greater than height

Upper to lower body ratio that is less than the average

Myopia

Ectopic lens

Elongated flexible digits

to 18-year-old group should be referred for further testing.[9] Head, ear, eyes, nose, and throat abnormalities and visual acuity are tested at a third station.

The athlete's cardiovascular, respiratory, and gastrointestinal systems are evaluated at a fourth station. Cardiovascular anomalies are the leading cause of sudden death in the young athlete. **Table 3-4** lists the cardiac conditions that contraindicate an athlete's participation in sports. At this station and independent of the medical history form, the patient should be asked, "Have you ever passed out, felt dizzy, or fainted during exercise?" Because cardiac abnormalities are very difficult to identify at a physical examination, an experienced professional skilled in the cardiovascular exam should perform this part of the examination. A decrease in cardiac return will accentuate the systolic murmur of hypertrophic cardiomyopathy, which is the most common cause of sudden death in the young athlete. The heart should be auscultated with the patient in the upright position as well as with Valsalva's maneuver. All systolic murmurs of grade 3 or greater, those that are accentuated with Valsalva's maneuver, and all diastolic murmurs should be referred for further evaluation.[8]

The musculoskeletal exam, which can be a brief screen completed in 2 to 3 minutes, is performed at a fifth station. **Table 3-5** presents the parts of the exam that should be performed for this cursory procedure, which suffices as a screening test for the preadolescent and school physical education exams. However, athletes involved in competitive team and individual sports in which greater physiologic and performance demands are required should be given a more formal and complete musculoskeletal exam, which can be accomplished by creating a physiologic profile for each athlete.

evaluation. Some other conditions that constitute an absolute or relative contraindication to sport-specific participation include atlantoaxial instability, acute illness, carditis, hypertension, congenital heart disease, impaired vision, hernia, absence of or enlargement of internal organs, musculoskeletal disorders, history of serious head or spinal injury, and poorly controlled convulsive disorder.

Vital signs are taken at a second station. Elevated systolic readings in the young athlete are usually anxiety related or as a result of a blood pressure cuff that is too small. All elevated readings need to be repeated, and the proper cuff size must be used. Some athletes with large arms may require a thigh blood pressure cuff for accurate readings. Accurate blood pressure readings greater than 130/75 mm Hg in the 6- to 11-year-old age group and 140/85 mm Hg in the 12-

TABLE 3-4
CARDIAC CONDITIONS THAT CONTRAINDICATE PARTICIPATION IN ATHLETICS

- Obstructive hypertrophic cardiomyopathy

- Congenital coronary artery abnormalities

- Marfan's syndrome

- Severe pulmonic stenosis (RV pressure > 75 mm HG)

- Aortic stenosis (pressure gradient > 40 mm HG)

TABLE 3-5
MUSCULOSKELETAL CURSORY EXAM

Cervical Range of Motion (ROM)

- Flexion/Extension (chin to chest/look to ceiling)
- Lateral bending (ear to shoulder)
- Lateral glance (look over shoulders)

Shoulder ROM

- Abduction/Adduction
- External/Internal rotation
- Extension/Flexion (scratch both scapulae with each hand from above and below)

Elbow ROM

- Supination/Pronation
- Extension/Flexion (with elbow at 90° fully flex and extend elbow, turn palms up and down)

Wrist ROM

- Extension/Flexion
- Ulnar/Radial deviation (fully flex and extend wrist)

Hand/Finger ROM

- Extension/Flexion
- Abduction/Adduction (hand grip, fully extend fingers)

Duck walk (functional screen, ROM, motor test)

- Knee, hip, and ankle

Heel/Toe walk (functional screen, ROM, motor test)

- Ankle/Foot

Toe touch (functional screen, ROM)

- Scoliosis
- Hamstring tightness

Hop test (functional screen, motor test, proprioception)

- Knee, hip, and ankle

Through standardized tests, all parameters of fitness, including flexibility, endurance, strength, and power, are documented in the *physiologic profile*.[10] The physiologic profile not only identifies biomechanical and physiologic deficits in the individual athlete that can be prehabilitated prior to the season, but also serves as a baseline measure to guide rehabilitation if the athlete is injured during the season. In addition, the profile develops a local normative database that can serve as a reference in future years. However development of such a database requires time and commitment to function in the setting of the preparticipation physical examination.

The physiologic profile testing should measure all the fitness parameters but concentrate on those that are more sport specific. Each specific sport will have a unique physiologic profile in conjunction with the demands of the sport. For instance, football requires more power, strength, and anaerobic endurance than basketball, but basketball requires more flexibility and endurance. The physiologic profile for football will include more strength and power tests than endurance tests; the profile for basketball will include more endurance and flexibility tests. Tests that measure overall flexibility include the following:

- sit reach
- knee flexion/extension
- iliotibial band (Ober's test)
- gastrocnemius/soleus

- shoulder rotations
- elbow and wrist flexibilities

When flexibility is graphed against injury, a J curve is created with two spikes of injury, one at the lower values for flexibility and one at the higher values for flexibility.[11] Injuries that occur at the lower values (inflexible) are usually muscular and tendinous strains; those that occur at the higher values (highly flexible) are sprains and dislocations. The range of motion of all major joints should be measured with special attention given to those joints that require increased flexibility for the sport involved—for instance, internal rotation in a throwing sport. **Table 3-6** lists the flexibility demands for some common sports.[12] Endurance is important in those sports that involve aerobic exercise, such as distance running and basketball. The timed distance 1- and 3-mile runs are good measures of aerobic endurance. Although aerobic endurance is the main parameter in long-distance running, such as in a marathon, strength and power training are believed to prevent injuries in these endurance sports. With a fatigued muscle, more force is transmitted to the tendon muscle allowing the tendon and bone to interface, thus predisposing that area to overuse injuries. Strength training may allow endurance muscles to fatigue less readily, thus providing a measure of protection. Strength and power parameters are important in sports such as football. Tests that measure strength and power include the following:

TABLE 3-6
FLEXIBILITY DEMANDS OF VARIOUS SPORTS

	Shoulder	Back	Hip	Groin	Thigh/ Knee	Calf/ Ankle	Elbow/ Wrist
Ballet		XX	X	X	XX	XX	
Baseball	XX	XX	X	X	X	XX	XX
Basketball	X	X	X	X	XX	X	X
Bicycling	X				XX	XX	X
Golf	X	X	X	X			
Football	XX	XX	X	XX	XX	XX	X
Marathon			X	X	X	XX	
Racquetball	XX	XX	X	X	X	XX	X
Skiing	X		X	X	X	X	
Swimming	XX	X	X	X	X	X	X
Tennis	XX	XX	X	X	X	XX	X
Triathlon	XX	X	X	X	X	X	
Volleyball	XX	XX	X	X	XX	X	X
Walking		X	X	XX	X	X	

(Adapted with permission from Micheli LJ (ed): *The Sports Medicine Bible: Prevent, Detect, and Treat Your Sports Injuries Through the Latest Medical Techniques.* New York, NY, Harper Perennial, 1995, p 24.)

- timed sit-ups
- push ups
- squats
- dips
- grip strength
- vertical jump
- medicine ball throw
- dynamometer testing

The 40-yard dash is a good test for anaerobic endurance. A rehabilitative conditioning program to reduce injuries and improve performance can be prescribed based on the physiologic profile and knowledge of the physiologic demands of the specific sport. Some of the common flexibility and strength deficits associated with specific sports injuries include rotator cuff tendinitis or strain, impingement syndromes, and labral tears associated with throwing sports, lateral epicondylitis associated with tennis, and patellofemoral pain, plantar fasciitis, Achilles tendinitis, and hip strains and tendinitis associated with running and endurance sports. Mechanical low back pain is associated with many sports.

ENVIRONMENTAL FACTORS

Several factors associated with the environment in which athletes participate can have a strong influence on injury prevention. Proper supervision, appropriate coaching, provision of medical care by qualified personnel, and adherence to the rules of each sport are the foundation of safe participation in athletics. The trampoline may show the best example of the value of proper supervision. Results of one study of injuries to the spine during trampoline activity showed no evidence that the participants were unfit for the activity, but rather that each injury was the result of instructor negligence.[13] A higher incidence of injuries is also seen in unorganized sports and during the early phases of participation than in organized sports.[14] Proper supervision by qualified personnel can prevent the occurrence of injury.

Changes in rules and regulations can also dramatically reduce the incidence and severity of injuries. The rules

FOCUS ON . . .

Environmental Factors

Environmental factors such as proper supervision, appropriate coaching, provision of medical care by qualified personnel, and adherence to the sport's rules can also prevent injury. A higher incidence of injuries is seen when instructors are negligent or sports are unorganized. Changes in rules can dramatically reduce injury incidence and severity; however, if coaches or athletes fail to comply with rules, or if the governing organization fails to support prevention programs, the potential benefits are lost.

adopted by the National Collegiate Athletic Association (NCAA) and the National Federation of State High School Associations (NFSHSA) include the following:

- No player shall intentionally strike a runner with the crown or top of the helmet.
- Spearing is the deliberate use of the helmet in an attempt to punish an opponent.
- No player shall deliberately use his or her helmet to butt or ram an opponent.

The addition of the above rules has significantly reduced injury to the cervical spine in football players.[15] Moreover, the development of and requirement to wear the helmet-face mask combination while playing ice hockey has reduced the incidence of facial injuries by 70%.[16]

Noncompliance with the rules on the part of coaches or athletes can dramatically reduce the effectiveness of injury prevention programs. For example, protective headgear worn during wrestling and required in competition has made the occurrence of "cauliflower ear" in wrestlers nearly nonexistent. However, this preventive measure is lost if coaches do not require wrestlers to wear the protective headgear during practice. Shin guards in soccer reduce the force transferred to the lower leg by 40% to 77%, but they are of no use if players do not wear them.[17] Mouthguards decrease the risk of damage to the teeth and, with traumatic mandibular closure, of oral laceration, mandibular fracture, and concussion.[18] Several sports organizations have mandated that mouthguards be a bright color to assist officials in detecting athletes attempting to compete without these protective devices.

Tradition can also obstruct the implementation of prevention programs. For example, protective eyewear is available specifically for use in women's lacrosse, yet the United States Women's Lacrosse Association (USWLA) does not mandate this eyewear for athletes competing in USWLA-sanctioned events.[19]

EQUIPMENT

The development of guidelines related to the quality, fitting, application, and maintenance of protective equipment plays an essential role in injury prevention. Most interscholastic sports programs operate under substantial budgetary restraints, as do some intercollegiate programs. However, the acquisition and maintenance of high-quality protective equipment is paramount to a sound injury prevention program. **Table 3-7** presents several considerations related to the use of protective equipment.[15]

Helmets

Helmets are designed to protect the head and, in some cases, the face and are required equipment for collision sports such as football and ice hockey. These helmets are designed to protect the head; however, they do not prevent injury to the cervical spine. The early use of helmets in football created a false sense of security among players, leading to a reduction of head injuries but an increase in catastrophic injuries to the cervical spine. Changes in rules related to the use of the head during blocking and tackling activities have significantly reduced the number of neck injuries in football. It is interesting to note that the development of the helmet-face mask combination in ice hockey has reduced the incidence of facial injuries by 70%, yet the incidence of catastrophic neck injuries has increased appreciably, a phenomenon that is eerily similar to what occurred in football.[16]

Only helmets bearing stickers of approval from agencies such as the Snell Memorial Foundation, the American National Standards Institute (ANSI), the American Society for Testing and Materials (ASTM), or the National Operating Committee on Standards for Athletic Equipment (NOCSAE) should be worn during participation in sports (**Figure 3-2**). As with any protective equipment, helmets should be properly fitted by qualified personnel and be worn in accordance with the manufacturer's instructions. **Table 3-8** presents guidelines for properly fitting a football helmet.[15]

Braces

A variety of braces proliferate in the marketplace and can be found for virtually every joint of the body. The joint that has received the greatest attention is the knee. Essentially, knee braces fall into three categories: rehabilitative, functional, and prophylactic. Rehabilitative knee braces are designed to provide protection and control motion during the healing and rehabilitative phases following injury or surgery. Functional braces are intended to provide stability to knees with ligamentous insufficiency, most often involving injury to the anterior cruciate

TABLE 3-7
GUIDELINES FOR PURCHASING AND USING PROTECTIVE EQUIPMENT

1. Buy protective sports equipment only from reputable manufacturers.

2. Buy only the best and safest equipment that available resources permit. Too often, athletes are allowed to participate with substandard equipment because financial limitations are considered before the safety of the participant.

3. Make sure that protective equipment fits properly according to the manufacturer's instructions. Even the highest-quality equipment may be dangerous and not adequately protect the participant as designed if not properly fitted.

4. Maintain the equipment according to the manufacturer's guidelines. Those who do not follow the manufacturer's recommendations for care and use of the equipment may risk liability in the event an athlete is injured.

5. Use the equipment only for the purpose for which it was designed.

6. Warn the participants who use the equipment of all the risks involved with equipment misuse or malfunction. Some schools and sponsoring sport groups, because of increasing litigation related to sport participation, not only warn their sport participants verbally, but request that they sign an "informed consent."

7. Use great caution in constructing or customizing any piece of sports protective equipment.

8. Do not use defective equipment. All equipment should be routinely inspected for defects, and all defective equipment should either be repaired or rendered unusable.

(Adapted with permission from Ellis TH: Sports protective equipment. *Prim Care* 1991;18:889-921.)

FIGURE 3-2

Helmets worn during sports participation should bear a sticker of approval from an agency such as this one from the National Operating Committee on Standards for Athletic Equipment (NOCSAE).

ligament. Prophylactic knee braces are intended to provide protection to the medial compartment of the knee against valgus forces and have received considerable attention in the sports medicine literature.

Considerable controversy exists among team physicians and athletic trainers regarding the effectiveness of prophylactic knee braces (PKBs). Results of some studies have shown a reduction in injury to the medial collateral ligament (MCL) while others have shown an increase. The interpretation of these studies is confounded by the fact that the players most likely to incur injury to the medial compartment of the knee, offensive and defensive linemen in football, are also more likely to elect to wear PKBs. In only one study were many of the potential confounding factors such as playing surface, shoe type, group assignment, compliance, and athlete exposure controlled.[20]

FOCUS ON . . .

Equipment

Equipment and facilities play important roles in injury prevention. Despite the budgetary restraints of many sports programs, it is essential that high-quality protective equipment be acquired and properly maintained. The equipment must fit correctly, be used only for the intended purpose, and either repaired or discarded when it becomes defective. Participants must be warned of the potential risks of equipment misuse or malfunction and may be required to sign informed consents. Construction or customizing of equipment must be done very carefully.

Helmets

Helmets are required for football and ice hockey players, and although they are designed to protect the head, they do not prevent injury to the cervical spine. However, changes in rules limiting the use of the head in blocking and tackling have significantly reduced neck injuries in football. Helmets must bear approval stickers from reputable testing agencies and must be fitted to the athlete by qualified personnel.

Braces

Braces are available for most joints of the body, but knee braces have received the most attention. Knee braces fall into three categories: rehabilitative (designed to provide protection and control motion during healing and rehabilitation after injury or surgery), functional (intended to stabilize ligament-deficient knees), and prophylactic (created to protect the medial compartment against valgus forces). The effectiveness of prophylactic knee braces is controversial and unproven.

Taping

Taping is used to prevent musculoskeletal injuries and as part of injury rehabilitation, but it is no substitute for sound strengthening, conditioning, and rehabilitation. Mechanically limiting excessive inversion and enhancing joint proprioception may be most useful in airborne sports such as volleyball and basketball. Applying tape correctly is a psychomotor skill acquired only with time and practice.

Because of the difficulty in establishing the usefulness of PKBs, the American Academy of Orthopaedic Surgeons (AAOS) released a position statement in 1987 stating that there was no proof of the brace's effectiveness in preventing injury.[21] The controversy continues today. The current state of affairs concerning the use of PKBs can be summarized as follows:[22]

- The efficacy of PKBs in reducing injury to the MCL remains in question.

- PKBs probably represent the least important factor influencing injury to the MCL.

- PKBs can provide 20% to 30% greater resistance to a lateral force.

- There is no evidence that PKBs put added valgus force on the knee.

- PKBs may slow sprint speed and cause early fatigue to the wearer.

Taping

Athletic taping can be used to prevent injuries to the musculoskeletal system and as an adjunct to injury rehabilita-

tion. From a preventive standpoint, the ankle joint is probably the most frequently taped body part. The advantages of applying tape to the ankle probably include a combination of some mechanical limitation of excessive inversion and enhancement of joint proprioception. These advantages would seem most important in airborne sports such as volleyball and basketball and have been seen in other activities as well.[23]

The application of athletic tape is a psychomotor skill that requires a substantial amount of time and practice before competence can be achieved.[24] At no time should tape be a substitute for sound strengthening, conditioning, and rehabilitation programs.

FACILITIES

The facilities in which athletes participate can play an important role in injury prevention. For example, more injuries leading to visits to the emergency department occur from participation in softball than in any other sport; however, the number and severity of injuries has decreased as a result of the use of breakaway bases.[25] Additional preventive measures should include deformable

TABLE 3-8
GUIDELINES FOR FITTING A FOOTBALL HELMET

1. Wet the player's hair to make the initial fit easier and more likely to assimilate playing conditions.

2. Measure the player's head approximately 1" above the eyebrow.

3. Convert the measurement in inches to hat size qand then to helmet size according to individual helmet manufacturer's specifications.

4 Make sure the helmet fits snugly around all parts of the player's head (front, side, and crown). The cheek or jaw pads should fit snugly and there should be no gaps between the pads and the head or face.

5. Make sure the helmet covers the base of the skull. The pads at the rear of the helmet should cradle the neck; however, the pads should not chafe the neck from too tight or too loose a fit.

6. The ear holes of the helmet should match the player's ears. If the helmet's ear holes are higher than the player's, then the helmet is too small or overinflated.

7. Make sure the helmet does not rotate while positioned on the head when the jaw or cheek pads are removed. Also, rotate the helmet up and down to check that the edge of the shell does not impinge on the neck. Use enough pressure to determine whether the skin on the forehead moves with the helmet.

8. For the final fit, put the helmet on and snap the chin straps. There should be no slack in the strap and the cup of the strap should fit approximately 1" (one to two finger widths) above the player's eyebrows. Try to rotate the helmet. It should not move.

(Adapted with permission from Ellis TH: Sports protective equipment. *Prim Care* 1991;18:889-921.)

walls and padded backstops and better coaching techniques that reduce player-to-player collisions.

Outdoor playing surfaces should be checked regularly for erosion, rocks, holes, and excessive moisture. Goalposts, scoring tables, and other hard objects should be padded to reduce the severity of impact injuries. Soccer goalposts that have fallen onto children have caused fatalities and catastrophic injuries.[26] Goalposts should be immobilized and immovable posts padded to reduce the severity of goalpost-player impacts.

A sound prevention program also includes the implementation of an emergency plan for the management of injuries. Facilities should be equipped with a communication system to summon emergency medical personnel, and all facilities should be accessible to emergency medical services (EMS) vehicles.

CONDITIONING IN INJURY PREVENTION

The three major components of a preseason conditioning program include flexibility, cardiovascular endurance, and strength. The value of these components should be emphasized to athletes and coaches, and they should be included as an ongoing part of every injury prevention program.

Flexibility

Optimal flexibility of the musculotendinous unit is paramount to a complete injury prevention conditioning program. Insufficient flexibility may predispose an athlete to muscle strain.[27] Stretching also increases muscle performance.[28]

The amount of flexibility necessary for safe and efficient performance varies with the demands of the sport.

Conditioning in Injury Prevention

A preseason conditioning program focuses on flexibility, cardiovascular endurance, and strength and is important to prevent injury. These components should be included as an ongoing part of every injury prevention program.

Flexibility

Flexibility demands vary among individual sports. Insufficient flexibility may render an athlete vulnerable to muscle strain. Correct stretching techniques increase muscle performance.

Types of stretching

The three primary forms of stretching are ballistic, static, and proprioceptive neuromuscular facilitation techniques. Ballistic stretching is rapid, repeated bouncing that stretches a muscle to its physiologic limit and produces a protective reflex contraction. This type of stretching is potentially injurious and should not be used. Static stretching applies tension to a lengthened muscle by contracting the agonist or by external force from gravity or a partner. The muscle is maximally stretched and held for 3 to 60 seconds without bouncing or movement. Proprioceptive neuromuscular facilitation combines alternating contraction and relaxation. The muscle is stretched to its pain-free physiologic limit, then is contracted isometrically for 10 seconds. After several seconds of relaxation, the sequence is repeated.

General recommendations for a flexibility program include teaching athletes and coaches correct techniques and encouraging their use before and after physical activity; tailoring the stretching program to the sport; preceding the sport with general warm-up activity to increase muscle temperature; stretching the target muscle to its maximum, pain-free physiologic limit; avoiding ballistic techniques; stretching statically for 10 to 30 seconds 3 to 5 times; and stretching all major muscle groups.

Endurance training

Endurance training improves cardiovascular endurance, which is the capacity to sustain prolonged exercise via efficient oxygen delivery to the working tissues. Cardiovascular endurance is measured in terms of the body's maximum ability to consume oxygen. Endurance training produces heart hypertrophy, increased stroke volume, decreased resting and submaximal exercise heart rate, increased cardiac output at maximal exercise levels, and increased blood flow to working muscles.

Endurance training also causes adaptations to the muscular system: increased number of capillaries supplying each muscle, increased muscle myoglobin content, increased size and number of mitochondria, and enhanced oxidative enzymatic activity. To produce these cardiovascular and muscular adaptations, endurance training must be of a volume and intensity that overloads the systems. Training should result in a heart rate that is 70% to 90% of the age-predicted maximum.

Strengthening

Basic strengthening principles are overload; progressive resistance; specificity; intensity, duration, frequency, and reversibility; and periodization.

Overload

The overload principle states that muscle strength, power, endurance, and hypertrophy increase only when the muscle performs workloads greater than those previously encountered. The overload principle has been incorporated into progressive resistance exercise by overloading the muscle in a progressive, gradual manner that avoids overtraining and fatigue.

Progressive resistance exercise

DeLorme's original progressive resistance exercise program was based on the 10-repetition maximum (RM), the maximum amount of weight a person can lift 10 times, and involves three sets of 10 repetitions, starting with one half the 10-RM weight. Once the individual successfully completes three sets of 10 lifts, the weight may be increased at the next training session.

(Continued)

FOCUS ON . . .

Conditioning in Injury Prevention (Continued)

Specificity

Specific adaptation to imposed demands (SAID) states that training must be relevant to the sport's demands, exercising the muscles in a way that resembles the movements performed during the activity while developing the predominant energy system. The muscles involved and the energy system must be analyzed before the program is designed.

Intensity, duration, frequency, and reversibility

Intensity is the degree of work or effort that the athlete exerts, duration is the time necessary to complete the desired exercise, and frequency is the number of workouts completed per unit of time or per week. Reversibility states that a muscle will atrophy from disuse and detrain without consistent training toward a set goal.

Periodization

Periodization is the division of the annual training plan into smaller segments, phases, or cycles. Periodization aims to improve athletic performance and prevent injury while timing the athlete's peak for the competitive season, varying exercise selection, intensity, volume, and load to decrease the possibility of overtraining. Depending on the sport, a training plan is divided into three or possibly four phases that include preparation, first transition, competition, and active rest.

Extrinsic and intrinsic risk factors

Intrinsic and extrinsic risk factors influence the occurrence of injury. Intrinsic factors are inherent in the individual's physical makeup and include previous injury, inadequate fitness or conditioning, anatomic or biomechanical variances, strength or flexibility imbalances, and illness or physiologic deficiency. Extrinsic factors are independent of the individual's physical makeup and include training errors; worn or inappropriate equipment, shoes, or clothing; environmental extremes; poor or inappropriate coaching; and improper technique. The most important environmental risk factors are heat and humidity. Heat illness most often affects individuals who are not acclimated to the weather and those who are very young, elderly, obese, unconditioned, and acutely ill. Over-the-counter cold medications, alcohol, illicit recreational drugs, heavy clothing, uniforms, and protective equipment can also interfere with heat regulation and predispose the athlete to heat illness. To prevent heat illness, athletes must replace fluids in adequate amounts. Weighing athletes before and after exercise is the best indicator of current and future fluid loss. Cold water is a good fluid replacement.

More informed and educated coaching staffs who rely on scientific and physiologic-based practices rather than tradition can prevent injuries. The athletic trainer is well suited to educate coaches regarding prevention.

For example, a wrestler or gymnast requires much greater overall body flexibility than a football player. Although some gymnasts consider themselves to be relatively inflexible, most athletes would be delighted to possess the flexibility characteristics of a gymnast.

Types of stretching

The three primary forms of stretching include ballistic, static, and proprioceptive neuromuscular facilitation techniques.[29] *Ballistic stretching* is a rapid and repeated bouncing technique that stretches a muscle to its physiologic limit. The short duration of the stretch produces a protective reflex contraction. This reflex contraction can potentially injure the muscle. Ballistic stretching is often used by athletes during unsupervised flexibility programs; however, its use is contraindicated, and it is considered the least desirable form of stretching.

In *static stretching*, tension is applied to a lengthened muscle (antagonist) by contraction of the agonist or by an external force from gravity or a partner. The muscle is placed in a position of maximum stretch and held without bouncing or movement. The duration of the stretch should be sufficient to activate the Golgi tendon organ, which will override impulses from the muscle spindle and cause relaxation of the muscle.[29] Duration of static stretching should range from 3 to 60 seconds. Results of one study indicated there is no difference in flexibility gains between 10 seconds, 20 seconds, and 30 seconds static stretching protocols, while results of another study indicated that the latter are an effective time of stretching to enhance flexibility.[30,31]

In *proprioceptive neuromuscular facilitation (PNF)* stretching techniques, some combination of alternating contraction and relaxation is used. Although many variations of the technique exist, the contract-relax technique is relatively simple and is effective in improving muscle flexibility.[32] Protocol for this technique includes stretching a muscle to its pain-free physiologic limit, followed by contracting the muscle isometrically for 10 seconds. After a few seconds of relaxation, the muscle is again stretched to its pain-free physiologic limit and held for 10 seconds. This procedure is repeated several times.

Athletes should be taught correct stretching techniques, which should then become an automatic part of any exercise program. General guidelines for a stretching program include the following:

1. Teach athletes and coaches the correct static or PNF stretching techniques and emphasize the value of using them before and after physical activity.

2. Tailor the stretching program to the needs of the sport.

3. Precede the stretching program with a period of general body warm-up activity such as light jogging or cycling to increase intramuscular temperature.

4. Make sure that the target muscle is stretched to its maximum, pain-free physiologic range without overstretching the muscle.

5. Avoid ballistic techniques.

6. Make sure the duration of the static stretch is from 10 to 30 seconds, and that the stretch is repeated 3 to 5 times.

7. Make sure that all major muscle groups, including agonists and antagonists, are stretched.

Figure 3-3 illustrates stretching techniques for the major muscle groups of the body.

Endurance Training

Endurance training produces positive adaptations to the muscular and cardiovascular systems. *Cardiovascular endurance* is the capacity to sustain prolonged bouts of exercise via the efficient delivery of oxygen to the body's working tissues. Cardiovascular endurance, also known as aerobic capacity, can be determined by measuring the body's maximal ability to consume oxygen ($VO_{2\,max}$). The adaptations to the cardiovascular system include the following:[33]

- hypertrophy of the heart and especially the left ventricle

- an increase in stroke volume

- a decrease in resting heart rate and the rate required for submaximal exercise

- an increase in cardiac output at maximal exercise levels

- an increase in blood flow to working muscles

The adaptations to the muscular system include the following:

- an increase in the number of capillaries supplying each muscle

- an increase in myoglobin content of the muscle

- an increase in the size and number of mitochondria

- enhancement of oxidative enzymatic activity

Endurance training requires a volume and intensity that sufficiently challenges the cardiovascular and muscular systems, which is known as the overload principle. An appropriate *training zone* can be determined based on an individual's maximum heart rate, which is approximately 220 beats per minute minus the person's age. The training stimulus should produce a heart rate that falls within 70% to 90% of the age-predicted maximum. For example, a 20-year-old athlete would have an age-predicted maximum heart rate of 200 beats per minute. The 70% to 90% training sensitive zone would be 140 to 180 beats per minute. Exercise producing heart rates at the lower end of the training zone would be considered moderate intensity activity. Training at the upper level of the training zone would produce greater gains in cardiovascular fitness. Cardiovascular and muscular endurance serve as the foundation for the development of sport-specific athletic fitness and skills and should be a component of every athlete's injury prevention program.[10]

Strengthening

The basic principles of strength training are overload; progressive resistance exercise; specificity; intensity, duration, frequency, and reversibility; and periodization.

Overload

Thousands of years ago, Milo of Croton began his routine by lifting a baby bull daily until it was fully grown. In the present day, the overload principle is employed similarly to develop strength and endurance in athletes. The *overload principle* states that strength, power, endurance, and hypertrophy of muscles can increase only when a muscle performs workloads greater than those previously encountered. The overload principle has been incorporated into what is now known as progressive resistance exercise.

Progressive resistance exercise

Progressive resistance exercise (PRE) was first formulated by DeLorme following World War II and is successful because it not only overloads the muscle, but it does so in a progressive, gradual manner that avoids the pitfalls of overtraining and fatigue.

DeLorme's original recommended program of progressive resistance exercise was based on the 10-repetition maximum (RM). The 10 RM is the maximum amount of weight a person can lift 10 times. DeLorme recommended lifting in three sets of 10, starting with one half

FIGURE 3-3

Correct stretching techniques should become an automatic part of any exercise program. **A** Seat straddle lotus. **B** Seat side straddle. **C** Seat forward straddle. **D** Seat stretch. **E** Leg stretch. **F** Leg crossover. **G** Knees to chest. **H** Forward lunges.

the 10-RM weight. Whenever an individual could successfully complete three sets of 10 lifts, he or she would progress to the next higher weight at the next training session.

Specificity

Specificity, also known as specific adaptation to imposed demands (SAID), is a training concept that states that training must be relevant to the demands of the sport. Training should exercise the muscles involved in the sport in a manner resembling the movements to be performed during the activity as well as develop the predominant energy system. Analysis of both the energy system and the muscles involved is necessary before a program is designed.

Intensity, duration, frequency, and reversibility

Intensity, duration, frequency, and reversibility are also terms commonly heard in relation to training. *Intensity* refers to the degree of work or effort exerted by the athlete. *Duration* is the time necessary to complete the desired exercise. *Frequency* is the number of workouts completed

per unit of time or how many workouts occur in a week. *Reversibility* states that a muscle will atrophy from disuse and detrain if it is not consistently trained toward a set goal.

Periodization

Periodization refers to the concept of dividing the annual training plan into smaller segments, phases, or cycles. This cycle-type of training appears to have originated in the Soviet Union during the 1950s. The goal of periodization is to improve athletic performance and prevent injury while allowing the athlete to peak during the competitive season rather than during a training phase.

Periodization varies exercise selection, intensity, volume, and load and helps to decrease the possibility of overtraining. Depending on the sport, a yearly training cycle normally can be divided into three or possibly four phases. A three-phase training cycle would consist of a preseason or preparatory phase, an in-season or competitive phase, and a postseason or transition phase. Matveyev's four-phase training cycle consists of a preparation phase, a first transition, a competition phase, and a second transition (active rest) [34] (**Figure 3-4**).

The preseason or preparatory phase is marked by high-volume, low-intensity workouts that focus on proper exercise technique and provide a foundation for later training. Sometimes the preparatory phase is divided into generalized and specialized phases. Strength-building exercises are introduced in the generalized preseason conditioning phase, and exercises more closely duplicating actual playing skills are employed in the specialized preseason phase. The specialized preseason phase shifts into higher-intensity workouts with lower volumes of work. In sports that are primarily anaerobic, power and strength workouts are introduced in the second half of the preseason phase, which is the first transition in the four-phase model.

As the in-season or competition phase approaches, more emphasis is placed on power workouts. For a generally anaerobic sport, anaerobic endurance should be emphasized. The overload principle is appropriate for this type of anaerobic workout.

During the in-season, or competition phase, focus is on technique during an event, bringing performance to its peak. Peak performance is maintained by high-intensity technique exercises during brief workouts. The goal during this phase is to maintain a level of intensity sufficient to prevent retrogression but not enough to lead to overtraining.

The postseason or transition phase, which corresponds with the second transition in the four-phase model, begins the termination of the competition season. This period is one of active rest in which the athlete engages in recreational physical activity so that a psychological, as well as a physiologic, break from competition occurs. Active rest consists of low-volume and low- to moderate-intensity work, which allows the athlete enough time to heal physically and to recover emotionally. **Figure 3-5** shows a periodization model for swimmers, and **Figure 3-6** shows a periodization model for wrestlers. Periodization models should also be created for track and field throwers, football players, pole vaulters, soccer and ice hockey players.

Extrinsic and Intrinsic Risk Factors

The occurrence of injury is influenced by risk factors, which can be divided into extrinsic and intrinsic factors. *Intrinsic risk factors* are inherent in the physical makeup of the individual. *Extrinsic risk factors* are those factors that are independent of the individual's physical makeup. The greatest intrinsic risk factor for developing a specific

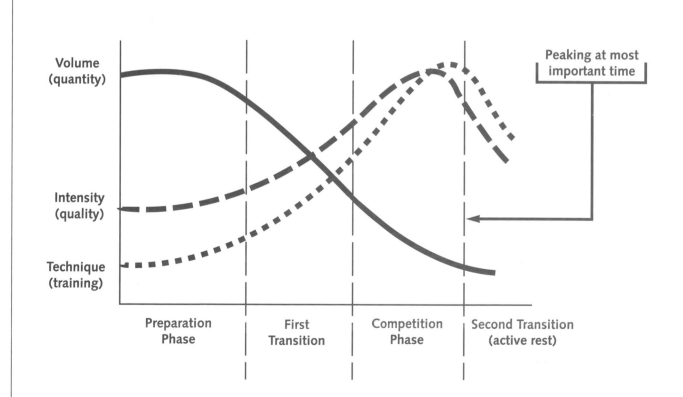

FIGURE 3-4

Periodization divides an annual training plan into smaller segments to improve athletic performance and prevent injury. Exercise selection, intensity, volume, and load are varied to help decrease the possibility of overtraining. (Reproduced with permission from the National Strength Conditioning Association, Lincoln, Nebraska.)

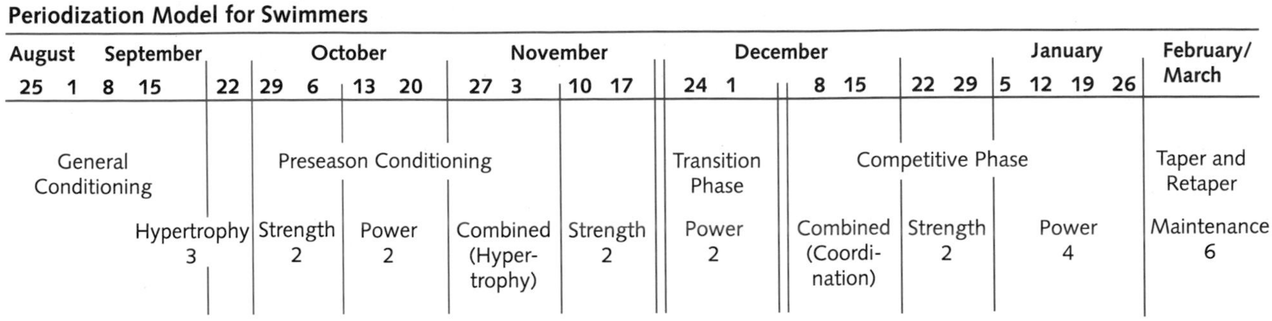

Periodization Model for Swimmers

August	September				October				November				December				January				February/March
25	1	8	15	22	29	6	13	20	27	3	10	17	24	1	8	15	22	29	5	12 19 26	
General Conditioning					Preseason Conditioning								Transition Phase		Competitive Phase						Taper and Retaper
		Hypertrophy 3		Strength 2		Power 2			Combined (Hyper-trophy)		Strength 2		Power 2		Combined (Coordi-nation)		Strength 2		Power 4		Maintenance 6

FIGURE 3-5

Different phases of a periodization model help swimmers improve athletic performance. (Reproduced with permission from Uebel R: Weight training for swimmers: A practical approach. Nat Strength Training Cond Assoc J 1987;3.)

injury is a history of previous injury. Other intrinsic risk factors include inadequate fitness or conditioning, anatomic or biomechanical variances, strength or flexibility imbalances, and illness or physiologic deficiency. Among extrinsic risk factors, training errors (too much, too fast, too soon) are the most frequently encountered. Training may be divided into three parameters: duration (too much), intensity (too fast), and frequency (too soon). Proper duration of a workout depends on the demands and fitness profile of the sport involved, but is kept generally at 1 hour. Intensity refers to the magnitude of the workout, tending toward anaerobic endurance. Intensity is the aspect of training that most affects performance improvement but also produces the most injuries. Frequency refers to the rate at which a workout occurs, such as three times a week, daily, or twice a day. To avoid injury, training should gradually increase generally no more than 10% per week in one or all of the training parameters. Pain and stiffness lasting more than 24 to 48 hours probably indicates overtraining. Other extrinsic risk factors include worn or inappropriate equipment, shoes, or clothing; environmental extremes; poor or inappropriate coaching; and improper technique.

No environmental risk factors are more significant than heat and humidity. Heatstroke is a true medical emergency that can usually be prevented. Individuals most susceptible to heat illness include those who are not acclimated to the weather, the very young, the elderly, the obese, the unconditioned, and the acutely ill. Many over-the-counter cold medications, alcohol, and illicit recreational drugs also interfere with heat regulation and predispose the athlete to heat illness. High temperature and humidity significantly affect the body's ability to control heat dissipation. Heavy clothing, uniforms, and protective equipment also compromise the body's ability to dissipate heat. Helmets are especially at fault because much of the body's heat dissipation occurs at the head. A comprehensive discussion about heat illness and thermal regulation is beyond the scope of this chapter, but it is nevertheless important for the athletic trainer to have a working knowledge of thermal regulation and illness. An athlete routinely sweats 1 to 2 L per hour during intense exercise in the heat. The most important factor in preventing heat illness is fluid replacement. Thirst is not a good indicator of fluid loss and the athlete must be reminded to drink every 15 to 20 minutes. Weighing oneself before and after exercise is the best indicator of fluid loss (1 L of water weighs nearly 1 lb) and is also a reliable method of estimating future fluid needs for exercise in similar conditions. For exercise sessions that last less than 4 hours, cold water is the best fluid replacement.

Recently, several collegiate wrestlers died while "making weight," which typically consists of the practice of water and nutrition deprivation combined with prolonged, intense exercise in a vinyl suit. This practice is dangerous and should be discouraged. In addition, the use of laxatives and diuretics to achieve similar goals should be condemned.

Poor coaching and improper techniques are other extrinsic risk factors. As coaching staffs become more informed and educated, scientific- and physiologic-based practices are gradually replacing many outdated and dangerous practices, such as withholding water during practice. Nevertheless, traditions fall hard and many unsafe practices are perpetuated through the "this is how we did it when I played" mentality. Those who are especially vulnerable to this type of thinking are the 2.5 million adults who volunteer annually to coach approximately 38 million youth in various sports teams. Too often, these volunteers' admirable dedication is matched with an equal amount of ignorance of sound scientific-based coaching techniques and practices. Although several national training programs for beginning coaches exist, an estimated 90% of all volunteers who coach youth sports have no formal education in coaching techniques, first aid, or injury prevention or care. This lack of training and education in

Periodization Model for Wrestlers

Off season I
Dates   June-August
Goal   Develop strength and power with emphasis on the legs, hips, and pulling muscles in the upper body.
Training Days   4 days per week.
Type of Training   Power training is conducted involving full body explosive lifts, such as power cleans, squats, push press, and weighted pull-ups. Rest between sets is 2-3 minutes.

Transition I
Dates   1 week
Goal   Allow the body and mind to recover from the previous mesocycle.
Type of training   Rest.

Off-season II
Dates   September-October
Goal   Same as I
Training Days   3 days per week.
Type of Training   Similar to I. Possibly substitute exercise with ones that are different but develop the same muscle groups.

Transition II
Dates   1 week
Goal   Allow the body and mind to recover from the previous mesocycle.
Type of Training   Wrestling drills with no weight training.

Preseason
Dates   November-December
Goal   Maintain strength and power developed during the off-season.
Training Days   2 days per week.
Type of Training   Similar to that used during the off-season with greater emphasis placed on technique work and exercise specificity.

Transition III
Dates   1 week during Christmas break.
Goal   Allow the body and mind to recover from training.
Type of Training   Wrestling drills and practice with no weight training.

In-season (Lactic Acid)
Dates   January-Mid February
Goal   Acclimate the body to the excessive amounts of lactic acid encountered during wrestling competitions.
Training Days   2 days per week.
Type of Training   The exercises are preexhaustive in nature; that is, a single joint exercise is immediately followed by a multiple joint exercise. Time between the single and multiple joint exercises is no more than 3 seconds, while the rest between sets is approximately 2 minutes. All sets are burnouts.

In-season (Circuit)
Dates   Mid February-March
Goal   To physically peak the wrestlers in muscular strength, endurance, and conditioning.
Training Days   2-3 days per week.
Type of Training   A circuit of 12 exercises is completed with the work/rest ratio of 45 sec/15 sec. After completing one set of the circuit, anaerobic running is performed followed by another set of the circuit.

Active rest
Dates   April-May
Goal   Restore the athlete's body and mind to rested conditions following the long competitive season.
Training Days   2-3 days per week.
Type of Training   Very light technique work on wrestling skills, along with participation in several recreational games.

FIGURE 3-6

A periodization model can help wrestlers improve performance and avoid overtraining. (Reproduced with permission from Palmieri G: Roundtable: Periodization, Part 3. Nat Strength Training Cond Assoc J 1987;9.)

coaches is a problem that is well suited for the athletic trainer to address. Common belief is that the quality of the youth sports experience is related directly to the quality of the adult supervision, specifically that of the coach.

PEDIATRIC SPORTS

Although participation in organized sports of some type is common, fewer than half of the nation's youth participate in an organized sport. The Surgeon General's recent report on physical activity and health documents the benefits of exercise in promoting health and well being, including decreased body fat, improved cardiovascular risk factors, increased self-esteem, reduced stress and anxiety, and improved fitness. However, the typical American youth does not exercise vigorously enough during the day to meet the criteria for aerobic fitness. Prevalence of excessive weight among adolescents has risen 6% in the last 15 years, from 15% to 21%.[35] Current fitness levels in the youth population are lower than in previous decades, a pattern that does not appear to be reversing as computer technology, video games, and television viewing command more of the youth's attention in this country.

The quality of the youth sport experience is in large part governed by the abilities of the adult supervision, especially those of the coach. Although society is indebted to the estimated 2.5 million adults who volunteer as coaches, the overwhelming majority of these volunteers have no formal training in technique, injury prevention, or care of injuries.[36]

Children are not miniature adults. There are major physical, psychological, emotional, social, and physiologic differences between children and adults. Physiologically, children have a reduced sweating capacity and a greater surface area-to-weight ratio, making them less tolerant of heat and more prone to heat illnesses. Emotionally, children typically are less concerned with top conditioning than with having fun. Psychologically, winning is less important to children than it is to adults. Surveys indicate that children would rather play on a losing team than a winning team if it meant more playing time.

In the preadolescent athlete, skill acquisition, technique training, and the enjoyment of sport and exercise should be emphasized. Intense, demanding workouts, which are considered essential for optimal performance in the adult world, can be detrimental in the pediatric world. Results of multiple studies support the contention that arduous, strenuous, and overly intense training in the pediatric population has no justifiable physiologic, psychological, or sociologic benefit.

Preadolescents have not fully developed the cognitive maturity to incorporate many aspects of competition that adults take for granted. The desire to compare skills, the role of an individual in a cooperative team process, and the ability to understand another's point of view are prerequisite to healthy competition. These psychological attributes are not developed until ages 8 to 10 years. Introducing preadolescents prematurely to an organized sports program that emphasizes competition and winning may contribute to frustration, discouragement, and low self-esteem.[37]

Because an active life offers abundant physical, psychological, and emotional benefits, emphasis at an early age should be directed toward participating, acquiring skill,

and enjoying the sport. The value of strength training in the pediatric population has been debated for years, but the consensus of many professional organizations suggests that properly supervised and instructed children can participate in an organized strength training program without adverse affect. **Table 3-9** lists the American College of Sports Medicine's recommendations and guidelines for strength training in children.[38]

THE FEMALE ATHLETE

During the last quarter century, opportunities for the female athlete have grown significantly. The passage of Title IX to the Education Amendments Act of 1972, enabled the female athlete's participation in organized sports to grow tenfold while male participation has remained the same or dropped.[39]

The increased opportunity and participation in women's sports paralleled an increased appreciation of the female athlete. A host of female athletes in a variety of sports were introduced to the nation at the 1996 Olympic Games in Atlanta. Gymnastics, softball, soccer, track and field, basketball, volleyball, and cycling were among the sports that gave generations of young female athletes role models to emulate. An increased interest in and opportunity for participation in sports for young female athletes was noted in the period following the 1996 Olympics, particularly in those sports that were highlighted by the media. Participation rates in women's sports still trails that of men; however, the rates are improving steadily. Girls tend to enter youth sports at a later age than boys (mean age of initial participation: girls, age 10 years; boys, age 8 years).

Girls also drop out of youth sports at a higher rate than boys, particularly in those sports that mandate co-ed participation. However, the greatest gender disparity lies in coaching and supervision of youth sports; 90% of the positions are held by men. Women in coaching and supervisory positions serve as teachers, mentors, and role models for the young female athlete, an important consideration to any young athlete.

Although participation in women's sports has improved, the change has not come without difficulty. Many decisions regulating participation of female athletes in sports were based on cultural bias and public opinion. Collected data were often incomplete, anecdotal, poorly controlled, or inaccurate. Consequently, many myths about the female athlete evolved and some still linger. At one time, female athletes were thought to be too frail to participate in strenuous exercise and were excluded from most endurance and contact sports. The 800-meter race for female participants was added to the 1928 Olympics for the first time. Given only 3 weeks to prepare, nine of 14 participants did not complete the race as a result of exhaustion. Because of this, long distance competition for women was barred until the 1984 Olympics when the marathon was added. Data from modern marathons show

FOCUS ON . . .

Pediatric Sports

Despite the many benefits of physical activity, most youth in the United States fail to exercise sufficiently to achieve aerobic fitness, and obesity among adolescents has increased in recent years. Children are physically, psychologically, emotionally, socially, and physiologically different from adults. The preadolescent athlete should focus on acquiring skills, training for technique, and enjoying sport and exercise. Intense, demanding workouts are unnecessary and can be detrimental to these athletes. Emphasizing competition and winning in young athletes may result in frustration, discouragement, and low self-esteem.

TABLE 3-9
ACSM'S GUIDELINES FOR EXERCISE TESTING AND PRESCRIPTION

- No matter how big, strong, or mature a young man or woman appears, remember that he or she is physiologically immature.

- Teach proper training techniques for all exercise movements involved in the program and proper breathing techniques (eg, no breath holding).

- Stress that exercise should be performed in a manner in which the speed is controlled, avoiding ballistic (fast and jerky) movements.

- Under no circumstances should a weight be used that allows less than eight repetitions to be completed per set; heavy weights can be potentially dangerous and damaging to the developing skeleton and joint structures. It is *not* recommended that resistance exercise be performed to the point of momentary muscular fatigue.

- As a training effect occurs, achieve an overload initially by increasing the number of repetitions, and then by increasing the absolute resistance.

- Perform one to two sets of eight to 10 different exercises (with 8 to 12 reps per set), ensuring that all of the major muscle groups are included.

- Limit strength-training sessions to twice a week and encourage children and adolescents to seek other forms of physical activity.

- Perform full-range, multijoint exercises (as opposed to single-joint exercises)

- Do not overload the skeletal and joint structures of adolescents with maximal weights.

- Most importantly, all strength-training activities should be closely supervised and monitored by appropriately trained personnel.

(Adapted with permission from Kenney WL, Humphrey RH, Bryant CX, Mahler DA (eds): *ACSM's Guidelines for Exercise Testing and Prescription*, ed 5. Baltimore, MD, Williams & Wilkins, 1995.)

FOCUS ON . . .

The Female Athlete

The participation of women in organized sports has increased dramatically. Girls tend to begin youth sports at approximately age 10 years, compared with age 8 years in boys, and they tend to drop out of sports at a higher rate than boys. At this time, most coaches and supervisors of youth sports are men, but it is important for women to serve as teachers, mentors, and role models for young female athletes.

Although, in the past, female sport participants sustained more injuries than their male counterparts, as conditioning for female athletes has improved, their injury rates have approached those of male athletes in the same sport. However, there are certain injuries for which female athletes remain at higher risk, including noncontact anterior cruciate ligament injuries, patellofemoral pain, carpal tunnel syndrome, lateral epicondylitis, and posterior tibial tendinitis. The underlying reasons for these higher incidences of injury are not yet clear and must be investigated in well-designed epidemiologic studies and multivariate analysis.

that women who are equally prepared as men compete in marathons with equal risk of injury as men.[40]

Results of early studies involving military training revealed that female recruits were injured as much as ten times more frequently than their male counterparts.[40] However, these early studies did not control for fitness, preparation, or other nongender-related risk factors. Results of later studies that did control for these risk factors show a much less dramatic difference in the injury rates of male and female military recruits.[41]

In the past, common belief was that all knee injuries in the exercising woman were of a patellofemoral origin. Expanding participation by female athletes in interscholastic and intercollegiate sports has shown that female athletes sustain the same injuries as male athletes. Female athletes appear to have a higher injury rate for some injuries, most notably noncontact ACL injuries. Explanations for this observation range from estrogen/progesterone influences of menstruation to a smaller intercondylar notch width, pelvis width, valgus knee, and size of the ACL. Other injuries that may be gender based include patellofemoral pain, carpal tunnel syndrome, lateral epicondylitis, and posterior tibial tendinitis; however, these observations must be studied systematically to identify risk factors. Well-designed epidemiologic studies and multivariate analysis are necessary to delineate gender differences and risk factors. Only then will it be possible to institute preventive measures to avoid injury, including regulatory and athletic policy. To eliminate mistakes made in the past, athletic policy and regulation must be based on objective, well-founded, scholarly, and scientific information.

CHAPTER REVIEW

Despite the medical system's traditional emphasis on the diagnosis and treatment of illness and injury, preventive efforts have been responsible for most of the improvements in our national healthcare morbidity and mortality statistics. Exercise is a common denominator in most health promotion initiatives. The relatively new focus on prevention, along with the emergence of managed care and the broadening of the athletic trainer's target population to include healthy individuals, will increase the athletic trainer's role in the healthcare system.

Models of health care include the disease model and the prevention model. The disease model focuses on the diagnosis and treatment of injury and illness. The consumer accesses the healthcare system only when symptoms occur, and resolution of symptoms is deemed curative. The healthcare provider is the primary medical practitioner. The prevention model takes a more proactive, multidisciplinary approach that emphasizes function and performance over symptoms. Functional deficits are identified and corrected before symptoms develop. Primary responsibility for the consumer's health care rests with the individual rather than the provider.

A standardized, focused, and directed preparticipation physical examination is an opportunity for the team physician and athletic trainer to identify structural, biomechanical, and physiologic deficits in the athlete that may be correctable before the season begins. Often required to fulfill insurance and legal requirements, the exam should take place 6 to 12 weeks before the sport's season and can be conducted either in a private office setting or in the group multiple-station setting. The multiple-station format includes stations devoted to the athlete's medical history; vital signs; head, ear, eyes, nose, and throat; cardiovascular, respiratory, and gastrointestinal systems and musculoskeletal system.

Environmental factors that can help to prevent injury include proper supervision, appropriate coaching, provision of medical care by qualified personnel, and adherence to the sport's rules. Equipment and facility modifications also play important roles in injury prevention. An emergency management plan is essential in the event of an injury.

Conditioning comprises flexibility, cardiovascular endurance, and strength training. Flexibility can be achieved safely through static stretching or proprioceptive neuromuscular facilitation. Based on the overload principle, endurance training promotes cardiovascular and muscular adaptations. Strengthening is also based on overload, which involves manipulating such factors as progressive resistance exercise; specificity; intensity, duration, frequency, and reversibility; and periodization. Intrinsic factors (for example, previous injury) and extrinsic risk factors (such as training errors) must be evaluated and addressed.

Pediatric athletes require proper training and supervision to participate in sports. Appropriate conditioning is just as important for female athletes as it is for male athletes. In general, female athletes sustain the same injuries as male athletes in a particular sport, but there are certain injuries to which female athletes appear more vulnerable. The results of ongoing epidemiologic studies may aid in the development of prevention programs to reduce the risk of injury.

1. Which of the following is the primary factor in health promotion of the healthy population?
   A. Exercise
   B. Cancer treatment
   C. Antibiotic therapy
   D. Hypertension control

2. Averting a major injury through early, accurate detection of a minor injury is known as:
   A. the disease model.
   B. the reactive approach.
   C. primary prevention.
   D. secondary prevention.

3. The physiologic profile testing of the preparticipation physical examination should be tailored to the:
   A. specific sport.
   B. physical setting.
   C. legal requirements.
   D. athlete's fitness level.

4. Which of the following is a test for anaerobic endurance?
   A. Sit-reach test
   B. 40-yard dash
   C. Vertical jump
   D. Medicine ball throw

5. Safe participation in sports is based on:
   A. aggressive coaching.
   B. minimal supervision.
   C. limiting changes in rules.
   D. available, qualified medical personnel.

6. The development of the helmet-face mask combination for ice hockey players has had which of the following effects on facial and catastrophic neck injury rates?
   A. Facial and catastrophic neck injury rates have decreased.
   B. Facial and catastrophic neck injury rates have remained unchanged.
   C. Facial injuries have decreased and catastrophic neck injuries have increased.
   D. Facial injuries have increased and catastrophic neck injury rates have decreased.

7. Which of the following techniques involves a rapid, repeated bouncing that forces a muscle to its physiologic limit?
   A. Static stretching
   B. Ballistic stretching
   C. Progressive resistance
   D. Proprioceptive neuromuscular facilitation

8. Which of the following terms represents the degree of work or effort exerted by the athlete?
   A. Intensity
   B. Duration
   C. Frequency
   D. Reversibility

9. Which periodization phase is characterized by an emphasis on power workouts or anaerobic endurance?
   A. Preparatory
   B. First transition
   C. Competition
   D. Second transition

10. Which of the following risk factors is extrinsic for injury?
    A. Previous injury
    B. Strength imbalance
    C. Improper technique
    D. Inadequate conditioning

Answers on page 891

References

1. Cantu RC (ed): *ACSM's Guidelines for the Team Physician: Vol 5. Rehabilitation and Return to Competition* [videotape]. Baltimore, MD, Williams & Wilkins, 1993.

2. Kibler WB: A framework for sports medicine. *Phys Med Rehab Clin North Am* 1994;5:1.

3. Ryan AJ: Editorial: Qualifying exams: A continuing dilemma. *Phys Sportsmed* 1980;8:10.

4. Risser WL, Hoffman HM, Bellah GG Jr, Green LW: A cost-benefit analysis of preparticipation sports examinations of adolescent athletes. *J Sch Health* 1985;55:270-273.

5. Fuller CM, McNulty CM, Spring DA, et al: Prospective screening of 5,615 high school athletes for risk of sudden cardiac death. *Med Sci Sports Exerc* 1997;29:1131-1138.

6. Cantu RC (ed): *ACSM's Guidelines for the Team Physician: Vol 2. The Musculoskeletal Preparticipation Examination* [videotape]. Baltimore, MD, Williams & Wilkins, 1993.

7. American Academy of Family Physicians, American Medical Society for Sports Medicine, American Orthopaedic Society for Sports Medicine, American Osteopathic Academy of Sports Medicine: *Preparticipation Physical Evaluation*, ed 2. Minneapolis, MN, 1997.

8. Hara JH, Puffer JC: The preparticipation physical examination, in Mellion MB, Walsh WM, Shelton GL (eds): *The Team Physician's Handbook*, ed 2. Philadelphia, PA, Hanley & Belfus, 1997, pp 295.

9. American Academy of Pediatrics, Committee on Sports Medicine: Recommendations for participation in competitive sports. *Pediatrics* 1988;81:737-739.

10. Kibler WB, Chandler TJ: Sport-specific conditioning. *Am J Sports Med* 1994;22:424-432.

11. Beaulieu JE: Developing a stretching program. *Phys Sportsmed* 1981;9:59-69.

12. Micheli LJ (ed): *The Sports Medicine Bible: Prevent, Detect, and Treat Your Sports Injuries Through the Latest Medical Techniques*. New York, NY, Harper Perennial, 1995, p 24.

13. Silver JR, Silver DD, Godfrey JJ: Trampolining injuries of the spine. *Injury* 1986;17:117-124.

14. Fountain JL, Meyers MC: Skateboarding injuries. *Sports Med* 1996;22:360-366.

15. Ellis TH: Sports protective equipment. *Prim Care* 1991;18:889-921.

16. Murray TM, Livingston LA: Hockey helmets, face masks, and injurious behavior. *Pediatrics* 1995;95:419-421.

17. Bir CA, Cassatta SJ, Janda DH: An analysis and comparison of soccer shin guards. *Clin J Sport Med* 1995;5:95-99.

18. Porter M, O'Brien M: The "Buy-Max" mouthguard: Oral, peri-oral and cerebral protection for contact sports. *J Ir Dent Assoc* 1994;40:98-101.

19. Livingston LA, Forbes SL: Eye injuries in women's lacrosse: Strict rule enforcement and mandatory eyewear required. *J Trauma* 1996;40:144-145.

20. Sitler M, Ryan J, Hopkinson W, et al: The efficacy of a prophylactic knee brace to reduce knee injuries in football: A prospective, randomized study at West Point. *Am J Sports Med* 1990;18:310-315.

21. Position Statement: The Use of Knee Braces. Park Ridge, IL, American Academy of Orthopaedic Surgeons, October 1987.

22. Albright JP, Saterbak A, Stokes J: Use of knee braces in sport: Current recommendations. *Sports Med* 1995;20:281-301.

23. Firer P: Effectiveness of taping for the prevention of ankle ligament sprains. *Br J Sports Med* 1990;24:47-50.

24. Perrin DH (ed): *Athletic Taping and Bracing*. Champaign, IL, Human Kinetics, 1995.

25. Janda DH, Wild DE, Hensinger RN: Softball injuries: Aetiology and prevention. *Sports Med* 1992;13:285-291.

26. Janda DH, Bir C, Wild B, Olson S, Hensinger RN: Goal post injuries in soccer: A laboratory and field testing analysis of a preventive intervention. *Am J Sports Med* 1995;23:340-344.

27. Safran MR, Seaber AV, Garrett WE Jr: Warm-up and muscular injury prevention: An update. *Sports Med* 1989;8:239-249.

28. Worrell TW, Smith TL, Winegardner J: Effect of hamstring stretching on hamstring muscle performance. *J Orthop Sports Phys Ther* 1994;20:154-159.

29. Shellock FG, Prentice WE: Warming-up and stretching for improved physical performance and prevention of sports-related injuries. *Sports Med* 1985;2:267-278.

30. Borms J, Van Roy P, Santens JP, Haentjens A: Optimal duration of static stretching exercises for improvement of coxo-femoral flexibility. *J Sports Sci* 1987;5:39-47.

31. Bandy WD, Irion JM: The effect of time on static stretch on the flexibility of the hamstring muscles. *Phys Ther* 1994;74:845-852.

32. Wallin D, Ekblom B, Grahn R, Nordenborg T: Improvement of muscle flexibility: A comparison between two techniques. *Am J Sports Med* 1985;13:263-268.

33. Wilmore JH, Costill DL (eds): *Physiology of Sport and Exercise*. Champaign, IL, Human Kinetics, 1994.

34. L. Matveyev: 1972. Periodisierang des sportlichen training. Berlin: Berles & Wernitz. Reprinted in Roundtable: "Periodization, Part 3,: *National Strength and Conditioning Association Journal 9*, no 3 (1987).

35. National Health and Nutrition Examination Survey, 1988-94. Hyattsville, Maryland; US Department of Health and Human Services, Public Health Service, CDC, 1994; DHHS publication no. (PHS)92-1387.

36. Kimiecik JC: Who needs coaches' education? US coaches do. *Phys Sportsmed* 1988;16:124-136.

37. President's Council on Physical Fitness and Sports Research Digest, Sept 1997;2:11.

38. Kenney WL, Humphrey RH, Bryant CX, Mahler DA (eds): *ACSM's Guidelines for Exercise Testing and Prescription*, ed 5. Baltimore, MD, Williams & Wilkins, 1995, p 225.

39. *Athletics Participation Survey*. Kansas City, MO, National Federation of State High School Associations, 1995.

40. Jones BH: American Running and Fitness Association Annual Sports Medicine Meeting, Bethesda, MD, October 1997.

41. Jones BH, Hansen BC (eds): *Injuries in the Military: A Hidden Epidemic*. Falls Church, VA, Directorate of Epidemiology and Disease Surveillance, Armed Forces, 1996.

2

Basic Concepts

Section Editor
Kevin M. Guskiewicz, PhD, ATC

techniques can be conducted on an as-needed basis following the clinical evaluation.

THE SUBJECTIVE EVALUATION PHASE

The subjective phase of the evaluation lays the foundation for the objective phase. During the subjective phase, the athlete provides the information, giving impressions regarding time, mechanism of injury, and site of injury. Attitude and emotion may influence this information, so the evaluator must react calmly. A previously established, trusting relationship between the athlete and evaluator may be helpful in this part of the evaluation process. If the athlete is unable to speak, witnesses may have to provide necessary details of the injury.

The evaluator uses the results of a careful and complete subjective evaluation, consisting of history, symptoms, and analyzing results, to plan a comprehensive objective evaluation, which will include the appropriate subphases.

History

The subjective phase begins with an interview with the athlete to determine the history of the present complaint. The athlete may be experiencing pain or discomfort, an inability or decreased ability to perform a movement or skill, concern about a previous injury or surgery, or any atypical sign or symptom that affects the body or performance. The athlete should try to isolate the problem to as small an area as possible, using one finger to point to the problem area. However, if the problem is systemic, this type of distinction may not be possible.[3] Symptoms

---

FOCUS ON . . .

The Subjective Evaluation Phase

The subjective evaluation phase focuses on the athlete's impressions (or those of witnesses if the athlete is unable to speak) of the time, mechanism and site of injury, and is conducted with easily understood terminology rather than scientific or medical jargon.

History

The evaluator interviews the athlete to determine the history of the complaint, including pain or discomfort, inability or reduced ability to perform a movement or skill, concern about a previous injury or surgery, and any unusual sign or symptom. Asking the athlete to point to the problem area with one finger can be helpful if the condition is localized, but many musculoskeletal problems are associated with poorly localized symptoms. The primary symptoms should be determined along with the area of involvement. Information about how the injury occurred; what happened, when, and where; and whether or not a specific incident caused the injury to occur comprises a complete history.

The subjective phase should be conducted in an orderly fashion with nonleading, open-ended questions. During this phase, the evaluator should also ask about any pertinent medical and family history.

Behavior of symptoms

The behavior of symptoms (general behavior, particular behavior, special behavior, duration of symptoms, and history of symptoms) is determined next. General behavior of the symptom deals with whether the symptom is present during rest or activity, during a certain time of day, and whether it fluctuates in intensity. An example of particular behavior is whether a type or speed of movement reproduces the symptoms. Special behavior can include dizziness, tingling, giving out, popping, or clicking. Duration of the symptom is how long the symptoms last. Asking the history of symptoms allows the athlete to tell what happened and if the injury is new or recurring (and if the latter, whether it has been managed successfully in the past).

Pain is the most commonly reported symptom of athletic injury. The mnemonic PQRST reminds the evaluator to obtain details about the provocation or cause of the pain (P), quality or description of the pain (Q), region of the pain (R), severity of the pain (S), and time the pain occurs or recurs (T). These descriptions can provide important clues regarding the athlete's condition. In addition, pain can be deep and dull (and thus, hard to localize) or referred (felt in an area away from the source of the injury).

Analyzing results

Once the history and behavior of symptoms have been investigated, the evaluator should analyze the results, determine the possible condition(s) that may be related to the subjective complaints, and plan the objective phase.

---

of greatest importance to the athlete should be determined.[2] During this interview, the evaluator should use easily understood questions and terminology and avoid using scientific and medical jargon. A complete history includes information about how the injury occurred, what happened, when it happened, where it happened, and whether or not a specific incident caused the injury to occur. The evaluator must also identify the area of involvement, or the provoked tissue.[1] Although the idea of attempting to identify the area of involvement may seem to be elementary, it is a necessary step because many musculoskeletal conditions appear to have poorly localized symptoms.

The subjective phase of the evaluation should be carried out in an orderly sequence and can begin with a question to the athlete about how the injury occurred. If the athlete responds that the injury occurred suddenly, the evaluator can then ask if there was an incident that brought about the injury. If this is the case, the evaluator should ask the athlete to describe the incident so that the evaluator can establish a mechanism of injury. This line of questioning would continue until the evaluator feels that all pertinent information was obtained. As in any good history, the evaluator should be cautious not to lead the athlete's answers. Early questions should be open ended. For example, the question, "Does throwing affect your pain?" would be a better choice than "Does throwing increase your pain?" An open-ended question allows the athlete to make a decision about the answer rather than leading the athlete to an answer. **Table 4-2** presents several pertinent questions that the evaluator can ask the athlete in the subjective phase of the evaluation. In addition to determining the history of the current injury, the evaluator should

---

TABLE 4-3
THE FIVE COMPONENTS OF THE BEHAVIOR OF SYMPTOMS

1. General behavior (When the symptom occurs and whether intensity fluctuates)

2. Particular behavior (Whether type or speed of movement reproduces the symptom)

3. Special behavior (Whether dizziness, tingling, giving out, popping, or clicking are present)

4. Duration of symptoms (How long the symptoms last)

5. History of symptoms (The athlete's statement of what happened and whether or not it has happened before)

---

always ask about any pertinent medical and family history during this phase. Additional history questions can be asked as needed throughout the evaluation process.

Symptoms

The second part of the subjective phase of the evaluation involves exploring the behavior of the important symptoms determined in the history. **Table 4-3** presents the five components that make up the behavior of the symptoms.

Identifying the general behavior of the symptom consists of determining whether the symptom is present during rest or activity, during the morning, afternoon, or evening, and whether the symptom appears to fluctuate in intensity. To identify the particular behavior of the symptom, the evaluator tries to determine its cause, for example, whether a type or speed of movement reproduces the symptoms. To identify special behavior, the evaluator must find out whether the athlete experiences dizziness, tingling, giving out, popping, or clicking. Duration of the symptom is determined by finding out how long the symptom lasts when provoked. The evaluator determines the history of the symptom by asking the athlete how the symptoms changed over time; for example, the athlete may tell the evaluator that he or she first heard a loud popping sound followed later by a click in the joint. During this part of the evaluation, the evaluator may ask whether the injury is new or recurring and, if recurring, whether it has been managed successfully in the past. While conducting this phase, the evaluator must be aware of symptoms that relate to a variety of common athletic injuries.

The most commonly reported symptom relative to athletic injury is pain, but pain may be particularly elusive

---

TABLE 4-2
PERTINENT QUESTIONS FOR THE SUBJECTIVE PHASE OF EVALUATION

What part of your body did you injure?

What sport do you play?

Did the injury occur slowly or suddenly?

What do you think caused the injury?

Was there an incident that led to the injury?

Is this a new injury, or has it happened before?

Was the injured area taped or braced?

Can you describe your pain?

and difficult to describe. For this reason, details regarding the pain should be obtained. The *PQRST* mnemonic (P = provocation or cause of the pain, Q = quality or description of the pain, R = region of the pain, S = severity of the pain, and T = time the pain occurs or recurs) provides the evaluator with an easy to remember guide of the descriptive information needed. Often, the quality and behavior of the pain will give the evaluator important clues to the athlete's condition, so careful attention should be paid to this part of the evaluation.

Determining the region of the pain may be difficult, for the deeper and duller the pain, the harder it is to localize. In addition, referred pain, which is pain that is felt in an area away from the source of injury, is commonly seen in musculoskeletal injuries. For example, an athlete may report pain in the area of the hamstrings but be unable to describe a history that is commensurate with the symptoms. The evaluator may be unable to document any signs of injury to the immediate area; however, the evaluator should suspect damage to a nearby joint or the nerve root that innervates the painful area.

Analyzing Results

After the evaluator has completed the history and behavior of symptoms portions of the subjective evaluation, he or she should analyze the results of the subjective evaluation. Asking, "What does this information mean, and what are the possible explanations for these results?" will help the evaluator determine what possible condition or conditions may be related to this pattern of subjective complaints. The evaluator should then plan the objective phase of the evaluation to clarify and differentiate the possible sources of the athlete's complaints and select the appropriate objective procedures and tests.

THE OBJECTIVE EVALUATION PHASE

Observation and Inspection

The first subphase of the objective evaluation consists of carefully observing and inspecting the injured athlete. The evaluator focuses attention on the athlete's overall appearance and to the specific regions of the body that were identified in the subjective phase of the evaluation as being related to the primary symptoms.

Inspection should include looking for signs of trauma, muscle atrophy or hypertrophy, obvious postural dysfunctions, and antalgic movements. The athlete's gait pattern and manner in which clothing is removed should be observed. An athlete who reports an injury to a muscle or joint may remove clothing in a guarded manner, often indicating the level of pain he or she is experiencing.

TABLE 4-4

SPECIFIC ITEMS TO INCLUDE IN THE OBSERVATION SUBPHASE

1. Overall posture

2. Guarding posture

3. Gait pattern

4. Obvious soft-tissue or bone deformity

5. Symmetry of limbs, chest, and shoulders

6. Comparison of limbs for size, shape, color, texture, and muscle hypertrophy or atrophy

7. Signs of inflammation (swelling, redness, and warmth)

8. Willingness to move the injured part, take off shoes, socks, tape, and uniform, and to get up on the examining table or sit on a chair

9. Facial expression that may indicate pain

Table 4-4 presents items to include in the observation subphase of the objective phase of the evaluation.

Information compiled during this subphase should be analyzed and related to the findings of the subjective phase. The evaluator can then refine the decision as to which procedures will be performed next. For example, if the evaluator notes atrophy in the posterior deltoid muscle in a rugby player and relates it to the subjective response, "My shoulder went out when I made a tackle," he or she would plan to perform a specific manual muscle test of the deltoid during the resistive testing subphase. In addition, shoulder instability tests would be performed as well as a segmental neurologic assessment in the appropriate subphases of the objective phase of the evaluation.

Palpation of Acute Injuries

If this is an initial evaluation of an acute injury, palpation should be performed at this time to detect any obvious but not visible soft-tissue or bony deformities that would warrant termination of the evaluation for referral to a physician. For subacute or chronic injuries, palpation can be performed later in the process.

Active and Passive Range of Motion Testing

In most situations involving joint injury, the range of motion subphase would follow observation. Active range of motion (AROM) and passive range of motion (PROM)

The Objective Evaluation Phase

Observation and inspection

The objective evaluation phase begins with observation and inspection. The evaluator observes the athlete's overall appearance and the specific body regions identified in the subjective phase as related to the primary symptoms. On inspection, the evaluator looks for signs of trauma, muscle atrophy or hypertrophy, obvious postural dysfunctions, and antalgic movements. By analyzing this information and relating it to the subjective phase findings, the evaluator decides which tests will be performed next.

Palpation of acute injuries

In an initial evaluation of an acute injury, palpation is performed next to detect obvious but not visible deformities. Palpation is performed later in the process for subacute or chronic injuries.

Active and passive range of motion tests

With a possible joint injury, active range of motion and then passive range of motion are tested. The evaluator may be able to localize a lesion biomechanically through selective tissue tension. Inert tissue pain usually occurs with active or passive range of movement in the same direction of the movement. Contractile tissue pain usually occurs with active or passive range of motion in the opposite direction of the movement. Active movements test all physiologic joint structures (and therefore, the evaluator must look for painful arcs and compensatory or substitution movements); passive movements test all inert or anatomic structures. Passive range of motion should be tested in three situations: during the assessment of end feels at the end of AROM with overpressure, when an injured athlete cannot complete full active range of motion, and when the evaluator suspects that limited active range of motion is from muscle tightness.

Resistive testing

Resistive testing is useful for assessing the physiologic components of a physiologic joint complex and determining the functional status of muscle, tendon, and appropriate nerve innervation. Midrange-of-motion muscle testing (MROMMT), manual muscle testing, and functional muscle testing are used to evaluate athletic injuries. MROMMT tests muscle, tendon, and nerve complexes. It is particularly helpful in an athlete with a suspected overuse syndrome and in evaluating muscle groups that perform a specific motion. Manual muscle testing is used to assess both the functional capacity of individual muscles and muscle-nerve innervation (in the neurologic examination). Functional testing of a specific muscle or muscle group can be accomplished with instrumented devices and functional activities.

Special tests

Special tests that may be useful in the evaluation include stability tests, functional tests, anthropometric measurements, and girth measurements.

Accessory motion and joint play testing

Accessory motions and joint play are small motions occurring within the joint along with physiologic movements that are necessary for normal biomechanical function of joint complexes. Accessory motions occur in two types: type I motions result from muscle contraction resistance, and type II motions result from gravitational force. Joint play describes the involuntary arthrokinematic motions of roll, glide, and spin that allow normal joint motion to occur.

Neurologic testing

Segmental neurologic testing is performed if nervous system involvement is suspected. Sensory and motor testing is commonly included. The evaluator must establish if a nerve root or peripheral nerve has been damaged. An athlete with an injured nerve root may have large areas of abnormal motor and sensory signs, while a more distal peripheral nerve injury will cause more localized abnormalities. The sensory distribution of a nerve root is the dermatome, which is tested with touch sensation and/or sharp and dull touch discrimination and compared with the uninvolved side. The motor distribution of the nerve root is the myotome, which is evaluated with muscle stress testing and deep tendon reflexes, when applicable; nerve root injury can cause a range of symptoms from muscle weakness to complete paralysis. Sensory and motor distributions of peripheral nerves are tested similarly, and damage results in localized signs.

(Continued)

FOCUS ON . . .

The Objective Evaluation Phase (Continued)

Functional assessment measures the athlete's readiness to return to participation. Joint stability, normal nervous system function and range of motion, and 85% to 90% of normal muscle strength are required. The athlete should be able to perform sport activities normally and without pain or significant swelling. If the athlete passes most but not all tests, gradual return to sport may be in order.

Palpation
The evaluator palpates the suspected pathologic tissue to assess quality; skin warmth, moisture, and texture; and swelling, deformity, and crepitance.

Diagnostic tests
As the evaluation proceeds, the physician may order diagnostic tests such as bone or MRI scans or radiographs. He or she interprets the results and shares them with the athletic trainer or physical therapist and the athlete.

TABLE 4-5

COMPONENTS OF A PHYSIOLOGIC JOINT COMPLEX

Physiologic	Anatomic
Nerve	Bone
Muscle	Ligament
Tendon	Capsule
	Bursae
	Periosteum
	Cartilage
	Fascia

(Adapted with permission from Hertling D, Kessler RD: *Management of Common Musculoskeletal Disorders*, ed 3. Philadelphia, PA, JB Lippincott, 1996, p 23.)

tests are used to assess the status of the physiologic and anatomic structures of the physiologic joint complex. **Table 4-5** shows the anatomic and physiologic components of a physiologic joint complex.[1] The physiologic components are nerve, muscle, and tendon, and the anatomic components are all of the other inert joint structures such as ligaments, articular surfaces, and cartilage. Proper patient positioning is very important for obtaining valid and reliable results from AROM and PROM techniques.

Active range of motion should be measured before passive range of motion. During AROM, the athlete moves the joint through the range of motion as requested by the evaluator. During PROM, the evaluator moves the joint through the range of motion while the athlete is relaxed.

To evaluate AROM and PROM differentially, the evaluator may be able to locate a lesion through biomechanical analysis by selective tissue tension (applying tension to all the tissues that might be a possible source of symptoms).[1] Inert tissue—the bones, joint capsule, ligaments, fascia, and cartilage—refer to the anatomic components of a physiologic joint complex (see Table 4-5).[1] Contractile tissue refers to the physiologic components of a physiologic joint complex. Contractile tissue can be assessed with midrange of motion muscle testing.

Pain that arises from inert tissue usually occurs with AROM or PROM in the same direction of the movement. Pain that arises from contractile tissue lesions usually occurs with AROM or PROM in the opposite direction of the movement. If movement is in flexion, the pain is perceived in the antagonist or opposite side, the extension side.

Active movements test all physiologic joint structures. Passive movements test all inert or anatomic structures. The evaluator must watch for painful arcs and compensatory or substitution movements during AROM assessment. At the conclusion of the active and passive range of motion testing, the evaluator should analyze the results and determine what procedures will be performed in the next subphase: resistive testing.

Passive range of motion tests are performed in the following three situations:

- The assessment of end feels that is usually performed at the end of AROM via the overpressure technique. (Overpressure is performed at the limitation of AROM or PROM and is a passive pressure applied by the evaluator.)

- An injured athlete is unable to complete full active range of motion due to pain or weakness

- The evaluator suspects that limited active range of motion is a result of muscle tightness

End feels
End feel refers to the "feel" of the joint at the end of the available range of motion that the evaluator encounters

TABLE 4-6

NORMAL AND ABNORMAL END FEELS

Normal (classic) end feels	Abnormal end feels
Bone-to-bone or hard	Springy block
Capsular	Spasm
Tissue approximation	Empty or pain
	Bone-to-bone or hard

when applying overpressure. Normal end feels vary depending on the joint complex that is being evaluated. Abnormal end feels are those that should not be present at that point of the range of motion. **Table 4-6** shows normal and abnormal end feels.

A bone-to-bone end feel is an abrupt halt to motion when two hard surfaces meet, as in the case of elbow extension. A capsular end feel is a "hard" end of movement with some give to the motion, as in shoulder external rotation. Tissue approximation is a "soft" end feel and refers to a gradual asymptomatic halt to movement when one body part encounters another, as in elbow flexion. These end feels are considered normal.

A springy block is a rebound at the end of the available range of motion. A spasm end feel is assessed when the evaluator encounters a steady resistance produced by involuntary muscle contraction; the resistance usually persists regardless of how carefully the evaluator moves the part. An empty end feel is encountered when pain prevents the body part from moving through the available range of motion, or the movement is clearly beyond the normal anatomic limit of the joint complex. These end feels are considered abnormal.

Capsular and noncapsular patterns

In some cases, the athlete will have a movement pattern that is a characteristic, proportional limitation of joint movement, usually as a result of inflammation or restriction of the joint capsule.[1] A capsular pattern is related to the joint that is being examined and is different in the various joint complexes. For example, a capsular pattern of the shoulder joint would be a limitation of abduction, with a greater percentage of loss of external rotation and a smaller percentage of loss of internal rotation. The capsular pattern of the knee is gross limitation of flexion and slight limitation of extension.[1,4] A noncapsular pattern is any limitation of motion in a joint except for the capsular pattern. Noncapsular patterns may be caused by ligamentous or extra-articular adhesions and internal derangements of the joint complex.

Goniometry

If range of motion limitation is discovered, the evaluator should objectively document the available range of motion with a goniometer. A goniometer is a measurement device and may be manual (the most popular type), electric, or work with gravity. Anatomic position is considered to be 0°; for example, full knee extension is 0° and knee flexion within normal limits would be between 120° and 135°.

Resistive Testing

Resistive testing is used to assess the physiologic components of a physiologic joint complex. The results of these tests guide the evaluator in determining the functional status of muscle, tendon, and appropriate nerve innervation.[5,6] Three types of resistive testing are used generally in the evaluation of athletic injuries.

As with all the subphases in the objective phase of the evaluation, the evaluator must analyze the results of resistive testing with the results of the previous objective subphases and the results of the subjective phase of the evaluation.

Midrange of motion muscle testing

Midrange of motion muscle testing (MROMMT) helps assess the status of the physiologic components of the joint complex.[1] Muscle, tendon, and nerve complexes are examined during this test. MROMMT is very useful in evaluating an athlete with a suspected overuse syndrome and is a screening evaluation that tests muscle groups that perform a specific motion such as shoulder abduction or knee flexion. The examination is performed at the approximate midrange of motion of the muscle-joint complex. The evaluator may explore various parts of the range of motion as long as resistance is not applied at the end ranges of motion. The evaluator assesses whether the motion is strong, weak, painful, not painful, or a combination of these. Muscle strength is not graded but is instead compared with the strength of the same groups on the uninvolved side. Although it is not necessary, pain may be graded.

Isometric contraction, or the so-called break test, is the resistance used in MROMMT.[1] If the athlete is experiencing pain, but motion is strong, the evaluator should suspect a possible first- or second-degree tendon injury. Weakness with no pain may indicate a nerve injury to one or more muscles in the group tested. For example, with a neurapraxic injury to the posterior cord of the brachial plexus, abduction and elbow extension of the shoulder may be painless but weak. However, weakness and a painful response indicate that a more significant injury, such as a fracture or more serious muscle injury, may have occurred.

Analysis of the results of MROMMT will determine whether the evaluator should perform a specific manual muscle test, a segmental neurologic exam, or both.

Manual muscle testing

Manual muscle testing (MMT) is used to assess the functional capacity of specific muscles, such as the rectus femoris, supraspinatus, and flexor digitorum sublimus. MMT is also used in the motor assessment portion of the neurologic subphase of the objective phase of evaluation to assess muscle-nerve innervation. However, MMT procedures do not necessarily eliminate stress on the anatomic joint components. If pain is encountered, the evaluator cannot clearly differentiate the site of the pain.

Although there are several methods of MMT, the break test method is used most often by athletic trainers and physical therapists and is considered to be the most objective and reliable test.[6,7] Results of MMT are graded objectively. **Table 4-7** presents the definitions of each grade.

The evaluator must understand kinesiology to be able to perform accurate and successful MMT procedures and pay careful attention to the location of the proximal and distal attachments and the angle of pull of each muscle-tendon complex tested. Generally, after the specific muscle is tested, the grade is noted as well as any pain or variations of the standardized test position.

TABLE 4-7
GRADING SCHEME FOR MANUAL MUSCLE TESTING

Muscle grade	Definition
5–Normal	Complete AROM against gravity with maximum resistance at a specified point in the range of motion
4–Good	Complete AROM against gravity with some resistance at a specified point in the range of motion
3–Fair	Complete AROM against gravity
2–Poor	Complete ROM with no gravity
1–Trace	Evidence of slight contraction with no joint motion
0	No evidence of contractility

Note: Plus and minus (+/−) grades may be used to reflect intermediate levels.

(Adapted with permission from Kendall, et al: *Muscle Testing and Function*, ed 4. Baltimore, MD, Williams and Wilkins, 1983; and from Daniels L, Worthingham C: *Muscle Testing, Techniques of Manual Examination*, ed 5. Philadelphia, PA, WB Saunders,

Functional muscle testing

In many situations, the evaluator may wish to assess the functional capacity of a specific muscle or muscle group. Functional activities such as toe hopping can help the examiner evaluate the capacity of the gastrocnemius-soleus complex, and unilateral squats can help the examiner evaluate the quadriceps muscle group. The single-leg hop test in ACL-reconstructed knees is useful in comparing functional return.

Special Tests

The evaluator may wish to employ a variety of special tests after performing the previous tests. Special tests have specific uses and may not be appropriate for all joint complexes or diagnoses. The athletic trainer can perform these tests during the initial clinical examination and report results or make referrals to an orthopaedist when indicated.

Stability tests assess the integrity of the ligamentous complexes of specific joints and usually apply only to a specified joint complex or ligamentous structure. For example, the Lachman test assesses the anterior cruciate ligament of the knee; the anterior apprehension test of the shoulder is used for a suspected instability of the glenohumeral joint. Passive tendon stretches assess shoulder rotator cuff and elbow joint injuries.[1] Functional tests assess the functional physiologic capacity of various organs and systems, such as stress tests for the cardiovascular system and jumping, throwing, or plyometric tests. Many functional tests are performed by the physician.

Anthropometric measurements assess body composition, stature, weight, and *somatotype* (physique or body type).[7] Anthropometric measurements are especially useful when the evaluator is responsible for sports such as wrestling and gymnastics in which weight control or physical appearance is important. The evaluator must be specially trained to administer anthropometric techniques. Girth measurements are appropriate to assess atrophy, hypertrophy, or swelling. Leg length and Q-angle measurements are often performed on athletes who report lower back pain or have signs or symptoms of patellofemoral pain syndrome (PFPS).

Accessory Motion and Joint Play Testing

Accessory motion and joint play are small motions that occur within the joint simultaneously with active or passive physiologic movements and are required for normal biomechanical function of joint complexes.[8-10]

There are two types of accessory motion: type I and type II. Type I motions are produced by resistance of muscle contraction, such as the rotation of the metacarpals when the functional hand and wrist position is assumed while gripping a ball or baseball bat. Type II motions are produced by the force of gravity, such as the downward glide of the humerus on the glenoid fossa during early abduction of the shoulder.

Joint play allows the joint to move with a combination of roll, glide, and spin. These motions, known as arthrokinematic motions, occur according to the shape of the joint surfaces.[11] The motions are involuntary but must be present for normal joint motion (as observed) to occur. The superior glide, rotation, and distraction of the tibiofibular joint that takes place during dorsiflexion of the ankle is an example of joint play.

The evaluator, who must be specially trained in this procedure, assesses these motions to ensure that they are present.

Neurologic Testing

The evaluator performs a segmental neurologic evaluation if results of previous subphases of the objective phase of the evaluation and results of the subjective phase indicate suspicion of nervous system involvement.[12]

Neurologic tests are performed when the evaluator suspects injury to the central or peripheral nervous system such as occurs with head or neck trauma, spine injury, fractures, dislocation, or complaints of altered sensations. Athletes complaining of numbness, tingling, burning, weakness, or pain inconsistent with the history of injury should be assessed for neurologic impairment. Therefore, the evaluator must understand the motor and sensory distribution of the peripheral and spinal nerves.

The nerve root is the segment of nerve that is connected to the spinal cord (**Figure 4-1**). The anterior and posterior sections of the nerve combine to form a single nerve root or spinal nerve. Because nerve roots depart through the vertebral foramen, they are named after the particular vertebra from which they exit. There are 31 pairs of nerve roots: eight cervical, 12 thoracic, five lumbar, five sacral, and one coccygeal. All cervical spinal roots, with the exception of C8, pass superior to the vertebrae for which they are named. The C8 nerve root passes inferior to the seventh cervical vertebrae. Following the C8 nerve root, each remaining nerve root passes inferior to its corresponding vertebrae.

Several nerve roots may join together to form one peripheral nerve, such as the femoral nerve, which includes L2, L3, and L4. In addition, several spinal nerve roots may combine to form a plexus such as the brachial plexus. Peripheral nerves are formed from this blending of spinal nerves.

The evaluator's challenge is to determine whether the problem is related to nerve root or peripheral nerve injury. Damage to one nerve root may result in abnormal sensory and motor signs in large areas. In contrast, damage to the more distal peripheral nerve will exhibit signs in the localized area innervated by the nerve. To document injury to the nerve root, the examiner can evaluate dermatomes and myotomes.

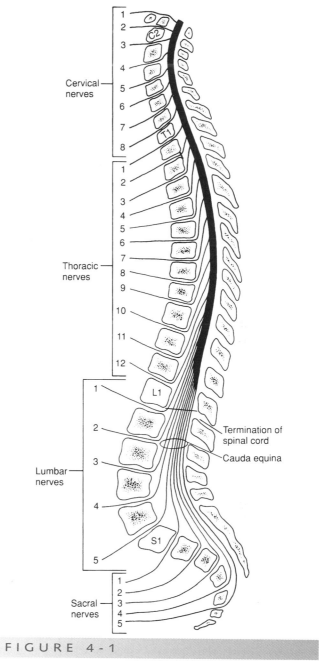

FIGURE 4-1

Nerve roots are connected to the spinal cord and depart through the vertebral foramen.

Dermatomes are the sensory distribution or the areas of skin supplied by the nerve root. The area of distribution will vary, and some areas will be larger than others. These distributions are regular and consistent but are subject to variability among the populations studied. In assessing dermatomes, the athlete's ability to discriminate between sharp and dull touch is tested. The distinction and quality of the sensation relative to the uninvolved side is compared for any abnormalities.

Myotomes are the motor equivalents to dermatomes. They represent the motor distribution of the nerve root or, in other words, the affected groups of muscles. Myotome testing is accomplished through muscle stress testing. Damage or injury to a single nerve root may result in a range of signs from muscle weakness to complete paralysis of the muscle groups.

Peripheral nerves may be assessed in much the same manner as nerve roots. The evaluator may test sensory and motor distribution; however, he or she must remember that peripheral nerve distributions are different from those for the nerve root. Unlike nerve root problems, peripheral nerve damage will result in signs only in the local area of distribution. For superficial peripheral nerves, special compression tests may be conducted to assess the nerve injury.

Functional assessment

The athlete's ability to return to practice or competition should be tested prior to participation. First, athletes must meet basic criteria that include joint stability, normal nervous system function, normal ROM, and 85% to 90% of normal muscle strength.[13] All athletes should demonstrate relatively pain-free and normal skill performance in their sport with minimal postactivity swelling. For most athletes, this assessment will include general abilities such as running, cutting, and jumping for lower leg injuries. It will also include sport-specific skills such as blocking, throwing, rebounding, and back peddling. Occasionally, an athlete may pass most but not all tests. When this occurs, it is sometimes appropriate to return the athlete to practice in a gradual and increasingly challenging process.

Palpation

At this point in the evaluation, the evaluator should have differentiated the normal tissue from the pathologic tissue and can proceed to specifically palpating the suspected pathologic tissue. Palpation assesses the quality of the specific injured tissue, structures, or complex. Palpation verifies the warmth, moisture, and texture of the skin, along with swelling, deformity, and crepitance. Trigger points should be assessed as well as bony contour. With practice, the evaluator can obtain valuable information about the pathologic tissue from the palpation process.

Diagnostic Tests

During the evaluation process, the physician may order various tests to help clarify and differentiate the normal and pathologic tissue. These tests are based on the physician's analysis of the results of the subphases of the subjective and objective phases of the evaluation. Tests may include bone scans, MRI scans, and other radiographs or electrodiagnostic procedures. The physician interprets the results of these tests and reports the results to the athletic trainer or physical therapist and to the athlete.

FOCUS ON . . .

Evaluation During Emergency Situations

Primary survey

In an emergency, the evaluation begins with a primary survey to determine if a life-threatening or serious illness or injury exists, and if so, how severe it is. Effective emergency responses require that emergency plans be in place, that actions be efficient, and that the healthcare professional remain composed at all times. Initially, the patient's airway, breathing, and circulation (ABCs) are checked; if necessary, cardiopulmonary resuscitation is started and the athlete is transferred to the emergency department as soon as possible.

Secondary survey

The secondary survey is more inclusive, focusing on diagnostic signs (pulse, respiration, blood pressure, body temperature, skin color, pupils, consciousness, movement, and pain reaction) and a more comprehensive examination. Any unusual findings are evaluated more thoroughly to determine what treatment should be instituted and how quickly.

EVALUATION DURING EMERGENCY SITUATIONS

The athletic trainer must be prepared to manage an emergency situation. Having an established emergency action plan is vital to a successful evaluation.

Primary Survey

All evaluations in emergency situations begin with a primary survey. This survey is used to determine the existence and severity of a life-threatening or serious illness or injury. Handling an emergency requires existing emergency plans, efficient action, and composure on the part of the medical provider. The initial screening of all situations begins with checking the patient's airway, breathing, and circulation (ABCs).[13] The athletic trainer must ensure that the athlete has an adequate airway, observe breathing by looking for the chest rise and fall, listening for breath sounds, and feeling the movement of air. Finally, the athletic trainer must confirm that the athlete's heart is circulating blood and that there is a pulse. If any one of the ABCs is absent, cardiopulmonary resuscitation (CPR) should be started and the athlete rapidly transported to the emergency department.

Secondary Survey

Once the ABCs are verified, the examiner should move on to a secondary survey. The secondary survey is more

Record Keeping

Appropriate record keeping that meets both medical and legal requirements is vital to an effective injury management program. The healthcare provider is ethically required to keep accurate, specific, and confidential records that describe the medical services provided and the athlete's response to treatment.

One way of maintaining these records is with SOAP notes, which also enables medical providers to communicate about the athlete's progress and eliminates duplication of services. Although it is generally used in the clinical setting, SOAP notes can be used throughout the treatment course; for example, an athlete injured on the field may need to be evaluated and managed emergently, but critical thinking and documentation are still necessary. Because only significant signs and symptoms and relevant objective test results are recorded, SOAP notes are useful for noting important daily changes. Another form is used for noting radiographic and other imaging test results.

Sports medicine professionals employ several formats to record the results of the evaluation. One such format, the SOAP (subjective, objective, assessment, plan) method, is an organizational technique for problem solving, decision making, and treatment documentation. Table 4-8 shows an outline of the SOAP method. An athlete's care is documented in the SOAP notes. SOAP notes are also a means of communication among healthcare providers, serving as a status report that updates other providers on an athlete's progress and thereby preventing a duplication of services.

The SOAP method may be applied throughout the course of the athlete's medical treatment. Although it is primarily used in the clinical setting, the process can be used in all phases of the sports injury evaluation, beginning with the injury on the field and progressing to the late stages of rehabilitation. On-the-field situations may necessitate communicating only the most essential information; however, the injured athlete should be afforded an appropriate evaluation, critical thinking, and, minimally, a short-term plan that may include emergency treatment, stabilization, and transportation.

The advantage of SOAP notes is that only significant symptoms and signs need be recorded and the evaluator

detailed and includes the documentation of diagnostic signs and a more thorough examination. Nine diagnostic signs that may be reviewed by the examiner as warranted include pulse, respiration, blood pressure, body temperature, skin color, pupils of the eye, state of consciousness, ability to move, and reaction to pain.[13] Any abnormal findings combined with a more detailed examination will determine the course of treatment and its urgency. Other parts of the body should be examined for trauma that may otherwise go unrecognized.

RECORD KEEPING

Adequate record keeping is essential to the success of any management program and plays a significant role in the present medical and legal environment. It is the ethical responsibility of the medical provider to maintain accurate, specific, and confidential records that document the medical services provided, the athlete's progress, and the efficacy of the treatment. Proper documentation and record keeping is also required by the NATA Board of Certification, Inc, and state athletic trainer practice acts. Identifying the significant symptoms and signs is a useful record keeping tool. When a significant symptom or sign is recorded, an asterisk is placed before the information in the written record so that the evaluator can find the information readily when reevaluating the injured athlete's progress. Therefore, during a reevaluation, the evaluator will only repeat those objective tests that produced the comparable signs with an asterisk.

TABLE 4-8
SOAP OUTLINE

Subjective evaluation
- Primary complaint
- History
- Behavior of symptoms

Objective evaluation
- Primary survey
  - ➤ ABCs

- Secondary survey
  - ➤ Visual inspection
  - ➤ Palpation (if this is an evaluation of an acute injury)
  - ➤ Range of motion
  - ➤ Muscle testing
  - ➤ Stress testing
  - ➤ Neurologic testing
  - ➤ Functional assessment
  - ➤ Palpation of subacute or chronic injuries

Assessment
- Suspected condition
- Suspected diagnosis

Plan
- Communication
- Treatment
- Meeting goals
  - ➤ Long-term goals
  - ➤ Short-term goals

only needs to record the objective test results that were performed. SOAP notes may be used to record significant changes on a day-to-day basis. SOAP notes are generally not used to record the results of radiographs and other imaging tests; a separate form is used for that purpose.

GOAL SETTING

Results of the evaluation process allow the physician and athletic trainer to set objective short- and long-term goals to govern the progress of the rehabilitation program. Goals are based on the information obtained during the evaluation and should be related to the athlete's signs and symptoms and restoration of functional capacity. **Table 4-9** lists some possible short- and long-term goals for an athlete who is recovering from a second-degree inversion ankle sprain. This procedure allows the physician and athletic trainer to monitor the progress of the rehabilitation program. If the short- or long-term goals are not met as set, the physician may decide that the injured athlete should be reevaluated.

CASE STUDIES

Case I: Peroneal Tendinitis

Subjective phase

History: A distance runner reports lateral ankle pain for the past 10 days that occurs at the start of the training run. There was no apparent incident and symptoms gradually developed.

Symptoms: The athlete reports pain inferior to the lateral malleolus. The athlete describes the pain as an ache. Pain decreases approximately 2 miles into the training run, but does not disappear. The lateral ankle

FOCUS ON . . .

Goal Setting

At the end of the evaluation, the physician and athletic trainer establish objective short- and long-term goals for the rehabilitation program designed to resolve or reduce signs and symptoms and promote functional return. These goals allow the medical providers to monitor the athlete's progress and alter the rehabilitation program if necessary.

region aches at night with rest; however, ice packs bring relief. The evaluator determines that the main symptom is pain below the medial malleolus that occurs with running.

Objective phase

Observation and inspection reveal a grade III valgus heel on the painful side of the ankle with grade II swelling under the lateral malleolus.

Active ROM tests reveal pain in plantarflexion and inversion that increase with overpressure.

Resistive testing: MROMMT produces pain but no weakness in eversion. All other motions are strong and pain-free. MMT of the peroneus brevis was 4/5 with pain.

Functional muscle testing reveals painful and weak toe hopping. Pain was reproduced during this test.

Special tests: Because there is no report of overt injury mechanism and no indication of nervous system involvement, neurologic testing is not indicated.

Joint play movements are within normal limits.

TABLE 4-9

EXAMPLE OF GOALS FOR AN ATHLETE RECOVERING FROM A SECOND-DEGREE INVERSION ANKLE SPRAIN

Short-term goals	Long-term goals
1. Decrease swelling by 25% in 3 days	Return to full competition with protective taping in 2 weeks
2. Increase AROM by 50% in 1 week	
3. Attain full weightbearing in 1 week	
4. Reduce acute pain by 50% in 3 days	
5. Increase strength by 50% in 3 weeks	
6. Improve agility and function by 50% in 1 week	

Palpation reveals swelling, pain, and crepitance over the peroneus brevis tendon as it passes inferior to the lateral malleolus.

Assessment

The principle signs are pain in AROM with overpressure in plantarflexion and inversion, pain with MROMMT in eversion, grade 4/5 strength of peroneus brevis muscle, and swelling and pain in the peroneus brevis tendon.

The athletic trainer determines that the peroneus brevis tendon is the pathologic tissue and notifies the physician, who examines the patient and diagnoses peroneus brevis tendinitis. The athletic trainer determines that the dysfunctions related to this condition are pain in plantarflexion and inversion and a grade I weakness in the peroneus brevis muscle. Short-term goals can be set, a prognosis determined, and a rehabilitation program planned to correct the dysfunctions.

Case II: Brachial Plexus Injury

Subjective phase

History: A rugby player reports pain in the upper extremity after making a tackle.

Symptoms: The athlete experienced shooting, burning pain that radiated to the hand after the initial blow to the shoulder during the tackle. The player reports paresthesia in the arm and hand, especially on the thumb side. The pain is constant and increases when the athlete tries to tackle. The patient reports that this is the first such incident. The evaluator determines that the main symptoms are the burning and paresthesia in the arm and hand.

Objective phase

Observation and inspection reveal no significant findings.

Active ROM tests of the upper extremity are within normal limits. The athlete reports generalized discomfort in the shoulder and neck with overhead movements; however, overpressure in the shoulder and neck is within normal limits.

Resistive testing: MROMMT produces weakness but no pain in shoulder abduction. MMT of the deltoid is 3+/5 and of the biceps brachii, 5/5. No pain is elicited with MMT.

Special tests: Results gathered in the subjective phase indicate there is no need for special tests.

Accessory motions: A shoulder quadrant maneuver to clear the glenohumeral joint reveals negative results.

Segmental neurologic testing reveals decreased sensation in the lateral arm and weakness in shoulder abduction but not in elbow flexion. Muscle stretch reflexes are within normal limits. Neurotension testing may be performed.

Palpation is not performed because the evaluator determined that a nerve injury occurred.

Additional tests: Results of a cervical spine-clearing test are negative. The athletic trainer reports the results of the evaluation to the physician, who orders radiographs of the cervical spine. Results of the radiographs are negative. The physician also repeats the segmental neurologic exam.

Assessment

The principle signs are weakness in the deltoid and decreased sensation on the lateral arm.

The physician diagnoses a neurapraxic injury (class I) of the posterior cord of the brachial plexus. The athletic trainer determines the dysfunctions related to this condition are pain in the upper extremity and a grade II weakness in the deltoid muscle. Short-term goals can be set along with a rehabilitation program.

Case III: Postsurgical ACL Reconstruction

Subjective phase

History: A basketball player reports to the athletic trainer after ACL reconstruction with a patella tendon graft. The physician had evaluated the athlete on the court immediately after the injury and determined the athlete had an acute, complete rupture of the ACL.

Symptoms: The athlete reports to the athletic training facility 7 days after surgery. The athlete ambulates on crutches with partial weightbearing. The athlete reports generalized pain in the knee region and that she is able to bend the knee to some extent with 2/5 pain over the surgical site. She is also able to walk short distances without using crutches. She has been using a continuous passive motion device since the day of surgery and has achieved 90° of flexion at the knee. The athletic trainer determines that the main symptom is pain with movement.

Objective phase

Observation and inspection reveal a 3+ swelling in the knee, which is confirmed by the wave test for swelling. The location and condition of the surgical incision is noted as is marked atrophy of the quadriceps musculature in 7 days. Because they affect the extent of available range of motion, modified palpation and patella joint mobility assessment are performed to assess the swelling and patella mobility before proceeding to the AROM assessment.

Active ROM tests reveal results of 0/10/90 (hyperextension/extension/flexion), determined by goniometry. Overpressure is not performed because it is contraindicated in postsurgical conditions. Ankle and hip motion is found to be within normal limits.

Resistive testing: MMT of the ankle and hip reveal motions within normal limits, except for the rectus femoris, which was 2/5. Proprioception of the quadriceps is poor.

Special tests: Stability testing is not appropriate at this time because the main symptom and previous AROM assessment indicate that a stability test cannot be performed accurately. Girth is measured on the thigh and calf bilaterally.

Neurologic testing is not indicated because there is no indication of nerve involvement at this time.

Palpation of the surgical scar is performed and other signs of inflammation are assessed.

Assessment

The principle signs are loss of AROM, inability to bear full weight functionally, decreased proprioception, and pain with motion.

The athletic trainer determines that the major dysfunctions are a lack of motion and full weightbearing and a decrease in proprioception and notifies the physician of these findings. Short-term goals can be set and a rehabilitation program planned.

Case IV: Inversion Ankle Sprain

Subjective phase

History: A volleyball player reports "rolling over" of her ankle during a match. As she landed after a block, she stepped on an opponent's foot, which came under the net.

Symptoms: The athlete reports pain on the lateral aspect of the ankle. She states that she heard a pop as her ankle turned over and that the ankle feels loose. The pain is sharp when she attempts full weightbearing. The athlete denies any prior ankle injuries.

Objective phase

Observation and inspection reveal the ankle is swollen (+3) over the lateral aspect, anterior to the lateral malleolus. The patient walked into the physician's office bearing weight on the toes and with an antalgic gait pattern; she was reluctant to move her ankle.

Active ROM tests reveal loss of motion in plantarflexion and inversion and restriction in dorsiflexion. Overpressure is not appropriate because the results of the subjective phase and observation analysis present an index of suspicion that a ligament injury has occurred.

Resistive testing: Resisted motion is not appropriate because previous phases of the evaluation indicate a high index of suspicion of ligament damage.

Special tests: Results of the inversion stress test and drawer test are both positive.

Neurologic testing: Evidence from the previous phases of evaluation did not indicate that there was nervous system involvement, so no neurologic testing is performed.

Palpation reveals tenderness over the anterior talofibular ligament. Palpation of the fibula reveals negative findings.

Other tests: The physician orders ankle stress radiographs; radiographs show an increase in talar tilt in the involved ankle.

Assessment

The principle signs are swelling, gait dysfunction, positive ligament stability test results, and positive results on stress radiographs. The physician bases a diagnosis of second-degree inversion ankle sprain on the results of the stress radiographs and the evaluation. The physician refers the athlete to the athletic trainer who determines that the dysfunctions that relate to this condition are pain, lack of AROM, inability to bear weight, and decreased proprioception. Short-term goals can be set, a prognosis determined, and a rehabilitation program planned to correct the dysfunctions.

CHAPTER REVIEW

The physician and athletic trainer must be knowledgeable about, and skilled in performing, an evaluation of neuromusculoskeletal injuries. Cooperation, communication, support, and mutual understanding of and respect for each other's role in athletic injury management will help the athlete return to sport as quickly and safely as possible.

The evaluation process is used in preventive strategies, on-site emergency procedures, subacute care, rehabilitation, and return to activity. As the findings of each phase are analyzed and accumulated, the pathologic tissues, organs, and systems are identified, and associated dysfunctions are recognized. The physician determines the diagnosis, and the athletic trainer uses it to characterize the dysfunction; both providers work together to set objective short- and long-term goals and create an effective management plan.

In an emergency situation, the primary survey includes checking the patient's airway, breathing, and circulation. Next is the secondary survey of the diagnostic signs. Abnormal findings may require the institution of cardiopulmonary resuscitation and other treatment.

Accurate record keeping is an ethical, medical, and legal responsibility of the medical provider. Not only can record keeping be used to monitor the athlete's progress, but it offers a way for the healthcare professionals involved in the athlete's care to communicate. SOAP notes are commonly used for record keeping.

Based on the results of the evaluation process, the physician and athletic trainer set objective short- and long-term goals for the rehabilitation program to safely return the athlete to activity. If the goals are not met, the athlete may need to be reevaluated by the physician or the program may need to be revised.

SELF-TEST

1. In order to evaluate musculoskeletal injuries appropriately, the athletic trainer must be able to:

   A. diagnose the injury.

   B. recognize dysfunctions related to the diagnosis.

   C. perform the subjective phase of the evaluation only.

   D. perform the objective phase of the evaluation only.

2. What does "SOAP" stand for?

   A. Sports Objective Assessment Process

   B. Systematic Objective Assessment Process

   C. Symptom Order Assessment Procedure

   D. Subjective Objective Assessment Plan

3. Which of the following items is included in the subjective phase of SOAP?

   A. History

   B. Observation

   C. Neurologic evaluation

   D. Range-of-motion assessment

4. Identifying the particular behavior of a symptom requires the examiner to:

   A. try to determine the cause of the symptoms.

   B. find out when the symptom first occurred.

   C. determine if the symptom varies in intensity.

   D. learn if dizziness, tingling, or popping occurs.

5. In the PQRST mnemonic, S refers to:

   A. shooting pain.

   B. severity of pain.

   C. symptom duration.

   D. speed of movement.

6. A "soft" end feel refers to:

   A. a rebound at the end of the available range of motion.

   B. an abrupt halt to motion when two hard surfaces meet.

   C. movement that is clearly beyond the normal anatomic limit of the joint complex.

   D. a gradual asymptomatic halt to motion when one body part encounters another.

7. When performing manual muscle testing, complete active range of motion against gravity is characteristic of which muscle grade?

   A. 5 (normal)

   B. 4 (good)

   C. 3 (fair)

   D. 2 (poor)

8. The motor distribution of a nerve root is known as the:

   A. plexus.

   B. foramen.

   C. myotome.

   D. dermatome.

9. Which of the following components is part of the primary survey in an emergency situation?

   A. Airway

   B. Skin color

   C. Temperature

   D. Consciousness

10. An advantage to SOAP notes is that they are used:

   A. to record significant daily changes.

   B. to record the results of imaging tests.

   C. only by the clinician who wrote them.

   D. primarily for the initial on-the-field injury.

Answers on page 891.

References

1. Cyriax J: *Textbook of Orthopedic Medicine*, ed 8. London, England, *Bailliere* Tindal, 1982.

2. Maitland GD: *Peripheral Manipulation*, ed 3. London, England, Butterworth, 1991, pp 71-73.

3. Arnheim DD, Prentice W: *Principles of Athletic Training*, ed 9. Madison, WI, Brown & Benchmark, 1997.

4. Magee DJ: *Orthopedic Physical Assessment*, ed 3. Philadelphia, PA, WB Saunders, 1997.

5. Kendall, et al: *Muscle, Testing and Function*, ed 4. Baltimore, MD, Williams & Wilkins, 1983.

6. Daniels L, Worthingham C: *Muscle Testing Techniques of Manual Examination*, ed 5. Philadelphia, PA, WB Saunders, 1986.

7. Carter JE, Lindsay JE, Honeyman-Heath B: *Somatotyping Development and Applications*. Cambridge, MA, Cambridge University Press, 1990.

8. Maitland GD: *Vertebral Manipulation*, ed 5. London, England, Butterworth, 1986, p 149.

9. Hertling D, Kessler RD: *Management of Common Musculoskeletal Disorders*, ed 3. Philadelphia, PA, Harper & Row, 1996.

10. Gross J, Fetto J, Rosen E: *Musculoskeletal Examination*. Cambridge, MA, Blackwell Science, 1996.

11. Williams P, Warwick R, Dyson M, Bannister L (eds): *Gray's Anatomy*, ed 37. Edinburgh, Scotland, Churchill Livingstone, 1989, pp 460-485.

12. Hoppenfeld S: *Orthopedic Neurology*. Philadelphia, PA, JB Lippincott, 1990.

13. Hunter-Griffin LY: *Athletic Training and Sports Medicine*, ed 2, Park Ridge, IL, American Academy of Orthopaedic Surgeons, 1991.

Anatomy and Physiology of the Musculoskeletal System

Bernard R. Bach, Jr, MD
Samer S. Hasan, MD, PhD

QUICK CONTENTS

- The anatomy of the bones, joints, and muscles.

- The biomechanics of the human body.

- The structure and function of normal tissue.

- The normal physiology of bone, cartilage, muscle, tendon, ligament, synovium, and peripheral nerves.

- The maintenance of connective tissue structure and function.

The main goal of sports medicine therapy is to minimize the adverse effects of trauma and promote proper tissue healing to expedite a safe return to activity. Understanding the underlying principles of wound healing and tissue repair is important. As a prelude to discussing connective tissue injury and repair, the various types of connective tissue that constitute the musculoskeletal system will be described both macroscopically and microscopically. Structure and function of the various tissues, including bone, cartilage, ligaments, muscles, tendons, synovial tissue, and nerves, will be emphasized. Some of the pertinent physiologic and biomechanical principles that govern the function of these tissues, under normal conditions and in response to injury, will also be discussed. Both general and tissue-specific injury response patterns will be presented. The chapter concludes with a brief discussion of clinical grading systems and the physiologic principles behind physical therapy and rehabilitation of injured connective tissues.

ANATOMY

Bone

The skeleton is made up of 206 bones arranged to protect vital internal organs, provide a scaffold that supports the human body, and facilitate muscle action and body movement (**Figure 5-1**). Joints link bones together and move under the influence of muscles that attach through tendons onto bone. Thus, the skeleton is at once a rigid framework that protects and a flexible framework that allows body parts to move by muscle contraction. The skeleton also enables the body to resist the pull of gravity and maintain an erect posture. The skeleton fulfills these functions because bone is rigid and unyielding. Yet bone is also dynamic, living tissue that grows as the body grows and is constantly being formed and replaced.

Bones may be classified according to morphology into long, short, and flat bones. Specific regions of a bone have their own names. For example, long bones are defined by their diaphysis, metaphysis, and epiphysis (**Figure 5-2**). The *diaphysis* is the shaft of the long bone, the *metaphysis* is the flare at either end, and the *epiphysis* is the rounded end at the joint. The epiphysis is separated from the metaphysis by the *physis*, a cartilaginous plate from which developing bone grows. Other terms are ascribed to parts of a bone depending on shape and function.

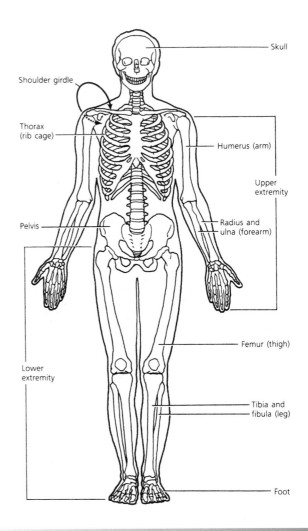

F I G U R E   5 - 1

The skeleton protects internal organs, provides support to the body, and facilitates muscle action and movement.

Joints

The ends of two adjacent bones connect to form a *joint*. Some joints, such as the hip or shoulder are triaxial, allowing a wide range of motion in all planes. Other joints, such as the acromioclavicular (AC) joint, allow more limited motion that is restricted to one or two planes. Still other joints, such as the joints between the bones of the skull (except for the mandible), fuse to prevent motion. Some joints are referred to by common names, such as shoulder, hip, knee, and wrist, while others are referred to by a combination of the names of the two bones that connect at that joint. One example is the metacarpophalangeal joint, which is the joint in the hand between the metacarpal bone and proximal phalanx.

A smooth, glistening surface of *articular cartilage* (hyaline cartilage) covers the ends of bones that articulate with each other to form an articulation. Some of these joints are also lined with interarticular fibrocarti-

FOCUS ON . . .

Anatomy

Bone

The 206 bones of the skeleton protect the vital internal organs, provide a scaffold to support the body, and offer a flexible framework to facilitate muscle action and body movement. The erect posture afforded by the skeleton resists the pull of gravity. The skeleton functions in this way because bone is rigid and unyielding; however, bone is also dynamic living tissue that forms, grows, and is replaced. Morphologically, bones are described as long, short, or flat. The parts of a long bone are called the diaphysis (shaft), metaphysis (flare at either end), epiphysis (rounded end at the joint), and physis (cartilaginous growth plate).

Joints

The ends of two adjacent bones come together to form a joint. Some joints allow a wide range of motion in all planes, while others have motion limited to one or two planes. Still others fuse to prevent motion. Some joints have common names, such as the hip and shoulder; others are described by the bones that connect at the joint, such as the metacarpophalangeal joints.

Articular cartilage covers the bone ends at the joint. Some joints also contain menisci, soft-tissue structures that distribute load, absorb shock, and lubricate the joint. The bony ends of moving joint are enveloped by a fibrous capsule. Joints take different forms: ball-in-socket (hip, shoulder), hinge (humeroulnar), and saddle (subtalar). All joints have limits beyond which normal motion cannot occur; forcing motion beyond this limit can break the bones or disrupt the capsule or ligaments.

Muscle

Muscles are classified as skeletal, visceral, or cardiac. Skeletal muscle, also known as striated or voluntary muscle, attaches one bone to another and forms the major muscle mass of the body. Skeletal muscles cause movement by acting on bone and across a joint. When a muscle contracts, it creates a line of force between the muscle origin and the insertion, bringing the ends of the bones closer together. Skeletal muscle is controlled by the central nervous system, mediated through the spinal cord and peripheral nerve signals. Visceral and cardiac muscles are involuntary muscles.

Joints move when the muscles on the side of the motion contract and those on the opposite side lengthen (relax). When the joint moves back to its original position, the lengthened muscles contract and the contracted muscles relax. Most often, several muscles work together synergistically. Agonist muscles produce body movement in the same direction, while antagonists produce motion in opposing directions. For example, the triceps extends the elbow and is the antagonist of the biceps brachii, which flexes the elbow.

lage, called a *meniscus*, which is a soft-tissue structure that provides load distribution, shock absorption, and joint lubrication.[1] Injury to a meniscus in the knee is common, and the resulting torn fragment may produce symptoms of locking or catching in the joint.

The bony ends of joints that allow motion are enveloped by a fibrous capsule. Bones are connected to each other by ligaments, which are tough, thick bands of capsule that resist stretching or bending. Joints that have relatively few or weak ligaments, such as the shoulder joint, allow greater motion in more directions than joints that are virtually surrounded by especially tough and thick ligaments, such as the sacroiliac joint. Ligamentous restraints as well as the geometry of the bone ends constrain the motion of a joint. The variability in bony and soft-tissue architecture leads to joints as diverse as the ball-in-socket joint, as in the hip and shoulder, the hinge joint, as in the humeroulnar joint, and the saddle joint, as in the subtalar joint in the foot.[2] All joints have a definite limit beyond which motion cannot normally occur. When a joint is forced beyond this limit, injury to some connective tissue structures invariably results. The bones forming the joint may break, or the supporting capsule and ligaments may be disrupted.

Muscle

Muscles are contractile connective tissues that affect movement and are a component of nearly all organs and body systems. Muscles can be classified as skeletal, visceral, or cardiac. Visceral and cardiac muscles are frequently called "special muscles." *Skeletal muscle* attaches from one bone to the other. It forms the major muscle mass of the body, and collectively accounts for approximately 40% to 45% of the body's weight, making it the heaviest organ in the body.[1]

Skeletal muscles cause movement by acting on bone, which functions as a lever, and across a joint, which acts as the pivot point or fulcrum. When a muscle contracts, a line of force or pull is created between the origin and the

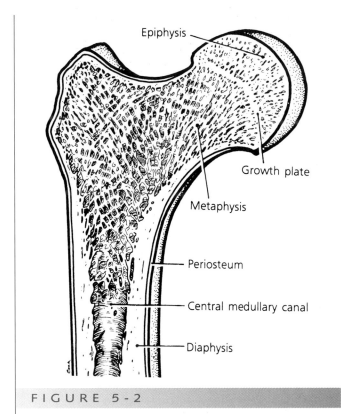

FIGURE 5-2

The diaphysis, metaphysis, and epiphysis define a long bone.

Epiphysis

Growth plate

Metaphysis

Periosteum

Central medullary canal

Diaphysis

insertion—that is, between the two bones to which the muscle is connected. Muscles can cross one, two, or more joints. In general, muscles that cross one joint are located close to the bone and tend to be stronger; however, they contract more slowly. Muscles that cross two joints are more superficial and contract more quickly but are less effective in producing tension over the full range of motion.

Skeletal muscle is attached through tendons to two or more bones to produce joint motion. Skeletal muscle originates from one bone and inserts on another. When skeletal muscle contracts, the ends of the bones spanned by the muscle are brought closer together to produce motion at the intervening joint. Skeletal muscle contains characteristic stripes or striations when it is viewed under a microscope and is also referred to as striated muscle.

Skeletal muscle is called voluntary muscle because it is under voluntary control of the central nervous system. Skeletal muscle can be contracted or relaxed at will to produce motion, such as in an arm or leg. Control of voluntary muscle is mediated through signals that travel down the spinal cord and along peripheral nerves to reach the muscle so that movements are voluntarily initiated and involuntarily coordinated. In contrast, special muscles are involuntary.

To produce joint motion, muscles on the side of the motion contract and those on the opposite side of the limb lengthen or relax. When motion in the opposite direction is desired, the lengthened muscles contract and the contracted muscles relax, rotating the joint back to its original position. Joint motion, and consequently body movement, is most often the result of several muscles contracting or relaxing synergistically. Muscles that produce body movement in the same direction are called *agonists*, and muscles that produce movement in opposing directions are called *antagonists*. For example, the triceps, which acts to extend the elbow, is the antagonist of the biceps brachii muscle, which acts to flex the elbow (**Figure 5-3**).

BIOMECHANICS

Force

The human body is subjected to a variety of mechanical loads during everyday activity. A *load* is defined as any force or combination of forces applied to the outside of a structure. A *force* is an action that changes the state or motion of a body to which it is applied. Forces may be external or internal. External forces include gravity, and internal forces include those generated by muscles, bone, and soft-tissue deformation. *Linear acceleration* is the change in an object's speed in a straight line. Most actions involve forces that act through a lever arm, producing a *moment of torque*, which is a force that acts through a distance, specifically the perpendicular distance from the application of the line of force to the center of motion or fulcrum of the structure. Forces are defined in terms of pounds of force or Newtons (N) in the metric system (where $1 \text{ N} = 1 \text{ kg m/s}_2$), and moments are defined in terms of foot-pounds or Newton-meters.

A delicate balance is needed between external and internal forces to provide the body with stability at rest and during movement. The study of these forces and their relationship to stability and motion is called *biomechanics* and is important in understanding both the mechanism of athletic injury and the principles of rehabilitation.[3] Large muscle forces generated during intense athletic activity place significant loads on bones, joints, ligaments, tendons, capsules, and muscles. Such factors as strength, elasticity, and the degree of deformation prior to failure determine whether or not these connective tissue structures are injured.

A force applied to a body has two effects. An external effect causes the body to accelerate, and an internal effect produces a deformation or state of mechanical strain in the body. For example, when a tennis racket hits a tennis ball, the external effect accelerates the tennis ball, and the internal effect or deformation changes the ball's shape when the racket's strings flatten one surface of the ball.

Four properties—magnitude, line of action, direction, and point of application—must be known to define a force uniquely[4] (**Figure 5-4**). Several forces acting in a given situation are called a *system of forces*. The resultant of a system of forces is the simplest system of forces that can replace the original system without changing its external

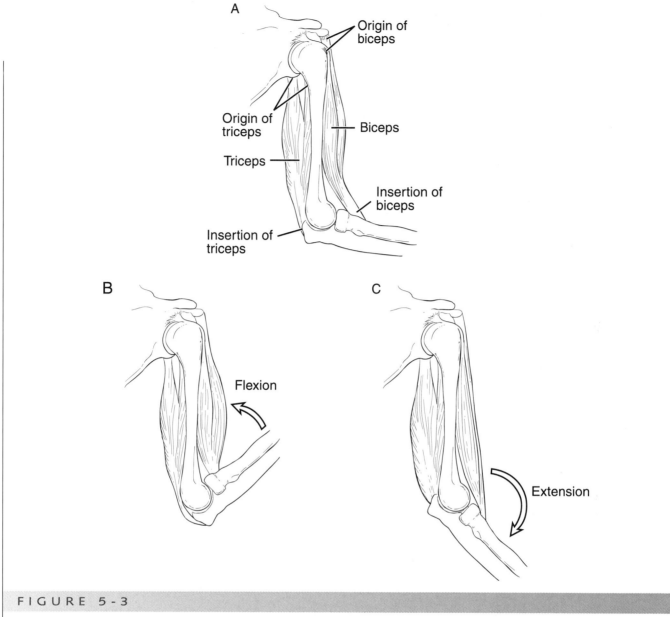

FIGURE 5-3

The triceps is the antagonist of the biceps brachii muscle.

effect on the body. The resultant of a system of force may be a single force, a single moment, or a force and moment. A *resultant force* is a single force representing the combined effect of two or more forces. Conversely, any single force may be replaced or resolved into two or more equivalent force vectors.

Resultant force

Determining the resultant force enables one to predict joint motion. If the resultant force of a system of forces passes through the center of motion, the moment arm is zero, and there is no motion. For example, if the resultant muscle force passes through the point of glenohumeral joint contact, no motion results if the forces are in the same plane. However, if the resultant force passes medial

to the joint contact point, an adduction moment of the humerus relative to the scapula results (**Figure 5-5**).

The study of the forces that produce movements is called *kinetics*. The relationship between force and motion is summed up in two mathematical relationships derived from Newton's second law, which states that the change in velocity (or acceleration) is proportional to the force:

$$F=ma,$$

where F is the applied force, m is the mass of the body, a is its linear acceleration, and

$$T=I\alpha,$$

where T is torque, α is the angular acceleration, and I is the mass moment of inertia, which is a property of the

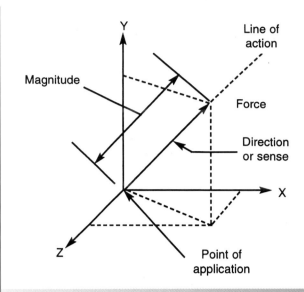

FIGURE 5-4

The four properties of a force define a force uniquely. (Reproduced with permission from Torzilli PA: Basic biomechanical principles: Forces, moments, and equilibrium, in DeLee JC, Drez D Jr (eds): *Orthopaedic Sports Medicine.* Philadelphia, PA, WB Saunders, 1994, pp 122-139.)

material and its shape and is a measure of resistance to change. Thus, by finding the linear acceleration, or angular acceleration, the forces and torques about a human joint during various athletic activities can be determined. The torque is a product not only of the mass moment of inertia and the angular acceleration of the body part, but also of the main muscle forces accelerating the body part and the perpendicular

distance of the force from the instance center of the joint. Therefore,

$$T=Fd,$$

where F is force and d is the perpendicular distance or, equivalently, the moment arm or lever arm.

An example illustrates the use of dynamic analysis to calculate the quadriceps muscle force exerted at a particular instant in time during a dynamic activity such as kicking a football. Results of knee and lower leg position data acquired using high-speed cameras during the kick showed that the maximal angular acceleration occurred at the instant the foot struck the ball, at which point the leg was almost vertical. From the kinematics data, the maximal angular acceleration was computed to be 453 radians per seconds squared (r/s^2) (one radian equals approximately 57.3°). From anthropometric data tables, the mass moment of inertia for the lower leg was determined to be 0.35 newton-meters (N·m) times seconds squared (s^2). The torque about the tibiofemoral joint was calculated according to the equation $T=I\alpha$:

$$T=(0.35 \text{ N·m·s}^2) (453 \text{ r/s}^2) = 158.5 \text{ N·m}.$$

Knowing that the perpendicular distance from the patellar tendon to the instant center for the tibiofemoral joint is 0.05 meter (m), the quadriceps muscle force acting on the joint via the patellar tendon can be determined from the equation T = Fd:

$$F = T/d = 158.5 \text{ N·m} / 0.05 \text{ m} = 3170 \text{ N}.$$

This maximal force exerted by the quadriceps muscle during the kicking motion is greater than four times the normal body weight of an adult man.

The moment arm is the most important muscle parameter because it influences the magnitude of the muscle

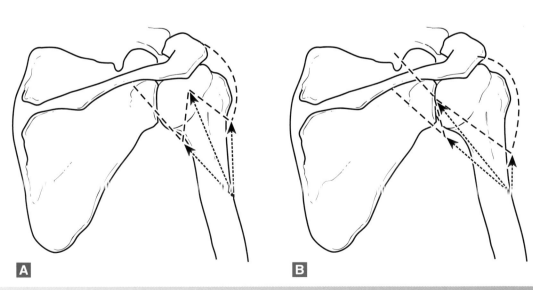

A   **B**

FIGURE 5-5

A resultant force that passes medial to the joint contact point results in an adduction moment of the humerus relative to the scapula.

FOCUS ON . . .

Biomechanics and Kinetics

Biomechanics is the study of the external and internal forces that provide the body with stability at rest and during movement. It also allows us to understand both the mechanisms of sports injury and the principles of rehabilitation. Mechanical loads, which are forces or combined forces, affect the human body every day. External forces include gravity, and internal forces are generated by muscles, bones, and soft-tissue deformation. A force applied to a body produces an external effect that causes the body to accelerate and an internal effect that produces deformation or mechanical strain in the body.

Kinetics is the study of the forces that produce movements. The force-motion relationships are described in mathematical equations derived from Newton's second law $F = ma$ (F = the applied force, m = the mass of the body, and a = its linear acceleration) and $T = I\alpha$ (T = torque, I = angular acceleration, and α = the mass moment of inertia). Torque reflects the mass moment of inertia, angular acceleration of the body part and the main muscle forces accelerating the body part, and the perpendicular distance of the force from the instant center of the joint: $T = Fd$ (F = force, d = the perpendicular distance or the moment or lever arm). The most important muscle parameter is moment arm because it influences the magnitude of the muscle forces. The smaller the moment arm, the greater the muscle force needed to resist an externally applied moment.

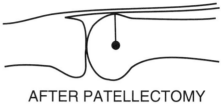

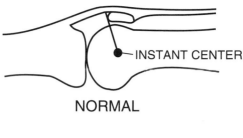

FIGURE 5-6

The patellar tendon in a knee from which the patella has been surgically removed lies closer to the center of motion of the tibiofemoral joint than it would in an intact knee.

forces. The smaller the moment arm, the greater the muscle force needed to resist an externally applied moment. For example, if the patella is surgically removed from the knee, the patellar tendon lies closer to the center of motion of the tibiofemoral joint than it would in an intact knee[5] (**Figure 5-6**). Acting with a shorter moment arm, the quadriceps muscle must produce even more force than is normally required to maintain a certain torque about the knee during the last 45° of extension. Full active extension of a knee following patellectomy may require up to 30% more quadriceps force than is normally required.[6]

During walking and running, the knee, hip, and ankle joints experience very high loads that exceed several times body weight. In level walking, the forces on the hip, knee, and ankle joints are three to five times body weight. With running and more rigorous activities, such as jumping, the forces rise even more.[1] The knee joint has a characteristic force pattern during normal gait, with the highest forces occurring at heel strike and at toe-off.[7] Even during the stance phase, the forces are at least as great as body weight.

Energy

Energy is another concept of great interest to the athletic trainer. The three types of energy are potential, kinetic, and work energy. *Potential energy (PE)* is the energy stored in a body by virtue of its position in space and is equal to the product of mass, gravitational acceleration, and the vertical height of the body. *Kinetic energy (KE)* is the energy of a moving body, and it equals one half the mass times the square of the velocity (v):

$$KE = \tfrac{1}{2}\,mv^2.$$

Work energy (WE) is the energy stored in a structure under deformation and is defined as the force times the distance a body is deformed:

$$WE = Fd.$$

During athletic activity, there is constant conversion of potential energy to kinetic energy to work energy back to kinetic or potential energy. For example, a skier standing on top of a hill has a great amount of potential energy owing to the height of the hill. He or she starts to ski down the hill by converting the potential energy to kinetic energy. As speed increases, the skier may feel uncomfortable and turn up into the hill again, converting some of the kinetic energy back into potential energy. Alternatively, some of the kinetic energy is converted into work energy by deforming the skis and the snow.

Kinesiology

Kinesiology is the study of motion of the human body. *Kinematics* is the study of the movement of rigid struc-

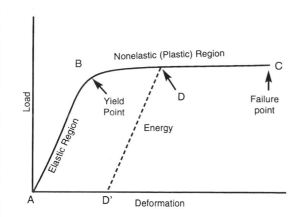

FIGURE 5-11

The load-deformation curve defines the parameters that determine the strength of a structure. The distance between A and D represents the amount of permanent deformation that occurs if the structure is loaded to point D and then unloaded. The point at which deformation occurs is represented by B. (Reproduced with permission from Frankel VH, Nordin M (eds): *Basic Biomechanics of the Skeletal System*, ed 2. Philadelphia, PA, Lea & Febiger, 1989.)

in terms of energy storage. The slope of the curve in the elastic region indicates the stiffness of the structure.[5]

The load-deformation curve is useful for determining the strength and stiffness of whole structures of various sizes, shapes, and material composition. However, to examine the mechanical behavior of the material that makes up a structure and to compare the mechanical behavior of different materials, test specimens and testing conditions must be standardized. When samples of standard size and shape are tested, the load per unit area and the amount of deformation in terms of length can be determined. The curve that is generated is termed the *stress-strain curve*.

Stress-strain curve

Stress is defined as the load per unit area that develops on the surface of a plane within a structure in response to externally applied loads. It is expressed in force units per area, which in the metric system is usually Newtons per meter squared (N/m^2), or Pascals (Pa). In the English system, the term pounds per square inch (psi) is used. *Strain* is the deformation in a structure under loading. Two basic types of strain exist: normal strain, which is a change in length, and shear strain, which is a change in angle. *Normal strain* is the amount of deformation, defined as the amount of lengthening or shortening divided by the structure's original length. It is a nondimensional parameter expressed as a percentage. *Shear strain* is the amount of angular deformation in a structure or change in the original angle of the structure in response to torque loading. Shear strain is expressed in radians. While normal

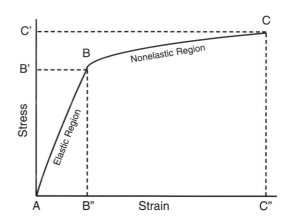

FIGURE 5-12

A stress-strain curve illustrates the strain that results from placing a standard specimen of tissue in a testing machine and loading it to failure. Yield point B represents the point past which some permanent deformation of bone occurs, yield stress B' represents the load per unit area that the bone sample sustained before nonelastic deformation, and yield strain B" represents the amount of deformation the sample sustained before nonelastic deformation. Ultimate failure point C is the point past which the sample failed, ultimate stress C' is the load per unit area the sample sustained before failure, and ultimate strain C" shows the amount of deformation that the sample sustained before failure. (Reproduced with permission from Frankel VH, Nordin M (eds): *Basic Biomechanics of the Skeletal System*, ed 2. Philadelphia, PA, Lea & Febiger, 1989.)

strain is typically a lengthening force, shear strain is typically a perpendicular force.

Stress and strain values can be obtained for materials such as bone by placing a standard specimen of tissue in a testing machine and loading it to failure. The strain that results can be illustrated in a stress-strain curve (**Figure 5-12**). The regions on the curve correspond to those on the load deformation curve. The stiffness of the material is represented by the slope of the curve in the elastic region so that stiffer materials have higher moduli. This slope is *Young's modulus of elasticity (E)*.[5] The *strength* in terms of elastic storage is represented by the area under the entire curve. This is called the *toughness* of the material.[1]

Stress-strain curves for metal, glass, and bone illustrate differences in their mechanical properties (**Figure 5-13**). Metal is the stiffest material so that it has the steepest slope.

Materials are classified as brittle or ductile, depending on the amount of deformation they undergo before failure. Glass, which is *brittle*, deforms little before failure, as indicated by the absence of a nonelastic (plastic) region on

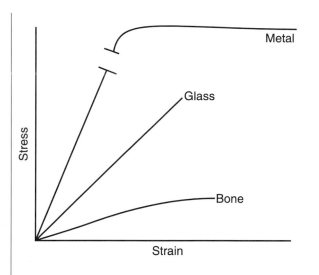

FIGURE 5-13

The different mechanical properties for metal, glass, and bone are illustrated in a stress-strain curve. (Reproduced with permission from Frankel VH, Nordin M (eds): Basic Biomechanics of the Skeletal System, ed 2. Philadelphia, PA, Lea & Febiger, 1989.)

the stress-strain curve (see Figure 5-13). Soft metal, which is *ductile*, deforms extensively before failure, as indicated by a long, nonelastic region on the curve. The fracture surfaces of the two materials reflect this difference in the amount of deformation.[5] A ductile material that is pieced together after fracture will not conform to its original shape, but a brittle material will.

Loading

All biologic materials are anisotropic such that their properties depend on the direction of loading. Bone is no exception. Forces and moments can be applied to bone in various directions, producing tension, compression, bending, shear, torsion, and combined loading (**Figure 5-14**). Bone is strongest in compression, weakest in shear, and intermediate in tension.[11] Bone is also viscoelastic because its properties are sensitive to the rate and duration of loading. Specifically, bone is stiffer and sustains a higher load prior to failure when loads are applied at higher rates. Cancellous bone is one fourth as dense, one tenth as stiff, and five times more ductile than cortical bone. Cortical bone is excellent at resisting torsion, whereas cancellous bone is excellent at resisting compressive and shear forces. The materials properties of bone are dynamic; stiffness increases and ductility decreases with aging, and strength decreases following immobilization. Moreover, loading of bone is complex because bones are constantly subjected to multiple indeterminate loads, and their geometry is irregular. For example, the complexity of loading patterns to the tibia during common physiologic activities such as walking and jogging has previously been

determined. During normal walking, the stresses were compressive during heel strike, tensile during the stance phase, and again compressive during push-off.

Bone fractures can be produced by a single load that exceeds the ultimate strength of the bone or by repeated applications of a lower magnitude load. A fracture caused by repeated applications of a lower magnitude load is called a fatigue fracture or stress fracture. The interplay of load and repetition for any material can be plotted on a fatigue curve. Fatigue fractures are usually sustained during prolonged strenuous physical activity, during which muscles fatigue and become less able to resist the stresses imposed on the bone.

Loading and soft tissue

The soft tissues that make up ligaments, tendons, and joint capsules also exhibit specific types of behavior under loading. When a ligament is loaded, microfracture occurs even before the yield point is reached. When the yield point is exceeded, the ligament begins to undergo gross failure at the same time the joint begins to displace abnormally. Other surrounding structures, such as the joint capsule and other ligaments, may be damaged as well.

As is the case for bone, soft tissues also exhibit viscoelastic behavior, including stress relaxation, creep, and hysteresis. *Stress relaxation* is the decrease in force required to maintain the tissue over time when it is subject to a constant deformation.[12] *Creep* is characterized by continued deformation in response to a maintained load.[1,12] The *hysteresis* response is the amount of relaxation, or variation in the load-deformation relationship, that takes place within a single cycle of loading and unloading.[12] In other words, the shape of the load-

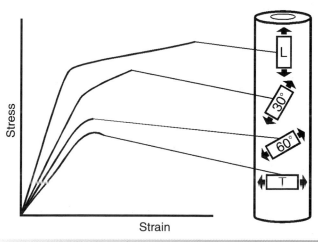

FIGURE 5-14

Forces and moments applied to bone in various directions produce tension, compression, bending, shear, torsion, and combined loading. (Reproduced with permission from Frankel VH, Nordin M (eds): Basic Biomechanics of the Skeletal System, ed 2. Philadelphia, PA, Lea & Febiger, 1989.)

deformation curve for viscoelastic soft tissues depends on the previous loading and unloading history (**Figure 5-15**). When tendons and ligaments are not under stretch, the collagen fibers display *crimp*, which is a regular undulation or wave-type pattern of cells and matrix.[13] Crimp is another property shared by ligaments and tendons. Crimp provides a buffer or shock absorber that protects the ligament from damage during elongation. Under loading, the tendon or ligament straightens out and the crimp disappears.[13]

STRUCTURE AND FUNCTION OF NORMAL TISSUE

Connective Tissue

Connective tissues are composed of two basic elements: cells and extracellular matrix. Cell composition varies greatly among the types of connective tissue. Cellular material occupies approximately 20% of the total tissue volume in tendon, ligament, and cartilage, and extracellular matrix accounts for the remainder. Because these tissues are relatively acellular, their response to injury relies on the migration of reparative cells. In contrast, bone, which is mostly organic and inorganic matrix, and muscle, which is relatively cellular, contain pluripotential cells that are available to initiate the repair process.

Extracellular matrix determines the form and function of connective tissues. Matrix may possess the ability to modulate protein synthesis by cells in response to loading or use. Approximately 70% of the extracellular matrix is composed of water, and 30% is solid. Collagen and proteoglycans are the two most abundant components of the extracellular matrix.

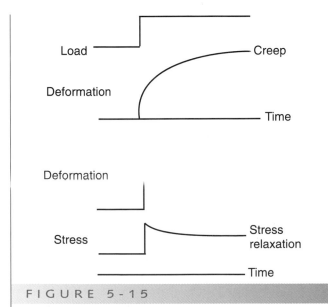

FIGURE 5-15

Previous loading and unloading history determine the shape of the load-deformation curve for viscoelastic soft tissues.

FOCUS ON . . .

Structure and Function of Tissue

Connective tissue

Connective tissues are composed of cells and extracellular matrix, but the amounts of each vary. In tendon, ligament, and cartilage, cells constitute 20% of the total tissue volume. The response of these tissues to injury relies on the migration of reparative cells. By contrast, bone and muscle contain pluripotential cells that initiate the repair process. Extracellular matrix, which is 70% water and 30% solid, determines the form and function of connective tissue and may modulate protein synthesis by cells in response to loading or use. The two most abundant components of the extracellular matrix are collagen and proteoglycans.

Collagen is made up of stiff, helical, insoluble protein macromolecules that provide scaffolding and tensile strength in fibrous tissues, and with added mineralization, rigidity in bone. Type I collagen, the most common type, is a component of tendon, ligament, muscle, and bone. Type II collagen is found in articular cartilage. Type III collagen has smaller fibrils and fewer cross-links than types I and II. Bone is formed by the mineralization of osteoid, which is an inorganic matrix synthesized by osteoblasts and composed of 70% type I collagen.

Proteoglycans retain water and contain a protein core with glycosaminoglycan side chains. Cartilage has large proteoglycans that aggregate with long chains of hyaluronic acid stabilized by link proteins. These aggregates are highly charged and bind water, which gives articular cartilage viscoelastic behavior and resistance to compression.

Collagen comprises a family of stiff, helical, insoluble protein macromolecules that are produced by fibroblasts that function as scaffolding and provide the tensile strength in fibrous tissues and, with the addition of mineralization, the rigidity in bone (**Figure 5-16**). Types I, II, and III collagen are most important in musculoskeletal tissue (**Figure 5-17**). **Table 5-1** shows the types and properties of collagen. *Type I collagen* is the most common collagen molecule and the fabric of tendon, ligament, muscle, and bone. *Type II collagen* is the principal collagen of articular cartilage. *Type III collagen* has smaller fibrils and fewer cross-links than types I and II collagen. Bone is formed by the mineralization of osteoid, which is an inorganic matrix synthesized by osteoblasts that is 70% type I collagen.[14]

Proteoglycans of various sizes are another component of the extracellular matrix that provide great water retention

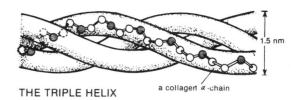

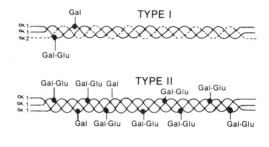

THE TRIPLE HELIX

a collagen α-chain

1.5 nm

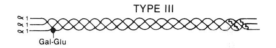

FIGURE 5-17

Types I, II, and III collagen are the most important types in musculoskeletal tissue. (Reproduced with permission from Gamble JG (ed): The Musculoskeletal System: Physiological Basics. New York, NY, Raven Press, 1988, p 61.)

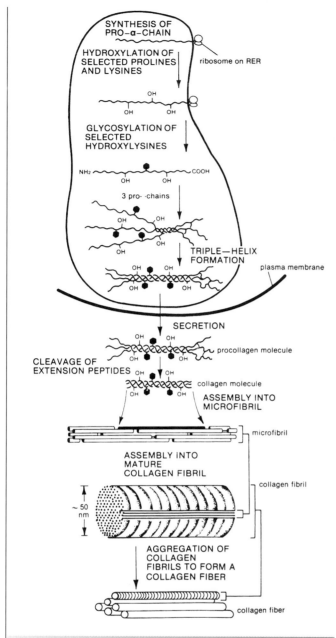

FIGURE 5-16

The rigidity of bone is determined by collagen, which comprises stiff, helical, insoluble protein macromolecules produced by fibroblasts that provide scaffolding and tensile strength in fibrous tissues, and mineralization. (Reproduced with permission from Gamble JG (ed): The Musculoskeletal System: Physiological Basics. New York, NY, Raven Press, 1988, p 63.)

Proteoglycan Aggregate

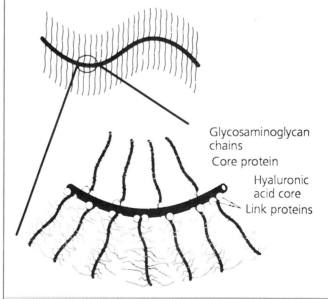

Glycosaminoglycan chains

Core protein

Hyaluronic acid core

Link proteins

FIGURE 5-18

Link proteins stabilize the aggregates of long chains of hyaluronic acid that are formed by the large proteoglycans of cartilage. (Reproduced with permission from Leadbetter WB, Buckwalter JA, Gordon SL (eds): Sports-Induced Inflammation: Clinical and Basic Science Concepts. Park Ridge, IL, American Academy of Orthopaedic Surgeons, 1990.)

capacity. Proteoglycans comprise a protein core to which one or more glycosaminoglycan (GAG) side chains are attached. The large proteoglycans of cartilage form aggregates with long chains of hyaluronic acid that are stabilized by link proteins (**Figure 5-18**). These aggregates, which are the largest such molecular structures in the body, are highly charged and function as enormous electrostatic sponges that bind water. This imparts articular

TABLE 5-1
TYPES AND PROPERTIES OF COLLAGEN

Type	Chains	Macromolecular Association	Aggregate Form	Localization
I	α 1(I), α 2(I)			Most abundant collagen: Ubiquitous— Bone, Tendon, Capsules,. Muscle, etc.
II	α 1(II)			Major cartilage collagen: Cartilage, Nucleus pulposus, Vitreous humor.
III	α 1(III)			Found in pliable tissues: Blood vessels, Muscle, Uterus, etc.

Adapted from Leadbetter WB, Buckwalter JA, and Gordon SL: *Sports-Induced Inflammation: Clinical and Basic Science Concepts.* Park Ridge, IL, American Academy of Orthopaedic Surgeons, 1990.

calage with viscoelastic behavior and effective resistance to compression.

TISSUE-SPECIFIC NORMAL PHYSIOLOGY

Bone

Bone is divided histologically into lamellar bone, which is arranged in layers, and nonlamellar bone, which is woven. Mature bone is *lamellar*; immature or pathologic bone is *nonlamellar*. At the macroscopic level, all bones are composed of two types of osseous tissue: cortical (or compact) bone and cancellous (or spongy or trabecular) bone (**Figure 5-19**). Cortical bone makes up 80% of the skeleton and forms the outer shell, or cortex, of the bone.[14] Cancellous bone within this shell is composed of thin plates, or trabeculae, arranged as a loose mesh. Because the lamellar structure and material composition of cancellous and cortical bone appear identical, the degree of porosity is the fundamental distinction between the two. The porosity ranges from 5% to 30% in cortical bone and from 30% to more than 90% in cancellous bone.[1] Consequently, the density of cancellous bone is a fraction of that of cortical bone. Cortical bone always surrounds cancellous bone, but the relative quantity of each type varies among bones and within individual bones according to functional demands.

At the microscopic level, lamellar bone is composed of tightly packed osteons or haversian systems. *Osteon* consists of a concentric series of layers (lamellae) of mineralized matrix surrounding the central canal, a configuration similar to growth rings in a tree trunk (**Figures 5-19 and 5-20**). At the center of the osteon is a small channel, called a haversian canal, that contains arterioles, venules, nerves, and other structures. Although both cortical and cancellous bone are arranged in concentric lamellae, cancellous bone does not contain haversian canals.

As with other connective tissue, bone is composed of cells and an organic extracellular matrix of fibers and ground substance produced by the cells. The distinguishing feature of bone is its high content of inorganic materials, in the form of a calcium phosphate mineral, that is part hydroxyapatite and part amorphous tricalcium phosphate. Bone matrix is made up roughly of one-third organic and two-thirds mineral components, although the exact composition depends on site, age, dietary history, and presence or absence of disease.[1] The organic matrix, which is known as *osteoid*, is mostly protein framework composed of collagen that allows growth and remodeling. The matrix also includes small amounts of water, proteoglycans (principally GAGs), and cells. The mineral component of bone matrix, *hydroxyapatite*, is deposited into the organic framework to make the bone hard and strong.

Bone cells include osteoblasts, osteocytes, and osteoclasts (**Figure 5-21**). Osteoblasts are the cells that form new bone; they deposit osteoid, which become mineralized over time. *Osteoblasts* are derived from precursor cells in the blood and migrate to areas where bone has been eroded by osteoclasts, laying down new bone in the cavities. Many osteoblasts become entrapped in the bone matrix and survive as osteocytes. These cells are relatively inert compared with osteoblasts and osteoclasts. *Osteoclasts* are bone-resorbing cells that also develop from precursor cells in the blood that collect at sites of bone resorption and fuse to form multinucleated cells. These osteoclasts erode any region of bone, especially those sites that have been damaged.

Bone growth

Bone growth occurs in one of two ways. *Enchondral ossification* is the manner in which long bones such as the femur or radius grow. A cartilage model is formed in utero and is invaded by osteoblasts to form primary centers of ossification. Secondary centers of ossification develop at the bone ends and form epiphyses or growth plates, which are responsible for longitudinal growth of immature bone.[15] During this process, bone replaces the cartilage model; cartilage is not converted to bone.

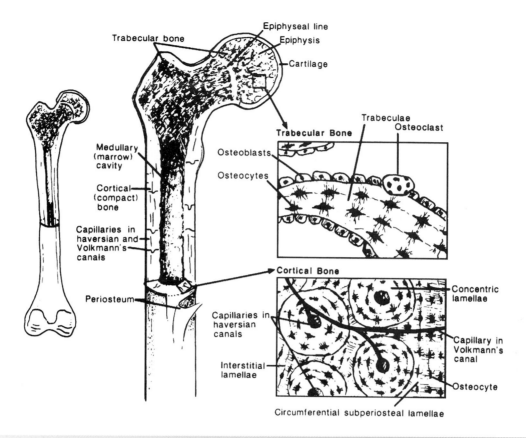

FIGURE 5-19

All bones are composed of cortical and cancellous tissue at the macroscopic level. (Reproduced with permission from Keaveny TM, Hayes WC: Mechanical properties of cortical trabecular bone. *Bone* 1993;7:285-344.)

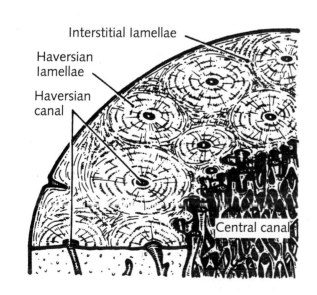

FIGURE 5-20

Osteon consists of concentric series of layers of mineralized matrix around a central canal; at the center of the osteon is the haversian canal.

The other manner of bone growth is *intramembranous ossification*, which occurs without a cartilage model. This process characterizes the in utero growth of flat bones as well as the growth in width of all bones. The diaphyseal portion of bone enlarges by the net proliferation of bone on its surfaces, beneath the periosteum.[15]

Bone formation and resorption

Bone formation and resorption are tightly coupled processes under the influence of humoral and mechanical factors that are normally in balance to maintain healthy tissue. In the constant cycle of resorption and formation, osteoclasts invade the bone surface and erode it by dissolving both mineral and matrix. Osteoblasts then build new bone by laying down collagen and mineral. Bone remodels according to *Wolff's law*, which states that bone is laid down where needed and resorbed where not needed in response to the mechanical demands or stresses placed on it.[1] Removing external stresses such as prolonged nonweightbearing can lead to significant bone loss or disuse osteopenia.

All bones are surrounded by *periosteum*, which is a dense connective tissue membrane. Several blood vessels and nerve fibers that pass into the cortex penetrate the outer layer of periosteum. An inner osteogenic layer

FOCUS ON . . .

Tissue-Specific Normal Physiology

Bone

Histologically, bone is composed of layered, mature (lamellar) bone and woven, immature or pathologic (nonlamellar) bone. Macroscopically, bone is composed of compact (cortical) bone and spongy or trabecular (cancellous) bone. Cortical bone comprises 80% of the skeleton, forming the outer shell (cortex) of bone. Cancellous bone within this shell is arranged in thin plates (trabeculae) in a loose mesh. Cortical bone always surrounds cancellous bone; the amount of each type varies among bones and within bones according to functional demands. Cortical and cancellous bone are distinguished by their degree of porosity, which ranges from 5% to 30% in cortical bone and from 30% to more than 90% in cancellous bone. As a result, cancellous bone is far less dense than cortical bone.

Osteoblasts, osteocytes, and osteoclasts are three types of bone cells. Osteoblasts form new bone by depositing osteoid, which becomes mineralized over time. They develop from precursor cells in the blood and migrate to areas of eroded bone; many osteoblasts become entrapped in the bone matrix and survive as osteocytes, which are relatively inert. Osteoclasts resorb bone and also derive from blood precursor cells; they collect where bone has been resorbed and fuse to form multinucleated cells.

Bone growth occurs via enchondral and intramembranous ossification. Enchondral ossification (important to long bones) is based on an in utero cartilage model that is invaded by osteoblasts to form primary centers of ossification. Secondary centers form at the bone ends to create growth plates (epiphyses), which provide longitudinal growth of immature bone as bone replaces cartilage. Intramembranous ossification is responsible for growth of flat bones, as well as for increasing width of all bones. This process occurs without a cartilage model; the diaphysis enlarges by the net proliferation of bone on its surfaces, beneath the periosteum.

To maintain healthy tissue, bone formation and resorption are tightly coupled under the influence of humoral and mechanical factors. Osteoclasts erode the bone surface by dissolving mineral and matrix. Osteoblasts then lay down collagen and mineral to form new bone. Wolff's law describes bone remodeling: bone is laid down where needed and resorbed where unneeded in response to the mechanical demands or stresses placed on it. For example, prolonged weightbearing can result in significant bone loss or disuse osteopenia.

Bone is surrounded by periosteum (a dense connective tissue membrane), which has an outer layer penetrated by blood vessels and nerve cells that supply the cortex. The inner osteogenic layer has bone cells that generate new bone during growth and repair. Periosteum covers the entire bone except for the joint surfaces, which are covered with articular cartilage. Oxygen and nutrients are provided to the bone by a rich blood supply. The blood supply is temporarily disrupted when a bone fractures, but increases within hours or days. The nerve supply in the periosteum is also extensive. Nerve irritation and hemorrhage result in the severe pain of a fracture.

Cartilage

There are many types of cartilage: physeal (growth plate), fibrocartilage (tendon and ligament), elastic (trachea), fibroelastic (meniscus), and articular or hyaline (joint). Articular cartilage decreases friction and distributes load. Its major component is water (65% to 80% of wet weight), which allows for cartilage deformation in response to stress. Collagen (10% to 20% of wet weight and more than 50% of dry weight) provides a framework for cartilage and offers tensile strength. Chondrocytes are cells that produce proteoglycans and secrete them into the extracellular matrix. Glycosaminoglycans trap water molecules, giving cartilage resiliency and contributing to its compressive strength. Histologically, cartilage is organized in several layers. In the tangential zone, collagen fibers are at right angles to each other and parallel to the articular surface, creating a strong, compression-resisting mesh.

Meniscus is specialized cartilage found in synovial joints such as the knee, hip, and glenohumeral joint. The meniscus is composed of fibrocartilage, a mesh of collagen fibers, proteoglycans, and glycoproteins interspersed with fibrochondrocytes. The extracellular matrix is primarily type I collagen (60% of dry weight), along with other types of collagen, proteoglycans, and glycoproteins (the latter two in smaller quantities than in hyaline cartilage). The knee meniscus has three layers: a mesh-like, radially oriented superficial layer, a middle layer or irregularly arranged collagen fibers, and a deep layer of parallel circumferential fibers (most of the meniscus). The vascular supply is to the outer third; the rest of the meniscus receives nutrition via the synovium. Innervation is to the peripheral two thirds of the meniscus only and may offer some nociceptive and proprioceptive function.

(Continued)

Tissue-Specific Normal Physiology (Continued)

Muscle

The basic structural unit of muscle is the muscle fiber. Fibers are arranged in bundles (fascicles), usually oriented obliquely to one another and to the longitudinal axis. Other muscle configurations are parallel, fusiform, unipennate, bipennate, and multipennate, with the orientation depending on the muscle's function. Fusiform muscles allow greater range of motion, while pennate muscles generate more power. A muscle's maximal force production is related to its cross-sectional area. The muscle fiber is an elongated cell, a fusion of many cells with many nuclei, and comprises arrays of parallel myofibrils. Each myofibril includes sarcomeres, which are the basic contractile elements of skeletal muscle.

Skeletal muscle is supplied with arteries, veins, and nerves, which bring oxygen and nutrients to the muscle and carries away waste produced by muscle contractions, processes without which the muscle cannot function. If insufficient oxygen or nutrients are available or waste products such as lactic acid accumulate, cramps result.

Muscle can contract fully or partially, leading to changes in muscle length or tension or both. Each individual fiber contracts either maximally or not at all, so increasing the force of contraction requires that additional fibers be recruited. A motor neuron innervates many muscle fibers that together form the motor unit. Recruiting additional motor units increases the force of contraction. An action potential from a motor neuron causes the entire motor unit to contract, producing a muscle twitch.

The contraction of many sarcomeres in series causes a muscle contraction. The motor neuron initiates the muscle contraction stimulus and sends an electrical impulse down the axon to the neuromuscular junction. At the motor endplate (muscle-nerve synapse), acetylcholine is released and diffuses across the synaptic cleft to bind on the muscle membrane, triggering the sarcoplasmic reticulum to release calcium. Calcium binds to troponin on the thin filaments, causing them to change the tropomyosin conformation and expose the actin filaments. Actin-myosin cross-bridges form, and as the breakdown of adenosine 5'-triphosphate (ATP) provides energy, the thick and think filaments slide past one another, causing contraction. With strenuous muscle activity, ATP and oxygen reserves are depleted. ATP must then be produced by anaerobic glycolysis, a less efficient process that releases lactic acid and causes oxygen debt. After exertion ends, extra oxygen is consumed and lactic acid is cleared from the muscle.

A muscle's passive and active tension resulting from stimulation vary with the muscle fiber's length. The resting muscle generates the greatest contractile force. A muscle that is passively stretched beyond its resting length develops increased passive and decreased active tension.

Histologically, muscles are composed mostly of type I (red) and type II (white) fibers. Type I (slow-twitch) fibers are rich in metabolic enzymes and myoglobulin. Type II (fast-twitch) fibers have high concentrations of anaerobic glycolytic enzymes and less myoglobin. Myoglobin, a protein storage site for oxygen, speeds the oxygen diffusion into the muscle fiber. Type I fibers contract slowly and are used for sustained work. Type II fibers contract rapidly and shortly and have fewer fibers per motor unit, making them better suited for fine-skilled movements. Different quantities of type I and II fibers among individuals may explain differences in athletic ability.

Tendon

Tendon is the tough, cable-like fibrous tissue that attaches muscle to bone and transmits tensile loads, thereby producing joint motion. Tendon must also be flexible enough to bend at joints and must dampen sudden shock to muscle damage. An aponeurosis is a broad, fibrous sheet that attaches one muscle to another. Tendon is composed of type I collagen fascicles in a proteoglycan matrix. Fibroblasts (the predominant cell type) are arranged in parallel rows between the collagen fibrils. The fascicles are separated by endotenon, surrounded by epitenon, and enclosed within either a tendon sheath or a paratenon, depending on the tendon and the location. Epitenon is the synovial-like membrane that envelops the tendon surface and is continuous on its inner surface with the endotenon, a thin layer of connective tissue containing lymphatics, blood vessels, and nerves. Tendons that move in a straight line and elongate have an epitenon surrounded by a paratenon (loose areolar tissue), which together form the peritendon. Tendons that bend sharply around a joint are enveloped by a tendon sheath (tenosynovium), two membrane layers lined by synovial cells, that acts as a pulley to direct the tendon's path. Where tendon and bone meet at the tenoperiosteal junction, the endotenon collagen fibers continue into bone as Sharpey's fibers. The tendon insertion into bone has four zones that increase stiffness and dissipate stress: tendon, fibrocartilage, mineralized fibrocartilage, and bone.

(Continued)

FOCUS ON . . .

Tissue-Specific Normal Physiology (Continued)

Tendon (Continued)

Vascular tendons are surrounded by a paratenon and receive vessels along their borders. Avascular tendons are surrounded by a tendon sheath. Connective tissue bands (mesotenons) that join the epitenon to the tendon sheath have conduits (vincula) that supply blood to the tendon.

The parallel tendon fibers allow the tendon to handle the high tensile loads of activity, making the tendon's tensile strength among the highest of any soft tissue (45 to 98 N/mm2, beginning to fail at 5% to 10% strain). On the stress-strain curve, the toe region is the collagen fibrils uncrimping during the initial stretch. The linear region is the elastic deformation with increasing strain, followed by plastic deformation. A viscoelastic material, tendon exhibits stress-relaxation, creep, and hysteresis, with the material properties dependent on time and rate change. With rapid loading, the tendon's elastic modulus (stiffness) and ultimate strength increase; with cyclical loading, the elastic modulus decreases.

Ligaments

Ligaments and joint capsules connect bone to bone. They enhance joints' mechanical stability, guide joint motion, prevent abnormal motion, provide proprioceptive feedback, and may initiate protective reflexes.

Ligament inserts into bone either directly (attaching to bone at right angles or tangentially in a transition similar to tendon, such as the tibial insertion of the medial collateral ligament) or indirectly (passing obliquely along the bone surface and inserting acutely into the periosteum, such as the femoral insertion of the medial collateral ligament). Some ligaments have more than one band of fibrils or bundles, which become taut as the joint moves through its range of motion, increasing flexibility. Blood is supplied to ligaments mainly at the insertion site, which also contains mechanoreceptors and free nerve endings that provide proprioception and may help to stabilize joints.

Synovium

Synovium, a complex, highly permeable, and vascular tissue, lines the inner surface of joint capsules along with bursae, tendons, and ligaments. Type A cells comprise 20% to 30% of the bursa, tendon sheath, and joint synovial linings and are active in phagocytosis (removing cellular debris), immunology, and inflammation. Type B cells are similar to fibroblasts and contribute to synovial fluid. Synovial fluid lubricates and nourishes chondrocytes. It contains proteinase, collagenase, hyaluronic acid, prostaglandins, and lymphocytes. The production of lysosomal enzymes increases in response to trauma; these enzymes degrade hyaluronic acid and decrease the synovial fluid viscosity. The concentration of lymphocytes and other injury-response cells is markedly increased in joint infections and some inflammatory conditions.

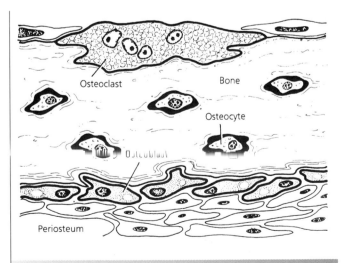

FIGURE 5-21

Bone cells are composed of osteoblasts, osteocytes, and osteoclasts.

contains bone cells responsible for generating new bone during growth and repair. The periosteum covers the entire bone except for the joint surfaces, which are covered with articular cartilage.

Bones are just as much living tissue as the tissues of muscle or skin. A rich blood supply constantly provides the oxygen and nutrients that bone needs. Following a fracture, the blood supply is disrupted initially but increases within hours to days in response to the injury. Bone has an extensive nerve supply, primarily in the periosteum. The combination of nerve irritation and hemorrhage from damaged blood vessels accounts for the severe pain produced by bone fracture.

Cartilage

The body contains several types of cartilage, as shown in **Table 5-2**. Articular cartilage, which decreases friction and distributes loading, is composed of water, collagen, proteoglycans, and cells. Water accounts for 65% to 80%

of the wet weight of cartilage and allows for cartilage deformation in response to stress.[14] Water content decreases with age; however, it increases with the presence of osteoarthritis. Collagen accounts for 10% to 20% of the wet weight of cartilage and more than 50% of the dry weight. Most of the collagen is type II collagen, which provides a framework for cartilage and accounts for its tensile strength. *Chondrocytes* are the cells in cartilage that produce proteoglycans, which are secreted into the extracellular matrix. The GAGs in proteoglycans trap water molecules, which impart resiliency to cartilage and contributes to its compressive strength. Adult chondrocytes do not undergo mitosis or cell division for new growth under normal conditions. Cartilage is organized histologically into several layers (**Table 5-3, Figure 5-22**). Collagen fibers in the tangential zone are arranged at right angles to each other and parallel to the articular surface, thereby creating a strong mesh that resists compression.

The *meniscus* is specialized cartilage found in various synovial joints including the knee. The meniscus broadens the contact area between the bony ends to distribute load (**Figure 5-23**). In the knee, the meniscus is responsible for transmitting 50% of the knee joint force in extension and 85% to 90% in flexion. The meniscus acts as a shock absorber, attenuating the stress wave produced by each heel strike. In addition, the anterior and posterior horns of the meniscus act as a secondary stabilizer to anteroposterior translation. In addition to the knee, menisci are found in joints such as the hip and glenohumeral joint, where they are referred to as the labrum, and in other joints of the body.

The meniscus is composed of *fibroelastic cartilage*. This tissue is a mesh of collagen fibers, proteoglycans, and glycoproteins, interspersed with specialized cells termed fibrochondrocytes. The extracellular matrix is made up of predominantly type I collagen (60% of dry weight), as well as other types of collagen, proteoglycans, and glycoproteins. Compared with hyaline cartilage, menisci have far fewer proteoglycans and glycoproteins.

In the knee, the meniscus is organized in three layers: a mesh-like radially oriented superficial layer, a middle layer of irregularly arranged collagen fibers, and a deep layer of parallel circumferential fibers that constitute the bulk of the tissue. The vascular supply is to the outer third of the meniscus. The remainder of the meniscus receives nutrition from the synovium. Innervation is restricted to the peripheral two thirds of the meniscus where free nerve endings and mechanoreceptors are found that may provide some nociceptive and proprioceptive function.

Muscle

The muscle fiber is the basic structural unit of muscle and is organized into bundles of fibers called *fascicles*. These may be parallel but are usually oriented obliquely to one another and to the longitudinal axis. The variability of fiber arrangement within the muscle accounts for different muscle configurations, including parallel, fusiform, unipennate, bipennate, and multipennate[1] (**Figure 5-24**). The orientation of muscle fibers depends on the specific function of the muscle. Fusiform muscles permit greater range of motion, whereas pennate muscles contain more short fibers working in parallel to generate more power (force of contraction). The maximal force production of a

TABLE 5-3

ARTICULAR CARTILAGE LAYERS

Layer	Width (μm)	Characteristic	Orientation	Function
Gliding zone	40	↑ Metabolic activity	Tangential	vs. Shear
Transitional zone	500	↑ Metabolic activity	Oblique	vs. Compression
Radial zone	1,000	↑ Collagen size	Vertical	vs. Compression
Tidemark	5	Undulating barrier	Tangential	vs. Shear
Calcified zone	300	Hydroxyapatite crystals		Anchor

↑Increased; ↓decreased

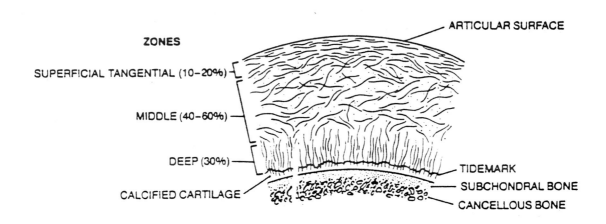

ZONES

SUPERFICIAL TANGENTIAL (10–20%)

MIDDLE (40–60%)

DEEP (30%)

CALCIFIED CARTILAGE

ARTICULAR SURFACE

TIDEMARK

SUBCHONDRAL BONE

CANCELLOUS BONE

FIGURE 5-22

Cartilage is organized histologically into several layers. (Reproduced with permission from Mow VC, Proctor CS, Kelly MA: Biomechanics of articular cartilage, in Nordin M, Frankel VH (eds): *Basic Biomechanics of the Skeletal System.* Philadelphia, PA, Lea & Febiger, 1989, p 34.)

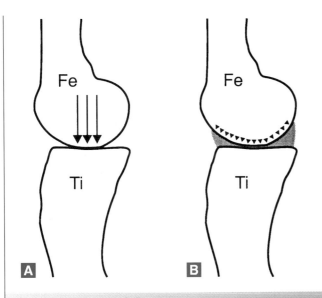

FIGURE 5-23

The contact area between the bony ends of the knee is broadened by the meniscus to distribute load. The sagittal section is shown through the femur (Fe) and tibia (Ti). **A** Shown without the meniscus. **B** Shown with the meniscus interposed. (Reproduced with permission from Adams LM: The anatomy of joints related to function, in Wright V, Radin EL (eds): *Mechanics of Human Joints: Physiology, Pathophysiology, and Treatment.* New York, NY, Marcel Dekker, 1993, p 37.)

muscle is related to its cross-sectional area.

Many muscle fibers are arranged within each fascicle, imbedded in delicate connective tissue. The muscle fiber is the basic structural element of skeletal muscle. It is a specialized elongated cell that is a fusion of many cells with multiple nuclei. The muscle fiber is composed primarily of arrays of parallel myofibrils. Each myofibril is a series of sarcomeres, which comprise the basic contractile element of skeletal muscle.[16] Muscle morphology depends on a fibrous connective tissue framework in addition to the arrangement of muscle fibers. Connective tissue surrounds whole muscle (epimysium), each fascicle or bundle of fibers (perimysium), and individual muscle fibers (endomysium)[1] **(Figures 5-25, A and B).** This connective tissue framework attaches to tendon and is essential for the efficient generation of force.

All skeletal muscles are supplied with arteries, veins, and nerves. Blood carries oxygen and nutrients to muscles and carries away the waste produced by muscle contractions. Muscles cannot function properly without both the continuous supply of nutrients and the continuous removal of waste. Cramps result when insufficient oxygen or nutrients are available or when waste products, such as lactic acid, accumulate.

Muscle contraction

Muscle may contract fully or partially, leading to a change in muscle length, tension, or both. Each individual muscle fiber contracts maximally or not at all. Increasing a muscle's force of contraction results from recruiting additional muscle fibers. A single motor neuron innervates many muscle fibers that together form a functional unit: the motor unit. Recruitment of additional motor units increases the force of contraction. Thus, a single action potential from a motor neuron causes the contraction of the entire motor unit, which is a muscle twitch.

Muscle contraction results from the contraction of many sarcomeres in series. The sarcomere is composed of intricately arranged thick and thin filaments that allow fibers to slide past each other **(Figure 5-25, C).** One type of protein aggregate, consisting of myosin, makes up thick filaments, and another type of protein

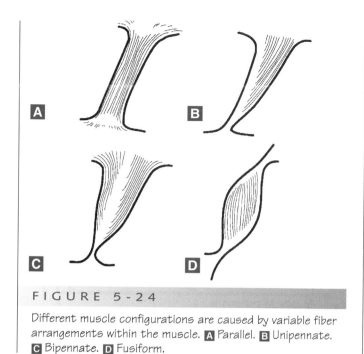

FIGURE 5-24

Different muscle configurations are caused by variable fiber arrangements within the muscle. **A** Parallel. **B** Unipennate. **C** Bipennate. **D** Fusiform.

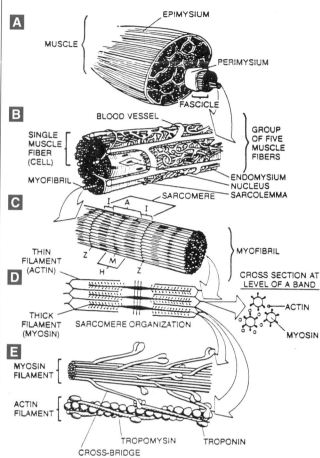

FIGURE 5-25

The structural organization of muscle consists of a connective tissue framework and arranged muscle fibers. **A** and **B** Connective tissue surrounds the epimysium, perimysium, and endomysium. **C** Intricately arranged thick and thin filaments allow fibers to slide past each other in the sarcomere. **D** Thick filaments are made up of a protein aggregate that consists of myosin, and thin filaments are made up of a protein aggregate that consists of actin, troponin, and tropomyosin. **E** Bands and zones make up the sarcomere, enabling effective and efficient muscle contraction at the subcellular or molecular level. (Reproduced with permission from Pitman MI, Peterson L: Biomechanics of skeletal muscle, in Frankel VH, Nordin M (eds): *Basic Biomechanics of the Skeletal System*, ed 2. Philadelphia, PA, Lea & Febiger, 1980, p 90)

aggregate, consisting mainly of actin, but also including troponin and tropomyosin, makes up the thin filaments (**Figure 5-25, D**). To enable effective and efficient muscle contraction at a subcellular or molecular level, the sarcomere is arranged into bands and zones (**Figure 5-25, E**). The H-zone contains only myosin filaments, and the I-band contains only actin filaments. The I-bands are attached to the Z-line, which borders individual sarcomeres and extends partially into the A-band.

The stimulus for a muscle contraction originates in the motor neuron and is carried toward the neuromuscular junction as an electrical impulse propagated down the entire length of the axon. Once the impulse reaches the motor end plate, which is a specialized synapse between muscle and nerve, the neurotransmitter acetylcholine is released[16] (**Figure 5-26**). The neurotransmitter diffuses across the synaptic cleft to bind a specific receptor on the muscle membrane, which in turn triggers the release of calcium from the sarcoplasmic reticulum (**Figure 5-27**). Calcium binds to troponin on the thin filaments, causing them to change the conformation of tropomyosin and expose the actin filaments. Actin-myosin cross-bridges form, and with the breakdown of the energy source adenosine 5'-triphosphate (ATP), the thick and thin filaments slide past one another in a ratchet-like manner, causing the muscle to contract.[16]

The energy source ATP is consumed to drive the conformational change in the two major protein constituents of muscles to produce contraction. ATP is synthesized by a complex series of metabolic pathways. During periods of strenuous muscle activity, ATP and oxygen reserves are depleted so that ATP is produced by a less efficient metabolic pathway, anaerobic glycolysis, which produces lactic acid and creates an oxygen debt. Once the exertion is complete, extra oxygen is consumed and the lactic acid is cleared from the muscle.

Both the passive tension and the active tension that a muscle develops when it is stimulated vary with the length of the muscle fiber. The greatest contractile force develops when the muscle is at its resting length. If the muscle is passively stretched beyond its resting length, the

tight as the knee extends.[8] Ligaments receive their blood supply mainly at the insertion site and harbor mechanoreceptors and free nerve endings that provide proprioception and may play an important role in stabilizing joints.

Synovium

Synovium, which is a complex, highly permeable, and vascular tissue, lines the inner surface of joint capsules, as well as that of bursae, tendons, and ligaments. A *bursa* is a very thin sac formed by two layers of synovial tissue that is located at sites where there is friction between tendon and bone or skin and bone. Examples include prepatellar bursa over the knee cap and olecranon bursa behind the elbow. Bursae are unappreciable on examination unless inflamed.

Synovial tissue contains two types of cells. Type A cells comprise 20% to 30% of the synovial lining of bursa, tendon sheaths, and joints. They are active in phagocytosis, which is the removal of cellular debris, and demonstrate immunologic and inflammatory activity.[14] Type B cells resemble fibroblasts and produce fluid that is combined with an ultrafiltrate of serum to form synovial fluid.

Synovial fluid provides lubrication and nutrients for joint chondrocytes. It has a very low coefficient of friction so that it acts as an excellent natural lubricant of joints. Synovial fluid contains proteinase, collagenase, hyaluronic acid, and prostaglandins. When produced in response to trauma, it contains high concentrations of lysosomal enzymes that degrade hyaluronic acid and decrease the fluid's protective viscosity. Synovial fluid also contains lymphocytes and other cells that react strongly to injury. The concentration of these cells is markedly increased in joint infections and some inflammatory conditions.

Peripheral Nerves

Peripheral nerves are highly organized structures that contain nerve fibers, blood vessels, and connective tissue. The different types of peripheral nerve fibers can be classified as type A, type B, and type C fibers. Type A fibers are heavily myelinated and fast, such as those fibers emanating from cutaneous pressure receptors.[1,14] Type C fibers are unmyelinated and slow, such as pain fibers. Type B fibers have intermediate properties.

A single nerve fiber is composed of a single axon that conducts the action potential or electrical impulse from the nerve cell or neuron body. Other parts of the neuron consist of the dendrites, which are thin processes that branch from the cell body to receive input from surrounding nerve cells, and the cell body, which is the neuron's metabolic center.

Peripheral nerve axons are myelinated if they are surrounded by myelin sheaths formed by Schwann cells. Myelinated fibers are faster than unmyelinated fibers because of saltatory conduction or action potentials that are conducted rapidly by jumping between the gaps between Schwann cells, known as nodes of Ranvier. Axons, coated with a fibrous tissue called *endoneurium*, are grouped into nerve bundles called fascicles. Individual fascicles are covered with connective tissue called *perineurium*. Peripheral nerves are composed of one to many fascicles and the surrounding areolar connective tissue or epineurium. Individual peripheral nerve branches contain both sensory and motor neurons.

MAINTENANCE OF CONNECTIVE TISSUE STRUCTURE AND FUNCTION

The process by which long-lived organisms replace obsolete components to preserve structural integrity and prolong normal function is called *morphostasis*.[17] At a tissue level, morphostasis involves the renewal of cell populations and extracellular matrix. For example, in connective tissues, morphostasis is responsible for the continual turnover of collagen.[17] Tissue loading and use are the primary mechanisms of connective tissue change in response to sports activity. In this context, use refers to both repeated movement and the accumulation of load over time. Consequently, the repetition seen in endurance sports may take the form of both cyclical loading and overuse, which lead to connective tissue injury.

Cells respond to increased load and use by modulating shape or composition, protein synthesis and breakdown, growth rate, and energy consumption.[16] Excessive overload or prolonged immobilization triggers protein breakdown or catabolism, which is prompted by an increase in the synthesis of matrix degradative enzymes. Maintenance of regular synthetic, homeostatic, and degradative cellular activity is conditional on a physiologic window of stress.

The adaptation to use or physical demand is a time-dependent cellular process. This is the foundation of the principle of transitional theory, which states that sports injury is most likely to occur when the athlete incurs

Maintenance of Connective Tissue Structure and Function

Morphostasis is the process by which long-lived organisms replace obsolete components, preserving structural integrity and prolonging normal function. This process involves the renewal of cell populations and extracellular matrix and the continual turnover of collagen in connective tissues. Connective tissue changes in response to sports activity occur primarily by tissue loading and use (repeated movement and accumulation of load over time), which can lead to injury. Increasing load and use cause cells to change shape or composition and increase protein synthesis and breakdown, growth rate, and energy consumption. Excessive overload or prolonged immobilization increase the synthesis of matrix degenerative enzymes, which cause protein breakdown (catabolism). Maintaining regular synthetic, homeostatic, and degradative cellular activity depends on a physiologic level of stress.

Transitional theory states that sports injury is most likely to occur when the athlete incurs any change in load or use of an involved part. Sudden activity changes (increase in level or duration of training, improper training, new running shoes, new running track) can trigger catabolism that exceeds the body's ability to repair itself. These transition changes are avoidable with proper coaching and supervision. The athlete's ability to adapt to load or use transitions is affected by aging and genetics. Aging reduces basal functional capacity and the ability to adapt and recover from environmental stress. Aging also increases collagen rigidity (making it less compliant and less resistant to tension) and decreases both its water content (decreasing resilience and deformation tolerance) and turnover. However, tissue healing is not slowed by age alone.

Genetic predisposition (perhaps a collagen abnormality) seems to be a factor in conditions such as rotator cuff complaints, lumbar disc degeneration, and Achilles tendon tears, which may reflect mesenchymal syndrome (increased risk of connective tissue breakdown with relatively benign load or use). Individuals with mesenchymal syndrome typically have severe tendinosis at multiple sites. Affected athletes must be counseled to train properly, avoid abusing training techniques, and be cautious during training transitions.

any change in load or use of an involved part.[17] Sudden activity change in training or during recovery from injury may trigger an undesired catabolic response in tissues that exceeds the reparative capacity. This commonly results in inflammation and pain. Examples include sudden increases in performance level or duration of training, improper training, and changes in equipment or environment, such as new running shoes or a new running track.[17] Injuries induced by transition can usually be avoided by proper coaching and training supervision that properly monitors rehabilitation and prevents overzealous return to activity.

Factors Influencing Adaptation

The athlete's ability to adapt to transitions in load or use is influenced by factors such as aging and genetics. Aging leads to a decrease in basal functional capacity and a reduced ability to adapt and recover from environmental stress. For example, the maximal increase in pulse with exercise becomes smaller with age for a given resting pulse rate, and the time required to return to basal heart rate is prolonged.[16,20]

Aging also adversely impacts the mechanical properties of connective tissue. Collagen undergoes a process called maturational stabilization, in which cross-linkages between collagen molecules become more molecularly bound. Up to a point, this actually enhances connective tissue strength, but in the later part of life, the increasing rigidity of collagen fibers actually results in less compliant, less tension-resistant tissue.[20] In addition, aging connective tissue undergoes a generalized decline in water content.[17,20] This leads to a loss of resilience and tolerance to deformation. Interestingly, although collagen turnover declines with age, overall tissue healing does not appear to be retarded by age alone.[20]

Genetic predisposition to injury has received little attention, but familial patterns have been identified in such conditions as rotator cuff complaints, lumbar disk degeneration, and Ac.hilles' tendon tears. The term *"mesenchymal syndrome"* describes a subset of sports trauma patients who are at risk for connective tissue breakdown following relatively benign load or use. These athletes may be plagued with multiple sites of chronic complaints usually referred to as "tendinitis," although as described later in this section, the term "tendinosis" is more appropriate because inflammation is not typically present. These athletes may complain of rotator cuff "tendinitis," lateral or medial tennis elbow or epicondylitis, and carpal tunnel syndrome, as well as patellar "tendinitis," Achilles' "tendinitis," and plantar fasciitis.[17]

Although this phenotype of susceptibility to injury is poorly defined, some form of collagen abnormality has been theorized.[17] In any case, the association of several of these diagnoses in one individual is striking and cannot otherwise be explained. Although the sites of injury are the same as would be seen in other populations of injured athletes, this subgroup has an inflammatory or degenerative reaction that is more severe than expected. Because of this increased susceptibility, affected athletes must be counseled to train properly, avoid abusive training techniques, and be aware of transitional risks.

CHAPTER REVIEW

In order to minimize the adverse effects of trauma and promote proper tissue healing to speed the safe return of the athlete to sport, the athletic trainer must understand the principles behind wound healing and tissue repair. Familiarity with the anatomy of bones, joints, and muscles and the biomechanics of the human body is essential. Recognizing the concepts of force, energy, and kinesiology, along with the mechanical properties of materials, allows one to comprehend how injuries occur and how they might be prevented. Along with the gross anatomy of the bones, joints, and muscles, the athletic trainer must assimilate the structure, function, and maintenance of connective tissue and the normal physiology of bone, cartilage, muscle, tendon, ligament, synovium, and peripheral nerves.

1. The flare at either end of a long bone is called the:

   A. diaphysis.

   B. metaphysis.

   C. epiphysis.

   D. physis.

2. What is the major muscle mass of the body?

   A. Skeletal

   B. Cardiac

   C. Visceral

   D. Special

3. Any force or combination of forces applied to the outside of a structure is known as:

   A. moment arm.

   B. torque.

   C. linear acceleration.

   D. load.

4. Of the following, which cells lay down new bone?

   A. Osteons

   B. Osteoblasts

   C. Osteocytes

   D. Osteoclasts

5. The thick filament of the sarcomere is composed of:

   A. actin.

   B. myosin.

   C. troponin.

   D. tropomyosin.

6. What is the name of the broad, fibrous sheet that attaches one muscle to another?

   A. Aponeurosis

   B. Tendon

   C. Ligament

   D. Synovium

7. Which of the following statements about type II muscle fibers is true?

   A. They are used primarily for sustained work.

   B. They have a high concentration of myoglobin.

   C They have low concentrations of enzymes.

   D. They are known as fast-twitch fibers.

8. The synovium-like membrane that envelops the tendon surface is known as:

   A. endotenon.

   B. epitenon.

   C. tenosynovium.

   D. paratenon.

9. The thin processes of neurons that branch from the cell body to receive input from surrounding neurons are called

   A. axons.

   B. Schwann cells.

   C. dendrites.

   D. nodes of Ranvier.

10. Mesenchymal syndrome refers to:

   A. connective tissue breakdown after relatively benign load.

   B. multiple sites of tendinitis.

   C. a less severe inflammatory reaction than expected after an injury.

   D. injury sites different from those seen in most injured athletes.

Answers on page 891.

References

1. Simon SR (ed): *Orthopaedic Basic Science*. Rosemont, IL, American Academy of Orthopaedic Surgeons, 1994.

2. Pansky, B: *Review of Gross Anatomy*, ed 5. New York, NY, Macmillan, 1984.

3. Peterson L, Renstrom P: *Sports Injuries: Their Prevention and Treatment*. Chicago, IL, Year Book Medical Publishers, 1986.

4. DeLee JC, Drez D (eds): *Orthopaedic Sports Medicine*. Philadelphia, PA, WB Saunders, 1994.

5. Nordin M, Frankel VH (eds): *Basic Biomechanics of the Musculoskeletal System*, ed 2. Philadelphia, PA, Lea & Febiger, 1989.

6. Kaufer H: Mechanical function of the patella. *J Bone Joint Surg* 1971;53A:1551.

7. Mow VC, Hayes WC (eds): *Basic Orthopaedic Biomechanics*, ed 2. New York, NY, Lippincott-Raven, 1997.

8. Fu FH, Harner CD, Vince KG (eds): *Knee Surgery*. Baltimore, MD, Williams & Wilkins, 1994.

9. Dye SF, Cannon WD: Anatomy and biomechanics of the anterior cruciate ligament. *Clin Sports Med* 1988;7:715-725.

10. Muller W: *The Knee: Form, Function, and Ligament Reconstruction*. New York, NY, Springer-Verlag, 1983.

11. Frankel VH, Burnstein AH: *Orthopaedic Biomechanics*. Philadelphia, PA, Lea & Febiger, 1970.

12. Zachazewski JE, Magee DE, Quillen WS (eds): *Athletic Injuries and Rehabilitation*. Philadelphia, PA, WB Saunders, 1996.

13. Almekinders LC (ed): *Soft Tissue Injuries in Sports Medicine*. Cambridge, MA, Blackwell Science, 1996.

14. Brinker MR, Miller MD: Basic sciences. *Rev Orthop* 1996:1-122.

15. Netter FH: *The CIBA Collection of Medical Illustrations – Musculoskeletal System*. Summit, NJ: CIBA-GEIGY, 1987, vol 8.

16. Guyton AC: *Textbook of Medical Physiology*, ed 6. Philadelphia, PA, WB Saunders, 1981.

17. Leadbetter WB, Buckwalter JA, Gordon SL (eds): *Sports-Induced Inflammation: Clinical and Basic Science Concepts*. Park Ridge, IL, American Academy of Orthopaedic Surgeons, 1990.

18. Windsor RE, Lox DM (eds): *Soft Tissue Injuries: Diagnosis and Treatment*. Philadelphia, PA, Hanely & Belfus, 1998.

19. Amiel D, Frank C, Harwood F, Fronek J, Akeson, W: Tendons and ligaments: A morphological and biomechanical comparison. *J Orthop Res* 1984;1:257-265.

20. Menard D, Stanish WD: The aging athlete. *Am J Sports Med* 1989; 17:187-196.

6

Sports-Related Injury and Tissue Response to Physical Injury

Bernard R. Bach, Jr, MD
Samer S. Hasan, MD, PhD

QUICK CONTENTS

- Tissue response to physical injury, including the inflammation-repair process, alternative responses to injury, and inflammatory-repair modifiers.

- The injury responses of bone, cartilage, muscle, tendon, tendon insertion, fascia, ligament, synovium, and nerve.

- The clinical grading systems in sports trauma.

OVERVIEW

It is important to understand the cellular response to injury to predict recovery or evaluate the efficacy of therapeutic intervention. The body's cellular response to sports trauma takes place in the context of a changing biochemical environment that is influenced by factors such as oxygen tension, nutrition, genetic endowment, and aging and modified by physical forces that trigger and govern communication to and between cells.

DEFINITION OF SPORTS INJURY

From the athlete's perspective, an injury is any painful problem that prevents or hampers usual sports performance. However, the diagnosis of injury, especially soft-tissue injury, by the sports medicine professional cannot be determined reliably from this definition. Instead, injuries have been objectively defined and classified using epidemiologic research by such variables as degree of structural tissue damage, duration of disability, and need for medical attention. In addition, tissue damage is defined as functional and structural defects resulting from biochemical, ultrastructural, microscopic, and macroscopic responses to trauma.

Based on the duration of disability, injuries are classified as either acute or chronic. Acute injury, such as a lateral collateral ligament sprain of the ankle or a fracture of the distal radius, is characterized by a sudden catastrophic event so that the inciting cause and moment of onset are clearly identifiable. Pain is often severe at the moment of injury but gradually decreases as inflammation is treated. The acute injury is followed by a fairly predictable, though often lengthy, resolution to healing. Ultimately, pain falls below an arbitrary threshold, at which time the patient feels "well."[1]

Chronic injuries differ from acute injuries in several important ways. A moment of injury manifested as noxious pain may be identified, but this is insidiously inhibited or becomes disabling over a period of time. In theory, subclinical injury and dysfunction, or microtrauma, precede the moment of recognizable injury. The implication is that tissue damage has been accumulating for a period of time before the injury is first recognized and medical treatment is first sought. Acute injury is different in that the traumatic event is closely followed by the initial treatment. In chronic inflammation, the accumulation of scar, degenerative change, and atrophy imply that recovery will be slower. Again, a period of vulnerability to reinjury results when conventional anti-inflammatory measures blunt the pain response

without enhancing structural integrity.[1] Chronic injury lasts months or even years and is characterized by persistent symptoms. Tendinitis, bursitis, and fasciitis are common examples of chronic injury. The subacute phase, which is a period that occurs between acute and chronic injury, typically takes place several weeks after the initial trauma.

THE INFLAMMATION-REPAIR PROCESS

A process common to all injuries, *inflammation (L. inflammatio; inflammari*—to set on fire) is a localized tissue response initiated by the injury or destruction of vascularized tissues that are exposed to excessive mechanical load.[1] It is a time-dependent, evolving process, characterized by complex and incompletely understood vascular, chemical, and cellular events that lead to tissue repair, regeneration, or scar formation. The inflammatory response may progress to resolution of the injury and repair of the damaged tissue, or it may persist as chronic inflammation.

Acute Inflammation

In Roman times, Celsus, and later Galen, identified four cardinal signs of acute inflammation: localized heat, redness, swelling, and pain.[1] In the 19th century, Virchow described the so-called fifth cardinal sign of inflammation—functi laesa or disturbed function.[1] Pain has limited use in quantifying the extent of inflammation, because it is a symptom of injury as much as it is, in the form of tenderness, a local sign of inflammation. This is especially true when localizing deep injury in complex regions of the body such as the lower back, shoulder, and knee. Nevertheless, many clinicians continue to refer to any painful site as being inflamed. This generalization is incorrect; some inflammations, such as the subtle intracapsular swelling or effusion associated with early joint trauma, are relatively painless while noninflammatory conditions such as some tendonopathies are exquisitely painful.

In addition to the classic inflammatory response following the initial vascular disruption, mounting evidence points to other injury responses caused by alterations in cell matrix. These various tissue responses may represent different stages in the overall response to a given sports injury[1] (**Figure 6-1**).

When significant tissue damage has occurred, inflammation is a required step in the activation of wound repair. The inflammatory process is initiated by tissue cell death or necrosis that results from damage and hypoxia at the site of injury. This nonspecific response to physical trauma resembles the body's response to infection and chemical or thermal injury. Inflammation is the body's attempt to limit the extent of injury, remove devitalized tissue from the wound, and initiate tissue repair.

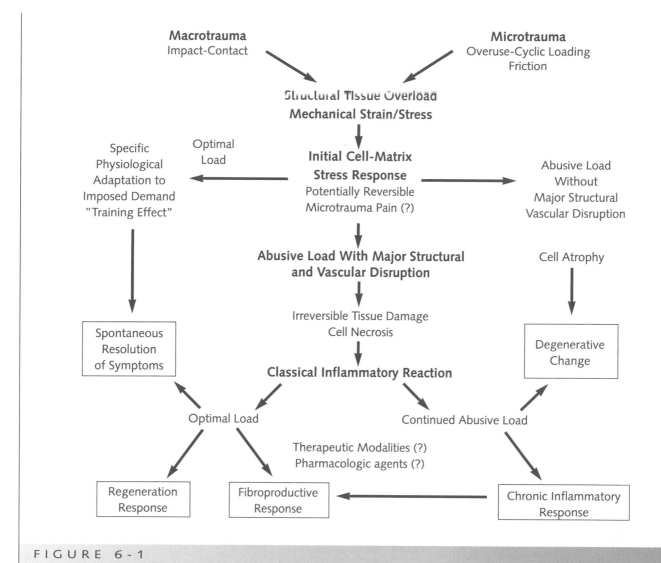

FIGURE 6-1

Tissue responses represent stages in the overall response to a sports injury.

Inflammation is not dose-related. Severe local inflammation can result from relatively minor trauma. In athletes, the sudden swelling of a bursa or tendon is a prime example of disproportionate inflammatory reactions. The inability to finely regulate the inflammatory process in these situations may further damage local tissues.

Repair is the replacement of damaged or lost cells and matrix with new cells and matrix that are not necessarily identical in structure and function to normal tissue. *Regeneration* produces tissue that is structurally and functionally identical to tissue damaged by injury. Repair and regeneration are necessary for the survival of all living organisms. In phylogenetically advanced organisms, the regenerative process has been replaced by a less complex healing process so that amphibians are the most advanced animals able to regenerate a lost extremity.[1]

Humans who sustain sports trauma maintain the capacity for only limited regeneration of epithelium, endothe-lium, and components of connective tissue.[1] Instead, healing occurs by tissue repair. This is often accomplished by *fibrous scar*, which is the typical patching material for wound repair. Inflammation and repair responses vary considerably in different injured tissues.

Inflammatory mediators

Inflammation and repair are complex processes involving the interplay of various cell types that comprise connective tissue. Specialized protein messengers mediate the cell-cell interactions that initiate the inflammatory response. These mediators include various *growth factors*, which are proteins that influence cell growth and division.[2] Growth factors are produced and released by one cell, then act on the same cell, adjacent cells, or remote cells. Growth factors may exhibit autocrine (effect on the same cell), paracrine (nearby cell), or hormonal (remote cell) activity. Types of growth factors include platelet-derived growth factor (PDGF), epidermal growth factor

(EGF), transforming growth factor beta (TGF-ß), and fibroblast growth factor (FGF), to name a few. Some factors attract other cells involved in the reparative process, other factors are mitogens that stimulate DNA production and cell division, and still others enhance the organization of granulation tissue and stimulate collagen and protein synthesis.[1,2] In addition to growth factors, other substances liberated in the initial inflammatory response to injury include histamine, complement, and coagulation factors.

Mediators act on cells by binding to specialized receptors on the cell wall. This induces a change in the three-dimensional molecular configuration (conformation) of the receptor. A small electrical charge is produced, which is the cue that activates the target cell to respond to the mediator, typically by initiating or inhibiting specific protein synthesis. The breakdown products of mediators can also act to modify cell activity. A mediator may have multiple actions depending on its interaction with other mediators, its concentration, and the timing of its arrival at the site of injury.[1,3]

Phases in the Normal Inflammation-Repair Process

Acute soft-tissue or bone injuries heal in three phases.[4] The first phase is a vascular inflammatory response, also referred to as the reaction phase, that begins within moments of injury. The second phase is the repair-regeneration or proliferative phase. The final phase involves remodeling and functional restoration and is also referred to as the remodeling-maturation phase.[1,4] The relative contributions of inflammation, proliferation, and maturation to tissue healing are functions of the size and location of the injury, the vascular supply, and local mechanical factors.

Phase I: Acute vascular inflammatory response

The inflammatory response to injury is triggered by a complex series of vascular, humoral, and cellular events that are controlled at all stages by chemical mediators[5] (Figure 6-2). The reaction phase is characterized by inflammatory cell mobilization triggered by mediators in response to blood vessel damage. The release of blood and plasma into the interstitial space results from damage to small and large blood vessels and lymphatics.[1] Blood collects locally and forms a hematoma, accompanied by cellular debris and early necrotic tissue. The extent of the initial hematoma and the area of devitalized tissue define the zone of primary injury. The extravasation of blood and plasma is followed by the initiation of coagulation, vasoconstriction, and platelet aggregation. Acute vasoconstriction lasts a few minutes and is followed by vasodilation, primarily of precapillary arterioles, that brings increased blood flow to the injured area.

The inflammatory response to injury is mediated by multiple interconnected humoral events that have been described as a "tangled web."[6] Clot formation or coagulation at the injury site is activated in part by collagen exposed in the walls of damaged blood vessels.[1] The clot comprises fibrin, platelets, red cells, and cell and matrix debris.[7] The clot acts to reduce blood loss and is the product of the coagulation cascade, a sequence of biochemical reactions involving various clotting factors and other substances.[3,8] Clot formation is balanced by fibrinolysis, which is the degradation of fibrin by enzymatic reaction to prevent widespread blood clotting.

Other mediators common to both the inflammatory and immune responses are also active. Factors resulting from the activation of the complement system enhance the inflammatory reaction. The complement system is a group of 20 plasma and five cell membrane proteins that work in a cascading sequence to amplify various aspects of the body's immune response and interface with other systems such as the coagulation system.[2,9] The complement system is activated by inflammatory mediators to produce special molecules called anaphylatoxins. One such anaphylatoxin is C5a, which is an important attractant of cells to the site of injury and an important stimulator of phagocytosis.[1]

The interconnections between the clotting, kinin, and complement systems are complex, but these mainly revolve around plasmin and the Hageman factor, which is factor XII of the clotting system. Plasmin digests fibrinogen and fibrin (fibrinolysis). It activates C1 and cleaves C3 to produce anaphylatoxic fragments. Plasmin also feeds back onto the clotting cascade to activate the Hageman factor, which in turn triggers kinin production.[1,6] Multiple other links in this web exist.

Mast cells and basophils are stimulated by the complement system to release histamine, causing a local increase in blood flow and vascular permeability.[1] Platelets, in addition to their role in clot formation, are the primary source of serotonin, which works with histamine to increase vascular permeability. The protein kallikrein generates low-molecular-weight vasoactive peptides referred to as kinins, most notably bradykinin, which is a potent vasodilator that increases capillary permeability.[1] Additionally, other substances called cytokines, which include interleukins and tumor necrosis factor, are released. These substances have an important but incompletely understood role that includes inhibitory effects on nearby cells.[5] In all, more than 300 cell-synthesized mediators have been identified.

The cellular response to injury is associated with vascular changes that occur at the postcapillary venule.[6] The lining of the venules develops gaps in response to the vasoactive mediators, such as C5a, histamine,

Phase I — The Acute Vascular Inflammatory Response

Blood vessel damage causes mediators to mobilize inflammatory cells. Blood and plasma from the damaged vessels and lymphatics are released into the interstitial space, and the blood forms a hematoma, accompanied by cellular debris and early necrotic tissue. At the injured vessel, coagulation, vasoconstriction (followed quickly by vasodilation, which increases blood flow to the area), and platelet aggregation occur.

A "tangled web" of humoral events mediates the inflammatory response. Exposed collagen in the damaged vessel walls activates clot formation or coagulation. Composed of fibrin, platelets, red cells, and cell and matrix debris, the clot reduces blood loss and is the product of the coagulation cascade. Fibrinolysis counteracts clot formation by degrading fibrin.

Activation of the complement system by inflammatory mediators produces anaphylatoxins. The C5a anaphylatoxin attracts cells to the site of injury and stimulates phagocytosis.

The complex interconnections among the clotting, kinin, and complement systems revolve around plasmin and Hageman factor (clotting factor XII). For example, plasmin digests fibrinogen and fibrin (fibrolysis); it activates C1 and cleaves C3 to produce anaphylatoxic fragments. Plasmin also feeds back onto the clotting cascade, activating the Hageman factor, which triggers kinin production.

The complement system stimulates mast cells and basophils to release histamine, causing local increases in blood flow and vascular permeability. Serotonin, largely supplied by the platelets, works with histamine to increase vascular permeability. Kallikrein generates kinins, low-molecular-weight vasodilators that increase capillary permeability. Cytokines inhibit nearby cells. More than 300 cell-synthesized mediators have been identified.

Vascular changes in response to injury occur at the postcapillary venule. Vasoactive mediators released from plasma and cells cause the venule lining to develop gaps. Mediator release is triggered by local ischemia from extrinsic pressure and major traumatic disruption of blood vessels and tissues. Vascular permeability changes cause fluid extravasation into the interstitial tissues, which presents as edema or swelling.

At the same time, leukocytes migrate through blood vessel walls toward increasing concentrations of mediators at the site of injury. Changes in electrostatic charge draw the leukocytes toward the vessel walls. Leukocytes produce platelet-activating factor, prostaglandins, and leukotrienes, which further increase vascular permeability. Leukocytes and macrophages act by phagocytosis to remove cellular debris at the injury site. Hydrolytic enzymes released by neutrophil granules break down cell membrane phospholipids, producing arachidonic acid. Prostaglandins, leukotrienes, thromboxane, eicosanoids, and slow-reacting substance of anaphylaxis are produced from arachidonic acid and are the targets of anti-inflammatory drugs. These chemicals and exudate cause the first clinical signs of inflammation, edema, and hypoxia and create the zone of secondary injury.

serotonin, bradykinin, leukotrienes, and prostaglandins, that are released from both plasma and cellular sources (**Figure 6-3**). Common initiating mechanisms for mediator release range from local ischemia produced by extrinsic pressure, such as that seen in shoulder impingement, to major traumatic disruption of blood vessels and tissue structure, such as that seen in severe tendon or muscle strains. These changes in vascular permeability lead to the extravasation of fluids into the interstitial tissues, which manifests as edema or swelling.

Leukocytes, which are white blood cells, pass through the blood vessel walls simultaneously and migrate unidirectionally toward increasing concentrations of mediators at the site of injury in a process called chemotaxis[6] (**Figure 6-4**). Mononuclear and polynuclear leukocytes

are drawn toward the walls of the blood vessels by changes in electrostatic charge caused by binding of mediators to specialized receptors. Leukocytes produce platelet-activating factor, prostaglandins, and leukotrienes, which further increase vascular permeability. Leukocytes and macrophages act by phagocytosis to remove cellular debris at the injury site. Granules within *neutrophils*, a type of leukocyte, release hydrolytic enzymes, which break down cell membrane phospholipids to produce arachidonic acid, a precursor of numerous inflammatory mediators, including prostaglandins, leukotrienes, thromboxane, eicosanoids, and slow reacting substance of anaphylaxis (SRS-A).[1,6] These mediators are produced from arachidonic acid by an enzymatic cascade and are the targets of current anti-inflammatory drug therapy. The intense

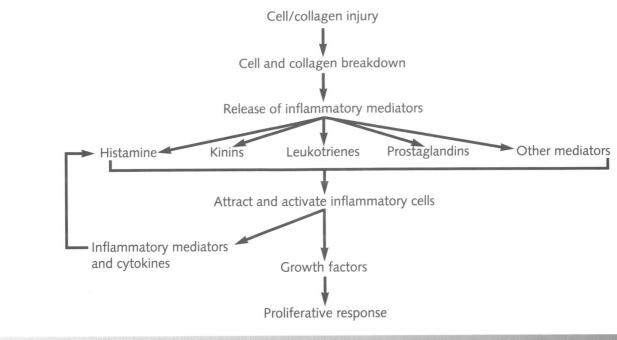

FIGURE 6-2

Chemical mediators control vascular, humoral, and cellular events that are triggered by the inflammatory response to injury.

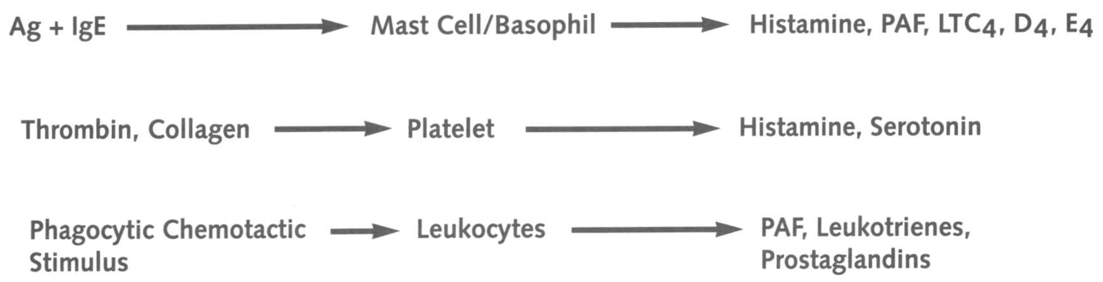

FIGURE 6-3

Changes in the postcapillary venules result as a response to cell-derived vasoactive mediators.

chemical activity and exudation during this phase produce the initial clinical signs of inflammation, edema, hypoxia, and pain create the zone of secondary injury (**Figure 6-5**).

Phase II: Matrix and cell proliferation

In the repair-regeneration phase of tissue healing, the wound hematoma becomes a fibrin clot that organizes by a cross-linking of fibrin and fibronectin within the clot. This provides some initial stability at the injury site without any significant tensile strength.[1] Beginning at 48 hours after injury and lasting up to 6 to 8 weeks, a second wave of cells consisting of fibroblasts begins the process of wound repair and collagen synthesis.[1] Proteolytic enzymes such as collagenase and elastase are released to degrade damaged tissue.[6]

At the same time, angiogenesis occurs, which is a process of vascular proliferation and ingrowth. Tiny blood vessels grow and form connections or anastomoses with each other to form a new capillary bed. Granulation tissue is the visible evidence of this process.[8] Various growth factors that promote this activity, including macrophage-, fibroblast-, nerve-, and platelet-derived growth factors (PDGF), have been identified. Of these factors, transforming growth factor-beta (TGF-ß) and PDGF stimulate the migration and differentiation of the endothelial, fibroblast, and myofibroblast cell populations that accumulate in the wound.[1] The hypoxia that occurs during phase I also stimulates vascular ingrowth and collagen synthesis.

The new collagen secreted by the fibroblasts, which begins to appear in wounds about 4 days after injury, is made up predominantly of immature type II collagen.[1]

Phase II — Matrix and Cell Proliferation

Phase II is the proliferation of matrix and cells. The hematoma becomes an organized, cross-linked fibrin-fibronectin clot that offers initial stability, but no significant tensile strength. At 48 hours and lasting up to 6 to 8 weeks, fibroblasts begin wound repair and collagen synthesis. Proteolytic enzymes degrade damaged tissue. Angiogenesis forms a new capillary bed, as evidenced by granulation tissue. Macrophage-, fibroblast-, nerve-, and platelet-derived growth factors promote angiogenesis. Transforming growth factor b and platelet-derived growth factor stimulate the migration and differentiation of the endothelial, fibroblast, and myofibroblast cell populations in the wound. The phase I hypoxia also stimulates vascular ingrowth and collagen synthesis.

The new collagen is mostly immature type II and initially soluble because tropocollagen cross-links are absent, increasing its susceptibility to enzymatic degradation. At first, fibroblasts are perpendicular to the lines of tensile force and their collagen deposition is disorganized. With wound maturation and increased cross-linking, collagen degradation decreases and the wound's tensile strength increases. Myofibroblast cells cause the wound to contract, decreasing ligament laxity and muscle flexibility.

In bone repair-regeneration, osteoclasts debride fractured bone surfaces, removing damaged bone. Periosteal blood vessel and bone periosteum mesenchymal cells proliferate and differentiate into osteoblasts to form collagen and into chondroblasts to form cartilage. Among these cells, capillaries form callus that bridges the gap between bone ends, a process known as enchondral bone healing. The new bone is weak until it is converted to lamellar bone during remodeling. Direct bone healing occurs when the broken bone ends are immobilized in contact, allowing direct deposit of woven bone without callus formation. Once a fracture has healed sufficiently to permit normal function, the repair-regeneration phase is completed.

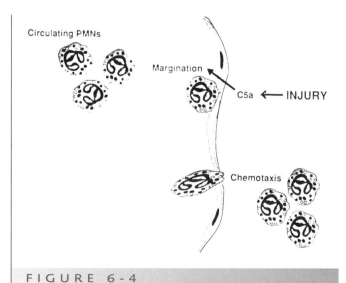

FIGURE 6-4

In chemotaxis, leukocytes migrate unidirectionally toward concentrations of mediators at the injury site.

Because it lacks cross-links between the constituent tropocollagen molecules, collagen is more susceptible to enzymatic degradation. In addition, the fibroblasts are initially oriented perpendicular to the lines of tensile force, and their deposition of collagen is disorganized.[10] As the wound matures and cross-linking increases, collagen degradation decreases and the wound's tensile strength increases.[1] During this phase, myofibroblast cells cause the wound to contract or shrink, which accounts for some of the decrease in ligament laxity and muscle flexibility following injury.[1]

In the repair-regeneration process of bone, osteoclasts perform the functions that are analogous to those carried out in soft tissue by macrophages and leukocytes. Osteoclasts debride fractured bone surfaces, removing damaged bone.[2] Mesenchymal cells from periosteal blood vessels and bone periosteum proliferate and differentiate into osteoblasts and chondroblasts to form collagen and cartilage respectively.[2] Capillaries grow among these cells, forming a fibrovascular tissue known as callus that bridges the gap between bone ends.[11,12] This process is known as enchondral bone healing. The new bone that is produced is relatively weak and is converted to lamellar or mature bone during later remodeling. Another kind of bone repair, direct bone healing, occurs when the broken bone ends are immobilized and are in contact, which allows direct deposit of woven bone without the intermediate step of callus formation.[11] Fractures that are not rigidly fixed by metal plates, screws, or rods undergo enchondral healing.[12,13] The stage at which a fracture has healed sufficiently to allow activity approaching normal function marks the end of this phase in the repair-regeneration process of bone.

Phase III: Remodeling-maturation

The final phase of remodeling and functional restoration, also referred to as the remodeling-maturation phase, is characterized by increased collagen density and organi-

FOCUS ON . . .

Phase III — Remodeling-Maturation

Phase III, remodeling-maturation, involves increased collagen density and organization, resulting in increased tensile strength. Cellularity and synthetic activity are decreased and the biochemical activity profile approaches normal. Type I collagen predominates in the extracellular matrix, and collagen turnover is near normal.

Factors influencing maturation are animal and tissue specific. Maturation of bone describes restoration of the original cortex. Maturation of soft tissue occurs with collagen remodeling as a response to mechanical load; fibroblasts and deposited collagen fibers reorient along the tensile force lines, a process that begins about 3 weeks after injury and may continue for a year or longer. Despite the predominance of type I collagen, the scar's ultimate tensile strength may be only 70% of the original tissue.

Electrical stimulation is useful in stimulating healing. In bone, load and the resulting piezoelectric effect direct osteoblasts to the electronegative side for bone deposition. Osteoclasts digest bone on the electropositive side. Bone remodeling is a form of accelerated bone turnover, resulting in restoration of normal shape, strength, and function.

An alternate response to injury is the cell atrophy-degeneration cycle, which does not involve leukocyte or macrophage infiltration. Atrophy is associated with decreases in cell size, function, and division; protein synthesis; energy production; storage; and contractility. Causes of cell atrophy include immobilization, inadequate oxygen supply or nutrition, hormonal deficiency, chronic inflammation, and aging. As tissue degenerates, it becomes more vulnerable to sudden dynamic or cyclic overload, which can lead to fatigue and failure. Traumatic disruption can injure vessels and stimulates renewed inflammation and repair. An atrophied cell needs balanced rest and physical stimulation to recover, and therefore, protected activity or controlled therapeutic exercise is preferred over complete rest.

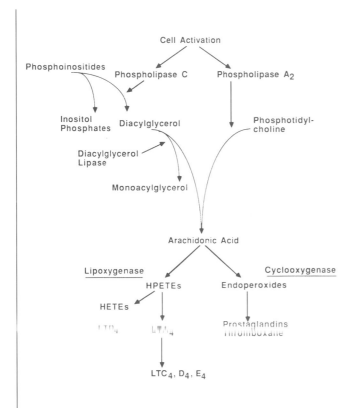

FIGURE 6-5

Chemical activity and exudation from production of mediators from arachidonic acid produce the initial signs of inflammation.

zation, and consequently, increased tensile strength. There is a tendency toward decreased cellularity, a concomitant decrease in synthetic activity, and a more normal biochemical activity profile. The extracellular matrix is characterized over time by increased type I collagen content, compared to the type III collagen that is formed initially, and the collagen turnover approaches normal levels. The increased content of type I collagen and glycosaminoglycans leads to increased tissue strength.

Maturation, which is the final stage of remodeling, is sometimes considered a fourth and separate phase of the injury-repair cycle; however, such a distinction appears to be arbitrary because both remodeling and maturation occur simultaneously without obvious demarcation. Maturation is quite variable in duration and arbitrary in end point.

The factors that influence maturation are animal- and tissue-specific. In bone, maturation implies the restoration of the original cortex. Bone healing follows *Wolff's law*, which states that bone remodels and adapts to the forces placed on it by increasing its strength along lines of mechanical stress or, more simply stated, that form follows function.[2,14] This process may continue for many years after fracture.[2] In the maturation of soft tissue, collagen remodeling proceeds under the influence of mechanical load, as fibroblasts and the deposited collagen fibers reorient along the lines of tensile force.[1,10] This process begins as early as 3 weeks following injury and continues for a year or longer.[10] During the remodeling-maturation phase, immature type III collagen is converted to the strong type I collagen.[1] However, the ultimate tensile strength of the scar may be as much as 30% less than that of the original tissue.[1]

Electric fields may also play a part in the orientation of soft-tissue collagen fibers; this is the basis for the electrical stimulation of healing.[1] In bone, the remodeling-maturation process is also affected by load and the resulting *piezoelectric effect,* which is the generation of electrical potential by the mechanical deformation of a solid material, in this case bone.[2] Following the fracture of a long bone, osteoblasts are directed by an electrical signal to the concave or compression bone surface. This site of local electronegativity becomes the site of greatest bone deposition. Conversely, osteoclasts digest bone on the electropositive side of the fracture, which is equivalently the convex or tension side.[2] The remodeling phase of bone healing is essentially an accelerated form of normal bone turnover that culminates in the restoration of normal shape, strength, and function.[12]

ALTERNATIVE RESPONSES TO INJURY

Not all sports injuries trigger an inflammation-repair reaction. In some cases of chronic injury of collagen in tendon, ligaments, or fascia, infiltration of leukocytes and macrophages does not occur. Theoretically, a cell atrophy-degeneration cycle may explain these observations.

Atrophy-degeneration

When atrophy occurs, cell size and function decrease in response to an environmental signal. Protein synthesis decreases, as does cell division, energy production, storage, and contractility. Immobilization is one cause of cell atrophy. Other causes include inadequate oxygen supply or nutrition, hormonal deficiency, chronic inflammation, and aging.

Tissue degeneration implies a weaker structure. Tissues become more vulnerable to sudden dynamic overload or cyclic overloading, which may lead to fatigue and failure. Traumatic disruption can cause vascular injury and initiate a renewed inflammation-repair process. Recovery of an atrophied cell requires a balance of rest and physical stimulation. An athlete who returns to sports activity after prolonged inactivity brought about by injury would do so without substantially improved tissue integrity and would be vulnerable to reinjury. For this reason, protected activity or controlled therapeutic exercise is usually a better treatment than complete rest to maintain musculoskeletal integrity.

Chronic inflammatory response

When the inflammatory response is unable to eliminate the injurious agent and restore injured tissue to its normal physiologic state, there may be a progression to chronic inflammation.[1] This characterizes certain overuse conditions such as lateral epicondylitis, commonly known as

tennis elbow. Although there is no sharp time limit between acute and chronic inflammation, the former typically lasts only a few hours or days, and the latter persists for a month or longer.[2,14]

The hallmarks of chronic inflammation are the production of additional connective tissue, termed granulation tissue, and the preponderance of mononuclear cells such as macrophages, lymphocytes, and macrophages over neutrophils and mast cells.[6] These cells are arranged in a highly vascularized and innervated loose connective tissue matrix. The macrophage is the pivotal cell in the chronic inflammatory response; it is an important source of inflammatory and immunologic mediators. Macrophages accumulate at the site of injury as a consequence of monocyte chemotaxis and subsequent differentiation in tissues to macrophages.[1] Many of the inflammatory mediators generated by macrophages are similar to those of the neutrophil and include degradative enzymes such as proteases and acid hydrolases and biologically active lipids, including platelet-activating factor and leukotrienes.[1] Macrophages also secrete cytokines that regulate fibroblast and endothelial cell proliferation and function.[1] A distinctive pattern of chronic inflammation defined as granulomatous inflammation may develop, but this is more typical of the tissue response to foreign bodies such as retained suture material and certain infectious diseases, such as tuberculosis than it is to typical sports injuries.[1,6]

The mechanisms that convert acute inflammation to chronic inflammation are not well understood, but overuse or overload, combined with cumulative microtrauma, is a contributing factor.[10] Chronic inflammation may also accompany atrophy and degeneration at the site of injury. It is marked by loss of function; the remaining cardinal signs need not be present.[14] In addition, some overuse sports injuries do not stimulate a chronic inflammatory response. For example, some chronic tendon injuries commonly referred to as chronic "tendinitis" are theorized to be an inflammatory reparative process following mechanical microtrauma.[1] However, histologic analysis of resected pathologic tendon tissue often fails to show evidence of a significant inflammatory reaction and, instead, demonstrates a degenerative process. This may be secondary to tensile overuse, fatigue, and weakness, and possibly to avascular change.[1] In this case, the term "tendinosis" is more appropriate than "tendinitis."[5]

INFLAMMATORY-REPAIR MODIFIERS

Modifiers of sports-induced inflammation are employed to decrease pain and the dysfunctional behavior it often causes, allowing earlier rehabilitation following injury. Modifiers are also used to mitigate the risk of "disuse atrophy, neurologic discoordination, and altered muscle function after injury."[1] As part of a comprehensive rehabilitation, a modifier can minimize such effects of immobilization as adhesions, joint stiffness, and cartilage degeneration. Modifiers decrease inflammation in freshly healed tissues during the period of retraining and reconditioning. They control the chronic inflammatory symptoms in overuse injuries, especially those stemming from degenerative sequelae of previous injuries.[1] Modifiers can also help limit the soft-tissue necrosis resulting from the "inflammatory overshoot" following acute trauma.[1]

Drug Modifiers

Nonsteroidal anti-inflammatory drugs

Nonsteroidal anti-inflammatory drugs (NSAIDs) are widely used in the management of pain following surgery and in the treatment of acute sports injuries, such as ligament and joint capsule sprains, and chronic overuse injuries, such as patellar or Achilles tendinitis. NSAIDs encompass a broad group of chemically heterogeneous drugs that includes aspirin, ibuprofen, indomethacin, naproxen, and others.[7] NSAIDs share important clinical and tissue effects: they all have some analgesic, antipyretic, and anti-inflammatory activity. Acetaminophen, a compound chemically related to NSAIDs, has analgesic and antipyretic properties but is not anti-inflammatory.[1] All NSAIDs share a variable potential for causing peptic bleeding and gastrointestinal ulceration and interfering with platelet function.[1] These effects, as well as the potential for liver toxicity, are well-known side effects that must be considered when these drugs are prescribed.

The mechanism of the anti-inflammatory activity of NSAIDs is the inhibition of cyclooxygenase, an enzyme in the arachidonic acid cascade that produces prostaglandins, which are potent inflammatory mediators released by damaged cells following injury (**Figure 6-6**).

NSAIDs thus act to limit the inflammatory response to injury. Paradoxically, the resultant decrease in prostaglandin synthesis may unmask other inflammatory mediators leading to potentially greater damage at the site of injury.[1]

NSAIDs decrease acute soft-tissue inflammation, and some clinical experience suggests that they decrease the pain associated with tissue injury and possibly stiffness as well.[1] Most studies fail to show a clear superiority of one NSAID over another in soft-tissue injuries. To obtain the maximal effect, NSAID use is initiated as soon as possible after injury and continued for several days. Once the injury has moved into the proliferative and maturation phase, the NSAID offers little advantage and can be discontinued.[5] Any residual pain can then be controlled with acetaminophen. Thus, the decision to use an NSAID for sports-related injuries should be driven by the need for anti-inflammatory relief rather than for pain relief alone.[1] The choice of a particular NSAID from a variety of agents grouped into five major classes is mainly dictated by the side effect profile. Until recently, all NSAIDs had a variable potential for causing gastrointestinal ulceration and interfering with platelet function, and many could cause other, less common side effects such as kidney toxicity and allergic reactions.[9,15] These toxicities are not shared by acetaminophen.[1] The cause of these side effects is the nonspecific inhibition of cyclooxygenase that affects the synthesis of thromboxane A_2 (TXA_2) and multiple prostaglandins that act on various sites in the body.[9] Thromboxane is necessary for platelet aggregation and clot formation, and some prostaglandins such as PGI_2 protect the gastrointestinal lining from ulceration.[9] Recently, two forms of cyclooxygenase (termed COX-1 and COX-2) have been discovered; COX-1 acts on the stomach, intestine, kidneys, and on platelets, and COX-2 acts on inflammatory sites.[15] This has prompted

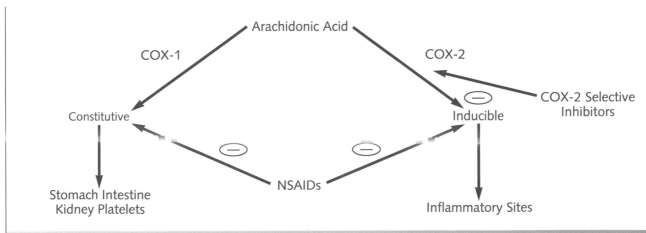

FIGURE 6-6

NSAIDs inhibit the production of prostaglandins to limit the inflammatory response to injury.

FOCUS ON . . .

Drug Modifiers

NSAIDs

Nonsteroidal anti-inflammatory drugs (NSAIDs) are a group of chemically heterogeneous agents used to manage pain after surgery and to treat both acute and chronic sports injuries. To varying degrees, they all have analgesic, antipyretic, and anti-inflammatory activity and can cause gastrointestinal ulceration, interference with platelet function, and liver toxicity. Acetaminophen, while chemically related to the NSAIDs, is not an anti-inflammatory medication.

NSAIDs act by inhibiting cyclooxygenase in the arachidonic acid cascade, which produces prostaglandins, potent inflammatory mediators released by damaged cells. While limiting the inflammatory response, the NSAID-triggered reduction in prostaglandin synthesis may also unmask potentially more damaging mediators. NSAIDs may also decrease the pain of tissue injury and perhaps stiffness. For maximum effect, the NSAID should be instituted as soon as possible after injury and continued for several days. However, once the proliferative and maturation phases begin, the NSAID is of little use, and acetaminophen will control pain. Therefore, an NSAID is used for a sports injury to relieve both inflammation and pain.

Corticosteroids

Corticosteroids, including cortisone, hydrocortisone, prednisone, and triamcinolone, are more potent anti-inflammatories that affect the arachidonic acid cascade at different sites of action. Corticosteroids are useful for chronic inflammatory musculoskeletal diseases, but because they can have serious side effects, their role in treating sports injuries is less clear. Corticosteroids suppress inflammation by inhibiting capillary dilation, inflammatory cell migration, tissue edema, capillary and fibroblast proliferation, and collagen synthesis. They may also reduce the zone of secondary injury and decrease adhesions after tendon injuries. As with NSAIDs, corticosteroids have not been shown to accelerate healing or return to normal function.

Oral corticosteroids are not generally used for sports injuries. However, injected corticosteroids are appropriate for a chronically inflamed synovial cavity, bursa, or tendon synovial sheath to suppress local mediators, diminish adhesions, and prevent further tissue injury. They should be given cautiously, by an experienced physician, and only after other conservative treatment modalities have failed. Injections should be limited to two or three to any area, spaced over several months and repeated only if the first injection was helpful. Injected corticosteroids should not be used after acute macrotrauma because of their catabolic effects, and they should not be injected directly into a tendon or ligament, where they can cause rupture. They should not be given right before a competitive event or in the presence of infection.

the development of COX-2 selective inhibitors that have analgesic and anti-inflammatory effects without the typical side effect profile.[15]

Despite the widespread use of NSAIDs in the treatment of sports injuries, they have not been shown to contribute significantly to the restoration of normal tissue function following injury or hasten a return to participation in sports.[7] Consequently, the efficacy of NSAIDs following sports injury remains to be clearly defined, although some believe it is greatest for chronic injury.[1,5,7]

Corticosteroids

Corticosteroids, such as cortisone, hydrocortisone, prednisone, and triamcinolone, also affect the arachidonic acid cascade, but at different sites of action than NSAIDs.[1,16] Corticosteroids have a far greater anti-inflammatory potency than NSAIDs; however, they also share a far greater frequency of serious complications following their use.[7] Although corticosteroids are frequently used in the treatment of chronic inflammatory diseases of the musculoskeletal system such as rheumatoid arthritis, their role in the treatment of sports injury is more ambiguous.[7]

Corticosteroids act to suppress inflammation by inhibiting capillary dilation, inflammatory cell migration, and tissue edema. They also inhibit capillary and fibroblast proliferation and collagen synthesis during the repair phase of healing.[1] Results of some studies have shown that corticosteroids reduce the zone of secondary injury and decrease scar tissue adhesions following tendon injuries.[7] However, these studies have not demonstrated accelerated healing or return to normal function following corticosteroid use.

The best indication for local corticosteroid injection appears to be certain chronic inflammatory processes in which suppression of local mediators may prevent further tissue injury.

Corticosteroids can be administered either orally or by injection. The administration of oral corticosteroids for

range of motion before physical activity.[14] If motion is limited by pain, then cryotherapy should be used; if motion is limited by stiffness, then thermotherapy is more appropriate.[14] In contrast to acute injuries, there are no consistent guidelines for the use of heat or cold in treating chronic inflammatory conditions. Some investigators advocate cryotherapy as long as pain persists, while others recommend heat before and cold after activity.[1]

Ultrasound

Although ultrasound has long been used to treat inflammatory conditions, its benefits and the underlying mechanisms have not been verified by well designed basic science experiments or clinical trials.[1] Higher intensities of ultrasound create heat and have limited use. Lower intensities, as in pulsed ultrasound do not create heat and are being used in the treatment of acute sports injuries.[7] Low-intensity ultrasound during bone repair also accelerates healing.[1] In soft tissues, ultrasound is believed to reduce edema, pain, and muscle spasms.[1,7]

The lower intensity sound waves of ultrasound alter cell membrane permeability to increase the flow of metabolites and ions, especially calcium. Ultrasound enhances the degranulation of mast cells by increasing the transport of calcium ions and releases chemotactic agents that draw cellular components of inflammation such as neutrophils and monocytes to the injury site.[1] These cells expedite tissue repair, by attracting macrophages, increasing collagen production, promoting wound contraction, and enhancing vascular ingrowth. During the proliferative phase of inflammation, ultrasound increases the entry of calcium ions into fibroblasts and endothelial cells. The calcium ions then signal the cells to enhance their metabolic machinery to a reparative mode.[1] The result is believed to be enhanced wound contraction, angiogenesis, and collagen production, leading to increased tensile strength.

Electrotherapy

The three commonly recognized applications of electrotherapy used in the treatment of soft-tissue injury include *transcutaneous electric nerve stimulation (TENS)* as an attempt to modulate pain, electrotherapy for muscle reeducation, which is a commonly employed postoperative rehabilitation technique, and electrotherapy to enhance soft-tissue healing.[7] Electrotherapy used to enhance soft-tissue healing is performed with high-voltage, pulsatile galvanic stimulation that provides an external electrical stimulation of more than 100 volts with a pulsatile waveform that lasts between 5 and 260 microseconds.[14] Although results of clinical observation suggest that electrical stimulation may increase local circulation, decrease edema, and modulate pain, there is a dearth of objective evidence in the literature about its efficiency in clinical situations.[7] Thus, although claims are made that electrochemical effects occur at both cellular and tissue levels, the effect of electrical stimulation on inflammation remains conjectural.

Therapeutic Exercise

The effects of rehabilitative therapeutic exercise provide the strongest rationale for use in the treatment of sports-induced inflammation and injury. Exercise should be of relatively high intensity to result in a strengthening effect. Cellular and biomechanical responses to exercise documented in tendon, ligament, and muscle include the following:[1]

- changes in collagen turnover rate
- changes in collagen cross-linking at the intramolecular and intermolecular levels
- alteration in tissue water and electrolyte content
- changes in the arrangement, number, and thickness of collagen fibrils

Collagen fibers may transmit physical signals under the effects of load that induce changes in cellular metabolism and synthesis of proteoglycans and matrix. Both tension and pressure modify cell synthesis in tendon and articular cartilage, and these changes can hasten the return of structural integrity. The response of soft tissues such as tendon, ligaments, and muscles to mechanical stress delivered during therapeutic exercise has been termed "Wolff's law of soft tissues."[1]

TISSUE-SPECIFIC INJURY RESPONSES

Bone Injury

Bone has an excellent capacity for self-repair because of its vascularity. Bone can alter its properties and configuration in response to changes in mechanical demand. For example, changes in bone density are commonly observed after periods of disuse and of greatly increased use; changes in bone shape are noted during fracture healing and after certain operations. The response of bone to injury is a continuum of processes: inflammation, repair with a soft callus followed by a hard callus, and remodeling. Bone injuries may be acute, as with a fracture, or chronic, as with an overuse injury that produces a stress fracture.

Although a discussion of the nonsurgical and surgical treatment of fractures is far beyond the scope of this chapter, one must appreciate that fracture healing is influenced by a variety of systemic and local factors (Table 6-1). In addition, the choice of treatment may influence the rate, method, and overall quality of bone healing. Bone healing may be described in general terms without dwelling on the specific treatment method.

Bone healing

Inflammation begins immediately after a fracture is sustained. Bleeding from the fracture site and surrounding soft tissues creates a hematoma and fibrin clot. Local

Local factors	Systemic factors
Degree of trauma	Age
Vascular injury	Hormones
Bone affected	Functional activity
Degree of bone loss	Nerve function
Infection	Nutrition
Local pathologic conditions	

TABLE 6-1
FACTORS INFLUENCING FRACTURE REPAIR

inflammatory mediators attract platelets, neutrophils, and monocytes or macrophages to the fracture site. Subsequently, fibroblasts, mesenchymal cells, and osteoprogenitor cells, which are the precursors of osteoblasts, appear at the fracture site. The mesenchymal and osteoprogenitor cells may arise from transformed endothelial cells in the medullary canal, the periosteum, and/or by osteogenic induction of cells within the surrounding muscle and soft tissue.[2] These cells form granulation tissue around the fracture ends. Some mesenchymal cells differentiate into osteoblasts, and these proliferate along with fibroblasts. The osteoblasts secrete osteoid, which is later mineralized, and the fibroblasts secrete the organic matrix.[2,12]

The primary callus response typically occurs within 2 weeks. The stages of soft and hard callus are somewhat arbitrary, because different regions within a given fracture may progress at different rates of repair.[2] The periphery of the external callus demonstrates cartilage formation, whereas regions closer to the bone ends demonstrate bone formation[2] (**Figure 6-7**). Nevertheless, it is convenient to define soft callus as beginning when pain and swelling subside and lasting until the bony fragments are no longer freely movable. During the stage of medullary or hard cal-

lus, which occurs later and more slowly, callus converts from cartilaginous tissue to woven bone.[2] The amount of callus formation is inversely proportional to the amount of immobilization of the fracture. The callus, specifically the amount of new bone connecting the fracture fragments, significantly increases the strength and stiffness of bone in bending and torsion during the healing period.[2]

Fracture healing varies with the method of treatment. With closed or nonsurgical treatment, the fracture ends of a typical long bone fracture are not in continuity. The healing of such a fracture exhibits both enchondral bone formation as in the external callus and intramembranous bone formation as in periosteal or bridging callus.[2] A third type of bone formation, direct primary bone healing, occurs without the formation of a visible callus.[2] This type of bone formation requires rigid immobilization, as with internal fixation, and anatomic (or near-anatomic) reduction.[12,13]

The remodeling phase of bone healing of an acute injury begins during the middle of the repair phase and continues for up to several years, long after the fracture has clinically healed.[2] Remodeling allows the bone to assume its normal configuration and shape based on the stresses to which it is exposed, in accordance with Wolff's law. Throughout this process, woven bone formed during the repair phase is replaced with lamellar bone. Fracture healing is complete when the marrow is repopulated with osteoprogenitor cells and hematopoietic stem cells that differentiate into the various types of blood cells.

Chronic overuse of bones

Chronic overuse results in a subtle stress reaction. In addition to sudden load shifts, such as a twisting injury or fall that causes a fracture, chronic cyclical accumulations of load may also cause bone fatigue and partial or complete fracture. Stress fractures are a consequence of abusive training that leads to bone overload. Stress fractures cause pain but no swelling. Effective treatment emphasizes load reduction and protected activity so that the bone may

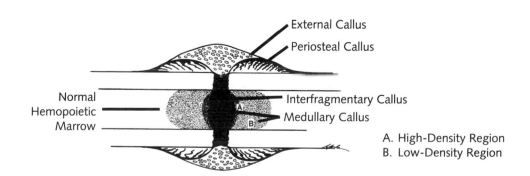

FIGURE 6-7

Bone is formed in regions close to the bone ends, and cartilage is formed at the periphery of the external callus.

FOCUS ON . . .

Fracture Healing

After a fracture, inflammation occurs. The fracture site and surrounding soft tissues bleed, creating a hematoma and fibrin clot. Local inflammatory mediators attract platelets, neutrophils, and monocytes or macrophages to the site. Later fibroblasts, mesenchymal cells, and osteoprogenitors appear at the site. The mesenchymal and osteoprogenitor cells may develop from medullary canal and periosteal endothelial cells or by osteogenic induction of surrounding muscle and soft tissue cells, or both and create granulation tissue at the fracture ends. Some mesenchymal cells differentiate into osteoblasts, proliferate with fibroblasts, and secrete osteoid, while fibroblasts secrete the organic matrix.

Primary callus occurs within 2 weeks. The hard and soft callus stages may occur in different regions of the fracture at the same time. The peripheral external callus forms cartilage, while the bridging callus forms bone. Soft callus begins when pain and swelling subside and lasts until the bony fragments are no longer freely moveable. Hard callus occurs as the callus converts from cartilage to woven bone, the amount of callus being indirectly proportional to the amount of fracture immobilization. During healing, callus significantly increases bone strength and stiffness in bending and torsion.

The treatment method affects fracture healing. With closed (nonsurgical) treatment, the bone ends are not continuous. Therefore, enchondral bone formation occurs in the external callus and intramembranous bone formation occurs in the bridging callus. With rigid immobilization of the fracture, reduction is near anatomic and direct primary bone healing takes place in the absence of a visible callus.

Remodeling begins during the repair phase and continues for years after clinical healing. Remodeling restores the bone's normal configuration and shape based on its exposed stresses (Wolff's law) as woven bone is replaced with lamellar bone. Fracture healing is complete when the marrow repopulates with osteoprogenitor and hematopoietic stem cells that differentiate into blood cells.

Chronic, cyclical load accumulations can fatigue and (partially or completely) fracture bone. Abusive training that causes bone overload can result in stress fractures, which cause pain without inflammation. Treatment focuses on reducing load and modifying activity to prompt the creation of a stronger, more durable bone structure. Remodeling is the most dangerous phase because accelerated bone resorption can lead to refracture. Other chronic overuse conditions include osteoperiostitis (painful periosteal inflammation) and shin splints (posterior tibial stress syndrome).

respond by producing a stronger and more durable structure. The athlete is especially vulnerable to reinjury during the remodeling phase of bone healing, because accelerated bone resorption may accompany remodeling, leading to microfracture. *Osteoperiostitis* is a frequently painful inflammation of the periosteum or lining of bone. *Shin splints*, or *posterior tibial stress syndrome*, is an overuse syndrome that results from cyclical loading at the posterior tibial and soleus muscle attachments onto the tibia. Chronic periosteal inflammation has been treated surgically after showing resistance to conservative therapy.

Cartilage Injury

Cartilage is protected from injury by a thin layer of synovial fluid that lubricates the opposing surfaces and keeps them apart. The underlying cancellous bone is also able to deform to protect the cartilage from injury. However, these protective mechanisms may fail and lead to wearing and damage of the cartilage. This damage occurs most frequently because of poor alignment and resulting abnormal forces on the cartilage.

Cartilage can be damaged either by a single high-impact load or multiple subthreshold loads that cause an accumulation of cartilage damage. Chondrocyte death, matrix damage, fissuring of the surface, injury to the underlying bone, and thickening of the tidemark region can occur.[2]

Articular cartilage has little capacity to repair itself following injury because it contains no blood vessels, lymphatics, or nerves. Partial-thickness cartilage injuries do not undergo repair. In contrast, full-thickness cartilage injuries in which the underlying subchondral bone is exposed or injured stimulate inflammation that leads to repair. These injuries include osteochondral fractures, which are common sports injuries such that the fracture extends through cartilage into the subchondral bone. The clot and repair tissue from bone, including inflammatory cells that migrate from the bone marrow, fill the cartilage defect and undergo the sequence of inflammation, repair, and remodeling as in the repair of other soft tissues.[7] Unlike ligaments and other soft tissues, the repair tissue that fills cartilage defects differentiates toward articular cartilage instead of dense fibrous tissue.[7] However, the new articular cartilage is not the native hyaline cartilage that lines the ends of bones but a fibrocartilage replacement that is neither as strong nor as durable.

Chondromalacia is the softening of the articular surface that results from exposure of normal cartilage to excessive pressure or shear. Chondromalacia may result from acute trauma or from repetitive microtrauma that has occurred over many years, leading to degenerative changes. Chondromalacia is graded using the Outerbridge classification in which grade I changes represent softening of the cartilage, grade II changes represent areas of fibrillation or fraying less than $1/2''$ in diameter, grade III changes represent larger areas of fibrillation, and grade IV changes represent erosion and exposure of subchondral bone.[18,19] Grade IV cartilage lesions or complete loss of articular cartilage is also referred to as eburnation. The inflammatory symptoms associated with cartilage injury may result from the shedding of enzymatically produced matrix breakdown products and secondary stimulation of the synovium. This is frequently manifest as pain, which is one of the hallmarks of degenerative joint disease or arthritis.

Muscle Injury

Acute traumatic injuries to muscle and tendon account for up to 50% of all injuries.[20] Muscle strain is probably the most common of these injuries. Clinically, muscle strains are most often associated with muscle stretching with a simultaneous forceful eccentric muscle contraction.[20] The mechanical strain occurs when load overcomes the muscle's ability to resist it during deceleration so that the spring-like or shock absorber function of the muscle fails.[1] The injury may be a break in a few myofibers, a tear in the fascia or aponeurosis, or a complete muscle rupture. Muscle strains produce symptoms such as pain on contraction and stretch, as well as ecchymosis and swelling with large or complete tears.[20] The ecchymosis results from bleeding that is not confined to the muscle proper and escapes to the subcutaneous space. A palpable defect corresponding to the site of muscle tear may be noted before or after the swelling peaks.

Muscle strains most commonly occur at or near the myotendinous or musculotendinous junction, which is the weak link in muscle.[20] The strains occur more frequently during powerful eccentric contractions in muscles, especially in those that cross two joints and contain an increased proportion of type II fibers, such as the hamstring or gastrocnemius muscles. Muscles that cross two joints are subject to greater stretch, and higher forces are possible with eccentric contraction. Muscle strains may be partial or complete, depending on the extent of muscle-tendon unit disruption, but partial tears are more common.[20] A muscle that is completely torn bulges with contraction toward the side of the musculotendinous unit that is still attached to bone.

Muscle strains elicit an inflammatory response similar to that seen in other soft tissues. Consequently, NSAIDs decrease the associated pain and inflammation in muscle without impairing the restoration of tensile strength.[1] Exercise-induced muscle soreness typically occurs hours after exercise and follows no identifiable injury. It is of shorter duration than a muscle strain, completely reversible, and may respond to NSAIDs.

Factors contributing to muscle strain

Multiple factors contribute to muscle strain injury, including inadequate flexibility, inadequate strength or endurance, uncoordinated muscle contraction, insufficient warm-up, or inadequate rehabilitation from previous injury.[20] Proper muscle stretching before activity is a mainstay of strain prevention. When a muscle is subjected to sustained stretch, the central nervous system receives information on the force and duration of the stretching action from sensory receptors within the muscle. Given enough information, the receptors trigger an inhibiting response causing the muscle to relax and lengthen.[7] A muscle stretch should be held or slowly increased over time to allow the time-dependent stress relaxation and creep to occur in the muscle. These viscoelastic properties allow muscle to lengthen. Ballistic stretching should be avoided because high velocities result in increased forces, and the resulting rapid muscle shortening does not allow the viscoelastic changes to occur.

A warm-up period prior to stretching is desirable and helps the athlete avoid some risk factors for muscle strain. Warm-up increases the temperature within muscles as a result of enhanced metabolic activity. Increased intramuscular temperature before stretching enhances the ability of collagen and the myotendinous junction to deform.[20] This ability enhances muscle extensibility and may protect against strains. The warmed muscle contracts more forcefully and relaxes more quickly so that speed and strength are both increased during exercise.[7] Following intramuscular warm-up, other stretching exercises such as static and ballistic stretching should be initiated. Fatigue predisposes muscle to injury because the ability of a fatigued muscle to generate force and absorb energy equivalently is diminished.[21] In addition, a previously or incompletely treated muscle strain or other injury might be a risk factor for reinjury.

The pain or discomfort in muscles that have undergone unaccustomed vigorous exercise, particularly involving eccentric muscle contractions, is commonly called *delayed-onset muscle soreness (DOMS)*.[7,20] DOMS is different from acute or injury-related muscle soreness in that the time course of pain follows the cessation of activity and continues for several days regardless of whether there is further activity. Typically, the soreness begins a few hours after exercise, becomes prominent 12 to 48 hours after activity, and may persist for several additional days.

FOCUS ON . . .

Muscle Injury

Muscle strain is the most common acute traumatic injury to muscle or tendon and occurs when muscle stretching is accompanied by a forceful eccentric muscle contraction. The load overcomes the muscle's resisting ability during deceleration and the muscle's spring-like or shock-absorbing function fails. The injury can range from breaks in a few myofibers to a fascial or aponeurotic tear to a complete rupture. Symptoms can include pain with contraction and stretch, ecchymosis, swelling, and a palpable defect.

Muscle strains usually occur at or near the musculotendinous junction, the weak link in the muscle, and happen with powerful eccentric contractions. In a complete tear, the muscle bulges toward the side of the musculotendinous unit still connected to bone; this injury, however, is less common than a partial tear. NSAIDs are helpful in reducing the pain and inflammation of muscle strain and soreness without impairing tensile strength restoration.

Warm-up before stretching reduces the risk of muscle strain injury by increasing the intramuscular temperature, thus improving the deformability of collagen and the myotendinous junction and enhancing muscle extensibility. The warm muscle contracts more forcefully and relaxes more quickly, increasing speed and strength. A fatigued muscle's force-generating ability declines, as does its capacity to absorb energy. Also, a previous or incompletely treated injury may be a risk factor for reinjury.

Delayed-onset muscle soreness (DOMS) is the muscle pain or discomfort that occurs after unaccustomed vigorous exercise. The soreness typically begins several hours after exercise, peaks between 12 and 48 hours, and may continue for several additional days. Clinically, the patient has tenderness, stiffness, and pain with movement. DOMS is the result of mechanical muscle damage and perhaps histologic myofiber damage from eccentric contractions. The classic inflammatory response is absent, and therefore, inflammatory modifiers may not be helpful. DOMS must be distinguished from the burning discomfort of maximal exercise that causes noxious substances to accumulate in muscle.

Immobilizing an extremity changes the number of sarcomeres at the myotendinous junction and accelerates the granulation response of the injured muscle. Prolonged disuse or abnormal motor unit recruitment can result in muscle atrophy. To reduce contracture and increase strength, the muscle should be immobilized in a lengthened position.

Exercise training is based on overload, specificity, and repetition. In endurance exercise, large muscle groups are activated, generating high metabolic demands that lead to respiratory and circulatory system and muscle metabolism adaptations. Specifically, the muscle's ability to consume oxygen to generate ATP increases sharply. Conversely, strength training relies on high-force, low-repetition exercises that increase muscle strength proportionally. Skeletal muscles enlarge, but whether this is due to hyperplasia of existing fibers or fiber splitting is unknown.

Clinically, tenderness, stiffness, and pain with movement characterize DOMS. DOMS results from mechanical damage to muscle and may be associated with histologic features of myofiber damage resulting from eccentric contractions such as hypercontracted sarcomeres leading to changes in the I-band.[20] Unlike other acute soft-tissue injuries, DOMS does not elicit the classic inflammatory response, which suggests that traditional inflammatory modifiers might not be effective in treating DOMS. Finally, DOMS must be distinguished from the "burning" experienced during and immediately following maximal exercise, which results from metabolic processes producing noxious substances such as lactic acid that accumulate in exercising muscles.[20]

Muscle lacerations

Another type of muscle injury is laceration, in which the muscle and overlying skin are transected as a result of penetrating trauma. Complete muscle disruptions, such as those resulting from laceration, typically heal with dense scarring.[7] However, regeneration is possible from the differentiation of reserve cells. Local inflammation is followed by fibrosis, the formation of fibrous tissue. Surgical repair of clean lacerations in the midbelly of skeletal muscle usually results in minimal regeneration of muscle fibers distally, scar formation at the laceration site, and recovery of about one half of muscle strength.

In addition to strains resulting from sudden stretch and lacerations resulting from sharp trauma, blunt direct trauma to muscle, such as that from contact sports, produces a muscle contusion. The quadriceps and gastrocnemius muscles are most susceptible to this injury. A *quadriceps contusion* is referred to as a *"charley horse."*[7] *Myositis ossificans* is the ossification of muscle tissue at the site of severe and/or repeated blunt injury. The heterotopic bone may resorb with time or may require excision once the bone has matured (after at least

12 months). *Myofascial pain syndrome* is a painful musculoskeletal response that may follow muscle trauma. *Fibrositis* is a diffuse multiple site complaint that does not result from trauma and is associated with emotional disturbances.

Treatment of muscle injuries

Immobilization of an injured extremity causes changes in the number of sarcomeres at the musculotendinous junction and acceleration of granulation tissue response in the injured muscle. In most cases, immobilization should be performed with the muscle in a lengthened position to decrease contracture and increase strength. Muscle atrophy can result from prolonged disuse or abnormal recruitment of motor units.

Exercise training programs are based on the principles of overload, specificity, and repetition. Overload means that a certain level of stimulus is necessary for adaptation to occur. Specificity of training implies that a specific stimulus for adaptation results in structural and functional changes in specific elements of skeletal muscle. Finally, reversibility implies that discontinuing training may result in detraining and a concomitant decrease in the adaptive changes that had occurred previously—in other words, that the effects of training can be reversed.

Endurance exercise activates large muscle groups that generate high metabolic demands resulting in adaptation of the respiratory and circulatory systems and the metabolic capacity of muscle. In particular, the ability of muscle to consume oxygen (oxygen uptake) to generate energy sources such as ATP increases sharply during endurance exercise. In contrast, strength training uses high-force, low-repetition exercises. This results in an increase in muscle strength that is proportional to the cross-sectional area of the muscle. Although it is generally accepted that skeletal muscles enlarge as a result of hypertrophy of preexisting muscle fibers, there is some controversy as to whether this is due to hyperplasia of existing fibers or to fiber-splitting.[1]

The proportion of type I and type II muscle fibers in each muscle is genetically determined.[22] Some individuals may have an unusually high percentage of slow-twitch or fast-twitch fibers in their muscles, predisposing them to specific athletic endeavors.[1,10] In addition, transformation of one type of muscle fiber to another in response to severe and sustained changes in activity has been reported, but remains controversial.[1]

Tendon, Tendon Insertion, and Fascia Injury

Several pathologic conditions may affect tendon and its surrounding tissues as a result of sports trauma and overuse, including paratenonitis, tendinitis, tendinosis, paratenonitis with tendinosis, and partial or complete tendon tears. Paratenonitis is inflammation of the paratenon, and is synonymous with peritendinitis, tenosynovitis, and tenovaginitis. Paratenonitis occurs because the tendon sheath is susceptible to repeated pressure and friction.

Tendinitis describes any injury that produces an inflammatory response within the tendon substance. For example, if acute tendon injury occurs without injury to the tendon sheath, a secondary reactive paratenonitis may occur in the sheath, but the primary site of injury remains the tendon. Tendinitis is usually symptomatic, and symptoms may be acute (present for less than 2 weeks), subacute (present for 2 to 6 weeks), or chronic (present longer than 6 weeks).[1]

In contrast, *tendinosis* is an avascular degenerative process that probably represents the result of failed tendon healing seen with aging or following repetitive microtrauma.[1] The omission of the "itis" suffix reinforces the fact that tendinosis does not incite an inflammatory response. Lateral epicondylitis or "tennis elbow" is a common example of tendinosis; other sites in which tendinosis has been reported include the Achilles tendon and rotator cuff. Histologically, tendinosis is characterized by fibroblast hypertrophy, abundant disorganized collagen, and atypical granulation tissue in which the vessels are abnormal or immature.[23]

Another condition, previously called chronic tendinitis, is characterized by both significant tendon degeneration and significant inflammation of the paratenon, but without inflammation of the tendon. This entity has been termed paratenonitis with tendinosis and is observed in patients with grossly visible partial tendon rupture. Insertional tendinitis, also called enthesopathy, is a subset of paratenonitis with tendinosis. Insertional tendinitis is inflammation at the bony insertion of the tendon and may result from overuse or following an acute injury in which the tendon fibers are torn directly off of their insertion.

Injury characteristics and healing

Histologically, tendon injury is characterized by mucoid degeneration, which is the loss of the normal cellularity and organized, crimped collagen fiber architecture that characterizes healthy tendon. Granulation tissue may also form, but as mentioned above, inflammatory cells are usually absent unless the tendon is at least partially torn. The inflammation that characterizes tendinitis and paratenonitis with tendinosis may result from associated local vascular disruption. The mechanism of tendon failure is believed to be inadequate production of maintenance collagen and matrix in response to increased loading. In addition, diminished vascularity also contributes by leading to decreased cellularity and consequently to decreased collagen production. It is not surprising that rotator cuff and Achilles tendon tears occur almost exclusively at watershed areas of decreased vascularity.[1] Fascial injuries resemble tendon injuries, but, additionally, chronic repetitive microtears, such as to the plantar fascia, may stimulate new bone formation in the form of bone spurs or osteophytes.

Tendon healing following injury is initiated by fibroblasts originating in the epitenon and macrophages that initiate healing and remodeling.[7] The repair process is a function of the specific treatment; tendon repairs are weakest at 7 to 10 days following repair, regain most of their original strength at 21 to 28 days following repair, and achieve maximum strength in 6 months. The effect of exercise on tendon properties remains inconclusive. It is possible that tendons have a variable capacity for adaptation; extensor tendons may have greater training potential than flexor tendons. Immobilization leads to increased collagen turnover and decreased tensile strength and stiffness.[20]

Ligament Injury

Ligament injury to patients with skeletally immature bone usually consists of an avulsion that occurs between the unmineralized and mineralized fibrocartilage layers. In contrast, ligament injury in adults is most commonly a midsubstance tear that is characterized by the tearing of sequential series of collagen fiber bundles.[1,7] Most ligaments sustain a 5% to 10% tensile strain prior to failure.

Ligament injuries can be partial or complete and are classified in three grades, according to the American Medical Association (AMA) Classification.[21] A grade I injury reveals mild stretching with no gross disruption of fibers, and no laxity, grade II reveals a partial tear without discontinuity with some degree of laxity, and grade III reveals a severe and complete tear. Hematoma and repair of soft-tissue inflammation follow ligament disruption. Newly synthesized collagen in the ligament scar following injury is usually type III collagen, which is later converted to type I. Full recovery may take longer than 1 year, and ultimate tensile strength may be reduced by 30% to 50%.

While immobilization usually is necessary during the acute (protective) phase, there is a potential for associated adverse effects on ligament properties; tensile strength and elastic modulus are decreased.[2] Immobilization leads to joint stiffness, which may result from new collagen fibrils forming abnormal connections that impede the normal parallel sliding of fibers in ligaments.[2] Immobilization also causes fibroblast cell atrophy and decreased metabolism. Consequently, immobilization decreases the rate of healing and the strength of repair, such as that following ligament surgery, and increases the rate of rerupture. In contrast, controlled exposure to load may accelerate ligament healing. The strength of an injured ligament returns more slowly to the insertion site than to the ligament midsubstance following mobilization. Consequently, avulsions at the insertion site are the most likely mode of ligament reinjury once the period of immobilization has passed. Short-term immobilization can be appropriate; however, in certain injuries, postoperative management (eg, quadriceps repair), and acute injuries, significant soft-tissue swelling can occur.

Synovial Injury

Both synovitis and bursitis are inflammations of synovial tissue lining a joint and bursa, respectively. Only a small amount of synovial fluid is normally present in a healthy bursa or uninjured joint, and up to a few cubic centimeters are present in large joints such as the knee. Bursae are appreciable on examination only if they are inflamed.

Trauma to the bursa or joint leads to vascular injury and bleeding, which then triggers the inflammatory process. The result is a frequently dramatic increase in the amount of joint or bursal fluid. Repetitive friction from an overlying tendon or external pressure triggers the inflammatory response to produce a bursitis, such as the olecranon bursitis of a dart thrower or prepatellar bursitis of a wrestler. If the inflammation in a bursitis is prolonged, the bursae walls may thicken, and sometimes the adjacent tendon degenerates or becomes calcified, causing a chemical bursitis. Synovitis in a joint can be secondary to multiple causes; in the knee, synovitis may result from a meniscal tear, a contusion, an osteochondral defect, or a subluxating patella. In the shoulder, it may be secondary to rotator cuff impingement or a torn glenoid labrum. The synovitis usually subsides if the underlying cause is identified and treated. In the absence of a history of trauma, other causes of acute synovitis and effusion, especially infection, must be eliminated, which usually requires joint aspiration.[1]

Inflammation of synovial tissue produces specific histopathologic appearances. Vascular endothelial cells in the synovium maintain nutrition and contribute to the inflammatory response. Connective tissue fibroblasts and macrophages assume the structure and function of cells of the synovial lining following injury. Lysosomal enzymes that damage exposed articular surfaces are released. Joint pain following injury is mediated by substance P, a neurotransmitter released from the dorsal sensory root cell bodies by afferent neurons to C-fiber axon terminals within the dorsal horn of the spinal cord in the synovium and joint capsule. Synovitis and other causes of joint pain are treated with NSAIDs.

Other specific conditions warrant mention. *Frozen shoulder* is a condition characterized by restricted shoulder movement resulting from acute trauma or a periarticular biceps or rotator cuff tendon injury. Adhesive capsulitis of the shoulder is a hypertrophic inflammatory synovitis associated with intra-articular and pericapsular adhesions. Inflammation of joints and recurrent traumatic insults may incite proliferative scar formation leading to significant joint contractures.

Nerve Injury

A variety of agents cause peripheral nerve injury. A nerve may be damaged by physical trauma in the form of compression, stretch, or friction.[2] Compression changes the

Tendon, Ligament, and Synovial Injuries

Tendon injuries

Several conditions may affect the tendon and its surrounding tissues. Paratenonitis is paratenon inflammation and occurs when the tendon sheath is subjected to repeated pressure and friction. Tendinitis is any injury that produces an inflammatory response of the tendon substance. Tendinosis is asymptomatic tendon degeneration from aging or accumulated microtrauma, or both, and occurs in the absence of an inflammatory response. Paratenonitis with tendinosis is characterized by significant tendon degeneration and paratenon inflammation without tendon inflammation. Grossly visible partial tendon rupture may be apparent. Insertional tendinitis is inflammation at the tendon's bony insertion, which can result from overuse or acute injury.

Histologically, tendon injury is typified by loss of normal cellularity and organized, crimped collagen fiber architecture and possibly granulation tissue. However, inflammatory cells usually are not present unless the tendon is at least partially torn. The inflammation of tendinitis and paratenonitis with tendinosis may result from associated local vascular disruption. Tendon failure is thought to result from inadequate production of maintenance collagen and matrix in response to increased loading, and reduced vascularity leads to decreased cellularity and collagen production. Rotator cuff and Achilles tendon tears tend to occur in areas of decreased vascularity. Chronic repetitive microtears to the fascia can stimulate new bone formation, leading to calcific tendinitis.

Fibroblasts and macrophages initiate tendon healing and remodeling. Tendon repairs are weakest at 7 to 10 days, regain most of their original strength at 21 to 28 days, and achieve maximum strength in 6 months. Exercise may cause some tendons to adapt, with extensor tendons being more adaptable than flexor tendons. Immobilization increases collagen turnover and decreases tensile strength and stiffness.

Ligament injuries

In skeletally immature patients, ligament injury usually results in an avulsion between the unmineralized and mineralized fibrocartilage layers. In adults, ligament injury is usually a midsubstance tear, with sequential tearing of collagen fiber bundles. Most ligaments sustain a 5% to 10% tensile strain before failing. Ligament injuries are classified according to the American Medical Association classification: grade I is mild stretching without gross fiber disruption, grade II is a partial tear without discontinuity, and grade III is a severe, complete tear. Once the ligament is disrupted, a hematoma forms and the repair process begins. Newly synthesized collagen in the scar is type III, later converted to type I. A year or more may be necessary for full recovery, and ultimate tensile strength can be reduced by 30% to 50%.

Immobilization reduces the ligament's tensile strength and elastic modulus and leads to joint stiffness. Fibroblast atrophy and decreased metabolism limit the rate of healing and the strength of repair after surgery, increasing the risk of rerupture. Exposure to controlled load, however, may accelerate healing.

Synovial injuries

Synovial injury includes synovitis and bursitis. Only a small amount of synovial fluid is normally present in a healthy bursa or joint. Trauma to the joint or bursa causes vascular injury and bleeding, triggering inflammation, which results in a dramatic increase in synovial fluid. Repetitive friction from an overlying tendon or external pressure produces bursitis. Prolonged bursitis can lead to thickening (granulation) of the bursal walls and degeneration or calcification of the adjacent tendon, or chemical bursitis. Synovitis usually resolves once the etiology is identified and treated; if no history of trauma exists, the synovitis may be acute and infected, requiring joint aspiration for diagnosis.

Anti-inflammatory medications treat synovitis by directly suppressing the arachidonic acid cascade. Specific examples of synovitis include frozen shoulder (restricted shoulder movement after acute trauma or periarticular biceps or rotator cuff tendon injury) and adhesive capsulitis of the shoulder (hypertrophic, inflammatory synovitis associated with intra-articular and pericapsular adhesions). Joint inflammation and recurrent trauma may allow scar to proliferate, producing significant joint contractures.

cross-sectional dimensions of nerve, and stretch increases its length. Some instances of nerve compression result from acute injuries producing immediate symptoms. Others result from chronic repetitive or sustained compression that leads to a delayed or gradual onset of symptoms. Friction-based injuries occur when a nerve glides through a limited space and rubs across a rough structure such as in the various entrapment syndromes.

3

Regional Pathology

Section Editors
Ronnie P. Barnes, MS, ATC
Jack B. Ryan, MD, FACS

7

Head Injuries

Kevin M. Guskiewicz, PhD, ATC
Jeffrey T. Barth, PhD, ABPP

QUICK CONTENTS

- The anatomy of the head, the scalp, and the brain.
- The types of traumatic brain injury.
- Assessment of traumatic brain injury.
- Return to competition after traumatic brain injury.

OVERVIEW

Despite the considerable amount of protective equipment available to and used by athletes today, the head and brain are still susceptible to injury during athletic competition. Unlike most injuries sustained in sports, injuries to the brain and spinal cord create the potential for catastrophic and irreversible damage because these tissues are largely incapable of regeneration. Sports medicine physicians and athletic trainers responsible for the care of athletes who may sustain head or neck trauma must be aware of the potential dangers of returning an athlete to competition following such an injury. This chapter will focus on injuries to the head, primarily those associated with the brain. Anatomy will be discussed first, followed by the most common mechanisms of injury, and various types (classifications) of trauma. The chapter will then explore sideline assessment and subsequent follow-up evaluation techniques, as well as considerations for return to sports participation.

ANATOMY OF THE HEAD

The Skull

The skull can be thought of as a natural helmet for the brain. It rests on the superior end of the vertebral column and includes two sets of bones: cranial bones and facial bones. The *cranial bones* serve to protect the brain and are more rigid and firm than the facial bones. The eight cranial bones include the frontal bone, two parietal bones, two temporal bones, the occipital bone, sphenoid bone, and ethmoid bone (**Figure 7-1**). The 14 bones of the face include two nasal bones, two maxillae, two zygomatic bones, the mandible, two lacrimal bones, two palatine bones, two inferior nasal conchae, and the vomer.

The *foramen magnum* is the large aperture at the base of the skull through which the medulla and spinal cord pass and enter into the bony spinal canal in the neck (Figure 7-2). The bones of the adult skull are constructed of firm outer and inner layers, or tables. Interspersed between these layers is softer bone, containing blood channels. Some of these larger vascular pathways are visible on radiographs of the skull.

Whenever an athlete sustains a severe blow to the head, a skull fracture should be suspected. Although the incidence of these fractures is low, they are potentially serious injuries. Skull fractures are described as depressed, linear, nondepressed, comminuted, and basal or basilar (**Figure 7-3**). A *depressed skull fracture* occurs when the fracture causes a portion of the skull to be indented toward the brain, and *linear* and *nondepressed skull fractures* involve minimal indentation of the skull toward the brain. A *comminuted skull fracture* is characterized by multiple fracture fragments, and a basal or basilar skull fracture involves the base of the skull.

Skull fractures may be difficult to diagnose clinically. Even a depressed skull fracture may be confused clinically with a deep scalp hematoma. Therefore, radiographic evaluation is crucial for detection and management of skull fractures. In evaluating athletes who have sustained skull fractures, the athletic trainer must always consider associated brain injury.

The Scalp

The scalp has energy-absorbing properties, thereby offering considerable protection for the skull. Without this protection, the skull would be fractured with significantly less force than is required to fracture it with the scalp attached. The scalp consists of five layers of soft tissue that cover the outer portion of the skull: skin, connective tissue, aponeurosis, loose connective tissue, and pericranium (**Figure 7-4**).

The first three layers, the skin, connective tissue, and aponeurosis, are called the "scalp proper" and are often clinically regarded as a single layer because they remain together when the scalp is torn away during accidents.

FOCUS ON . . .

Skull

Composed of the cranial and facial bones, the skull rests on the superior end of the vertebral column. The foramen magnum is the large basal skull aperture, through which the medulla and spinal cord pass and enter the bony spinal canal. The adult skull bones are constructed of firm outer and inner layers (tables), with softer bone and blood channels interspersed.

Scalp

The energy-absorbing scalp offers considerable skull protection. The scalp consists of five soft tissue layers that cover the outer portion of the skull: skin, connective tissue, aponeurosis, loose connective tissue, and pericranium.

Scalp lacerations generally bleed profusely and most commonly require surgical care. Lacerations must be treated carefully to prevent scalp infection, which can spread to the underlying bones and cranial cavity.

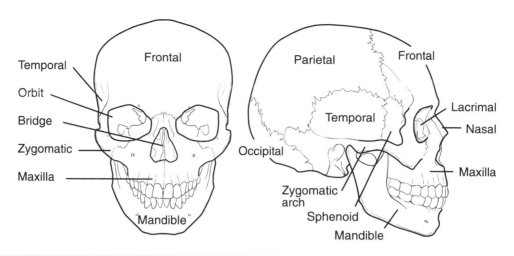

FIGURE 7-1

The skull contains two different sets of bones: cranial bones and facial bones. Lateral view of the skull (right). Anteroposterior view of the skull (left).

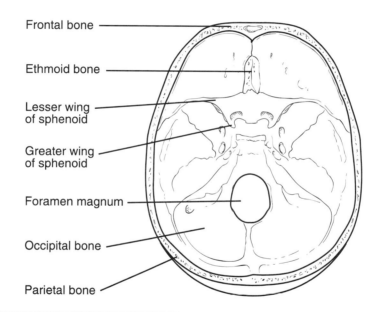

FIGURE 7-2

The foramen magnum is an opening at the base of the skull through which the medulla and spinal cord pass.

The skin of the scalp is thin except in the occipital region. The skin contains many sweat and sebaceous glands and hair follicles. It has an abundant arterial supply and good venous and lymphatic drainage systems. The connective tissue is rather dense and acts to bind the skin above to the aponeurosis of the epicranius muscle below. If this layer is lacerated, it tends to bleed profusely because the blood vessels are firmly anchored by connective tissue and cannot retract. The aponeurosis epicranialis is a very dense and strong membrane that serves as the tendon of the epicranius muscle. The epicranius muscle consists of four parts, the two occipital bellies (occipitalis) and the two frontal bellies (frontalis). Scalp wounds do not gape unless this layer is cut.

The loose connective tissue is somewhat like a sponge because it contains innumerable potential spaces that are capable of becoming distended with fluid. It is this loose connective tissue that allows free movement of the scalp

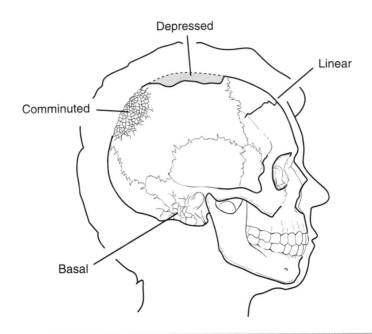

An athlete can sustain various types of skull fractures, some of which include depressed, linear, comminuted, and basal fractures.

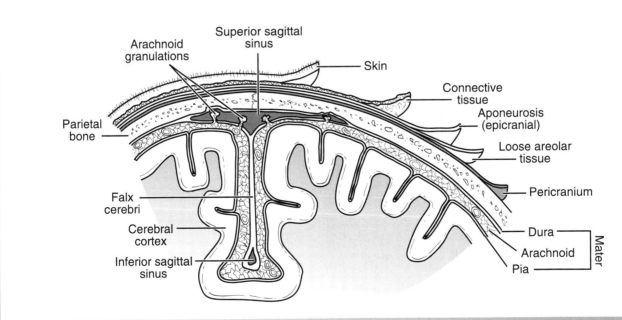

The five soft-tissue layers of the scalp are the skin, connective tissue, aponeurosis, loose connective tissue, and pericranium. The meninges comprise the dura mater, arachnoid, and pia mater.

proper. Injury to this layer of the scalp is considered to be dangerous because pus or blood can spread easily in it. Infection in this layer can be transmitted to the cranial cavity by the emissary veins that connect the large venous sinuses inside the skull with the superficial scalp veins that traverse this area. Thus, when the aponeurosis is cut and the loose connective tissue is exposed, the athlete should be referred to a physician for careful debridement, irrigation, and closure of the wound.

The pericranium is the fifth and deepest layer of the scalp. It is a dense layer of specialized connective tissue that is firmly attached to the surface of the skull. If this

FOCUS ON . . .

The Brain

Layers

The meninges (dura mater, arachnoid, and pia) are the layers of nonnervous tissue that form the venous drainage system and surround and protect the brain and spinal cord. The dura mater, a tough, fibrous membrane, lies just under the bone and contains venous sinuses that carry blood from the brain to the neck veins. The dura mater covering the spinal cord is separated from the bone by the epidural space, which contains fat and small veins.

The arachnoid is a thin, cellular membrane separated from the dura mater by the narrow subdural space. This layer is closely connected to the pia mater by a mesh of connective tissue strands. The pia mater loosely covers the brain and sheaths the blood vessels entering the brain. The subarachnoid space between the arachnoid and the pia mater contains the cerebrospinal fluid.

Parts

The cerebrum is the largest part of the brain, a large mass of nerve tissue with folds (convolutions) on its surface. The diencephalon lies between the two hemispheres, forming the upper part of the brain stem. The brain contains four paired lobes and the brain stem, which connects the cerebral hemispheres with the spinal cord at the foramen magnum. The cerebral cortex controls language, speech, visuospatial problem solving, and motor and sensory functions: the highest cognitive and behavioral activities of humans. The thin cerebral cortex is composed of gray matter (nerve cell bodies), whereas the interior of the cerebral hemispheres is composed of white matter (nerve cell processes and fibers) and basal ganglia (well-demarcated masses of gray matter).

The cerebellum, lying underneath the cerebral tissue, functions with the cerebral cortex and brain stem to automatically regulate movement and posture. This fissured mass of gray matter is located at the posteroinferior cranium and attaches to the brain stem by three pairs of peduncles. The cerebellar cortex is composed mainly of white matter.

The brain stem, fixed between the more movable cerebral hemispheres above and the spinal cord below, has three parts: the medulla oblongata, pons, and midbrain. The medulla contains the centers for the cranial and other nerves, which govern respiration, circulation, and other visceral activities, and is often referred to as the most vital part of the brain. The pons is involved in the refinement of motor functions and postural movements. Injury to the midbrain can result in loss of consciousness and coma.

Cerebrospinal Fluid, Cerebral Blood Supply, and the Cranial Nerves

The ventricles of the brain contain the choroid plexus, in which an almost protein-free cerebrospinal fluid forms. This fluid circulates through the ventricles, enters the subarachnoid space, and filters back into the venous system. The fluid acts as a shock absorber and cushions and protects the brain by converting focally applied external stresses to a more uniform compressive stress.

The vertebral and internal carotid artery cerebral branches supply blood to the brain, and the middle meningeal branch of the maxillary artery mainly supplies blood to the meninges. Vertebral arteries and segmental arteries supply the spinal cord and spinal roots, with small branches supplying the peripheral nerves. Oxygenated blood from the vertebral, basilar, and internal carotid arteries flows to the circle of Willis and is then distributed to the cerebrum via bilateral anterior, middle, and posterior cerebral arteries.

Twelve pairs of special cranial nerves are associated with the brain and mediate sensory and motor functions.

---

layer is torn as a result of a skull fracture, intracranial hemorrhage can leak into and collect in the subaponeurotic space of the scalp. Accumulation of blood in this space, instead of inside the skull, may for a time prevent compression of the brain.

Scalp injury

Scalp lacerations are the most common type of head injury that requires surgical care. These wounds usually bleed profusely because communicating arteries enter around the periphery of the scalp and, because the scalp is tough, the vessels do not retract when lacerated. Lacerations must be treated carefully because scalp infection may develop and spread into the underlying bones of the skull, causing osteomyelitis. The infection can also spread to the cranial cavity, producing an extradural abscess, or meningitis. In the event of a scalp laceration with an expected brain concussion, the source of bleeding should be located, and the bleeding controlled by direct pressure before evaluation of the head is continued.

The Brain
The meninges

Layers of the nonnervous tissue that form the venous drainage system, collectively termed the *meninges*, surround and protect the brain and spinal cord. These layers comprise the dura mater, arachnoid, and pia mater, which is nearest the brain (see Figure 7-4). The *dura mater* is a tough fibrous membrane that lies immediately inside the bone. It contains venous channels, or sinuses, that carry blood from the brain to the veins in the neck. The portion of the dura mater that covers the spinal cord is separated from the bone by the epidural space, which contains fat and small veins.

The *arachnoid*, so-called because it resembles a spider web, is a thin, cellular membrane that is separated from the dura mater by the narrow subdural space. The arachnoid is very closely connected to the innermost meningeal layer, the pia mater, by a meshwork of connective tissue strands. The *pia mater* is a loose tissue that covers the brain and sheaths the blood vessels as they enter the brain. The space between the arachnoid and the pia mater is the *subarachnoid space*, which contains the cerebrospinal fluid. The arachnoid and pia mater are more widely separated from each other around the spinal cord than over the brain.

The cerebrum

The largest part of the brain is the *cerebrum*, which is a mass of nerve tissue that is distinguished by folds or convolutions over much of its surface. The bulk of the brain is formed by two cerebral hemispheres. The *diencephalon* lies between these hemispheres and forms the upper part of the brain stem, the unpaired stalk or stem that descends from the base of the brain. The brain contains four paired lobes—the frontal, parietal, temporal, and occipital lobes—plus the brain stem, which connects the cerebral hemispheres with the spinal cord at the foramen magnum (**Figure 7-5**).

The *cerebral cortex*, the outer layer of the cerebral hemispheres, controls language and speech, visuospatial problem solving, and motor and sensory functions. The highest cognitive and behavioral activities of humans are performed by the cerebral cortex. The cerebral cortex is only a few millimeters thick and is composed of gray matter, which consists of the bodies of nerve cells. In contrast, the interior of the cerebral hemispheres is composed partly of white matter, which consists largely of the processes or fibers of the nerve cells. This interior portion, which includes the diencephalon, also contains well-demarcated masses of gray matter, known collectively as *basal ganglia*.

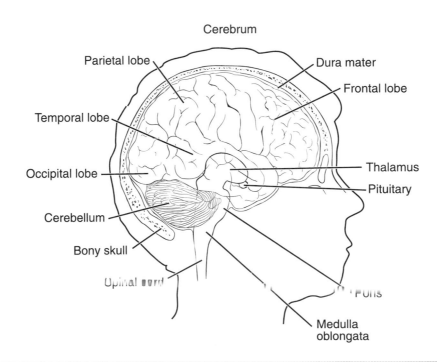

FIGURE 7-5

The cerebrum is the largest part of the brain and contains two cerebral hemispheres. Four paired lobes and the brain stem are contained within the brain.

The cerebellum and brain stem

The *cerebellum*, sometimes called the "little brain," lies underneath the great mass of cerebral tissue. The cerebellum is important to the automatic regulation of movement and posture and functions in concert with the cerebral cortex and the brain stem. It is a fissured mass of gray matter that occupies the posteroinferior part of the cranium and is attached to the brain stem by three pairs of peduncles (stalks or bands). The cortex of the cerebellum, like that of the cerebral hemisphere, is composed mainly of white matter.

The *brain stem* is a fixed functional area between the more movable cerebral hemispheres above and the spinal cord below. The brain stem is made up of three parts, the *medulla oblongata, pons,* and *midbrain.* Disruption to the medulla caused by a blow to the head that sets the brain into motion often leads to neurologic symptoms associated with either a brain concussion or diffuse axonal injury. Because the medulla contains the centers for the cranial nerves and nerves governing respiration, circulation, and other visceral activities, it is often referred to as the most vital part of the entire brain. Severe contusions to this area that result in actual tissue damage and hemorrhage may cause death. The midbrain houses the major portion of the reticular activating system, which is responsible for wakefulness and alertness, consciousness, and some aspects of muscle tone. Insult to this area can result in loss of consciousness and coma. The pons, which is located superior to the medulla and inferior to the midbrain, is involved in the refinement of motor functions and postural movements.

Cerebrospinal fluid

The ventricles (communicated cavities) of the brain contain a vascular portion of the pia mater, the choroid plexus, in which an almost protein-free *cerebrospinal fluid (CSF)* forms. This fluid circulates through the ventricles, enters the subarachnoid space, and eventually filters back into the venous system (**Figure 7-6**). CSF acts as a shock absorber, cushioning and protecting the brain as it follows the brain contours and converts focally applied external stresses to a more uniform compressive stress.

Pressure of the CSF, when it is removed during a lumbar puncture or spinal tap, is usually quite low, between 100 and 200 millimeters of water (mm H_2O). Certain anesthetics, as well as contrast radiographic material for determining the positions of masses, tumors, ruptured disks, and displaced fracture fragments, can be introduced into the space occupied by the fluid.

Cerebral blood supply

The cerebral branches of the vertebral and internal carotid arteries supply blood to the brain (**Figure 7-7**). The main function of the middle meningeal branch of the maxillary artery is to supply blood to the meninges. Vertebral arteries and segmental arteries supply the spinal cord and spinal roots, and a number of small branches

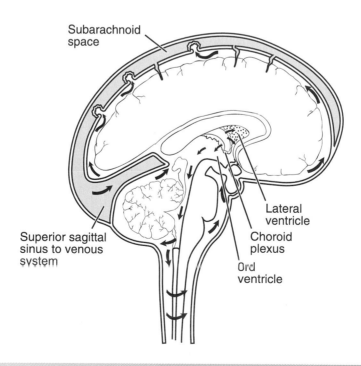

Subarachnoid space

Superior sagittal sinus to venous system

Lateral ventricle

Choroid plexus

Ord ventricle

FIGURE 7-6

Cerebrospinal fluid circulates through the ventricles of the brain and subarachnoid space before filtering back into the venous system.

along the course of the nerves supply the peripheral nerves. Oxygenated blood from the vertebral, basilar, and internal carotid arteries flows to the circle of Willis where it is distributed to the cerebrum via bilateral anterior, middle, and posterior cerebral arteries.

Cranial nerves

The large cranial nerves consist of 12 pairs of special nerves that are associated with the brain (**Figure 7-8**). The fibers in the cranial nerves mediate the following sensory and motor functions:

- Cranial nerve I: olfactory (smell)
- Cranial nerve II: optic (visual acuity)
- Cranial nerves III, IV, and VI: oculomotor, trochlear, and abducens (motor nerves that control movement of the eyes and pupil constriction)
- Cranial nerve V: trigeminal (sensation of the head, face, and movement of the jaw)
- Cranial nerve VII: facial (special sensory, motor, and autonomic nervous components that allow taste, facial movements, and secretion of tears and saliva)
- Cranial nerve VIII: vestibulocochlear (helps with equilibrium [vestibular] and hearing [cochlear])
- Cranial nerve IX: glossopharyngeal (sensory and motor components dealing with taste, sensation in and movement of the pharynx, autonomic function in secretion of saliva, and sensory components in visceral reflexes)
- Cranial nerve X: vagus (controls taste and sensation to the pharynx, larynx, and tracheobronchial tree; important in the movements of the pharynx and larynx, secretions of the thoracic and abdominal viscera and visceral reflexes)
- Cranial nerve XI: spinal accessory (motor nerve concerned with movements of the pharynx, larynx, head, and shoulders)
- Cranial nerve XII: hypoglossal (primarily a motor nerve concerned with the movements of the tongue)

Because signs and symptoms related to more serious injuries can be detected through a basic cranial nerve assessment, clinicians should have a clear understanding of the role for each cranial nerve.

FOCUS ON . . .

Types of Traumatic Brain Injury

Traumatic brain injury is classified as focal or diffuse. Focal lesions include subdural hematomas, epidural hematomas, cerebral contusions, and intracerebral hemorrhages and hematomas. Diffuse injuries can result in widespread or globally disrupted neurologic function, but are not usually associated with macroscopically visible brain lesions, except for cerebral edema.

Diffuse injuries

Diffuse injuries are usually caused by an acceleration-deceleration motion in a linear or rotational plane, which produces a shaking of the brain within the skull. The speed of the head, time of deceleration, and the load placed on the head (force) are the key elements. Most diffuse brain injuries are caused by rotational or rotational acceleration-deceleration injuries. Structural diffuse axonal injury is the most severe type of diffuse injury; axonal disruption can disrupt breathing, heart rate, consciousness, memory, and cognition. Nonstructural diffuse injuries such as cerebral concussions tend to be less severe than structural injuries because the anatomic integrity of the central nervous system remains intact, but they can affect consciousness, memory, and cognition and raise the individual's risk for second-impact syndrome.

Coup and contrecoup injuries

A forceful blow to the resting, movable head usually produces maximum brain injury beneath the point of impact (coup injury), unlike the moving head hitting an unyielding object, which produces maximum brain injury opposite the side of impact (contrecoup injury) as the brain bounces within the cranium and to the opposite side. With acceleration of the head before impact, the brain lags toward the trailing surface, squeezing away the cerebrospinal fluid, which maximizes the shearing force at this site. The cerebrospinal fluid thickens under the point of impact from the brain lag, averting a coup injury. Conversely, if the head is stationary before impact, brain lag does not occur and the cerebrospinal fluid remains evenly distributed, producing a coup injury. A skull fracture can absorb trauma energy (thus eliminating the possibility of either a coup or contrecoup injury) or directly injure brain tissue. In this case, a focal lesion is most common at the frontal and temporal lobe anterior tips and inferior surfaces.

A force applied to the brain can cause compressive (crushing so that the tissue cannot absorb any additional force or load), tensile (tissue pulling or stretching), or shearing (a force moving across the parallel tissue) stress.

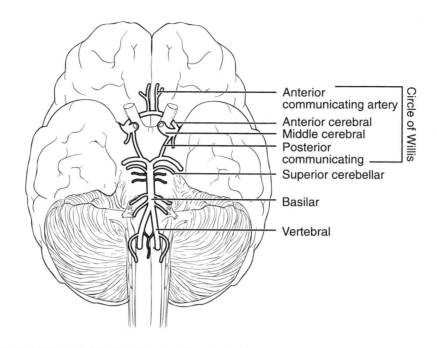

FIGURE 7-7

The cerebral branches of the vertebral and internal carotid arteries supply blood to the brain, spinal cord, spinal roots, and peripheral nerves.

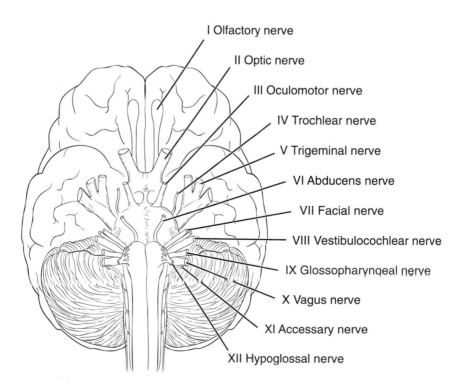

FIGURE 7-8

The cranial nerves comprise 12 pairs of special nerves with specific sensory and motor functions.

TRAUMATIC BRAIN INJURY

The immediate management of the athlete with a head injury depends on the nature and severity of the injury. There are two classifications of *traumatic brain injury (TBI)*: focal and diffuse. Focal or posttraumatic intracranial mass lesions include subdural hematomas, epidural hematomas, cerebral contusions, and intracerebral hemorrhages/hematomas. *Diffuse brain injuries* can result in widespread or global disruption of neurologic function and are not usually associated with macroscopically visible brain lesions; however, cerebral edema may be noted. Most diffuse injuries involve an acceleration-deceleration motion either within a linear plane or in a rotational model. In either case, lesions are caused when the brain is shaken within the skull. For example, with a linear acceleration-deceleration mechanism, the head experiences a violent, side-to-side or front-to-back movement before potential impact. The key elements are how fast the head moves (acceleration and deceleration speed), how long deceleration takes, and how much load is placed on the head (force). Rotational injuries or rotational acceleration-deceleration injuries are believed to be the primary injury mechanism for diffuse brain injuries.[1,2] Structural diffuse brain injury, or *diffuse axonal injury (DAI)*, is the most severe type of diffuse injury because axonal disruption occurs and can result in impairment. Such injuries can result in disruption to centers of the brain responsible for breathing, heart rate, consciousness, memory, and cognition. Nonstructural diffuse injuries such as cerebral concussions are typically less severe than structural brain lesions because the anatomic integrity of the central nervous system is maintained. Although nonstructural injuries are less severe, they may still result in disruption of consciousness, memory, or cognition and can place the individual at higher risk for second impact syndrome.

Mechanisms of Traumatic Brain Injury

A forceful blow to the resting head usually produces a *coup injury*, which is a maximum brain injury that occurs beneath the point of cranial impact. Impact of a moving head with an unyielding object usually produces a *contrecoup injury*, which is a maximum brain injury that occurs opposite the site of cranial impact as the brain bounces within the cranium. When the head is accelerated prior to impact, the brain lags toward the trailing surface, thus squeezing away the CSF and allowing the shearing forces to be maximal at this site. This brain lag actually thickens the layer of CSF under the point of impact, which explains the lack of coup injury in the moving head injury. On the other hand, when the head is stationary prior to impact, there is neither brain lag nor disproportionate distribution of CSF, accounting for the presence of coup injury and absence of contrecoup injury. If the skull is fractured, the individual will sustain neither

a coup nor a contrecoup injury because the bone itself, either transiently (linear skull fracture) or permanently (depressed skull fracture) displaced at the moment of impact, may absorb much of the trauma energy or may directly injure the brain tissue. Because the associated cranial bones have irregular surfaces, focal lesions are most common at the anterior tips and the inferior surfaces of the frontal and temporal lobes.[3]

In a brain injury, an applied force can generate three different types of stresses: *compressive*, *tensile*, and *shearing*. Compression involves a crushing force so that the tissue cannot absorb any additional force or load. Tension involves pulling or stretching of tissue, and shearing involves a force that moves across the parallel organization of the tissue. Uniform compressive stresses are fairly well tolerated by neural tissue, but shearing stresses are very poorly tolerated.[4]

Classification of Traumatic Brain Injury

Athletic trainers and team physicians must develop a high sensitivity to the various presentations of TBI. All medical personnel must understand the immediate, delayed, and associated findings, as well as the known complications. An injury that initially appears to involve minor pathology may gradually worsen and reveal signs and symptoms of a more serious injury.

Cerebral Concussion

The most common sport-related injury to the brain is also the least severe. *Cerebral concussion* is a clinical syndrome characterized by immediate and transient impairment of neural functions, such as alteration of consciousness, disturbance of vision, and equilibrium, that is due to brain stem involvement. An athlete who has sustained a concussion does not necessarily experience a loss of consciousness. The definition is often expanded to include mild (grade 1), moderate (grade 2), and severe (grade 3) forms of cerebral concussion. Although these distinctions may be valuable for treatment and prognosis, they are less important than previously believed. The clinician should focus more on the presentation of overall signs and symptoms.

Several grading scales have been proposed for classifying and managing cerebral concussions.[2,5-11] None of these scales has been universally accepted or followed with any consistency by the sports medicine community. Some scales are more conservative than others; however, most are useful in the management of concussion. Athletic trainers and team physicians who work together should choose one scale and ensure consistent use of that scale. Most scales are based primarily on level of consciousness and amnesia; however, because most concussions will not involve loss of consciousness or observable amnesia, other signs and symptoms associated with con-

FOCUS ON . . .

Classifying Traumatic Brain Injuries

Traumatic brain injury must be classified so that all medical personnel understand the athlete's current condition and what to expect over time. Cerebral concussion is the most common sport-related brain injury and the least severe. It involves immediate, transient neural function impairment, but the athlete need not have lost consciousness. Several grading scales for concussion exist, but none are universally accepted or followed. The athletic trainer and team physician should select one scale to use consistently.

Mild concussion

A mild concussion is the most difficult to recognize and assess and is often not reported until after the practice or game. Consciousness is not lost, but the athlete may experience some alteration of consciousness and impaired mental function, especially for remembering recent events (posttraumatic amnesia) and in assimilating and interpreting new information, along with dizziness and tinnitus. Headache is common; the intensity and duration can reflect the direction of the injury.

Moderate concussion

A moderate concussion may be associated with transient mental confusion, tinnitus, moderate dizziness, unsteadiness, blurred vision, nausea, prolonged posttraumatic amnesia, and momentary loss of consciousness.

Severe concussion

A severe concussion is characterized by more signs and symptoms than a mild or moderate injury, along with blurred vision, nausea, tinnitus, markedly impaired neuromuscular coordination, severe mental confusion, dizziness, posttraumatic amnesia of more than 24 hours, and retrograde amnesia. Any prolonged loss of consciousness means that the concussion is severe. Because these signs and symptoms can also reflect serious and progressive brain injury, the athletic trainer must carefully monitor the athlete.

Cerebral contusion

A cerebral contusion (bruise) occurs when an object hits the skull or the skull hits an object, causing injured vessels to bleed. Signs and symptoms can include prolonged loss of consciousness, partial paralysis or hemiplegia, one-sided pupil dilation, and altered vital signs. Progressive swelling may injure brain tissue not affected by the original trauma. Recovery without surgery is usual, but the prognosis can be affected by the emergency care provided, including necessary basic life support, proper transport techniques, and prompt expert evaluation.

Cerebral hematoma

Cerebral hematomas (blood clots) are either epidural or subdural and cause increased intracranial pressure and shifting of the cerebral hemispheres away from the clot. As the hematoma forms, neurologic signs and symptoms deteriorate.

An epidural hematoma in an athlete is usually the result of a severe blow that produces a temporoparietal fracture and can injure the middle meningeal artery. Neurologically, the athlete may not deteriorate for 10 to 20 minutes or more. Immediate surgery may be needed to decompress the hematoma and control the bleeding artery.

A subdural hematoma occurs when a blow to the skull thrusts the brain against the point of impact, tearing the subdural vessels. The low-pressure bleeding slowly clots, but symptoms may not appear until much later, when the clot absorbs fluid and expands and may need to be evacuated (drained). Therefore, an athlete who has lost consciousness or experienced altered mental status should be monitored for several days.

An artery torn by a depressed skull fracture, penetrating wound, or acceleration-deceleration injury can result in a collection of blood within the brain itself, causing an intracerebral hematoma. Neurologic deterioration is often rapid, and death may occur before the athlete reaches the emergency facility.

Second Impact syndrome

Second impact syndrome occurs when an athlete who has sustained head trauma incurs a second injury before symptoms from the first have resolved. Brain swelling and herniation are rapid from loss of blood supply autoregulation. The brain stem fails within 2 to 5 minutes, resulting in dilated pupils, loss of eye movement, respiratory failure, and coma. If the athlete is on the field, the helmet and pads should be removed to allow intubation. While the incidence of second impact syndrome is low, the 50% mortality rate and 100% morbidity rate demand that return-to-play decisions be made cautiously in even mildly head-injured athletes.

The mechanism of the subdural hematoma is more complex. The force of a blow to the skull thrusts the brain against the point of impact. As a result, the subdural vessels tear, resulting in venous bleeding. Because bleeding produces low pressure with slow clot formation, symptoms may not become evident until hours, days, or even weeks later when the clot may absorb fluid and expand. Treatment of any athlete who has lost consciousness or experienced altered mental status should include prolonged observation and monitoring for several days, because slow bleeding will cause subsequent deterioration of mental status. In such a case, surgical intervention may be necessary to evacuate (drain) the hematoma and decompress the brain.

Intracerebral hematoma

Bleeding from a torn artery that results from a depressed skull fracture, penetrating wound, or acceleration-deceleration injury may lead to a collection of blood within the brain substance itself. The athlete who has sustained an intracerebral hematoma usually has no lucid interval after the injury, and the hematoma often progresses rapidly.

Death often occurs before the injured athlete can be moved to an emergency facility. Sometimes, an autopsy will reveal a congenital lesion, indicating that the cause of death was ultimately unavoidable.

Second Impact Syndrome

Over the past decade, there has been an increased incidence of *second impact syndrome (SIS)* in athletes.[4,5,9,11-14] SIS is a special condition that occurs when an athlete who has sustained an initial head trauma, most often a concussion, sustains a second head injury before symptoms associated with the first have totally resolved. Often, the first injury was unreported or unrecognized. SIS usually occurs within 1 week of the initial injury and involves rapid brain swelling and herniation as a result of the brain's loss of autoregulation of its blood supply. Brain stem failure develops in a matter of 2 to 5 minutes and causes rapidly dilating pupils, loss of eye movement, respiratory failure, and eventually, coma. On-the-field management of SIS should include removal of any helmet or pads so the athlete can be rapidly intubated, depending on the status of and possible

---

FOCUS ON . . .

Treatment of Brain Injuries

Most cerebral concussions involve no loss of consciousness, only transient loss of alertness or mental confusion, causing the athlete to be dazed, dizzy, and disoriented. When caring for an athlete with a head injury, it is essential to recognize the injury and its severity, determine if additional attention or assessment is needed, and decide when the athlete can return to play. A carefully prepared protocol is key to the successful initial evaluation of an injured athlete and may differ if the athlete is down or ambulatory. A head-injured athlete is preferably initially evaluated on the playing field.

A primary survey should be performed to immediately assess respiration and cardiac status. Once a life-threatening condition has been ruled out, a secondary survey is performed. A thorough history should be taken to evaluate any mental confusion, loss of consciousness, and amnesia.

Level of consciousness should be monitored with a neural watch chart. An athlete who is unconscious or regaining consciousness should be treated as if he or she has a cervical spine injury and transported from the field on a spine board with the head and neck immobilized. Vital signs should be monitored at regular 1- to 2-minute intervals, and, even if the athlete appears lethargic, stuporous, or unconscious, he or she should be spoken to. To avoid worsening a cervical spine injury, the athlete should not be shaken. If the loss of consciousness lasted less than 1 minute and the rest of the examination is normal, the athlete should be observed on the sideline and referred for physician evaluation later. Unconsciousness lasting longer than 1 minute requires immobilization and transfer to an emergency facility for a thorough neurologic examination.

The athletic trainer should test for amnesia by asking the athlete the first thing he or she remembered after the injury and requesting a description of the play before the injury or the name of last week's opponent. Name, date, time, and place questions do not discriminate between injured and noninjured athletes. Instead, turning the athlete away from the field and asking for the name of the opponent can be useful. Also, the athletic trainer should ask if the athlete has any ringing in the ears, blurred vision, or nausea, and use a concussion symptom checklist to record signs and symptoms.

While asking the athlete questions, the athletic trainer should observe for any facial deformities or abnormal expressions, respirations, and extremity movement, and listen to the speech pattern. He or she should gently palpate the athlete's skull and cervical spine to rule out a fracture. A helmet need not be removed unless ventilation is compromised; removing the facemask or strap may provide adequate airway access. An unconscious player should be moved carefully on a spine board and the neck gently but firmly supported.

necessity to immobilize the cervical spine. Unfortunately, the mortality rate of SIS is 50%, and the morbidity rate is 100%. Although the number of reported cases is relatively low, the potential for SIS to occur in athletes with mild head injuries should be a major consideration when making decisions about return to play.[0]

ASSESSING TRAUMATIC BRAIN INJURY

Recognition of a mild traumatic brain injury is straightforward if the athlete has a loss of consciousness. However, 90% to 95% of all cerebral concussions involve no loss of consciousness but only a transient loss of alertness or the presence of mental confusion.[10] The athlete will likely appear dazed, dizzy, and disoriented. Injuries in which the athlete does not lose consciousness are more difficult to recognize and even more challenging to classify given the numerous grading scales available and the inability to quantify most of the signs and symptoms.

The three primary objectives for the athletic trainer who encounters an athlete with a head injury are recognizing the injury and its severity, determining if the athlete requires additional attention or assessment, and deciding when the athlete may return to sports activity. The first objective can be met by performing a thorough initial evaluation. A well-prepared protocol is the key to the successful initial evaluation of an athlete who has sustained a head injury or any other type of trauma. During the secondary survey, a seven-step protocol (history, observation, palpation, special tests, active/passive range of motion, strength tests, and functional tests) should be strictly followed to ensure that nothing has been overlooked.

Initial On-Site Assessment

The athletic trainer's approach to the initial assessment depends on whether an "athlete-down" condition or an "ambulatory" condition exists. An athlete-down condition exists when the athletic trainer or team physician responds to the athlete on the field or court. An ambulatory condition exists when the athlete is seen by the athletic trainer at some point following the injury. Head trauma in an athletic situation requires immediate assessment for appropriate emergency action, and, if at all possible, the athletic trainer or team physician should perform the initial evaluation of the athlete at the location where the injury occurred.

A primary survey to determine whether basic life support measures are necessary should be performed first. This survey is easily accomplished and usually takes only a matter of 10 to 15 seconds. Respiration and cardiac status are assessed to rule out a life-threatening condition. Once the primary survey has been completed, the secondary survey can begin.

A thorough history taken by the athletic trainer begins the secondary survey. The history is the most important

step of the evaluation process because it can narrow down the assessment very quickly. The athletic trainer should try to obtain as much information as possible about any mental confusion, loss of consciousness, and amnesia. Confusion can be determined quickly by noting whether the athlete's facial expression is dazed, stunned, or glassy-eyed and whether the athlete is exhibiting inappropriate behavior such as running the wrong play or returning to the wrong huddle. **Table 7-2** presents a neural watch chart, which helps the athletic trainer monitor the athlete's level of consciousness.

If the injured athlete is unconscious or regaining consciousness but still disoriented and confused, the athletic trainer may not be able to totally rule out an associated

TABLE 7-2
NEURAL WATCH CHART

Unit			Time
I	Vital signs	Blood pressure	_____
		Pulse	_____
		Respiration	_____
		Temperature	_____
II	Conscious and oriented		_____
		Disoriented	_____
		Restless	_____
		Combative	_____
III	Speech	Clear	_____
		Rambling	_____
		Garbled	_____
		None	_____
IV	Will awaken to	Name	_____
		Shaking	_____
		Light pain	_____
		Strong pain	_____
V	Nonverbal reaction to pain	Appropriate	_____
		Inappropriate	_____
		"Decerebrate"	_____
		None	_____
VI	Pupils	Size on right	_____
		Size on left	_____
		Reacts on right	_____
		Reacts on left	_____
VII	Ability to move	Right arm	_____
		Left arm	_____
		Right leg	_____
		Left leg	

cervical spine injury. Therefore, the unconscious athlete should be treated as if cervical spine injury has occurred and should be transported from the field or court on a spine board with the head and neck immobilized. This is performed by either the athletic trainer or emergency medical technicians, depending on the program's policy. Vital signs should be monitored at regular intervals (every 1 to 2 minutes) as the athletic trainer talks to the athlete in an attempt to help bring about full consciousness. If the athlete is in a state of lethargy or stupor and appears to be unconscious, the athlete should not be shaken in an attempt to arouse him or her. Shaking the patient is contraindicated when a cervical spine injury is present. If loss of consciousness is brief, lasting less than 1 minute, and the remainder of the examination is normal, the athlete may be observed on the sideline; however, the athlete should be referred to a physician at a later time. Prolonged unconsciousness lasting more than 1 minute requires immobilization and transport to the emergency department so the athlete can undergo a thorough neurologic examination.

The athletic trainer can perform amnesia testing by first asking the athlete simple questions directed toward recent memory and progressing to more involved questions. Asking the athlete what the first thing was that he or she remembered after the injury will test for length of post-traumatic amnesia. Asking what the play was before the injury or who the opponent was last week will test for retrograde amnesia. Retrograde amnesia is generally associated with a more serious head injury. Questions of orientation (name, date, time, and place) may be asked; however, such questions may not be good discriminators between injured and noninjured athletes. Facing the athlete away from the field and asking the name of the team being played may be helpful. The athletic trainer should also ask the athlete whether he or she is experiencing any tinnitus, blurred vision, or nausea. **Table 7-3** presents a concussion symptom list that can be used to facilitate the follow-up assessment of signs and symptoms.

Portions of the observation and palpation steps should take place during the initial on-site evaluation. The athletic trainer should observe the athlete for any deformities or abnormal facial expressions that might indicate an injury to cranial nerve VII. The athletic trainer should also observe speech patterns, respirations, and movement of the extremities at the same time that he or she is asking

TABLE 7-3
CONCUSSION SYMPTOM CHECKLIST

Symptom	Time of Injury	Postcontest	24 Hours Postinjury	48 Hours Postinjury	72 Hours Postinjury
Headache					
Nausea					
Vomiting					
Dizziness					
Poor balance					
Sensitivity to noise					
Ringing in the ears					
Sensitivity to light					
Blurred vision					
Poor concentration					
Memory problems					
Trouble sleeping					
Sleeping too much					
Fatigue					
Sadness/depression					
Irritability					

the athlete questions. Additionally, the athletic trainer should gently palpate the skull and cervical spine to rule out an associated fracture. The athlete who is conscious or who was momentarily unconscious should be transported to the sidelines or locker room for further evaluation after the initial on-site evaluation. Any moving and positioning of the athlete must be done carefully, assuming possible associated cervical spine injury. Motion of the patient's neck must be avoided by using gentle, firm support. The patient should be transported from the field on a spine board. A helmet does not have to be removed at this time unless it in some way compromises maintenance of adequate ventilation. Often, an adequate airway can be maintained just by removing the facemask or chin strap.

Assessment at the Sideline

A more detailed examination can be conducted on the sideline or in the training room once the helmet has been removed. At this time, the athletic trainer can continue with the observation and palpation phase of the evaluation. A quick cranial nerve assessment should be conducted first. Visual acuity (cranial nerve II: optic) can be checked by asking the athlete to read or identify selected objects at both near and far range. Eye movement (cranial nerves III and IV: oculomotor and trochlear) should be checked for coordination and a purposeful appearance by asking the athlete to track a moving object (**Figure 7-10**).

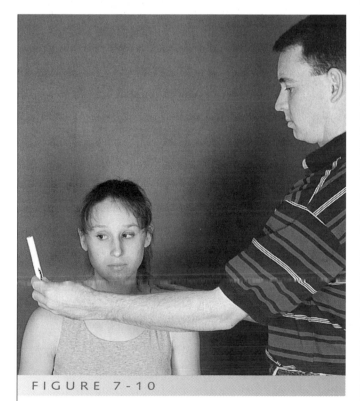

Asking an athlete to track a moving object with the eyes helps determine coordination of eye movement.

FOCUS ON . . .

Assessment at the Sideline

Once the helmet is removed on the sideline or in the training room, the cranial nerves should be quickly assessed. Visual acuity can be checked by asking the athlete to read or identify near and far objects. Eye movement should be evaluated for coordination and purposefulness by having the athlete track a moving object, and the pupils should be checked for equal size and constriction in response to light. Abnormal eye movement or size or light-reaction changes are often a sign of increased intracranial pressure.

Signs of a basilar skull fracture include Battle's sign, cerebrospinal fluid otorrhea, cerebrospinal fluid rhinorrhea, and raccoon eyes. The pulse and blood pressure should be checked if the athlete's condition appears to be worsening; a slow heartbeat or increased pulse pressure may indicate increasing intracranial involvement.

The pupils also should be observed to determine whether they are equal in size and equally reactive to light; the pupils should constrict when light is shined into the eyes. Observation of the pupils also assesses the oculomotor nerve. Abnormal movement of the eyes, changes in pupil size, or reaction to light often indicate increased intracranial pressure. The athletic trainer should also look for any signs indicating a potential basilar skull fracture, including *Battle's sign* (posterior auricular hematoma), *otorrhea* (CSF draining from the ear canal), CSF *rhinorrhea* (CSF draining from the nose), and *raccoon eyes* (periorbital ecchymosis secondary to blood leaking from the anterior fossa of the skull). The athletic trainer should check the patient's vital signs if the athlete's condition appears to be worsening. An unusually slow heart rate or an increased pulse pressure (increased systolic and decreased diastolic pressures) after the athlete has calmed down may be signs of increasing intracranial involvement.

Special Tests for Assessment of Coordination

Balance tasks and finger-to-nose tests can be used to assess the injured athlete's coordination. A moderate or severe cerebral concussion will likely produce balance deficits (a positive Romberg's sign). To test for *Romberg's sign*, the athlete is told to stand with the feet together, arms at sides, and eyes closed. A positive sign is determined if the athlete begins to sway, cannot keep the eyes closed, or falls away from the base of support. If the athlete successfully completes Romberg's test, the test can be made more

FOCUS ON . . .

Testing Coordination and Cognition

Special tests assess coordination and cognition. Coordination should be evaluated with balance tasks and finger-to-nose tests. Romberg's test involves asking the athlete to stand with feet together, arms at the sides, and eyes closed. Computerized forceplate systems and sensory organization testing are more sophisticated ways to measure balance deficits and are recommended for making return-to-play decisions, particularly when preseason baseline measurements are available. The finger-to-nose test assesses acuity and depth perception; inability to perform these tasks may reflect physical disorientation from intracranial involvement.

For the cognitive evaluation, the athlete should be told three words to remember and recall later. Concentration should be tested first, then orientation and recent memory. The number of correct responses is helpful in assessing ability to return to play. The Standardized Assessment of Concussion (SAC) is also useful for sideline testing.

Other cognitive tests may prove useful for follow-up exams. Athletes with mild cerebral concussion may show significant cognitive declines immediately after the injury that clear by about 10 days.

If the athlete performs well on the special tests and same-day return to play is anticipated, sensory and range-of-motion testing, followed by strength testing, should be performed. Normal sensory and motor function suggest that the brachial plexus has not been injured.

An athlete who has been asymptomatic for 15 minutes and has passed all tests should undergo functional testing, including exertional tests on the sideline. If the athlete has a concussion, these tests may increase intracranial pressure and cause symptoms to appear. Documentation of all findings is essential.

Consensus is lacking as to the best grading scale for concussion severity and return-to-play guidelines; however, experts agree that a symptomatic athlete should not return to play. The athletic trainer and team physician should select one system and use it consistently. Return-to-play decisions are made on an individual basis. An athlete whose confusion resolves within 20 minutes and who has no symptoms at rest or during or after functional testing may be able to return to play, but any loss of consciousness disqualifies an athlete from returning to play that day. When making the return-to-play decision, the athlete's previous history of concussion should be considered, along with whether the sport is contact or noncontact, the availability of experienced personnel to observe and monitor the athlete during recovery, the need for early follow-up to determine when a disqualified athlete can return to participation, the importance of repeated assessments, and the urgency of neurologic evaluation or hospital admission for any athlete whose symptoms deteriorate.

An athlete who has been unconscious for a period of time or who has headaches should be evaluated and monitored by a physician. Although most head trauma resolves without deficit or the need for surgery, head trauma can be life threatening. An athlete who has sustained a second concussion should be withheld from competition for 1 to 3 additional weeks; an athlete who has sustained a third concussion is terminated from play for the season.

challenging by having the athlete perform a single leg Romberg or tandem (heel-to-toe) Romberg (Figure 7-11). More sophisticated balance assessment using computerized forceplate systems and sensory organization testing (SOT) has identified balance deficits in athletes up to 3 days after a mild concussion.[12,15] These tests can help the athletic trainer make return-to-play decisions, especially when preseason baseline measurements are available for comparison.

The athlete performs the *finger-to-nose test* by standing with the eyes closed and arms out to the side. The evaluator then asks the athlete to touch the index finger of one hand to the nose and then to touch the index finger of the other hand to the nose (**Figure 7-12**). The evaluator asks the athlete to open his or her eyes and touch the evaluator's index finger, which is placed at varying ranges in the ath-

lete's peripheral view. This test is performed to determine the athlete's acuity and depth of perception. Inability to perform any of these tasks may be an indication of physical disorientation secondary to intracranial involvement.

Special Tests for Assessment of Cognition

The cognitive evaluation begins when the athlete is given three unassociated words to remember (for example, raccoon, yellow, and table). He or she will be asked to recall the words at the conclusion of the assessment. **Table 7-4** presents a sample test of concentration that should be performed first. **Table 7-5** presents an orientation and recent memory test that should follow the concentration test. The athletic trainer should document the number of correct responses and use the results in making a return-to-

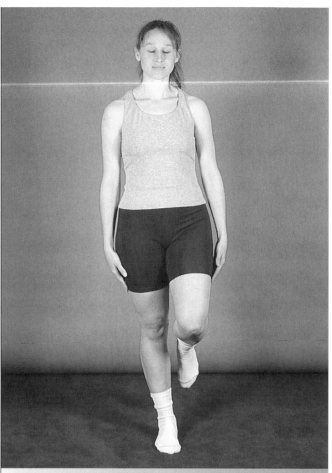

FIGURE 7-11

A single-leg Romberg test helps assess balance deficits in an athlete.

FIGURE 7-12

The finger-to-nose test is performed to assess the athlete's acuity and depth of perception.

TABLE 7-4
CONCENTRATION TEST

Questions	Correct Response?
1. Recite the days of the week backward beginning today	
2. Recite the months of the year backward beginning with this month.	
3. Serial 3s—count backward from 100 by 3 until you get to single digits	
4. Serial 7s—count backward from 100 by 7 until you get to single digits	

TABLE 7-5
ORIENTATION AND RECENT MEMORY TEST

Questions	Correct Response?
1. Where are we playing (name of field or site)?	
2. Which quarter (period, inning, etc.) is it?	
3. Who scored last?	
4. Who did we play last week?	
5. Who won last week?	
6. Recite the three words given at the start of the exam.	

play decision. A similar protocol called the Standardized Assessment of Concussion (SAC) has been proposed for use during sideline examinations.[16] The SAC identifies significant differences between athletes with concussions and those without a concussion as well as between preseason baselines and postinjury scores.

Other neuropsychological (cognitive) tests have been used for both identifying and managing traumatic brain injury in athletes.[12,17] Although most of these tests are difficult to administer as part of a sideline examination, they have proved useful for subsequent follow-up exams. At 24 hours after trauma, one study revealed cognitive decline from preseason levels in areas of attention, concentration, and rapid complex problem-solving in comparison to control subjects.[17] These mild deficits were directly correlated with reported symptoms of increased headaches, dizziness, and memory problems. The deficits and symptoms began to clear by the fifth day after injury and were essentially identical to the control group by the tenth day after injury. These results revealed that young, healthy, well-motivated athletes who experienced mild cerebral concussion could experience significant cognitive decline immediately following their injury. Therefore, the athletic trainer and team physician should consider neuropsychological testing as part of the overall evaluation process. **Table 7-6** lists several tests that neuropsychologists use in cooperative efforts with athletic trainers and team physicians to evaluate recovery of neurocognitive function in symptomatic players.

If the athlete successfully completes the special tests and return to participation is anticipated on the same day , sensory (dermatome) testing, range of motion (ROM) testing, and strength testing should be performed to ensure that the athlete has normal sensory/motor function. Sensory/motor function could have been compromised by associated brachial plexus injury. The tests can be performed in a systematic order, as described for upper and lower quarter screenings. If the athlete has been asymptomatic for at least 15 minutes and has passed all tests up to this point, functional tests should be performed to assess the athlete's readiness to return to participation. Functional testing should include exertional tests on the sideline such as sit-ups, pushups, short sprints, and sport-specific tasks. The objective of these tests is to seek evidence of early postconcussive symptoms. Often, these exercises will increase intracranial pressure in the athlete with a head injury and cause symptoms to appear.

The athletic trainer must document and record the initial findings and subsequent monitoring of any athlete with a head injury.

RETURN TO COMPETITION AFTER TRAUMATIC BRAIN INJURY

Over the past two decades, a number of grading scales for severity of concussion and return to play have been proposed.[5-7,9,13] The lack of consensus among experts lies in the fact that none of the scales or guidelines is derived from conclusive scientific data; rather, they have been developed from anecdotal literature and clinical experience. The one guideline that all experts agree on is that no athlete should return to participation while still symptomatic. Most experts agree that all of the proposed guidelines are safe but disagree on which one is the safest and most practical. The National Athletic Trainers' Association (NATA) does not support or recommend any one grading scale or return to play guideline, nor does the National Collegiate Athletic Association (NCAA) or any of the professional sports associations. It is important that the team physician and athletic trainer agree on one system and ensure consistent use of that system.

The question of return to competition after a head injury is handled on an individual basis, although conservatism seems the wisest course in all cases. The athlete

TABLE 7-6
SELECTED NEUROPSYCHOLOGICAL TESTS

Test	Ability Evaluated
Hopkins Verbal Learning Test (HVLT)	Verbal memory
Trail Making Test—A and B	Visual scanning, mental flexibility, attention
Stroop Test	Mental flexibility, attention
Wechsler Digit Span	Attention span
Symbol Digit Modalities	Visual scanning, attention
Grooved Pegboard Test	Motor speed/coordination
Paced Auditory Serial Addition Test (PASAT)	Attention, concentration, immediate memory recall, rapid mental processing

whose confusion resolves promptly (within 20 minutes) and who has no associated symptoms at rest or during or following functional testing may be considered a candi- date for return to play. *Any loss of consciousness should eliminate a player from participation that day.* **Table 7-7** offers a guide to making restricted and unrestricted return-

---

TABLE 7-7
GUIDELINES FOR RETURN TO PLAY AFTER CONCUSSION

Mild (Grade 0)	Remove from contest. Examine immediately and at 5-minute intervals for development of abnormal Cs (cranial nerves, cognition, coordination) or other postconcussive symptoms at rest and with exertion. May return to contest if examination is normal and no symptoms develop for at least 20 minutes. If any symptoms develop within the initial 20 minutes, return on that day should not be permitted.
(Grade 1)	If the athlete is removed from participation as a result of developing symptoms, follow-up evaluations should be conducted daily. May return to restricted participation when the athletic trainer and team physician are assured the athlete has been asymptomatic* at rest and with exertion for at least 2 days, followed by return to unrestricted participation if asymptomatic for 1 additional day. Neuropsychological assessment and balance/coordination testing are valuable criteria, especially if preseason baseline measures are available.
Moderate (Grade 2)	Remove from contest and prohibit return on that day. Examine immediately and at 5-minute intervals for signs of evolving intracranial pathology. Reexamine daily. May return to restricted participation when the athletic trainer and team physician are assured the athlete has been asymptomatic at rest and with exertion for at least 4 days, followed by return to unrestricted participation if asymptomatic* for an additional 2 days. The performance during restricted participation should be used as a guide for making the decision for unrestricted participation. Neuropsychological assessment and balance/coordination testing are valuable criteria, especially if preseason baseline measures are available.
Severe (Grade 3)	Treat on field/court as if there has been a cervical spine injury. Examine immediately and at 5-minute intervals for signs of evolving intracranial pathology. Reexamine daily. Return to play is based on how quickly the athlete's initial symptoms resolve: 1. If symptoms totally resolve within the first week, athlete may return to restricted participation when the athletic trainer and team physician are assured the athlete has been asymptomatic at rest and with exertion for at least 10 days. The athlete may return to unrestricted participation if asymptomatic for an additional 3 days. 2. If symptoms fail to totally resolve within the first week, athlete may return to restricted participation when the athletic trainer and team physician are assured the athlete has been asymptomatic at rest and with exertion for at least 17 days. The athlete may return to unrestricted participation if asymptomatic for an additional 3 days. The performance during restricted participation should be used as a guide for making the decision for unrestricted participation. Neuropsychological assessment and balance/coordination testing are valuable criteria, especially if preseason baseline measures are available. ***Note:** "Asymptomatic" involves no abnormal Cs and no headache. If the athlete sustains a second concussion within a 3-month period after the first concussion, the athlete must rest for two times the maximum number of days for the respective severity level.

to-play decisions following concussion. **Table 7-8** presents a list of factors that the athletic trainer and team physician should consider when making decisions regarding an athlete's readiness to return to play following a head injury.

Athletes who are unconscious for a period of time or who have headaches require evaluation and monitoring by a physician. Although most individuals with head trauma recover without any permanent neurologic deficit or need for surgery, head trauma can be very serious and perhaps life-threatening. Several guidelines have been proposed for return to play following multiple head injuries in the same season.[5,6] Most experts agree that athletes should be held from competition for extended periods of time (1 to 3 additional weeks) following a second concussion to ensure that all postconcussive symptoms have resolved. Participation in contact sports should be terminated for the season after an athlete has sustained three concussions.

TABLE 7-5

FACTORS TO CONSIDER FOR RETURN-TO-PLAY DECISION-MAKING

- Athlete's previous history of concussion

- The sport of participation (contact or noncontact)

- Availability of experienced personnel to observe and monitor the athlete during recovery

- Early follow-up to determine when a disqualified athlete can return to participation

- Repeated assessment. The athletic trainer and team physician must be assured that the athlete is asymptomatic before a return to participation is permitted. This can be done through the use of neuropsychological testing and postural stability assessment

- Loss of consciousness. Any athlete who has experienced loss of consciousness should not be permitted to return to play on that day

- A concussion that evolves downward, where intensity and frequency of signs and symptoms increase. The athlete should be sent for neurologic evaluation or admitted to the hospital

CHAPTER REVIEW

Despite the protective equipment for the head and brain available to today's athletes, these areas remain vulnerable to injury during sport, a particular problem because the brain and spinal cord do not regenerate. Therefore, injury can cause catastrophic and irreversible damage. The athletic trainer must understand the anatomy of the head, scalp, and brain, the types of traumatic brain injury, how to assess traumatic brain injury, and how to make the decision about when an athlete with a head injury can return to play.

The skull is formed by eight cranial bones and 14 facial bones, with firm outer and inner layers interspersed with softer bone and blood channels. A severe blow to the head can fracture the skull and injure the brain. The scalp comprises five layers of soft tissue that cover the outer portion of the skull. Scalp lacerations can bleed profusely and must be treated cautiously to avoid the development of an infection, which can spread into the skull bones and the cranial cavity.

The brain is surrounded by the meninges and includes the cerebrum, the cerebellum, and brain stem. The cerebral cortex controls the highest cognitive and behavioral activities, the cerebellum regulates movement and posture, and the brain stem coordinates respiration, circulation, and consciousness. The cerebrospinal fluid, which circulates through the ventricles and the subarachnoid space, is a shock absorber for the brain. The brain is supplied with blood by the vertebral and internal carotid arteries; the meninges are supplied by the middle meningeal branch of the maxillary artery. Twelve sets of cranial nerves mediate sensory and motor functions.

Traumatic brain injury is classified as focal or diffuse. Coup injury describes a forceful blow to the resting, movable head, which produces maximum brain injury beneath the point of cranial impact. Contrecoup injury occurs when the moving head hits an unyielding object, producing maximum brain injury opposite the site of cranial impact. Compressive, tensile, and shearing forces can be generated by an applied force to the head; uniform compressive forces are well tolerated by neural tissue, unlike shearing forces. Types of traumatic brain injury include cerebral concussion, cerebral contusion, cerebral hematoma, and second impact syndrome.

In assessing traumatic brain injury, the athletic trainer must recognize the injury and its severity, determine if the athlete requires additional attention or assessment, and decide when the athlete may return to play. The initial on-site assessment involves a primary survey and a secondary survey. The assessment should be carefully documented, along with each follow-up. The sideline assessment consists of evaluating the cranial nerves, looking for signs of a basilar skull fracture, and continuation of the secondary survey, including special tests of coordination and cognition, sensory testing, range-of-motion testing, strength testing, and functional testing.

An athlete who is symptomatic should not return to participation, and any loss of consciousness disqualifies an athlete from playing for the rest of the day. Other factors to be considered when making the return-to-play decision include the athlete's previous history of concussion, whether the sport is contact or noncontact, availability of experienced medical personnel, early follow-up to reevaluate a disqualified athlete, repeated assessments to track the athlete's progress, and the urgent need for medical attention if an athlete's condition worsens.

Most head injuries resolve without permanent neurologic deficits or the need for surgery, but because head trauma can be life threatening, these injuries should always be taken seriously and treated appropriately.

1. The large aperture at the base of the skull through which the medulla and spinal cord pass is called the:
   A. vomer.
   B. palatine.
   C. foramen magnum.
   D. aponeurosis epicranialis.

2. What is the deepest layer of the scalp?
   A. Pericranium
   C. Aponeurosis
   D. Connective tissue
   B. Loose connective tissue

3. The highest cognitive and behavioral activities of humans are controlled by which of the following areas in the brain?
   A. Brain stem
   B. Arachnoid
   C. Diencephalon
   D. Cerebral cortex

4. Which of the following structures regulates movement and posture?
   A. Pons
   B. Midbrain
   C. Cerebellum
   D. Medulla oblongata

5. What is the most severe type of nonfocal brain injury?
   A. Cerebral contusion
   B. Epidural hematoma
   C. Subdural hematoma
   D. Diffuse axonal injury

6. What is the classification of the most common type of concussion, characterized by slight confusion that resolves within 10 minutes?
   A. Mild, grade 0
   B. Mild, grade 1
   C. Moderate, grade 2
   D. Severe, grade 3

7. What is the most important step of the secondary survey?
   A. History
   B. Observation
   C. Special tests
   D. Functional tests

8. Testing for retrograde amnesia in an athlete with a head injury involves asking the athlete:
   A. time of day and the place.
   B. his or her name and the date.
   C. the name of the team being played.
   D. the first thing he or she remembered after the injury.

9. The oculomotor nerve is assessed by:
   A. looking for otorrhea.
   B. asking the athlete to identify near objects.
   C. asking the athlete to identify far objects.
   D. determining if the pupils are equal in size and reaction to light.

10. Which of the following statements about return to play criteria for an athlete with a traumatic brain injury is true?
    A. Return to restricted play is allowed if confusion resolves within 45 minutes.
    B. Return to full play is allowed if confusion resolves within 45 minutes.
    C. An athlete who loses consciousness must not return to participation that day.
    D. An athlete who loses consciousness must not return to participation until the next season.

Answers on page 891.

References

1. Hugenholtz H, Richard M: Return to athletic competition following concussion. *Can Med Assoc J* 1982; 127:827–829.

2. Ommaya A: Biomechanical aspects of head injuries in sports, in Jordan B, Tsairis P, Warren R (eds): *Sports Neurology*. Rockville, MD, Aspen Publishers, 1990.

3. Cantu R: Reflections on head injuries in sport and the concussion controversy. *Clin J Sports Med* 1997; 7:83–84.

4. Cantu R: Athletic head injuries. *Clin Sports Med* 1997;16:531–542.

5. American Academy of Neurology, QSS: Practice Parameter: The management of concussion in sports (summary statement). *Neurology* 1997; 48:581–585.

6. Cantu R: Guidelines for return to contact sports after a cerebral concussion. *Phys Sports Med* 1986;14:75–83.

7. Jordan B: Head injuries in sports, in Jordan B, Tsairis P, Warren R (eds): *Sports Neurology*. Rockville, MD, Aspen Publishers, 1981.

8. Nelson W, Jane J, Gieck J: Minor head injuries in sports: A new system of classification and management. *Phys Sports Med* 1984;12:103–107.

9. Roberts W: Who plays? Who sits? Managing concussion on the sidelines. *Phys Sports Med* 1992;20:66–72.

10. Torg J (ed): *Athletic Injuries to the Head, Neck and Face*. St. Louis, MO, Mosby-Year Book, 1991.

11. Wilberger JJ, Maroon J: Head injuries in athletes. *Clin Sports Med* 1989; 8:1–9.

12. Guskiewicz K, Riemann B, Perrin D, Nashner L: Alternative approaches to the assessment of mild head injuries in athletes. *Med Sci Sports Exerc* 1997;29(suppl):S213–S221.

13. Kelly J, Nichols J, Filley C, Lillehei K, Rubinstein D, Kleinschmidt-Demasters B: Concussion in sports: Guidelines for the prevention of catastrophic outcome. *JAMA* 1991; 226: 2867–2869.

14. Saunders R, Harbaugh R: The second impact in catastrophic contact-sports head injuries. *JAMA* 1984; 252:538–539.

15. Guskiewicz K, Perrin D, Gansneder B: Effect of mild head injury on postural sway. *J Athlet Train* 1996; 31:300–306.

16. McCrea M, Kelly JP, Kluge J, Ackley B, Randolph C: Standardized assessment of concussion in football players. *Neurology* 1997;48:586–588.

17. Barth J, Alves W, Ryan T, Macciocchi S, Rimel R, Jane J, et al: Mild head injury in sports: Neuropsychological sequelae and recovery of function, in Levin H, Eisenberg H, Benton A (eds): *Mild Head Injury in Sport*. New York, NY, Oxford University Press, 1989, pp 257–275.

8

Facial Injuries

Jaime R. Garza, MD, DDS
David Carrier, MA, ATC

QUICK CONTENTS

- The anatomy of the face.

- The examination of the face and related structures.

- Evaluation and management of soft-tissue injuries affecting the face.

- Assessment and treatment of facial fractures.

- Protective devices available and how they prevent injury.

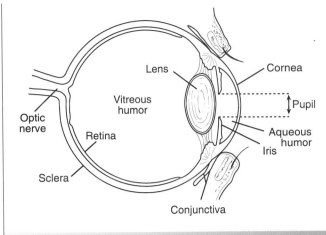

FIGURE 8-2

The major soft-tissue components of the eye are supported by the conical shape of the periorbital rim and interior bony walls.

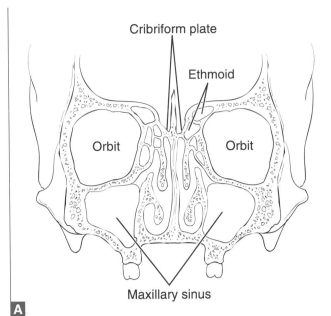

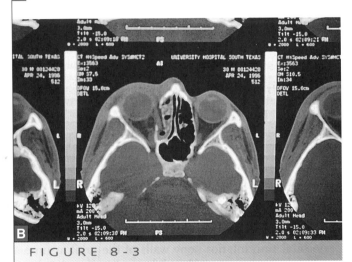

FIGURE 8-3

The walls of the orbital structures are made up of delicate bones.
A The orbital walls separate the orbit and its contents from the various sinuses of the face.
B A CT scan demonstrates a fracture of the medial wall of the orbit with its contents communicating with the ethmoid sinus.

Because of this abundant blood supply, devascularization of the skin as a result of traumatic injury is infrequent. Contained within this soft-tissue envelope is a plexus of nerves, both sensory (cranial nerve V) and motor (cranial nerve VII), that contribute to sensation and facial animation. The natural movements of the underlying facial muscles account for the "wrinkle" lines or relaxed skin tension lines seen about the face. These lines of expression typically run perpendicular to the action of the underlying muscles and become more prominent with age. The lines are seen as "normal" by the casual observer, and any lines that go counter to these "normal" expression lines are readily detected. The relaxed skin tension lines, therefore, constitute the basis for elective incision lines, repair of lacerations, and scar revision surgery.

EXAMINATION OF THE FACE AND RELATED STRUCTURES

Examination of the facial skeleton and related soft-tissue structures of the injured athlete should be thorough and consistent. Examination of the injured face involves visual inspection and manual palpation.

Visual Inspection

Bruising and swelling are signs of possible underlying hematomas or fractures. Contour changes of the facial structures may be related to fractures of underlying bone. Inspection of facial animation will allow the examiner to assess the facial nerve function. The patient should be asked to animate the facial muscles by elevating the eyebrows, tightly closing the eyes, and showing the teeth. Any asymmetry or obvious muscle weakness could be a sign of an underlying facial nerve injury. The examiner must pay close attention to the level of the pupils and the motion of the eyes in all fields of vision. Any restriction of gaze or appearance of asymmetry may be the result of ocular damage or a fracture of the periorbital bony framework. If an ocular injury is suspected, a thorough eye examination should be performed. This examination includes a visual acuity check, pupillary reflexes to light and accommodation, and visual inspection of the cornea and sclera to rule out lacerations, abrasions, or foreign bodies. Foreign bodies should be carefully removed by inverting the upper lid and lifting out the foreign body with a sterile cotton swab (**Figure 8-6**). The anterior chamber of the eye should be

FOCUS ON . . .

Examination of the Face

Examination of the face and related structures consists of visual inspection and manual palpation. On visual inspection, look for bruising and swelling that may suggest a hematoma or fracture; changes in the contour of the facial structures may reflect a fracture. Ask the athlete to animate the facial muscles by elevating the eyebrows, tightly closing the eyes, and showing the teeth. Any asymmetry or muscle weakness may indicate a facial nerve injury.

Observe the level of the pupils and eye motion in all fields of vision. Any restricted gaze or apparent asymmetry may be the result of ocular damage or a fracture of the periorbital rim. If an ocular injury is suspected, perform a thorough eye examination, including a visual acuity check; pupillary reflexes to light and accommodation; visual inspection of the cornea and sclera for lacerations, abrasions, or foreign bodies; and check the anterior chamber to rule out blood or a change in the shape of the iris. If there are any abnormalities, the athlete should consult an ophthalmologist.

Intraoral examination of the teeth and soft tissues may show bruising, particularly in the anterior sublingual region, which is diagnostic for a mandible fracture. Ask the athlete to bring the teeth together to determine whether the bite feels "normal"; any discrepancy may indicate a fracture of the maxilla, mandible, or dentoalveolar structures. Pain with mouth opening or closing indicates injury to the temporomandibular joints.

Manually palpate the facial skeleton, beginning at the cranium and extending to the mandible, including the temporomandibular joints. Crepitance and movement of the bones suggests a fracture. Assess maxillary stability by placing the palm of the hand on the athlete's forehead, grasping the anterior maxillary teeth and bone, and trying to move the maxilla in all directions; crepitance or motion indicate a fracture. Evaluate mandible stability by placing the thumbs on each lingual (inside) surface of the mandible and pushing outward; if the bone is fractured, this maneuver will cause pain.

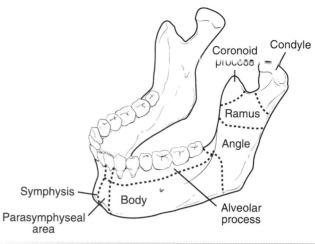

FIGURE 8-4

The bony mandible and its associated dental structures make up the lower third of the face.

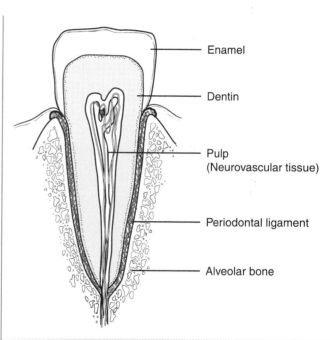

FIGURE 8-5

The dentoalveolar process includes the tooth, alveolar bone, and the periodontal ligament.

inspected to rule out the presence of blood or a change in the shape of the iris. If any of the above signs is noted, an ophthalmologist should be consulted.

Intraoral examination should include inspection of the teeth and soft tissues for injuries. Intraoral bruising, particularly in the immediate anterior sublingual region, is a pathognomonic sign of a mandibular fracture. The simple act of bringing the teeth into contact, or **occlusion**, will allow the athlete to determine if his or her bite "feels right" (**Figure 8-7**). Any discrepancy in the bite suggests a possible fracture of the maxilla, the mandible, or the associated dentoalveolar structures. Pain while opening or closing the mouth may also indicate fracture or injury to the temporomandibular joints (TMJ).

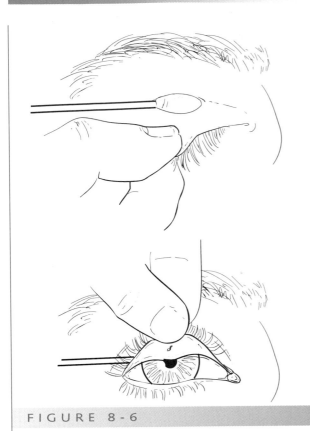

FIGURE 8-6

A foreign body should be removed by inverting the upper lid and, while holding the lid and stick in place with one hand, using a sterile cotton swab to remove the foreign body.

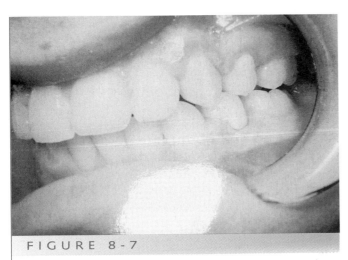

FIGURE 8-7

The simple act of bringing the teeth into contact or occlusion allows the patient to determine if his or her bite is out of alignment or in a malocclusion.

Palpation

The entire facial skeleton should be palpated manually, beginning at the cranium (skull) and extending to the mandible. Palpation should include the TMJs (**Figure 8-8**). Crepitance and movement of the underlying bones indicate a fracture. The examiner should assess the stability of the maxilla and mandible by placing the palm of one hand on the athlete's forehead, grasping the anterior maxillary teeth and bone with the other hand, and attempting to move the maxilla in all directions. By placing a thumb on each *lingual surface* (inside surface) of the mandible and simultaneously pushing outward, the examiner can easily rule out a mandibular fracture (**Figure 8-9**). Because the mandible is a continuous arch, this simple maneuver will elicit discomfort at the site of a fracture. In addition, any crepitance or motion indicates a fracture.

Although it is not important where the examination starts, it is important that it be consistent and thorough every time.

SOFT-TISSUE INJURIES

When the athlete's face comes into direct contact with an opposing player, equipment, or the playing surface, contusions, abrasions, and lacerations generally result. The anatomy of the underlying facial skeleton is a prime contributor to many common soft-tissue injuries.

Universal Precautions

The athletic trainer should follow universal precautions when treating an athlete with a bleeding wound or when contact with other body fluids such as saliva is likely.[8] **Table 8-1** presents a list of universal precaution procedures that are designed to reduce concerns about the dissemination of infectious diseases such as HIV and hepatitis that are spread through body fluid. Protective items usually include gloves, eyewear, and gowns. Not every wound requires that the caregiver wear all of these items, but the caregiver should certainly exercise caution. At the least, gloves should be worn any time contact with blood or other body fluids is likely.

Contusions and Abrasions

Contusions and abrasions of the face are managed much like those elsewhere on the body. Elevation of the affected body part and application of ice are the mainstays of treatment for facial contusions. Other than these straightforward measures, most contusions require no further treatment and will spontaneously resolve over several days to a few weeks.

Abrasions are essentially partial-thickness skin losses that occur secondary to shearing forces. The athletic trainer should clean any abrasions with mild soap and debride them of any foreign matter to prevent permanent discoloration of the skin. Aseptic dressings are used to prevent secondary infections. Healing is generally rapid and reepithelialization of the abrasion occurs over a period of several days. The development of an infection can convert a superficial abrasion injury into a full-thickness skin loss, resulting in delayed healing and more severe scarring.

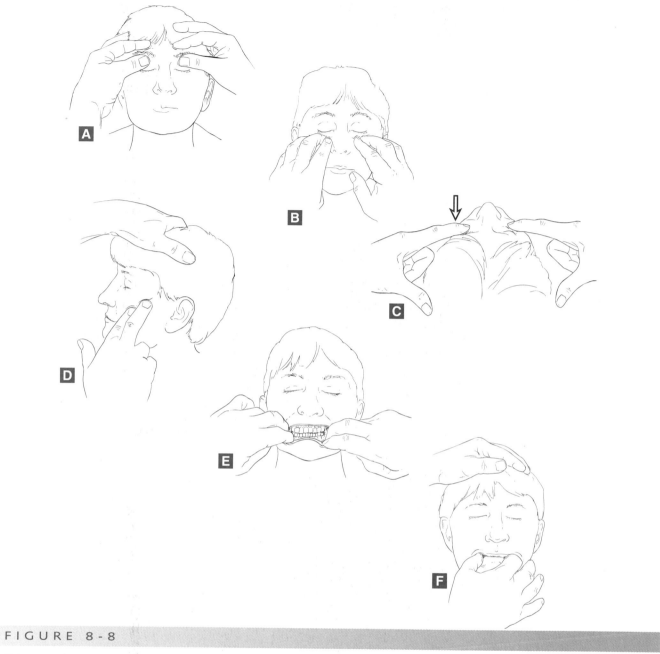

FIGURE 8-8

Palpation of the entire facial skeleton. **A** Palpating for step-offs or irregularities of the supraorbital rims. **B** Palpating for step-offs or irregularities of the inferior orbital rims and zygomatic complex (cheekbones). **C** Comparing the projection of the cheekbones. **D** Palpating for step-offs or irregularities of the zygomatic arch. **E** Visually inspecting the gross dentition and occlusion. **F** Manually assessing the stability of the maxillae by stabilizing the head with one hand and attempting to move the maxillae by grasping it with the opposite hand.

Lacerations

Lacerations are the most common sports-related facial injuries.[9] Blunt trauma to the soft tissues of the face compresses them against the underlying bony prominences and can cause a "burst type" laceration. This type of injury typically occurs over the brow, cheek, chin, or teeth. Burst-type lacerations differ from lacerations caused by a sharp object. In a *burst laceration*, the skin is compressed at impact, and a jagged opening of the skin occurs with a variable amount of skin ischemia and necrosis. If the laceration is not properly treated, the long-term sequelae of excessive scar tissue and an unacceptable cosmetic result are difficult to correct.

Hemostasis

Because of the abundant blood supply to the facial soft tissues, bleeding from a laceration can be brisk and significant. When a facial laceration occurs, immediate

FIGURE 8-9

The mandibular stress test consists of placing the thumbs on the inside (lingual) surfaces of the mandible and pushing outward, which will elicit discomfort at the site of a fracture.

TABLE 8-1

INFECTION CONTROL PROCEDURES IN THE SPORTS SETTING

1. A player who is bleeding or has excessive blood on the uniform must be removed from the competition until the bleeding has stopped and the wound is covered. Return to play is dictated by the rules of individual sports.

2. The athletic trainer treating the wound should wear protective medical-quality gloves and other protective clothing such as eyewear and a gown.

3. The wound should be cleaned with an antibacterial solution such as Betadine™, an antibiotic cream or ointment should be applied, and the area should be protected with a bandage and dressing.

4. If the athlete's uniform contains any blood, it must be replaced by a clean one. Contact with the bloody clothing should be avoided until it can be laundered properly.

5. If the playing surface or equipment is bloody, it should be cleaned with a solution of ten parts water and one part chlorine bleach before play resumes.

6. The athletic trainer should wash his or her hands with soap immediately after removing gloves, and any skin area that comes into contact with blood or body fluids should be washed immediately.

7. Any potentially infectious materials, such as bandages, towels, gloves, gowns, mouthguards, and any other articles that contain blood or body fluids, must be disposed of in accordance with the regulations of the facility.

attention should be directed to hemostasis. The athletic trainer should apply direct manual pressure to the bleeding area with a sterile gauze pad. Because of the close proximity of nerves and salivary ducts to the larger blood vessels of the face, clamping of bleeding vessels in the wound should be avoided. Indiscriminate clamping can cause unnecessary damage to these neighboring structures.

Once bleeding is controlled, the athletic trainer should then rule out an underlying bone fracture. Direct visualization or direct palpation with a sterile glove through the laceration is usually adequate. If there is any doubt, the athlete should be referred to a physician for appropriate radiographs and further evaluation.

Cleansing

If there are no apparent underlying fractures, the wound should be irrigated with sterile saline solution using an 18-gauge needle attached to a 30-mL syringe to generate approximately 7 psi to 11 psi of force. This level of force is beneficial for debridement of bacteria and foreign material from the wound and is not deleterious to the normal cellular structures.

The athletic trainer should pay special attention to cleaning lacerations that occur during a boxing competition. During a boxing competition, the ringside corner-man often coats a bleeding wound with a homemade ointment to obtain hemostasis and allow the boxer to continue the competition. This treatment is not acceptable as a standard of care in medical practice. Such ointments may contain eucalyptus, Gelfoam, thrombin, microfibrillar collagen hemostat, and even superglue (P. Saenz, personal communication, 1997). The athletic trainer should suspect that these illicit substances are likely to have been applied to any wounds that occurred during a boxing competition. Therefore, the wound should be thoroughly cleansed before it is closed.

Repair

After they are cleansed with sterile saline, superficial and small lacerations can be reapproximated with simple Steri-strips® or butterfly bandages. A liquid adhesive such as a compound benzoin tincture applied to the undamaged skin surrounding the laceration will help keep the tapes in place and effectively splint the wound closed.

A physician who is skilled in the management of soft-tissue injuries of the face should treat larger or more complex lacerations. Sharp debridement of the ischemic, contused skin margins converts the burst laceration to one analogous to a sharp laceration, which allows better primary healing and lessens the formation of scar tissue **(Figure 8-10)**.

In repair of facial lacerations, the physician should first precisely align and approximate the aesthetic anatomic landmarks, such as the lip vermilion border, eyebrow, nasal alae, helical rim of the ear, and eyelids, with fine

FOCUS ON . . .

Soft-Tissue Injuries

Soft-tissue injuries such as contusions, abrasions, and lacerations are usually caused by direct contact of the athlete's face with an opposing player, equipment, or playing field surface. In these instances, universal precautions should be followed. Depending on the nature of the wound, protective items may include gloves, eyewear, and a gown.

Contusions and abrasions

Elevating the affected body part and applying ice is the treatment of choice for contusions and abrasions on the face. Most contusions require no further treatment and heal spontaneously over several days to a few weeks. Cleanse abrasions with mild soap to debride any foreign matter and prevent permanent skin discoloration. Apply an aseptic dressing to prevent secondary infection.

Lacerations

Lacerations may bleed significantly because of the abundant facial blood supply. The first step in management is to apply manual pressure with a sterile gauze pad directly on the bleeding area. Once the bleeding is controlled, rule out a fracture with direct visualization or direct palpation with a sterile glove through the laceration. If there is any doubt, the athlete should be referred to a physician. If there is no fracture, irrigate the wound with sterile saline.

Superficial and small lacerations can be reapproximated with Steri-strips or butterfly bandages. A liquid adhesive applied to the undamaged skin surrounding the wound will help keep the tapes in place and splint the wound closed. Larger or more complex lacerations should be handled by a physician with expertise in the management of these injuries on the face.

If treated properly, most facial lacerations do not require antibiotics. However, if the wound is heavily contaminated, has remained open for several hours, or resulted from a human bite, 7 to 10 days of appropriate antibiotics are suggested. Tetanus prophylaxis guidelines should also be followed.

If the sport allows the athlete to resume play once the laceration has been sutured, the immediate goals are to obtain hemostasis, approximate the skin edges to prevent further contamination, and prevent extension of the laceration.

Injuries to the ear

Ear hematoma, or wrestler's ear, can result from blunt trauma to the ear causing a hematoma between the cartilage and the overlying perichondrium, commonly called a "cauliflower" deformity. Once created, this deformity is difficult to correct, and therefore, early drainage is recommended. This can be accomplished with a needle and syringe, but incision and drainage under sterile technique is preferred. After evacuation of the hematoma, the ear contours should be packed with a lubricated sterile dressing (eg, Xeroform gauze, Vaseline gauze strips, or cotton balls impregnated with mineral oil or an antibiotic ointment) and a circumferential head dressing covering the affected ear applied. The wrap is removed within 24 hours for a check of the hematoma for reaccumulation or infection and then replaced for 24 hours. Using properly fitted and adjusted ear protectors can prevent ear injury and minimize hematoma formation.

Return to play criteria

The athlete's return to competition after the repair of a soft-tissue wound depends on the location and severity of the laceration and the potential for repeated injury to the site. Repaired skin wounds gain strength at 14 to 21 days after repair. Most athletes with lacerations that have been repaired and dressed can return to competition.

---

sutures. The remainder of the laceration should then be closed in layers. The physician may use absorbable sutures in the deeper layers such as muscle, fascia, and dermis. Simple, fine, interrupted or subcuticular monofilament sutures are then used to simply approximate the epidermis (**Figure 8-11**). Facial skin sutures are typically removed within 5 days and the wound is splinted with liquid adhesive and sterile tape for another 7 days. Lacerations over

aesthetic landmarks are best directed to a plastic surgeon for definitive closure to ensure the best functional and aesthetic outcome.

Intraoral lacerations should be treated much like skin lacerations. The physician should approximate the intraoral mucosa with an absorbable suture. Through-and-through lacerations of the lip or cheek should be irrigated thoroughly and closed in layers from the inside out.

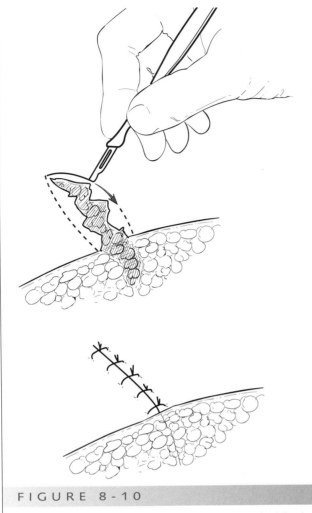

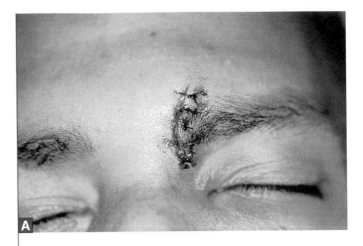

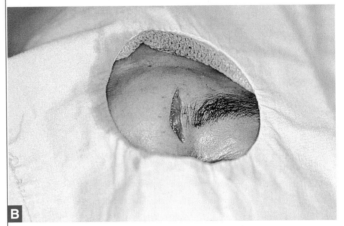

FIGURE 8-10

Contused, jagged wound edges should be sharply debrided to allow for better and faster healing of the laceration.

Because delayed healing and excessive scar tissue formation can occur, mucosal lacerations, including tongue lacerations, should not be left open to heal secondarily.

In some sports, such as hockey and boxing, an athlete is allowed to resume play after the laceration has been sutured. The goals of immediate suturing are to obtain hemostasis, approximate the skin edges to prevent further contamination, and prevent the laceration from becoming larger. In a study of ringside suturing, one or two figure-of-8 4-0 braided nonabsorbable sutures were used to close lacerations.[10] The repaired wounds were noted experimentally and clinically to withstand repeated blows with a gloved fist without disruption of the repair. Definitive repair of the laceration was then performed after the competition.

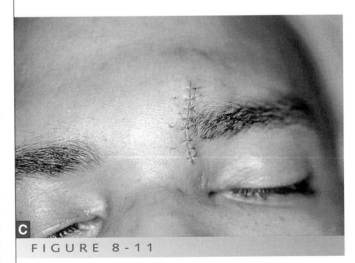

FIGURE 8-11

Monofilament sutures are used to approximate the epidermis. **A** Hastily repaired laceration illustrating overlapping and jagged skin margins. **B** Wound edges cleaned and sharply debrided. **C** Precise layered repair allows for better healing and a more acceptable cosmetic outcome.

Ear Hematoma (Wrestler's Ear)

A hematoma can form from blunt trauma to the ear because blood accumulates between the cartilage and its overlying perichondrium.[11] The combined effects of pressure and the formation of free radicals from the coagulated blood cause ischemia and necrosis of the underlying cartilage. Eventual fibrosis and deformation of the cartilage result in a loss of the normal architecture of the ear and the formation of a "cauliflower" deformity. This late deformity is extremely difficult to correct.

Prudent treatment is early drainage of the hematoma. A physician may aspirate the hematoma under sterile conditions with an 18-gauge needle and a syringe. However, a more reliable treatment choice is incision and drainage of the hematoma as soon as possible. Sterile technique is mandatory when draining the hematoma because contamination can cause a devastating bacterial chondritis.[12] The incision should be made in a dependent and inconspicuous location, such as the helical or antihelical fold. This ensures drainage of the hematoma and any further bleeding. The resulting scar from the incision is camouflaged within the fold and not easily detected (**Figure 8-12**).

Once the hematoma has been evacuated, the contours of the ear should be packed with a lubricated sterile dressing such as Vaseline gauze strips or cotton balls impregnated with mineral oil or an antibiotic ointment. A circumferential head dressing that covers the affected ear should be applied. The wrap can be removed within 24 hours and the ear inspected for reaccumulation of the hematoma or early signs of infection. A second circumferential head dressing should be applied and left on for another 24 hours. The use of properly fitted and adjusted ear protectors can prevent damage to the ears during competition and minimize the formation of hematomas.

Antibiotics

The use of antibiotics to treat facial lacerations is controversial.[13-15] The abundant blood supply and lymphatic drainage of the face decreases the potential for infection, and in most cases, adherence to good wound care princi-

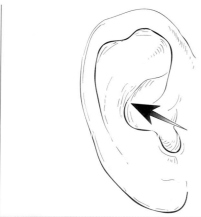

Hematoma of the ear can cause a loss of the normal intricate anatomy. The arrow indicates a proper location for incising and draining the blood.

ples precludes the need for antibiotics. However, in a heavily contaminated wound, such as one that has remained open for several hours or a wound that is the result of a human bite, the athlete should probably be placed on a 7- to 10-day course of appropriate antibiotics and monitored closely. Tetanus prophylaxis guidelines should be followed.

Return to Competition

The decision to return the athlete to competition after a soft-tissue wound has been repaired should be based on the location and severity of the laceration and the potential for repeated injury to the repaired site. Repaired skin wounds gain strength at 14 to 21 days after repair and reach peak tensile strength at approximately 60 days. Over several months to years, the healed wound will achieve 80% of the unbroken skin's tensile strength and plateau at that level, rarely achieving greater strength.[16] Most sports-related lacerations can be bandaged with a dressing after repair and the athlete allowed to resume competition.

FACIAL FRACTURES

Most athletes who have sustained soft-tissue injuries to the face can return to competition shortly after their injury. The same is not true for athletes with broken facial bones. A second impact to an unhealed facial fracture can be potentially severe, even after fixation of the initial fracture with plates and screws.[6]

Airway management, control of bleeding, and systematic evaluation for associated injuries, particularly of the head and neck, are the first issues to be resolved when an athlete is injured and take precedence over examination to rule out suspected facial fractures.[17] A number of definitive texts address the management of these life-threatening injuries.[18,19] All caregivers, including athletic trainers, must be certified in basic life support measures.

When treating an athlete with a facial fracture, the athletic trainer should be able to accurately identify the condition, assist in the prevention of further injury, and refer the patient to an appropriate specialist to manage the injury. The goals for management of all facial fractures are the same: make an accurate diagnosis; obtain precise anatomic reduction of the fracture; stabilize the fracture to achieve facial contour, symmetry, and primary healing of the bones; and reestablish the pretraumatic dental occlusion. The definitive treatment of more severe fractures is beyond the scope of this text; however, the more common sports-related facial fractures will be discussed.

Nasal Fractures

Because of its prominent location on the face, the nose is the most commonly fractured facial structure. Nasal fractures account for approximately 50% of sports-related facial fractures.[20] Of even greater concern is that 15% of these fractures are recurring.[20] Because nasal injuries occur so frequently, most physicians tend to underestimate their severity and, therefore, undertreat them. The late effects of poorly managed nasal fractures can lead to functional breathing difficulties and an unacceptable cosmetic appearance that can ultimately have a negative psychological effect on the athlete. In this era of media-driven sports and product endorsements by athletes, a poor cosmetic result can have a negative financial effect as well.

Trauma to the nose generally comes from one of two directions (**Figure 8-13**). A frontal blow causes the nasal bones to splay apart, much like the pages of an open book, giving the nose a widened appearance. The more common nasal fracture occurs when the impact comes from a lateral direction, causing the nose to deviate to the side away from the direction of the blow. The nasal bone on the side of the impact is forced inward, and if the blow is severe enough, the opposite nasal bone is pushed outward. Because of the intimate relationship between the septum and nasal bones, if the nasal bones fracture, the septum will generally deviate and can also be fractured. Deviation of the septum, nasal bones, or lateral cartilages can have a profound effect on nasal appearance as well as nasal airflow.

Examination and diagnosis

The diagnosis of a nasal fracture is made clinically. Radiographs are not routinely helpful; 60% of radiographs of the nasal bone result in a false negative interpretation.[20] The examination should rule out associated injuries including head trauma, fractures of the adjacent periorbital framework, and injuries in the mouth. The most common findings in a nasal fracture include *epistaxis* (nosebleeds), swelling and tenderness of the nasal dorsum, bruising around the eyes, and an obvious nasal deformity (**Figure 8-14**). Palpation of the nasal bones can demonstrate mobility or crepitance, which usually indicates a nasal fracture. If the injured athlete complains of nasal obstruction during inspiration, the examiner should strongly suspect a nasal/septal fracture or dislocation. If the diagnosis of a fracture is still questionable, radiographs of the nasal bones can be obtained and a surgeon should be consulted.

The intranasal examination should be conducted with proper lighting, and a nasal speculum and, if necessary, suction should be used (**Figure 8-15**). The examiner should spray the intranasal structures with a vasoconstrictor such as phenylephrine. The examiner should also evaluate the septum for deviation or fractures severe enough to occlude or obstruct the airway and identify intranasal lacerations.

Particular emphasis should be placed on diagnosing a septal hematoma. Trauma to the nose can cause blood to accumulate between the septal cartilage and the overlying mucoperichondrium, much like what occurs with a hematoma of the ear. The septum bulges and may appear darker than the surrounding nasal mucosa as a result of

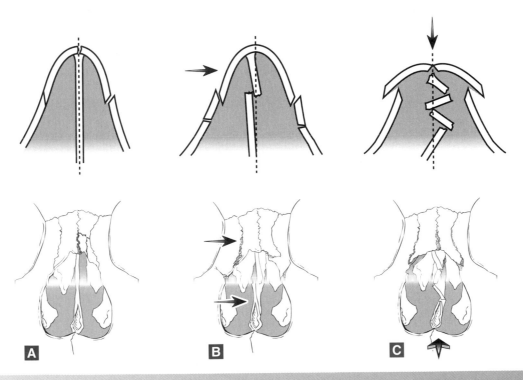

FIGURE 8-13

Trauma to the nose can take on a variety of forms. **A** Isolated nasal bone fracture with no septal displacement. **B** Lateral forces that result in a fracture of nasal bones and septal deformation. **C** Frontal blow that result in splayed fractures of the nasal bones and septum.

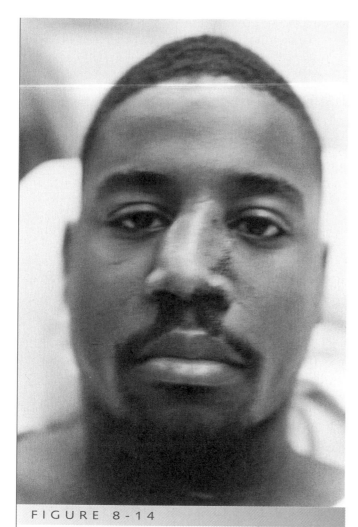

FIGURE 8-14

Swelling and gross deviation of the nasal dorsum indicate an obvious nasal deformity.

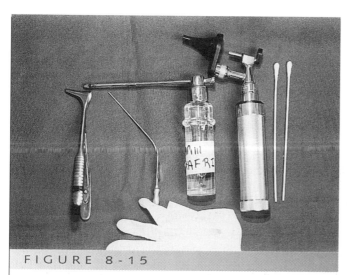

FIGURE 8-15

Useful instrumentation for intranasal examination of the traumatized nose includes gloves, a nasal speculum, suction, good lighting, a vasoconstrictor, and cotton swabs.

the accumulation of blood. This condition demands immediate attention. If the septal hematoma is not diagnosed, the septal cartilage can become ischemic and necrotic, leading to collapse of the nasal dorsum with a resultant "saddle nose" deformity. A physician should incise the affected mucosa and evacuate the hematoma. The nasal passage should then be packed with petrolatum-impregnated gauze and appropriate precautions taken to avoid toxic shock syndrome.

Several blood vessels that supply the nose join together on the anterior septum in a confluence known as Little's area or Kiesselbach's plexus. This confluence of blood vessels is readily subject to environmental insults such as excessive heat and dryness and trauma; 90% of all nosebleeds occur in the anterior portion of the septum.[21] Epistaxis as a result of nasal trauma is usually of a limited nature and can almost always be controlled with digital pressure on the anterior nose. Nasal packing is rarely needed in this setting. However, if the athletic trainer is unable to control a nosebleed with digital compression, the athlete should be taken to an area that has adequate lighting and instrumentation for an intranasal exam, and physician input should be sought.

Treatment

The indications for treatment of nasal/septal injuries by a physician are nasal airway obstruction or obvious external nasal deformity. Open wounds that expose cartilage or bone should be treated as an open fracture. The wound should be thoroughly irrigated and the patient placed on appropriate antibiotics.

Acute management of nasal/septal fractures or displacement should occur within a couple of hours of injury. Swelling that occurs over time obscures the deformity and makes an accurate repair difficult. If swelling has occurred, it is usually prudent to wait at least 4 to 7 days for the swelling to subside. The athlete can then be reexamined and definitive repair performed if needed. Repair can be limited to a simple closed reduction of the nasal bones using topical and local anesthesia in a physician's office setting or be a more involved open reduction of a fractured or severely dislocated septum in the operating room. The realigned nasal bones or septum are then splinted externally and internally (**Figure 8-16**). The splints are usually removed in 7 to 10 days. **Table 8-2** presents some practical tips for treating nasal injuries.

The decision to return the athlete to competition and the need for nasal protection should be carefully weighed. The nasal bones will generally heal sufficiently within 4 to 8 weeks, allowing the athlete to return to competition in contact sports. A protective facial device of sufficient strength to prevent further injury should be used if the athlete resumes competition soon after repair (**Figure 8-17**). Because repeated nasal injuries are possible, prophylactic use of a protective facial device should be considered after a nasal fracture has occurred.

FOCUS ON . . .

Managing Nasal Fractures

The nose is the most commonly fractured facial structure, accounting for 50% of all sport-related facial fractures. Treatment should focus on preventing functional breathing difficulties and avoiding an unacceptable cosmetic appearance. A frontal blow causes the nose to splay, giving it a widened appearance. More often, the impact is lateral, causing the nose to deviate to the side away from the blow. If the nasal bones fracture, the septum usually deviates and can also fracture.

A nasal fracture is usually evident on physical examination. Epistaxis, swelling and tenderness of the nasal dorsum, bruising around the eyes, and obvious nasal deformity are characteristic. Mobility or crepitance, or both, may be evident with palpation of the nasal bones. Nasal obstruction during inspiration suggests a nasal or septal fracture or dislocation. Check for septal deviation and fracture and intranasal lacerations. Radiographs generally are not helpful and may be negative even when the nose is fractured. If the diagnosis remains unclear, the athlete should be evaluated by a plastic surgeon.

Epistaxis tends to occur anteriorly in the septum at Little's area, which is vulnerable to environmental factors such as excessive heat and dryness and trauma. Epistaxis in nasal trauma is usually limited and easily controlled with digital pressure on the anterior nose. If bleeding cannot be controlled in this way, the athlete should be examined further.

Nasal fractures with airway obstruction or obvious deformity require treatment within several hours of injury, preferably before swelling has occurred. If that is not possible, the athlete should be re-examined after at least 4 to 7 days, at which time definitive repair can be performed if needed. Open wounds with exposed cartilage or bone are treated as open fractures with thorough irrigation and appropriate antibiotics. A strong protective facial device is needed to prevent further injury if the athlete returns to competition soon after repair and should be considered after a nasal fracture.

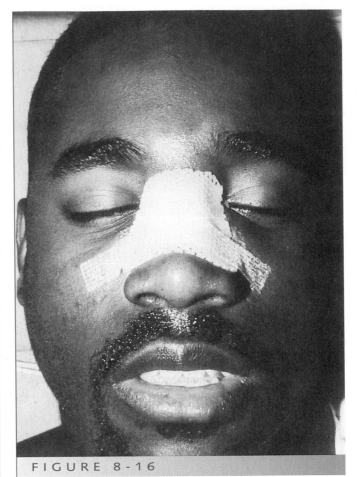

FIGURE 8-16

The displaced nasal bones and septum are realigned and splinted to help maintain proper alignment during the healing process.

Orbital Injuries

Although they are a common injury in athletes, eye injuries can almost always be prevented with the use of protective eyewear. The degree of the risk of injury to the eye is almost totally related to the sport.[22] Low-risk sports are those that do not involve a thrown or hit object or close, aggressive play with body contact. High-risk sports include games with high-speed objects, sticks, or bats or aggressive, intentional body contact.

Examination and diagnosis

When an injury occurs in the vicinity of the eye, a thorough eye examination should be performed. A visual acuity check should be performed using a hand-held eye chart positioned approximately 14" from the eyes. The soft tissues of the orbit should be inspected closely for signs of abrasions, lacerations, or foreign bodies. Changes in the pupillary dimension or reaction to light should be noted. Any change in the athlete's visual acuity, evidence of blood in the anterior chamber, or change in the shape of the iris warrants a consultation with an ophthalmologist.

A circumferential bony framework protects the vital structures of the orbital complex. The aperture of the circumferential bony rim does not allow objects with a radius greater than 5 cm to penetrate to the globe.[4] During the examination, the circumferential bony rim should be palpated. Fractures of the orbital rim can occur at any point on the rim; however, fractures of the inferior rim are most

TABLE 8-2
PRACTICAL TIPS FOR EVALUATION AND MANAGEMENT OF PATIENT WITH NASAL INJURIES

1. The key to diagnosis and treatment of nasal injuries is visualization of both the external and internal nose during the initial examination.

2. Septal hematomas, especially if undrained, can cause permanent cartilage damage, which results in both cosmetic and functional problems.

3. All foreign materials should be cleaned from the wound at the initial evaluation, using a scrub brush if necessary, to prevent permanent tissue tattooing.

4. The diagnosis of a nasal fracture is essentially clinical. Further diagnostic studies may help delineate the injury and rule out other injuries.

5. A nasal fracture should be reduced immediately after the injury before swelling occurs, if possible. If not, reduction should be delayed until swelling abates. Nondisplaced fractures do not need reduction; however, protective splinting for 7 days limits edema and prevents accidental nasal bone displacement.

6. Management of the septum is the key to preventing long-term complications from nasal fractures. Diagnosis of a hematoma or dislocated septum must be made early to direct later treatment.

(Reproduced with permission from Schendel SA: Sports related nasal injuries. *Phys Sports Med* 1990;18:72.)

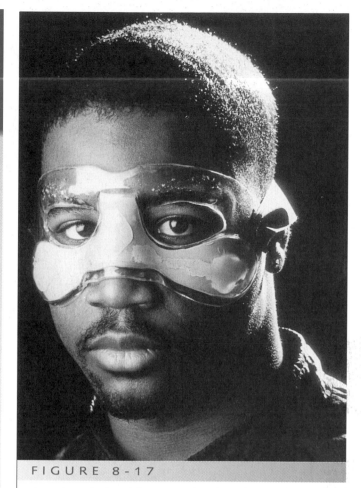

FIGURE 8-17

A custom-designed protective facial mask can protect the nose and allow the athlete to resume competition, and can also protect the nasal structures from repetitive injury.

common. These fractures can occur independently or in combination with interior wall fractures; interior wall fractures can also occur alone. A direct blow to the orbital rim may be of insufficient force to fracture the bony rim, however, it can cause an increase in intraorbital pressure that is sufficient to fracture the thin interior bones (**Figure 8-18**). The thin interior bones that are most commonly fractured are the bones of the inferior medial portion, or the floor of the orbit. This type of injury is called a *"blowout fracture."* It can present with ecchymosis (bruising), *enophthalmos* of the globe (sunken eyeball), *vertical dystopia* (a change in the vertical position of the pupil in relation to the unaffected side), and numbness of the area on the ipsilateral cheek supplied by the infraor-

bital nerve[4] (**Figure 8-19**). *Diplopia* (double vision) on upward gaze can be due to a restriction of movement of the eye because of direct entrapment of the inferior rectus muscle in the floor fracture or to swelling or contusion of the muscle. A CT scan with coronal views is ideal for evaluating the interior walls of the orbit and can accurately diagnose a blowout fracture (see Figure 8-19). A forced duction test, performed by a physician, can help to determine if limitation of ocular movements is due to entrapped soft tissues or to edema or contusion of a motor nerve or muscle. In this test, the affected eye is anesthetized with a topical anesthetic, the sclera is grasped with a fine toothed forceps at the level of the insertion of the inferior rectus muscle, and the eye is gently moved in a superior and inferior direction. If the globe moves easily, entrapment of the ocular contents can be ruled out.

Treatment
Because soft-tissue swelling, hemorrhage, or damage to the ocular motor nerves can mimic orbital floor fracture signs and symptoms, the surgical correction of a blowout

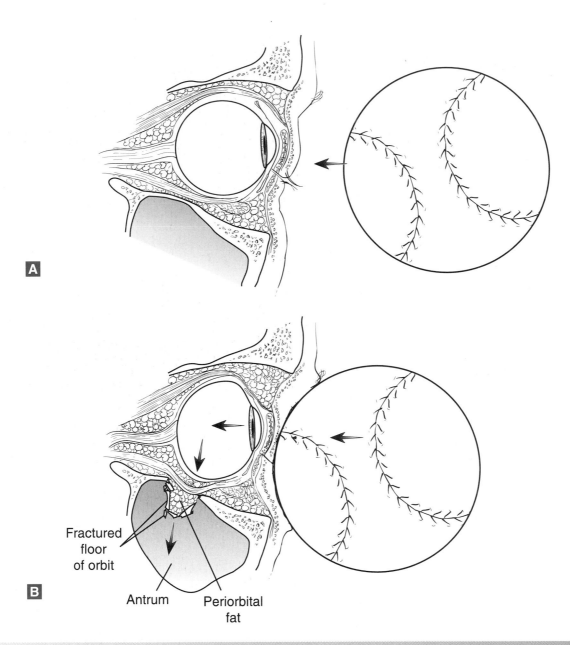

A

B

Fractured
floor
of orbit

Antrum   Periorbital
fat

FIGURE 8-18

Orbital rim fractures can occur at any point on the rim. **A** The opening of the periorbital rim does not allow objects with a radius of greater than 5 cm to penetrate. **B** The force generated at impact causes a "blowout" type fracture of the thin, bony walls of the floor of the orbit sparing the outer bony framework.

fracture is controversial.[?] Often, the combinations of findings on the CT scan, clinical examination including limited upward gaze, and significant enophthalmos leads to the decision to surgically repair the orbital floor defect. Absolute indications for repair include enophthalmos, limitation in extraocular movements, and diplopia related to entrapment of the orbital contents in the fracture line.

A blowout fracture is surgically repaired through a standard lower eyelid aesthetic incision. The periosteum of the inferior orbital rim is incised, the contents of the orbit are delivered back into the orbit, and the hole in the floor is repaired with an overlay of either autologous bone or cartilage grafts or a sheet of alloplastic material. Orbital rim fractures are repaired with open reduction techniques through aesthetic incisions and stabilized with miniplates and screws.

Protective facial devices sufficient to prevent reinjury should be used if the player returns to competition before

Managing Eye Injuries

The risk of eye injury is almost totally related to the sport. When an athlete sustains an injury to or near the eye, a thorough eye examination is necessary, including assessment of visual acuity and any changes in pupil dimension or reaction to light, inspection of orbital soft tissues for abrasions, lacerations, or foreign bodies, presence of blood in the anterior chamber, or change in the shape of the iris. The latter findings require consultation with an ophthalmologist.

Fractures of the inferior orbital rim are the most common and can occur independently or in combination with interior wall fractures. A direct blow to the orbital rim that fails to fracture the rim can increase intraorbital pressure enough to fracture the thin interior bones, producing a "blowout" fracture. Signs and symptoms can include ecchymosis, enophthalmos, vertical dystopia numbness of the cheek area supplied by the infraorbital nerve, and diplopia on upward gaze. A CT scan is often needed to confirm the diagnosis.

Treatment of a blowout fracture is typically surgical. Orbital rim fractures are repaired by open reduction and stabilization. The athlete who returns to competition before 4 to 8 weeks should wear a facial protective device. Most injuries can be prevented by wearing such a device.

4 to 8 weeks have passed. When protective eyewear has been used in racquet sports and face protection devices in hockey, eye injuries have been eliminated.[22]

Zygomaticomaxillary Complex Fractures

The bones of the zygomaticomaxillary complex (ZMC) (cheekbone) make up the prominence of the face known as the cheekbone. Fractures of this bony complex account for approximately 10% of sports-related facial fractures.[5] The zygomatic bone articulates with the frontal bone, maxilla, temporal bone, and the wing of the sphenoid, and fractures of this complex usually involve several of these articulations. This type of fracture typically occurs when significant force is directed at the prominent cheekbone. The bony complex is forced posteriorly and rotates laterally and inferiorly (**Figure 8-20**). Although several attempts have been made to classify the various patterns of ZMC fracture, Manson's classification system, based on CT scan findings, is possibly the most straightforward and sensible.[23] The fracture patterns most commonly found

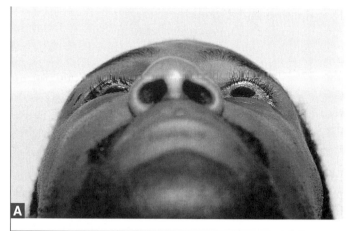
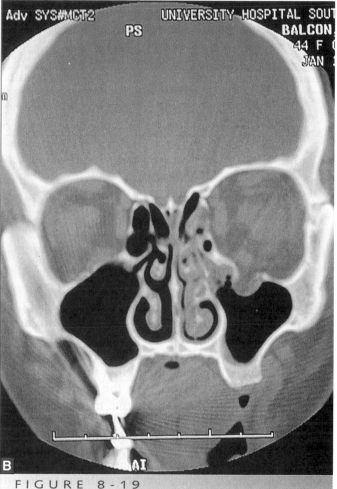

FIGURE 8-19

A proper evaluation can detect an orbital fracture. **A** Worm's eye view demonstrating enophthalmos or a sunken globe of the patient's right eye after a fracture of the orbital floor. **B** A CT scan showing an orbital floor fracture with displacement of the orbital soft tissues into the maxillary sinus.

on CT scan are classified as low velocity, medium velocity, or high velocity. Most sports-related cheekbone fractures are low- or medium-velocity injuries.

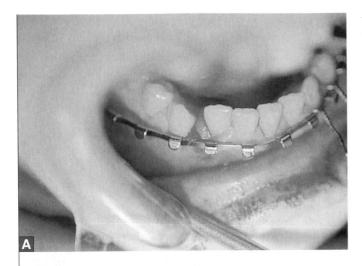

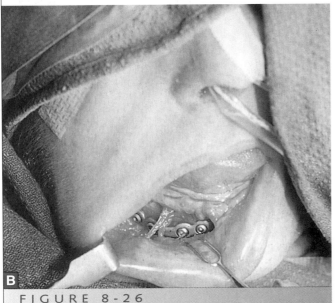

FIGURE 8-26

Management of a displaced fracture should include maxillomandibular fixation. **A** Arch bars and wires placed on the upper and lower teeth can be used to fixate the jaws into proper occlusion and allow for healing of minimally displaced or nondisplaced fractures over a 4- to 8-week period. **B** Rigid fixation of the fracture with titanium plates and screws allows for immediate postsurgical movement of the jaws.

nourishment and maintenance of the periodontal ligament of the tooth. If the periodontal ligament fibers become desiccated, necrotic, or are removed as a result of rough handling, the tooth may undergo resorption or can ankylose (fuse) to the surrounding bone and ultimately be lost. Gentle handling of the root of the tooth where the ligaments are attached is imperative (**Figure 8-27**). The athletic trainer should not scrub or brush the root of the avulsed tooth, but instead should gently handle the tooth by its crown and irrigate it with normal saline. If the tooth cannot be immediately replanted into its socket, it should be cleansed gently and simply placed in the *buccal*

vestibule of the mouth (between the cheek and gum), and the athlete should be transported immediately to a dentist. If the athlete is unable to hold the tooth in this way, the tooth should be placed in fresh cold milk, sterile saline, or cool tap water.[26] Milk is an ideal storage medium; mitotic activity in periodontal cells has been maintained for up to 6 hours when a tooth is stored in milk.[25] Commercially available transport systems for avulsed teeth are also available. Treatment by a dentist involves replanting the tooth into its socket, splinting the tooth, prescribing a diet of soft foods and the use of analgesics and antibiotics, and close follow up. Often the tooth will require *endodontic therapy* (root canal treatment) for ultimate salvage.

Dentoalveolar fractures

A *dentoalveolar fracture* is a fracture of the alveolar bone and the associated teeth. The involved teeth may or may not have associated fractures of the crown or root, or they may be luxated or avulsed. Dentoalveolar fractures should be treated as open fractures. A specialist should pay attention to tetanus prophylaxis, antibiotic coverage, and reduction and fixation of the fracture.

PROTECTIVE FACIAL DEVICES

Although restoring function and aesthetics is important, prevention of injuries should be the primary focus. The use of protective facial devices has decreased the incidence of facial injuries when use is enforced.[27] Prior to 1960, 50% of football injuries involved the facial/dental regions.[27] Face masks became mandatory for football players in 1959. In a 1988 study, the incidence had dropped to

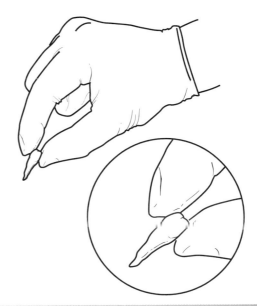

FIGURE 8-27

The avulsed tooth should be handled by the crown to prevent damage to the periodontal fibers that are attached to the root of the tooth.

FOCUS ON . . .

Managing Tooth Injuries

Almost 40% of all dental injuries are related to sport; 80% of these affect the four anterior maxillary teeth. Any trauma to the lower face, including lacerations to the lips and intraoral mucosa and mandible and maxilla fractures, can affect the teeth. Physical examination may reveal intraoral bleeding, tooth malposition, malocclusion, mobility of the affected structures, pain, and altered sensation of the teeth. Always count the athlete's teeth after this type of injury; missing teeth may be lodged in the lips, tongue, or airway or may be aspirated into the lungs. Airway precautions should be followed and radiographs obtained.

Tooth fractures

Tooth fractures can involve the crown or the root. Crown fractures do not require urgent attention unless the neurovascular tissue or pulp is involved, exposing the nerve center and causing pain. Cover the exposed pulp and dentin with calcium hydroxide paste and an acid-etched composite resin to relieve discomfort and allow healing. A superficial fracture of the crown with a sharp edge can be gently filed with an emery board. Root fractures should be suspected if a tooth is mobile or pain occurs with palpation or movement. The athlete should be referred to a dentist for radiographs, evaluation, and management.

Tooth luxation

Tooth luxation is obvious when a tooth is malpositioned in its bone socket. Gently manipulate the tooth into position and palpate the surrounding alveolar bone for fractures. Treatment, which should be provided by a dentist, may involve splinting the affected tooth. The long-term prognosis depends on the amount of displacement.

Tooth avulsion

Tooth avulsion is a partial or total separation of the tooth from the alveolus. This injury is considered an urgent situation: the longer the tooth remains out of its socket, the less chance of successful replantation. The tooth should be replanted within 20 minutes to 2 hours for continued nourishment and maintenance of the periodontal ligament. If rough handling causes desiccation, necrosis, or removal of the periodontal ligament fibers, the tooth may be resorbed or ankylosed to the surrounding bone and ultimately lost.

Handle the tooth gently by its crown and irrigate with normal saline. Do not scrub or brush the root. If the tooth cannot be immediately replanted into its socket, cleanse it gently, place it between the athlete's cheek and gum, and transport the athlete immediately to a dentist. If the athlete is unable to keep the tooth in the mouth, place the tooth in fresh cold milk (ideal), sterile saline, cool tap water, or a commercially available system. Treatment is replanting and splinting the tooth in its socket, a soft diet, analgesics, antibiotics, and close follow-up. The tooth will often require root canal treatment for ultimate salvage.

approximately 1.4%.[28] The use of full-face protection and helmets has also decreased the rate of facial injuries in ice hockey.[29] As mentioned earlier, when protective eyewear has been used, eye injuries have been almost totally eliminated. Helmets afford the athlete protection of the cranium and have been instrumental in decreasing the morbidity and mortality from cranial injuries. However, they afford little, if any, protection for the middle and lower face.[30] Results of an Austrian study revealed a high incidence of lower facial injuries in cycling and skiing, sports in which athletes often wear helmets.[24] Many professional skiers now wear racing helmets with an extension that covers the lower jaw and may reduce the incidence of facial fractures (**Figure 8-28**).

The use of mouthpieces and the reduction of injuries to the oral/facial regions is well documented.[26] A properly fitting mouthguard functions like a shock absorber on impact.[26] The well-constructed, well-fitted mouthguard separates the upper teeth from the lower teeth approximately 3 to 4 mm, displaces the mandibular condyles from their articulation with the base of the cranium, and minimizes damage to the teeth and their supporting structures. In addition, results of some studies have indicated that mouthguards that are properly constructed can aid in reducing concussive injuries to the head and cervical spine injuries.[26]

The various types of mouthguards range from inexpensive, off-the-shelf mouthpieces to more elaborate, high-heat, pressure-laminated custom mouthguards. The pressure-laminated guards reportedly have a predictable long-term fit that does not degenerate in thickness over time. Proper fit, the ability to speak with the mouthguard in place, and comfort are important if the athlete is going to wear the mouthguard on a regular basis.

FIGURE 8-28

A protective helmet with an attachment to protect the lower third of the face may reduce the incidence of facial fractures.

Injury Prevention

Preventing injuries should be our primary focus in sports. The enforced use of protective facial devices has dramatically decreased the incidence of facial injuries in football and hockey. Helmets also protect the cranium, but they afford little, if any, protection for the middle and lower face. Cyclists and skiers have a high incidence of lower facial injuries, but these may be reduced with the use of a lower jaw extension to the helmet.

Properly constructed and fitted mouthguards can substantially reduce injuries to both the oral and facial regions and the cranial and cervical regions by absorbing shock on impact, separating the teeth slightly, displacing the mandibular condyles from their articulation with the cranial base, and minimizing damage to the teeth and their supporting structures. Mouthguards range from inexpensive, off-the-shelf models to elaborate, high-heat, pressure-laminated custom versions that are reported to fit predictably and not degenerate over time. Proper fit, ability to speak with the mouthpiece in place, and comfort are important.

Appropriate, well-fitted protective eye devices have reduced the incidence of eye injuries. Protective eyewear should be made of a shatterproof, lightweight polycarbonate material and should not interfere with the athlete's vision. To prevent injuries to the middle face (cheekbones, nose, dentoalveolar structures), a custom-made plastic face shield can be worn. An improvement on this device is a custom-fabricated face mask composed of a shatterproof outer polycarbonate shell lined with energy-absorbing and energy-dissipating viscoelastic polymer, which can reduce impact force by more than 30%.

Although the designs of protective facial devices continue to advance in both function and aesthetics, if the athlete refuses to wear the equipment, the risk of injury has not been reduced. The sports medicine team must educate athletes about the importance of protective equipment and encourage the use of these devices to enhance safety.

Appropriate, well-fitted eye protective devices have reduced the incidence of injuries to the eyes.[31] Protective eyewear should be constructed from a polycarbonate material that is shatterproof and lightweight.[4] It should also be constructed so as not to interfere with the athlete's direct or peripheral vision.

Although protective eyewear can theoretically protect the immediate periorbital bony framework, it cannot afford protection for the midface, including the cheekbones, nasal region, and dentoalveolar structures. The most commonly used protective device for the prevention of injuries to the midface, particularly the nose, is a custom-made plastic face shield. When such a shield is used following an injury, it is typically designed to cover the area of the face that is injured while not touching it. This simple design has been improved by a patented face mask that is composed of two layers of protective materials: a shatterproof outer shell of polycarbonate lined with an energy-absorbing and energy-dissipating viscoelastic polymer. This mask is custom fabricated to the individual's face and injury. The mask is designed to take advantage of the naturally protective design of the bony facial buttresses and reinforces them to further decrease the amount of energy that reaches the injured site. This mask design has been used by players in the National Basketball Association (NBA) for protection of nasal fractures and fractures of the orbit.

The designs of protective facial devices are improving in both function and aesthetics. However, no matter how good the protection is, if the athlete will not wear the protective equipment, then the risk of injury has not been lessened. Noncompliant athletes have a higher recurrence rate of injury than do those who are compliant.[32] All members of the sports healthcare team should educate athletes about the importance of protective equipment and encourage the use of all protective devices to ensure the athlete's safety.

CHAPTER REVIEW

The face is the most vulnerable part of an athlete's body and is also often the least protected. Sport-related facial injuries account for many of the facial injuries evaluated in the emergency department. The healthcare professional must understand the anatomy of the facial region and the evaluation and management of the most common injuries sustained to this area. The ultimate goal is to return the athlete to competition as quickly and as safely as possible, with minimal risk of further injury.

Anatomically, the facial skeleton can be divided into thirds: the upper third contains the strongest facial bones and has the lowest incidence of fractures; the middle third contains the nose, cheekbones, maxillae, upper teeth, and their dentoalveolar processes; the lower third contains the mandible, lower teeth, and their dentoalveolar processes. The face has an abundant blood supply, which reduces the risk of skin devascularization from traumatic injury.

Examination of the athlete with a facial injury should be thorough and consistent, using visual inspection and manual palpation. Universal precautions are necessary when the athlete is bleeding or when contact with other body fluids is likely. Lacerations are the most common sport-related facial injuries; if not properly treated, excessive scar tissue may form, producing an unacceptable cosmetic result. Other possible injuries include contusions, abrasions, and ear hematomas, all of which also require correct treatment for the best outcome. Facial fractures can affect the nose, the orbit, the cheekbone, the mandible, and the dentoalveolar complex. Depending on the nature and severity of the fracture, the athlete may be able to return to competition before healing is complete with a well-fitted, well-constructed protective facial device. Not only are these devices, which include helmets, mouthguards, eyewear, and face shields, helpful to injured athletes, but they are also effective in preventing injury, and their use should be encouraged.

SELF-TEST

1. The upper jaw is known as the _____, and the lower jaw is called the _____.

- A. Maxilla, mandible
- B. Frontal bone, orbit
- C. Periorbital rim, zygoma
- D. Septum, dentoalveolar process

2. Which of the following cranial nerves provide sensation and animation to the face?

- A. I, III
- B. II, IV
- C. V, VII
- D. VI, VIII

3. Which of the following signs is diagnostic of a mandibular fracture?

- A. Restricted gaze
- B. Intraoral bruising
- C. Asymmetric facial animation
- D. Inability to elevate the eyebrow

4. What are the most common sport-related facial injuries?

- A. Abrasions
- B. Contusions
- C. Lacerations
- D. Hematomas

5. Which of the following structures is injured most often?

- A. Lip
- B. Ear
- C. Eye
- D. Nose

6. Enophthalmos is characterized by:

- A. double vision.
- B. sunken eyeball.
- C. blowout fracture.
- D. change in position of the pupil.

7. Of the following, which diagnostic study is the most accurate in diagnosing a cheekbone fracture?

- A. CT scan
- B. Panorex
- C. MRI scan
- D. Plain radiographs

8. A tooth malpositioned in its socket is known as:

- A. a luxation.
- B. an avulsion.
- C. a root fracture.
- D. a crown fracture.

9. Which of the following procedures offers the best chance of replanting a tooth that has been torn from its socket?

- A. Placing the tooth in ice water
- B. Storing the tooth in hot water
- C. Vigorous brushing of the tooth to remove dirt
- D. Placing the tooth between the athlete's cheek and gum

10. How has the regular use of facial protection by athletes affected the rate of facial, dental, and eye injuries?

- A. Increased
- B. Decreased
- C. No change
- D. Facial and dental injuries have decreased, but eye injuries have increased.

Answers on page 891

References

1. Crowe RW: Diagnosis & management of sports-related injuries to the face. *Clin North Am* 1991;35.

2. Linn EW: Facial injuries sustained during sports and games. *J Maxillofac Surg* 1986;14–83.

3. Lebescond Y: Mountain sports: Their role in 2200 facial injuries occurring over 4 years at the University Hospital Center in Grenoble. *Rev De Stomotologie et De Chirugie Maxillo-Faciale* 1992;93:185–186.

4. Guyette RF: Facial injuries in basketball players. *Clin Sports Med* 1993; 12:247–264.

5. Torg JS (ed): *Athletic Injuries to the Head, Neck and Face*, ed 2. Philadelphia, PA, Lea & Fibiger, 1991, pp 611–649.

6. Garza JR, Baratta RV, Odinet K, et al: Impact tolerances of the rigidly fixated maxillofacial skeleton. *Ann Plastic Surg* 1993;30:212–216.

7. Nahum AM: The biomechanics of maxillofacial trauma. *Clin Plastic Surg* 1975;2:59–64.

8. Managing wounds: Playing it safe. *UPMC Sports Med* 1993;5:4–5.

9. Schultz RC, de Camara DL: Athletic facial injuries. *JAMA* 1984;252: 3395–3398.

10. Millard DR: Closure of boxing lacerations between rounds. *Arch Sur* 1963;86:295–298.

11. Griffin CS: Wrestler's ear: Pathophysicology and treatment. *Ann Plastic Surg* 1992;28:131–139.

12. Kaufman B, Heckler FR: Sports-related facial injuries. *Clin Sports Med* 1997;16:545–562.

13. Roberts AH, Teddy PJ: *Br J Surg* 1977;64:394–396.

14. Thirlby RC, Blair AJ, Thal ER: *Surg Gynecol Obste* 1983;156:212–216.

15. Ryan AJ: *Post Grad Med* 1976;59:259–262.

16. Levenson SM: The healing of rat skin wounds. *Ann Surg* 1965;161:293.

17. Hunter JG: Pediatric maxillofacial trauma. *Pediatr Clin North Am* 1992;39:1127–1143.

18. Nevore EE, Mattox KL, Feliciano DV: General principles of trauma, in *Trauma*, ed 2. Appleton and Lange, 1991.

19. Baxt WG: *Trauma: The First Hour*. Norwalk, CT, Appleton-Centry-Crofts, 1985.

20. Schendel SA: Sport-related nasal injuries. *Physic Sports Med* 1990;18:59–74.

21. Friedrich G: Therapy of recurring epistaxis of the anterior nasal septum. *Arch Otorhinolaryngol* 1982;236: 131–134.

22. Eye injuries and eye protection in sports: A position statement from the International Federation of Sports Medicine. *Br J Sports Med* 23:59–60.

23. Manson PN: Toward CT-based facial fracture treatment. *Plast Reconstr Surg* 1990;85:202.

24. Emshoff R: Trends in the incidence and cause of sport-related mandibular fractures: A retrospective analysis. *J Oral Maxillofac Surg* 1997;55: 585–592.

25. Camp JH: Diagnosis and management of sports-related injuries to the teeth. *Dent Clin North Am* 1991;35:733–756.

26. Padilla RR, Felsenfeld AL: Treatment and prevention of alveolar fractures and related injuries. *J Cranio-Maxillofac Trauma* 1997;3:22–27.

27. Ranalli DN: Prevention of cardio facial injuries in football. *Den Clin North Am* 1991;35:4.

28. Best face forward, athletic facial injuries. *UPMC Sports Med* 1993;5:2.

29. Rampton J: Head, neck and facial injuries in ice hockey: The effect of protective equipment. *Clin J Sport Med* 1997;7:162–167.

30. deRoche R: Facial injuries in bicyclists: Epidemiologic analysis and prophylactic consequences. *Zeitschrift fur Unfallchirugie und Versicher Ungs Medizin* 1991;84:132–139.

31. Easterbrook M: Eye protection in racquet sports. *Clin Sports Med* 1988;7:253–266.

32. Ellis TH: Sports protective equipment: Primary care. *Clin Office Prac* 1991:18:889–921.

9

Cervical Spine Injuries

Clayton F. Holmes, EdD, PT, ATC
Elliott B. Hershman, MD
Sean E. McCance, MD

QUICK CONTENTS

- The anatomy of the cervical spine.

- The biomechanics of the cervical spine.

- General considerations in the evaluation and treatment of the cervical spine.

- The mechanism of injury, assessment, and management of specific pathologies affecting the cervical spine, including catastrophic injuries.

An understanding of the cervical spine is critical to providing quality care to athletes. In the past, focus on the cervical spine has rightly been on the traumatic and sometimes life-threatening events such as cervical subluxations and dislocations or injuries involving the spinal cord. This chapter begins with a description of the anatomy of the cervical spine, followed by discussions of both traumatic and nonemergency injuries to the cervical spine. Discogenic problems, facet syndrome, and "stingers" and "burners" are also discussed. The chapter concludes with summary of catastrophic cervical spine injuries.

ANATOMY

Osseous Structures

The *cervical spine* consists of seven mobile vertebrae (C1 through C7) that extend from the base of the occiput to the first thoracic vertebra. Cervical vertebrae are the smallest of the true vertebrae and have a relatively large range of motion (ROM) because of their unique construction.[1] The typical cervical vertebra consists of a vertebral body anteriorly, lamina, and a spinous process posteriorly (**Figure 9-1**). The *foramen* is the space between the pedicles of two adjacent vertebrae, through which the nerve root exits at each level in the cervical spine. There is an intervertebral disk between each pair of vertebrae, except between the C1 and C2 articulation (see Figure 9-1). Normally, the bones of the cervical spine are aligned in a position of lordosis, or concave posteriorly, when viewed in the sagittal plane. The upper cervical spine (C1 and C2 vertebrae) has anatomic structures that are completely different from the lower cervical vertebrae (C3 through C7), making them completely separate areas.

The vertebrae provide stability and protection to the spinal cord and support the occiput, as well as allow for motion. These functions depend on the structural integrity of the bones, disks, and ligaments of the cervical spine, as well as on normal muscle activity.

Upper cervical spine

The C1 vertebra, also known as the "*atlas*," lacks a true anterior body. During embryonic development, the body of C1 fuses with C2 so that by birth, it is ring-like structure. The atlas can be divided into five separate regions: an anterior arch, two lateral masses, and two posterior arches. The anterior articular facet is concave from side to side, is found on the posterior surface of the anterior arch, and corresponds to the articular process of the superior portion

Anatomy

The cervical spine contains seven vertebrae (C1 through C7), which are the smallest of the vertebrae and have a relatively larger range of motion as a result of their construction.

The atlas (C1) lacks a true anterior body, but has a ring-like structure from its embryonic fusion with the axis (C2). The atlas has five regions: the anterior and two posterior arches and the two lateral masses. The concave anterior articular facet on the posterior surface of the anterior arch corresponds with the superior articular C2 process (the dens). The largest and most solid portions of the atlas are the lateral masses, which contain facets. The occipital condyles form the atlanto-occipital joint. The inferior facets face inferiorly and laterally. The transverse processes contain foramina that hold the vertebral arteries. C2 is the thickest and strongest cervical vertebra. The anterior surface of the dens articulates with the atlas' anterior arch posterior surface.

The lower cervical vertebrae (C3 through C7) have sagittal diameters smaller than their transverse diameters and the bodies are the same height. Fibrocartilaginous disks separate the vertebral bodies below C2. The vertebral bodies, transverse processes, and foramina increase slightly in size at C7. Both C6 and C7 have relatively larger spinous processes than the upper vertebrae, and the C7 spinous process is most prominent posteriorly.

of the C2 vertebra.[2] A very small tubercle is located on the anterior surface of the midpoint of the anterior arch, which serves as the attachment site for the two longus colli muscles.[2] A slightly larger tubercle is located on the back of the midpoint of the posterior arch and serves as the attachment for the rotator muscles. The lateral masses are the largest and most solid portions of the atlas; both have

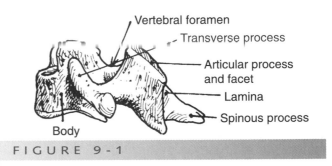

The typical cervical vertebra consists of a vertebral body, lamina, and spinous process.

facets on their inferior and superior surfaces.[2] The concave superior facets face superiorly and medially, and hold the occipital condyles to form the atlanto-occipital joint. The inferior facets face inferiorly and laterally. The transverse processes of the atlas are slightly longer than those of other cervical vertebrae; each transverse process contains a foramen for transmission of the vertebral arteries. Cervical vertebrae have smaller bodies relative to their larger neural arches.

The C2 vertebra, known as the *"axis,"* also has a unique anatomy. Anteriorly, the vertebral body is attached to the *odontoid process*, or "dens," a superior bony projection that sits just posterior to the atlas (**Figure 9-2**). The posterior surface of the anterior arch of the dens is separated from the anterior arch of the atlas by a synovial cavity.[1] Another synovial cavity is found between the dens and the transverse ligament of the atlas. The dens form during embryonic development when the C1 vertebral body fuses to, and eventually becomes a part of, the C2 vertebra.[1] The anterior surface of the dens has a convex articular facet for articulation with the posterior surface of the anterior arch of the atlas; this articulation forms a pivot around which the atlas and the head rotate.[1]

Posteriorly, the axis has a large, bifid spinous process, palpable on physical examination, that extends from the lamina. Small transverse processes project from each side of the axis. Ligamentous stability is provided by the transverse, the apical, and the alar ligaments (**Figure 9-3**). The transverse ligament passes from the ring of the atlas posterior to the odontoid process, and thereby prevents significant anterior translation of the atlas. The apical and alar ligaments stabilize the occipito-atlantoaxial joint complex, because they attach to both the occiput and the odontoid process. Additional stability is provided by the anterior and posterior atlanto-occipital membranes, which resist hyperflexion and extension of the occiput on the atlas.

Lower cervical spine

The lower cervical spine, from C3 through C7, is more anatomically uniform. The vertebrae consist of an anterior body, pedicle, lamina, and spinous process posteriorly, and articular superior and inferior facet joints bilaterally (**Figure 9-4**). The sagittal diameters of these vertebrae are smaller than their transverse diameters, and the anterior and posterior height of the bodies are equal.[1] The cranial surface is concave transversely; mediolateral and posterolateral margins of the superior surface form the uncinate process, an upward projecting lip on either side of the vertebral body.[1] The superior surface fits the convex inferior surface of the vertebra above it. The two uncinate processes of each vertebra fit well into a small concavity on the posterior lateral surface of the supra-adjacent vertebra to hold its lateral edges.[1] In addition to these two areas of contact, vertebral bodies below C2 are separated by fibrocartilaginous disks. The closeness of fit between vertebrae further increases after puberty; as maturation occurs, the anterior margin of the inferior surface of each cervical vertebra forms a downward lip, which conforms to the rounded anterior superior margin of the vertebra below. Short pedicles, which extend posteriorly and later-

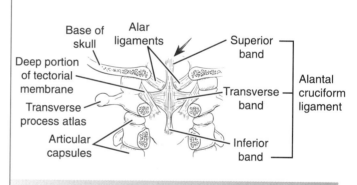

FIGURE 9-3

The transverse, apical, and alar ligaments provide ligamentous stability.

ally, are located posteriorly at the middle of cervical vertebrae.[2] In the lower cervical spine, vertebral bodies, transverse processes, and foramina are approximately the same, with a slight increase in the size of these components at C7.[2]

The C6 and C7 vertebrae have significantly larger spinous processes than C3 through C5. The spinous processes from C2 through C6 are bifid, unlike those of C7. The spinous process of C7 is easily palpable on physical examination and is called the *"vertebra prominens."* All of the articular facets in the cervical spine are lined by hyaline cartilage and function as synovial diarthrodial joints. The ligaments of the lower cervical spine are similar to those ligaments throughout the remainder of the spine.

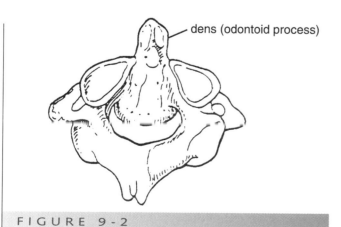

FIGURE 9-2

The odontoid process or dens is a bony projection that sits posterior to the atlas. (Reproduced with permission from An HS, Simpson JM (eds): *Surgery of the Surgical Spine.* London, England, Martin Dunitz, 1994, p 2.)

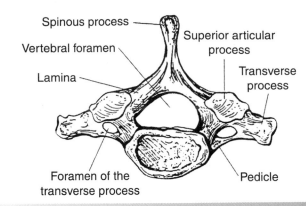

FIGURE 9-4

The lower cervical spine is anatomically more uniform than the upper cervical spine. Superior and lateral views of the seventh cervical vertebra. (Reproduced with permission from Cramer GD, Darby SA (eds): *Basic and Clinical Anatomy of the Spine, Spinal Cord, and ANS.* St Louis, MO, Mosby Year-Book, 1995, p 126.)

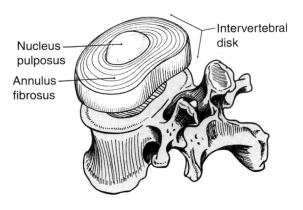

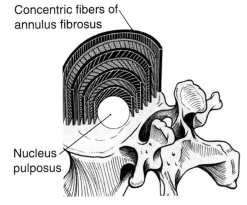

FIGURE 9-5

Thick intervertebral disks, containing nucleus pulposus and annulus fibrosus, hold together vertebrae C2 through C7. (Reproduced with permission from Kapandji IA: *The Physiology of the Joints,* ed 3. New York, NY, Churchill Livingstone, 1974.)

The anterior longitudinal ligament is a broad band that covers the anterior and anterolateral surfaces of the vertebral bodies and provides stability against hyperextension. The posterior longitudinal ligaments course along the posterior aspects of the vertebral bodies and provide stability in flexion. The interspinous ligaments course between the adjacent spinous processes posteriorly and provide further resistance to flexion.

Articular Disks

Bodies of the individual vertebrae from C2 through C7 are held together by thick intervertebral disks. There is no disk between C1 and C2. Each disk has two regions, the *nucleus pulposus* and the *annulus fibrosus*, that form a single dynamic unit.[3] The softer nucleus pulposus is located toward the posterior end of the disk and functions as a shock absorber against axial loads. The annulus fibrosus, which consists of concentric layers of fibers that cross each other obliquely, provides support for the nucleus.[4] The annulus is anchored to the ring epiphyses of the vertebral body[3] (**Figure 9-5**).

Ligaments

Strong anterior and posterior longitudinal ligaments provide significant stability at and distal to C2. The *anterior longitudinal ligament* is a very broad, strong ligament that runs from the occiput to the sacrum. This ligament is firmly attached to each vertebral body and prevents anterior derangement of the disk, excessive backward bending, and anterior shearing forces.[2] The *posterior longitudinal ligament* is located posterior to the vertebral body and anterior to the spinal canal. Although this ligament controls excessive flexion, it is neither as broad nor as strong as the anterior longitudinal ligament. Posteriorly, the *ligamentum flavum* are broad, fairly elastic ligaments that run

from the posterior inferior border of the laminae above to the posterior superior border of the laminae below.[5] The interspinous ligaments that attach from the root to the apex of each process connect adjacent spinous processes. The supraspinous ligament begins in the ligamentum nuchae, a firm fibrous band extending on the midsagittal plane from the occiput to the C7 spinous process.[5] The round, slender supraspinous ligament continues down the points of the spinous processes to reach the sacrum (**Figure 9-6**).

The upper cervical spine also houses the atlantal cruciform complex and the alar ligaments[4] (see Figure 9-7). This additional ligamentous structure provides a great deal of both stability and mobility to the upper cervical spine.

Muscles

The *erector spinae* muscles extend into the cervical spine. Specifically, the iliocostalis cervicis, the longissimus cervicis, the spinalis cervicis, and the spinalis capitis muscles make up the most superficial layer of muscles. These muscles attach to and are generally responsible for extension and lateral flexion of the spinal column. The deep muscles of the cervical spine, the *transversospinalis* group, include the semispinalis cervicis, the semispinalis capitis, the multifidus, the rotatores cervicis, the interspinalis, and the intertransversarii. As the name of this group implies, the fibers of these muscles run in a transverse direction. The primary function of these muscles is to rotate the spine, and they have been implicated as primary stabilizers of the spine.[6,7]

Deep to these muscles is a group of muscles called the *suboccipital muscles:* the rectus capitis posterior major, the rectus capitis posterior minor, the obliquus capitis superior, and the obliquus capitis inferior (**Figure 9-7**). These muscles allow forward thrust of the chin such as in nodding (**Figure 9-8**). In addition, they have been implicated as muscles that are "tight" when the forward head posture is present.[6]

Overlying these muscles posteriorly is the trapezius muscle and the *levator scapulae muscles.* These muscles are also often areas of sensitivity frequently referred to as trigger points.[8]

F O C U S   O N . . .

Ligaments and Musculature

Significant stability distal to C2 is provided by the anterior longitudinal and the posterior longitudinal ligaments. The ligamentum flavum runs from the posteroinferior lamina border above to the posterosuperior lamina border below. The interspinous ligaments from the root to the apex of each process connect adjacent spinous processes. The supraspinous ligament begins in the ligamentum nuchae and continues down the spinous processes to the sacrum. The upper cervical spine also has the atlantal cruciform complex and alar ligaments, which offer stability and mobility.

The superficial erector spinae muscles (iliocostalis cervicis, longissimus cervicis, and spinalis cervicis and capitis) extend and laterally flex the cervical spine. The deep transversospinalis muscles (semispinalis cervicis and capitis, multifidus, rotatores cervicis, interspinalis, and intertransversarii) run transversely and rotate and primarily stabilize the spine. Deeper still are the suboccipital muscles (rectus capitis posterior major and minor, and obliquus capitis superior and inferior). Overlying the suboccipital muscles are the trapezii and levator scapulae. The three scalene muscles laterally flex the cervical spine and contain the upper extremity neurovascular bundle. Anteriorly is the sternocleidomastoid muscle, which laterally flexes and rotates the occiput.

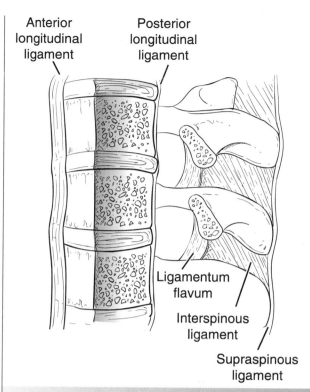

FIGURE 9-6

The strong anterior and posterior longitudinal ligaments provide stability to the vertebrae at and distal to C2. Other ligaments include the ligamentum flavum and the interspinous and supraspinous ligaments. (Reproduced with permission from Kapandji IA: *The Physiology of the Joints,* ed 3. New York, NY, Churchill Livingstone, 1974.)

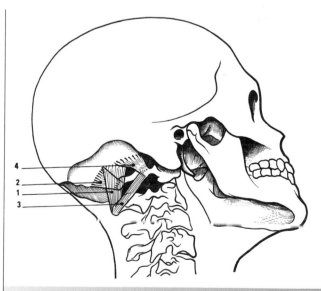

FIGURE 9-7

The suboccipital muscles. **1** Rectus capitis posterior major, **2** rectus capitis posterior minor, **3** obliquus capitis superior, **4** obliquus capitis inferior. (Reproduced with permission from Kapandji IA: *The Physiology of the Joints,* ed 3. New York, NY, Churchill Livingstone, 1974.)

Laterally, at the floor of the cervical triangle are the three scalene muscles. These muscles perform lateral flexion, but, perhaps more importantly, the neurovascular bundle of the upper extremities courses through these muscles. When pathologically tight, these muscles can be a contributing factor to some radiating symptoms. When the pulse is diminished, this condition is called thoracic outlet syndrome (TOS). Just anterior to the scalenes is the *sternocleidomastoid muscle*, which performs lateral flexion and rotation of the occiput[6] (**Figure 9-9**).

Biomechanics

The anatomic structure and surface geometry of the vertebrae define the motion of the spine and its related biomechanical responses to movement. The head and neck form a kinematics chain consisting of eight links. Each link has 6° of freedom; connecting joints limit the degrees

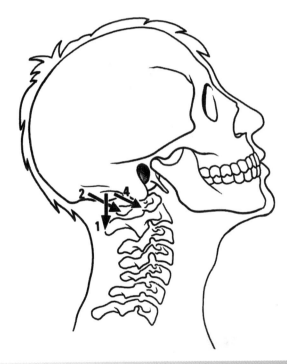

FIGURE 9-8

Bilateral simultaneus contraction of the suboccipital muscles allows for extension and forward thrust of the chin. Muscles involved include, 1 rectus posterior major, 2 rectus posterior minor, and 4 obiquus capitis superior. (Reproduced with permission from Kapandji IA: *The Physiology of the Joints*, ed 3. New York, NY, Churchill Livingstone, 1974.)

of freedom and the amount of motion available. An analysis of the movement of the cervical spine should consider the upper (C1 and C2) and lower (C3 through C7) cervical sections separately.[9]

Upper cervical spine

The atlanto-occipital joint primarily allows flexion and extension (nodding) in a sagittal plane with a coronal axis (**Figure 9-10**). However, the atlanto-occipital joint also allows a small amount of rotation and lateral flexion, or bending to the side. Flexion is limited by contact between the foramen magnum and the dens; extension is limited by several structures, particularly the spinous processes. Movement at C1 and C2 includes flexion, extension, lateral flexion, and rotation.[9]

Flexion and extension are considered pure movements because they occur alone. In contrast, rotation and lateral flexion are considered coupled motions because they occur together (**Figure 9-11**). For example, for an athlete to bend to the side or laterally flex the cervical spine to the right, the spine must both rotate and bend to the right. Although the direction of vertebral rotation that occurs with right or left lateral flexion has recently been called into question, many manual interventions are based on the simple biomechanical principles known as the *Laws of Freyette*.[10,11] These principles assume that the spine is

FOCUS ON . . .

Biomechanics

The vertebrae's anatomic structure and surface geometry define the motion of the spine. The head and neck form a kinematic chain with eight links, each having 6° of freedom that are limited by the connecting joints and the amount of motion available.

Upper cervical spine

The atlanto-occipital joint primarily allows flexion and extension in a sagittal plane with a coronal axis and a small amount of rotation and lateral flexion. C1 and C2 movements include flexion, extension, lateral flexion, and rotation. The Laws of Freyette assume that the spinal position is upright and the top segment is always moving on the bottom segment. At the occipito-atlantal articulation, rotation and sidebending occur to opposite sides, whereas the atlanto-axial articulation is the only spinal segment for which rotation and sidebending do not occur together. From C2 through T2, rotation and sidebending occur to the same side.

Lower cervical spine

Spinal movements are based on the shape of the vertebral articulations, primarily the posterior facets. With flexion, the lower articulations of the upper vertebra move on the upper articulations of the lower vertebra, producing the arthrokinematic motion of slide or glide. Extension causes the opposite movements.

in an upright (standing) position, which allows for the top segment to move on the bottom segment. According to the Laws of Freyette, rotation and sidebending occur to opposite sides at the occipito-atlantal articulation; the only segment in the spine where rotation and sidebending do not occur together is the atlanto-axial articulation, because the ring-like structure of the atlas allows only rotation to occur; and rotation and sidebending occur to the same side from the C2 vertebra to the T1 vertebra. The atlanto-axial articulation allows only rotation to occur; this is the site of up to half of all cervical rotation.

Lower cervical spine

Movement in the lower cervical spine depends on the shape of the vertebral articulations. The posterior facet articulations are of primary consideration because most of

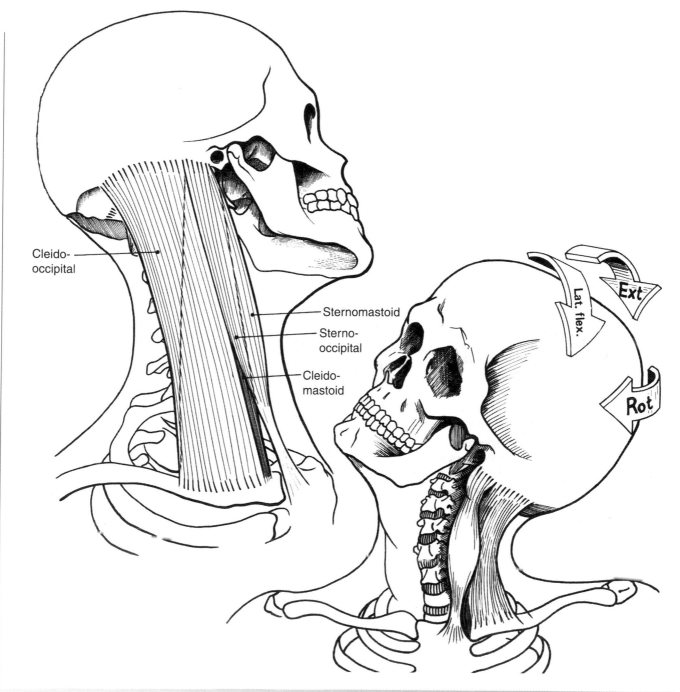

FIGURE 9-9

The four distinct bands of the sternocleidomastoid muscle perform lateral flexion and rotation of the occiput.
(Reproduced with permission from Kapandji IA: *The Physiology of the Joints*, ed 3. New York, NY, Churchill Livingstone, 1974.)

PRACTICE SESSION 9-1
ASSESSING ACTIVE RANGE OF MOTION

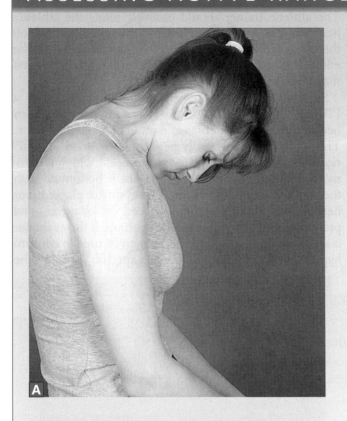

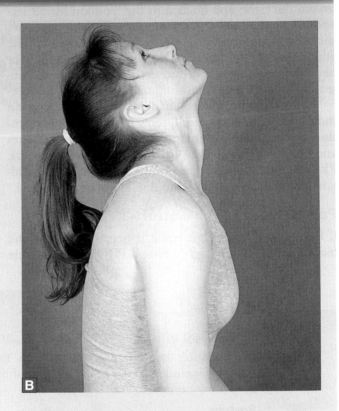

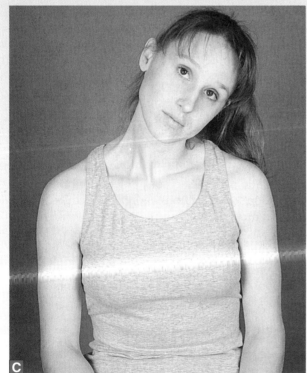

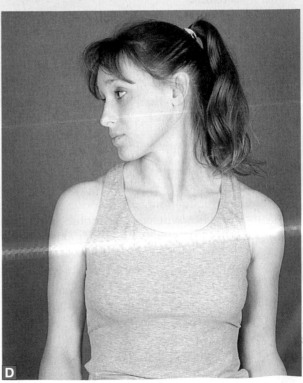

To assess active range of the cervical spine, the athletic trainer should evaluate the seated athlete for quantity, quality, and symptom reproduction. **A** Forward flexion. **B** Extension. **C** Sidebending. **D** Rotation.

PRACTICE SESSION 9-2
THE VERTEBRAL ARTERY TEST

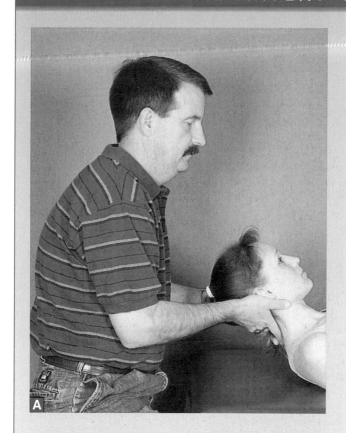

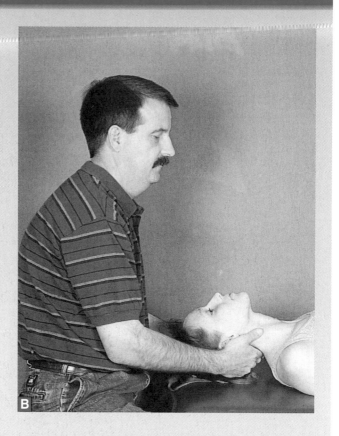

Before passive range of motion can be assessed, the athletic trainer should determine the integrity of the athlete's vertebral arteries. **A** Cervical forward bending. **B** Cervical backward bending. **C** Cervical rotation.

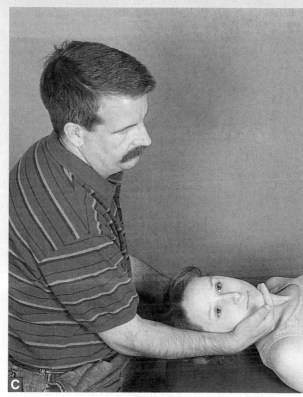

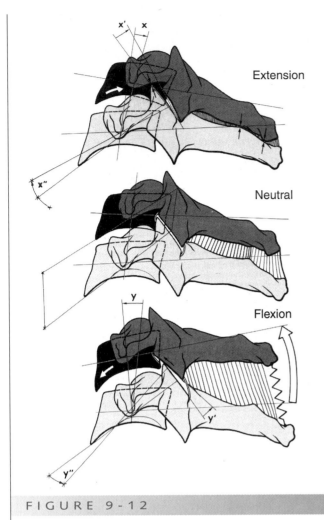

FIGURE 9-12

During extension, the bottom articulation of the top verte-bra moves posteriorly on the top articulation of the bottom vertebra. During flexion, the opposite occurs. (Reproduced with permission from Kapandji IA: *The Physiology of the Joints,* ed 3. New York, NY, Churchill Livingstone, 1974.)

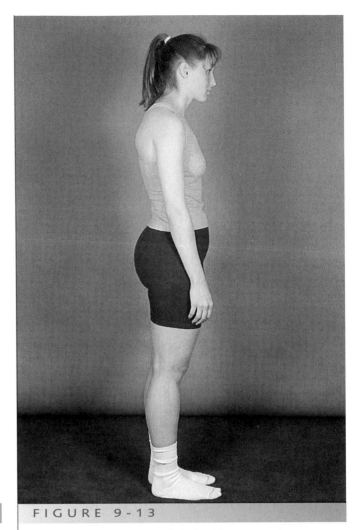

FIGURE 9-13

Thoracic kyphosis, or rounded shoulders, is common in athletes.

segment in question is compared to the one above it and the one below it to distinguish dysfunction. Only an individual who has specific training in manual evaluation and treatment should perform this test.

Quadrant Test

The *quadrant test* is the most common special test used to diagnose cervical spine dysfunction and is frequently used to reproduce symptomatic pain. In this test, the standing athlete extends and rotates his or her head to one side, which closes the facet on that side. Next, the athlete repeats the motion to the opposite side, closing the corresponding facet. Finally, the athlete rotates and bends to one side in flexion, maximally opening the facet opposite the motion. These movements should be done in all four quadrants so that the athlete's pain responses in each can be compared[18] (**Figure 9-15**).

Mobility-based Treatment

If the clinician accepts the concept that segmental dysfunction can occur in the facet, the disk, or both structures at the same time, the focus should shift to simply identifying hypomobile or hypermobile segments and treating each dysfunction accordingly. Hypomobile segments should be mobilized, and hypermobile segments stabilized. This general guideline should be followed until more serious symptoms such as motor involvement or weakness appear.

Because athletes may have one or more hypomobile segments as well as one or more hypermobile segments concurrently, correctly identifying which segments have which disorder is essential. Modalities such as heat, cold, transcutaneous electrical nerve stimulation, and diathermy may be an important part of the clinical management of dysfunctional spinal segments, but such passive forms of treatment are no substitute for manual

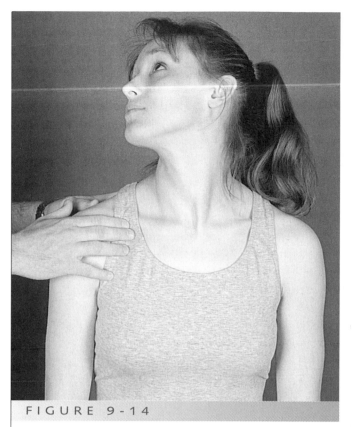

FIGURE 9-14

Assessing passive range of motion.

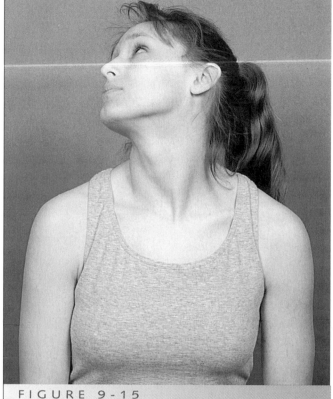

FIGURE 9-15

The quadrant test for the cervical spine reproduces symptomatic pain and should be performed in all four quadrants.

treatment or active exercise when symptoms permit. Manual therapy has been shown to be an effective treatment modality for spine pathology.[24,25] The primary goal of these techniques is to restore full spinal function. Exercise regimens, which are specifically designed to promote segmental stabilization by selectively strengthening the muscles that surround the facet joints, can be used effectively to treat hypermobile segments.

General mobilization principles
Manual interventions aim to facilitate normal joint motion and can be used in treating the hypomobile segment. Typically, mobilization are separated into grades I through V.[26] (**Figure 9-16**). The mobilization grade selected for use is based on the amount of range of passive motion that is needed at the segment.

The central posterior/anterior (PA) glide is commonly used to treat facet hypomobility. This technique is simply the spring test performed with grades of mobilization (**Figure 9-17**). The transverse glide is performed with the thumbs over the spinous process of the segment in question to introduce rotation. This mobilization may also be applied in grades I through IV, with the lower grades used for more acute dysfunctions (**Figure 9-18**).

General stabilization principles
Exercise programs designed to strengthen stabilizing muscles are crucial to the proper treatment of hypermobile

spinal segments. These programs should also be a part of proper follow-up care, after hypomobile segments have been effectively mobilized by the clinician and the athlete is able to achieve normal ROM.

When the athlete can maintain a neutral spine, movement is introduced, particularly of the arms and legs (**Figure 9-19**). This is an extremely difficult maneuver for the athlete to achieve in the early stages of any stabilization program; however, with minimal training, the athlete can generally learn to maintain a neutral spine while in motion. Once this skill is mastered, the stabilization program is relatively simple. The athlete begins by superimposing easy movements over the neutral spine and progresses in sequence to more difficult maneuvers. Stabilization exercises for the cervical spine requires movements of the upper extremities. In one exercise, the athlete assumes a prone position on an inflated exercise ball while slowly rotating the shoulders (**Figure 9-20**).

SPECIFIC PATHOLOGIES

Stinger or Burner Syndrome

The "*stinger*" or "*burner*" is a relatively common syndrome in athletes, particularly in football players. In the

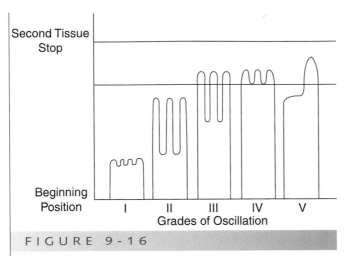

FIGURE 9-16

Mobilizations are typically separated into five grades. Use of the first four are within the scope of the athletic trainer. (Reproduced with permission from Edmond SL: *Manipulation and Mobilization, Extremity and Spinal Techniques.* St. Louis, MO, Mosby Year-Book, 1993.)

past, the condition has been called a brachial plexus stretch; however, more recently, nerve root pathology is one cause of the problem.[27,28] Symptoms occur immediately after contact about the head or neck, and can be either sensory, motor, or both. Sensory symptoms include a tingling numbness and sharp, hot pain that may radiate down one of the upper extremities. These symptoms may or may not follow a dermatome. Pain is usually so severe that dermatome distinction is not possible. Initial motor findings may not be valid because of the severe sensory symptoms. After the initial pain subsides, motor deficit can range from normal to poor.

Initial evaluation

The initial evaluation should focus on determining return-to-play status. Two criteria must be met before the athlete can return to participation. First, cervical spine pathology must be ruled out. Both dermatomes and range of motion should be evaluated; in addition, the cervical spine should be palpated to identify areas of tenderness; light compression and distraction of the occiput should be performed. An increase in radiating symptoms during light compression is positive and rules out palpation until further imaging studies can be obtained. The second criterion requires that the athlete have normal strength in the upper extremities before returning to play. This is done by evaluating upper extremity myotomes. Without normal strength, the athlete would be unable to protect him- or herself and would be highly susceptible to further injury. Any athlete suspected of having a cervical spine injury should not be allowed to return to play that day.

Rehabilitation

Immediate treatment of a stinger or burner should include ice and physical agents, such as electrical stimulation, that

are designed to decrease muscle spasm in the upper back and shoulder area. However, these modalities are only palliative and should not be the focus of long-term treatment of this or any other condition of the cervical spine. Rest and a soft cervical collar may also be indicated. Manual interventions should focus on general manual traction while the athlete is in a comfortable position, such as with some lateral cervical flexion usually to the side of the pathology.

The stinger or burner syndrome occasionally returns after the initial episode and may become chronic. A treatment scheme based on the Maitland approach to treatment of acute and chronic nerve root pathology is indicated.[15] With this approach, manual traction should be performed initially at the angle in which the cervical spine is found. This means that acutely, not much move-

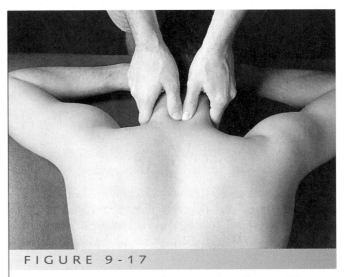

FIGURE 9-17

The central PA glide is used to treat facet hypomobility.

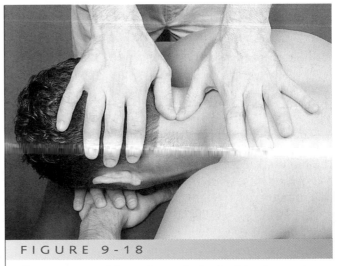

FIGURE 9-18

The transverse glide on the cervical spine introduces rotation in the spinous process of a segment.

FIGURE 9-20

One stabilization exercise for the cervical spine requires the athlete to be prone on an inflated exercise ball.

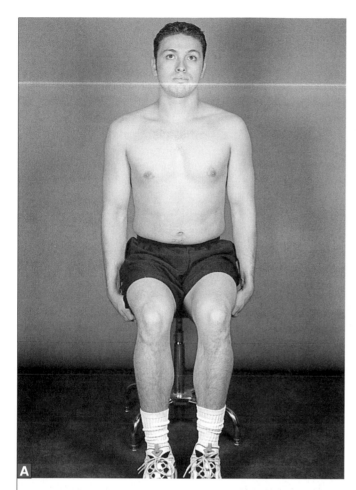

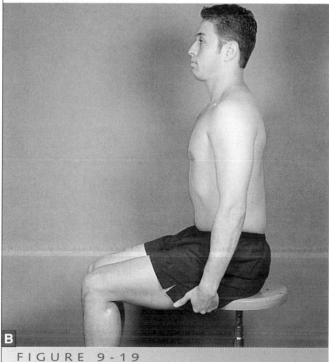

FIGURE 9-19

Movement of the arms and legs is introduced when the injured athlete achieves a neutral spine. **A** Front view. **B** Side view.

ment is indicated. The cervical spine is generally found laterally flexed to the side of the pathology. If it is laterally flexed to 15°, manual traction should be performed. As time elapses and symptoms permit (ie, less pain with range of motion), lateral flexion and rotation to the opposite side is indicated. For example, if the pathology is on the left side, then there should be a slow progression to right lateral flexion and right rotation. As the condition becomes chronic, palliative measures can progress to moist heat rather than ice, and, as pain permits, traction should progress to the neutral position. In addition, rotation away from the side of the pathology should be initiated and continued until the athlete has full, pain-free motion, rotation, and lateral flexion away from the condition. The athlete's activity status should depend on the daily neurologic exam. Athletes can return to play when they demonstrate full, pain-free range of motion in the cervical spine and have no strength deficiencies in the upper extremities.

Facet Dysfunction (Impingement)

As mentioned previously, the facets of the vertebral body can become hypomobile or hypermobile, depending on the type of dysfunction that occurs. The athlete who suffers from a "locked" segment probably has a *hypomobile facet*. The mechanism of injury for this dysfunction can be backward bending, sidebending, or rotation. A "locked" facet is typically more painful at rest and becomes less painful with movement. Pain and a significant restriction in the normal ROM may be evident in the acute stages.[12] In addition, the patient may be able to point to the exact spot of the facet pain (usually about a thumb's width lateral to the spinous processes). Although hypomobile facet symptoms do not normally include decreased motor function and radiating sensory pain, the facet may be implicated in *radiculopathy* (nerve root disease). Radiating sensory symptoms during a straight leg raise test may not necessarily indicate that intervertebral disk material is pressing on a nerve root, and motor involvement in the extremity may be necessary to implicate the nerve root.[29]

Treatment

Regardless of whether the symptoms are central or peripheral to the injury, the focus of treatment of a facet dysfunction should be on manual intervention and exercise. A central PA glide is a common technique, performed with the thumbs and minimal pressure directly over the spinous process. The four grades of mobilization may be performed; however, the lower grades should be used in the cervical spine. As with all manual techniques, the PA glide should only be performed by a trained professional. Other general techniques such as the manual traction techniques described for stingers and burners may also be performed. Gentle passive, assisted, and active ROM exercises should be part of the treatment. Initially, passive rotation should be emphasized. None of the exercises or manual interventions should cause the athlete to feel pain.

In addition, palliative modalities may be used as adjunct treatments. Ice and cryotherapy may be used initially, with a shift to heat-producing agents as symptoms become chronic.

Disk Disease

Because athletics involves extremely high forces, disk derangement occurs from time to time.[30] Although the etiology of disk diseases is not completely known, it may be that any activity affecting the inherent stability of a vertebral segment can affect the disk. The possible results of disk instability include facet synovitis, breakdown of the annulus, and mechanical or chemical irritation of the nerve roots or spinal cord because of the leakage of nuclear material from the disk and surrounding ligaments.[31]

Clinical findings are not always an accurate means of diagnosing disk disease. However, traditionally accepted signs of this dysfunction include radiating sensory or motor symptoms down the upper extremity, sometimes following a dermatomal distribution. Abnormal findings during PIVM testing may also indicate disk changes. However, medical imaging remains the most important way of diagnosing disk disease.[32]

Repeated injury to the cervical intervertebral disks may be associated with degenerative changes at the involved levels. Disk degeneration occurs with the normal aging process, but may be accelerated by repeated injury. The degenerative process can also lead to symptoms such as neck pain and stiffness that are secondary to arthritis of the neck. These changes are often seen on radiographs as narrowing of the disk space and osteophyte formation. Occasionally, the arthritic changes will encroach into the spinal canal and compress the nerve root or spinal cord to produce impingement symptoms.

Treatment of cervical disk disease depends on whether the condition is postsurgical or nonsurgical; if surgery has been performed, the type of surgery will be crucial in determining the appropriate rehabilitation. Regardless of these variables, some general guidelines should be followed. For example, immediately after surgery there should be a period of maximal protection, followed by a period of deliberate AROM with moderate protection; depending on the surgeon's preference. Then, isometrics in all planes can be initiated and stabilization exercises using a neutral position and upper extremity movements can begin. Surgical treatment usually results in a return to activity for the athlete; however, with nonsurgical treatment, return to competition is tenuous at best.

Acute cervical intervertebral disk herniation

An acute *cervical intervertebral disk herniation*, which is caused by an acute loading injury of violent motions of the head and neck, may occur in sports. In this injury, some of the disk material pushes against or ruptures the annulus fibrosus to impinge against the spinal cord or nerve root in the region of the herniation. If the spinal cord is significantly displaced or compressed, the athlete may experience diffuse weakness, paralysis, or other signs of spinal cord dysfunction. However, impingement against a single nerve root most commonly occurs, resulting in a more localized pain pattern involving just that nerve.

The athlete may present with acute and severe neck pain or milder forms of neck pain that resemble the pain of a strain or sprain. The main complaint with an acute cervical disk herniation is usually severe shooting pain or "electric shocks" down the arm into the forearm or hand. The pain may be accompanied by feelings of numbness, tingling, or weakness. Placing the hand of the affected arm behind the head may somewhat relieve the symptoms.

The diagnosis of disk herniation is based on the patient's complaints (in a dermatomal pattern), the symptom complex, and objective findings. Physical examination may reveal specific areas of decreased sensation in the upper extremity, weakness of specific muscle groups in the arm, or loss of reflexes. A cervical radiographic series should be obtained to rule out any fracture or vertebral subluxation or dislocation, but the definite diagnostic test is a magnetic resonance image (MRI), which should be obtained if the clinical signs and symptoms suggest a cervical disk herniation.

If the athlete does have a symptomatic disk herniation, conservative treatment should be used. Treatment includes the use of NSAIDs, cervical collar immobilization as tolerated, rest from activity and sports, physical therapy, and a gradual return to activity. Symptoms from a cervical disk herniation can often be successfully treated with these measures, but surgery may be necessary in some cases if symptoms cannot be relieved.

Spurs, soft disks, and degenerative changes

The process of *spur formation* is part of the degenerative cascade that occurs with degenerative disk disease and normal aging-related changes in the neck. When cervical segments are injured or degenerate, spurs form along the vertebral end plates in an attempt to "autostablize" the vertebral motion in that segment. These spurs occasionally become symptomatic if they impinge on neural structures. An athlete with this problem may report some neck pain and stiffness or arm symptoms such as shooting pain, numbness, or weakness. If the athlete has degenerative changes in the neck associated with limited ROM, evaluation by a physician is required to determine the appropriateness of participation in contactsports.

Spinal stenosis

In *spinal stenosis*, or developmental narrowing of the cervical spine, the width of the cervical canal is smaller than average, leaving less room for the spinal cord. It is diagnosed by radiographic evaluation of the width of the spinal canal. These athletes may be at increased risk for transient *neurapraxia*, a temporary condition lasting from less than 15 minutes to 36 hours or more. The condition involves different degrees of neurologic loss, from mild sensory changes to complete quadriplegia.[33] Current recommendations permit an athlete who experiences a single episode of transient cervical cord neurapraxia to return to full contact sports without greater risk of permanent neurologic injury. However,

---

FOCUS ON . . .

Specific Pathologies

Stinger or burner syndrome

Specific pathologies affecting the cervical spine include stinger or burner syndrome. Symptoms can include severe, sharp, hot pain radiating down one upper extremity; tingling; and numbness. Treatment includes ice, physical agents, electrical stimulation, rest, and a soft cervical collar to reduce muscle spasm, but manual intervention is the primary therapy. Over time, moist heat can be substituted for cryotherapy, traction progresses to the neutral position, and rotation away from the side of discomfort is started.

Impingement

Facets can become hypomobile or hypermobile. A locked segment may be hypomobile and the result of injury can be backward bending, sidebending, rotation, or a combination of these. Pain is worse with rest and improves with movement. Range of motion may be markedly limited. The facet may also be a factor in radicular symptoms. Treatment involves manual intervention by a trained individual and should include the central posteroanterior glide or manual traction. The primary treatment is manual intervention, exercise, or both, although modalities (cold at first, heat later) can be helpful in relieving symptoms.

Disk disease

Disk disease can result from any activity that affects the inherent stability of a segment. Clinical findings may not be diagnostic, but can include radiating sensory or motor symptoms into the upper extremity. Medical imaging is the definitive method of diagnosing disk disease. Treatment depends on etiology (postsurgical or nonsurgical) and location (anterior or posterior). After surgery, maximal protection is indicated, followed by deliberate, active range of motion with moderate protection and then isometrics and strengthening, progressing to stabilization exercises for the upper extremities in neutral position. If the condition is nonsurgical, these phases are also appropriate.

Acute cervical intervertebral disk herniation

Acute cervical intervertebral disk herniation can occur to an athlete as a result of acute loading injury from violent motions to the head and neck. Here, disk material is pushed against or ruptures the annulus fibrosus and impinges against the spinal cord or nerve root. The athlete may have acute and severe neck pain, with severe shooting pain down the arms. A disk herniation diagnosis is based on the patient's complaints, the symptom complex, and objective findings. If the athlete has a symptomatic disk herniation, conservative treatment should be implemented.

Anomalies

Anomalies in the cervical spine may require restriction from participation in contact sports. Ondontoid anomalies can lead to an inherent instability between C1 and C2. This condition is a contraindication for contact sports. Atlanto-occipital fusion is a rare condition that is characterized by congenital fusion of the ring of the occiput's atlas. This is a contraindication to participation in contact sports. A Klippel-Feil anomaly refers to the congenital fusion of two or more vertebrae, and may be associated with short neck, low posterior hairline, limited neck range of motion, scapular anomalies, or other anomalies. An orthopaedic surgeon of neurosurgeon should evaluate patients with spinal stenosis.

there is a 56% recurrence rate of transient neurologic loss, and multiple episodes are considered an absolute contraindication for return to contact sports.[33] Associated degenerative changes in the cervical spine are considered a relative contraindication. In addition, any episode that is associated with ligamentous instability or has neurologic findings that last more than 36 hours is an absolute contraindication for return to contact sports.

Anomalies

Various anomalies in the cervical spine occur and may require restrictions on athletic participation in contact sports. The following management guidelines are suggested:[33]

- *Odontoid anomalies:* Any developmental anomaly of the odontoid process that results in a malformation can lead to an inherent instability between C1 and C2. This condition is an absolute contraindication for contact sports because any violent impact can lead to a catastrophic injury to the cervical spinal cord.

- *Atlanto-occipital fusion:* This rare condition is characterized by congenital fusion of the ring of the atlas to the occiput. When it occurs, either in isolation or in conjunction with other anomalies, it is an absolute contraindication to participation in contact sports.

- *Klippel-Feil anomaly:* This condition refers to the congenital fusion of two or more vertebra, and may be associated with a short neck, low posterior hairline, limited neck ROM, scapular anomalies, or other anomalies. The congenital cervical fusion may involve only one or two interspaces, or it may be a mass fusion involving many vertebral segments. The mass fusion type of anomaly is always an absolute contraindication to participation in contact sports. If the limited fusion variety is associated with degenerative changes in the cervical spine, other anomalies, or limited cervical motion, participation in contact sports is also contraindicated. However, if a limited congenital fusion occurs at C3 or below and has no other associated anomalies, degenerative changes, or limitations of motion, participation in contact sports may be permitted. An orthopaedic surgeon or neurosurgeon should meticulously evaluate all patients with spinal stenosis to make proper decisions about the patient's ability to participate in sports.

CATASTROPHIC CERVICAL SPINE INJURIES

Pathomechanics

The position of the cervical spine at the moment of impact affects fracture or dislocation patterns. In addition, *axial compression*, which is a force directed along the vertical axis of the cervical spine, is a part of almost every serious injury. This component of *axial loading*, which is a load directed vertically along the axis of the cervical spine during a compression force such as occurs with "spearing" or a head-on collision impacts the entire spine and can be catastrophic. An axial compression force of only 319 lb combined with flexion or rotation can produce almost any cervical spine fracture or dislocation. Epidemiologic and video analyses show that axial loading is the most common biomechanical cause of catastrophic cervical spine injuries in football.[34] After this was determined, techniques such as "spearing" were identified and banned in 1976. The ban continues, but this type of impact still occasionally occurs. To demonstrate appropriate management of a potential spinal cord injury, several potential situations will be reviewed.

The unconscious athlete

The athletic trainer faced with an unconscious athlete on the playing field should assume that a cervical spine injury exists. In this case, the athletic trainer should first log roll the athlete into a supine position while stabilizing the cervical spine. The next step is to check for vital signs and ensure an airway. In a sport such as football, the athletic trainer may have to cut off the athlete's face mask to gain access to the airway, but his or her helmet should not be removed. There are some arguments for removing the helmet, but there is no evidence in the literature that suggests this is advisable on the playing field, and it is almost never done.

If cardiopulmonary resuscitation (CPR) is indicated, the athlete's jersey and the lacing on the anterior chest pad should be cut so that CPR can be administered. Even in this instance, the helmet and shoulder pads should not be removed because they help to stabilize the athlete's neck. Recent radiographic analysis has shown that removal of either the helmet or the shoulder pads permits a significant amount of extension and flexion to occur in the cervical spine. Although increasing cervical lordosis is not considered as dangerous as decreasing cervical lordosis, it is very difficult to keep other cervical spine motions from occurring in conjunction with these motions, particularly to the high degrees reported.[34] Finally, the athletic trainer can proceed with spinal cord injury transport such as with a backboard while keeping the head stabilized. The helmet and shoulder pads should not be removed until radiographs are obtained.

The down, but conscious, athlete

A second scenario involves the player who is down on the field, but conscious. In this case, a history and physical examination, including dermatomes and myotomes, can be performed. There are four indications for spinal cord injury: point tenderness in the region of the cervical spine; severe neck pain, which limits motion; abnormal neurologic signs secondary to a dermatome and myotome check; and neurologic signs or symptoms such as numbness or weakness in the lower extremity along a dermatome or myotome distribution. In addition, any pain, tingling, or weakness in the lower extremity indicates that the athlete should be transported after appropriate immobilization. However, if the player can move his or her neck with little or no pain and has only transitory arm symptoms that resolve quickly, the athlete may be allowed to walk off the field.

TABLE 9-1
GUIDELINES FOR THE APPROPRIATE CARE OF THE SPINE-INJURED ATHLETE

General guidelines

- Any athlete suspected of having a spinal injury should not be moved and should be managed as though a spinal injury exists.

- The athlete's airway, breathing, and circulation, neurologic status and level of consciousness should be assessed.

- The athlete should not be moved unless absolutely essential to maintain airway, breathing, and circulation.

- If the athlete must be moved, to maintain airway, breathing, and circulation, the athlete should be placed in a supine position while maintaining spinal immobilization.

- When moving a suspected spine-injured athlete, the head and trunk should be moved as a unit. Once accepted technique is to manually splint the head to the trunk.

- The Emergency Medical Services (EMS) system should be activated.

Face mask removal

- The face mask should be removed prior to transportation, regardless of current respiratory status.

- Those involved in the prehospital care of injured football players should have the tools for face mask removal readily available.

Football helmet removal

- The athletic helmet and chin strap should only be removed:

- If the helmet and chin strap do not hold the head securely, such that immobilization of the helmet does not also immobilize the head.

- If the design of the helmet and chin strap is such that even after removal of the face mask the airway cannot be controlled, or ventilation be provided.

- If the face mask cannot be removed after a reasonable period of time.

- If the helmet prevent immobilization for transportation in an appropriate position.

Helmet removal

- Spinal immobilization must be maintained while removing the helmet

- Helmet removal should be frequently practiced under proper supervision.

- Specific guidelines for helmet removal need to be developed. In most circumstances, it may be helpful to remove cheek padding and/or deflate air padding prior to helmet removal.

Equipment

- Appropriate spinal alignment must be maintained.

- There needs to be a realization that the helmet and shoulder pads elevate an athlete's trunk when in the supine position.

- Should either be removed, or f only one is present, appropriate spinal alignment must be maintained.

- The front of the shoulder pads can be opened to allow access for CPR and defibrillation.

Note: The Task Force encourages the development of a local emergency care plan regarding the prehospital care of the athlete with a suspected spinal cord injury. This plan should include communication with the institution's administration and those directly involved with the assessment and transportation of the injured athlete.

All providers of prehospital care should practice and be competent in all of the skills identified in these guidelines before they are needed in an emergency situation.

Delayed symptoms

The third treatment scenario involves a player who has walked off the field and removed the helmet before complaining of arm and neck pain. The athletic trainer should obtain a history and perform a physical examination with the athlete sitting on the bench. If the examination reveals any abnormal or neurologic symptoms or limited ROM, the athletic trainer should immobilize the cervical spine and arrange for transport to a hospital for a radiographic examination by a physician.

Treatment

If the athlete is unconscious, the athletic trainer should assume that a spinal cord injury has occurred and activate the EMS system for transport to the emergency department. **Table 9-1** lists the guidelines of the 1998 Inter-Association Task Force for Appropriate Care of the Spine-Injured Athlete. A spinal cord injury should be suspected if the athlete has neck point tenderness or neck pain severe enough to limit active cervical motion; has an abnormal neurologic examination (numbness or weakness); complains of burners; experiences transient symptoms in the upper extremities lasting longer than 15 minutes; or has any neurologic signs in the lower extremity after a cervical spine insult. An athlete may return to play if he or she has full, pain-free cervical ROM, a normal neurologic exam and normal strength, and no history of sensory problems.

Although much progress has been made regarding the care of an athlete with a spinal cord injury, controversy continues over issues such as predisposing conditions and helmet removal. In any case, the care of the athlete on the field dictates that he or she be moved as little as possible. In addition, evidence suggests that cervical spine motion does indeed occur if the helmet or shoulder pads are removed.[34]

CHAPTER REVIEW

Cervical spine injuries can be life threatening and must be managed correctly. The athletic trainer must be familiar with the anatomy and biomechanics of the cervical spine, the general guidelines for evaluating and treating an athlete with a cervical spine condition, and specific pathologies affecting the region.

The cervical spine contains seven vertebrae, including C1 (the atlas) and C2 (the axis), which are structurally different from the other cervical vertebrae. Except for C1 and C2, the cervical vertebrae are held together by disks. Strong anterior and posterior longitudinal ligaments offer significant stability to the cervical spine, and the extra ligaments of the upper cervical spine provide both stability and mobility. The cervical spine muscles flex, extend, laterally flex, and rotate the cervical spine.

Biomechanically, the head and neck form a kinematic chain with eight links, each with 6° of freedom that are constrained by the connecting joints and the available motion. When the spine is upright, the upper segment moves on the lower segment, producing an arthrokinematic slide or glide during flexion and the opposite motion during extension. Spinal movements are based on the shape of the vertebral articulations.

In evaluating the athlete with a cervical spine condition, the athletic trainer should take the history, check posture, assess range of motion, and perform special tests as indicated. Treatment depends on whether the segments are hypomobile (and should be mobilized) or hypermobile (and should be stabilized). Modalities can be helpful, but the focus should be on manual treatment or active exercise, or both, to restore full spinal function.

Specific cervical spine pathologies that can affect the athlete include stinger or burner syndrome, facet dysfunction, disk disease, and catastrophic injuries. The athletic trainer should be familiar with the mechanism of injury, evaluation, and treatment of each of these conditions. Some athletes with cervical spine injuries will need to be properly immobilized to prevent further injury before they are transported to the emergency department.

1. Which of the following statements about the atlas is true ?

A. The superior facets are convex.

B. There are two posterior arches.

C. The lateral masses are the smallest portions of the atlas.

D. The transverse processes are slightly smaller than those of the other cervical vertebrae.

2. Which of the following vertebrae is the thickest and strongest?

A. C1

B. C2

C. C3

D. C4

3. An extra ligament found in the cervical spine that provides both stability and mobility is the:

A. alar ligament.

B. ligamentum flavum.

C. supraspinous ligament.

D. anterior longitudinal ligament.

4. Each link of the head and neck chain has how many degrees of freedom?

A. 2°

B. 4°

C. 6°

D. 8°

5. Which of the following treatments is the most effective for an athlete with a dysfunctional spinal segment?

A. Diathermy

B. Cryotherapy

C. Manual therapy

D. Electrical stimulation

6. How much upper extremity strength should an athlete recovering from a "stinger" regain before returning to play?

A. 25%

B. 50%

C. 75%

D. 100%

7. Which of the following motions can cause a hypomobile facet?

A. Extension

B. Sidebending

C. Forward bending

D. Axial compression

8. Which of the following exercises is introduced first after surgical treatment of disk disease?

A. Isometrics

B. Strengthening

C. Active range of motion

D. Stabilizing in neutral position

9. What should an athletic trainer do first when evaluating an unconscious athlete on the playing field?

A. Remove the helmet.

B. Check for vital signs and an airway.

C. Arrange for transport to the emergency department.

D. Log roll the athlete into a supine position while stabilizing the cervical spine.

10. If an athlete is down on the field, but is conscious, which of the following signs or symptoms may be associated with a spinal cord injury?

A. Mild neck pain

B. Cervical spine point tenderness

C. Upper extremity neurologic signs or symptoms

D. Abnormal neurologic signs in a nondermatome distribution

Answers on page 892

References

1. Newman J: Medical Imaging of trauma to the upper cervical spine. *Radiol Technol* 1997;68:201-207.

2. O'Malley KF, DeLong WG: Cervical spine considerations in head and trunk trauma. *Topics Emer Med* 1991;13:8-16.

3. Bowden RE: The applied anatomy of the cervical spine and brachial plexus. *Proc Roy Soc Med* 1966;59:1141-1146.

4. Kapandji IA: *The Physiology of the Joints*, ed 3. New York, New York, Churchill Livingstone, 1974.

5. Goel VK, Clark CR, McGowan D, Goyal S: An in-vitro study of the kinematics of the normal, injured, and stabilized cervical spine. *J Biomech* 1984;17:363-376.

6. Williams PL, Warwick R, Dyson M, et al (eds): *Gray's Anatomy*, ed 37. New York, NY, Churchill Livingstone, 1989.

7. Norris C: Spinal stabilization: 3. Stabilization mechanisms of the lumbar spine. *Physiotherapy*. 1995;81:72-78.

8. Travell, J, Simons D: *Myofacial Pain and Dysfunction: The Trigger Point Manual*. Baltimore, MD, Williams & Wilkins, 1983.

9. Norkin CC, Levangie PK: *Joint Structure & Function: A Comprehensive Analysis*, ed 2. Philadelphia, PA, FA Davis, 1992.

10. Panjabi M, Oxland T, Takata K, et al: Articular facets of the human spine: Quantitative three-dimensional anatomy. *Spine* 1993;18:1298-1310.

11. Brown L: Treatment and examination of the spine by combined movements: II *Physiotherapy* 1990;70:66-74.

12. Saunders HD, Saunders R: Evaluation, in *Treatment and Prevention of Musculoskeletal Disorders*, ed 3. Bloomington, MN, Educational Opportunities, 1993.

13. Cyriax JH, Cyriax PJ: *Illustrated Manual of Orthopaedic Medicine*. London, England, Butterworths, 1983.

14. McKenzie RA: *The Lumbar Spine, Mechanical Diagnosis and Therapy*. Upper Hutt, New Zeland, Spinal Publications, 1981.

15. Maitland GD: *Vertebral Manipulation*, ed 4. London, England, Butterworths, 1977.

16. Kaltenborn FM: *The Spine*, ed 2. Oslo, Norway: Olaf Norlis,1993.

17. Grieve GP: *Mobilization of the Spine*, ed 5. London, England, Churchill Livingstone, 1991.

18. Magee DJ: *Orthopedic Physical Assessment*, ed 2. Philadelphia, PA, Harcourt Brace, 1992.

19. Mennell JM: *The Musculoskeletal System, Differential Diagnosis from Symptoms and Physical Signs*. Gaithersburg, MD, Aspen Publishers, 1992.

20. Twomey LT, Taylor JR: *Physical Therapy of the Low Back*, ed 2. New York, New York, Churchill Livingstone, 1994.

21. Greenman PE: *Principles of Manual Medicine*. Baltimore, MD, Williams & Wilkins, 1989.

22. Hoppenfeld S: *Physical Examination of the Spine and Extremities*. East Norwalk, CT, Appleton-Century-Crofts, 1976.

23. Garfin SR, Vaccaro AR (eds): *Orthopaedic Knowledge Update: Spine*. Rosemont, IL, American Academy of Orthopaedic Surgeons, 1997, pp 3-17.

24. DiFabio RP: Efficacy of Manual Therapy. *Phys Ther* 1992;72:853-864.

25. Koes BW, Bouter LM, vanMameren H, et al: The effectiveness of manual therapy physiotherapy, and treatment by the general practitioner for nonspecific back and neck complaints: A randomized clinical trial. *Spine* 1992;17:28-35.

26. Edmond SL: *Manipulation & Mobilization, Extremity and Spinal Techniques*. St. Louis, MO, Mosby-Year Book, 1993.

27. Clancy WGR, Brand RL, Bergfeld JA: Upper trunk brachial plexus injuries in contact sports. *Am J of Sports Med* 1977;5:209-216.

28. Cantu RC: Neurologic athletic head and neck injuries. *Clin Sports Med* 1998;17:1-97.

29. Mooney V, Robertson J: The facet syndrome. *Clin Orthop* 1976; 115: 149-156.

30. Alexander MJL: Biomechanical aspects of lumbar spine injuries in athletes: A review. *Can J Appl Sport Sci* 1985;10:1-20.

31. Young JL, Press JM, Herring SA: The disc at risk in athletes: Perspectives on operative and nonoperative care. *Med Sci Sports Exerc* 1997;29:S222-S232.

32. Wheeler A: Diagnosis and management of low back pain and sciatica. *Am Fam Phys* 1995;52:1333-1341.

33. Torg JS, Ramsey-Emrhein JA: Management guidelines for participation in collision activities with congenital developmental or post-injury lesions involving the cervical spine. *Clin J Sports Med* 1997:7:273-291.

34. Swenson TM, Lauerman WC, Blanc RO, Donaldson WF, Fu FH: Cervical spine alignment in the immobilized football player: Radiographic analysis before and after helmet removal. *Am J Sports Med* 1997;25.

10

Shoulder Injuries

William O. Thompson, MD
Russell F. Warren, MD
Ronnie P. Barnes, MS, ATC
Shawn Hunt, MSPT, ATC

QUICK CONTENTS

- The anatomy of the shoulder.

- The biomechanics of the shoulder.

- The mechanisms of injury to the shoulder and initial assessment and management of an athlete with a shoulder injury.

- The evaluation and treatment of specific shoulder injuries.

- The principles and phases of shoulder rehabilitation.

- An interval throwing program.

The highly mobile shoulder is subject to a variety of athletic injuries from acute trauma as well as from overuse. This chapter begins with a discussion of the normal anatomy and biomechanics of the shoulder, which are essential for evaluating and treating athletic shoulder injuries. Mechanisms of injury are described next, as well as the initial assessment and management of an athlete with a shoulder injury. Specific shoulder injuries, their evaluation, and treatment guidelines are then presented. Finally, shoulder rehabilitation is described, including guiding principles, phases, and important considerations. The chapter concludes with examples of rehabilitation programs for athletes in several sports.

ANATOMY

The shoulder possesses a high degree of mobility, but not as much osteoarticular stability as other joints such as the hip (**Figure 10-1**). This anatomy allows the hand to be placed in the infinite number of positions required for activities of daily living and sport, but it renders the shoulder susceptible to both acute traumatic and overuse injuries. The shoulder is a complex system consisting of three bones (the clavicle, scapula, and humerus), four articulations, and more than 26 muscles (**Figure 10-2**). This coordinated system is responsible for moving the arm. Understanding the interrelationship of the bones, joints, and muscles is critical for the athletic trainer to evaluate the injured shoulder.

Bones

Clavicle

The *clavicle*, or collarbone, appears straight when viewed from the front and S-shaped when viewed from above. The obvious processes on each end of the clavicle are called the *medial* and *lateral articular surfaces*. The clavicle articulates with the sternum medially, and with the medial aspect of the acromion process on the scapula laterally. The broad surface of the clavicle is the site of many muscular attachments, including the trapezius and the subclavius. Four muscles have their origins on the clavicle: the deltoid; the pectoralis major; the sternocleidomastoid (SCM), and the sternohyoid. Because the medial clavicular growth plate fuses late in development (not until age 22 to 25 years in men), an epiphyseal fracture at the sternoclavicular joint may be mistaken for a dislocation in a young male athlete.

Anatomy

The high degree of shoulder mobility comes at the expense of stability. Three bones, four articulations, and more than 26 muscles comprise the shoulder. The bones include the clavicle, scapula, and humerus, while the articulations are the acromioclavicular (AC), sternoclavicular (SC), glenohumeral (GH), and scapulothoracic joints.

Scapula

The *scapula* is a thin, triangular sheet of bone that is the attachment site for the rotator cuff and other muscles (**Figure 10-3**). The bone condenses along its margins to form superior and inferior angles as well as a thickened lateral border. Other thickenings form the scapular spine, the coracoid and acromion processes, and the glenoid. The scapular spine divides the posterior scapula into two fossae, which are named for their relation to it: the *supraspinatus fossa* and the *infraspinatus fossa*. The scapular spine converges with the glenoid and the coracoid processes to form the *suprascapular notch* at the base of the coracoid and the *spinoglenoid*, or greater scapular notch, at the base of the scapular spine. These notches can be sites of potential nerve compression. The cora-

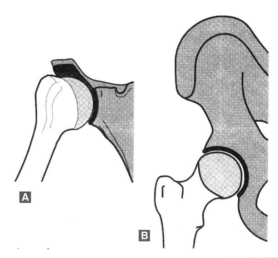

FIGURE 10-1

The shoulder does not have as much osteoarticular stability as other joints. **A** Negligible congruence of the glenohumeral joint. **B** Significant congruence of the hip joint. (Reproduced with permission from Matsen FA III, Thomas SC, Rockwood CA, Wirth MA: Glenohumeral instability, in Rockwood CA Jr, Matsen FA III (eds): *The Shoulder*, ed 2. Philadelphia, PA, WB Saunders, 1998, p 622.)

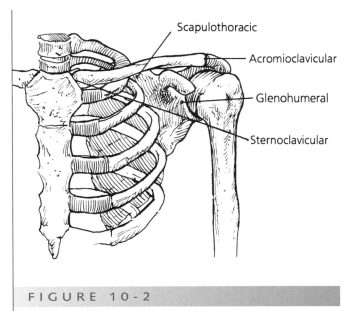

FIGURE 10-2

Three bones, four articulations, and more than 26 muscles make up the shoulder complex.

Labels in figure: Scapulothoracic, Acromioclavicular, Glenohumeral, Sternoclavicular

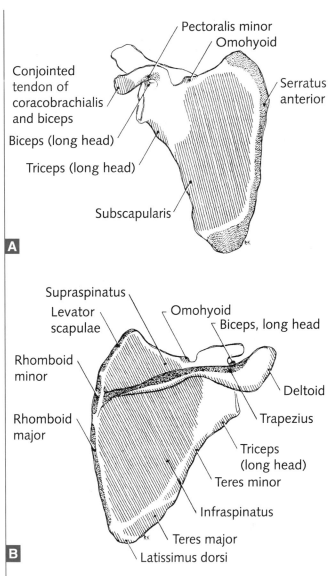

FIGURE 10-3

The scapula is a thin, triangular sheet of bone. **A** Anterior view. **B** Posterior view. (Reproduced with permission from Jobe CM: Gross anatomy of the shoulder, in Rockwood CA Jr, Matsen FA III (eds): *The Shoulder*, ed 2. Philadelphia, PA, WB Saunders, 1998, p 44.)

Labels in figure A: Pectoralis minor, Omohyoid, Conjointed tendon of coracobrachialis and biceps, Serratus anterior, Biceps (long head), Triceps (long head), Subscapularis

Labels in figure B: Supraspinatus, Levator scapulae, Omohyoid, Biceps, long head, Rhomboid minor, Deltoid, Trapezius, Rhomboid major, Triceps (long head), Teres minor, Infraspinatus, Teres major, Latissimus dorsi

coacromial and suprascapular ligaments arise and insert on the scapula. The coracoacromial ligament helps shape the lateral *coracoacromial arch,* a roof over the lateral shoulder that is implicated in subacromial impingement. The transverse scapular ligament forms the roof of the spinoglenoid notch and may be implicated in suprascapular nerve compression.

The *coracoid process* arises from the anterior scapula at the base of the glenoid neck and projects anterolaterally. It is the origin of several muscles and ligaments, including the conjoined tendon of the short head of the biceps brachii, the coracobrachialis, and the pectoralis minor muscles, as well as the coracohumeral and coracoacromial ligaments. A prominent, laterally directed coracoid might impinge on the humeral head in the adducted, forward flexed, and internally rotated arm.

The lateral condensation of bone that forms the *acromion process* is one of the most important structures of the scapula. It is the attachment site for the lateral and posterior two thirds of the deltoid muscle. The lateral length of the acromion process relative to the medial glenoid process gives the deltoid muscle an important mechanical advantage in elevating the arm. The acromion process and the coracoacromial ligament form the coracoacromial arch. The area between the superior lateral humeral head and the coracoacromial arch is called the supraspinatus outlet, and is the site of superior rotator cuff tendinitis and bursitis. The shape of the acromion is associated with the development of rotator cuff pathology. Three distinct acromial morphologies have been described: a type I acromion has a flat under-surface and the lowest risk of impingement and its sequelae, a type II acromion is gently curved, and a type III acromion has a sharply hooked undersurface that is highly associated with subacromial disease[1] (**Figure 10-4**).

The fusion of several growth centers forms the acromion. If the fusion is incomplete, an *os acromiale* or unfused acromial epiphysis may result. The name and functional relevance of the os acromiale depends on its position relative to the scapular spine. A basi-acromion is

FOCUS ON . . .

The Clavicle, Scapula, and Humerus

The clavicle, appearing straight when viewed from the front and S-shaped as seen from above, contains processes at each end, the medial and lateral articular surfaces. The clavicle articulates with the sternum medially and with the medial acromion laterally. Muscles inserting on the clavicle include the trapezius and subclavius. Muscles originating on the clavicle are the deltoid, pectoralis major, sternocleidomastoid (SCM), and sternohyoid.

The thin, triangular scapula is the attachment site for the rotator cuff and other muscles. The scapula contains bone condensations along its margins and thickenings that form the spine, coracoid, acromion, and glenoid processes. The spine divides the posterior scapula into the supraspinatus and infraspinatus fossae. The spine, coracoid, and glenoid converge to form the suprascapular notch and spinoglenoid notch, which can be sites of nerve compression. The coracoacromial and suprascapular ligaments arise and insert on the scapula. The coracoacromial ligament helps to form the lateral coracoacromial arch, while the transverse scapular ligament forms the spinoglenoid notch roof.

The coracoid process, arising from the anterior scapula at the base of the glenoid neck and projecting anterolaterally, is the origin of several muscles and ligaments, including the conjoined tendon of the short head of the biceps brachii, coracobrachialis, and pectoralis minor muscles, and the coracohumeral and coracoacromial ligaments.

The acromion process is the attachment for the lateral and posterior two thirds of the deltoid. Its length laterally relative to the medial glenoid offers the deltoid a mechanical advantage in arm elevation. With the coracoacromial ligament, the acromion process forms the coracoacromial arch. The supraspinatus outlet (the area between the superior lateral humeral head and coracoacromial arch) is the site of superior rotator cuff tendinitis and bursitis.

Incomplete fusion of the growth centers that form the acromion can result in an os acromiale. A basi-acromion is located at the spine-acromion junction, a meta-acromion in the posterior half, a meso-acromion in the midportion, and a preacromion at the anterior acromial margin. An os acromiale, while rare, can actively deform and narrow the supraspinatus outlet and cause arthritis in the older athlete.

The glenoid articular surface is directed 3° to 9° posteriorly relative to the transverse scapular axis and inclined 5° superiorly relative to the medial border. The glenoid and neck peripheral margins are attachment sites for the medial GH joint capsule, GH ligaments and labrum, and long heads of the biceps and triceps muscles.

The humeral articular surface approximates a sphere. On the anterolateral surface are the anterior lesser tuberosity and the greater tuberosity. The bicipital groove at the junction between the tuberosities contains the long head of the biceps as it travels to insert on the supraglenoid tubercle. The bicipital groove, bounded superiorly by the transverse humeral ligament, is important in the development of biceps tendinopathy and as a surgical landmark. Humeral head blood supply is primarily from the anterolateral ascending branch of the anterior humeral circumflex artery, which enters the bone in the lateral bicipital groove or a tubercle.

---

located at the spine-acromion junction; a meta-acromion is located in the posterior half of the acromion; a meso-acromion is located in the middle portion, and a preacromion is located at the anterior margin of the acromion. Although an os acromion is rare, it may lead to active deformity and narrowing of the supraspinatus outlet and the pseudojoint it creates may become arthritic in the older athlete.

The glenoid articular surface is directed approximately 3° to 9° posteriorly (retroverted) relative to the transverse axis of the scapula, and it inclines superiorly 5° relative to the medial border of the scapula. The peripheral margin of the glenoid and the glenoid neck serve as the attachment sites for the medial glenohumeral joint capsule, the glenohumeral ligaments, and the labrum, as well as for the long heads of the biceps and triceps muscles.

Humerus

The articular surface of the humerus, or upper arm bone, approximates a sphere with a radius of curvature of 22.5 mm. The orientation of the humeral articular surface is retroverted approximately 30° in relation to the transepicondylar axis of the elbow and inclined approximately 130° to 140° relative to the humeral shaft (Figure 10-5). On the anterolateral surface, two tuberosities form the attachment sites for the rotator cuff tendons. The long head of the biceps travels through the *bicipital groove*, formed at the junction of the tuberosities, to insert on the supraglenoid tubercle of the glenoid. The bicipital groove is bounded superiorly by the transverse humeral ligament and is important both in the development of biceps tendinopathy and as a surgical landmark, because the anterolateral ascending branch of the anterior humeral

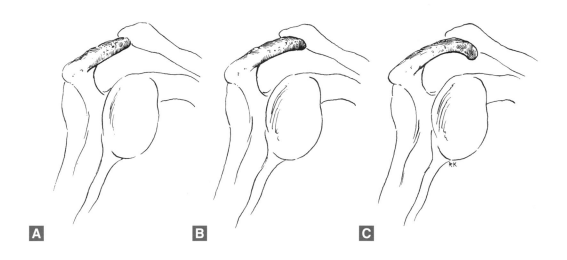

FIGURE 10-4

Three types of acromial morphology have been described. **A** A type I acromion is flat. **B** A type II acromion is gently curved. **C** A type III acromion is sharply hooked. (Reproduced with permission from Jobe CM: Gross anatomy of the shoulder, in Rockwood CA Jr, Matsen FA III (eds): *The Shoulder*, ed 2. Philadelphia, PA, WB Saunders, 1998, p 45.)

circumflex artery, which supplies blood to the humeral head, enters the bone in the lateral intertubercular groove or one of the tubercles.

Joints

Acromioclavicular joint

The acromioclavicular (AC) joint is the only articulation between the clavicle and the acromion. The AC capsule contains a *diarthrodial joint* (an articulation that permits free movement) incompletely divided by a fibrocartilagenous disk. The disk is often perforated in its center and is thicker superiorly, anteriorly, and posteriorly. The AC joint capsule generally controls the anteroposterior stability of the AC joint, and the coracoclavicular ligaments (the conoid and the trapezoid ligaments) contribute to vertical stability of the joint.

Sternoclavicular joint

The sternoclavicular (SC) joint is a saddle joint formed by the sternum and the medial clavicle. It is the only true articulation between the thorax and the shoulder girdle. The joint is diarthrodial, and a complete fibrocartilagenous disk is interposed between the two bones in almost all individuals. The bony surfaces of the SC joint are relatively flat, and much of its stability comes from strong ligamentous structures between the medial aspect of the clavicle, the sternum, and the first rib **(Figure 10-6)**. These same ligaments also resist rotation of the clavicle.

The relationships of the great vessels, which are immediately posterior to the SC joint, are of prime importance **(Figure 10-7)**. A posterior dislocation of the clavicle on the sternum, although rare, may injure the underlying great vessels and compromise the airway and trachea and precipitate a surgical emergency.

Glenohumeral Joint

The glenohumeral (GH) joint, a *spheroidal joint* (ball-and-socket), is the principal articulation of the shoulder and is supported by the GH ligaments and the labrum, a fibrous structure surrounding the periphery of the glenoid. The three GH ligaments (inferior, middle, and superior) are discrete thickenings of the joint capsule that serve to limit motion of the joint at its extremes. The inferior glenohumeral ligament has an anterior band, a posterior band, and an interval axillary pouch, and serves as a major stabilizer of the joint, particularly when the arm is abducted.

The articular geometry of the bone and cartilage surfaces of the GH joint is highly congruent, even to within 2 mm, with the articular cartilage of the humeral head, thickest at its center, and the articular cartilage of the glenoid, thickest at its periphery. This may help explain why data from plain radiographic studies show a larger radius of curvature to the glenoid compared with the humeral head. The articular surface geometry of the GH joint approaches congruency in most individuals.

Scapulothoracic articulation

The scapula slides over the thoracic rib cage. The scapular rotator muscles, particularly the serratus anterior muscle, control its stability and motion. The serratus anterior compresses the medial scapula to the chest wall and exhibits more muscle activity than any other scapular muscle throughout the range of motion. Scapular rotation is critical for the GH joint to maintain a position of maximum stability.

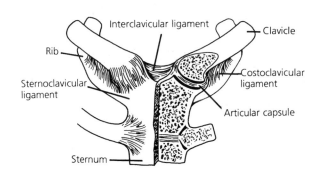

FIGURE 10-6

Much of the sternoclavicular joint's stability is from strong ligamentous structures.

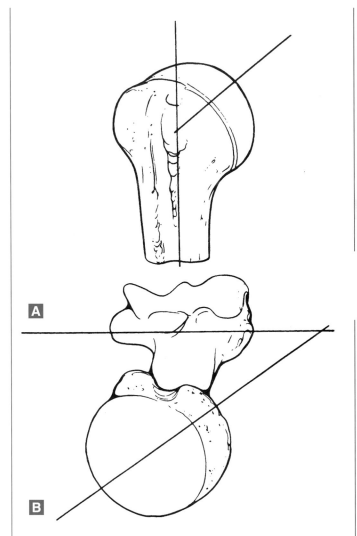

A **B**

FIGURE 10-5

The humeral articular surface is retroverted approximately 30° and inclined approximately 130° to 140°. **A** Neck shaft angle. **B** Head retroverted 30° to the long axis of the humeral shaft and epicondyles. (Reproduced with permission from Jobe CM: Gross anatomy of the shoulder, in Rockwood CA Jr, Matsen FA III (eds): *The Shoulder*, ed 2. Philadelphia, PA, WB Saunders, 1998, p 13.)

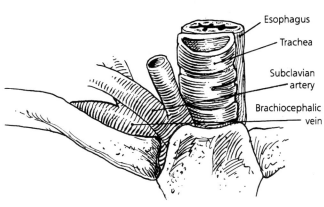

FIGURE 10-7

The relationship of the great vessels to the sternoclavicular joint is important because of the threat of injury to the vessels following a posterior clavicle dislocation.

The scapulothoracic articulation can be divided into two triangular spaces. The serratus anterior space is bordered anteriorly by the rib cage, posteriorly by the serratus anterior muscle, and medially by the rhomboid muscles. A well-defined bursa, which may become inflamed and thickened, fills this space. This bursa is implicated in the so-called *"snapping scapula,"* which is a sensation of snapping as the scapula glides against the chest wall. The lesser subscapularis space is bounded anteriorly by the serratus anterior muscle, posteriorly by the subscapularis, and laterally by the axilla.

Capsulolabral complex

The capsulolabral complex of the GH joint is of prime importance to the static stability of this joint and bears separate mention.

The labrum is triangular in cross section in the superior portion of the joint and becomes more rounded and less elevated on the inferior glenoid. The attachment of the labrum to the underlying glenoid varies in different individuals. The long head of the biceps inserts into the superior labrum, and there is usually a *synovial reflection* (a small cleft between the labrum and stenoid articular cartilage that is lined with synovial tissue) beneath the labrum superiorly, under the area of biceps attachment.

The middle or inferior glenohumeral ligament may originate on the anterosuperior labrum rather than on the

FOCUS ON . . .

Joints

The capsule of the AC joint (the only clavicle-acromion articulation) contains a diarthrodial joint incompletely divided by a fibrocartilagenous disk (often perforated in the center) that is thicker superiorly, anteriorly, and posteriorly. The AC ligaments control anteroposterior stability of the AC joint, and the medial coracoclavicular ligaments contribute to vertical joint stability.

The diarthrodial, saddle SC joint between the sternum and medial clavicle is the only true articulation between the thorax and shoulder girdle. A complete fibrocartilagenous disk is interposed between the bones in most individuals. The SC joint surfaces are relatively flat, and stability comes from the strong ligaments connecting the medial clavicle, sternum, and first rib, which stabilize the joint and resist clavicular rotation. The great vessels immediately posterior to the SC joint can be injured by a posterior clavicular dislocation, precipitating a surgical emergency.

The spheroidal GH joint is the principal shoulder articulation, supported by the GH ligaments and labrum. Discrete joint capsule thickenings, the GH ligaments limit extremes of motion and contribute significantly to joint stability, particularly in abduction. Glenohumeral bone-cartilage surface geometry is congruent with the humeral head articular cartilage, which is thickest at its center, and that of the glenoid, which is thickest at its periphery.

Scapulothoracic movement and stability are controlled by the scapular rotators. The serratus anterior compresses the medial scapula to the chest wall and is the most active scapular muscle throughout the range of motion. Scapular rotation is critical to maximizing GH joint stability. The scapulothoracic articulation is divided into two triangular spaces: the serratus anterior space and lesser subscapularis space.

The GH capsulolabral complex is of prime importance to static shoulder stability. The labrum is triangular in cross section superiorly and becomes more rounded and less elevated on the inferior glenoid. Labrum-glenoid attachment varies among individuals. The long head of the biceps inserts into the superior labrum, with a synovial reflection beneath the labrum superiorly at the extension of the articular cartilage over the glenoid rim. The anterosuperior labrum can be the site of origin for the middle glenohumeral ligament (MGHL) or inferior glenohumeral ligament (IGHL). The anterior glenolabral attachments vary at the equator, with a sublabral hole communicating with the subscapularis recess in some individuals. The superior labrum tends to be more mobile and more loosely attached than the inferior labrum.

Although the posterior shoulder joint capsule is relatively thin without identifiable thickenings, the superior glenohumeral ligament (SGHL), MGHL, and IGHL are identifiable at the anteroinferior capsule. The SGHL is visible only from the articular side of the capsule, variably sized, and present in most patients. Originating from the superior glenoid rim at the supraglenoid tubercle just anterior and inferior to the biceps tendon, it inserts onto the lesser humeral tuberosity medial to the bicipital groove. The SGHL is a restraint to inferior translation and external rotation in adduction. The MGHL varies in orientation and presentation, originating from the labrum in most individuals; however, in some individuals it originates from the glenoid rim. The MGHL represents a distinct band in some shoulders, while it is joined with the capsule in the remainder. The MGHL enhances anterior stability and limits external rotation in midabduction. The IGHL, the most consistent in orientation and presentation of the GH ligaments, consists of a thick anterior band and a thinner, inconsistent posterior band separated by an intervening pouch. The anterior IGHL stabilizes the humeral head in abduction and external rotation.

glenoid itself. The anterior glenolabral attachments are variable at the *equator* (an imaginary line that divides a surface into two approximately equal areas), with a sublabral hole communicating with the subscapularis recess in some individuals. The superior labrum is generally more mobile and is attached more loosely to the glenoid than is the inferior labrum.

The labrum increases the depth of the glenoid socket by approximately 50%, the contact surface area of the GH joint by 38% in the long axis and 36% in the short axis, and the area of humeral head coverage by 72% in the long axis and 59% in the short axis in comparison with a glenoid without labrum. The labrum contributes approximately 20% to glenohumeral stability when the humeral head is compressed onto the glenoid in the absence of capsule and musculature.

The shoulder joint capsule is a complex structure reinforced with distinct thickenings. The posterior capsule is relatively thin with no obvious thickenings; however, the anteroinferior capsule has thickenings that have been identified as the superior, middle, and inferior glenohumeral ligaments.

The *superior glenohumeral ligament (SGHL)* is visible only from the articular side of the capsule, varies in size, and is present in most individuals. The SGHL originates from the superior rim of the glenoid at the supraglenoid tubercle just anteroinferior to the biceps tendon and inserts onto the lesser tuberosity of the humerus medial to the bicipital groove. The SGHL restrains inferior translation and external rotation in the adducted shoulder position.[2]

The *middle glenohumeral ligament (MGHL)* varies considerably in orientation and presentation. It originates from the labrum most often; however, in some individuals, it originates from the glenoid rim. The MGHL represents a distinct band in some shoulders and joins with the capsule in others. The MGHL contributes to anterior stability in the midabducted shoulder and limits external rotation in this position.[3] In the midranges of motion, capsular mechanisms of joint restraint seem to play a small role in GH joint stability.

The *inferior glenohumeral ligament (IGHL)* is the most consistent in orientation and presentation, appearing in all individuals. The IGHL consists of a thick anterior band and a thinner, inconsistent posterior band separated by an intervening pouch.[4] The anterior IGHL complex stabilizes the humeral head from excessive translation when the arm is abducted and externally rotated. This is key for anterior instability.

Muscles

A discussion of muscle action about the shoulder must be based on a clear definition of joint motions. Using the plane of the scapula as the reference point for motion of the upper extremity, the following movements can be defined (**Figure 10-8**):

- *Abduction* is movement of the upper extremity away from the body.
- *Adduction* is movement of the upper extremity toward the body.
- *Flexion* is movement of the upper extremity anterior to or in front of the plane of the scapula.
- *Extension* is movement of the upper extremity posterior to or behind the plane of the scapula.
- *Internal rotation* is the medial rotation of the upper extremity relative to the thorax and is typically used in reference to the adducted upper extremity, although a similar motion can occur in both abduction and forward flexion.
- *External rotation* is the lateral rotation of the upper extremity relative to the thorax and typically refers to the adducted upper extremity, although a similar motion can occur in both abduction and forward flexion.

Scapulothoracic (periscapular) muscles

The largest and most superficial of the scapulothoracic muscles is the *trapezius.* It originates from the spinous processes of the C7 to T12 vertebrae and inserts over the distal third of the clavicle. It functions primarily as a scapular rotator, with the upper fibers elevating the lateral angle. The accessory spinal nerve (cranial nerve XI) is the motor supply, although C2, C3, and C4 also contribute some sensory branches.

The two *rhomboids* function similarly to the trapezius. The rhomboid minor arises from the lower ligamentum nuchae C7 and T1 and inserts on the posterior portion of the medial base of the scapular spine. The rhomboid major originates from T2 to T5 and inserts inferior to the rhomboid minor along the posterior medial scapula to the inferior angle. The rhomboids primarily retract and secondarily elevate the scapula. The innervation of the rhomboids is the dorsal scapular nerve (C5).

The *levator scapulae* originates from the posterior tubercles of the transverse processes of C1 to C3 and, occasionally, C4. It inserts on the superior angle of the scapula and, in conjunction with the serratus anterior, provides upward elevation of the scapula. It derives innervation from C3 and C4. The *serratus anterior* muscle originates from the first through ninth anterior lateral thoracic ribs and inserts on the anterior medial aspect of the scapula. This important stabilizer protracts or extends the scapula and assists the levator scapulae muscle in elevating the scapula. It is mainly active in forward flexion of the humerus. Absence of serratus activity, usually secondary to paralysis, produces *winging* of the scapula (lifting off of the medial border of the scapula from the chest wall) with forward flexion and loss of strength in that motion. It derives innervation from the long thoracic nerve (C5, C6, C7).

The *pectoralis minor* muscle originates from the second through fifth anterior ribs and inserts onto the base of the medial coracoid. It actively counteracts scapular retraction and upward rotation. In other words, it will extend the retracted scapula and depress the upwardly rotated scapula. It has little impact on the resting scapula. Perhaps its most important function is as a superficial landmark of the underlying brachial plexus during surgical approaches in this area. Innervation is from the medial pectoral nerve (C8, T1).

The *subclavius* crosses the SC joint. It originates from the first rib and cartilage, inserts on the inferior surface of the medial clavicle, and is innervated by the nerve to the subclavius. It stabilizes the SC joint during intense activity, such as hanging from a bar.

Glenohumeral muscles

The deltoid, the largest and most important glenohumeral muscle, forms one component of the superficial layer of

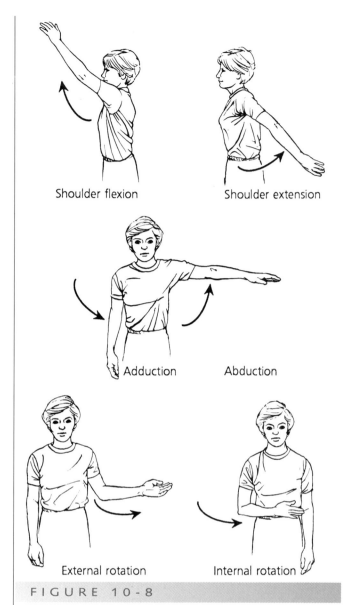

Shoulder flexion   Shoulder extension

Adduction   Abduction

External rotation   Internal rotation

FIGURE 10-8

The six joint motions at the glenohumeral joint are abduction, adduction, flexion, extension, internal rotation, and external rotation.

thirds. The anterior and middle thirds of the deltoid elevate the humerus in the scapular plane, with some contribution from the posterior third if elevation extends beyond 90°. Activation of the posterior third contributes to extension of the arm.

The *rotator cuff muscles*—the supraspinatus, infraspinatus, teres minor, and subscapularis muscles—arise from the scapula and insert on the proximal humerus in a nearly continuous manner (**Figure 10-9**). These muscles act in concert to steer or rotate the proximal humerus.

The *supraspinatus muscle* arises from the supraspinatus fossa along the superior scapula and inserts on the lateral greater tuberosity of the humerus. It helps initiate glenohumeral abduction in the scapular plane, contributes to forward elevation, compresses the humeral head into the glenoid to enhance stability of the joint, and assists the subscapularis and infraspinatus in resisting the superior shear force of the deltoid during early abduction. Because the supraspinatus tendon has a tenuous blood supply and must pass through a narrow outlet before reaching its insertion point, it is easily subject to attritional wear and rupture. Innervation is derived from the suprascapular nerve C5, with some innervation from C6. The suprascapular nerve is subject to compression as it enters the supraspinatus fossa through the suprascapular notch at the base of the coracoid process. Degenerative ganglion of the superior labrum may also compress the nerve as it travels to the supraspinatus muscle.

The *infraspinatus* is the second most active rotator cuff muscle. It originates from the infraspinatus fossa and inserts on the greater tuberosity of the humerus just posterior to the supraspinatus. Its primary action is to externally rotate the humeral head, and it provides approximately 60% of the external rotation torque of the shoulder. It also functions as a humeral head depressor. The infraspinatus buttresses the humeral head against a posterior subluxation force in internal rotation, while it resists anterior translation in the abducted, externally rotated position. The suprascapular nerve innervates the infraspinatus muscle. Denervation of this muscle may result if the nerve is compressed as it traverses the spinoglenoid notch.

The *teres minor muscle* arises from the lower posterior border of the scapula and inserts on the lower portion of the greater tuberosity, inferior to the infraspinatus tendon. Its inferior surface forms the roof of the quadrilateral space through which the axillary nerve and the posterior humeral circumflex artery pass. The space is further defined by the teres major muscle inferiorly, the long head of the triceps muscle medially, and the humeral shaft laterally. The teres minor produces approximately 40% of external rotation torque, and its eccentric contractions during the follow-through phase of the baseball pitch further stabilizes the GH joint and helps prevent anterior

shoulder muscles. The other muscles that form this layer are the trapezius and the pectoralis major. The anterior third of the deltoid originates from the lateral third of the clavicle, the middle third arises from the lateral acromion, and the posterior third originates from the posterior lateral scapular spine. The muscle continues inferiorly to a single insertion on the deltoid tubercle of the lateral humeral shaft. The innervation of the deltoid comes from the axillary nerve (C5, C6), which splits so that the posterior branch supplies the posterior one third of the muscle, while the other branch enters the deltoid along its deep surface and continues anteriorly to supply the anterior two

FOCUS ON . . .

Muscles

Upper extremity motion is described relative to the scapular plane. Abduction is movement of the upper extremity away from the body, and adduction is movement toward the body. Flexion is movement of the upper extremity anterior to the scapular plane, and extension is movement posterior to the scapular plane. Internal rotation is medial rotation of the upper extremity relative to the thorax, and external rotation is lateral rotation.

The scapulothoracic (periscapular) muscles are the trapezius, rhomboids, levator scapulae, serratus anterior, pectoralis minor, and subclavius. The trapezius is the largest and most superficial of these muscles. A primary scapular rotator, the trapezius elevates the lateral angle with its upper fibers. The rhomboids retract and secondarily elevate the scapula. The levator scapulae elevates the superior scapular angle and with the serratus anterior, elevates the scapula upward. The serratus anterior protracts and helps to elevate the scapula, mainly in forward flexion. Absent serratus activity (usually from paralysis) causes scapular winging and loss of strength with forward flexion. The pectoralis minor protracts the retracted scapula and depresses the upwardly rotated scapula, but has little effect on the resting scapula. It serves as a superficial surgical landmark of the underlying brachial plexus. The subclavius stabilizes the SC joint during intense activity.

The glenohumeral muscles are the deltoid, rotator cuff, teres major, and coracobrachialis. The deltoid is the largest and most important GH muscle and, with the trapezius and pectoralis major, forms the superficial shoulder muscles. Humeral elevation in the scapular plane is produced by the anterior and middle deltoid, with some contribution from the posterior third beyond 90° of elevation. The posterior third also contributes to extension.

The rotator cuff muscles include the supraspinatus, infraspinatus, teres minor, and subscapularis. The supraspinatus contributes to the initiation of GH abduction in the scapular plane and to forward elevation, compresses the humeral head into the glenoid to enhance stability, and assists in humeral head depression (with the subscapularis and infraspinatus) to resist superior shear deltoid force during early abduction. The infraspinatus is the next most active rotator cuff muscle and externally rotates the humeral head, providing 60% of the shoulder's external rotation torque, and depresses the humeral head. Depending on humeral head rotation, the infraspinatus buttresses the humeral head against posterior subluxation force in internal rotation while resisting anterior translation in abduction and external rotation. The teres minor produces 40% of external rotation torque and further stabilizes the GH joint by eccentrically contracting during follow-through of a baseball pitch to prevent anterior subluxation. The subscapularis is a strong internal rotator that also passively stabilizes the GH joint anteriorly. The inferior fibers assist in humeral head depression, while the superior fibers assist in elevation in external rotation. The teres major internally rotates, adducts, and extends the humerus. The coracobrachialis flexes and adducts the GH joint.

subluxation. The posterior branch of the axillary nerve (C5, C6) innervates the teres minor.

The *subscapularis muscle* originates on the anterior surface of the scapula and inserts on the lesser tuberosity of the humerus. It is a strong internal rotator that also acts as a passive anterior stabilizer of the GH joint. The lower fibers assist in humeral head depression during abduction, and the superior fibers assist in elevation in external rotation. The muscle is innervated by two nerves: the upper subscapular nerve (C5) in the superior portion, and the lower subscapular nerve (C5, C6) in the inferior portion.

The *teres major muscle* originates on the posteroinferior aspect of the lateral scapula, rotates 180°, and inserts on the humeral shaft. It internally rotates, adducts, and extends the humerus and is innervated by the lower subscapular nerve (C5, C6).

The *coracobrachialis* inserts with the short head of the biceps on the anterolateral aspect of the midhumerus as the conjoined tendon of the coracoid. It assists in flexion and adduction of the GH joint and is innervated by the musculocutaneous nerve (C5, C6). The nerve enters the muscle approximately 1.5 cm to 8 cm from the tip of the coracoid, which is a useful reference during surgery to avoid injury to this nerve.

Multiple-Joint Muscles

Several muscles cross two joints and provide motor power to both the GH joint and the other joint, usually the scapulothoracic articulation.

The pectoralis major muscle consists of three portions. The upper or clavicular portion arises from the medial two thirds of the clavicle and runs parallel to insert on the lateral lip of the bicipital groove of the humerus. The midportion arises from the *manubrium* (the upper two thirds of the body of the sternum) and the second through fourth ribs and runs parallel to insert directly posterior to the clavicular portion on the humerus. The inferior portion arises

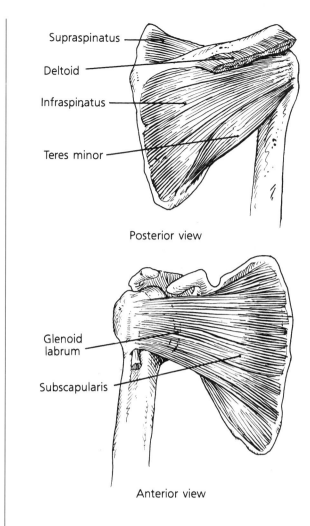

- Supraspinatus
- Deltoid
- Infraspinatus
- Teres minor

Posterior view

- Glenoid labrum
- Subscapularis

Anterior view

FIGURE 10-9

The rotator cuff is made up of the supraspinatus, infraspinatus, teres minor, and subscapularis muscles.

from the distal body of the sternum, the fifth and sixth ribs, and the external oblique abdominal fascia. The inferior portion rotates 180° to insert with the other two portions on the humerus. The action of the pectoralis major depends on its starting position; for example, the clavicular portion assists the anterior deltoid in flexion, and the lower portions antagonize this action. The pectoralis major is active in internal rotation against resistance and will extend the shoulder from a flexed position until the neutral position is achieved. It is also a powerful adductor of the GH joint and indirectly depresses the scapula laterally. The muscle is innervated by two sources: the lateral pectoral nerve (C5, C6, and C7) in the clavicular portion, and the medial pectoral nerve (C8, T1) in the mid- and inferior portions.

The latissimus dorsi originates near the large, broad aponeuroses from the dorsal spinous processes of T7 to L5 and the iliolumbar fascia. The muscle wraps around the

teres major and inserts on the medial crest and the floor of the bicipital groove. The latissimus dorsi adducts, internally rotates, and extends the arm and indirectly rotates the scapula inferiorly. The thoracodorsal nerve (C6 and C7) innervates the muscle.

The long head of the biceps brachii originates on the supraglenoid tubercle, and the short head arises lateral to and in common with the coracobrachialis. It inserts on the radial tuberosity laterally and via the lacertus fibrosis aponeurosis medially. At the elbow, the biceps brachii flexes and supinates the forearm; at the shoulder, it may contribute to humeral head depression in external rotation and resist external rotation torsion. The musculocutaneous nerve (C5, C6) supplies innervation.

The triceps brachii originates in the shoulder through the long head, which attaches to the infraglenoid tubercle. It inserts in an aponeurotic manner on the olecranon of the ulna. The long head of the triceps, unlike the long head of the biceps, is not intra-articular. However, fibers of its attachment blend with and reinforce the inferior glenoid labrum. Its main function at the shoulder is to stabilize the inferior glenoid, and at the elbow, the long head promotes elbow extension.

The Neurovascular Supply of the Shoulder Girdle

The primary blood supply of the upper extremity arises from the subclavian artery, which emerges from between the scalenus anterior and medius muscles and becomes the axillary artery as it courses over the outer border of the first

FOCUS ON . . .

Multiple-Joint Muscles

Muscles that cross two joints and provide motion to the GH and one other joint (often the scapulothoracic articulation) include the pectoralis major, latissimus dorsi, biceps brachii, and triceps brachii. The upper portions assist the anterior deltoid in flexion, and the lower portions antagonize this action. The pectoralis major is active in internal rotation against resistance and can extend the shoulder from flexion to neutral. It is a powerful GH joint adductor and also indirectly depresses the lateral scapula. The latissimus dorsi adducts, internally rotates, and extends the arm. It also indirectly rotates the scapula inferiorly. The biceps brachii flexes and supinates the forearm at the elbow and contributes to humeral head depression in external rotation and resists external rotation at the shoulder. The triceps brachii is not intra-articular, but its attachment fibers blend in and reinforce the inferior glenoid labrum.

FOCUS ON . . .

Static Stabilizers

The GH joint allows more motion than any other human joint, but at a cost of stability, making the shoulder the most frequently dislocated joint. Instability is associated with pain or instability symptoms, while laxity is not associated with symptoms.

Static stabilizers of the GH joint include the humerus, glenoid fossa, surface area and articular conformity, glenoid labrum, intra-articular pressure, GH ligaments and capsule, SGHL, coracohumeral ligament, MGHL, and IGHL. The proximal humerus articular surface is inclined superiorly, with neck shaft angles from 130° to 140°. Also, the humeral head is retroverted 30° relative to the elbow transepicondylar axis.

At rest, the scapula is oriented 30° to 45° anterior to the coronal plane, and the glenoid fossa is oriented 7° posterior to the scapula, usually with a 5° superior tilt. This tilt helps to control inferior humeral head translation.

The large humeral head and small glenoid articulating surfaces, while different in size, conform closely. Also, humeral head contact with the glenoid surface is relatively uniform throughout shoulder motion. The GH joint generally behaves as a ball-and-socket, with limited translation opposite to the plane of motion except at the extremes. Thus, anterior translation accompanies forward flexion, and posterior translation accompanies abduction and external rotation.

The glenoid labrum is a fibrocartilagenous anchor for the capsuloligamentous structures that increases both the socket depth (buttressing the humeral head against dislocation) and the surface area available for humeral head contact. The Bankart lesion, the most common pathology, occurs below the equator and is associated with tension loss in the MGHL and IGHL and resultant anterior instability.

Normally, the GH joint is a closed system of finite volume with a slightly negative intra-articular pressure. Distracting the normal GH joint pulls the articular surfaces apart, further decreasing the pressure and enhancing joint stability. Negative intra-articular pressure may also help to center the humeral head, particularly in neutral or early motion ranges with the arm at the side. Multidirectional instability (resulting in increased capsular volume) or a capsular (rotator interval) defect compromises stability.

Histologically, the GH ligaments are formed of collagen fiber bundles in several layers of different thicknesses and orientation. The SGHL is found in the rotator interval parallel to the coracohumeral ligament. The SGHL is a primary restraint to external rotation in adduction or slight abduction and to inferior translation in adduction and a secondary restraint to posterior translation in adduction, flexion, and internal rotation.

The coracohumeral ligament (CHL) is an extra-articular, dense, fibrous structure that originates from the lateral border of the coracoid process base and divides into a band that inserts into the greater tuberosity and tendinous anterior supraspinatus edge and another band that inserts on the lesser tuberosity and superior subscapularis border. The CHL is a primary restraint to inferior translation in adduction and external rotation and to posterior translation in adduction, forward flexion, and neutral to internal rotation.

The MGHL is a primary stabilizer to anterior translation in 45° of abduction and is important in limiting external rotation at 60° and abduction at 90°. It may be a secondary stabilizer for inferior translation in adduction.

The IGHL is a triangular structure of varying thickness with a superior band originating from the glenoid labrum between 2:00 and 4:00 and a posterior band (if present) originating from 7:00 to 9:00. The IGHL courses laterally to the humeral head between the subscapularis and triceps. The IGHL restrains anterior translation in external rotation and abduction while it restrains posterior translation in internal rotation. The superior band provides static restraint to anteroinferior translation in abduction and external rotation.

tion at 60° and 90° of abduction. The MGHL may be a secondary stabilizer for inferior translation in the adducted arm.[3]

The IGHL is a triangular structure of varying thickness that comprises the inferior shoulder capsule. The superior band originates from the glenoid labrum in the 2:00 to 4:00 positions and the posterior band, if present, from the 7:00 to 9:00 positions. The IGHL courses laterally to the humeral head between the subscapularis and the triceps. In the abducted shoulder, external rotation places the IGHL anteriorly to restrain anterior translation of the

humeral head. Correspondingly, internal rotation directs the IGHL posteriorly to restrain posterior translation of the humerus. The superior band of the IGHL is a significant static restraint to anteroinferior translation of the humeral head in the abducted and externally rotated humerus.

Dynamic Stabilizers

The muscles of the rotator cuff and the long head of the biceps muscle provide dynamic stability to the GH joint in a variety of ways.

Joint compression

Rotator cuff muscle contraction compresses the humeral head into the glenoid, so that a greater force is needed to translate the humeral head. Agonist-antagonist muscle pairs also act in concert to provide a joint compressive force without joint rotation. This arrangement of muscle force is called a *"force couple"* and is vital to GH joint stability. Rotator cuff activation and the resultant joint compression effect may be more important for stabilizing the GH joint than static capsular constraints. Individual components of the rotator cuff may play important roles in maintaining glenohumeral stability, particularly in the unstable shoulder. Electromyography reveals that throwing athletes with anterior instability have demonstrable weakness during internal rotation. Because older patients with recurrent dislocations often have ruptures of the subscapularis, the subscapularis may play a role in preventing anterior instability, particularly in the lower ranges of abduction, and the infraspinatus and teres minor may have similar effects on posterior instability.

Proprioception

Specialized nerve endings may provide the GH joint with proprioception, another component of dynamic stabilization. Individuals with clinical laxity have significantly less shoulder proprioception than individuals with no laxity. Additionally, proprioception is enhanced when the shoulder nears its limits of motion and during external rotation. Patients with known anterior instability have less proprioceptive ability than those with no instability; however, proprioception can be restored after surgical repair. Proprioception, through reflex or cortical mechanisms, may play an important role in GH stability, particularly in the abducted and externally rotated shoulder.

The biceps tendon

The long head of the biceps can increase joint compression, resulting in an increase in the force required to translate the humeral head. Sectioning the long head of the biceps tendon in the abducted externally rotated arm increases the strain on the IGHL. The stabilizing role of the biceps tendon seems to depend on the position of the arm. When the arm is internally rotated, tension on the biceps tendon decreases anterior humeral head translation. In contrast, when the arm is externally rotated, the biceps tendon limits posterior translation. The biceps tendon appears to have a greater impact on shoulder stability when the arm is in the lower and middle elevation angles. Like the supraspinatus, the biceps tendon restrains inferior translation.

The scapular rotators

The glenoid is a small platform that supports the humeral head. Its position relative to the humeral head and the forces that may create instability is critical. The scapular rotators connect the scapula to the torso and control the position of the scapula. They include the trapezius, rhom-

boids, latissimus dorsi, serratus anterior, and levator scapulae. Abnormal functioning of these muscles that results in altered scapulothoracic motion may be related to GH instability. Scapular winging has been noted in patients with anterior instability. Alteration in scapulothoracic motion is a factor in rotator cuff disease and anterior glenohumeral instability.[5]

Relative Importance of the Various Components of Glenohumeral Stability

Many components contribute to GH stability. Nevertheless, the position of the arm is critical in determining the relative importance of various factors. When the arm is in a neutral position, intra-articular pressure and muscles play a major role. In the midrange of motion, the role of the rotator cuff increases, and in extremes of motion, the glenohumeral ligaments become important.

THE THROWING MECHANISM

The athlete in a sport that involves overhead throwing presents a challenge to the athletic trainer. Any overhead throwing act, such as hitting a tennis ball, pitching a baseball, or throwing the javelin, is a very complex activity with a velocity of up to 7000° per second. The act of throwing places great stress on the anterior and posterior structures of the shoulder, frequently resulting in overuse injuries. The complex mechanics of overhead throwing may be illustrated by considering the five phases involved in throwing a baseball (**Figure 10-11**).

- The wind-up phase initiates the rhythm and coordination of the throwing act.

- The pitcher begins wind-up from either a full position or a stretch position to generate the force necessary to propel the ball toward the plate.

- The cocking phase, which can be further divided into early and late phases, begins when the ball and glove separate and ends when the shoulder is at the extreme of external rotation. At this point, the pitcher's hips are rotated, and the lower extremities begin to rotate forward as the body starts to move forward. A synchronized chain of movements, beginning with the lower extremities and progressing to the upper extremities, occurs during this phase. The rotator cuff and deltoid muscles bring the arm into an externally rotated, abducted position. As a general rule, the shoulder is positioned at approximately 90° of abduction, with as much as 135° to 165° of external rotation, and 15° of horizontal abduction. The angle at the shoulder stays the same, whether the pitcher throws from an overhead position, three-quarters position, or side-arm position. It is the lean of the body that determines the type of delivery.

- In the acceleration phase, the anterior muscles horizontally adduct and internally rotate the humerus, as does the momentum of the derotation of the rest of the body, and the arm is brought forward for ball release. The rotator cuff is relatively inactive during this stage; angular momentum and the triceps extend the elbow from 90° to about 30°.

- Ball release occurs in just a few milliseconds; at this point, the hand is moving as fast as the ball is.

- Follow-through occurs once the ball is released. The rapid deceleration by the rotator cuff muscles stops horizontal adduction and internal rotation of the humerus and stabilizes the humerus in the glenoid. Concurrently, the biceps brachii muscle stops elbow extension by pulling anteriorly across the shoulder. This eccentric maneuver places the rotator cuff under great strain.

Other sports that involve overhead movements, such as throwing a football, serving a tennis ball, or making overhead racquetball shots, involve variations of these five basic phases. The motions have different mechanics but can be

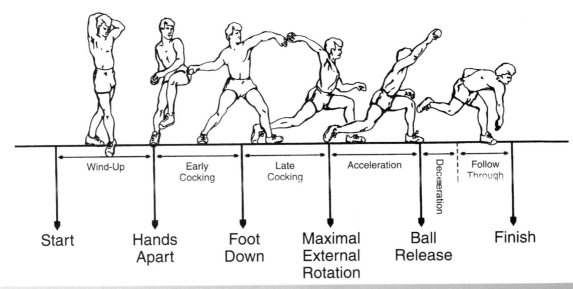

Wind-Up | Early Cocking | Late Cocking | Acceleration | Deceleration | Follow Through

Start | Hands Apart | Foot Down | Maximal External Rotation | Ball Release | Finish

FIGURE 10-11

The phases of the baseball pitch include wind-up, cocking, acceleration, ball release, and follow-through. (Reproduced with permission from DiGiovine NM, Jobe FW, Pink M, et al: An electromyographic analysis of the upper extremity in pitching. *J Shoulder Elbow Surg.* 1992;1:15–25.)

FOCUS ON . . .

The Throwing Mechanism

Throwing comprises five phases. Wind-up initiates the rhythm and coordination as the pitcher generates the necessary force to propel the ball toward the plate. Cocking begins when the ball and glove separate and ends when the shoulder is in extreme external rotation. The hips are rotated, and the lower extremities are beginning to rotate forward as the body moves forward. In acceleration, the anterior muscles horizontally adduct and internally rotate the humerus, as does the derotation momentum of the body as the arm comes forward for ball release. At ball release, the hand is moving as fast as the ball. Follow-through begins once the ball is released.

analyzed from this example. In the crawl stroke in swimming, for example, the humerus abducts above neutral, and irritation to the rotator cuff from impingement can occur if the muscles are not strong enough to hold the humeral head firmly in the glenoid fossa. In tennis, impingement can occur when the player abducts the humerus greater than 90° during a serve or with overhead strokes.

MECHANISMS OF INJURY

Shoulder injuries can be caused by acute trauma or by movements repeated over time.

Acute Trauma from a Direct Force

Strictly differentiating between direct and indirect forces in a specific injury may be difficult; however, it is informative about the mechanism of injury. For example, AC joint dislocations classically result from falling directly onto the point of the acromion. The force of the fall drives the clavicle upward and disrupts the stabilizing ligament of this joint. A posterior GH joint dislocation is more likely to result from a direct blow to the anterior aspect of the shoulder when the arm is held in internal rotation; the humeral head is forced back out of its shallow glenoid. Direct blows can also cause fractures of the scapular body and the clavicle.

Acute Trauma from an Indirect Force

Indirect forces are classically involved in the anterior shoulder dislocation. The humeral head is levered anteriorly as the arm is brought into extremes of abduction, extension, and external rotation. This injury may occur during an arm tackle in football. Another example of indirect injury to the shoulder is a fall on the outstretched hand, which can result in a fracture of the humeral head or a superior labral tear.

Chronic Overload by Repetitive Movements

Any injury caused by repetitive submaximal stress that surpasses the tissue's natural repair processes is termed an *overuse injury*. For example, repetitive abduction and internal rotation of the humerus can result in impingement syndrome, causing swelling and scarring in the rotator cuff and the subacromial bursa. Once swollen, this thickened, edematous tissue can be further impinged under the anterior rim of the acromion and the coracoacromial ligament. Such repetitive trauma may eventually lead to actual tears in the cuff. Internal impingement is another example of an overuse injury resulting from subtle anterior instability in the overhead athlete.

INITIAL ASSESSMENT AND MANAGEMENT OF SHOULDER INJURY

An assessment of the shoulder should take place immediately following injury. Because cervical spine injuries often present with distal neurologic deficits and can confuse the clinical picture, the athletic trainer must evaluate and eliminate cervical spine trauma before moving the injured athlete or removing a helmet or shoulder pads. After obtaining a brief history of the mechanism of injury, the athletic trainer should conduct a vascular assessment of the upper extremity before removing any of the athlete's clothing or protective equipment. The athletic trainer should palpate and assess both radial and ulnar arterial pulses and conduct a sensory examination of the entire upper extremity, especially in obvious GH dislocations. Next, the athletic trainer should assess motor function. If there is any evidence of neurovascular compromise of the

FOCUS ON . . .

Shoulder Injury

Shoulder injuries can result from acute trauma or repetitive movements. Acute trauma from direct force can produce AC joint dislocations, posterior GH joint dislocations, and scapular body and clavicular fractures. Acute trauma from indirect force can cause anterior shoulder dislocations, humeral head fractures, superior labral tears. Chronic overload from repetitive movements can result in impingement.

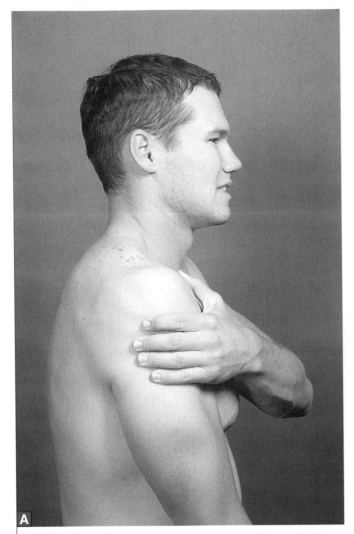

FIGURE 10-12

Pathology in organ systems may mimic shoulder girdle symptoms. A. True shoulder pathology appears as referred pain in the deltoid. B. Cervical disk disease pain radiates from the trapezius down into the shoulder.

upper extremity, the athlete should be transported immediately to a medical facility. If the athlete is neurovascularly intact, the athlete's clothing and protective equipment can be removed, and the athletic trainer can perform a more thorough neurovascular examination.

After assessing neurovascular status, the athletic trainer should examine the shoulder area for any obvious deformity, lacerations, abrasions, hemorrhage, or swelling that would indicate damage to underlying structures. The athletic trainer then palpates the area of injury to determine the location of tenderness and the presence of any obvious bony deformity that might indicate fracture or dislocation. If possible, the athletic trainer should measure passive range of motion by trying to move the shoulder through a complete range of motion. If the athlete has full passive range of motion, the athletic trainer should then assess active range

---

FOCUS ON . . .

Initial Assessment and Management

Shoulder assessment begins immediately after injury, once cervical spine injury has been ruled out. A brief history of the mechanism of injury should be obtained and a cursory upper extremity vascular examination performed before the protective equipment and clothing in the area are removed. The radial and ulnar arterial pulses should be checked and a sensory examination of the extremity conducted, followed by a motor examination. If neurovascular compromise is evident, the athlete should be transported immediately to a medical facility. If the athlete is neurovascularly intact, the athlete's protective equipment and clothing should be removed and a more thorough neurovascular examination performed.

The athletic trainer should observe the shoulder for obvious deformity, lacerations, abrasions, hemorrhage, or swelling, which can indicate underlying damaged structures. The injured area should be palpated to determine the location of tenderness and the presence of obvious bony deformity, and, if possible, the shoulder should be moved passively through a complete range of motion before the athlete is asked to move the shoulder actively through the complete range. Painful limitations of motion should be documented. If pain is significant, the shoulder should be immobilized in a sling and swathe for protection pending a more thorough evaluation and ice applied to decrease pain and swelling.

of motion by having the athlete move the shoulder through its entire range. Painful limitations of motion should be documented. If the athlete experiences significant pain, the athletic trainer should immobilize the shoulder in a sling and swathe for protection until a more thorough evaluation can be performed off the field. Ice applied to the injured area can help decrease pain and swelling.

EVALUATION OF A PAINFUL SHOULDER

Often an athlete complains of shoulder pain of variable duration. Chronic complaints often present differently from an acute traumatic episode. Steps in the evaluation include taking a history, inspecting the shoulder, palpating the painful area, assessing both active and passive range of motion and strength, and conducting provocative tests.

During evaluation of an injured shoulder, the athletic trainer must remember that pathology in other organ systems may mimic shoulder girdle symptoms. Cardiac abnormalities may present with left shoulder pain. Pain from cervical disk disease with radiculopathy and cervical osteoarthritis is frequently referred to the posterior shoulder, primarily the trapezius muscle. Unlike primary shoulder pain, which emanates primarily from the shoulder, the pain of cervical disk disease will radiate from the trapezius down into the shoulder (**Figure 10-12**). A stretched brachial plexus nerve in the thoracic outlet can also present as shoulder pain.

Apical lesions in the lung can present as either anterior or posterior shoulder pain, with pain that typically worsens with time, despite conservative care. The athletic trainer should suspect pulmonary lesions if the athlete feels pain deep within the shoulder and the painful area cannot easily be palpated or reproduced on examination of the athlete's shoulder.

Visceral abdominal injuries, such as injuries of the spleen and gallbladder, can result in shoulder pain, but these intra-abdominal problems more typically generate reports of pain in the posterior thoracic region.

History

A detailed history should include the onset of symptoms, the relationship of symptoms to sport performance and activities of daily living, and any prior injury or shoulder pain. The athletic trainer should ask for the location of pain, whether the location varies with the time of day or the activity, and a description of the pain. For example, the athletic trainer should find out whether the pain is throbbing, aching, sharp, stabbing, or burning and note the duration of symptoms. He or she should also determine whether the symptoms have progressed over time, whether there are associated symptoms such as tingling,

weakness, snapping, radiation, or catching, and what factors aggravate or relieve the pain.

Inspection for Deformity

When inspecting the shoulder, the athletic trainer should examine the relationship of the acromion to the clavicle at the AC joint and determine whether there is any separation, scapular winging from a long thoracic nerve palsy, or atrophy of the deltoid, supraspinatus, or infraspinatus muscles.

Palpation

The athletic trainer should palpate the shoulder systematically, noting any deformity or painful points. The examination generally begins at the SC joint and proceeds laterally. Both the AC joint and GH joint should be palpated, assessed for laxity, and put through a range of motion. Any clicks, such as might occur with abduction (external rotation of the shoulder as the humeral head rolls over an irregular glenoid rim) should be noted. The athletic trainer can frequently locate the point of maximal tenderness during this phase of the examination. The biceps tendon should be palpated for congruity and for localized tenderness. Palpating the clavicle can reveal any irregularities that are secondary to an old fracture.

Assessing Range of Motion

Both active and passive range of motion (ROM) should be noted, as well as the coordination of motion. Forward elevation, abduction, and extension should be assessed. External rotation at 0° and 90° of abduction, internal rotation (thumb to highest vertebral spinous process), and internal rotation at 90° of abduction should also be noted. The athletic trainer can observe scapulohumeral rhythm by standing behind the patient. Normally, the GH joint moves primarily in the first 30° in a 4:1 ratio with the scapulothoracic joint. This ratio decreases to a 2:1 GH to scapulothoracic joint movement ratio overall during the full arc of motion.[6] Various conditions can alter the contributions of the scapulothoracic and GH joint to overall shoulder motion. For example, a rotator cuff tear may decrease the GH component of scapulohumeral rhythm, and instability will typically increase the GH contribution to motion. In addition, the athletic trainer should test the strength of all the muscles about the athlete's shoulder.

Provocative Testing

The athletic trainer can use an array of provocative stress tests for assessing a painful shoulder in conjunction with the history and routine physical examination to further clarify an athlete's shoulder pathology. A routine examination will include several of these tests, although others are rarely used. ROM testing of the cervical spine and a complete neurologic assessment

FOCUS ON . . .

Evaluation

Evaluation of a painful shoulder includes taking the history, inspecting for deformity, palpating, assessing range of motion and strength, and conducting provocative tests.

A detailed history of symptom onset, relationship of symptoms to sport activity and activities of daily living, and any history of prior injury or shoulder pain should be obtained. The athletic trainer should ask how long the symptoms last, whether they have progressed or are associated with tingling, weakness, snapping, radiation, or catching, the location and nature of the pain, and whether the location varies with the time of day or activity. The athletic trainer should also find out what factors worsen or improve the pain.

Next, the athletic trainer should inspect for deformity to find out whether there is any separation between the acromion and the clavicle at the AC joint, scapular winging, or deltoid, supraspinatus, or infraspinatus muscle atrophy.

The shoulder should be palpated systematically and any deformity or tenderness noted. The examination begins with the SC joint and proceeds laterally to the AC and GH joints. The clavicle can be palpated for irregularities secondary to an old fracture and the AC and GH joints assessed for laxity and range of motion. Any clicks should be documented. The biceps tendon should be palpated for congruity and localized tenderness.

Both passive and active range of motion and the coordination of that motion should be assessed, including forward elevation, abduction, extension, external rotation at 0° and 90° of abduction and internal rotation, and internal rotation at 90°. Scapulothoracic rhythm shoud be observed by standing behind the patient.

Provocative tests can help to elucidate shoulder pathology. The athletic trainer must recognize that laxity is not synonymous with instability. Instability is excessive laxity accompanied by pain or feelings of instability. An accurate and successful instability examination requires patient cooperation and comfort. The athlete should be comfortably attired to allow access to both shoulders while maintaining modesty. Movements should be slow, deliberate, and explained to the patient to prevent reflex muscular contractions that may mask instability. If the shoulder is too painful or the athlete too apprehensive to comply, examination under anesthesia may be needed.

Glenohumeral instability tests include the load-and-shift test, apprehension test, relocation test, posterior apprehension test, and sulcus sign. The load-and-shift test demonstrates translation of the humeral head, the apprehension test determines glenohumeral stability, and the relocation test is a companion to the apprehension test. The posterior apprehension test produces a positive result if the humeral head subluxates or dislocates or the athlete reports apprehension or pain. Often, a clunk can be felt if the shoulder is unstable. The sulcus sign test determines if the shoulder has inferior laxity.

Impingement tests can be performed in patients with instability to detect associated rotator cuff tendinopathy. Impingement tests include the Neer impingement test and the Hawkins test.

To test for disease in the AC joint, cross-body adduction can be performed. An athlete with AC joint disease will have focal pain with direct compression of the AC joint. This test can also be positive in the presence of cuff, labral, biceps, or capsular pathology.

The Yergason test evaluates biceps tendon stability. The Speed test also evaluates the long head of the biceps tendon. The Popeye sign indicates rupture of the long head of the biceps. The clunk and O'Brien tests are performed to test the superior labrum.

---

should be performed on all patients who have shoulder symptoms.[7]

Glenohumeral Instability Tests

Before testing for GH instability, the athletic trainer must recognize that GH laxity is not the same as GH instability.[8] Athletes with either congenital or acquired joint laxity do not necessarily have unstable joints. *Glenohumeral instability* is defined as excessive shoulder laxity accompanied by pain or feelings of instability. An accurate and successful instability examination also requires that the patient be both cooperative and comfortable. Clothing should allow access to both shoulders while allowing the patient to maintain modesty. Movements should be slow and deliberate, and the athletic trainer should explain the movements to the patient to avoid reflex muscular contractions that will mask any sense of instability. If the athlete is in too much pain or too apprehensive to follow the athletic trainer's instructions, adjuvant testing and/or examination under anesthesia may be necessary. Because shoulder instability may be a manifestation of generalized ligamentous laxity, the athletic trainer should examine the athlete for generalized ligamentous laxity. If the athlete can meet three of the four following criteria, the athletic trainer can conclude that there is generalized ligamentous laxity:

1. Thumb abduction to touch the volar forearm with the wrist flexed
2. Hyperextension of the little finger metacarpophalangeal joint beyond 90°
3. Elbow hyperextension beyond 10°
4. Knee hyperextension beyond 10°

Athletes in this category generally do not respond as favorably to surgical intervention as do athletes with traumatic instability and may benefit more from rehabilitation. In testing for laxity, the athletic trainer should always test both shoulders and compare the results of the injured shoulder with those of the contralateral asymptomatic shoulder.

Anterior and posterior instability in the GH joint may be assessed by various methods. **Table 10-1** presents the system used to grade instability in the GH joint. Results obtained must be compared with the contralateral asymptomatic shoulder.

The load and shift test demonstrates translation of the humeral head (**Figure 10-13**). Before beginning the test, the athletic trainer must ensure that the humeral head is located in the glenoid cavity and not translated anteriorly, posteriorly, or inferiorly. To achieve a stable, reduced starting position, the athletic trainer grasps and "loads" the abducted arm, neutrally rotated with the elbow flexed, then applies a translational force to the proximal humerus and attempts to ride the humeral head out of the glenoid socket. Using the instability criteria provided in Table 10-1, the athletic trainer applies a stability grading to the shoulder. If the GH ligaments are competent, rotating the arm to

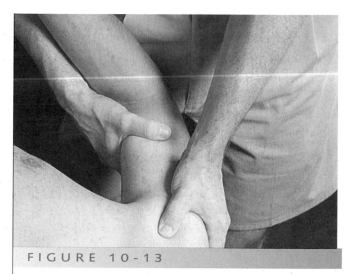

FIGURE 10-13

Translation of the humeral head is demonstrated by the load and shift test.

tighten them (external rotation tenses the anterior IGHL) may lessen the magnitude of translation.

The apprehension test is used to determine glenohumeral instability (**Figure 10-14**). This test is highly specific when apprehension as well as pain are presenting symptoms.[9] Generally, the athlete with anterior shoulder laxity will become apprehensive and resist further attempts at rotation when the shoulder is abducted, extended, and externally rotated. This apprehension is generally exacerbated when the athletic trainer places an anteriorly directed force on the posterior proximal humerus. The test can be performed with the athlete supine or upright and must be performed slowly and deliberately so that the athletic trainer does

TABLE 10-1
GRADED ANTERIOR AND POSTERIOR GH JOINT INSTABILITY

Grade 0	No evidence of glenohumeral translation.
Grade 1+	Subluxation is less than 50% of the humeral head diameter. A clinical appreciation of laxity is noted but without an accompanying clunk.
Grade 2+	Dislocation with spontaneous reduction. The athletic trainer can transiently dislocate the humeral head over the glenoid rim and can feel an associated clunk as the humeral head dislocates over the glenoid rim. The humeral head spontaneously reduces when the deforming translational force is removed.
Grade 3+	Frank dislocation of the joint. As with grade 2+ laxity, the humeral head rides over the glenoid rim and dislocates; however, it does not spontaneously reduce when the translating force is removed. The patient will rarely be relaxed enough for the athletic trainer to successfully evaluate grade 3+ laxity.

FIGURE 10-14

Glenohumeral instability is determined by the apprehension test.

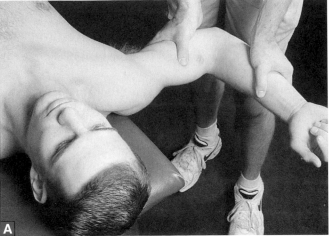

A

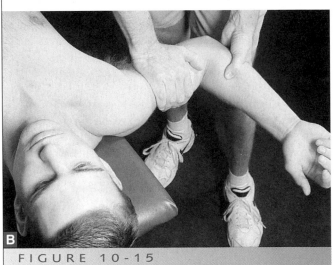

B

FIGURE 10-15

The apprehension and relocation tests are companion tests that determine anterior instability. **A** Apprehension test. **B** Relocation test.

not inadvertently dislocate the shoulder. This maneuver mimics the position of anterior dislocation and causes reflexive guarding by the athlete.

The relocation test is a companion test to the apprehension test and is performed with the patient supine (**Figure 10-15**). The athletic trainer applies a posterior translational force to the anterior proximal humerus at the point of external rotation when the athlete feels apprehensive. The test result is positive if this maneuver relieves the apprehension symptoms. The athletic trainer may continue passive external rotation of the arm while maintaining the posterior translation force until apprehension symptoms recur. Test results may be positive in patients with posterior rotator cuff tendinitis, and the athletic trainer must be careful not to falsely interpret findings of pain relief alone for findings of instability.

A posterior apprehension test is performed with the patient supine and the arm in 90° of forward flexion. The athletic trainer internally rotates the arm while applying a posteriorly directed force. With a positive result, the athletic trainer may feel the humeral head subluxate or dislocate, or the patient will complain of apprehension or pain during this maneuver. Often, the athletic trainer will feel a clunk such as is felt in anterior instability. If the loaded arm is slowly extended and abducted at about 30° to 45°, the humeral head will reduce itself and produce a definitive clunk.

The sulcus sign test can determine if there is inferior laxity. The athlete sits with the involved arm at the side in neutral rotation, and the athletic trainer applies an inferior distraction force along the humerus. If there is laxity, dimpling may occur over the subacromial space as the humeral head is translocated inferiorly. The distance between the lateral humeral head and the acromion is measured and a laxity grade of from 0 to 3+ is assessed. A

grade of 0 represents no pathologic increase in humeral translation and demonstrates less than 1 cm of inferior glenohumeral translation. Grade 1+ represents less than 1 cm of inferior laxity; a grade 2+ sulcus has between 1 cm and 2 cm of inferior glenohumeral translation; and a grade 3+ sulcus has more than 2 cm of inferior laxity. Grade 3+ is believed to be pathognomonic for multidirectional instability.[10] Instability in this position is typically related to a rotator interval defect or SGHL laxity. The IGHL complex stability is tested by looking for an inferior sulcus with the arm in 90° of abduction. The amount of laxity can be physiologic and should be compared with the contralateral uninvolved shoulder and correlated to the patient's symptom complex.

Impingement tests

Impingement tests to detect associated rotator cuff tendinopathy may be performed even in patients who exhibit joint instability. In the Neer impingement test, the athletic trainer places one hand on the posterior aspect of the scapula to stabilize the shoulder girdle, and, with the other hand, takes the patient's internally rotated arm by the wrist, and places it in full forward flexion (**Figure 10-16**). If there is impingement, the patient will report pain in the range of 70° to 120° of forward flexion as the rotator cuff comes into contact with the rigid coracoacromial arch.[11] For the Hawkins test, the athletic trainer places the athlete's arm in 90° of forward flexion and forcefully internally rotates the arm, bringing the greater tuberosity in contact with the lateral acromion (**Figure 10-17**). A positive test result is indicated if pain is reproduced during the forced internal rotation of the arm in the provocative position. Often, an injection of the subacromial bursa (impingement test) can be both diagnostic and therapeutic in these patients when the injection is a mixture of cortisone and lidocaine. A patient with bursitis often will demonstrate greater strength and/or increased active motion. A negative

impingement test result will elicit no pain relief or pain relief without an impingement in manual strength testing or active abduction.

Acromioclavicular joint

To test for disease in the AC joint, the athletic trainer should conduct the cross-body adduction test by asking the athlete to abduct the arm 90° and internally rotate it. The athletic trainer then brings the athlete's arm across the body in adduction toward the opposite shoulder (**Figure 10-18**). This test theoretically compresses the AC joint, causing pain in the athlete who has AC joint disease. Unfortunately, this maneuver also elicits complaints about the rotator cuff, labral, biceps, and capsule. The most accurate way to assess AC joint pathology is to directly compress the joint to elicit focal

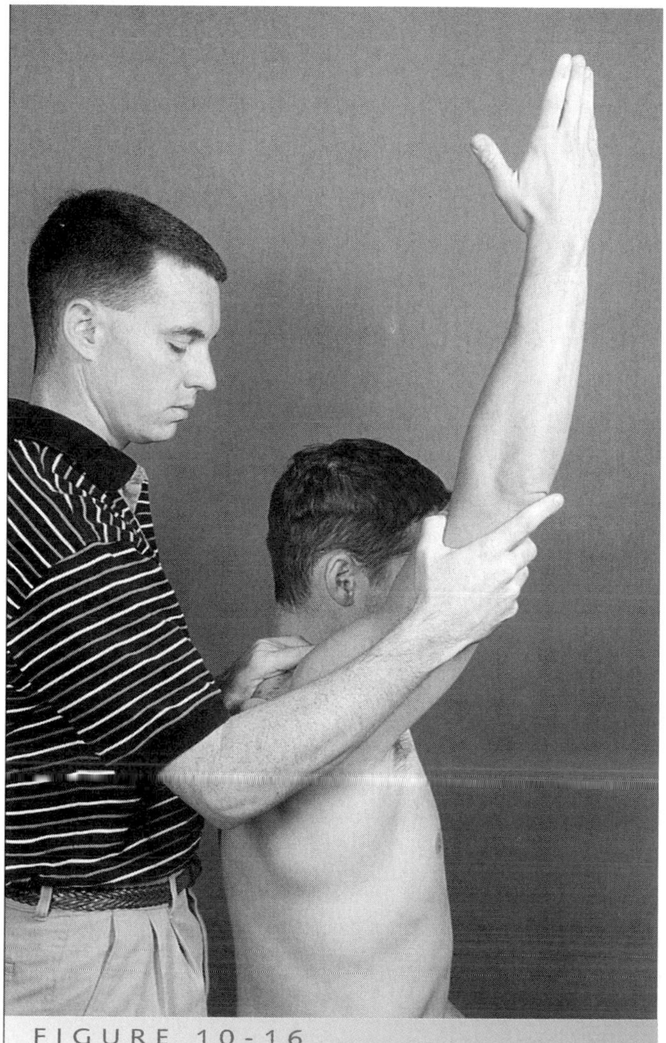

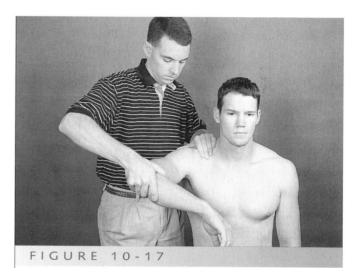

FIGURE 10-17

The Hawkins test determines whether impingement has occurred.

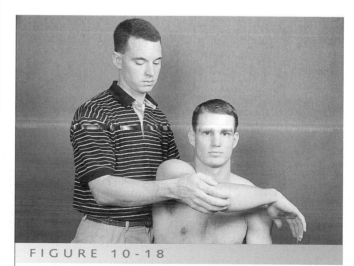

FIGURE 10-18

Disease in the acromioclavicular joint can be determined by the cross-body adduction test.

FIGURE 10-16

The patient will report pain in 70° to 120° range of forward flexion during the Neer test.

pain. Pain can be relieved with a plain lidocaine injection, if necessary.

Biceps tendon

The Yergason test is used to evaluate biceps tendon stability and is performed with the athlete standing or sitting. The elbow is flexed to 90°, and the forearm is pronated. While the athletic trainer holds the athlete's wrist, the athlete actively supinates the forearm against the athletic trainer's resistance. If this maneuver produces pain localized to the bicipital groove, disease in the long head of the biceps tendon is possible.

The Speed test also evaluates the long head of the biceps tendon. The athlete extends the arm in the frontal plane (**Figure 10-19**). The athletic trainer places an inferiorly directed force on the athlete's wrist while the athlete attempts to forward flex the arm. With a positive test result, pain will be elicited in the bicipital groove.

The classic appearance of rupture of the long tendon of the biceps is distal migration of the biceps muscle belly, creating a bulbous appearance distally, called the Popeye sign.

Superior labrum

The clunk test is used to determine glenoid labrum tears. The athlete lies supine, and the athletic trainer places one hand on the anterior surface of the GH joint. With the other hand exerting gentle pressure at the elbow, the athletic trainer externally rotates and abducts the athlete's arm 160°. The athletic trainer can rotate the arm internally and externally in the abducted position. As the arm is put through this range of motion, the athletic trainer may occasionally feel the humeral head clicking, popping, or clunking over an irritated glenoid. This test can be compared with the Apley compression test of the knee to elucidate meniscal pathology.

In the O'Brien test, superior labral pathology is examined as the athlete tries to elevate the extended, pronated arm from a starting position of 90° forward flexion and 20° to 30° of adduction against resistance[12] (**Figure 10-20**). Resisted flexion, adduction, and internal rotation will cause more pronounced symptoms. The

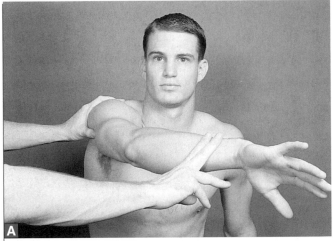

FIGURE 10-20

The O'Brien test examines superior labral pathology.
A Resisted flexion, adduction, and internal rotation of the extended arm cause more pronounced symptoms. **B** Labral symptoms decrease with the arm in external rotation.

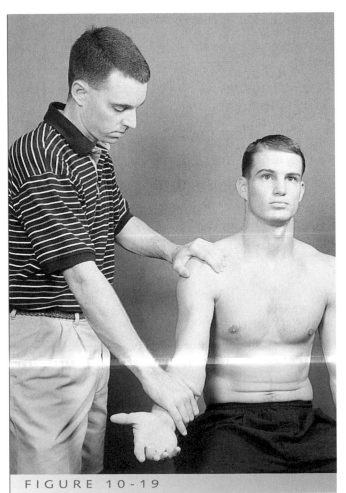

FIGURE 10-19

The Speed test evaluates the long head of the biceps tendon.

result is considered positive if symptoms are relieved with resisted forward elevation when the test is repeated with the arm supinated. Because any superior glenohumeral pathology may elicit symptoms, rotator cuff tendinitis and AC joint pathology must first be ruled out.

EVALUATION AND TREATMENT OF SPECIFIC INJURIES

When the upper extremity is subjected to abnormal forces, the resulting injuries may be to bone or soft tissue. The injury depends primarily on three elements: the direction, magnitude, and speed of the applied force. In general, the bony shoulder girdle has a rich blood supply that enables rapid healing, so bony injuries may heal even if there is some movement at the fracture site. Ligaments and tendons of the shoulder are not as well vascularized, and consequently, have a longer healing time.

Sternoclavicular Joint Injuries

In the skeletally mature athlete, an injury to the SC joint does not usually involve an associated fracture. The injury typically consists of a torn SC joint capsule and may range from a mildly symptomatic sprain to a complete SC dislocation with disruption of the entire anterior capsule and its restraining ligaments. A posterior SC joint dislocation may be a surgical emergency and requires a thorough examination of the trachea and vasculature.

Sternoclavicular joint sprain

A mild SC joint sprain represents a stable situation. Treatment involves the application of ice for the first 12 to 24 hours, followed by heat applications. A moderate sprain is typified by subluxation of the joint, and should also be treated with ice followed by heat. Figure-of-eight bandaging and a sling will help stabilize the joint. The shoulder should be protected for 4 to 6 weeks. Persistent popping and grinding may indicate the need for surgery.

Anterior sternoclavicular dislocation

The most common type of SC dislocation is anterior. This dislocation is easily recognized clinically by the anterior prominence of the proximal clavicle on the involved side. Radiographic documentation of an anterior SC joint dislocation is difficult, but the injury can be confirmed by special views. Computed tomography (CT) scanning helps evaluate almost all injuries at the SC joint, and both SC joints should be visualized. Although an anterior dislocation of the SC joint may initially cause considerable distress, the symptoms usually subside rapidly, with little or no loss of shoulder function. Because of the high complication rate of open procedures at the SC joint, closed reduction under intravenous sedation or general anesthesia may be necessary. If a stable reduction is achieved, figure-of-eight bandaging and a sling are used to immobilize the joint for 6 weeks, followed by 2 weeks of protection (limitation of motion, particularly abduction/extension motions, and avoiding contact). However, the reduction is usually unstable, and the joint should remain immobilized with bandaging and a sling until symptoms subside.

Posterior sternoclavicular dislocation

Although less common than anterior dislocation of the SC joint, posterior SC dislocation has a higher morbidity and can involve potential injury to the great vessels, the esophagus, and the trachea. Symptoms vary from mild to moderate pain in the SC joint region to hoarseness, difficulty swallowing, or severe respiratory distress. Subcutaneous emphysema from tracheal injury is possible. Special radiographic views or a CT scan is necessary to confirm the diagnosis. An aortagram may be combined with CT scanning to assess possible compromise to the great vessels.

Closed reduction of a posterior dislocation is successful and stable in most instances, particularly when performed early. As with any dislocation, a reduction attempt is the domain of medical professionals. To achieve reduction, the physician places a pillow under the upper back of the supine athlete and applies gentle traction with the shoulder held in 90° of abduction and in maximum extension. Occasionally, open reduction or surgical manipulation under general anesthesia is required.

Epiphyseal fracture of the clavicle

In athletes younger than age 25 years, SC injuries typically represent epiphyseal fractures rather than true joint dislocations. Clinically, medial clavicular epiphyseal fractures may appear as dislocations, especially if some displacement is present. Reduction of the fracture is not usually required unless the displacement is severe. Typically, these fractures are not associated with growth deformities and remodeling occurs readily. Treatment of symptoms such as pain, swelling, and limitation of motion until the athlete is pain free is all that is required.

Occasionally, a young athlete will report an enlarging mass at the SC joint several weeks after a fall. The mass is generally firm and may be slightly tender, depending on the length of time elapsed since the injury occurred. This mass is probably a healing callus of a clavicular epiphyseal fracture. Radiographs will confirm the diagnosis.

Clavicular fractures

Clavicular fractures that occur during sport participation rarely involve the underlying neurovasculature, despite the proximity of vital structures. Accompanying soft-tissue pathology is also rare. Midclavicular fractures occur most often, followed by distal clavicle fractures, then by proximal clavicle fractures. Most fractures of the shaft of the clavicle heal uneventfully.

Although a serious neurovascular complication, such as a tear of the subclavian artery or injury to the brachial plexus, is rare, the athletic trainer must

FOCUS ON . . .

Sternoclavicular Joint Injuries

Sternoclavicular injuries include SC joint sprain, anterior and posterior SC dislocation, and clavicular fracture. The skeletally mature athlete rarely fractures the SC joint but more often tears the SC joint capsule, which can result in an injury ranging from a mild sprain to a complete dislocation. A thorough cardiopulmonary examination should be performed in all athletes with suspected SC joint injury.

A mild (stable) SC joint sprain is treated with ice for 12 to 24 hours, followed by heat. A moderate sprain (subluxation) is also treated with ice followed by heat and a figure-of-eight bandage and sling for 4 to 6 weeks. Rarely, persistent popping and grinding require surgical management.

The anterior SC dislocation, the most common SC dislocation, is clinically apparent with the anterior prominence of the involved proximal clavicle. Radiographic documentation is difficult; special views and CT scans may be needed. Although distress can be considerable initially, symptoms usually subside rapidly, with little or no functional loss. If the joint does not spontaneously reduce, closed reduction under IV sedation or general anesthesia may be required. If a stable reduction is achieved, a figure-of-eight bandage and sling for 6 weeks, then 2 weeks of protection are recommended. If the reduction is unstable, the joint is immobilized until symptoms subside. Closed treatment is preferred because of the high complication rate of open SC joint procedures.

Posterior SC dislocation, although far less common, has a higher rate of complications from potential injury to the great vessels, esophagus, and trachea. Symptoms include mild to moderate SC joint pain, hoarseness, difficulty swallowing, severe respiratory distress, and subcutaneous emphysema. Special radiographic views, CT, or aortogram may be needed to confirm the diagnosis. Early closed reduction is usually successful and stable.

Athletes younger than age 25 years typically sustain clavicular epiphyseal fractures rather than true joint dislocations. Clinically, medial clavicular epiphyseal fractures may present as dislocations, especially if displaced. Growth deformities are rare and remodeling is likely. Fracture reduction is usually unnecessary unless displacement is severe, and treatment is symptomatic until the athlete is pain free. A young athlete who fell on the shoulder may report several weeks later a firm, slightly tender SC joint mass, which usually represents a healing callus. This can be confirmed with radiographs.

Clavicular fractures rarely involve the underlying neurovasculature or surrounding soft tissue. Midclavicular fractures are most frequent, followed by the distal clavicle, then the proximal clavicle. Most clavicular shaft fractures heal without incident. However, a careful neurovascular examination is important to rule out a neurovascular injury.

A fracture through the clavicle causes the shoulder to sag forward. The SCM pulls the proximal fragment superiorly. In the older child or adult, bone size and muscle development can hinder the reduction. Distal clavicular fractures, which are more common in older athletes, may be associated with coracoclavicular ligament tears.

Treatment of middle and proximal clavicular fractures is figure-of-eight strapping, tightened periodically to maintain shoulder position. The strap is a reminder to the athlete not to let the shoulder sag forward, but should not be so tight as to put significant pressure on the axilla. A sling may help to support the extremity in the first few days after injury. Distal clavicular fractures may be better reduced with a Kenny Howard splint to depress the clavicle. Factors preventing or delaying healing and precipitating a bony nonunion include inadequate immobilization, trauma severity, and fracture location. Once the fracture has healed, range-of-motion and strengthening exercises are instituted. Return to play should not be permitted until shoulder strength has normalized. Special braces or pads are usually not needed.

remember the potential for such an injury when evaluating and treating clavicular fractures. As with SC dislocations, a neurovascular examination during the initial evaluation is very important. Pulses in the distal part of the upper extremity, strength, and sensation should all be noted carefully.

Because the clavicle is a single, bony structure that fixes the shoulder girdle to the thorax, a fracture through it causes the shoulder to sag down and forward. The pull of the SCM muscle displaces the proximal fragment superi-

orly. In an older child or an adult, the size of the bone and the muscular development may make it difficult to achieve and maintain reduction. In addition, distal fractures of the clavicle, more common in older age groups, may involve tears of the coracoclavicular ligament.

Clavicular fractures are classified by their location and the possible involvement of the attached lateral coracoclavicular ligaments, as shown in **Table 10-2**.

Middle and proximal clavicular fractures in all age groups are usually treated with figure-of-eight strapping, which must be tight enough to maintain good shoulder position without putting significant pressure on the axilla (armpit). Athletes should understand that the strap is a reminder not to allow the shoulder to sag forward. During the first few days after injury, a sling on the affected side may also be used to support the extremity. In distal clavicular fractures, using an AC joint splint, such as the Kenny Howard splint, to depress the clavicle may achieve better reduction results. Factors that can prevent or delay healing and precipitate a bony nonunion include inadequate immobilization, severe trauma (disruption of the soft-tissue envelope), and location of the fracture.

After the clavicular fracture has healed, range-of-motion and strengthening exercises should be initiated, and the athlete should not be allowed to return to play until preinjury shoulder strength returns. Generally, no special braces or pads are used when the athlete returns to play.

Acromioclavicular Joint Injuries

Acromioclavicular separations or sprains vary in severity, depending on the extent of injury to the stabilizing ligaments and capsule. A type I injury results from a mild blow that produces a partial tear of the AC ligament. In a type II injury, the AC ligament is completely torn but the coracoclavicular (CC) ligament remains intact, and there may be subluxation or partial displacement. The subluxation is not always obvious on physical examination, but the diagnosis can be confirmed by a weighted shoulder radiograph, in which 10-lb weights are attached to both of the athlete's wrists, rather than held in the hands. When the force is severe enough to tear the CC ligament as well as the AC ligament and capsule, a type III injury occurs. The resulting joint displacement is often obvious on observation and can be confirmed by a shoulder radiograph.

The weighted shoulder radiograph uses weights attached to the athlete's wrists rather than held in the hands because the increased muscular effort required to hold the weights may mask the degree of separation. An anteroposterior (AP) radiograph of the entire upper thorax enables a comparison of the vertical distance between the coracoid and the clavicle on both the involved and uninvolved sides. An increase in this distance on the weighted radiograph compared with an "unweighted" radiograph indicates incompetence of the CC ligaments and categorizes the injury as a type III separation. By contrast, a type II injury typically will not show a widening of the coracoclavicular space because the CC ligaments are functionally intact and only minor stretching occurs. Three other

FOCUS ON . . .

Acromioclavicular Joint Injuries

Acromioclavicular joint separations or sprains vary in severity with the extent of injury to the stabilizing ligaments and capsule. A mild blow produces only a partial tear to the AC ligament and a first-degree injury. A torn AC ligament with an intact CC ligament produces a second-degree injury that involves subluxation or partial displacement. Force severe enough to tear the AC and CC ligaments and the capsule results in a third-degree injury with resulting joint displacement. More severe injury with posterior, superior, or inferior clavicular displacement is typically the result of a motor vehicle accident rather than sport.

The athlete with an AC joint injury leaves the field holding the arm close to the side. The mechanism of injury should be reviewed with the athlete to determine whether the fall was on the outstretched arm or (more often) on the lateral shoulder point. A direct superior acromial blow results in focal pain. When checking for AC joint laxity, the clavicle midshaft should be manipulated rather than the AC joint. A severe injury is often easier to detect than a mild injury. Athletes with type I injuries usually have focal AC joint pain on palpation, minimal pain with arm motion, and no pain on direct CC ligament palpation. Type II injuries are characterized by moderate to severe joint pain, mild distal clavicular prominence, an unstable clavicle, moderate pain with arm motion, increased anteroposterior motion on AC joint stress with midshaft clavicle manipulation, and moderate acute discomfort on CC ligament palpation. Grade III injuries present with shoulder depression, lateral clavicle elevation, the arm kept at the side with the elbow supported, pain with any shoulder motion at the AC joint and CC ligament interspace and along the superior quarter of the lateral clavicle, and a palpably unstable clavicle with manual inferior translation.

Treatment of first- and second-degree AC joint sprains initially is ice and a sling until pain subsides (usually 2 to 4 weeks), then a rehabilitation program to restore normal range of motion and strength. Treatment of third-degree sprains or complete dislocations can be surgical or nonsurgical. Ice and other modalities decrease initial soreness. Range-of-motion and strengthening exercises are gently and gradually instituted as pain permits. Return to play is allowed when range of motion is full and painless, tenderness is absent with direct AC joint palpation, and manual traction does not cause pain.

TABLE 10-2
CLASSIFICATION OF CLAVICULAR FRACTURES

Class	Location	Ligament Involvement
Group I	Middle one third of the clavicular shaft	Strong, underlying soft-tissue attachments secure both the proximal and distal segments. These are the most common fractures, relatively stable, and heal uneventfully.
Group II	Lateral one third of the clavicle	Cause the most problems; functionally similar to an AC joint separation. Further divided into subcategories: Types I, II (IIA, IIB), III
• Type I	Interligamentous fracture between the medial coracoclavicular and lateral coracoclavicular ligaments.	Minimally displaced fracture. Most common type, with a stable configuration. Ligaments prevent fracture displacement, rotation, or tilting.
• Type II	Medial to the coracoclavicular ligament	Prone to nonunion secondary to opposing forces at the fracture site
➤ Type IIA		Both medial and lateral coracoclavicular ligaments intact.
➤ Type IIB		Torn medial coracoclavicular ligament; intact lateral coracoclavicular ligament.
• Type III	Articular portion of distal clavicle	May be confused with a grade I AC joint sprain and can progress to AC joint arthritis.
Group III	Medial one third of the clavicle	Difficult to detect on radiographs because of overlapping adjacent ribs; may be misdiagnosed as SC joint dislocation in the skeletally immature athlete.

grades denote more severe injuries with either posterior, superior, or inferior clavicular displacement; however, these injuries occur more commonly in motor vehicle accidents.

An athlete with an AC joint injury will typically leave the field with the involved arm held close to the side. The athletic trainer should review the mechanism of injury with the athlete to determine whether the athlete fell on the outstretched arm or, more typically, on the lateral point of the shoulder. A direct blow to the superior acromion will demonstrate focal pain in the area, whether there is a sprain or just a contusion. When checking for laxity of the AC joint, the athletic trainer should manipulate the clavicle at midshaft rather than at the AC joint itself to avoid being confused by pain from a contusion to the area. Occasionally, there is an obvious deformity or easily detected motion at the AC joint that makes it easy to diagnose the injury.

The mild injury may be more difficult to diagnose. Athletes with type I injuries usually have focal AC joint pain on palpation, minimal pain with arm motion, and no pain on direct palpation of the CC ligaments, as noted by palpating the anterior region between the superior coracoid and the inferior midlateral clavicle. Type II injuries are notable for moderate to severe pain at the joint and a mild prominence of the distal clavicle. The clavicle may seem unstable and free floating on palpation. Moving the arm causes moderate pain, and the joint may exhibit increased anteroposterior motion when the midshaft of the clavicle is manipulated. Palpation of the CC ligaments may reveal moderate acute discomfort. Type III injuries represent a complete suspensory disruption of the CC ligaments and the AC joint capsule. The shoulder is typically depressed by the weight of the arm, and the lateral clavicle appears elevated when compared with the uninjured shoulder. The athlete will usually keep the arm at the side and support the elbow. Any shoulder motion, particularly abduction, exacerbates the pain, which is present at the AC joint, in the CC ligament interspace, and along the superior quarter of the lateral clavicle. The lateral clavicle is palpably unstable, and manual inferior translation has been described as similar to depressing a piano key.

Management of AC joint injuries depends on their severity. Type I and II sprains of the joint frequently can be successfully managed by applying ice initially and wearing a sling until discomfort dissipates, usually within 2 to 4 weeks. This is followed by a rehabilitation program to restore normal range of motion and strength to the upper extremity. An athlete should have full range of painless motion and no tenderness on direct palpation of the AC joint or pain when manual traction is applied to it before returning to play.

The treatment of type III sprains or complete dislocations can be surgical or conservative. Surgical repair of acute type III dislocations may be indicated for young, active individuals, for heavy overhead laborers, and for athletes who participate in noncontact sports that involve overhead movements. But type III sprains may also be treated nonsurgically, and many athletes can and do function well with complete dislocation of the AC joint. Surgery, when performed, is generally directed at reconstructing the CC ligaments and excising the distal clavicle. Nonsurgical treatment can be a sling for comfort or a Kenny Howard-type AC sling to try to achieve reduction of the dislocation. The athletic trainer or physician must carefully monitor the athlete to ensure that the pressure applied by the sling to the distal clavicle is sufficient to

afford reduction but not great enough to cause compromise of the skin. Ice and other modalities are used to decrease initial soreness in an acute AC joint injury. Pain initially limits the athlete's ability to perform range-of-motion and strengthening exercises, and progress is determined by the achievement of full active range of motion, a process that must be carried out gently and gradually. Isometric exercises can begin when range of motion is still limited, but isotonic strengthening exercises should not be initiated until full range of motion is achieved.

Before an athlete can return to play with a mild injury, he or she should have full range of painless motion and no tenderness on direct palpation of the AC joint or pain when manual traction is applied to the joint.

Rotator Cuff Impingement

Athletes who participate in overhead sports such as throwing, swimming, tennis, and volleyball subject their shoulders to significant repetitive stresses when the arm is in extremes of motion. These athletes are vulnerable to injury, and they present with a variety of problems, including subacromial bursitis, rotator cuff tendinitis, impingement, and possible rotator cuff tear. Repetitive overhead stress to the shoulder may cause cumulative microtraumatic injury to the rotator cuff and overlying bursa. In addition to microtrauma, isolated macrotrauma to the shoulder may result in an acute rotator cuff strain, rupture, or contusion. Shoulder complaints in the athlete are often best divided into two categories based on the athlete's age. In athletes younger than age 35 years, instability and impingement are intimately related and present as a spectrum of complaints such as internal impingement. Athletes older than age 35 years are subjected to more classic, primary outlet impingement.

Internal or glenoid impingement may be associated with subtle anterior instability in young athletes who participate in overhead activities.[13] Arthroscopic findings reveal a subacromial space that appears normal and does not fit with the traditional description of outlet impingement. Instead, there are intra-articular findings of injury to one or more of the following: the undersurface of the posterior rotator cuff (posterior supraspinatus and anterior infraspinatus tendon) (fraying), posterior superior labrum, and, occasionally, the anterior labrum. These findings may help explain the poor results of open and arthroscopic acromioplasties in these young athletes.[14]

Internal impingement occurs between the posterior superior labrum and the articular surface of the rotator cuff. The process of internal impingement begins with the extreme position of the abducted and externally rotated humerus that impacts the posterior superior labrum during the late cocking phase of throwing. This repetitive stress stretches the anterior capsuloligamentous restraints, resulting in mild anterior subluxation of the GH joint. In

FOCUS ON . . .

Rotator Cuff Impingement

Rotator cuff injuries can affect throwing, swimming, tennis, and volleyball athletes whose shoulders are repeatedly stressed at the extremes of motion. Overuse injuries include subacromial bursitis, rotator cuff tendinitis, impingement, and rotator cuff tear. Acute traumatic injuries can cause acute rotator cuff strain, rupture, or cuff contusion.

Overhead athletes younger than age 35 years tend to experience recurrent anterior instability and internal impingement. Arthroscopically, the subacromial space is normal, but the superior labrum, posterior rotator cuff tendon, greater tuberosity, inferior GH ligament or labrum, or superior glenoid rim may be damaged. Acromioplasties (whether open or arthroscopic) are associated with poor results in younger athletes.

The athlete with internal impingement often reports shoulder pain and decreased throwing velocity, but the associated instability may be so subtle that it is only detectable with a positive relocation test result and clinical suspicion. The diagnosis is confirmed by examination under anesthesia, positive drive-through sign on arthroscopy, normal subacromion, and intra-articular findings as described earlier. Treatment is to decrease inflammation and strengthen the rotator cuff and scapular stabilizers. Persistent symptoms require that the primary instability be addressed in addition to the intra-articular pathology. Subacromial depression alone is unlikely to be successful.

Individuals age 35 years and older have more classic primary outlet impingement with narrowing of the supraspinatus outlet or the space beneath the coracoacromial area. Rotator cuff and subacromial bursal compression by the coracoacromial arch usually is associated with AC arthritis, anterolateral acromial spurring, or acromial variations. Partial bursal surface tears or full-thickness rotator cuff tears and subacromial space fibrosis and adhesions are seen. The age-related degenerative processes affecting the rotator cuff may be an important causative factor.

Symptoms include pain with overhead activity, subacromial crepitance, loss of strength in elevation and external rotation at 90°, and night pain. The athletic trainer should palpate the AC joint to rule out AC joint arthritis and test the rotator cuff muscles for strength.

An anteroinferior subacromial spur on a 30° caudal tilt AP radiograph reflects primary impingement. The supraspinatus outlet view is useful in classifying acromial morphology and estimating coracoacromial arch narrowing. MRI scans may show acromial morphology and subacromial bursal inflammation and thickening, but is more useful in rotator cuff disease.

Treatment is to decrease inflammation and pain while maintaining range of motion. NSAIDs, occasional subacromial bursa corticosteroid injections, phonophoresis, and iontophoresis can be used. Pendulum and passive range-of-motion pulley exercises are instituted, avoiding any painful positions. Once motion is restored, supine stick exercises are initiated to facilitate a full, painless arc of motion. A tight posterior capsule may need stretching to limit nonoutlet impingement (anterosuperior humeral migration in the subacromial space during forward flexion when the posterior capsule is tight).

The second phase emphasizes progressive rotator cuff, deltoid, and scapular stabilizer strengthening. Capsular stretching in increasing abduction is performed as tolerated. The third phase begins when the patient has minimal to no symptoms, strength is near normal, and motion is full. The goal of unrestricted, symptom-free activity is accomplished with continued active range of motion and gradual progression to overhead and sport-specific activities. To avoid recurrent symptoms, some modification of activity may be necessary.

If the athlete continues to have painful limitation of motion after 3 to 6 months of rehabilitation, arthroscopic subacromial debridement and acromioplasty are recommended. Although these procedures can be done open with similar results, pain is less and return to throwing is earlier with the arthroscopic approach. After surgery, range of motion is achieved before strengthening is started.

an effort to compensate and stabilize the joint, the dynamic restraints (rotator cuff and scapular stabilizers) work harder. Muscular fatigue ensues, which intensifies the occult instability and internal impingement. The primary essential instability, which is often subtle and clinically silent, may progress to rotator cuff tendinitis or tearing, which has a more dramatic clinical appearance.

Thus, the instability complex in throwing athletes is a continuum from mild anterior subluxation to internal impingement to rare rotator cuff tendon tearing.

The athlete with internal impingement will often report shoulder pain and a decrease in throwing velocity. The associated instability is often so subtle that it is only detectable with a positive relocation maneuver and a clinical suspicion. The diagnosis is usually confirmed by an examination under anesthesia, an arthroscopic positive drive-through sign (the ability to "drive" the scope from the back "through" the glenohumeral joint to the anterior capsule), absence of subacromial abnormality, and intra-articular injury findings as previously described. Treatment aims to decrease inflammation and strengthen the rotator cuff and scapular stabilizer muscles. If symptoms persist, the primary lesion of instability should be addressed, and intra-articular pathology debrided. Subacromial decompression alone is unsuccessful in this patient population.

Posterior capsular contracture may exacerbate nonoutlet impingement, another form of impingement often seen in the throwing athlete. If the posterior capsule is tight or contracted, an obligate anterosuperior migration of the humeral head in the subacromial space can occur during forward flexion, resulting in impingement.[15]

Athletes older than age 35 years are subjected to more classic, primary outlet impingement, in which the supraspinatus outlet (the space beneath the coracoacromial area) narrows as a result of age-related degenerative processes, including thinning of tendons and decreased vascularity. Compression of the rotator cuff and subacromial bursa by the coracoacromial arch usually is related to acromioclavicular arthritis, anterolateral acromial spurring, or variations in the shape or slope of the acromion. Partial tears of the bursal surface or full-thickness tears of the rotator cuff, as well as fibrosis and adhesions in the subacromial space, can occur. Symptoms include pain with overhead activity, subacromial crepitance, and loss of strength in elevation and external rotation at 90°, often accompanied by night pain. Provocative test results, such as from the Neer and Hawkins tests, are positive. The AC joint should be palpated to rule out possible AC joint arthritis.

The athletic trainer should manually test the athlete's rotator cuff muscles for strength. The athletic trainer can test the infraspinatus/teres minor (posterior cuff) by having the athlete resist external rotation with the arm adducted against the trunk and the elbow flexed to 90°. Jobe's supraspinatus test tests for weakness specifically in the supraspinatus tendon (**Figure 10-21**). The athlete stands with arms extended at the elbows and abducted in the scapular plane and with thumbs pointed to the floor. In this position, the infraspinatus, subscapularis, and teres minor muscles are comparatively silent. The examiner applies downward pressure to the arms and the athlete attempts to resist.

The subscapularis should also be evaluated, using the Gerber modified lift-off test (**Figure 10-22**). Athletes with subscapularis tears have an increase in passive external rotation and a weakened ability to resist internal rotation. With the athlete's hand on the small of the back, the arm is extended and internally rotated. The athletic trainer then passively lifts the hand off the small of the back,

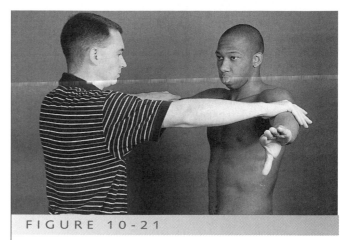

FIGURE 10-21

Supraspinatus tendon weakness is determined by Jobe's supraspinatus test.

placing the arm in maximal internal rotation, then releases it. If the hand falls onto the back because the subscapularis is unable to maintain internal rotation, the test result is positive.

The impingement test is an important confirmatory step in evaluating primary impingement and rotator cuff disease. A single injection of 10 mL of 1% plain lidocaine in the subacromial space will eliminate the pain of primary impingement and allow full, painless range of shoulder motion with restoration of strength. If the injection relieves pain, but with residual limited strength, a rotator cuff tear is generally indicated. The athletic trainer must assess both passive and active range of motion prior to, as well as after the injection. Impingement and isolated rotator cuff disease do not generally limit passive motion. Subacromial scarring and intracapsular and extracapsular contractures will limit passive motion after a successful impingement test and will need to be addressed before the athlete can resume activities.

Radiography

Primary impingement is correlated by plain film radiographs with the presence of an anteroinferior subacromial spur on the 30° caudal tilt AP radiograph. The supraspinatus outlet view can classify acromial morphology and estimate narrowing of the coracoacromial arch. Magnetic resonance images (MRI) may reveal acromial morphology and subacromial bursal inflammation and thickening, but are generally more useful in rotator cuff disease.

Treatment

Initial treatment of primary impingement aims to decrease inflammation and pain and to maintain range of motion. A number of adjunctive modalities may be used, including nonsteroidal anti-inflammatory drugs (NSAIDs), occasional corticosteroid injections into the subacromial bursa, phonophoresis, and iontophoresis. Pendulum exercises and passive range of motion pulley exercises that avoid any painful arcs (impingement positions) can also be used. When full range of motion is

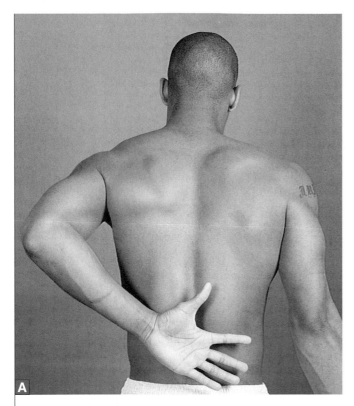

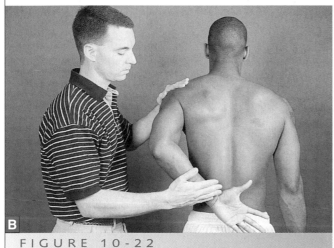

FIGURE 10-22

The Gerber modified lift-off test evaluates the subscapularis.
A The athlete places his or her hand on the small of the back. **B** The athletic trainer places the athlete's arm in maximal internal rotation.

restored, the athlete may progress to supine stick exercises to further facilitate a full painless arc of motion. Posterior capsular contracture may exacerbate another form of impingement, nonoutlet impingement, which is often seen in the throwing athlete. In nonoutlet impingement, the posterior capsule is often tight and may need to be stretched.

The second phase of rehabilitation is characterized by progressive strengthening of the rotator cuff, deltoid, and scapular stabilizers. Capsular stretching continues, with

increasing degrees of abduction as tolerated. Elastic tubing allows the patient to progress with increasing resistance exercises as tolerated. The patient should attempt five to 10 repetitions each of external rotation, extension, internal rotation, and flexion. Jobe's position of abduction (abduction of the scapular plane with the arm in internal rotation) should be avoided. Proximal integrity of the shoulder girdle is fundamental in the rehabilitation of a rotator cuff tear or impingement. Therefore, strengthening of the periscapular muscles (trapezius, serratus anterior, rhomboids, and levator scapulae) is essential for full recovery. Wall push-ups and shoulder shrugs with low weights are employed to isolate these muscles.

When symptoms are minimal or absent, strength approaches normal, and no restriction of motion exists, phase III may be initiated. The goal of phase III is unrestricted, symptom-free activity. Active range-of-motion exercises continue, gradually progressing to overhead activities and sport-specific exercises. Modification of sport may be necessary early to avoid a recurrence of symptoms.

If this protocol fails to return the athlete to preinjury level within 3 to 6 months, and a painful limitation of motion continues, surgical intervention is recommended. A shoulder arthroscopy may be performed to rule out any confounding intra-articular pathology. The subacromial space, including the bursa, is debrided and an acromioplasty is performed. An open approach to this procedure will yield similar long-term results. However, arthroscopic subacromial decompression yields a lower perioperative morbidity with less pain and an earlier return-to-throwing program at 6 to 8 weeks.[16] After any surgical procedure, the athlete should achieve full range of motion before beginning any strengthening exercises.

Rotator Cuff Tears

Rotator cuff tearing represents a continuum of pathology. A **rotator cuff tear** is described as acute or chronic and partial or full thickness and is further classified by estimated size. The cuff may be torn in a single traumatic event, as in the case of the contact athlete, or it may fail over a longer period of time and present in an insidious manner. Overhead athletes typically present with a partially torn, articular-sided rotator cuff, while older athletes may present with a full-thickness, chronic rotator cuff tear.

Acute rotator cuff rupture is typically seen in the contact athlete younger than age 40 years. These patients commonly recall a single traumatic event and present with shoulder pain, weakness, and a positive shrug sign (shrugging the shoulder with an attempted abduction of the arm). Rehabilitation should be attempted but is not often successful in this population; instead, arthroscopic evaluation and treatment is indicated, with a high rate of return to play expected. A small subset of patients may present with a similar clinical picture, but will have an intact cuff and a thickened, inflamed, and fibrotic subacromial bursa. Pathologically, a subacromial hemorrhage sec-

FOCUS ON . . .

Rotator Cuff Tears

Rotator cuff tears are described as acute or chronic and partial or full thickness, as well as by size. The cuff can tear in a single traumatic event or as a result of cumulative microtrauma. Overhead athletes generally have partial articular-side tears, while older athletes tend to have chronic, full-thickness tears.

Acute rotator cuff tear is typical in the contact athlete younger than age 40 years who recalls a single traumatic event and presents with shoulder pain, weakness, and a positive shrug sign. Arthroscopic evaluation and treatment produce good results. At arthroscopy, a subgroup of these patients demonstrates an intact cuff but a markedly thickened, inflamed, and fibrotic subacromial bursa. This finding is likely the result of subacromial hemorrhage from a rotator cuff contusion and strong inflammatory response; arthroscopic subacromial decompression is indicated.

Partial rotator cuff tears in the overhead athlete related to secondary impingement are debrided and the instability corrected. Tears involving less than 50% of the tendon thickness can be debrided arthroscopically, while larger tears may require repair. Usually a tear that does not respond to rehabilitation can be treated arthroscopically. An acute rupture in a young athlete, however, should be treated surgically, as rehabilitation is unlikely to be successful.

The causes of chronic rotator cuff tears include extrinsic cuff compression, age-related intrinsic cuff degeneration and hypovascularity, and repetitive activity. A relatively minor injury can cause a full-thickness tear in an athlete with mild or moderate tendon degeneration.

Symptoms of a chronic tear include gradual loss of strength in abduction and external rotation with increasingly persistent pain, night pain, and pain with overhead activity. Although difficult to localize, the pain is described as deep and at the lateral deltoid or midhumerus.

Rehabilitation after rotator cuff repair requires 6 to 12 months of gradually increasing exercises. The exact program depends on the extent of the tear and the type of repair. Initially, only isometric exercises are permitted. Shoulder shrugs are then added, along with elbow, hand, and grip strengthening, and pendulum exercises, followed by progressive flexion and external rotation exercises, then gentle, active strengthening exercises against gravity for flexion and external rotation sidelying. The goals are for the athlete to perform resistive exercises and to obtain functional range of motion.

ondary to a rotator cuff contusion with a robust inflammatory response is suspected and is treated very well with arthroscopic subacromial decompression.[17]

Partial rotator cuff tears in the overhead athlete are treated according to the associated pathology. Tears related to secondary impingement are debrided and the instability corrected. Tears that involve less than 50% of the tendon thickness respond to arthroscopic debridement; larger tears may require repair. In general, if a tear does not respond to the impingement therapy protocol outlined above, arthroscopic evaluation and treatment should be initiated. The one exception is an acute rupture in the young athlete. Conservative, nonsurgical therapy is generally not beneficial in these cases and surgical intervention is recommended.

Many factors can contribute to chronic rotator cuff tears. Extrinsic compression of the cuff results from a decrease in height of the coracoacromial arch. Additionally, age-related intrinsic cuff degeneration and hypovascularity compromise the cuff's ability to repair itself. Repetitive activity, especially in the athlete with a restricted subacromial space, may also be a contributing factor. A minor traumatic event, such as a fall on the outstretched arm that causes the humeral head to be impacted against the acromion, may cause a full-thick-

ness tear in an athlete who already has mild or moderate tendon degeneration. The older athlete with a chronic rotator cuff tear may describe a gradual loss of strength in abduction and external rotation, with increasingly persistent pain in this range. Night pain is common, as is pain with overhead activity. The pain is difficult to pinpoint but is usually described as being deep and localized to the lateral deltoid or midhumerus. Plain radiographs will reveal signs of impingement as well as possible cystic or sclerotic changes in the greater tuberosity and possible superior humeral head migration. MRI is useful to characterize the rotator cuff tear morphology and assess the quality of the rotator cuff musculature. Occult lesions, such as an os acromiale or glenohumeral osteoarthritis, may also be identified. The treatment program outlined above should be followed.

Rehabilitating the shoulder after a rotator cuff repair requires 6 months to a year of gradually increasing exercises until full function returns. The program selected will vary, depending on the extent of the tear and the type of repair performed. In general, initially following repair, only isometric exercises are done. The athlete then progresses to shoulder shrugs; elbow, hand, and grip strengthening; and pendulum exercises. At 4 weeks, progressive flexion and external rotation in the supine position on the table or floor can usually begin. The athlete should avoid exercises that load the supraspinatus in isolation, such as scapular plane abduction exercises. At 6 weeks, the athlete may be able to begin some gentle, active strengthening exercises against gravity for flexion, and external rotation sidelying with the athlete lying on the unaffected side and gradually flexing to 90°. The goals are to enable the athlete to perform resistive exercises and to obtain functional range of motion.

Glenoid Labrum Injuries

The *glenoid labrum* is the soft fibrous rim surrounding the glenoid fossa that deepens the socket and provides stability for the humeral head. Glenoid labrum tears can occur from repetitive shoulder motion or from acute trauma, and can be above (superior) or below (inferior) the glenoid equator. Inferior labrum tears occur in the athlete with repeated anterior dislocation or subluxation of the shoulder, may result from anterior instability during the acceleration phase of throwing, and will be considered as part of the anterior instability complex. Superior tears occur during the deceleration phase of the throwing act, from the biceps pulling on the anterior labrum. An injury to the biceps tendon anchor and/or superior labrum is called a *SLAP (Superior Labral, Anterior to Posterior) lesion*.[18] The four types of SLAP lesions include type I, focal labral degeneration and fraying; type II, detachment of the biceps anchor; type III, bucket handle tear with an intact biceps anchor; and type IV, a type II or III lesion

that extends into the biceps tendon (**Figure 10-23**). SLAP lesions increase anterior shoulder laxity.[19]

A glenoid labrum tear may develop in athletes who are weight training with repetitive bench pressing and overhead pressing. Weakness in the posterior rotator cuff can aggravate this pathology. Glenoid labrum tears can occur from acute trauma, such as falling on an outstretched arm; they also occur in the leading shoulder of batters or golfers who ground their bats or clubs.

Unfortunately, there are no unique signs for lesions of the superior labrum. The history may vary widely, from falls onto the lateral aspect of the shoulder to a sudden inferior force applied to an extended, supinated arm, or a vague discomfort with overhead use. Athletes with these injuries often report pain, limited endurance with use of the shoulder, and popping or sliding, exacerbated by overhead use. Night pain may also be a feature.

Examination of the shoulder generally reveals more specific findings. Range of motion (active and passive) is usually normal. Standard Neer and Hawkins impingement signs are often positive because of secondary posterior rotator cuff irritation. Although the apprehension test result may be positive for pain and not instability, the relocation test result is usually negative. A palpable (audible) click may be heard and felt with forced external rotation of the arm in the 90° abducted position. Manual muscle testing may show associated weakness in the rotator cuff. O'Brien's

---

FOCUS ON . . .

Glenoid Labrum Injuries

Glenoid labrum injuries can occur from acute trauma or repetitive shoulder motion. An athlete with repeated anterior dislocation or subluxation or anterior instability during acceleration may sustain a labral tear below the glenoid equator. The biceps' pulling on the anterior labrum during deceleration can cause a superior tear. Superior labral injury, anterior to posterior, is also known as a SLAP lesion and describes an injury to the biceps tendon anchor or the superior labrum, or both. SLAP lesions increase anterior shoulder laxity. Glenoid labrum tears can occur in weight trainers from repetitive bench and overhead pressing, as a result of acute trauma, and in batters or golfers who ground bats or clubs.

The history may include a fall onto the lateral shoulder, a sudden inferior force applied to an extended and supinated arm, or vague discomfort with overhead activity. Pain (especially at night), limited shoulder endurance, popping, and sliding may be noted. On examination, range of motion is normal. Neer and Hawkins test results may be positive secondary to posterior rotator cuff irritation. The apprehension test result may be positive for pain (not instability), but the relocation test is negative. A palpable or audible click may be evident with forced external rotation in 90° of abduction. Rotator cuff weakness may be observed. The O'Brien test result is positive in the absence of frank impingement signs and AC joint tenderness.

Treatment is NSAIDs and rotator cuff rehabilitation exercises to decrease symptoms. Rotator cuff and periscapular exercises that limit forward flexion to less than 90° are often beneficial. If symptoms persist, arthroscopic labral debridement may be indicated. A shoulder immobilizer is applied postsurgically, to be removed for showers and for gentle, passive, pain-free range-of-motion exercises beginning on the first postsurgical day. After 3 weeks, the immobilizer is discarded and an active shoulder exercise program begun. After 6 weeks, a sport-specific conditioning program is introduced to permit normal function by 10 to 16 weeks.

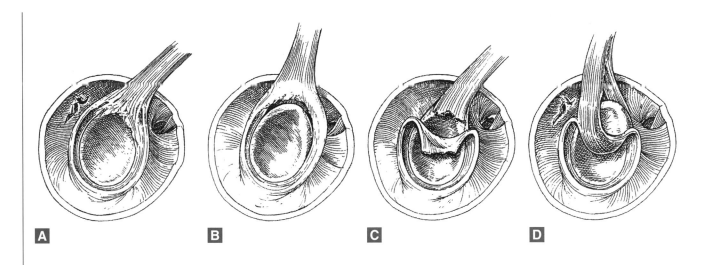

FIGURE 10-23

A SLAP lesion is an injury to the biceps tendon anchor or superior labrum. **A** Type I (focal labral degeneration and fraying). **B** Type II (detachment of the biceps anchor). **C** Type III (a bucket handle tear with an intact biceps anchor). **D** Type IV (a type II or III lesion that extends into the biceps tendon). (Reproduced with permission from Snyder SJ, Karzel RP, Del Pizzo W, et al: SLAP lesions of the shoulder. Arthroscopy 1990;6:274-279.)

test result is generally positive in the absence of frank impingement signs and AC joint tenderness. Injecting the joint with saline or gadolinium prior to an MRI scan helps detect tears and avulsions frequently not seen on regular studies. Additionally, the smooth contour noted as a normal anatomic variance can be visualized with these more refined tests, decreasing the incidence of false-positive results. A dedicated shoulder coil and an experienced orthopaedic radiologist will also improve accuracy.

Selective use of NSAIDs and rotator cuff rehabilitation exercises may significantly decrease symptoms in many patients, obviating the need for surgical intervention. Emphasizing rotator cuff and periscapular exercises that limit forward flexion to less than 90° is often beneficial. If conservative range-of-motion exercises and gradual return to activity are not successful, arthroscopic debridement of the labrum may be performed. If the biceps anchor is disrupted or the superior labrum is grossly loose, it is typically debrided of its frayed, degenerated margin and reattached to the bone with resorbable tacks, suture anchors, or transglenoid sutures. Simply debriding a SLAP lesion without reattachment shows a poor rate of return to sport. During an arthroscopy, excessive debridment of the inferior or anterior superior labrum must be avoided, or the risk of anterior shoulder instability and anterior shoulder dislocation will increase.[19,20] Unstable flap tears should be removed as necessary. After surgery, the patient should wear a shoulder immobilizer, removing it only for showers and for gentle passive range-of-motion exercises within a pain-free arc beginning on the

first day after surgery. After 3 weeks, the immobilizer may be discarded, and an active shoulder exercise program initiated. After 6 weeks, sport-specific conditioning programs are introduced so that normal function is achieved by 10 to 16 weeks. However, when a transrotator cuff approach is used to repair a SLAP lesion, cuff dysfunction may persist for some time.

The athlete who undergoes debridement of a small superior or middle glenoid labrum tear may be ready to enter a throwing program 2 or 3 weeks after surgery and be ready to throw in a game within 3 months.

Bicipital Tendinitis

The same mechanism that initiates the impingement syndrome symptoms in rotator cuff injuries can inflame the long tendon head of the biceps as it passes under the acromion, producing bicipital tendinitis. Bicipital tendinitis may also result from subluxation of the tendon out of its groove in the proximal humerus. This condition occurs with rupture of the transverse ligament and superior subscapularis tendon.

The symptoms of bicipital tendinitis, whether a result of impingement or tendon subluxation, are essentially the same. Pain is localized to the proximal humerus and the shoulder joint. Because the primary function of the biceps is supination, resisted supination of the forearm will aggravate the pain. Pain may also occur on manual muscle testing of the elbow flexors and on palpation of the tendon itself. The Yergason test for instability of the long head of the biceps in its groove often yields falsely negative results.

If bicipital tendinitis is associated with the shoulder impingement syndrome, therapy directed to the impingement syndrome may result in spontaneous resolution of the bicipital tendinitis. If subluxation of the tendon within its groove is the cause of irritation, conservative treatment includes modalities, followed by activity restriction, with slow resumption of activity after a period of rest lasting 1 to 3 weeks. Strengthening muscles that assist the biceps in elbow flexion and forearm supination may also be helpful. Subacromial corticosteroid injections should be used judiciously because they may promote tendon degeneration if used in excess. If symptoms persist, surgical options include tenodesis of the biceps tendon directly into bone or repair of the subscapularis and repair of the transverse humeral ligament in the case of subluxation.

Scapular Fractures

Scapular fractures, which account for less than 1% of all fractures, are usually the result of severe blunt trauma. In many patients, nonsurgical treatment results in satisfactory outcomes. Scapular fractures may be divided into three groups: those of the glenoid, those of the spine and acromion, and those of the scapular body. Fractures involving the glenoid are most frequent, and those of the body are least common. Fractures of the glenoid usually involve the rim and are often associated with dislocation or subluxation of the shoulder. They are usually minimally displaced, and treatment is dictated by the shoulder subluxation and percentage involvement of the glenoid, not by the scapular fracture.

Infrequent fractures of the acromion may occur in connection with AC separations and should be treated in the same manner. Occasionally, a markedly displaced acromial fracture with substantial AC disruption requires surgical treatment. Radiographs of the scapula are indicated any time severe trauma occurs to the shoulder or crepitus or acute tenderness is localized over the scapula. The athletic trainer should refer the athlete to the team physician for evaluation.

Fractures of the body and spine of the scapula can be treated in the same manner as injuries to the surrounding soft tissue, that is, by cold applications for the first 48 hours to minimize bleeding, followed by heat and early mobilization. Displacement is not incompatible with a good result and can be accepted. Typically, the vast muscular envelope holds the bony fragments in position and fracture union is the rule. Once the fracture is stabilized, the athlete should begin range-of-motion and strengthening exercises for the shoulder girdle muscles to facilitate a return to the previous level of activity.

Shoulder Dislocations

The GH joint is notable for its mobility at the expense of static stability. Osteoarticular contact is minimal, and the capsular ligaments are lax in all but the extremes of shoulder motion. Consequently, joint control is provided primarily by the dynamic stabilization of the muscles. When forces driving the GH joint toward the limits of its normal

FOCUS ON . . .

Bicipital Tendinitis and Scapular Fractures

The same mechanism that precipitates impingement symptoms in rotator cuff injuries can irritate the biceps tendon subacromially and produce biceps tendinitis. Tendon subluxation out of its proximal humerus groove can also cause tendinitis when the transverse ligament and superior subscapularis tendon are ruptured. Symptoms include pain localized to the proximal humerus and shoulder joint, with manual elbow flexor testing, and on tendon palpation. The Yergason test result is often falsely negative.

Treatment of bicipital tendinitis that is associated with shoulder impingement should be directed at the impingement, which may result in spontaneous resolution of the tendinitis. If tendon subluxation within the groove is the cause, treatment is modalities, initial restriction of activities with gradual return to sport, and strengthening muscles that assist the biceps in elbow flexion and forearm supination. Subacromial corticosteroid injections should be used cautiously because they can promote tendon degeneration. Persistent symptoms may require tenodesis of the tendon into bone or repair of the subscapularis muscle and transverse humeral ligament.

Scapular fractures are rare, usually result from severe blunt trauma, and are generally treated conservatively. Fractures involving the glenoid commonly affect the rim, are associated with dislocation or subluxation, are minimally displaced, and are treated for the subluxation rather than the fracture. Fractures of the acromion are rare and may occur with AC separations; they are treated as AC separations. Infrequently, a markedly displaced acromial fracture with substantial AC disruption requires surgical intervention. Any severe shoulder trauma or crepitus or acute tenderness localized to the scapula requires a scapular radiograph. Scapular body and spine fractures are treated with cold applications for 48 hours to minimize bleeding, followed by heat and early mobilization. Displacement does not compromise a good result, but the muscular envelope tends to hold the bony fragments in position and promote union. Once the fracture is stable, the athlete begins range-of-motion and strengthening exercises.

FOCUS ON . . .

Shoulder Dislocations

Displacement of the humeral head from the GH joint occurs when the forces driving the GH joint toward its limits of motion exceed the restraining strength of the shoulder muscles and capsular ligaments. Most GH dislocations and subluxations are anterior and inferior to the glenoid rim.

Anterior Dislocation

Anterior GH dislocation is caused by an external rotation and abduction force on the humerus or a direct posterior or posterolateral blow great enough to displace the humeral head. The anterior capsule is stretched or torn within its substance or avulsed from its anterior glenoid attachment, or both. The head can be displaced into the subcoracoid, subglenoid, subclavicular, or intrathoracic position. A Bankart lesion is an anterior capsulolabral injury associated with an anteroinferior glenoid labrum tear and sometimes an anteroinferior glenoid fracture. A Hill-Sachs lesion is an indentation or compression fracture of the posterior, superior, lateral humeral head articular surface created by the sharp anterior glenoid edge as the humeral head dislocates over it. Both lesions compromise GH mechanical stability in abduction and external rotation and can predispose the joint to recurrent dislocations.

Injuries associated with anterior GH dislocation in the young athlete are greater tuberosity avulsion fractures from the humerus caused by eccentric rotator cuff traction and axillary nerve injury. The axillary nerve can be contused, stretched, or torn during the dislocation, resulting in denervation of the deltoid muscle. Most often, the nerve recovers, but function should always be tested before and after reduction.

On presentation, the athlete is distressed, reports acute pain, and holds the arm against the body with the opposite hand in internal rotation and abduction and states that the shoulder feels as if it has slipped out of joint. The physician should obtain an accurate description of the mechanism of injury, including arm position and estimate of forces.

The physician should be able to distinguish between acute and recurrent dislocations. An acute dislocation is usually the result of considerable trauma and may be associated with fractures and nerve injuries. The exception is the athlete who has congenital laxity or a history of a previous GH joint dislocation.

If possible, radiographs should be obtained before reduction to rule out a fracture that could complicate or preclude a reduction attempt. Reduction before the onset of muscle spasm can be tried if a dislocation is witnessed, but it should be done quickly and gently to avoid further injury.

After reduction, the neurovascular examination should be repeated and radiographs obtained for comparison with the initial films to evaluate the reduction and any resulting injury. Physical examination should be repeated within 10 days of injury, at which time much of the acute pain and apprehension will have resolved and the soft tissues can be assessed.

After an initial dislocation, the shoulder is immobilized in internal rotation for 3 to 6 weeks. As soon as pain permits, rotator cuff and deltoid muscle isometric exercises can begin. Strengthening exercises in the scapular plane minimize tension on the injured anteroinferior capsular ligamentous structures and allow healing. Rotator cuff and scapular stabilizer strengthening can begin at week 3 or 4. Return to competition, unlikely before 6 weeks, can occur when the athlete has regained normal strength and range of motion without pain.

Despite adequate immobilization and rehabilitation, redislocation rates are significant for athletes younger than age 25 years. Patients older than age 40 years tend to have a lower recurrence rate and are treated nonsurgically.

To prevent recurrent dislocation, restraining devices that keep the arm from abduction, extension, and external rotation are effective, but restrict shoulder motion. Surgical reconstruction may be advisable for the athlete with recurrent dislocation after the number of episodes, circumstances of each, and involvement of the dominant arm are considered.

Athletes with recurrent anterior shoulder instability report limited power and motion in the late cocking position and repeated dislocations. The apprehension and relocation test results are positive. Early dislocations require reduction, but later dislocations may spontaneously reduce. Dislocations are treated with limited immobilization to reduce inflammation and then rotator cuff and periscapular strengthening. Conservative treatment may allow the athlete to complete the season, but open or arthroscopic correction is ultimately recommended.

Postsurgically, the arm is immobilized and pendulum exercises are permitted. Range-of-motion exercises begin at week 4, with the goal of achieving the 90°-90° position by the end of week 8. The throwing athlete should try to achieve this position by week 6. By week 12, athletes who are progressing appropriately can begin weight training, avoiding exercises that stress the anterior capsule.

(Continued)

dislocation is the scapular manipulation method, which begins with the athlete prone on an examination table or bench. The athlete should be relaxed with the arm hanging as the physician places the right hand under the lateral border of the inferior angle of the scapula (for a left GH dislocation) and the left hand on the superior lateral aspect of the acromion. The physician then anteriorly and medially rotates the scapula to position the glenoid under the humeral head to achieve reduction. This method can be used without significant traction on the arm or sedation; however, forceful reduction attempts must be avoided because of the risk of fracture or neurovascular injury.

After the reduction maneuver, the physician should repeat the neurovascular examination and document the results. In addition, postreduction radiographs should be obtained and compared with the initial radiographs to evaluate the adequacy of the reduction and to determine whether further injury occurred during the reduction maneuver. A repeat physical examination should be performed within the first 10 days afte injury. By then, much of the acute pain and apprehension will have resolved, and a thorough examination may reveal occult soft-tissue injuries.

After an initial dislocation, the shoulder should be immobilized in internal rotation for 3 to 6 weeks. The first phase of rehabilitation should emphasize soft-tissue healing and preserving a protected range of motion while avoiding external rotation. Rotator cuff and deltoid muscle isometric exercises may proceed as soon as pain permits. Strengthening exercises in the plane of the scapula may minimize the tension applied to the injured anteroinferior capsular ligamentous structures and allow healing of the soft tissues. Rotator cuff and scapular stabilizer strengthening may begin at 3 to 4 weeks after dislocation, but the late cocking position should be avoided. It will probably be 6 weeks before the athlete can return to competition, and healing may take longer. The athlete should regain normal strength without pain and have normal range of motion before returning to play and should avoid wide grips on the bench press and deep shoulder dips during routine weight-training activities. Any activity that increases stress on the anterior capsule should be modified. With recurrent shoulder dislocations, minimal immobilization until pain subsides is generally recommended. Range-of-motion and strengthening exercises can then begin.

Despite an organized physical therapy program and adequate immobilization, recurrence rates for dislocation are significant for athletes younger than age 25 years. Studies at the United States Military Academy report that acute arthroscopic repair of an initial anterior dislocation was successful in 86% of patients, and nonsurgical treatment resulted in recurrent instability in 80% of patients.[23] The advantages of arthroscopic surgery include a significantly decreased incidence of recurrent instability (when com-

pared with nonsurgical treatment, yet a higher incidence when compared with open repair), low surgical morbidity, and faster return to preinjury athletic activity in the noncontact athlete. Open stabilization is typically recommended for the contact athlete. Surgical correction of an initial, traumatic dislocation is recommended for an initial dislocation that requires a reduction; an athletic, high-demand patient younger than age 25 years who is unwilling or unable to modify his or her lifestyle; no prior shoulder subluxation or impingement history; no neurologic injuries; and no greater tuberosity fractures. Patients older than age 40 years are generally treated without surgery and have a significantly lower rate of recurrent instability. Initial indications for surgical treatment of anterior shoulder dislocations remain controversial.

Restraining devices that attempt to keep the arm from going into abduction, extension, and external rotation are available to prevent recurrent dislocations. These devices can be effective, but the restriction on the athlete's shoulder motion is a disadvantage in certain sports, especially if the affected extremity is dominant. For an athlete who has sustained multiple dislocations, surgical reconstruction of the shoulder joint may be advisable, but only after all other factors are considered, including the number of dislocations, the circumstances of each dislocation, and involvement by the dominant arm.

Recurrent anterior shoulder instability

Traumatic anterior shoulder instability can result in recurrent anterior instability. Typically, patients with recurrent anterior instability will complain of limitation of power and motion in the late cocking position, accompanied by recurrent dislocations. Both the apprehension and relocation test results will be positive. In the early stages of instability, the dislocations will require medical assistance for reduction, but as the frequency of dislocations increases, spontaneous reduction may occur. Each dislocation episode should be treated with a limited period (1 week) of immobilization to reduce inflammation; however, prolonged immobilization may not be effective. Rotator cuff and periscapular strengthening form the basis for a rehabilitation program. Nonsurgical treatment of this disorder is not usually adequate, but it may allow the athlete to complete the season. A frank discussion of the risk of repeated dislocation and its consequences should be undertaken among the athletic trainer, treating physician, athlete, and athlete's family.

Recurrent anterior instability may be corrected through open or arthroscopic means. Arthroscopy has two advantages over open repair: decreased morbidity and the ability to repair a Bankart lesion without detaching the subscapularis muscle. However, a stretched anterior IGHL cannot be properly tightened during arthroscopy. Open capsulolabral reconstruction is the treatment of choice, especially for the athlete who participates in contact sports. Various methods of reconstructing the capsulolabral complex are available to the orthopaedic surgeon.[10,24,25] Overall, results of anterior instability reconstruction are favorable. The surgeon must have an appreciation of the underlying pathology and soft-tissue reconstruction design to successfully reattach the labrum and balance the GH ligaments.

After surgery, the arm should be immobilized. Pendulum exercises are permitted. In postsurgical weeks 4 through 8, range-of-motion exercises are encouraged to achieve 90° of abduction and 90° of external rotation (the 90°–90° position) at the end of 8 weeks. The throwing athlete who requires more abduction and external rotation should aim to achieve the 90°–90° position 6 weeks after surgery. By 12 weeks after surgery, athletes who have progressed well with their initial program can begin a variety of weight-training activities, as long as exercises that stress the anterior capsule are avoided.

Posterior glenohumeral dislocation

Although posterior and anterior GH dislocations result from different sets of forces, they share a similar pathology. The posterior capsule is stretched, torn, or disrupted from the posterior glenoid, creating a reverse Hill-Sachs lesion on the anterior articular surface by the posterior lip of the glenoid. With an anterior GH dislocation, the rotator cuff or its bony attachment at the greater tuberosity may be injured by stretching; with a posterior dislocation, the subscapularis or its insertion on the lesser tuberosity may be injured.

The posterior GH dislocation may be difficult to detect. An athlete with a posterior dislocation may present with a normal anterior contour to the shoulder. Chest muscles appear intact, and it may be difficult to see that the shoulder is depressed. A cardinal sign of a posterior shoulder dislocation is prominence of the humeral head in the shoulder posteriorly and a prominent coracoid process anteriorly, but this prominence may be masked by heavy deltoid musculature. What cannot be masked, however, is that the shoulder is held in internal rotation and cannot be externally rotated.

All shoulder injuries sustained on the playing field should first be evaluated by observation, gentle palpation, and attempts at bringing the joint carefully and gently through a full range of motion. Restriction of joint motion indicates that the athlete should be transferred to a medical facility for radiographic examination. Even with the aid of standard radiographs, posterior dislocations may go unrecognized. Thus, if the physician notes that the shoulder cannot be rotated externally during a careful physical examination, the athlete may still need additional radiographs to document the position of the humeral head relative to the glenoid and to ascertain the presence of a possible fracture.

A posterior dislocation of the GH joint is reduced by applying traction in the line of the adducted deformity with concomitant direct anterior pressure on the humeral head. If the maneuver is done gently after total body relaxation, reduction should be atraumatic. For an initial dislocation, immobilization for 3 to 6 weeks with the arm in neutral rotation at the side is warranted. The recurrent dislocation should be treated symptomatically, and surgical treatment may be considered.

Multidirectional instability

Multidirectional instability (MDI) is defined as symptomatic GH instability in more than two directions. True MDI is a global type of instability, which can occur in one of three patterns: anteroinferior dislocation with posterior subluxation, posteroinferior dislocation with anterior subluxation, or dislocation in all three directions (anterior, posterior, and inferior). Although hyperlaxity may occur in normal asymptomatic individuals, MDI represents excessive symptomatic multiplanar translations.

There is no single etiology for MDI, but a number of factors have been implicated including inherent ligamentous laxity, recurrent macrotrauma (which is rare), and cumulative, repetitive microtrauma. Many patients with MDI of the shoulder possess generalized ligamentous laxity, although a significant subset has only "loose shoulders." Frequently, these athletes repeatedly stress the shoulder capsule with overhead sports activities, such as throwing, gymnastics, or swimming, that selectively stretch out the shoulder ligaments. Another subgroup of patients with MDI can reproduce the instability by placing the shoulder in a provocative position. These "positional dislocators" must be differentiated from willful voluntary dislocators, whose shoulder instability indicates an underlying emotional or psychiatric problem.[26]

MDI can be seen in a variety of ways. Pain with carrying objects is often accompanied by paresthesia secondary to brachial plexus traction with inferior shoulder subluxation. Pushing a heavy door with the arm flexed, internally rotated, and adducted will stress a lax posterior capsule and may produce posterior subluxation. Athletes with symptoms during the follow-through phase of a throw or swimming stroke may have some posterior instability as well. Subtle anterior instability noted during a tennis serve or the late cocking phase of a pitch may cause a reflex inhibition of the plexus called the "dead arm" sensation.

During the examination, the physician should investigate any evidence of gross hyperlaxity. Range of motion and strength testing are generally normal. Careful attention to laxity and apprehension signs will denote the primary and secondary direction of the instability. Plain radiographs are often normal, and MRI scans may reveal capsular redundancy.

The initial treatment of MDI is nonsurgical and combines activity modification (avoiding provocative activities) with a prolonged exercise program.[27] Deltoid and rotator cuff muscle strengthening below the horizon are initiated, as well as periscapular muscular conditioning to stabilize the scapula. Rehabilitation is generally successful in shoulders with involuntary atraumatic MDI treated by conservative measures. In rare instances, subacromial inflammation will develop in a patient with MDI. A subacromial corticosteroid injection to reduce symptoms will also enable the patient to continue the exercise program.

Surgical treatment is recommended for the athlete with significant, disabling pain and instability despite a prolonged period of rehabilitative exercises.[28,29] The most common surgical repair is a modified inferior capsular shift procedure aimed at rebalancing the GH ligaments and reducing capsular redundancy. Postsurgically, the arm is immobilized in a brace for 6 weeks with the shoulder positioned in neutral flexion/extension, neutral rotation, and slight abduction. During this period, only gentle isometric exercises and elbow range-of-motion exercises are allowed. When the brace is removed, range-of-motion exercises for the shoulder can begin. Progressive resistive exercises are initiated approximately 8 to 12 weeks postsurgically. Rehabilitation after an inferior capsular shift for MDI is intentionally slower, so that motion is regained gradually over several months, to decrease the likelihood of stretching out the repair. Recurrent instability is generally more of a problem than is postsurgical stiffness. Participation in sports is restricted for 9 to 12 months after repair.

Mild to moderate GH laxity in one or more planes can now be addressed arthroscopically through arthroscopic capsular suture plication or thermal capsular shrinkage. However, these techniques are currently practiced at only a few centers, and long-term follow-up is necessary before their widespread use is advocated.

Proximal Humerus Fractures

Fractures of the proximal humerus occur infrequently in sports. Occasionally, fractures are associated with dislocation of the humerus in the glenoid; the injury is then termed a fracture-dislocation of the shoulder. Healing of these injuries depends on the number of fragments, the degree of displacement of the fragments, and the extent of disruption of the blood supply to the fragments. In the young athlete, epiphyseal (growth plate) injuries to the proximal humerus can occur. Fracture separations of this area can occur at any age until the growth plate closes, at about age 20 to 22 years. Fractures in this area usually do not arrest growth and are treated with a period of rest.

In the mature athlete, primary healing of proximal humeral fractures with conservative treatment (sling or sling and swathe) is usually the rule unless the fracture fragments are significantly displaced. Stiffness, even in young people, remains a threat following these injuries because the soft tissues that envelop the shoulder joint lose their range of excursion with injury and immobilization. Pendulum exercises can begin early to avoid or minimize postinjury stiffness. As healing progresses, active and

FOCUS ON . . .

Proximal Humerus Fractures

Proximal humerus fractures are rare in sports. Also, the humeral growth plate that remains open until age 20 to 22 years can be fractured, although growth is unaffected and treatment is rest. Occasionally, fractures are associated with humeral dislocation (a fracture-dislocation). Healing depends on the number of fragments, their degree of displacement, and the disruption of their blood supply. Conservative treatment of a sling or sling and swathe is appropriate unless the fragments are significantly displaced. Post-injury stiffness is a concern because the soft tissues enveloping the shoulder joint lose flexibility with injury and immobilization. Pendulum exercises should be introduced early, followed by active and then passive range-of-motion exercises and strengthening for the shoulder girdle muscles.

then passive range-of-motion exercises are initated and later are coupled with strengthening exercises for all the shoulder girdle muscles.

NEUROVASCULAR INJURIES TO THE ATHLETE'S SHOULDER

Suprascapular Nerve Palsy

Suprascapular nerve palsy is perhaps one of the most common compressive neuropathies of the shoulder. The course of the suprascapular nerve takes it through the suprascapular notch.[30] Stenosis may compress the nerve at the suprascapular notch, resulting in atrophy of the supraspinatus and infraspinatus muscles. If the nerve is compressed as it travels through the spinoglenoid notch at the back of the shoulder, the result is isolated infraspinatus atrophy. A final mechanism of compression is by an expanding degenerative labral ganglion of the superior shoulder. Patients with a suprascapular nerve lesion generally have a history of trauma to the area or perform repetitive activities that require a wide excursion of the shoulder. Activities such as baseball, volleyball, tennis, and weightlifting can predispose the athlete to this injury.

The athlete with suprascapular nerve palsy will typically report a poorly localized, deep ache in the posterolateral shoulder. The pain may radiate for a short distance but does not progress distally. Shoulder weakness is common,

Neurovascular Injuries to the Athlete's Shoulder

Neurovascular injuries to the athlete's shoulder include suprascapular nerve palsy, burner (stinger) syndrome, thoracic outlet syndrome, long thoracic nerve injury, quadrilateral space syndrome, axillary artery occlusion, and venous thrombosis. Suprascapular nerve palsy can result if the nerve is compressed at the suprascapular notch, at the spinoglenoid notch, or by an expansile, degenerative labral ganglion in the superior shoulder. Usually, there is a history of trauma or repetitive, wide-shoulder excursion. Symptoms include poorly localized, deep aching in the posterolateral shoulder, radiating slightly without progressing distally; shoulder weakness, particularly with abduction and external rotation; and wasting of the spinati muscles (a late finding). Examination reveals suprascapular or spinoglenoid notch tenderness with reduced active abduction and external rotation power. A careful, thorough history and physical examination, along with electromyography showing delayed conduction velocity and fibrillation potentials, confirm the diagnosis. Conservative treatment consists of rest, analgesics, physical therapy, and sometimes corticosteroid injections. Nerve entrapment caused by acute trauma rather than anatomic compression is most likely to improve on nonsurgical treatment. An athlete with persistent pain despite such treatment or one who has no nerve recovery in 1 to 2 months with atrophy may require surgical release of the nerve. Long-standing atrophy, however, is likely to persist.

Burner (stinger) syndrome is an acute injury to the upper trunk brachial plexus from head, neck, or shoulder contact in football. The shoulder is driven away from the body and the head or neck (or both) are forced in the opposite direction, stretching the plexus. The athlete reports sharp, burning shoulder pain radiating to the arm and hand. An athlete with bilateral burner syndrome is treated as though a cervical spine injury is present until it can be ruled out. Pain or weakness lasting more than 2 weeks signals a more severe injury; the athlete can return to sport once strength has returned to normal. Cervical muscle strengthening and cowboy collar pads reduce the risk of burners.

Thoracic outlet syndrome is caused by trauma and anatomic changes from throwing, resulting in brachial plexus or subclavian vessel compression in the thoracic outlet. Symptoms include coolness, paresthesia, weakness, heaviness, and easy fatigability of the arm. The modified Adson's test, or Wright, is designed to elicit symptoms. Early fatigue and symptom reproduction are consistent with thoracic outlet syndrome. Treatment is NSAIDs and physical therapy. If rehabilitation fails and specific anatomic factors are causing the symptoms, surgery may be appropriate.

The long length and superficial location of the long thoracic nerve leave it vulnerable to trauma (from a blow or from traction), resulting in serratus anterior muscle paralysis. Clinically, the athlete has a deep, dull ache, winged scapula, and reduced active shoulder function. If the athlete is asked to perform an internally rotated wall push with the arms extended, the medial scapular border becomes prominent. Conservative treatment of physical therapy and rest from sport are usually successful.

The quadrilateral space is defined by the teres minor superiorly, teres major inferiorly, long head of the triceps medially, and humeral shaft laterally. Compression of the axillary nerve and posterior humeral circumflex artery in this area characterizes quadrilateral space syndrome. Throwers are susceptible, and the poorly localized shoulder pain typical of this condition is reproduced by the late cocking position. Intermittent, nonspecific upper arm paresthesia is noted, and throwing is impaired. Subclavian arteriogram confirms the diagnosis. If conservative treatment of gentle internal rotation stretching, horizontal stretching in adduction, and rotator cuff strengthening is unsuccessful, surgical decompression may be indicated.

Transient axillary artery occlusion from pectoralis minor muscle pressure can occur during the cocking phase of throwing in a pitcher. Pain, pectoralis minor tenderness, claudication, upper extremity fatigue, diminished pulses, and cyanosis reproduced by placing the arm in the late cocking position are typical. Angiography confirms axillary artery occlusion or aneurysmal dilation, and surgery is recommended.

Axillary or subclavian vein (effort) thrombosis can affect the weightlifter or any athlete who performs repetitive, vigorous activities, or it can result from blunt trauma and direct or indirect injury. Symptoms include aching pain, numbness, arm heaviness, and significant swelling of the upper extremity. Neurovascular examination is normal, and the diagnosis is confirmed with duplex Doppler venous imaging or venography. Treatment is elevation and anticoagulation medications.

particularly with abduction and external rotation. Wasting of the spinati muscles, depending on the site of compression, is a late finding and is more commonly absent, which makes the diagnosis more difficult.

On examination, tenderness over the suprascapular notch, in the triangle between the clavicle and the scapular spine, is almost invariably present. The power of active abduction and external rotation is usually reduced. The pain accompanying suprascapular nerve entrapment at the spinoglenoid notch is usually milder than that related to entrapment at the suprascapular notch and is generally located at the infraspinatus area. Tenderness over the spinoglenoid notch, located about 4 cm from the posterolateral point of the acromion along the scapular spine, is marked.

The diagnosis of suprascapular nerve entrapment is based on a careful, thorough history, physical examination, and electromyography. Electromyographic findings such as delayed conduction velocity and fibrillation potentials are definitive.

Conservative treatment includes rest, analgesics, physical therapy, and perhaps local corticosteroid injections. Nerve entrapment caused by acute trauma without any marked anatomic compression may improve with conservative treatment.[31]

Persistent pain despite conservative treatment or a lack of nerve recovery in 1 to 2 months in athletes with atrophy is an indication for surgical treatment. Surgical release of the nerve shows good improvement in strength; however, an atrophy that persists for many years very seldom disappears.

Burner (stinger) syndrome

Burner (stinger) syndrome is an acute upper trunk brachial plexus injury resulting from head, neck, or shoulder contact in football. During contact, as the shoulder is driven away from the body and/or the head and neck are forced in the opposite direction, the plexus, which is fixed proximally in the neural foramen and distally in the arm, stretches. Typically, the athlete feels a sharp, burning shoulder pain that radiates to the arm and hand. Pain or weakness that persists for more than 2 weeks indicates more severe brachial plexus injury. The athlete should be restricted from sports participation until strength returns to normal. All athletes with bilateral burner syndrome should be treated as though they have a cervical spine injury until spinal injury can be ruled out. Cervical muscle strengthening and cowboy collar pads decrease the incidence of burners. There is an increased risk of complications from a stinger injury in athletes with a relatively narrow spinal canal.[32]

Thoracic Outlet Syndrome

Thoracic outlet syndrome is also associated with trauma and the anatomic changes that can occur in the shoulder as a result of throwing mechanics. Injuries to the shoulder musculature can cause secondary compression of the brachial plexus or subclavian vessels in the thoracic outlet. Symptoms are usually associated with a specific throwing motion and include coolness and paresthesia of the involved arm. Patients may report that their arm is weak, heavy, or easily fatigued.

The modified Adson's test, also called the Wright test, is designed to elicit symptoms. In this test, the athlete's arm is abducted, extended, and externally rotated. The head and neck are extended and laterally rotated toward the opposite shoulder. The radial pulse is palpated before and during this maneuver, and a diminution of the radial pulse or reproduction of symptoms typifies a positive test result. In another test, the athlete places both arms in the late cocking position and rapidly opens and closes the fists. Early fatigue and reproduction of symptoms are consistent with thoracic outlet syndrome. Treatment involves using NSAIDs to relieve pain and physical therapy to correct posture and strengthen shoulder and scapular muscles. Surgical treatment to correct the specific anatomic factors that cause the symptoms is indicated only if rehabilitation fails.

Long Thoracic Nerve Injury

Injury to the long thoracic nerve resulting in serratus anterior muscle paralysis can occur in a number of sports. Because of its length and superficial location, the long thoracic nerve is predisposed to traumatic injury caused by a blow or traction. Clinically, the athlete often reports a deep dull ache, winging scapula, and decreased active shoulder function. Having the athlete perform an internally rotated wall push with the arms extended will demonstrate the injury clinically. The medial border of the scapula will become significantly prominent with this maneuver.

Nonsurgical treatment is preferred and includes physical therapy (range of motion and scapular stabilization exercises) and rest from the involved sport. The prognosis is generally good.

Quadrilateral Space Syndrome

The quadrilateral space is delineated by the teres minor (superiorly) and major (inferiorly) muscles, the long head of the triceps medially, and the humeral shaft laterally. *Quadrilateral space syndrome* involves compression of the axillary nerve and the posterior humeral circumflex artery as they course through this area. The syndrome has been reported in throwing athletes with poorly localized shoulder pain and intermittent, nonspecific (no dermatomal pattern) paresthesia of the upper arm without associated trauma. The pain is reproduced in the late cocking position and impairs throwing.

The diagnosis is confirmed by subclavian arteriogram. When the arm is abducted and externally rotated, the posterior humeral circumflex artery becomes occluded in the quadrilateral space.

Conservative treatment is gentle internal rotation, stretching, horizontal stretching in adduction, and rotator cuff strengthening. If this fails, surgical decompression may be indicated.

Axillary Artery Occlusion

Transient arterial occlusion, typically caused by pressure from the pectoralis minor muscle, can occur during the cocking phase of throwing in pitchers. Symptoms, such as pain, pectoralis minor tenderness, vascular *claudication* (a sensation of coolness with pain), upper extremity fatigue, diminished pulses, and cyanosis, can be reproduced by placing the arm in the late cocking position. Angiography will confirm the diagnosis, showing evidence of axillary artery occlusion or aneurysmal dilation. Surgery usually is required for effective treatment. Procedures include thrombectomy, synovectomy, excision and bypass grafting, and angioplasty.

Venous Thrombosis (Effort Thrombosis)

Thrombosis of the axillary or subclavian vein can occur in the weightlifter or other athlete who performs repetitive, vigorous activities. It may also occur after a blunt trauma that results in indirect or direct injury to the vein. Symptoms include aching pain, numbness, and a feeling of arm heaviness in association with a significantly swollen upper extremity. The neurovascular examination is typically normal. The diagnosis is confirmed with duplex Doppler venous imaging or venography. Effort thrombosis is treated nonsurgically with elevation and anticoagulation medications.

PRINCIPLES OF SHOULDER REHABILITATION

Shoulder rehabilitation has advanced significantly over the past decade, primarily because of the advances in orthopaedic medicine and increased focus on the shoulder girdle and its function. The entire shoulder complex and upper extremity must be considered when a shoulder rehabilitation program is being planned. Shoulder treatment strategies involve an understanding of the force couple at the GH joint and the synchronous movement of the entire shoulder complex. The structure of the shoulder complex provides a high degree of mobility and depends on a balance of muscular force couples for stability.[33]

Rehabilitation goals should always be stated in a very broad and comprehensive manner. Because the shoulder is a highly muscle-dependent joint, strength and power are essential to all rehabilitation plans. Controlling pain, reestablishing full range of motion, and gaining flexibility, coordination, and endurance are also important goals of rehabilitation efforts. These goals are common to all shoulder dysfunction, but the starting point varies widely,

FOCUS ON . . .

Rehabilitation Principles

A shoulder rehabilitation program should include the entire upper extremity. The shoulder's high degree of mobility depends on balanced muscular force couples for stability. Rehabilitation goals should be stated broadly and comprehensively and must include restoration of strength and power, control of pain, and return of full range of motion, flexibility, coordination, and endurance. The rehabilitation starting point depends on the pathologic process, type of treatment, and other injuries or deficits. A complete, accurate diagnosis is important.

Exercises should be selected based on mode (open versus closed kinetic chain patterns), contraction type, motion speed, and joint angle. A functional exercise program results from constant and timely interaction of these variables with soft-tissue healing and improved motor capabilities. The athlete's most important goal is successful return to sport, which occurs if all the functional exercise goals are mastered at the correct time and sport-specific activities are emphasized in the late stages. Functional testing at the end of rehabilitation is necessary to establish whether the athlete has met the stated goals.

depending on the pathologic process (macrotrauma or microtrauma), type of treatment (rest, immobilization, or surgery), and associated alterations (other injuries, inflexibility, or strength deficit). A complete and accurate diagnosis is very important and aids in determining a starting point for rehabilitation.[34]

Exercises during shoulder rehabilitation should be implemented based on the interaction of the exercise mode (open versus closed kinetic chain patterns), contraction type, speed of motion, and joint angle. A functional exercise progression therefore results from a constant interplay of exercise variables applied with proper timing to coincide with healing of the soft tissue and improvement in the patient's motor capabilities.[35] These goals, as well as the pathology and relative status of the patient, should be considered when a rehabilitation program is being developed.

Return to participation is the most important goal of the athletic patient. A successful return to play will be ensured if the athlete masters all the functional exercise goals at the appropriate time and tailors the late stages of the rehabilitation program to sport-specific activities. Restoration of proper function is determined by functional testing at the end stage of the rehabilitation program.

Many shoulder protocols that are presently available overlap and have limited scientific basis for their conclusions. Early range of motion and specific exercises documented by electromyelographic (EMG) studies have supplanted older protocols.

THE PHASES OF SHOULDER REHABILITATION

The three phases of shoulder rehabilitation include exercises and protocols that should be adapted to the specific pathology of the patient.

Phase 1

The starting point of all rehabilitation programs includes controlling pain while increasing range-of-motion. Passive and active-assisted range of motion exercises, such as Codman pendulums, circumduction, flexion, abduction, extension, external rotation, and internal rotation, are incorporated during this phase. Because of gravity's assistance, exercises performed while the patient is in a supine position are less difficult. A pulley system can be used to increase elevation in the scapular plane. As pain and surgical considerations permit, range of motion should be increased. Enhancements to the program include proper warm-up activities, heat and ultrasound modalities, and application of pre- and postexercise ice to control pain and prevent inflammation. Joint mobilization exercises should be used in low grades for pain modulation, joint nutrition, and prevention of contractures, especially posterior GH contractures.

During the first phase of shoulder rehabilitation, passive, active-assisted, and active range-of-motion exercises are included as tolerated. For shoulder abduction and external rotation, stress to the joint capsule should be avoided by positioning the shoulder in the scapular plane, approximately 30° to 40° forward of the coronal plane. Isometric exercises and rhythmic stabilization in this position of function improve strength and neuromuscular control while they limit capsular stress. Scapular stabilization and mobility are established, and elbow and wrist ranges of motion are maintained.

Phase 2

The rotator cuff, deltoid, and scapular rotators are addressed in the second phase of shoulder rehabilitation. The rotator cuff and deltoid are strengthened progressively with increasing resistance and avoidance of the impingement arc. Isometric exercises that progress from neutral to functional positions in flexion, extension, abduction, and

---

FOCUS ON . . .

Shoulder Rehabilitation Phases

Shoulder rehabilitation consists of three phases. Phase 1 focuses on controlling pain while increasing range of motion. Range of motion should be increased as pain and surgical considerations permit. Proper warm-ups, heat and ultrasound modalities, and ice before exercise are beneficial. Low-grade joint mobilization exercises are used to control pain, nourish the joint, and prevent contractures (especially those of the posterior GH joint).

In phase 2, the rotator cuff and deltoid are strengthened with increasing resistance (avoiding the impingement arc). Isometric exercises progress from neutral to functional positions. Normal scapulohumeral mechanics are reestablished by strengthening the scapular stabilizers. Active isotonic shoulder internal and external rotation exercises with the arm in neutral or in the scapular plane progress to functional overhead and elevated positions as tolerated. Posterior rotator cuff and capsular stretches reestablish normal range of motion and joint mechanics. Elbow and wrist strengthening exercises are continued, and joint mobilization techniques are progressed to normalize joint play. Isokinetic strengthening, endurance and flexibility exercises, and total body conditioning are introduced. Abdominal strength, posture, and lower extremity strength are restored.

The athlete begins phase 3 when symptoms have disappeared. Range of motion is monitored and maintained. Isotonic and isokinetic exercises advance as tolerated. Return to sport is the goal of phase 3, and the athlete prepares by performing sport-specific movement patterns for throwing, shooting, and swinging and impact progressions for collision sports. Positioning the upper extremity toward 90° of abduction progressively strengthens the internal and external rotators and increases the functional demands on the joint. PNF patterns and inflated ball exercises are useful for enhancing strength and range of motion in throwing patterns, and plyometric exercises further increase the demands on the shoulder. Progressive shoulder girdle endurance activities and total-body fitness training are incorporated, along with creative sport-specific exercises and skill mastery training. Duration, force, and velocity of functional activities advance to competition level, and a maintenance program continues as the athlete returns to full participation.

internal and external rotation are included. Scapulo-humeral rhythm is evaluated, and efforts to reestablish normal mechanics are directed toward strengthening the scapular stabilizers. Shoulder shrugs; wall, knee, and traditional push ups; rowing motions, depressions, and protraction of the scapula increase scapular mobility and dynamic stability to prevent impingement symptoms.

Active isotonic shoulder internal and external rotation exercises are performed with the arm positioned in neutral or in the scapular plane and progress toward functional positions, such as overhead and elevated positions, as tolerated.

During this phase, shoulder stretches may be implemented based on the pathology. Posterior rotator cuff and capsular stretches are indicated to reestablish normal range of motion and joint mechanics. Strengthening exercises for the wrist and elbow should be continued, and joint mobilization exercises such as posterior glides should be used in increasing grades to improve joint play to normal. Isokinetic strengthening, total body conditioning, and endurance exercises may be incorporated during this stage as well as flexibility exercises as needed. Abdominal strength, normal posture, and lower extremity strengthening, which also contribute to throwing, should be normalized or augmented.

Phase 3

The third phase of shoulder rehabilitation begins when the athlete is asymptomatic. Range of motion is monitored and maintained, and isotonic and isokinetic exercises for shoulder flexion, extension, abduction, adduction, and horizontal abduction and adduction progress as tolerated. The upper extremity should be positioned toward 90° of abduction to progressively strengthen the internal and external rotators and increase the functional demands on the shoulder.

Proprioceptive neuromuscular facilitation (PNF) patterns and medicine ball exercises may be used for increasing strength and range of motion in the throwing patterns. Plyometrics exercises further increase the demands on the shoulder.

During phase 3, progressive endurance activities for the shoulder girdle and fitness training for the total body are incorporated. Sport-specific exercises and skill mastery training may also be instituted. This component should be creative to recreate increasingly demanding activities.

The goal of phase 3 is a gradual return to sports activities. Sport-specific movement patterns are used for throwing, shooting, and swinging progressions, and impact progressions are used for collision sports. Duration, force, and velocity of functional activities progress from submaximal to competition levels. A maintenance program must continue throughout the athlete's return to full activity.

IMPORTANT FACTORS IN SHOULDER REHABILITATION

A starting point for rehabilitation is determined by an examination and assessment of the injured athlete. The athletic trainer or physical therapist gathers information about the athlete's current status, which is essential in the overall care of the shoulder. The athlete generally demonstrates needs in the following specific areas:

- Joint and soft-tissue mobility
- Range of motion and flexibility
- Strength
- Proprioception and kinesthesia
- Endurance
- Functional skills and coordination

Joint Mobility and Mobilization

Joint mobilization refers to techniques that are used to treat joint dysfunctions such as stiffness, reversible joint hypomobility, and pain.[36]

Joint mobilization is a passive movement performed by the athletic trainer or physical therapist at a speed slow enough for the patient to stop the movement. The stretch technique may be applied with an oscillatory motion or a sustained stretch intended to decrease pain or increase mobility.[36,37] Stretch techniques may include physiologic movements that the patient can perform voluntarily, such as flexion and abduction, or accessory movements, which are component motions or joint play. *Component motions,* such as the upward rotation of the scapula and clavicle that occurs with shoulder flexion, accompany voluntary motions but are not under voluntary control. *Joint play* is capsular laxity that allows movement at the joint that may be demonstrated passively but cannot be actively performed by the patient. Joint play motions include but are not limited to glide, distraction, and spin. The athletic trainer or physical therapist must be able to recognize when a particular technique is indicated. Indiscriminate use of joint mobilization techniques could lead to potential harm to the patient's joints.[38] Contraindications to joint mobilization include hypermobility and inflammation with joint effusion that causes the joint capsule to be distended to accommodate the extra fluid. The loss of motion is the result of extra fluid volume rather than adaptive shortening of capsule fibers.[36]

Precautions must be taken when the following conditions are present:

- Malignancy
- Bone disease detectable on radiographs
- Unhealed fracture (The location of the fracture and stabilization provided affect the choice of mobilization.)
- Excessive pain

FOCUS ON . . .

Important Rehabilitation Factors

Shoulder rehabilitation focuses on joint and soft-tissue mobility, range of motion and flexibility, strength, proprioception and kinesthesia, endurance, and functional skills and coordination. Joint mobilization techniques are used to treat joint dysfunctions (eg, stiffness, reversible joint hypomobility, and pain) through passive movements performed by the athletic trainer or physical therapist at speeds slow enough for the patient to stop the movements. The stretch technique is applied with either an oscillatory motion or a sustained stretch and is designed to decrease pain or increase mobility. Included are voluntary physiologic movements and component motions or joint play. Component motions accompany voluntary motions without being under voluntary control. Joint play describes capsular laxity that is evident on passive joint movements but cannot be actively performed by the patient.

Joint mobilizations must be used appropriately to avoid causing harm. Hypermobility and inflammation with joint effusion and a distended joint capsule are contraindications to these techniques. Joint mobilization must be applied cautiously in the presence of malignancy, radiographically evident bone disease, unhealed fracture (depending on fracture location and stability), excessive pain, associated joint hypermobility, and total joint replacement. These techniques are useful in inhibiting pain, moving synovial fluid and exchanging nutrients, and maintaining or elongating tissue length.

Joint mobilization provides sensory input to joint mechanoreceptors and produces neurophysiologic effects. Joint receptors are classified in four types: types I through IV.

The two systems of joint mobilization involve oscillations and sustained translatory joint-play techniques, each with its own grading system for dosage of mobilization (grades I through IV for oscillation and grades I through III for sustaining joint play).

Combining mobilization with passive, active, or overpressured movements may correct post-injury "positional faults" that restrict motion and cause pain. For example, a mobilizing force directed 90° to the plane of movement helps to reestablish motion and normal movement patterns.

The time at which pain was experienced determines which techniques should be used. If pain occurred before tissue limitation, then gentle grade techniques without stretching are implemented. If the pain was concurrent with tissue limitation, cautious stretching to increase movement (but not pain) is appropriate. If pain occurred after tissue limitation, aggressive higher grade techniques to stretch tissue and increase motion are employed.

The convex humeral head in the concave GH joint means that the component motion of sliding occurs in the direction opposite to the angular movement of the humerus, while rolling occurs in the same direction. Bone surface motion within a joint is a balance of rolling, sliding, and spinning. Rolling is not used to mobilize because it causes joint compression, while the sliding component of GH motion is used passively in the normal direction as a translatory glide. Because the shoulder's treatment plane is in the concave glenoid surface, traction is applied perpendicularly and glides are applied in parallel (ie, the direction opposite to the physiologic motion being treated). The proximal clavicle, the moving segment in the SC joint, is convex superiorly to inferiorly and concave anteriorly to posteriorly. Therefore, to retract or protract the clavicle, the mobilization is in the same direction as the movement, but for elevation or depression, the force is applied in the opposite direction. Mobilizing the clavicle on the acromion or applying scapular gliding forces increases joint play in the same direction.

- Hypermobility in associated joints (Associated joints must be properly stabilized.)
- Total joint replacements (Although the joint capsule may be present, the mechanism of the joint replacement is self-limiting.)

Joint mobilization can be used to produce neurophysiologic pain inhibition, synovial fluid movement and nutrient exchange, and tissue length maintenance or elongation.[36-40]

Neurophysiologic effects of joint mobilizations are secondary to providing sensory input to articular mechanoreceptors. **Table 10-3** presents classifications of joint receptors.[40,41]

Grading joint mobilization

There are two systems of joint mobilization; one involves oscillations and the other sustained translatory joint-play techniques.[36,37] Each system has its own grading system for the dosage of mobilization. **Table 10-4** presents the grading system for the oscillation techniques.[38]

Table 10-5 shows the grading system for the sustained translatory joint-play technique.[36]

Recently, descriptions of the combination of mobilizations with movement (MWMs) have indicated that movements can be passive, active, or occur with overpressure.[42] Certain "positional faults" occur after injury to a joint, resulting in movement restrictions and/or pain. A mobi-

TABLE 10-3
CLASSIFICATION OF JOINT RECEPTORS

Type I
- Sense of static position
- Sense of speed of movement
- Sense of direction of movement
- Regulation of muscle tone
- Low threshold, slow adapting, tonic reflexogenic effect on shoulder

> Note: Type I joint receptors are found in a superficial joint capsule and appear with greater density in proximal joints such as the shoulder. They are the only mechanoreceptors that relay information to the cortex of the brain and thus affect conscious awareness.

Type II
- Change of speed of movement
- Regulation of muscle tone
- Fast adapting, phasic reflexogenic effect on lumbar spine, foot, hand, and jaw

> Note: Type II joint receptors are found in deep layers of capsule and articular fat pads and are more prevalent in distal joints such as the ankle.

Type III
- Sense of direction of movement
- Regulation of muscle tone
- Active at extreme ranges of motion
- Slow adapting, identical in structure to Golgi tendon organ
- Respond to stretch at end range of motion
- Result in reflex muscle inhibition

> Note: Type III joint receptors are found in deep and superficial layers of joint ligaments.

Type IV
- Nociception
- High-threshold, tonic reflexogenic with continuous activity
- Respond to deformation, temperature change, and chemical stimuli

> Note: Type IV joint receptors are found in fibrous capsule, ligaments, articular fat pads, periosteum, and walls of blood vessels.

TABLE 10-4
GRADED OSCILLATION TECHNIQUES

Grade I Small amplitude rhythmic oscillations are performed at the beginning of the range of motion. Grade I oscillations are used for their inhibitory effect on the perception of painful stimuli via type II mechanoreceptors.

Grade II Large amplitude rhythmic oscillations are performed within the range of motion that does not reach the limit. Grade II oscillations are used for their inhibitory effect on the perception of painful stimuli via type II mechanoreceptors.

Grade III Large amplitude rhythmic oscillations are performed up to the limit of the available motion. Grade III oscillations are used as a stretching maneuver and may cause inhibition via type III mechanoreceptors.

Grade IV Small amplitude rhythmic oscillations are performed at the limit of the available motion. Grade IV oscillations are used as a stretching maneuver and muscle relaxation technique via type III mechanoreceptors.

cated. The relationship of pain to the limitation determines whether mobilization should be used to relieve pain or to stretch a joint limitation.[37,43] **Table 10-6** shows the factors that will aid in the clinical decision-making process.

Arthrokinematics

The convex-concave rule for each joint determines the direction of the mobilizing force that the athletic trainer or physical therapist applies. Because of the convexity of the humeral head in the GH joint, the component motion of sliding occurs in the opposite direction of the angular movement of the humerus. Rolling occurs in the same direction as the angular movement. Motion of the bone surfaces within the joint is a variable combination of rolling, sliding, or spinning.[36,39,44] Because it causes joint compression, the rolling motion is not used as a mobilizing force. The passive use of the sliding component of glenohumeral motion in the direction that it normally occurs is used as a translatory glide.[36] The treatment plane of the shoulder lies in the concave surface of the glenoid. Traction is applied perpendicular to the treatment plane, and glides are performed parallel to the treatment plane.[38] Thus, mobilization forces or glides in the GH joint are in the opposite direction of the physiologic motion that is being addressed.[36] The proximal clavicle is the moving

lizing force directed 90° to the plane of movement aids in reestablishing motion and normal movement patterns. Clinically, the results of such treatments appear promising, but have yet to be scientifically validated.[42]

Application of joint mobilization

Assessment of the patient's shoulder function and pain patterns determines whether a mobilization technique is indi-

segment in the SC joint and is convex superiorly to inferiorly and concave anteriorly to posteriorly. Thus, for retraction or protraction of the clavicle, the mobilizing force is in the same direction as the movement of the clavicle. However, for elevation or depression of the clavicle, the mobilizing force is applied opposite the movement of

the clavicle. Clavicular mobilization on the acromion increases general joint play in the direction of mobilization. Scapular gliding mobilization forces are also in the same direction as the motion that is being addressed.

JOINT MOBILIZATION TECHNIQUES

The following joint mobilization techniques aid in treating pain, stiffness, and reversible joint hypomobility and are passive movements that are performed by the athletic trainer or physical therapist.[36,37,45]

Inferior Glide of the Clavicular Head

The inferior glide of the clavicular head is indicated as a component motion for shoulder elevation. The patient is supine, and the athletic trainer stands above the patient's head. The athletic trainer places his or her thumb pad in contact with the most superior/proximal surface of the clavicle. The opposite thumb is placed on top of the other thumb, and inferior force is exerted diagonally away from the patient's midline.

Posterior Glide of the Clavicular Head

The posterior glide of the clavicular head is indicated as a component motion for shoulder retraction and horizontal abduction. The patient is supine, and the athletic trainer stands to the side of the patient. The athletic trainer places his or her thumb pad in contact with the anterior/proximal surface of the clavicle. The opposite thumb is placed on top of the other thumb, and posterior force is exerted (**Figure 10-25**).

Posterosuperior and Anteroinferior Glide of the Clavicle on the Acromion

The posterosuperior and anteroinferior glide of the clavicle on the acromion is indicated as a joint-play motion that is necessary for shoulder complex movement. The

---

TABLE 10-5

GRADED SUSTAINED TRANSLATORY JOINT-PLAY TECHNIQUES

Grade I	Small II amplitude joint traction is employed where no stress is placed on the capsule. Grade I techniques are used with gliding motions to relieve pain via stimulation of type I mechanoreceptors.
Grade II	Enough traction or glide of the joint surfaces is employed to tighten the tissues around the joint. This is also known as "taking up the slack." Grade II techniques are used to assess the sensitivity of the joint to mobilization so that dosage may be increased or decreased accordingly.
Grade III	Traction or glide of the joint surfaces of an amplitude large enough to place a stretch on the joint capsule and surrounding periarticular structures is employed. Grade III techniques are used to stretch the joint structures and increase joint play. Muscle relaxation occurs via type III mechanoreceptors.

TABLE 10-6

FACTORS THAT AID IN THE CLINICAL DECISION-MAKING PROCESS

Time at which pain is experienced	Techniques to be used
Before tissue limitation	• Gentle grade techniques with no stretching
Concurrent with tissue limitation	• Cautious stretching (to increase movement but not pain)
After tissue limitation	• Aggressive higher-grade techniques (to stretch tissue and increase motion)

Note: A subluxation or dislocation of one bony part on another or a torn loose structure within the joint that blocks normal motion calls for manipulative techniques that are beyond the scope of this text.

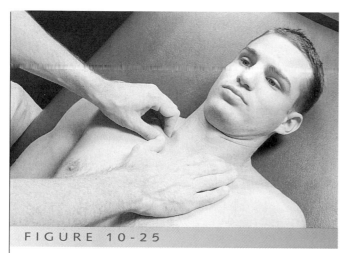

FIGURE 10-25

The posterior glide of the clavicular head is a component motion for shoulder retraction and horizontal abduction.

patient is supine, and the athletic trainer stands facing the patient. The athletic trainer grasps the anterior surface of the humerus with one hand while the opposite thumb contacts the anterolateral surface of the clavicle. He or she then exerts a force in a posterior/superior/medial direction through the thumb as well as exerting an anterior/inferior/lateral directional force (**Figure 10-26**).

Distraction of the Scapula

Distraction of the scapula is indicated as a joint-play motion that is necessary for shoulder complex movement. The patient is prone, and the athletic trainer stands facing the patient. The athletic trainer grasps the anterior surface of the patient's humerus with one hand, pulling posteriorly. He or she rests the opposite proximal phalanx on the thoracic wall and squeezes under the inferior angle of the scapula (**Figure 10-27**).

Superior and Inferior Glide of the Scapula

The superior and inferior glide of the scapula is indicated as a joint-play motion that is necessary for shoulder complex movement. The patient is lying on his or her side, and the athletic trainer stands facing the patient. The humerus is maintained against the athletic trainer's abdomen as he or she moves the scapula superiorly and inferiorly (**Figure 10-28**).

Lateral and Medial Rotation of the Scapula

Lateral and medial rotation of the scapula is indicated as a joint-play motion that is necessary for shoulder complex movement. The patient is lying on his or side, and the athletic trainer stands facing the patient. The humerus is maintained against the athletic trainer's abdomen as he or she moves the scapula medially and laterally in the directions of rotation (**Figure 10-29**).

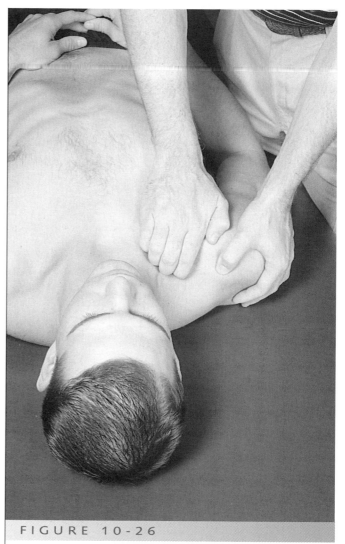

FIGURE 10-26

The posterosuperior and anteroinferior glide of the clavicle on the acromion is a joint-play motion for shoulder complex movement.

Anterior Humeral Glide

The anterior humeral glide is indicated as a component motion for glenohumeral external rotation, extension, and abduction. The patient is prone, and the athletic trainer stands facing the patient and holds the patient's arm in a loose packed position. The athletic trainer holds one hand around the proximal humerus while the other hand is distal to the acromion. Force is applied in an anterior direction (**Figure 10-30**).

Inferior Humeral Glide

The inferior humeral glide is indicated as a component motion for flexion and abduction. The patient is supine, and the athletic trainer stands at the patient's side. The athletic trainer places the proximal phalanx of his or her index finger against the neck of the scapula while the other hand contacts the lateral/distal surface of the humerus. The athletic trainer exerts an inferior

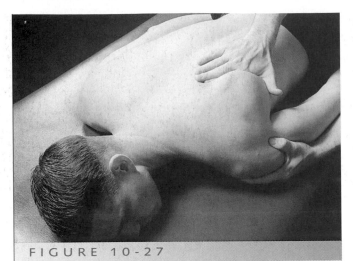

FIGURE 10-27

Distraction of the scapula is a joint-play motion for shoulder complex movement.

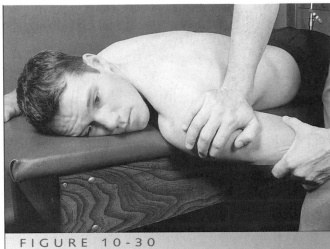

FIGURE 10-30

The anterior humeral glide is a component motion for gleno-humeral external rotation, extension, and abduction.

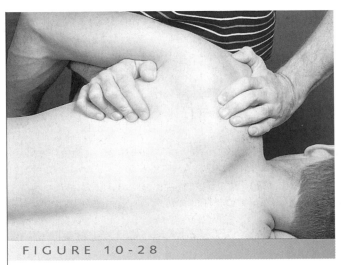

FIGURE 10-28

The superior and inferior glide of the scapula is a joint-play motion for shoulder complex movement.

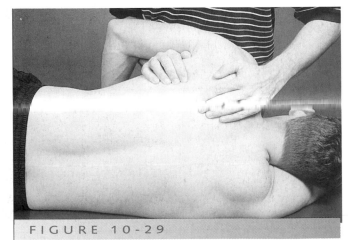

FIGURE 10-29

Lateral and medial rotation of the scapula is a joint-play motion for shoulder complex movement.

force through the contact on the distal humerus (**Figure 10-31**).

Lateral Distraction of the Humeral Head

Lateral distraction of the humeral head is indicated as a joint-play motion for shoulder complex movement. The patient is supine, and the athletic trainer stands at the side of the patient's shoulder. The athletic trainer's outside hand grasps the anterior/distal part of the humerus, and the hand nearest the patient is placed so that the proximal phalanx of the index finger and the first web space contact the medioproximal surface of the humeral neck. The athletic trainer exerts a lateral force with the inside hand's index finger and web space (**Figure 10-32**).

Posterior Glide of the Humeral Head

The posterior glide of the humeral head is indicated as a component motion for internal rotation and flexion. The patient is supine, and the athletic trainer stands at the patient's shoulder facing the patient. The athletic trainer grasps the anterior/distal surface of the humerus with one hand, while the opposite hand contacts the anterior surface of the humerus. The athletic trainer exerts a posterior force (**Figure 10-33**).

SELF-MOBILIZATION TECHNIQUES

Lateral Glide

The patient is seated in a chair at the side of the table with the involved extremity resting in the sagittal plane on the table. The uninvolved hand is placed on the medial humerus just below the axilla. The patient applies gentle force in the lateral direction with the uninvolved hand (**Figure 10-34**).

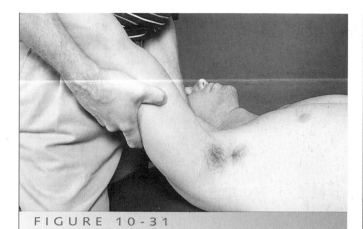

FIGURE 10-31

The inferior humeral glide is a component motion for flexion and abduction.

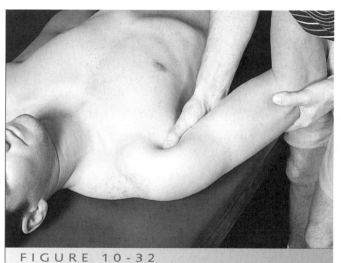

FIGURE 10-32

Lateral distraction of the humeral head is a joint-play motion for shoulder complex movement.

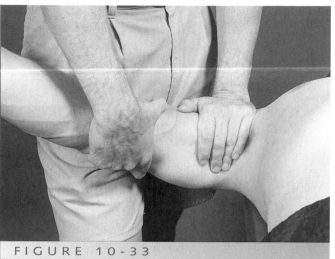

FIGURE 10-33

The posterior glide of the humeral head is a component motion for internal rotation and flexion.

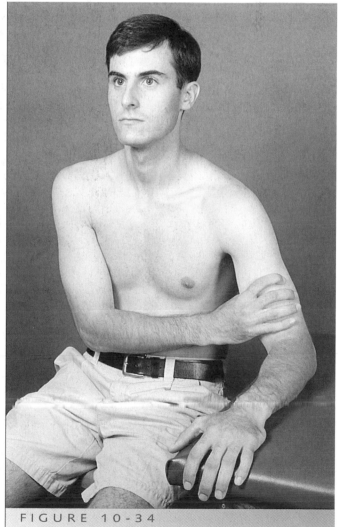

FIGURE 10-34

The lateral glide is a self-mobilization technique in which the patient applies gentle force to the involved arm with the uninvolved hand.

Inferior Glide

The patient stands at the edge of the table, and the involved hand grasps the edge of the table. The patient leans away from the edge of the table while maintaining the grasp (**Figure 10-35**).

Alternative methods include the following:

- The patient sits in a chair with the involved extremity resting in the coronal plane on the table and places the uninvolved hand on the lateral aspect of the humerus over the deltoid. The patient applies gentle force in the inferior direction with the uninvolved hand.

- The patient stands with the involved upper extremity in neutral position, and the uninvolved hand grasps the humerus just above the epicondyles. The patient then applies gentle force in the inferior direction with the uninvolved hand.

Posterior Glide

The patient is prone on the table and rests his or her weight on the elbows before allowing the body weight to shift downward (**Figure 10-36**).

Anterior Glide

The patient is supine on the table with shoulders extended and rests on flexed elbows before allowing the body weight to shift downward (**Figure 10-37**).

SOFT-TISSUE MOBILIZATION

The soft tissues of the shoulder should be addressed beyond the joint capsule. Skin, fascia, muscle, tendons, and ligaments may be shortened, lack mobility, or experience contracture, particularly following surgical intervention with subsequent scarring and immobilization. Standard massage techniques, such as effleurage and pétrissage, and specific techniques, such as transverse friction massage all play a role in increasing soft-tissue mobility.

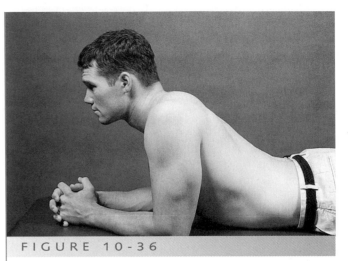

FIGURE 10-36

The posterior glide is a self-mobilization technique in which the patient allows his or her body weight to shift downward while lying prone on the table.

RANGE-OF-MOTION EXERCISES

Passive Range-of-Motion Exercises with a Wand

The following range-of-motion exercises are performed using a wand.

Shoulder flexion

The patient stands or is supine and holds the wand at waist level with palms supinated. The patient lifts both upper extremities directly overhead in the sagittal plane, guiding the involved extremity with the uninvolved extremity (**Figure 10-38**).

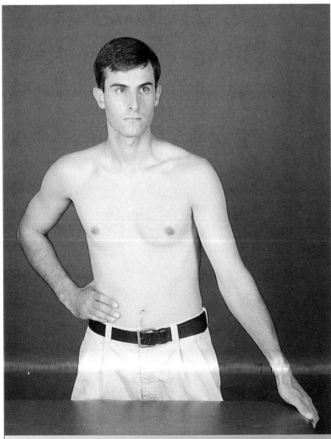

FIGURE 10-35

The inferior glide is a self-mobilization technique in which the patient applies gentle force to the involved arm in the inferior direction.

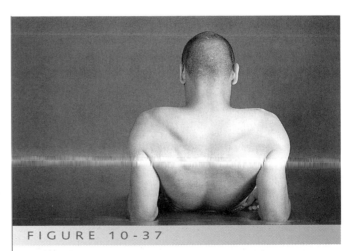

FIGURE 10-37

The anterior glide is a self-mobilization technique in which the patient allows his or her body weight to shift downward while lying supine on the table with the elbows flexed.

Shoulder abduction

The patient stands or is supine and holds the wand at waist level with the involved hand supinated and the uninvolved hand pronated. The patient guides the involved upper extremity with the uninvolved extremity and moves it overhead in a lateral direction in the coronal plane (**Figure 10-39**).

Shoulder internal/external rotation

The patient stands or is supine and holds the wand at the umbilical level with elbows flexed to 90°. The patient guides the involved hand with the uninvolved hand to move it laterally in the transverse plane (**Practice Session 10-1**).

The patient stands or is supine and holds the wand at chest level with shoulders abducted to 90° and elbows flexed to 90°. The patient guides the involved hand with the uninvolved hand to move it inferiorly and superiorly from the waist to the overhead position with the forearms moving in the sagittal plane.

Shoulder horizontal abduction

The patient stands or is supine and holds the wand at chest level with the involved hand supinated. The patient guides the involved hand with the uninvolved hand to move it laterally and medially in the transverse plane.

Shoulder extension

The patient stands and holds the wand on the involved side at waist level with the hand in neutral position. The uninvolved hand is held in horizontal adduction with the hand at waist level. The patient guides the involved hand with the uninvolved hand to move it posteriorly in the sagittal plane (**Figure 10-40**).

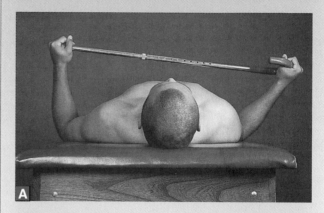

PRACTICE SESSION 10-1
SHOULDER INTERNAL/EXTERNAL ROTATION

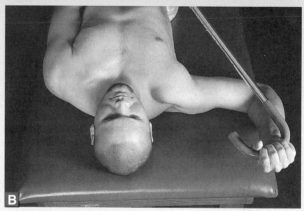

Shoulder internal/external rotation. **A** The patient is supine with the wand at the umbilical level, then guides the involved extremity laterally with the uninvolved hand. **B** The patient is supine with the wand at chest level, then guides the involved extremity inferiorly and superiorly with the uninvolved hand.

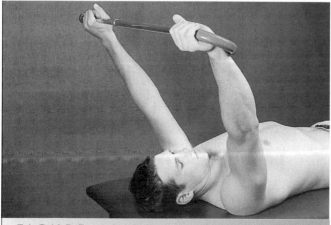

FIGURE 10-38

Shoulder flexion is a range-of-motion exercise with a wand in which the patient lifts both upper extremities and guides the involved extremity with the uninvolved extremity.

Pendulum Exercises

Shoulder pendulum exercises

The patient stands flexed at the waist and supports the uninvolved side by leaning on the table. The involved extremity is allowed to hang in a relaxed position free from support. Using a rocking motion of the entire body, the patient oscillates the involved extremity through flexion, extension, horizontal adduction, horizontal abduction, and circumduction (**Figure 10-41**).

FIGURE 10-39

Shoulder abduction is a range-of-motion exercise with a wand in which the patient moves the involved upper extremity overhead in a lateral direction.

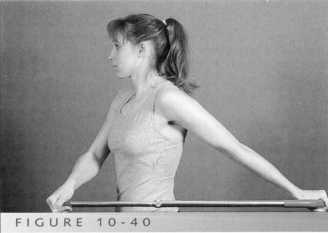

FIGURE 10-40

Shoulder extension is a range-of-motion exercise with a wand in which the patient moves the involved hand posteriorly.

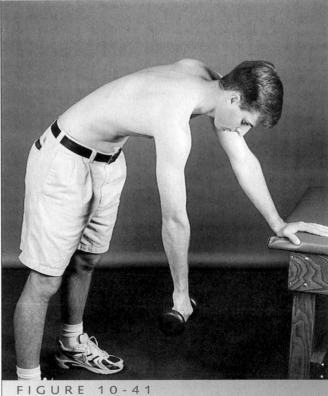

FIGURE 10-41

In shoulder pendulum exercises, the patient oscillates the involved extremity through various movements.

Wall Exercises

Shoulder flexion
The patient stands facing the wall and, with the palm facing the wall, slides the involved hand upward along the wall (**Figure 10-42**).

Shoulder abduction
The patient stands with the involved upper extremity nearest the wall and, with the palm facing the patient, slides the hand upward along the wall (**Figure 10-43**).

Shoulder horizontal abduction
The patient stands facing the wall with the involved shoulder abducted to 90° and the palm flat against wall. The patient then turns the trunk away from the shoulder until he or she feels a stretch (Figure 10-44).

Shoulder external rotation
The patient stands facing a corner or door frame with the involved elbow flexed 90° and the hand against the wall. The patient turns the trunk away from the wall until he or she feels a stretch (**Figure 10-45**).

Wheel or Inflated Ball Exercises

Shoulder flexion (wheel)
The patient stands facing the wall with both hands grasping the wheel handles with the wheel midline at the waist level. The patient guides the uninvolved extremity to roll the wheel to the overhead position.

Alternatively, the patient stands facing the table with both hands grasping the wheel handles with the wheel midline at the waist level. The patient guides the uninvolved extremity to roll the wheel away anteriorly on the surface of the table.

Shoulder flexion (ball)

The patient stands facing the wall, holding the ball on the wall with the involved shoulder flexed to 90°. The patient then rolls the ball up the wall by moving closer to the ball with the entire body as the upper extremity moves along the ball superiorly in the sagittal plane (**Figure 10-46**).

Alternatively, the patient stands facing the ball, which is on the table surface, and rests the involved hand low on the ball. The patient then rolls the ball away by leaning the trunk forward, allowing the involved hand to move superiorly as the ball rolls forward.

Shoulder abduction (ball)

The patient stands with the involved shoulder holding the ball to the wall at 90° of abduction. The patient rolls the ball up the wall by moving the entire body closer to the ball, allowing the involved extremity to move superiorly in the coronal plane (**Figure 10-47**).

Alternatively, the patient stands at the side of the table with the involved upper extremity resting on the ball, which is on the table surface. The patient rolls the ball laterally by leaning the trunk, allowing the involved hand to move along the ball superiorly in the coronal plane.

Strengthening Techniques

Strength is defined as the force or tension a muscle or muscle group can exert against a resistance in one maximal effort.[46] Strength is developed through progressive-resistance exercise. Progressive-resistance exercises can be isolated movements or combined movement patterns. An isolated movement is used to strengthen a particular weak muscle. A common isolated movement is the "empty can," which isolates the supraspinatus muscle. Combined patterns such as PNF shoulder D2 flexion and extension exercises are used to reestablish, encourage, and strengthen a specific functional movement.[47]

FIGURE 10-42

Shoulder flexion is a wall exercise in which the patient faces the wall and slides the involved hand up along the wall.

FIGURE 10-43

Shoulder abduction is a wall exercise in which the patient turns the palm away from the wall and slides the hand up along the wall.

FIGURE 10-44

Shoulder horizontal abduction is a wall exercise in which the patient faces the wall with the involved shoulder abducted and palm flat against the wall, then turns away.

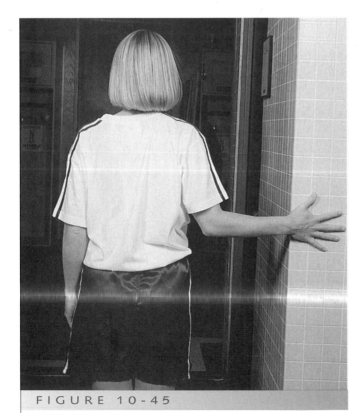

FIGURE 10-45

Shoulder external rotation is a wall exercise in which the patient faces a corner door frame with the involved elbow flexed and palm flat against the wall, then turns away.

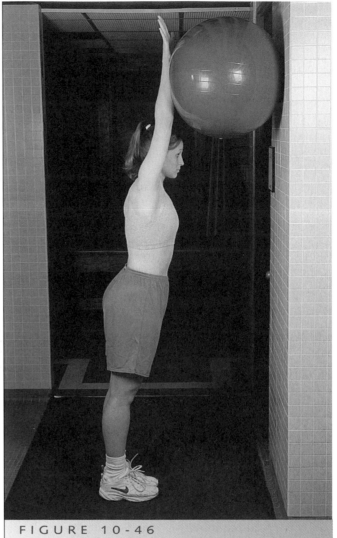

FIGURE 10-46

Shoulder flexion with a ball is an exercise that can be performed either on a table surface or against a wall.

All exercises can be performed with limb weight, body weight, manual resistance, dumbbells, elastic bands, barbells, or machines and should be performed in pain-free range of motion or as allowed by precautions.

Isometric Shoulder Exercises

Abduction

The patient stands with the involved upper extremity next to a wall, with the elbow flexed 90°. The patient presses a pillow or rolled towel into the wall with the elbow held away from the body in the coronal plane (**Figure 10-48**).

Adduction

The patient stands with a pillow or rolled towel held between the trunk and involved elbow with the elbow flexed 90°. The patient presses the elbow toward the trunk in the coronal plane (**Figure 10-49**).

FIGURE 10-47

Shoulder abduction with a ball is an exercise that can be performed either on a table surface or against a wall.

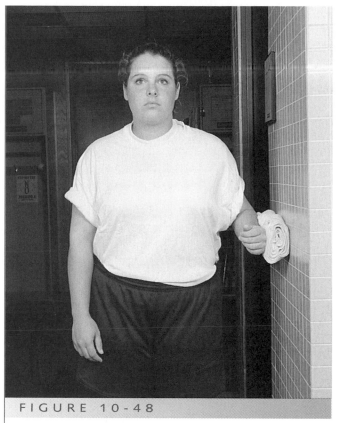

FIGURE 10-48

Shoulder abduction is an isometric exercise in which the patient presses a pillow or rolled towel into the wall.

Flexion

The patient stands facing the wall with the involved elbow flexed 90° and presses the fist anteriorly in the sagittal plane into a pillow or rolled towel held against the wall (**Figure 10-50**).

Extension

The patient stands facing away from the wall with the involved elbow flexed 90° and presses the elbow posteriorly in the sagittal plane against the wall or into a pillow or rolled towel held against the wall (**Figure 10-51**).

Internal rotation

The patient stands facing the corner of the wall with the involved elbow flexed 90° and presses the fist medially in the transverse plane into the wall or against a pillow or rolled towel held against the wall (**Figure 10-52**).

External rotation

The patient stands facing the corner of the wall with the involved elbow flexed 90° and presses the dorsum of the hand or fist laterally in the transverse plane into the wall or against a pillow or rolled towel held against the wall (**Figure 10-53**).

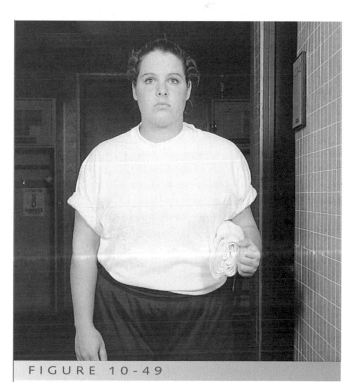

FIGURE 10-49

Shoulder adduction is an isometric exercise in which the patient presses a pillow or rolled towel against his or her trunk with the elbow.

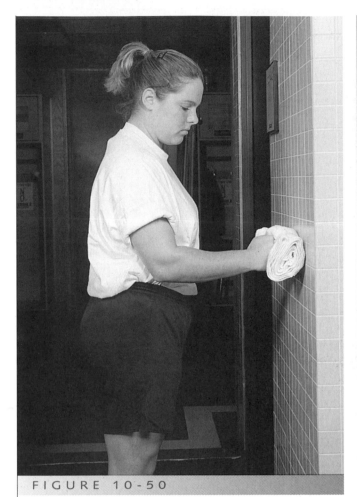

FIGURE 10-50

Shoulder flexion is an isometric exercise in which the patient presses his or her fist into a pillow or rolled towel held against the wall.

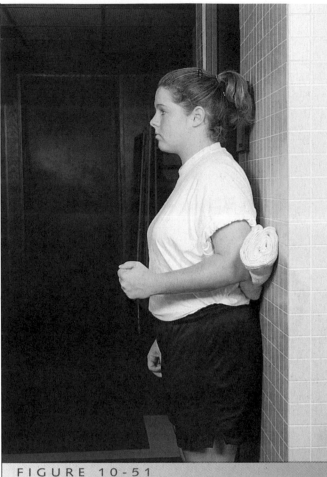

FIGURE 10-51

Shoulder extension is an isometric exercise in which the patient presses the elbow posteriorly against the wall.

Horizontal adduction

The patient stands facing the corner of the wall with the involved shoulder and elbow flexed 90° and presses the medial forearm medially in the transverse plane into the wall or against a pillow or rolled towel held against the wall.

Horizontal abduction

The patient stands facing the corner of the wall with the involved shoulder and elbow flexed 90° and presses the lateral forearm laterally in the transverse plane into the wall or against a pillow or rolled towel hold against the wall.

Progressive Resistive Shoulder Exercises

Flexion

The patient stands or sits with the upper extremity in a neutral position at the side and lifts the upper extremity in the sagittal plane forward from the body in a pain-free arc (**Figure 10-54**).

Abduction

The patient stands or sits with the upper extremity in a neutral position at the side. The patient then lifts the upper extremity in the coronal plane away from the body (**Figure 10-55**).

Extension

The patient stands or sits with the upper extremity in a neutral position at the side. The patient then lifts the upper extremity in the sagittal plane backward from the body (**Figure 10-56**).

Alternatively, the patient lies prone on the table with the upper extremity in a relaxed position over the edge of the supporting surface. The patient lifts the upper extremity in the sagittal plane toward the midline of the body and continues beyond the neutral position, if possible.

External rotation

The patient stands or sits with the upper extremity at the side and the elbow flexed to 90° (**Figure 10-57**). The

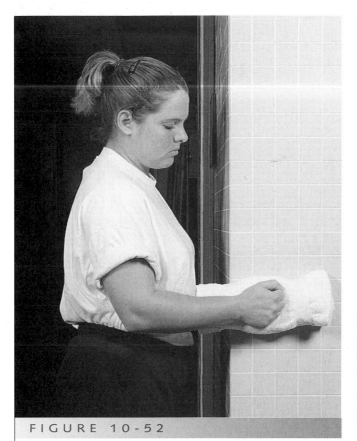

FIGURE 10-52

Shoulder internal rotation is an isometric exercise in which the patient presses the fist medially against a pillow or rolled towel held against the wall.

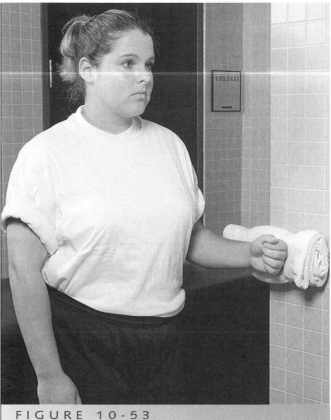

FIGURE 10-53

Shoulder external rotation is an isometric exercise in which the patient presses the dorsum of the hand or fist laterally into a pillow or rolled towel held against the wall.

patient pulls the tubing by moving the hand away from the midline of the body in the transverse plane.

Alternative methods include the following:

- The patient lies on the uninvolved side, with the involved upper extremity at the side and the elbow flexed to 90°. The patient lifts a weight by moving the hand away from the midline of body in the transverse plane.

- The patient lies on the involved side with the involved upper extremity in a relaxed position over the edge of the supporting surface. While holding a weight in the involved hand, the patient turns the upper extremity outward as a unit in the transverse plane of the limb.

- The patient stands or sits with the upper extremity abducted to 90° and the elbow flexed to 90° and stabilized in this position by a supporting surface. The patient pulls the tubing by moving the hand posteriorly in the sagittal plane.

Internal rotation

The patient stands or sits with the upper extremity at the side and the elbow flexed to 90° (**Figure 10-58**). The

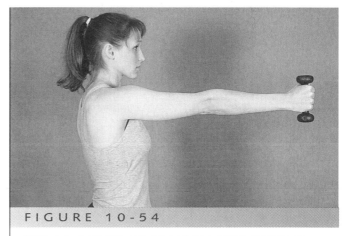

FIGURE 10-54

Flexion is a progressive resistive shoulder exercise in which the patient lifts the upper extremity forward in a pain-free arc.

patient pulls the tubing by moving the hand toward the midline of the body in the transverse plane.

Alternative methods include the following:

- The patient lies on the involved side of the body with the involved upper extremity at the side and

FIGURE 10-55

Abduction is a progressive resistive shoulder exercise in which the patient lifts the upper extremity away from the body.

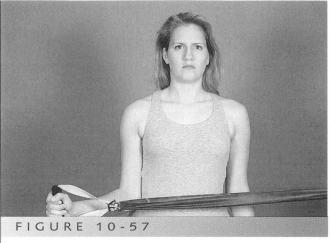

FIGURE 10-57

External rotation is a progressive resistive shoulder exercise in which the patient pulls tubing by moving the hand away from the midline.

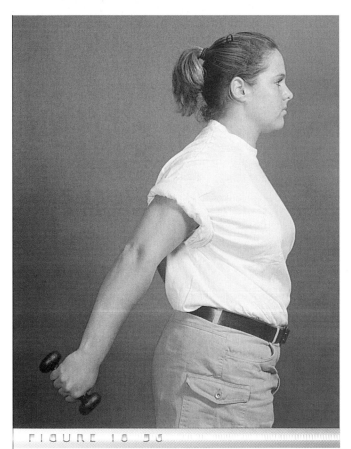

FIGURE 10-55

Extension is a progressive resistive shoulder exercise in which the patient stands, sits, or lies prone, then lifts the upper extremity.

the elbow flexed to 90°. The patient lifts a weight by moving the hand toward the midline of the body in the transverse plane.

- The patient lies on the involved side with the involved upper extremity in a relaxed position over the edge of the supporting surface. The patient holds a weight and turns the upper extremity inward as a unit in the transverse plane of the limb.

- The patient stands or sits with the upper extremity abducted to 90° and the elbow flexed to 90°. This position is stabilized by a supporting surface. The patient pulls the tubing by moving the hand anteriorly in the sagittal plane.

Seated rows

The patient sits with the trunk in neutral, the shoulders flexed from 70° to 90°, the elbows fully extended, and the hands holding the tubing with a neutral grip. The patient pulls the tubing to the umbilicus by retracting the scapulae, extending the shoulders, and flexing the elbows.

Latissimus pull-downs

The patient sits with the shoulders in full flexion and the elbows fully extended and holds the resistance with a supinated grip. The patient pulls the resistance downward to chest level by retracting and depressing the scapulae, extending the shoulders, and flexing the elbows.

Alternatively, the patient sits with the shoulders flexed to 90°and the elbows flexed to 90° and holds the resistance with a supinated grip. The patient pulls the resistance downward to chest level by retracting and depressing the scapulae, extending the shoulders, and flexing the elbows.

Shoulder press

The patient stands or sits while holding weights at shoulder height, with the hands shoulder-width apart and grip pronated (**Practice Session 10-2**). The patient pushes the

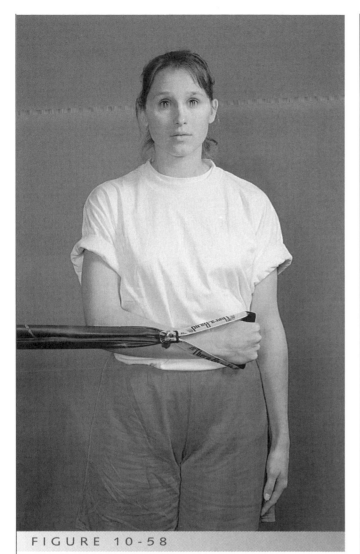

FIGURE 10-58

Internal rotation is a progressive resistive shoulder exercise in which the patient pulls tubing my moving the hand toward the midline.

weights upward to a position of shoulder abduction, flexion, and elbow extension.

Supraspinatus empty can
The patient stands with the involved upper extremity at the side in internal rotation and holds a weight with a pronated grip (**Figure 10-59**). The patient then abducts the upper extremity in the scapular plane approximately 30° anterior to the coronal plane to no higher than 90°.

Supraspinatus open can
The patient stands with the involved extremity at the side in a neutral position and holds a weight with a neutral grip (**Figure 10-60**). The patient abducts the upper extremity in the scapular plane approximately 30° anterior to the coronal plane.

PRACTICE SESSION 10-2
SHOULDER PRESS

Shoulder press. **A** The patient holds weights at shoulder height with the hands shoulder-width apart. **B** The patient pushes the weights upward.

Supraspinatus press
The patient stands with the shoulders abducted in the scapular plane to 90°, externally rotated to 90°, and with the elbows flexed to 90° and holds a weight in each hand. The patient moves the weights in a short arc from chin height to head height.

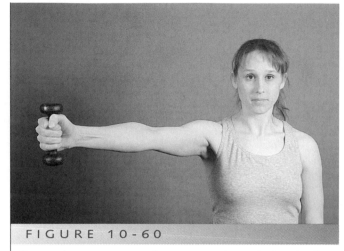

FIGURE 10-59

Supraspinatus empty can is a progressive resistive shoulder exercise in which the patient stands with the involved arm internally rotated and abducts the upper extremity.

FIGURE 10-60

Supraspinatus open can is a progressive resistive shoulder exercise in which the patient stands with the involved extremity in a neutral position and abducts the upper extremity.

Bench press

The bench press can be used in the standard form or in limited ranges of motion. Range limits can be set using spotting racks or padded rolls on the bar itself. Chest press machines or dumbbells can be used for unilateral motions.

Push-up

The patient performs a push-up in the standard or modified position. On reaching the top position of the movement, the patient protracts the scapulae to push beyond the normal stopping position (**Figure 10-61**).

Hughston Prone Series

The Hughston Prone Series includes three steps.

Position A: The patient lies prone on a table with the involved extremity abducted to 90° and the thumb pointed toward the head. The patient lifts the extremity away from the floor, pauses for 2 seconds, and repeats the movement.

Position B: The patient lies prone on a table with the involved extremity abducted so that the hand is at eye level. The thumb is pointed toward the head. The patient lifts the extremity away from the floor, pauses for 2 seconds, and repeats the movement.

Position C: The patient assumes position A, but with the thumb pointed toward the ceiling. The patient lifts the extremity away from the floor, pauses for 2 seconds, and repeats the movement. The patient then assumes position B, but with the thumb pointed toward the ceiling. The patient lifts the extremity away from the floor, pauses for 2 seconds, and repeats the movement.

FIGURE 10-61

The push-up is a progressive resistive shoulder exercise in which the patient performs a push-up and protracts the scapulae beyond the normal stopping point.

PROPRIOCEPTIVE NEUROMUS-CULAR FACILITATION SHOULDER PATTERNS

Proprioceptive neuromuscular facilitation (PNF) involves mass movement patterns that incorporate spiral or diagonal motions that facilitate selective irradiation (resisting strong muscle groups at specific times in a pattern to facilitate the contractions of weaker muscle groups in the same pattern).[48,49] These patterns closely resemble movements that occur in sport and work activities. Each spiral and diagonal pattern includes a three-component motion with respect to all the joints or pivots of action participating in the movement. These three components include flexion or extension, adduction or abduction, and rotation. The optimal performance of a pattern involves sequential contractions described as a "chain" of muscles moving in synergy. The agonistic pattern is the pattern of muscles having components of action that are exactly opposite of those of the agonistic pattern.[49]

Rhythmic Initiation

Rhythmic initiation is used to improve the patient's ability to initiate movement. This technique involves voluntary relaxation, passive movement, and isotonic contractions of major muscle components of the antagonistic pattern.[49]

Repeated Contractions

The stretch reflex is facilitated and coupled with repetitive voluntary isotonic contractions to enhance the patient's effort to initiate movement. As the patient's ability to produce an isotonic contraction improves, an isometric hold at weaker points in the range may be added to advance the treatment.[49]

Reversal of Antagonists

Stimulation of the agonist contraction is achieved when the patient first resists an isometric or isotonic contraction of the antagonist followed by resistance of the agonist movement as the antagonistic pattern is reversed.[49]

Slow Reversal: An isotonic contraction of the antagonist is followed by an isotonic contraction of the agonist.

Slow Reversal Hold: The antagonist performs an isotonic contraction followed by an isometric contraction, then the agonist performs an isotonic contraction followed by an isometric contraction.

Rhythmic Stabilization: An isometric contraction of the antagonist is followed by an isometric contraction of the agonist resulting in co-contraction of both groups.

Relaxation Techniques

Relaxation techniques are used to gain range of motion via the relaxation or inhibition of a pattern's antagonist.[49]

Contract-Relax: The athletic trainer moves the patient's body part passively into the agonistic pattern to the point where the patient feels limitation, at which point the athletic trainer instructs the patient to contract isotonically in the antagonistic pattern. As the patient feels the relaxation, the athletic trainer then moves the limb again into the agonistic pattern until the patient again feels limitation.

Hold-Relax: The athletic trainer moves the patient's body part in the same sequence as in the contract-relax technique. At the point of limitation, the athletic trainer instructs the patient to perform a maximal isometric contraction, then instructs the patient to voluntarily relax. As the patient feels the relaxation, the athletic trainer then moves the limb into the agonistic pattern to a new point of limitation.

Hold-Relax: The range-limiting pattern)antagonistic) performs an isotonic contraction, followed by an isometric contraction of the same pattern against the athletic trainer's resistance. After a brief, voluntary relaxation, an isotonic contraction of the agonsitic pattern is then performed.

Direction 1 (Flexion)

Component motions

- Fingers: Extend and abduct toward the radial side
- Thumb: Extends, adducts, and externally rotates toward the radial side
- Wrist: Supinates and extends toward the radial side
- Elbow: Flexes
- Shoulder: Flexes, abducts, and externally rotates
- Scapula: Rotates, adducts at the medial angle, elevates posteriorly
- Clavicle: Rotates and elevates anteriorly away from the sternum

Hand position

The athletic trainer places his or her left hand in the palm of the patient's right hand, so that the patient may grasp it with fingers and thumb, and so that the patient may resist wrist flexion toward the radial side. To control external rotation and proximal components of motion, the athletic trainer places the palmar surface of the patient's right arm on the anterior medial surface of his or her own left arm (**Figure 10-62**).

Timing/sequence

Movement is distal to proximal: first at fingers, thumb, wrist/forearm, then at shoulder, scapula, and clavicle.

Commands

The athletic trainer prepares the patient by saying, "You are to squeeze my hand, turn it, and bend your elbow, then pull my hand up and across your face."

The athletic trainer initiates action by saying, "Pull!" "Squeeze my hand!" "Turn it!" "Bend your elbow!" "Pull up across your face!"

Direction 1 (Extension)—Antagonist Pattern

Component motions

- Fingers: Flex and adduct toward ulnar side
- Thumb: Flexes, abducts, and internally rotates toward ulnar side
- Wrist: Pronates and flexes toward ulnar side
- Elbow: Remains straight
- Shoulder: Extends, adducts, and internally rotates
- Scapula: Rotates, abducts at the medial angle, and depresses anteriorly
- Clavicle: Rotates and depresses anteriorly toward the sternum

Hand position

The athletic trainer cups the palmar surface of his or her left hand and fingers over the dorsal ulnar aspect of the fingers and wrist of the patient's left hand. To control

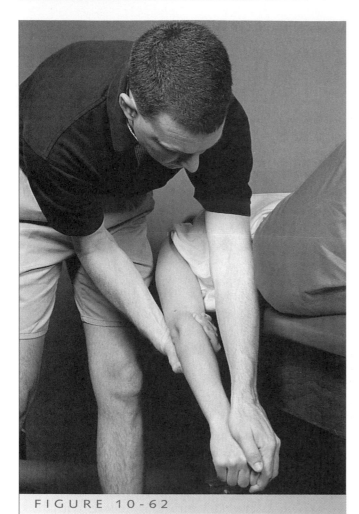

FIGURE 10-62

Direction 1 (flexion) is a PNF exercise in which the patient tries to resist wrist flexion toward the radial side.

internal rotation and proximal components of motion, the athletic trainer places the palmar surface of his or her right hand on the posterolateral surface of the patient's arm (Figure 10-63).

Timing/sequence
Movement is distal to proximal: first at fingers, thumb, wrist/forearm, then at shoulder, scapula, and clavicle.

Commands
The athletic trainer prepares the patient by saying, "You are going to open your hand, turn it, and push it down and away from your face."

The athletic trainer initiates action by saying, "Push! "Open your hand!" "Turn it!" "Keep your elbow straight!" "Push it down toward me!"

Direction 2 (Flexion)

Component motions
- Fingers: Flex and adduct toward radial side
- Thumb: Externally rotates, flexes, and adducts toward the radial side

- Wrist: Supinates and flexes toward the radial side
- Elbow: Flexes slightly
- Shoulder: Flexes, abducts, and externally rotates
- Scapula: Rotates, abducts at the inferior angle, elevates anteriorly
- Clavicle: Rotates and elevates anteriorly to approximate the sternum

Hand position
The athletic trainer cups the palmar surface of his or her right hand and fingers over the dorsoradial aspect of the fingers and wrist of the patient's right hand. To control external rotation and proximal components of motion, the athletic trainer places the palmar surface of his or her left hand on the anterolateral surface of the patient's right arm (Figure 10-64).

Timing/sequence
Movement is distal to proximal: first at fingers, thumb, wrist/forearm, then at shoulder, scapula, and clavicle.

Commands
The athletic trainer prepares the patient by saying, "You are going to open your hand, turn it, and lift it up and out toward me, keeping your elbow straight."

The athletic trainer initiates action by saying, "Lift!" "Open your hand!" "Turn it!" "Keep your elbow straight!" "Lift it up toward me!"

Direction 2 (Extension)— Antagonistic Pattern

Component motions
- Fingers: Extend and abduct toward ulnar side
- Thumb: Internally rotates, extends, and abducts toward ulnar side

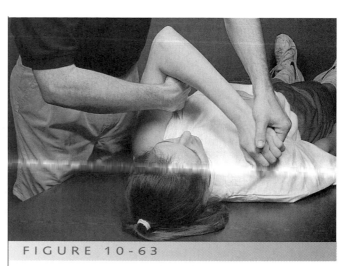

FIGURE 10-63

Direction 1 (extension) antagonistic pattern is a PNF exercise in which the athletic trainer tries to control internal rotation and proximal components of motion.

- Wrist: Pronates and extends toward ulnar side
- Elbow: Extends
- Shoulder: Extends, abducts, and internally rotates
- Scapula: Rotates, adducts at the inferior angle, and depresses posteriorly
- Clavicle: Rotates and depresses anteriorly away from the sternum

Hand position

The athletic trainer places his or her right hand in the palm of the patient's right hand, so that the patient may grasp it with fingers and thumb and so that the patient's wrist may flex toward the ulnar side. To control internal rotation and proximal components of motion, the athletic trainer places the palmar surface of his or her left hand on the postero-medial surface of the patient's arm (**Figure 10-65**).

Timing/sequence

Movement is distal to proximal: first at fingers, thumb, wrist/forearm, then at shoulder, scapula, and clavicle.

Commands

The athletic trainer prepares the patient by saying, "You are going to squeeze my hand, turn it, and pull it down toward your left hip, keeping your elbow straight."

The athletic trainer initiates action by saying, "Pull!" "Squeeze my hand!" "Turn it!" "Keep your elbow straight!" "Pull it down toward your left hip!"

PROPRIOCEPTION AND KINESTHESIA

Proprioception is the term used to define the perception of joint position and limb "heaviness."[49] *Kinesthesia* is the term used to define the body's ability to detect positional changes. Although the terms are not interchangeable,

they are closely related. Articular mechanoreceptors, golgi tendon organs, muscle spindles, the vestibular system, the visual system, and cerebellar function all contribute to the body's conscious and unconscious positional awareness.

The athletic trainer's goal is to integrate these systems to work in conjunction across a variety of functional activities and positions. Progressive activities should move from slow speed (nonfunctional) to high speed (functional), from positions of high scapular stability to low scapular stability, and from below shoulder height to overhead positions. Activities should be repetitious enough to promote automatic behavior patterns of the shoulder complex.

PROPRIOCEPTIVE/KINESTHETIC/ STABILIZATION EXERCISES

Rhythmic Stabilization

Drop/catch ball

The patient stands and uses the involved upper extremity to drop and catch a ball or weighted medicine ball as quickly and with as little motion as possible while maintaining a stable position (**Figure 10-66**). To increase the difficulty, the patient progresses from positions of 0° of flexion and abduction into flexion and abduction.

Inflated exercise ball walkouts

The patient lies prone over an inflated exercise ball. The patient walks forward and backward using his or her hands, maintaining balance and stability as the body rolls across the ball. To increase stability, the patient should hold the lower extremities and trunk rigid (**Figure 10-67**).

Minitramp push-up

The patient performs standard or modified push-ups while his or her hands are supported on the surface of

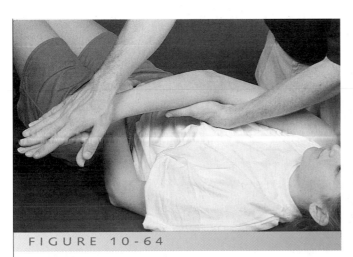

FIGURE 10-64

Direction 2 (flexion) is a PNF exercise in which the athletic trainer tries to control external rotation and proximal component motions.

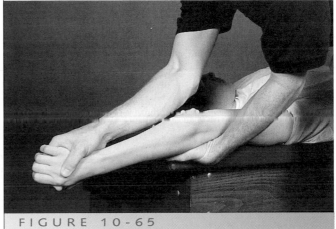

FIGURE 10-65

Direction 2 (extension) antagonistic pattern is a PNF exercise in which the athletic trainer tries to control internal rotation and proximal components of motion.

FIGURE 10-66

Drop/catch ball involves dropping and catching a weighted ball quickly with little motion.

FIGURE 10-67

Inflated exercise ball walkouts involve the athlete walking forward and backward using his or her hands while lying prone over the ball.

FIGURE 10-68

Inflated exercise ball push-ups involve the athlete performing push-ups with his or her hands supported on the ball.

the miniature trampoline. The mobility of the supporting surface increases the stabilization demand on the shoulders.

Inflated exercise ball push-up

The patient performs standard or modified push-ups while his or her hands are supported on the inflated exercise ball (**Figure 10-68**). The mobility of the ball increases the stabilization demand on the shoulders.

Isokinetic repositioning

The patient uses an isokinetic device to reproduce a specific position repetitively.

Slide board movements

The patient is in a quadruped position with the involved extremity bearing weight as tolerated on the slide board. While wearing a slide board slipper on the involved hand, the patient performs rapid, small circles in clockwise and counterclockwise directions (**Figure 10-69**). The initial position of the exercise is below shoulder level (less than 90° of flexion) and progresses by increasing time, weight-bearing, circle circumference, and positions (to greater than 90° of flexion).

FIGURE 10-69

Slide board movements involve the athlete moving his or her hand in rapid, small circles on the board.

Endurance

Muscular endurance is defined as the capacity of a muscle group to perform repeated contractions against a load or sustain a contraction for an extended period of time.[47]

The mechanics of performing an activity often change as the body becomes fatigued.[50] Endurance activities can be performed on upper body cycles, rowing machines, overhead climbing machines, and stepper machines.

FUNCTIONAL PROGRESSIONS

Plyometrics

Plyometrics is defined as exercises that enable a muscle to reach maximum strength in as short a time as possible.[51] Implements such as weighted balls, basketballs, elastic bands, and rebounders can be used for various catch or throw drills. Exercises such as power drops, backward throws, overhead throws, pullover passes, and side throws can increase shoulder girdle response to functional demands. Sport-specific programs are recommended and patterns can be mixed with jumping and catching drills. Some of these programs include interval throwing, mound pitching, golf, tennis, and swimming.[52]

CHAPTER REVIEW

The shoulder's high degree of mobility is at the expense of stability, rendering the shoulder vulnerable to acute traumatic and overuse injuries. The athletic trainer must understand the anatomy and biomechanics of the shoulder complex to comprehend injury mechanisms and the evaluation, management, and rehabilitation of an athlete with a shoulder injury.

The shoulder consists of three bones (clavicle, scapula, and humerus), four articulations (acromioclavicular, sternoclavicular, glenohumeral, and scapulothoracic), and 26 muscles. The glenoid labrum deepens the glenoid socket and serves as an attachment site for the biceps muscle and several glenohumeral ligaments (which originate at the capsule). Shoulder joint motions are abduction and adduction, flexion and extension, and internal and external rotation.

Static stabilizers of the shoulder include the humerus, glenoid, surface area and articular conformity, glenoid labrum, intra-articular pressure, glenohumeral ligaments and capsule. Dynamic stabilizers consist of joint compression, proprioception, the biceps tendon, and scapular rotators. Depending on the position of the arm, these components work together in different ways to stabilize the shoulder. The throwing mechanism, consisting of wind-up, cocking, acceleration, ball release, and follow-through, stresses the shoulder's anterior and posterior structures significantly, frequently causing overuse injuries. Other sport injuries can occur acutely, from direct or indirect forces.

An athlete who has injured the shoulder must be presumed to have cervical spine trauma until proven otherwise. After obtaining a brief history of the mechanism of injury, a cursory vascular examination should be conducted, followed by an evaluation of sensory and motor function. The athletic trainer should observe for obvious deformities and palpate the area, then try to move the shoulder passively and actively through the complete range of motion. Strength and instability should be assessed, and the appropriate provocative tests performed.

Sternoclavicular injuries include joint sprain, anterior dislocation, posterior dislocation, and clavicular fracture. Acromioclavicular injuries consist of separations or sprains. Rotator cuff injuries present as subacromial bursitis, impingement, or rotator cuff tendinitis, strains, ruptures, contusions, or tears. Tears of the glenoid labrum can occur inferiorly or superiorly (SLAP lesion). Other shoulder injuries include bicipital tendinitis, scapular fractures, anterior or posterior glenohumeral dislocation, multidirectional instability, proximal humerus fractures, and neurovascular injuries (suprascapular nerve palsy, burner syndrome, thoracic outlet syndrome, long thoracic nerve palsy, quadrilateral space syndrome, axillary artery occlusion, and venous thrombosis).

Whether treatment of a shoulder injury is conservative or surgical, rehabilitation of the entire shoulder complex is essential to returning the athlete safely to sport. Restoration of strength, power, full range of motion, flexibility, coordination, and endurance, along with pain control, are important goals. The athlete who masters all functional exercise goals at the appropriate time and tailors the late stages of the rehabilitation program to sport-specific activities will ensure a successful return to play.

Shoulder rehabilitation progresses in three phases. Phase 1 focuses on controlling pain while increasing range of motion. Joint mobilization techniques are helpful to modulate pain, nourish the joint, and prevent contractures. Phase 2 includes rotator cuff, deltoid, and scapular rotator strengthening; wrist and elbow strengthening; joint mobilization to normalize joint play; total body conditioning; and endurance exercises. Phase 3 begins when the athlete is asymptomatic. Range of motion is maintained, and shoulder strengthening and functional demands progress. Proprioceptive neuromuscular facilitation and plyometric exercises may be useful, and shoulder endurance activities and total body fitness are emphasized, along with sport-specific exercises and skill mastery training.

The appropriate shoulder program for an individual athlete depends on the diagnosis, which is determined after a thorough examination and assessment. Specific areas to be addressed may include joint and soft tissue mobility, range of motion and flexibility, strength, proprioception and kinesthesia, endurance, and functional skills and coordination. The athlete's position and sport may require the pursuit of a particular functional progression (for example, an interval throwing program) to allow safe return to sport.

SELF TEST

1. The supraspinatus, infraspinatus, and teres minor tendons insert on which of the following structures?
   A. Acromial process
   B. Supraspinatus outlet
   C. Greater scapular notch
   D. Greater humeral tuberosity

2. The structure that increases glenoid socket depth and glenohumeral joint contact surface area is the:
   A. capsule.
   B. labrum.
   C. clavicle.
   D. humerus.

3. Which of the following statements about shoulder joint proprioception is true?
   A. Proprioception is unrecoverable after surgical repair.
   B. Proprioception is reduced when the shoulder is near the limits of motion.
   C. Individuals with anterior instability have more proprioception than individuals with no instability.
   D. Individuals with clinical laxity have significantly less shoulder proprioception than individuals with no laxity.

4. Which phase of the throwing mechanism is characterized by separation of the ball and glove?
   A. Cocking
   B. Wind-up
   C. Acceleration
   D. Follow-through

5. Which of the following statements about the initial assessment and management of an athlete with a shoulder injury is true?
   A. Motor function should be evaluated before sensory function.
   B. The helmet and shoulder pads should be removed immediately.
   C. Cervical spine trauma must be ruled out before the athlete is moved.
   D. Neurovascular evaluation can wait until the patient arrives at the medical facility.

6. Results of which of the following tests are positive with relief of symptoms with resisted forward elevation?
   A. Clunk test
   B. Yergason test
   C. O'Brien test
   D. Impingement test

7. Anterior prominence of the proximal clavicle is typical of which of the following injuries?
   A. Rotator cuff impingement
   B. Clavicular epiphyseal fracture
   C. Anterior sternoclavicular dislocation
   D. Posterior sternoclavicular dislocation

8. A factor implicated in multidirectional instability is:
   A. inherent ligament tightness.
   B. a single episode of acute trauma.
   C. cumulative repetitive microtrauma.
   D. sport activities below shoulder height.

9. Which of the following statements about shoulder rehabilitation is true?
   A. Shoulder rehabilitation can begin before a diagnosis is determined.
   B. Only the damaged structures of the shoulder are targeted for rehabilitation.
   C. The starting point of shoulder rehabilitation is the same for all patients.
   D. Strength and power are essential to rehabilitation of the highly muscle-dependent shoulder.

10. A passive movement performed by the athletic trainer or physical therapist at a speed slow enough for the patient to stop the movement is known as:
    A. joint mobilization.
    B. reversal of antagonists.
    C. soft-tissue mobilization.
    D. proprioceptive neuromuscular facilitation.

Answers on Page 892

References

1. Bigliani LU, Morrison DS, April EW: The morphology of the acromion and rotator cuff tears. *Orthop Trans* 1986;10:288.

2. Warner JJ, Deng XH, Warren RF, et al: Static capsuloligamentous restraints to superior-inferior translation of the glenohumeral joint. *Am J Sports Med* 1992;20:675–685.

3. Turkel SJ, Panio MW, Marshall JL, Girgis FG: Stabilizing mechanisms preventing anterior dislocation of the glenohumeral joint. *J Bone Joint Surg* 1981;63A:1208–1217.

4. O'Brien SJ, Neves MC, Arnoczky SP, et al: The anatomy and histology of the inferior glenohumeral ligament complex of the shoulder. *Am J Sports Med* 1990;18:449–456.

5. Paletta GA Jr, Warner JJ, Warren RF, et al: Shoulder kinematics with two-plane x-ray evaluation in patients with anterior instability or rotator cuff tearing. *J Shoulder Elbow Surg* 1997;6:516–527.

6. Poppen NK, Walker PS: Normal and abnormal motion of the shoulder. *J Bone Joint Surg* 1976;58A:195–201.

7. Hawkins RJ, Bokor DJ: Clinical evaluation of shoulder problems, in Rockwood CA Jr, Matsen FA III (eds): *The Shoulder*. Philadelphia, PA, WB Saunders, 1990, pp 149-177.

8. Lippitt SB, Harris SL, Harryman DT II, et al: In vivo quantification of the laxity of normal and unstable glenohumeral joints. *J Shoulder Elbow Surg* 1994;3:215–223.

9. Speer KP, Hannafin JA, Altchek DW, et al: An evaluation of the shoulder relocation test. *Am J Sports Med* 1994;22:177–183.

10. Altchek DW, Warren RF, Skyhar MJ, et al: T-plasty modification of the Bankart procedure for multidirectional instability of the anterior and inferior types. *J Bone Joint Surg* 1991;73A:105–112.

11. Neer CS: Anterior acromioplasty for the chronic impingement syndrome in the shoulder: A preliminary report. *J Bone Joint Surg* 1972;54A:41–50.

12. O'Brien SJ, Pagnani MJ, Fealy S, et al: The active compression test: A new and effective test for diagnosing labral tears and acromioclavicular joint abnormality. *Am J Sports Med* 1998;26:610–613.

13. Davidson PA, Elattrache NS, Jobe CM, et al: Rotator cuff and posterior-superior glenoid labrum injury associated with increased glenohumeral motion: A new site of impingement. *J Shoulder Elbow Surg* 1995;4:384–390.

14. Payne LZ, Altchek DW, Craig EV, et al: Arthroscopic treatment of partial rotator cuff tears in young athletes: A preliminary report. *Am J Sports Med* 1997;25:299–305.

15. Harryman DT II, Sidles JA, Clark JM, et al: Translation of the humeral head on the glenoid with passive glenohumeral motion. *J Bone Joint Surg* 1990;72A:1334–1343.

16. Altchek DW, Carson EW: Arthroscopic acromioplasty: Current status. *Orthop Clin North Am* 1997;28:157–168.

17. Blevins FT, Hayes WM, Warren RF: Rotator cuff injury in contact athletes. *Am J Sports Med* 1996;24:263–267.

18. Snyder SJ, Karzel RP, Del Pizzo W, et al: SLAP lesions of the shoulder. *Arthroscopy* 1990;6:274–279.

19. Pagnani MJ, Deng XH, Warren RF, et al: Effect of lesions of the superior portion of the glenoid labrum on glenohumeral translation. *J Bone Joint Surg* 1995;77A:1003–1010.

20. Payne LZ, Jokl P: The results of arthroscopic debridement of glenoid labral tears based on tear location. *Arthroscopy* 1993;9:560–565.

21. Speer KP, Deng X, Borrero S, et al: Biomechanical evaluation of a simulated Bankart lesion. *J Bone Joint Surg* 1994;76A:1819–1826.

22. Rockwood CA, Green DP (eds): *Fractures in Adults*, ed 2. Philadelphia, PA, JB Lippincott, vol 3, 1984.

23. Arciero RA, Wheeler JH, Ryan JB, et al: Arthroscopic Bankart repair versus nonoperative treatment for acute, initial anterior shoulder dislocations. *Am J Sports Med* 1994;22:589–594.

24. Rowe CR: Prognosis in dislocations of the shoulder. *J Bone Joint Surg* 1956;38A:957–977.

25. Jobe FW, Giangarra CE, Kvitne RS, et al: Anterior capsulolabral reconstruction of the shoulder in athletes in overhand sports. *Am J Sports Med* 1991;19:428–434.

26. Rowe CR, Pierce DS, Clark JG: Voluntary dislocation of the shoulder: A preliminary report on a clinical, electromyographic, and psychiatric study of twenty-six patients. *J Bone Joint Surg* 1973;55A:445–460.

27. Burkhead WZ Jr, Rockwood CA Jr: Treatment of instability of the shoulder with an exercise program. *J Bone Joint Surg* 1992;74A:890–896.

28. Cooper RA, Brems JJ: The inferior capsular-shift procedure for multidirectional instability of the shoulder. *J Bone Joint Surg* 1992;74A:1516–1521.

29. Neer CS II, Foster CR: Inferior capsular shift for involuntary inferior and multidirectional instability of the shoulder: A preliminary report. *J Bone Joint Surg* 1980;62A:897–908.

30. Warner JP, Krushell RJ, Masquelet A, et al: Anatomy and relationships of the suprascapular nerve: Anatomical constraints to mobilization of the supraspinatus and infraspinatus muscles in the management of massive rotator cuff tears. *J Bone Joint Surg* 1992;74A:36–45.

31. Meyer SA, Schulte KR, Callaghan JJ, et al: Cervical spinal stenosis and stingers in collegiate football players. *Am J Sports Med* 1994;22:158–166.

32. Martin SD, Warren RF, Martin TL, et al: Suprascapular neuropath: Results of nonoperative treatment. *J Bone Joint Surg* 1997;79A:1159–1165.

33. Nicholson GG: Rehabilitation of common shoulder injuries. *Clin Sports Med* 1989;8:633–655.

34. Kibler WB, Herring SA, Press JM (eds): *Functional Rehabilitation of Sports and Musculoskeletal Injuries: Rehabilitation of the Shoulder*. Gaithersburg, MD, Aspen Publishers, 1998.

35. Andrews JR, Wilk KE (eds): *The Athlete's Shoulder*. New York, NY, Churchill Livingstone, 1994.

36. Kaltenborn FM, Morgan D (eds): *Mobilization of the Extremity Joints: Examination and Basic Treatment Techniques*. Oslo, Norway, Olaf Norlis, 1980.

37. Maitland GD: *Peripheral Manipulation*, ed 2. Boston, MA, Butterworth, 1977.

38. Norkin C, Levangie P(eds): *Joint Structure and Function: A Comprehensive Analysis*, ed 2. Philadelphia, PA, FA Davis, 1992, pp70–72.

39. Kessler R, Hertling D (eds): *Management of Common Musculoskeletal Disorders: Physical Therapy Principles and Methods*. Philadelphia, PA Harper and Row, 1983.

40. Wyke B: The neurology of joints. *Ann R Coll Surg* 1967; 41:25.

41. Wyke B: Articular neurology: A review. *Physiotherapy* 1972;58:94–99.

42. Mulligan BR (ed): *Manual Therapy: SNAGS, NAGS, MWMS*, ed 3. Wellington, New Zealand, Plane View Services; 1995.

43. Cyriax J, Russel G (eds): *Textbook of Orthopaedic Medicine: The Diagnosis of Soft Tissue Lesions*, ed 6. Baltimore, MD, Williams & Wilkins, vol 1, 1975.

44. Kisner C, Colby L: *Therapeutic Exercise: Foundations and Techniques*. Philadelphia, PA, FA Davis, 1997.

45. Saunders DH: *Orthopaedic Physical Therapy: Evaluation and Treatment of Musculoskeletal Disorders*. Minneapolis, MN; 1982.

46. Fox E, Bowers R, Foss M: *The Physiological Basis for Exercise and Sport*: ed 5. Madison, WI, WC Brown Communications, 1993.

47. Wilk KE, Arrigo C: Current concepts in the rehabilitation of the athletic shoulder. *J Orthop Sports Phys Ther* 1993; 18:371–372.

48. Sherrington C: *The Integrative Action of the Nervous System*, ed 2. New Haven, CT, Yale University Press, 1961.

49. Knott M, Voss DE: *Proprioceptive Neuromuscular Facilitation: Patterns and Techniques*, New York, NY, Hoeber, 1956.

50. Davies GJ, Dickoff-Hoffman S: Neuromuscular testing and rehabilitation of the shoulder complex. *J Orthop Sports Phys Ther* 1993;18:449–458.

51. Chu DA (ed): *Jumping Into Plyometrics*. Champaign, IL, Leisure Press, 1991.

52. Wilk KE, Andrews JR: Rehabilitation following arthroscopic subacromial decompression. *Orthopaedics*, 1993; 16:349.

11

Elbow Injuries

Kevin E. Wilk, PT
James R. Andrews, MD
Craig Levitz, MD
Wendy Hurd, PT

QUICK CONTENTS

- The anatomy of the elbow.

- The biomechanics of the elbow.

- The common injuries affecting the elbow and their associated pathomechanics.

- The clinical examination of the elbow.

- The nonsurgical treatment of elbow pathologies.

- Surgical indications and commonly performed procedures.

- Rehabilitation after the various types of elbow surgery.

OVERVIEW

The elbow joint complex is frequently injured in sports, and the athletic trainer must be prepared to evaluate and manage elbow injuries. This chapter begins with descriptions of the bony and soft-tissue anatomy and a discussion of biomechanics in activities of daily living and sports. Common injuries and their associated pathomechanics are addressed next, followed by the clinical examination. Nonsurgical and surgical treatment of elbow pathologies are explained, and the chapter concludes with rehabilitation programs for the throwing athlete who has undergone surgery.

ELBOW INJURIES

The elbow joint complex is a frequent site of injury in individuals who participate in sport activities. These injuries may occur as a result of macrotraumatic forces, which may result in dislocations, fractures, and ligamentous failures. The elbow joint and surrounding structures may also sustain injury from repetitive microtraumatic forces such as throwing a baseball or hitting a tennis serve. Often, these injuries appear as overuse tendinitis, musculotendinous failure, and articular cartilage degeneration.

ANATOMY

Osseous Structures

The elbow joint complex is composed of the humeroulnar, humeroradial, superior radioulnar, and inferior radioulnar articulations. The superior and inferior radioulnar junctions function essentially as one complex, although only the superior radioulnar joint has a direct association with the other counterparts in the elbow complex. A single joint capsule encloses the elbow joint proper and the superior radioulnar joint.

Humeroulnar articulation

The humeroulnar joint is a uniaxial, diarthrodial joint with primarily 1° of freedom, flexion, and extension. Although it is generally described as a hinge joint, the humeroulnar joint is probably more appropriately designated as a modified hinge joint with small amounts of internal and external rotation (approximately 5°), which occurs at the extremes of flexion and extension.[1]

The osseous structures of the humeroulnar joint include the distal humerus and the proximal ulna (**Figure 11-1**). The hourglass-shaped trochlea is the anterior aspect of the distal humerus. Its articular surfaces

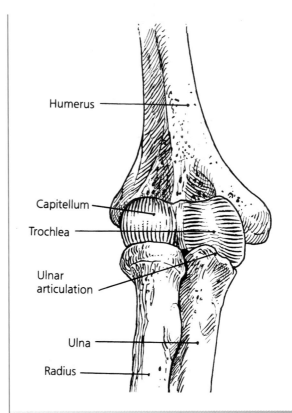

FIGURE 11-1

The elbow joint is composed of various structures, including the distal humerus and proximal ulna.

are covered with articular cartilage from the olecranon posteriorly to the coronoid fossa anteriorly. The central depression of the trochlea is called the *trochlear groove* and is bound on either side by two unequal convex segments of bone. The trochlear groove is arranged obliquely, running anteriorly to posteriorly. The obliquity of the trochlear groove has individual variations. The distal end of the humerus is rotated anteriorly 30° with respect to the long axis of the humerus. A similar 30° angular arrangement is seen at the proximal ulna. The ulnar rotation is angled 30° posterior with respect to the shaft of the ulna. This matching anatomic relationship has biomechanical implications in that it promotes elbow flexion motion from 145° to 150° and allows elbow static stability when fully extended.[2]

The coronoid fossa is a bony depression that is located immediately above the articular surface of the anterior and posterior humerus. This fossa receives the coronoid process of the ulna during flexion. Posteriorly, the olecranon fossa receives the olecranon process of the ulna during extension. The proximal ulna contains a central ridge that runs between two bony projections, the olecranon posteriorly and the coronoid process anteriorly. The structural congruency of these articular surfaces makes the humeroulnar joint one of the most stable joints in the human body.[3]

Anatomy

The elbow joint complex has three articulations: humeroulnar, humeroradial and superior (proximal) radioulnar. A joint capsule encloses the elbow joint proper and the superior radioulnar joint. The humeroulnar joint, a uniaxial, diarthrodial joint with 1° of freedom (flexion and extension), is a modified hinge joint with 5° of internal and external rotation at the flexion and extension extremes. The distal humerus and proximal ulna form the humeroulnar joint.

The humeroradial joint, also a uniaxial, diarthrodial joint, glides around a coronal axis to perform flexion and extension with the humeroulnar joint and pivots around a longitudinal axis to perform rotation with the superior radioulnar joint. The humeroradial joint is referred to as a hinge-pivot joint and is also described as the radiocapitellar articulation.

The superior and inferior radioulnar joints supinate and pronate the forearm. The superior radioulnar joint is a uniaxial, diarthrodial joint that includes the convex rim of the radial head and the concave radial notch of the ulna. The inferior radioulnar joint, also a uniaxial, diarthrodial joint, is formed by the articulation of the ulnar head with the ulnar notch of the radius at the wrist. A fibrocartilaginous disk, the triangular fibrocartilage complex, between the lower ends of the radius and ulna assists in holding the radius and ulna congruent.

The elbow carrying angle is measured in the frontal plane with the elbow extended. The angle in men averages 11° to 14° and in women, 13° to 16°. The carrying angle diminishes in flexion and increases in extension.

The *medial epicondyle*, a bony prominence located proximal and medial to the trochlea, is another significant anatomic feature related to the humeroulnar articulation. The medial epicondyle serves as the attachment site for the flexor-pronator muscle group and the ulnar collateral ligament. Its size and prominence provide an important mechanical advantage for the medial collateral ligament complex and flexor-pronator muscle groups.[4] This prominence continues superiorly to form the medial supracondylar ridge. Just posterior to the medial epicondyle is the cubital tunnel or ulnar groove, a bony depression that protects and houses the ulnar nerve.

Humeroradial articulation

The humeroradial joint or radiocapitellar articulation, like the humeroulnar joint, is a diarthrodial, uniaxial joint. However, the joint performs a dual role by rotating around a coronal axis to perform flexion and extension with the humeroulnar joint and pivoting around a longitudinal axis to perform rotational movements (pronation-supination) in association with the superior radioulnar joint. Thus, the humeroradial joint is often referred to as a hinge-pivot joint.[5]

The articular surfaces of the humeroradial joint include the proximal radius and the distal lateral aspect of the humerus. The distal humerus contains the *capitellum*, which is a spheroidal prominence that lies lateral to the trochlea. The capitellum is not a complete sphere, but is actually the anterior half of a sphere.[6] The *capitulotrochlear groove* separates the capitellum from the trochlea. The rim of the radial head is guided by this groove as it moves in flexion and extension.

The *radial fossa* is a depression that lies immediately above the capitellum on the anterior aspect of the humerus. This fossa receives the anterior tip of the radial head in the fully flexed position. Lateral to the radial fossa is a bony prominence known as the *lateral epicondyle*, which is the origin of several wrist extensor muscles. The lateral epicondyle extends superiorly at the lateral supracondylar ridge.

The *radial head*, which is a slightly oval concave depression, tops the proximal radius. The radial head and the surrounding rim narrow distally to form the radial neck. Just below the radial neck is a bony prominence called the *radial tuberosity* or bicipital tuberosity, which represents the insertion of the biceps tendon.

Superior radioulnar joint

The *superior radioulnar joint* functions with the inferior radioulnar joint to produce rotation of the forearm, or supination and pronation. The superior radioulnar joint is a uniaxial, diarthrodial joint that comprises the convex medial rim of the radial head and the concave radial notch of the ulna. During rotational movements, very little motion actually occurs at the ulna. During pronation-supination movements, the radius rotates around the ulna. During supination and pronation, the head of the radius rotates within a ring formed by the annular ligament and radial notch of the ulna.

Inferior radioulnar joint

The *inferior radioulnar joint* functions with the superior radioulnar joint to produce supination and pronation. The inferior radioulnar joint, which is a uniaxial, diarthrodial joint, is formed by the articulation of the head of the ulna with the ulnar notch of the radius. This L–shaped joint includes a fibrocartilaginous articular disk, the triangular fibrocartilage complex (TFCC), between the lower ends of the radius and ulna, which assists in holding the radius and ulna congruent. During supination and pronation, the ulnar notch and the articular disk rotate on the head of the ulna.

The *middle radioulnar joint* is a fibrous joint or syndesmosis formed by the interosseous membrane that connects the shafts of the radius and ulna bones. This interosseous membrane of the forearm is a thin but strong fibrous sheet. The fibrous bands are oriented downward and medially from the radius to the ulna. They provide an attachment to the deep muscles of the forearm and connect the radius and ulna.

The Carrying Angle

The *carrying angle of the elbow* is defined as the angle formed by the long axis of the humerus and ulna resulting in an abducted position of the forearm relative to the humerus. This angle is measured in the frontal plane with the elbow extended. In men, the angles average approximately 11° to 14° and in women, about 13° to 16°.[7,8] The angular relationship between the humerus and ulna changes as the humeroulnar joint is flexed. The carrying angle changes linearly with flexion and extension; it diminishes in flexion and increases in extension.

Ligamentous Restraints

The elbow *joint capsule* is a relatively thin but significantly strong structure. The anterior capsule is normally a thin transparent structure that allows visualization of the bony prominence when the elbow is fully extended. The anterior capsule inserts proximally above the coronoid and radial fossae. Distally, the capsule attaches to the anterior margin of the coronoid medially and to the annular ligament laterally. Posteriorly, the capsule attaches just above the olecranon fossa and distally along the medial and lateral margins of the trochlea. The capsule exhibits significant strength from the transverse and obliquely directed fibrous bands. The anterior capsule is taut into extension and lax with elbow flexion. The greatest capacity occurs at approximately 80° of flexion.[9] The synovial membrane lines the joint capsule and is attached anteriorly above the radial and coronoid fossae to the medial and lateral margins of the articular surface and posteriorly to the superior margin of the olecranon fossa.

The ligaments of the elbow consist of specialized parts of the medial and lateral capsules that thicken to form medial and lateral collateral ligament complexes.

The Medial Collateral Ligament Complex

The *ulnar collateral ligament (UCL)* is located on the medial side of the elbow. This ligamentous complex consists of the anterior oblique, posterior oblique, and transverse portion (Figure 11-2). The anterior oblique or anterior bundle originates from the inferior surface of the medial epicondyle just posterior to the axis of rotation of the elbow and can be readily distinguished from the medial joint capsule. The anterior bundle inserts at the medial aspect of the coronoid process. The humeral origin is eccentrically located in relation to the axis of rotation and permits tautness of the ligament throughout the range of motion (ROM). Functionally, the ligament

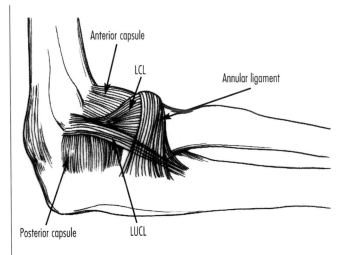

FIGURE 11-2

The radial collateral ligament originates from the lateral epicondyle and extends distally to insert into the annular ligament. (Reproduced with permission from Hwang J, Ramsey HL, Yamaguchi K: Elbow reconstruction, in Beaty JH (ed): *Orthopedic Knowledge Update 6*. Rosemont, IL, American Academy of Othopaedic Surgeons, 1999, pp 337–346.)

can be subdivided into two bands: the anterior band, which is taut in extension, and the posterior band, which is tight in flexion.[10,11] The anterior oblique portion of the UCL represents the major ligamentous support to the medial aspect of the elbow. Compromise of this structure results in gross instability during functional activities, especially throwing.

The transverse bundle of the UCL complex originates from the medial olecranon and inserts into the coronoid process of the ulna. The bundle cannot be separated from the medial joint capsule. This portion of the medial ligament complex contributes little, if at all, to elbow stability.[3,11]

The posterior oblique bundle originates from the medial epicondyle posteriorly and inferiorly to the axis of rotation. The posterior oblique bundle is fan-shaped and inserts into the posteromedial aspect of the olecranon. This band becomes taut in flexion, especially at 60°.[3] Sectioning of this ligament does not significantly affect medial elbow stability.[10]

Lateral Ligamentous Complex

Unlike the medial collateral ligament complex with its rather consistent pattern, the lateral ligaments of the elbow joint are less discrete, and some individual variation is common. Several components make up the lateral ligament complex: the radial collateral ligament, the annular ligament, the accessory lateral collateral ligament, and the lateral ulnar collateral ligament.

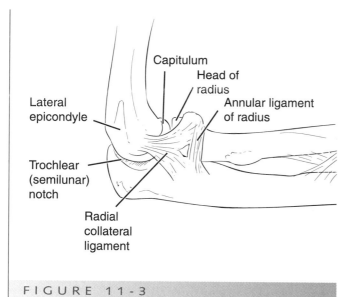

FIGURE 11-3

The ulnar collateral ligament complex consists of the anterior, posterior, and transverse portions.

The radial collateral ligament

The *radial collateral ligament (RCL)* is not as well defined as the UCL. The RCL originates from the lateral epicondyle and extends distally in a fan shape to insert into the annular ligament (**Figure 11-3**). The origin of the RCL is directly at the axis of rotation; thus, little change in ligament length is noted throughout elbow flexion and extension ROM. The average length of this structure is 20 mm, and the average width is approximately 8 mm.

Annular ligament

The *annular ligament* is a strong fibro-osseous ring that encircles and stabilizes the radial head in the radial notch of the ulna. Its origin and insertion occur anteriorly and posteriorly relative to the radial notch of the ulna. The shape of the ligament is somewhat like a funnel and comprises four fifths of a circle. The anterior portion of this ligament becomes taut with supination, and the posterior portion becomes taut with pronation.[12]

The accessory lateral collateral ligament

The *accessory lateral collateral ligament (ALCL)* originates from the inferior margin of the annular ligament and inserts discretely into the tubercle of the supinator crest. The ALCL further stabilizes the annular ligament during varus stress.[13]

The lateral ulnar collateral ligament

The *lateral ulnar collateral ligament (LUCL)* was first described in 1985.[11] The LUCL originates at the midportion of the lateral epicondyle and inserts into the tubercle of the crest of the supinator of the ulna. This ligament provides stability to the humeroulnar joint; deficiency of

this ligament produces posterolateral rotary instability of the joint.[14]

Other ligamentous structures that exhibit a stabilizing role for the superior radioulnar joint include the quadrate ligament and the oblique cord. The function of these structures has been debated in the literature.

Neurologic Structures of the Elbow

The four nerves that play significant roles in normal elbow function and pathologies are the median, ulnar, radial, and musculocutaneous nerves (**Figure 11-4**). Frequently, anatomic variations exist in many of these structures; however, these variations are not within the scope of this chapter.

Median nerve

The *median nerve* arises from branches of the lateral and medial cords of the brachial plexus. Nerve root levels include C5 to C8 and T1. This nerve proceeds distally over the anterior medial portion of the brachium, passing beneath the brachial fascia and over the brachialis muscle. It continues in a straight descent to the medial aspect of the antecubital fossa, where it lies medial to the biceps brachii tendon. From the antecubital fossa, the median nerve continues its course under the bicipital aponeurosis and passes most often between the two heads of the pronator teres. Just inferior to the border of the pronator teres,

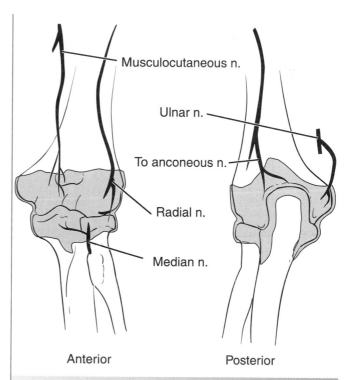

FIGURE 11-4

The neurologic structures of the elbow include the median, ulnar, radial, and musculocutaneous nerves.

Neurologic Structures of the Elbow

The median, ulnar, radial, and musculocutaneous nerves supply the elbow. The median nerve arises from branches of the lateral and medial cords of the brachial plexus and originates from C5 to C8 and T1. Compression of the median nerve between the two heads of the pronator teres or by the bicipital aponeurosis results in either pronator syndrome or anterior interosseous syndrome. Repetitive, strenuous pronation can lead to median nerve entrapment. The ulnar nerve originates from the C8 and T1 levels and descends into the proximal aspect of the upper extremity from the medial cord of the brachial plexus. The radial nerve originates at the posterior cord of the brachial plexus from C6 to C8 with variable contributions from C5 and T1.

The musculocutaneous nerve originates at the lateral cord of the brachial plexus from C5 to C7. Compression between the biceps tendon and the brachialis fascia can entrap the nerve.

the anterior interosseous branch arises and descends along the anterior aspect of the interosseous membrane. This portion of the median nerve innervates the pronator quadratus, flexor pollicis longus, and lateral portion of the flexor digitorum profundus muscles. The median nerve can be compressed between the two heads of the pronator teres or by the bicipital aponeurosis, resulting in either pronator syndrome or anterior interosseous syndrome. Although relatively uncommon, highly repetitive and strenuous pronation movements of the forearm can lead to entrapment of the median nerve.[15]

Ulnar nerve

The *ulnar nerve* emanates from the C8 and T1 levels and descends into the proximal aspect of the upper extremity from the medial cord of the brachial plexus. The ulnar nerve passes from the anterior to posterior compartments of the brachium through the arcade of Struthers. This arcade represents a fascial bridging between the medial head of the triceps and the medial intermuscular septum. The nerve continues distally, passing behind the medial epicondyle and through the cubital tunnel. At the cubital tunnel, bony anatomy provides little protection for the nerve. Ulnar nerve injury, which can occur by compression or stretching, takes place most frequently in the cubital tunnel. The roof of the cubital tunnel has been defined recently by a structure called the cubital tunnel

retinaculum.[14] The cubital tunnel retinaculum is not continuous with the forearm fascia and is not always present. Absence of the cubital tunnel retinaculum accounts for congenital subluxation of the ulnar nerve. The cubital tunnel retinaculum flattens with elbow flexion, thus decreasing the capacity of the cubital tunnel. This can be noted clinically as stimulating nerve symptoms when osteophytes are present on the ulna or medial epicondyle.[16] During elbow extension, the cubital tunnel retinaculum relaxes, allowing greater accommodation of the ulnar nerve. Injury to the medial capsular ligaments can result in increased traction forces against the medial elbow, resulting in a change in length of the ulnar nerve. This change in length may result in ulnar neuropathy or ulnar nerve subluxation. At the level of the cubital tunnel, a few small branches of the ulnar nerve innervate the elbow joint capsule. The nerve enters the forearm by passing between the two heads of the flexor carpi ulnaris and continues distally between the flexor digitorum profundus and the flexor carpi ulnaris.

Radial nerve

The *radial nerve* originates from the posterior cord of the brachial plexus and derives its nerve supply from the C6, C7, and C8 levels with variable contributions from the C5 and T1 levels. At the midportion of the brachium, the radial nerve descends laterally through the radial groove of the humerus and continues in a path laterally and distally to penetrate the lateral intermuscular septum. The nerve then descends inferiorly and anteriorly behind the brachioradialis and brachialis muscles, and at the level of the joint, the nerve divides into the posterior interosseous and superficial radial branches.

Musculocutaneous nerve

The *musculocutaneous nerve* originates from the lateral cord of the brachial plexus at nerve root levels C5 to C7. The nerve passes between the biceps and brachialis muscles to pierce the brachial fascia lateral to the biceps tendon. The nerve continues distally to terminate as the lateral antebrachial cutaneous nerve, which provides sensation over the anterolateral aspect of the forearm. Compression between the biceps tendon and the brachialis fascia can cause entrapment of the musculocutaneous nerve. **Table 11-1** shows the effects of injury to specific peripheral nerves.

Cutaneous Innervation of the Elbow

Five sensory nerves innervate the elbow cutaneously. Sensory function around the elbow is derived from four nerve root levels: C5, C6, T1, and T2 (**Figure 11-5**).

Muscles

The musculature that directly affects the elbow joint can be subdivided functionally into four groups consisting of

TABLE 11-1

THE EFFECTS OF INJURY TO SPECIFIC PERIPHERAL NERVES

Musculocutaneous nerve (C_5, C_6, C_7)

Sensory supply	• Lateral half of the anterior surface of the forearm from the elbow to the thenar eminence
Effect of injury	• Severe weakness of elbow flexion
	• Weakness of supination
	• Loss of biceps deep tendon reflex
	• Loss of sensation, cutaneous distribution

Radial nerve (C_5, C_6, C_7, C_8, T_1)

Sensory supply	• Back of the arm, forearm, wrist, radial half of the dorsum of the hand, back of the thumb, index finger, and part of the middle finger
Effect of injury	• Loss of triceps reflex
	• Weakness of elbow flexion
	• Loss of supination (when the elbow is extended)
	• Loss of wrist extension
	• Weakness of ulnar and radial deviation
	• Loss of extension at the MCP joints
	• Loss of extension and abduction of the thumb

Median nerve (C_5, C_6, C_7, C_8, T_1)

Sensory supply	• Radial half of the palm; palmar surface of the thumb; index, middle, and radial half of the ring finger; and on dorsal surfaces of the same fingers
Effect of injury	• Loss of complete pronation (brachioradialis can bring the forearm to midpronation, but not beyond)
	• Weakness with flexion and radial deviation (ulnar deviation with wrist flexion)
	• Loss of flexion at the MCP joints
	• Loss of thumb opposition or abduction, loss of flexion at IP or MCP joints

Ulnar nerve (C_7, C_8, T_1)

Sensory supply	• Dorsal and palmar surfaces of the ulnar side of the hand, including the little finger and ulnar half of the ring finger
Effect of injury	• Weakness of wrist flexion and ulnar deviation (radial deviation with wrist flexion)
	• Loss of flexion of DIP joints of ring and little fingers
	• Inability to abduct or adduct fingers
	• Inability to adduct thumb
	• Loss of flexion of fingers, especially ring and little fingers at the MCP joints
	• Loss of extension of fingers, especially ring and little fingers at the IP joint

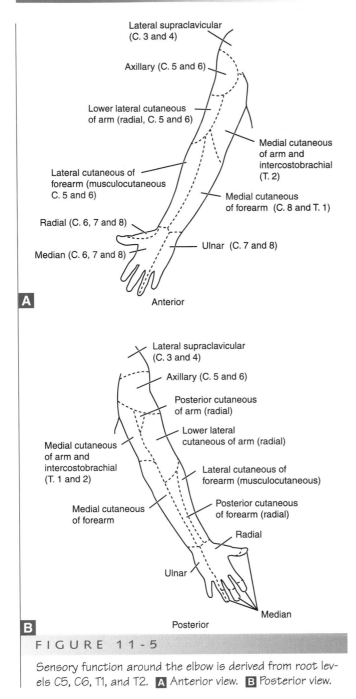

A Anterior

Labels (Figure A):
- Lateral supraclavicular (C. 3 and 4)
- Axillary (C. 5 and 6)
- Lower lateral cutaneous of arm (radial, C. 5 and 6)
- Medial cutaneous of arm and intercostobrachial (T. 2)
- Lateral cutaneous of forearm (musculocutaneous C. 5 and 6)
- Medial cutaneous of forearm (C. 8 and T. 1)
- Radial (C. 6, 7 and 8)
- Median (C. 6, 7 and 8)
- Ulnar (C. 7 and 8)

B Posterior

Labels (Figure B):
- Lateral supraclavicular (C. 3 and 4)
- Axillary (C. 5 and 6)
- Posterior cutaneous of arm (radial)
- Lower lateral cutaneous of arm (radial)
- Medial cutaneous of arm and intercostobrachial (T. 1 and 2)
- Lateral cutaneous of forearm (musculocutaneous)
- Medial cutaneous of forearm
- Posterior cutaneous of forearm (radial)
- Radial
- Ulnar
- Median

FIGURE 11-5

Sensory function around the elbow is derived from root levels C5, C6, T1, and T2. **A** Anterior view. **B** Posterior view.

the elbow flexors, the elbow extensors, the flexor-pronators, and the extensor-supinators. The primary supinator and pronator muscles will be discussed separately.

Elbow flexors

The three primary flexor muscles of the elbow include the biceps brachii, the brachioradialis, and the brachialis. The *biceps brachii* covers the brachialis muscle anteriorly and usually consists of two heads. On rare occasions, three heads may be present.[17] The long head of the biceps brachii originates on the supraglenoid tubercle, and, in most cases, it attaches directly to the glenoid labrum. The long head passes directly through

the glenohumeral joint capsule and through the intertubercular groove until it joins with the short head. The short head of the biceps brachii originates from the apex of the coracoid process of the scapula. Insertion of the biceps brachii occurs at the posterior portion of the radial tuberosity and via the bicipital aponeurosis, which attaches to the anterior capsule of the elbow joint. The biceps is a significant elbow flexor when the forearm is supinated and generates its highest torque values when the elbow is flexed between 80° and 100°.[5] The biceps brachii also functions as a supinator of the forearm, primarily when in a flexed position.

The brachialis muscle, which exhibits the longest cross-sectional area of all the elbow flexors, originates from the lower half of the anterior surface of the humerus and the medial and lateral intermuscular septum. The brachialis muscle extends distally to cross the anterior aspect of the elbow joint and inserts into the ulnar tuberosity and coronoid process. Some of the fibers attach directly to the anterior capsule and retract the capsule during elbow flexion. The brachialis muscle is active in flexing the elbow in all positions of the forearm.[18] It is also the shortest flexor of the elbow.

The *brachioradialis* muscle originates from the proximal two thirds of the lateral supracondylar ridge of the humerus and along the lateral intermuscular septum distal to the spiral groove. The brachioradialis muscle inserts into the lateral aspect of the base of the styloid process of the radius. The brachioradialis muscle inserts a long distance from the joint axis; therefore, this muscle exhibits a significant mechanical advantage as an elbow flexor.[5] The function of the brachioradialis during supination and pronation remains questionable.[19]

Elbow extensors

The two muscles that serve as primary extensors of the elbow are the triceps brachii and the anconeus muscles. The *triceps brachii* is a large three-headed (long, lateral, and medial) muscle that comprises almost the entire posterior brachium. The long head of the triceps originates from the infraglenoid tubercle; thus, the long head crosses the shoulder joint. The other two heads, the lateral and medial heads, originate from the posterior and lateral aspects of the humerus. At the distal portion of the humerus, the three heads converge to form a common muscle that inserts into the posterior surface of the olecranon.

The small *anconeus muscle* originates from a broad area on the posterior aspect of the lateral epicondyle and inserts into the olecranon. The anconeus muscle covers the lateral portion of the annular ligament, the radial head, and the posterior surface of the proximal ulna. Electromyographic (EMG) activity of the anconeus muscle during the early phase of elbow extension has been noted, and this muscle appears to have a stabilizing role during pronation/supination movements.[20]

FOCUS ON . . .

Muscles

The elbow musculature includes the elbow flexors, elbow extensors, flexor-pronators, and extensor supinators. The primary elbow flexors are the biceps brachii, brachioradialis, and brachialis muscles. The biceps brachii covers the brachialis muscle anteriorly and usually has two (occasionally three) heads. The brachialis muscle has the largest cross-sectional area of all the elbow flexors and is the strongest elbow flexor. The brachioradialis muscle originates from the proximal two thirds of the lateral supracondylar ridge of the humerus and along the lateral intermuscular septum distal to the spiral groove and inserts into the lateral aspect of the base of the radial styloid process. The brachioradialis muscle's insertion far from the joint axis provides it with a significant mechanical advantage as an elbow flexor.

The primary elbow extensors are the triceps brachii and anconeus muscles. The triceps brachii is a large muscle with long, lateral, and medial heads that comprises almost the entire posterior brachium. The small anconeus muscle originates from a broad area on the posterior lateral epicondyle to insert on the olecranon. The anconeus muscle plays a stabilizing role in pronation and supination.

The flexor-pronator muscles include the pronator teres, flexor carpi radialis, palmaris longus, flexor carpi ulnaris, and flexor digitorum superficialis, which originate from the medial epicondyle. They primarily function as wrist extensors and supinators and serve secondarily as elbow flexors and dynamic medial stabilizers against valgus stress. The extensor-supinator muscles include the brachioradialis, extensor carpi radialis brevis and longus, supinator, extensor digitorum, extensor carpi ulnaris, and extensor digiti minimi muscles, which originate at or near the lateral epicondyle. These muscles move the wrist and hand and provide dynamic support to the lateral elbow. The pronator muscles are the pronator teres and quadratus, brachioradialis, and flexor carpi radialis. The pronator quadratus is a significant pronator in all positions. The pronator teres generates its highest contractile force during rapid or resisted pronation, but its strength diminishes in full extension. The brachioradialis and flexor carpi radialis muscles are secondary pronators.

The primary supinator muscles are the biceps brachii and the supinator, with the biceps brachii and brachioradialis muscles functioning as secondary supinators. Although the supinator is a significant supinator, it is weaker than the biceps muscle and less affected by elbow position, acting alone only with unresisted slow supination and with unresisted fast supination in extension. The supinator muscle may support or stabilize the lateral elbow.

Flexor-pronator muscles

The *flexor-pronator muscles* include the pronator teres, flexor carpi radialis, palmaris longus, flexor carpi ulnaris, and flexor digitorum superficialis. All these muscles originate completely or in part from the medial epicondyle, and all serve secondary roles as elbow flexors. Their primary roles are associated with the wrist and hand. This muscle group provides dynamic stability to the medial aspect of the elbow against valgus stress.[21] This muscle group is susceptible to microtraumata and overuse injuries such as tendinitis.

Extensor-supinator muscles

The *extensor-supinator muscles* include the brachioradialis, extensor carpi radialis brevis and longus, supinator, extensor digitorum, extensor carpi ulnaris, and extensor digiti minimi muscles. Each muscle originates near or directly from the lateral epicondyle of the humerus. The insertion for each muscle varies. The primary functions of the extensor-supinator muscles involve the wrist and hand and provide dynamic support over the lateral aspect of the elbow. As are the wrist flexor-pronator muscles, this muscle group is susceptible to various overuse muscle strain injuries.

Pronator muscles

Two primary muscles act on the radioulnar joints to produce pronation movements: the pronator teres and the pronator quadratus. Two other muscles that play a minor role in pronation are the brachioradialis and the flexor carpi radialis.

The pronator quadratus originates from the anterior surface of the lower one fourth of the ulna. Insertion occurs at the distal one fourth of the lateral border of the radius. The pronator quadratus acts as a significant pronator in all positions of the elbow and forearm.

The pronator teres, which possesses humeral and ulnar heads, originates from the medial epicondyle and coronoid process of the ulna. The two heads join together and insert along the middle of the lateral surface of the radius. The pronator teres is a strong pronator muscle that generates its highest contractile force during rapid or resisted pronation.[19] However, the pronator teres' strength to pronate diminishes when the elbow is positioned in full extension.[5] The flexor carpi radialis and brachioradialis also act as secondary pronators.

Supinator muscles

The biceps brachii and the supinator muscle are the primary supinators of the forearm. The brachioradialis muscles also act as accessory supinators. The *supinator muscle* originates from four separate locations: the lateral epicondyle, the proximal anterior crest and depression of the ulna distal to the radial notch, and the radial collateral and annular ligaments. The supinator muscle then winds around the radius to insert into the dorsal and lateral surfaces of the proximal radius. The supinator muscle is a significant supinator of the forearm, but it appears to be weaker generally than the biceps.[1] The supinator acts alone only with unresisted slow supination in all elbow/forearm positions and with unresisted fast supination with the elbow extended.[6] The effectiveness of the supinator is not altered by elbow position; however, elbow position does significantly affect the biceps. A portion of the supinator originates at the radial collateral and annular ligaments, suggesting that the muscle may act as a supportive or stabilizing muscle to the lateral aspect of the elbow.

The anatomic features of the elbow joint complex suggest a high degree of joint congruency. The ligamentous structures and the neuromuscular system assist in providing dynamic joint stability. The elbow musculature provides movement and normal use of the elbow, wrist, and hand. A thorough understanding of the anatomic structures will ensure that the clinician assesses and treats various elbow disorders appropriately.

BIOMECHANICS

During sport participation and activities of daily living, normal use of the hand depends largely on a well functioning elbow joint. The elbow is a complex joint that serves as a link in the kinetic chain that positions the hand and acts as a fulcrum for forearm and hand function. Functional use of the elbow joint depends on a balance between mobility and stability of the elbow joint. During sport activities, the elbow joint receives tremendous stresses and strains and may be susceptible to specific injuries.

Kinematics

The elbow joint complex possesses 2° of freedom: flexion-extension and supination-pronation. Because of the significant congruity of the humeroulnar articulation and surrounding soft-tissue constraint, the elbow joint has been considered generally to allow only hinge motion. However, three-dimensional studies of passive motion at the elbow have revealed that the elbow does not function as a simple hinge joint.[22,23] Rather, a helical motion of the flexion axis occurs that is probably the result of the obliq-

uity of the trochlear groove. Therefore, approximately 3° to 4° of varus-valgus occurs during elbow flexion.

Elbow flexion ranges from 0°, or slight hyperextension, to approximately 150° of flexion in the normal elbow. Average forearm rotation is from about 75° of pronation to 85° to 90° of supination. Normally, during elbow flexion, the elbow has a soft-tissue end point; during elbow extension, it has a bony end point.[24]

The factors that limit elbow joint extension may be the impact of the olecranon process on the olecranon fossa and tension of the anterior capsule and flexor muscles.[6] Tautness of the anterior bundle of the UCL serves as a checkrein to elbow extension.[25] Structures that limit elbow flexion include the anterior muscle bulk of the arm/forearm, a tight or contracted triceps muscle, a coronoid process that is impacted against the coronoid fossa, and a radial head that is impacted against the fossa.

The resting position or maximum *loose-packed position* of a joint is described as the position in which the joint capsule is most relaxed and the greatest amount of joint play is possible.[26] In the resting position of the humeroulnar joint, the elbow is flexed to approximately 70°, and the forearm is supinated approximately 10°. In the resting position of the humeroradial joint, the elbow is extended and the forearm supinated. In the resting position of the proximal radioulnar joint, the elbow is flexed to 70° and supinated approximately 35°.

Conversely, the *close-packed position* is described as a joint position in which the joint capsule and ligaments are tight or normally tensed. In addition, there is maximal contact between the articular surfaces, and the articular surfaces cannot be separated substantially by traction forces.[26] The close-packed position of the humeroulnar joint is full elbow extension and forearm supination. In the close-packed position of the humeroradial joint, the elbow is flexed to 90°, and the forearm is supinated approximately 5°. In the close-packed position of the radioulnar joint or forearm, the forearm is supinated approximately 5°, and the interosseous membrane is at its tightest.

A *capsular pattern* is a lesion that affects the synovium and joint capsule. When a capsular pattern occurs, the whole capsule is shortened and becomes clinically manifested as a characteristic pattern of decreased movements at a joint. The capsular pattern is always present when the entire capsule is affected, such as in patients with arthroses. However, limitation of movement that is the result of capsular shortening does not necessarily follow a typical pattern. For example, only one part of a capsule might be shortened as a result of trauma, localized lesion, or surgery. In these cases, limitation of movement will be evident only with movements that stretch the affected portion of the capsule. The capsular pattern of the elbow joint is a significant restriction of flexion of 90° and a limitation of extension of 10°.[24] The capsular pattern of the radioulnar joint is an equal restriction of supination and pronation.

The arthrokinematics of the humeroulnar and humeroradial joint are somewhat straightforward. The articular surfaces of the humeroulnar joint include the *trochlea* (the convex-shaped distal segment of the humerus) and the *trochlear notch* (the concave-shaped proximal segment of the ulna). The articulating surfaces of the humeroradial joint include the *capitellum* (the convex distal humerus) and the radial head (the concave proximal radius). During flexion and extension of the elbow, both moving surfaces, the trochlear notch and radial head, are concave surfaces. Thus, the swing of the two bones is accompanied by gliding of the articular surfaces in the same direction.[27] At the extremes of flexion and extension, the gliding movement also occurs in the same direction as the swing of the bones.[27,28] The rolling movement accounts for the displacement of the joint's axes of rotation.[29]

Elbow Stability

The elbow joint is one of the most congruous joints in the human body and as such is one of the most stable. The structures that provide stability are soft-tissue constraints and the articular surfaces. The static soft-tissue stabilizers include the collateral ligament complexes and the anterior capsule. During elbow flexion and extension, different portions of the UCL complex are taut at different positions of elbow flexion (**Figure 11-6**). The tautness occurs because the UCL has two discrete components,

---

FOCUS ON . . .

Biomechanics

The elbow is a link in the kinetic chain that positions the hand and acts as a fulcrum for forearm and hand function, and normal elbow function requires a balance between mobility and stability.

Kinematics

The elbow joint complex possesses 2° of freedom: flexion-extension and supination-pronation. The elbow functions not as a simple hinge joint, but rather with a helical motion of the flexion axis that probably is due to the oblique trochlear groove, producing 3° to 4° of varus and valgus during flexion. Elbow flexion ranges from 0° or slight hyperextension to about 150°, with forearm rotation ranging from 75° of pronation to 85° to 90° of supination. In flexion, the elbow's end point is soft tissue; in extension, the endpoint is bony.

Extension constraints include the impact of the olecranon process on the olecranon fossa, tension of the anterior capsule and flexor muscles, and tautness of the anterior portion of the ulnar collateral ligament. Flexion constraints include the anterior muscle bulk of the arm and forearm, a tight or contracted triceps muscle, and the impact of the coronoid process against the coronoid fossa and the radial head against the fossa.

The resting, or maximum loose-packed position, is 70° of flexion and 10° of forearm supination for the humeroulnar joint, extension and supination for the humeroradial joint, and 70° of flexion and 35° of supination for the proximal radioulnar joint. The tense, or close-packed, position is extension and supination for the humeroulnar joint, 90° of flexion and 5° of supination for the humeroradial joint, and 5° of supination for the radioulnar joint.

A capsular pattern lesion affects the synovium and joint capsule, shortening the capsule and limiting motion. When the entire capsule is affected (eg, by arthrosis), the capsular pattern is present. However, if only one part of the capsule is affected (eg, from trauma or surgery), only movements that stretch the affected portion will be limited.

The humeroulnar articular surfaces include the trochlea and the trochlear notch. The humeroradial (radiocapitellar) articular surfaces include the capitellum and the radial head. During elbow flexion and extension, the trochlear notch and the radial head are concave surfaces; thus, the movement of the two bones glides the articular surfaces in the same direction. The rolling movement displaces the joint's axes of rotation.

Elbow stability

The elbow is one of the most congruous and stable joints in the body. The soft-tissue constraints, the articular surfaces, the collateral ligament complexes, and the anterior capsule provide stability. Different portions of the ulnar collateral ligament are taut at different positions of flexion because neither of the ligament's components originates at a site on the axis of rotation. The lateral collateral ligament, which lies on the axis of rotation, exhibits uniform tension throughout the range of motion.

Sport biomechanics

The elbow is susceptible to injury during sport activities. Overhead throwing can cause macrotraumatic and microtraumatic damage. The significantly high forces generated at the elbow joint during pitching can cause elbow injuries.

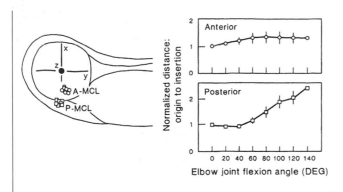

FIGURE 11-6

Biomechanically, different portions of the ulnar collateral ligament complex are taut at different positions of elbow flexion. (Reproduced with permission from Morrey BF: Anatomy of the elbow, in Morrey BF (ed): *The Elbow and Its Disorders*. Philadelphia, PA, WB Saunders, 1985, pp 7–40.)

TABLE 11-2
RESTRAINING FORCES FOR VARIOUS DISPLACEMENTS

	Stabilizing structure	Distraction (%)	Varus (%)	Valgus (%)
Extension	UCL	12		31
	LCL	10	14	
	Capsule	70	32	38
	Articulation		54	31
Flexion	UCL	78		54
	LCL	10	9	
	Capsule	8	13	13
	Articulation		75	33

(Reproduced with permission from Morrey BF: Anatomy of the elbow, in Morrey BF (ed): *The Elbow and Its Disorders*. Philadelphia, PA, WB Saunders, 1985, pp 7–40.)

neither of which originates at a site that lies on the axis of rotation.[11] The lateral collateral ligament lies on the axis of rotation; thus, it exhibits uniform tension throughout the range of motion.

Table 11-2 summarizes the influence of the ligamentous and articular components on the elbow joint. When the elbow is in full extension, the anterior capsule provides approximately 70% of the soft-tissue restraint to distraction, whereas the UCL provides approximately 78% of the distraction restraint at 90° of elbow flexion. The restraint to valgus displacement varies significantly depending on the elbow flexion angle. When the elbow is in full extension, the capsule provides 38% of the restraint, the UCL provides 31%, and the articulation provides 31%. Conversely, at 90° of flexion, the primary valgus restraint is the UCL, which provides 54% of the restraint, followed by the lateral articulation, which provides 33%, and the capsule, which provides 13%. Varus stress is controlled in extension by the joint articulation (54%) and the soft tissue, LCL (14%), and capsule (32%).[11]

Sport Biomechanics and Muscle Activity

During specific sport activities, especially overhead throwing, the elbow joint is subjected to significant forces. Additionally, during these sport activities, the muscles of the elbow and forearm exhibit significant muscular activity. Because of these increased forces and high muscular activity, the elbow is susceptible to various specific types of injuries.

The overhead throwing athlete is susceptible to both macrotraumatic and microtraumatic injuries to the elbow. The baseball pitcher is particularly susceptible to elbow injuries because of the significantly high forces generated at the elbow joint complex. Tennis players are most susceptible to overuse injuries about the elbow, such as tendinitis.

Significant forces are generated at the elbow joint during an overhead throw. A large valgus stress, approximately 64 Nm, is generated during the acceleration phase of the overhead throw.[30] This valgus stress is maximal at 70° to 90° of elbow flexion and produces tension across the medial aspect of the elbow, specifically at the UCL. During early acceleration, an extension torque of 60 Nm is generated at the initiation of elbow extension.[30,31] Immediately following release of the ball, a compressive force of approximately 800 to 1,000 N is generated within the elbow joint.[30] This force occurs at an extremely rapid rate. The angular velocity of the elbow joint is in excess of 2,400° per second during the acceleration phase of the overhead throw.[30,31]

Specific muscles of the arm, forearm, and wrist are active during the overhead throw. These muscles act in a synchronous and well-coordinated fashion. During the cocking phase of throwing, most muscles of the wrist and elbow exhibit mild to moderate muscle activity, but the wrist extensors (extensor carpi radialis longus and brevis and the extensor digitorum communis) exhibit moderately high levels of EMG activity.[32,33] During the acceleration phase, the triceps brachii acts to forcefully extend the elbow joint, while the wrist flexors act at an extremely high level to flex the wrist joint. The pronator teres is also extremely active during the acceleration phase. Because the biceps brachii and brachioradialis muscles act to control or decelerate elbow extension, peak EMG activity of these muscles occur during the deceleration phase. Thus, a sequential muscular firing pattern is necessary to successfully accomplish the overhead throwing motion.

The difference in muscular activity levels between a fastball and curveball is most evident during the late cocking and acceleration phases. Significantly greater wrist extensor muscle activity is apparent during the late cocking, acceleration, and follow-through phases of a curveball throw.[34] Different hand positions are used in the late cocking phase of curveball and fastball throws.[35] In addition, the forearm is held in more degrees of supination and slightly less wrist extension for a curveball than for a fastball.[34,35]

Greater activation of the extensor carpi radialis longus, extensor carpi radialis brevis, flexor carpi radialis, pronator teres, and triceps muscles was noted in pitchers with UCL instability.[36] This increase in muscular activity may stabilize the elbow joint or change the arm position to minimize stress on the UCL.

The tennis serve can be divided into four phases: windup, cocking, acceleration, and follow-through. During the cocking phase, most of the muscular activity is in the biceps, extensor carpi radialis brevis, and extensor digitorum communis muscles. During the acceleration, the most active muscles include the pronator teres, flexor carpi radialis, extensor carpi radialis brevis, triceps, and biceps.[37] The follow-through phase is not characterized by extremely high levels of activity in the muscles crossing the elbow, forearm, and wrist.

The tennis forehand and backhand ground strokes may be separated into three phases: preparation, acceleration, and follow-through. Except for activity of the wrist extensors during the forehand ground stroke, muscle activity is quite low during the preparation phase of both the forehand and backhand.[37] The acceleration phase of the forehand produces very high EMG activity of the wrist extensors, biceps, and brachioradialis muscles. The acceleration phase of the backhand ground stroke consists of high activity in the extensor carpi radialis longus and brevis and extensor communis muscles. During the follow-through phase of both ground stroke movements, the extensor carpi radialis brevis muscle illustrates high levels of EMG activity. The backhand also exhibits moderate levels of biceps activity during the follow through.

In one study, EMG activity of the forearm in 22 competitive tennis players was compared.[38] Eight of the players exhibited lateral epicondylitis while they performed a backhand ground stroke. When compared with players with no injury, the players with lateral epicondylitis exhibited significantly greater EMG activity in the extensor carpi radialis longus and brevis, pronator teres, and flexor carpi radialis muscles.[38]

The golf swing may be divided into four specific phases: take-away, forward swing, acceleration, and follow-through. During the take-away phase, the wrist flexors exhibit minimal EMG activity, whereas the wrist extensors exhibit 33% of a maximum voluntary isometric contraction (MVIC).[39] The forward swing is characterized by increased muscle activity of both the wrist extensors,

which exhibit 45% MVIC, and the wrist flexors, which exhibit 35% MVIC. At ball contact, the wrist flexor activity significantly increases to 91% MVIC. Additionally, the wrist extensors exhibit EMG activity of approximately 58% MVIC. During follow through, the wrist extensor EMG activity is approximately 60% to 70% MVIC.[39] Results of a study of the muscular activity patterns of golfers with medial epicondylitis and golfers with no injury indicated significantly greater wrist flexor muscle activity in the golfers with medial epicondylitis during the take-away, forward swing, and acceleration phases.[39]

COMMON INJURIES AND ASSOCIATED PATHOMECHANICS

Repetitive overuse injuries that result in inflammation and traumatic injuries such as tendinitis, sprains, contusions, lacerations, and fractures or dislocations are common conditions that affect the elbow. Understanding the mechanism of injury is essential for proper clinical evaluation and rehabilitation.[40] Elbow pathology is normally separated into four groups for discussion purposes based on the four compartments of the elbow joint: anterior, lateral, medial, and posterior. A fifth grouping categorizes general conditions such as fractures that commonly affect multiple compartments.

Anterior Compartment

A repetitive overhead throwing motion can lead to problems with elbow motion. Anterior capsule sprains, flexor-pronator muscle strains, and bicipital tendinitis can lead to incomplete elbow extension, which occurs secondary to pain associated with stretching of the structures as the arm is brought into extension.[40,41] The protective response of avoiding painful extension can result in a flexion contracture.

A sprain of the anterior capsule of the elbow joint is most commonly caused by hyperextension of the elbow joint. Collision trauma may lead to the injury such as when a defensive football player extends the arm to make a tackle at the same time the ball carrier runs through the tackle. The injury also occurs commonly in gymnastics because the elbow is prone to hyperextension during handspring and walkover stunts, particularly if the gymnast's muscles are fatigued. Anterior capsulitis can also occur as a repetitive overuse injury. Inflammation of the anterior capsule results from repetitive hyperextension in athletes with hyperlaxity, insufficient strength, or poor biomechanics. Excessive hyperextension injuries can lead to osteochondritis of the trochlear groove, osseous hypertrophy, and osteophyte formation of the coronoid process of the ulna resulting in additional loss of motion and a decrease in flexion secondary to a mechanical block. Once osteophyte formation or osteochondritis of the trochlea has occurred, symptoms persist even with rest. This situation is seen most commonly in football players who play offensive and defensive line because their

FOCUS ON . . .

Anterior Compartment Injuries

Anterior compartment injuries include anterior capsule and flexor-pronator muscle strains and bicipital tendinitis. Pain with stretching of the injured structures results in incomplete extension and can produce a flexion contracture. Anterior capsule sprain is usually caused by elbow hyperextension, often from a collision or a gymnastics handspring or walkover, particularly if the athlete is fatigued. Anterior capsulitis can also result from repetitive overuse, such as hyperextension in a hyperlax athlete, insufficient strength, or poor biomechanics. Hyperextension injury can lead to trochlear groove osteochondritis, osseous hypertrophy, and coronoid process osteophyte formation, resulting in additional motion loss and decreased flexion from a mechanical block. At this point, symptoms persist even with rest.

Distal biceps tendon rupture can occur when athletes use excessively heavy hand weights in eccentric, forceful hyperextension or repetitive supination and pronation against a bony prominence. Symptoms include the sudden onset of sharp pain and tenderness in the antecubital fossa, sometimes preceded by burning pain, with marked weakness in resisted supination. Ulnar coronoid fractures can be associated with elbow dislocations.

Lateral elbow pain is most often the result of lateral epicondylitis (tennis elbow), which is characterized by pain directly over the lateral epicondyle, made worse by wrist and middle finger extension. Osteochondrosis and osteochondritis dissecans of the capitellum and radius from repetitive compressive forces can affect the immature elbow. Lateral compartment pressure during the late cocking and acceleration throwing phases and deceleration shearing forces in the pronated forearm can lead to vascular disruption, irregular ossification patterns, capitellar flattening, loose body formation, and arthritic changes. Pitchers sustain overuse injuries with radial head compression on the capitellar convexity from valgus stress. Repeated compression with the arm abducted, extended, and externally rotated can damage the articular cartilage and produce subchondral necrosis and loose body formation.

A direct blow to the lateral elbow can result in a contusion, radial head fracture or dislocation, and possibly an ulnar fracture, or lateral condylar or capitellar fracture. The radial nerve can be injured by direct contusion, fracture, or compression in the radial tunnel or under the fibrous arcade of the triceps, causing weak supination. Lateral collateral ligament complex injury (usually from posterior elbow dislocation, but sometimes with repeated subluxations and sprains) causes posterolateral rotatory instability, which can lead to pain and subluxation.

blocking and rushing techniques lead to repetitive hyperextension injuries with resultant osteophyte formation and loss of motion.[40]

A more devastating injury is a rupture of the distal biceps tendon, which often occurs when athletes use excessively heavy hand weights such as when performing curls. This injury can also occur with eccentric, forceful hyperextension or repetitive supination and pronation against a bony prominence such as abutting the soft tissues against the biceps tuberosity. A sudden onset of sharp pain and tenderness in the antecubital fossa that is associated with marked weakness in resisted supination usually indicates rupture of the distal biceps tendon. A history of a burning pain in the antecubital fossa may precede the actual rupture.[41]

Coronoid fractures of the ulna may be associated with elbow dislocations. The symptoms and treatment depend on the degree of coronoid involvement.

Lateral Compartment

The most frequent cause of lateral elbow pain is *lateral epicondylitis* or "tennis elbow." Lateral epicondylitis is characterized by pain directly over the lateral epicondyle. The pain is accentuated with wrist and middle finger

extension. Lateral epicondylitis most commonly affects golfers and tennis players as torque is increased in an already contracted extensor muscle mass when the club contacts the ground or the racquet the ball. The most involved area of the extensor muscle mass is the origin of the extensor carpi radialis brevis muscle. Because the extensor muscle origin becomes inflamed secondary to overuse or poor mechanics leading to overload of the extensor muscle group, lateral epicondylitis is an example of a classic overuse injury.[42]

Osteochondrosis and osteochondritis dissecans of the capitellum and radius secondary to repetitive compressive forces can develop in the immature elbow.[43] Compression in the lateral compartment during the late cocking and acceleration phases of throwing along with shearing forces in the pronated forearm during the deceleration phase combine to produce injury. Repetitive overload of the young thrower's elbow can lead to vascular disruption, irregular ossification patterns, flattening of the capitellum, and if not halted, loose body formation and eventual arthritic changes.[40]

An overuse pattern in pitchers occurs when the radial head is compressed on the convexity of the capitellum as a result of valgus elbow stress. Repeated episodes of compression with the arm abducted, extended, and externally rotated can cause damage to the articular cartilage and lead to subchondral necrosis and/or the formation of loose bodies.

The lateral elbow is fairly susceptible to trauma from a direct blow. The energy absorbed by the elbow will dictate the degree of injury. The elbow's thin soft-tissue covering makes contusions fairly common. More forceful trauma can produce a radial head fracture or dislocation. It is important to look for an associated ulnar fracture when a radial head dislocation is encountered. Fractures of the lateral condyle and capitellum are rare in the athlete, but because surgical intervention is usually warranted for these injuries, prompt recognition is important.

Although the radial nerve is not a frequent cause of symptoms in the athlete's elbow, it can be injured by direct contusion, fractures, or compression of the nerve in the radial tunnel or under the fibrous arcade of the triceps. Radial tunnel syndrome has been reported in throwing sports, golf, tennis, and weight lifting; however, it is a rare diagnosis. Compression of the nerve occurs most commonly beneath the supinator muscle, and the patient may experience weakness in supination.[44]

Injury to the lateral collateral ligament complex, which is made up of the radial collateral ligament, annular ligament, accessory collateral ligament, and lateral ulnar collateral ligament, leads to posterolateral rotatory instability. Symptoms can range from lateral elbow pain to the sensation of subluxation resembling the sensation that patients complain about when they have instability of the shoulder. The most common cause of this injury is a posterior dislocation of the elbow; however, it can also occur with repeated subluxations and sprains.[45]

Medial Compartment

Medial epicondylitis, ulnar collateral ligament sprains and tears, strain of the flexor-pronator mass, and ulnar nerve neuritis are the most common causes of medial elbow pain.[40]

The UCL is the primary medial stabilizer of the elbow and commonly becomes injured in activities such as pitching, batting, forehand tennis strokes, and repetitive valgus load to the trailing arm of batters. A sudden, sharp medial pain associated with a pop following a hard throw in throwers with no previous symptoms may indicate injury to the UCL. Arm wrestling and collegiate wrestling may also lead to trauma of the ligament. Repetitive valgus stress leads to ultimate tensile failure of the ligament because the bony architecture of the elbow provides little stability during the throwing motion. This injury is rare in nonathletes, although the ligament can be strained or torn during an elbow dislocation.[40,46]

Medial epicondylitis appears differently in the immature skeleton than in the mature skeleton. Repetitive tension across the medial epiphyseal growth plate secondary to overuse from excessive pitching leads to medial elbow

FOCUS ON . . .

Medial Compartment Injuries

Medial elbow pain is usually caused by medial epicondylitis, ulnar collateral ligament sprain or tear, flexor-pronator mass strain, or ulnar nerve neuritis. The ulnar collateral ligament is often injured with pitching, batting, forehand tennis strokes, repetitive valgus load to the batter's trailing arm, or an elbow dislocation. Symptoms can include sharp, sudden medial pain associated with a pop after a hard throw or arm or collegiate wrestling.

Medial epicondylitis in the young athlete from excessive pitching produces medial apophyseal pain made worse with valgus stress and pitching, tenderness, swelling, and decreased extension. The growth plate is most often injured in these patients. Adults sustain inflammatory changes at the flexor-pronator muscle origin.

Flexor-pronator strain can occur with similar pathomechanics. High tensile loads during acceleration and deceleration cause pain, tenderness, and sometimes a palpable rupture. In the gymnast, an increased carrying angle and hyperlaxity can overload the muscle.

Ulnar nerve injury can result from traction, friction, compression, or contusion, producing symptoms of numbness, tingling, and medial pain. Fibrous cubital tunnel compression, flexor carpi ulnaris hypertrophy with nerve compression, or friction from nerve subluxation in the groove can occur.

Median nerve injury causes symptoms of pronation loss, radial deviation, weakness, loss of proximal interphalangeal finger flexion and thumb opposition, and atrophy of the thenar muscles. Direct trauma or throwing sports that require forceful pronation or grip can cause a pronator syndrome, resulting in pain at the pronator teres, flexor sublimis arch, or lacertus fibrosis or, in cheerleaders and gymnasts, aching pain between the radius and ulna.

pain over the medial apophysis that is worsened with valgus stress and the pitching motion.[43,47,48] Tenderness, swelling, and decreased extension can also occur. Although the flexor-pronator mass and the UCL also attach to the medial epicondyle, the growth plate is the weak link and the most commonly injured structure in the immature athlete. Avulsion of the medial epicondyle can be seen as either an acute or chronic injury.

In the adult, medial epicondylitis resembles lateral epicondylitis in that repetitive overuse leads to inflammation. The inflammatory changes occur at the flexor-pronator muscle origin. Although medial epi-condylitis is less common than lateral epicondylitis, the incidence of occurrence may increase among golfers. Medial epicondylitis, often called "golfer's elbow," is seen most commonly in golfers secondary to poor mechanics and overreliance on the right hand in the right hander's golf swing. Medial epicondylitis is also seen in young gymnasts with increased carrying angles and elbow recurvatum secondary to repetitive elbow flexor-pronator strain that occurs during tumbling.[46]

The pathomechanics of flexor-pronator strain are similar to those of medial epicondylitis, although with flexor-pronator strain, athletes experience more distal pain localized over the flexor-pronator muscle belly. The flexor-pronator group is active during the throwing motion as it assists the UCL in stabilizing the medial elbow. The flexor-pronator group is subject to high tensile loads during the acceleration phase of throwing and even higher stress during deceleration. In the early stages of flexor-pronator strain, the athlete experiences pain and tenderness with throwing; however, muscle ruptures exhibiting a palpable defect have been reported in the early stage. An increased valgus-carrying angle combined with hyperlaxity of the elbow can result in overload of the flexor-pronator muscle group in the gymnast.[46]

The ulnar nerve crosses the elbow joint superficially below the medial epicondyle. Symptoms of ulnar nerve injury, such as numbness into the fourth and fifth digits, tingling, and medial elbow pain, may be caused by traction, friction, compression, or contusion of the ulnar nerve. The most common cause of these symptoms is fibrous compression in the cubital tunnel, muscular hypertrophy of the flexor carpi ulnaris with resultant nerve compression, or friction resulting from the nerve subluxating from its groove. Repetitive valgus stress of the elbow during the throwing motion accentuates any pathology and contributes to a traction injury. Repetitive elbow flexion and cubitus valgus deformity also predispose athletes to symptomatic injury.[47,48]

Common symptoms of median nerve injury include loss of pronation, radial deviation, weakness, loss of proximal interphalangeal finger flexion and thumb opposition, and atrophy of the thenar muscles. A pronator syndrome can be caused by direct trauma or throwing sports that require forceful pronation or grip. The athlete experiences pain in the pronator muscle group with the throwing motion. Pain is most often caused by median nerve compression at the pronator teres, flexor sublimis arch, or lacertus fibrosis. Pronator syndrome is different from "forearm splints," which are similar to shin splints of the leg. Cheerleaders and gymnasts complain of aching pain between the radius and ulna that is aggravated by weight-bearing activities of the upper extremity such as cartwheels and handstands.

Posterior Compartment

Incomplete extension usually indicates posterior elbow pathology in the athlete. With repetitive overhead motions such as throwing and swimming, the olecranon compresses against the medial wall of the olecranon fossa of the humerus leading to valgus extension overload syndrome. Pain is present with forced extension and valgus stress. The combination of valgus and extension forces during the acceleration and deceleration phases of throwing leads to chronic changes in the posterior compartment of the elbow. Loose bodies and osteophytes of the olecranon tip are the most common findings. In addition, football linemen are prone to the development of posterior osteophytes from repeated valgus extension stress.[40]

Forced elbow extension such as what occurs during the follow-through phase of pitching can produce a contraction apophysitis and nonunion of the secondary ossification center of the olecranon. These conditions occur as a result of repetitive stress generated in the triceps tendon insertion. In the mature adult, avulsion of the triceps at its insertion can occur. Occasionally, an asymptomatic nonunion of the olecranon that developed secondary to a traction apophysitis will separate later in life leading to the equivalent of an olecranon fracture. A stress fracture of the olecranon is not uncommon in the gymnast or throwing athlete. Isolated triceps tendinitis and rupture of the triceps tendon are also seen.[46]

Traumatic olecranon fractures can occur from a direct blow with a stick or ball or, more commonly, with the combination of a fall on a hard surface associated with forceful contraction of the triceps. Motion is limited, and pain and swelling are severe. Less traumatic falls on the tip of the olecranon can lead to contusions of the soft tissue over the tip of the bone. Falls can also produce inflammation and bleeding into the olecranon bursa and a subsequent olecranon bursitis. The bursitis is a reaction of the bursal tissue to the swelling and discomfort.

Multicompartment Injuries

Displaced fractures and elbow dislocations are not as common as overuse injuries in athletes, but their sequelae can be severe. These injuries may result in neurovascular complications, arthrofibrosis, heterotopic ossification, and posttraumatic arthritis. These complications are usually related to the initial traumatic disruption of bone, muscle, ligaments, and capsule but may be worsened by failure to obtain early motion of the elbow joint. The elbow joint is prone to the deleterious effects of extended immobilization.

FOCUS ON . . .

Posterior Compartment and Multicompartment Injuries

Posterior compartment injury is characterized by incomplete flexion. Repetitive overhead motions compress the olecranon against the medial olecranon fossa wall, creating valgus extension overload syndrome. Valgus and extension forces during the acceleration and deceleration phases cause pain, loose bodies, and olecranon tip osteophytes. Also, posterior osteophytes can develop in football linemen from repeated valgus extension stress.

Contraction apophysitis and nonunion at the olecranon secondary ossification center can occur with forced elbow extension and triceps tendon insertion stress. The mature adult may have a triceps insertion avulsion or an olecranon fracture from an asymptomatic nonunion earlier in life. Gymnasts and throwing athletes can experience olecranon stress fractures, isolated triceps tendinitis, and triceps tendon rupture.

Traumatic olecranon fractures from a direct blow or a fall on a hard surface with a forceful triceps contraction result in limited motion and severe pain and swelling. A less severe injury to the olecranon tip can produce a contusion or olecranon bursitis.

Multicompartment Injuries

Multicompartment injuries include displaced fractures and dislocations, which are less common than overuse injuries in athletes, but can have severe sequelae with neurovascular complications, heterotopic ossification, and posttraumatic arthritis. Although they result from the initial trauma, these sequelae can be worsened by failing to achieve early range of motion.

CLINICAL EXAMINATION

Observation and Inspection

The patient should completely expose the trunk and both arms for an adequate physical examination. Muscular hypertrophy of the sports-dominant arm should be noted. Comparison of the asymptomatic elbow to the symptomatic elbow is essential. The skin should be examined for areas of contusion, ecchymosis, scars, and any evidence of systemic vascular disease such as petechiae or venous congestion. Swelling over the olecranon as can be seen with olecranon bursitis should be noted.

The carrying angle in men is approximately 12° to 13°; in women, it is 13° to 16°. The dominant arm of the pitcher may demonstrate 10° to 15° of increased valgus compared to the nondominant arm after adaptive remodeling from repetitive stress. Previous fractures can lead to excessive valgus or varus.[48]

Palpation

The prominence of the medial epicondyle can be palpated subcutaneously. Tenderness localized to this area is often associated with epicondylitis. The medial supracondylar ridge of the humerus can be palpated proximal to the medial epicondyle. Osteophytic or congenital bony processes that may entrap the median nerve can be palpated along this ridge. The examination of the medial side continues with palpation of the soft tissue. The ulnar nerve, the UCL, and the flexor pronator mass are the most important structures deserving attention during examination of the medial elbow.

The stability of the ulnar nerve in its groove should be examined with the arm abducted and externally rotated and the elbow flexed between 20° and 70° (**Figure 11-7**). Any dislocation or subluxation should be noted. To determine whether the subluxation is associated with pain or paresthesia in the symptomatic elbow, the examiner should tap gently over the course of the nerve in an attempt to elicit a Tinel's sign. A Tinel's sign indicates irritability of injured nerve fibers and the possibility of nerve compression or the presence of a neuroma.[47]

The UCL is difficult to palpate directly, but tenderness along its course from the medial epicondyle to the sublime tubercle of the ulna can sometimes be elicited. Tenderness just distal to the medial epicondyle is seen in overuse of the flexor-pronator mass. Posteriorly, the olecranon is most prominent and is best palpated in flexion. The presence of a fluid-filled bursa can be detected easily. Osseous changes secondary to valgus extension overload can also be detected. The triceps tendon should be palpated for defects if a rupture is suspected.

The radial head and the radiocapitellar articulation can be palpated in the soft spot of the elbow, which lies in a triangle formed by the lateral epicondyle, the tip of the olecranon, and the lateral border of the radial head. The articulation can be palpated easily by pronating and supinating the forearm. The muscle mass of the brachioradialis and the extensor carpi radialis longus and brevis can be palpated and examined for tenderness. Tenderness directly over the lateral epicondyle is the hallmark of lateral epicondylitis.

Anteriorly, the biceps tendon is most prominent as it crosses the cubital fossa. The pulse of the brachial artery can be palpated medial to this tendon.

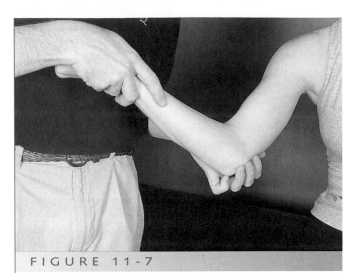

FIGURE 11-7

The athletic trainer can examine the stability of the ulnar nerve in its groove when the athlete's arm is abducted and externally rotated and the elbow is flexed between 20° and 70°.

Range of Motion

Every elbow exam should include documentation of range of motion in flexion, extension, pronation, and supination. Active and passive motion should be assessed, and a side-to-side comparison is essential. The feel of the endpoints of motion should be carefully evaluated and documented.[49]

Muscle Testing

Complete testing of the muscles around the elbow joint includes evaluation of active elbow flexion and extension, forearm pronation and supination, and wrist flexion and extension.

The individual elbow flexors can be isolated depending on the position of the forearm. Flexion in pronation depends mostly on the brachialis, whereas the biceps is the dominant flexor in supination. The brachioradialis can be tested with the forearm in a neutral position.[50]

Resisted extension of the triceps can be tested with the arm stabilized and the elbow flexed to 90°. Resisted pronation and supination is performed with the patient seated, arm at the side, elbow flexed to 90°, and the forearm in neutral.[51] Resistance is offered at the distal forearm preventing pronation, then supination. Any pain with resisted pronation, which is seen often in throwers, should be noted.[52]

Wrist flexors and extensors should be examined when a patient reports medial or lateral elbow pain. Pain over the lateral epicondyle with resisted wrist extension is a classic symptom of lateral epicondylitis. Pain is caused most commonly by inflammation of the origin of the extensor carpi radialis brevis and is isolated by resisting middle finger extension. Pain that occurs with resisted index finger extension is associated more commonly with pathology

involving the extensor carpi radialis longus. Resisted pronation or wrist flexion exacerbates the medial elbow pain associated with medial epicondylitis (pain directly over the muscle origin) or flexor-pronator syndrome (pain distal to the muscle origin). Isolation of the specific muscle group involved becomes important when a treatment protocol is established.[51]

Neurologic Exam

Branches of the axillary nerve from the C5 nerve root innervate the lateral arm. The lateral forearm is innervated by the musculocutaneous nerve and the C6 nerve root. The antebrachial cutaneous nerve arising from the C8 nerve root innervates the medial forearm, and the brachial cutaneous branch of the T1 nerve root innervates the medial arm. Sensory innervation is usually tested by pinprick or light touch. More sensitive techniques are reserved for those patients with ambiguous examination results. Eliciting the deep tendon reflexes of the biceps, brachioradialis, and triceps can also test the C5, C6, and C7 nerve roots, respectively. Abnormalities in the neurologic exam should alert the examiner to the possibility of cervical spine pathology as the source of elbow pain.[4,47]

Diagnostic Tests

Stability of the ulnar collateral ligament can be tested with the elbow flexed to 25° (**Figure 11-8**). Valgus stress is applied to the flexed elbow joint to assess the integrity of the ligament. The ligament can be palpated by holding the upper extremity in 25° to 30° of flexion and blocking external rotation of the humerus. This test can be performed either in a supine or prone position; however, testing may be more effective in the prone position. A UCL instability can be diagnosed if there is an excessive opening of the medial elbow joint when compared to the

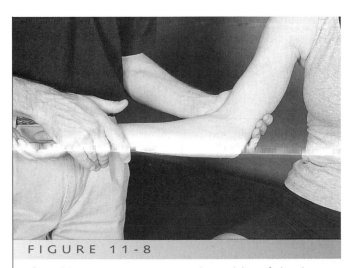

FIGURE 11-8

The athletic trainer can assess the stability of the ulnar collateral ligament with the athlete's elbow flexed to 25°.

opposite side. The amount of opening as well as the endpoint should be noted. Pain may be associated with stress testing in those patients with a UCL injury.[48,49]

The valgus extension overload test is used to confirm the presence of a posteromedial osteophyte that abuts the medial margin of the olecranon fossa. Impingement in this area is a common finding in throwers and football linemen. The patient experiences posterior elbow pain or loss of motion. To perform the valgus extension overload test, the examiner places the patient's arm in forced extension and exerts a valgus stress, simulating the position of the arm during the acceleration phase of pitching (**Figure 11-9**). The examiner can also palpate crepitation from a loose body and elicit tenderness by placing a finger over the posteromedial olecranon tip. Pain over the posterior and posteromedial olecranon process indicates a positive test result.[53]

The clinical examination for radiocapitellar chondromalacia or radiohumeral degenerative changes may be performed by gently supinating and pronating the patient's elbow with various degrees of elbow flexion. The radial head should also be palpated in full extension. With motion, the examiner should palpate the head of the radius for crepitus, popping, or pain.[48,49,54]

Radiographic Examination of the Elbow

Routine radiographic examination of the elbow should include an anteroposterior and lateral view. These views will determine joint integrity and identify fractures or loose bodies. Oblique views can be added if posterior pathology is suspected. If a UCL injury is suspected, bilateral valgus stress views should be obtained.

Magnetic resonance imaging (MRI) supplemented with intra-articular dye or saline injections may be used as a diagnostic test in those patients with suspected UCL injuries. The ligament can be viewed easily. A UCL tear

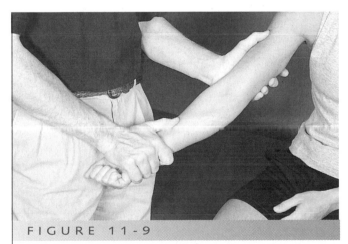

FIGURE 11-9

In the valgus extension overload test, the athletic trainer simulates the position of the athlete's arm during the acceleration phase of pitching.

is indicated by leakage of dye along the medial side of the elbow. The dye may leak both proximally and distally along the medial olecranon. This radiographic finding has been referred to as the "T-sign".[55]

NONSURGICAL TREATMENT OF ELBOW PATHOLOGIES

Many of the previously mentioned elbow pathologies can be successfully managed with nonsurgical treatment programs.

As with any sport-specific program, several basic principles of rehabilitation should be recognized and instituted. The effects of immobilization must be minimized, and healing tissue must not be overstressed. The patient should fulfill certain criteria to progress through the phases of rehabilitation. The program must be based on current scientific and clinical research. The process should be adapted to each patient and his or her goals for return to sport. Finally, the rehabilitation program must be a team effort by the physician, physical therapist, athletic trainer, and patient. Ongoing communication with all involved individuals is essential for a speedy and successful outcome. Compliance with the rehabilitation program is enhanced by proper patient education. Because more knowledge is available today regarding anatomy, pathophysiology, and biomechanics of the elbow joint, more effective rehabilitation techniques can be implemented for prevention and nonsurgical treatment.

Ulnar Neuropathy

The nonsurgical treatment program for ulnar neuropathy focuses on diminishing ulnar nerve irritation with night splinting, enhancing dynamic medial joint stability, and gradually returning the athlete to throwing. Once the athlete has been evaluated and a diagnosis of ulnar neuritis has been made, the athlete is instructed to discontinue overhead sports such as throwing for approximately 4 to 5 weeks. However, this time period varies greatly depending on the severity of symptoms. A program consisting of isometric exercises to strengthen the wrist, forearm, and arm musculature and exercises to strengthen the shoulder is initiated. Flexibility exercises to prevent muscular tightness and restore normal motion are begun. The initial acute phase of the injury usually lasts approximately 2 weeks.

The second phase of treatment is considered the advanced strengthening period. The goals of this phase include improving strength, power, and muscular endurance; enhancing dynamic elbow joint stability; and initiating higher speed special muscular training drills such as plyometrics. During the second phase, the athlete continues the isotonic-strengthening program, but a greater emphasis is placed on eccentric exercises. Additionally,

FOCUS ON . . .

Nonsurgical Treatment of Elbow Pathologies

Nonsurgical treatment of many elbow pathologies is often successful if basic rehabilitation principles are followed. The rehabilitation program must be a team effort that is based on current scientific and clinical research and adapted to the individual patient and the specific return-to-sport goals.

Nonsurgical treatment of ulnar neuropathy includes diminishing ulnar nerve irritation, improving dynamic medial joint stability, and gradually returning the athlete to throwing. Medial epicondylitis and flexor-pronator tendinitis are treated by diminishing the tendinitis and gradually improving muscle strength. Nonsurgical management of an ulnar collateral ligament strain or tear is somewhat controversial and can involve immobilization or immediate motion.

Rehabilitation of lateral epicondylitis comprises three sequential stages. The first phase is designed to reduce inflammation and pain, promote tissue healing, and retard muscle atrophy and minimize aggravating activities. The goals of the second phase are to restore flexibility, gradually improve muscle strength, and increase functional activities. Goals of the third phase include returning to sport activities and continuation of strengthening, flexibility, and endurance activities. Any deficiencies in sport techniques should be corrected.

Osteochondritis dissecans is treated depending on clinical and radiographic findings and the stage of the lesion. Nonsurgical treatment is rest and elbow immobilization and is indicated if no loose bodies are present. If nonsurgical treatment fails or a loose body is evident, arthroscopic abrasion and drilling of the lesion is indicated, with fixation or removal of the fragment. Nonsurgical treatment of valgus extension overload focuses on reducing posterior elbow pain, soreness, and inflammation while improving eccentric strength of the biceps, brachioradialis, and brachialis muscles and enhancing control of the elbow flexors. If nonsurgical treatment fails, surgical excision of the posterior and posteromedial olecranon tip is indicated. Nonsurgical treatment of olecranon stress fracture begins with restriction from aggravating activities and includes stretching and range-of-motion exercises, along with upper extremity isometric and light isotonic strengthening exercises. If nonsurgical treatment fails, internal fixation (with or without bone graft) is indicated.

Nonsurgical treatment of degenerative joint disease focuses on diminishing pain and inflammation, then improving range of motion and flexibility, and finally enhancing muscle strength and endurance. If nonsurgical treatment is unsuccessful, joint debridement is indicated. Initial treatment of synovitis is activity modification and NSAIDs (if not contraindicated). Rehabilitation focuses on restoring and maintaining elbow extension.

TABLE 11-3
ISOKINETIC ASSESSMENT

Bilateral comparison

	180° per second	300° per second
Elbow flexion		
Elbow extension	110% to 120%	105% to 115%
	105% to 115%	100% to 110%
Flexion/extension ratio	70% to 80%	63% to 69%

The athlete is allowed to initiate a throwing program if the following criteria are met:

- full range of motion with no pain
- satisfactory results of the clinical exam with no neurologic symptoms and with adequate medial stability
- satisfactory muscular performance

Table 11-3 illustrates the criteria to determine muscular performance based on an isokinetic assessment.

Once the athlete fulfills these criteria, the throwing program can be initiated. **Table 11-4** shows the first phase of an interval throwing program. Throwers are started on an interval long-toss program beginning with light tossing from 45′. Progression of the throwing program is based on the distance, intensity, and number of throws that are increased gradually over the next several weeks. Once the thrower successfully completes step 8 of phase 1, phase 2, which is throwing from the pitching mound, can be initiated. **Table 11-5** shows the second phase of the interval throwing program. During this return-to-activity phase, the thrower begins the strengthening program referred to as the "thrower's 10 program." Once the

dynamic stability drills are initiated for the elbow stabilizers. Plyometric exercise drills are initiated to prepare the athlete for throwing. This phase usually takes 2 to 4 weeks to prepare the athlete for the return-to-activity phase.

TABLE 11-4
PHASE 1 OF AN INTERVAL THROWING PROGRAM[83]

45' Phase:

Step 1:
- A. Warm-up throwing
- B. 45' (25 throws)
- C. Rest 15 minutes
- D. Warm-up throwing
- E. 45' (25 throws)

Step 2:
- A. Warm-up throwing
- B. 45' (25 throws)
- C. Rest 10 minutes
- D. Warm-up throwing
- E. 45' (25 throws)
- F. Rest 10 minutes
- G. Warm-up throwing
- H. 45' (25 throws)

60' Phase:

Step 3:
- A. Warm-up throwing
- B. 60' (25 throws)
- C. Rest 15 minutes
- D. Warm-up throwing
- E. 60' (25 throws)

Step 4:
- A. Warm-up throwing
- B. 60' (25 throws)
- C. Rest 10 minutes
- D. Warm-up throwing
- E. 60' (25 throws)
- F. Rest 10 minutes
- G. Warm-up throwing
- H. 60' (25 throws)

90' Phase:

Step 5:
- A. Warm-up throwing
- B. 90' (25 throws)
- C. Rest 15 minutes
- D. Warm-up throwing
- E. 90' (25 throws)

Step 6:
- A. Warm-up throwing
- B. 90' (25 throws)
- C. Rest 10 minutes
- D. Warm-up throwing
- E. 90' (25 throws)
- F. Rest 10 minutes
- G. Warm-up throwing
- H. 90' (25 throws)

120' Phase:

Step 7:
- A. Warm-up throwing
- B. 120' (25 throws)
- C. Rest 15 minutes
- D. Warm-up throwing
- E. 120' (25 throws)

Step 8:
- A. Warm-up throwing
- B. 120' (25 throws)
- C. Rest 10 minutes
- D. Warm-up throwing
- E. 120' (25 throws)
- F. Rest 10 minutes
- G. Warm-up throwing
- H. 120' (25 throws)

150' Phase*

Step 9:
- A. Warm-up throwing
- B. 150' (25 throws)
- C. Rest 15 minutes
- D. Warm-up throwing
- E. 150' (25 throws)

Step 10:
- A. Warm-up throwing
- B. 150' (25 throws)
- C. Rest 10 minutes
- D. Warm-up throwing
- E. 150' (25 throws)
- F. Rest 10 minutes
- G. Warm-up throwing
- H. 150' (25 throws)

180' Phase:

Step 11:
- A. Warm-up throwing
- B. 180' (25 throws)
- C. Rest 15 minutes
- D. Warm-up throwing
- E. 180' (25 throws)

Step 12:
- A. Warm-up throwing
- B. 180' (25 throws)
- C. Rest 10 minutes
- D. Warm-up throwing
- E. 180' (25 throws)
- F. Rest 10 minutes
- G. Warm-up throwing
- H. 180' (25 throws)

Step 13:
- A. Warm-up throwing
- B. 180' (25 throws)
- C. Rest 10 minutes
- D. Warm-up throwing
- E. 180' (25 throws)
- F. Rest 10 minutes
- G. Warm-up throwing
- H. 180' (25 throws)

Step 14:
Begin throwing off the mound or return to respective position

*Pitchers progress to flat ground throwing from windup at 60', then progress to Phase 2 of the interval throwing program.

TABLE 11-5

PHASE 2 OF AN INTERVAL THROWING PROGRAM STARTING OFF THE MOUND[83]

Stage 1: Fastball only

Step 1:   Interval throwing
          15 throws off mound 50%

Step 2:   Interval throwing
          30 throws off mound 50%

Step 3:   Interval throwing
          45 throws off mound 50%

Step 4:   Interval throwing
          60 throws off mound 50%

Step 5:   Interval throwing
          30 throws off mound 75%

Step 6:   30 throws off mound 75%
          45 throws off mound 50%

Step 7:   45 throws off mound 75%
          15 throws off mound 50%

Step 8:   60 throws off mound 75%

Stage 2: Fastball only

Step 9:   45 throws off mound 75%
          15 throws in batting practice

Step 10: 45 throws off mound 75%
          30 throws in batting practice

Step 11: 45 throws off mound 75%
          45 throws in batting practice

Stage 3: Fastballs and breaking balls

Step 12: 30 throws off mound 75%
          15 throws off mound 50% breaking balls
          45 to 60 throws off mound 75%

Step 13: 30 throws in batting practice (fastball only)
          30 breaking balls 75%
          30 throws in batting practice

Step 14: 30 throws off mound 75%
          60 to 90 throws off mound 75%

Step 15: Simulated game: progressing by 15 throws per work-out (use interval throwing to 120' phase as warm-up). All throwing off the mound should be done in the presence of the pitching coach to stress proper throwing mechanics (use of a speed gun may aid in effort control).

throwing program is completed successfully, the thrower may gradually return to play.

Medial Epicondylitis/Flexor-pronator Tendinitis

The nonsurgical treatment approach for athletes who have flexor-pronator tendinitis focuses on diminishing the tendinitis inflammatory response and gradually improving muscular strength. Initially, the treatment may consist of a warm whirlpool, ultrasound with hydrocortisone cream (phonophoresis), stretching exercises, light strengthening to maintain musculature, high-voltage galvanic stimulation to promote tendon healing, and ice massage. Once the patient's symptoms are significantly diminished, an aggressive strengthening exercise program that uses concentrics, eccentrics, and isometrics may be initiated. Once suitable levels of strength and endurance have been reached, an aggressive strengthening program using plyometrics and a light tossing program may be initiated. If the patient's throwing mechanics contributed to the condition, an analysis of those mechanics may be necessary.

Ulnar Collateral Ligament Strain/Tear

The nonsurgical treatment program for throwers who have strained or partially torn the UCL is somewhat controversial, especially pertaining to the question of whether to use immobilization or immediate motion.

Table 11-6 illustrates a program that employs restricted motion of the elbow from 20° to 90° immediately following injury. This program allows inflammation of the torn tissue to calm and proper collagen to form and become aligned. Most commonly, the elbow is placed in a brace to prevent a valgus stress to the joint. Isometric exercises to strengthen the wrist and elbow joint musculature are performed. The injured athlete is instructed to ice his or her elbow 4 to 6 times per day to control inflammation and pain.

Restoration of full motion and gradual improvement of the patient's strength and endurance are the primary goals of the second phase of this program. During this phase, motion is increased by 5° to 10° per week for both flexion and extension. Therefore, by 6 weeks, the patient should exhibit full motion. Additionally, during the second phase, isotonic muscle strengthening drills are initiated for the entire upper extremity. Rhythmic stabilization drills are performed in this phase to enhance neuromuscular control of the surrounding elbow musculature to enhance dynamic joint stability.

The advanced strengthening phase is usually initiated approximately 6 to 7 weeks after injury. The primary goals of this phase are to enhance muscular strength, power, and endurance and to gradually initiate higher speed drills in the throwing position. During this time frame, the athlete performs an isotonic strengthening program referred to as the thrower's 10 program, which should be

TABLE 11-6

NONSURGICAL TREATMENT FOLLOWING ULNAR COLLATERAL SPRAINS OF THE ELBOW

Phase 1: Immediate motion phase (weeks 1 and 2)

Goals:

- Increase range of motion
- Promote healing of ulnar collateral ligament
- Retard muscular atrophy
- Decrease pain and inflammation

  ❑ ROM:
  - ➢ Brace (optional) for pain-free ROM (20° to 90°)
  - ➢ Active assisted range of motion (AAROM) and passive range of motion (PROM) elbow and wrist (pain-free range)

  ❑ Exercises:
  - ➢ Isometric (wrist and elbow musculature)
  - ➢ Shoulder strengthening (no external rotation strengthening)

  ❑ Ice and compression

Phase 2: Intermediate phase (weeks 3 through 6)

Goals:

- Increase range of motion
- Improve strength/endurance
- Decrease pain and inflammation
- Promote stability

  ❑ ROM:
  - ➢ Gradually increase motion 0° to 135° (increase 10° per week)

  ❑ Exercises:
  - ➢ Initiate isotonic exercises
    - Wrist curls
    - Wrist extension
    - Pronation/supination
    - Biceps/triceps
    - Dumbbells (external rotation, deltoid, supraspinatus, rhomboids, and internal rotation)

  ❑ Ice and compression

Phase 3: Advanced phase (weeks 6 and 7 through weeks 12 and 14)

Criteria to progress to this phase:

- Full ROM
- No pain or tenderness
- No increase in laxity
- Strength 4/5 of elbow flexors/extensors

Goals:

- Increase strength, power, and endurance
- Improve neuromuscular control
- Initiate high-speed exercise drills

  ❑ Exercises:
  - ➢ Initiate exercise tubing, shoulder program:
    - Thrower's 10 program
    - Biceps/triceps program
    - Supination/pronation
    - Wrist extension/flexion
    - Plyometric throwing drills

Phase 4: Return-to-activity phase (weeks 12 through 14)

Criteria to progress to this phase:

- Full pain-free ROM
- No increase in laxity
- Isokinetic test fulfills criteria
- Satisfactory clinical exam

Goals:

- Gradual return to competition
- Maintain strength, power, and endurance

  ❑ Exercises:
  - ➢ Initiate interval throwing
  - ➢ Continue thrower's 10 program
  - ➢ Continue plyometrics

modified based on the patient's weakness and deficiencies. In addition, a plyometric program is initiated to prepare the athlete for throwing. The plyometric program can include several specific plyometric drills such as the two-hand overhead soccer throw, two-hand chest pass, two-hand side-to-side throw, two-hand overhead side throw, and the one-hand baseball throw.

An interval throwing program is initiated once the patient has achieved the criteria to begin throwing: full pain-free ROM, satisfactory results of the clinical examination, and satisfactory muscular performance based on isokinetic testing (see Table 11-3). As soon as the patient exhibits this criteria, the long toss program can be initiated (see Table 11-4). However, throwers with a UCL sprain usually need 3 to 4 months before they can return to play. Once the throwing program is completed, the athlete may return to competition. If symptoms persist, then reassessment is indicated and possible surgical reconstruction of the UCL may be required.

Lateral Epicondylitis

The rehabilitation program for lateral epicondylitis progresses through three sequential stages. The primary goals of the first phase, the acute phase, are to diminish the inflammation and pain of the involved tissues, promote tissue healing, retard muscular atrophy, and minimize activities that aggravate the condition. Modalities such as cryotherapy, high-voltage galvanic stimulation, ultrasound, iontophoresis, and whirlpool can be effective in reducing acute inflammation and pain. Gentle stretching exercises are performed to normalize motion. Submaximal strengthening exercises can be performed during this phase to prevent muscular atrophy. Frequently, isometric exercises can be initiated, followed by isotonic exercises. Painful movements and aggravating activities should be avoided or minimized in an attempt to reduce inflammation and repetitive microtraumatic stresses.

During phase 2, the subacute phase, emphasis is placed on restoring flexibility, the gradual progression of muscular strength, and increasing functional activities. Strengthening exercises are progressed to use concentric and eccentric muscle loading. The patient is encouraged to use caution with excessive gripping activities.

Phase 3, the chronic phase, is marked by the patient's return to the sport activities that have aggravated the condition in the past. The patient is encouraged to continue strengthening, flexibility, and endurance exercises. Often the patient is encouraged to alter body mechanics or sports movements to prevent symptoms from recurring.

Osteochondritis Dissecans

Treatment options for osteochondritis dissecans depend on clinical and radiographic findings. Three stages of lesions have been identified for purposes of classification and treatment.[56] Stage 1 lesions include those with no radiographic evidence of subchondral displacement or fracture. Stage 2 lesions show evidence of subchondral detachment or articular cartilage fracture. Stage 3 lesions involve chondral or osteochondral fragments that have become detached, resulting in an intra-articular loose body or bodies.[56] Nonsurgical treatment is indicated if there are no findings consistent with detachment of subchondral bone, articular cartilage, or loose body. Nonsurgical treatment should consist of rest and immobilization of the elbow until irritability has resolved followed by institution of a rehabilitation program.

Treatment begins with 3 to 6 weeks of immobilization with the elbow flexed at 90°. The patient is instructed to perform ROM exercises 3 to 4 times per day. Once the symptoms are resolved, a gentle strengthening program can be initiated. The patient begins performing isometric strengthening exercises for approximately 1 week before progressing to isotonic strengthening exercises. During this phase, the patient also performs stretching exercises for the entire upper extremity with emphasis on the wrist and elbow musculature. Plyometric strengthening drills, eccentric muscle strengthening exercises, and aggressive strengthening exercises can be initiated. Once these are successfully completed, the patient can begin an interval throwing program and progress to a return to throwing from the pitching mound.

If nonsurgical treatment fails or there is evidence of an impending or documented loose body, surgery is indicated. Surgical treatment consists of arthroscopic abrading and drilling of the lesion with fixation or removal of the loose body.[57] However, long-term follow-up of patients who have had surgery has not indicated that drilling or reattaching the lesions has a favorable effect on symptoms or radiographic changes.[58,59] Prevention and early detection appear to be the best form of treatment.

Posterior Pathology

Valgus extension overload in baseball pitchers occurs during the acceleration and deceleration phases of throwing.[53,60] During these phases, excessive valgus forces coupled with medial elbow stresses cause the olecranon to wedge into the medial wall of the olecranon fossa. Repetitive extension stresses from contraction of the triceps also contribute to this condition. A posterior osteophyte eventually develops on the olecranon process. The osteophyte is responsible for the pain elicited posteriorly. Valgus instability of the elbow may further enhance osteophyte formation. Repetitive impact of the spur within the olecranon fossa may cause fragmentation and eventually loose body formation within the joint. These changes are mainly seen in baseball pitchers, but they also occur in javelin throwers who use the overhead throwing style.

A nonsurgical treatment program frequently is attempted before any surgical intervention is considered. The program focuses initially on diminishing any pain, soreness, or inflammation in the posterior elbow region. The rehabilitative approach also attempts to improve eccentric strength and control of the elbow flexors. By enhancing the eccentric strength efficiency of the biceps, brachioradialis, and brachialis muscles, the rapid elbow extension that occurs during the deceleration phase of throwing might be controlled. This may be helpful in reducing the magnitude of the compressive load posteriorly. Occasionally, a young thrower who develops valgus extension overload may need to undergo a biomechanical pitching analysis to determine if faulty or undesirable pitching mechanics are present. Alterations in the throwing mechanics can then be suggested by the player's pitching coach or a biomechanist.

If nonsurgical treatment fails, surgical excision of the posterior and posteromedial olecranon tip is indicated. Surgery can be performed through an open approach or arthroscopically, which minimizes soft-tissue involvement and allows for more aggressive rehabilitation.

Stress fracture

Stress fracture of the olecranon has been reported in throwers and can occur in any part of the olecranon, especially in the midarticular area.[60] The stress fracture is likely caused by repetitive extension stresses from triceps contraction during the acceleration, deceleration, and follow-through phases of throwing. The patient typically experiences an insidious onset of pain in the posterolateral elbow during or after a throw. Symptoms are similar to triceps tendinitis; however, there is usually tenderness over the involved site of the olecranon. Bone scan or MRI scan may be required to confirm the diagnosis if plain radiographs are normal.

Nonsurgical treatment begins with 6 to 8 weeks of restriction of aggressive strengthening exercises such as heavy lifting, participating in sport activities, or any other activities that aggravate elbow symptoms. During this time, the patient is instructed to perform stretching and ROM exercises to maintain motion. Additionally, isometric exercises and light isotonic strengthening exercises are initiated for the entire upper extremity musculature. The patient is told to discontinue any exercise that causes pain near the stress fracture site and to contact the athletic trainer, physical therapist, or physician. Usually by 6 to 8 weeks, the patient can begin a swimming program, which promotes upper extremity strength and endurance. Aggressive strengthening exercises such as heavy weight one-hand lifting, plyometrics, or sports-related drills are not allowed until bony healing is seen on clinical and radiographic evaluation. Bony healing may not occur until 8 to 12 weeks after the onset of symptoms. At that time, a light throwing program may be initiated. The throwing program consists of a long toss program that progresses to a throwing program from the pitching mound. Complete recovery usually requires 3 to 6 months.

If nonsurgical treatment fails, surgery is indicated for internal fixation of the stress fracture with or without bone graft. Bony union can be expected in approximately 95% of cases with surgical treatment.

Other Injuries

Degenerative joint disease

Degenerative joint disease of the elbow can occur prematurely in certain athletes, such as throwers and football linemen. Repetitive loading to the articular surfaces of the elbow joint can lead to an acceleration of wear and osteophyte formation. Loose body formation may be the result, which will, in turn, cause pain and limited motion of the elbow. Although the disability may not be enough to compromise routine activities of daily living, it may restrict or prohibit further participation in sports.

The conservative treatment goals are focused first on diminishing the patient's pain and inflammatory process. Second, an improvement in range of motion and flexibility should be emphasized. Last, overall enhancement of elbow muscle strength and endurance is undertaken.

Initially, a warm whirlpool can be used to diminish pain and to promote soft-tissue stretching. The patient is then instructed to perform stretching exercises, especially those that improve elbow extension and forearm supination and pronation. Therapeutic techniques to enhance motion include stretching; contract-relax techniques to relax the muscles; joint mobilization; and low-load, long-duration stretching. Patients with degenerative joint disease must improve flexibility, especially capsular extensibility, to help slow the degenerative joint process and control elbow pain. In addition, the athletic patient is placed on a strengthening exercise program for all muscles in the upper extremity. If possible, the athlete is instructed to use lighter weights for weight lifting exercises. Exercises such as the bench press, triceps push-downs, triceps French curls, press-ups, and other exercises that place high compressive and shear forces onto the humeroulnar joint may be helpful.

If the nonsurgical approach does not improve symptoms, open or arthroscopic debridement is indicated. Arthroscopic debridement allows an accelerated rehabilitation program to be undertaken.

Synovitis

Generalized synovitis may result from a repetitive throwing motion. On physical examination, the patient does not localize the pain to any specific area. The soft-tissue inflammation within the joint usually results in a flexion contracture. Initial treatment includes a modification of activity and, if not contraindicated, administration of nonsteroidal anti-inflammatory drugs (NSAIDs).

The rehabilitation program is focused on the restoration and maintenance of elbow extension. Thus, ROM and strengthening exercises should be initiated immediately to prevent further loss of motion. Care must be taken not to become too aggressive with early exercise that may contribute to the inflammatory synovial reaction. Early in the rehabilitation program, a tepid to warm whirlpool may be beneficial for motion enhancement and pain relief. Cryotherapy and contrast treatments (cold to warm) also may be beneficial. Strengthening exercises in the form of submaximal subpainful isometrics are performed with care. Isotonic strengthening is not initiated until the inflammatory response has decreased significantly. Once the patient has achieved a proper strength level and the results of the clinical examination are satisfactory, a sports rehabilitation program consisting of throwing and lifting can be instituted.

Shoulder Program

Any elbow rehabilitation program is not complete without a shoulder program. Shoulder exercises should be initiated most appropriately in the second or subacute phase and no later than the final stage of the elbow program. Rotator cuff strengthening should be emphasized with specific focus on the abductors and external rotators.

This program includes the concept of total arm strength in which proximal stability and distal mobility are developed or maintained to ensure adequate strength and neuromuscular performance. Thus, the rehabilitation program should include scapular muscle training and a glenohumeral muscle exercise program to help accomplish these goals. The exercise program should focus on specific muscle groups that are active in the throwing motion.

SURGICAL TREATMENT

Surgical treatment of the elbow is reserved for those patients who fail to respond to nonsurgical treatment programs. Depending on the pathology, surgery may involve arthroscopy, open surgery, or both approaches.

Surgical Arthroscopic Procedures

The removal of loose bodies is one of the most common indications for elbow arthroscopy. Surgical arthroscopy is performed with the patient in a supine position with the arm suspended freely over the edge of the table to allow for full access to the elbow. A needle is inserted into the soft spot of the elbow. Fluid egress through the needle verifies intra-articular positioning. Various portals are established, so that different compartments can be examined and accessed.[61,62]

With osteochondritis dissecans, the anterior and posterior compartments should be examined for loose bodies and loose cartilage is debrided from the radiocapitellar joint. Excision of the fragment and debridement of the base provide the best results. Although arthroscopic reduc-

tion and fixation can be attempted, it is a technically demanding procedure and results are no better than with simple debridement.[63]

Repetitive stress may cause osteophytes to form in both the anterior and posterior compartments of the elbow. The anterior, lateral, and posterior compartments are examined, and osteophyte formation and soft tissue are debrided if necessary. Once the olecranon spur can be visualized, it is removed from the tip and posterior aspect of the olecranon in a biplanar fashion, and any remaining osteophyte is contoured and debrided.

Treatment of chronic synovitis of the elbow begins with a complete examination of the joint. Any lateral synovial plicas should be resected, and hypertrophic synovium should be removed.[64] Synovial biopsies should be obtained. Debridement along the medial gutter should be cautious to prevent injury to the ulnar nerve.[63]

Elbow joint contractures can also be treated with the arthroscope; however, an overzealous release can increase the risk of injury of the neurovascular structures. Osteophytes should be debrided. The elbow is manipulated once the debridement is complete and range of motion is measured intraoperatively.[65]

Open Surgical Procedures

Transposition of the ulnar nerve is indicated in throwing athletes with persistent ulnar nerve symptoms as a result of nerve compression or recurrent subluxation.[66] The nerve is usually transferred to a subcutaneous position. A second surgical procedure may be needed at some point during the athlete's career, and the nerve may be difficult to expose because of scarring in a submuscular position.

A medial approach is used for this surgery. Soft tissue is dissected until the nerve is free. After the procedure, the elbow is placed in a splint in 90° of flexion.

The UCL is reconstructed with an open procedure after an arthroscopic stress test is performed to evaluate stability.[66] The ulnar nerve is transposed and the UCL muscle is dissected. The tear is identified, and the graft is harvested. The graft is passed through the bone tunnels in a figure-of-eight manner. After the graft is sutured and the elbow is tensioned in 30° of flexion and varus stress, the ligament is sutured closed and the ulnar nerve transposition is completed subcutaneously and the wound closed.[66]

Surgical treatment of medial epicondylitis is similar to reconstruction of the UCL. Care should be taken not to disrupt the attachment of the flexor tendons from the medial epicondyle. The medial epicondyle can be drilled to stimulate healing. The ulnar nerve should be protected.[66]

A distal biceps rupture involves surgical treatment through either a one- or two-incision technique. In the two-incision technique, the lateral incision is made distal to the lateral epicondyle over the radial head.[67] The soft tissues are split to expose the radial tuberosity. The posterior interosseous nerve is at risk and should be protected.

Rehabilitation Following Elbow Surgery in the Throwing Athlete

Rehabilitation plays a vital role in restoring full, unrestricted arm function following elbow surgery in the athlete. Because of the excessive forces that are transferred across the joint, the elbow joint is susceptible to a variety of repetitive stress injuries. Often, these injuries require surgery to restore full pain-free function. The unique orientation of the elbow joint complex and the high degree of joint congruency may account for much of the difficulty experienced by the rehabilitative specialist in obtaining full motion and preinjury function. Therefore, postsurgical complications such as loss of motion, persistent elbow pain, and muscular weakness may be attributed, in part, to the postsurgical rehabilitation program.

Rehabilitation following elbow surgery is a sequential and progressive multiphase approach. The ultimate goal of this process is to return the athlete to sport as quickly and safely as possible. The athlete may be allowed to gradually return to sport-specific training and a progressive interval throwing program when the elbow exhibits the following criteria: full pain-free range of motion, no pain or tenderness, satisfactory muscular strength, and satisfactory results of a clinical examination.

Rehabilitation Following Elbow Arthroscopy

Elbow arthroscopy performed for diagnostic purposes or for procedures such as debridement, loose body removal, or synovial resection generally causes minimal postsurgical pain and stiffness. **Table 11-7** shows a somewhat aggressive postsurgical rehabilitation program for patients following elbow arthroscopy.

The goals of phase 1, the immediate motion phase, are to reestablish full pain-free ROM, diminish pain and inflammation, and retard muscular atrophy. The exercises used during this phase are designed to restore motion, prevent the formation of adverse collagen tissue, and respect the healing constraints of the tissue involved.

Early motion exercises are performed to assist in collagen organization and synthesis, pain reduction, and articular cartilage nourishment.[68-71] Active-assisted and passive motion exercises for the humeroulnar joint and supination and pronation exercises for the humeroradial and radioulnar joints are performed to restore flexion and extension. Because arthroscopic elbow surgery appears to minimize tissue morbidity, aggressive motion exercises can be performed immediately following most arthroscopic elbow procedures. Reestablishing full elbow extension is a primary and critical goal during the initial phase of the rehabilitation program. Elbow flexion contracture, which can be deleterious in the overhead throwing athlete, is a common side effect that occurs when full elbow extension is not successfully accomplished. A flexion contracture can place repetitive abnormal stress patterns on various elbow structures that can lead to further microtraumatic or macrotraumatic injuries.[72,73]

Factors that may contribute to the development of an elbow flexion contracture include the intimate congruency of the elbow complex, especially of the humeroulnar joint; the tightness of the elbow joint capsule; and the tendency of the anterior capsule to scar and become adhesive. The anterior capsule is relatively thin and very sensitive to injury. These factors may lead to many alterations in the anatomy of the anterior capsule that adversely affect normal elbow motion. Normal joint motion can also be severely compromised by rupture, contracture, and occasional calcification of the medial and lateral ligamentous structures. Posttraumatic thickening of the lateral ligamentous structure can often cause impingement and snapping during active elbow movements.[73] Significant scar formation has been reported within the anterior, posterior, and lateral capsule of the elbow joint capsule in patients with posttraumatic dislocated elbows that exhibit loss of motion.[65] In addition, the anterior anatomy of the elbow is unique because the brachialis muscle may also cause functional splinting of the elbow as a result of pain. Once motion is limited or lost, changes can occur to the sarcomere of the muscle, which may lead to an additional loss in motion and prolonged motion restriction.[74,75]

To counteract potential capsular restrictions, immediate motion and joint mobilization may be performed.[68-73] To promote the restoration of full motion, joint mobilization should be performed to the humeroulnar and radioulnar joints also.[26] Another extremely effective technique designed to regain motion and improve elbow extension is a low-load, long-duration stretching technique (**Practice Session 11-1**). This stretch is performed for 10 to 12 minutes. Reports in the literature indicate that the low-load, long-duration stretching principle produces a plastic response within the collagen tissue that will result in permanent elongation.[76-79] This type of stretching, which may be used successfully at home, can be extremely beneficial and superior to other techniques in restoring elbow motion.

Gentle joint mobilization techniques, oscillation of the joint, and gentle motion can be beneficial as neuromodulators of pain by stimulating the type I and type II articular receptors of the joint.[26] In addition, modalities such as ice, high-voltage pulsed galvanic stimulation, ultrasound, whirlpool, and transcutaneous neuromuscular stimulation can help decrease pain and inflammation.

Muscular strengthening exercises for the wrist and elbow musculature are initiated during this phase to prevent muscular atrophy. Patients are instructed to perform submaximal pain-free isometric exercises for the elbow flexors and extensors, wrist flexors and extensors, and pronators and supinators.

The primary goal of the first phase of elbow rehabilitation is to restore motion, particularly full elbow extension.

TABLE 11-7
REHABILITATION FOLLOWING ELBOW ATHROSCOPY

Phase 1: Immediate motion phase (week 1)

Goals:

- Full wrist and elbow ROM
- Decrease swelling
- Decrease pain
- Retardation of muscle atrophy

- ❏ Day of surgery
  - ➤ Begin gently moving elbow in bulky dressing

- ❏ Postsurgical days 1 and 2
  - ➤ Remove bulky dressing; replace with elastic bandages
  - ➤ Immediately begin postsurgical hand, wrist, and elbow exercises

    - ▪ Putty/grip stretching
    - ▪ Wrist flexor stretching
    - ▪ Wrist extensor stretching
    - ▪ Wrist curls
    - ▪ Reverse wrist curls
    - ▪ Neutral wrist curls
    - ▪ Pronation/supination
    - ▪ Active range of motion (AROM) and AAROM elbow extension/flexion

- ❏ Postsurgical days 3 through 7
  - ➤ ROM elbow extension/flexion
  - ➤ Begin progressive resistance exercises (PRE) with 1-lb weight

    - ▪ Wrist curls
    - ▪ Reverse wrist curls
    - ▪ Neutral wrist curls
    - ▪ Pronation/supination
    - ▪ Broomstick roll-up

Phase 2: Intermediate phase (weeks 2 and 3)

Goals:

- Improve muscular strength and endurance
- Normalize joint arthrokinematics

- ❏ Week 2
  - ➤ Add biceps curl and triceps extension
  - ➤ Continue to progress to PRE weight and repetitions as tolerated

- ❏ Week 3
  - ➤ Initiate biceps and triceps eccentric exercise program
  - ➤ Initiate rotator cuff exercise program

Phase 3: Advanced phase (weeks 4 through 8)

Criteria to progress to this phase:

- Full pain-free ROM
- No pain or tenderness
- Isokinetic test that fulfills criteria to throw
- Satisfactory clinical exam

Goal:

- Prepare athlete to perform functional activities

- ❏ Weeks 4 through 6
  - ➤ Continue maintenance program, emphasizing muscular strength, endurance, and flexibility
  - ➤ Initiate phase 1 of interval throwing program

- ❏ Weeks 7 through 8
  - ➤ Progress to throwing program
  - ➤ Continue strengthening program
  - ➤ Gradual return to competition when ready

FOCUS ON . . .

Rehabilitation Following Surgery

After elbow surgery, the throwing athlete must pursue an appropriate rehabilitation program to restore full, unrestricted arm function. Rehabilitation is a sequential, progressive, multiphase approach with the ultimate goal of returning the athlete to sport quickly and safely. Gradual return to sport-specific training and a progressive interval-throwing program may be instituted once range of motion is full and pain free, pain and tenderness have resolved, muscle strength is adequate, and the clinical examination results are satisfactory.

Elbow arthroscopy for diagnosis or debridement, loose body removal, or synovial resection usually results in minimal pain and stiffness. A somewhat aggressive rehabilitation program starts with phase 1 (immediate motion) with the goals of reestablishing full, pain-free range of motion, diminishing pain and inflammation, and retarding muscle atrophy. The second (intermediate) phase emphasizes improving mobility, strength, endurance, and neuromuscular control. The third phase, advanced strengthening, focuses on preparing the athlete for return to sport. Specific goals include increasing total arm strength, power, endurance, and neuromuscular control. Once these goals are achieved, a gradual return to throwing and hitting is permitted.

Rehabilitation after ulnar collateral ligament reconstruction varies with the type of surgery, the method of ulnar nerve transposition, and the extent of joint injury. In one program, range-of-motion exercises begin after 2 weeks of immobilization, with full range of motion achieved by 3 to 4 months. In another program, the athlete's elbow is placed in a posterior splint in 90° of flexion for 1 week to allow initial healing, and submaximal isometric elbow and wrist contractions and gripping exercises are started. Extension and flexion are increased over the course of the next several weeks and by the end of week 6, the athlete should have full range of motion.

Rehabilitation after arthroscopic elbow arthroplasty for posterior olecranon osteophyte excision is slightly more conservative than after elbow arthroscopy. Elbow extension may be achieved more slowly because of pain. Range of motion progresses as quickly as pain and patient tolerance allow. Throwers with valgus extension overload should train to control the rapid elbow extension of acceleration and deceleration and dynamically stabilize the elbow against the valgus strain of acceleration.

Rehabilitation after isolated, subcutaneous ulnar nerve transposition with fascial slings must be initially nonsurgical to allow soft-tissue healing. A posterior splint immobilizes the elbow in 90° of flexion, preventing extension and tension on the nerve. Removal of the splint and range-of-motion exercises follow. Full range of motion is normally achieved by weeks 3 or 4.

Arthroscopic arthrolysis may be needed after a fracture or dislocation if nonsurgical treatment fails to reestablish motion. Rehabilitation after this surgery begins with hourly range-of-motion exercises, with special attention to restoring full extension. Full motion should be obtained quickly, but without inflaming the joint capsule (which can result in further pain and reflex splinting). Full passive range of motion is usually restored within 10 to 14 days with the aid of low-load, long-duration stretching.

By attaining this goal, the most common postsurgical complication, an elbow flexor contracture, is prevented. Stretching should be performed with caution to ensure that the healing tissues are not overstressed or that pain is not exacerbated.

The second phase, the intermediate phase, emphasizes the advancement of elbow mobility and improvement of strength, endurance, and neuromuscular control of the elbow complex. To progress to this phase, the patient must have achieved full ROM, minimal pain and tenderness, and at least a good manual muscle test grade (4/5) for the elbow flexors and extensors during phase 1. If the patient has not accomplished these criteria, phase 1 activities should be continued until all are met.

During the second phase, stretching exercises to maintain full elbow and wrist ROM are continued. Because elbow extension and forearm pronation are important components of the thrower's elbow, making them flexible is paramount. In addition, wrist and shoulder flexibility stretching exercises are performed.

Muscular strengthening is advanced using isotonic contraction (concentrics/eccentrics) exercises. Dumbbell isotonic progressive resistive exercises or elastic tubing exercises are performed for the entire arm musculature. During this phase, the muscles of the shoulder complex are also placed on a strengthening program with a special focus on the rotator cuff musculature, abductors, and adductors. To ensure adequate muscular performance and dynamic joint stability and encourage strengthening of the whole arm, proximal stability and distal mobility are used. In addition, neuromuscular control exercises are performed to enhance dynamic stability and proprioceptive

PRACTICE SESSION 11-1
THE LOW-LOAD, LONG-DURATION STRETCHING TECHNIQUE

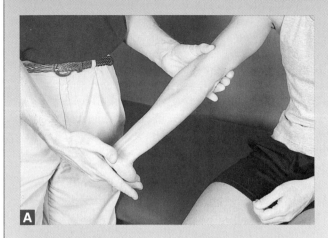

A

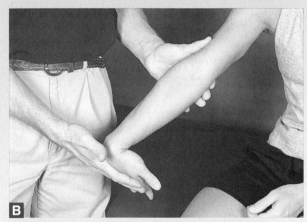

B

C

In this technique, the athlete stretches the injured extremity against resistance for 10 to 12 minutes. **A** Elbow extension, wrist dorsiflexion. **B** Elbow extension, wrist palmar flexion. **C** Elbow flexion.

skill. These exercise drills include proprioceptive neuromuscular facilitation exercises such as rhythmic stabilization and slow reversal holds that can progress as tolerated to rapid diagonal movements.

The third phase, the advanced strengthening phase, focuses on progressively increasing activities that prepare the athlete for a return to sport. The specific goals of this phase are to increase the patient's total arm strength, power, endurance, and neuromuscular control. Meeting these goals means a gradual return to sport-related activities such as throwing and hitting.

To progress to this phase, the patient must have achieved full, pain-free ROM and strength that is 70% of that of the contralateral side with no pain or tenderness. These criteria should be fulfilled before the specific exercises in phase 3 are initiated because of the explosive and aggressive movements that are required to perform them.

Advanced strengthening exercises designed specifically for the patient are emphasized during this phase. These exercises generally include high-demand strengthening exercises such as plyometrics and high-speed, high-energy strengthening exercises, in addition to concentric and eccentric muscle loading.[80]

During this phase, muscular training for the elbow extensors and wrist musculature and eccentrics for the elbow flexors are incorporated. The elbow extensors act concentrically to rapidly accelerate the arm during the acceleration phase, whereas the elbow flexors act eccentrically to decelerate the elbow and prevent elbow hyperextension or the potentially pathologic abutting of the olecranon into its fossa during follow through. Thus, exercises are specifically designed to simulate these specific muscle functions. Plyometric training drills can be performed specifically for baseball overhead throwing to appropriately train the elbow flexors and extensors.

Plyometric muscle training is an extremely beneficial form of exercise used to rehabilitate the overhead-throwing athlete.[80] The basic principle of plyometric exercise is to use an eccentric muscle contraction to prestretch the muscle before using a concentric muscular contraction. This stretch stimulates the muscle spindle that facilitates a greater or enhanced concentric contraction during the exercise. Thus, plyometric neuromuscular training encompasses three phases: a stretch phase (eccentric loading), an amortization phase, and the response phase or concentric contraction. The throwing motion is an example of a plyometric movement, whereas cocking the arm produces a stretch on the anterior muscles to stimulate the acceleration (concentric) phase of the throw. Almost all sport movements use a plyometric form of muscular contraction.

Weighted balls may be used to perform plyometric exercise drills for the entire upper extremity and body.[80] **Practice session 11-2** shows plyometric exercise drills that can be used to replicate the throwing motion.

Exercises that improve flexibility also teach the patient how to transfer weight and use the legs to accelerate the arm. The drills can be performed with a weighted ball that is rebounded from a wall back to the athlete. A wide variety of upper extremity plyometric activities are available for use during this phase.[80]

During phase 3, the shoulder complex musculature, especially the rotator cuff and scapular muscles, is placed on an aggressive exercise program. The thrower's 10 program was designed specifically for the overhead-throwing athlete.[83] The exercises in the thrower's 10 program are based on the collective works of numerous investigators and electromyographic studies of the shoulder and arm musculature during exercise.[82-86] These exercises include 1) a diagonal pattern D2 extension and flexion,

2) external and internal rotation at 0° abduction and 90° abduction, 3) shoulder abduction to 90°, 4) scaption, internal rotation, 5) prone horizontal abduction at neutral and full external rotation, at 100° abduction, 6) press-ups, 7) prone rowing, 8) push-ups, 9) elbow flexion and extension, and 10) wrist extension, flexion, supination, and pronation.

The fourth phase of the rehabilitation program is the return-to-activity phase. The goal of this phase is to ensure that adequate motion, strength, and functional drills are performed to prepare the thrower to return to a specific sport and position. An interval throwing program ensures a gradual progression to unrestricted throwing activities. The interval throwing program progressively increases the demands on the shoulder, elbow, and arm by controlling the intensity, duration, distance, type, and number of throws performed.

To progress to this phase, the patient must achieve full ROM, experience no pain or tenderness, perform an isokinetic test that fulfills set criteria, and achieve a satisfactory clinical examination.

The specific criteria of the isokinetic test are part of an ongoing study. Routinely, the throwing elbow is tested at 180° and 300° per second in the seated position. The throwing arm's elbow flexors should be 10% to 20% stronger and the dominant extensors 5% to 15% stronger when compared with the nonthrowing arm during the bilateral comparison at 180° per second. This data may be useful in providing objective muscular performance data regarding the thrower.

The immediate and primary goal following elbow arthroscopy is to reestablish full elbow ROM as quickly and expeditiously as possible. Immediately following surgery, emphasis is placed on full elbow extension to prevent the formation of scar tissue and an elbow flexion contracture. The rehabilitation program following elbow arthroscopy is designed so that the patient regains full motion as quickly and safely as possible. In most cases, this is to be accomplished by 10 to 12 days after surgery. The advanced strengthening phase normally extends from week 3 or 4 following surgery until week 7 or 8. In addition, the athlete may initiate an interval throwing program between 3 and 6 weeks after surgery, depending on the severity of the pathology.

Rehabilitation Following Ulnar Collateral Ligament Reconstruction

The rehabilitation program following UCL reconstruction varies significantly based on the type of surgery performed, the method of transposition of the ulnar nerve, and the extent of injury within the elbow joint. A limited number of rehabilitation programs following UCL reconstruction have been described in the literature.[87,88]

In one published rehabilitation program following UCL reconstruction using a palmaris longus tendon graft and

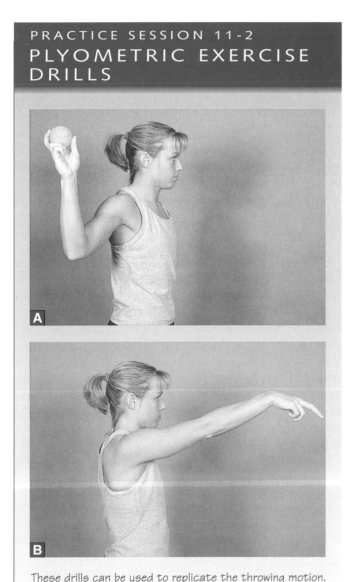

PRACTICE SESSION 11-2
PLYOMETRIC EXERCISE DRILLS

These drills can be used to replicate the throwing motion.
A Overhead throw. **B** Ball release.

transposition of the ulnar nerve within the flexor muscle mass, investigators reported that ROM exercises can be initiated after 2 weeks of elbow immobilization.[87] Full ROM should be obtained by 3 or 4 months following surgery. Strengthening exercises for the elbow and wrist musculature are initiated 4 weeks after surgery. Throwing is initiated between 3 to 5 months and throwing from the windup is performed at 6 months. The thrower may be ready for competition 1 year following surgery.

Another rehabilitation program is based on the surgical technique described earlier in this chapter.[88] Following UCL reconstruction, the patient is placed in a postoperative posterior splint and the elbow is immobilized at 90° flexion for 1 week to allow initial healing of both the UCL graft and soft tissue of the fascial slings for the transferred ulnar nerve. The wrist is free to move, and submaximal isometric muscle contractions are initiated for the wrist and elbow musculature. The patient also performs gripping exercises and uses cryotherapy with a bulky compression dressing to control inflammation and pain. At the end of the second week, the patient is placed in a ROM brace that is adjusted to allow motion from 30° to 100° of flexion. During the third week, the brace is opened to allow 15° to 110° of motion. Every week thereafter, motion is increased by 5° of extension and 10° of flexion. By the end of the sixth week, the patient should exhibit full ROM of the elbow joint (0° to 145°). Usually at the end of the fifth or sixth week, the brace is discontinued. **Table 11-8** shows the complete rehabilitation program following UCL reconstruction.

Immediately following surgery and for the next several weeks, the physician or rehabilitation specialist must assess the status of the transferred ulnar nerve. Results of two studies indicate a 31% and 22% occurrence of ulnar neuropathy following UCL surgery with ulnar nerve transposition.[89,90] Sensory changes of the little finger and ulnar half of the ring finger or the inability to adduct the thumb, weakness of the finger abductor/adductors, and abduction of the little finger or the flexor carpi ulnaris may suggest possible ulnar nerve injury. Often the patient conveys a slight sensory change along the ulnar side of the hand, but this is usually transient and should be resolved within 7 days. Often, immediately following surgery, the compression dressing may be too tight and simply loosening the wrap may alleviate the symptoms.

Strengthening exercises for the elbow, forearm, and wrist musculature are initiated immediately after surgery in the form of pain free submaximal isometrics to prevent muscular atrophy. At 4 weeks, light resistance isotonic strengthening exercises are initiated for the wrist and elbow musculature. By 6 weeks, the patient should perform concentric/eccentric strengthening exercises for the entire upper quadrant. At approximately 8 to 9 weeks, sport-specific muscle training is emphasized. The exercise program is designed to emphasize the muscle training and specificity of muscle contraction required by the muscle during the throwing motion.

During the intermediate and advanced strengthening phases, specific muscles are emphasized based on their role during the overhead throwing motion. The flexor carpi radialis, flexor digitorum superficialis, flexor carpi ulnaris, triceps brachii, and pronator teres muscles play an important role during the acceleration phase of throwing; these muscles should be exercised concentrically. The elbow flexors should be exercised in an eccentric training program. The flexor carpi ulnaris and flexor digitorum superficialis muscles directly overlay the anterior band of the ulnar collateral ligament and may provide a synergistic support to the ligament.[91] Because of this anatomic feature, rhythmic stabilization exercises for the elbow are preformed to train these and other muscles about the elbow to provide dynamic support to the joint and perhaps dynamically unload the UCL. Posterior shoulder girdle and scapular strengthening exercises are performed as well to assist in preventing compressive, valgus, and extension torques from injuring the elbow.

During the intermediate phase (weeks 4 through 8), the rehabilitation specialist and physician must continuously assess the patient's motion progression for contractures and joint stiffness, particularly the development of an elbow flexion contracture. A flexion contracture can develop readily following any surgery of the elbow. In addition, a flexion contracture is a common occurrence in the overhead pitcher. Thus, prevention of elbow flexion contracture is ensured through early intervention and progressive motion and stretching exercises. Occasionally, a patient's elbow may become stiff. To negate joint stiffness, particularly a flexion contracture, the patient may be placed in a splint that is worn night and day. A static splint can be used to hold the joint at the end of the available range of motion, or a dynamic splint that uses a spring to exert a force to create a progressive stretch can be used. The patient is encouraged to remove the brace and perform motion and strengthening exercises 2 to 3 times daily. The patient is instructed to perform elbow stretching exercises at least 5 to 6 times per day for approximately 10 to 15 minutes. Three vital components of the stretch are emphasized: duration (10 to 15 minutes), intensity (low to moderate), and frequency (5 to 6 times per day).

The advanced strengthening phase (weeks 9 through 14) is initiated only when the patient achieves specific criteria. During this phase, an aggressive strengthening program that consists of plyometrics, eccentrics, concentric muscular contractions, and neuromuscular control drills is instituted. Elbow flexor/extensor and shoulder strength are emphasized. An interval throwing program can be initiated approximately 4 months following surgery. In most cases, throwing from the mound can be performed approximately 6 weeks later and return to competitive throwing can occur at approximately 6 to 7 months following surgery.

TABLE 11-8
REHABILITATION FOLLOWING UCL RECONSTRUCTION

Phase 1: Immediate postsurgical phase (weeks 0 through 3)

Goals:

- Protect healing tissue
- Decrease pain/inflammation
- Retard muscular atrophy
- Establish limited range of motion

❑ Week 1

- ➤ Posterior splint at 90° elbow flexion
- ➤ Wrist AROM extension/flexion
- ➤ Elbow compression dressing (2 to 3 days)
- ➤ Exercises such as gripping exercises; wrist ROM; shoulder isometrics, except shoulder external rotation (ER) for the first 14 days; biceps isometrics
- ➤ Cryotherapy

❑ Week 2

- ➤ Apply functional brace at 30° to 100°
- ➤ Initiate shoulder ER isometrics (day 14)
- ➤ Initiate wrist isometrics
- ➤ Initiate elbow extension isometrics
- ➤ Continue all exercises listed above

❑ Week 3

- ➤ Advance brace 15° to 110° (gradually increase ROM; 5° extension/10° flexion per week)
- ➤ Initiate light isotonics using only the weight of the arm
- ➤ Initiate tubing external/internal rotation at 0° abduction
- ➤ Continue ROM and gripping exercises

Phase 2: Intermediate phase (weeks 4 through 8)

Goals:

- Gradual increase in range of motion
- Promote healing of repaired tissue
- Regain and improve muscular strength

❑ Weeks 4 and 5

- ➤ Set functional brace (10° to 120°)
- ➤ Begin light resistance exercises for arm (1 lb)
- ➤ Progress to shoulder program, emphasize rotator cuff strengthening

❑ Weeks 6 and 7

- ➤ Set functional brace (0° to 130°) (discontinue brace at end of week 6); AROM 0° to 145° (without brace)
- ➤ Progress to wrist and elbow strengthening exercises
- ➤ Initiate thrower's 10 program
- ➤ Progress to shoulder program

❑ Week 8

- ➤ Continue stretching program for elbow and wrist ROM
- ➤ Gradually progress in strengthening program

(Continued)

Returning the competitive thrower to a preinjury level is a significant challenge for the physician, physical therapist, athletic trainer, and athlete. Results of one study of patients with a surgically corrected UCL indicated that 10 of 16 patients (63%) returned to the previous level of throwing.[92] In a later study of 68 patients, 14 UCLs were repaired and 54 were reconstructed. Average follow-up was 6.3 years.[93] Thirty-eight of the 54 patients (71%) with reported reconstructions returned to throwing at their previous level. Only seven of the 14 patients (50%) in the group that underwent UCL repair were able to return to their previous athletic level.

Appropriate rehabilitation is vital to the successful outcome following UCL surgery. Early motion should be used to prevent complications resulting from loss of motion. An advanced strengthening program that

TABLE 11-8 (CONTINUED)
REHABILITATION FOLLOWING UCL RECONSTRUCTION

Phase 3: Advanced strengthening phase (weeks 9 through 14)

Goals:

- Increase strength, power, endurance
- Maintain full elbow ROM
- Gradually initiate sporting activities

❏ Weeks 9 and 10

➤ Initiate eccentric elbow flexion/extension

➤ Initiate PRE triceps strengthening

➤ Continue isotonic program for forearm and wrist

➤ Continue shoulder program, thrower's 10 program

➤ Initiate manual resistance diagonal patterns

➤ Initiate plyometric exercise program

❏ Weeks 11 through 14

➤ Continue all exercises listed above

➤ Begin light sport activities such as golf and swimming

➤ Initiate plyometric exercise program

Phase 4: Return-to-activity phase (weeks 15 through 26)

Goals:

- Continue to increase strength, power, and endurance of upper extremity musculature
- Gradual return-to-sport activities

❏ Weeks 14 through 21

➤ Initiate phase 1 of interval throwing program (week 16)

➤ Continue strengthening program

➤ Emphasize elbow and wrist strengthening and flexibility exercises

❏ Weeks 22 through 26

➤ Progress to interval throwing program (phase 2)

➤ Upon completion of phase 2, progress to competitive throwing

includes strengthening exercises to enhance joint stability, arm speed, power, and endurance should be initiated before a throwing program is begun. Because the flexor carpi ulnaris and flexor digitorum superficialis muscles are located directly over the anterior band of the UCL, they are emphasized to provide dynamic support to the UCL. In addition, the biceps brachii are emphasized to control elbow extension, and the shoulder/arm scapular muscles, especially the posterior rotator cuff, are stressed to provide proximal stability.

Rehabilitation Following Posterior Olecranon Osteophyte Excision

The rehabilitation program following arthroscopic elbow arthroplasty (debridement) is similar to the rehabilitation program following elbow arthroscopy; however, the program is slightly more conservative.[94] Elbow extension is often slightly slower to normalize and is usually sec-

ondary to postsurgical pain. **Table 11-9** outlines the entire rehabilitation program.

Range of motion progresses as expeditiously as pain and patient tolerance allow. Usually, ROM should be at least 15° to 100° by 10 days following surgery, and 10° to 110° by 14 days. In most cases, full ROM (0° to 145°) is achieved by 20 to 25 days following surgery. Motion progression is often retarded because of osseous structure pain and synovial joint inflammation. If full motion is restored before 21 days, the pain and inflammation are not a concern.

The strengthening program is similar to the other previously discussed programs, with performance of isometric strengthening exercises during the first 10 to 14 days and isotonic strengthening exercises during weeks 3 to 6. In throwers, a shoulder-strengthening program should be instituted by weeks 2 through 4 and progressed to a thrower's 10 program at week 6. In most cases, a throwing athlete can begin an interval throwing

TABLE 11-9

REHABILITATION FOLLOWING ELBOW ARTHROSCOPY

Phase 1: Immediate motion phase

Goals:

- Improve and regain full range of motion
- Decrease pain and inflammation
- Retard muscular atrophy

❑ Days 1 through 4

- ➤ ROM to tolerance (extension/flexion and supination/pronation) (often, full elbow extension is not possible because of pain)
- ➤ Gentle overpressure into extension
- ➤ Wrist flexion/extension stretches
- ➤ Gripping exercises (putty)
- ➤ Isometric wrist extension/flexion
- ➤ Isometric elbow extension/flexion
- ➤ Compression dressing, ice 4 to 5 times daily

❑ Days 5 through 10

- ➤ ROM exercises to tolerance (at least 15° to 100°)
- ➤ Overpressure into extension
- ➤ Joint mobilization to reestablish ROM
- ➤ Wrist flexion/extension stretches
- ➤ Continue isometric exercises
- ➤ Continue use of ice and compression to control swelling

❑ Days 11 through 14

- ➤ ROM exercises to tolerance (at least 10° to 110°)
- ➤ Overpressure into extension (3 to 4 times daily)
- ➤ Continue joint mobilization techniques
- ➤ Initiate light dumbbell program (PRE): biceps, triceps, wrist flexion/extension, and supinators/pronators
- ➤ Continue use of ice postexercise

Phase 2: Intermediate phase

Goals:

- Improve strength, power, and endurance
- Increase range of motion
- Initiate functional activities

❑ Weeks 2 through 4

- ➤ Full ROM exercises (4 to 5 times daily)
- ➤ Overpressure into elbow extension
- ➤ Continue PRE program for elbow and wrist musculature
- ➤ Initiate ER and rotator cuff (RTC) shoulder strengthening program
- ➤ Continue joint mobilization
- ➤ Continue use of ice postexercise

❑ Weeks 4 through 7

- ➤ Continue all exercises listed above
- ➤ Initiate light upper body program
- ➤ Continue use of ice postexercise

Phase 3: Advanced strengthening program

Criteria to progress to this phase:

- ➤ Full pain-free range of motion
- ➤ Strength greater than 75% of contralateral side
- ➤ No pain or tenderness

Goals:

- Improve strength, power, and endurance
- Gradual return to functional activities

❑ Weeks 8 through 12

- ➤ Continue PRE program for elbow and wrist
- ➤ Continue stretching for elbow and shoulder
- ➤ Initiate interval throwing program and gradually return to sport activities

program at 10 to 12 weeks following surgery. Again, the rate of throwing progression should be advanced individually and closely monitored by the physician and rehabilitation specialist.

The nonsurgical and postsurgical rehabilitation programs should attempt to train throwers who have been diagnosed with valgus extension overload to control the rapid elbow extension that occurs during the acceleration and deceleration phases of throwing. These patients should also dynamically stabilize the elbow against the valgus strain that occurs during arm acceleration. The wrist flexor-pronator muscles play an important role in dynamic elbow joint stability in patients with valgus stress. Additionally, the elbow flexors, particularly the biceps brachii, brachioradialis, and brachialis contract eccentrically to control the rapid rate of elbow extension and the abutting of the olecranon within the medial aspect of its fossa. Thus, in the rehabilitation program, this type of muscle control must be emphasized. In a study of 72 professional baseball players, 47 patients (65%) exhibited a posterior olecranon osteophyte.[92] Additionally, 25% (11 patients) of the individuals who had an isolated olecranon resection later required a UCL reconstruction.[92] This may suggest that in some throwers, subtle medial laxity may accelerate the osteophytic formation on the olecranon.

Rehabilitation Following Ulnar Nerve Transposition

The subcutaneous ulnar nerve transposition uses fascial slings to stabilize the relocated ulnar nerve. Thus, the rehabilitation must be fairly conservative initially to allow soft-tissue healing to occur. A posterior splint can immobilize the elbow at 90° flexion to prevent elbow extension and, thus, tension on the ulnar nerve. During week 2, the patient removes the splint and performs ROM exercises; by weeks 3 and 4, full ROM is normally restored. Vigorous strengthening exercises are restricted until week 4. An isotonic program for the entire arm can then be initiated 5 weeks following surgery. Between weeks 7 and 8, an aggressive strengthening program can safely be initiated. An interval throwing program may be initiated at 8 to 9 weeks, if all the previously outlined criteria have been met. A return to competitive throwing can usually be resumed between 12 and 16 weeks after surgery.

Rehabilitation Following Arthroscopic Arthrolysis

The elbow is one of the joints of the body that most commonly develops loss of motion.[65,72] The elbow may be subjected to significant trauma such as a fracture or dislocation, which may cause both intra-articular and extra-articular injury. Periarticular soft tissue may be injured and thus become edematous and hemorrhagic. Thus, the elbow flexes in response to pain and the ensuing hemarthrosis. The periarticular soft tissue and joint capsule become shortened, fibrotic, and loss of motion develops. Once this clinical sequela develops, nonsurgical treatment is used. If the nonsurgical treatment fails, then an arthroscopic arthrolysis may be necessary in selected patients.[65]

Table 11-10 shows an aggressive rehabilitation program used to reestablish full elbow motion following arthroscopic arthrolysis of the elbow capsule. During the first week following surgery, the patient is instructed to perform hourly ROM exercises, paying special attention to restoring full elbow extension.[94] During the first week, treatment for restoring full elbow motion is "cautiously aggressive." Full motion should be obtained quickly; however, care should be taken so that the joint capsule does not become inflamed. Inflammation of the joint capsule may lead to further pain and reflex splinting. During week 2, usually by 10 to 14 days, full passive ROM is restored. The low-load, long-duration stretching technique is extremely beneficial in restoring motion. Isometric strengthening exercises are used during the first 2 weeks, followed by isotonic dumbbell exercises during the third and fourth week. Once the patient achieves full ROM, a motion maintenance program should be used. To ensure that full motion is maintained following an arthroscopic arthrolysis, the patient should perform stretching exercises several times a day for 2 to 3 months, especially before and after sport activities.

TABLE 11-10
REHABILITATION FOLLOWING ARTHROLYSIS

Phase 1: Immediate motion phase

Goals:

- Improvement of ROM
- Reestablish full passive extension
- Retard muscular atrophy
- Decrease pain and inflammation

❑ Days 1 through 3
- ➢ ROM to tolerance hourly (elbow extension/flexion; 2 sets of 10)
- ➢ Overpressure into extension (at least 10°)
- ➢ Joint mobilization
- ➢ Gripping exercises with putty
- ➢ Isometrics for wrist and elbow
- ➢ Compression and ice hourly

❑ Days 4 through 9
- ➢ ROM extension/flexion (at least 5° to 120°)
- ➢ Overpressure into extension using 5-lb weight with elbow in full extension (4 to 5 times daily)
- ➢ Joint mobilization
- ➢ Continue isometrics and gripping exercises
- ➢ Continue use of ice

❑ Days 10 through 14
- ➢ Full passive ROM
- ➢ ROM exercises hourly (2 sets of 10)
- ➢ Stretch into extension
- ➢ Continue isometric exercises

Phase 2: Motion maintenance phase

Goals:

- Maintain full ROM
- Gradually improve strength
- Decrease pain and inflammation

❑ Weeks 2 through 4
- ➢ ROM exercise (4 to 5 times daily)
- ➢ Overpressure into extension, 2-minute stretches 3 to 4 times daily
- ➢ Initiate PRE program (light dumbbells)
- ➢ Elbow extension/flexion
- ➢ Wrist extension/flexion
- ➢ Continue use of ice postexercise

❑ Weeks 5 through 7
- ➢ Continue all exercises listed above
- ➢ Initiate interval throwing sport program

82. Moseley JB Jr, Jobe FW, Pink M, et al: EMG analysis of the scapular muscles during a shoulder rehabilitation program. *Am J Sports Med* 1992; 20:128–132.

83. Townsend H, Jobe FW, Pink M, Perry J: Electromyographic analysis of the glenohumeral muscles during a baseball rehabilitation program. *Am J Sports Med* 1991;19:264–269.

84. Blackburn TA, McLeod WD, White B: EMG analysis of posterior rotator cuff exercises. *Athlet Training* 1990; 25:40–45.

85. Jobe FW, Moynes DR: Delineation of diagnostic criteria and a rehabilitation program for rotator cuff injuries. *Am J Sports Med* 1982;10:336–339.

86. Pappas AM, Zawacki RM, McCarthy CF: Rehabilitation of the pitching shoulder. *Am J Sports Med* 1985; 13:223–235.

87. Seto JL, Brewster CE, Randall CC, Jobe FW: Rehabilitation following ulnar collateral ligament reconstruction of athletes. *J Orthop Sports Phys Ther* 1991;14:100–105.

88. Wilk KE, Arrigo C, Andrews JR: Rehabilitation of the elbow in the throwing athlete. *J Orthop Sports Phys Ther* 1993;17:305–317.

89. Jobe FW, Stark H, Lombardo SJ: Reconstruction of the ulnar collateral ligament in athletes. *J Bone Joint Surg* 1986;68A:1158 1163.

90. Conway JE, Jobe FW, Glousman RE: Medial instability of the elbow in throwing athletes. *J Bone Joint Surg* 1992;74:67–83.

91. Davidson PA, Pink M, Perry J, Jobe FW: Functional anatomy of the flexor pronator muscle group in relation to the medial collateral ligament of the elbow. *Am J Sports Med* 1995;23:245–250.

92. Andrews JR, Timmerman LA: Outcome of elbow surgery in professional baseball players. *Am J Sports Med* 1995;23:407–413.

93. Azar FM, Andrews JR, Wilk KE, Groh D: Operative treatment of ulnar collateral ligament injuries of the elbow in athletes. *Am J Sports Med* 2000;28:16–23.

94. Wilk KE: Rehabilitation of the elbow following arthroscopic surgery, in Andrews JR, Soffer SR (eds): *Elbow Arthroscopy*. St. Louis, MO, Mosby Year Book, 1994, pp 109–116.

12

Hand and Wrist Injuries

Arthur C. Rettig, MD
Mark S. De Carlo, MHA, MS, PT, SCS, ATC

QUICK CONTENTS

- The anatomy of the hand and wrist, including the bones, tendons, and ligaments and the neurovascular supply.

- The nomenclature of hand injuries.

- Treatment of injuries to the fingertip, proximal finger joint, thumb, palmar and dorsal hand, wrist, and skin.

- A rehabilitation program for an athlete with an injured hand or wrist.

- Fashioning an RTV-11® playing cast.

Most athletic trainers will encounter many hand and wrist injuries during their career. "Baseball finger," "jersey finger," "coach's finger," and "gamekeeper's thumb" are some of the more common sprains, fractures, and musculotendinous injuries experienced by athletes, but many other injuries to the bones, tendons, and ligaments of the wrist and hand also occur. This chapter discusses the anatomy of this region, as well as information about the diagnosis, management, and rehabilitation of common hand and wrist injuries.

ANATOMY

Bones, Tendons, and Ligaments

The distal ulna and radius form the base for the *wrist joint*. The ulnar styloid and radial styloid are the prominent ends of the bones, which are easily palpable at the wrist (**Figure 12-1**). Eight carpal bones form the wrist, which are interconnected by a complex system of joint capsules and ligaments and joined by ligaments to the radius and ulna proximally and to the metacarpals distally. The five *metacarpals* lying distal to the carpals form the palm of the hand. The *phalanges* make up the finger bones (three in each finger and two in the thumb).

Tendons flex and extend the metacarpophalangeal joints on the dorsal (back) and palmar surfaces (**Figure 12-2**). At the proximal levels, intrinsic muscles of the hand also produce motion to both sides. Muscles and tendons that produce flexion, extension, abduction, adduction, rotation, or

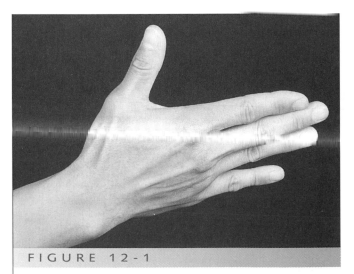

FIGURE 12-1

Posterior view of the forearm, wrist, and hand.

Anatomy

Bones, tendons, and ligaments

The distal radius and ulna form the base of the wrist joint, with their respective styloids easily palpable at the wrist. The eight carpal bones of the wrist are interconnected by joint capsules and ligaments; ligaments also join the carpals to the radius and ulna proximally and the metacarpals distally. Five metacarpals distal to the carpals form the palm of the hand, and three phalanges make up each finger bone (two in the thumb).

Except for the carpals, flexor and extensor tendons on the dorsal and palmar surfaces join each bone. The proximal intrinsic muscles move the hand from side to side. At the wrist, muscles and tendons produce flexion, extension, abduction, adduction, and rotation, as well as opposition of the thumb. For normal function, the four fingers must move as a unit. Axial rotation is the most difficult alignment to evaluate and maintain. To assess rotation, the athlete should flex all the fingers and bring them as close together as possible; the fifth finger should point to the middle of the wrist.

Neurovascular supply

The radial and ulnar arteries branch into the superficial and deep volar arches, which anastomose and send common branches to the fingers. The radial nerve innervates the dorsal hand and the muscles that extend the fingers at the metacarpophalangeal joints, and with the ulnar nerve, controls wrist extension. The ulnar nerve also supplies the little finger and the ulnar side of the ring finger on the dorsal and volar surfaces. In addition, it innervates the intrinsic finger abductors and adductors in full extension and ring and little finger dorsal interphalangeal (DIP) joint flexion. The median nerve controls wrist flexion, supplies the opposing muscles of the thumb, and controls thumb and middle fingers distal and proximal interphalangeal (PIP) joint flexion.

Nomenclature

For consistency, metacarpal injuries are identified by number (first, second, third, fourth, fifth) and digital injuries by their names (thumb, index, middle or long finger, ring finger, little finger).

combinations of varus muscles and tendons provide the same possibilities for motion at the wrist. In addition, the thumb is opposable, which makes the hand and wrist a versatile and functional unit.

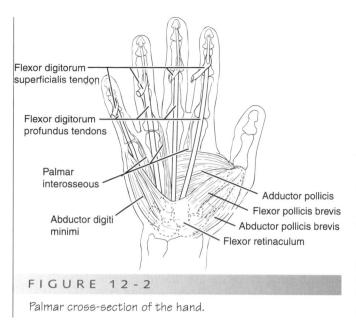

FIGURE 12-2

Palmar cross-section of the hand.

The four fingers move as a unit. The longitudinal and rotational alignments must be maintained to grasp and manipulate small objects within the palm. Axial rotation is the most difficult alignment to evaluate and maintain. Failure to correct a malrotation, such as in a metacarpal fracture, causes one finger to overlap another when a fist is made. The easiest way for an athletic trainer to assess a possible rotation problem is to ask the athlete to flex all the fingers, positioning them as close together as possible. If there is proper alignment, the fifth finger will point toward the middle of the wrist. As part of the examination, the athletic trainer should compare the alignment with the unaffected hand.

Neurovascular Supply

A network of the branches of the radial and ulnar arteries and their accompanying veins supply blood to the hand. After entering the hand, the radial and ulnar arteries divide into two branches that form the superficial and deep volar arches, which anastomose and send common branches to the fingers. The radial, ulnar, and median nerves innervate the muscles of the hand and provide sensory distribution in a fairly regular pattern, subject to some variations (**Figure 12-3**). The *ulnar nerve* innervates the little finger and the ulnar side of the ring finger on both front and back surfaces. It also supplies the intrinsic muscles that move the fingers apart (abduct) or together (adduct) when they are held in full extension as well as the muscles that flex the distal interphalangeal (DIP) joint of the ring and little fingers. The *median nerve* innervates the remainder of the volar (front) surface of the hand and fingers and controls the muscles that oppose the thumb to the fingers and control flexion of the thumb and the muscles of the middle fingers at the DIP

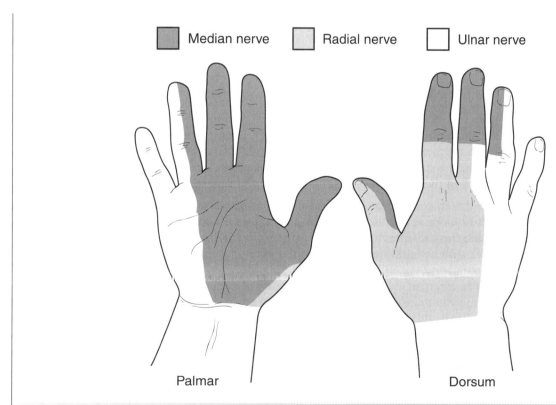

FIGURE 12-3

The radial, ulnar, and median nerve distribution to the hand.

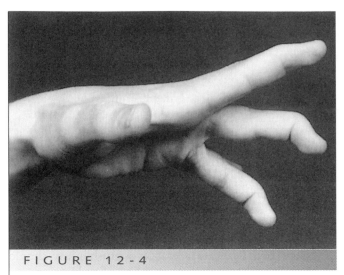

FIGURE 12-4

Mallet finger injury.

splint at night and during part of the day. If an extension lag develops, the splinting program for the DIP joint should be started again. As healing progresses, the exercises can be increased and passive flexion and grip strength exercises with putty or a hand gripper can begin 2 weeks after the immobilization period.

If allowed by the sport, the splint may be taped and padded, enabling the athlete to return to full participation immediately. However, some positions such as pitcher or quarterback may require that the athlete take time off. Surgery is usually not required unless a large fracture of the joint has significant displacement or subluxation has occurred.

The opposite of the mallet finger, the *"jersey" finger,* is caused by a sudden, forceful extension of the flexed DIP, typically when a tightly held jersey is torn off of the grasp of a would-be tackler. An avulsion of the long flexor tendon

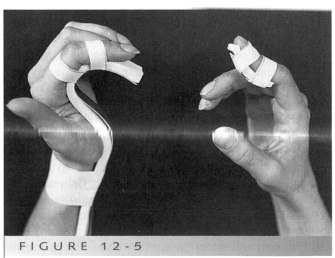

FIGURE 12-5

When immobilizing the DIP joint, the splint should allow full flexion of the PIP joint.

from its attachment to the distal joint can result. On examination, the athlete cannot flex the DIP joint, although the athletic trainer can passively flex it. It is important to recognize jersey finger injuries early, so the athlete can be immediately evaluated by a physician. A delay in treatment may compromise healing and result in the need for a tendon graft rather than primary repair of the injured tendon.

Proximal Finger Joint Injuries

Injuries of the PIP joint can occur in a similar fashion as fingertip injuries. In addition, forceful twisting injuries may result from grabbing, being grabbed, or catching fingers on opponents' clothing or equipment.

Hyperextension injury

One of the most common injuries of the PIP joint is the hyperextension injury, in which the finger is bent forcibly backward, resulting in either the stretching of, or rupturing of, the volar plate on the palmar side of the joint. In more severe PIP injuries, dorsal dislocations, rupture of the collateral ligaments, or fractures may occur. In a simple hyperextension injury with no torn structures, the joint will swell much like a direct compression injury to the PIP joint. On examination, the palmar side of the joint will be tender, and attempts to hyperextend the joint will cause pain. The injury evaluation should include a stress examination of the collateral ligaments to ensure that they are intact. Finger hyperextension injuries associated with significant pain or swelling should be referred for radiographic evaluation to rule out the possibility of an associated fracture.

Initial treatment for hyperextension injuries include the application of ice while keeping the hand elevated. Splinting should be performed if there is an avulsion fracture of the volar surface of either the DIP or the PIP joint. Generally, splinting at a slight flexion for 10 to 14 days is preferred. Subsequently, the affected finger is buddy taped to the adjacent finger and ROM exercises to achieve full extension and flexion are encouraged. It is important for these injuries to be splinted and supervised until they are completely healed. If left unsupervised, a painful, stiff finger with a fixed-flexion deformity of the joint, frequently called *"coach's finger,"* may develop. Surgery is rarely required to correct hyperextension injuries unless fractures involving the joints, subluxation, or marked instability of the collateral ligaments also exist.

Dislocations

In a PIP joint dislocation, the athlete's middle phalanx usually dislocates dorsally on the proximal phalanx. The cause is most often a hyperextension force, and the dislocation is an extension of the simple hyperextension injury. Typically, the finger is foreshortened with obvious swelling and deformity.

An athletic trainer can treat many of these dislocations immediately with simple, longitudinal distraction that produces successful and prompt reduction. Nevertheless, a physician should evaluate the integrity of the athlete's collateral ligaments and obtain radiographs to check for associated fractures and to ensure that the reduction is satisfactory. If the joint is stable, it should be splinted at 20° to 30° of flexion for 1 week, iced several times a day, and treated with Coban wraps to control edema.[2] Buddy taping the injury will permit an athlete to return to play, and should be continued until full, pain-free ROM is obtained.[3,4] To prevent stiffness, the athlete should be encouraged to perform ROM exercises with the finger out of the splint early during the postinjury period. Unless there is a serious fracture of the joint surface or persistent subluxation, surgery is rarely required.

Collateral ligament tears

Hyperextension injuries can also cause tears of the collateral ligaments, although these tears are more commonly associated with force applied to the sides of the fingers. Joint swelling is common, but obvious deformity is rare. To assess the integrity of the collateral ligaments, the athletic trainer should apply a lateral force to the joint; first with the joint fully extended and then with it flexed at approximately 30°. Minor tears may produce joint laxity up to 10° with a definite end point. Greater laxity is apparent with a complete rupture. After an acute injury, application of stress may be too painful for the athlete to tolerate, and his or her attempts to guard against the pain may compromise the examination. Careful examination will reveal localized tenderness to the side of the ligament rupture.

Most ligament tears can be treated by splinting the joint at 20° of flexion or by taping the injured finger to the adjacent finger. ROM exercises should be initiated, and the athlete may return to play as the pain becomes tolerable. More severe or complete ruptures may require surgical repair.

Boutonniere deformity

A *boutonniere deformity* is caused by rapid, forceful flexion at the PIP joint (**Figure 12-6**). Here, the central slip of the extensor tendon of the middle phalanx ruptures, along with separation and palmar displacement of the lateral band. This injury leaves no effective, active extensor mechanism at the joint. As a result, the PIP joint flexes, and the DIP joint tends to hyperextend, which produces the deformity.

Initial treatment is to splint the PIP joint in full extension for 6 weeks (**Figure 12-7**). During this time, the DIP should be stretched several times a day, and the athlete may return to sports with a padded splint and the injured finger buddy taped. After the immobilization period, active ROM exercises are initiated for the PIP joint and the athlete should continue to wear the splint at night and between exercises. Passive ROM exercises are added and continued until full extension is attained.[3] Grip strength exercises are initiated approximately 8 weeks after the

injury. Because surgical repair is occasionally required to restore full functioning, early evaluation by a physician is recommended. As with other finger injuries, radiographs to detect associated fractures are recommended.

Phalanx fractures

Phalanx fractures require both a physical assessment and a radiographic evaluation. Treatment varies depending on which phalanx is fractured. The clinical diagnosis is obvious if there is a gross deformity; however, in many occult or nondisplaced fractures, clinical diagnosis may be difficult to determine. The most reliable sign of injury is localized tenderness, but this is not sufficient for positive diagnosis. When a fracture is suspected, the safest course for proper diagnosis is to refer the athlete to a physician for radiographic evaluation. The adages of "It's not broken if you can move it" or "It's not broken if it doesn't swell" are unreliable.

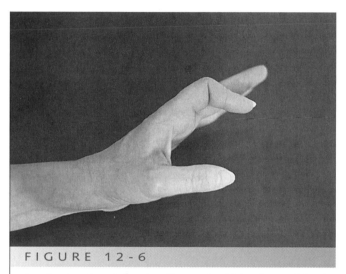

FIGURE 12-6

In a boutonniere deformity, the proximal joint flexes while the distal joint hyperextends.

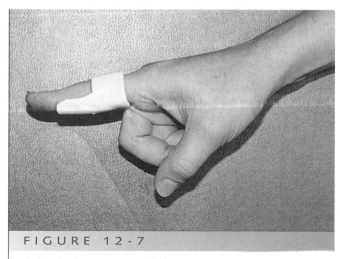

FIGURE 12-7

Splint for boutonniere deformity.

Most fractures of the phalanges are stable and can be treated with protective splinting of the injured finger in extension and buddy taping. Depending on the stability of the fracture and the position the athlete plays, the use of a padded splint and buddy taping will usually enable the athlete to return to play after the first week of treatment. Fractures of the proximal portion of the proximal phalanx require a well-molded, hand-based splint fitted to the adjacent finger (**Figure 12-8**). Stable intra-articular fractures of the PIP joint are also treated with a hand-based splint, and unstable fractures typically require surgery.[3]

Thumb Injuries

The thumb is a unique digit because it has only two phalanges and one IP joint. Generally, with the exception of the boutonniere deformity, all of the injuries described for the fingers can also affect the thumb.

Rupture of the ulnar collateral ligament is a characteristic injury of the MCP joint of the thumb. The common name for this injury, *gamekeeper's thumb*, originated because the injury was first described in gamekeepers who chronically stressed this ligament when wringing the necks of rabbits. Today, it is seen in skiing and in many contact sports such as football and wrestling.[5] Gamekeeper's thumb is caused by forceful abduction of the thumb away from the hand while the MCP joint is in extension. There is usually local tenderness on the ulnar side of the MCP joint on examination. Diagnosis is confirmed by stressing the joint laterally, first while it is in extension and at 30° of flexion. With partial ligament tears, a definite end point is felt, and only modest lateral laxity on the ulnar side is noted. In more severe, or complete tears, joint laxity of 45° or more on the ulnar side is noted, and no discrete end point is felt. In all cases, the laxity of the involved thumb must be compared with that of the uninvolved thumb to determine what is normal for that athlete.

Stability of the ulnar collateral ligament is critical to normal hand function, and particularly for fine pinching such as in grasping a key between the thumb and index finger. Therefore, a physician should evaluate all cases of collateral ligament injuries in the thumb. A radiograph should be obtained to reveal fractures or volar subluxation of the joint. Grade I and II injuries are typically treated conservatively with a thumb spica splint for 2 to 5 weeks, depending on the severity of the injury and the possibility of a partial tear of the ligament. While wearing the splint, the patient should exercise the thumb's IP joint to maintain full motion. After pain and swelling have subsided (often as early as within 1 week of the injury), the athlete may return to sports participation wearing a padded splint or playing cast. Strengthening exercises may begin after the period of immobilization and once the athlete is pain free.[3]

Grade III injuries, which require surgical intervention, involve a complete tear of the ulnar collateral ligament and may also include a Stenar lesion, in which the ligament is displaced outside of the tendon hood, or a displaced intra-articular fracture. After surgery, the joint should be immobilized for 3 to 4 weeks and, depending on the sport and position involved, the athlete may return to play in 2 to 3 weeks with the use of a playing cast. As with less severe injuries, the athlete should exercise the IP joint during immobilization with active ROM exercises of the wrist and thumb beginning 3 to 4 weeks after surgery. Approximately 6 weeks after surgery, the patient may begin passive ROM and strengthening exercises.[3]

Palmar and Dorsal Hand Injuries

Midhand contusions

Simple contusions of the hand produce a soft, painful, bluish discoloration of the dorsum (top) of the hand and must be differentiated from metacarpal fractures. The latter should be suspected if examination reveals acute localized tenderness, crepitus, and weakness. Treatment includes ice, compression, and elevation of the hand. Disability seldom lasts longer than 2 or 3 days.

Thenar and hypothenar eminence contusions

Contusions of the thenar and hypothenar eminences are most often associated with athletes who participate in baseball, hockey, and handball. These contusions follow trauma and appear as tender, painful swelling of the fleshy areas at the base of the thumb or the little finger and can be confused with a tendon sheath infection or a carpal or metacarpal fracture. Treatment includes ice, compression, elevation, and protective padding such as a sponge rubber doughnut. Splinting to rest the injured muscles may be needed, and disability may last 4 days or longer if the injury is severe.

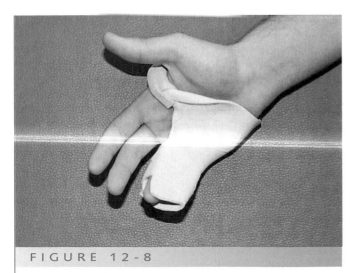

FIGURE 12-8

Hand-based splint used in the treatment of a fracture of the proximal phalanx.

FOCUS ON . . .

Palmar and Dorsal Hand Injuries

Midhand contusions
Palmar and dorsal hand injuries include midhand contusions, which produce soft, painful, bluish discoloration of the dorsal hand. Treatment is ice, compression, and elevation, with return to play after 2 to 3 days.

Thenar and hypothenar eminence contusions
Thenar and hypothenar eminence contusions are tender, painful swellings of the fleshy areas at the base of the thumb and little finger. Treatment is ice, compression, elevation, protective padding, and a splint, if necessary. Disability can last 4 days or longer.

Dislocation of the metacarpophalangeal joints
Metacarpophalangeal joint dislocations usually follow hyperextension injuries, with the proximal phalanx dislocating dorsally. A simple injury may be reduced by closed means. A dimple on the palmar skin indicates an irreducible dislocation, which requires open reduction. Physician referral is needed for all metacarpophalangeal joint dislocations.

Rupture of the transverse metacarpal ligament
Transverse metacarpal ligament rupture is caused by a spreading force to the fingers that spreads the interior metacarpal joints and can rupture the intrinsic muscle attachments. Treatment includes splinting, progressing to buddy taping and early ROM exercises.

Metacarpal fractures
Axial compression, twisting stress, or a direct blow can cause metacarpal fractures. The metacarpal joint is depressed, and the dorsal hand is tender, swollen, and angulated. Physician referral is needed. Metacarpal shaft fractures are splinted to the adjacent finger and early, active ROM exercises are begun once the fracture is stable. If surgery is required, active and gentle passive ROM exercises can start in the first week. Once the fracture is stable, passive exercises, taping the fingers in flexion, and dynamic splinting can increase passive flexion. Oblique fractures into the joint at the first metacarpal base are usually unstable and result in a fracture-dislocation of the carpometacarpal joint, requiring surgical correction. Fractures that do not penetrate the joint surface can be treated with closed reduction and casting for 4 to 6 weeks.

Dislocation of the metacarpophalangeal joints
Metacarpophalangeal (MCP) joint dislocations usually follow hyperextension injuries, with the proximal phalanx dislocating dorsally in respect to the metacarpal head. The joint remains hyperextended and foreshortened, with obvious deformity. Simple injuries may be reduced by closed means. Occasionally, a dimple may be apparent on the skin of the palm, which indicates a "complex" irreducible (by closed nonsurgical means) dislocation. This dislocation will not respond to closed manipulation because the surrounding soft tissues of the volar plate are interposed within the joint and entrap the metacarpal head. Because complex dislocations ordinarily require open surgical reduction, a physician should evaluate all suspected MCP joint dislocations.

Rupture of the transverse metacarpal ligament
Rupture of the transverse metacarpal ligament is an unusual injury caused by a force that spreads the fingers such as a faulty catch that forces the fingers apart and spreads the interior metacarpal joints. The intrinsic muscle attachments can also be ruptured. Physical examination of the athlete's hand will reveal tenderness and swelling over the area where the ligament attaches. Stress testing will reveal a loss of stability. Primary treatment for this injury includes rest, first with the hand in a splint, and later with buddy taping and early ROM exercises. Frequent monitoring of the hand is necessary to ensure that stability is being maintained.

Metacarpal fractures
Metacarpal fractures, particularly of the neck of the fifth metacarpal, are relatively common. The fifth metacarpal can fracture with a direct blow to the MCP joint with the fist clenched such as when striking a hard object. Ordinarily, the MCP joint is depressed, with tenderness, swelling, and angulation on the back of the hand. Referral to a physician for further evaluation, including radiographs, is important. Axial compression, twisting stress, or direct blows can also cause metacarpal fractures. Generally, the metacarpal shafts are splinted to one another and are more stable than phalanges when fractured.

Early motion is frequently initiated to help prevent extensor tendon adherence to the fracture site and to minimize contractures. The athlete may begin active ROM exercises as soon as the physician determines the fracture is stable. If surgery is required, active and gentle passive ROM exercises may be initiated within the first week. Passive exercises, taping the fingers into flexion, and dynamic splinting may all be used to increase passive flexion once the fracture is stable. However, shortening and rotation can occur, necessitating surgical fixation to restore alignment and length.

Oblique fractures into the joint at the base of the first metacarpal are usually unstable and result in a fracture dislocation of the carpometacarpal joint. These fractures typically require surgical correction and pin fixation to maintain a reduced position. If the fracture does not penetrate the joint surface, closed reduction and cast immobilization for 4 to 6 weeks or until healing is complete may be adequate treatment. Some angular deformity, but no rotational deformity, is acceptable in these injuries.

Wrist Injuries

The following wrist injuries often present pitfalls in diagnosis. These injuries may result in chronic pain and disability, and the seriousness of the injury may be easily overlooked initially.

Carpal scaphoid fractures

Fractures of the carpal scaphoid may occur when an athlete falls on an outstretched hand and are most often seen in football, basketball, and soccer.[6] Most scaphoid fractures are nondisplaced and stable, and may be difficult to see on a radiograph.[7,8] Therefore, if the athlete has significant pain or swelling in the anatomic snuffbox, splint immobilization (using a thumb spica) is recommended. Radiographs should be repeated in 10 to 14 days when bone absorption at the fracture site makes the injury more apparent on a radiograph. A bone scan can provide a definitive diagnosis in less than 10 days. If a fracture is present, the bone scan will show increased uptake of tracer at the navicular.[9] Stable fractures are immobilized in a short arm thumb spica cast and usually take 10 to 12 weeks to heal, but unstable fractures may take 20 to 24 weeks to heal. Depending on the athlete's sport and playing position, a playing cast may be fabricated to permit an early return to play.[3,4,10,11]

The scaphoid proximal pole has a tenuous blood supply; therefore, nonunion of the middle and proximal pole is a common problem. Because of this, close monitoring of the injury is needed. Surgery is usually recommended for displaced scaphoid fractures, and many physicians recommend surgical stabilization of the nondisplaced unstable fracture.[3,12]

Base of second and third metacarpal fractures

Fractures of the base of the second and third metacarpals are related to the wrist rather than to the hand because their symptoms are closely involved with wrist function. These fractures often are associated with subluxation of the carpometacarpal joint and result in tenderness in this area. A fall on the volar-flexed wrist is the usual mechanism of this injury. Radiographs may or may not show a small flake of bone just dorsal to the base of the metacarpal. CT scans may be needed to localize fractures and detect any subluxation; reduction of the subluxated metacarpal is necessary to restore normal function.

Rotatory dislocation of the radioulnar joint

Rotatory dislocation of the radioulnar joint is a hyperpronation injury. Pain and disability with movement and a shift of the ulnar styloid to the center of the bone on AP radiographs may be the only signs of this injury. There may be a click on supination of the wrist. Cast immobilization in supination for approximately 4 weeks is generally recommended, as the dislocation will stay reduced when immobilized in this position.

Hamate hook fractures

Hamate hook fractures can occur as a result of a strong, twisting force or from a direct blow and are commonly seen in baseball, racquet sports, and golf.[7,8] The repetitive pressure on the hypothenar eminence as a result of repeated strikes can produce a stress fracture.[1] An athlete with a hamate hook fracture will have tenderness over the hypothenar eminence and an inability to perform twisting motions such as a golf swing. A radiograph of the wrist (carpal tunnel view) will help in diagnosing this disabling fracture.

Although some physicians immobilize the wrist in a cast for 6 to 12 weeks, many physicians prefer to excise the hook fragment.[3,13] The wrist is typically immobilized for 2 to 3 weeks after the excision; ROM exercises can begin as early as 1 week after surgery.[7,14] Because the incision may be hypersensitive, the splint may need to be padded. Light strengthening exercises may be initiated 2 weeks after surgery. The athlete may begin a gradual return to sports activity at 3 weeks with return to full play at 6 to 10 weeks. If necessary, a pad may be worn inside the athlete's glove.[3] Scar massage and desensitization exercises should be performed after the wound is healed.

Radiocarpal joint injuries

Although it is possible to sprain the radiocarpal joint, it rarely dislocates except at the distal radioulnar joint. If the force applied, often as a result of a fall on the outstretched arm with the hand extended, is severe, the radius and the tip of the ulna may fracture, resulting in the so-called Colles' fracture. This same mechanism may produce other injuries in the upper extremity, and in the developing child, the epiphyseal plate can be injured. Angular

FOCUS ON . . .

Wrist Injuries

Carpal scaphoid fractures

Wrist injuries include carpal scaphoid fractures, which usually occur after a fall on the outstretched hand. The athlete may have significant pain or swelling, or both, in the snuffbox. Most stable fractures are immobilized in a short arm thumb spica cast for 10 to 12 weeks; unstable fractures usually require 20 to 24 weeks of immobilization. Surgery is recommended for displaced scaphoid fractures and for some nondisplaced, unstable fractures. Depending on the sport and position, the athlete may return to activity in a playing cast.

Base of second and third metacarpal fractures

Second and third metacarpal base fractures typically result from a fall on the volar-flexed wrist and are often associated with carpometacarpal joint subluxation. Tomography may be needed if radiographs are nondiagnostic, and the subluxed metacarpophalangeal joint must be reduced.

Rotatory dislocation of the radioulnar joint

Rotatory dislocation of the radioulnar joint from a hyperpronation injury can result in pain and disability with wrist movement. Wrist supination may cause a click. Treatment is cast immobilization in supination for 4 weeks.

Hamate hook fractures

Hamate hook fractures can occur from a strong twisting force or a direct blow; stress fractures can result from repetitive pressure on the hypothenar eminence from a bat, racquet, or golf club. Some physicians cast the wrist for 6 to 12 weeks. Others excise the fragment and then immobilize the wrist in a padded splint. ROM exercises can be started at 1 week and light strengthening at 2 weeks. Scar massage and desensitization exercises are performed after the wound heals. Gradual return to play can begin at 3 weeks, with full play allowed at 6 to 10 weeks.

Radiocarpal joint injuries

The radiocarpal joint can be sprained or dislocated, but a severe fall on the outstretched arm and extended hand usually fractures the radius and the tip of the ulna (Colles' fracture). In the growing child, an epiphyseal plate injury must be diagnosed and treated to prevent future problems. A lunate or perilunate dislocation should be suspected if swelling is significant, motion is restricted, and median nerve paresthesias are present. Immediate physician referral is needed.

A sudden twisting injury to the wrist can tear the triangular fibrocartilaginous complex. Physician referral is needed. Stable injuries without associated fractures are splinted for 4 to 6 weeks, followed by strengthening and a functional progression for return to sport. Persistent pain or a displaced tear may require surgical intervention. ROM scar massage (once the wound is healed), hand strengthening (at 1 to 4 weeks), and wrist strengthening (at 4 to 6 weeks) exercises are instituted.

Traumatic subluxation of the extensor carpi ulnaris

Traumatic subluxation of the extensor carpi ulnaris can occur with forceful supination, ulnar deviation, and flexion, which can tear the extensor carpi ulnaris sheath at the distal ulna. A popping sound may be felt with the tendon subluxation. Acute injuries are immobilized, but chronic injuries usually require surgery. A cast is worn for 4 to 6 weeks, followed by a splint for 2 to 3 weeks as the athlete begins active and passive ROM exercises for the wrist and forearm. At about 8 weeks, strengthening exercises are added with the support of a soft wrist brace, which also helps promote functional return to sport, with full return (with wrist taping) at 10 to 12 weeks.

Dorsal ganglion

Dorsal ganglion cysts seem to result from chronic stress to the wrist. Treatment is wrist immobilization for 10 to 21 days, gradual institution of ROM exercises, and strengthening exercises as pain decreases. The splint can be padded for play and its use decreased as full, pain-free motion returns. Persistent pain may require surgical excision. ROM exercises are started at 1 week, and a splint is worn for 3 weeks (as needed). Strengthening is started at 3 weeks and advanced functionally to return to sport.

deformity may result if these injuries are not diagnosed and treated properly.

Radiocarpal joint dislocations other than at the distal joint are rare and usually take the form of a dislocation of the lunate or perilunate. These injuries should be suspected if an athlete has a significant amount of swelling and restriction of motion. Paresthesias in the median nerve distribution (thumb, index and middle fingers, and radial aspect of the ring finger) also may be present. These injuries require immediate attention, and referral to a physician for radiographic evaluation and treatment is imperative (**Figure 12-9**).

Severe sprains of the radiocarpal joint that include significant swelling, pain, and restricted ROM also require referral to a physician. Complete ruptures of the scapholunate ligament or the lunotriquetral ligament also may occur. These require special imaging studies for appropriate diagnosis (**Figure 12-10**).

A sudden twisting injury to the wrist may tear its articular disk. This is a small, fibrocartilaginous structure called the *triangular fibrocartilaginous complex (TFCC)*, which is located between the distal end of the ulna and the carpals. Injury to the TFCC results in point tenderness just distal to the ulna and pain during wrist motion. Routine radiographs are usually performed, and an arthrogram is necessary for diagnosis.[15] The athlete should be referred to a physician if a TFCC injury is suspected. Stable injuries with no associated fractures are splinted at slight flexion and ulnar deviation for 4 to 6 weeks, which usually allows for peripheral tears to properly heal. Strengthening and a functional progression for return to sports may follow if the patient is free of pain.

Athletes who continue to have pain after the immobilization period, or who have a displaced tear, require surgical intervention, which usually includes debridement of the centrum. Ulnar shortening may also be necessary to unload a portion of the wrist.[16] After surgery, the wrist is immobilized in a splint to restrict forearm rotation. Subsequently, ROM exercises are initiated, and once the wound is healed, scar massage is introduced to prevent adhesions. Hand strengthening may begin 1 to 4 weeks postoperatively, depending on the type of surgery performed. Wrist strengthening exercises such as with light weights or resistance tubing can be initiated 4 to 6 weeks postoperatively. Activities such as wall push-ups and gradual weightbearing are slowly introduced as tolerated.[3] For athletes in sports such as gymnastics and cheerleading a supportive wrist brace is recommended, and a radial-ulnar brace is suggested in sports such as tennis (**Figure 12-11**).

Traumatic subluxation of the extensor carpi ulnaris

The tendon of the *extensor carpi ulnaris (ECU)* is secured to the distal ulna by the tendon sheath. Forceful supination, ulnar deviation, and flexion, as in a tennis player's forehand stroke, can lead to a tear of the ECU sheath at the distal ulna, resulting in subluxation of the ECU ulnarly and volarly with ulnar deviation of the wrist in supination.[8] The athlete may experience a popping sensation as the tendon subluxates across the ulnar styloid.

Acute injuries are usually treated with immobilization, but chronic injuries with more pronounced symptoms generally do not respond well to conservative treatment and require surgery.[8] After surgery, a cast is applied for 4 to 6 weeks, after which time a splint is fabricated and worn for 2 to 3 weeks between exercises as the patient begins active and passive ROM for the wrist and forearm.[3]

Approximately 8 weeks after surgery, strengthening exercises may begin. The use of a soft wrist brace provides added support during strengthening exercises and enables a functional progression for return to sports. A full return to sports with the wrist taped usually can occur 10 to 12 weeks after surgery.

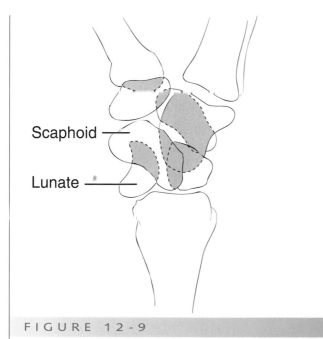

FIGURE 12-9

A volar lunate dislocation (stage IV perilunate dissociation) caused by disruption of the radiocarpal ligaments.

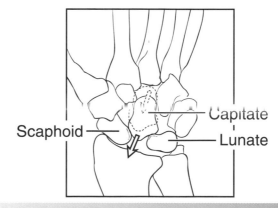

FIGURE 12-10

One mechanism of injury is the compressive effect of the capitate directly into the scapholunate joint.

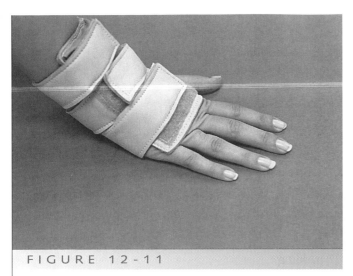

FIGURE 12-11

Support wrist brace.

Dorsal ganglion

Generally, ganglion cysts appear over time as a result of chronic stress and are common in sports such as gymnastics in which stress is repeatedly applied to the wrist.[1] An athlete with this condition may report pain over the scapholunate ligament, which is made worse by extremes of flexion and extension.[4] Sports participation may lead to chronic pain with limited motion and a weakened grip.

Conservative treatment includes wrist immobilization for 10 days to 3 weeks, with gradual initiation of ROM exercises. As pain decreases, strengthening exercises may be added.[7] The splint may be padded for play and its use gradually decreased as the patient gains full, pain-free ROM.[3]

Athletes who continue to have persistent pain require surgical excision of the ganglion. ROM exercises can start 1 week postoperatively. A splint should be worn for 3 weeks after surgery to allow the dorsal capsule to heal; subsequently, it should only be worn as a protective aid. If scarring on the dorsum of the wrist occurs, weighted wrist stretches may be used to increase passive flexion. A strengthening program should be started at 3 weeks, followed by a functional progression program before returning to sports.

Injuries to the Skin: Lacerations and Abrasions

Hand abrasions should be completely cleaned and all foreign matter removed. The entire hand should be scrubbed with surgical soap and the abrasion washed with a prepared iodine solution. All imbedded foreign matter should be removed from the abrasion. This can be accomplished by scrubbing the hand with a prepackaged sterile brush that contains a water-soluble iodine compound. The abrasion should be dressed with a nonadherent dressing and inspected daily for signs of infection. Soaking wounds in hydrogen peroxide may help to clean abrasions.

Superficial lacerations of the fingers and the back of the hand may be treated with careful scrubbing, removal of debris, and loose closure using butterfly tape. Because a cut may spread as a result of motion, splinting of the joint may be required during the first few days of healing if the laceration crosses a joint on the dorsal surface. All deep lacerations, particularly those of the palm of the hand, should be referred to a physician promptly.

Evaluating the extent of the laceration, including nerve status, vascular status, and tendon injury, is essential. The evaluation should include sensory testing using a pin on each side of the digit distal to the laceration to determine whether the palmar and digital nerves are intact. In most cases, an evaluation using touch only is deceptive, because the athlete thinks he or she feels touch when the sense is actually transmitted through proprioceptive elements within the joints. Therefore, evaluation with a sterile pin is recommended. As previously noted, sensory innervation of the hand may vary slightly, which the examiner should be aware of.

To assess the integrity of the tendons, the examiner should observe the injured hand in the resting position. Normally, all fingers flex slightly at rest; with loss of a flexor tendon, one or more fingers remain extended. To test for continuity of the long flexors of the thumb or fingers (flexor profundus), the examiner holds the proximal joints straight while the athlete bends the distal joints (**Figure 12-12**). The athlete can do this only if the long flexor tendon is intact. To examine the short flexor tendons (flexor sublimis), the athlete should hold all fingers extended except for the finger being examined. When the athlete flexes the injured digit, the long flexors will remain tethered, and only the flexor sublimis of the finger being examined will be able to cause flexion of the PIP joint. It is important to assess each of the four fingers separately.

Puncture wounds may appear trivial, but a small puncture wound of the skin may be associated with a more serious injury to deeper structures. Furthermore, puncture wounds have a high incidence of infection. When evaluating an athlete with a puncture wound, the examiner must carefully check for nerve and tendon function disturbances, particularly if the wound is on the palm side. Treatment includes a thorough cleaning, which consists of soaking the hand in warm water that contains a germicidal agent, followed by the application of a sterile dressing and referral to a physician. A tetanus toxoid booster is needed if the athlete's tetanus immunization is not current. Puncture wounds of the fingertip can produce a felon, a fingertip injury discussed earlier in this chapter.

REHABILITATION OF HAND AND WRIST INJURIES

Proper rehabilitation of the injured hand is important to achieve a good functional outcome after an injury. In complex injuries, failure to follow through with rehabili-

1. The prominent ends of the bones that form the base for the wrist joint are called:
   A. phalanges.
   B. ulna and radius.
   C. carpals and metacarpals.
   D. ulnar and radial styloids.

2. Which alignment of the hand and wrist is the most difficult to evaluate and maintain?
   A. Flexion
   B. Rotation
   C. Extension
   D. Opposition

3. The _____ nerve innervates the dorsum of the hand, and the _____ and _____ nerves control flexion of the wrist.
   A. Ulnar, digital, radial
   B. Radial, median, ulnar
   C. Ulnar, radial, median
   D. Median, digital, radial

4. An injury to the middle finger may also affect which of the following metacarpals?
   A. 2nd
   B. 3rd
   C. 4th
   D. 5th

5. It is easier to mobilize a finger joint that has been fixed in _____ for several weeks than a joint that has been fixed in _____.
   A. Flexion, extension
   B. Extension, flexion
   C. Abduction, adduction
   D. Adduction, abduction

6. Which of the following conditions is a fingertip pulp infection?
   A. Felon
   B. Contusion
   C. Paronychia
   D. Subungual hematoma

7. To assess the integrity of the collateral ligaments, the athletic trainer should apply which type of force to the joint?
   A. Lateral
   B. Medial
   C. Anterior
   D. Posterior

8. When can an athlete with a grade II ulnar collateral ligament rupture safely return to sports if protected with a splint or playing cast?
   A. At 2 weeks
   B. At 6 weeks
   C. When strength is 90% of normal
   D. When pain and swelling have subsided

9. When the hand is at rest, what is the normal alignment of the fingers?
   A. Slightly flexed
   B. Maximally flexed
   C. Slightly extended
   D. Maximally extended

10. The goals of hand and wrist rehabilitation are:
    A. 50% strength and minimal swelling.
    B. 80% strength and quick return to sport.
    C. minimal swelling and early mobilization.
    D. early mobilization and quick return to sport.

Answers on page 892

References

1. McCue FC, Mayer V: Rehabilitation of common athletic injuries of the hand and wrist. *Clin Sports Med* 1989;8:731–776.

2. Kahler DM, McCue FC: Metacarpophalangeal and proximal interphalangeal joint injuries of the hand, including the thumb. *Clin Sports Med* 1992;11:57–76.

3. Alexy C, De Carlo MS: Rehabilitation and use of protective devices in hand and wrist injuries. *Clin Sports Med* 1998;17:635–655.

4. Rettig AC, Patel DV: Wrist and hand injuries in athletes, in Kibler WB (ed): *ACSM's Handbook for the Team Physician.* Philadelphia, PA, Lippincott Williams & Wilkins, 1996.

5. Rettig AC: Hand injuries in football players. *Phys Sports Med* 1991;19:55–64.

6. Riester JN, Baker BE, Mosher JF, Lowe D: A review of scaphoid fracture healing in competitive athletes. *Am J Sports Med* 1985;13:159–161.

7. Zemel NP: Carpal fractures, in Strickland J, Rettig AC (eds): *Hand Injuries in Athletes.* Philadelphia, PA, WB Saunders, 1992, pp 155–173.

8. Rettig AC, Adsit WS: Athletic injuries of the hand and wrist, in Griffin LY (ed): *Orthopaedic Knowledge Update: Sports Medicine.* Rosemont, IL, American Academy of Orthopaedic Surgeons, 1994, pp 205–224.

9. Ganel A, Engel J, Oster Z, Farine I: Bone scanning in the assessment of fractures of the scaphoid. *J Hand Surg* 1979;4:540–543.

10. Rettig AC, Weidenbener EJ, Gloyeske R: Alternative management of mid-third scaphoid fractures in the athlete. *Am J Sports Med* 1994;22:711–714.

11. De Carlo MS, Malone K, Darmelio J, Gerig B: Casting. *Sport J Athl Train* 1994;29:37–43.

12. Herbert TJ, Fisher WE: Management of the fractured scaphoid using a new bone screw. *J Bone Joint Surg* 1984;66B:114–123.

13. Stark HH, Jobe FW, Boyes JH, Ashworth CR: Fracture of the hook of the hamate in athletes. *J Bone Joint Surg* 1977;59A:575–582.

14. Prosser R, Herbert TJ: The management of carpal fractures and dislocations. *J Hand Ther* 1996;9:139–147.

15. Dell PC: Traumatic disorders of the distal radioulnar joint. *Clin Sports Med* 1992;11:141–159.

16. Rettig AC: Wrist problems in the tennis player. *Med Sci Sports Exerc* 1994;26:1207–1212.

17. De Carlo MS, Darmelio J, Rettig AC, Malone K: Perfecting a playing cast for hand and wrist injuries. *Phys Sports Med* 1992;20:95–104.

OVERVIEW

No matter what the cause, chest injuries are serious and potentially fatal because of the likelihood of internal bleeding and direct or indirect injury to the heart or lungs. This chapter begins with a discussion of chest injuries, including classification, initial care, and types (with signs, symptoms, and treatment) and the conditions resulting from chest injuries. Next, the anatomy and biomechanics of the thoracic spine and rib cage are addressed, followed by a description of the assessment and treatment of various rib dysfunctions. Discussions of thoracic spine fractures, instability, and disk herniations follow, and the chapter concludes with the treatment of segmental and facet joint dysfunction.

CLASSIFICATION AND INITIAL CARE OF CHEST INJURIES

Chest injuries may result from numerous types of trauma, including motor vehicle accidents (MVA), gunshot wounds, stab wounds, and compressive or concussive forces. Whatever their cause, chest injuries are serious because of the likelihood of internal bleeding and of direct or indirect injury to the heart or lungs. Serious chest trauma is uncommon in young, healthy athletes; however, chest injuries, unless properly recognized and treated, may be fatal.

FOCUS ON . . .

Classification and Initial Care of Chest Injuries

Chest injuries are classified as open or closed. In an open injury, the chest wall has been penetrated, allowing air to enter the pleura. Intrapleural pressure increases, producing a pneumothorax (accumulation of air in the pleural cavity) and a collapsed lung. Major blood vessels can be lacerated, causing a hemothorax (accumulation of blood in the pleural cavity). A closed chest injury is usually caused by blunt, compressive trauma, and although the skin remains intact, serious internal damage may still have occurred. Initial care of a chest injury includes quick recognition, accurate assessment of the situation and the injury, and proper emergency care.

Surrounding the chest and giving it shape and support are the ribs and the thoracic spine. Soft-tissue injuries, as well as fractures or herniated disks, are common in this area.

Chest injuries are categorized as either open or closed. In *open chest injuries*, the chest wall has been penetrated, such as by a knife, broken glass, or bullet.[1] An opening in the chest wall allows air to enter the pleura, causing intrapleural pressure to increase and subsequently producing a pneumothorax (**Figure 13-1**).

Pneumothorax refers to the presence of air within the chest cavity in the pleural space. The increased pressure from the build-up of air causes the lung to separate from the chest wall and collapse. As the degree of pneumothorax increases, respiratory distress occurs because of the lung's diminished capacity to exchange oxygen and carbon dioxide with the blood resulting from diminished lung volume.

An open or penetrating chest injury may also lacerate major blood vessels, producing a hemothorax (**Figure 13-2**). *Hemothorax* refers to the presence of blood in the pleural space outside of the lung. A hemothorax may occur in open or closed chest injuries. If bleeding is severe, the athlete may show signs of shock from blood loss.

In *closed chest injuries*, the skin is not broken but there may still be serious internal damage. Closed chest injuries are usually caused by blunt chest trauma of a compressive nature such as occurs in an MVA or when a football player is tackled by several opponents.

An athletic trainer is often the first to respond to an injured athlete. A possible chest injury requires initial quick recognition, accurate assessment of the situation and injury, and proper emergency medical care. **Table 13-1** reviews the steps that should be taken when an athlete has a chest injury.

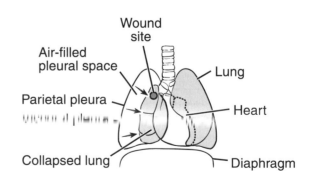

FIGURE 13-1

Pneumothorax occurs when air enters the pleura from an opening in the chest wall and causes intrapleural pressure to increase.

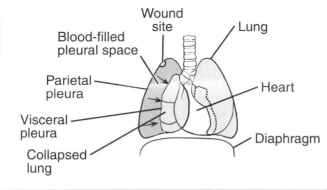

FIGURE 13-2

Hemothorax occurs when major blood vessels are lacerated and blood is present in the pleural space outside the lung.

TABLE 13-1
INITIAL CARE OF CHEST INJURIES

The following steps should be taken when treating an athlete with a chest injury:

- Make sure the patient has an adequate airway, breathing, and circulation (ABCs), and be prepared to maintain the ABCs.

- Assess the patient for any head or spinal injury.

- Be prepared to administer artificial ventilation or cardiopulmonary resuscitation (CPR).

- Observe and record the patient's vital signs every 5 minutes.

- Control all obvious external bleeding.

- Cover open or penetrating chest wounds with an occlusive dressing sealed on three sides only.

- Do not remove any objects that may be penetrating the chest wall; however, trim objects to allow for transport.

- Activate emergency medical services (EMS) and arrange for immediate transport to the emergency department.

TYPES OF CHEST INJURIES

Several different types of chest injuries with varying degrees of severity can be sustained from a traumatic event. The most common causes of chest injuries are MVAs, direct blows to the chest, high-velocity impacts, and falls.

Flail Chest

Flail chest injuries, the most serious of chest wall injuries, are defined as a fracture of at least four consecutive ribs in two or more places[2,3] (**Figure 13-3**). A functional definition is an incompetent segment of chest wall large enough to impair the patient's respiration.[3] Significant respiratory distress results. The most common causes of flail chest are MVAs and falls. Normally, the chest wall expands during inhalation and contracts during exhalation. With a flail chest injury, the flail segment (that portion of the chest wall between the fractures) will collapse during inhalation and protrude during exhalation. This opposite movement, termed "paradoxical motion," is extremely painful and results in inefficient expansion of the thorax and a significant expenditure of energy for breathing. The flail chest causes difficulty in breathing because of the damage to underlying pulmonary tissue; the paradoxical movement of the flail segment and the pain from the fractures leads to decreased chest expansion and shallow breathing.[4]

Flail chest injuries are relatively easy to diagnose through observation and palpation. The chest does not rise properly and there may be an observable and/or palpable deformity. The initial treatment is to ensure adequate breathing, including the use of supplemental oxygen if available. A pillow can be placed over the flail segment to help stabilize the segment and decrease pain.[2] Vital signs should be monitored, and the athlete should be transported immediately by EMS to the emergency department. Inpatient treatment of flail chest involves aggressive pulmonary management and pain control.[3] The decision to surgically stabilize the chest wall is based on the judgment of the surgeon. A patient who cannot be weaned from a ventilator or who manifests a persistent chest wall deformity may benefit from the surgical approach.[3]

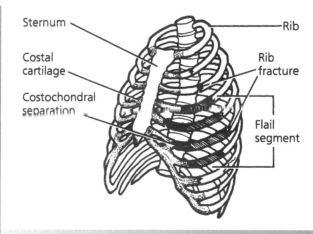

FIGURE 13-3

Flail chest occurs when four or more consecutive ribs are fractured in two or more places.

FOCUS ON . . .

Anatomy and Biomechanics of the Thoracic Spine and Rib Cage

Functional anatomy of the thoracic spine

The thoracic spine offers spinal column stability between the relatively mobile cervical and lumbar regions, protects the spinal cord and internal organs in the thoracic cavity, and assists the lungs and rib cage mechanically. Because the anterior vertebral posture height is shorter than posterior vertebral body height, the kyphotic thoracic spine between the lordotic cervical and lumbar spines gives the spinal column its S-shaped appearance and increased flexibility and shock-absorbing capacity while maintaining adequate stiffness and stability. As opposed to the transitional upper (T1 to T4) and lower (T4 to T8) segments, which resemble the adjacent cervical and thoracic spines, the midthoracic spine (T4 to T8) is anatomically different, with less space and a more precarious blood supply for the spinal cord in this region. Here, the spinous processes are long and slender and appear shingled from above.

Musculature of the thoracic spine

The superficial muscles are the longest and comprise the trapezius, latissimus dorsi, and rhomboids. The intermediate transversocostalis muscles span medial to lateral as they ascend the back and include the sacrospinalis and spinalis, which extend and laterally flex the trunk and rotate to the same side. The deep transversospinalis muscles ascend the back from lateral to medial and include the semispinalis, multifidus, and rotators, which extend and laterally flex the trunk and rotate to the opposite side. The superficial splenius capitis and cervicis muscles extend from T1 to T6 superiorly; they extend the head and neck and rotate the head to the same side.

The rib cage

The rib cage acts as a protective barrier to the spine; stiffens and strengthens the spine, increasing resistance to displacement; increases the thoracic spine's transverse dimension; and adds to the spine's strength and energy-absorbing capacity during trauma. Motions of the ribs are inhalation, exhalation, and torsion. Normal rib motion requires mobility at the costovertebral and costotransverse joints and the costochondral articulations.

Stability of the thoracic spine

The thoracic spine posterior elements are the supraspinous and interspinous ligaments, bilateral facet joints, and ligamentum flavum. The facet joints are important stabilizers (resisting anterior shear loads) and can be a direct source of pain. In this region, the facet joints are oriented more coronally and angulated, as opposed to the corresponding cervical and lumbar facet joints.

The costovertebral joints are synovial joints with articular capsules, formed by the articulation between the head of the rib and the sides of the corresponding vertebrae and the one above. The rib's tubercle articulates with the transverse process of the corresponding vertebrae to form the costotransverse joint.

Musculature of the Thoracic Spine

Generally, the name of the muscle group also specifies its location in the back musculature. There are three layers of back muscles: superficial, intermediate, and deep. In general, the superficial layer contains the longest muscles; the muscles in the intermediate layer are somewhat shorter, and the shortest muscles lie immediately against the vertebrae in the deep layer. The superficial muscle group comprises the upper, middle, and lower portions of the trapezius, the latissimus dorsi, and the rhomboids. The transversocostalis muscle group is an intermediate muscle group that spans medial to lateral as it ascends the back. The muscles included in this group are the sacrospinalis (erector spinae), composed of the iliocostalis and longissimus, and the spinalis. These muscles function to extend the trunk, to flex the trunk laterally, and to rotate the trunk to the same side. The transversospinalis muscle group is a deep muscle group with fibers running lateral to medial as it ascends the back. This muscle group includes the semispinalis, the multifidus, and the rotators. These muscles function as trunk extensors, lateral flexors, and rotators to the opposite side. The splenius capitis and splenius cervicis are superficial muscle groups that run superiorly from the spinous processes of the lower cervical and thoracic regions (approximately T1 to T6). These muscles extend the head and neck and rotate the head to the same side. Thus, moving from the superficial layer to the deep layer, the back musculature is composed of the splenius, sacrospinalis, semispinalis, multifidi, and rotators.

The Rib Cage

The rib cage has several biomechanical functions related to the spine. It acts as a protective barrier; stiffens and strengthens the spine, thus providing greater resistance to

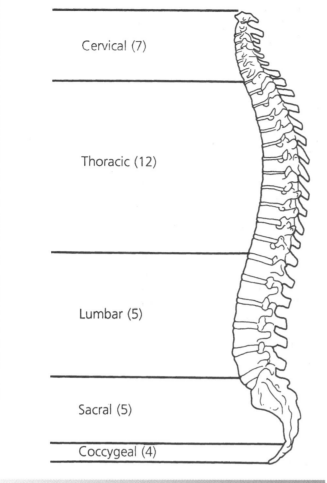

FIGURE 13-9

Stability of the spinal column is provided by the thoracic spine, which is the transitional region between the relatively mobile cervical and lumbar regions. The spinal column's S-shaped appearance is caused by the connection of the lordotic curves of the cervical and lumbar spines with the kyphotic curves of the thoracic spine.

displacement; increases the transverse dimension of the thoracic spine, and provides additional strength and energy-absorbing capacity during trauma.[9]

The characteristic motions of the ribs are the up-and-out movement of inhalation and the down-and-in movement of exhalation. Another motion of the ribs is called rib torsion and accompanies the rotation of the thoracic spine.[12] When two thoracic vertebrae are involved in rotation, the attached ribs also demonstrate a torsional movement.[12] For normal motion of the ribs to occur, there must be mobility at the costovertebral joints, costotransverse joints, and costochondral articulations.[12]

Stability of the Thoracic Spine

The thoracic spine is noted for its stability and rigidity as opposed to the more mobile cervical and lumbar spinal

regions.[9] Structures such as the posterior elements, costovertebral joints, sternum, and rib cage all play an essential role in the stability of the thoracic spine.

Posterior elements

Posterior elements of the thoracic spine consist of the supraspinous and interspinous ligaments, bilateral facet (zygapophyseal) joints, and ligamentum flavum.[4] The posterior elements contribute to the stability of the spine. Clinically, the facet joints are important because they are a direct source of pain and they are important stabilizing structures.[9] The facet joints of the thoracic spine have a more coronal orientation and angulation than those of the cervical and lumbar spines.[13] The superior and inferior facets arise from the upper and lower parts of the pedicles of the thoracic vertebrae, respectively. Studies have shown that the facets play an important role in stabilizing the thoracic spine during loading.[13] They also have an important role in resisting anterior shear loads, carrying an estimated one third of the anterior shear load while the disk carries two thirds.[9] Results of a study of the role played by the posterior elements in restricting physiologic motions of the spine indicated that motion in the upper thoracic region increased significantly in flexion and extension, and that lower thoracic motion increased with axial rotation and, to a lesser degree, lateral bending, flexion, and extension.[9] When dealing with a hypermobile or hypomobile facet or a facet dysfunction, the athletic trainer should keep in mind the important load-carrying capacity of the facet and its contribution to the overall stability of the spine.

Costovertebral joints

The costovertebral and costotransverse joints connect the thoracic spine to the rib cage. The costovertebral joint is formed by the articulation between the head of the rib and the sides of the corresponding vertebrae and the one above. This is a synovial joint with an articular capsule. The tubercle of the rib articulates with the transverse process of the corresponding vertebrae to form the costotransverse joint.

ASSESSMENT AND TREATMENT OF VARIOUS RIB DYSFUNCTIONS

Rib cage dysfunctions, other than rib fractures, are difficult to recognize. However, rib cage dysfunction is a component of musculoskeletal system dysfunction.[12] Alterations in rib cage function can influence respiratory activity, circulatory activity, and neural activity.[12] An athletic trainer or other healthcare professional dealing with athletes after a rib fracture or other injury to the thoracic region must pay close attention to the rib cage. Signs and symptoms of rib dysfunctions may be referred to the anterior chest (sternal area), posterior thorax, or thoracic vertebrae. If pain in the area of the thoracic vertebrae shows no significant improvement with treatment, a possible rib dysfunction should be suspected. A proper and thorough assessment of the rib cage by the athletic trainer may help ensure timely care of an athlete injured in the thoracic region.

Assessment of the Rib Cage

An athletic trainer evaluating the thoracic spine should assess the rib cage as well because of the direct relationship between the ribs and the thoracic spine. As with any other area being assessed, the athletic trainer looks for asymmetry, altered range of motion (ROM), and tissue texture abnormalities.[12] The assessment should include observation, inspection, palpation, ROM, and joint mobility. The athletic trainer should observe and inspect the injury site from all directions, looking for any visible deformities, discoloration, or asymmetry. The athletic trainer should palpate for the symmetry and contour of the rib cage anteriorly, posteriorly, and laterally, with the patient prone, sitting, or supine if sitting is difficult[12] (**Figure 13-10**). Palpation should include the costochondral articulations and the rib interspaces, and any tenderness or asymmetry should be noted.[12] Tissue texture abnormalities, especially hypertonicity, should be noted as should tenderness of the muscles attaching to the ribs.[12] The iliocostalis muscle group attaches to the rib angle and is frequently tense and tender in the presence of a rib dysfunction.[12] To assess range of motion, the athletic trainer places his or her hands symmetrically over the individual ribs or groups of ribs and follows the inhalation and exhalation patterns, both quiet and forced.[12] Gentle compressive forces can be applied to the rib cage anteriorly, posteriorly, and then laterally to determine the presence and location of pain and also the quality of flexibility of the rib cage (see Figure 13-5). Assessing the mobility of the costochondral and costovertebral joints with a posterior/anterior glide will also provide vital information about tissue reactivity and mobility (**Figure 13-11**).

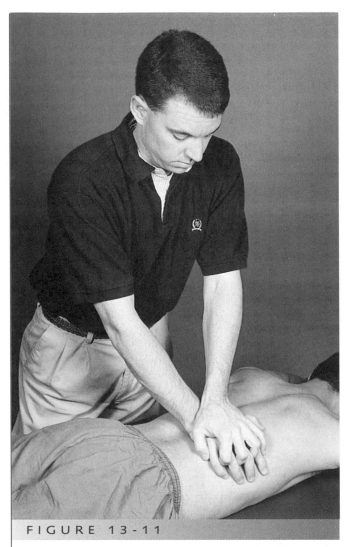

FIGURE 13-11

Vital information about tissue reactivity and mobility can be found during an assessment of the costochondral and costovertebral joints using a posterior/anterior glide.

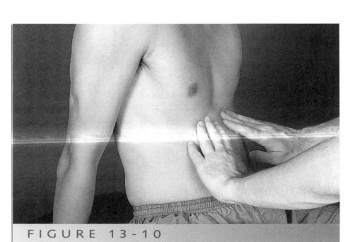

FIGURE 13-10

The athletic trainer should palpate the athlete's rib cage anteriorly, posteriorly, and laterally and observe the symmetry and contour of the rib cage.

Classifications of Rib Dysfunctions

There are two classifications of rib dysfunction: structural and respiratory.[12] Structural dysfunctions are of four types: rib subluxation (anterior, posterior, or superior), rib torsion, rib compression, and laterally flexed rib.[12]

Rib subluxations, also referred to as positional faults, can occur in the anterior, posterior, and, in the first rib, superior directions. With anterior and posterior subluxations, there is frequently a complaint of intercostal neuralgia at the adjacent interspace as well as a marked decrease in motion of the rib cage on inhalation and exhalation.[12] A superiorly subluxated first rib may present with marked tenderness of its superior aspect and hypertonic ipsilateral scalene muscles.[12]

Rib torsion usually accompanies dysfunctions of the thoracic spine.[12] On palpation, the athletic trainer may notice a widened intercostal space above the dysfunctional rib, and a narrowed intercostal space below it. There may be respiratory motion restrictions.[12] The athletic trainer should first focus on treating the thoracic dysfunction; the rib torsion then usually resolves.[12]

Rib compression dysfunctions are rare and usually follow traumatic events that cause an anteroposterior compression of the rib cage, such as hitting the steering wheel in an MVA or sustaining a compressive force in a sporting activity.[12]

The laterally flexed rib behaves as though the anterior and posterior ends were fixed and the rib flexes up and down.[12]

Respiratory rib dysfunctions demonstrate restrictions in either inhalation or exhalation and can affect a single rib or a group of ribs.[12] The term "key rib" is used in respiratory dysfunctions to refer to the major restrictor of the motion.[12]

Treatment

The sequence to follow in treating rib dysfunctions is to first treat any thoracic spine dysfunctions, then structural rib dysfunctions, and finally, respiratory rib dysfunctions.[12]

Numerous techniques are used to manually treat any type of soft-tissue or structural dysfunction. Two of the best known techniques are joint mobilization and muscle energy, both of which incorporate breathing and guidance techniques to facilitate the proper response. The muscle energy technique also involves voluntary contraction of the patient's muscle(s) in a controlled and precise manner against a distinct counterforce applied by the athletic trainer.[14]

THORACIC SPINE FRACTURES

Classification of Thoracic Spine Fractures

A classification system of spinal fractures, based on a better understanding of these injuries, is available to help with more precise treatment and prognosis. A modified classification system divides spinal fractures into three categories based on the severity of injury (extent of soft-tissue and bony involvement), planes of disruption, number of columns involved, and close relationship between fracture morphology and neurologic deficits.[15] Type A fractures are compression injuries primarily involving the vertebral body; they are the most stable fractures and have the least amount of neurologic deficit. Type B fractures are distraction injuries affecting anterior and posterior elements. Type C fractures are multidirectional injuries with translation that also affect anterior and posterior elements; they are unstable and have the greatest degree of neurologic deficit. Type C fractures usually require surgical treatment.[15] Subdivisions of these categories are also used in the classification process to determine fracture stability, increase in neurologic deficits, and whether surgery is indicated.

FOCUS ON . . .

Thoracic Spine Fractures

Classification of thoracic spine fractures

Spinal fractures can be classified into three categories: type A (compression injuries involving the vertebral body), type B (distraction injuries to the anterior and posterior elements), and type C (multidirectional translation injuries to the anterior and posterior elements). Subdivisions reflect fracture stability, neurologic deficits, and the need for surgical treatment.

Characteristic injury patterns and indirect signs
The well-protected, stable thoracic spine is less likely to fracture than the cervical or lumbar spine, but once injured, can result in a worse outcome because of the larger thoracic spinal cord relative to the smaller spinal canal and the greater force required to cause an injury. Indirect signs of thoracic spine injury include sternal and posterolateral or posteromedial rib fractures.

Common spinal injuries in athletes
Most thoracic spine fractures in athletes are compression injuries caused by high-velocity sports. Treatment is bracing to prevent flexion and close monitoring. Once the fracture is healed, the athlete can return to sport. With cord compression, once the surgical fusion is healed, the athlete can return to sport. Repetitive twisting and turning sports can cause disk degeneration or facet joint arthritis; treatment is reconditioning, stabilization, and sport-specific exercises, and reducing stress on the injured area.

Radiography and imaging
Adequate thoracic spine imaging may include overpenetrated anteroposterior views with special breathing techniques, CT scan (especially for costovertebral dislocations), and MRI scan (for the spinal cord and extraosseous structures). MRI findings must correlate with clinical findings to be useful.

Treatment of thoracic spine fractures
Nonsurgical treatment of thoracic spine fractures may be feasible, if the posterior column is intact and the athlete is clinically stable. Bed rest for 1 to 2 weeks, an orthosis, and ambulation for exercise are followed by physical therapy for spinal muscle strengthening, postural education, and body mechanics. Surgery to decompress or stabilize the area may be necessary if the patient is neurologically compromised or instability is diagnosed.

Characteristic Injury Patterns and Indirect Signs

Fractures of the thoracic spine are less common than fractures of the cervical and lumbar spines because the thoracic spine is well protected by the rib cage and associated articulations. When a fracture does occur in the thoracic area, the outcome may be worse because greater force is required to cause an injury and the size of the thoracic spinal cord is much larger relative to the smaller spinal canal.[7]

The athletic trainer should be aware of the indirect signs of a possible thoracic spine injury. Sternal fractures, as mentioned previously, can indicate not only the presence of a thoracic spine fracture, but also an increased risk of instability.[7] Fracture of the posterolateral or posteromedial ribs with or without an associated costovertebral joint dislocation is another indirect sign of a fracture or instability in the thoracic spine.[7]

Common Spinal Injuries in Athletes

Most thoracic spine injuries in athletes result from high-velocity sports, such as racing and skiing. Most fractures seen in the athletic field are compression fractures, with or without associated disruption of the surrounding soft tissue.[16] Treating an athlete for such an injury involves bracing to prevent flexion and reduce the chances of an increased kyphosis.[16] The healing process and potential kyphotic development must be monitored. After the fracture has healed, the athlete can usually return to normal sporting activity.[16] If the fracture involves spinal cord compression, surgical intervention is required, but the athlete can return to competition without any increased risk of injury after the fusion has healed.[16]

Sports that involve repetitive twisting and turning can take their toll and cause disk degeneration or facet joint arthritis.[16] This type of injury is usually treated with reconditioning, stabilization, and sport-specific exercises as well as modifications to decrease the stress on the involved area.

Radiography and Imaging

Thoracic spine fractures can be more difficult to diagnose than fractures in the cervical or lumbar region because of the stabilizing function of the rib cage and sternum. Standard anteroposterior (AP) or posteroanterior (PA) chest radiographs are not sufficient for adequate visualization of the thoracic spine.[7] A dedicated AP and lateral thoracolumbar spine radiographic series enables better visualization of the vertebrae.[7]

Other imaging techniques enable the physician to be more accurate in diagnosing spinal fractures and soft-tissue lesions of the thoracic spine. A computed tomography (CT) scan provides significantly more diagnostic information than does a plain radiograph, and it detects costovertebral dislocations that are not seen on ordinary radiographs.[7] Magnetic resonance imaging (MRI) enables excellent visualization of extraosseous structures around the spinal cord and shows spinal cord pathology.[7] The high specificity of MRI can pick up abnormalities that may not be the primary cause of pain; indeed, MRI presents a high rate of asymptomatic abnormalities in the thoracic spine. Athletic trainers and physicians must be aware that the use of MRI findings may assist in the diagnostic process, but only if they correlate to clinical findings.

Treatment of Thoracic Spine Fractures

The debate over surgical or nonsurgical treatment of thoracic spine fractures has persisted for years. Some physicians have found that the nonsurgical approach yields acceptable alignment of the fractured site, equivalent neurologic recovery, avoidance of late deformity, and a lower complication rate than does surgery.[17,18] Nonsurgical management of thoracic spine fractures includes postural reduction, bed rest, bracing (usually with a thoraco-lumbar-sacral orthosis or TLSO), and early mobilization.[18] Through immobilization, bracing reduces the stress on the injured area as it is healing. But the nonsurgical approach is not appropriate for all thoracic spine fractures. Studies have indicated that the nonsurgical approach can yield good recovery if the integrity of the posterior column (posterior elements) is intact.[18]

Some physicians believe that surgery to decompress and stabilize the spine is a better approach for treating thoracic spine fractures. They believe that surgery enables earlier mobility and rehabilitation, reduces anatomic fractures, restores spinal alignment, and improves neurologic function.[17-19] If the patient is neurologically compromised or if instability is diagnosed, surgery is necessary to decompress and stabilize the area.

Appropriate rehabilitation after the fracture heals is essential for normal recovery in either surgical or nonsurgical approaches. If a patient is evaluated and determined to be clinically stable, treatment usually entails bed rest for 1 to 2 weeks, appropriate bracing to immobilize and allow healing, ambulation as exercise, followed by physical therapy for strengthening spinal musculature, postural education, and body mechanics.

THORACIC DISK HERNIATION

Thoracic disk herniation is rare, making up only approximately 0.25% to 0.75% of total disk ruptures, primarily because of the inherent stability of the thoracic spine.[20,21] Results of studies have shown that disk herniations in the thoracic region appear to follow a course similar to those in the cervical and lumbar regions, a slow progression that often starts with pain and sequentially develops sensory, motor, gait, and sphincter dysfunction.[20,22]

FOCUS ON . . .

Thoracic Disk Herniation

Thoracic disk herniation is rare and slowly progressive. Thoracic disk herniations appear to follow a similar course to disk herniations in the cervical and lumbar regions, beginning with pain and progressing to sensory, motor, gait, and sphincter dysfunction. Mechanisms of injury include excessive torsion, combined torsion and lateral bending, and hyperflexion with sudden axial compression.

Signs and symptoms of disk herniation

Among the signs and symptoms of disk herniation are dull, deep retrosternal or retrogastric pain, "band-like" anterior chest pain, interscapular or back pain, lower extremity paresthesia, muscle weakness, and bowel and bladder dysfunction.

Magnetic resonance imaging is the most sensitive diagnostic test. CT scan and myelography are also used for diagnosis.

Nonsurgical treatment of thoracic disk herniation

Nonsurgical treatment includes rest, nonsteroidal anti-inflammatory drugs, and controlled therapy of modalities, education, and proper body mechanics. The McKenzie technique uses repetitive motion for pain centralization. The Maitland technique uses specific methods of oscillation or sustained holds to eliminate reproducible signs of pain. Once associated muscle guarding and pain have decreased and pain is centralized, reconditioning begins with general aerobic exercise, such as walking, and strengthening of the back extensors and scapular muscles, progressing to work- or sport-related reconditioning. Close monitoring for progress and neurologic stability is necessary.

Intervertebral Disk

The intervertebral disk (IVD) is composed of an inner nucleus pulposus, outer annulus fibrosus, and cartilaginous end-plates. The nucleus pulposus functions to distribute compressive forces, whereas the annulus fibrosus acts to withstand tension within the disk. The IVDs constitute 20% to 33% of the entire height of the vertebral column and are responsible for carrying all the compressive load to which the trunk is subjected.[9] The usual mechanisms of injury for disk herniation are excessive torsion, a combination of torsion and lateral bending, and

sudden axial compression while hyperflexed. When a disk is injured, the mechanical behavior of the disk is significantly affected.[9]

Signs and Symptoms of Disk Herniation

The duration of symptoms of a thoracic disk herniation is usually long, averaging 1 to 2 years before presentation.[21] Many times, referred pain from a thoracic disk herniation mimics pulmonary, cardiac, or intra-abdominal disorders and can be misdiagnosed.[21] Some common signs and symptoms are dull, deep retrosternal or retrogastric pain; "band-like" anterior chest pain; interscapular pain; lower extremity paresthesia; muscle weakness; back pain; and bowel and bladder dysfunction.[20,21] Symptoms can be referred to nerve roots in the lower extremity, but they also can entail signs of myelopathy (cord compression) and can assist in determining the necessary course of treatment.

The MRI is the most sensitive method for diagnosing a thoracic disk herniation.[20] Other tests used in the diagnosis are CT scan and myelography.[21]

Surgical Treatment of Thoracic Disk Herniation

Indications for surgical intervention in thoracic disk herniations are still not clear. There is evidence that, as in cervical and lumbar disk disease, symptoms of thoracic disk herniations often stabilize within time.[20] If there is evidence of neurologic deficits, surgery may be the alternative of choice; however, if there is simply pain, surgical management is controversial because the disk herniation may be incidental.[22]

Nonsurgical Treatment of Thoracic Disk Herniation

Nonsurgical treatment of thoracic disk herniations is often recommended initially if there are no neurologic signs of myelopathy. As in the cervical and lumbar regions, radicular symptoms in the thoracic region are known to stabilize with time.[20] Conservative treatment often comprises a regimen of rest, nonsteroidal anti-inflammatory drugs, and controlled therapy.[20]

Rehabilitation for a thoracic disk herniation focuses on indirectly facilitating the healing process. After a period of rest and once the acute inflammation and pain have been addressed by the physician, rehabilitation can begin. Initially, rehabilitation consists of modalities, such as ice, heat, ultrasound or massage, to assist in pain relief from associated muscle spasms and postural guarding. Early education is very important so that the patient accepts responsibility for recovery. Teaching proper body mechanics with a formal back school emphasizing thoracic spine extension and avoiding a kyphotic position is a priority so that an improper movement does not trigger an acute episode. At least half of one clinical session should be spent educating the patient about the body mechanics of the entire vertebral column and upper extremities, either one-on-one, or through educational booklets. Proper lifting techniques, proper support of the shoulder girdles to decrease the work on the scapulothoracic muscles, and proper posture must all be covered in detail (**Figure 13-12**).

Poor posture is very common in today's society and typically results in muscle imbalances. College students, desk workers, and even healthcare professionals exhibit the usual "slumped" posture. A very slumped thoracic/shoulder girdle area leads to elongated and stretched posterior soft-tissue structures (scapula, paraspinal muscles, ligaments, and joints) and tight anterior soft-tissue structures (pectoralis muscles, ligaments, and joints). Constantly elongating and stretching soft tissue leads to weakness and hypermobility. The goal of postural correction is to balance the anterior and posterior structures.

There is no set protocol for good posture. Proper posture is individual, requires minimal energy for maintenance, minimizes stresses and strains on the body tissues, and is maximally functional.[23] Static and dynamic posture as well as posture in different positions (sitting, standing, lying) should be addressed. The musculature in the thoracic spine region (especially the scapular muscles) are primarily postural muscles. Supporting the upper extrem-

ities and decreasing the amount of unsupported upper extremity use will assist in decreasing the workload of these muscles and prevent spasms.

Numerous methods of treating a single injury have developed from different philosophies of treatment. The athletic trainer who learns various techniques according to different philosophies can select from them to maximize treatment sessions.

The McKenzie technique uses repetitive motion for centralization of pain.[23] Clinically, prone press-ups and prone on elbows with the use of breathing are used to centralize pain with thoracic disk herniations (**Practice Session 13-2**)

The Maitland technique uses specific degrees of oscillation or sustained holds to eliminate reproducible signs of pain[23] (**Practice Session 13-3**). Graded oscillations of I through V are directed at pain relief; grades I and II focus solely on reducing pain, and grades III through V also trigger mechanical effects. The oscillations fire both type I postural and type II dynamic mechanoreceptors (position- or pressure-sensitive neurons) to reduce pain and muscle guarding.[23]

Once the athletic trainer is able to centralize the pain, decrease associated muscle guarding, and assist in decreasing the associated pain, reconditioning needs to occur. The athletic trainer must always stress continued maintenance of good posture and body mechanics during this phase. General aerobic exercise, especially walking, is

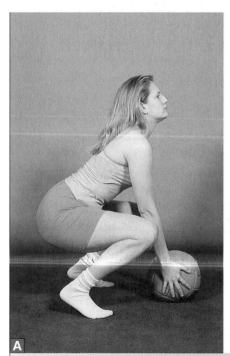

FIGURE 13-12

Education of the patient should include proper lifting techniques. **A** The athlete should keep the head and back straight while placing weight on the balls of the feet. **B** With feet flat, the athlete should lift the object, keeping the back straight. **C** The athlete completes the lift, still keeping the back straight and weight balanced on the feet.

PRACTICE SESSION 13-2
THE McKENZIE TECHNIQUE

A The athlete lies prone. **B** The athlete raises him- or herself using only arm strength so that the back muscles are relaxed. The pelvis remains on the table; only the upper part of the body raises. Exercises are repeated until the pain centralizes in the lower back.

PRACTICE SESSION 13-3
THE MAITLAND TECHNIQUE

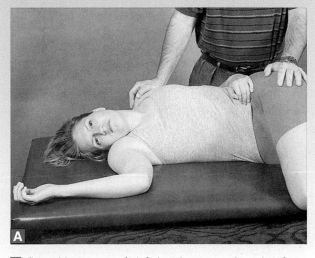

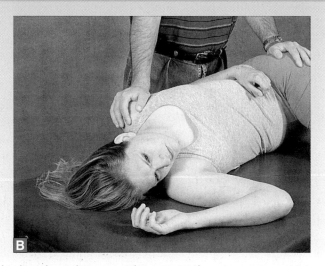

A The athletic trainer's left hand rotates the pelvis forward and indirectly applies an axial torque to the thoracic and lumbar spine. The right hand steadies the thorax. **B** The same procedure seen from a different angle.

beneficial. Strengthening the back extensors and scapular musculature is required to assist in supporting and stabilizing the area. Because these muscles are postural in function, an exercise regimen of low weights and high repetitions is recommended. After initial reconditioning has taken place, work-related or sport-specific reconditioning can begin to enable the person to return to his or her normal activities of daily living.

Athletic trainers must be aware that the conservative approach may not yield 100% success in every case. Constant reevaluation must take place to determine if progress is being made and neurologic signs are still stable.

Treatment of Segmental or Facet Dysfunction

"Segmental dysfunction" and "facet dysfunction" are common terms heard in the clinical setting. By definition, a dysfunction is "any disturbance, impairment, or abnormality of function," and a joint dysfunction is the state of altered mechanics or presence of an abnormal movement.[23] A discussion of segmental dysfunction will focus primarily on the facet joints, which are synovial joints with a fibrous capsule.[24] Synovial fluid, secreted by the synovial membrane, lubricates the joint. The principal function of a facet joint is to permit, guide, and limit motion of the segments of functional segmental units (FSUs) it connects.[24] The facet capsule and capsular ligaments limit the amount of free movement allowed by the facet joint itself.[24] Pain associated with facet injury is transmitted through nerve endings within the capsule and ligaments.[24]

Facet joint injuries, such as osteoarthritis, instability, and aftereffects of sprains and strains, are dysfunctions as opposed to diseases. Physicians diagnose and treat disease, but athletic trainers evaluate and treat dysfunction. Joint dysfunctions are usually divided into three main categories: hypomobile, hypermobile, and unstable.

Hypomobility

Hypomobility is defined as a decrease in normal motion. Hypomobility in a segment can occur as a result of poor posture or injury that causes immobilization in that segment. If an athletic trainer directs a patient's treatment solely to increasing range of motion and stretching soft-tissue structures in the cardinal planes and does not address the underlying joint hypomobility, total recovery may not occur.

Joint hypomobility can effectively be treated with manipulation. *Joint manipulation*, which is also called joint mobilization, is defined as skilled, passive movement of a joint (or spinal segment) either within or beyond its active range of motion.[25] Joint manipulation can restore normal joint motion and lead to improved overall function and performance, increased tolerance to further insult, decreased pain, restoration of proper nutrition, and repair of joint structures.[23] Although the use of joint manipulation has many benefits for problems such as hemarthrosis, muscle guarding, and for patients with joint replacements, certain precautions must be taken. Precautions include a clear understanding of the underlying abnormality or diagnosis. The physician must rule out abnormalities of the joint that require surgical correction. Other treatments, such as muscle energy, gentle oscillations, sustained stretching, and thrust can be included with joint manipulation.[25]

Some of the philosophies based on normalizing joint mobility include osteopathic medicine, Paris, Maitland, Mulligan, and muscle energy techniques.[12, 23,26] The philosophy behind osteopathic medicine is to mobilize and manipulate the joints and body structures to increase motion.[23] The Paris philosophy emphasizes restoration of normal arthrokinematics, especially joint-play motion, and deemphasizes pain.[23] Maitland's approach uses oscillatory or sustained mobilizations for pain control and restoration of joint motion. Mulligan combines mobilization with movement in emphasized, pain-free techniques. The more functional postures of weightbearing are emphasized during these techniques and a sustained natural apophyseal glide (SNAG) is recommended in treating thoracic segmental dysfunctions.[26] In a SNAG, the technique is sustained and combined with active or passive movements and overpressure is applied at the end of the range.[26]

Muscle energy is a manual technique involving voluntary muscle contraction by the patient in a controlled direction against a distinct counterforce applied by the athletic trainer.[12] *Muscle energy techniques* involve two types of dysfunctions: group dysfunctions that involve three or more motion segments, and single segmental dysfunctions that involve only one vertebral motion segment.[12] The term used for a dysfunction with the muscle energy technique is "positional fault." The key elements of muscle energy techniques are accurate diagnosis of the restriction, accurate localization, appropriate patient effort and counterforce by the athletic trainer, repositioning and localization into the barrier or pathologic area, and two or three repetitions of each movement.[12]

In addition to restoring normal joint range of motion, the athletic trainer must also stretch tight associated soft-tissue structures and recondition the total patient. The first aim of reconditioning is to restore normal general body reconditioning, balance, and coordination; task-specific activity reconditioning comes later.[24]

Hypermobility

Hypermobility is defined as an increase in normal motion. Treatment of a hypermobile joint is not to manipulate it, but to stabilize it. The athletic trainer must be aware that a hypermobile joint can still be stable. One common cause of hypermobility in one segment is compensation for an adjacent hypomobile segment. For example, when a fusion occurs, the segments above and below the fused segment compensate for its lack of motion by becoming hypermobile. Other causes of hypermobility include an individual's genetic make-up and response to repeated stress.[23] Treatment includes postural education and correction, stabilization exercises, and correction of any associated hypomobile segments of adjacent joints. Manipulation can assist to decrease pain and muscle guarding, but it should not be directed toward the end ranges of joint motion.

Instability

Instability is defined as looseness, unsteadiness, or an inability to withstand normal physiologic loading without mechanical deformation. Some clinical signs of instability include the following: history or demonstration of tissue relaxation or creep; inability to maintain a single position for long periods of time; pain that worsens with normal use and is relieved by movement or rest; inappropriate increase in muscle tone with altered positions; palpable evidence of joint subluxation, particularly with changing of positions; and shaking (jittering) with movement. Treating instability may involve bracing or the use of an orthosis to allow healing as therapy is taking place. Rehabilitation includes body mechanics, postural education and correction, and stabilization exercises.

Stabilization

"Stabilization" is a common term used in rehabilitation today. Stabilization is either "static" or "dynamic."[31] *Static stabilization* involves preparing the body for a task, such as lifting a heavy object.[23] *Dynamic stabilization* involves muscle strength and, more importantly, muscle coordination during performance of activities.[23] Both types of stabilization should be incorporated into the rehabilitation of a patient with hypermobility or instability. The stabilization program should address the back extensors, deep rotators, stabilizers close to the spine, and scapular stabilizers through endurance-strengthening exercises and functional closed-chain exercises.

CHAPTER REVIEW

Chest injuries can be open or closed and can result from many types of trauma, including motor vehicle accidents, gunshot and stab wounds, and compressive and concussive forces. These injuries are likely to injure the heart or lungs and can be fatal unless properly recognized and promptly treated. Flail chest, sternal fractures, chest wall contusions and hematomas, and rib fractures can occur from a traumatic event. Conditions that can result from these injuries include sucking chest wounds, pneumothorax, spontaneous tension pneumothorax, hemothorax, hemopneumothorax, subcutaneous emphysema, pericardial tamponade, dyspnea, pulmonary and myocardial contusions. The athletic trainer should recognize the potential seriousness of these conditions and ensure rapid transport to a hospital.

The thoracic spine is well protected by the rib cage and its associated articulations. However, although thoracic spine pain syndromes and injuries are less frequent than those affecting the cervical and lumbar spine, they may be more serious. A clear understanding of the anatomy and biomechanics of the thoracic spine and rib cage is necessary, including the posterior elements, the costovertebral joints, and the sternum. The assessment and classification of rib cage dysfunction are important in appreciating how such conditions are treated. Treatment of rib dysfunctions follows treatment of thoracic spine dysfunctions and precedes treatment of respiratory rib dysfunctions. Joint mobilization and muscle energy are useful manual treatment techniques.

Thoracic spine fractures usually result from high-velocity sports and are generally compression fractures with or without associated soft-tissue disruption. The decision to proceed conservatively or surgically depends on the athlete's neurologic status, the fracture morphology and classification, sagittal plane deformity, and associated injuries. Nonsurgical treatment comprises postural reduction, limited bed rest, bracing, and early mobilization.

Thoracic disk herniation is rare. Its natural history is slowly progressive, and sensory, motor, gait, and sphincter dysfunction may occur. Symptoms may stabilize over time. Surgical management is, therefore, definitely indicated only for those with signs of spinal cord compression. Conservative treatment consists of rest, nonsteroidal anti-inflammatory drugs, and controlled therapy.

Segmental or facet dysfunction describes disturbed, impaired, or abnormal function and is classified as hypomobile, hypermobile, or unstable. Hypomobility is treated with manipulation, hypermobility with stabilization, and instability with bracing or an orthosis, body mechanics, postural education and correction, and stabilization exercises.

1. The presence of air within the chest cavity but outside the lung is called:
   A. dyspnea.
   B. pneumothorax.
   C. pulmonary contusion.
   D. subcutaneous emphysema.

2. Which of the following statements about a flail chest injury is true?
   A. A flail chest injury is difficult to diagnose without surgery.
   B. A flail chest injury is often pain-free and the athlete may not be aware of it.
   C. A flail segment collapses during inhalation and protrudes during exhalation.
   D. A flail segment protrudes during inhalation and collapses during exhalation.

3. The muscles that function as trunk extensors, lateral flexors, and rotators to the opposite side are the:
   A. splenius, capitis, and cervicis.
   B. semispinalis, multifidus, and rotators.
   C. trapezius, latissimus dorsi, and rhomboids.
   D. sacrospinalis, iliocostalis, longissimus, and spinalis.

4. A biomechanical function of the rib cage related to the thoracic spine is to:
   A. protect the spine.
   B. increase the mobility of the spine.
   C. allow displacement during trauma.
   D. decrease the transverse dimension of the thoracic spine.

5. In resisting anterior shear loads, the facet joint carries about _____ of the load, while the disk carries _____.
   A. One quarter, three quarters
   B. Three quarters, one quarter
   C. One third, two thirds
   D. Two thirds, one third

6. With which of the following structural rib dysfunctions is intercostal neuralgia often noted?
   A. Rib torsion
   B. Rib subluxation
   C. Rib compression
   D. Laterally flexed rib

7. If spinal cord pathology is suspected, what is the best method for imaging this area?
   A. CT scan
   B. MRI scan
   C. Ultrasound
   D. Plain radiographs

8. How many weeks of bed rest are indicated during initial nonsurgical treatment of a stable thoracic spine fracture?
   A. 1 to 2
   B. 2 to 4
   C. 4 to 6
   D. 6 to 8

9. An athlete with a thoracic disk herniation may have pain in which of the following areas?
   A. Anterior chest
   B. Retroperitoneal area
   C. Upper extremity
   D. Lower extremity

10. With which of the following methods can lack of motion in a facet joint be effectively treated?
    A. Bracing
    B. Stabilization
    C. Manipulation
    D. Postural correction

Answers on page 892

References

1. Pate J: Chest wall injuries. *Surg Clin North Am* 1989;69:59-70.

2. Prentice D, Ahrens T: Pulmonary complications of trauma. *Crit Care Nurs Q* 1994;17:24-33.

3. Mayberry JC, Trunkey DD: The fractured rib in chest wall trauma. *Surg Clin N Am* 1997;7:239-261.

4. Oda I, Abumi K, Lu D, Shono Y, Kaneda K: Biomechanical role of the posterior elements, costovertebral joints, and rib cage in the stability of the thoracic spine. *Spine* 1996; 21:1423-1429.

5. Berg EE: The sternal-rib complex: A possible fourth column in thoracic spine fractures. *Spine* 1993;18:1916-1919.

6. Jackimczyk K: Blunt chest trauma. *Emerg Med Clin North Am* 1993;11:81-93.

7. Brandser EA, el-Khoury GY: Thoracic and lumbar spine trauma. *Radiol Clin North Am* 1997;35:533-557.

8. Hills MW, Delprado AM, Deane SA: Sternal fractures: Associated injuries and management. *J Trauma* 1993; 35:55-60.

9. White A, Panjabi M: *Clinical Biomechanics of the Spine*, ed 2. Philadelphia, PA, JB Lippincott, 1990.

10. Irwin, S, Tecklin, JS: *Cardiopulmonary Physical Therapy*, ed 2. St. Louis, MO, CV Mosby, 1990.

11. Wood KB, Garvey TA, Gundry C, Heithoff KB: Magnetic resonance imaging of the thoracic spine: Evaluation of asymptomatic individuals. *J Bone Joint Surg* 1995;77A:1631-1638.

12. Greenman PE: *Principles of Manual Medicine*. Baltimore, MD, Williams & Wilkins, 1989.

13. Ebraheim NA, Jabaly G, Xu R, Yeasting RA: Anatomic relations of the thoracic pedicle to the adjacent neural structures. *Spine* 1997;22:1553-1557.

14. Mitchell F: An Evaluation and Treatment Manual of Osteopathic Muscle Energy Procedures. 1979.

15. Gertzbein SD: Spine update: Classification of thoracic and lumbar fractures. *Spine* 1994;19:626-628.

16. Hodge B: Common spinal injuries in athletes. *Nursing Clin North Am* 1991;26:211-221.

17. Hartman MB, Chrin AM, Rechtine GR: Non-operative treatment of thoracolumbar fractures. *Paraplegia* 1995;33:73-76.

18. Cantor JB, Lebwohl NH, Garvey T, Eismont FJ: Non-operative management of stable thoracolumbar burst fractures with early ambulation and bracing. *Spine* 1993;18:971-976.

19. Benli IT, Tandogan NR: Cotrel-Dubousset instrumentation in the treatment of unstable thoracic and lumbar spine fractures. *Arch Orthop Trauma Surg* 1994;113:86-92.

20. Brown CW, Deffer PA, Akmakjian J, Donaldson DH, Brugman JL: The natural history of thoracic disc herniation. *Spine* 1992;17(suppl):S97-S102.

21. Simpson JM, Silveri CP, Simeone FA, Balderston RA, An HS: Thoracic disc herniation: Re-evaluation of the posterior approach using a modified costotransversectomy. *Spine* 1993;18:1872-1877.

22. Currier BL, Eismont FJ, Green BA: Transthoracic disc excision and fusion for herniated thoracic discs. *Spine* 1994;19:323-328.

23. Paris SV, Loubert PV: *Foundations of Clinical Orthopaedics*. St. Augustine, FL, Institute Press, 1990, pp 99, 131-135, 294-303.

24. Prokop LL, Wieting JM: The use of manipulation in sports medicine practice. *Phys Med and Rehab Clin of North Am* 1996;7:915-932.

25. Paris SV: Spinal manipulative therapy. *Clin Orthop* 1983;101:55-61.

26. Mulligan BR: *Manual Therapy* "NAGS,""SNAGS," "MWMS" etc. ed 3. Wellington, New Zealand, Hutcheson Bowman & Stewart, 1995, pp 58-61.

14

Lumbar Spine Injuries

Clayton F. Holmes, EdD, PT, ATC

QUICK CONTENTS

- The anatomy of the lumbar spine.

- The biomechanics of the lumbar spine.

- The athlete with a lumbar spine condition.

- Symptom patterns that influence the treatment of a lumbar spine injury.

- The evaluation and treatment of facet joint dysfunction, degenerative disk disease, and spondylolysis and spondylolisthesis.

- The anatomy, biomechanics, and evaluation and treatment of sacroiliac and pelvic dysfunction.

cates segmental hypomobility. Facet dysfunction is often painful during active extension. In addition, motions may cause radiating symptoms either into the buttock or leg.

Next, passive range of motion, often called passive intervertebral motion (PIVM), should be assessed using a posteroanterior (PA) glide over the spinous process the *spring test*. The test is performed with the athlete prone. The clinician gently presses the spinous process in a posteroanterior fashion with the pisiform of his or her hand. A skilled evaluator will be able to confirm hypomobility or hypermobility at a segment. The segment in question is compared with the segment above and below to distinguish dysfunction.

Passive range of motion can also be evaluated with the athlete lying on his or her side. The examiner should hold the top leg and place his or her hand in between the two spinous processes to be evaluated. Next, the examiner flexes the patient's leg at the hip until motion at the segment is noted. This motion is compared with the segment above and below for hypomobility or hypermobility. In the absence of other clinical data, these evaluation measures are not reliable.[25, 26] However, when coupled with patient feedback such as a report of pain as each segment is tested in turn, reliability increases significantly. These tests are sometimes considered to be more valuable in simply determining pathology in a specific segment.[26]

Perhaps the two most common special tests used to determine lumbar spine dysfunction are the straight-leg raise and the quadrant tests. The *straight-leg raise* may be the most traditional lumbar spine evaluation technique (Figure 14-9). The patient is supine, and the clinician passively brings the whole leg into hip flexion with the knee extended. A positive test result is indicated by radiating pain down the leg. Radiating sensory symptoms do not necessarily indicate nerve root compression from disk protrusion.[27] However, sensory symptoms, particularly when present above the knee, may indicate SI or facet dysfunction.

The *quadrant test* is used frequently to reproduce symptomatic pain. The athlete stands and extends and rotates to one side. This motion closes the facet on the side toward which the patient is rotating. Next, the patient repeats the motion to the opposite side, closing the corresponding facet. Finally, the patient rotates and bends to one side in flexion, maximally opening the facet opposite the motion, and then rotates and bends to the other side. This test is performed in all quadrants, and the patient's pain responses in each are compared (**Figure 14-10**).

EVALUATION AND TREATMENT BASED ON MOBILITY

In the past, treatment of the lumbar spine depended on which school of thought the clinician subscribed to—

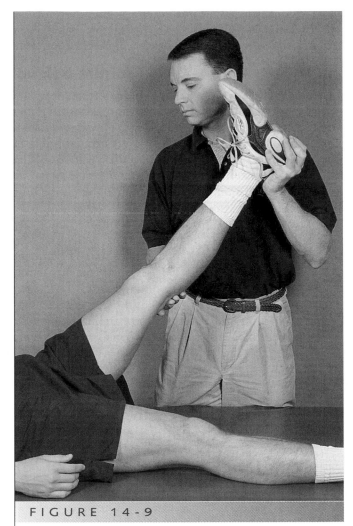

FIGURE 14-9

The straight raise may be the most traditional lumbar spine technique.

whether the facet or disk was the primary site of pathology. Now, however, if the clinician believes that segmental dysfunction can occur in either structure or both at the same time, he or she may simply focus on identifying hypomobile or hypermobile segments and treat such dysfunctions accordingly. This general guideline should be followed unless more frank symptoms such as motor involvement or weakness appear.

In addition, symptom patterns should influence the choice of technique in treatment. For example, traction is usually indicated if symptoms are central and bilateral. However, techniques that involve rotation or unilateral posteroanterior or transverse glides are indicated if symptoms are unilateral.

Athletes may have one or more hypomobile segments and one or more hypermobile segments concurrently, and the correct identification of these segments is essential. Modalities such as heat, cold, transcutaneous electrical nerve stimulation, and diathermy may be an

chapter is on grades 1 through 4. The mobilization grade is selected based on the desired amount and range of passive motion to be gained at the segment.

The *central PA glide* is commonly performed in the treatment of facet hypomobility. This technique is simply the spring test performed with grades of mobilization.

The *unilateral PA glide* may help to introduce rotation in a hypomobile segment. Pressure is applied over the opposite facet, typically one thumb-width lateral to the spinous process. This pressure is applied in a posteroanterior fashion using grades 1 and 2 for the more acute patient and 3 and 4 for the patient with less pain. The clinician uses the pisiform to apply pressure (**Figure 14-11**).

The *transverse glide* is applied with the thumbs over the spinous process to introduce rotation to the segment in question (**Figure 14-12**). This mobilization may also be applied using grades 1 through 4. The lower grades are used for the more acute dysfunctions.

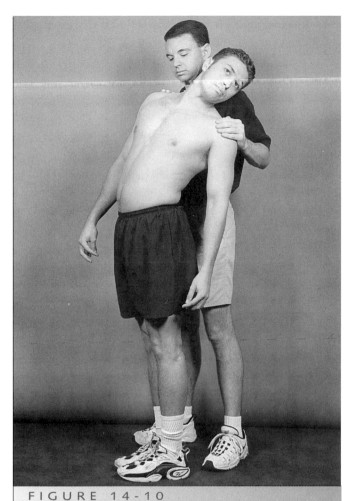

FIGURE 14-10

The quadrant test is performed in all four quadrants, and pain responses in each quadrant are compared.

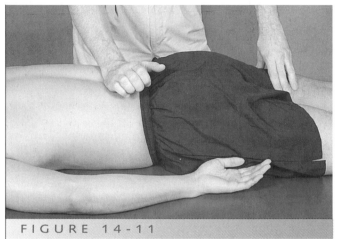

FIGURE 14-11

The pisiform is used to apply pressure in the unilateral PA glide.

important part of the clinical management of dysfunctional spinal segments; however, such passive forms of treatment are no substitute for manual treatment or active exercise when symptoms permit. Manual intervention is an effective treatment modality for lumbar spine pathology.[28,29] The primary goal of these techniques is restoration of full spinal function. On the other hand, specifically designed exercise regimens promote segmental stabilization by selectively strengthening the muscles that surround the facet joints. These exercise programs may be used effectively to treat hypermobile segments.

General Mobilization Principles

Manual interventions aim at the facilitation of normal joint motion and should be used to treat the hypomobile segment. Mobilizations are typically graded and are commonly separated into grades 1 through 4.[30] There is a fifth grade that represents a high-velocity thrust, commonly called a manipulation. The focus of treatment in this

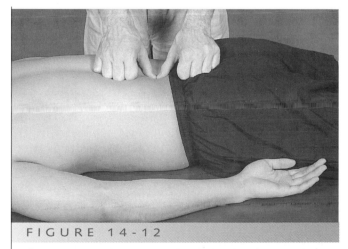

FIGURE 14-12

The transverse glide is applied with the thumbs over the spinous process.

General Stabilization Principles

Exercise programs designed to strengthen stabilizing muscles are crucial to the proper treatment of hypermobile spinal segments. These programs should also be considered a part of proper follow-up care once hypomobile segments have been effectively mobilized and possess range of motion within normal limits. Strengthening must target those muscles that provide the greatest support to the spine if stabilization is to be effective. The rotatores, multifidus, and oblique muscles of the trunk are the primary stabilizers of the spine[11] (see Figure 14-5). Intra-abdominal pressure, which increases with increased tension of the rectus abdominis, is a secondary stabilizer at best. In addition, an increase in intra-abdominal pressure is associated with increases in blood pressure; therefore, it is not always advisable (ie, increasing strength in the abdominal muscles does not necessarily increase intra-abdominal pressure by heavy lifting). Although abdominal muscle strength is important in the stabilization of the lumbar spine, it does not provide the primary means of stabilization. In fact, multiple repetitions of crunch-type sit-ups may actually cause hypermobility of the lumbar spine. Stabilization exercises are performed by superimposing motion over a neutral spine (the normal lordosis position). The athlete should not experience pain in this position, which may be attained using an inflated exercise ball with the athlete sitting or supine in a bridge position.

Once the athlete has found a neutral spine position, he or she should maintain this position while moving the arms and legs. This is an extremely difficult maneuver for the athlete to achieve during the early stages of a stabilization program; however, with minimal training, the athlete can generally maintain neutral spine while in motion. Once this skill has been mastered, the stabilization program is relatively simple. The athlete begins by superimposing easy movements over the neutral spine and progresses in sequence to more difficult maneuvers. **Table 14-1** lists the basic principles of lumbar stabilization, and **Table 14-2** shows a typical exercise regimen for stabilization of a hypermobile segment.

SPECIFIC PATHOLOGIES

Facet Dysfunction (Impingement)

As mentioned earlier, the type of dysfunction that occurs determines whether a facet becomes hypomobile or hypermobile. The athlete who has a "locked" segment quite possibly has a hypomobile facet. The mechanism of injury for this dysfunction can be backward bending, side bending, and/or rotation. A locked facet is more painful typically at rest and becomes less painful with movement. Pain and the restriction of normal range of motion may be quite significant in the acute stages.[14] In addition, the athlete may be able to point to the exact spot of the facet pain, usually about a thumb-width lateral to the spinous processes. Although decreased motor function and radiating sensory pain are not normally considered facet symptoms, some researchers do implicate the facet in radiculopathy. These researchers assert that radiating sensory symptoms that occur during a straight-leg raise test do not necessarily indicate that intervertebral disk material is pressing on a nerve root. In fact, they claim that motor involvement in the extremity is necessary to implicate the nerve root.[27]

Lumbar Disk Disease

Fortunately, injury or degeneration of the lumbar intervertebral disk is only one of the possible explanations of why low back pain and sciatica occur.[31] However, because sport activities involve extremely high forces, disk derangement does occur from time to time.[32] Although the etiology is not completely known, some researchers believe that any activity that affects inherent stability of a segment can affect the disk. Possible results of such instability include development of facet synovitis, breakdown of the annulus, and migration of nuclear material beyond the confines of the disk and surrounding ligaments. These developments may lead to a mechanical or chemical irritation of the nerve roots or spinal cord.[31]

Clinical findings have not always been an accurate means of diagnosing disk disease. However, the traditionally accepted sign of this dysfunction has been radiating sensory and/or motor symptoms that usually extend below the knee. Such symptoms could include paresthesia down the back of the leg and possibly into the foot. In addition, motor findings can include weakness in foot dorsiflexion and great toe extension and flexion, which may occur because the myotomes are innervated by nerves that exit

---

TABLE 14-1
BASIC PRINCIPLES OF LUMBAR STABILIZATION

1. Identify full excursion of lumbo-pelvic motion.

2. Determine and maintain functional position.

3. Practice mass body movement.

4. Superimpose extremity motion.

5. Maintain stabilization during complex activities.

(Adapted with permission from Morgan D: Concepts in Functional Training and Postural Stabilization. *Top Acute Care Trauma Rehabil* 1988;2:8-17.)

the intervertebral foramen at the level of L4 to L5 and L5 to S1. These levels are most commonly affected by lumbar disk disease. The significance of this symptom as a diagnostic tool has diminished in importance in recent years. In fact, results of recent studies have suggested that individuals who are asymptomatic can have disk changes that may be identified with medical imaging.[31] Bearing this in mind, the presence of sciatica in an athlete does not necessarily indicate lumbar disk disease.[31]

Although it is theoretically possible that abnormal findings during passive intervertebral motion testing could indicate disk changes, medical imaging, such as MRI scans, remains the only certain way of diagnosing lumbar disk disease. Even after diagnosis is certain, traditional conservative rehabilitation measures may be all that is needed as treatment.[31,33]

FOCUS ON . . .

Specific Pathologies

Specific pathologies include facet dysfunction, lumbar disk disease, and spondylolysis and spondylolisthesis.

Facet Dysfunction

Facet dysfunction, or impingement, can result from backward bending, side bending, and/or rotation. Facet dysfunction restricts range of motion and causes pain that may worsen with rest and improve with movement. Treatment includes mobilization or manual or mechanical traction (preceded by heat or massage), passive rotation of the hypomobile segment, and rocking the supine athlete's knees from side to side.

Lumbar Disk Disease

Lumbar disk disease, or disk derangement, can result from injury or degeneration and typically causes radiating sensory and/or motor symptoms extending below the knee. Degenerative disk disease is typically treated with the McKenzie regimen, which attempts to indirectly move the nucleus of a herniated disk centrally, reducing the symptomatic bulge and the radiating lower extremity symptoms (although lumbar spine pain may increase). Spinal stabilization is instituted once the radiating symptoms have lessened.

Spondylolysis and Spondylolisthesis

Spondylolysis (a defect in the pars interarticularis) and spondylolisthesis (forward slippage of one vertebral body on the next) can be caused by the continuous hyperextension required in certain sports and typically produce nonspecific low back pain. Treatment consists of stabilization exercises not extending beyond the neutral position. If slippage has occurred, all aggravating sporting activities must be stopped.

Spondylolysis and Spondylolisthesis

Spondylolysis refers to a defect (possibly a type of stress fracture) in the pars interarticularis of the vertebrae. *Spondylolisthesis* is a more serious condition in which the pars defect has caused forward slippage of one vertebral body onto the next. A significant slippage can narrow the spinal canal and increase the likelihood of spinal cord damage.[34,35] These two conditions can occur at any lumbar level, but defects and possible impingement as a result of slippage are most common at the L4 and L5 levels.[34] Although the exact cause of these conditions is unknown, some individuals believe that a stress fracture may result, at least in part, from continuous hyperextension common in sports such as gymnastics, weight lifting, football, and hockey.[3,34]

The clinical evaluation of athletes with these conditions is often unremarkable. Nonspecific low back pain is often the major complaint. The pars defect itself has been implicated in production of pain.[3] Passive intervertebral motion findings should indicate a significant hypermobility at the segment in question. Imaging studies such as bone scans may be indicated.[34]

TREATMENT OF SPECIFIC PATHOLOGIES

Facet Dysfunction

A specific diagnosis of facet impingement implies that the segment in question is hypomobile. The pathology is generally treated with mobilization and manual or mechanical traction. Heat or massage may help prepare soft tissue for mechanical treatment. In addition, passive rotation of the specific segment may provide some relief (**Figure 14-13**). Finally, as with most lumbar spine pathology, the pelvic rock exercise, in which an experienced clinician rocks the athlete's knees side to side while he or she is supine, may help alleviate pain (**Figure 14-14**).

Degenerative Disk Disease

Medical intervention for a specific diagnosis of Herniated nucleus pulposus (HNP) has ranged from complete bed rest to surgery.[34] During rehabilitation, the patient's pathology is typically treated with the McKenzie regimen.[15] Three McKenzie positions can be used depending on the stage of the treated condition[15] (**Practice Session 14-1**). In one position, a patient with an acute condition may simply lie prone, which allows normal lumbar lordosis and some degree of spinal extension. In the second position, the athlete remains prone but lifts the chest and extends the back by rising up on the elbows with the elbows flexed and forearms resting. In the third position, the athlete extends the back further by fully extending the elbows. These positions are to be held for no longer than 15 to 20 seconds. These exercises indirectly move the

TABLE 14-2
TYPICAL EXERCISE REGIMEN TO STABILIZE A HYPERMOBILE SEGMENT

The athlete advances to higher levels if he or she can complete a predetermined number of repetitions in lower levels without difficulty.

Supine Progression
Start position: The athlete is supine with knees bent and feet flat on support surface. The athlete finds and maintains a functional spine position throughout the exercise.

Levels	Action
1	Contract abdominal muscles—hold and release
2	Contract gluteal muscles—hold and release
3	Co-contract gluteal and abdominal muscles—hold and release
4	Co-contract muscles, alternate sides: raise and lower heels
5	Co-contract muscles, alternate sides: raise and lower toes
6	Co-contract muscles, lift both legs off surface and alternately extend knees
7	Co-contract muscles, lift both arms together over head and back down
8	Co-contract muscles, alternate sides: lift arms up over head and back down
9	Co-contract muscles, lift both legs together, combine arm motions from Level 8 with alternating knee extension

Prone Progression
Start position: The athlete is prone with a pillow placed for support under the pelvis and abdomen and arms resting overhead. The athlete finds and maintains a neutral spine position throughout the exercise.

Levels	Action
1	Contract abdominal muscles—hold and release
2	Contract gluteal muscles—hold and release
3	Co-contract abdominal and gluteal muscles—hold and release
4	Co-contract abdominal and gluteal muscles, contract adductors—hold and release
5	Co-contract abdominal and gluteal muscles, first contract adductors and then hip extensors to alternately raise legs
6	Co-contract abdominal and gluteal muscles, first contract adductors and then bilateral hip extensors to raise both legs at once
7	Co-contract abdominal and gluteal muscles, alternate sides: lift one arm up over head and lower, then the other arm
8	Co-contract abdominal and gluteal muscles, combine levels 5 and 7—the arm and leg on opposite sides are raised and lowered together (raise left arm and right leg and lower, then raise right arm and left leg and lower)

(Continued)

TABLE 14-2 (CONTINUED)
TYPICAL EXERCISE REGIMEN TO STABILIZE A HYPERMOBILE SEGMENT

Quadruped Progression
Start position: The athlete is on hands and knees and finds and maintains a neutral spine position throughout the exercise.

Levels	Action
1	Contract abdominal muscles—hold and release
2	Contract gluteal muscles—hold and release
3	Co-contract gluteal and abdominal muscles—hold and release
4	Co-contract abdominal and gluteal muscles, shift weight anterior and posterior
5	Co-contract abdominal and gluteal muscles, alternate sides: straighten and extend one leg and return to start position, then the other
6	Co-contract abdominal and gluteal muscles, alternate sides: straighten and extend one arm in front, then the other
7	Co-contract abdominal and gluteal muscles, alternate sides: extend and straighten opposite arm and leg simultaneously

Bridging Progression
Start position: The athlete is supine with knees bent and feet flat on support surface. The athlete lifts the pelvis off the surface (the abdomen and pelvis should form a "flat" surface) and finds and maintains a neutral spine position throughout the exercise.

Levels	Action
1	Contract abdominal muscles—hold and release
2	Contract gluteal muscles—hold and release
3	Co-contract abdominal and gluteal muscles—hold and release
4	Co-contract abdominal and gluteal muscles, alternate sides: lift heels off surface and lower
5	Co-contract abdominal and gluteal muscles, alternate sides: lift toes off surface and lower
6	Co-contract abdominal and gluteal muscles, alternate sides: lift foot off surface and lower
7	Co-contract abdominal and gluteal muscles, alternate sides: extend knee, lower leg to surface, slide heel back to start position
8	Same as for Level 7, but without letting the leg touch the floor

Standing Progression
Start position: The athlete stands with the feet shoulder width apart and finds and maintains a neutral spine position thoughout the exercise.

Levels	Action
1	Contract abdominals—hold and release
2	Contract gluteals—hold and release
3	Co-contract abdominal and gluteal muscles—hold and release
4	Maintain co-contraction in walking
5	Maintain co-contraction while performing semi-squats (not more than 30° to 40° of hip flexion)

Note: When alternating sides, the athlete performs the action first on one side and then on the other. Adapted from the Dynamic Lumbar Stabilization Program, The San Francisco Spine Institute, 1989.

Treatment of Specific Pathologies

Facet Dysfunction

Treatment of facet dysfunction includes mobilization or manual or mechanical traction (preceded by heat or massage), passive rotation of the hypomobile segment, and rocking the supine athlete's knees from side to side.

Degenerative Disk Disease

Degenerative disk disease is typically treated with the McKenzie regimen, which attempts to push the nucleus of a herniated disk centrally, reducing the symptomatic bulge and the radiating lower extremity symptoms (although lumbar spine pain may increase). Spinal stabilization is instituted once the radiating symptoms have lessened.

Spondylolysis and Spondylolisthesis

Spondylolysis and spondylolisthesis are treated with stabilization exercises not extending beyond the neutral position. If slippage has occurred, all aggravating sporting activities must be stopped.

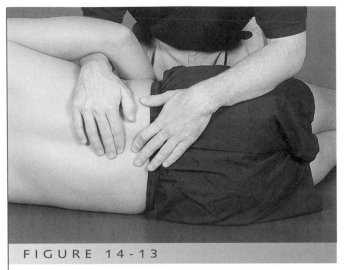

FIGURE 14-13

Passive rotation of the specific dysfunctional facet may provide some relief.

nucleus of a herniated disk centrally, reducing the symptomatic bulge. If this effect is achieved, a "centralization phenomena" should be seen in which the symptoms radiating down the lower extremity should decrease while the pain in the lumbar spine region may actually intensify.[15] Because an unstable pars defect may allow the vertebra to slip and compromise the spinal cord during extension, these exercises are contraindicated in the athlete with spondylolysis or spondylolisthesis.[11]

Once radiating symptoms have decreased, the next step in rehabilitation is spinal stabilization to strengthen the muscles that are intrinsic to the spine.

Spondylolysis and Spondylolisthesis

Medical interventions for dysfunctions involving pars defects can range from orthoses to fusion. Before conservative rehabilitative treatment of these dysfunctions is initiated, the clinician must determine if the athlete has spondylolysis or spondylolisthesis. If slippage has occurred, all sporting activities that aggravate the condition must be stopped. Such instability often occurs in the adolescent athlete; by the time he or she reaches adulthood, the pars defect is usually stable.[3]

Rehabilitation of athletes with spondylolysis or spondylolisthesis should be approached with caution. The McKenzie (or extension) exercises typically ordered for rehabilitation of low back pain are contraindicated in these athletes. Rehabilitation, when appropriate, should

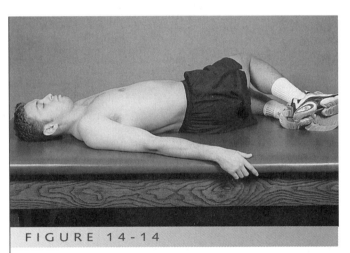

FIGURE 14-14

Rocking the athlete's knees from side to side may help alleviate pain.

consist of a stabilization program that involves no extension beyond the neutral position.

SACROILIAC/PELVIC DYSFUNCTION

Anatomy

Although lumbar spine dysfunction alone may be responsible for low back pain, some pain may result from SI/pelvic dysfunction. To be able to identify different problems and treat each appropriately, the clinician must understand the anatomy of the pelvis and SI joints and the motions that can occur at pelvic joints. The bony anatomy of the pelvis is relatively simple. The pelvis is composed of the sacrum (located centrally and most posterior) and two hemipelvic

McKENZIE POSITIONS

Three McKenzie positions are used during different stages of treatment.

Position 1—The athlete lies prone.

Position 2—The athlete lifts the chest and extends the back.

Position 3— The athlete fully extends the elbows to further extend the back.

orly at the symphysis pubis. In this arrangement, the sacrum and two innominates form a closed kinematic chain (**Figure 14-15**). The sacrum is shaped like a shield with fulci toward the midline of the bottom edge of the shield, referred to as inferior lateral angles (ILA).

Biomechanics

As with the lumbar spine, the biomechanical implications of this kinematic arrangement are significant to pathology. For this reason, normal SI/pelvic motion should be reviewed. If movement of one innominate occurs in one direction, then movement of the contralateral innominate will occur in the opposite direction. Innominate motion typically occurs during normal walking or running. For example, if the left leg moves forward, the left innominate rotates posteriorly and the right innominate rotates anteriorly. Then, as the right leg moves forward, the right innominate rotates posteriorly and the left innominate rotates anteriorly.

The sacrum also possesses a minimal capacity for movement. The two sacral motions are nutation (sacral flexion) and counternutation (sacral extension). Nutation of the sacrum occurs when the lumbar spine extends, increasing

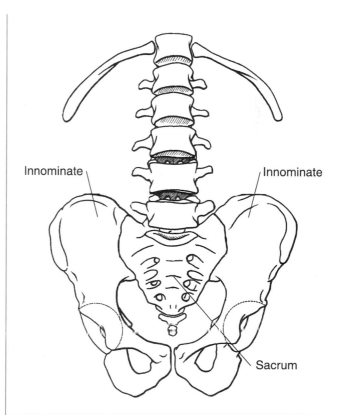

The sacrum and two innominates form a closed kinematic chain. (Reproduced with permission from Kapanji A: *The Physiology of the Joints: Annotated Diagrams of the Mechanics of the Human Joints*, ed 3. New York, NY, Churchill Livingstone, 1974.)

bones (one located on each side of the sacrum). The hemipelvic bones are each composed of the fused ilium, ischium, and pubis. Each *hemipelvis,* or innominate, articulates with the spine at the sacral level via the SI joint. In addition, the innominates articulate with each other anteri-

Sacroiliac/Pelvic Dysfunction

Anatomy

Sacroiliac and pelvic dysfunction can also cause low back pain. The pelvis is composed of the sacrum and two hemipelvic (innominate) bones, each containing the fused ilium, ischium, and pubis. Each innominate articulates with the spine at the sacroiliac joint and with the other innominate anteriorly at the symphysis pubis.

Biomechanics

As one innominate moves, the other innominate moves in the opposite direction. The sacrum nutates (flexes) when the lumbar spine extends and counternutates (extends) when the lumbar spine flexes. Sacral dysfunction can occur if one of the bones becomes hypomobile, causing sacroiliac joint or groin pain.

Evaluation and Treatment

A nutated sacrum has deep sacral sulci and superficial inferior lateral angles. A counternutated sacrum has superficial sulci and deep inferior lateral angles. Treatment for a nutated sacrum is a graded, direct, posteroanterior force on the lower sacrum; treatment for a counternutated sacrum is force on the sacral promontory near the superior aspect.

Hemipelvic asymmetry can be identified by iliac spine or crest asymmetry. Treatment consists of muscle energy techniques that attempt to realign the structure using the patient's own muscle strength.

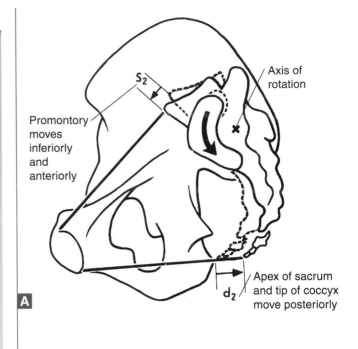

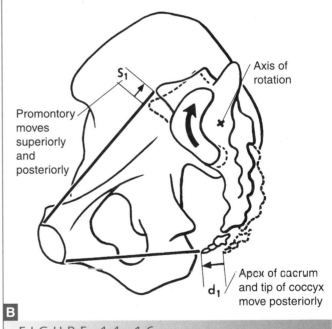

FIGURE 14-16

Nutation and counternutation. **A** Nutation of the sacrum occurs when the lumbar spine extends. **B** Counternutation of the sacrum occurs when the lumbar spine is flexed. (Reproduced with permission from Kapandji A: The Physiology of the Joints: Annotated Diagrams of the Mechanics of the Human Joints, ed 3. New York, NY, Churchill Livingstone, 1974.)

the lordotic curve. Counternutation of the sacrum occurs when the lumbar spine is flexed, decreasing the lordotic curve (**Figure 14-16**). Some researchers believe that the sacrum rotates about an oblique axis, and more advanced treatment "techniques," such as muscle energy techniques, have been developed to address the dysfunctions that may result from sacral rotation.[13]

Sacral dysfunction may occur if the bones become hypomobile or "stuck" to each other during nutation or counternutation. If this happens, pain will occur typically over one of the two SI joints or in the groin region.

Evaluation and Treatment

With a nutated sacrum, the sacral sulci will be relatively deep and the inferior lateral angles (ILAs) will be more superficial. Conversely, with a counternutated sacrum, the sulci will be more superficial and the ILAs will be deeper. These are examined by palpation with the athlete in a prone position.

A nutated sacrum can be distinguished by palpation, which should be performed gently, using the same range of mobilization grades that are used in the treatment of the lumbar spine.

Treatment of a nutated sacrum includes a direct posteroanterior force on the lower sacrum between the two ILAs using graded mobilization to gain a counternutated position (**Figure 14-17**). If the sacrum is counternutated, a similar force should be applied in a graded fashion to the sacral promontory near the superior aspect of the sacrum (**Figure 14-18**). The athlete's stage of dysfunction should be considered.

Using careful observation and palpation, the clinician must also assess hemipelvic alignment. The accurate assessment of hemipelvic rotation depends on the identification of bilateral symmetry or asymmetry of the PSISs, ASISs, and iliac crests.

Treatment of hemipelvic asymmetry generally consists of muscle energy techniques that attempt to realign structures by using the athlete's own muscle strength. For example, a high left PSIS and a low left ASIS might indicate that the left innominate is rotated anteriorly. In this instance, the hip extensors can be used to rotate the innominate posteriorly. A low left PSIS and high left ASIS indicates that the innominate is rotated posteriorly. In this case, the hip flexors would be used to rotate the innominate anteriorly (**Figure 14-19**).

Although the above pathologies represent some of the more common dysfunctions, others may be present. If pain persists despite treatment, a specialist in this area should be consulted.

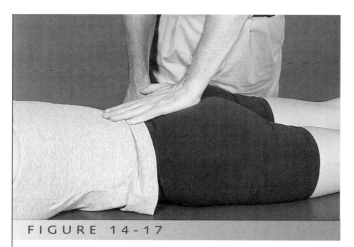

FIGURE 14-17

Treatment of a nutated sacrum includes a PA glide over the inferior sacrum.

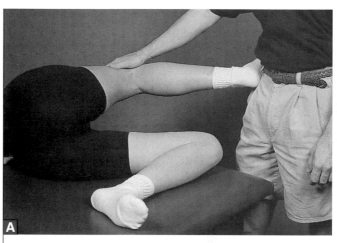

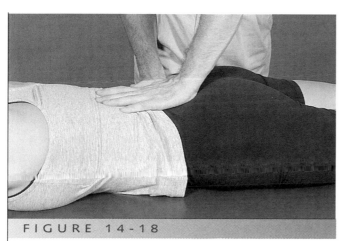

FIGURE 14-18

Treatment of a counternutated sacrum includes a PA glide over the superior sacrum.

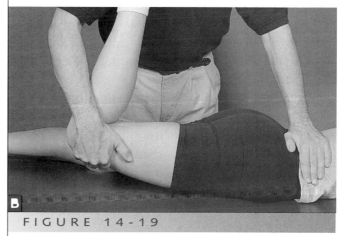

FIGURE 14-19

Treatment of hemipelvic asymmetry. **A** When the innominate is rotated anteriorly, the athlete's hip extensors can be used to rotate the innominate posteriorly. **B** When the innominate is rotated posteriorly, the athlete's hip flexors can be used to rotate the innominate anteriorly.

CHAPTER REVIEW

Low back pain is a symptom affecting many athletes, and, therefore, the clinician must be familiar with the anatomy of the lumbar spine. There are five lumbar vertebrae, separated by intervertebral disks containing the annulus fibrosus and the nucleus pulposus. The four zygapophyseal facets on the posterior arch of each vertebra articulate with the corresponding surfaces of the superior and inferior vertebrae. The descending arrangement of the facets from the frontal to the sagittal plane allows for maximal L4 to L5 and L5 to S1 flexion-extension, but also carries more potential for dysfunction at this level. The spinous and transverse processes serve as attachments for the multifidi and rotatory muscles. The lumbar spine ligaments provide much passive stability, limiting flexion when taut. The muscles extend, laterally flex, and control forward flexion of the lumbar spine, and the deep muscle group provides primary stabilization. The main function of the vertebral column is to house the spinal cord.

Osteokinematic motions of the lumbar spine include flexion, extension, rotation, and lateral flexion. Arthrokinematic motion in this region consists of sliding or gliding of the superior vertebra onto the inferior one. A hypomobile or hypermobile facet or disk disease can cause dysfunction of the entire segment. Rotation and lateral flexion are almost always coupled motions; one does not occur without the other.

Multiple philosophies exist regarding lumbar spine evaluation, but patient history and physical examination (including posture, active and passive range of motion, and special tests) should be included. Treatment is based on mobility: a hypomobile segment should be mobilized and a hypermobile segment stabilized. Graded manual intervention and active exercise of the primary stabilizers are combined to restore full spinal function.

Specific pathologies that can affect the lumbar spine include facet dysfunction, lumbar disk disease and spondylolysis and spondylolisthesis. Facet joint dysfunction can occur when a facet becomes hypomobile from backward or lateral bending or rotation, or a combination of these. Pain, restricted range of motion, and sometimes radiating sensory symptoms may be present. Treatment includes manual (mobilization) techniques, preceded by passive agents designed to enhance the soft-tissue environment. Passive rotation of the affected segment performed by an experienced clinician and exercises such as the pelvic rock may also be helpful.

Lumbar disk disease, or disk derangement, can result from injury or degeneration and result in sensory, motor symptoms, or both extending below the knee. Typical treatment includes the McKenzie extension regimen, which aims to push the herniated disk centrally, reducing the symptomatic bulge and, presumably, the radiating symptoms. Spinal stabilization exercises are also commonly a component of treatment.

Spondylolysis (pars interarticularis defect) and spondylolisthesis (forward slippage of one vertebral body on the next) typically occur at L4 and L5 or L5—S1 and may result from the continuous hyperextension required in certain sports. Nonspecific low back pain is often the major complaint. Treatment is a stabilization program that involves no extension beyond neutral. In this instance, McKenzie extension exercises beyond the neutral position of the spine are contraindicated. If slippage has occurred, all aggravating sporting conditions must be stopped.

Sacroiliac and pelvic dysfunction can also cause low back pain. The bony pelvis consists of the sacrum and the two hemipelvic (innominate) bones; the latter articulate with the spine at the sacroiliac joint and with each other at the symphysis pubis, forming a closed kinematic chain. Sacral movements include nutation and counternutation.

1. Which of the following structures courses within the intervertebral canal posteriorly and connects the laminae of adjacent vertebrae?

   A. Spinalis muscle

   B. Multifidus muscle

   C. Ligamentum flavum

   D. Posterior longitudinal ligament

2. Which of the following is an arthrokinematic motion of the lumbar spine?

   A. Flexion

   B. Gliding

   C. Rotation

   D. Side bending

3. Which of the following is a coupled osteokinematic motion of the lumbar spine?

   A. Flexion

   B. Gliding

   C. Extension

   D. Side bending

4. Which of the following statements about a "locked" facet is true?

   A. It often produces radiating sensory pain.

   B. It may have resulted from forward flexion.

   C. It can cause significantly restricted range of motion.

   D. It is usually more painful with movement than while at rest.

5. Forward slippage of one vertebral body onto the next is called:

   A. spondylolysis.

   B. spondylolisthesis.

   C. facet impingement.

   D. lumbar disk disease.

6. An athlete with an acute herniated nucleus pulposus should be treated with the McKenzie regimen in which position?

   A. Prone

   B. Supine

   C. Sitting

   D. Standing

7. What restrictions are given for an athlete with spondylolisthesis to participate in sports?

   A. No restrictions

   B. Participation as tolerated

   C. Participation after 6 months' rest

   D. No participation

8. What type of movement occurs as an athlete's right leg moves forward?

   A. The right innominate rotates posteriorly, and the left innominate rotates anteriorly.

   B. The right innominate rotates anteriorly, and the left innominate rotates posteriorly.

   C. The left innominate rotates posteriorly, and the right innominate rotates anteriorly.

   D. The left innominate rotates anteriorly, and the right innominate rotates posteriorly.

9. Which of the following movements can the sacrum perform?

   A. Flexion and extension

   B. Extension and rotation

   C. Side bending and flexion

   D. Rotation and side bending

10. A counternutated sacrum should be treated with a:

    A. medial force on the sacrum.

    B. medial force on the sacral promontory.

    C. posteroanterior force on the sacrum.

    D. posteroanterior force on the sacral promontory.

Answers on page 892.

References

1. Harvey J, Tanner S: Low back pain in young athletes: A practical approach. *Sports Med* 1991;12:394-406.

2. Congeni J, McCulloch J, Swanson K: Lumbar spondylolysis: A study of natural progression in athletes. *Am J Sports Med* 1997;25:248-253.

3. Letts M, Smallman T, Afanasiev R, Gouw G: Fracture of the pars interarticularis in adolescent athletes: A clinical-biomechanical analysis. *Pediatr Orthop* 1986;6:40-46.

4. DiFabio RP, Mackey G, Holte JB: Physical therapy outcomes for patients receiving workers' compensation following treatment for herniated lumbar disc and mechanical low back pain syndrome. *Orthop Sports Phys Ther* 1996;23:180-187.

5. Craft RC: *A Textbook of Human Anatomy*, ed 2. New York, NY, John Wiley & sons, 1979.

6. Cailliet R: Biomechanics of the spine. *Phys Med Rehab Clin North Am* 1992;3:1-28.

7. Norkin CC, Levangie PK, Crane LD: Joint Structure and Function: A *Comprehensive Analysis*, ed 2. Philadelphia, PA, FA Davis, 1992.

8. Bogduk N, Twomey LT: *Clinical Anatomy of the Lumbar Spine*, ed 2. London, England, Churchill Livingstone, 1991.

9. Soderberg GL: *Kinesiology: Application to Pathological Motion*, ed 2. Bloomingdale, NY, Williams & Wilkins, 1997.

10. Kapandji IA: *Physiology of the Joints: The Trunk and the Vertebral Column*, ed 2. New York, NY, Churchill Livingstone, 1974, vol 3.

11. Norris C: Spinal stabilization: Stabilization mechanisms of the lumbar spine. *Physiotherapy* 1995;81:72-78.

12. Hertling D, Kessler RM: *Management of Common Musculoskeletal Disorders: Physical Therapy Principles and Methods*, ed 2. St Louis, MO, JB Lippincott, 1990.

13. Greenman PE: *Principles of Manual Medicine*. Baltimore, MD, Williams & Wilkins, 1989.

14. Saunders HD, Saunders R: *Evaluation, Treatment, and Prevention of Musculoskeletal Disorders*, ed 3. Bloomington, MN, Educational Opportunities, 1993.

15. Brown L: Treatment and examination of the spine by combined movements. *Physiotherapy* 1990;70:66-74.

16. Cyriax JH, Cyriax PJ: *Illustrated Manual of Orthopedic Medicine*. London, England, Butterworths, 1983.

17. McKenzie RA: *The Lumbar Spine: Mechanical Diagnosis and Therapy*. Upper Hutt, New Zealand, Spinal Publications Limited, 1981.

18. Maitland GD: *Vertebral Manipulatio*, ed 4. London, England, Butterworths, 1977.

19. Kaltenborn FM: *The Spine, ed 2*. Oslo, Norway, Olaf Norlis, 1993.

20. Grieve GP: *Mobilisation of the Spine: A Primary Handbook of Clinical Method*, ed 5. Edinburgh, Scotland, Churchill Livingstone, 1991.

21. Magee DJ: *Orthopedic Physical Assessment*, ed 2. Philadelphia, PA, WB Saunders, 1992.

22. Mennell JM: *The Musculoskeletal System: Differential Diagnosis From Symptoms and Physical Signs*. Gaithersburg, MD, Aspen Publishers, 1992.

23. Twomey LT, Taylor JR: *Physical Therapy of the Low Back*, ed 2. New York, NY, Churchill Livingstone, 1994.

24. Hoppenfeld S: *Physical Examination of the Spine and Extremities*. New York, NY, Appleton-Century-Crofts, 1976.

25. Brinkley J, Stratford PW, Gill C: Interrater reliability of lumbar accessory motion mobility testing. *Phys Ther* 1995;75:786-762.

26. Maher C, Adams R: Reliability of pain and stiffness assessments in clinical manual lumbar spine examination. *Phys Ther* 1994;74:801-811.

27. Mooney V, Robertson J: The facet syndrome. *Clin Orthop* 1976;115:149-156.

28. DiFabio RP: Efficacy of manual therapy. *Phys Ther* 1992;72:853-864.

29. Koes BW, Bouter LM, Knipschild PG, et al: The effectiveness of manual therapy, physiotherapy, and treatment by the general practitioner for nonspecific back and neck complaints: A randomized clinical trial. *Spine* 1992;17:28-35.

30. Edmond SL: *Manipulation and Mobilization: Extremity and Spinal Techniques*. St Louis, MO, Mosby-Year Book, 1993.

31. Young JL, Press JM, Herring SA: The disc at risk in athletes: Perspectives on operative and nonoperative care. *Med Sci Sports Exerc* 1997;29:S222-S232.

32. Alexander MJ: Biomechanical aspects of lumbar spine injuries in athletes: A review. *Can J Appl Sport Sci* 1985;10:1-20.

33. Wheeler AH: Diagnosis and management of low back pain and sciatica. *Am Fam Physician* 1995;52:1333-1341,1347-1348.

34. Skinner HB: *Diagnosis and Treatment in Orthopedics*. Norwalk, CT, Appleton & Lange, 1995.

35. Schneiderman GA, McLain RF, Hambly MF, Nielsen SL: The pars defect as a pain source: A histologic study. *Spine* 1995;20:1761-1764.

15

Pelvis, Hip, and Thigh Injuries

John D. Campbell, MD
Rob Higgs, MS, ATC
Ken Wright, DA, ATC
Deidre Leaver-Dunn, PhD, ATC

QUICK CONTENTS

- The anatomy and biomechanics of the pelvis, hip, and thigh.

- The pathophysiology and treatment of injuries to the pelvis, hip, and thigh.

- Wrapping the pelvis, hip, and thigh for support.

- Rehabilitating the athlete with a pelvis, hip, or thigh injury.

OVERVIEW

*S*ports injuries to the pelvis, hip, and thigh, although very common, are often frustrating to both the athletic trainer and the athlete. The complexity of the anatomy, physiology, and biomechanics of this region leads to unique and often difficult injuries.

This chapter will cover the anatomy, pathophysiology, treatment, and rehabilitation of injuries to the pelvis, hip, and thigh.

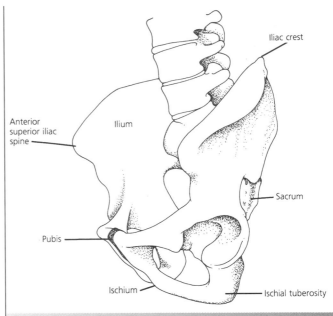

FIGURE 15-1

The pelvis, which comprises several large, flattened bones that form a ring, is a major support structure of the human skeleton.

ANATOMY

The pelvis houses several vital structures. In addition, the pelvic ring transfers forces from the axial skeleton to the lower extremities. The hip and thigh are subject to significant forces that may predispose them to injury. These portions of the body—pelvis, hip, and thigh—challenge the most talented caregiver working to return an athlete to competitive status as soon as possible.

Pelvis

The *pelvis* is composed of several large, flattened bones that form a ring and function as a major support structure of the human skeleton (**Figure 15-1**). The pelvis has adapted to allow upright posture and gait. The ring formed by the pelvis supports the abdominal contents, contains the birth canal in women, and allows the passage of excretory canals. The *sacrum*, which is a flattened fusion of five bones from the spinal column, forms the posterior aspect of the pelvic ring and is the base of the upright spinal column. Attached to the lateral sides of the sacrum are two paired coxal bones (the hip bones) formed by the fusion of the ilium, ischium, and pubis. The two paired coxal bones form a fibrous articulation with the sacrum and curve anteriorly to unite and form an anterior fibrous joint called the *symphysis pubis* or pubic symphysis. The ilium, ischium, and pubis also form the *acetabulum*, the articular side of the femoral head. Distal to the sacrum are three to five fused vertebrae, called the *coccyx*.

Anteriorly and posteriorly, the sacrum and ilium are held together by the ventral sacroiliac, interosseous, and dorsal sacroiliac ligaments. Two other supporting ligaments of the pelvis are the sacrospinous and sacrotuberous ligaments. The sacrospinous ligament originates on both the sacrum and the coccyx and attaches to the ischial spine of the ischium, and the sacrotuberous ligament spans from the sacrum and coccyx to the ischial tuberosity of the ischium. The iliolumbar ligament secures the pelvis (sacrum) to the fifth lumbar vertebra. The *iliac crest*, the most superior and lateral portion of the pelvis, serves as an attachment point for abdominal musculature. Four iliac spines, the anterior superior iliac, anterior inferior iliac, posterior superior iliac, and posterior inferior iliac spine, serve as origins of muscles that function across the hip. Both the sacrum and the ilium have attachment points for paraspinous muscles and for muscles that extend to the thigh. The most inferior prominence of the pelvis is the ischial tuberosity, the point of origin for three of the four hamstring muscles. The pubic tubercle and pubic crest, which are located just lateral to the pubic symphysis, are the most anterior parts of the paired coxal bones. Posteriorly on the pelvis, the greater sciatic notch is a posterior protrusion of the ischium, located between the posterior inferior iliac spine and the ischial spine. The lesser sciatic notch is also positioned on the posterior aspect of the pelvis, between the ischial spine and the ischial tuberosity. The ramus of the ischium and the inferior ramus of the pubis arc to join inferiorly and medially to the acetabulum, forming the obturator foramen and serving as the origin of several muscles that function at the hip.[1-3]

The Femur

The femur, which has an almost perfectly cylindrical cross section, is the largest, longest, and strongest bone in the body (**Figure 15-2**). The femoral head articulates at the pelvis through the acetabulum. From the head, the femur extends lateral to the greater trochanter. The area between the head and the greater trochanter is the femoral neck. Just medial to the greater trochanter is the trochanteric fossa. The lesser trochanter is located on the posteromedial

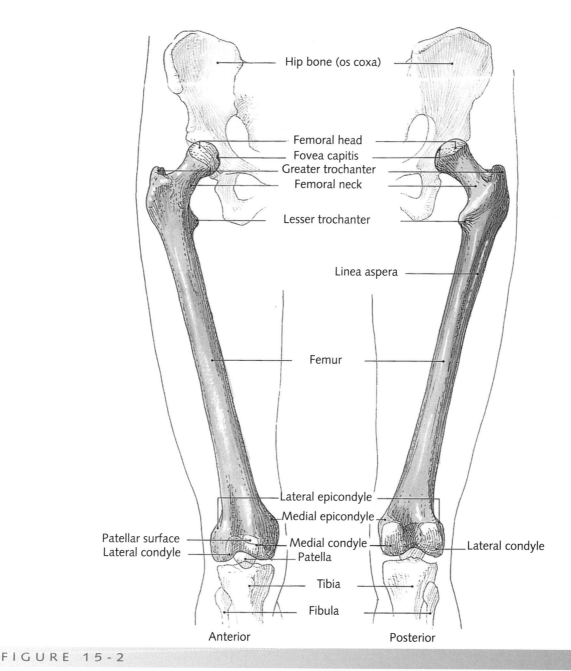

Femoral head
Fovea capitis
Greater trochanter
Femoral neck

Hip bone (os coxa)

Lesser trochanter

Linea aspera

Femur

Lateral epicondyle
Medial epicondyle

Patellar surface
Lateral condyle

Medial condyle
Patella

Lateral condyle

Tibia

Fibula

Anterior

Posterior

FIGURE   15-2

The femur is the largest, longest, and strongest bone in the body. (Reproduced with permission from Carola R, Harley JP, Noback CR (eds): *Human Anatomy and Physiology.* New York, NY, McGraw Hill, 1990, p 194.)

aspect of the femur, inferior to the greater trochanter. Both the greater and lesser trochanters are insertion sites for muscles. The body of the femur extends distally until it expands to become the medial and lateral epicondyles. The medial and lateral condyles, which are the articular surfaces of the femur at the knee, are inferior to the epicondyles. The adductor tubercle is positioned superior to the medial epicondyle. The linea aspera on the posterior aspect of the femoral shaft is a major area for muscular attachment.[1-3]

Articulation of the femur and pelvis

The hip joint is formed by the articulation of the femur with the pelvis. The acetabulum of the pelvis, which is a deep notch that receives the head of the femur, is reinforced by a strong fibrocartilaginous rim, the acetabular labrum. The ligamentum teres is a supporting structure within the hip joint and lies between the femoral head and the acetabulum. A tough fibrous capsule of synovial tissue encases the hip joint and provides vascularity to the femoral head. The strong iliofemoral, pubofemoral, and

FOCUS ON . . .

The Pelvis

The pelvis provides major support for the skeleton and has adapted for upright posture and gait and supports the abdominal contents. The sacrum forms the posterior pelvic ring and provides the upright spinal column's base support. The ilium, ischium, and pubis attach to the lateral aspects of the sacrum and create a fibrous articulation with the sacrum that curves anteriorly to form the symphysis pubis (pubic symphysis).

The coccyx consists of three to five fused vertebrae distal to the sacrum. The sacrum and ilium are held together by the ventral sacroiliac, interosseous, and dorsal sacroiliac ligaments.

The most superior and lateral portion of the pelvis, the iliac crest, is an attachment point for the abdominal muscles. Four iliac spines are the origins of the hip muscles. The sacrum and ilium are attachment points for the paraspinous and thigh muscles. The ischial tuberosity is the most inferior pelvic prominence and the attachment point for three of the four hamstring muscle origins. The ischial ramus and inferior pubic ramus arc to join inferiorly and medially at the acetabulum, forming the obturator foramen and serving as the origin of several hip muscles.

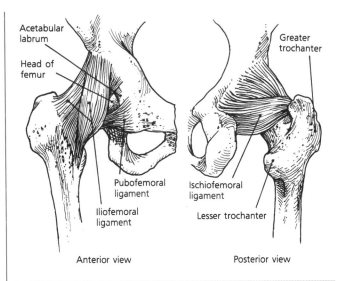

FIGURE 15-3

The three ligaments of the hip joint are the pubofemoral, iliofemoral, and ischiofemoral ligaments.

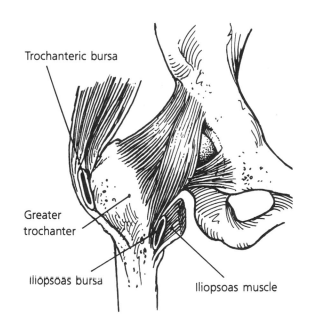

FIGURE 15-4

The trochanteric and iliopsoas bursae are located about the hip.

ischiofemoral ligaments surround the joint and reinforce the capsule. The iliofemoral ligament is often referred to as the "Y" (**Figure 15-3**) ligament, because of the configuration of its fibers in two main branches. Its fibers originate inferior to the anterior inferior iliac spine of the ilium and spiral in a medial direction to insert anteriorly on the femur between the two trochanters. The pubofemoral ligament originates on the anterior rim of the acetabulum and projects to the femur. The ischiofemoral ligament begins on the ischial rim of the acetabulum and proceeds anteriorly to its insertion point at the neck of the femur.[1-3]

Bursae

Numerous bursae, including the trochanteric bursa and the iliopsoas bursa, are located about the hip. The trochanteric bursa is located posterior to the greater trochanter and deep to the gluteus maximus and tensor fascia lata muscles. The iliopsoas bursa is positioned deep in the anterior part of the hip between the iliopsoas muscle and the capsule of the hip joint (**Figure 15-4**).

Musculature

The rectus abdominis, internal and external obliques, and transverse abdominis help support the abdominal contents

within the pelvis. These four muscles flex and rotate the trunk and compress the contents of the abdomen.[1-3] The rectus abdominis inserts on the pubis, while the internal and external obliques and transverse abdominis attach to the aponeurosis of the abdominis and the crest of the pelvis. All four muscles attach to the inguinal ligament via their involvement with the aponeurosis. The inguinal ligament, which runs from the anterior superior iliac spine to the pubic tubercle, forms the lower boundary of the abdomen about the anterior pelvis.

The *erector spinae* are a group of muscles about the posterior pelvis that extend the spinal column. These muscles originate at the sacrum, the lumbar and thoracic vertebrae, and the iliac crest and proceed superiorly to insert at other places on the axial skeleton. The quadratus lumborum, which is also located about the lateral pelvis, runs from the medial portion of the iliac crest to the last rib and along the transverse process of the lumbar vertebrae. The quadratus lumborum laterally flexes the pelvis and trunk. The latissimus dorsi is another muscle that originates on the crest of the ilium.[1-3]

The iliopsoas, located deep within the abdomen and thigh, flexes, externally rotates, and adducts the hip. The iliopsoas is actually two separate muscles, the psoas major and the iliacus, that share one common tendon at their insertion. The psoas major originates on the lumbar vertebrae, and the iliacus originates on the anterior surface of the iliac. The psoas minor, which anteriorly rotates the pelvis, is just anterior to the iliopsoas and originates on the last thoracic and first lumbar vertebrae. The pectineus is responsible for adduction and flexion of the thigh and is sometimes included in the adductor or anterior medial thigh group.[1-3] The pectineus courses from the superior ramus of the pubis to an area on the femur below the lesser trochanter.

The sartorius and quadriceps are the anterior muscles of the thigh. The *sartorius*, which flexes, abducts, and externally rotates the thigh, is the most superficial muscle and runs from the anterior superior iliac spine to the medial surface of the tibia in a lateral to medial course across the anterior thigh (**Figure 15-5**). The *tensor fasciae latae*, which assist in flexion, abduction, and internal rotation at the hip, originate on the iliac crest and insert into the iliotibial band, a strong, long, wide band of connective tissue that inserts on the lateral aspect of the tibia.[1-3]

Four individual muscles form the quadriceps: the rectus femoris, vastus medialis, vastus lateralis, and vastus intermedius. Each muscle has a unique origin; however, all four unite to form a common tendon and insert at the tibial tuberosity via the patella. The rectus femoris, which begins at the anterior inferior iliac spine and is the most anterior muscle, flexes the thigh at the hip and, in

FOCUS ON . . .

Musculature

The rectus abdominis, internal and external obliques, and transverse abdominis muscles support the abdominal contents and attach to the inguinal ligament. These muscles flex and rotate the trunk and compress the abdominal contents. The inguinal ligament runs from the anterior superior iliac spine to the pubic tubercle and, with the anterior pelvis, forms the lower abdominal boundary.

The erector spinae muscles extend the spinal column. The quadratus lumborum laterally flexes the pelvis and trunk. The iliopsoas, located deep within the abdomen and thigh, flexes, externally rotates, and adducts the hip and is actually two muscles: the psoas major and the iliacus. The pectineus adducts and flexes the thigh.

The sartorius, tensor fasciae latae, and quadriceps are the anterior thigh muscles. The sartorius is the most superficial and flexes, abducts, and externally rotates the thigh. The tensor fascia lata assists in hip flexion, abduction, and internal rotation.

The quadriceps muscles in the anterior thigh form a common tendon and insert at the tibial tuberosity via the patella. The rectus femoris originates at the anterior inferior iliac spine; it flexes the thigh at the hip and assists the other quadriceps muscles in extending the knee. The vastus medialis originates on the medial linea aspera, and the vastus lateralis originates on the lateral linea aspera. The vastus intermedius is the deepest of the quadriceps.

The anterior medial thigh muscles (adductor group) include the gracilis, adductor brevis, adductor magnus, adductor longus, and obturator externus, which adduct, flex, and rotate the thigh. Medially, the gracilis is the most superficial muscle. Deep to the gracilis is the adductor longus. The smallest adductor is the adductor brevis, and the largest adductor is the adductor magnus.

Posteriorly, the most superficial buttock muscle is the gluteus maximus, which extends and externally rotates the hip. Deep to this are the gluteus medius and gluteus minimis, which abduct, flex and extend, and internally and externally rotate the thigh, depending on the hip position. External rotators of the thigh from the buttock are the piriformis, obturator internus, superior and inferior gemelli, quadratus femoris, and obturator externus. The piriformis abducts and adducts the thigh. The obturator internus unites with the superior and inferior gemelli and may abduct the flexed thigh. The quadratus femoris adducts the thigh.

The hamstrings, which extend the hip and flex the knee, consist of the semimembranosus, semitendinosus, and biceps femoris.

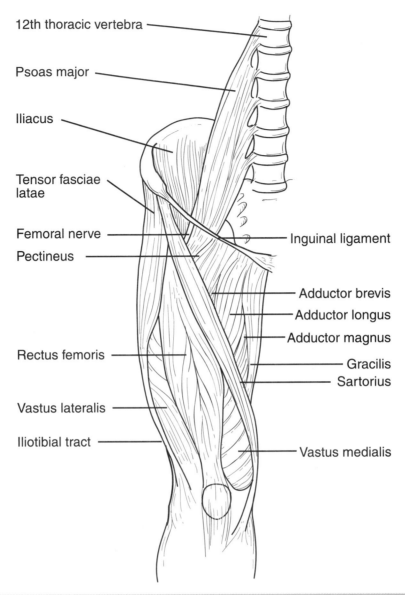

12th thoracic vertebra

Psoas major

Iliacus

Tensor fasciae latae

Femoral nerve

Pectineus

Inguinal ligament

Adductor brevis

Adductor longus

Adductor magnus

Rectus femoris

Gracilis

Sartorius

Vastus lateralis

Iliotibial tract

Vastus medialis

FIGURE 15-5

The anterior muscles of the thigh include, among others, the sartorius, quadriceps, and tensor fasciae latae.

combination with the three other quadriceps, extends the knee. The vastus medialis originates on the medial portion of the linea aspera, and the vastus lateralis originates on the lateral portion of the linea aspera. The vastus intermedius is the deepest of the quadriceps and has its origin in the body of the femur.[2,3]

The anterior medial musculature of the thigh includes the gracilis, adductor brevis, adductor magnus, adductor longus, and obturator externus. These muscles are collectively known as the adductor group and adduct, flex, and rotate the thigh. The gracilis, which is the most superficial muscle, originates on the inferior rami of the pubis and ischium and inserts on the medial anterior surface of the tibia. The adductor longus, which originates at the pubic

tubercle and inserts on the linea aspera, is deep to the gracilis. The adductor brevis, the smallest adductor, originates at the inferior ramus of the pubis and inserts on the femur between the lesser trochanter and a superior portion of the linea aspera. The largest adductor, the adductor magnus, has three separate identifiable origins: the inferior ramus of the pubis, the ramus of the ischium, and the ischial tuberosity. Insertion of this muscle is almost the entire distance of the linea aspera. In addition to adduction, rotation, and flexion, the adductor magnus can also extend the thigh, depending on neural input and the position of the thigh.[2,3]

Posteriorly, the most superficial muscle of the buttock is the gluteus maximus, which originates at the sacrum and inserts at the greater trochanter. The gluteus maximus extends and externally rotates the hip. The gluteus medius and gluteus minimis, which abduct the thigh, are deep to the gluteus maximus. Depending on the position of the hip, these two muscles can produce flexion/extension or internal/external rotation. Both muscles originate on the lateral portion of the ilium and insert on the greater trochanter. The piriformis, obturator internus, superior and inferior gemelli, quadratus femoris, and obturator externus are muscles deep within the buttocks that externally rotate the thigh. The piriformis originates at the sacrum and inserts on the greater trochanter and largely fills the greater sciatic foramen. The piriformis may also abduct or adduct the thigh. The obturator internus is attached to the lesser sciatic foramen, where it unites with the superior and inferior gemelli to insert at the trochanteric fossa. The superior gemellus originates on the ischial spine, and the inferior gemellus originates on the ischial tuberosity. These muscles may also abduct the flexed thigh. The quadratus femoris, which adducts and externally rotates the thigh, originates on the ischial tuberosity and inserts between the lesser and greater trochanters. The obturator externus, often mentioned with the anterior medial musculature, originates on the outer edge of the obturator foramen and extends laterally and posteriorly around the femur, before inserting superiorly at the trochanteric fossa.[1,2]

The *hamstrings* are three muscles (four muscle bodies) in the posterior region of the buttock and thigh that originate at the ischial tuberosity and provide an extension force at the hip and a flexion force at the knee (**Figure 15-6**). These muscles are more appropriately named the semimembranosus, semitendinosus, and biceps femoris (short and long heads). The short head of the biceps femoris originates on the linea aspera, and inserts on the head of the fibula. The semitendinosus shares many fibers with the biceps femoris at the origin, but it inserts through a common tendon on the tibia just medial to the tibial tuberosity. The semimembranosus has a much wider and thicker origin and muscle belly than the semitendinosus, arises from the lateral portion of the ischial tuberosity, and inserts through multiple sites on the medial femoral tibial condyle.[1-3]

Nerve and Blood Supply

The lumbosacral plexus, made up of the lumbar plexus and the sacral plexus, supplies the myotomes and dermatomes about the pelvis, hip, and thigh (**Figure 15-7**). The lumbar plexus, made up of ventral nerve roots from the first four lumbar vertebrae, supplies the anterior and medial aspects of the thigh. The sacral plexus supplies the buttocks and posterior thigh and is made up of parts of the anterior branches from the ventral rami of two lumbar and four sacral nerves. As the sacral plexus descends, it becomes the sciatic nerve, passes through the greater sciatic foramen and runs lateral to the ischial tuberosity

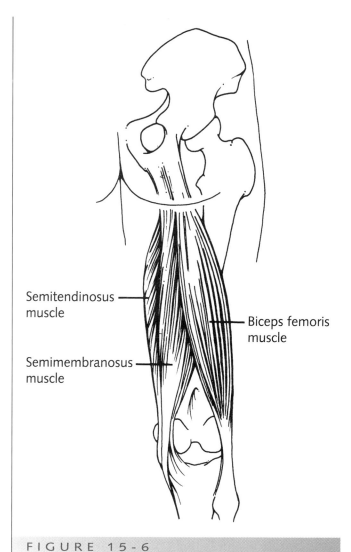

Semitendinosus muscle

Biceps femoris muscle

Semimembranosus muscle

FIGURE 15-6

The hamstrings comprise the semitendinosus, semimembranosus, and biceps femoris muscles.

between the hip joint and the piriformis to innervate the posterior thigh musculature. At the knee, the sciatic nerve divides into the tibial and peroneal nerves. The obturator and femoral nerves supply the adductors and quadriceps respectively and are direct branches of the lumbar plexus.[1,2] The superior and inferior gluteal nerves innervate the gluteal muscles of the buttocks.

Near the superior crest of the pelvis, the abdominal aorta divides into the right and left common iliac arteries, which further divide into external and internal iliac arteries to supply the pelvis and posterior musculature of the hip. At the anterior thigh, the external iliac artery becomes the *femoral artery*. The femoral nerve, artery, and vein course anteriorly to the femoral triangle, which is formed by the inguinal ligament (superior border), the gracilis (medial border), and the sartorius (lateral border). They then branch out and infiltrate individual muscles and areas of skin on the anterior and medial portions of the

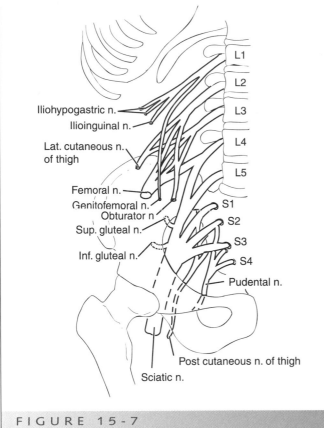

Iliohypogastric n.
Ilioinguinal n.
Lat. cutaneous n. of thigh
Femoral n.
Genitofemoral n.
Obturator n
Sup. gluteal n.
Inf. gluteal n.

L1
L2
L3
L4
L5
S1
S2
S3
S4
Pudendal n.
Post cutaneous n. of thigh
Sciatic n.

FIGURE 15-7

The lumbosacral plexus supplies the pelvis, hip, and thigh's dermatomes and myotomes.

thigh. The femoral artery branches into the profunda femoris; however, just before the profunda femoris, a few small branches come off the femoral artery and supply the lower part of the abdomen. The femoral artery continues inferiorly after branching into the medial and lateral circumflex arteries. It then descends through the adductor canal, which is formed by the fascia from the adductor and quadriceps groups, and the adductor hiatus into the posterior thigh where it becomes the *popliteal artery*. The femoral artery and its perforating branches supply all of the muscles of the anterior, anterior medial, and posterior thigh; the greater saphenous vein drains this area.[2,3] The external rotators are supplied by the medial femoral circumflex; the gluteal muscles receive their blood supply from perforating branches of the superior and inferior gluteal arteries.

BIOMECHANICS

The importance of a normal hip in any athletic activity is underscored by the role this joint plays in movement and weightbearing. The hip is a structurally sound joint, constructed for weightbearing, that also allows for multidirectional motion. As a triaxial joint, the hip allows motion in the three primary planes, sagittal, transverse, and coronal, as flexion-extension, abduction-adduction, and inter-

nal-external rotation motions. The hip is also capable of transverse or horizontal abduction/adduction and flexion/extension, making it possible to achieve circumduction by including all motions in a single movement pattern. As the structural link between the lower extremities and the axial skeleton, the hips not only transmit forces from the ground up but also carry forces from the trunk, head and neck, and upper extremities. Furthermore, the hips must be able to bear forces that are several times the weight of the individual.[4,5]

INJURIES OF THE PELVIS

The Iliac Crest

Pain in the area of the iliac crest is referred to as a *hip pointer* and may have several different causes, including contusions, periostitis, avulsion injuries to the iliac apophysis, and avulsion of the muscles that insert along the iliac crest. Contusions are the most common cause of a hip pointer. If an athlete receives a contusion in this area, ice should be applied immediately, and a return to play may be possible after padding is applied. To decrease the chances of infection, a hematoma that develops is usually not drained. Repeated injury may result in *periostitis*, an inflammation of the periosteum, which can be frustrating to the athlete because of the extended heal-

FOCUS ON . . .

Injuries to the Iliac Crest

Iliac crest pain (hip pointer) is caused by contusions, periostitis, iliac apophysis avulsion injuries, or iliac crest muscle insertion avulsions. Contusions are the most common cause, and ice should be applied immediately for this type of injury. The athlete may be able to return to play quickly with padding. To limit the chance of infection, any hematoma that develops is usually not drained. Periostitis occurs with repeated injuries and can take a long time to heal. Treatment is rest, heat before and ice after activity, stretching, NSAIDs, and occasionally a corticosteroid injection. Avulsion of the iliac crest muscle insertions (or apophyses in adolescents) results from violent contractions of these muscles. Surgical repair may be needed if displacement is significant, but conservative therapy is usually effective. Trauma or stress to the iliac crest can produce a fracture. Conservative treatment is indicated because of the vast blood supply to this area. Stress fractures from repetitive impact or muscle contractions may require bone scan or magnetic resonance imaging for diagnosis; they are treated with rest, then a gradual increase in activity.

ing period required. Rest, heat before activity, ice after activity, stretching, nonsteroidal anti-inflammatory drugs (NSAIDs), and occasional corticosteroid injection usually resolve this problem.[6,7]

The muscles that insert along the iliac crest can be torn by violent contractions, and in adolescents, such contractions may tear the apophysis. If the muscle or bone is significantly displaced in an avulsion injury, surgical repair may be necessary, but conservative treatment usually is indicated.[6,7] Displacement of more than 1 cm typically is needed before surgery would be considered.

Fractures can result from trauma or stress in the iliac crest and will usually heal readily with conservative treatment because of the excellent blood supply to this area. A direct blow is the most common mechanism of traumatic fractures. The athletic trainer should also be aware of other concurrent injuries that may be associated with this type of trauma, such as abdominal trauma or trauma to other major body systems. Stress fractures are often seen with repetitive impact or muscle contractions. Bone scans or magnetic resonance imaging (MRI) are often necessary to confirm the diagnosis of stress fracture. Stress fractures are best treated with rest initially, followed by a gradual increase in activity within the limits of pain. For runners, increasing mileage by 10% per week will often allow continued healing.[6,7]

The Pelvis

Avulsion fractures, caused by a violent muscle contraction or sudden passive stretch, may also occur in other apophyses around the pelvis. The most common areas are the anterosuperior iliac spine (ASIS), the insertion of the sartorius, the anteroinferior iliac spine, the insertion of the superior head of the rectus femoris, the ischial tuberosities, and the insertion of the hamstrings. Athletes will report severe immediate pain in the involved area and may try to keep the hip flexed (with anterior avulsions), or the knee flexed (with posterior avulsions). Radiographs help confirm the diagnosis. If the fragment is only minimally displaced, treatment consists of keeping the extremity in a comfortable position and using crutches as necessary. If displacement is greater than 1 or 2 cm, open reduction may be indicated. Most athletes may return to competition approximately 3 months after surgical treatment of this type of injury; if treatment is nonsurgical, then the athlete can return 3 months after the injury.[6,9]

Sacrum, Coccyx, and Sacroiliac Joint

Stress or traumatic fractures can also occur in the sacrum and coccyx. Treatment of these stress fractures is similar to that described above: rest until the pain improves, followed by a slow return to sport at increments of 10% increase per week.[10] Traumatic injury to the sacrum may result in neurologic compromise of the sacral nerves and a careful neurologic examination is indicated. Plain radiographs and computed tomography (CT) may be indi-

cated with these injuries. Sacroiliac sprains or dislocations may also occur from trauma, although these are relatively uncommon in sports. Symptoms may include an inability to walk and reports of pain in the lower back, hip, or groin regions because of muscle splinting. Pain may result from compression or distraction of the iliac wings. Plain radiographs or CT should be obtained to confirm the diagnosis. Unstable sprains are often treated surgically with open reduction and internal fixation.[6,7]

Buttocks and Perineum

The buttocks are quite susceptible to injury in most sports, commonly from direct blows to the area. Symptoms include complaints of pain in the area, difficulty extending the hip, walking uphill, or running. Ice, rest, stretching, and a gradual return to activity usually resolve the problem. Some athletes in contact sports may need to wear special padding. An occasional complication resulting from a blow to the buttock is a *compartment syndrome*. This condition occurs when the amount of swelling and/or bleeding in a muscle compartment causes pressure that is greater than the capillary pressure and results in ischemia. The patient will report severe pain in the gluteal compartments, may have sciatic nerve abnormalities, and often will experience pain with passive stretching of the gluteal muscles. Compartment pressure measurements should be taken immediately, and if pressures warrant, surgical decompression should be performed.[11] Chronic compartment syndrome is rare, and usually can be treated with stretching; however, *fasciotomy* (a surgical incision of the fascia) may be indicated in recalcitrant cases.[6,7]

Sciatic nerve injury can also be sustained from a direct blow to the buttocks, but most sciatic nerve injuries resolve with time.[6,7] Patients present with pain or paralysis in the sciatic nerve distribution. Rarely, a hematoma may compress the nerve and require surgical decompression. This diagnosis can be verified with an MRI scan.

Stress fractures and traumatic injuries can also occur to the pubic rami and ischial tuberosities. Although these fractures often occur in distance runners and long and triple jumpers, swimmers can also sustain these injuries. Treatment consists of rest, low-impact activities, and a gradual return to sport as symptoms improve.[12] Ischial bursitis may develop in patients who experience repeated trauma in this area. Radiographs may show calcification around the ischial bursa. Treatment consists of ultrasound, hamstring stretching, NSAIDs, and, occasionally, corticosteroid injections. If symptoms persist, resection of the bursa may be indicated.[6,7]

Osteitis pubis, or an inflammation of the pubis symphysis, is a relatively uncommon problem that affects endurance athletes. One large study reported that it occurred frequently in runners, soccer players, ice hockey players, and tennis players.[13] Athletes with osteitis pubis may experience a gradually increasing groin discomfort and report popping in the symphysis pubis area. The pain may radiate into the thigh. The athlete will experience tenderness in the symphysis pubis and pain with adductor stretch or manual muscle testing and range of motion of the hip. Treatment involves rest, NSAIDs, and stretching and strengthening exercises. When treating anyone with osteitis pubis, the physician should first rule out an infectious process.[14]

Pudendal nerve palsy, which is a numbness in the distribution of the peroneal area, has been reported in cyclists. More severe cases may cause mild urinary or bowel incontinence, and in men, mild sexual dysfunction. Treatment consists of rest and modification of the bicycle seat.[6,7]

The Groin Area

Contusions are a relatively common cause of groin pain that usually resolve without problems. If they occur in the area of the femoral triangle, they may lead to traumatic phlebitis or atraumatic femoral nerve palsy.[15] Treatment of phlebitis consists of observation or anticoagulation therapy. For femoral nerve palsy, observation is indicated, with possible electromyography if the condition persists for more than 6 weeks. Other causes of groin pain are adductor or iliopsoas muscle strains, avulsion fractures (often of the lesser trochanter), and hip avulsions. **Table 15-1** describes the treatment of all avulsion injuries of the pelvis.

TABLE 15-1
PHASES OF TREATMENT IN A PELVIC AVULSION INJURY

Treatment phase	Days after injury	Subjective pain	Palpation (subjective— pain; objective— tissue)	Range of motion	Muscle strength	Level of activity	Radiographic appearance
I	0 to 7	Moderate	Moderate to severe	Very limited	Poor	None, protected gait	Osseous separation
II	7 to 14-20	Minimal	Moderate	Improving with guided exercise	Fair	Protected gait, guided exercise	Osseous separation
III	14-20 to 30	Minimal with stress	Moderate	Improving with gentle stretch	Good	Guided exercise, resistance	Early callus formation
IV	30 to 60	None	Minimal	Normal	Good to normal	Limited athletic participation	Maturing callus
V	60 to return	None	None	Normal	Normal	Normal	Maturing callus

(Reproduced with permission from Metzmaker JN, Pappas AM: Avulsion fractures of the pelvis. *Am J Sports Med* 1985;13:555.)

Chronic groin pain can be challenging to the athletic trainer. The incidence of chronic groin pain seems to be higher in athletes who participate in soccer, ice hockey, and tennis than in those who participate in other sports.[16,17] The most common mechanism is reinjury to the adductor muscle complex. Treatment includes rest, stretching, NSAIDs, ultrasound, and myofascial release of trigger points. If symptoms persist for more than 3 months, surgical treatment may be indicated. Surgical exploration and either tenotomy or excision of the granulation tissue yields good or excellent results in more than 90% of patients.[18] The rectus abdominis can become inflamed with recurrent injury, as with the adductor muscle group and should be treated in a similar fashion, including surgical treatment if necessary. Nonmuscular causes of groin pain that must be considered include inguinal hernia, prostatitis, orchitis, tumors, and systemic arthritis. Testicular torsion, which has been reported in long-distance runners and bicycle riders, is a urologic emergency and should be treated immediately by a urologist.[6,7]

The Greater Trochanter

The hip and greater trochanter have their own unique characteristic injuries. Contusion is the most common injury to the greater trochanter, which is a prominent structure with only skin, subcutaneous tissue, and bursae over the bone. Athletes with a trochanter contusion will experience pain and should be treated with ice, rest, and iliotibial band stretching in the presence of a positive Ober test. Persistent pain raises the possibility of trochanteric bursitis, which may not be seen on radiographs or may show as calcification in the area. Trochanteric bursitis may be treated with ultrasound, stretching, NSAIDs, and, if the condition persists, a corticosteroid injection. If symptoms persist, resection of the bursa is occasionally indicated.[6,7]

Patients may report a popping or snapping sensation in the hip area. There are two varieties of snapping hip syndrome: external and internal. The external type, which is caused by the iliotibial band popping over the greater trochanter of the hip, is more common. Initial treatment is the same as for greater trochanteric bursitis. If this treatment fails, surgical treatment may help. Several surgical techniques are available, including resection of the bursa, iliotibial band, or gluteus maximus, or an elliptical removal of the center portion of the iliotibial band. The internal variety of snapping hip syndrome is less common and is caused by the iliopsoas tendon snapping over the iliopectineal eminence of the hip. Patients will often report more medial pain with no tenderness over the greater trochanter. Treatment consists of stretching, myofascial trigger point relief of the musculotendinous junction, NSAIDs, corticosteroid injections, and if pain persists, surgical intervention. The most common surgical treatment is lengthening of the iliopsoas tendon.

FOCUS ON . . .

Injuries to the Greater Trochanter

The most common injuries to the greater trochanter are contusions because of the structure's bony prominence, resulting in pain. Treatment is ice, rest, and iliotibial band stretching. Persistent pain may suggest trochanteric bursitis, which may be reflected in calcification on radiographs. Treatment is ultrasound, stretching, NSAIDs, and perhaps a corticosteroid injection. Bursal resection may be indicated if symptoms are persistent.

Snapping hip syndrome can be external (caused by the iliotibial band popping over the greater trochanter) or internal (caused by the iliopsoas tendon snapping over the iliopectineal eminence). The external type is most common and is treated with ultrasound, stretching, NSAIDs, and sometimes a corticosteroid injection. If these measures fail, surgical treatment may help. The internal type is less common and causes more medial pain without greater trochanter tenderness. Treatment is stretching, NSAIDs, corticosteroid injections, and surgical intervention if pain persists.

Intra-articular causes of snapping hip include synovial chondromatosis, loose bodies from trauma or osteochondritis dissecans, osteocartilaginous exostoses, acetabular labral tear, or inverted labrum. Computed tomography, magnetic resonance imaging, arthrography, or hip arthroscopy can help to make the diagnosis.

Muscle strains and ligament sprains also cause pain in the area of the greater trochanter. Treatment is rest, ice, and gradual stretching as pain permits. Partial or complete avulsion of the greater trochanter can occur with a violent contraction of these muscles; significant displacement calls for open reduction and internal fixation. Fracture of the greater trochanter from a direct blow is usually minimally displaced and treated with crutch ambulation and progression of activities as the fracture heals.

Resection of a portion of the lesser trochanter has also been reported.[6,7]

There are several intra-articular causes of snapping hip syndrome, including synovial chondromatosis, loose bodies secondary to trauma or osteochondritis dissecans, osteocartilaginous exostoses, acetabular labral tear, and inverted labrum. Diagnosis can be aided by CT and MRI, arthrography, or hip arthroscopy.[19,20]

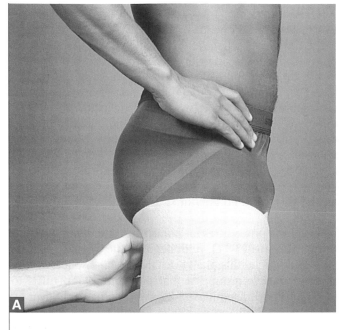

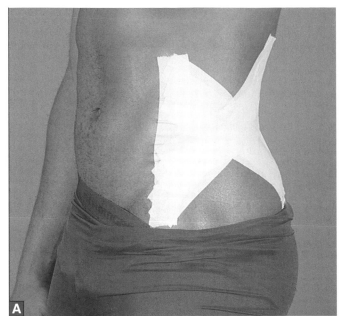

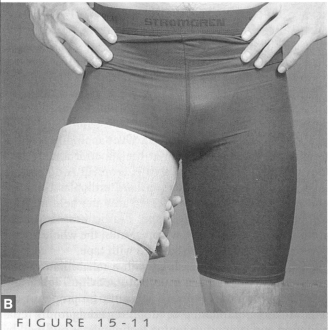

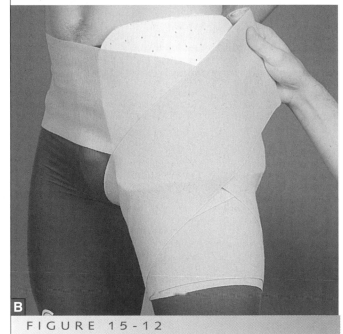

FIGURE 15-11

Hamstrings and quadriceps wrapping procedures are similar, both beginning at the proximal end of the thigh and angling diagonally to the distal aspect of the affected muscle group, before being wrapped in an upward spiral around the thigh, ending at the proximal end of the thigh. **A** Hamstrings wrap. **B** Quadriceps wrap.

FIGURE 15-12

The hip pointer wrap, which supports and protects contused tissue of the iliac crest, begins with vertical anchor strips 4″ to 6″ anteriorly and posteriorly of the affected area. An "X"-pattern of tape covers the area, followed by horizontal strips and a hip pointer pad. **A** Hip pointer taping. **B** A hip pointer pad.

crossover, which states that exercising the noninjured leg can have beneficial effects on the injured leg, is an important concept in rehabilitation. The setting of short- and long-term goals is important to provide positive reinforcement during all phases of the rehabilitation process. Intact joints and muscles, control of swelling and pain, range of motion, strength, muscular endurance, speed, power, coordination and agility, cardiovascular fitness, and psychological confidence are all areas that need attention during the rehabilitation process. All members of the healthcare team—physician, physical therapist, athletic trainer, and patient—should agree on a well thought out and progressive rehabilitation program.[4,38]

Because the hip serves as the articulation point of the lower kinetic chain with the axial skeleton, the musculature of the abdomen and lower back must not be forgotten during rehabilitation of injuries to the pelvis, hip, and thigh. Because many of the muscles in this region are postural, proper sitting, standing, and lifting should be emphasized to ensure a complete rehabilitation. Proper execution of exercises and timing increases in the intensity of the exercises must be carefully monitored at all times.

Isometrics, isotonics, and isokinetics are three types of resistive exercises that can be used in rehabilitation. Manual resistance may also be used for strengthening. Concentric and eccentric muscle contractions as well as open-chain and closed-chain exercises should be included at appropriate times. When rehabilitating an athlete, it is also important to identify and simulate components of the competitive activity or activities within the regimen.[4,38] A wide variety of exercises should be incorporated into a rehabilitation program for the pelvis, hip, and thigh, including abdominal, low back, and stretching exercises.[4,38]

Abdominal and Low Back Exercises

Exercises such as the pelvic tilt, single and double knee-to-chest stretches, prone propping on elbows, back press and release, bridging, partial curl-up, prone push-up, quadruped, and lumbar roll benefit the abdominal and low back areas. A minimum of five to 10 repetitions is recommended for each of the exercises described.

Pelvic tilt

The athlete lies supine with knees bent and feet flat on the table, then tightens the abdomen and buttocks, pressing the small of the back into the table (**Figure 15-13**). This is a small, subtle movement that is held for a count of three to five, then released. The athlete should then progress to a knees-extended position.

Single knee-to-chest stretch

The athlete lies supine with knees bent and feet flat on the table, then tightens the abdomen and buttocks, pressing the small of the back into the table. The athlete places his or her hands behind one knee, slowly pulls it in toward the chest, and holds for a count of six to 10 (**Figure 15-14**).

The athlete releases the leg and lowers it completely to the table. The athlete alternates legs for a total of five to 10 stretches per leg.

Double knee-to-chest stretch

As in the single knee-to-chest stretch, the athlete lies supine with knees bent and feet flat on the table, tightening the abdomen and buttocks, and pressing the small of the back into the table. With the right hand behind the right knee, the athlete slowly pulls the knee in to the chest. Then, the athlete places the left hand behind the left knee and pulls it in also (**Figure 15-15**). This position is held for a count of six to 10, then the athlete releases the right leg and lowers it to the table and releases the left leg and lowers it.

Prone propping on elbows

The athlete lies prone with knees extended and forearms flat on the table at shoulder level. While keeping the neck in neutral and the hips and abdomen pressed against the table, the athlete presses up on his or her forearms. The position is held for a count of six to 10, then the athlete slowly lowers his or her body to the original position.

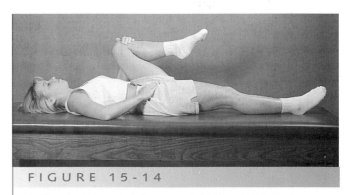

FIGURE 15-14

In the single knee-to-chest stretch, the athlete pulls one knee to the chest for a count of six to 10 before alternating legs.

FIGURE 15-13

In the pelvic tilt, the athlete lies supine with knees bent and the feet flat.

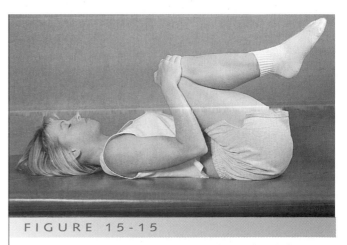

FIGURE 15-15

In the double knee-to-chest stretch, the athlete pulls one knee, then the other in to the chest, holding both in that position for a count of six to 10.

Back press and release

The athlete assumes an all-fours position with knees and hands evenly spaced and neck in neutral position and presses his or her back upward by tightening the abdomen and buttocks (**Practice Session 15-1**). The position is held for a count of six to 10 before the athlete relaxes the abdomen and buttocks. The athlete then continues to relax the abdomen and buttocks, allowing the back to sag while keeping weight evenly distributed. This position is held for a count of six to 10 before the athlete returns to the original position. The knees and hands should be kept stationary.

Bridging

The athlete lies supine with knees bent and feet flat on the table, then tightens his or her abdomen and buttocks, pressing the small of the back into the table. While keeping the abdomen and buttocks contracted, the back straight, and the body in a straight line from the knees to the shoulders, the athlete lifts the hips up from the table (**Figure 15-16**). The position is held for a count of three to five, then released.

Partial curl-up

The athlete lies supine with knees bent and feet flat on the table, then tightens his or her abdomen and buttocks, pressing the small of the back into the table. The athlete crosses his or her arms across the chest and keeps the neck in a neutral position. Keeping the abdomen and buttocks in the pelvic tilt position, he or she slowly curls up until the shoulder blades are off the table, then slowly lowers to the original position, making sure to breathe regularly and curl up without twisting (**Figure 15-17**).

Prone push-up

The athlete lies prone with the knees extended and forearms flat on the table at shoulder level, then presses up on

PRACTICE SESSION 15-1
BACK PRESS AND RELEASE

A The athlete assumes an all-fours position, presses the back up by tightening the abdomen and buttocks, and hold the position for a count of six to ten. **B** The athlete relaxes the abdomen and buttocks.

FIGURE 15-16

In the bridging exercise, the athlete lifts the hips from the table, keeping the body in a straight line from the knees to the shoulders.

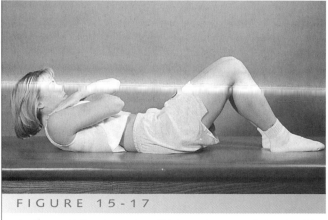

FIGURE 15-17

In the partial curl-up, the athlete curls up until the shoulder blades are off the table.

the forearms while keeping the neck in a neutral position. Keeping the hips against the table, the athlete extends the elbows until the arms are straight and the abdomen is lifted off the table (**Figure 15-18**). The position is held for a count of six to 10, then the athlete lowers his or her body slowly to the original position.

FIGURE 15-18

In the prone push-up, the athlete lifts the abdomen off the table by extending the elbows until the arms are straight.

Quadruped

The athlete assumes an all-fours position with knees and hands evenly spaced and neck in neutral position, tightening the abdomen and buttocks (**Practice Session 15-2**). He or she supports the weight evenly between one hand and both knees while raising one arm to shoulder level. This position is held for 6 to 10 seconds, then the athlete lowers the arm to the table and repositions his or her weight evenly among the hands and knees. The movement is repeated using the opposite arm. Arms are alternated for a total of five to 10 lifts per arm. The athlete then makes sure that his or her weight is supported evenly between both hands and one knee while extending one leg to hip level. This position is held for 6 to 10 seconds; the athlete then lowers the leg to the table and repositions his or her weight evenly among hands and knees. The movement is repeated using the opposite leg. Legs are alternated for a total of five to 10 lifts on each leg. For a further progression, the athlete supports his or her weight evenly between one hand and the opposite knee while raising the second arm and extending the second leg. The

PRACTICE SESSION 15-2
QUADRUPED

A The athlete assumes an all-fours position with hands and knees evenly spaced. **B** The athlete raises one arm to shoulder level for a count of 6 to 10 seconds.

C The athlete extends one leg to hip level for a count of 6 to 10 seconds. **D** The athlete raises one arm and extends the opposite leg for a count of 6 to 10 seconds.

position is held for 6 to 10 seconds, then the athlete lowers the arm and leg to the table and repositions his or her weight evenly among hands and knees. The exercise is repeated with the other arm and leg, and alternations are continued for a total of five to 10 lifts on each side.

Lumbar roll

The athlete lies supine with knees bent and feet flat on the table, then tightens his or her abdomen and buttocks, pressing the small of the back into the table (**Figure 15-19**). He or she drops the knees to one side while keeping the upper body flat. Extending the arm on the side opposite the direction of rotation may help stabilize the upper body and improve the stretch. The position is held for a count of six to 10, then the athlete returns his or her legs to the original position. The exercise is repeated on the opposite side, and alternations are continued for a total of five to 10 times per side.

Stretching Exercises

Exercises such as the sidelying and standing quadriceps stretches; hip flexor stretch; standing and sidelying ITB stretches; adductor stretch; supine, seated, and standing hamstrings stretches; piriformis stretch; and internal and external rotators stretches focus on a particular muscle group. Again, each exercise should be repeated a minimum of six to 10 times.

Sidelying quadriceps stretch

The athlete lies on one side, keeping weight supported on the elbow. Then he or she slowly bends the upper knee and stretches the quadriceps by pulling on the same ankle with the free hand (**Figure 15-20**). The position is held for a count of 20 to 30, then the athlete extends the knee and returns to the original position. An entire series of repetitions should be completed before the athlete rolls over to the other side and repeats the exercise.

Standing quadriceps stretch

The athlete stands, using a wall or table for hand support, bends one knee, and holds the same foot behind the body with the same hand (**Figure 15-21**). The position is held

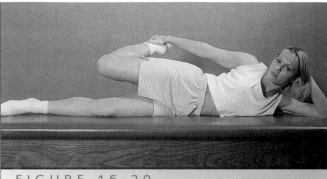

FIGURE 15-20

In the sidelying quadriceps stretch, the athlete supports his or her weight on the elbow and slowly bends the upper knee, pulling on the ankle with the free hand for a count of 20 to 30 before extending the knee and returning to the original position.

FIGURE 15-21

In the standing quadriceps stretch, the athlete stands with his or her hand supported on the wall or a table and bends the knee and holds the foot behind the body with one hand for a count of 20 to 30 before extending the knee and returning to the original position.

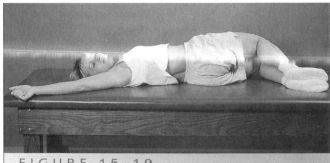

FIGURE 15-19

In the lumbar roll, the athlete lies supine with knees bent and tightens the buttocks and abdomen before dropping the knees to one side and keeping the upper body flat.

for a count of 20 to 30, then the athlete extends the knee and returns to the original position. An entire series of repetitions should be completed before the athlete turns and repeats the exercise.

Hip flexor stretch

The athlete kneels and extends one leg backward until the knee is straight, keeping the toes in contact with the floor or turned under (**Figure 15-22**). The front knee is bent with the weight centered over the hips, and the front knee is always behind the front foot. The athlete pushes the hips forward until he or she feels a stretch, increasing the stretch by keeping the trunk erect or in slight extension. The position should be held for a count of 20 to 30, then the athlete returns to the original position. The exercise should be repeated using the opposite leg, and alternations continue for a total of six to 10 repetitions on each leg.

Standing iliotibial band stretch

The athlete stands next to a wall with the leg to be stretched closer to the wall, crossed behind the opposite leg. He or she leans the hip inward toward the wall until a stretch is felt. The position is held for a count of 20 to 30, then the athlete returns to the original position. An entire series of repetitions is completed before the athlete turns to the other side and repeats the exercise.

Sidelying iliotibial band stretch

This exercise requires assistance from another person. The athlete lies on his or her side at the edge of a table with the affected leg off the table (**Figure 15-23**). The assistant holds the athlete's pelvis stable with one hand and places stress below the knee of the affected leg with the other hand. The amount of flexion in the hip and knee varies until the athlete feels the appropriate stretch.

Adductor stretch

The athlete is seated with the knees bent and the soles of the feet together (**Figure 15-24**). The athlete slides the

feet toward the buttocks and pulls the knees toward the floor until a stretch is felt. The position is held for a count of 20 to 30, then the athlete returns to the original position.

Supine hamstrings stretch

The athlete lies supine with the knees bent and feet flat, then pulls one knee toward the chest until the hip is flexed to 90°. The athlete supports the leg with a hand behind the knee and slowly extends the knee until a stretch is felt (**Figure 15-25**). The position is held for a count of 20 to 30, then the athlete returns to the original position. The legs are alternated for a total of six to 10 repetitions on each leg.

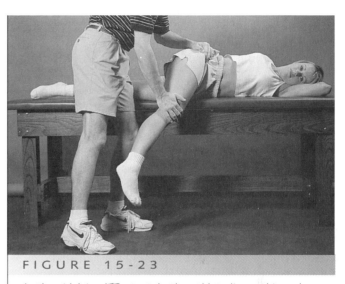

FIGURE 15-23

In the sidelying ITB stretch, the athlete lies on his or her side at the edge of the table while an assistant holds the pelvis stable with one hand and places stress below the knee with the other hand.

FIGURE 15-22

In the hip flexor stretch, the athlete kneels and extends one leg backward, keeping the front knee bent, and pushes the hips forward until a stretch is felt.

FIGURE 15-24

In the adductor stretch, the athlete sits with the knees bent and soles of the feet together, then slides the feet toward the buttocks, pulling the knees toward the floor until a stretch is felt.

FIGURE 15-25

In the supine hamstrings stretch, the athlete lies with knees bent and pulls one knee toward the chest, then supports the leg with his or her hand and slowly extends the knee until a stretch is felt.

FIGURE 15-26

In the seated hamstrings stretch, the athlete sits with one knee bent and the opposite knee extended, then leans forward until a stretch is felt.

FIGURE 15-27

In the piriformis stretch, the athlete lies with the knees bent, crosses one ankle on the opposite leg's knee, and pulls both knees into the chest until a stretch is felt.

Seated hamstrings stretch

The athlete is seated with one knee bent and the opposite knee extended (**Figure 15-26**). Keeping the knee extended, chin lifted, and back straight, the athlete leans forward from the hips until a stretch is felt. The toes of the extended foot should be pointed straight toward the ceiling. The position should be held for a count of 20 to 30, then the athlete returns to the original position. An entire series of repetitions should be completed before performing the exercise with the other leg.

Standing hamstrings stretch

The athlete stands with one heel supported on a step or stool (not more than 2' tall). Keeping the knee extended and toes pointed straight toward the ceiling, chin lifted, and back straight, the athlete leans forward from the hips until he or she feels a stretch. The foot of the supporting leg must be pointed straight ahead. The position is held for a count of 20 to 30, then the athlete returns to the original position. The exercise should be repeated six to 10 times on each leg.

Piriformis stretch

The athlete lies supine with the knees bent and feet flat, then he or she crosses one ankle on the knee of the opposite leg (Figure 15-27). Holding this position, the athlete pulls both knees into the chest until he or she feels a stretch. The position is held for a count of 20 to 30, then the athlete returns to the original position. The exercise is repeated six to 10 times on each leg.

Internal rotators stretch

This exercise requires assistance from another person. The athlete sits at the edge of the table, and the assistant places a hand distal to the flexed knee and puts external rotational force on the hip until the athlete feels a stretch on the internal rotators (**Figure 15-28**). The position is held

for a count of 20 to 30, then the athlete returns to the original position. The exercise is repeated six to 10 times on each leg.

External rotators stretch

This exercise is similar to the internal rotators stretch, except that internal rotational force is placed on the hip until the athlete feels a stretch on the external rotators (Figure 15-29)

Strengthening Exercises

Exercises such as forward step-ups, standing hamstring curls, standing hip extensions, sidelying hip abduction and adduction, prone hip external and internal rotations, and co-contractions are examples of initial strengthening exercises for rehabilitating the musculature about the hip and thigh. These exercises focus on using the weight of the extremities, body weight, or manual resistance for resistance. Co-contractions use isometric contractions from strengthening.[29,33] The minimum number of repetitions and sets or time for each exercise should be determined individually, according to the needs of the athlete.

Forward step-ups

The athlete stands behind a 6" to 8" box and places one foot on the box (**Figure 15-30**). He or she then extends the knee to raise the body up, pauses, and slowly lowers to the original position. The exercise is repeated, beginning with two to three sets of 10 repetitions and progressing to five sets of 10 repetitions.

Standing hamstring curls

The athlete stands with the quadriceps pressed against the table and flexes the knee, bringing the heel toward the buttocks (**Figure 15-31**). He or she then pauses and lowers the foot to the floor, completely extending the knee. The exercise is repeated, beginning with two to three sets of 10 repetitions and progressing to five sets of 10 repetitions.

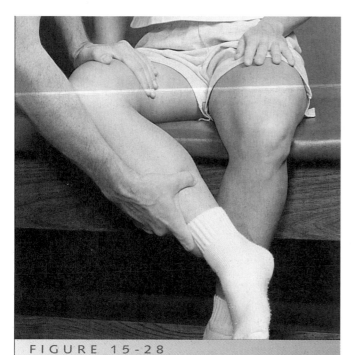

FIGURE 15-28

In the internal rotators stretch, the athlete sits at the edge of a table as an assistant places one hand distal to the flexed knee and applies external rotational force on the hip until the athlete feels a stretch on the internal rotators.

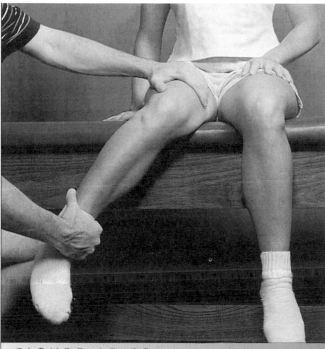

FIGURE 15-29

In the external rotators stretch, the athlete sits at the edge of a table as an assistant places one hand distal to the flexed knee and applies internal rotational force on the hip until the athlete feels a stretch on the external rotators.

FIGURE 15-30

In forward step-ups, the athlete stands behind a box, places one foot on the box, and extends the knee to raise the body up before slowly returning to the original position.

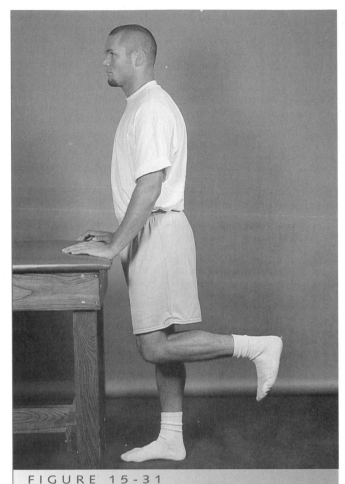

FIGURE 15-31

In standing hamstring curls, the athlete stands while flexing the knee, and brings the heel toward the buttocks before lowering the foot to the floor.

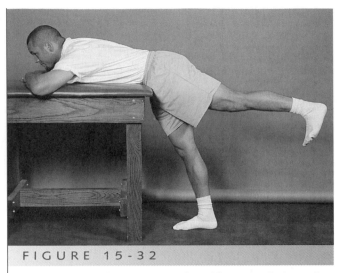

FIGURE 15-32

In the standing hip extension, the athlete stands, leans forward with the upper body supported on the table then extends the hip while keeping the knee straight.

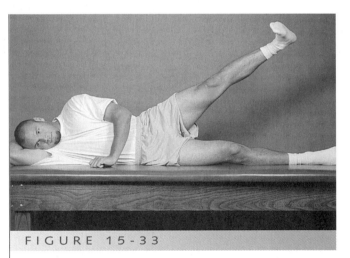

FIGURE 15-33

In the sidelying hip abduction, the athlete lies on his or her side with the upper leg extended, raises the leg toward the ceiling, before pausing and lowering the leg to the original position.

Weights can be added in increments of 1 lb; however, the athlete must begin with two sets of 10 repetitions after any increase.

Standing hip extension

The athlete stands and leans forward with the upper body supported on the table (**Figure 15-32**). While keeping the knee straight, the athlete extends the hip by raising the leg toward the ceiling, extending the hip only as far as can be done without externally rotating it. He or she then pauses and lowers the foot to the floor. The exercise is repeated, beginning with two to three sets of 10 repetitions and progressing to five sets of 10 repetitions. Weights can be added in increments of 1 lb; however, the athlete must begin with two sets of 10 repetitions after any increase.

Sidelying hip abduction

The athlete lies on the side with the upper leg extended and, keeping the knee straight, raises the upper leg toward the ceiling, making sure to lead with the outside of the ankle so the hip does not rotate (**Figure 15-33**). He or she

then pauses and lowers the leg to the original position. The exercise is repeated, beginning with two to three sets of 10 repetitions and progressing to five sets of 10 repetitions. Weights can be added in increments of 1 lb; however, the athlete must begin with two sets of 10 repetitions after any increase.

Sidelying hip adduction

The athlete lies on the side with the upper leg extended and supported on a chair (**Figure 15-34**). Keeping the lower leg extended, he or she raises it toward the ceiling, pauses, then lowers the leg to the original position. The exercise is repeated, beginning with two to three sets of 10 repetitions and progressing to five sets of 10 repetitions.

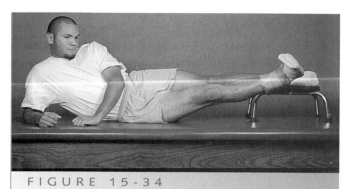

FIGURE 15-34

In the sidelying hip adduction, the athlete lies on the side with the upper leg extended and supported on a chair, then raises the extended lower leg toward the ceiling before pausing and lowering the leg to the original position.

Weights can be added in increments of 1 lb; however, the athlete must begin with two sets of 10 repetitions after any increase.

Prone hip external rotation

The athlete lies prone with the knee flexed to 90° and internally rotated. Manual resistance is placed at the medial aspect of the leg. While keeping the knee flexed, the athlete rotates the hip against resistance until the foot is across the midline of the body, to the furthest internally rotated position possible. The athlete then relaxes and returns to the starting position. The exercise is repeated, beginning with two to three sets of 10 repetitions and progressing to five sets of 10 repetitions.

Prone hip internal rotation

The athlete lies prone with the knee flexed to 90° and externally rotated. Manual resistance is placed at the lateral aspect of the leg. While keeping the knee flexed, the athlete rotates the hip against resistance until the foot is lateral of the midline of the body, to the furthest externally rotated position possible. The athlete then relaxes and returns to the starting position. The exercise is repeated, beginning with two to three sets of 10 repetitions and progressing to five sets of 10 repetitions.

Co-contractions

The athlete sits in a chair with the foot on the floor, then tightens the quadriceps and hamstrings by pushing the foot forward on the floor. The position is held for a count of three to five. The athlete then relaxes and returns to the starting position. The exercise is repeated, beginning with two to three sets of 10 repetitions and progressing to five sets of 10 repetitions.

Proprioceptive Neuromuscular Facilitation

Proprioceptive neuromuscular facilitation (PNF) is defined as a therapeutic exercise technique that is designed on the principles of functional human anatomy and neurophysiology. Improvements in functional output are achieved when proprioceptive, cutaneous, and auditory input are used in the rehabilitative setting. The stretch reflex is the primary neurophysiologic mechanism on which PNF is based. Autogenic inhibition and reciprocal inhibition are two neurophysiologic phenomena used to describe a neuromuscular system's ability to be facilitated and inhibited.

There are two patterns, D1 and D2, for the lower extremity, which are further divided into two subdivisions: D1 moving into flexion, D1 moving into extension, D2 moving into flexion, and D2 moving into extension (**Figure 15-35**). These patterns involve diagonal and rotational movements. Each pattern begins when the musculature that will be active is placed in a stretched position and ends when the musculature has obtained a shortened position after contraction. Resistance is supplied manually. These patterns incorporate gross muscle activity, not individual or isolated muscular activity. Many daily and sports-related activities are simulated through these patterns. It can be beneficial for athletes to learn these patterns prior to using resistance.

Table 15-2 describes the D1 lower extremity movement patterns, and **Practice Session 15-3** shows the movement pattern. **Table 15-3** describes the D2 lower extremity movement patterns, and **Practice Session 15-4** shows the movement pattern.

Plyometric Exercises

Plyometric exercises are defined as those exercises that allow a muscle to obtain its maximum strength or produce a maximum amount of force as rapidly as possible. Safety is of great concern when using plyometrics. Progression, frequency, volume, intensity, and recovery must be considered. A good base for strengthening and conditioning is needed before initiating a program of low-intensity, in-place plyometrics. Recovery for plyometrics can range from 5 to 10 seconds between repetitions and 2 to 3 minutes between sets. The frequency at which plyometrics is done depends on the athlete's level of conditioning and ability, as well as the intensity at which the exercises are done. Large amounts of high-intensity plyometric exercise should be done only twice weekly to allow for ample recovery, along with other conditioning exercises. Volume is another way to measure plyometrics and is usually measured as the number of foot contacts made during one workout. Volume for a beginner should be limited to 80 to 100 contacts per session. Advanced athletes can have as many as 120 to 140 contacts per session, depending on the intensity of the exercise.

These advanced exercises are used to improve strength and speed and require great kinesthetic ability. Appropriately used, plyometrics can further complete the rehabilitation process. General categories of plyometrics for the lower body include jumps in place, standing jumps, hops, bounds, and shocks. Jumps in place are the lowest inten-

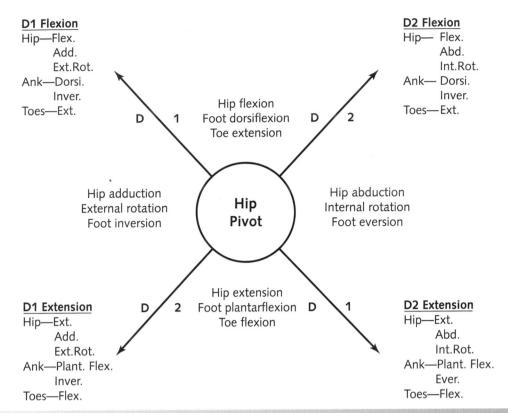

FIGURE 15-35

D1 and D2 proprioception neuromuscular facilitation patterns for the lower extremity are divided into D1 moving into flexion, D1 moving into extension, D2 moving into flexion, and D2 moving into extension. (Reproduced with permission from Prentice W: *Rehabilitation Techniques in Sports Medicine*, ed 2. St. Louis, MO, Mosby Yearbook, 1994.)

TABLE 15-2

D1 LOWER EXTREMITY MOVEMENT PATTERNS

	Moving into Flexion		Moving into Extension	
Body Part	**Starting Position**	**Terminal Position**	**Starting Position**	**Terminal Position**
Hip	Extended Abducted Internally rotated	Flexed Adducted Externally rotated	Flexed Adducted Externally rotated	Extended Abducted Internally rotated
Knee	Extended	Flexed	Flexed	Extended
Position of tibia	Externally rotated	Internally rotated	Internally rotated	Externally rotated
Ankle and foot	Plantarflexed Everted	Dorsiflexed Inverted	Dorsiflexed Inverted	Plantarflexed Everted
Toes	Flexed	Extended	Extended	Flexed
Hand position for sports therapist*	Right hand on dorsimedial surface of foot Left hand on anteromedial thigh near patella		Right hand on lateral plantar surface of foot Left hand on posterolateral thigh near popliteal crease	
Verbal command	Pull		Push	

*For athlete's right leg. (Reproduced with permission from Prentice W: *Rehabilitation Techniques in Sports Medicine*, ed 2. St. Louis, MO, Mosby Yearbook, 1994.)

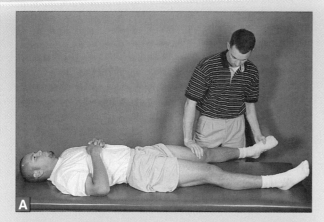

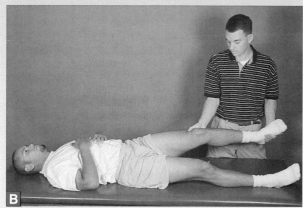

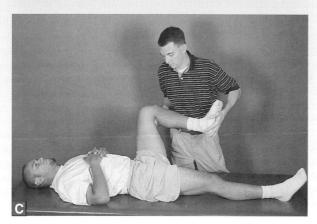

A The D1 lower extremity movement pattern. **B** Moving into flexion. **C** Moving into further flexion.

sity exercises; shocks are the highest. Vertical, horizontal, and lateral movements can be performed while the athlete is doing plyometric exercises.[4,38,39]

Squat jump
In this low-intensity plyometric exercise, the athlete assumes a half-squat position with hands behind the head,

jumps vertically, and, on landing, returns to the half-squat position to repeat the same series without pause (**Figure 15-36**). A minimum of 10 repetitions per set should be performed.

Split squat jump
In this low-intensity plyometric exercise, the athlete assumes a lunge position with one foot forward, jumps vertically to land in a lunge position, and repeats the series without pause (**Figure 15-37**). A minimum of 10 repetitions with each foot forward should be performed.

Standing triple jump
In this medium-intensity level exercise, the athlete begins in a partial squat position and jumps horizontally and vertically, using the arms for balance, and lands on one foot. Without pausing, the athlete jumps off that foot to land on the opposite foot, and again without pausing, jumps and lands on both feet. Two sets of six jumps each should be performed, with a 30- to 60-second rest period between sets.

Double leg hop
In this medium-intensity level exercise, the athlete stands with feet shoulder width apart and jumps horizontally and vertically, using his or her arms for balance and momentum. The jump is repeated without pause on landing. Ten repetitions are performed for short response or a distance of 30 meters or more. The number of sets depends on the number, intensity, and volume of the exercises.

Single leg hop
In this high-intensity level exercise, the athlete, with arms at sides, places one leg slightly in front of the other as if taking a step. He or she then jumps horizontally and vertically from one leg, using arms for balance and momentum. The nonjumping knee is driven up and held. The athlete lands on the same leg used in take-off. The jump is repeated without any pause on landing. Ten repetitions are performed for short response or a distance of 30 meters or more. The number of sets depends on the number, intensity, and volume of the exercises.

Alternate leg bound
In this medium-intensity level exercise, the athlete, with arms at sides, places one leg slightly in front of the other as if taking a step. He or she then jumps horizontally and vertically from one leg, using arms for balance and momentum. The nonjumping knee is driven up. The athlete lands on the opposite leg, then cycles from one leg to the other without pausing. Either alternate arm action or double arm action can be used. Ten repetitions are performed for short response or a distance of 30 meters or more. The number of sets depends on the number, intensity, and volume of the exercises.

Combination bound
In this medium-intensity level exercise, the athlete, with arms at the sides, places one leg slightly in front of the other as if taking a step. He or she then jumps horizontally

TABLE 15-3
D2 LOWER EXTREMITY MOVEMENT PATTERNS

Body Part	Moving into Flexion		Moving into Extension	
	Starting Position	Terminal Position	Starting Position	Terminal Position
Hip	Extended Adducted Externally rotated	Flexed Abducted Internally rotated	Flexed Abducted Internally rotated	Extended Adducted Externally rotated
Knee	Extended	Flexed	Flexed	Extended
Position of tibia	Externally rotated	Internally rotated	Internally rotated	Externally rotated
Ankle and foot	Plantarflexed Inverted	Dorsiflexed Everted	Dorsiflexed Everted	Plantarflexed Inverted
Toes	Flexed	Extended	Extended	Flexed
Hand position for sports therapist*	Right hand on dorsilateral surface of foot Left hand on anterolateral thigh near patella		Right hand on medial plantar surface of foot Left hand on posteromedial thigh near popliteal crease	
Verbal command	Pull		Push	

*For athlete's right leg.

(Reproduced with permission from Prentice W: *Rehabilitation Techniques in Sports Medicine*, ed 2. St Louis, MO, Mosby Year-Book, 1994.)

and vertically from one leg, using the arms with double arm action. On the leg that will be landed on, the knee should be driven up and out. The athlete will land on the opposite leg after this jump, for example—right, right, left or left, left, right. Ten repetitions are performed for short response or a distance of 30 meters or more. The number of sets depends on the number, intensity, and volume of the exercises.

In-depth jump
In this high-intensity level exercise, the athlete stands on a box approximately 0.3 to 0.9 m, then steps off the box landing on both feet and flexing the knees. Without pausing, the athlete then jumps either vertically or horizontally using double arm action and extends the body. Five to 10 repetitions are performed.

Box jumps
In this high-intensity level exercise, the athlete stands in front of a box in a semisquat position, jumps up on a box approximately 0.3 to 0.9 m, and immediately on contact, jumps off (**Figure 15-38**). As soon as contact is made with the ground, the athlete jumps up or out, using double arm action. Two to four sets of 5 to 10 repetitions are performed.

Kinesthetic Exercises
Kinesthetic training for balance, coordination, and agility is incorporated at all levels of the rehabilitation process, from balancing on the injured extremity to running at top speed and changing direction. As the athlete progresses through rehabilitation, an increasing level of difficulty in terms of joint positioning should be included. Kinesthetic training helps condition both conscious and unconscious neural pathways to increase joint and limb awareness so that skilled movement patterns can be achieved and injuries can be decreased. More advanced exercises to increase kinesthetic awareness may have the athlete balance on unstable surfaces while performing a sport-specific skill. Exercises and equipment that help train balance, agility, and coordination are all integral parts of increasing kinesthetic awareness.[4,38,39]

Kinesthetic exercises include exercises on the floor and on equipment such as a minitrampoline, proprioception board, and slide board. Sport cords and inflated exercise balls may also be used.

Single leg squat
The athlete squats on one leg and balances for up to 30 seconds or longer, if possible (**Figure 15-39**). This exercise should be performed with the affected leg flexed and/or extended at various joint angles to change the center of gravity. The number of repetitions can vary.

Minitrampoline
The athlete can perform several exercises on the minitrampoline, including balancing on one foot, stepping on and off the tramp, hopping on and off the tramp, and hopping on the tramp and holding the position before hopping off. The number of repetitions can vary.

A The D2 lower extremity movement pattern moving into extension. **B** Moving into flexion. **C** Internal rotation of the hip. **D** External rotation of the hip.

Proprioception board

The athlete stands on the proprioception or wabble board, and tries to balance or trace the edge of the board. Varying levels of difficulty can be achieved by changing the height or size of half balls attached to the platform as with the proprioception board. The athlete also can perform the exercise using front-to-back or side-to-side motions (**Figure 15-40**). The number of repetitions can vary.

Slide board

The athlete stands on the slide board and moves laterally on the surface with a skating-like motion. The resistance between the surface of the board and the covering placed on the feet decreases friction, allowing the athlete to glide on the slide board (**Figure 15-41**). Repetitions can be counted as the number of times the athlete glides side to side or the number of times the exercise is done in a specific time period.

Sport cord exercises

Many exercises can be done with a sport cord (elastic tubing). The athlete should hold the sport cord behind, in front of, or at the side and then perform specific exercises against the resistance of the cord. Functional tasks such as walking, shuffling, and jogging can be done with varying resistance from the sport cord. This resistance occurs as the athlete moves away from or toward the place that the cord is attached. These exercises require that the athlete constantly maintain his or her balance. Repetitions can be counted as the number of specific exercises done or the number of times an exercise is done in a specific time period.

Wall squats

The athlete assumes a squatting position with his or her back facing a wall and holds an inflated exercise ball against the wall with his or her back. The position is held for up to 30 seconds or longer, if possible. The number of repetitions can vary.

FUNCTIONAL EXERCISES

Exercises that are often used to determine if an athlete is ready to return to a higher level of activity or sports com-

Half-squat position   Vertical jump

FIGURE 15-36

In the squat jump, the athlete assumes a half-squat position with hands behind the head, jumps vertically, returns to the original position, and repeats the series without pause.

petition are frequently called "functional exercises."[4,38-40] Functional activities include everything from walking to sport-specific drills. These are often timed and are only limited by the imagination.

The T-Test is a timed functional exercise that uses four cones, set in a T-formation. Cone A, at the base of the T, is the start and finish. Cone B is 10 yards away at the top of the T, cone C is 5 yards to the right of cone B, and cone D is 5 yards to the left. The athlete runs from cone A to touch the base of cone B, then shuffles to touch cone C, shuffles back past cone B to touch cone D, returns to cone B and races for cone A.

Other functional exercises include jogging, running backward, zig-zag running, running circles or figures of eight, and side shuffles.

Cardiovascular Exercises

A rehabilitating athlete must work on cardiovascular fitness. In the early stages of rehabilitation, an athlete with a lower extremity injury to the pelvis, hip, or thigh may not be able to use the injured extremity to condition. Therefore, he or she must find a way to continue cardiovascular exercises to maintain or increase the level of cardiovascular fitness. Many cardiovascular exercises will also improve range of motion and strength.[4,38] An athlete's cardiovascular system can be exercised during different stages of the rehabilitation process by using a stationary bicycle, upper body exerciser, stair stepper, or rowing machine. Swimming or other water-supported exercises are also useful

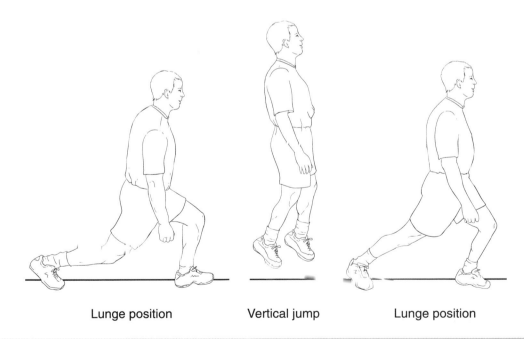

Lunge position   Vertical jump   Lunge position

FIGURE 15-37

In the split squat jump, the athlete begins in a lunge position, jumps vertically, and lands in the lunge position, repeating the exercise without pause.

Starting position   Jump onto box   Jump from box

FIGURE 15-38

In box jumps, the athlete jumps onto a box from a semi-squat position, then jumps down using double arm action.

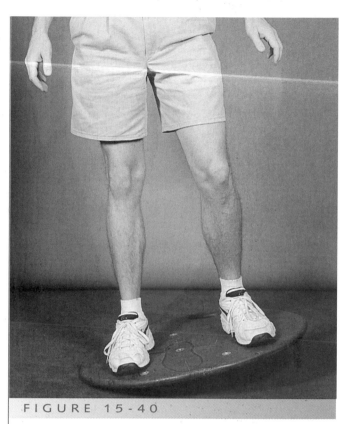

FIGURE 15-40

The athlete steps from side to side on the proprioception board.

FIGURE 15-39

In the single leg squat, the athlete squats on one leg at various joint angles.

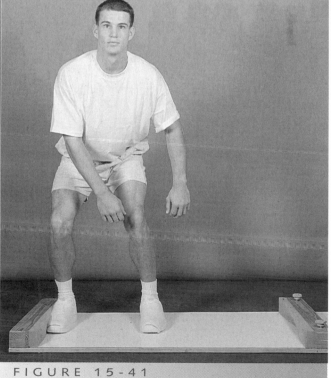

FIGURE 15-41

Using a slide board, the athlete moves laterally on the surface with decreased resistance.

CHAPTER REVIEW

The complex anatomy, physiology, and biomechanics of the pelvis, hip, and thigh lead to unique and often difficult-to-treat athletic injuries. The athletic trainer must understand how these injuries arise and the recommended treatment for each, including appropriate rehabilitation.

The pelvis is a major support structure of the skeleton that allows upright posture and gait, supports the abdominal contents, contains the birth canal in women, and permits the passage of excretory canals.

Muscles about the pelvis include the rectus abdominis, internal and external obliques, and transverse abdominis; the erector spinae; the quadratus lumborum; the iliopsoas; and the psoas minor. Among the anterior thigh muscles are the sartorius; the tensor fasciae latae; the quadriceps; and the adductor group. Posteriorly in the buttock are the gluteus maximus; the gluteus medius and minimis; the piriformis; the obturator internus and superior and inferior gemelli; the quadratus femoris; and the hamstrings.

The lumbosacral plexus supplies nerves to the pelvis, hip, and thigh, while the sacral plexus supplies the buttock and posterior thigh. Blood is supplied to these areas by the common iliac arteries, the external iliac arteries, the femoral artery, the medial femoral circumflex, and the superior and inferior gluteal arteries. The greater saphenous vein drains blood from the thigh.

The hip joint is capable of multidirectional motion in three primary planes (sagittal, transverse, and coronal) in flexion-extension, abduction-adduction, and internal-external rotation. Also possible are transverse or horizontal abduction-adduction or transverse or horizontal flexion-extension. Circumduction occurs when all these motions are combined. The hip is very structurally sound and well constructed for the forces it must sustain.

Athletic injuries can affect any of the structures about the pelvis, hip, and thigh. The athletic trainer must understand the etiology, clinical presentation, and management of each of these injuries. Conditions affecting the iliac crest include a hip pointer, muscle or bone avulsion, and traumatic and stress fractures, while the pelvis is vulnerable to avulsion fractures. The sacrum, coccyx, and sacroiliac joint can sustain traumatic or stress fractures and sacroiliac sprains or dislocations. The buttocks and perineum can sustain a number of injuries. Contusions, strains, fractures, and illness can affect the groin. The greater trochanter is subject to contusions, bursitis, strains and avulsions, sprains, and fractures. Hip joint conditions include traumatic and stress fractures and illness. The thigh can be injured by contusions, myositis ossificans, compartment syndrome, muscle strains and ruptures, and traumatic and stress fractures. Among the miscellaneous conditions of the pelvis, hip, and thigh are iliotibial band syndrome, vastus lateralis calcific tendinitis, meralgia paresthetica, piriformis syndrome, hamstring syndrome, and femoral nerve palsy.

Once a physician completes a thorough injury evaluation, a qualified healthcare professional can make recommendations about the application of protective devices and wraps that support and compress the affected body part, aid in muscle function and support, and reduce excessive range of motion. Supportive techniques are combined with a rehabilitation program to enhance an athlete's return to activity. Rehabilitation focuses on the intact joints and muscles, control of swelling and pain, range of motion, strength, muscular endurance, speed, power, coordination and agility, cardiovascular fitness, and psychological confidence. Components of such a program might include abdominal and low back exercises; stretching and strengthening exercises for the thigh, hip, and groin; proprioceptive neuromuscular facilitation; plyometrics; kinesthetics; functional exercises; and cardiovascular exercises. All members of the healthcare team should agree on a carefully considered, progressive rehabilitation program that will allow the athlete to return safely to sport.

1. The pelvic articulation for the femoral head is the:

A. coccyx.

B. sacrum.

C. acetabulum.

D. obturator foramen.

2. The most inferior prominence of the pelvis is the:

A. iliac crest.

B. sciatic notch.

C. pubic symphysis.

D. ischial tuberosity.

3. The muscle that laterally flexes the pelvis and trunk is the:

A. iliopsoas.

B. pectineus.

C. rectus abdominis.

D. quadratus lumborum.

4. Which muscle flexes, abducts, and externally rotates the thigh?

A. Sartorius

B. Rectus femoris

C. Vastus medialis

D. Tensor fascia latae

5. Which artery supplies the muscles of the anterior, anterior medial, and posterior thigh?

A. Femoral

B. External iliac

C. Common iliac

D. Superior gluteal

6. A violent muscle contraction or sudden passive stretch that results in severe immediate pain such that the athlete keeps the hip or knee flexed is characteristic of:

A. a hip pointer.

B. osteitis pubis.

C. a sacroiliac sprain.

D. a pelvic avulsion fracture.

7. A direct blow to the buttock that results in pain or paralysis in the distribution of the nerve that innervates the posterior thigh is characteristic of which injury?

A. Sciatic nerve injury

B. Meralgia paresthetica

C. Pudendal nerve palsy

D. Stress fracture of the pubic rami

8. Which of the following studies is the most sensitive and specific for diagnosis of a femoral neck stress fracture?

A. Bone scan

B. Radiography

C. Arthrography

D. Magnetic resonance imaging

9. Severe pain in the anterior thigh with inability to extend the knee or ambulate is typical of which injury?

A. Hamstring strain

B. Myositis ossificans

C. Quadriceps rupture

D. Compartment syndrome

10. To improve strength and speed after a pelvis, hip, or thigh injury, which of the following rehabilitation techniques would most likely be used?

A. Plyometrics

B. Kinesthetics

C. Functional exercises

D. Proprioceptive neuromuscular facilitation

Answers on page 892

References

1. Anderson JE: *Grant's Atlas of Anatomy*, ed 8. Baltimore, MD, Williams & Wilkins, 1983.

2. Hollinshead W, Jenkins D: *Functional Anatomy of the Limb and Back*, ed 5. Philadelphia, PA, WB Saunders, 1981.

3. Tortora GJ, Anagnostakos NP: *Principles of Anatomy and Physiology*, ed 4. New York, NY, Harper & Row, 1984.

4. Kisner C, Colby LA: *Therapeutic Exercise: Foundations and Techniques*, ed 3. Philadelphia, PA, FA Davis, 1996.

5. Kreighbaum E, Barthels KM: *Biomechanics: A Qualitative Approach for Studying Human Movement*, ed 4. Needham Heights, MA, Allyn & Bacon, 1996.

6. Campbell JD, Ryan JB, Feagin JA Jr: Injuries of the pelvis, hip, and thigh, in Grana WA, Kalanck A (eds): *Clinical Sports Medicine*. Philadelphia, PA, WB Saunders, 1991, pp 413-426.

7. Campbell JD: Injuries to the pelvis, hip, and thigh, in Griffin L (ed): *Orthopaedic Knowledge Update: Sports Medicine*. Rosemont, IL, American Academy of Orthopaedic Surgeons, 1994, pp 239-253.

8. Metzmaker JN, Pappas AM: Avulsion fractures of the pelvis. *Am J Sports Med* 1985;13:349-358.

9. Woolton JR, Cross MJ, Holt KWG: Avulsion of the ischial apophysis: The case for the open reduction and internal fixation. *J Bone Joint Surg* 1990;72B:625-627.

10. Atwell EA, Jackson DW: Stress fractures of the sacrum in runners: Two case reports. *Am J Sports Med* 1991;19:531-533.

11. Schmalzried TP, Neal WC, Eckardt JJ: Gluteal compartment and crush syndromes: Report of three cases and review of the literature. *Clin Orthop* 1992;277:161-165.

12. Hill PF, Chatterji S, Chambers D, Keeling JD: Stress fracture of the pubic ramus in female recruits. *J Bone Joint Surg* 1996;78B:383-386.

13. Fullerton LR Jr, Snowdy HA: Femoral neck stress fractures. *Am J Sports Med* 1988;16:365-377.

14. McMurtry CT, Avioli LV: Osteitis pubis in an athlete. *Calcif Tissue Int* 1986;38:76-77.

15. Berlusconi M, Capitani D: Post-traumatic hematoma of the iliopsoas muscle with femoral nerve entrapment: Description of a rare occurrence in a professional cyclist. *Ital J Orthop Traumatol* 1991;17:563-566.

16. Karlsson J, Sward L, Kalebo P, Thomee R: Chronic groin injuries in athletes: Recommendations for treatment and rehabilitation. *Sports Med* 1994;17:141-148.

17. Tucker AM: Common soccer injuries: Diagnosis, treatment, and rehabilitation. *Sports Med* 1997;23:21-32.

18. Akermark C, Johansson C: Tenotomy of the adductor longus tendon in the treatment of chronic groin pain in athletes. *Am J Sports Med* 1992;20:640-643.

19. Caudle RJ, Crawford AH: Avulsion fracture of the lateral acetabular margin: A case report. *J Bone Joint Surg* 1988;70A:1568-1570.

20. Ikeda T, Awaya G, Suzuki S, et al: Torn acetabular labrum in young patients: Arthroscopic diagnosis and management. *J Bone Joint Surg* 1988;70B:13-16.

21. Shin AY: The superiority of magnetic resonance imaging in differentiating the cause of hip pain in endurance athletes. *Am J Sports Med* 1996;24:168-176.

22. Haddad FS, Bann S, Hill RA, Jones DH: Displaced stress fracture on the femoral neck in an active amenorrhoeic adolescent. *Br J Sports Med* 1997;31:70-72.

23. Johansson C, Ekenman I, Tornkvist H, et al: Stress fractures of the femoral neck in athletes: The consequence of a delay in diagnosis. *Am J Sports Med* 1990;18:524-528.

24. Aronen JG, Chronister R, Ove PN, et al: Thigh contusions: Minimizing the length of time before return to full athletic activities with early immobilization in 120 degrees of knee flexion. *Orthop Trans* 1991;15:77-78.

25. Kahan JS, McClellan RT, Burton DB: Acute bilateral compartment syndrome of the thigh induced by exercise: A case report. *J Bone Joint Surg* 1994;76A:1068-1071.

26. Klasson SC, Vander Schilden JL: Acute anterior thigh compartment syndrome complicating quadriceps hematoma. *Orthop Rev* 1990;19:421-427.

27. Winternitz WA Jr, Metheny JA, Wear LC: Acute compartment syndrome of the thigh in sports-related injuries not associated with femoral fractures. *Am J Sports Med* 1992;20:476-478.

28. Rougraff BT, Reeck CC, Essenmacher J: Complete quadriceps tendon ruptures. *Orthopedics* 1996;19:509-514.

29. Hershman EB, Lombardo J, Bergfeld JA: Femoral shaft stress fractures in athletes. *Clin Sports Med* 1990;9:111-119.

30. Volpin G, Hoerer D, Groisman G, et al: Stress fractures of the femoral neck following strenuous activity. *J Orthop Trauma* 1990;4:394-398.

31. Barber FA, Sutker AN: Iliotibial band syndrome. *Sports Med* 1992;14:144-148.

32. Orchard JW, Fricker PA, Abud AT, Mason BR: Biomechanics of iliotibial band friction syndrome in runners. *Am J Sports Med* 1996;24:375-379.

33. Macnicol MF, Thompson WJ: Idiopathic meralgia paresthetica. *Clin Orthop* 1990;254:270-274.

34. Williams PH, Trzil KP: Management of meralgia paresthetica. *J Neurosurg* 1991;74:76-80.

35. Barton PM: Piriformis syndrome: A rational approach to management. *Pain* 1991;47:345-352.

36. Parziale JR, Hudgins TH, Fishman LM: The piriformis syndrome. *Am J Orthop* 1996;25:819-823.

37. Wright K, Whitehill W: *The Comprehensive Manual of Taping and Wrapping Techniques*. Cramer Products Inc., 1995.

38. Prentice WE: *Rehabilitation Techniques in Sports Medicine*, ed 2. St Louis, MO, Mosby-Year-Book, 1994.

39. Baechle TR (ed): *Essentials of Strength Training and Conditioning/National Strength and Conditioning Association*. Champaign, IL, Human Kinetics, 1994.

40. Torg JS, Vegso JJ, Torg E: *Rehabilitation of Athletic Injuries: An Atlas of Therapeutic Exercise*. Chicago, IL, Year Book Medical Publishers, 1987.

16

Knee Injuries

K. Donald Shelbourne, MD
Bart P. Rask, MD
Shawn Hunt, MSPT, ATC

QUICK CONTENTS

- The bony and soft-tissue anatomy of the knee and the palpable structures.

- The biomechanics of the knee.

- Evaluation of an athlete with a knee injury, including the physical examination and radiographs.

- The various types of acute knee injuries, recognizing at-risk groups, mechanisms of injury, history, physical examination, radiographs, and treatment.

- Pediatric athletic injuries of the knee.

- Functional knee pain.

- Principles of knee rehabilitation.

- Complications of knee rehabilitation.

- Phases of knee rehabilitation.

OVERVIEW

The knee joint is a very complex structure that is vulnerable to injury in practically all sports activities. The coach or athletic trainer, who must make a determination regarding the seriousness of the injury, first evaluates most knee injuries in athletic situations. Because muscle spasm and joint swelling often develop following knee injuries, the athletic trainer's initial examination may be more reliable than a subsequent exam. Therefore, it is imperative that the athletic trainer understands the basic anatomy of the knee joint and the various mechanisms of knee injury.

This chapter begins with a detailed review of the functional anatomy, biomechanics, and joint stability of the knee. It then describes how to evaluate an injured knee, and reviews specific knee problems, including ligament tears, fractures, dislocations, and overuse injuries. An explanation of how to test for knee instabilities follows. The chapter concludes with a discussion on management of knee injuries, rehabilitation principles, and rehabilitation exercises.

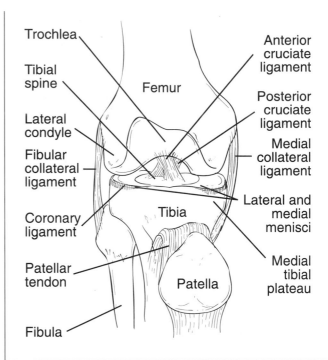

FIGURE 16-1

The knee comprises two joints made up by the femur, tibia, and patella. The four major ligaments of the knee are the medial, lateral, anterior, and posterior collateral ligaments. The tibia is partially covered by menisci.

ANATOMY

Bony Anatomy

The knee consists of two separate joints made from three bones: the femur superiorly, the tibia inferiorly, and the patella anteriorly (**Figure 16-1**). The tibiofemoral joint is the larger of the two joints and contains two compartments, medial and lateral. These compartments correspond to the medial and lateral femoral condyles, which articulate with the medial and lateral tibia plateaus. In the second joint, the patellofemoral joint, the patella articulates with the femoral trochlea only.[1]

Soft-Tissue Anatomy

Proximal to the patella is the quadriceps muscle, consisting of four compartments: the *vastus lateralis* (laterally), the *rectus femoris* (anterior and superficial), the *vastus intermedius* (anterior, deep), and the *vastus medialis* (medially) (**Figure 16-2**). The most distal and medial part of the vastus medialis consists of obliquely oriented fibers attached to the patella and is differentiated as the *vastus medialis obliquus (VMO)*.

Inferior to the patella is the patellar ligament, often referred to as the patellar tendon; the former term is the classic name, and the latter is more commonly used in clinical texts. In this text, it is referred to as the patellar tendon because it attaches the quadriceps muscle to the tibial tubercle and extends superficially to the patella. Deep to the patellar tendon is the infrapatellar fat pad.

The quadriceps mechanism is continuous with the medial and lateral retinacula, which attach to and run on either side of the patella before inserting onto the tibia. The retinacula are strong sheet-like structures attached to the iliotibial band laterally and the VMO medially.

Four major ligaments are involved in knee stability. The *medial collateral ligament (MCL)* provides medial stability against valgus stress; the *lateral collateral ligament (LCL)* provides lateral stability against varus stress; the *anterior cruciate ligament (ACL)* provides stability against anterior stress applied to the tibia, and the *posterior cruciate ligament (PCL)* provides stability against posterior stress applied to the tibia (see Figure 16-1). The ACL originates on the tibial plateau anterior and lateral to the medial tibial spine and inserts onto the medial aspect of the lateral femoral condyle. The PCL originates on the lateral aspect of the medial femoral condyle and inserts on the posterior aspect of the tibia 2 cm below the jointline.

Although the MCL is the primary source of medial stability in the knee, the LCL is only one of many structures

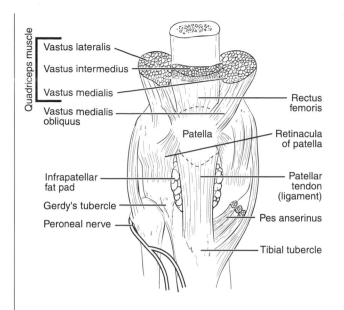

FIGURE 16-2

The musculature of the knee includes the quadriceps, sartorius, gracilis, and semitendinosus muscles. The quadriceps consists of the vastus lateralis, rectus-femoris, vastus intermedius, and vastus medialis.

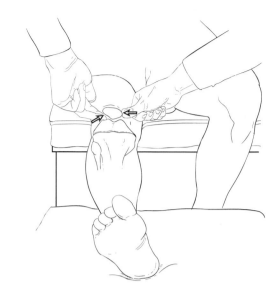

FIGURE 16-3

The patella can be easily palpated, then pushed medially and laterally so that the underlying facet can be palpated.

that contribute to lateral stability. From front to back, the sources of lateral stability in the knee include the iliotibial band, the lateral capsule, the popliteus muscle, the LCL, the biceps femoris muscle, and the lateral head of the gastrocnemius muscle.

The surface of the tibia is partially covered by the medial and lateral menisci, which are tough, flexible structures made of fibrocartilage. The menisci attach to the tibia via the coronary ligaments (see Figure 16-1). The articular surfaces of the femur, tibia, and patella are covered with smooth hyaline cartilage.[1]

Palpable Structures

The patella is a sesamoid bone, easily palpated, that looks like an ovoid structure when viewed from the front. When the knee is extended and the thigh muscles are relaxed, the patella can be pushed medially and laterally so that the underlying and corresponding facet can also be palpated (**Figure 16-3**). The quadriceps tendon attaches to the superior portion of the patella, and the band-like patellar tendon extends inferiorly toward the tibial tubercle. The prepatellar and superficial infrapatellar bursae lie over the patella and patellar tendon, respectively. The bursae enable the overlying skin to move easily over the deeper structures, thus permitting unobstructed knee motion.

The medial femoral epicondyle is palpable just above the jointline and serves as the attachment site for the MCL. The epicondyle is prominent 3 to 4 cm above the

jointline at the highest point of the medial aspect of the medial femoral condyle. The articular part of the medial femoral condyle is palpable medial to the lower half of the patella when the knee is flexed.

The tibiofemoral jointline can be more easily felt when the knee is slightly flexed, so that the overlying skin is pulled taut (**Figure 16-4**). Jointline tenderness medially and laterally is a common sign of a meniscal tear in knees without an acute ACL tear.

The superficial MCL is an indiscreet structure that can be palpated medially, slightly on the posterior half of the knee. The MCL runs from the medial epicondyle, crosses the jointline, and inserts 5 to 7 cm distally on the tibia. The deep MCL is at the jointline and is not palpable as a discrete structure. The LCL, which runs from the lateral femoral epicondyle to the fibular head, is easily palpable as a discrete structure when the legs are crossed in a figure-four position. The popliteus tendon inserts just anterior and distal to the femoral LCL attachment.

The medial and lateral tibial plateaus are palpable just beneath their corresponding femoral condyles. *Gerdy's tubercle*, the attachment site for the iliotibial band, is located laterally on the tibia just below the jointline and is the bump on the tibia lateral to the insertion point of the patellar tendon on the tibial tubercle. One fingerbreadth posterior and lateral to Gerdy's tubercle is the prominent, round fibular head. In thinner individuals, the common peroneal nerve can be palpated just distal to the fibular head as it crosses the fibular neck. Anteriorly, the tibial tubercle is prominent and is the insertion site for the patel-

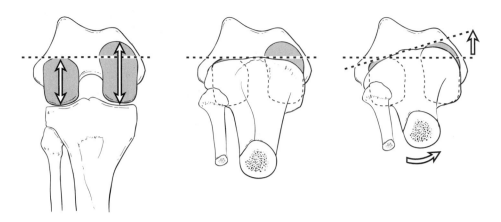

FIGURE 16-6

The screw home mechanism of knee extension occurs because the medial femoral condyle has a larger circumference than the lateral femoral condyle.

the tibial articular surfaces and may predispose the athlete to early arthrosis. If a portion of the meniscus is removed, the risk of arthrosis is unknown but is probably proportional to the amount removed.[5] The menisci do not play a significant role in shock absorption because the chondral surfaces of the femur and tibia contact each other within the center of the concave part of each meniscus.

With normal walking, forces across the knee joint range from two to four times body weight, and 50% to 100% of this force is transmitted through the meniscus. Flexion places more weight on the posterior horns of both menisci. The medial meniscus translates 2 mm in the anteroposterior direction with extension, but up to 5 mm with flexion. The lateral meniscus, which is not tethered by the LCL, moves 9 to 11 mm in the anteroposterior direction. Most of the movement occurs in the part of the meniscus posterior to the popliteus tendon because there are no coronary ligament attachments there.[6]

On the medial side, load is shared equally between the medial meniscus and the articular surface. However, the lateral meniscus must bear most of the lateral side load transmission alone. Therefore, degenerative changes are more likely after partial lateral meniscectomies than after partial medial meniscectomies.[4,7]

Knee Stability

The medial meniscus provides more knee stability against anteroposterior motion than the lateral meniscus. But human cadaver studies show that both menisci provide this function in the ACL-deficient knee. The menisci also assist the ligaments and the capsule in providing condylar geometric conformity during weight-bearing to decrease laxity when loaded. Functional loading by body weight and muscle forces also contribute to knee stability.[6]

Knee flexion is limited by a combination of ligaments and leg and thigh muscles. Extension is limited by ligaments and joint compression.[6] The superficial MCL provides 57% of total valgus restraint at 5° of flexion; at 25° of flexion, it provides 78% of total valgus restraint. The posteromedial capsule is the main secondary restraint at 5° of flexion, but its effect lessens as flexion increases. The PCL plays a significant role in valgus restraint at full extension, and the ACL has a minor role.[3,6]

The LCL is the major primary static restraint to varus stress. Significant static primary lateral stability is also supplied by the lateral capsule, and dynamic lateral stability comes from the iliotibial band, biceps femoris, popliteus muscle, and lateral head of the gastrocnemius muscle. The ACL and PCL are secondary stabilizers and provide some resistance to varus stress if most of the primary stabilizers have been disrupted.[3,6]

The ACL is the primary restraint against anterior tibial translational force. At 90° of flexion, the ACL provides 85% of anterior restraining force, and this contribution increases as flexion decreases. Other structures contributing to anterior restraint include the iliotibial band, the medial and lateral capsules, and the collateral ligaments.[3,6]

The PCL provides 94% of restraint against posteriorly directed force at 90° of flexion, but this contribution lessens slightly as extension increases. Both collateral ligaments and the medial capsule have a smaller role in posterior stability[3,6] (**Figure 16-7**). PCL laxity probably leads to a decrease in medial meniscal load transmission with knee flexion.

The Patellofemoral Joint

The *patellofemoral joint* has four major functions. By increasing the length of the lever arm, it increases the efficiency of the quadriceps mechanism. Because the patella

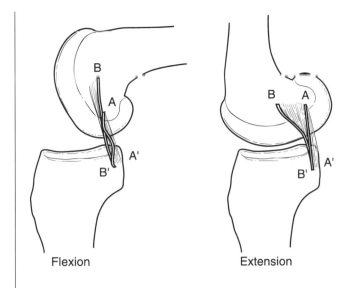

FIGURE 16-7

The insertion of the posterior cruciate ligament extends 2 cm below the tibial plateau surface on its posterior aspect. With flexion, the bulk of the ligament (B-B') becomes taut.

serves as an opposing force against the distal femur, it provides functional stability for the knee under load. It allows the quadriceps force to be transmitted around an angle without significant energy loss from friction. Finally, it protects the articular surface of the trochlea.

As the knee flexes, the patella makes contact with the trochlea at approximately 20° of flexion. Contact begins at the inferior pole and gradually includes more superior parts of the patella as flexion increases. At 90° of flexion, the superior pole of the patella makes contact with the trochlea. The lateral patellar facet remains in contact with the trochlea at all positions, but the medial facet of the patella does not make contact until 30° of flexion. The odd facet, the smallest and most medial articular portion of the patella, does not make contact with the trochlea until after 90° of flexion.[3,6] Because the patella centers into the trochlea with increasing flexion, the steepness of the lateral trochlea contributes to patellofemoral stability.[3,6]

The forces across the patellofemoral joint vary, depending on the type of activity. During level walking, the patellofemoral joint reactive force is one half of body weight (BW). Climbing up or down stairs generates a force of 3.3 BW, or seven times greater than for walking. This explains why patients with patellofemoral damage experience symptoms more frequently when climbing stairs than when level walking. For deep knee bends the force is 7.6 BW.[3,6] With extension against resistance, as in open chain exercises, the patellofemoral joint reactive force increases as the angle of flexion decreases. There-

fore, with less patellar articular surface area, the stresses are concentrated even further.

The quadriceps angle (Q-angle) is formed by three points: the anterior superior iliac spine, the patella center, and the tibial tubercle (**Figure 16-8**). A normal Q-angle is less than 20°. A Q-angle of more than 20° suggests that the quadriceps mechanism is exerting increased lateral pulling forces on the patellofemoral joint, which may be a factor in patellofemoral dysplasias. The vastus medialis and medial patellofemoral ligaments act as counterforces against this lateral drift.

EVALUATION OF KNEE INJURIES

Role of the Athletic Trainer

The athletic trainer is usually the first caregiver to see an athlete after a knee injury. The athletic trainer should use observation and history-taking skills to determine the

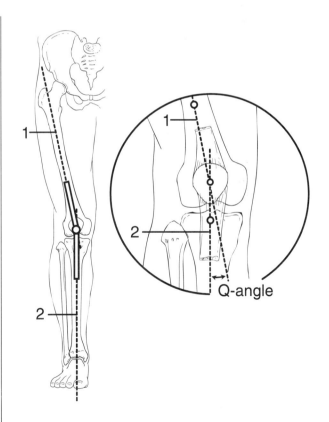

FIGURE 16-8

Three points (the anterior superior iliac spine, patella center, and tibial tubercle) form the quadriceps angle. The line of the quadriceps pull (1) is approximated by a line extending from the anterior superior iliac spine through the center of the patella and (2) from the tibial tubercle to the center of the patella. A normal Q-angle is less than 20°.

severity of the injury and to decide on the need for further evaluation by a physician. Many knee injuries can be accurately diagnosed by history alone. Athletic trainers who understand the typical appearances, causes, and mechanisms of injury will quickly be able to determine the severity of the injury and will know when it is important to refer the athlete for additional medical care.

An athletic trainer faces several different injury scenarios during the year, and the evaluation process differs depending on whether the injury is acute or chronic. In every situation, the athletic trainer should attempt to examine the athlete under the best possible conditions, resulting in the best possible evaluation.

An acute injury occurs when a specific event causes structural damage that is immediately noticed by the athlete. An acute injury usually causes the athlete to stop playing. A chronic injury develops gradually, with increasing pain but often without any specific injury. Onset of a chronic injury is frequently related to the beginning of a new sport season or a change in routine. Usually, pain from a chronic injury does not result from structural damage but from simple overuse, resulting in a sore knee.

Acute Knee Injury Evaluation

An immediate evaluation on the field enables the athletic trainer to decide whether the injury requires immediate medical attention by a physician or immediate transport to the emergency department. Signs of a serious injury include gross lower extremity deformity, a pale foot, or the inability to move the foot or toes, which suggest a fracture or dislocation about the knee. Although these injuries are rare in sports, when they do occur, the athletic trainer should not attempt a manipulation but should alert a physician immediately. If a physician is not available, the extremity should be splinted and the athlete carried off the field and immediately transported to the nearest emergency department.

If the injury is not considered an emergency, the athletic trainer should calm the athlete and move him or her to a more quiet environment off the field for further eval-

FOCUS ON . . .

Evaluation of Knee Injuries

The athletic trainer evaluating a player with an acute injury must determine the severity of the injury and if the athlete should be referred to a physician; these determinations can be made largely on the basis of good observation and history-taking skills.

An athlete on the playing field who displays gross lower extremity deformity, a pale foot, or inability to move the foot or toes (suggesting a knee dislocation) requires immediate attention by a physician or transport to the emergency department. If a physician is not available, the extremity should be splinted for transport.

If the injury is not an emergency, the athletic trainer should calm the athlete and remove him or her from the playing field, at the same time observing the athlete's reaction, how much weight the athlete can place on the leg, and how much pain he or she appears to have. The athletic trainer should allow the athlete to freely describe the injury, and then ask specific questions to help determine whether the injury precludes the athlete from returning to play. General observations of the knee for asymmetry can detect hemarthrosis or soft-tissue swelling. A hemarthrosis may become apparent over several hours and requires that the athlete be referred to a physician. If the athlete can walk normally and the injury appears minor, agility running can determine the possibility of returning to play. If the athlete is limping or unable to bear weight on the leg, a cold compression device and perhaps an immobilizer should be applied until a complete evaluation can be performed.

Ideally, the athlete should be examined in the training room, which can occur at halftime or game's end. The athlete should wear shorts that expose most of the thigh. After taking the history and observing the knee, the athletic trainer should perform only those tests or maneuvers that will confirm the suspected diagnosis in case the athlete is too uncomfortable to tolerate a full examination. If the athlete cannot relax for the examination, physician referral is needed. If the need for referral is unclear, the examination can be repeated the next day, when a hemarthrosis or other signs and symptoms may have developed. In the interim, ice, splinting, compression, rest, and elevation are recommended. If a repeat examination is required, the athletic trainer should observe the athlete's gait and again ask about the mechanism of injury. The normal knee should be evaluated first to establish baselines and to limit apprehension. Again, only those tests needed to confirm the suspected diagnosis should be performed.

When evaluating a player with a chronic injury, the athletic trainer should observe, take the history, examine the normal knee, and then examine the injured knee. Before the examination, the athletic trainer should observe the athlete's gait and stance, ask about major and minor past injuries, which activities improve or worsen symptoms, and if the knee has ever swollen (if so, how quickly and after what activities?).

uation. Generally, there is no reason to perform a knee examination on the playing field, nor is it usually necessary to perform physical tests or maneuvers to determine the severity of injuries on the playing field. Instead, understanding typical history patterns of injuries and observing usual signs and symptoms are sufficient for recognizing when an athlete needs an examination on the field or by a physician.

As the athlete is helped to the sidelines, the athletic trainer can observe the athlete's reaction to the injury. How much weight can the athlete place on the leg? Does the athlete appear to be in pain? The athletic trainer should get the athlete's impression of the injury. During the history taking, the athlete should be allowed to describe the event in his or her own words, instead of responding to a series of restrictive questions. After the athlete describes the injury, the athletic trainer can ask specific questions, but should limit these to only the most pertinent issues. Because the athlete may be in physical and emotional distress, the athletic trainer should focus on determining whether the injury precludes a return to play.

The athletic trainer can discover the mechanism of injury by asking the athlete the following questions: 1) Was your foot planted when the injury occurred? 2) Did your knee twist? If so, which way did it twist? 3) Did you feel or hear a "pop"? 4) Did you land on your knee?

After talking with the athlete, the athletic trainer can make some general observations by viewing both knees simultaneously to see whether a hemarthrosis is developing, based on any asymmetry of knee contour. The athletic trainer must be able to recognize and differentiate between a hemarthrosis and soft-tissue swelling. A *hemarthrosis* is an intra-articular accumulation of blood in the joint. Soft-tissue swelling, or edema, is extra-articular. A hemarthrosis is not always apparent immediately after a knee injury but may appear a few hours later. All athletes with a hemarthrosis should be referred to a physician.

If the athlete can walk normally and the injury appears minor, the athletic trainer should have the athlete do some agility running to determine whether he or she can return to play. If the athlete is limping or is not able to bear weight on the leg, further evaluation is necessary. If it is obvious that the athlete will not be returning to the game, the athletic trainer can postpone any further evaluation and apply a cold compression device and possibly an immobilizer for comfort until the evaluation can be completed in a comfortable location. The athlete's family, if present, should be notified of the evaluation plan.

Ideally, the examination should be completed in the athletic training room, either at halftime or at the end of the game. The athlete should wear shorts that expose most of the thigh so the knee can be fully observed and should lie on an examining table. Based on the observations and history of the injury, the athletic trainer should perform only those tests or maneuvers that will confirm the suspected diagnosis because the athlete may be in too much discomfort to tolerate a full knee examination. If the athlete will not relax for the examination, the athletic trainer should make a referral to a physician for an examination. If there is some uncertainty about the necessity for a referral, the athletic trainer can wait until the next day and try to perform the knee examination again. At 12 to 24 hours after the injury, the athlete's knee may have developed a hemarthrosis, or the athlete may be walking differently and have different pain or soreness. Until then, the athletic trainer should apply ice, splinting, and compression to the knee and advise the athlete to elevate and rest the extremity.

An examination on the day after the injury provides the opportunity to obtain more information from the athlete. The athletic trainer should observe the athlete's gait as he or she walks, wearing shorts. Is the walk normal, on the toe, or straight-legged? What is the athlete's impression of the injury now? By asking specific questions about the mechanism of injury, the athletic trainer may get answers that differ from those of the previous day.

With the athlete lying on the examining table, the athletic trainer should do a full examination of the contralateral normal knee to establish what is normal for that athlete. The athlete should know why the normal side is being examined to avoid anxiety or apprehension. Only those tests needed to confirm the suspected diagnosis should be performed on the injured knee. Any suspected injury to the ligaments, menisci, or joint surface should be referred to a physician.

Chronic Knee Injury

When the athlete complains of a minor or nuisance knee injury, the athletic trainer should be able to perform a complete physical examination of the knee. First, the athletic trainer should conduct the evaluation in the best possible environment. The evaluation includes observation, history, a physical examination of the contralateral knee, and a physical examination of the injured knee.

The athlete should wear shorts that expose most of the thigh so atrophy, effusion, and other signs of asymmetry can be observed. Before the physical examination, the athletic trainer should observe the athlete's gait and stance, talk with the athlete, and listen to what is said about the knee. The athletic trainer should ask questions so the athlete can explain the duration of the problem and describe the type and the location of pain or soreness. These questions might include the following:

- Have you had a major injury to the knee in the past where you could not continue to play?

- Was there a particular minor injury when the knee started hurting?

- What activities aggravate or alleviate symptoms?

- Has the knee ever appeared swollen and, if so, how quickly and after what activities did swelling occur?

lateral view can be used to assess tibiofemoral alignment and patella tendon length and to identify tibia tubercle ossicles or fractures. The Merchant view assesses the patellofemoral joint space and alignment.[17]

Although magnetic resonance imaging (MRI) can be useful as a diagnostic tool to evaluate soft-tissue injuries, it is costly, inconvenient, and rarely necessary. Most soft-tissue injuries of the knee can be identified from the history, observation, and physical examination. MRI is very sensitive and requires careful clinical correlation. The incidence of false-positive readings in one study was 14% for tears of the medial meniscus, 24% for tears of the lateral meniscus and for ACL tears, and less than 1% for PCL tears.[18]

FOCUS ON . . .

Radiographic Examination

Radiographs detect fractures, dislocations, and other bony deformities, including joint space narrowing, patellofemoral malalignment, osteochondritis dissecans, loose bodies, tumors, and cysts. Three views are needed: (1) a bilateral, standing, posteroanterior weightbearing view at 45° of flexion, (2) a lateral view at 60° of flexion, and (3) a Merchant view of the patella at 30° of flexion. Magnetic resonance imaging is useful for diagnosing soft-tissue injuries, but it is rarely necessary, is inconvenient and expensive, and has a high incidence of false-positive findings.

COMMON ACUTE KNEE INJURIES

This section describes acute knee injuries that athletic trainers commonly see during athletic practices and events. The risk group and type of sports involved, mechanism of injury and typical history, the typical physical signs, radiographic features, and treatment will be described for each injury.

Anterior Cruciate Ligament Tears

Risk group: *Anterior cruciate ligament tears* commonly occur in basketball, football, soccer, volleyball, gymnastics, and skiing. An ACL tear can also occur in jumping hurdles because the athlete must land on one foot in a sometimes unpredictable manner. An ACL tear is uncommon in hockey because these athletes do not fix their feet to the ground, which is a necessary part of the mechanism of injury. Age is not a factor except that younger athletes are more involved in high-risk activities.

Mechanism of injury and history: ACL tears most frequently occur during sports that require twisting, jumping, and pivoting. Usually, these are noncontact injuries. The foot is planted, the knee is flexed, and, as the athlete makes a sudden change in direction, a valgus force is applied to the knee with the lower leg in external rotation, resulting in an immediate disability. The same mechanism also occurs in contact sports, such as a clipping injury in football that occurs when a player's foot is planted and the player is hit on the posterolateral part of the knee. Less often, an ACL tear can occur with the knee in hyperextension and the leg internally rotated.[12]

ACL tears usually occur when the athlete is reacting to or is "bumped" by an opponent and are rare in individual sports other than downhill skiing and gymnastics. Athletes shooting baskets on their own or hitting a tennis ball against a wall will not tear the ACL because their movements are predictable and do not require responding to another player's actions.[12]

Almost all athletes who tear the ACL will be unable to continue playing. In describing the injury, most believe that the injury was major and about half will report hearing or feeling a "pop" in the knee. The athlete will usually need help to get up and off the field, and full knee extension will be difficult and painful on the following day because the ACL stump, which is trapped outside of the intercondylar notch, blocks extension.[12]

Physical examination: After an ACL tear, the athlete will walk with a bent-knee gait, if he or she is able to tolerate any weightbearing. A hemarthrosis develops within 6 to 12 hours after the injury and is usually moderate to severe. The Lachman test result will be positive. A positive pivot shift test can also indicate an ACL tear but should not be performed with an acute injury because it is too painful. The athletic trainer should also check for associated MCL or LCL injuries. If there is jointline tenderness with an acute ACL tear, this does not necessarily indicate meniscal tears.[19]

Radiographic examination: A plain radiograph eventually should be obtained for presurgical planning, but one is not necessary to make the diagnosis of an ACL tear. In rare cases, an avulsion of the tibial spine will occur that would affect the definitive treatment plan. An MRI scan usually is not necessary to make the diagnosis.

Treatment: The athletic trainer may first suspect an ACL tear based on observation and history, but the diagnosis should be confirmed by a physician who will also initiate a treatment plan. The athletic trainer can help relieve initial symptoms by attempting to reduce swelling, regain motion, and normalize gait. The athlete's knee typically will feel more normal in about 2 weeks, after the hemarthrosis subsides and range of motion returns. At this point, the athlete may want to return to sports. The athletic trainer should caution patients not to return to play until a physician approves the move. Returning to sports too quickly may result in repeat tears and could result in permanent loss of meniscal or articular cartilage.

Anterior Cruciate Ligament Tears

Among the acute knee injuries athletic trainers often see are ACL tears. At-risk athletes are those who participate in basketball, football, soccer, volleyball, gymnastics, skiing, and track hurdles. ACL tears most often occur during sports that require twisting, jumping, and pivoting and usually are noncontact injuries when the athlete is reacting to or bumped by an opponent. Most athletes who tear the ACL will have known that the injury was major, will have heard or felt a pop, will be unable to continue to play, will walk with a bent-knee gait (if at all), and will develop a hemarthrosis over 6 to 12 hours. The next day, full extension will be difficult and painful because the ligament stump is trapped outside the intercondylar notch.

On physical examination, the athlete walks with a bent-knee gait and has a moderate to severe hemarthrosis and a positive Lachman test result and may have associated medial or lateral ligament injuries.

Once the diagnosis is confirmed by a physician, the athletic trainer can begin setting goals to reduce swelling, regain motion, and normalize gait. The athlete must be cautioned not to return to play before being cleared by the physician to avoid subsequent giving-way episodes and permanent loss of meniscal or articular cartilage.

Athletes who wish to continue participating in competitive, high-risk, cutting, or jumping sports need surgical reconstruction of the ACL. Those who are willing to modify their lifestyle and restrict themselves to noncutting sports (eg, running, weightlifting, biking, swimming) can do well without an anterior cruciate ligament.

Surgery should be performed after the knee has regained normal motion and swelling has diminished (typically 2 to 5 weeks) to avoid complications such as arthrofibrosis and anterior knee pain. Rehabilitation emphasizes resolving swelling and preserving physiologic hyperextension, then regaining flexion, and finally, recovering strength. Return to sport must be individualized, depending on the patient's lifestyle and goals and the surgeon's philosophy of rehabilitation, and bracing is not necessary.

Athletes involved in cutting or jumping sports will need surgical reconstruction to continue a high level of play. Studies of athletes who have an ACL deficiency show that continued play in competitive high-risk sports almost always results in repetitive giving-way episodes, which can lead to meniscal tears and arthrosis.[20] Patients who are willing to restrict themselves to noncutting sports, such as running, weightlifting, biking, or swimming, can do well with an ACL-deficient knee.

Surgery is most successful when performed after the knee has returned to normal motion and has minimal swelling, about 2 to 5 weeks after the injury. Postsurgical problems, such as arthrofibrosis and anterior knee pain, are more likely to develop if surgery is performed on a swollen knee that has not regained full motion.[21,22]

Rehabilitation after ACL reconstruction should first focus on reducing swelling and preserving physiologic hyperextension, then on regaining flexion, and finally on recovering strength. The time it takes to return to sports depends partially on the athlete's lifestyle and goals and partially on the surgeon's philosophy of rehabilitation. Regardless of when the athlete returns, play for the first 2 to 3 months will be awkward. Bracing after successful ACL reconstruction has no proven physical benefit and can be an unnecessary burden to the athlete.[23]

In a child with a midsubstance ACL tear, reconstruction should be delayed until the child reaches Tanner stage 3. Reconstruction before this time may disturb the child's growth, because the surgery involves drilling across growth plates for graft insertion. Until the surgery can be done, the child should abstain from high-risk sports to avoid the risk of meniscal tears.[24]

Medial Collateral Ligament Injuries

Risk group: Isolated MCL injuries or combined ACL/MCL injuries are seen frequently in football players and snow skiers. There is probably no risk differential between the sexes, except that more men play football.

Mechanism of injury and history: Isolated **medial collateral ligament injuries** are commonly second-degree valgus laxity. First-degree injuries are less frequent, and third-degree injuries are usually accompanied by disruption of the ACL and/or the PCL. An athlete with an MCL injury will report medial-side knee pain that is too severe to continue play.

The mechanism of injury is a direct blow to the lateral side of the knee when the foot is planted, resulting in a valgus force. If the foot is not planted, a lateral blow will more likely result in a lateral knee contusion instead of an MCL injury. An isolated MCL injury without contact is uncommon but can occur in snow skiers. These mechanisms should be distinguished from a noncontact torsional injury that results in a combined ACL/MCL injury.[25,26] Another mechanism of injury involves a valgus force to the knee with the tibia externally rotated and foot fixed but unloaded, resulting in a PCL/MCL injury. This type of injury can occur when a football player is on the ground and sustains a valgus external rotation injury to the knee.[27]

Pure MCL injuries rarely have associated meniscal tears because injury to the collateral ligament is due to a distraction force, whereas meniscal injury requires compression force.[25] Meniscal tears do occur with combined ACL/MCL injuries. Medial meniscus tears occur 10% of the time; whereas lateral meniscus tears occur 32% of the time with grade III injuries and 71% of the time with grade II injuries.[26]

Physical examination: On physical examination, the MCL will be tender, and valgus stress will illicit medial pain. Full extension can be obtained easily unless the MCL is injured near its femoral origin or there is an associated ACL tear. Swelling, if present, will be localized to soft-tissue edema medially. The examiner should palpate to determine whether MCL tenderness is located over the femoral or tibial attachments because the treatment will differ depending on the tear site. Both Lachman and posterior drawer tests should be performed to rule out associated cruciate injury.[14]

FOCUS ON . . .

Medial Collateral Ligament Injuries

Isolated MCL or combined MCL/ACL injuries are seen often in football players and snow skiers. Usually the injury results from a direct blow to the lateral side of the knee while the foot is planted, causing a valgus force. Meniscal tears are rarely associated with isolated injuries because of the distraction force (meniscal injury requires compression), but do occur with combined ACL/MCL injuries.

Physical examination reveals tenderness over the MCL and pain with valgus stress. Extension is full unless the ligament is injured near its femoral origin or there is an associated ACL tear. Swelling, if present, is located to soft-tissue edema medially. It is important to determine if the ligament tenderness is over the femoral or tibial attachment because the treatment differs. Radiographs are usually not necessary.

Isolated MCL tears are treated nonsurgically, with the emphasis on resolving pain and swelling, preserving motion, and restoring normal gait. A femoral origin tear (most common) should not be immobilized except for the athlete's comfort, and range-of-motion exercises should begin immediately to avoid stiffness. The athlete can return to play when pain has decreased and motion and strength have improved enough that he or she is comfortable with sport-specific activity. A slow recovery demands that the athlete be reevaluated for associated cruciate ligament tears.

Radiographic examination: For an acute injury, plain radiographs usually are negative, but are useful in ruling out a fracture.

Treatment: All isolated MCL tears can be treated nonsurgically. Treatment should be based on the symptoms with emphasis on reducing pain and swelling, preserving motion, and restoring a normal gait. If the tear has a femoral origin (as with most of these injuries), immobilization should be avoided except for comfort. Range-of-motion exercises should begin immediately because femoral-side tears are more prone to stiffness. If the tear is from the tibial attachment and is a grade III or a loose grade II injury, the knee should be immobilized for 1 to 2 weeks or the MCL may retain some residual laxity.[14] Strengthening exercises can begin after the swelling has resolved and normal range of motion is attained. Weightbearing is allowed as tolerated and bracing usually is not needed. A hinged brace can be worn for comfort and during competition if it makes the athlete feel more secure.[14] Grade I and mild grade II injuries need only symptomatic treatment.

The athlete can return to play when pain, motion, and strength have resolved enough so that he or she is comfortable with sport-specific activity. More severe MCL injuries are associated with a longer time to return to sports. If the recovery seems slow, the knee should be reevaluated for associated PCL and/or ACL tears.

In a study of 51 college football players with grades I and II MCL sprains, those with grade I injuries returned to full play after an average of 10.6 days; those with grade II injuries returned to full play after an average of 19.5 days.[28] Another study reported that 22 out of 24 high school football players with grade III MCL tears and treated with an off-the-shelf brace were stable at the end of 4 weeks and able to return to sports after 5 weeks.[29]

Lateral Side Complex Injuries

Risk group: The risk group for *lateral side complex injury* includes athletes involved in contact team sports and wrestling.

Mechanism of injury and history: The LCL, lateral capsule, popliteus tendon, biceps femoris tendon, iliotibial band, and lateral head of the gastrocnemius all contribute to lateral knee stability. The LCL is not the main lateral stabilizer, and an injury will rarely affect just one of the lateral structures. The one exception is with wrestlers, who can incur an isolated LCL injury when the leg is subjected to an excessive "figure-four" force.[14] Injury to the lateral side complex is rare because it requires the unusual mechanism of a medial blow to the knee when the foot is planted. The athlete will report lateral knee pain and instability.[30]

Physical examination: A varus stress test at 30° flexion is performed and compared with that of the normal knee (see Figure 16-11). A grade III injury is seen primarily with an associated ACL tear, but it can also be seen with a combined ACL and PCL tear (knee dislocation), resulting in lateral laxity in full extension. Peroneal nerve function should be documented because a traction injury can occur with grade III laxity in 30% to 56% of injuries.[30] The integrity of the peroneal nerve can be tested by evaluating the athlete's ability to dorsiflex the ankle or great toe.

Radiographic evaluation: Plain radiographs should be obtained if the patient has a grade III lateral injury to rule out an associated fibular head fracture.

Treatment: Isolated LCL tears, grade I, and possibly grade II lateral-side injuries can be treated symptomatically. Nonsurgically treated grade II injuries may heal with some residual laxity but will still retain good functional results. Grade III lateral complex injuries require surgical reattachment within 10 to 14 days because spontaneous proximal retraction of structures prevents healing in the anatomic position.[14,31]

An 8-year follow-up of patients with grade II and grade III lateral complex injuries who were treated nonsurgically showed that 82% of the patients with grade II injuries and 75% of the patients with grade III injuries were able to return to sports at the same level as before the injury.[31] It is likely that many of the grade III injuries also had associated but unrecognized and untreated ACL or PCL tears, which contributed to the poor prognosis. Chronic lateral complex laxity is a problem because there are no good reconstructive procedures that can enable an athlete to return to high levels of activity. Prompt recognition of this injury is therefore imperative.[14,31]

Tibial Spine Fractures

Risk group: In children, the subchondral bone at the ligament insertion is weaker than the ligament itself. Thus, ACL disruption with an avulsion of the tibial spine occurs more frequently in children than it does in adults.

Although 60% of all *tibial spine fractures* occur in the pediatric age group, midsubstance tears are still more common than avulsions in children.[32] The sports that lead to tibial spine avulsions are the same ones that lead to midsubstance ACL tears: basketball, football, soccer, volleyball, gymnastics, and skiing.

Mechanism of injury and history: The ACL attaches to the fossa anterior of the medial intercondylar eminence (or medial tibial spine) and blends with the anterior horn of the lateral meniscus. The mechanism of injury and history for a tibial spine fracture are the same as for midsubstance ACL tears.

Physical examination: The physical examination of tibial spine avulsions is the same as for midsubstance ACL tears.

Radiographic examination: Plain radiographs are necessary to confirm the diagnosis and will be helpful in making treatment decisions, which depend on the amount of displacement. Radiographs, however, may not reveal the full extent of the injury because a significant portion of the avulsed spine may be chondral. In these cases, arthroscopic examination is sometimes necessary.[33]

Treatment: Minimally displaced fractures can be immobilized and casted in extension for 2 to 6 weeks. Displaced fractures or those that do not allow full extension require open or arthroscopic reduction, with or without internal fixation. The prognosis is good, although there may be occasional symptomatic laxity and an extension block from overgrowth of the spine during healing.[34]

Posterior Cruciate Ligament Tears

Compared to ACL injuries, PCL injuries are neither as common nor as disabling. However, PCL injuries are often missed or misdiagnosed and are probably more

---

FOCUS ON . . .

Lateral Side Complex Injuries

Athletes involved in contact team sports and wrestling are most at risk for lateral side complex injuries. Isolated lateral structure injuries are rare, but the LCL can be damaged when the knee is subjected to an excessive figure-four force, as in wrestling. Lateral complex injuries are rare because they result from a medial blow to the knee with the foot planted.

On physical examination, a varus stress test at 30° of flexion reveals the degree of laxity (grading is as for MCL tears). A grade III injury usually occurs in association with an ACL tear, but can also occur with a combined ACL/PCL (knee dislocation) and results in lateral laxity in full extension. Peroneal nerve function should be checked because traction forces are common with grade III injuries. Plain radiographs are necessary to rule out a fibular head fracture.

Isolated LCL tears and grade I and some grade II lateral complex injuries can be treated symptomatically. Nonsurgically treated grade II injuries heal with some residual laxity, but good functional results. Grade III injuries require surgical repair within 10 to 14 days. Anterior or posterior cruciate ligament tears associated with grade III injury may go unrecognized and untreated, leading to a poor prognosis. There are no reliable reconstructive procedures for chronic lateral complex laxity, and therefore, prompt recognition and treatment are essential.

Tibial Spine Fractures

Subchondral bone at ligament insertions in children is weaker than the ligament itself (in contrast to adults), causing ACL tears to often be associated with tibial spine avulsions. Still, midsubstance tears are more common than avulsions in children. The at-risk sports, mechanism of injury, and physical examination are as for midsubstance ACL tears. Radiographs are necessary, but may not reveal the full extent of injury, in which case arthroscopic examination may be helpful. Minimally displaced fractures are treated with casts in extension for 2 to 6 weeks. Displaced fractures or those not allowing full extension require open or arthroscopic reduction and may need internal fixation.

prevalent than once believed. Patients with PCL insufficiency are often asymptomatic and many probably do not present to the medical team. Therefore, the true incidence of PCL injuries is unknown.[15]

Risk group: PCL injuries can occur in any sport in which the athlete can fall onto the knee with the foot plantar flexed, but are most common in football and soccer.

Mechanism of injury and history: There are three common mechanisms of PCL injury in sports. The first is a direct blow to the anterior proximal tibia that occurs when a player falls onto the knee with the foot plantar flexed. Direct blows can also occur when an opposing player strikes the proximal tibia of an athlete who has the foot planted. The second mechanism is a twisting injury (isolated PCL), and the third is a lateral blow (PCL/MCL).[35] Hyperflexion is a possible fourth cause.[36]

An injury that results in a PCL rupture initially may be dismissed or overlooked by the athlete. It is often possible to continue to play immediately after the injury. Pain will not be severe, and an effusion, if present, may be mild. The athlete will note that something seems wrong with the knee, but walking will be normal and instability usually is not noted. One or 2 weeks later, the athlete may report anterior knee pain when running as he or she approaches full stride, and the posteriorly subluxated tibia abuts the femoral condyles in full extension. The athlete may also have difficulty running at full speed or slowing down from running. Symptoms usually resolve in 3 to 6 weeks.[15]

A PCL injury contrasts with an ACL injury in several ways. First, PCL tears are usually interstitial and can heal spontaneously, but ACL tears are usually complete and do not heal most of the time. Second, PCL disruption occurs with what is perceived as a relatively mild-to-moderate

force, with barely enough energy to disrupt the fibers, and the knee usually has a mild effusion. ACL tears, on the other hand, result from a severe force that is much greater than necessary to disrupt the ligament, are perceived as major incidents, and create a large effusion in the knee. Third, patients with isolated PCL insufficiency usually will be asymptomatic or have mild medial compartment pain. Instability symptoms related to the amount of residual laxity are not usually reported.[12,15] Meniscal pathology

Posterior Cruciate Ligament Tears

PCL tears, often missed or misdiagnosed, are probably more common than once believed, but they are less frequent and less disabling than ACL tears. At-risk sports include football and soccer, but a tear can occur anytime the athlete falls onto the knee with the foot in plantar flexion. A twisting injury can cause an isolated PCL injury, and a lateral blow can cause a PCL/MCL injury. Hyperflexion is another possible cause. The athlete may continue to play, even while knowing that something is "wrong," and pain and effusion may be mild. Other symptoms (which resolve within 3 to 6 weeks) include anterior knee pain when approaching full stride and difficulty slowing down from running or running at full speed. PCL tears are usually interstitial and can heal spontaneously, unlike ACL tears. The athlete is typically asymptomatic, but may have mild medial compartment pain without instability. Meniscal pathology is rarely associated.

On physical examination, the athlete may have minimal pain, a mild effusion, full range of motion, and a contusion or abrasion over the tibial tubercle. The athlete's feet should be flat on the table, with the knees bent. The athletic trainer should note the contour of the tibial tubercles; the tubercle of the PCL-deficient knee is less prominent. The posterior drawer sign is positive (but must be differentiated from a pseudopositive anterior drawer test by a firm anterior endpoint and a soft posterior endpoint), as is the quadriceps active test. MCL integrity should be assessed. Plain radiographs and magnetic resonance imaging are not needed.

Treatment involves resolving swelling and maintaining normal motion, then progressing to strengthening. Return to play can occur at 3 weeks if the athlete passes agility tests and has regained confidence. A brace may make the athlete feel more comfortable or stable. Most athletes are able to return to full activities with conservative treatment.

associated with PCL tears is rare.[15] ACL insufficiency, however, will leave the athlete with a knee that feels unstable and that gives out with cutting and jumping sports. Symptoms do not resolve until stability is surgically restored.

Physical examination: PCL laxity should always be evaluated during all knee examinations. It is important that the examiner recognize the common combination of PCL/MCL injury because the management of this injury differs from treatment of isolated PCL injuries. A mild effusion may develop, unlike the tense hemarthrosis of an ACL rupture. The athlete may have minimal pain and full range of motion. A contusion or abrasion over the tibial tubercle should alert the athletic trainer to a PCL tear.

During the physical examination, the athlete should lie supine on the examining table with both knees bent up and feet flat on the table. The examiner should note the contour of the tibial tubercles because the PCL-deficient knee will have a less prominent contour. The posterior drawer sign will be positive, but the athletic trainer should differentiate this from a "pseudopositive" anterior drawer sign in which excessive anterior motion of the tibia is interpreted as subluxation of an ACL-deficient knee rather than reduction of a PCL-deficient knee. A positive posterior drawer sign for a PCL-deficient knee would be a firm endpoint anteriorly and a soft endpoint with a posteriorly directed force. The examiner should also test for MCL laxity because of the common association with PCL injury.[27]

During the posterior drawer test, the examiner should note the relationship between the tibial plateau and femoral condyles as shown in Table 16-1. Because both tests begin with the athlete in the same position, the quadriceps active drawer test can be performed at the same time as the posterior drawer test. The athlete attempts to contract his or her quadriceps isometrically as the examiner prevents extension. When PCL laxity exists, a gross anterior motion of the proximal tibia to the reduced position will be seen.[35]

Radiographic examination: Plain radiographs may not be necessary to diagnose a PCL injury. An MRI scan can accurately demonstrate an acute PCL injury but cannot evaluate laxity and is not needed. An MRI scan of chronic PCL tear injuries can be interpreted as normal because the ligament can heal.[17]

Treatment: Most PCL tears are interstitial and heal with time, developing a firm endpoint although in a lax position.[15]

Injury management should first emphasize reducing swelling and maintaining normal motion, followed by a prescribed strengthening program. The specific type of rehabilitation program is not significant for the final result, but it can influence the timing of return to activities. The athlete may return to unrestricted play when he or she can pass agility tests and regains confidence, which

can take as little as 3 weeks after injury. A PCL brace can be used to help the athlete feel more stable or comfortable during play. Most athletes are able to return to full activities with nonsurgical therapy.[37]

Current reconstructive procedures cannot reproduce normal PCL kinematics and have proven no better than nonsurgical care.[15,38-40] Arthroscopic evaluation is not needed for evaluation or treatment. Long-term follow-up after nonsurgical care has revealed that most patients rate the knee as good and are able to return to sports.[15,36,37,40]

Combined Ligament Injuries

Combinations of two, three, or even four ligaments can be disrupted depending on the direction and severity of the force. One of the most common combined injuries is the ACL/MCL tear, which results from a lateral blow to the knee with the foot planted. A more severe lateral blow can cause an ACL/MCL/PCL injury. The MCL is the most common ligament tear associated with PCL disruption, because of the combined valgus and external rotation stresses to the flexed knee on the unloaded foot.[27] Combined ligament injuries involving the lateral side complex are less common.

In two-ligament injuries that involve both a collateral and a cruciate ligament, varus or valgus stress will demonstrate collateral ligament laxity with no endpoint at 30° of flexion. However, the leg will be stable in full extension, as it is with isolated complete collateral injuries. Complete disruption of at least one collateral and both cruciates is necessary before laxity in full extension is apparent. Physical examination can sometimes be difficult, but an MRI scan may help identify the torn structures.[27,41]

Medial meniscal tears occur in only 8% of combined ACL/MCL injuries because they have two different mechanisms of injury. The ligament injury is caused by medial distraction, but injury to the menisci requires compression. In contrast, lateral meniscal tears occur in 32% of combined ACL/MCL injuries.[42] These data contradict the classic O'Donahue triad of ACL, MCL, and medial meniscal tears.[43]

Treatment: The treatment approach for combined ligamentous injuries should consider each injury separately. For example, in a combined complete MCL/cruciate injury, the extremity should be treated conservatively until the MCL heals. For a combined ACL/MCL injury, the ACL reconstruction can be performed when motion and swelling normalize after the MCL heals. The indications and timing of surgery in a combined ACL/MCL tear are the same as for an isolated ACL injury.[41]

For combined lateral side complex/cruciate ligament injuries, the lateral complex needs to be repaired within 7 to 10 days or retraction and scarring will make reapproximation difficult. In one study, six out of 10 patients with ACL/lateral side injuries had some peroneal nerve dysfunction.[41] If the athlete requires an ACL reconstruction, the two procedures should be done simultaneously. Acute treatment should be rest and elevation with a cold compression device to decrease swelling. Splinting can be used for ambulation, which should be limited. Surgery should be performed after the inflamed appearance of the knee has resolved.[41]

Knee Dislocations

Probably the most serious knee injury in athletics is a dislocation of the tibiofemoral joint. This is an emergency because of the potential for vascular disruption. The close proximity of the popliteal artery to the proximal tibia means that it can easily become obstructed by an anterior or posterior dislocation.[44]

Risk group: Knee dislocations are most common in football, but rare in other sports.

Mechanism of injury and history: Dislocations can occur in any direction and are named for the direction of tibia displacement. In sports, the most common direction is posterior with a mechanism similar to that for PCL disruption but with greater force, such as when a football player is tackled by several players. Almost any combination of ligaments can be injured, depending on the direction of force, but the ACL and PCL are always involved.[45] After a knee dislocation, the athlete will be unable to stand and will realize that the injury is a major injury.

Physical examination: Frequently upon presentation, the knee may have spontaneously reduced. The diagnosis can be obvious in athletes who have thin legs because the tibia will be grossly displaced and skin tenting will be evident over a prominent part of the tibial plateau. The diagnosis can be more difficult in athletes who have large legs, because the examiner may just note an enlarged swollen knee. The presence or absence of the dorsalis pedis and posterior tibialis pulses should be noted. Both the tibial and the peroneal branches of the sciatic nerve should be tested to ensure their continued functioning (toe extension tests the peroneal branch; toe flexion tests the tibial branch). Common peroneal nerve injury is frequent with lateral and posterolateral dislocations. Presence of a pulse does not rule out a popliteal artery injury.[44]

Treatment: Before the athlete is carried off the field, the leg should be splinted. Emergency transportation to the hospital is imperative. If a few minutes are available until the transport team arrives, a physical examination can be performed by a physician on the sideline.

If time is still available until transport and the examiner is comfortable with the diagnosis, a single quick attempt at reduction can be made by a physician. Gentle longitudinal traction is applied until a "clunk" is felt. If the first attempt at reduction is unsuccessful, no further attempts should be made until the athlete arrives at the emergency department and radiographs are obtained. After reduction,

an objective evaluation of the popliteal artery, either by doppler ultrasound or arteriography, should be done.

Arterial evaluation and repair take precedence over ligament management. Arterial disruption that lasts longer than 6 hours results in a high amputation rate because of muscle *ischemia* (tissue deprived of a blood supply). The patient should be admitted to the hospital and observed for signs of *compartment syndrome*, which is ischemia of the muscles and nerves of the leg secondary to swelling and poor perfusion.[44] An MRI scan should be obtained after the vascular status is stable to determine ligament damage.

The management of ligament damage is controversial. At some institutions, after clearance from the vascular surgery team, dislocations are treated as combined ligamentous injuries.[41,45]

FOCUS ON . . .

Knee Dislocations

A tibiofemoral joint dislocation is an emergency because of the potential for vascular disruption. Knee dislocation is rare in most sports, but common in football. The dislocation can occur in any direction and is named for the direction of tibial displacement. In sports, the most common force is posterior, with the mechanism as previously described for a PCL tear, but with greater force. The ACL and PCL are always involved; other ligaments can also be affected. The athlete is unable to stand.

On physical examination, the knee may have spontaneously reduced. If not, an athlete with thinner legs will have a grossly displaced tibia, noted by skin tenting over the tibial plateau. In athletes with larger legs, the only obvious abnormality may be a swollen knee. Treatment is immediate splinting of the extremity before the athlete is transported off the field and to the hospital. If time permits, a physician can attempt a single, quick reduction with gentle longitudinal traction applied until a "clunk" is felt. If this attempt is unsuccessful, reduction should be delayed until radiographs are obtained. After reduction, the athlete requires either doppler ultrasound or arteriography of the popliteal artery. If the artery must be repaired, this procedure takes precedence over treatment of the ligament injuries. Arterial disruption lasting longer than 6 hours carries a high amputation rate because of muscle ischemia. The athlete is admitted to the hospital and observed for compartment syndrome (ischemia of the muscles and nerves from swelling and poor perfusion). Once the vascular status is stable, an MRI scan should be obtained to assess ligament damage.

Acute Patellar Dislocations

Risk group: One third to two thirds of patients who sustain an acute patellar dislocation have an anatomic predisposition, such as *patella alta* (an abnormally high patella), shallow trochlea, high Q-angle, tight lateral retinaculum, severe *genu valgum* (knock knees), *femoral anteversion* (intoeing), pronated feet, or generalized ligamentous laxity. The injury occurs primarily in sports that require cutting, pivoting, and contact, and commonly presents during adolescence.[46]

Mechanism of injury and history: Patellar dislocations are always lateral. A direct blow that forces the knee into valgus can cause an acute patellar dislocation. The athlete may notice that the patella is positioned laterally or that "something" (the uncovered femoral condyle) has popped out on the medial side. The athlete may also feel or hear one or two "pops." The first pop is the dislocation and the second is the reduction. The patella will stay dislocated as long as the knee is flexed, but will frequently spontaneously reduce if the athlete extends the knee. During the dislocation, the VMO or the medial retinaculum can tear away from the patella unless the athlete has significant malalignment factors that would prevent tearing of these structures.[46]

Chondral or osteochondral fractures can occur either as the patella is forced out or as it relocates in the trochlear groove. These fractures can result in defects at the medial facet of the patella and/or the lateral aspect of the trochlea and may create loose bodies that can cause recurrent locking and effusions.[46]

Physical examination: If the patella is still dislocated at the time of the physical examination, the knee will be flexed and the examiner will note a gross prominence laterally and the bare trochlea medially. If the athlete presents with the patella reduced, as is often the case, there will be a large effusion with tenderness over either the medial retinaculum or the VMO. If the athlete has significant anatomic predisposing factors, an effusion may not be present because the dislocation occurred without tearing the medial soft tissues. Because most acute hemarthroses are associated with ACL tears, the examiner must first rule out injury to the ACL by checking passive extension. If an ACL tear exists, the examiner will not be able to fully extend the knee because of the ligament stump impinged in the joint. After a patellar dislocation, the knee can be passively extended. The J-sign, in which the patella shifts laterally out of the trochlear groove as the knee is fully extended, should be observed as it is a sign of patella alta undergoing lateral dislocation or subluxation during active extension.[47,48]

FOCUS ON . . .

Acute Patellar Dislocations

Some patients with acute patellar dislocations have an anatomic predisposition, such as patella alta, shallow trochlea, large Q-angle, tight lateral retinaculum, severe genu valgus, femoral anteversion, pronated feet, or generalized ligamentous laxity. Cutting, pivoting, and contact sports also increase the risk. Most patients are adolescents.

Patellar dislocations are always lateral. A direct blow forces the knee into valgus, and one or two "pops" are felt or heard: the dislocation and then the reduction. The patella may be positioned laterally or the athlete may note that something "popped out" medially (the medial femoral condyle). The patella remains dislocated while the knee is flexed, but will often spontaneously reduce with knee extension. During dislocation, the vastus medialis obliquus (VMO) or the medial retinaculum can tear. Chondral or osteochondral fractures can occur with either the dislocation or the reduction and may result in loose bodies that cause recurrent locking and effusions.

On physical examination, if the patella remains dislocated, the knee is flexed, with a gross prominence laterally and a bare trochlea medially. If the patella is reduced, there is a large effusion with medial retinacular or VMO tenderness. However, in the presence of significant anatomic predisposing factors, effusion may be absent if tearing of medial soft tissues was not necessary for the dislocation to occur. A Merchant view allows assessment of the patella when the quadriceps is relaxed. The Insall ratio estimates patellar height. The reduced patella is usually more laterally displaced than the normal patella.

Treatment is patellar reduction. With the athlete supine, gentle, passive extension should be attempted by lifting the foot while supporting the distal thigh; a "clunk" will be felt or heard as the patella returns to the trochlea. Physician referral is needed, along with radiographs. If effusion is minimal and there are no signs of malalignment and a negative J-sign, treatment is conservative. Brief splinting in extension, a cold compression device, elevation, and a normal gait are recommended. Once swelling resolves, quadriceps-strengthening exercises can begin. The athlete can return to practice and competition when comfortable. A neoprene knee sleeve with a patellar cutout can relieve symptoms and improve the athlete's confidence level. Loose bodies from osteochondral fractures frequently are reabsorbed, and arthroscopic removal is needed only if crepitation or effusions persist. To prevent future problems, surgery may be justified in those athletes with a high risk for recurrent dislocation.

Radiographic evaluation: A Merchant radiographic view allows the physician to observe the alignment of the patellae when the quadriceps are relaxed. The dislocated patella will usually be more laterally displaced than the opposite normal patella. Evidence of a shallow trochlea and an abnormal congruence angle can also be seen on the Merchant view.[48] The Insall ratio can be measured on the lateral radiographic view as an estimate of patella height.[46] On a lateral radiograph, with the knee at 30°, the longest lengths of the patella and patellar tendon are measured. Normally, the measurement of the two lengths is about equal.

Treatment: The athlete should immediately be helped to the sideline or athletic training room before a complete evaluation or treatment is initiated. An immediate referral to a physician should be made. Initial treatment is to reduce the patella. The athlete should be relaxed and lying supine on the examining table. The physician gently attempts passive extension of the knee by slowly lifting the foot with one hand while supporting the distal thigh with the other. As the knee extends, gravity should allow the patella to "clunk" back into the trochlea.

After the game, a radiographic evaluation should be obtained. If the knee looks benign and has minimal effusion, no signs of malalignment, and a negative J-sign, conservative therapy should be used.[46,49] Symptoms may be relieved with a few days of splinting in extension, use of a cold compression device, and elevation. The athlete should be encouraged to walk with a normal gait. After swelling resolves, quadriceps strengthening exercises can commence. An athlete can return to sports practice and competition when he or she feels comfortable doing so. A neoprene knee sleeve with a patella cutout provides symptomatic relief in many patients and may help the athlete feel more confident when returning to sports.[49] A nonrandom study showed that patellar dislocations treated with initial immobilization in a posterior splint for approximately 3 weeks had a lower recurrence rate than those without immobilization.[50]

To prevent future morbidity and chondral surface damage, an acute surgical patellar stabilization may be justified in those athletes with a high chance of recurrence. Candidates for early surgical therapy include patients with a grossly abnormal congruence angle of greater than +16°, more than five malalignment factors, and persistent VMO atrophy after rehabilitation.[48]

For other patients, surgery should probably be delayed until recurrent dislocations become annoying. Loose bodies from osteochondral fractures sustained during the dislocation or reduction can be present in the knee but frequently become trapped in the synovium and are reabsorbed. Arthroscopic removal is needed only if crepitation or effusions persist.[47]

Recurrent Patellar Dislocations

Recurrent patellar dislocations can begin in individuals as young as age 5 years, but usually they do not present until adolescence, or even as late as the third decade.[46] The tendency to redislocate is greater if the primary dislocation occurred before the athlete attains age 20 years, and redislocations rarely occur after the athlete attains age 30 years.[51] Osteochondral fractures may result in loose bodies that can cause recurrent locking and effusions. Following a patellar dislocation that has reduced, the athlete may walk with the knee slightly flexed to avoid the position of instability. The patella is often hypermobile and can sometimes be manually pushed out to the lateral side; the apprehension test result will be positive.[46]

If redislocations occur only rarely and under unusual circumstances, there is no need to decide whether to operate until crepitation or effusions develop. If redislocations occur frequently enough to affect the athlete's lifestyle or if they are disabling, surgery is indicated. Surgical options include an arthroscopic lateral release, a tibial tubercle realignment, a medial soft-tissue tightening, or some combination of the three procedures.

Recurrent patellar dislocations generally occur less frequently as the patient ages.[51] In one study, 21 patients were treated with physical therapy for recurrent dislocations at an average age of 25 years (range age 13 to 54 years). After a mean of 14 years follow-up, only four patients continued to have dislocations.[51]

Meniscal Injuries

Risk group: An isolated acute meniscal tear is unusual in a young athlete who has an intact ACL. Therefore, if a meniscal tear is suspected in a patient under age 20 years, the examiner must rule out an ACL tear. However, wrestlers are an exception to this rule. These athletes spend much of their time kneeling and hyperflexing their knees, which squeezes the meniscus between the tibia and femur posteriorly. Other athletes at risk are weightlifters who perform leg curls and dead lifts.[52,53] Any activity that causes shear or compression can result in an isolated meniscal tear in an athlete older than age 30 years because of predisposing degeneration. Athletes with chronic ACL deficiency are at risk for displaced bucket handle meniscal tears (meniscus tears that displace into the intercondylar notch), which are usually medial. Displaced bucket-handle meniscal tears rarely occur in conjunction with acute ACL tears.[54]

Mechanism of injury and history: An acute meniscal tear occurs when the tibiofemoral joint subluxes, and shear and twisting forces damage the meniscus, such as what occurs with ACL disruption. Recent data reveal that 70% of patients with acute ACL tears also have meniscal tears: 30% have lateral meniscal tears; 17% have medial menis-

Meniscal Injuries

Although wrestlers and weightlifters are at risk for isolated meniscal tears, a young (younger than age 20 years) athlete with a meniscal tear should also be evaluated for an ACL tear. Players older than age 30 years can sustain isolated meniscal tears more easily as a result of tissue degeneration. Chronic ACL deficiency places the athlete at risk for displaced bucket-handle meniscal tears. An acute meniscus tear occurs when the tibiofemoral joint subluxes, as with an ACL disruption. Most patients with ACL tears also have meniscal tears; however, these tears are more likely to heal because they are traumatic tears in the peripheral region, unlike the degenerative tears not associated with ACL deficiency.

On physical examination, the athlete has jointline pain, made worse with weightbearing, squatting, and hyperflexion, and may have an effusion. Radiographs are necessary to rule out fractures and osteochondritis dissecans. An MRI scan is very accurate in young patients with traumatic tears.

Medial meniscal tears are more often symptomatic than lateral meniscal tears; most tears occur in the posterior load-bearing area, causing medial and posteromedial jointline pain and effusion. Anteromedial pain with a mechanical block to extension reflects a displaced bucket-handle or ACL tear.

If the ACL is intact, rehabilitation emphasizes the return of hyperextension and full flexion and strength. Pain-producing maneuvers should be avoided. If symptoms do not improve, MRI or arthroscopic evaluation may be appropriate. An acutely displaced bucket-handle tear in an athlete with an ACL tear requires arthroscopic repair or excision.

Lateral meniscal tears are less common, even in the older athlete, because the lateral meniscus is more mobile and degenerative tears are less frequent. Half of lateral meniscal tears are associated with an effusion, but most produce middle-third jointline pain. A false-positive McMurray test can reflect patellofemoral subluxation and normal lateral meniscus hypermobility and must be interpreted cautiously. Lateral meniscal tears often heal or become asymptomatic without surgical treatment. Symptomatic tears are treated with arthroscopic repair or partial excision. The lateral compartment is more prone to degeneration than the medial compartment, and therefore, as much of the lateral meniscus should be preserved as possible.

cal tears, and 23% have both medial and lateral tears.[19] Meniscal tears associated with ACL tears are more likely to heal because they are traumatic tears that usually occur in the peripheral portion of the meniscus. In contrast, tears not associated with ACL injuries do not heal as well because the major factor in the injury is the degenerative component of the meniscus.[54]

Knowing the mechanism of injury is important for ruling out the possibility of a meniscal tear. For example, in a complete MCL tear, the medial side of the joint is distracted, which protects the medial meniscus. The athlete may have pain over the medial jointline, but it is from the MCL tear and not the meniscus.[42] Meniscal tears require a compressive force with the foot loaded. An athlete with a meniscal tear will present with pain at the jointline that worsens with weightbearing, squatting, and hyperflexion.

Physical examination: A knee effusion may or may not be present, but most patients will have jointline tenderness. Displaced bucket handle tears, which usually occur with chronic ACL deficiency, will cause the knee to be locked in flexion.[54] The examiner can diagnose a meniscal tear based on a positive history that includes pain with squatting, effusion, limited flexion as a result of pain, limited extension if displaced, and medial or lateral jointline tenderness.[55] The most frequently described provocative test is the McMurray test (see Figure 16-15).

Radiographic examination: Radiographic evaluation should be obtained in all athletes with suspected meniscal tears to rule out osteochondral fractures of the tibial plateau or femoral condyle and osteochondritis dissecans, which can have a similar presentation. An MRI scan is nearly 100% accurate in diagnosing meniscal tears in young patients with traumatic rather than degenerative tears. In an older population, an MRI scan can detect an asymptomatic meniscal tear.

Medial meniscal tears

Medial meniscal tears are more commonly symptomatic than lateral meniscal tears, and most occur in the posterior half, the load-bearing area of the meniscus.[56] Pain will be medial to posteromedial. Pain in the anterior third is not from a medial meniscal tear, because no weightbearing occurs there, and anterior medial meniscal tears are extremely rare. Patients with a displaced bucket-handle-type medial meniscal tear may exhibit anteromedial pain with a mechanical block to extension, in which they cannot straighten the knee because it is mechanically blocked by the meniscus that has been displaced into the intercondylar notch. In these patients, an ACL disruption should be ruled out because ACL disruptions have a similar appearance and can also block extension. A physical examination will reveal medial to posteromedial jointline tenderness. Most knees with symptomatic medial meniscal tears have an effusion.[55]

Treatment: Nonsurgical treatment should first be tried for a patient who has an ACL-intact knee, no mechanical block to extension, and a suspected meniscal tear. Rehabilitation should emphasize the return of hyperextension, full flexion, and strength. The athlete should avoid pain-producing actions such as jumping, pivoting, twisting, and other high-impact activities. If nonsurgical therapy is unsuccessful, the physician should reconsider the diagnosis with an MRI scan or arthroscopic evaluation; outpatient arthroscopic excision or repair may be required.[55,57] After an arthroscopy, a functional rehabilitation program can be initiated.

Patients who have an ACL deficiency and a locked, "bent" knee with an acutely displaced bucket handle tear should undergo arthroscopic repair or excision of the meniscus. Knee rehabilitation should occur before the patient has an ACL reconstruction as a second-stage procedure. There is a higher incidence of arthrofibrosis when both procedures are performed simultaneously.[54] Cutting and pivoting sports should be avoided until the ACL is reconstructed. Bracing will not adequately protect the meniscus during these activities.

Lateral meniscal tears
Symptomatic isolated lateral meniscal tears are not common, even in the older athlete. Because the lateral meniscus is more mobile and therefore more accommodating to stress than the rigidly fixed medial meniscus, degenerative tears are much less frequent. The examiner should rule out the more common patellofemoral pain syndromes because these can often present as pain on the lateral side.[55,56]

Physical examination: Upon physical examination, less than one half of patients with symptomatic tears will have an effusion. Jointline tenderness is at the site of the symptomatic tear, usually in the middle third of the meniscus. Tears that occur behind the popliteus are so mobile that they are rarely symptomatic. Results of a lateral McMurray sign should be interpreted with caution because false positives can occur if there is misleading patellofemoral subluxation and normal lateral meniscus hypermobility.[55,56]

Treatment: Lateral meniscal tears usually heal or become asymptomatic without surgical excision or repair. Often, lateral meniscal tears are discovered incidentally during ACL reconstruction or arthroscopy, but these are rarely symptomatic, especially if they are posterior to the popliteus tendon. Asymptomatic tears do not need treatment, and symptomatic lateral meniscal tears can be treated with arthroscopic repair or partial excision if the repair is not possible.[56,58] As much meniscus as possible should be preserved because the lateral compartment is more prone than the medial side to joint degeneration when the meniscus is removed.[5]

Discoid Lateral Meniscus
A *discoid meniscus* is a congenital deformity in which the lateral meniscus lacks the usual concavity that faces the intercondylar notch. Thus, the lateral meniscus covers a greater surface area of the lateral tibial plateau.

Risk group: In a series of 347 arthroscopies for meniscal lesions in children and adults, the incidence of a discoid meniscus was 5.2%, of which 20% were bilateral.[59,60] In the athletic child, symptoms can begin as early as age 7 or 8 years, or they may not present until adolescence when the intensity of sports participation increases.[61]

Mechanism of injury and history: Discoid menisci are thicker, poorly vascularized, and more prone to mechanical stress and tears from any sport or routine daily activity. Common symptoms include pain with ordinary activity, limping, giving way, snapping, swelling, and locking. Snapping is present in only 39% of these patients. A history of trauma may or may not be elicited.[61]

Physical examination: There may be a positive McMurray sign, as well as jointline tenderness, an effusion, a locked knee, or loss of physiologic hyperextension.[61]

Radiographic examination: Radiographs are normal in 90% of patients with a discoid meniscus; 10% may show widening of the lateral compartment and squaring of the lateral femoral condyle.[59] The diagnosis is usually evident clinically, but an MRI scan is sometimes necessary for confirmation.[62]

Treatment: Immediate specialty referral is indicated for athletes with a locked knee. Treatment consists of arthroscopic excision of the excess meniscus and, in some cases, stabilization may also be necessary because some discoid menisci can be hypermobile.[61]

ACUTE FRACTURES

Patellar Fractures
Patellar fractures are uncommon in sports. When a fracture does occur, it usually results from direct trauma such as a fall onto a hard surface with the knee flexed and foot dorsiflexed. Indirect trauma, such as from a violent quadriceps contraction, is rarely the cause. In these cases, a pre-existing patella stress fracture should be ruled out.[63]

Physical examination: Athletes with nondisplaced fractures will have tenderness directly over the patella and a large hemarthrosis. With displaced fractures, there will be a palpable gap at the fracture site. The athlete's ability to perform a straight leg raise does not rule out a displaced patella fracture if the medial and/or lateral retinaculae are intact. Extension typically will lag at least 10° to 30°.[63]

Treatment: Specialty referral is indicated for all athletes with suspected fractures. Plain radiographs should be ordered to establish the diagnosis and aid in the treatment decision. The neurovascular status should be checked to rule out a knee dislocation, which can have a similar appearance in larger legs with a tense hemarthrosis.

The lower extremity should be splinted in extension. Nondisplaced fractures may be immobilized until tenderness is gone. Fractures displaced more than 2 to 4 mm require surgical reduction and fixation.[63]

Distal Femur and Proximal Tibia Fractures

Distal femur and proximal tibia fractures rarely occur as a result of a sports-related injury because these fractures require a great deal of force. The athlete may suspect a fracture because of the swelling. Immediate evaluation by a physician is imperative. Initial management includes splinting the knee in the position found and immediately transporting the athlete to the emergency department.

Radiographs are required for diagnosis (**Figure 16-14**). Minimally displaced fractures can usually be treated nonsurgically. Significantly displaced fractures may require surgical reduction and fixation.[63]

Osteochondral Fractures

Mechanism of injury and history: Patellar dislocation is probably the most common cause of acute osteochondral fractures. A fragment generated during the dislocation produces a lateral femoral condyle fracture; one generated during reduction produces a medial patellar facet fracture. Another common cause is a direct blow to the knee, such as a fall onto a hard surface with foot dorsiflexed. If osteochondral fractures become displaced, they can behave as loose bodies within the joint, and cause mechanical symptoms such as locking, crepitation, and recurrent effusions.[64]

Physical examination: During the physical examination of an acute osteochondral fracture, the examiner must first rule out a dislocated patella that has reduced. A large effu-

---

FOCUS ON . . .

Acute Fractures

Patellar fractures

Uncommon in sports, patellar fractures can occur from direct trauma with the knee flexed and the foot dorsiflexed. On physical examination of a nondisplaced fracture, the athlete will have tenderness over the patella and a large hemarthrosis. A displaced fracture will demonstrate a palpable gap at the fracture site. The extremity should be splinted in extension and the athlete referred to a physician. Radiographs aid in determining the appropriate treatment: immobilization for a nondisplaced fracture, surgical reduction and fixation of a displaced fracture.

Distal femoral and proximal tibial fractures

Rare in sports, these fractures require a great deal of force. Swelling in or about the knee can be mild or marked. The knee should be splinted as it is and immediate transport to the emergency department provided. Radiographs will help determine appropriate treatment: nonsurgical management for minimally displaced fractures, surgical reduction and fixation for significantly displaced fractures.

Osteochondral fractures

Patellar dislocation is the most common cause of acute osteochondral fractures, generating fragments either during dislocation (lateral femoral condyle fracture) or during reduction (medial patellar facet fracture). A direct blow to the knee, as from a fall onto a hard surface with the foot dorsiflexed, can also cause an osteochondral fracture. If the fracture is displaced, it can cause loose body symptoms of locking, crepitation, and recurrent effusion.

On physical examination, the athletic trainer should check for a reduced patella. A large effusion can accumulate rapidly, but a mobile patella can permit palpation of the patellar facets. Patellofemoral tracking for crepitation and the medial femoral condyle for tenderness with knee flexion should be evaluated, in addition to ligament stability and range of motion. Radiographs, including the Merchant view, are necessary, and computerized tomography may be of benefit to learn the size and location of the fracture fragment.

An athlete with a large effusion must be cleared by a physician before returning to play. The knee should be splinted in extension, a cold compression device applied, and the athlete referred to a physician. If no mechanical block to knee motion exists, physical therapy may prompt reabsorption of the fragment. However, with blocked motion or crepitation, arthroscopy may be needed to remove or reattach fragments.

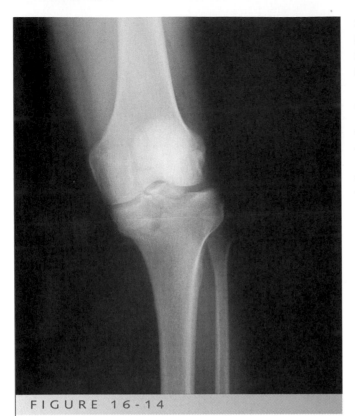

FIGURE 16-14

Radiographs are required for diagnosis of a proximal tibia fracture.

sion may develop rapidly. If the patella is mobile enough, palpating the patellar facets may elicit tenderness suggesting an osteochondral fracture. Patellofemoral tracking should be evaluated for crepitation. The medial femoral condyle can be palpated for tenderness with the knee flexed. Ligament stability should always be examined in patients with an effusion because the most common cause of a traumatic hemarthrosis is an ACL tear. Limitations to range of motion should be checked.[49,64]

Radiographic examination: Plain radiographs, including a Merchant view, are imperative before treatment commences. Computed tomography may be needed to delineate the size and location of the fracture fragment.

Treatment: If a large effusion is present, the athlete should not return to play until he or she receives clearance from a physician. The knee should be splinted in extension, a cold compression device should be applied, and the patient should be referred to a physician. In cases where there is no mechanical block to knee motion, nonsurgical physical therapy to treat the symptoms is an option because the loose osteochondral fracture bodies are frequently trapped within knee synovium and reabsorbed. If motion is blocked or if crepitation is present, arthroscopic surgery may be necessary to remove or fix the fragments. Large fragments in the weightbear-

ing area will probably be reattached, and return to play should be delayed until the fragment heals. If the fragment is removed, the athlete can return to play as soon as symptoms will permit.[49]

OVERUSE INJURIES

Overuse injuries are caused by chronic, repetitive microtrauma usually related to sports, causing submaximal insults to local tissues and resulting in the onset of pain.[65] The result is a painful knee that has no damaged or broken structures. Overuse injuries to the knee are common in athletes, usually because of a training error such as doing too much too quickly. A common training error scenario involves the adolescent who had been sedentary, but suddenly tries out for the track team and begins training as a middle distance runner. Focused training year-round for the same sport is another common cause of overuse injuries.

Overuse injuries can be treated nonsurgically. Surgical intervention should be attempted only when there is a surgically correctable deformity or when it is clear that further nonsurgical care will not help.[65]

Prevention of Overuse Injuries

The preparticipation physical evaluation presents both the physician and the athletic trainer with opportunities to prevent overuse sports injuries. The athlete should also undergo a physical evaluation before adjusting his or her level of competition. Increases in activity duration, frequency, and intensity should be gradual. For running sports, the "10% per week" rule (an increase in activity by 10% each week) can be used as a guideline in increasing the duration and intensity of training. Athletes who have a history of overuse injury may benefit from stretching and strengthening programs as well as from an assessment of the need for orthotics to correct lower extremity malalignment.[65]

Patellofemoral Dysplasia

Patellofemoral dysplasia (PFD) is a clinical diagnosis describing a spectrum of disorders that involve anterior knee symptoms in athletes who may or may not have signs of patellofemoral malalignment. PFD is the most common overuse injury and can be described as one of five types based on the degree of malalignment. The mildest form, overuse PFD, is anterior knee pain from overuse in athletes who have no malalignment. The other four types, in increasing degrees of malalignment, are lateral patellar compression syndrome, chronic subluxating patella, recurrent dislocating patella, and chronic dislocating patella, which is rarely present in athletes.[66]

Risk group: PFD is most common in adolescent athletes involved in running and jumping sports.[66]

FOCUS ON . . .

Overuse Injuries

Overuse injuries caused by chronic, repetitive microtrauma, usually related to sports, result in submaximal local tissue insults and pain. A common cause of overuse is training errors. Overuse injuries are treated nonsurgically unless there is a surgically correctable deformity that cannot be improved by conservative care. To prevent overuse injuries, the athlete should be evaluated before an anticipated change in competition level; increase duration, frequency, and intensity of activity gradually; and incorporate stretching and strengthening programs and orthotics as needed.

Patellofemoral dysplasia

Patellofemoral dysplasia, the most common overuse injury, is the clinical diagnosis for a spectrum of disorders involving anterior knee pain. It is divided into five types, depending on the amount of malalignment: (1) no malalignment, (2) lateral patellar compression syndrome, (3) chronic subluxing patella, (4) recurrent dislocating patella, and (5) chronic dislocating patella (rare in athletes). Adolescent athletes involved in running and jumping sports are most likely to be affected. Malalignment factors that may predispose the athlete to this condition include a Q-angle of more than 15° to 20°, patella alta or lateral patellar tilt, tight lateral retinaculum, generalized ligamentous laxity, femoral anteversion, pronation, genu valgum or varum, and femoral condyle hypoplasia.

On physical examination, the athletic trainer should look for signs of malalignment and perform the apprehension test. Radiographs, including the standing 45° weightbearing PA view, lateral view, and Merchant view should be obtained to look for patella alta, lateral patellar tilt, shallow trochlea, laterally displaced patella, and abnormal congruence angle.

Overuse patellofemoral dysplasia presents as overuse anterior knee pain in athletes without malalignment. It is common in those who participate in marathons, basketball, and other running sports and is usually caused by training errors. Pain occurs during activity and may persist after the activity ends. Physical examination and radiographs are normal. Treatment is to decrease the duration, frequency, or intensity (or a combination of these) of the offending activity, while substituting other activities (eg, stair-stepping, cycling, swimming, rowing) to maintain fitness. As conditioning improves, the offending activity can gradually be returned to the regimen in most athletes.

Lateral patellar compression syndrome is the mildest form of patellofemoral dysplasia and causes the insidious onset of vague, poorly localized pain on the anterior aspect of the knee that is increased with activity, stairs, sports, and prolonged sitting with the knee flexed. Rest or walking short distances relieves symptoms. Locking, crepitus, giving way, and swelling may occur at more advanced stages.

Physical examination reveals patellofemoral tenderness and a tight lateral retinaculum. The Merchant view may be normal or may show a laterally tilted or subluxated patella or an abnormal congruence angle. Treatment is initially nonsurgical, with a three-phase rehabilitation program: pain control, stretching the hamstrings and quadriceps muscles and strengthening the extensor mechanism, and functional progressive exercises. When nonsurgical treatment fails, arthroscopic release of the lateral retinaculum may be beneficial in athletes with a tight lateral retinaculum, patellar tilt, and an abnormal congruence angle. With a large Q-angle, genu valgum, J-sign, or lateral subluxation, a tibial tubercle medialization procedure (ie, Elmslie-Trillat) may be indicated.

Symptoms of chronic subluxating dysplasia can be vague: the patella partially dislocates and then snaps back into place. Subluxation is more likely to occur during quadriceps muscle contraction with the knee flexed and the foot fixed to the ground and externally rotated. Associated chondromalacia may become severe.

On physical examination with the knee flexed to 30°, the patella may be easily subluxated laterally as the knee is extended. With the athlete seated, the patella may be oriented laterally, suggesting lateral malalignment, and proximally, suggesting patella alta. The Merchant view usually reveals an increased congruence angle and patellar tilt. Conservative treatment is successful in most patients. However, athletes with mechanical symptoms from a loose osteochondral fragment may require arthroscopic removal of the loose body.

(Continued)

Mechanism of injury and history: The severity of lower extremity malalignment has been correlated to the severity of the patellofemoral dysplasia symptoms.[67] Malalignment factors that may predispose athletes to PFD include a Q-angle of greater than 15° to 20°, patella alta or lateral tilt, tight lateral retinaculum, generalized ligamentous laxity, femoral anteversion, pronation, genu valgus or varum, and femoral condyle hypoplasia. Anterior knee pain develops in some patients with normal alignment, but this pain usually is caused by overuse or a training error.[67,68] The

FOCUS ON . . .

Overuse Injuries (Continued)

Patellar tendinitis (jumper's knee)

Patellar tendinitis is common in athletes who participate in jumping sports, especially basketball and volleyball, and is due to overuse of the patellar tendon from jump landings or planting the foot hard to change directions quickly. Chronic tendinitis is less likely to heal because of hyaline degeneration, endothelial hyperplasia, and collagen fiber disorganization.

The athlete presents with insidious-onset pain at the inferior pole of the patella, made worse with jumping. The hamstrings may be tight. Phase 1 involves pain only after activity; phase 2 describes pain during and after activity, although the athlete is able to perform at a functional level; and phase 3 indicates pain during and prolonged after activity, with the athlete unable to perform at a functional level. Radiographs should be obtained in athletes with phase 3 symptoms.

Nonsurgical treatment, consisting of abstinence from high-impact activities, substitution of pain-free low-impact exercises, hamstring stretching, modalities, and NSAIDs, is usually successful for patients with phase 1 and phase 2 pain. Low-level sports can be attempted after several weeks with warm-up and stretching. Corticosteroids are not injected into the tendon because they can cause collagen breakdown and predispose the tendon to spontaneous rupture.

Athletes with phase 3 symptoms should be considered for off-season local debridement of the posterior tendon. After debridement, the tendon hypertrophies and should become stronger with healing. Gradual return to sports is permitted once symptoms have resolved.

Quadriceps tendinitis

Quadriceps tendinitis causes activity-related pain at the tendon insertion just proximal to the patella and is frequent in athletes who participate in running and jumping sports that involve changing directions and in those older than age 30 years. Tight quadriceps and hamstrings may result in quadriceps mechanism overuse.

Physical examination reveals tenderness localized to the quadriceps insertion. Long-standing cases may be associated with quadriceps atrophy. Radiographs may be necessary if the history and physical examination are not diagnostic. MRI scans are rarely necessary. Treatment is as for patellar tendinitis. Those few individuals who fail to improve with nonsurgical therapy should have an MRI scan, and surgical debridement may be helpful if part of the tendon is diseased.

Patellar stress fractures

Insidious-onset, activity-related patellar pain in an athlete who plays volleyball or basketball, particularly during a summer training camp, may reflect a patellar stress fracture. The demands of repetitive microtrauma or overuse exceed the body's ability to heal the bone. Stress fractures are usually transverse, reflecting a longitudinal or tension load. The athlete's pain is typically relieved with rest.

Physical examination reveals focal tenderness over the patella with minimal soft-tissue swelling and loss of full flexion because of pain. If the condition is chronic, quadriceps atrophy is present. Radiographs may be normal or equivocal. A bone scan will show the fracture, but is not necessary to treatment. Treatment involves eliminating or modifying the offending activity and predisposing factors. Swimming, bicycling, or stair-stepping can be substituted for running as long as they are pain free. Once pain and tenderness have completely resolved, activity can be gradually resumed.

(Continued)

correlation between the severity of PFD symptoms and the degree of chondromalacia is weak. The etiology of pain from chondromalacia is unknown because there are no nerve fibers in articular cartilage.[69]

The athlete with PFD typically presents with anterior knee pain that worsens after activity. Those with more severe symptoms will have pain during activity as well as pain that lingers for hours after activity has ceased.

The natural history of patellofemoral knee pain secondary to malalignment is controversial. Some physicians believe the condition is serious and reflects early tissue injury from maltracking that places abnormal pressures on the articular surface. These physicians believe that the pain will persist unless steps are taken to correct the train-

FOCUS ON . . .

Overuse Injuries (Continued)

Osteochondritis dissecans

Osteochondritis dissecans is a focal area of necrotic subchondral bone of varying etiologies and is a common cause of loose bodies. Men are three times more likely to have osteochondritis dissecans than women, and the condition most often presents in the second and third decades. The cause is believed to be disruption of end arterioles to subchondral bone from repetitive microtrauma, causing local areas of ischemia. Trauma has occurred to about half of patients, although this may be incidental. There are four stages: intact lesion, but softening of subchondral bone; early separation; partially detached lesion; and completely detached lesion, resulting in a loose body. Pain may be vague and insidious or acute from trauma. If the lesion is detached, locking, catching, and effusion may be present.

On physical examination, an effusion may signal a detached fragment. Quadriceps muscle atrophy is common. If the lesion is in the lateral aspect of the medial femoral condyle, flexing the knee to 90° and internally rotating the tibia causes pain that is then relieved by external rotation (Wilson's sign). Tenderness over the jointline (as with a meniscal tear) must be differentiated from tenderness over the involved condyle or other articular surface. Radiographs, including a tunnel view, show most lesions. An MRI test is sensitive and specific.

Stage 1 and stage 2 lesions that occur before skeletal maturity tend to heal spontaneously in 6 to 12 months. Pain-producing sports should be avoided until symptoms resolve. Radiographs can be used to document healing of the lesion.

Lesions that occur after skeletal maturity and most stage 3 and 4 lesions are less likely to heal and may require arthroscopic excision. The prognosis may be poor if the fragment is large and in a weightbearing area. Reattaching the fragment has proved impractical to date.

Bipartite patella

A bipartite patella has an accessory bony fragment connected to the body of the patella by a line of cartilage. It occurs in a small portion of the population and is usually an incidental finding on radiographs, and very few of these become symptomatic (often during adolescence). Pain begins with either repetitive microtrauma from sports or acute trauma. Symptoms are generally due to a cartilaginous incomplete fracture between the body of the patella and the bipartite fragment or a traction apophysitis from quadriceps muscle overuse. The athlete notes anterior pain and occasional catching with stair climbing or other activities.

On physical examination, the athletic trainer should try to reproduce symptoms by attempting to elicit motion at the synchondrosis site. Pain, local tenderness, and a history of trauma help to make the diagnosis, but other causes of pain should be ruled out. Radiographs are needed when there is a history of trauma, and a bone scan may be useful. Treatment is restriction from pain-producing activities. If nonsurgical treatment is unsuccessful, surgical excision of the fragment can be considered in older adolescents and young adults who wish to continue competitive sports. Lateral retinacular release has also proved helpful in relieving symptoms and achieving bony union. The natural history of the bipartite patella is probably self-limiting.

Iliotibial band friction syndrome

Iliotibial band friction syndrome describes lateral knee pain that occurs almost exclusively in distance runners. It is likely due to inflammation of the intra-articular synovium or iliotibial band fascia from repetitive rubbing of the tight band over the lateral condyle. Pain is well localized over the lateral femoral condyle and occurs at a predictably specific time or distance during a run, preventing the athlete from continuing. Walking relieves symptoms. Athletes with advanced cases may walk with a stiff-knee gait to avoid rubbing the iliotibial band over the condyle.

On physical examination, tenderness may not be reproducible. The athletic trainer should perform the Noble compression test by having the athlete lie supine and placing the thumb over the lateral epicondyle during active flexion and extension. Treatment is complete abstinence from running. Walking, bicycling, stair-stepping, swimming, tennis, and basketball may be substituted. Iliotibial band stretching, ice, NSAIDs, and corticosteroid injections, along with correction of overuse risk factors, can be beneficial. Athletes with genu varum or excessive pronation may be helped by orthotics. Running can be slowly resumed after symptoms have completely resolved. If nonsurgical treatment fails, surgical release is recommended.

ing errors, to restore normal alignment, or both. However, a study of 54 adolescent girls with anterior knee pain who were treated with benign neglect showed that 95% still had pain after 2 to 17 years, 13% said the pain was worse, 48% had no sports restrictions, and 17% had restricted sports activity.[70] These results may be interpreted as either benign and self-limiting or disappointing.[71]

Physical examination: Athletes with suspected PFD should eventually be evaluated by a physician. Other diagnoses that have similar presentations include osteochondritis dissecans and patella stress fractures. When examining for PFD, the athletic trainer should look for a positive apprehension test result and for signs of malalignment (**Figure 16-15**). The patella normally engages into the trochlea from the lateral position at 20° of flexion and should centralize at 30° to 45° of flexion.[72] A positive J-sign indicates patella alta with a high Q-angle, because the patella slips out of the trochlea laterally during active terminal knee extension from 20° of flexion.

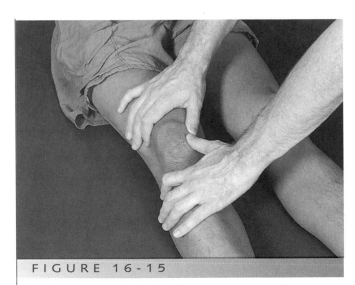

FIGURE 16-15

A positive result of the apprehension test can indicate patella subluxation or recurrent dislocation.

Signs of patellofemoral articular damage include palpable crepitation when the knee is flexed at an angle greater than 30° or during active extension.[73] Frequently, radiographs will not show signs of malalignment or patellofemoral articular damage in athletes with activity-related anterior knee pain. In these individuals, the diagnosis is likely overuse PFD.

Radiographic examination: Radiographic evaluation should include three views: standing 45° weightbearing PA view, lateral view, and Merchant view. Features that may be present in some athletes with PFD include patella alta, a lateral patellar tilt, a shallow trochlea, a laterally displaced patella, and an abnormal congruence angle.[48,67,71]

Overuse Patellofemoral Dysplasia

Overuse PFD is anterior knee pain caused by overuse in athletes without signs of malalignment. This is a common source of disability in athletes who participate in marathons, basketball, and other running sports. The cause is training error resulting from a sudden increase in duration, frequency, or intensity of activity. Anterior knee pain will occur at variable times after the onset of activity depending on its severity and will be present for minutes to hours after activity has ceased. Results of the physical examination and radiographs are normal.

Treatment involves decreasing the duration, frequency, and/or intensity of the offending activity, while substituting other exercises to help maintain fitness. The substitution activities should be relatively painless and can include such low-impact exercises as stair-stepping, bicycling, swimming, or rowing. As conditioning improves, the original activity can gradually replace the low-impact exercises. Some athletes, however, will continue to feel anterior knee pain above a certain activity level and may wish to consider making a permanent change in training habits. Permanent patellofemoral damage probably will not occur in athletes who continue to run despite pain.

Lateral patellar compression syndrome

Lateral patellar compression syndrome (LPCS) is the mildest form of patellofemoral dysplasia involving some degree of malalignment. Symptoms include insidious onset of vague, poorly localized pain on the anterior aspect of the knee that usually increases with activities such as stair climbing, sports, and prolonged sitting with the knee flexed. Symptoms are relieved with rest or short walks. Locking, crepitation, giving way, and swelling may be present at more advanced stages, but are rare at initial presentation.[73]

Physical examination: Results of the physical examination may be normal, but some patellofemoral tenderness may be evident. The examiner will be unable to push the patella medially secondary to a tight lateral retinaculum.

Radiographic examination: The Merchant view may be normal or may show that the patella is tilted, subluxated laterally, or has an abnormal congruence angle.[68,73]

Treatment: Initial treatment of LPCS should be nonsurgical. The rehabilitation program can be divided into three phases. Phase 1, pain control, is necessary to make a strengthening program effective and involves cryotherapy, rest, cushioned insoles to reduce ground reaction forces, and taping. Phase 2 involves stretching the hamstrings and quadriceps muscles. Quadriceps strengthening for athletes with quadriceps atrophy can be beneficial. The best exercises provide general strengthening of the extensor mechanism and should include closed chain exercises that make a short flexion arc, such as bicycling, stair-stepping, and leg presses. Exercises should be managed to keep pain to a minimum and prevent effusions. Straight leg raises with increasingly heavier ankle weights are cumbersome and of questionable effectiveness. Leg extensions (open chain) and long arc exercises may aggravate symptoms and should be individualized. Phase 3 rehabilitation involves functional progressive exercises.[71]

If the athlete has symmetric extremities, no effusion, and pain with activity, overuse should be suspected and specific exercises will probably not be useful. The athlete should be reassured that there is no structural knee damage and advised to decrease the frequency and duration of the sport until symptoms are tolerable.

Neoprene elastic sleeves with a patella cut out may provide physical and psychological comfort to some athletes. However, in some athletes, the elastic sleeves can irritate the skin, making them less effective.[74] Orthotics may help correct minor lower extremity malalignment and relieve symptoms.[75] The athlete can learn to apply McConnell taping to pull the patella medially and use it throughout the day.[76] One or two strips of tape placed on the front of the knee completely cover the patella. Another strip of tape is placed at the center. (**Figure 16-16**). The effectiveness of taping, however, may be short term, because the tape will begin to loosen after 16 minutes of sweating and motion from exercise.[77]

Nonsurgical therapy has a 70% to 93% success rate in rendering patients asymptomatic with return to full athletic activity.[78] Whether success depends on a particular exercise protocol or simply rest is unknown because of the lack of controlled studies. If nonsurgical therapy fails and the physician believes that surgery may be beneficial, the type of surgical procedure to perform is controversial. An arthroscopic release of the lateral retinaculum (lateral release) may help patients who have a tight lateral retinaculum and patellar tilt with an abnormal congruence

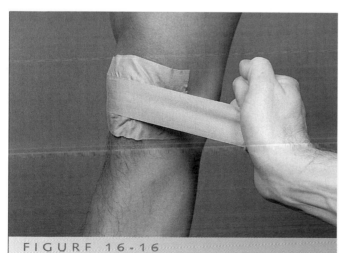

FIGURE 16-16

The McConnell taping technique pulls the patella medially.

angle.[79] If malalignment signs such as a high Q-angle, genu valgum, J-sign, or lateral subluxation are present, a tibial tubercle medialization procedure (Elmslie-Trillat) may be indicated.[80] Arthroscopic shaving of damaged articular cartilage is of unclear benefit.

Chronic subluxating patella

A *chronic subluxating patella* is the next stage in the continuum of patellofemoral dysplasias. This condition is often difficult to diagnose because symptoms can be vague. The patella partially dislocates out of the intercondylar groove and snaps back into place rather than completely dislocating. Subluxation is more apt to occur during quadriceps muscle contraction with the knee flexed and the foot fixed to the ground in an externally rotated position. Associated chondromalacia over time may be severe.[66,73]

Physical examination: With the knee flexed 30°, the patella may be hypermobile so that the examiner can easily subluxate the patella laterally as the knee is extended. The examiner may also note a lateral or upwardly oriented patella when the patient is seated, suggestive of lateral malalignment and patella alta, respectively.[73]

Radiographic examination: Radiographic findings on the Merchant view will probably reveal an increased congruence angle and patellar tilt.[68,73]

Treatment: Nonsurgical treatment as discussed for LPCS is successful in 80% to 90% of patients and should be attempted first. The number of subluxations dramatically decreases as the patient approaches age 30 years.[68] Patients who have mechanical symptoms, such as locking, crepitation, effusions, or a mechanical block to motion, may have a loose osteochondral fragment caused by subluxation episodes. Arthroscopic removal or replacement of these loose bodies may be necessary. However, replacing loose bodies has not yet been proven more beneficial than removing them and involves the added postsurgical morbidity of restricted weightbearing for several weeks, resulting in a longer delay in returning to activities than removal does.[81]

Whether to use a proximal or distal realignment procedure is another surgical controversy. Distal realignment procedures such as tibial tubercle medialization are preferred because they correct the high Q-angle, which is usually the most significant anatomic disorder. Proximal realignment procedures such as VMO advancement rely on the dynamic action of the muscle to help pull the patella medially. However, the procedure is not as successful in achieving patella centralization on radiographs as the distal transfer procedure. Elevation of the tubercle may relieve pain by decreasing the joint reactive forces at the patellofemoral joint, but is of unproven benefit over tubercle medialization alone.

Patellar Tendinitis (Jumper's Knee)

Risk group: Patellar tendinitis is a common problem in jumping sports, especially basketball and volleyball.

Mechanism of injury and history: Patellar tendinitis results from overuse of the patellar tendon, presumably from the repetitive eccentric contractions involved in landing from a jump or from planting the foot hard to change directions quickly. Histologic analysis of patients who have long-standing symptoms reveals that the posterior region of the tendon is usually symptomatic. This region is less vascular and reveals focal areas of hyaline degeneration, endothelial hyperplasia, and collagen fiber disorganization, which give it a low healing potential.[82]

The athlete presents with insidious onset of pain at the inferior pole of the patella that becomes worse with jumping activities. Symptoms can be divided into three phases based on severity.[83] Phase 1 involves pain only after activity; phase 2 involves pain during and after activity, but the pain does not prevent the athlete from performing at a functional level; and phase 3 involves pain that is more prolonged during and after activity and inhibits the athlete from performing at a functional level.

Physical examination: The athlete typically will have tenderness localized to the inferior pole of the patella and possibly tight hamstrings.

Radiographic examination: Radiographs usually are not necessary, but should be obtained in patients with phase 3 symptoms to rule out other diagnoses. An MRI scan will show thickening of the anterior patellar tendon with increased intratendinous signal intensity in the posterior patellar region suggestive of localized degeneration. It is not yet known, however, if MRI can be useful in making management decisions.[82]

Treatment: Nonsurgical therapy usually is successful for patients with either phase 1 or phase 2 pain. The athlete should completely abstain from high-impact activities. Low-impact exercises that do not cause pain can be substituted to maintain fitness. Hamstring stretching will ease the tension placed on the extensor mechanism. The athlete can return to a lower level of sports after a few weeks and should continue preparticipation stretching and warming up. Cryotherapy and nonsteroidal anti-inflammatory drugs (NSAIDs) are also helpful.[83]

Corticosteroids should never be injected around or into the tendon because they cause collagen breakdown that weakens the tendon and predisposes it to spontaneous rupture. Modalities such as heat, ultrasound, electrical stimulation, phonophoresis, and iontophoresis may provide some temporary relief.[84]

Some athletes may get relief by wearing patellar tendon straps during the offending activity, but others cannot tolerate the discomfort in the popliteal fossa region. The patellar tendon strap works like a tennis elbow strap and assumes some of the patellar tendon forces that would be transmitted to its origin.[84] Patellar taping with the McConnell technique to correct for posterior tilt of the distal patella can be effective in some patients.[76,84]

Athletes with phase 3 symptoms that persist throughout the season and make playing difficult should consider off-season surgery, especially if rehabilitation during the previous off-season did not lessen the problem. Surgery involves a local debridement of the diseased posterior part of the tendon, which can be enucleated without significant disruption of the anterior portion, thus preserving extensor mechanism integrity. After debridement, the tendon becomes hypertrophic and presumably stronger as it heals. A gradual return to sports can be attempted in 3 to 6 months, after symptoms and tenderness have resolved.[83-85]

Quadriceps Tendinitis

Risk group: Tendon insertion pain just proximal to the patella is indicative of *quadriceps tendinitis.* This condition is common in athletes who participate in running and jumping sports that involve changing directions, such as soccer, football, and basketball. It is more common in patients older than age 30 years. Possible predispositions to this condition include tight quadriceps and hamstrings that may result in an overuse of the quadriceps mechanism. The athlete typically will report an insidious onset of pain at variable times during the activity. Pain is relieved with rest but may linger in more severe cases.[86]

Physical examination: The athlete will have tenderness localized to the quadriceps insertion at the proximal pole of the patella. Quadriceps atrophy will be present if the condition is long-standing. The examiner must rule out a patellar stress fracture by ensuring that the patella is not tender.

Radiographic examination: Radiographs may be necessary if the physical examination and history are equivocal. An MRI scan may demonstrate an area of inflammation but is rarely necessary for guiding treatment.

Treatment: Treatment of quadriceps tendinitis is the same as that for patellar tendinitis: complete abstinence from high-impact activities, low-impact exercises for fitness, hamstring stretching, cryotherapy, and NSAIDs. If nonsurgical therapy is unsuccessful, MRI is indicated to determine whether part of the tendon is diseased. Surgical debridement of this area usually is successful.[86]

Patellar Stress Fractures

Risk group: Patellar stress fractures should be suspected with activity-related patellar pain in an athlete in high-risk sports such as volleyball or basketball. Stress fractures are common during summer training camps when the athlete begins a sudden, intense workout program.[86] The incidence of patellar stress fractures is probably higher than suspected because many inferior pole patellar stress fractures are misdiagnosed as patellar tendinitis.

Mechanism of injury and history: Stress fractures result from a failure of normal bone equilibrium because of the excessive demands made by repetitive microtrauma or overuse, coupled with inadequate rest and insufficient healing time. The resulting microfractures can cause a clinical stress fracture if there is an inadequate rest period. Stress fractures are usually transverse, indicating a longitudinal or tension load.[86] The patient has insidious onset of anterior knee pain, which is worse with activity and relieved with rest. A history of an abrupt increase in training intensity and/or duration is common.[86]

Physical examination: The physical examination reveals focal tenderness over the bony patella, minimal soft-tissue swelling, and loss of full flexion because of patellar pain from stressing the fracture. Quadriceps atrophy will be present if the condition is chronic.[65] A patellar stress fracture should be differentiated from patellar tendinitis, which has tenderness present over the proximal patellar tendon instead of over the bone.

Radiographic examination: Early radiographs are normal or equivocal, and in fact, may never be positive. Lateral views sometimes show a small line along the inferior pole. A technetium Tc 99m bone scan allows early diagnosis but will not alter treatment. Therefore, the diagnosis is usually made clinically with a positive bone scan.[65]

Treatment: The athlete should eliminate or modify the offending activity and predisposing factors to break the cycle and allow bone healing. Swimming, bicycling, or stair-stepping can substitute for running activities, if these do not cause pain. Activity can be gradually resumed after pain and tenderness have completely resolved.[65] Occasionally, an acute transverse displaced fracture can occur at the site of a preexisting stress fracture. Surgical reduction and fixation is recommended, although healing will be slower than in typical acute traumatic patellar fractures.

Osteochondritis Dissecans

Osteochondritis dissecans (OCD) is a focal area of necrotic subchondral bone of varying etiologies (**Figure 16-17**). OCD is most commonly located on the lateral aspect of the medial femoral condyle or on the weight-bearing surface of the posterior lateral femoral condyle. Although other parts of the condyles and the patella can be involved, only one lesion usually is present. Osteochondritis dissecans is a common cause of loose bodies within the joint.[87]

Risk group: The incidence of OCD is three times greater in men than in women and most commonly affects individuals in high school or college sports.[88]

Mechanism of injury and history: OCD may be caused by the disruption of end arterioles to subchondral bone from

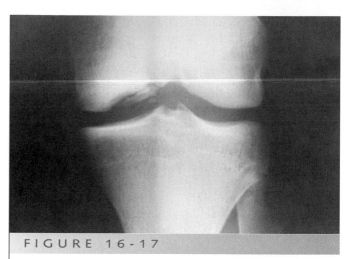

FIGURE 16-17

Osteochondritis dissecans is most commonly located on the lateral aspect of the medial femoral condyle.

repetitive microtrauma, resulting in local areas of ischemia.[89] A history of trauma will be present in 46% of patients but this may be incidental.[88] Four stages of OCD have been described: 1) intact lesion but softening of subchondral bone; 2) early separation; 3) partially detached lesion; and 4) completely detached lesion, resulting in a loose body.[87] Pain may be vague and insidious or more acute if onset is associated with trauma. If the lesion is detached, the athlete may have symptoms of locking, catching, and effusions.

Physical examination: An effusion may be present if fragments are detached. Quadriceps muscle atrophy is common. The examiner should differentiate between true jointline tenderness, as with a meniscal tear, and OCD tenderness over the involved condyle or other articular surface. If the lesion is in the lateral aspect of the medial femoral condyle, pain can be elicited by flexing the patient's knee 90° and internally rotating the tibia to force the tibial spine against the lesion. External rotation will relieve the pain (Wilson's sign).[90]

Radiographic examination: Radiographs, including a tunnel view, will show most lesions. An MRI scan is the most sensitive and specific test.[91]

Treatment: Stage 1 and 2 lesions that occur prior to skeletal maturity nearly always heal spontaneously in 6 to 12 months. Treatment should focus on preventing symptoms and avoiding pain-producing sports. The return to sports should be gradual and as symptoms allow. Radiographs used to document healing of the lesion can be reassuring to the patient and family.[92]

Most lesions that occur after skeletal maturity and nearly all mature and immature stage 3 and 4 lesions are less likely to heal and may eventually require arthroscopic intervention.[93] When symptoms become severe enough to preclude activity or when the athlete begins to develop effusions with activity, arthroscopy may be warranted. Excision of a loose fragment or debridement of a partially detached fragment is the treatment of choice. This will result in immediate improvement, but if the fragments are large and in a weightbearing area, the long-term prognosis may be poor. Replacing and fixing the fragment is an attractive idea but has not proven to prevent arthrosis and may be impractical in athletes because of the required long-term postsurgical weightbearing restrictions.

Bipartite Patella

A *bipartite patella* has an accessory bony fragment connected to the body of the patella by a line of cartilage.

Risk group: The incidence of bipartite patella is 2% to 3% and is usually an incidental finding on radiographs. Of the population with bipartite patella, 40% to 50% will have the condition bilaterally, primarily at the superolateral pole. Only 2% of patients will have symptoms, usually during adolescence.[94]

Mechanism of injury and history: Pain usually begins with the repetitive microtrauma of athletic activities or acute trauma. Symptoms usually are due to an incomplete cartilaginous fracture, which may act like a symptomatic nonunion, between the body of the patella and the bipartite fragment. A symptomatic bipartite patella may also represent a traction apophysitis from quadriceps muscle overuse. The most common complaint is anterior pain, and stair climbing or other activities may result in occasional catching.[95]

Physical examination: The examiner should attempt to reproduce symptoms by trying to elicit motion at the synchondrosis site. The diagnosis of a painful bipartite patella requires a clinical correlation of pain, local tenderness, and, occasionally, a history of trauma. Because most athletes are asymptomatic, other causes of pain, specifically the more common patellofemoral dysplasias, must first be ruled out.[95]

Radiographic examination: Radiographs should be obtained and critically evaluated to rule out a fracture when there is a history of trauma. A negative technetium Tc 99m bone scan can rule out a symptomatic bipartite patella with an injured synchondrosis.[73]

Treatment: Refraining from participating in pain-producing activities is frequently effective. Surgical excision of the fragment can be considered when it is evident that nonsurgical treatment is not working, especially with patients involved in jumping sports. Excision of the smaller fragment can decrease symptoms but is indicated only for older adolescents and young adults who wish to continue competitive sports. A lateral retinacular release can be successful in relieving symptoms and in achieving bony union because it relieves excessive lateral pressure.[96] The natural history of the bipartite patella is not clear but is probably self-limiting.[95]

Iliotibial Band Friction Syndrome

Risk group: Iliotibial band (ITB) friction syndrome is lateral knee pain that occurs almost exclusively in distance runners.[97,98]

Mechanism of injury and history: This condition is probably caused by inflammation of the intra-articular synovium or ITB fascia because the tight ITB repeatedly rubs over the lateral condyle as it moves posteriorly with flexion and anteriorly with extension during running. Once the condition develops, the pain remains well localized over the lateral femoral condyle, occurs fairly predictably at a specific time or distance during a run, and will prevent the athlete from continuing. Walking usually relieves the symptoms but pain quickly returns when the athlete resumes running.[98] In advanced cases, the athlete may walk with a stiff knee gait to avoid causing motion of the ITB over the condyle.[97]

Physical examination: Physical examination of the knee may be normal, and tenderness is frequently unreproducible. The compression test of Noble can occasionally elicit pain. With the patient lying supine, the examiner places his or her thumb over the lateral epicondyle during active flexion and extension. Pain reproduces at about 30°, when the ITB rubs against the most prominent part of the lateral femoral condyle during impact activities.[97]

Treatment: Treatment consists of complete abstinence from running. The athlete can substitute walking, bicycling, stair-stepping, swimming, or other activities that can maintain fitness without causing pain. Nonrepetitive running sports such as tennis and basketball may be tolerated, but distance running is not. ITB stretching, ice, NSAIDs, and corticosteroid injections can be helpful along with correction of overuse risk factors. Orthotics may be helpful in patients with genu varum or excessive pronation. Running can be resumed only after symptoms are completely resolved, beginning with low mileage and slowly advancing the distance. If nonsurgical therapy fails, surgical release (relaxation incision) can be successful.[97]

KNEE INJURIES IN PEDIATRIC ATHLETES

Patellar Sleeve Fractures

The patella in a newborn is composed entirely of cartilage. Ossification begins at age 5 or 6 years, from the center to the periphery, and is not complete until late adolescence. In pediatric athletes, therefore, the peripheral bone is the least mature and most susceptible to fracture.[99] A

patellar sleeve fracture is an avulsion of unossified distal patella from a sudden forceful quadriceps contraction with the knee flexed. It occurs in older children or young adolescents, most commonly with jumping sports.[100]

Physical examination may show a palpable gap at the inferior pole of the patella. The athlete may be able to do a straight leg raise if fibers of the medial and/or lateral retinaculum are intact. Even if a straight leg raise can be performed, there will be an extension lag.[100]

Immediate physician referral is necessary. Initially, the leg should be splinted in extension. Plain radiographs and sometimes MRI scans are mandatory for diagnosis. Surgical reapproximation may be necessary unless there is minimal displacement that can be treated with immobilization.[100]

Physeal Fractures

The two major growth plates, or physes, of the lower extremity are the distal femoral and proximal tibial physes, which account for 70% of lower extremity growth.[101]

Risk group: The physes are weakest and most susceptible to injury when growth is most rapid; for boys, this period is between ages 12 and 16 years, and for girls, between ages 8 and 12 years, or Tanner stage III. The incidence of these injuries in sports is uncommon, but physeal fractures can occur in contact sports such as football and hockey.[101]

Mechanism of injury and history: Proximal to the knee, both collateral ligaments originate at the distal femoral epiphysis, but distally, they insert onto the tibial and fibular metaphyses. Because the proximal tibial epiphysis is somewhat protected by the collateral ligaments, disruption at the distal femoral physis is more common.[102]

The physis is the weak link in the integrity of the rapidly growing knee, because bone is stronger than the ligament, which, in turn, is stronger than the growth plate cartilage. Therefore, blows to the knee will preferentially disrupt at the physis. The mechanism usually is by direct contact, with the foot planted and under severe varus or valgus stress. Hyperextension stress is more likely to result in a proximal tibial physeal disruption.[102]

Physical examination: There may be gross angular deformity of the lower extremity, or alignment may be normal. There will be gross laxity with varus or valgus stressing similar to a collateral ligament tear. With children, physeal disruption must be considered first. Documenting the distal pulses is crucial because the close proximity and tight adherence of the popliteal artery put it at risk in a proximal tibial physeal disruption. Peroneal nerve function should also be documented because varus injuries put the nerve at risk.[101]

Radiographic examination: Plain radiographs with varus or valgus stress views are diagnostic.

Treatment: If a physeal fracture about the knee is suspected, the lower extremity should be splinted to prevent further soft-tissue (popliteal artery and nerve) damage before the athlete is transported to the emergency department. Physician referral is urgent. Nondisplaced fractures can be casted, but displaced fractures require anatomic surgical reduction and fixation.[102]

The prognosis worsens as the degree of initial displacement increases. Repeated reduction attempts may cause more physeal damage. Angular deformities and shortening from the damaged growth plate can begin to develop as late as 2 years after the injury. Therefore, long-term follow-up of these injuries is necessary.[102]

Tibial Tubercle Avulsions

Risk group: Tibial tubercle avulsions typically occur in male basketball players who are age 14 to 16 years and nearing the end of their growth. Up to 40% have preexisting Osgood-Schlatter disease. The incidence of those with Osgood-Schlatter disease who get an avulsion after age 16 years is unknown, but it is probably low.[103]

Mechanism of injury and history: Avulsions of the tibial tubercle occur through its open physis from a violent quadriceps contraction, usually during jumping activities.[103]

Physical examination: The athlete can have a patella alta with a mass over the anterior proximal tibia from the displaced tubercle with an associated hematoma. A straight leg raise may be possible because of intact medial and lateral retinaculum, but a significant extension lag will be present. Radiographs are diagnostic.

FOCUS ON . . .

Tibial Tubercle Avulsions

Tibial tubercle avulsions typically occur in the 14- to 16-year-old male basketball player at the end of his growth, and as many as 40% have preexisting Osgood-Schlatter disease. The tibial tubercle can avulse through its open physis from a violent quadriceps contraction, usually during jumping.

On physical examination, patella alta may be evident, with a mass over the anterior proximal tibia and an associated hematoma. Straight-leg raising may be possible if the retinaculum is intact, but the extension lag is significant. Radiographs are diagnostic. Initial management is application of a knee immobilizer or splint before transport to the emergency department. Nondisplaced avulsions are treated with a cylinder cast, while displaced fractures require surgical reduction with internal fixation. The prognosis is excellent.

FOCUS ON . . .

Osgood-Schlatter Disease

Osgood-Schlatter disease, or tibial osteochondrosis, is the most common traction apophysitis and exertion injury in the adolescent knee. Most at risk is the 13- to 14-year-old boy and the 10- to 11-year-old girl who participates in jumping sports. In some, the condition is bilateral. Repetitive microtrauma is responsible and causes insidious-onset, low-grade, activity-related aching of the tibial tubercle. Pain is relieved with rest and worsened by acceleration and deceleration forces.

On physical examination, tenderness and sometimes swelling are present over the tibial tubercle. A bony or cartilage prominence may be evident. Pain is reproduced with resisted extension from 90°, and tight quadriceps and hamstrings may be noted. Radiographs are usually normal, but can be helpful in ruling out other conditions. Treatment is avoidance of aggravating activities and relative rest for 2 to 3 weeks, although some patients require 12 to 24 months before symptoms resolve. Bicycling, stair-stepping, and swimming can be substituted if they are pain free. Cryotherapy, hamstring stretching, and a patellar tendon strap or neoprene knee sleeve may be helpful. Severe symptoms may be relieved by a cylinder cast for 2 to 4 weeks. Symptoms may recur with resumption of excessive activity, and many athletes continue to have some symptoms that will resolve when growth stops, but the risk of avulsion is low. Kneeling and resisted knee extension may continue to be painful. Surgical excision of ossicles or debridement of the bony prominence, or both, are options for recalcitrant cases, although the efficacy of these procedures has not been established.

Treatment: To prevent further displacement of the tubercle, a knee immobilizer or other long leg splint should be applied for comfort before the athlete is transported to the emergency department. The athlete should be referred to a physician, but this can wait until the game is over, if the athlete so desires. Nondisplaced avulsions are treated with a cylinder cast. Displaced fractures require surgical reduction with internal fixation and have an excellent prognosis.[102,103]

Overuse Injuries

Overuse injuries in children have increased because of the increasing participation of children in sports. In skeletally immature athletes, microtrauma can place traction stress at the sites of tendon insertions (the apophysis) on the bone growth plate. This results in a chronic traction apophysitis, the pediatric counterpart of an adult's tendinitis.[65]

Musculotendinous imbalance from rapid bone growth during adolescence may contribute to childhood overuse injuries but probably is not a significant factor. In one prospective study, 446 children with anterior knee pain were compared with asymptomatic, age-matched controls, and no significant difference in lower extremity alignment or joint mobility was found. The only difference between the two groups was the amount of sports participation, and training error with repetitive overload from increased sports participation was considered the major etiologic factor.[65]

In assessing children suspected of having an overuse injury, the athletic trainer should ask about prior injuries and predisposing factors such as changes in distance, speed, surface, or technique. The child's growth over the last year also should be documented. The physical examination should include an evaluation of asymmetry, atrophy, and tightness for both muscles and tendons.[65]

Osgood-Schlatter Disease

Osgood-Schlatter disease, or tibial osteochondrosis, is the most common traction apophysitis and exertion injury in the adolescent knee.[104]

Risk group: Symptoms typically appear in adolescents at the onset of a growth spurt, coupled with regular physical activity that usually involves jumping sports. In boys, it appears at about age 13 or 14 years, although it can appear anytime between ages 10 and 15 years; in girls, the range at onset is from age 8 to 13 years, usually at age 10 or 11 years. One study found an incidence of 21% in athletically active boys, compared with a 4.5% incidence among nonathletic controls.[104] Girls are often involved with gymnastics, soccer, or other jumping sports, and 20% to 33% of cases are bilateral.[101]

Mechanism of injury and history: The condition develops from repetitive microtrauma to the tibial tubercle apophysis, usually in jumping sports. Rarely, vigorous jumping may lead to complete displacement of the apophysis.[101] Symptoms include an insidious onset of a low-grade aching that is associated with activity and localized to the area of the tibial tubercle. The pain is relieved with rest and aggravated by acceleration and deceleration forces, such as sudden stopping during running and jumping.[101]

Physical examination: The athlete typically has tenderness and occasional swelling over the tibial tubercle. Often, a bony or cartilaginous prominence is present. Pain is reproduced with resisted extension from 90°. Occasional associated findings are tight quadriceps and hamstring muscles. The knee does not have an effusion. The diagnosis is made clinically.[105]

Radiographic examination: Plain radiographs are usually normal and are sometimes needed to rule out other processes. Occasionally, bony ossicles are present, but these may or may not correlate with symptoms.[105]

Treatment: Activity limitations and relative rest for 2 to 3 weeks will usually alleviate symptoms. Patients should avoid sports that require running, jumping, or kneeling until all symptoms are resolved. Cross training with bicycling, stair-stepping, and swimming should be encouraged if these activities do not cause pain.[46] Frequently, up to 3 months of rest from the offending sport may be required, and 70% of patients will have some degree of restriction over 10 months. Both the athlete and parents should be advised that it may take a 12- to 24-month period for symptoms to resolve with nonsurgical therapy.[101] Cryotherapy is useful in controlling pain and swelling after activity.

Hamstring stretching will help reduce overuse by lessening the antagonistic force acting on the extensor mechanism. A patellar tendon strap or neoprene knee sleeve with a patella cut out sometimes provides comfort.[46] If symptoms are severe, a cylinder cast for 2 to 4 weeks may be indicated. Anti-inflammatory medication is not helpful in children. A corticosteroid injection is contraindicated because the etiology is not inflammatory, and a steroid injection can result in skin thinning and weakening of the tendon.[105]

After successful nonsurgical treatment, the athlete and parents should be advised that the process might recur if excessive activity is resumed. Up to 60% of patients may continue to have some symptoms; however, symptoms are self-limiting and will stop when growth stops. In the long term, some patients may be unable to kneel without discomfort and may continue to have pain with resisted knee extension.[101,105]

If nonsurgical therapy is unsuccessful and the child wishes to remain active, surgical excision of ossicles and/or debridement of the underlying bony prominence can be done, although the efficacy of these procedures has been questioned.[106] The child may also safely remain active regardless of symptoms because the risk of avulsion is rare.[105]

Sinding-Larsen-Johanssen Syndrome

Sinding-Larsen-Johanssen syndrome, or patellar osteochondrosis, is an overuse traction apophysitis caused by repetitive microtrauma at the insertion point of the proximal patellar tendon onto the lower patellar pole. Sinding-Larsen-Johanssen syndrome is the same condition as Osgood-Schlatter disease, except that it occurs at the opposite end of the patellar tendon. It is analogous to jumper's knee of the skeletally mature athlete. A displaced fracture of the distal patellar pole may result, but this is rare.

Risk group: The condition is most common in adolescents from age 10 to 14 years who participate in jumping sports.[65]

Physical examination: The presentation and history are similar to that of Osgood-Schlatter disease, but the pain is

FOCUS ON . . .

Sinding-Larsen-Johanssen Syndrome

Sinding-Larsen-Johanssen syndrome, or patellar osteochondrosis, is an overuse traction apophysitis from repetitive microtrauma at the proximal patellar tendon insertion into the inferior patellar pole. The condition is most common in adolescent jumping athletes age 10 to 14 years. Many athletes report a single episode of trauma, and pain is worse with running, jumping, and climbing stairs. Tenderness is present over the distal pole of the patella and the adjacent patellar tendon origin. The quadriceps are often tight and weak. Lateral radiographs may reveal elongation of the distal pole of the patella or fragmentation of multiple ossicles. Treatment is as for Osgood-Schlatter disease, and symptoms are usually self-limiting.

at the distal pole of the patella. A high percentage of patients will report a single episode of trauma, such as a fall, that significantly increased the symptoms. Pain is worse with running, jumping, or climbing stairs.[46]

The diagnosis is made clinically. Physical examination reveals tenderness over the distal pole of the patella and over the adjacent patellar tendon origin. Frequently, the quadriceps will be tight and relatively weak.[46]

Radiographic examination: Lateral radiographs may show elongation of the distal pole of the patella or fragmentation of multiple ossicles.

Treatment: Treatment is the same as that for Osgood-Schlatter disease. Symptoms are usually self-limiting.[46,65]

INFLAMMATORY AND NEOPLASTIC CONDITIONS

Nontraumatic causes of knee pain include malignant and benign tumors as well as inflammatory conditions. The sexually transmitted gonococcal arthritis is the most common knee infection in young adults. The onset of juvenile rheumatoid arthritis can range from age 2 to 17 years.

Bone and soft-tissue neoplasms about the knee can occur at any age but most commonly occur during the second decade when children begin school sports. Malignant and benign primary bone tumors usually are located on the distal femur or the proximal tibia. These conditions should be suspected if the athlete has pain with no antecedent trauma or obvious overuse; exhibits night pain, weight loss, fever, anorexia, effusions, or does not respond to therapy; or sustains a fracture with minimal trauma. A family history may or may not be present. These conditions are rare, and more common etiologies of pain should be sought first. If a neoplastic or inflammatory condition is suspected, urgent physician referral is mandatory.[107]

FUNCTIONAL KNEE PAIN

Constitutional or *functional knee pain* is a diagnosis given to an athlete who experiences pain without any anatomic pathology to reduce anxiety and enable the athlete to cope with the demands of his or her environment. This condition is sometimes referred to as emotional burnout and is commonly found in children and adolescents who are pressured into too many activities by demanding parents.[108] In a study of 28 consecutive adolescents who presented with knee pain, five (18%) were found to have no demonstrable organic cause of their pain after an extensive work-up.[109]

Predicting functional knee pain is difficult. Factors such as personality profile, obesity, bilateral pain, night pain, missing school or physical education class, or single versus multiple orthopaedic problems are not predictive. The only factor found to correlate more with functional pain than with organic causes of pain was duration of symptoms for more than 6 months. Without a reliable indicator for functional knee pain, athletes with pain of unknown etiology should be referred for physician evaluation. If organic causes are ruled out, a psychiatric referral may be necessary. If the cause is burnout, both the child and parents should receive counseling.[109]

KNEE REHABILITATION

Rehabilitation of the knee should be approached with the same principles used in all extremity rehabilitation. The athletic trainer and physical therapist must understand the anatomy of the knee, the biomechanics of the kinetic chain of the lower extremity, the pathophysiology of the particular injury, and tissue healing. Increased biomechanical understanding, as well as improvements and changes in arthroscopic surgical techniques are advancing knee rehabilitation. Early motion and weightbearing are the keystones to superior rehabilitation outcomes.

Inflammation occurs to the knee joint in both injury and surgical intervention. Managing the inflammatory response pre- and postsurgically includes controlling pain and swelling and regulating motion both in the initial phase and throughout the entire rehabilitation process. Ice, elevation, compression, and other treatment modalities are used to manage pain and swelling. Attention to the inflammatory response encourages patient progress.

Individualized rehabilitation programs following knee injury or surgery should be developed based on the knee structures injured, the severity of the injury, the surgical technique, and the goals of the patient, athletic trainer, and physical therapist. The overall psychological make-up of the athlete should also be considered before developing a framework of rehabilitation parameters and phases. Sequential time frames are important in any rehabilitation program to allow for proper healing, but certain goals must be reached within each time frame before the athlete can progress to the next stage. As the patient advances from one phase of rehabilitation to the next, the time needed for tissue healing must be balanced with the functional progress attained. Range of motion and muscle function, including strength, tone, and muscle control, tend to prevail as benchmarks for phase progression in functional rehabilitation of the knee. Assessing knee joint flexion, extension, range of motion, and strength is paramount in knee rehabilitation protocols. Although the knee joint is classically referred to as a hinge joint, it actually has 6° of freedom in a three-axis system. Internal and external rotation of the leg at the knee does not normally occur once the knee is in complete extension because of the screw home mechanism of the knee. Although the patellofemoral joint appears to be a simple plane joint, it is actually a joint that undergoes an intricate combination of flexion, slide, tilt, and rotation during knee motion. Rehabilitation programs for the knee must consider the impact of the exercise on both articulations. Quality and quantity of motion must be continually assessed.[110] This complex interaction of translational and rotational forces is referred to as coupled motion and most accurately describes knee kinematics.[111]

Complications in Rehabilitation

Infection, an infrequent complication, can occur during the rehabilitation process. Although infection is rare, it can be a major obstacle to functional rehabilitation and threaten the patient's life and limb. Wound management after trauma or surgery should be closely monitored.

The most common complication is loss of motion, which can result from a variety of reasons including late movement postsurgically, contracture, arthrofibrosis, inadequate inflammation management, and poor patient compliance. Typical complications following ACL reconstruction are extension loss and anterior knee pain.[112-114] Early motion in knee trauma and postsurgical cases can generally prevent deterioration in range of motion and possible subsequent postsurgical manipulations under anesthesia.

To reduce the frequency of rehabilitation complications after ACL reconstruction, rehabilitation should aim to attain greater than 90° of flexion, full extension, minimal swelling, and active quadriceps control of the knee no later than 1 week following surgery.[23] Similar goals should be set and attained posttrauma and presurgically for prevention of arthrofibrosis. Particular attention to patellar entrapment should be observed. Poor patella mobilization, quadriceps lag, and patellar pain are early warning signs of ROM complications.

Phases of Knee Rehabilitation

Phase 1 involves acute posttraumatic or postsurgical management of swelling, pain, inflammation, and joint dysfunction. This phase may involve joint protection by immobilization, bracing, and limiting weightbearing until the patient can walk without a limp. Modality use, early limited motion, low-grade joint mobilization, and low-level strengthening are used to control pain and edema and to maintain an optimal healing environment.

Phase 2 reestablishes full ROM and joint mobility. Strengthening progresses within tissue-healing constraints. Weightbearing advances according to strength and level of healing. Endurance exercises are used to maintain or reestablish fitness. Proprioception and balance advance from low-level, stable-surface training to high-level, unstable-surface training. Light functional activities can begin.

The athlete continues advanced progressive resistive exercises, functional activities, and implements speed and power training during phase 3. Plyometrics, dynamic balance and proprioception, agilities and sport-specific activities are used; protections and limitations gradually decrease.

Phase 4 involves return-to-play criteria. Simulated competition, limited practices, and skill refinement are important to return to play in a competitive environment. The athlete's return to play should be based on his or her satisfactory performance on various tests, including an isokinetic evaluation, manual muscle testing, negative clinical exam, functional tests, and psychological state of readiness.

Rehabilitation programs should follow a protocol of ongoing pain and swelling control to aid in establishing and maintaining early range of motion and progressive weightbearing.

Each phase of rehabilitation may involve the performance of isometrics, isotonics, isokinetics, balance and proprioception, endurance, power, and functional or sport-specific activities. Appropriate activities are selected based on the individual athlete's stage of healing and functional capability. Open and closed chain activities should be judiciously implemented throughout the functional rehabilitation process based on the needs of the athlete.

Important Factors in Knee Rehabilitation

A starting point for rehabilitation is determined by an examination and assessment of the injured athlete. The athletic trainer or physical therapist gathers information about the athlete's current status, which is essential in the overall care of the knee. The athlete generally demonstrates needs in the following specific areas:

- Range of motion and flexibility
- Strength
- Proprioception and kinesthesia
- Endurance
- Functional skills and coordination

Range-of-Motion Exercises

Heel slide

The patient lies supine on a table with the involved lower extremity straight, then slides the involved heel along the surface of the table, moving the knee into flexion until he or she feels pain or restriction in motion. The patient then performs a slow controlled return to the starting position. The patient may use a stretching strap, belt, or towel to assist the motion to higher levels (**Figure 16-18**).

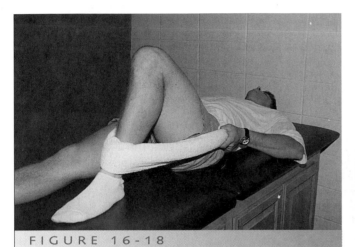

FIGURE 16-18

The heel slide is a range-of-motion exercise in which the patient slides the involved heel along the table before moving the knee into flexion.

Wall slide

The patient lies supine on a table that is perpendicular to the wall, with the involved lower extremity supported by the wall. The patient lets his or her foot slide down the wall assisted by gravity until he or she feels pain or restriction. The patient then returns the foot to the starting position.

Continuous passive motion

A continuous passive motion (CPM) device gently moves a limb through a specified ROM. Although a CPM device can increase early motion, most athletic trainers prefer to involve the patient in active rehabilitation as early as possible. CPM should not be used as a substitute for active and active-assistive ROM unless a specific diagnosis or postsurgical restrictions are imposed by the surgeon. Although a CPM device may promote early motion, it typically does not maintain full extension or achieve full flexion.

Bicycle

The bicycle is an effective active or active-assistive form of ROM. The stationary bicycle has lower ACL stresses than normal walking.[115] With no resistance, a patient can use the uninvolved extremity to move the involved extremity. Oscillating partial revolutions can be performed if the patient has inadequate knee flexion and cannot perform a full revolution. The seat height can also be manipulated to vary the range of knee flexion as needed, depending on the patient's tolerance or postsurgical precautions.

Prone hangs

The patient lies prone on a table with thighs supported just proximal to the patella. Gravity pulls the tibia into extension as the patient relaxes. Low weights can be added to the ankle of the involved limb to increase the stretch. Higher loads should be avoided because patient guarding may occur (**Figure 16-19**).

Towel propping

The patient sits on the table with a towel roll under the ankle of the involved extremity. The knee is unsupported and gravity pulls it into extension. The patient can manually assist the extension by gently pressing the thigh toward the table with his or her hands. An active quadriceps set can also be performed in this position (**Figure 16-20**).

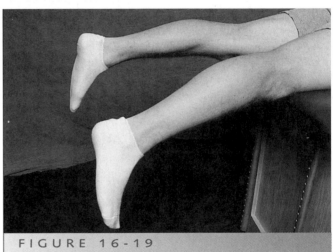

FIGURE 16-19

In prone hangs, the prone athlete relaxes as gravity pulls the tibia into extension.

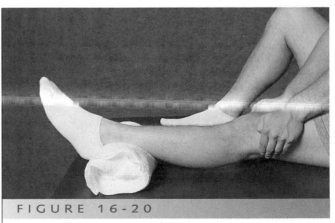

FIGURE 16-20

In the towel propping exercise, gravity pulls the athlete's unsupported knee into extension.

Strengthening Techniques

Strength is defined as the force or tension a muscle or muscle group can exert against a resistance in one maximal effort.[116] Strength is developed through progressive-resistance exercises. Exercise selection by the athletic trainer should be based on the patient's position, the amount of weightbearing the patient can tolerate, and specific ranges of motion that provide the most benefit with the least risk of complications. Specific ranges of knee motion have their advantages and disadvantages, determined by the needs of the individual patient. For example, closed kinetic chain (CKC) exercises develop high tibiofemoral joint contact forces, but low shearing forces because of compression and the co-contractions of the quadriceps and hamstring muscles. Open kinetic chain (OKC) exercises, on the other hand, result in lower tibiofemoral compression, higher anterior shearing with quadriceps activity, and higher posterior shearing with hamstring activity. **Table 16-2** provides the results of analyses of joint forces in various positions and ranges.[115,117-130]

TABLE 16-2
ANALYSIS OF JOINT FORCES

Knee Position	Joint Forces	Knee Position	Joint Forces
0° (Full extension)	• Minimal stress on the ACL and PCL • Minimal patellofemoral joint contact forces and stability • High quadriceps activity with isometrics and moderate activity with single leg raising	60° to 90°	• Low PFJ contact forces • No ACL stress as a result of anterior shear forces from quadriceps or hamstring activity in OKC or CKC • High PFJ stability • High PFJ contact forces • High PCL stress as a result of posterior shearing forces with hamstring activity in OKC or CKC • Highest hamstring EMG activity in CKC
0° to 30° (Terminal knee extension)	• High anterior shear forces with quadriceps activity in both OKC and CKC • Highest quadriceps EMG activity with OKC (all groups) • Minimal PCL stress as a result of posterior shear forces with quadriceps activity in both OKC and CKC		
0° to 60°	• Increased PFJ stability at 30° • Low ACL stress as a result of anterior shear forces with hamstring activity in OKC • Low PCL stress as a result of posterior shear forces with hamstring activity • OKC and CKC	90° to 105°	• Highest posterior shearing forces in both OKC and CKC • Highest tibiofemoral compressive forces • Highest quadriceps EMG activity in CKC

Isometric Exercises

Quad sets

The patient lies supine, sits, or stands with the involved knee in full extension. The patient contracts the quadriceps muscles, "setting" the muscle, and holds it for 10 seconds (**Figure 16-21**). The use of an electrical muscle stimulator (EMS) or biofeedback unit can aid the patient in holding the contraction. Low-intensity, portable home EMS units are less effective than high-intensity, clinic units in regaining quadriceps strength.[131] The patient should be monitored for proper muscle activation patterns so that the gluteals and hamstrings do not substitute for the quadriceps activity.

Hamstring sets

The patient sits or lies supine and presses the heel of the involved extremity into the supporting surface using the hamstring muscles. The patient should be monitored so that gluteal substitution patterns are avoided.

Quadriceps and hamstring co-contraction

The patient sits or lies supine with the involved extremity in full extension. The patient contracts or sets the quadriceps and simultaneously uses the hamstrings to press the involved heel into the supporting surface.

Multi-angle isometrics

The quadriceps and hamstrings can be exercised isometrically at various degrees of knee flexion. These angles will ultimately be determined by the patient's diagnosis, post-surgical precautions, and tolerance. The level of shearing forces on the ACL and PCL, the patellofemoral joint reaction forces, and the levels of patellar stability vary with different positions. The athletic trainer will judiciously determine what positions are safest and appropriate for the patient at each stage of rehabilitation.

Isotonic Exercises

Straight leg raises

Initially, these exercises can be performed using only the weight of the extremity. As the athlete's strength improves, external weights can be added to the thigh, knee, or ankle.

Flexion: The patient lies supine with the uninvolved extremity flexed and the involved extremity in full extension. The patient first sets the involved quadriceps and then lifts the heel from the table (**Figure 16-22**).

Abduction: The patient lies on the uninvolved side with the uninvolved knee flexed and the involved extremity in full extension. The patient first sets the quadriceps and then lifts the involved extremity away from the table (**Figure 16-23**).

Extension: The patient lies prone with knees in full extension. The patient first sets the involved quadriceps

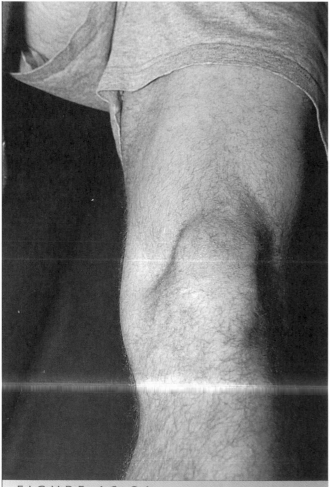

FIGURE 16-21

Quad sets are isometric exercises in which the athlete contracts the quadriceps muscles and holds for 10 seconds.

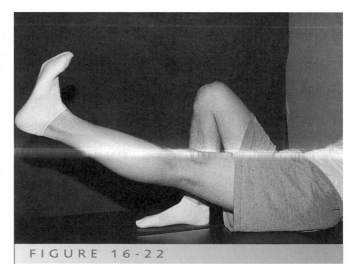

FIGURE 16-22

Straight leg raises (flexion) are isotonic exercises in which the athlete sets the involved quadriceps and lifts the heel away from the table.

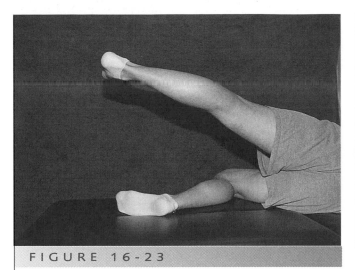

FIGURE 16-23

Straight leg raises (abduction) are isotonic exercises in which the athlete sets the quadriceps and lifts the involved extremity away from the table.

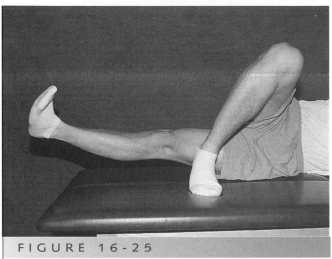

FIGURE 16-25

Straight leg raises (adduction) are isotonic exercises in which the athlete sets the involved quadriceps and lifts the extremity away from the table.

and then lifts the involved extremity away from the table (**Figure 16-24**).

Adduction: The patient lies on the involved side with the involved knee in full extension and the uninvolved extremity crossed over the involved extremity. The patient first sets the involved quadriceps, and then lifts the involved extremity away from the table (**Figure 16-25**).

Squat

The squatting motion can be performed in numerous ways with various apparatus including free weights, gym balls, resistive bands, walls, and shuttles. It can be performed in limited ROM as needed by the individual athlete. Hamstring activity is facilitated by trunk flexion.[118,125]

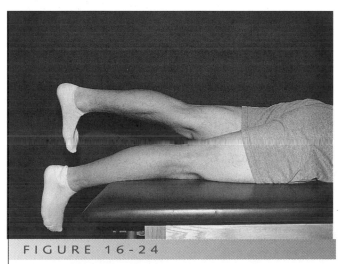

FIGURE 16-24

Straight leg raises (extension) are isotonic exercises in which the athlete sets the quadriceps and lifts the involved extremity away from the table.

Step-ups and step-downs

These exercises begin at low heights and are advanced as ROM and strength improve. Forward, lateral, and backward vectors of movement can be used. The patient begins by stepping up on a short stool, first with one foot, then the other, then stepping down in the same order.

Closed chain terminal knee extension

The patient stands with the involved knee in approximately 30° of flexion. The resistance is placed behind the knee proximal to the popliteal fossa, and the patient straightens the knee by setting the quadriceps (**Figure 16-26**). The athletic trainer should monitor the patient for gluteal substitution.

Leg curl: The patient lies prone, and resistance is placed proximal to the ankle posteriorly (**Figure 16-27**). Limited arcs of motion can be used.

Leg extension: The patient is seated, and resistance is placed proximal to the ankle anteriorly (**Figure 16-28**). Limited arcs of motion can be used.

Abduction/adduction/flexion/extension: The patient stands, and the resistance is placed proximal to the knee or ankle laterally, medially, anteriorly, and posteriorly (**Practice Session 16-1**). The hip is abducted, adducted, flexed, or extended against the resistance.

Calf raise: The patient is seated with the resistance placed over the thigh proximal to the knee as the ankle is plantarflexed against the resistance (**Figure 16-29**). An alternate position is for the patient to stand with the weight across the shoulders or held in the hands.

Isokinetics

Isokinetics is a useful strengthening and testing modality for speed-specific training. However, isokinetics involves a

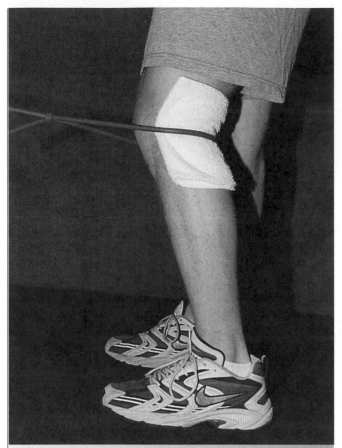

FIGURE 16-26

Closed chain terminal knee extensions are isotonic exercises in which the athlete straightens the knee by setting the quadriceps against resistance.

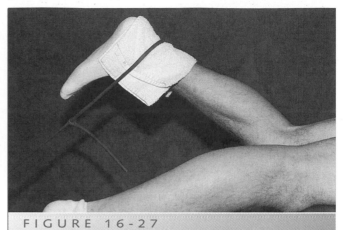

FIGURE 16-27

In leg curls, the athlete lies prone and uses limited arcs of motion against resistance.

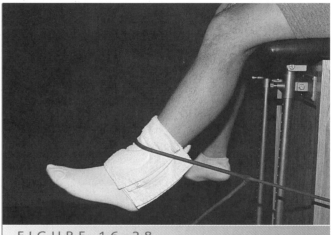

FIGURE 16-28

In leg extensions, the athlete sits and uses limited arcs of motion against resistance.

computerized, electromechanical device that is not readily available to many athletic trainers because of space requirements and prohibitive cost. Exercise velocity, exercise volume, contraction type (concentric, eccentric, isometric, and isotonic), and ROM can be varied according to the needs of the patient. Although isokinetic exercise is versatile, it is not a panacea or replacement for a comprehensive rehabilitation progression.

PROPRIOCEPTION AND KINESTHESIA

Proprioception is the term used to define the perception of joint position and limb "heaviness."[132] Kinesthesia is the term used to define the body's ability to detect positional changes. Although the terms are not interchangeable, they are closely related. Articular mechanoreceptors, golgi tendon organs, muscle spindles, the vestibular system, the visual system, and cerebellar function all contribute to the body's conscious and unconscious positional awareness.

Proprioceptive/Kinesthetic/Stabilization Exercises

Standing tubing/band kicks
The patient stands single-legged on the involved extremity. Tubing or a band is wrapped around the uninvolved ankle and foot, and the patient kicks the uninvolved extremity against the tension of the tubing or band as he or she attempts to maintain balance. Patterns of hip flexion, adduction, abduction, extension, or diagonals may be used.

Stork stands
Stork stands can be done with or without movement of the uninvolved leg. The patient stands single-legged on the involved leg and attempts to maintain his or her balance for as long as possible. Visual cueing may be used at first

PRACTICE SESSION 16-1
ABDUCTION/ADDUCTION/FLEXION/EXTENSION

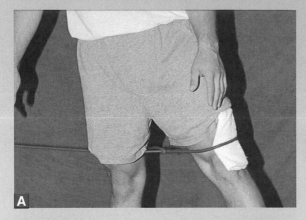

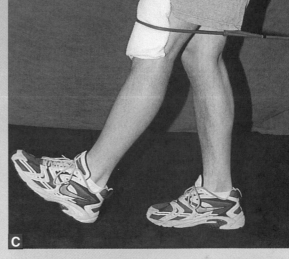

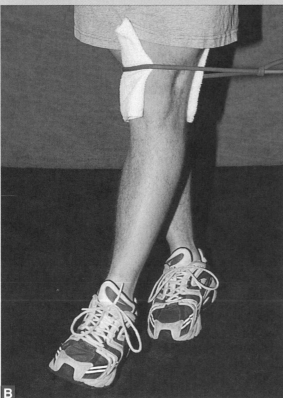

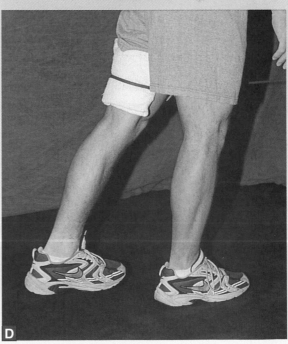

In abduction/adduction/flexion/extension, the athlete stands as resistance is placed proximal to the knee or ankle laterally, medially, anteriorly, and posteriorly and abducts, adducts, flexes, or extends the hip against resistance. **A** Abduction. **B** Flexion. **C** Adduction. **D** Extension.

to enhance performance. Later, the patient can perform the same exercise with the eyes closed to increase difficulty. Movement of the uninvolved leg can also increase difficulty. Incorporating movements such as catching, throwing, object manipulation, or medicine ball activities by the uninvolved upper extremity causes reactionary

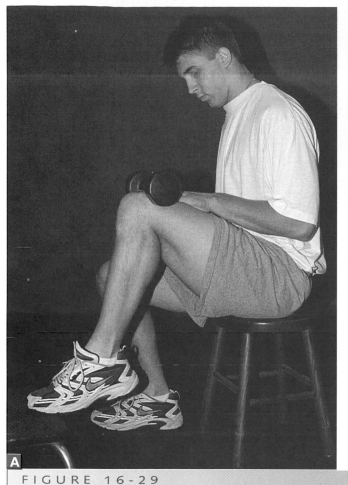 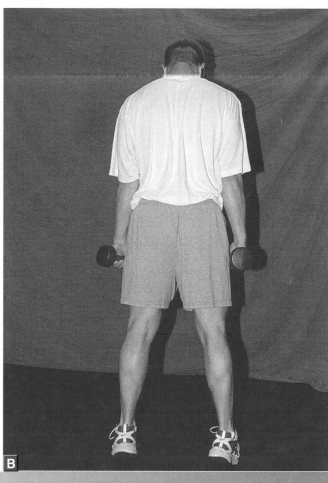

FIGURE 16-29

The calf raise can be performed in two ways. **A** The athlete sits and plantar flexes the ankle against resistance placed over the thigh. **B** The athlete stands with the weight across the shoulders or in the hands.

forces back through the body that increase the difficulty of the activity as well.

Minitramp
The patient can perform stork stands while standing on the moving surface of a miniature trampoline. Here, too, visual cues and movement of the upper extremities can increase the difficulty of the activity.

Balance beam
The balance beam presents the patient with the difficulty of maneuvering on a narrow base of support. Static and dynamic balance can be challenged by doing variations of the stork stand and by walking forward, backward, side-stepping, and heel to toe.

Vestibular board
The vestibular board typically challenges the patient in two directions: forward-backward and side-to-side. Because it has a larger surface area than other unstable surface trainers, the patient can perform activities that involve wider stances or kneeling and can focus on controlling two directions of movement.

Rhythmic stabilization
Rhythmic stabilization can be performed in functional positions such as in a squat, on stairs, or in a downhill skier's tuck. The patient holds the position while the athletic trainer attempts to move him or her from the position with perturbations. The force applied by the athletic trainer can be individualized to the patient's tolerance (Figure 16-30).

Endurance
Muscular endurance is defined as the capacity of a muscle group to perform repeated contractions against a load or sustain a contraction for an extended period of time.[116] The mechanics of performing an activity often change as the body becomes fatigued.[133] Endurance activities can be performed on treadmills, cycles, skier machines, stairsteppers, elliptical runners, and other machines.

FIGURE 16-30

In rhythmic stabilization, the athlete holds a functional position as the athletic trainer attempts to move the athlete from the position.

Functional Progressions

Quantitative functional testing is an effective way for the athletic trainer to determine a patient's limitations. Functional tests can be used to document progress, set limits in exercise programs, or determine if a patient is ready to advance to the next phase of rehabilitation or return to play. There are four functional one-legged hop tests for ACL rehabilitation; the two described have the highest specificity.[134]

One-legged single hop for distance

The patient stands on one leg, hops as far as possible, and lands on the same leg. The total distance is measured. Each leg is tested twice, and the results for each leg are averaged. The average for the involved leg is divided by the average for the noninvolved leg, and the result is multiplied by 100 to obtain a percentage.

One-legged timed hop

The patient hops on one leg a distance of 6 meters as quickly as possible. The total time to cover the distance is recorded to the nearest one hundredth of a second. Each leg is tested twice, and an average score for each leg is calculated. The average time for the noninvolved leg is divided by the average time for the involved leg, and the result is multiplied by 100.

Running

Running progressions should begin with low intensities and short distances on smooth, even surfaces such as a treadmill. The degree of activity and the length of rest periods should be determined by the initial fitness level of the athlete and gradually progress toward the competitive requirements of the individual's sport, whether it be marathons or gymnastics.

Agilities

Agilities combine speed, power, and skill. The patient should begin with simple, well-controlled tasks such as forward and backward running or side-shuffling at low intensities. As the patient improves, the agilities can progress to more complex patterns such as figure eights, bag drills, or obstacle courses. As with all other rehabilitation programs, agilities should be designed to meet the functional requirements of the individual athlete's sport.

Plyometrics

Plyometrics is defined as exercises that enable a muscle to reach maximum strength in as short a time as possible.[135] Lower extremity plyometrics typically involve jump training. Each activity can be varied in intensity and volume as needed by the athlete. Cones, boxes, mats, hurdles, stairs, and medicine balls are used for plyometric activities. Exercises are categorized by activity, according to the following categories:

- Jumps-in-place
- Standing jumps
- Multiple hops and jumps
- Bounding
- Box drills
- Depth jumps

CHAPTER REVIEW

The knee consists of the femur, tibia, and patella, which form the tibiofemoral and patellofemoral joints. The major ligaments contributing to knee stability are the medial collateral, lateral collateral, anterior cruciate, and posterior cruciate. The medial and lateral menisci partly cover the tibial surface, while hyaline cartilage covers the articular surfaces of the femur, tibia, and patella.

The cruciate ligaments enable the knee to roll and slide for maximum motion while maintaining contact and stability. The screw-home mechanism permits axial rotation. Contact surface area between the femur and the tibia is increased by the menisci, which play an important role in load transmission. The patellofemoral joint improves quadriceps mechanism efficiency, provides functional knee stability under load, transmits quadriceps force around an angle with little energy loss, and protects the trochlear articular surface.

In evaluating a player with an acute knee injury, the athletic trainer must determine the severity of the injury and if physician referral is needed. Gross deformity, a pale foot, or inability to move the foot or toes requires immediate physician attention. A nonemergent injury allows time for observation, talking with the athlete about the nature of the injury, and performing a physical examination as tolerated.

When evaluating an athlete with a chronic knee injury, the athletic trainer should observe, take the history, and assess the knee for swelling, range of motion, and stability. Radiographs are necessary to rule out bony deformities, and magnetic resonance imaging may be helpful in certain situations.

Acute knee injuries can affect the bones and the soft tissues. The athletic trainer should understand predisposing factors, mechanism of injury, history, physical examination, radiographs, and treatment of anterior cruciate ligament tears, medial collateral ligament tears, lateral complex injuries, tibial spine fractures, posterior cruciate ligament injuries, combined ligament injuries, knee dislocations, acute patellar dislocations, recurrent patellar dislocations, meniscal injuries, discoid lateral menisci, patellar fractures, distal femoral and proximal tibial fractures, and osteochondral fractures.

Overuse injuries are caused by chronic, repetitive microtrauma, often from training errors. Among the overuse injuries commonly seen in athletes are patellofemoral dysplasia, chronic subluxating patella, patellar tendinitis, quadriceps tendinitis, patellar stress fracture, osteochondritis dissecans, bipartite patella, and iliotibial band friction syndrome. The athletic trainer should be familiar with the predisposing factors, mechanism of injury, history, physical examination, radiographs, and treatment of each of these conditions.

Certain knee injuries affect only pediatric athletes, among them patellar sleeve fractures, physeal fractures, tibial tubercle avulsions, Osgood-Schlatter disease, and Sinding-Larsen-Johanssen syndrome. The mechanism of injury, history, physical examination, radiographs, and treatment of each injury are important for the athletic trainer to understand.

Inflammatory and neoplastic causes of knee pain include gonococcal and juvenile rheumatoid arthritis and malignant and benign bone and soft-tissue tumors. If the athletic trainer suspects any of these conditions are present, the athlete must be referred to a physician immediately.

Functional knee pain is diagnosed in the athlete who experiences pain in the absence of anatomic pathology in order to cope with the environment and reduce anxiety. It is common in children and adolescents who are pressured into too many activities by demanding parents. If organic causes are ruled out, psychiatric referral may be necessary.

The principles of knee rehabilitation are the same for all extremities, and the athletic trainer must understand anatomy, biomechanics, pathophysiology of an injury, and healing. The four phases of knee rehabilitation are acute posttraumatic or postsurgical management, reestablishing full ROM and joint mobility, continuing advanced progressive resistive exercises and activities, and return-to-play criteria.

SELF-TEST

1. The attachment site for the medial collateral ligament is the:
   A. patella.
   B. fibular head.
   C. tibial tubercle.
   D. medial femoral condyle.

2. Which structures permit maximum motion (rolling and sliding) of the knee while maintaining contact and stability?
   A. Tibiofemoral joint, patellofemoral joint
   B. Popliteus tendon, biceps femoris tendon
   C. Prepatellar bursa, superficial infrapatellar bursa
   D. Anterior cruciate ligament, posterior cruciate ligament

3. What is one of the functions of the patellofemoral joint?
   A. Protects the trochlear articular surface
   B. Enhances stability by allowing the patella to work with the distal femur
   C. Decreases the lever arm, increasing the efficiency of the quadriceps mechanism
   D. Contains the quadriceps force and prevents it from being transmitted to other structures

4. The accumulation of blood within the knee joint is known as:
   A. edema.
   B. hemarthrosis.
   C. soft-tissue swelling.
   D. intra-articular effusion.

5. What is the name of the diagnostic test in which the patient's hips are externally rotated, the knee flexed, and the tibia pulled anteriorly to assess the endpoint to anterior translation?
   A. Lachman test
   B. Pivot shift test
   C. Varus stress test
   D. Posterior drawer test

6. An athlete with an ACL-deficient knee who does not wish to undergo surgical reconstruction is most likely to be able to participate in which of the following sports?
   A. Soccer
   B. Football
   C. Bicycling
   D. Basketball

7. Anatomic predisposition to acute patellar dislocation includes a:
   A. deep trochlea.
   B. small Q-angle.
   C. femoral anteversion.
   D. loose lateral retinaculum.

8. Anterior knee pain caused by overuse in an athlete without apparent structural malalignment may reflect:
   A. patellar tendinitis.
   B. patellar stress fracture.
   C. patellofemoral dysplasia.
   D. bipartite patella.

9. Which of the following signs or symptoms characterizes iliotibial band friction syndrome?
   A. Pain relieved by walking
   B. Walking with a flexed-knee gait
   C. A negative compression test of Noble
   D. Pain localized over the medial femoral condyle

10. In which of the following groups is Osgood-Schlatter disease often seen?
    A. In boys ages 8 to 9 years
    B. In girls ages 13 to 14 years
    C. In adolescents at the onset of a growth spurt
    D. In sedentary adults

Answers on page 892.

References

1. Wilson SA, Vigorita VJ, Scott WN: Anatomy, in Scott WN (ed): *The Knee*. St Louis, MO, Mosby-Year Book, 1994, pp15–54.

2. Hoppenfeld S: Physical examination of the knee, in Hoppenfeld S (ed): *Physical Examination of the Spine and the Extremities*. New York, NY, Appleton-Century-Crofts, 1976, pp 171–196.

3. Rosenberg A, Mikosz RP, Mohler CG: Basic knee biomechanics, in Scott WN (ed): *The Knee*. St Louis, MO, Mosby-Year Book, 1994, pp 75–94.

4. Walker SP, Erkman MJ: The role of the menisci in force transmission across the knee. *Clin Orthop* 1975;109:184–192.

5. Cox J, Cordell L: The degenerative effects of medial meniscus tears in dogs' knees. *Clin Orthop* 1977;125:236–242.

6. Beynnon BD, Johnson RJ: Knee: Relevant biomechanics, in DeLee JC, Drez D Jr (eds): *Orthopaedic Sports Medicine: Principles and Practice*. Philadelphia, PA, WB Saunders, 1994, vol 2, pp1113–1133.

7. Allen PR, Denham RA, Swan AV: Late degenerative changes after meniscectomy: Factors affecting the knee after operation. *J Bone Joint Surg* 1984;66B:666–671.

8. Eiskjaer S, Larsen ST, Schmidt MB: The significance of hemarthrosis of the knee in children. *Arch Orthop Trauma Surg* 1988;107:96–98

9. DeCarlo MS, Sell KE: Normative data for range of motion and single leg hop in high school athletes. *J Sports Rehab* 1997;6:246–255.

10. Shelbourne KD, Johnson G: Evaluation of knee extension following anterior cruciate ligament reconstruction. *Orthopaedics* 1994;17:205–206.

11. Torg JS, Conrad W, Kalen V: Clinical diagnosis of anterior cruciate ligament instability in the athlete. *Am J Sports Med* 1976;4:84–93.

12. Shelbourne KD, Foulk DA, Nitz PA: Anterior cruciate ligament injuries, in Reider B (ed): *Sports Medicine: The School-Age Athlete*, ed 2. Philadelphia, PA, WB Saunders, 1996, pp 329–347.

13. Bach BR Jr, Warren RF, Flynn WM, et al: Arthrometric evaluations of knees that have a torn anterior cruciate ligament. *J Bone Joint Surg* 1990;72A:1299–1306.

14. Rettig AC, Rubinstein RA: Medial and lateral ligament injuries of the knee, in Scott WN (ed): *The Knee*. St Louis, MO, Mosby-Year Book, 1994, pp 803–722.

15. Shelbourne KD, Rubinstein RA: Methodist Sports Medicine Center's experience with acute and chronic isolated posterior cruciate ligament injuries. *Clin Sports Med* 1994;3:531–543.

16. Rosenberg TD, Paulos, LE, Parker RD, et al: The forty-five-degree posteroanterior flexion weight-bearing radiograph of the knee. *J Bone Joint Surg* 1988;70A:1479–1483.

17. Merchant AC, Mercer RL, Jacobsen RH, et al: Roentgenographic analysis of patellofemoral congruence. *J Bone Joint Surg* 1974;56:1391–1396

18. Fischer SP, Fox JM, Del Pizzo W, et al: Accuracy of diagnosis from magnetic resonance imaging of the knee. *J Bone Joint Surg* 1991;73A:2–10.

19. Shelbourne KD, Martini DJ, McCarroll JR, et al: Correlation of joint line tenderness and meniscal lesions in patients with acute anterior cruciate ligament tears. *Am J Sports Med* 1995;23:166–169.

20. Kannus P, Jarvinen M: Conservatively treated tears of the anterior cruciate ligament. *J Bone Joint Surg* 1987;69A:1007–1012.

21. Shelbourne KD, Trumper RV: Preventing anterior knee pain after anterior cruciate ligament reconstruction. *Am J Sports Med* 1997;25:41–47.

22. Shelbourne, KD, Wilckins JH, Mollabashy A, DeCarlo M: Arthrofibrosis in acute anterior cruciate ligament reconstruction. The effect of timing of reconstruction and rehabilitation. *Am J Sports Med* 1991;19:332–336.

23. Shelbourne KD, Gray T: Anterior cruciate ligament reconstruction with autogenous patellar tendon graft followed by accelerated rehabilitation: A two- to nine-year follow-up. *Am J Sports Med* 1997;25:786–795.

24. Shelbourne KD, Patel DV, McCarroll JR: Management of anterior cruciate ligament injuries in skeletally immature adolescents. *Knee Surg Sports Traumatol Arthrosc* 1996;4:68–74.

25. Indelicato PA: Non-operative treatment of complete tears of the medial collateral ligament of the knee. *J Bone Joint Surg* 1983;65A:323–329.

26. Shelbourne KD, Patel DV: Management of combined injuries of the anterior cruciate ligament and medial collateral ligament. *J Bone Joint Surg* 1995;77A:800–8060.

27. Shelbourne KD, Mesko JW, McCarroll JR, et al: Combined medial collateral ligament-posterior cruciate rupture: Mechanism of injury. *Am J Knee Surg* 1990;3:42–44.

28. Derscheid GL, Garrick JG: Medial collateral ligament injuries in football: Nonoperative management of grade I and grade II sprains. *Am J Sports Med* 1981;9:365–368.

29. Jones RE, Henley MB, Francis P: Nonoperative management of isolated Grade III collateral ligament injury tears in high school football players. *Clin Orthop* 1986;213:137–140.

30. DeLee JC, Riley MB, Rockwood CA Jr: Acute straight lateral instability of the knee. *Am J Sports Med* 1983;11:404–411.

31. Kannus P: Nonoperative treatment of Grade II and III sprains of the lateral ligament compartment of the knee. *Am J Sports Med* 1989;17:83–88.

32. Hayes JM, Masear VR: Avulsion fracture of the tibial eminence associated with severe medial ligamentous injury in an adolescent: A case report and literature review. *Am J Sports Med* 1984;12:330–333.

33. Warner JP, Micheli LJ: Pediatric and adolescent musculoskeletal injuries, in Grana WA, Kalenak A (eds): *Clinical Sports Medicine*. Philadelphia, PA, WB Saunders, 1991, pp 490–498.

34. Baxter MP, Wiley JJ: Fractures of the tibial spine in children: An evaluation of knee stability. *J Bone Joint Surg* 1988;70B:228–230.

35. Clancy WG Jr, Shelbourne KD, Zoellner GB, et al: Treatment of knee joint instability secondary to rupture of the posterior cruciate ligament. *J Bone Joint Surg* 1983;65A:310–325.

36. Fowler PJ, Messieh SS: Isolated posterior cruciate ligament injuries in athletes. *Am J Sports Med* 1987;15:553–557.

37. Torg JS, Barton TM, Pavlov H, Stine R: Natural history of posterior cruciate ligament-deficient knee. *Clin Orthop* 1989;246:208–216.

38. Bianchi M: Acute tears of the posterior cruciate ligament: Clinical study and results of operative treatment in 27 cases. *Am J Sports Med* 1983;11:308–314.

39. L'Insalata JC, Harner CD: Treatment of acute and chronic posterior cruciate ligament deficiency. New approaches. *Am J Knee Surg* 1996;9:185–193.

40. Parolie JM, Bergfeld JA: Long term results of nonoperative treatment of isolated posterior cruciate ligament injuries in the athlete. *Am J Sports Med* 1986;14:35–38.

41. Rubinstein RA Jr, Shelbourne KD: Management of combined instabilities: Anterior cruciate ligament/medial collateral ligament and anterior cruciate ligament/lateral side. *Oper Tech Sports Med* 1993;1:66–71.

42. Shelbourne KD, Nitz PA: The O'Donoghue triad revisited: Combined knee injuries involving anterior cruciate and medial collateral ligament tears. *Am J Sports Med* 1991;19:474–477

43. O'Donoghue D: Surgical treatment of fresh injuries to the major ligaments of the knee. *J Bone Joint Surg* 1950;32A:721–738.

44. McCoy GF, Hannon DG, Barr RJ, et al: Vascular injury associated with low-velocity dislocations of the knee. *J Bone Joint Surg* 1987;69B:285–287

45. Shelbourne KD, Porter DA, Clingman JA, et al: Low velocity knee dislocation. *Orthop Rev* 1991; 20: 995–1004.

46. Micheli LJ: Patellofemoral disorders in children, in Fox JM, Del Pizzo W (eds): *The Patellofemoral Joint.* New York, NY, McGraw-Hill, 1993, pp 105–121.

47. Post WR, Fulkerson JP: Surgery of the patellofemoral joint: Indications, effects, results, and recommendations, in Scott WN (ed): *The Knee.* St Louis, MO, Mosby-Year Book, 1994, pp 441–468.

48. Shelbourne KD, Porter DA, Rozzi W: Use of a modified Elmslie-Trillat procedure to improve abnormal patellar congruence angle. *Am J Sports Med* 1994;22:318–323.

49. Cash JD, Hughston JC: Treatment of acute patellar dislocation. *Am J Sports Med* 1988;16:244–249.

50. Mäenpää H, Lehto MU: Patellar dislocation: The long-term results of nonoperative management in 100 patients. *Am J Sports Med* 1997;25:213–217.

51. Arnbjörnsson A, Egund N, Rydling O, et al: The natural history of recurrent dislocation of the patella: Long-term results of conservative and operative treatment. *J Bone Joint Surg* 1992,74B:140–142.

52. Brady TA, Cahill BR, Bodnar LM: Weight training-related injuries in the high school athlete. *Am J Sports Med* 1982;10:1–5.

53. Risser WL: Weight-training injuries in children and adolescents. *Am Fam Phys* 1991;44:2104–2108.

54. Shelbourne KD, Johnson GE: Locked bucket-handle meniscal tears in knees with chronic anterior cruciate ligament deficiency. *Am J Sports Med* 1993;21:779–782.

55. Steiner ME, Grana WA: The young athlete's knee: Recent advances. *Clin Sports Med* 1988;7:527–546.

56. Fitzgibbons RE, Shelbourne KD: "Aggressive" nontreatment of lateral meniscal tears seen during anterior cruciate ligament reconstruction. *Am J Sports Med* 1995;23:156–159.

57. Shelbourne KD, Patel DV, Adsit WS, Porter DA: Rehabilitation after meniscal repair. *Clin Sports Med* 1996,15:595–612.

58. Sprague NF III: Arthroscopic meniscal resection, in Scott WN (ed): *The Knee.* St Louis, MO, Mosby-Year Book, 1994, pp 527–557.

59. Bellier G, Dupont JY, Larrain M, et al: Lateral discoid menisci in children. *Arthroscopy* 1989;5:52–56.

60. Dickhaut S, DeLee JC: The discoid lateral meniscus syndrome. *J Bone Joint Surg* 1982;64A:1068–1073.

61. Hayashi LK, Yamaga H, Ida K, et al: Arthroscopic meniscectomy for discoid lateral meniscus in children. *J Bone Joint Surg* 1988;70A:1495–1500.

62. Silverman JM, Mink JH, Deutsch AL: Discoid menisci of the knee: MR imaging appearance. *Radiology* 1989;173:351–354.

63. Hohl M, Johnson EE, Wiss DA: Fractures of the knee, in Rockwood CA, Green DP, Bucholz RW (eds): *Fractures in Adults,* ed 3. Philadelphia, PA, JB Lippincott, 1991, pp1725–1797.

64. Milgram JE: Tangential osteochondral fracture of the patella. *J Bone Joint Surg* 1943;25A:271–280.

65. O'Neill DB, Micheli LJ: Overuse injuries in the young athlete. *Clin Sports Med* 1988;7:591–610.

66. Merchant AC: Classification of patellofemoral disorders. *Arthroscopy* 1988;4:235–240.

67. Reider B, Marshall JL, Warren RF: Clinical characteristics of patellar disorders in young athletes. *Am J Sports Med* 1981;9:270–274.

68. Aglietti P, Insall JN, Cerulli G: Patellar pain and incongruence: I. Measurements of incongruence. *Clin Orthop* 1983;176:217–224.

69. Insall JN, Aglietti P, Tria AJ Jr: Patellar pain and incongruence: II. Clinical application. *Clin Orthop* 1983;176:225–232.

70. Sandow MJ, Goodfellow JW: The natural history of anterior knee pain in adolescents. *J Bone Joint Surg* 1985;67B:36–38.

71. Shelbourne KD, Adsit WS: Conservative care of patellofemoral pain, in Scuderi GR (ed): *The Patella.* New York, NY, Springer-Verlag, 1995, pp 127–141.

72. Schutzer SF, Ramsby G, Fulkerson JP: The evaluation of patellofemoral pain using computerized tomography: A preliminary study. *Clin Orthop* 1986;204:286–293.

73. Yates C, Grana WA: Patellofemoral pain: A prospective study. *Orthopedics* 1986;9:663–667.

74. Finestone A, Radin E, Lev B, et al: Treatment of overuse patellofemoral pain: Prospective, randomized controlled clinical trial in a military setting. *Clin Orthop* 1993; 293:208–210.

75. Eng JJ, Pierrynowski MR: Evaluation of soft foot orthotics in the treatment of patellofemoral pain syndrome. *Phys Ther* 1993;73:62–70.

76. McConnell JS: The management of chondromalacia patella: A long term solution. *Aust J Physiother* 1986;32:215–223.

77. Larsen B, Andreasen E, Urfer A, et al: Patellar taping: A radiographic examination of the medial glide technique. *Am J Sports Med* 1995;23:465–471.

78. Kannus P, Niittymaki S: Which factors predict outcome in the nonoperative treatment of patellofemoral pain syndrome? A prospective follow-up study. *Med Sci Sports Exerc* 1994;26:289–296.

79. Fulkerson JP, Schutzer SF: After failure of conservative treatment for painful patellofemoral malalignment: Lateral release or realignment? *Orthop Clin North Am* 1986;17:283–288.

80. Brown DE, Alexander AH, Lichtman DM: The Elmslie-Trillat procedure: Evaluation in patellar dislocation and subluxation. *Am J Sports Med* 1984;12:104–109.

81. Anderson AF, Pagnani MJ: Osteochondritis dissecans of the femoral condyles: Long-term results of excision of the fragment. *Am J Sports Med* 1997;25:830–834.

82. Popp JE, Yu JS, Kaeding CC: Recalcitrant patellar tendinitis: Magnetic resonance imaging, histologic evaluation, and surgical treatment. *Am J Sports Med* 1997;25:218–222.

83. Blazina ME, Kerlin RK, Jobe FW, et al: Jumper's knee. *Orthop Clin North Am* 1973;4:665–678.

84. Walsh WM: Patellofemoral joint, in DeLee JC, Drez D Jr (eds): *Orthopaedic Sports Medicine: Principles and Practice.* Philadelphia, PA, WB Saunders, 1994, pp 1163–1248.

85. Ferretti A, Ippolito E, Mariani P, Puddu G: Jumper's knee. *Am J Sports Med* 1983;11:58–62.

86. Schmidt DR, Henry JH: Stress injuries of the adolescent extensor mechanism. *Clin Sports Med* 1989;8:343–355.

87. Guhl JF: Arthroscopic treatment of osteochondritis dissecans. *Clin Orthop* 1982;167:65–74.

88. Aichroth P: Osteochondritis dissecans of the knee: A clinical survey. *J Bone Joint Surg* 1971;53B:440–447.

89. Enneking WF (ed): *Clinical Musculoskeletal Pathology.* Gainesville, FL, Storter Printing, 1977, p 147.

90. Wilson JN: A diagnostic sign in osteochondritis dissecans of the knee. *J Bone Joint Surg* 1967;49A:477–480.

91. Gylys-Morin VM, Hajek PC, Sartoris DJ, et al: Articular cartilage defects: Detectability in cadaver knees with MR. *AJR Am J Roentgenol* 1987;148:1153–1157.

92. Federico DJ, Lynch JK, Joki P: Osteochondritis dissecans of the knee: A historical review of etiology and treatment. *Arthroscopy* 1990;6:190–197.

93. Hughston JC, Hergenroeder PT, Courtenay BG: Osteochondritis dissecans of the femoral condyles. *J Bone Joint Surg* 1984;66A:1340–1348.

94. Beaty JH: Congenital anomalies of the lower and upper extremities, in Canale ST, Beaty JH (eds): *Operative Pediatric Orthopaedics.* St Louis, MO, Mosby-Year Book, 1991, pp 73–186.

95. Bourne MH, Bianco AJ Jr: Bipartite patella in the adolescent: Results of surgical excision. *J Pediatr Orthop* 1990;10:69–73.

96. Mori Y, Okumo H, Iketani H, et al: Efficacy of lateral retinacular release for painful bipartite patella. *Am J Sports Med* 1995;23:13–18.

97. Noble CA: Iliotibial band friction syndrome in runners. *Am J Sports Med* 1980;8:232–234.

98. Orava S: Iliotibial tract friction syndrome in athletes: An uncommon exertion syndrome of the lateral side on the knee. *Br J Sports Med* 1978;12:69–73.

99. Grogan DP, Carey TP, Leffers D. et al: Avulsion fractures of the patella. *J Pediatr Orthop* 1990;10:721–730.

100. Gardiner JS, McInerney VK, Avella DG, et al: Injuries to the inferior pole of the patella in children. *Orthop Rev* 1990;19:643–649.

101. Stanitski CL: Management of sports injuries in children and adolescents. Orthop Clin North Am 1988;19:689–698.

102. Roberts JM: Operative treatment of fractures about the knee. *Orthop Clin North Am* 1990;21:365–379.

103. Wiss DA, Schilz JL, Zionts L: Type III fractures of the tibial tubercle in adolescents. *J Orthop Trauma* 1991;5:475–479.

104. Ogden JA, Southwick WO: Osgood-Schlatter's disease and tibial tuberosity development. *Clin Orthop* 1976;116:180–189.

105. Smith JB: Knee problems in children. *Pediatr Clin North Am* 1986;33:1439–1456.

106. Trail IA: Tibial sequestrectomy in the management of Osgood-Schlatter disease. *J Pediatr Orthop* 1988;8:554–557

107. Gebhardt MC, Ready JE, Mankin HJ: Tumors about the knee in children. *Clin Orthop* 1990;255:86–110.

108. Speer DP: Differential diagnosis of knee pain in children. *Ariz Med* 1977;34:330–332.

109. Fritz GK, Bleck EE, Dahl IS: Functional versus organic knee pain in adolescents: A pilot study. *Am J Sports Med* 1981;9:247–249.

110. Andrews JR, Harrelson GL, Wilk KE (eds): *Physical Rehabilitation of the Injured Athlete,* ed 2. Philadelphia, PA, WB Saunders, 1998, pp 330–331.

111. Richard DB, Kibler WB: Rehabilitation of knee injuries, in Kibler WB, Herring SA, Press JM (eds): *Functional Rehabilitation of Sports and Musculoskeletal Injuries.* Gaithersburg, MD, Aspen Publishers, 1998, p 244.

112. Fu FH, Woo SL, Irrgang JJ: Current concepts for rehabilitation following anterior cruciate ligament reconstruction. *J Orthop Sports Phys Ther* 1992;15:270-278.

113. Shelbourne KD, Nitz P: Accelerated rehabilitation after anterior cruciate ligament reconstruction. *J Orthop Sports Phys Ther* 1992;15:256-264.

114. Wilk KE, Andrews JR, Clancy WG: Quadriceps muscular strength after removal of the central third patellar tendon for contralateral anterior cruciate ligament reconstruction surgery: A case study. *J Orthop Sports Phys Ther* 1993;18:692-697.

115. Henning CE, Lynch MA, Click KR: An in vivo strain guage study of elongation of the anterior cruciate ligament. Am J Sport Med 1985;13:22.

116. Fox E, Bowers R, Foss M (eds): *The Physiological Basis for Exercise and Sport*, ed 5. Madison, WI, Brown & Benchmark, 1993.

117. Lutz G, Palmitier RA, An KN, Chao EY: Comparison of tibiofemoral joint forces during open-and closed kinetic-chain exercises. *J Bone Joint Surg* 1993; 75A: 732-739.

118. Wilk K, Escamilla RF, Fleisig G, et al: A comparison of tibiofemoral joint forces and electromyographic activity during open and closed kinetic chain exercises. *Am J Sports Med* 1996;24:518–527.

119. Henche R, Kunzi HU, Morscher E: The areas of contact pressure in the patello-femoral joint. *Int Orthop* 1981;4:279–281.

120. Norkin C, Levangie PK (eds): *Joint Structure and Function: A Comprehensive Analysis*, ed 2. Philadelphia, PA, FA Davis, 1992, pp 337–378.

121. Shelton GL, Thigpen LK: Rehabilitation of patellofemoral dysfunction: A review of literature. *J Orthop Sports Phys Ther* 1991;14:243-249.

122. Grood ES, Suntay WJ, Noyes FR, et al: Biomechanics of the knee extension exercise: Effect of cutting the anterior cruciate ligament. *J Bone Joint Surg* 1984;66A:725–734.

123. Hungerford DS, Barry M: Biomechanics of the patellofemoral joint. *Clin Orthop* 1979;144:9-15.

124. Irrgang JJ, Safran MR, Fu FH: The Knee: Ligamentous and meniscal injuries, in Zachazewski JE, Magee DJ, Quillen WS (eds): *Athletic Injuries and Rehabilitation*. Philadelphia, PA, WB Saunders, 1996.

125. Ohkoshi Y, Yasuda K, Kaneda K, et al: Biomechanical analysis of rehabilitation in the standing position. *Am J Sport Med* 1991;19:605–611.

126. Wilk KE: Rehabilitation of isolated and combined posterior cruciate ligament injuries. *Clin Sports Med* 1994;13:649–677.

127. Schutzer SF, Ramsby GR, Fulkerson JP: Computerized tomographic classification of patellofemoral pain patients. *Orthop Clin North Am* 1986;17:235–248.

128. Paulos LE, Stern: Rehabilitation after anterior cruciate ligament surgery, in Jackson DW (ed): *The Anterior Cruciate Ligament: Current and Future Concepts*. New York, NY, Raven Press, 1993.

129. Fulkerson JP, Hungerford DS, Ficat RP (eds): *Disorders of the Patellofemoral Joint*, ed 2. Baltimore, MD, Williams & Wilkins, 1990.

130. Ahmed A, Burke D: In vitro measurement of static pressure distribution in synovial joints: part I. Tibial surface of the knee. *J Biomech Eng* 1983;105:216–225.

131. Snyder-Mackler L, Ladin Z, Schepsis AA, Young JC: Electrical stimulation of thigh muscles after reconstruction of the anterior cruciate ligament. *J Bone Joint Surg* 1991;73A:1025.

132. Sherrington CS (ed): *The Integrative Action of the Nervous System*. New Haven, Yale University Press, 1961.

133. Davies GJ, Dickoff-Hoffman S: Neuromuscular testing and rehabilitation of the shoulder complex. *J Orthop Sports Phys Ther*. 1993;18:449–458.

134. Barber SD, Noyes FR, Mangine R, DeMaio M: Rehabilitation after ACL reconstruction: Function testing. *Orthopaedics* 1992;15:969.

135. Chu DA (ed): *Jumping Into Plyometrics*. Champaign, IL, Leisure Press, 1991.

17

Leg, Ankle, and Foot Injuries

Dale A. Funk, MD
Thomas O. Clanton, MD
Christine M. Bonci, MS, ATC

QUICK CONTENTS

- The anatomy, normal function, gait, and common injuries and conditions affecting the leg.

- The physical examination and specific injuries of the leg.

- The anatomy, normal function, and common injuries and conditions involving the ankle.

- The anatomy, normal function, and common injuries and conditions affecting the foot.

- The rehabilitation of the ankle and foot.

The leg, the portion of the lower extremity between the knee and the ankle, is vital for locomotion. The ankle is the linking joint between the foot and the leg and is crucial to the performance of all running and jumping sports. The foot is the terminal appendage of the lower extremity and functions as the contact point between the body and the terrain.

Athletic competition places a great deal of stress on the leg, ankle, and foot. The athletic trainer's understanding of the anatomy of this region and possible injuries, as well as patient care during rehabilitation, can make a great difference in the success of recovery. This chapter covers the anatomy of the leg, ankle, and foot, as well as possible injuries and rehabilitation techniques.

THE LEG

The leg includes the tibia, the fibula, and the associated muscles that are necessary for locomotion (**Figure 17-1**). Because the leg is a very common site for athletic complaints, the athletic trainer must understand its function and the pathologic conditions that affect it.

Anatomy

Osseous structures

The tibia is slightly concave at both the knee and the ankle to accommodate the articulations with the femur and the talus, respectively. At the ankle, it widens and extends medially to become the medial malleolus, which provides bony stability to the ankle joint. Because the tibia is protected only by skin along its anterior and medial borders, it is readily accessible to palpation and examination throughout its length. This exposure also makes it vulnerable to frequent injury by direct impact blows such as contusions and fractures.

The fibula is a long, slender bone lying posterior and lateral to the tibia and connected to the tibia in three ways: by a true joint at its proximal end (knee); by the *interosseous membrane* (a thick, sheet-like ligament) along its length; and by strong ligaments at its distal end (ankle). It can also be palpated with relative ease proximally at the fibular head and neck, and then again along its distal third where it ends as the lateral malleolus. In thin individuals, the common peroneal nerve can be "rolled" over the neck of the proximal fibula with the examiner's finger approximately 3 cm from the tip of the fibular head (at the knee). The nerve is very close to the skin surface at this location and vulnerable to compression

by straps, wraps, and direct blows. Such compression would be manifested early by a decrease in sensation on the dorsum (top) of the foot and then by progressive motor loss of ankle dorsiflexion, toe dorsiflexion, and foot eversion with more severe or long-lasting injury.

Soft-tissue structures

The leg is divided by distinct fascial connection into four compartments: the anterior, lateral, superficial posterior, and deep posterior. The anterior compartment, which is most commonly involved in exertional compartment syndromes, contains the tibialis anterior muscle and the extensor muscles to the great and small toes (the extensor hallucis longus and the extensor digitorum longus). The deep peroneal nerve runs together with the anterior tibial artery deep within the anterior compartment. It provides the motor supply to the anterior compartment muscles and the sensory supply to the first web space in the foot.

The lateral compartment contains only two muscles, the peroneus longus and peroneus brevis, which plantar flex and evert the ankle. The superficial peroneal nerve is the only major neurologic structure in the lateral compartment. It innervates these two muscles and provides sensation to most of the dorsal foot.

The superficial posterior compartment contains two muscles: the gastrocnemius and the soleus. The muscles of the deep posterior compartment include the tibialis

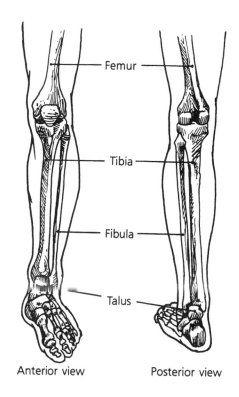

FIGURE 17-1

The bones of the leg consist of the tibia and fibula.

posterior (which plantar flexes and inverts the hindfoot); the flexor digitorum longus (long flexor of the toes); and the flexor hallucis longus (long flexor of the great toe). The tibial nerve, posterior tibial artery, and peroneal artery are also contained in the deep posterior compartment and supply its structures.

Normal Function and Gait

An understanding of athletic injuries to the lower extremities requires a basic knowledge of biomechanics and the normal gait cycle. The body planes of motion give a reference point to movement and position. The frontal plane sections the body into front and back and the horizontal or transverse plane divides the body into top and bottom. The sagittal plane separates the body into right and left sides. Motion of a body part occurs within these planes. Movements within a single plane include dorsiflexion/plantarflexion (sagittal plane), inversion/eversion (frontal plane), and abduction/adduction (horizontal or transverse plane). Other terms are used to describe deformities that occur in these planes; for example, varus describes a position toward the midline in the frontal plane. When motion or deformity involves more than one plane, it is described as *triplane*. Triplane most commonly refers to supination (adduction, plantarflexion, and inversion) and pronation (abduction, dorsiflexion, and eversion). **Table 17-1** presents the terminology for motion, instability, and deformity.

In locomotion, a complex series of movements through the various joints absorbs and dissipates forces as the joints adapt to the walking surface. The lower leg serves as a transitional link between the ankle and knee and is subject to tremendous loads and demands during athletic play. As a result, most injuries in the leg are strains and

FOCUS ON . . .

Normal Function and Gait

To understand lower extremity athletic injuries, it is important to recognize the biomechanics of normal gait, which requires knowledge of the body planes of motion. Single plane movements include dorsiflexion and plantarflexion (sagittal plane), inversion and eversion (frontal plane), and abduction and adduction (horizontal plane). Motion or deformity involving more than one plane is described as triplane.

During gait, forces are absorbed and dissipated as the body adapts to the walking surface. Most leg injuries are strains, tears, or overuse syndromes from cumulative impact loading. In normal running, the lateral aspect of the foot strikes the ground with the tibia externally rotated. As the stance phase progresses, body weight is carried over the foot. With pronation, the foot contact forces are dissipated. As the stance phase continues, the foot reaches midstance. Halfway through midstance, the nonweightbearing leg swings forward and the pelvis rotates, externally rotating the weightbearing leg. Foot supination through the subtalar joint creates a rigid foot in preparation for the toe off.

Excessive foot pronation is associated with medial tibial stress syndrome and tibial and fibular stress fractures. One possible explanation is that the medial soleus muscle causes calcaneal inversion with concentric contraction and then undergoes eccentric contraction as the foot is pronated, which can alter an athlete's normal running mechanics.

TABLE 17-1

COMMONLY USED TERMINOLOGY FOR MOTION, INSTABILITY, AND DEFORMITY

Plane	Motion	Position	Deformity
Sagittal	Dorsiflexion	Dorsiflexed	Calcaneus
	Plantarflexion	Plantar flexed	Equinus
Frontal	Inversion	Inverted	Varus
	Eversion	Everted	Valgus
Transverse	Adduction	Adducted	Adductus
	Abduction	Abducted	Abductus
Triplane description	Pronation	Pronated	Pronatus
	Supination	Supinated	Supinatus

tears or overuse syndromes from the cumulative impact of loading. For example, vertical loading, such as in running jumps, can be up to seven times an individual's body weight. Other loading forces include fore and aft shear, and torque or rotational forces.

The normal gaits of walking and running are each divided into a *stance phase* and a *swing phase*. In normal running, the lateral aspect of the foot strikes the ground first, with the tibia externally rotated. As stance phase progresses, the weight of the body is carried over the foot, and the tibia rotates internally, producing rapid heel inversion and pronation through the subtalar joint of the ankle. This *pronation*, or flattening of the foot, dissipates the contact forces, provides a smooth transition, and adapts to varying surfaces. At midstance, the foot is bearing full body weight. As heel-lift occurs, the toe-off or propulsion part of the stance phase begins, culminating with the toes leaving the ground to initiate the swing phase of gait. At about the halfway point in midstance, the nonweightbearing leg (in swing phase) swings forward and the pelvis rotates, resulting in external rotation of the weightbearing leg. This rotation produces supination of the foot through the subtalar joint and results in a rigid foot that acts as a lever for propulsion at the end of the stance phase.

Excessive foot pronation has frequently been associated with pathologic entities in the lower extremity, particularly medial tibial stress syndrome and stress fractures of the tibia and fibula.[1,2] The pathomechanics may be related to muscle activity. For example, the medial soleus muscle produces inversion of the calcaneus with concentric contraction and, therefore, undergoes eccentric contraction as the foot is pronated.[3] If this happens excessively (either by frequency or velocity), the muscle will become fatigued and the athlete will change the normal mechanics of running (compensation). The tibia will absorb the forces placed on the leg and foot, and an overuse syndrome such as stress fracture can develop.

Physical Examination

An examination of the leg is relatively straightforward and should include an evaluation of the joints above and below the site of injury or symptoms. The tender areas must be visually inspected, palpated, and compared with the normal opposite leg. The athletic trainer should check for subtle anatomic abnormalities such as limb-length discrepancy; excessive femoral anteversion (increased internal rotation of the hip and little external rotation); hamstring tightness (limited straight leg raise); *genu varum* (bowlegs) or *genu valgum* (knock-knees); foot overpronation; and excessive Q-angle (**Figure 17-2**). The entire extremity should be evaluated for a complete understanding of the causative factors in an athlete's lower leg complaint.

How to determine leg alignment to the heel and heel alignment to the forefoot deserves special mention. To

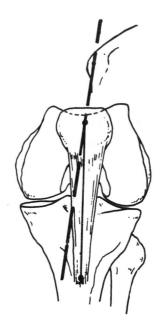

FIGURE 17-2

Quadriceps angle at 90° knee flexion. An excessive Q-angle is an anatomic abnormality the athletic trainer should look for during an examination of the leg. Lateral distal patella vector is consistent with values greater than 8°.

determine leg alignment to the heel, the athletic trainer should sit behind the standing athlete with the athlete's heel positioned directly under the tibia in a symmetrical fashion. The athletic trainer should imagine two vertical lines, one bisecting the calf and the Achilles tendon and the other bisecting the posterior heel. The intersection of these two lines determines the valgus angle (mean = 7°) (**Figure 17-3**).

Measuring the alignment of the forefoot to heel to determine forefoot varus or valgus is done with the athlete in both standing and sitting positions. Ideal forefoot position demonstrates a neutral alignment with respect to the perpendicular axes of the heel. An examiner positioned behind the athlete will be able to see a positive "too many toes" sign for unilateral flatfoot deformity (**Figure 17-4**). When the longitudinal arch is collapsed and viewed from behind, more toes on the affected side can be seen than on the opposite side. This sign usually indicates a posterior tibial tendon dysfunction or a spring ligament injury that causes compensatory motion through the subtalar (talocalcaneal) joint or transverse tarsal joint (talonavicular and calcaneocuboid joints). However, these findings are rare in the young athlete, whose overly pronated foot position is more commonly a bilateral dynamic deformity that occurs during the stance phase of walking and running. Symptoms secondary to overly pronated feet can often be alleviated with the use of an orthosis that has a semirigid arch support and slight medial heel posting.[4]

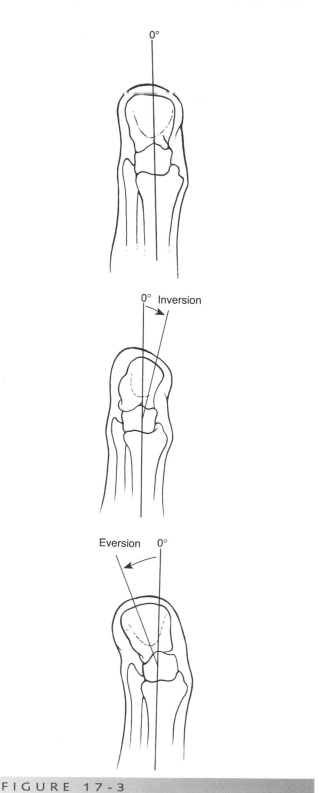

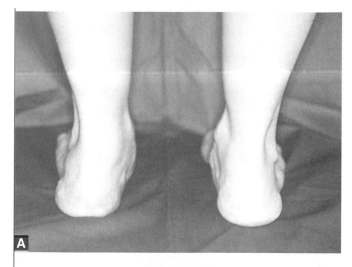

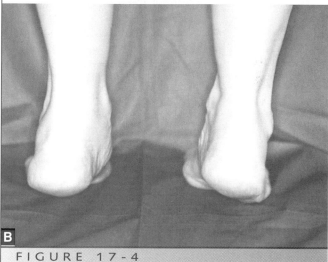

FIGURE 17-4

A The "too many toes" sign is demonstrated in the left foot with advanced posterior tibial tendon dysfunction. **B** Heel rise shows heel inversion on the right normal foot with continued eversion on the left stressed foot.

FIGURE 17-3

To determine the leg-to-heel-to-forefoot alignment, the athletic trainer should view the leg from behind and imagine two vertical lines, one that bisects the calf and Achilles tendon and one that bisects the posterior heel. The average valgus angle of the heel with respect to the leg is 7°. (Reproduced with permission from Greene WB, Heckman JD (eds): *The Clinical Measurement of Joint Motion*. Rosemont, IL American Academy of Orthopaedic Surgeons, 1994.)

Common Injuries and Conditions

Some of the more common conditions that affect the leg include exertional compartment syndrome, medial tibial stress syndrome, stress fractures of the tibia and fibula, gastrocnemius-soleus strains, Achilles tendinitis and rupture of the Achilles tendon, tibial contusions, and nerve entrapment syndromes. In a study of 150 patients with exercise-induced leg pain, 33% of patients had chronic (exertional) compartment syndrome, 25% had stress fractures, 14% had muscle strains, 13% had medial tibial stress syndrome, and 10% had nerve entrapments.[5]

Most overuse injuries are attributable to sudden increases in training, excessive mileage or duration of training sessions, or training errors and improper mechanics. When performing the initial assessment of an injury, the athletic trainer's in-depth knowledge of the individual

FOCUS ON . . .

Injuries and Conditions of the Leg

Specific injuries affecting the lower leg include compartment syndrome, medial tibial stress syndrome, tibial and fibular stress fractures, gastrocnemius-soleus disorders, and superficial peroneal nerve entrapment.

Compartment syndrome describes elevated tissue pressure within a closed space, resulting in decreased blood perfusion and compromised neuromuscular function, and can be acute or chronic. Tibial fractures and muscle ruptures are the most common athletic injuries that cause acute compartment syndrome. The acute compartment syndrome must be corrected surgically within 6 hours of onset to avoid irreversible cell damage and neuromuscular dysfunction. Definitive diagnosis requires the measurement of elevated compartment pressures before and after exercise, with a delay in return to normal resting pressure after exercise.

Medial tibial stress syndrome describes an overuse syndrome of the medial soleus fascia as it originates on the posteromedial tibial periosteum. Symptoms include exertional pain that may ease with continued running or warming up, but returns at the end of or after running. Treatment is relative rest, with emphasis on nonweight-bearing exercise, orthotics if the medial arch has collapsed, cryotherapy, and NSAIDs. If several trials of conservative therapy are unsuccessful, localized fasciotomy may be beneficial.

Tibial and fibular stress fractures usually result from repetitive loads on the bone that cause an imbalance between bone resorption and formation. Typically, the athlete has recently increased or changed his or her workout routine. Tibial stress fractures are the most common stress fractures in athletes. A pneumatic leg brace is helpful in protecting a tibial stress fracture, allowing for a faster return to play. Fibular stress fractures generally occur several centimeters above the ankle joint, are point tender to palpation, and may have associated swelling. A distal fibular stress fracture can be protected with a pneumatic stirrup brace. Stress fractures are also treated with rest from the offending activity, with a gradual return to activity. Anterior tibial stress fractures with an obvious fracture line usually require surgery.

Gastrocnemius-soleus disorders include overuse tendinitis, strains, and ruptures. The mechanism of injury is usually eccentric load on the gastrocnemius-soleus unit while the ankle is dorsiflexed and the knee extended. Treatment is rest, ice, compression, and elevation, with weightbearing as tolerated and gentle passive calf stretching.

Superficial peroneal nerve entrapment is the most common nerve entrapment in the athlete. With entrapment, the athlete's numbness and paresthesia follow the distribution of the nerve. A history of ankle sprains or leg trauma is a predisposing factor. Physical examination commonly reveals local muscle and fat herniation. Conservative treatment is relative rest, cross-training, NSAIDs, selective injections, and ankle braces. If conservative methods fail, surgical release of the nerve from the fascia is indicated.

sport will be very helpful and enables him or her to ask the appropriate questions during the history segment.

Specific Injuries and Conditions

Compartment syndrome

Compartment syndrome is a condition in which elevated tissue pressure (for example, within the muscles or nerves) exists within a closed space, resulting in reduced blood perfusion and compromised neuromuscular function[6] (Figure 17-5). Compartment syndrome is either acute, which is usually secondary to significant trauma, or chronic, which is mostly exertional. In chronic compartment syndrome, symptoms may be absent until the athlete has exercised above a threshold level.

In sports, the two situations that are most likely to produce an acute compartment syndrome in the leg are tibial fracture and muscle rupture.[6] The clinical features of an acute compartment syndrome include a firm, tense swelling over the involved compartment (usually the

anterior compartment), pain out of proportion to the apparent clinical situation, marked tenderness to palpation, and severe pain with passive movement of the involved compartment's muscles (such as passive plantarflexion of the ankle and toes in anterior compartment syndrome). Decreased pulses and altered sensation in the foot can occur, but these are late findings and should not be relied for the diagnosis. Immediate treatment involves immobilizing the extremity, including the knee and ankle (usually with a splint and elastic wrap), icing the involved areas, and elevating the leg slightly above the level of the heart. The athlete should be transported to the hospital for a physical examination by a physician and possible surgery. Acute compartment syndrome is a surgical emergency and needs to be corrected within about 6 hours of onset to avoid irreversible cell damage and neuromuscular dysfunction.

More commonly, symptoms may develop that are consistent with chronic (exertional) compartment syndrome, and

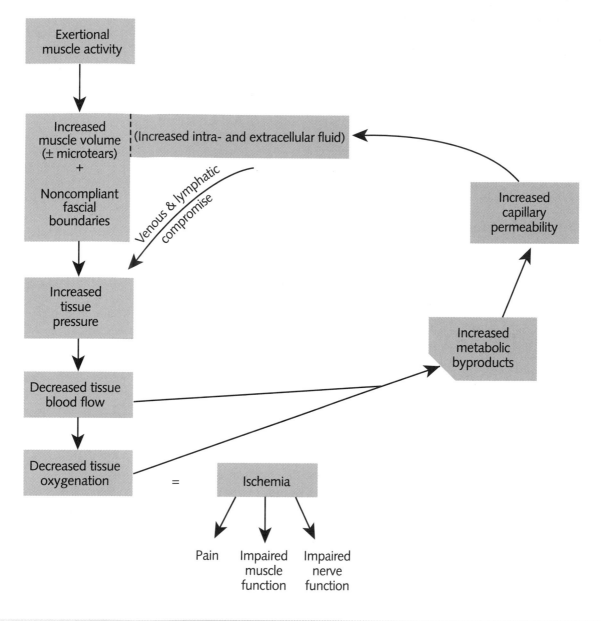

FIGURE 17-5

Flow chart depicting how compartment syndrome develops. (Reproduced with permission from Clanton TO, Schon LC: Athletic injuries to the soft tissues of the foot and ankle, in Mann RA, Coughlin MJ (eds): *Surgery of the Foot and Ankle.* St. Louis, MO, CV Mosby, 1993, pp 1095–1224.)

the athlete may report pain during or immediately following exercise. Related aching or cramping pain is typically located over the involved compartment and usually develops after a certain distance, duration, or speed is attained. The pain will often persist after the activity has ended. Clearly, knowledge of the compartment anatomy is essential for proper diagnosis because the contents of the involved compartment(s) help in determining potential neurologic symptoms.[5] Approximately 80% of all cases of chronic compartment syndrome in the leg are located in the anterior compartment and the deep posterior compartment.[3]

Most athletes diagnosed with chronic or exertional compartment syndrome are runners; results of one study indicated that three fourths of patients requiring surgery to alleviate their symptoms were runners.[7] A physical examination of the resting athlete is often unremarkable, and the pain is usually localized to the involved compartment and its contents. Importantly, certain conditions have been associated with chronic compartment syndrome, including muscle herniation through fascial defects, periostitis (inflammation of the bone covering), and certain nerve entrapments.

The definitive diagnosis involves actually measuring compartment pressures with a catheter inserted into each compartment under question. Most authors recommend the following criteria to establish the diagnosis of chronic compartment syndrome: elevated compartment pressures before and after exercise, and in particular, a delay in return to normal resting pressure after exercise.[3]

Unless the athlete is willing to decrease his or her activities to a more tolerable and less symptomatic level, treatment alternatives for chronic compartment syndrome are limited. Ice, medications, shoe modifications, cross training, orthoses, and rehabilitation are of little permanent benefit for the athlete who wishes to continue at a higher level of training. For these athletes, surgery is the only potential long-term solution. According to most studies, surgical decompression by releasing the encompassing fascia of the compartment, has a success rate of 80% to 90%.[5]

Medial tibial stress syndrome

Medial tibial stress syndrome (MTSS) is an overuse syndrome of the fascia of the medial soleus as it originates on the periosteum of the posteromedial tibia. In the past, the term "shin splints" has been commonly used to refer to this condition, but because "shin splints" is vague and can describe a number of other conditions involving pain that develops with exercise, its use should be avoided in medical settings. MTSS usually occurs when there has been a significant increase in the athlete's activity level. Complaints associated with this are invariably consistent and include pain on exertion that may be relieved with continued running or warm-up activities. However, the pain usually returns near the end of the run or afterwards as a dull ache or soreness along the posteromedial distal third of the tibia. Physical examination reveals a band of tenderness along the posteromedial distal tibia that starts about 4 cm above the medial malleolus and extends toward the knee for up to 12 cm.[1] In many cases there is also slight swelling of the tibia in the area of maximum tenderness. Routine radiographs are generally normal, but bone scans will show uptake on delayed images along the posteromedial border of the tibia, extending up to a third of the length of the tibia.[2]

Treatment of MTSS focuses on relative rest with emphasis on nonweightbearing exercises such as cycling, swimming, and pool running early in the treatment period. Orthotic devices are often useful if there is also excessive pronation of the foot and collapse of the medial arch. Cryotherapy (icing) to the affected area and nonsteroidal anti-inflammatory drugs (NSAIDs) help reduce swelling and pain. Return to activity may be gradually resumed after 1 to 2 weeks of rest, but the timing depends on the severity and duration of the symptoms. Initially, the athlete should resume training using only one half of his or her typical pace and distance to help avoid recurrence of the symptoms.[6] Surgery is rarely indicated for MTSS, but it has been successful if the more conservative treatment of relative rest and gradual resumption of activities has been tried and failed several times. In such incapacitating circumstances, a localized fasciotomy will usually improve the situation.

Stress fractures of the tibia and fibula

Running and jumping are activities that can lead to stress fractures of the lower extremity, which develop from repetitive loads on the bone that cause an imbalance of bone resorption over formation. Other sports frequently associated with stress fractures of the tibia and fibula include soccer, basketball, cross-country, track and field, dancing, and aerobics. Dancers and basketball players have a higher incidence of anterior midtibial stress fractures, which are reported to heal poorly with nonsurgical treatment.[8] The increased relative risk of stress fractures in female athletes ranges from 3.8 to 10.0 times higher than the average.[9] Contributing factors for this increased risk may be menstrual irregularities or amenorrhea, the smaller bone structures of women, eating disorders, or poor nutrition.[10]

In the classic stress fracture presentation, the athlete with pain will note a recent increase or change in the workout routine: increased duration or frequency of running, different footwear, altered running surface, or change of speed. The pain is localized to the area of the stress fracture and occurs with a gradual onset over several weeks. Symptoms usually are apparent about 4 or 5 weeks after a change in training regimen.[11,12] Pain typically begins during or after a stressful activity and can progress until the athlete feels it when performing daily activities and, eventually, during rest. *Tibial stress fractures* are the most common stress fractures in the athlete, and the differential diagnosis should include both MTSS and exertional compartment syndrome. Tibial stress fractures differ from MTSS in several ways: the area is usually more proximal (midshaft or above) and tends to be localized on exam and by complaint; the pain develops more gradually; and the injury is reflected in a positive bone scan in all three phases (MTSS is only positive in delayed images) with more localized uptake.[13] Exertional compartment syndrome can be differentiated from a stress fracture, even though it also occurs during exercise, because it is frequently accompanied by paresthesia, and the postexercise pain diminishes faster than that of a stress fracture.

Certain generalities can be stated about the relationship between the location of tibial stress fractures and particular sports: runners tend to sustain middle-distal third junction fractures; jumping sports (basketball, volleyball) tend to produce more proximal fractures; and dancers often sustain midshaft stress fractures.[9] A pneumatic leg brace is helpful for treating tibial stress fractures and enabling the athletes to return to play quickly.[4,9]

Fibular stress fractures are generally located a few centimeters above the ankle joint, but may occur anywhere along its length. They are point tender to palpation and occasionally have associated swelling. The differential diagnosis includes exertional compartment syndrome and superficial peroneal nerve entrapment. One-legged hopping and percussion of the bone will recreate the pain of stress fractures of the tibia and fibula, and ultrasound frequently exacerbates the symptoms.

Relative rest is essential in treating stress fractures. Symptoms often abate immediately once the athlete discontinues the offending activity. If pain has progressed to the point of being severe with daily activities, the leg should not bear any weight at all. Distal fibular stress fractures may be successfully treated with a pneumatic stirrup brace to improve symptoms, and tibial stress fractures also often respond to this mode of protection, which allows an earlier return to sports participation. A rehabilitation protocol similar to that described for MTSS can be used for stress fractures of the tibia and fibula. However, the relative rest period is usually longer (2 to 4 weeks) and the return to activities should be slightly more gradual to prevent recurrence of symptoms. Anterior tibial stress fractures that have the "dreaded black line" usually require surgery to promote adequate healing and prevent a complete fracture of the tibia. This transverse line appears on the lateral radiograph in the anterior cortex of the tibia. Tibial stress fractures with this finding on radiographs usually do not heal with nonsurgical treatment. Surgical treatments that yield good results include percutaneous drilling with bone grafting, intramedullary rodding, and electrical stimulation.[2,9,14] Surgical treatment of fibular stress fractures is rarely, if ever, indicated.[14]

Gastrocnemius-soleus disorders

Overuse tendinitis, strains, and ruptures of the calf musculotendinous unit are very common, especially in the middle-aged athlete. The sports most commonly involved with these injuries include basketball, racquet sports, running, and skiing. The injuries are secondary to eccentric (lengthening) loads on the gastrocnemius-soleus unit while the ankle is dorsiflexed and the knee is extended. *Gastrocnemius-soleus strains* usually involve the medial side of the complex and are commonly labeled "tennis leg" because of the prevalence of this injury in middle-aged tennis players.[15] Sudden pain with a popping sensation in the calf is usually followed by swelling and ecchymosis in the posterior region of the leg. The athlete is treated with rest, ice, compression, elevation (RICE), weightbearing as tolerated, and gentle passive stretching of the calf. The injury can be debilitating, but it has a universally good outcome with appropriate eccentric rehabilitation. Normally, the athlete is at least partially restricted from full competition for 2 weeks to several months.

Achilles tendinitis is another common chronic sports injury that typically affects mature athletes involved in running and jumping activities. Causes for this injury can be related to increased activity (duration, frequency, or intensity), improper footwear (inadequately supported hindfoot), cavus (high-arched) feet, or tight hamstrings.[16] Training errors are a frequent etiologic factor. Complaints are localized to the portion of the tendon just above its insertion onto the calcaneus. Swelling and a decreased range of motion (ROM) in the ankle may be present. If the tendinitis is severe and present for a significant period of time, the tendon can develop a nodular appearance. Initial management should include a change in footwear if indicated, rest, icing, NSAIDs for pain relief, and liberal stretching of the heel cord. Surgery should be considered only in severe and recalcitrant cases. If surgery is necessary, it involves localizing the pathology through a physical examination with magnetic resonance imaging (MRI) to confirm the diagnosis, excising the inflammatory scar tissue, and reconstructing the defect with local tissue. In some cases a local tendon transfer may be necessary.

Acute Achilles tendon ruptures occur most commonly 2 to 6 cm above the calcaneus and have greater than a 20% chance of being missed by a physician who has not previously seen the athlete.[17] The Achilles rupture produces a pop that can be felt by the athlete and is similar to that felt in a medial gastrocnemius-soleus tear/strain, but in a more distal location. Pain may not be too severe at first, but the onset of edema and ecchymosis may mean that the athlete is unable to return to activity. If the athletic trainer focuses primarily on the ankle or foot, the diagnosis of an Achilles tendon rupture can be easily missed. A palpable defect will be present at the tear site, and in most cases, the athlete will be unable to bear weight. The diagnosis of a rupture can be confirmed by placing the patient prone on the table and squeezing the calf (Thompson test). If normal plantarflexion of the ankle fails to occur, the tendon is ruptured.

Initial management consists of wearing a short leg splint with the ankle and foot in a comfortable position, elevating the foot, applying ice, eliminating weightbearing activities, and urgent referral to an orthopaedist. Active athletic patients should undergo primary surgical repair of the tendon (**Figure 17-6**). Nonsurgical treatment carries a higher recurrence rate and can lead to lower ultimate performance.[18] Nevertheless, the difference in outcome between surgical treatment and nonsurgical treatment with cast immobilization and crutches is minimal, making either treatment method a reasonable alternative. If the athlete and the surgeon choose surgery, the postsurgical rehabilitation protocol is as follows:

- nonweightbearing for 2 weeks, but early active ROM (plantarflexion and limited dorsiflexion) out of the splint (two sets of five, three times daily)

- progressive ROM and weightbearing by the third week, as well as gentle, passive stretching

- weightbearing with some heel elevation device (cast, cam-walker, heel insert) for 6 to 8 weeks

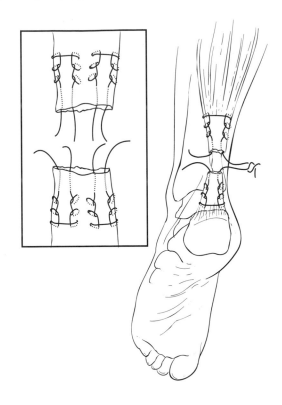

FIGURE 17-6

Primary surgical repair of the Achilles tendon may be more beneficial because nonsurgical treatment carries a higher recurrence rate. (Adapted with permission from Soma CA, Mandelbaum BR: Achilles tendon disorders. *Clin Sports Med* 1994;13:811–823.)

- jogging along with progressive resistance exercises, beginning in the third or fourth month after surgery
- return to some athletic activities for most athletes by the fifth or sixth month[16]

Return to full skill level can take 9 to 18 months. Rehabilitation of athletes with these injuries is a prolonged undertaking and must proceed at a much slower pace when nonsurgical treatment is selected. Regular stretching of the gastrocnemius-soleus group is required for up to 18 months following injury to prevent contractures and rerupture.

Superficial peroneal nerve entrapment

Superficial peroneal nerve entrapment is the most common of all nerve entrapment syndromes in the athlete.[5] The entrapment typically occurs where the nerve pierces the deep fascia of the lateral compartment of the leg, about 10 to 12 cm above the tip of the lateral malleolus (**Figure 17-7**). The superficial peroneal nerve divides into two branches, with the intermediate dorsal cutaneous nerve providing sensation to the dorsolateral aspect of the foot, and the medial dorsal cutaneous nerve providing sensation over the dorsomedial aspect of the ankle and

foot. This anatomy is important because some athletes will report numbness and paresthesia along the distribution of the entrapped nerve and some will indicate direct points of tenderness where the nerve passes through the fascia. Usually, pain intensifies with activity and eases with rest. However, entrapment may present with vague aching discomfort over the anterolateral aspect of the ankle and foot with no specific neurologic symptoms. One key element is a history of ankle sprains or trauma to the leg that appears to predispose an athlete to the condition.[19] Physical examination often reveals local herniation of muscle and fat and point tenderness directly where the superficial peroneal nerve pierces the fascia. In thin athletes, the nerve can readily be seen and palpated. Percussion of the nerve (Tinel's sign) elicits pain, paresthesia, or both. In addition, plantarflexion and inversion can also recreate the athlete's symptoms.[20] Exertional compartment syndrome should always be part of the differential diagnosis and should be ruled out in all cases prior to making any surgical decision.

Conservative treatment involves relative rest, cross-training activities, NSAIDs, selective cortisone injections of the nerve as it exits from the leg fascia, and ankle braces. Although these methods should be attempted, the treating physician and athletic trainer should realize that conservative treatments have limited abilities in providing lasting relief.[21] When conservative methods fail, the nerve can be surgically released from its fascial constriction and the athlete can usually resume competition within 3 to 6 weeks.

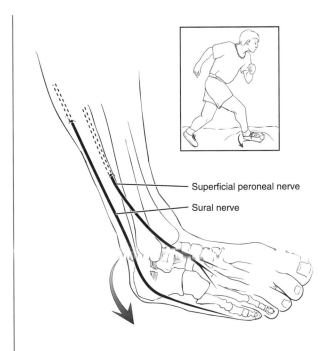

Superficial peroneal nerve

Sural nerve

FIGURE 17-7

Superficial peroneal nerve entrapment occurs where the nerve pierces the deep fascia of the lateral compartment.

THE ANKLE

Because the ankle is the most commonly injured area in the athlete, the athletic trainer must be completely comfortable with identifying injuries and treating this critical area. The care provided by the athletic trainer, particularly during rehabilitation, makes a considerable difference in the athlete's outcome. This section covers the anatomy of the ankle, as well as current diagnosis and management guidelines for the common conditions seen in the athletic training room.

Anatomy

Osseous structures

Three bones form the ankle joint proper: the tibia, fibula, and talus. However, the calcaneus (the heel bone of the foot) sits underneath the talus and provides the ankle with both a firm foundation and another joint (subtalar or talocalcaneal) for inversion and eversion. The distal end of the tibia (plafond and medial malleolus), the distal end of the fibula (lateral malleolus), and the body of the talus make up the ankle mortise. The mortise provides the ankle with its bony stability, primarily on the lateral side because of the inferior projection of the lateral malleolus (the bony prominence on the outside of the leg at the ankle). The subtalar joint is the articulation between the talus and the calcaneus and is a frequent area of symptoms overlooked in lateral ankle sprains.

Ligaments of the ankle

Three sets of ligaments provide most of the soft-tissue stability to the ankle: the lateral ligamentous complex, the syndesmosis ligaments (laterally), and the deltoid ligament (medially). The lateral ligamentous complex consists of the anterior talofibular ligament (ATFL), the posterior talofibular ligament (PTFL), and the calcaneofibular ligament (CFL) (**Figure 17-8**). The ATFL is approximately 20 mm long, 10 mm wide, and 2 mm thick, and runs from the anterior distal margin of the lateral malleolus to the body of the talus at a 75° angle to the floor. The PTFL is the strongest ligament of this complex and the least injured. It measures approximately 30 mm long, 5 mm wide, and 8 mm thick and runs from the posterior medial margin of the lateral malleolus to the posterior talus. The CFL is 2.5 times stronger than the ATFL; measures approximately 25 mm long, 4 mm wide, and 5 mm thick; and attaches to the lateral wall of the calcaneus before traveling anteriorly and proximally to insert just below the ATFL on the lateral malleolus just anterior to its most distal tip.

Although the subtalar ligamentous complex is less studied and less discussed than the lateral ligamentous complex, it is a very crucial stabilizing system of ligaments. This complex includes the CFL (which is part of both the lateral and subtalar ligament complexes), the inferior extensor retinaculum, the lateral talocalcaneal ligament, the cervical ligament, and the interosseous ligament. All but the interosseous ligament are lateral to the axis of rotation for the subtalar joint and provide stability to inversion stress. Therefore, these subtalar ligamentous structures are frequently injured at the same time as the other lateral ligaments of the ankle, creating the potential for further instability and long-term problems (**Figure 17-9**).

The tibiofibular syndesmosis is composed of the anterior inferior tibiofibular ligament (AITFL), the posterior inferior tibiofibular ligament (PITFL), the interosseous ligament, and the interosseous membrane. This strong group of ligaments maintains the relationship of the fibula to its groove in the distal tibia and, therefore, is a major contributor to ankle stability.

The deltoid ligament is a fan-shaped ligament on the medial side of the ankle that has both superficial and deep layers. It has insertions onto the navicular and calcaneus bones of the foot as well as the talus bone of the ankle, and is the strongest of the three ligament complexes. The primary function of the deltoid ligament is to limit abduction of the ankle. Because of its strength and the uncommon mechanism for its injury, the deltoid ligament is the least frequently injured ligament of the ankle.

Musculotendinous structures

The lateral dynamic stabilizers of the ankle include the peroneus brevis and longus muscles. Both pass behind the fibula in a groove and are contained within a single sheath en route to their insertions: the peroneus brevis at the base of the fifth metatarsal and the peroneus longus on the plantar aspect of the first metatarsal base and medial cuneiform of the foot. The peroneus tendons provide the ankle with active eversion and pronation. Injury to the peroneus tendons or the superior retinaculum frequently accompanies lateral ankle injury. Instability symptoms can be produced by injury to one or both structures (tendons or ligaments).

The dynamic stabilizers of the medial ankle include the tibialis posterior tendon, flexor digitorum longus, and flexor hallucis longus tendons. Each of these tendons passes behind the medial malleolus (the bony projection on the inside of the leg at the ankle joint) and provides a small but important stabilizing function for the ankle and hindfoot.

Normal Function

Stability of the ankle is provided to a large degree by the bony architecture and its supporting ligaments. The lateral malleolus and its associated ligaments appear to be key in supporting the ankle and maintaining the tibiotalar relationship. Talar displacement within the ankle joint of greater than 2 mm is considered pathologic, a circumstance that shows just how tightly this joint is maintained.[22] Normal motion between the fibula and tibia during gait occurs in the lateral and posterior planes, as well as in the vertical axis and in rotation.[23] The tibia

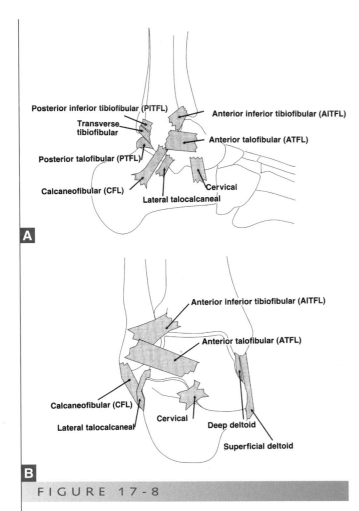

A Lateral view (top image)

Posterior inferior tibiofibular (PITFL)
Transverse tibiofibular
Anterior inferior tibiofibular (AITFL)
Posterior talofibular (PTFL)
Anterior talofibular (ATFL)
Calcaneofibular (CFL)
Cervical
Lateral talocalcaneal

B Anterior view (bottom image)

Anterior inferior tibiofibular (AITFL)
Anterior talofibular (ATFL)
Calcaneofibular (CFL)
Cervical
Deep deltoid
Lateral talocalcaneal
Superficial deltoid

FIGURE 17-8

Most soft-tissue stability to the ankle is provided by three sets of ligaments. **A** Lateral view of the ankle and subtalar joint ligaments. **B** Anterior view of the ankle and subtalar joint ligaments. (Reproduced with permission from Lutter LD, Mizel MS, Pfeffer GB (eds): *Orthopaedic Knowledge Update: Foot and Ankle.* Rosemont, IL, American Academy of Orthopaedic Surgeons, 1994.)

transmits approximately 80% of the weight of the leg, the fibula approximately 17%, and the interosseous membrane the remaining 3%.[24]

The normal biomechanics of the ankle and foot absorb and direct the forces that occur during heel strike, foot flat, and push off. The series of movements that produces pronation of the foot and enables this to happen occurs in a regular sequence: initial contact, followed by internal rotation of the tibia with concomitant eversion of the subtalar joint, followed by dorsiflexion of the ankle, and lastly, abduction of the foot. If this progression is interrupted by injury, or if the sequence is altered by anatomy, the forces generated by walking will be absorbed by different portions of the lower extremity, and injuries will result. Ankle conditions that can alter the normal biomechanics of gait include limited subtalar motion, inadequate dorsiflexion (such as from a tight Achilles tendon or anterior ankle spurs), weakness of the

plantar flexor muscles (such as the gastrocnemius-soleus complex), and an overly pronated foot.[25]

Physical Examination

Examining the ankle includes attention to the ankle joint, the subtalar joint, and the structures supporting them. The examination by the athletic trainer is invaluable because it is usually the first and best examination. An examination immediately after the injury can isolate the injury to a specific area based on the degree of tenderness with palpation. This becomes more difficult as the time frame between injury and examination increases. The athletic trainer can subsequently convey specific information to the physician who usually firsts sees the patient more than 24 hours after the injury occurred, when hemorrhage, edema, and inflammation have caused the entire ankle to become tender.

The first step of the examination is to assess the athlete's ankle stability. This should be done before palpation to determine maximal tenderness so that the patient does not tense up and guard against any further movement. The *anterior drawer maneuver* is performed with the patient sitting, the knee flexed at 90°, and the ankle plantar flexed. With the tibia stabilized, the athletic trainer should grasp the athlete's heel and pull it forward[26,27] (**Figure 17-10**). A soft end point and increased anterior excursion compared with the opposite ankle suggest a rupture of the ATFL. The *talar tilt test* assesses the integrity of the CFL. The examiner stabilizes the tibia by supporting the medial aspect of the distal tibia in one hand and placing the opposite hand on the lateral aspect of the heel. With the ankle in neutral dorsiflexion, talar tilt is determined by turning

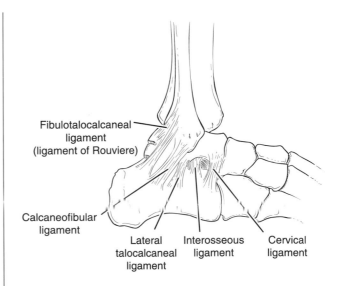

Fibulotalocalcaneal ligament (ligament of Rouviere)
Calcaneofibular ligament
Lateral talocalcaneal ligament
Interosseous ligament
Cervical ligament

FIGURE 17-9

The subtalar joint ligaments are frequently injured when other lateral ligaments are injured, creating the potential for further instability.

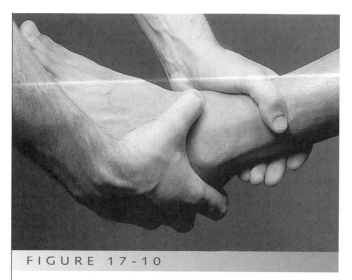

FIGURE 17-10

When performing the anterior drawer maneuver, the patient should be seated, the knee flexed at 90°, and the ankle plantar flexed.

ver and avoids resisting the examiner's inversion stress, the examiner can conclude that there is damage to the peroneal retinaculum.

Common Injuries and Conditions

Ankle injuries, especially sprains, are ubiquitous in the athletic arena and demand that the athletic trainer be familiar and comfortable identifying these injuries and planning management. Common ankle injuries include sprains, fractures, tendon injuries, impingement syndromes, and nerve entrapments. If the examiner is knowledgeable about ankle anatomy and has basic examination skills, these injuries become relatively straightforward to diagnose and their care and treatment can be rewarding.

Specific Injuries and Conditions

Ankle sprains

There are different types of ankle sprains that are based on both the location and the severity of the sprain. Lateral

the heel inward. The degree of tilt must be compared with the athlete's normal side because great variability exists among individuals. Ligamentously lax patients often have an "increased" test compared with other patients, but this can be normal for some patients.

After ankle stability is assessed, the areas of maximum tenderness are defined by specific palpation of the entire fibula, ATFL, CFL, PTFL, syndesmosis, calcaneocuboid joint, peroneal and posterior tibial tendons, fifth metatarsal shaft and base, and the medial and lateral malleoli. The presence of ecchymosis and swelling indicates a probable ligament tear or fracture. Syndesmosis injuries are diagnosed by the presence of tenderness over the syndesmosis, located just anterior to the lateral malleolus and proximal to the ATFL. Another diagnostic test is the squeeze test, performed by compressing both the fibula and tibia at the midportion of the lower leg[28] (**Figure 17-11**). Pain in the distal syndesmosis is considered a positive test result, indicating a potential syndesmosis tear. The external rotation stress test can also be used to determine the possibility of a syndesmosis sprain.[29] This test is performed with the patient sitting and the knee flexed at 90°. The examiner externally rotates the foot while the ankle is in slight dorsiflexion. Pain at the level of the syndesmosis and possibly radiating proximally is a good indicator of a syndesmotic sprain.

The peroneal tendons should also be examined for subluxation or dislocation in both acute and chronic ankle complaints. The examiner places the ankle in a dorsiflexed and everted position (toes up and out) and attempts to turn the ankle inward, with the patient resisting the movement. If the peroneal retinaculum is damaged, the tendons will subluxate or dislocate out of the fibular groove and should reproduce the patient's symptoms. Likewise, if the athlete is apprehensive during this maneu-

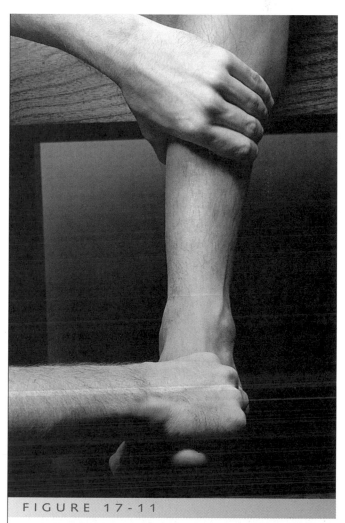

FIGURE 17-11

A squeeze test is performed by compressing the fibula and tibia at the midportion of the lower leg. Pain in the area of the distal syndesmosis may indicate a syndesmosis tear.

ankle sprains are the most common, and 85% of these are inversion sprains of the lateral ligaments.[30,31] Deltoid ligament and medial ligament eversion sprains constitute about 5% of ankle sprains, and syndesmosis injuries account for the remaining 10%.[31]

Lateral ankle sprains are caused by an inversion mechanism and often involve both joint complexes on this side: the ankle joint (tibiotalar) and the subtalar joint (talocalcaneal). The classic mechanism occurs when the ankle is inverted forcefully on a plantarflexed ankle. This frequently occurs in basketball and volleyball when one player lands on another player's foot after a jump. The severity of the sprain is graded from I to III, or mild, moderate, and severe. The injuries can also be classified as stable or unstable, based on the absence or presence of a positive anterior drawer test. Generally, the two classification systems interrelate well; grade I sprains are stable, and grade II and grade III sprains are unstable.

Grade I injuries usually involve minor stretching of the ATFL with no or minimal swelling or hemorrhage and only mildly restricted ROM. Examination reveals no instability, and the athlete should be able to bear full weight with little discomfort and return to full activity within 7 to 10 days.[27] A grade II sprain is frequently a complete tear of the ATFL and a partial tear of the CFL. Instability may or may not be present, motion should be restricted, and moderate, localized swelling, tenderness, and ecchymosis should be present. Usually, the patient can bear weight, but does so with considerable discomfort and a limp. A grade III sprain implies a complete rupture of the ATFL, CFL, and capsule and has accompanying generalized swelling and ecchymosis. Moderate to severe laxity is present, and the athlete will usually be unwilling or unable to bear weight. Radiographs of more severe injuries are necessary to rule out occult fractures and to help diagnose or confirm any pattern of instability.

Treatment of grades I and II injuries includes ice, compression, early weightbearing and ROM, and functional rehabilitation. Disability is generally limited to 1 week with grade I injuries and from 2 to 4 weeks with grade II sprains. Although there is some controversy concerning treatment of grade III sprains in high-level athletes, most authors agree that grade III ankle sprains in a typical athlete should be treated with a short period (3 to 4 days) of crutch walking and immobilization, followed by early, but protected, weightbearing in a walking boot or cast for 3 to 6 weeks. At this time, a program of functional rehabilitation crucial to the long-term outcome should begin (**Practice Session 17-1**). Prognosis for recovery in grade III injuries is excellent in 80% to 90% of cases, but the ankle must be protected for the remainder of the season with taping or bracing to prevent reinjury.[32] High-level athletes may occasionally elect primary surgical repair to decrease the possibility of persistent instability after nonsurgical treatment.

Syndesmosis sprains are generally more disabling than routine lateral ankle sprains. They are often diagnosed late because the athlete is not recovering as quickly as expected from an initially diagnosed "routine sprain." However, an athletic trainer can identify the hallmarks of a syndesmosis sprain within 30 to 60 minutes after an injury. A combination of a positive squeeze test, a positive external rotation stress test, and point tenderness over the AITFL (less commonly over the PITFL) indicates a syndesmosis sprain. Radiographs are mandatory to rule out *diastasis* (separation of the distal tibia and fibula). If the radiographs confirm a diastasis, surgical treatment is essential to reestablish the normal position.

In most patients, syndesmosis sprains are treated like grade III lateral sprains. Initial immobilization should be kept to a minimum, and motion should be instituted as soon as the athlete can tolerate the discomfort. As the ligaments and capsule begin to heal, a nighttime resting ankle dorsiflexion splint should be prescribed to keep the ankle in a neutral position. This will help reduce the incidence and severity of secondary Achilles tendinitis that commonly accompanies more severe sprains. Syndesmosis sprains are among the most severe and disabling injuries to the ankle, usually 4 to 8 weeks of recovery must pass before the athlete can return to full activity, even when there is no diastasis. The most common difficulties encountered once an athlete returns to his or her sport are pushing off and cutting maneuvers on the affected ankle.[33]

Medial ankle sprains are the least common sprains of the ankle, but they can be quite troublesome for the athlete. They occur with a pronation-eversion mechanism, although the deltoid ligament is rarely disrupted completely (grade III) because of its high load to failure strength.[34] Isolated deltoid ligament sprains are extremely rare. Most occur in association with lateral ligamentous injuries, fibular fractures, or syndesmosis sprains. Thus, the athletic trainer must assess the entire ankle and use the findings to determine the need for further evaluation and treatment. In general, if the athlete is unable to bear weight or has extreme tenderness, radiographs should be taken and the athlete referred to a physician. If the ligament is completely disrupted, if it is an isolated injury, and if the radiographs do not show widening of the mortise, then a short leg walking cast or walking boot can be used for 4 to 8 weeks, based on the athlete's reliability. Afterward, an aggressive ROM and strengthening program can begin. It typically takes longer for an athlete to return to competition after a medial ankle sprain than after a lateral ankle sprain of similar severity. The athletic trainer, physician, athlete, and coaches must be patient.

The athlete with chronic lateral ankle symptoms following an ankle sprain merits special mention. Careful evaluation is needed to detect any bony, tendinous, ligamentous, cartilaginous, or neurologic pathology. **Table 17-2** presents common sources of chronic pain or

FOCUS ON . . .

Common Injuries and Conditions of the Ankle

Ankle injuries are common in athletics. Common ankle injuries include sprains, fractures, tendon injuries, impingement syndromes, and nerve entrapments. These injuries can be straightforward to diagnose.

Most ankle injuries are sprains, and most sprains are inversion injuries of the lateral ligaments. Sprains are graded from I (mild) to III (severe) and by stability based on the anterior drawer test. Treatment of grades I and II injuries includes ice, compression, early weightbearing and range of motion, and functional rehabilitation. Treatment of grade III sprains should include crutch walking and immobilization, followed by early, protected weightbearing in a walking boot, and functional rehabilitation.

Syndesmosis sprains are often more disabling than lateral ankle sprains and are frequently diagnosed late. The most definitive signs of a syndesmosis sprain are a positive squeeze test, positive external rotation test, and anterior inferior tibiofibular ligament point tenderness. Medial ankle sprains are the least common type and occur with pronation and eversion. Chronic symptoms after a lateral sprain deserve careful evaluation to diagnose any treatable problems undetectable by patient history and physical examination.

Tendon injuries of the ankle can affect the peroneal or posterior tibial tendons. Peroneal tendon injuries are common. Peroneal tendinitis usually occurs posteriorly at the lateral malleolus or more distally where the peroneus longus passes around the cuboid. A less aggressive physical therapy program with periods of rest is indicated and should include NSAIDs, immobilization, heel cord and peroneal muscle stretching, cold and heat modalities, and relative rest. Corticosteroid injections are rarely warranted.

Ankle fractures (including medial and lateral malleolus, osteochondral talar, and tibial fractures) cause immediate swelling, ecchymosis, inability to bear weight, severe tenderness, and often deformity. The athletic trainer should immobilize the ankle in a splint, elevate the injury site, apply ice, and immediately arrange for transport to the emergency department.

Impingement syndromes can result in anterior, anterolateral, or posterior symptoms. Swelling may or may not be present with anterolateral impingement. Treatment is relative rest, NSAIDs, and bracing; if these fail, arthroscopic debridement may be needed. Anterior impingement often results from an osteophyte on the distal tibial's anterior lip. Severe impingement may require open or arthroscopic osteophyte excision. Posterior impingement causes pain at the back of the ankle when the toe is pointed. Rest, NSAIDs, and local corticosteroid injection are recommended; if these fail to relieve symptoms, surgical excision of the bony prominence is indicated.

Tarsal tunnel syndrome is posterior tibial nerve entrapment in the lower leg, medial ankle, and medial heel and can occur after an injury or spontaneously. Treatment is avoidance of the inciting activity, an arch support, toe flexor and tibialis posterior tarsal strengthening, NSAIDs, and ankle stirrup bracing. If these measures fail to relieve symptoms, the investing tarsal tunnel fascia can be surgically released.

instability after an ankle sprain. Special radiographs, computed tomography (CT) scans, MRI scans, or bone scans can help discover treatable entities that the patient's history and a physical examination alone might not detect. Initial emphasis should be on correcting any deficiencies in proprioception, strength, and flexibility through a well-supervised program with the athletic trainer. If this does not alleviate the symptoms, the next step is surgery, including examination under anesthesia, stress radiographs, arthroscopy of the ankle, and ligament reconstruction when indicated.

Tendon injuries

Peroneal tendon injuries are common and include tendinitis, acute and chronic dislocations, longitudinal tears, and tendon ruptures. Peroneal tendinitis can occur at several sites along the peroneal tendon sheath, but is usually present posteriorly at the lateral malleolus or more distally

where the peroneus longus passes around the cuboid (outer bone of the tarsus). Symptoms include pain, tenderness, and swelling along the tendons and are aggravated by passive plantarflexion and inversion or by active, resisted eversion of the foot. It is very common for the athlete recovering from a lateral ankle sprain to develop peroneal tendinitis secondary to the sprain. This occurs because the body "recruits" the tendons for a more important role in ankle stabilization until the ligaments heal, resulting in overuse of the tendons. The athletic trainer should be aware of this pattern and institute less aggressive physical therapy programs with periods of rest in this situation. Nonsurgical treatment measures are usually successful and include NSAIDs, immobilization, stretching the heel cord and peroneal muscles, cold and heat modalities, and relative rest. Because of the risk of tendon rupture, corticosteroid injections are rarely warranted.

PRACTICE SESSION 17-1
FUNCTIONAL REHABILITATION

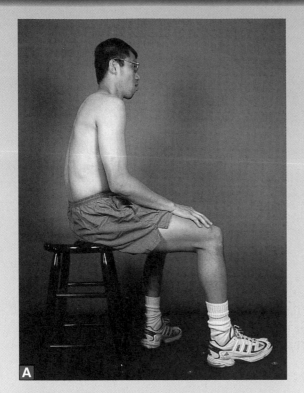

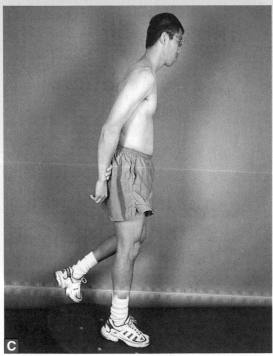

Functional rehabilitation after an ankle sprain includes proprioception training.

A Proprioception board seated position.

B Partial weightbearing position.

C Full weightbearing position.

Peroneal tendon intrasubstance tears were once considered rare, but improved diagnostic methods and basic science research have confirmed that the superior peroneal retinaculum and the peroneal tendons are easily injured through the same mechanism that results in lateral ankle ligament sprains. Surgeons who perform lateral ligament

TABLE 17-2
COMMON SOURCES OF CHRONIC PAIN OR INSTABILITY AFTER AN ANKLE SPRAIN

Articular injury	Chondral fractures
	Osteochondral fractures
Nerve injury	Superficial peroneal
	Posterior tibial
	Sural
Tendon injury	Peroneal tendon (tear or dislocation)
	Posterior tibial tendon
Other ligamentous injury	Syndesmosis
	Subtalar
	Bifurcate
	Calcaneocuboid
Impingement	Anterior tibial osteophyte
	Anterior inferior tibiofibular ligament
Miscellaneous conditions	Failure to regain normal motion (tight Achilles)
	Proprioceptive deficits
	Tarsal coalition
	Meniscoid lesions
	Accessory soleus muscle
Unrelated ongoing pathology masked by routine sprain	Unsuspected rheumatologic condition
	Occult tumor

(Adapted with permission from Clanton TO, Schon LC: Athletic injuries to the soft tissues of the foot and ankle, in Mann RA, Coughlin MJ (eds): *Surgery of the Foot and Ankle.* St. Louis, MO, CV Mosby, 1993, pp 1095–1224.)

reconstruction on athletes who have symptoms of chronic lateral instability with coexisting pain and tenderness over the peroneal tendons should also routinely check for peroneal tendon tears. MRI can usually confirm a diagnosis.

Acute dislocation of the peroneal tendons is uncommon and is attributed to a forceful dorsiflexion and eversion of the ankle with a violent reflex contraction of the peroneal tendons.[35] Diagnosis is usually not difficult, but such a dislocation is often overlooked because it is assumed that the athlete has sustained an ankle sprain. However, pain is posterior to the fibula, not anterior, as occurs in a typical lateral sprain. To check ankle stability, the athletic trainer should ask the patient to try to dorsi-flex the foot while the athletic trainer holds it in a plantarflexed, everted position. If this maneuver elicits a painful subluxation or dislocation of the peroneal tendons, the test result is positive. Plain radiographs should be taken in all cases to ensure that no bone fragment has been avulsed from the fibula where the retinaculum attaches. In the ankle with a retinacular injury and a stable, relocated tendon, nonsurgical treatment is justified. A cast should be applied to the foot and ankle in a slightly plantarflexed position until the sheath heals. Surgical treatment in the higher-demand athlete may be indicated because nonsurgical management has a higher chance of residual instability and symptoms. Surgical repair of symptomatic, chronically unstable peroneal tendons yields predictably good results.

Posterior tibial tendon dysfunction can occur in young athletes, but most of the literature on this subject focuses on partial and complete tears in older individuals. The spectrum of injury in younger athletes can include tenderness as a result of an accessory navicular, tenosynovitis and longitudinal tearing, and rupture or avulsion with subsequent arch collapse. The posterior tibial tendon is subjected to a great amount of stress just after heel strike because it controls the hindfoot movement from a position of eversion into increased inversion, producing the rigid foot necessary for toe-off.[36] As a result, tenosynovitis can result, particularly in sports that require rapid changes in direction such as basketball, tennis, soccer, and ice hockey. Also, training errors such as running on a banked track or road can place excessive loads on the foot. A physical examination will reveal tenderness over the course of the posterior tibial tendon from the medial malleolus to the navicular; swelling in this region is sometimes present. Pain can be reproduced with the "single heel rise test," which tests the functional integrity of the tendon. Treatment is aimed at resting the tendon through decreased activity, orthosis, and immobilization if symptoms are severe. Preventive measures include stretching techniques, using a semirigid arch support and slight medial heel posting, and wearing running shoes with a flared heel, which should be replaced after 400 to 500 miles of use.

One of the more common entities encountered in the younger athlete is the accessory navicular. For this condition, the average age at diagnosis is 12 years and the female-to-male ratio is almost 3:1, respectively.[37] Point tenderness and erythema over the tarsal navicular tuberosity confirm the diagnosis, which can be further documented with a radiograph of the accessory bone. Generally, the symptoms will resolve with rest and the use of a semirigid orthosis. Occasionally, surgical excision of the accessory bone is needed.

Ankle fractures

Ankle fractures in the athlete can include obvious medial or lateral malleoli fractures or more subtle osteochondral fractures of the talus or tibia. Acute fractures of the ankle can be readily diagnosed because of the immediate swelling and ecchymosis, inability to bear weight, severe tenderness, and often some degree of deformity. Treatment by the athletic trainer involves rigid immobilization in a splint, elevation, ice, and consultation with a physician. Most, but not all, ankle fractures require surgery as dictated by the injury type and the amount of displacement shown on radiographs.

Fracture-dislocations can be recognized by severe deformity at the ankle and require careful evaluation of the neural and vascular integrity of the foot. If either is compromised, a trial reduction is warranted and is performed with longitudinal traction on the foot in an attempt to reverse the deforming force. That is, if the foot was turned inward, reduction is attempted with longitudinal force and the foot pulled outward. After reduction, the ankle is splinted and elevated, ice is applied, and the athlete is immediately transported to an emergency facility.

Osteochondral fractures of the dome of the talus are a common result of ankle sprains because the talus impinges on the surrounding malleoli. The bone and its overlying cartilage can be chipped, which results in a free fragment that irritates the joint. This type of fracture is usually not recognized until it is determined that the ankle sprain is not healing as expected. Here, pain, swelling, and intermittent popping, clicking, or locking (if the fragment is loose) persist beyond the time expected for normal healing of a sprain. If the injury is diagnosed as an acute fracture, a nonweightbearing cast should be applied for approximately 6 weeks to allow healing. If the fracture is chronic and symptomatic, the ankle should be arthroscopically examined or opened so that the fragment can be excised or replaced. Other possible ankle fractures that may occur include occult fractures of the talar neck, lateral talar process, posterior talar process, or anterior process of the calcaneus. These will have point tenderness at the injury site and not in the region of the ATFL or CFL, as with the typical ankle sprain. Management of these fractures is more conservative and often involves a period of nonweightbearing. Displaced fractures require surgery.

Impingement syndromes

Chronic ankle pain from impingement can present in a variety of ways and can involve anterior, anterolateral, or posterior symptoms. Anterolateral impingement in the gutter between the lateral talus and fibula may represent synovitis and scarring from either repetitive injury such as a number of minor sprains or a single, more severe lateral ankle sprain. The athlete will report symptoms in the region of the ATFL or sinus tarsi, which will be tender. Swelling in this region is variable because most of the pathology is intra-articular. Treatment includes relative rest, NSAIDs, and bracing, but arthroscopic debridement may be necessary if nonsurgical treatment fails.

Anterior impingement is seen frequently in basketball and football players as well as in dancers. An osteophyte (bony outgrowth) on the anterior lip of the distal tibia is the most common cause of anterior impingement. The bony impingement of the distal tibia on the neck of the talus causes the pain, which can also be elicited by the examiner with maximal dorsiflexion of the ankle. If the impingement is severe, it can be relieved by open or arthroscopic excision of the osteophyte from the distal tibia.

Posterior impingement is far more common in ballet dancers. Pain is felt at the back of the ankle when the toe is pointed. The pain is the result of the presence of a bony prominence such as an os trigonum on the back of the talus that pinches the soft tissue when the ankle is in plantarflexion. Diagnosis is confirmed by reproducing the patient's pain with forced passive plantarflexion. If the pain is not relieved with rest, NSAIDs, or a local corticosteroid injection, the bony prominence can be surgically excised. Tenosynovitis in the flexor hallucis longus tendon, with the occasional finding of triggering or locking of the great toe, is another impingement syndrome that can be diagnosed if there is posterior ankle pain with resisted flexion of the tip of the great toe. Longitudinal tears of the tendon are sometimes found at the time of surgical exploration.

Nerve entrapments

Tarsal tunnel syndrome is a well-described entity that refers to the entrapment of the posterior tibial nerve in the lower quarter of the leg, medial ankle, and medial heel.[10] In some ways, it resembles carpal tunnel syndrome at the wrist. Classic tarsal tunnel syndrome occurring in athletes usually follows an injury or other pathology (for example, tenosynovitis of the posterior tibial tendon), but many cases are spontaneous.[21] Physical findings are often subtle and mostly consist of discomfort or paresthesia when the nerve is palpated and percussed along its length. It may be necessary to examine the athlete shortly after the offending activity to recognize the location of the problem. Conservative treatment includes avoiding the inciting activity, strengthening the toe flexor and tibialis posterior tarsals, using NSAIDs and accommodative arch support and ankle stirrup bracing. Surgical release of the investing tarsal tunnel fascia is usually successful if conservative management fails. A variety of other nerve entrapment syndromes, which are less common, occur around the ankle and can be suspected if the examiner has a firm grasp of the relevant anatomy.

THE FOOT

The foot with its many articulations is a complex array of bone and soft-tissue structures that undergo a great deal of stress, particularly in athletes. The athletic trainer may hear more complaints about this region than about any other except the ankle. A large portion of the energy absorbed by the body is dissipated by the foot, and any athlete who presents with a complaint from the hip down should undergo a physical examination of the foot to ensure that no subtle underlying foot pathology is contributing to the complaint.

Anatomy

Osseous structures

The skeleton of the foot is composed of 26 bones (**Figure 17-12**). The foot is subdivided into the hindfoot, midfoot, and forefoot. The hindfoot includes the talus and the calcaneus and their midtarsal articulations with the navicular and the cuboid, respectively. The midfoot is composed of the navicular, the cuboid, and three cuneiforms num-

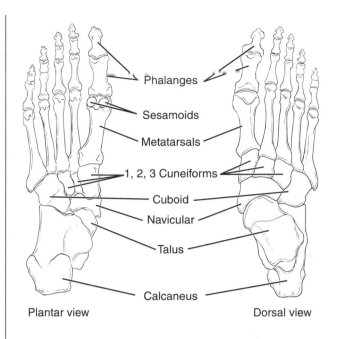

FIGURE 17-12

The foot is composed of 26 bones.

bered from medial to lateral. The metatarsals (MT) and phalanges compose the forefoot. Not included in the 26 bones are the two sesamoid bones located beneath the first metatarsal head that function as weightbearing structures and leverage points in flexing the great toe. There are other sesamoid or accessory bones in the foot, but these are rarely the source of symptoms.

The foot is constructed with a longitudinal arch and a transverse arch, each held together by a complex system of ligaments (static) and muscle-tendon units (dynamic). The plantar fascia runs from the plantar calcaneal tuberosity to the phalanges and acts as a bowstring for the longitudinal arch and a support for the plantar musculature. Approximately one sixth of body weight is borne on each of the lateral four MT heads of the transverse arch, and the first metatarsophalangeal (MTP) joint bears the remaining one third of body weight.

Soft-tissue structures

Musculotendinous structures from all four compartments of the lower leg cross the ankle joint to insert onto the foot. The calcaneus receives the insertion of the Achilles tendon; the tibialis posterior tendon has a broad insertion on the navicular. The flexor digitorum longus flexes the lateral four toes, and the flexor hallucis longus flexes the great toe (**Figure 17-13**). The peroneus brevis and peroneus longus traverse behind the lateral malleolus from the lateral compartment of the leg and insert onto the bases of the fifth and first MT, respectively, and plantar flex and evert the foot. The peroneus longus plantar flexes the first ray (**Figure 17-14**). From the

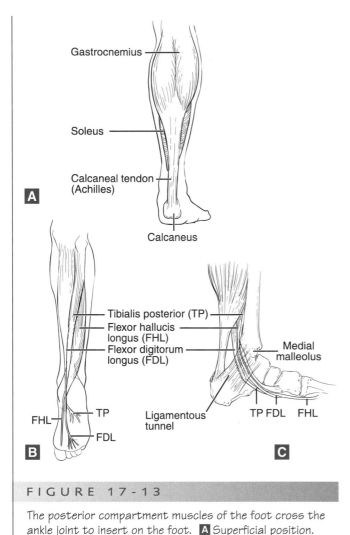

Gastrocnemius

Soleus

Calcaneal tendon
(Achilles)

A

Calcaneus

Tibialis posterior (TP)
Flexor hallucis
longus (FHL)
Flexor digitorum
longus (FDL)

Medial
malleolus

FHL — TP
— FDL

Ligamentous
tunnel

TP FDL   FHL

B

C

FIGURE 17-13

The posterior compartment muscles of the foot cross the ankle joint to insert on the foot. **A** Superficial position. **B** Deep portion. **C** Medial view.

midtarsal joints absorbs and dissipates the force of the heel strike. As the foot progresses to toe-off, it launches the leg into the swing phase and the other foot begins the same cycle. In running, the same movements and biomechanics are done at a higher velocity; however, there is a float phase during which neither limb is on the ground and there is no period of double limb support. An understanding of the normal mechanics of walking and running makes it easier for the examiner to detect the subtle changes that produce pathologic gait and to diagnose athletic injury and compensation patterns that can produce secondary symptoms.

Physical Examination

Examining the injured foot requires an understanding of the topical anatomy and the mechanisms by which particular injuries occur. A systematic examination has five parts: a visual inspection for swelling, discoloration, or deformity with shoes off both feet; manual palpation of the bony prominences and tendinous structures; active and passive ROM of the joints of the foot; observation of gait, if possible; and examination of the neural and vascular structures to ensure that no deficits exist. Each particular injury will have history and physical findings specific to its presentation.

anterior compartment comes the tibialis anterior, which inserts on the first cuneiform; the extensor digitorum longus, which inserts on the dorsum of small toes, and the extensor hallucis longus, which inserts on the dorsum of the great toe.

The tibial nerve supplies most of the protective sensation to the plantar foot and all of the motor supply to the intrinsic muscles of the foot. It enters the foot in the tarsal tunnel behind the medial malleolus. The posterior tibial artery accompanies the nerve and is the major blood supply to the foot. It has some anastomoses with the dorsal pedis artery, which is a continuation of the anterior tibial artery of the leg.

Normal Function

In walking, as stance phase passes from heel strike to midstance, weightbearing forces are carried along the lateral border of the foot to the MT heads. During midstance, the foot goes from inversion at heel strike to pronation. This complex series of movements through the subtalar and

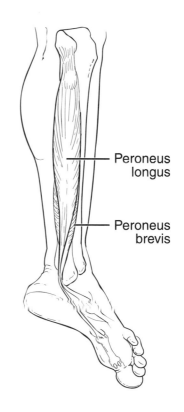

Peroneus
longus

Peroneus
brevis

FIGURE 17-14

The peroneus longus plantar flexes the first ray of the foot.

Common Injuries and Conditions

Common conditions found in an athlete's foot can be divided into regions. Most of the pathology presented to the athletic trainer will be in the forefoot, including nail disorders, corns and calluses, blisters, generalized forefoot pain (*metatarsalgia*), turf toe and hallux rigidus, neuromas, sesamoiditis, hallux valgus deformity, and stress fractures of the metatarsals. Midfoot injuries can be somewhat difficult to diagnose and include fractures of the base of the fifth MT, stress fractures of the navicular, and midfoot (Lisfranc joint) sprains and dislocations. In these injuries, diagnostic radiographs usually dictate the appropriate treatment. Plantar fasciitis and stress fractures of the calcaneus frequently affect the hindfoot.

Each of these conditions can be treated by a variety of nonsurgical and surgical techniques. It is important that the athletic trainer know when to continue conservative modalities and when to recommend more aggressive treatment.

Specific Injuries and Conditions

Skin and nail disorders

Treatment of ingrown toenails is based on the severity and cause of the irritation and infection. Ingrown toenails are usually limited to the great toe and commonly involve the fibular (lateral) side of the nail groove. Prevention is the ideal treatment because many ingrown toenails develop as a result of improperly fitted shoes, improper clipping habits, a congenital overcurvature of the nail plate, or a combination of these factors. Early, mild cases can be treated by gently packing absorbent cotton or lamb's wool (soaked in camphor and phenol for pain relief) under the infected nail plate to lift the plate up and keep it from embedding into the nail fold. The packing should be changed daily, and the foot soaked in warm saline or water three times a day, with a reevaluation after 5 to 7 days. Proper nail hygiene consists of cutting the nail plate squarely, distal to the nail groove, and perpendicular to the axis of the toe.[38] Moderate and advanced cases with a purulent infection and granulation tissue surrounding the nail plate require administration of antibiotics and excision of both the granulation tissue and a portion of the nail plate. In chronic cases, germinal matrix should be excised to prevent recurrence.

Fungal infections of the toenail (onychomycosis) generally cause the nail to thicken and become yellow and woody or white and crumbly. Treatment strategies to eradicate the infection are prolonged, varied, and include oral medications and topical gels. In most cases, the nail plates should be trimmed and filed down, and the athlete should live with the condition unless cosmesis or secondary bacterial infection is an important concern.

Subungual hematomas from crush injuries to the toenail can be very painful because of the pressure of the expanding blood in a confined space. These hematomas are easily decompressed with a disposable electrocautery device, a hot paper clip, or a nail drill. The nail plate should be preserved, if at all possible, to prevent the development of clubbing of the nail, which sometimes occurs with its removal.[38] *Black toe* ("jogger's toe") is a variant of this condition and is merely a chronic subungual hemorrhage that gives the nail a black appearance and is often caused by hyperextension of the toes or improper shoe fit, which allows the foot to slide forward with repeated starts and stops. Hyperextension of the toes can be treated with a metatarsal pad in the shoe, and a tighter shoe vamp can help prevent the foot from sliding forward. The athletic trainer and physician should not dismiss black toe without seeing improvement because this condition can be difficult to distinguish from a subungual melanoma.

Infection of the toe web space is commonly known as *athlete's foot*, which is a form of tinea pedis that most often affects the lateral toes where they are closest together when confined by a shoe. Successful treatment is directed against fungal, bacterial, and moisture factors. It may be necessary to use a potent astringent such as 30% aluminum chloride or gentian violet to eradicate the infection.[39] Drying measures and long-term use of a topical antifungal cream or spray can help prevent recurrence. Antibiotics are used when secondary bacterial cellulitis occurs.

Common afflictions of the foot's skin seen in athletes include blisters, calluses, corns, fissures, and ulcers. These conditions are primarily the body's means of adapting to pressure or abnormal stress on the skin from an internal or external source. Blisters are caused by frictional forces and are epidemic during the beginning of a new sports season. Properly fitted shoes are essential to prevent blisters. Reducing friction through the use of double socks, powder, lubricant cream, or moleskin or other skin coverings can also help prevent blisters. When blisters occur, they can be drained sterilely by using a syringe and needle, leaving the overlying skin as a protective covering. Tincture of benzoin, zinc oxide, and innumerable home remedies have also been found useful.

Callusing is a hyperkeratotic skin condition usually found overlying bony prominences, with most occurrences plantar at the MT heads. Calluses can be either discrete or diffuse and can be quite bothersome. Black calluses at the borders of the heel, forefoot, and great toe are frequently seen in football running backs and other athletes in running sports that involve quick cuts and changes in direction such as tennis and basketball. These are friction-related calluses with bleeding at their depth, which can be very painful.

Corns are the smallest hyperkeratotic skin conditions and appear as areas of thickened skin over the interphalangeal joints of the toes or between the toes. Treatment of all hyperkeratotic lesions begins conservatively by paring the lesion and placing a metatarsal pad proximal to the bony prominence or using a circular relief pad. Corns can also be treated by wearing shoes that have extra depth,

FOCUS ON . . .

Common Injuries and Conditions of the Foot

Specific injuries and conditions involving the foot include skin and nail disorders, great toe conditions, fractures and dislocations, forefoot disorders, and heel pain. Among the skin and nail disorders affecting the foot are ingrown toenails, fungal nail infections, subungual hematomas, athlete's foot, blisters, fissures, ulcers, corns, and calluses. Ingrown toenails usually involve the great toe on the fibular side of the nail. Early, mild cases are treated with gentle packing of absorbent cotton or lamb's wool. If purulent infection develops and granulation tissue surrounds the nail plate, the athlete should be treated with antibiotics and excision of the granulation tissue and a portion of the nail plate.

Onychomycosis is a fungal toenail infection that causes the nail to thicken and turn yellow and woody or white and crumbly. Oral medications and topical gels are available, but often trimming the nail plate and keeping it filed down is appropriate. Subungual hematomas from toenail crush injuries can be very painful, but are easily decompressed. Black, or jogger's, toe is a chronic subungual hematoma in which the nail appears black, often the result of toe hyperextension or sliding of the foot forward in the shoe with repeated starts and stops. Treatment consists of use of a metatarsal pad and a tighter shoe vamp, which can prevent the foot from sliding forward.

Great toe conditions include hallux valgus, turf toe, hallux rigidus, and sesamoid problems. Hallux valgus deformity describes lateral deviation of the proximal first MTP joint. Conservative treatment, such as shoes made of a soft material that have a lower heel, a wider toe box, and no seam over the medial eminence, is recommended. Contributing factors of turf toe, or sprain of the first MTP joint, include playing on a hard artificial surface, increased turf-shoe friction, and a shoe forefoot that is too flexible. Treatment is rest, ice, compression, and elevation, followed by contrast whirlpool baths and early range of motion. Pain is controlled with analgesics and NSAIDs. Reducing shoe wear flexibility or using a stainless steel spring plate insole will limit forefoot stresses and prevent MTP hyperextension.

Hallux rigidus is the painful loss of MTP joint motion with walking and is usually caused by arthrosis. Treatment consists of NSAIDs, activity modification if possible, and use of a shoe with a stiffer sole and an enlarged toe box. If these methods fail to relieve pain, the spur can be surgically excised. Sesamoid problems in the athlete can be disabling. Treatment is a J-shaped pad to unload the sesamoid, NSAIDs, rest, and occasionally a corticosteroid injection. Trauma can cause acute fracture (usually of the medial sesamoid). Treatment is protected weightbearing in a short leg case with a toe plate or walking boot.

Fractures and dislocations of the foot include tarsal navicular and metatarsal stress fractures and tarsometatarsal injuries. The Jones fracture occurs with an inversion injury of the foot. An acute fracture is treated with a short nonweightbearing leg cast, followed by limited activity. Surgical fixation may be appropriate if the athlete is likely to be noncompliant or if nonweightbearing is difficult.

Forefoot disorders include interdigital neuromas and Freiberg's disease. Interdigital (Morton) neuroma is a painful lesion of the forefoot digital nerves. Treatment includes shoe modification to increase forefoot space and a lower heel, metatarsal pads to relieve pressure, and corticosteroid and anesthetic injections. Painful neuromas, especially those present for more than 1 year, require surgical excision or decompression. Freiberg's disease is an osteochondrosis of the metatarsal head. Treatment aims to minimize the metatarsal head deformity with reduced activity, limited weightbearing, and a slow return to athletic activity with a metatarsal pad or bar. If a lengthy course of conservative treatment fails to relieve symptoms, surgery may be needed.

Inferior heel pain can result from plantar fascia rupture or inflammation, calcaneal stress fracture, or nerve compression in the heel. Plantar fasciitis causes pain on the medial aspect of the plantar fascia and responds to stretching and reduced activity. Nonsurgical treatment of the heel cord and plantar fascia includes stretching, NSAIDs, heel cups, longitudinal arch supports, and night splinting. Plantar fascia rupture is rare and is typically treated with protected weightbearing and stretching exercises. Os calcis stress fractures present with a dull, nagging inferior heel pain. Reduced activity is recommended.

stretching the toe box of existing shoes, using lamb's wool padding between the toes, and the use of circular corn pads. Surgery to remove an underlying spur or prominence or elevate a metatarsal head (in the case of a plantarflexed metatarsal with a diffuse callus) is rarely necessary.

Fissures and ulcers can be signs of a more serious systemic disease process or merely the result of neglected foot care. Foot ulcers can develop in athletes with poor foot sensation, such as those with peripheral neuropathies. Often, these athletes are not aware of the problem unless their feet are examined. Other athletes ignore the warning sign of pain and allow a soft corn to erode the skin, leading to an ulceration and even secondary infection. Timely foot care can prevent almost all these problems from becoming serious, and athletic trainers should be sure to educate the athletes in their charge.

Conditions of the great toe

Hallux valgus (bunion) deformity of the great toe involves deformity at the first MTP joint where the proximal phalanx deviates laterally and causes increased pressure and pain over the medial portion of the joint. It affects women more frequently than men, and it is generally believed that women's shoes play a dominant role in the development of this deformity. One hypothesis is that the increased demands placed on the medial side of the foot in athletes, especially in dancers, may contribute to an increased incidence of hallux valgus deformity, but there is little evidence to support this theory. Hereditary predisposing factors such as anatomic variation of the first MTP joint, generalized ligamentous laxity, and the overall posture of the foot (for example, the overly pronated foot) may also play a role. The differential diagnosis includes hallux rigidus, bursitis over the medial eminence, neuritis of the dorsal or plantar medial nerve, sesamoid pathology, or a metabolic disorder such as gout. Conservative treatment is most commonly prescribed for the athlete with a bunion deformity because surgical success in this population is uncertain.[40] Conservative treatment involves changing to shoes that have a lower heel, a wider toe box, a seam pattern that does not cross over the medial eminence, and a softer material that better accommodates the deformity. In the case of excessive pronation, a soft orthosis with medial posting may help relieve the pain.

Turf toe is a sprain of the first MTP joint that occurs in sports and is related to the shoe-surface interface.[4] This injury is typically seen in football players who play on artificial grass, but also occurs in soccer, tennis, basketball, and wrestling athletes. One survey found that 45% of active NFL players sustained this injury at some time in their career.[41] The mechanism of injury is primarily hyperextension of the first MTP joint, which damages the plantar capsular and ligamentous structures and impacts the dorsal articular surface of the metatarsal head. Contributing factors include hard artificial playing surfaces, increased friction between the turf and shoe, and a shoe that is too flexible in the forefoot.

Turf toe sprains, like lateral ankle sprains, can be graded into three types based on their severity (W Pedowitz, unpublished data, 1998). Grade I (minor) sprains have localized plantar tenderness and swelling with minimal restriction of motion, and the athlete is typically able to continue playing with only slight discomfort. Grade II sprains are characterized by more pain and moderate swelling, restricted joint motion, and difficulty bearing weight. A grade III sprain causes severe pain with plantar and dorsal tenderness, marked swelling and ecchymosis. Athletes with grade III sprains are rarely able to bear weight because of pain. Severe restriction of MTP motion is present with these more severe sprains. Radiographs should be obtained to rule out bony injury. The athlete with a severe turf toe sprain can be disabled from play for up to 6 weeks. Initial treatment is rest, ice, compression, and elevation during the first 48 hours, followed by contrast whirlpool baths and early ROM exercises. The toe can be taped or wrapped, and pain can be controlled with analgesics and NSAIDs. Reinjury can be prevented by modifying the shoe or placing a stainless steel spring plate insole into the shoe to reduce its flexibility. This will help to reduce the stresses across the forefoot and prevent MTP hyperextension. If the athlete does not tolerate the insole, or if the condition is more chronic, a custom insole with better contour fitting and a Morton's extension can be formulated from a stiff material to limit first MTP motion. The athletic trainer and athlete must be patient with this injury, which can be annoying and sometimes disabling. The majority of MTP joint sprains, regardless of grade, will heal in 3 to 4 weeks if properly treated and protected.

Hallux rigidus is defined as a painful loss of motion of the great toe MTP joint, caused primarily by arthrosis of the joint. This loss of joint motion causes the development of a dorsal metatarsal head *exostosis* (a spur or bony overgrowth) that restricts dorsiflexion. Pain is usually present with walking because dorsiflexion during gait causes impingement at the MTP joint. Evaluation should include an assessment of ROM for the foot and ankle. The normal ROM of the hallux MTP joint is 70° of dorsiflexion and 20° of plantarflexion. Athletic activities generally require at least 45° of dorsiflexion; anything less will be painful and restricting. Conservative management consists of NSAIDs, activity modification (if possible), and changes to the shoe (a stiffer sole and an enlarged toe box). If the symptoms become resistant to conservative therapy and radiographs show spurring and degeneration of the joint, surgical management with spur excision is indicated.

Although sesamoid problems in athletes are relatively uncommon, they can be disabling because of the vital weightbearing role of the sesamoids in the plantar capsuloligamentous complex under the hallux MTP joint. The medial and lateral sesamoids modify pressure, alter the direction of muscle pull, and diminish friction. When they are injured, the mechanism of injury is usually a fall from a height, repetitive stress (in runners and dancers), or forced dorsiflexion as occurs with turf toe in football.

Sesamoiditis, an inflammation of the sesamoid, can be either acute or chronic. It is diagnosed by pain on direct palpation and is usually treated successfully with a J-shaped pad to reduce the load on the sesamoid, NSAIDs, rest, and, in some cases, a corticosteroid injection. Acute fractures of the sesamoid as a result of a traumatic event occur more commonly on the medial sesamoid and usually require special radiographs or a bone scan for a definitive diagnosis. Treatment is protected weightbearing for 3 to 6 weeks in a short leg cast with a toe plate or a walking boot. Subsequently, a stiff-soled shoe with the toe taped until the pain subsides should be used for return to play. Stress fractures also occur more commonly on the medial sesamoid and can be difficult to diagnose. A bone scan is the best means of supporting this diagnosis. Excision of the involved sesamoid should be considered if symptoms persist.

Fractures and dislocations

Stress fractures of the foot are most commonly found in the metatarsals (MT) and the tarsal navicular. One of the more common injuries seen in athletes, particularly in basketball players, is the "Jones fracture," which occurs at the base of the fifth MT. This is an inversion injury of the foot. If the athlete experiences discomfort along the lateral border of the foot for 2 or more weeks before the injury actually occurs, a stress fracture is indicated. Symptoms include tenderness and localized swelling over the lateral aspect of the fifth MT at the fracture site, and the athlete is either unable to bear weight or does so only with great pain. For the acute fracture with no signs of chronicity, a nonweightbearing short leg cast is the treatment of choice. The athlete should not bear any weight for 8 weeks, followed by 6 more weeks of limited activity. Because refracture is common, many sports medicine specialists favor acute, surgical fixation in the athlete who fails to comply with these requirements (R Mann, unpublished data, 1998). However, even with this aggressive approach, it is difficult for an athlete to return to full competition in less than 8 to 10 weeks.

Another troublesome variety of stress fracture occurs at the base of the second MT in dancers. Prolonged immobilization is often necessary and electrical stimulation or ultrasound is an adjunctive consideration. Other MT stress fractures are not as difficult to manage, usually occur along the neck or diaphysis of the bone, and most commonly involve the second or third toe. Rest and wearing hard-sole shoes are the focus for treatment, and return to sports can be achieved in 4 to 6 weeks.

Navicular stress fractures occur with repetitive stress activities and have a typical presentation: insidious medial foot pain; tenderness over the dorsal navicular; no swelling; and a rapid decrease in symptoms with rest. Most runners with navicular stress fractures can jog, but avoid striking the forefoot because of the pain.[42] It is very important to recognize a navicular stress fracture as a possible cause of insidious onset midfoot pain because prompt diagnosis minimizes the chance of developing a nonunion or traumatic arthritis. The fractures are usually in the central one third of the bone and in the sagittal plane. If radiographs are inconclusive, which is common, a diagnosis can be made based on a positive bone scan. A CT scan

will better delineate the severity and completeness of the fracture line. If the margins are not *sclerotic* (hard), treatment in a nonweightbearing cast for 6 to 8 weeks is sufficient in most patients.[43] If the CT scan demonstrates sclerotic margins or conservative treatment fails, surgical management with reduction, bone grafting, and internal fixation is indicated.

Tarsometatarsal (Lisfranc) injuries are the most important midfoot injuries for the athletic trainer and physician to recognize because the injury may present in subtle ways or appear insignificant, only to progress to severe deformity and chronic pain. The second through fifth MTs are connected by a series of strong plantar intermetatarsal ligaments, but the base of the first MT has no direct connection to the lateral four MTs. The keystone of the stability for the tarsometatarsal joints is the second MT base, which is recessed within the medial and lateral cuneiforms. A large ligament extends from the base of the second MT to the medial cuneiform (Lisfranc's ligament) and connects the first ray to the lateral four MTs. Because of this anatomy, it is a frequently injured area. The most common mechanism of injury is an axial load applied to a plantarflexed foot, which ruptures the dorsal tarsometatarsal ligaments, fractures the plantar MT bases or plantar capsules, and displaces the metatarsals dorsally.[44] This is the typical scenario of a high-energy injury and is not usually seen in routine athletic competition. More subtle injuries (sprains) commonly occur during sports and are caused by extreme plantarflexion of the foot and ankle, as might occur in football "pile-ups" and gymnastic landings (**Figure 17-15**).

Clinical diagnosis of severe injuries is not difficult because of the intense pain and swelling at the midfoot and the athlete's inability to bear weight. However, sprains without fracture-dislocations may be more subtle, with delayed swelling and ecchymosis, mild to moderate pain, and limited difficulty with normal weightbearing. Specific radiographs are mandatory in all suspected cases of Lisfranc injuries to assess for any diastasis between the medial aspect of the middle cuneiform and that of the second MT base. Those injuries that maintain their anatomic relationships on weightbearing radiographs can be treated with a nonweightbearing cast for 4 to 6 weeks, followed by protected weightbearing (for example, in a walking boot). A full-length, custom-molded orthosis to provide long term support to the midfoot and rigidity to the shoe will enable the athlete to return to activity. If any abnormal anatomic gaps that indicate complete ligament rupture are detected by the radiographs, most sports medicine experts agree that surgical treatment is warranted for the best chance at achieving a successful outcome. Both moderate and severe sprains of the Lisfranc complex are usually season-ending injuries for the athlete because of the prolonged treatment time and the risk of reinjury if return to play is hastened. This fact should be discussed

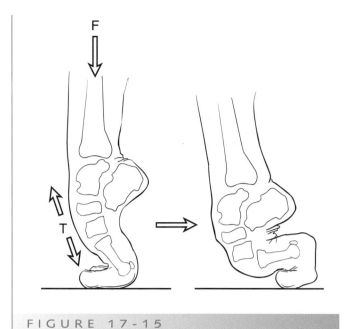

FIGURE 17-15

Plantarflexion injuries of the foot and ankle commonly occur during sports. Body weight (F) acts as a deforming force, which contributes to tension (T) across the dorsum of the tarsometatarsal joint.

with the athlete and coaching staff from the outset of the treatment program so that everyone understands the gravity of the injury.

Forefoot disorders

Forefoot pain in the athlete is quite common. This pain occurs in the area of the foot composed of the metatarsals, MTP joints, interphalangeal joints, flexor and extensor tendons, and digital nerves. Both the plantar and dorsal aspects of the foot should be examined for abnormal forces applied to the skin. The ball of the foot contains specialized tissue adapted to absorbing the stresses placed on this area. When the forefoot is squeezed into an excessively tight shoe, an abnormal force results. Because this is a common etiologic factor in both athletes and nonathletes, proper shoe fit should be confirmed in the evaluation process of any patient who reports with foot complaints.

Morton's neuroma (interdigital neuroma) is a painful lesion of the digital nerves in the forefoot and most commonly occurs in the interspace between the third and fourth MT heads, with the next most common location being the interspace between the second and third toes. This lesion is caused by excessive pressure exerted on the digital nerves by the intermetatarsal ligament as the toes are extended. Scarring around the nerve (*perineural fibrosis*) causes a very painful condition that is exacerbated by wearing narrow shoes and high heels. The patient reports pain localized to the ball of the foot, which worsens when walking while wearing shoes, and is

relieved by resting and removing the shoes. Up to one third of patients also complain of paresthesia and occasional numbness in the toes.[45] Up to 90% of patients with this problem are women.[46] Initial treatment should include modifying the shoe to provide more space for the forefoot and wearing a shoe with a low heel. Both metatarsal pads to relieve pressure on the nerve and a corticosteroid plus anesthetic injection around the nerve are useful in diagnosing and treating perineural fibrosis and should be tried before surgery is considered. Most neuromas that cause a significant amount of discomfort and remain present for longer than 1 year should be surgically excised or decompressed.

Freiberg's disease, an osteochondrosis or osteonecrosis of the metatarsal head, may be diagnosed in young active patients with unexplained forefoot pain. Up to 80% of cases occur in the second MT head.[47] The typical patient is a young woman in her late teens or early 20s who has pain and limited ROM in the involved MTP joint. Tenderness over the affected area is often accompanied by soft-tissue thickening secondary to synovitis. To minimize the deformity of the MT head, treatment includes a prompt reduction in activity, limited weightbearing (often in a cast), and a very gradual return to full athletic activity with a metatarsal pad or metatarsal bar to reduce pressure in the affected area (J Nunley, unpublished data, 1998). This conservative treatment can take time, possibly years; surgical treatment can be undertaken if significant improvement in symptoms is not achieved.

Heel pain

The four major causes of inferior heel pain are rupture of the plantar fascia, inflammation of the plantar fascia, stress fracture of the calcaneus, or compression of nerves in the heel[48] (**Figure 17-16**). Occasionally, metabolic and inflammatory arthritic conditions can cause pain around the heel, but these are not very common. The most common cause of inferior heel pain is *plantar fasciitis*, which is frequently present in joggers. The pain is usually on the medial aspect of the plantar fascia, and is worse in the morning or when the athlete first gets out of bed. It eases with stretching and reduced activity. Most patients will respond to conservative treatment that includes stretching of the heel cord and plantar fascia five to seven times a day for 20 seconds; NSAIDs; heel cups or longitudinal arch supports; and night splinting for persistent symptoms. Entrapment of the first branch of the lateral plantar nerve is often associated with plantar fasciitis. Nerve entrapment causes the pain to radiate into the distal lateral aspect of the foot; conservative treatment responds well to this in most cases. Rupture of the plantar fascia rarely occurs in athletes; when it does, conservative treatment with protected weightbearing and stretching exercises can result in a return to full sports in 1 to 2 months.

Stress fractures of the os calcis can usually be seen on an oblique radiograph of the calcaneus or on a bone scan.

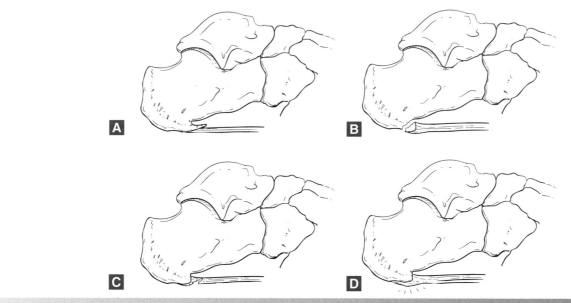

FIGURE 17-16

Nerve entrapment can also cause heel pain. Heel pain is usually seen with one of four conditions. **A** Heel spur. **B** Stress fracture. **C** Fascial rupture. **D** Plantar fasciitis.

The athlete reports a dull, nagging pain in the inferior heel with activity that is relieved with rest. Pain on direct side-to-side compression of the calcaneal head is usually present. Treatment consists of reducing activity until the athlete is completely asymptomatic, complete healing may take 6 to 8 months.

REHABILITATION OF THE ANKLE AND FOOT

Successful injury rehabilitation requires that the ankle and foot be treated as a functional unit. Bones, joints, muscles, and connective soft tissue link together to provide coordinated flexibility in the function of these structures during gait cycle.[49]

The Ankle

The goal of every ankle injury rehabilitation program is to obtain a stable, painless, and supple ankle that can withstand the rigors of sports participation. The following will focus on ankle sprains because they comprise most injuries to the ankle.[39] The literature supports an aggressive three-phase treatment plan that results in early weightbearing and quicker restoration of ROM, strength, and motor control.[50-56]

Phase I: Acute

Phase I of the treatment plan, initiated immediately after the onset of the injury, is designed to reduce inflammation and to protect the traumatized tissues until they heal sufficiently to permit early mobilization. Inappropriate treatment can exacerbate the symptoms of pain and swelling associated with the inflammatory response and create a less

than optimal healing environment within the affected tissues, delaying the restoration of optimal joint functioning.

An appropriate treatment plan begins with ice, compression, elevation, and active rest, with cross-training activities. **Cross training** is the substitution of one activity for another to maintain cardiovascular conditioning and to exercise similar muscle groups to allow the injured area to heal. The use of a functional orthosis or brace to support the ankle in an optimal healing position so that ROM and protected weightbearing can occur in stable planes will complement this treatment and promote a rapid return to function.

Unfortunately, emergency department personnel commonly advise an inappropriate treatment strategy for routine lateral ankle sprains. For example, use of a compression wrap and crutches, along with instructions to the patient to "stay off" of the injured extremity, can often increase the recovery time. This combination of factors maintains the foot and ankle in a dependent position, plantarflexed and inverted, which contributes to a loss of ankle motion.[55] In this position, increased venous and lymphatic return to the muscle is limited. The joint is subjected to a vicious cycle of increasing edema, less use, loss of ROM, and muscle deconditioning.

One of the primary factors contributing to recurrent ankle injuries and disability is inadequate restoration of motion, specifically in dorsiflexion. The dorsiflexion range for normal ambulation is approximately 10° during walking and 20° during running.[55] Any restriction in this range suggests not only ankle pathology, but also heel cord tightness. Adequate length-tension properties of the heel cord are essential for the athlete to resume play at the previous level of function. A supple heel cord is necessary for adequate dorsiflexion and normal walking and running gaits. During ambulation, the heel cord lengthens as it eccentrically controls dorsiflexion at the ankle joint. Just prior to heel lift, it reaches its greatest length, and the subtalar joint inverts through the mediolateral plane.[57] Contracture of the heel cord may be accompanied by increased foot pronation. In more extreme cases, it may also be accompanied by midfoot and subtalar subluxation and instability with dorsiflexion occurring through the foot and not the ankle.[49] Compensatory actions increase the pathology, leading to altered mechanics in walking and running gaits.

Depending on the severity of the injury, gentle ROM exercises to restore dorsiflexion may be initiated within the first 24 hours after the injury. Stationary cycling with the forefoot placed directly on the pedal to encourage ankle dorsiflexion can be started immediately after the injury to enhance venous return and decrease swelling.[58] Additionally, active ROM exercises in the anterior posterior plane on a teeterboard can be initiated with the athlete in a seated position behind the board. The goal of these activities is to reestablish at least 100° of dorsiflexion as quickly and safely as possible. This allows for early, pain-free ambulation during walking, which is the key to accelerating the recovery time.

Once weightbearing can be tolerated, the athletic trainer can assess the degree of motion restriction in dorsiflexion and provide a basis for selecting and sequencing additional ROM/stretching in dorsiflexion.[55,56] During the evaluation, the athlete assumes a parallel stance with bare feet on the floor, hip width apart, and then flexes both knees and both ankles while keeping the feet flat on the floor. Asymmetry of horizontal alignment at the knee level indicates restriction in the ankle motion. Active-assisted range of motion (AAROM) exercises can facilitate restoration of dorsiflexion with weightbearing stresses. Proper exercise technique includes weightbearing with the knee flexed and extended (**Figure 17-17**). In addition, to supination and pronation of the subtalar joint should be included. Athletes should be instructed to comply with the AAROM exercise regimen up to three times daily.

During phase I of rehabilitation, activities to normalize gait are introduced. Retraining the normal heel-to-toe gait cycle begins with retropulsion or backward walking because it places decreased demands on the ankle joint in dorsiflexion.[58] The athlete can progress to forward walking only after the retropulsion activities can be done without pain. During all ambulation activities, the patient should wear an adhesive strapping or a functional ankle orthosis for medial-lateral support.

A functional ankle brace or support helps control swelling and allows activity to occur in stable planes, which facilitates an early return to weightbearing activities. The pneumatic compression brace or air cast is a traditionally popular choice for establishing early return to

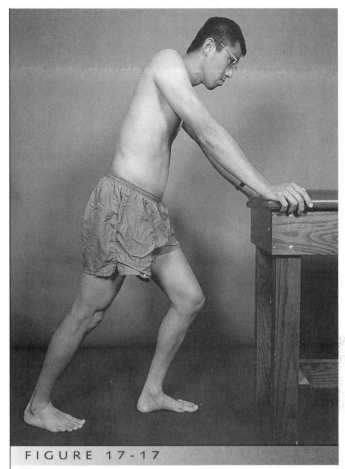

FIGURE 17-17

In ankle range of motion and heel cord stretching using a table for support, the athlete assumes a lunge position with the injured ankle/leg forward. Body weight is shifted from the back leg to the injured extremity until a stretch is felt in the anterior aspect of the ankle or the heel cord. The stretch should be held for a minimum of 10 seconds and repeated 15 to 20 times.

function after routine injuries. For complicated cases of soft-tissue injuries of the ankle and foot, a new orthotic treatment, ankle stabilizing boots, is beginning to receive attention. Initial research on the efficacy of these devices is encouraging.[58,59]

The design features of ankle stabilizing boots include dual medial and lateral removable stabilizers that maintain stability in the mediolateral plane while allowing dorsiflexion and plantarflexion in the anteroposterior plane; a firm, reinforced, cardboard-leather combination heel cup; a lacing system with nylon webbing that inserts distally at the plantar aspect of the boot, and a sole design that is torsion-resistant in the mediolateral plane, with flexibility in the anteroposterior plane. D-shaped eyelets made from one-piece, punched out, sheath metal are located at the proximal end. This system is constructed to provide an even distribution of instep pressure over the entire dorsal aspect of the foot. Ankle stabilizing boots with these fea-

FOCUS ON . . .

Rehabilitation of the Ankle

The goal of ankle rehabilitation is a stable, painless, supple ankle that can withstand the rigors of sport participation. Most ankle injuries are sprains, for which a three-phase treatment plan is recommended.

Phase I: Acute

Phase I (the acute phase) is designed to reduce inflammation immediately after injury and to protect the damaged tissues until healing is sufficient for early mobilization. Ice, compression, elevation, active rest, and a functional orthosis or brace are recommended. Restricted motion may reflect ankle pathology and heel cord tightness. Heel cord flexibility contributes to adequate dorsiflexion and normal walking, running, and sports participation. To assess dorsiflexion, any asymmetry of horizontal alignment at the knee level reflects restricted ankle motion. Active-assisted range of motion exercises can restore dorsiflexion with weightbearing stresses. These exercises should be done up to three times per day.

Normalizing gait involves reestablishing the normal heel-toe gait cycle and begins with retropulsion. Once retropulsion is pain free, the athlete can progress to forward walking. During ambulation, the patient should wear an adhesive strapping or a functional ankle orthosis for mediolateral support. An ankle-stabilizing boot may be helpful for more complex injuries.

Phase II: Recovery

Phase II (recovery) continues the use of modalities to control pain and swelling and progressive exercises to reestablish full range of motion and weightbearing. Exercises are introduced to reestablish muscle strength and joint proprioception. Ankle stabilizer strengthening should begin as soon as exercise is pain free. Manual muscle testing will help to assess contractile tissue integrity, neuromuscular status, and movement coordination.

Strengthening exercises at submaximal effort within the patient's pain-free range of motion and tolerance can begin with isometrics. Isotonic and isoflex exercises have concentric and eccentric components that work the muscle through a range of motion and can be used to strengthen the tibialis anterior in dorsiflexion, triceps surae in plantarflexion, peroneals in eversion, and tibialis posterior in inversion. Once strength improves, isokinetics are introduced to provide maximum dynamic loading through a velocity spectrum.

Because sensory deficits have been reported in patients with ankle stability, proprioception is important to rehabilitation. Both open and closed kinetic chain exercises should be incorporated. Motor control must be reestablished through dynamic weight shifting closed kinetic chain activities before the athlete can return to sport-specific activities.

Phase III: Sport-specific

Phase III (sport-specific) activities include the reestablishment of lower extremity muscle firing patterns to generate and regulate force. Drills should be performed in a controlled setting with linear foot and ankle stress and become more difficult with circular patterns and lateral movements. Once the athlete masters contested maneuvers, full participation may be possible. Lower extremity functional performance can be quantified by a series of tests to assess dynamic stability including co-contraction semicircular maneuver, carioca maneuver, shuttle run, and hop test.

tures can be a viable substitute for casting and other commonly used orthotic modalities.

Phase II: Recovery

The recovery phase of the treatment plan continues the efforts to control swelling and pain and employs progressive exercises to reestablish full ROM and weightbearing capacity. In addition, exercises to reestablish muscular strength and joint proprioception are introduced to restore an efficient mechanism for shock absorption, stability, and propulsion.

Muscle deconditioning occurs immediately after injury because of relative inactivity. Therefore, strengthening of the ankle stabilizers to enhance dynamic muscular compensation should begin as soon as pain-free exercise is possible. Because no single ligament is dominant in stabilizing the ankle, the athletic trainer must rely on the direction of applied forces and the position of the ankle at the time of injury to determine which muscular stabilizers should be addressed in the initial strengthening phase.[60] For example, inversion-plantarflexion injuries require eversion exercises to emphasize the peroneus longus and brevis and dorsiflexion exercises to strengthen the tibialis anterior. As the strength of these muscle groups improves, exercises for the posterior tibialis, gastrocnemius, and soleus can be added for muscle balance. Manual muscle testing (MMT) can be used to determine whether the exercise prescription is meeting the patient's special needs. MMT has the potential to provide information on the integrity of contractile tissues, neuromuscular status, and movement coordination.

Strengthening exercises at submaximal effort should be incorporated within the patient's available pain-free ROM and tolerance levels. Isometric exercises can be highly effective during the early phases of rehabilitation when the patient has a limited ROM. The rule of tens (10 repetitions of an exercise with a 10-second hold performed 10 times each day) provides a good general guideline for isometric exercises to rebuild static strength.[61] Isometrics can be complemented with the use of electrical stimulation to assist in muscular recruitment during exercise performance.[58]

Rhythmic stabilization, a form of isometric exercise using manual resistance, can improve dynamic joint stability through co-contractions of the ankle musculature. This technique strengthens and improves coordination of muscle groups by alternating between isometric contraction of the agonist muscles and isometric contraction of the antagonist muscles. Low forces are applied initially; as the quality of movement improves, higher forces can be applied rapidly and randomly to challenge the joint. Later, isotonic, isoflex or elastic tubing, and isokinetic exercises can be developed and practiced to retrain integrated muscle action and build dynamic muscle strength.

Isotonic and isoflex exercises have both concentric and eccentric components that provide work through a ROM. The goals of increasing muscular strength and endurance are initially accomplished by a high-repetition, low-resistance program. The athletic trainer should alter the number of repetitions, sets, and degree of resistance to maintain the appropriate workload throughout the rehabilitative phases. Isotonic and isoflex exercises can strengthen the extrinsic muscles of the lower leg: the tibialis anterior in dorsiflexion, the triceps surae in plantarflexion, the peroneals in eversion, and the tibialis posterior in inversion (**Figure 17-18**). Additionally, the extrinsic and small intrinsic muscles of the foot should not be neglected. Effective exercises to reestablish motor control and strength of these muscles include towel gathering, marble pick-up, and toe extension. As the strength of the unstable extremity improves, isokinetic exercises can be introduced to further challenge the joint. This exercise mode can be incorporated in the advanced stages of rehabilitation to provide maximum dynamic loading through a velocity spectrum.

Strengthening exercises should progress in both open kinetic chain (OKC) and closed kinetic chain (CKC) conditions. OKC exercises are traditionally used to strengthen the ankle musculature for stabilization. However, because OKC exercises are limited to isolated joint movements in a single plane of motion, their capacity for functional and proprioceptive training is limited.

A comprehensive approach to rehabilitating the unstable ankle combines both OKC and CKC activities. In CKC activities, the body moves over the ankle and foot with consequent synchronous movement of all joints of the lower extremity. CKC activities, beginning with simple balance activities on a stable platform and progressing to dynamic weight shifting exercises that require sudden changes in joint positioning, are an effective method for reestablishing normal neurologic patterns for joint stabilization.

Proprioceptive training is essential in the rehabilitation process. The function of the proprioceptive system is to conduct sensory reports to the central nervous system through specialized neurosensory cells or receptors located in the articular and musculotendinous anatomy. Stimulation of the receptors contributes to the sensory awareness of limb positions and movements, often called kinesthetic awareness or sense. An intact proprioceptive system permits athletes to change directions rapidly when participating in activities involving running, cutting, and jumping maneuvers or to run on uneven terrain without having to stare at the ground continuously.[51,54] Sensory deficits in patients with ankle instability have been reported.[62, 63]

A safe program for proprioception training begins in the early stages of rehabilitation with simple two-to-one-legged balance exercises on a stable base with support. Once the athlete can balance him- or herself on one leg for 30 seconds with the eyes open while using a table for support, the degree of exercise difficulty can be enhanced by adding extrinsic loading such as holding hand-held weights or using elastic tubing. Balance exercises from a stable base can then be transferred to unstable platforms such as a wobble or proprioception board. The proprioception board has many accessories and can be modified to prevent ankle motion in the mediolateral plane during the early stages of rehabilitation. Once the patient's ROM, strength, and motor control improve, the BAPS board can be used to challenge the ankle in all planes of motion to its full ROM.

Reestablishing motor control through dynamic weight-shifting CKC exercises is a prerequisite for advancing the athlete to sport-specific reentry activities. Activities that challenge the stabilizing mechanisms of the joint to respond to the high-speed and high-energy loads characteristic of running, jumping, and cutting maneuvers must be incorporated in the rehabilitation process. The athlete's predisposition for ankle and foot injuries may be attributable to the level of biomechanical stresses placed on individual components. For example, the ankle and foot must be able to withstand stresses equivalent to 125% of body weight during walking and 200% during running, with an even greater degree of stress in diagonal patterns resulting from lateral motion.[64] Preparing the athlete for a return to unrestricted sports participation requires that functional, multiplane, and high-speed activities be incorporated into the later stages of rehabilitation.

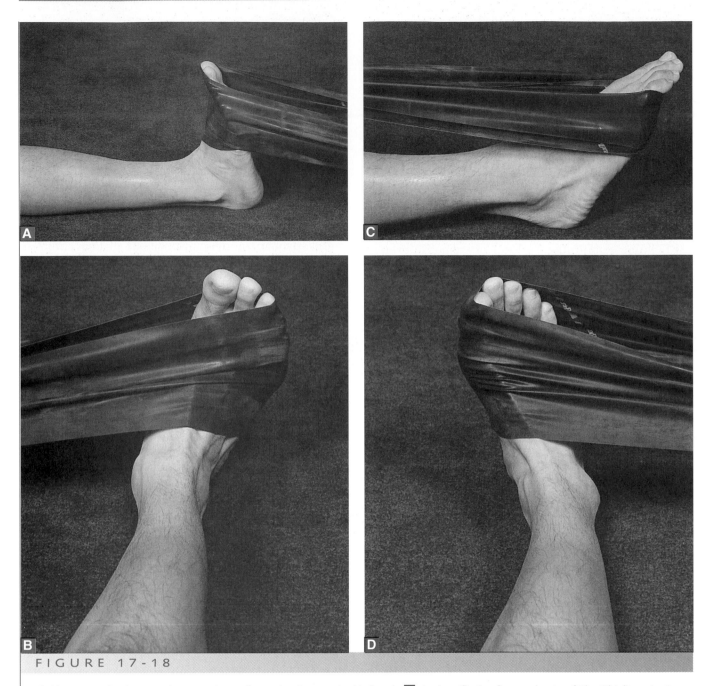

FIGURE 17-18

Ankle strengthening exercises can be performed using an elastic band. **A** In dorsiflexion for emphasis of the tibialis anterior. **B** In eversion for emphasis of the peroneals. **C** In plantarflexion for emphasis of the triceps surae. **D** In inversion for emphasis of the tibialis posterior.

Phase III: Sport-specific

Muscle firing patterns inherent in lower extremity function must be reestablished in the organization of force generation and force regulation patterns.[65] To accomplish this goal, repetitious drills that contain sports-specific movement patterns should be included in the rehabilitation process. The sequence of activities begins in a controlled setting with drills that impart linear stress on the foot and ankle and become increasingly more difficult as circular patterns and lateral movements are added. Examples of drills with emphasis on planned responses include forward and backward jogging, figure-of-eights, carioca crossover maneuvers, zig-zag running, and right-angle cuts. Once the athlete is able to perform these drills at full speed, without pain or disturbances in gait, playing situations characterized by uncontested offensive and defensive maneuvers such as fielding baseballs or softballs, dribbling and shooting a soccer ball, receiving and passing a volleyball, and guarding an opponent with controlled speed can be introduced. Contested maneuvers follow and serve as a stepping stone for full participation clearance. An appropriate functional rehabilitation plan for the lower extremity emphasizes cutting and agility-proprioception activities in addition to sport-specific drills.[66]

In the functional activity phase of rehabilitation, an objective method for determining when the athlete is ready for return to unrestricted sports participation must be established. A series of lower extremity functional performance tests can be used to assess dynamic stability. One series of tests consists of a co-contraction semicircular maneuver, a carioca maneuver, a shuttle run, and a hop test.[66] Figure-of-eight running, running up and down a slope, and running up and down a staircase for distance or time can also be used.

Criteria for return to play should be based on normal clinical evaluation, normal ankle and foot kinetics, normal kinetic chain integration, and completed progression.[66]

The Foot

Specific rehabilitation procedures unique to a particular foot injury have already been discussed. However, to prevent deconditioning, the intrinsic and extrinsic musculature of the foot must not be neglected. If a musculotendinous unit of the foot becomes contracted or weakened, the athlete is at increased risk for new or further injury. To prevent this, several exercises for the foot and toes can be initiated as soon as pain and swelling allow.

Active and passive ROM of the toes and midtarsal joints can be performed with the athlete seated and the foot suspended or on the floor. If the injury is stable, light weights can be placed on the athlete's lap. Toe curls with a towel and weights will help with plantarflexion motion as well as strength (**Figure 17-19**). The marble pick-up exercise uses 10 or 20 marbles. In this exercise, the athlete picks up the marbles with his or her toes and places them into a bowl. This exercise should be repeated three times during each rehabilitation session. Using the injured foot to "write" the alphabet also helps with intrinsic strengthening.

As soon as it is physically possible, the athlete with a foot injury should begin cross-training activities to maintain cardiovascular fitness. Depending on the severity and location of the injury to the foot, cross-training activities can include bicycling, swimming, roller-skating, and cross-country skiing. For example, for an athlete with a stress fracture, running on a pool treadmill can minimize the impact loads of gravity, which will benefit the athlete during rehabilitation. Obviously, if any activity causes symptoms, it should be curtailed or discontinued.

For a runner with a foot injury, rehabilitation can be particularly frustrating for both the athletic trainer and the athlete. If the injury is minor and relatively acute, merely a decrease in mileage or a change of surface may be all that is necessary. If the symptoms are more severe and

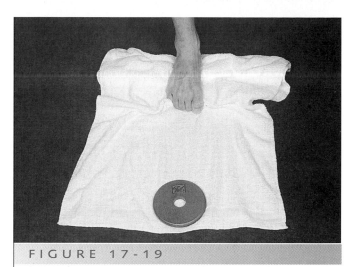

FIGURE 17-19

Exercises such as toe curls with a towel and weights will help with plantarflexion motion.

FOCUS ON . . .

Rehabilitation of the Foot

When rehabilitating an athlete with a foot injury, it is important to include the intrinsic and extrinsic foot musculature with active and passive toe and midtarsal joint range of motion, toe curls with a towel and weights, marble pick-ups, and alphabet writing. The athlete should begin cross-training as soon as possible to maintain cardiovascular fitness as long as the activities do not cause discomfort. Once the athlete is completely asymptomatic with daily activities and cross-training, a gradual return to activity is possible. Orthotics may be helpful to protect the injured area and prevent reinjury.

require the athlete to stop running, alternate activities should be performed to maintain fitness. Once the injured area is completely asymptomatic during daily activities and cross-training exercises, a gradual return to running may be initiated. Both the athletic trainer and the physician must make the athlete realize that a quick return to his or her regular mileage and intensity will only delay the return to competition. A reasonable schedule would be to run every other day for half of the normal preinjury mileage, and to continue cross-training activities on the alternate days. If the athlete is symptom-free after 2 weeks on this schedule, mileage and frequency can gradually be increased until preinjury levels are reached, about 4 to 8 weeks later, depending on the severity and type of injury. Orthotic prescriptions by the physician are often indicated as protection for the injury as well as for prophylaxis against further injuries.

CHAPTER REVIEW

The lower extremity between the knee and ankle, the leg (which includes the tibia, fibula, and muscles needed for locomotion) is a very common location for athletic complaints. The soft-tissue structures of the lower leg are contained in four compartments (anterior, lateral, superficial posterior, and deep posterior). The anterior compartment contains the tibialis anterior, extensor hallucis longus, and extensor digitorum muscles, plus the extensor muscles to the great and small toes, along with the deep peroneal nerve and the anterior tibial artery. The lateral compartment contains the peroneus longus and brevis muscles and the superficial peroneal nerve. The superficial posterior compartment contains the gastrocnemius and soleus muscles, and the deep posterior compartment contains the tibialis posterior, flexor digitorum longus, and flexor hallucis longus muscles, plus the tibial nerve and the posterior tibial and peroneal arteries. Normal gait and running require a complex and coordinated series of movements involving the bones and soft-tissue structures of the lower leg.

Common conditions affecting the lower leg include exertional compartment syndrome, medial tibial stress syndrome, tibial and fibular stress fractures, gastrocnemius-soleus strains, Achilles tendinitis and rupture, tibial contusions, and nerve entrapment syndromes. The athletic trainer must know how to evaluate the athlete with a lower leg complaint, be knowledgeable of the signs and symptoms typical of these conditions, and know how to manage these conditions.

The ankle is a critical linkage between the leg and the foot and is the most commonly injured area in the athlete. The ankle is formed by the tibia, fibula, and talus, with the lateral ligamentous complex, syndesmosis ligaments, and deltoid ligaments providing soft-tissue stability. The peroneus brevis and longus muscles provide lateral dynamic stability, and the tibialis poste-

rior, flexor digitorum longus, and flexor hallucis longus tendons provide medial dynamic stability.

If normal ankle function is disrupted, walking and running may alter the distribution of forces and cause additional injuries.

Common injuries to the ankle include sprains, fractures, tendon injuries, impingement syndromes, and nerve entrapments. The athletic trainer's initial examination, before hemorrhage, edema, and inflammation have set in, can be invaluable in determining the nature of the injury, and therefore, it must be thorough and systematic. The athletic trainer must be familiar with the characteristic presentations of these injuries and their treatment.

After the ankle, the foot is the most frequently injured area in sports. The foot is composed of 26 bones and is divided into the hindfoot (the talus and calcaneus and their midtarsal articulations with the navicular and cuboid), midfoot (the navicular, cuboid, and three cuneiforms), and forefoot (metatarsals and phalanges). The soft-tissue structures of the foot include the musculotendinous insertions of the Achilles, tibialis posterior, flexor digitorum longus, flexor hallucis longus, peroneus brevis and longus, tibialis anterior, and extensor hallucis longus. The tibial nerve and the posterior tibial and dorsalis pedis arteries supply the foot.

Common injuries and conditions affecting the foot include skin and nail disorders, great toe conditions, fractures and dislocations, forefoot disorders, and heel pain. The athletic trainer should be able to examine the foot and recognize the typical presentations of these conditions, along with their management.

Ankle and foot rehabilitation is key to returning the athlete to sport successfully after an injury. The athletic trainer should be able to develop an appropriate, progressive program for the injured athlete that will culminate in full ROM, strength, and flexibility.

1. The peroneus longus and brevis muscles and the superficial peroneal nerve are contained in which of the following compartments?

   A. Lateral

   B. Anterior

   C. Deep posterior

   D. Superficial posterior

2. Which of the following conditions is an overuse condition of the medial soleus fascia as it originates on the posteromedial tibial periosteum?

   A. Achilles tendinitis

   B. Tibial stress fracture

   C. Compartment syndrome

   D. Medial tibial stress syndrome

3. The most common stress fracture in athletes affects which of the following areas?

   A. Tibia

   B. Talus

   C. Fibula

   D. Navicular

4. The anterior talofibular, posterior talofibular, and calcaneofibular ligaments comprise the:

   A. deltoid ligaments.

   B. syndesmosis ligaments.

   C. lateral ligamentous complex.

   D. subtalar ligamentous complex.

5. Which of the following tests is used to assess calcaneofibular ligament integrity?

   A. Squeeze test

   B. Talar tilt test

   C. Anterior drawer test

   D. External rotation stress test

6. Which of the following ligaments is most often involved in ankle sprains?

   A. Lateral

   B. Medial

   C. Deltoid

   D. Syndesmosis

7. The talus and calcaneus are bones in which of the following areas?

   A. Midfoot

   B. Hindfoot

   C. Ankle mortise

   D. Longitudinal arch

8. Painful loss of motion at the great toe metatarsophalangeal joint often caused by arthrosis is referred to as which of the following?

   A. Turf toe

   B. Sesamoiditis

   C. Hallux valgus

   D. Hallux rigidus

9. Inferior and medial heel pain that is worse in the morning is characteristic of which of the following conditions?

   A. Plantar fasciitis

   B. Nerve compression

   C. Plantar fascia rupture

   D. Calcaneal stress fracture

10. After an ankle sprain, the athlete can usually begin which of the following exercises within 24 hours?

   A. Isokinetics

   B. Forward walking

   C. Gentle range of motion

   D. Proprioceptive training

Answers on page 893

References

1. Detmer DE: Chronic shin splints: Classification and management of medial tibial stress syndrome. *Sports Med* 1986;3:436-446.

2. Brill DR: Sports nuclear medicine: Bone imaging for lower extremity pain in athletes. *Clin Nuc Med* 1983;8:101-106.

3. Pedowitz RA, Hargent AR, Mubarak SJ, et al: Modified criteria for the objective diagnosis of chronic compartment syndrome of the leg. *Am J Sports Med* 1990;18:35-40.

4. Clanton TO, Solcher BW: Chronic leg pain in the athlete. *Clin Sports Med* 1994;13:743-759.

5. Conti SF: Posterior tibial tendon problems in athletes. *Orthop Clin North Am* 1994;25:109-121.

6. Andrish JT: The leg, in Delee J, Drez D (eds): *Orthopaedic Sports Medicine: Principles and Practice.* Philadelphia, PA, WB Saunders, 1994, pp 1603-1631.

7. Detmer DE, Sharp EK, Sufit RL, et al: Chronic compartment syndrome: Diagnosis, management and outcomes. *Am J Sports Med* 1985;13:162-170.

8. Blank S: Transverse tibial stress fractures: A special problem. *Am J Sports Med* 1987;15:597-602.

9. Sullivan D, Warren RF, Parlor H, et al: Stress fractures in 51 runners. *Clin Orthop* 1984;187:188-192.

10. Kadel NJ, Teitz CC, Krommal RA: Stress fractures in ballet dancers. *Am J Sports Med* 1992;20:445-449.

11. Goldberg B, Pecora C: Stress fractures: A risk of increased treating in freshmen. *Phys Sports Med* 1994;22:68-78.

12. McKenzie DC, Clement DB, Tucenton JE: Running shoes, orthotics, and injuries. *Sports Med* 1985;2:334-337.

13. Matheson GO, Clement DB, McKenzie DC, et al: Stress fractures in athletes: A study of 320 cases. *Am J Sports Med* 1987;15:1650.

14. Hershman EB, Mailly T: Stress fractures. *Clin Sports Med* 1990;9:183-214.

15. Rupani HD, Holder LE, Espinola DA, et al: Three phase radionuclide bone imaging in sports medicine. *Radiology* 1985;156:187-196.

16. Monteleone GP Jr: Stress fractures in the athlete. *Orthop Clin North Am* 1995;26:423-432.

17. Swenson FJ, DeHaven KE, Sabastianelli, et al: Pneumatic leg brace after tibial stress fracture for faster return to play. *Am J Sports Med* 1997;25:322-328.

18. Clanton TO, Schon LC: Athletic injuries to the soft tissues of the foot and ankle, in Mann RA, Coughlin MJ (eds): *Surgery of the Foot and Ankle,* ed 6. St. Louis, MO, Mosby-Year Book, 1993, pp 1095-1224.

19. Clanton TO, Solcher BW, Baxter DE: Treatment of anterior midtibial stress fractures. *Sports Med Arthroscopy Rev* 1994;2:293-300.

20. Millar AP: Strains of the posterior calf musculature ("tennis leg"). *Am J Sports Med* 1979;7:172-174.

21. Soma CA, Mandelbaum BR: Achilles tendon disorders. *Clin Sports Med* 1994;13:811-823.

22. Bradley JP, Tibone JE: Percutaneous and open surgical repairs of Achilles tendon ruptures: A comparative study. *Am J Sports Med* 1990;18:188-195.

23. Schon LC: Nerve entrapment, neuropathy, and nerve dysfunction in athletes. *Orthop Clin North Am* 1994;25:47-59.

24. Styf J: Entrapment of the superficial peroneal nerve: Diagnosis and results of decompression. *J Bone Joint Surg* 1989;71B:131-135.

25. Cetti R, Andersen I: Roentgenographic diagnoses of ruptured Achilles tendons. *Clin Orthop* 1993;286:215-221.

26. Schon LC, Baxter DE: Neuropathies of the foot and ankle in athletes. *Clin Sports Med* 1990;9:489-508.

27. Kibler WB, Goldberg C, Chandler TJ: Functional biomechanical deficits in running athletes with plantar fasciitis. *Am J Sports Med* 1991;19:66-71.

28. Ramsey PL, Hamilton W: Changes in tibiotalar area of contact caused by lateral talar shift. *J Bone Joint Surg* 1976;58A:356-357.

29. Lundberg A: Kinematics of the ankle and foot: In vivo roentgen stereophotagrammetry. *Acta Orthop Scand* 1989;60:1-24.

30. Lambert K: The weight-bearing function of the fibula: A strain gauge study. *J Bone Joint Surg* 1971;53A:507–513.

31. Anderson KJ, Lecocq JF, Lecocq EA: Recurrent anterior subluxation of the ankle. *J Bone Joint Surg* 1952;34A:853-860.

32. Lassiter TE, Malone TR, Garrett WE: Injury to the lateral ligaments of the ankle. *Orthop Clin North Am* 1989;20:629-640.

33. Hopkinson WJ, St. Pierre P, Ryan JB, et al: Syndesmosis sprains of the ankle. *Foot Ankle* 1990;10:325-330.

34. Boytim MJ, Fischer DA, Neuman L: Syndesmotic ankle sprains. *Am J Sports Med* 1991;19:294-298.

35. Lin SH, Jason WJ: Lateral ankle sprains and instability problems. *Clin Sports Med* 1994;13:793-809.

36. Balduini FC, Tetzlaff J: Historical perspectives on injuries of the ligaments of the ankle. *Clin Sports Med* 1982;1:3-12.

37. Kannus P, Renstrom P: Treatment for acute tears of the lateral ligaments of the ankle. *J Bone Joint Surg* 1991;73A:305-312.

38. Taylor DC, Englehardt DL, Bassett FH: Syndesmosis sprains of the ankle: The influence of heterotopic ossification. *Am J Sports Med* 1992;20:146-150.

39. Attarian DE, McCrackin HJ, DeYito DP, et al: Biomechanical characteristics of human ankle ligaments. *Foot Ankle* 1985;6:54-58.

40. Marti B, Vaderi JP, Minder CE, et al: On the epidemiology of running injuries: The Bern Gran-prix study. *Am J Sports Med* 1988;16:285-294.

41. Grogan DP, Gasser SI, Ogden JA: The painful accessory navicular: A clinical and histopathological study. *Foot Ankle* 1989;10:164-169.

42. Bowers KD Jr, Martin RB: Turf-toe: A shoe-surface related football injury. *Med Sci Sports Exerc* 1976;8:81-83

43. Rodeo SA, O'Brien S, Warren RF, et al: Turf-toe: An analysis of metatarsophalangeal joint sprains in professional football players. *Am J Sports Med* 1990;13:731-741.

44. Clanton TO, Ford JJ: Turf toe injury. *Clin Sports Med* 1994;13:731-741.

45. Torg JS, Balduini FC, Zelko RR, et al: Fractures of the base of the tibia metatarsal distal to the tuberosity. *J Bone Joint Surg* 1984;66A:209-214.

46. Mann RA: Entrapment neuropathies of the foot, in DeLee JC, Drez D (eds): *Orthopaedic Sports Medicine.* Philadelphia, PA, WB Saunders, 1994, pp 1838-1840.

47. Mindrebo N, Shelbourne D, Van meter CD, et al: Outpatient percutaneous screw fixation of the acute Jones fracture. *Am J Sports Med* 1993;21:720-723.

48. Khan KM, Fuller PJ, Brukner PO, et al: Outcome of conservative and surgical management of navicular stress fracture in athletes: Eighty-six cases proven with computerized tomography. *Am J Sports Med* 1992;20:657-666.

49. Reynolds JC: Functional examination of the foot and ankle, in Sammarco GM (ed): *Rehabilitation of the Foot and Ankle.* St Louis, MO, Mosby, 1995, pp 57-75.

50. Garrick JG: When can I ...? A practical approach to rehabilitation illustrated by treatment of ankle injury. *Am J Sports Med* 1987;15:258-259.

51. Geiringer SR: Sports: Management of the athletic ankle sprain. *Biomech* 1997;4:25-31.

52. Hunter S: Rehabilitation of ankle injuries, in Prentice WE (ed): *Rehabilitation Techniques in Sports Medicine.* St Louis, MO, Times Mirror/Mosby, 1990, pp 331-338.

53. Jackson DW, Ashley RL, Powell JW: Ankle sprains in young athletes: Relation of severity and disability. *Clin Orthop* 1974;101:201-215.

54. Lephart SM, Pincivero D, Giraldo J, Fu F: The role of proprioception in the management and rehabilitation of athletic injuries. *Am J Sports Med* 1997;25:130-137.

55. Torg JS, Vegso JJ, Torg E: *The Ankle. Rehabilitation of Athletic Injuries: An Atlas of Therapeutic Exercise.* Chicago, IL, Yearbook Medical Publishers, 1987, pp 26-68.

56. Vegso JJ, Harmon LE: Non-operative management of athletic ankle injuries. *Clin Sports Med* 1982;1:85-98.

57. Gray GW: Functional kinetic chain rehabilitation. *Sports Med Update* 1993;7:19-24.

58. Vogelbach WD: Biomechanical approach to the treatment of ankle sprains. *Sports Med Update* 1983;8:12-21.

59. Adrian AP, Mose S: Clinical outcomes of an orthopedic ankle-stabilizing boot. *J Prosth Orthot* 1998;10:33-41.

60. McBryde AM: The acute ankle sprain, in Harris M, Williams C, Standish WD, Micheli LJ (eds): *Oxford Textbook of Sports Medicine.* New York, NY, Oxford University Press, 1996, pp 487-493.

61. Sobel J, Pettrone FA, Nirschl RP: Prevention and rehabilitation of racquet sports injuries, in Nicholas JA, Poser MA (eds): *The Upper Extremity in Sports Medicine.* St Louis, MO, Mosby, 1995, pp 805-823.

62. Freeman MA: Instability of the foot after injuries to the lateral ligament of the ankle. *J Bone Joint Surg* 1965;47B:669-677.

63. Lephart SM, Henry TJ: The physiological basis for open and closed kinetic chain rehabilitation for the upper extremity. *J Sports Rehab* 1996;5:71-87.

64. Fiore RD, Leard JS: Functional approach in the rehabilitation of the ankle and rear foot. *Athletic Train* 1980;231-235.

65. Kiebler WB: Shoulder rehabilitation: Principles and practice. *Med Sci Sports Exerc Clin* 1998;30:40-50.

66. Lephart SM, Borsa PA: Functional rehabilitation of knee injuries, in Fu F, Vince (eds): *Knee Surgery.* Baltimore, MD, Williams & Wilkins, 1994, pp 527-539.

Other Medical Issues

Section Editor
Chad Starkey, PhD, ATC

18

Sports Psychology

Jerry R. May, PhD
Colleen Capurro, MD

QUICK CONTENTS

- The psychological factors that can affect injury onset.

- The psychological sequelae of injury.

- The psychological components of rehabilitation.

- The need for psychological consultation.

- General principles and specific guidelines for psychological rehabilitation.

OVERVIEW

Early detection of the athlete's emotional reaction to injury, quick intervention, establishment of a positive relationship, continuity of care, moderation of intensity and activity levels, proper communication, and providing support are all important aspects in helping an athlete to rehabilitate after an injury.

This chapter begins with a discussion of the athlete's psychological status, including personality, personal life events and experiences, and emotional and arousal state, and how it can influence the onset of injury. Following this is a description of the psychological factors that may be associated with the onset of injury as well as the psychological sequelae following injury. Psychological treatment and rehabilitation considerations are discussed as are the need for psychological consultation and a prescription for psychological intervention. The chapter closes with specific guidelines for psychological rehabilitation, including how the practitioner can understand the dynamics of injury, assess development issues, and help the injured athlete develop fun, pleasant activities.

PSYCHOLOGICAL STATUS

The athlete's *psychological status*, consisting of personality, personal life events and experiences, and emotional and arousal state, can influence the onset of injury. Psychological factors can affect the onset, sequelae, and rehabilitation of athletic injuries. Factors such as stress, perceived pain, and parental expectations can influence the athlete's ability to concentrate on a specific sport-related task, flexibility of movement, experience of fun, sports performance, and health status. Once injured, the athlete will experience psychological reactions that can be debilitating and vary considerably. Anxiety, depression, loss of self-esteem, loss of the peer group, and perception of aging can have a major impact on the athlete's rehabilitation.

Assisting the injured athlete during rehabilitation requires an understanding of the individual's emotional status and interpretation of the injury. Several of the mental skills techniques used to assist athletes enhance performance in sport are also beneficial in assisting an injured athlete during recovery. The athlete's ability to experience the emotion of fun is also crucial to the athlete's return to well-being.

When athletes become injured or ill, their ability to participate in sports is impaired or their level of performance suffers. Many individuals, including health professionals, may have the misperception that all athletes are in peak physical and psychological health. Another myth shared by the general public is that athletes become injured or ill with less frequency than the general population and are able to cope with an injury more effectively and rehabilitate more quickly. A study of certified athletic trainers indicated that 47% of the respondents believed that every injured athlete experiences some form of psychological trauma.[1]

All athletes run a relatively high risk of sustaining an injury when participating in sports. Approximately 17 million sports-related injuries occur annually in the United States; roughly one third of the nation's 15 million joggers sustains a musculoskeletal injury each year.[2] More than 1,000 swimmers sustain spinal cord injuries in diving accidents annually, and nearly 15% of these injuries result in a minimum of 3 weeks of lost time.[3] Most advanced athletes who have participated in a sport for 3 to 5 years have sustained an injury significant enough to cause them to miss either practice or an important event.[4] Understanding and identifying factors that contribute to injury and implementing preventive measures to avoid them is a central focus of sports medicine programs. **Table 18-1** shows the factors that influence the onset of injury. Because no

FOCUS ON . . .

Psychological Status

Psychological status, which includes personality, personal life events, and emotional and arousal state, can influence the onset, sequelae, and rehabilitation of athletic injuries. Once an athlete is injured, he or she will experience psychological reactions that may be debilitating, and anxiety, depression, and loss of self-esteem are some of the factors that can have a major impact on rehabilitation.

The practitioner must understand an athlete's emotional status and interpretation of the injury during rehabilitation. An ill or injured athlete may have an impaired ability to participate in sports, or their level of performance may suffer.

All athletes run a relatively high risk of sustaining an injury during sports participation. A central focus of sports medicine programs is to identify factors that contribute to injury and implement preventive measures. Variable factors can influence the onset of injury, including sport-specific, participant, environmental, coaching, and consequences such as the statistical probability that injury will occur regardless of preventive measures taken.

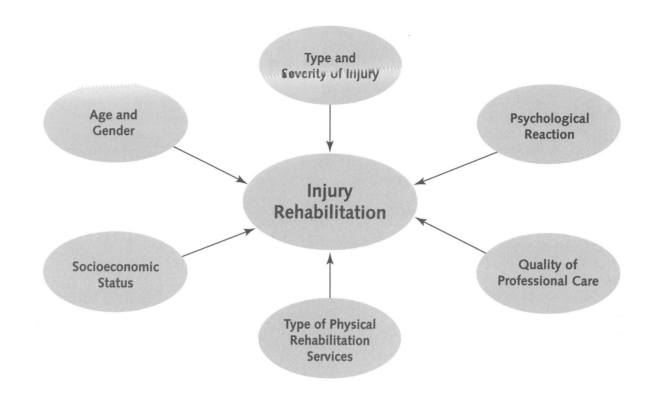

FIGURE 18-1

FIGURE 18-1

An accurate understanding of the significant components of injury and rehabilitation is needed to identify factors that influence the rehabilitation program.

single variable influences the cause, rehabilitation, and prevention of athletic injuries, a more comprehensive and accurate understanding of the significant components of injury and rehabilitation is needed (**Figure 18-1**).

PSYCHOLOGICAL FACTORS IN THE ONSET OF INJURY

The basic energy of the human psyche creates the potential for injury, and aggression plays a definite causal role in the theoretical relationship between psychology and sports injury.[5] The central concept of this theory is that young athletes who are under- or over-aggressive develop "*magical thinking*," which may lead them to believe they could not be injured by participating in daring or dangerous activities. As a result, young athletes frequently take unnecessary risks, leading to a higher probability of injury. The increased popularity of high-risk sports such as bungee jumping and the emergence of extreme games indicates that many individuals may seek risky and dangerous activities through sports. The athlete who regularly participates in an extreme sport such as street luge or sky surfing may not be taking as great of a risk as it may appear because of the high skill level of the individual. However,

TABLE 18-1
FACTORS INFLUENCING THE ONSET OF INJURY

Variables	Examples
Sport-specific	Rules of the game, equipment design, type of sport
Participant	Age, experience, physical conditioning, and psychological status of the athlete; nature of the competition
Environmental	Weather and playing surface
Coaching	Quality, type, and extent of coaching rendered
Consequences	Statistical probability that injury will occur, regardless of preventive measures taken; "freak" accidents

FOCUS ON . . .

Psychological Factors in the Onset of Injury

Many psychological factors can play a role in injury onset, among them counterphobia; validation of masculinity; masochism; injury as a weapon, escape or concoction; and psychosomatic injury. Young athletes who are under- or overaggressive can develop magical thinking, causing them to believe they will not be injured while participating in daring or dangerous activities. These athletes frequently take unnecessary risks that lead to a higher probability of injury.

High stress levels can be induced and inner conflict created by competition or anticipation of competition. Athletes who are vulnerable to stress can lose their composure and experience more negative thinking than less vulnerable athletes.

the novice athlete participating in an extreme sport may go beyond his or her skill level and become injured.[6]

Table 18-2 shows several psychological variables that may further account for the inattentiveness or miscalculation that leads to injury during athletic performance, or general athletic "injury proneness." In many athletes, the inner conflict created by competing in sports or the anticipation of competing can induce high stress levels, especially among highly motivated athletes.[7] Athletes who are vulnerable to stress tend to lose composure more easily and experience more negative thinking than those who are less vulnerable. Various fears or phobias could precipitate this vulnerability to stress.

Other conditions that are not directly associated with athletic competition can also predispose an athlete to trauma. For example, *depression* (inward aggression) and the fear of success can decrease an athlete's performance while increasing the likelihood of sustaining a real or perceived injury.[8]

THEORETICAL OBSERVATIONS OF THE ONSET OF INJURY

Guilt/Parent Pressure

Repeated injuries or accident proneness may be an athlete's way of manifesting guilt. A clinical example of this involved an 11-year-old "injury prone" boy who entered therapy. The patient was trying to be a superb athlete because his father, an avid sports spectator, was an amputee and was unable to participate in sports. The son became a devoted athlete, not out of a desire to fulfill his own needs but rather to fulfill his father's needs. Having

TABLE 18-2
CHARACTERISTICS LEADING TO INJURY PRONENESS

Trait	Characteristic
Injury resulting from counter-phobia	This individual finds the competitive nature of sport to be anxiety-inducing and counteracts the anxiety by confronting it.
Masculinity	The male athlete may use injuries to validate his courage and masculinity, yet he may lack self-confidence.
Injury as a result of masochism	The individual suffers from inward-directed anger and hostility and feels a level of satisfaction and pleasure when injured.
Injury as a weapon	The athlete may be getting back at a domineering parent. The injury can allow the athlete to avoid undesired competition and frustrate the parent.
Injury as an escape	The athlete may feel inferior or afraid, and the injury gives him or her a reason to withdraw without losing face.
Psychosomatic injury	The athlete complains of injury with no concurrent physical findings.
Injury as a concoction	The athlete makes up injuries to avoid training or disrupt the team.

(Adapted with permission from Sanderson FH: The psychology of the injury prone athlete. *Br J Sports Med* 1978;11:56-57.)

developed a "win at any cost" attitude, the patient's injury proneness was ultimately attributed to the child's feeling of guilt.[8]

"The eager parents syndrome" has been traced to young athletes whose parents place excessive demands on them to perform at levels that would be acceptable for adults, but unacceptable for young athletes.[9] Some young athletes may injure themselves on purpose or either feign or

Guilt/Parent Pressure and Exercise Addiction

Guilt or parental pressure (the "eager parents" syndrome) and exercise addiction (exercising beyond one's recuperative capacity) can influence onset of injury. Negative exercise addiction occurs when the individual perceives that survival is contingent on exercising and is typified by required daily exercise to cope with stress, regardless of the consequences, and withdrawal symptoms when unable to exercise because of medical, vocational, or personal reasons. When unable to train, exercise-addicted individuals may become depressed, irritable, anxious, and restless. They may be unable to stop exercising, even when it is contraindicated, take medications before exercising, and ignore pain during exercise. Exercise-addicted individuals often incur overuse injuries. Similarly, overtraining can result in loss of competitive drive, decreased enthusiasm for training, aversion to sport, and general "staleness."

Overzealous and untrained coaches and parents may be the unintentional instigators of these types of behaviors. Children's participation in sport activity should be consistent with their level of physical, social, and psychological maturity, with the emphasis on developing interest in sport and having fun rather than winning. Educational workshops and clinics for coaches and parents can offer training guidelines, and keeping accurate records of athletic injuries and fitness history will help to identify young athletes who are at risk.

TABLE 18-3
SIGNS AND SYMPTOMS OF EXERCISE ADDICTION

- Hyperirritability
- Increased sensitivity to loud noise
- Problems in concentrating and memory recall
- Absentmindedness
- Social withdrawal
- Anxiety
- Depression
- Sexual inhibition or inadequacy
- Repetitive nightmares of the injury experience

(Adapted with permission from Morgan WP: Negative addiction in runners. *Phys Sports Med* 1979;7:57-70.)

exaggerate an injury. Others may believe themselves to be injured when they are not. A significant feature of this syndrome is that no amount of medical encouragement will convince the young athlete that he or she does not have a serious injury. Most athletes are anxious to get back into play, whereas the athlete with a fictitious injury is not. The athlete's family system must be observed to assess the dynamics and relations among the athlete and other family members to make the appropriate diagnosis.

Exercise Addiction

Exercise addiction is a commonly accepted overuse model used by sports medicine professionals to describe athletes who exercise at a level beyond their recuperative capacity.[10] **Table 18-3** shows the signs and symptoms associated with exercise addiction.

Regular exercise is usually portrayed as a positive addiction, but can become negative when an athlete perceives that his or her survival is contingent on exercising. *Negative exercise addiction* is characterized by two traits. In one trait, daily exercise is required to cope with stress, and the exercise routine occurs regardless of the consequences. An example of this trait is when an athlete continues to exercise even when injured. In the second trait, the athlete demonstrates withdrawal symptoms when unable to exercise because of medical, vocational, or personal reasons.[11] As shown in **Table 18-4**, exercise-addicted individuals who are unable to train because of an injury will have a wide range of clinical signs and symptoms. The addicted individual may search specifically for a physician who is willing to provide symptomatic relief for the condition, such as administration of a cortisone injection.

Exercise-addicted athletes often sustain common overuse injuries such as stress fractures, tendinitis, and other musculoskeletal conditions.[12] Likewise, overtraining can result in a loss of competitive drive, decreased enthusiasm for training, an aversion to the sport, and a general athletic "staleness."[13,14]

Just as the eager parents syndrome is characterized by adult pressure, exercise addiction and overtraining tendencies can be instilled in young athletes by overzealous and untrained coaches.[15] Many coaches lack a basic knowledge of the causes of injury, as well as injury-prevention methods, and are not formally educated in effective training methodologies. As a result, many coaches may overtrain an athlete. These conditions are often related to young athletes who are managed as if they were adults. Preparation for sport activity should be commensurate with the athlete's level of physical, social, and psychological maturity. Early emphasis should be on developing an interest in sports and having fun, not on perfection and performance. Children should be allowed to stop a physical activity when they recognize their limitations rather than be driven by adults to succeed in a sport despite its psychological costs.[15]

Coaches and parents can learn much from educational workshops and clinics that teach guidelines for training young athletes.[15] Accurate records of athletic injuries and a fitness history for each athlete can assist coaches in identifying young athletes who are at risk for overuse injuries or exercise addiction. The risks of exercise addiction and overtraining are compelling reasons for young athletes to receive adequate health care.

TABLE 18-4

SIGNS AND SYMPTOMS OF WITHDRAWAL FROM EXERCISE ADDICTION

- Depression
- Increased irritability
- Decay of personal relationships
- Anxiety
- Restlessness
- Insomnia
- Generalized fatigue
- Muscle tension
- Soreness
- Decline of appetite
- Constipation
- Continuation of exercise when contraindicated
- Ignoring pain
- Medication use, such as the use of an analgesic prior to exercise

(Adapted with permission from Morgan WP: Negative addiction in runners. *Phys Sports Med* 1979;7:57-70.)

Optimal Performance Model

The Arousal Theory of Injury Proneness, based on the Yerkes-Dodson principle, is frequently used to demonstrate the relationship of arousal and stress to athletic performance (**Figure 18-2**).[16,17] This relationship also helps explain injury. When an athlete experiences low levels of arousal, concentration, perceptive acuity, and awareness, and when motivation is low, the athlete may make errors when participating in sports and may increase the risk of injury. As the athlete's arousal level reaches a

---

FOCUS ON . . .

Optimal Performance Model

The Arousal Theory of Injury Proneness, based on the Yerkes-Dodson principle, states that when an athlete experiences low levels of arousal, concentration, perceptive acuity, awareness, and motivation, errors may increase the risk of injury. As arousal increases to a moderate point, performance is maximized and errors are minimized, leading to low injury rates. As arousal increases further, performance diminishes and both errors and injuries increase.

Among the strongest injury predictors are low levels of coping ability and social support, which interact to predict vulnerability or resistance to injury. As pressure and anxiety increase, psychological and physical flexibility decrease and heart rate, blood pressure, respiratory rate, and (most significantly) muscle tension increase, elevating the risk of injury.

A comprehensive, multicomponent stress injury model relating stress, personality, history of stress, coping resources, interventions, and injury to the athlete's balance between perceived sport demands and perceived resources has been proposed, although it has not yet been rigorously tested. However, progressive relaxation and imagery training have been shown to reduce injuries in some athletes.

Demographic and descriptive studies

Other factors that may contribute to injury include more time-consuming and more strenuous training, inattentiveness, miscalculation, fatigue, poor visibility, poor environmental conditions, and race fever.

---

moderate point, his or her psychological factors normalize, allowing for maximum performance while minimizing error and potentially reducing injury rates. Moreover, as an athlete's arousal becomes too intense, performance level again diminishes, and the error and injury rates begin to accelerate. Each athlete has an individual zone of optimal performance. Although injuries may still be more frequent when stress or arousal levels fall at either end of the continuum, some athletes function well under lower or higher degrees of arousal than described by the Yerkes-Dodson model.[18,19]

Reports based on both observation and laboratory evidence suggest that athletes who sustained major injuries immediately following an acute outburst of anger or stress experience substantial decreases in peripheral vision during stress. Individuals who scored high on life stress scales may also experience this.[20,21] Some of the strongest predictors of injury are low levels of coping

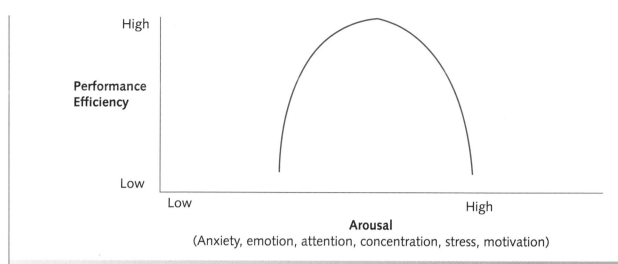

High

Performance
Efficiency

Low

Low   High

Arousal
(Anxiety, emotion, attention, concentration, stress, motivation)

FIGURE 18-2

The Yerkes-Dodson principle describes the relationships among arousal, stress, and athletic performance.

ability and low social support, which interact to predict vulnerability or resistance to injury.[22,23] Progress relaxation and imagery training reduced injuries in a group of swimmers by 52% and among football players by 33%.[24] Here, athletes were taught how to deeply relax and produce visual images and sensations of carrying out the physical movement of their sport.

As pressure and anxiety increase, psychological and physical flexibility are reduced, and heart rate, blood pressure, respiration rate, and, most significantly, muscle tension are increased.[25] These effects result in the athlete's reduced control over fine muscle coordination and timing. Increasing psychological pressure produces rigidity in the perceptual process, potentially increasing the likelihood of injury.

A comprehensive multicomponent stress injury model has been proposed in which the athlete's stress level, personality, history of stress, coping resources, intervention activities, and injury are shown to impact on the athlete's optimal balance between perceived demands of the sport and his or her perceived resources (**Figure 18-3**).[26] Although this model appears to be accurate, most of the reports using this model are based on observation with little systematic controlled data-gathering. However, according to clinical observation, a growing research database supports the use of a multicomponent stress model.[21]

Demographic and Descriptive Studies

Investigators have begun to use standardized procedures and instruments to evaluate the psychosocial status of an individual and its influence on the likelihood of injury. Review of the literature demonstrates that an athlete's ability to moderate thoughts, feelings, and behavior is an important component in the possible prevention of injury. Currently, many of these theoretical postulates are being substantiated.[27-30]

Intercollegiate athletes sustain injuries at a much greater rate than their intramural counterparts. Results of one study indicate that a male intercollegiate athlete is nine times more likely to sustain an injury than a male intramural athlete.[27] This increased incident rate was attributed to the fact that intercollegiate athletes train longer and harder than intramural athletes. Unlike intramural sports, another finding of this study was that intercollegiate injury rates seem to peak at midseason. This may be associated with increased intensity of competition as playoffs approach.

In alpine skiing, 79% of female participants and 87% of male participants sustained at least one injury serious enough to affect the athlete's health for at least 20 days, with the likelihood of injury being 25 times greater during practice than during competition.[28] Most skiing injuries took place in the lower third of the hill, followed by the middle and upper thirds. Injuries were attributed to inattentiveness, miscalculation of the course, fatigue, poor visibility, and poor race course conditions. Failure in skiing technique was seldom the cause of an injury.[28] In another study that examined the frequency of ski injuries, the injury rate was 4.7 injuries per 1,000 ski sessions.[29]

Race fever is also considered an injury factor.[30] Race fever is a feeling that an athlete is running faster than the speeds at which he or she trained. The athlete thinks he or she is running harder than usual, but, in fact, the athlete is running at normal speed. Researchers who studied 27 heat-injury patients discovered interesting physical and psychological facts.[30] First, individuals who sustained heat injuries were not overweight or untrained. Most had been running for approximately 2 years and were averaging about 20 miles a week in their training. Also in this study, there was no correlation between fluid intake and the probability of heat injuries. The researchers suggested that more information was needed regarding a runner's moti-

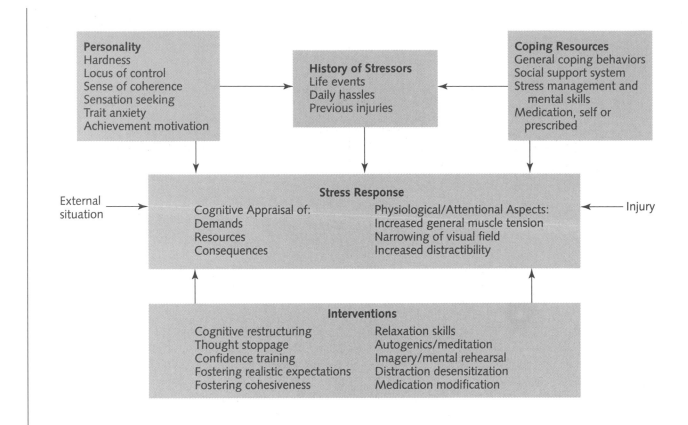

FIGURE 18-3

A comprehensive, multicomponent stress injury model that depicts the relationship among stress and injury, personality, history of stress, coping resources and interventions that impact on the balance of perceived demands, and the athlete's perceived resources. (Reproduced with permission from Anderson MD, Williams JM: A model of stress and coping and athletic injury: Prediction and prevention. *J Sport Exerc Psychol* 1988;10:294-306.)

vation before a race and its relationship to heat injury. The authors also suggested that T-shirts or souvenirs awarded to individuals who finish a race might increase the probability of race fever. By distributing T-shirts and souvenirs prior to an event, the occurrence of race fever may decrease.

Research of Life Events and General Well-Being Scale

An athlete's health can be negatively affected when he or she experiences too many changes, when life events are too close together, or when both emotional and personal life is not pleasant and appears to be out of control. The Social and Athletic Readjustment Rating Scale (SARRS) is a commonly used instrument to systematically assess the psychosocial influence on athletes' health problems.[31] SARRS is an adaptation of the Social Readjustment Rating Scale (SRRS) that measures social events and life situations in nonathletic individuals.[32] Significant life events include the death of a close family member, a jail term, trouble with in-laws, changes in eating habits, or a vacation. When the SRRS was revised to the SARRS,

modifications were made to make the scale more relevant to the athletic population. Additional measurements introduced to the SARRS scaling system include entering college, trouble with a coach, a sibling leaving home, changing to a new athletic position, and loss of playing time because of injury or illness. The sum score of the SARRS can be used as a measure of turmoil and stress in the athlete's life; the greater the SARRS score, the more likely an athlete will sustain an injury.

The possible relationship between athletic injuries and the magnitude of significantly perceived life change events has been investigated within a collegiate football team.[33] The injured group was defined as those players who missed three or more practices or one or more games because of a specific injury. Players who suffered from a major time-loss injury had significantly higher SARRS scores than uninjured players. The injury rate for players with low SARRS scores (0 to 399) was 30%; with medium scores (400 to 799), the injury rate was 50%; and with high scores (800 or greater), the injury rate was 73%. The researchers found a positive correlation between the scores on the SARRS and the probability of injury.

FOCUS ON . . .

Research of Life Events and General Well-Being Scale

Life events are also contributors to injury. The Social and Athletic Readjustment Rating Scale (SARRS) is an adaptation of the Social Readjustment Rating Scale that measures social events and life situations. Players with major injuries have shown higher SARRS scores than noninjured players, and athletes with high scores had more frequent (but not more severe) injuries than those with low scores.

When SARRS was administered to athletes in a variety of different sports, the findings included the fact that the greater the life change score, the more likely the player was to become ill or injured during the season. Athletes with higher SARRS scores performed more poorly than those with lower scores. Thus, the frequency of an athlete's health problems appeared to be more sensitive to life change events than either duration or severity of injury. Negative life events seemed to be more strongly associated with health problems than positive events, but the SARRS is heavily weighted for negative events. Also, scores differed by sport: for example, basketball players had higher scores than figure skaters. Age was another factor: younger athletes had higher scores, and each sport had a predictive age range (therefore, the difference between sport groups was more a function of age than of sport). Younger athletes who have not yet learned the physical and psychological coping skills needed to overcome setbacks in performance, injury, stress, and illness, should be taught these skills.

The US Alpine Ski Teams were studied with the SARRS, the Life Events Scale for Adolescents (LESA), the General Well-Being Scale (GWBS), the Zung Depression Scale (ZDS), and the Health, Injury, and Performance Survey. Scores on the SARRS and LESA predicted the frequency of ear, nose, and throat problems, which are common in skiers. High life change scores were also associated with the use of tobacco and drugs. Scores on the GWBS were negatively correlated with health problems, and depression scores were significantly correlated with the amount of time the individual spent worrying and with increased use of nonprescription substances. Higher scores on the life change scales were related to greater duration of ear, nose, and throat problems, headaches, musculoskeletal leg injuries, and sleep problems. However, positive well-being was associated with a shorter duration of ear, nose, and throat problems, headaches, anxiety, digestive problems, sleep disturbances, and neurologic conditions. Overall, the scales predicted seven of the 10 most frequent health and injury problems in these skiers. The GWBS was the most sensitive instrument for subsequent health problems and injuries during the competitive season. Based on the ZDS, 22% of the athletes were clinically depressed, and they were more than twice as likely to drop off the team as the nondepressed athletes. The athlete's general well-being correlated with performance such that athletes with higher scores tended to maintain their positions or move up and those with lower scores showed performance reductions. The researchers concluded that life changes, depression, uncontrolled emotions, increased tension, and lower life satisfaction may affect an athlete's injury, illness, and performance potential, but even though these variables were statistically and clinically significant, they did not account for a large amount of the variance. Therefore, these psychological factors were only some of the potential contributors in the overall change in athletes' health status.

Injuries related to life events may be the second most significant source of injury because of impaired concentration on environmental cues that are crucial in the athletic arena.

Three additional hypotheses related to SARRS scores have been tested.[33] The first hypothesis predicted that SARRS scores for injured athletes would be significantly greater than scores for uninjured athletes. The second hypothesis predicted that football players with high SARRS scores would experience a greater frequency of injury than football players with lower scores. The third hypothesis predicted that football players with high SARRS scores experienced more severe injuries than football players with low stress scores. The mean stress score (total points on the SARRS) for uninjured players was 467.

The mean stress score for injured players was 622. Players who have scores that are less than the median of 500 points were injured 38.5% of the time. Players whose scores were greater than the median were injured 68% of the time. The researchers concluded that college football players who experienced a high level of change were at greater risk for injury than were players who experienced a low level of change.

Based on the above data, the results of this research project supported two of the three hypotheses. A high level of change did predispose college football players to a greater risk of sustaining multiple injuries during the season, but a high level of life change did not place college football players at a greater risk of sustaining a major injury than players whose life change levels were low.

Another modification of SARRS is the Life Events Scale for Adolescents (LESA).[34] This scale provides a score for family life events, undesirable events, desirable events, and an object loss score. The object loss score is the sum of the weighted items that relate to the possible or real loss of a person close to the athlete. Research findings involving high school football players indicated that players who experienced more family instability were more likely to sustain a significant injury.[34] This was particularly true for those athletes who experienced parental illness, separation, divorce, and death.

The Athletic Life Experience Survey (ALES) is a modification of the LESA.[35,36] The ALES is composed of various positive and negative life events. A major goal of this study was to examine the effect of several moderator variables. A moderator variable is a variable that affects another variable, specifically general trait anxiety, competitive trait anxiety, and locus of control.[37-39] The subjects consisted of 104 college varsity football players from two universities. One group was from a Division II institution, and the other group was from a Division I school, which tend to have more talented athletes. Athletic injury was determined by time lost from practice and games. The results of this study showed that the moderator variables did not assist in predicting the rate of injury. When the two teams were examined separately, the Division II school demonstrated a positive correlation between increasing negative life changes and injury. There was also a trend toward a significant positive relationship when object loss was considered. However, the Division II school athletes did not demonstrate a significant relationship between any of the isolated variables. Although it was not an original hypothesis, this study was able to confirm that total life change scores for the Division II team demonstrated a predictive relationship between life events scores and injury. This relationship has been supported in other studies.[31] However, no such relationship existed for the athletes from the Division I institution. The researchers concluded that life events scales were not predictive of injury potential. This was a confusing statement because, for unknown reasons, a different scale was used in other studies to measure life event changes.[35]

Originally, all investigators employing the life event model had examined only football players in the United States and had only evaluated injuries. The SARRS is now administered to a diverse range of athletes.[40] Participants include members of the national gymnastics, figure skating, basketball, biathlon, and race walking teams training at the US Olympic Training Center. One year after taking the SARRS, participants are mailed a Health, Injury, and Performance Survey that was specifically developed for this study and, subsequently, is correlated with the scores on the SARRS. Significant relationships have been found between the SARRS and the Health, Injury, and Performance Survey indicating that the greater an individual's life change scores, the more likely it is that the individual will become ill or injured during the season.[40] A significant statistical correlation has been found between life change scores and frequency of headaches, musculoskeletal leg and foot problems, anxiety, weight changes, and use of nonprescription substances. Duration and severity of musculoskeletal problems and nonprescription substance use have been associated with increased changes in life events. In addition, individuals with higher SARRS scores perform more poorly than athletes whose lives are more stable. The frequency of an athlete's health problems appears to be more sensitive to life change events than to duration or severity of injury.

Results of a study that examined the function of life events as a predictor of future health, injury, and performance difficulties statistically indicated that negative life changes seemed to be more strongly related to health problems than positive life changes.[40] However, the researchers suggested that the SARRS may be heavily weighted toward negative events. Consequently, a conclusion could not be established concerning the influence of negative events on athlete injury. An additional finding determined that athletes' scores on the life event rating scale differed by sport; for example, basketball players had a mean SARRS score of 773, and figure skaters had a mean score of 371. Younger athletes had higher scores, and each sport had a predictive age range. The different SARRS mean scores between sport groups was a function of age rather than of the actual sport. The study suggests that younger athletes might be more vulnerable to stress. This finding contradicts previous theories that suggest that older individuals are more susceptible to illness and injury as a result of an accumulation of significant life events.[40] Younger athletes may not have yet learned the physical and psychological coping skills necessary to overcome injury, stress, illness, and setbacks in performance. In order to cope with such events, coaches should train young athletes to improve their coping skills as an effective means of helping them decrease stress and thus avoid injury, illness, and performance decrements.

Besides life events, other significant psychological factors have been correlated to an athlete's health and injury.[41] The SARRS, LESA, the General Well-Being Scale (GWBS), the Zung Depression Scale (ZDS), and the Health, Injury, and Performance Survey have been used in several studies to quantify a range of psychosocial variables.[42,43] The GWBS is a screening instrument that assesses an individual's concern for physical health problems, energy level, life satisfaction, cheerfulness, tension, and degree of emotional control. The Health, Injury, and Performance Survey gathers information from athletes regarding illness, injury, and performance level throughout the course of their competitive season. Athletes with higher scores on the LCES or lower scores on the GWBS are expected to experience a greater number of health and injury problems. Athletes with higher GWBS scores and lower SARRS scores experience a smaller number of health and injury problems. No specific predictions regarding depression were made in the use of the ZDS. The men's and women's US Alpine Ski Teams provided the researchers with a sample of internationally successful athletes with whom they had maintained a high level of contact and rapport, allowing for more accurate and consistent reporting.[41]

Results of this study indicated that life events, general well-being, and depression scale scores were significantly related to many health or injury problems reported on the Health, Injury, and Performance Survey.[41] Specifically, scores on the SARRS and the LESA predicted the frequency of ear, nose, and throat problems, which are common illnesses for skiers. The study also showed a significant correlation between life change scores and an athlete's use of nonprescription substances such as tobacco and drugs. GWBS scores were negatively correlated with health problems; high well-being scores were related to better health. Depression scores were significantly correlated with the amount of time the athlete spent worrying and with increases in the use of nonprescription drugs and substances. Findings regarding the duration of health and injury problems were particularly high. Higher scores on the life change scales were related to greater duration of ear, nose, and throat problems, as well as headaches, musculoskeletal leg injuries, and sleep problems. Conversely, positive well-being was associated with a shorter duration of ear, nose, and throat problems, and headaches, anxiety, digestive problems, sleep disturbances, and neurologic conditions. Overall, the four scales predicted seven of the 10 most frequent health and injury problems of alpine skiers.

Of the various methodologies used, the GWBS was the most useful scale in predicting potential injury and health problems experienced by athletes during the competitive season.[41] Based on scores obtained using the ZDS, an above average number of athletes (22%) were clinically depressed. The depressed athletes, as assessed before the season, had a dropout rate of 50% from the sport in comparison to a 21% dropout rate for athletes who were not identified as depressed. Moreover, the athletes' general well-being also correlated with performance during the season; individuals with a higher well-being score generally maintained their position on the team or moved to a higher position. Athletes whose performance decreased had lower well-being scores at the beginning of the season.

The authors of this study suggest that elite athletes are as susceptible as nonathletes to the emotional stresses and concurrent depression that all populations experience, and are, perhaps, more susceptible. Athletes are individuals first and athletes second. Although they do not account for a large degree of variance, life changes, depression, uncontrolled emotions, increased tension, and lower life satisfaction may have an effect on an athlete's injury, illness, and performance potential. These psychological variables are only a few examples of potential contributing factors that may influence the health status of an athlete. How these psychological factors play a role in an overall psychological program is part of a proposed consultation model.44-47 It is important to examine how these factors affect the athlete's health and performance rather than just superficially teaching him or her performance-enhancing skills.

Personality Studies

Certain personality characteristics have been studied as they relate to injury predisposition; however, this evidence is less convincing than the evidence related to an athlete's life events and general well-being. In one study, physiologic and psychological components of injury in 110 football players from six high schools were evaluated.[48] Joint flexibility was not a significant predictor of future injury. The 16PF Personality Inventory yields 16 scores representing different personality traits and has been employed to predict football injuries.[49] The personality variables are contrasted so that an individual is identified as being on one side of a continuum or on the other. For example, the scales include reserved versus outgoing, assured versus apprehensive, and trusting versus suspicious demeanors. One significant difference between

FOCUS ON . . .

Personality Studies

The 16PF Personality Inventory has been used to predict injuries. Tender-minded, dependent, overprotected, and sensitive football players were more likely to be injured than the tough-minded, self-reliant, and no-nonsense players. Also, players who were reserved had more severe injuries than those who were outgoing. When undergraduate runners were studied, and sex was considered a variable, three personality factors predicted injury: humbleness versus assertiveness, practicality versus imagination, and lack of discipline versus control. The author suggested that female athletes were more assertive and practical, but less disciplined when compared with male athletes, and therefore experienced more injuries.

A follow-up study of male runners at the end of a race demonstrated that injured runners were less tough-minded than uninjured runners. Also, injured runners appeared to be less forthright than uninjured runners.

Most studies to date support the notion that the individual athlete's psychological status plays a significant role in the onset of health and injury problems, but more research is needed.

injured and uninjured players was that the tender-minded, dependent, overprotected, and sensitive players were more likely to be injured than were the tough-minded, self-reliant, and no-nonsense players. A second difference was that athletes with a reserved demeanor experienced more severe injuries than players with outgoing demeanors.

In another study in which the 16PF Inventory was used, 42 male and 24 female undergraduate students who were actively participating in running sports were examined.[50] Each group was divided into injured and uninjured subgroups. According to the study, a greater percentage of female runners were injured than male runners. When gender was excluded as a factor, there were no measures significantly correlated to injury. However, when considering gender as a variable, three personality factors appear to be predictive of injury. The first factor was a humble versus assertive demeanor. Male runners fell into the normal range on this scale with a mean score of 5.5. Female runners tended to be more assertive than male runners concerning this factor with a mean score of 6.4. The next factor, practical versus imaginative demeanor, had the same type of relationship. Men fell into the average range with a mean score of 5.2, whereas women were more practical with a mean score of 4.3. For the third factor, undisciplined versus controlled scale, the men's mean score was 6.3, indicating greater control than the women, who had a mean score of 4.4. These results suggest that women are more assertive and practical, but less disciplined, when compared to men and may experience more injuries.

In a follow-up study that used the 16PF Inventory scale, 41 male runners responded to a questionnaire that was distributed at the end of a race.[51] In this study, injured runners were classified as being less tough-minded than uninjured runners. The average score on the tough-minded versus tender-minded measure was 6.03 for the injured runners and 4.53 for uninjured runners. A second injury-related variable used in this study was a forthright versus shrewd demeanor. Injured runners appeared to be less forthright and had a mean score of 5.20. Uninjured runners had a mean score of 3.80. However, these variables were not reflected in the previous study using the 16PF Personality Inventory.

Most studies support the notion that the psychological status of the individual athlete plays a significant role in the onset of injury and health problems. More research is needed with specific focus on the psychology of the athlete and improved assessment techniques when evaluating his or her physical injuries or health problems.

PSYCHOLOGICAL SEQUELAE OF INJURY

There has been minimal amounts of research performed investigating psychological reactions to injury. One of the possible explanations for lack of research in this area is that the physical impact of injury is more apparent and therefore becomes the focus of care. Nevertheless, compassionate, empathic athletic trainers, physicians, physical therapists, or coaches are typically aware of an athlete's emotional reactions. Lack of compassion and empathy can worsen an athlete's psychological reaction to an injury. Athletes usually become depressed following injury, experiencing fear of reinjury or future injuries. Many injured athletes have concerns about being able to return to their prior level of function in the sport. Also, they may experience a distorted body image and lowered self-esteem following an injury. Frequently, practitioners who treat such athletes may mistake these reactions as normal, take them for granted, or believe them to be temporary and insignificant and that the emotional reactions will just spontaneously cease or that addressing psychological reactions is not critical to the rehabilitation process.

Another possible explanation for lack of research about psychological reaction to injury is that the health professionals who treat injuries may tend to be technical in their assessment and treatment approach, overlooking the athlete's emotional status or viewing it as irrelevant. This group of practitioners tend to only focus on caring for the injury. The athlete is viewed only as a body or a piece of mechanical equipment.

A third possible reason for the lack of research regarding psychology and injury is that an injured athlete has little motivation to be evaluated psychologically for research purposes. Understandably, the athlete wants to recover from the injury or illness and return to his or her sport as soon as possible rather than dwell on the negative experience. Once injured, the athlete's psychological reactions can be quite varied and debilitating. Anxiety, depression,

FOCUS ON . . .

Psychological Sequelae of Injury

There is surprisingly little controlled research investigating psychological reactions to injury, which may be due to the focus on the physical impact of injury, the mechanistic approach of the health professional, or the athlete's desire to recover and return to play rather than dwelling on the psychological impact.

One model describing the psychological impact of injury is the ABC model: affect (feelings and sensations shaping the quality of life), behavior (the injury itself and the related activity after the injury occurred), and cognition (conscious and unconscious thoughts). The goal for recovery is synchronization of these spheres within each injured athlete, without allowing one sphere to dominate.

loss of self-esteem, loss of peer group, and changes in perception of aging can have a major impact on an injured athlete. The injured athlete must realize that these are common reactions to injury and that it is important to remain optimistic during recovery by recognizing and paying attention to basic psychological factors.

One such model of basic psychological factors is the ABCs of Psychology and Rehabilitation from Injury as shown in **Table 18-5**[52] ABC stands for "Affect," "Behavior," and "Cognitions," which helps identify the patient's feelings, actions, and thoughts. The goal for recovery is to synchronize the three ABC psychological spheres during rehabilitation. At times, too much focus is put on how the injury occurred or just the physical part of rehabilitation. At other times, the clinician's own feelings become too intense and too negative, and the patient gets discouraged or gives up. In addition, an athlete's thoughts about the injury and returning to sport can be consuming, draining time and energy that are needed for recovery. Each area of the ABCs must be tracked to make sure the patient is improving in a balanced psychological fashion.

Emotional manifestations of injury have been outlined clinically.[53-59] **Table 18-6** presents a checklist that reviews some of the physical, emotional, and behavioral signs and symptoms the injured athlete may experience. The list is by no means exhaustive; however, the table emphasizes the significance of potential symptoms, problems, and clinical significance of the psychological ramifications of injury.[60,61] The frequency, intensity, and duration of these factors vary, but this checklist can be effectively used to evaluate the athlete's psychological reaction to an injury.

SEQUENCE OF EMOTIONAL REACTIONS

Injured individuals tend to follow five basic steps of a core emotional reaction that is independent of the nature or origin of the injury.[62]

Step 1. The individual experiences shock and numbness characterized by a lack of anxiety about the injury, which is due to a lack of comprehension about the severity and permanence of the injury.

Step 2. The athlete implicitly denies the severity of the injury and is not highly motivated to participate in treatment. The athlete also experiences excessive optimism about recovery potential.

Step 3. The athlete experiences an increased emotional liability, particularly depression and anxiety.

Step 4. The athlete becomes partially adapted to and gradually accepts the body's limitations.

Step 5. The athlete adapts and accepts the injury and moves on with his or her life.

During periods of depression and anxiety, the athlete typically experiences sadness, mourning the loss of previous capabilities. The athlete is also anxious about recovery, the ability to return to the sport, and the effects the injury has on the family.[62]

Table 18-7 shows the characteristics of Kubler-Ross' five emotional stages following a traumatic event.[63] Although these reactions are very common in injured athletes, it is not always a stepwise progression. These stages give the athletic trainer broad categories to be aware of when assessing an injured athlete, but response varies with each injured athlete and the stages may not apply to all situations or all athletes. It is more important to be aware of the emotional reactions of the individual patient.

The psychological response to injury depends on three factors. The first factor, prior level of psychological functioning, suggests that the better an individual was functioning before the injury, the better he or she will function after the injury. The second factor takes into consideration the nature and duration of the disability and the lifestyle changes that result from it. The third factor focuses on the meaning of the disability to the patient. These variables

---

TABLE 18-5
ABCs OF PSYCHOLOGY AND REHABILITATION FROM INJURY

Trait	Definition	Example
Affect	Feelings and sensations shaping the quality of life	Negative emotions associated with injury or positive emotions associated with recovery
Behavior	The actual injury and the related activity after the injury occurred	What can be done to recover during rehabilitation
Cognition	Conscious and unconscious thoughts	Thoughts and dreams during recovery

TABLE 18-6
SIGNS AND SYMPTOMS OF PSYCHOLOGICAL REACTIONS TO PHYSICAL INJURY

Physical signs and symptoms	Emotional/cognitive signs and symptoms	Behavioral signs and symptoms
Pain	Mood fluctuations	Continues to train even though medically, vocationally, or socially contraindicated
Muscle spasm	Distractibility	Tendency to overtrain
Hypersensitivity to pain	Hyperexcitation	Difficulty training
Ignoring pain	Guilt	Decrease in athletic performance
Pounding of the heart	Fear	Isolation
Dryness of the throat or mouth	Frustration	Increased use of alcohol
Insomnia, an inability to fall or stay asleep, or early awakenings	Dependency	Increased use of nonprescription drugs
Frequent or lingering cold viruses	Depression	Increased use of various medications, such as tranquilizers or amphetamines
	Boredom	
Trembling and nervous tics	Restlessness	Shopping for a physician
Grinding of the teeth	Stagnation	Taking analgesics before exercise
Increase or decrease in appetite	Overpowering urge to cry, run, or hide	Increased use of tobacco
Increased sweating		Less time for recreation
Frequent need to urinate	Difficulty relaxing	Less time for intimacy with others
Diarrhea	Need to generate excitement over and over	Less vacation time
Constipation		Overworked, but cannot say no to more work without feeling guilty
Indigestion, stomach queasiness	Feeling unappreciated or used	
Vomiting	Inability to laugh at own self	
Increased premenstrual tension	Increased feeling or expression of anger or being cynical	Hypermotility (increased tendency to move about without any reason)
Missed menstrual cycle	Inability to concentrate	
Headache	Disenchantment	Inability to take a physically relaxed attitude, sitting quietly in a chair or lying on a sofa
Weakness	Feeling of unreality	
Dizziness	Feeling life is not much fun	
Weight gain or loss	Not enjoying the sport	Feeling that sexual intimacy is more trouble than it is worth
Shortness of breath	Denial that anything is wrong	
Stuttering or other speech difficulties	Reduced body image	Feeling sexually inadequate
Increased pitch in voice	Reduced vigor	
Nervous laughter	Reduced self-esteem	
	Feeling ashamed	

(Continued)

are related to several of the factors discussed earlier regarding the onset of health and injury problems and reinforce the need to view and treat the whole person rather than the isolated physical injury.[62]

In a multifaceted, practical, comprehensive model of response to injury from which the injured athlete can be evaluated, the role of several moderator variables, such as personality, coping resources, history of stressors, and intervention, are considered (**Figure 18-4**).[64] This model describes several mediators that affect the process from injury to physical and psychological outcome, such as injury characteristics and individual differences, sport-specific factors, and interaction with the sports medicine team. Finally, the model outlines how the individual assesses the injury and how he or she emotionally and behaviorally responds to it.

Early research recognized the significance and benefits of holistic treatment approaches by emphasizing treating the mind as well as the body.[65] An important link exists between self-esteem and body image. When individuals lose control of their body, such as through injury, self-image becomes markedly decreased, especially in young

TABLE 18-6
SIGNS AND SYMPTOMS OF PSYCHOLOGICAL REACTIONS TO PHYSICAL INJURY (CONTINUED)

Physical signs and symptoms	Emotional/cognitive signs and symptoms	Behavioral signs and symptoms
Muscle tension	Feeling vulnerable	Speaking up less and less at gatherings and then only speaking negatively
Soreness	Vivid imagination	Difficulty setting goals
	Distrust	A tendency to be easily startled by small sounds
	Desire to quit the team	Finding oneself farther behind at the end of each day
	Feeling afraid of things such as loss of position on the team, permanent injury, or reduction of physical activity	Forgetting deadlines and appointments
	Free-floating anxiety; the athlete is afraid of something but does not know exactly what it is	Accident proneness
	Feeling pressure to always succeed	Making foolish mistakes
	Hyperalertness, a feeling of being "keyed up"	Poor workout
	Automatic expression of negative feelings	Blaming equipment for poor performance
	Disappointment in him- or herself or others	Decay in interpersonal relationships
	Increased rationalization	Withdrawal from sport, teammates, peers
	Feeling indispensable or dispensable	Social withdrawal
	Obsessed with recurring thoughts	
	Unable to enjoy or compliment colleagues' successes	
	Fault finding	
	Nightmares	
	Excessive concern for physical health	
	Grief response to loss/injury	

athletes. During childhood and adolescence, body image is a significant component of self-identity because other personal traits important to self-esteem, such as linguistic abilities, writing skills, or professional skills, have yet to be developed. If an athlete loses necessary gross or fine motor control because of injury or illness, a decreased sense of self-esteem can occur secondary to a reduced body image. Even if this alteration is only temporary, its impact on rehabilitation and performance may be great. Rehabilitation programs designed for younger populations assist injured athletes in building or restoring self-esteem. By restoring control over the body, the young athlete is better able to regain skills critical to participation in his or her sport.

The relationship of injury, body image, and self-esteem continues throughout life. The impact of aging on body image during midlife and health-related problems experienced later in life has major emotional implications and affects treatment compliance and rehabilitation. Older recreational athletes frequently experience marked changes in psychological status and body image as they cease athletic activity or become injured. Active participa-

TABLE 18-7

KUBLER-ROSS EMOTIONAL STAGES FOLLOWING A TRAUMATIC EVENT

Stage	Characteristic
1—Shock and Denial	Patient disavows the injury or understates its magnitude; he or she fails to accept the physician's diagnosis.
2—Anger	Frustration, irritability, or anger manifesting the feeling of "Why me?"
3—Bargaining	The patient attempts to negotiate with the physician, athletic trainer, or even a higher being in return for a cure (for example, the athlete makes promises, gives to charity, or promises to go to church).
4—Depression	The patient demonstrates clinical signs of depression such as withdrawal, psychomotor retardation, sleep disturbance, hopelessness, or suicidal ideation.
5—Acceptance	Patient realizes the extent of the trauma and accepts the rehabilitation and functional limitations. The patient's mood may vary from neutral to euphoric.

tion in sport is a symbol of youth and vitality. Injury and lack of participation may signify aging and deterioration. This relationship may help explain why athletes with similar injuries often recover at different rates.[66,67]

POSTTRAUMATIC REACTIONS

Posttraumatic states experienced by individuals can be described in terms of functional and nonfunctional emotional reactions.[68] *Functional emotional reactions* are often associated with the possibility of receiving cash settlements or other types of financial or legal reimbursement and are reinforced by the individual feigning symptoms to increase the amount of the award. *Nonfunctional emotional reactions* are those directly related to the trauma and are characterized by the appearance of the symptoms 2 to 8 weeks after injury. **Table 18-8** presents a list of psychological posttraumatic reactions to injury.

Posttraumatic reactions do not appear to be related to gender, age, injury location, or personality. However, some distinct differences have been identified between individuals who experience posttraumatic reactions and those who do not. Individuals who experience posttraumatic reactions tend to be less prepared for an injury.[68] In addition, skiers tend to be injured on the last day of a holiday; industrial workers are most often injured on the last day of the week or just prior to a vacation. The injury, therefore, prevents individuals from returning to work or interferes with vacation plans.

Injured athletes who demonstrated posttraumatic reactions had more experience in their sport and tended to be in better condition than injured athletes who did not demonstrate posttraumatic reaction.[68] Injuries

sustained by athletes while skiing are often viewed as symbols of courage and audacity, which serves a counterphobic function.[68]

Fitness Fanatics

"Fitness fanatics," or individuals with athletic neurosis, are typically characterized as being men who are approximately age 40 years, who, unlike most athletes, do not report a long interest in physical achievement or athletic perfection. This population tends to have a history of significant childhood illnesses and disturbed interpersonal relationships.[69] When a fitness fanatic sustains an injury, the emotional reaction is marked by depression and anxiety, often proceeding to a psychological debilitating state. These patients are more resistant to various types of therapy, possibly because of psychological defense mechanisms and the inability to address crucial issues and implement appropriate changes.

PSYCHOLOGICAL TREATMENT AND REHABILITATION CONSIDERATIONS

Many physical symptoms that follow an injury can be exacerbated by psychological factors. Minor symptoms experienced by an athlete may resolve more quickly if the associated psychological problems are resolved.[70] Psychological factors that may influence an athlete should be evaluated. Engaging an athlete in conversation to find out about the athlete and his or her ambitions or speaking with the athlete's coach or teammates may provide valuable insight about the individual's psychological makeup.

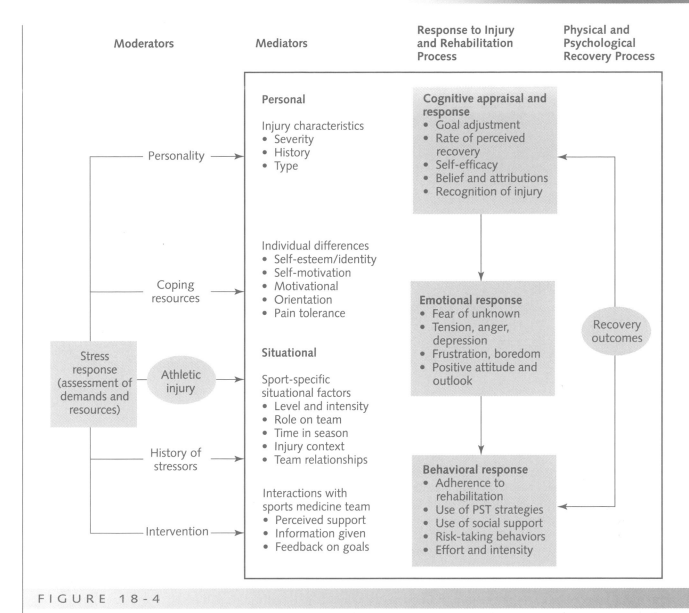

FIGURE 18-4

A multifaceted, comprehensive model of response to injury considers the role of several moderator variables. Abbreviation: T= psychological skills training. (Reproduced with permission from Wiese-Bjornstal DM, Smith AM, LaMott EE: A model of psychological response to athlete injury and rehabilitation. Athlet Train Sports Healthcare Perspect 1995;1:16-30.)

To gain an understanding of an athlete's potential psychological reactions that are experienced after an injury, it is important to understand what the physical symptoms mean to the patient.[70]

The rate of compliance, recovery, and performance is enhanced when the injured athlete develops trust in the caregiver.[70] Spending extra time speaking with the athlete to gain a complete history of the injury, symptoms, and any problems may be more useful in the rehabilitation process than a battery of medically related tests. Interpersonal communication between the patient and the caregiver leads to improved attitude, builds empathy, provides much needed emotional support, and makes the patient an active participant in the recovery process.[71] In contrast, factors that influence patient noncompliance fall into the categories of psychological factors, environmental and social factors that impact on the patient, characteristics of the therapeutic regimen, and properties of the physician-patient interaction.[72]

Educating and helping the patient become an informed and knowledgeable consumer is important to the rehabilitation process. The athlete needs to understand how the injury occurred, what to expect during and after rehabilitation, and how to assist in the recovery. Providing specific

TABLE 18-8

PSYCHOLOGICAL POST-TRAUMATIC REACTIONS TO INJURY

- Fatigue
- Irritability
- Sleep disturbances
- Difficulty concentrating
- Memory lapses
- Episodes of confusion
- Depression
- Gastrointestinal complaints

rehabilitation goals such as progressive range of motion targets and strength increases are also useful.[73] Factors that may interfere with effective rehabilitation include the following:[74]

- Lack of knowledge about the rehabilitation process
- Lack of skills at a particular rehabilitation task
- Perception that the risk of treatment outweighs the benefits
- Lack of social support

Social support can be enhanced through the following means:[75.]

- Developing a network of individuals with whom to share thoughts and feelings
- Nurturing and developing relationships
- Integrating social support systems into an ongoing program rather than using them only during the time of crisis

FOCUS ON . . .

Psychological Treatment and Rehabilitation Considerations

Psychological treatment and rehabilitation considerations include many factors specific to the individual. To learn about these, athletes should be engaged in conversation about themselves and their ambitions and speak with the coach and teammates.

The rate of compliance, recovery, and performance is enhanced when the injured athlete trusts the caregiver. Interpersonal communication provides much-needed emotional support and enlists the athlete as an active participant in the recovery process.

The athlete needs to understand what went wrong, what to expect, and what to do to assist in the recovery. Specific goals are useful. Factors that can interfere with effective rehabilitation include lack of knowledge about the rehabilitation process, lack of skills for a particular rehabilitation task, perception that the risk of treatment outweighs the benefits, and lack of social support. Social support can be enhanced by developing a network of individuals with whom to share thoughts and feelings, developing and nurturing relationships, and providing social support functions as part of an ongoing program rather than simply a reaction to crisis.

Athletes who adopt a positive mental attitude toward rehabilitation and assume an active role (setting goals and self-directing practice) feel in control and can view the injury and recovery as a learning process.

In a study of patients after knee surgery, three categories were included for successful rehabilitation: physical rehabilitation of the injured extremity, physiologic rehabilitation, and psychological rehabilitation. Lifestyle changes because of injury resulted in important physiologic and psychological consequences that needed to be addressed immediately after surgery. An important psychological component was the athletes' loss of control of their physical body or environment.

Three primary components make up the essential ingredients of rehabilitation. The first relates to physical factors. The athlete's physical status should be discussed before and after surgery in enough detail not to become overwhelming to the athlete; the possibility of returning to activity should be discussed as well. The second component involves vigorous exercise of uninjured parts of the body; this step is good for psychological rehabilitation. The third component involves active exercise of the injured extremity. The second and third components usually occur concurrently; however, implementation of the third component depends on the injury's severity and the complexity of the surgery.

An athlete's personality traits can affect the rehabilitation process. These traits include information seeking, altered level of self-confidence or self-esteem, varied speed of decision making, and extroversion-introversion.

Individuals who adopt a positive attitude toward rehabilitation and who assume an active role in rehabilitation tend to recover more quickly.[67] Goal-setting and self-directed practice resembling mental training are paramount in this process, providing the athlete with a sense of control.[67] An individual's sense of control over his or her destiny is the basis of the Model of Self Efficiency.[76,77] Viewing the injury and the subsequent rehabilitation as a learning process can help some athletes return to their sport with a high level of performance.[66]

Based on scores obtained from the Minnesota Multiphasic Personality Inventory (MMPI), nonathletic patients who scored high on the hysteria and hypochondriasis scales, although not reaching the pathologic level, showed less improvement 1 to 3 years after surgery than patients who had lower scores.[78] An additional finding of this study was that patients who expected to receive compensation or who were receiving compensation for their injury showed significantly worse results than those who were not expecting an award.[78]

In a study of patients after knee surgery, successful rehabilitation comprised three categories.[79] The first was the physical rehabilitation of the operated extremity. Second was the physiologic rehabilitation of the patient. Third was psychological rehabilitation. Changes in lifestyle brought on by the injury resulted in important physiologic and psychological consequences that required immediate postoperative attention. An important psychological component noted was that the athletes were no longer in control of their physicality or environment. It was important to the athletes to resume their exercise program immediately to recover their strength and stamina and feel in control.

The essential ingredients of rehabilitation include three primary areas.[80] The first component relates to physical factors. Before and immediately after surgery, the athlete's physical status should be discussed in detail without overwhelming the individual with too much information and the possibility of returning to activity should be explored.[81] Athletes should express their emotional reactions and discuss their fears regarding the injury and surgery. The athlete should also be provided with preliminary realistic information regarding the severity of the injury and what to expect in rehabilitation. The second stage, which begins immediately after surgery, involves vigorous exercise of the uninjured parts of the body. The purpose for this is partially for psychological rehabilitation; the exercises reestablish body image, self-esteem, and physical activity to combat fear, anxiety, and depression. The third component involves active exercise of the injured extremity, not only for physical conditioning. Although the second and third components usually occur concurrently, implementation of the third component is dependent on the severity of the injury and the complexity of the surgery.

In a study in which hand and wrist rehabilitation was examined, the most important psychological factor was to return the patient to his or her sport as soon as prudently possible.[82]

Because an athlete may experience extreme pressure while recovering from an injury, some personality traits may become more negative and rigid than normal and affect the relationship between the rehabilitation specialist and the athlete. The following are some of the psychological factors in athletes that impact the relationship with the physician, psychologist, coach, or athletic trainer:[25]

1. *Information seeking.* The athlete's desire to know what is happening is increased.

2. *Alteration of the level of confidence or self-esteem.* Self-confident individuals have difficulty trusting and listening to the opinion of others. They usually do things their own way, and when they are injured, this tendency may increase. Consequently, input from the care provider may be disregarded or devalued.

3. *Variation in speed of decision making.* Some individuals need more time to assimilate the information about their injury and rehabilitation, whereas others are better able to accept facts and continue with life more easily. The care provider must know the patient.

4. *Extroversion and introversion.* The more quiet and socially withdrawn an athlete is, the more this trait increases when the athlete is injured. Although the individual's need for isolation and privacy must be respected, the potential for depression must be evaluated and a complete patient history must be gathered. The extroverted athlete may exercise denial, become overly talkative, and appear jovial in an attempt to avoid the seriousness of the injury. A moderate amount of denial can be helpful in coping, unless it interferes with compliance.[3]

PAIN

Pain is a central negative feature associated with an injury and has a major effect on an athlete's emotional status, rehabilitation, and potential sport performance. Unfortunately, the effect of pain is often overlooked in the sports psychology literature. The International Association for the Study of Pain defines pain as a "sensory and emotional reaction that could be precipitated by an actual or anticipated injury."[83] Pain can be a result of damage to tissue or nerves and can be exacerbated by increased pressure on the injury site, inflammation, or muscle spasm. It can also result from a tenderness of the tissue. Pain may be dull or sharp and may be localized to the injury site or referred to

FOCUS ON . . .

Pain

Pain can result from damage to tissue or nerves and be made worse by pressure on the injury site, inflammation or muscle spasm. It begins as a biologic event that gives rise to a psychological perception of distress. Pain provides protective feedback, and how tolerant an individual is to pain can reflect how the person perceives pain. The longer pain lasts, the more likely is increased chronic psychological impairment (anxiety, fear, hopelessness, despair, depression). The individual with pain can feel out of control, which can be debilitating to self-esteem and confidence, and can experience problems with sleep, appetite, and sexuality. How well the athlete learns to cope with the pain will influence compliance with the physical rehabilitation program and return to sport.

The athlete's tolerance to pain increases as more information is provided and the athlete knows what to expect. Quantitative and qualitative assessments of pain are helpful to the healthcare professional in understanding the athlete's experience.

In addition to pharmacologic management of pain, psychological techniques are essential for recovery from injury. These include external focus of attention, pleasant activities, mental imagery, rhythmic cognitive activities, pain acknowledgment, and dramatized coping.

other areas of the body. Pain begins as a biologic event that leads to a psychological perception of distress.

Pain provides protective feedback to the injured individual. The perception of pain is a complex, subjective process that links together sensory input and personal interpretation.[60,73] The individual's ability to tolerate pain largely depends on how he or she perceives the pain experience.[84] In all sport activities, athletes must discriminate between the pain of exacerbation of minor aches and pains, the pain of an acute injury, and the recurring pain of an overuse injury or a chronic injury.

The longer the duration of the pain, the greater the probability of chronic psychological impairment. The sense of being out of control because of pain can be very debilitating to the athlete's self-esteem and confidence. Individual perception plays an important role in the experience of pain. The psychological impact of injury includes an increase in anxiety, fear, hopelessness, despair, and depression. Uncontrolled pain can affect sleep, appetite, and expression of sexuality. Ultimately, the athlete's ability to cope with pain may influence compli-

ance or noncompliance of the physical rehabilitation program, as well as his or her recovery and return to activity.

Helping the injured athlete attribute the discomfort to a normal and safe physiologic and psychological process, rather than taking it as a sign of possible damage or permanent disability, increases his or her pain tolerance.[85] When the procedure to be performed and the time frame necessary for recovery are described to the patient, pain tolerance tends to increase.[86,87] The more information an athlete understands about the rehabilitation treatment program, especially as it relates to the likelihood of causing pain and the effort needed for rehabilitation, the greater the individual's tolerance of pain and the greater the adherence to the rehabilitation program.

Pain perception can be described and assessed in both quantitative and qualitative terms.[60,73] A scale that measures pain quantitatively from 1 (no pain) to 10 (greatest possible pain) can be used, and the athlete can keep a daily pain log or the athletic trainer can record pain levels in the patient's medical file. Any specific activities that increase or decrease the level of pain should also be noted. Open-ended questions about the description of the pain will give an excellent qualitative evaluation of what the athlete is experiencing. Individual qualitative statements such as "like an electric shock," "feels numb," and "excruciating deep pain" will assist in evaluating what the athlete is experiencing. The experience of pain is a perception; therefore, the athlete's experience must be recognized. Nonverbal cues such as grimacing and muscular tightness also reflect the intensity of the pain and the individual's perception of it. Tolerance to pain is highly individual, and understanding the uniqueness of the pain reactions for each patient is critical to the psychological and physical rehabilitation.

Psychological and pharmacologic management of pain is essential for recovery from injury. Many sports psychology techniques used for performance enhancement can be applied to help control pain. Mental imagery, relaxation, goal setting, cognitive restructuring, stop-think, interpersonal conflict resolution, and active rest have been used for pain control and injury rehabilitation.[46] Clinical psychology techniques of systematic desensitization and repetitive positive affirmations are also beneficial for pain management and injury rehabilitation. The following six categories of pain management techniques have been identified:[8]

1. External focus of attention
2. Pleasant activities
3. Mental imaging
4. Rhythmic cognitive activities
5. Pain acknowledgment
6. Dramatized coping

Patients experiencing pain can gain relief by learning to redirect attention away from the experience of pain toward external environmental events and to employ an internal focusing technique such as the use of pleasant imagery. Having the patient engage in repetitive or systematic mental tasks (affirmations) also assists in pain control.[60,73,88]

Having injured athletes identify and engage in pleasant, fun activities during their rehabilitation program assists with the psychological adjustment and helps to decrease pain.[89] Social networking and interaction, whether perceived as support, fun, distracting, or time consuming, can also be very beneficial to pain management and rehabilitation. The pain of injury is inevitable; suffering can be reduced if the psychology of pain is understood and addressed during an athlete's rehabilitation.

PSYCHOLOGICAL CONSULTATION

On occasion, referral to a psychologist is not only beneficial, it is an ethical imperative. The following questions have been designed to assist health practitioners when deciding whether to refer an athlete to a psychologist. A "Yes" response to any of the following questions warrants referral to an appropriate professional:

1. Is the personality makeup of the athlete such that the support he or she needs is beyond my scope?

2. Is my own personality such that I prefer not to work with the psychological component after it reaches a certain level of complexity?

3. Does the patient's depression, anxiety, or fear appear to be of sufficient magnitude to warrant the help of a specialist?

During rehabilitation of an injury, addressing the psychological and social significance of athletics in the injured person's life is critical.[90] Narcissism must also be considered when conducting therapy with individuals who have suffered an orthopaedic injury. An injury may be perceived as a direct assault on the athlete's self-esteem, because the athlete may begin to perceive him- or herself as defective in some way. In addition, a person with an orthopaedic injury must adjust to a different body image, at least temporarily. Inactivity because of the injury results in a change in body style and may be difficult for a narcissistic individual to cope with, particularly when a large portion of the athlete's emotional stability and security are contingent on being physically fit.

In middle-aged adults, injury may also symbolize a person's declining personal and physical adequacy. Therapy for injured athletes should include a discussion of the role of athletic activity within the psychological and social adaptive pattern in the patient's life. Athletes should become aware of their physical self and how it relates to their personal development.

The meaning and connotations of the actual injury as interpreted by the patient must be identified. These

FOCUS ON . . .

Psychological Consultation

Psychological consultation is not only beneficial, but ethically imperative when the health practitioner answers "yes" to any of the following questions:

1. Is the athlete's personality such that the support needed is beyond my scope?

2. Is my own personality such that I prefer not to work with the psychological component once it reaches a certain level of complexity?

3. Do the depression, anxiety, or fears of the patient appear to be of sufficient magnitude to warrant the help of a specialist?

An injury may be perceived as an obvious defect, and thus, a direct assault on the athlete's self-esteem. The new (even if temporary) body image requires adjustment, and inactivity may result in a change in body style, which can be difficult for a narcissistic individual, especially when much of the athlete's emotional stability and security relied on physical fitness. Injury in middle-aged adults may symbolize declining personal and physical adequacy.

The meaning and connotations of the injury must be identified. These include interpretations of loss, fear of dependency, narcissistic disfigurement, fortified self-esteem, and incompetence. The healthcare practitioner must understand the role of the athlete's injury and, when necessary, assist the individual by identifying a broader range of personal strengths and competencies.

include the athlete's interpretation of loss, fear of dependency, narcissistic disfigurement, fortified self-esteem, and incompetence. The athlete's thoughts regarding the injury must be examined, and how the athlete perceives the meaning and symbolic importance of the injury and athletics as a whole must be understood. Practitioners should assist athletes who experience difficulty adapting to an injury by identifying a broader range of the patient's strengths and competencies.[90] This strategy allows the individual to be aware that self-esteem can be developed and maintained through other means. Occasionally, an athlete's career can be terminated by an injury. In this instance, the psychological transition from active involvement with a specific event or sport can be difficult.

PRESCRIPTION FOR PSYCHOLOGICAL INTERVENTION

Various strategies implemented by the health practitioner can help the athlete through the rehabilitation process

FOCUS ON . . .

Prescription for Psychological Intervention

General principles of psychological rehabilitation

General principles of psychological rehabilitation include early detection and intervention, establishing a positive relationship, providing continuity of care, offering small doses of information, and providing support throughout the rehabilitation process.

Specific guidelines for psychological rehabilitation

Specific guidelines include the need for medical evaluation, understanding the dynamics of exercise and the consequences of injury to the athlete, assessing developmental issues, exploring existing coping skills, and supporting moderation in rehabilitation and training.

Setting positive short-term, intermediate, and long-term goals with specific ways of achieving them will help the athlete develop a regular routine. Focus should be on the process, methods, and tasks of achieving goals rather than on their attainment.

Goals can be divided into two categories. Wish or performance goals help to motivate and give a sense of mission, but thinking about them does not produce direct improvement. Process or task goals are measurable and fall into four types: physical conditioning, sport-specific technique, mental skills, and personal and social.

Social support is crucial, not only maintaining the pre-injury network, but also developing new interests and social contacts. Optional thinking allows athletes to keep their minds open to possibilities rather than limitations, to consider new ideas, and to be creative in solving problems. Both the athlete and the healthcare professional should become more aware of pleasant activities and fun outside of sport. Fun experiences bring many positive benefits for life and rehabilitation, and people who know how to have fun have more satisfying relationships and enjoy life to the fullest.

Thinking optimistically allows the athlete to progress successfully through the rehabilitation process. Guiding the individual to task-relevant activities, such as relaxation for pain control and physical exercise for the uninjured portion of the body, promotes physical activity and maintains self-esteem.

Visualizing a sport and practicing it mentally prepares the athlete for return to sport, as does paying attention to diet, fitness, and healthy lifestyle behaviors. Providing reading material about the psychology of injury can also be helpful.

and, potentially, prevent injuries from occurring. The practitioner can target many of these techniques at reducing the athlete's negative feelings associated with the perceived loss of self-control.

General Principles of Psychological Rehabilitation

Early detection and intervention

Changes in physical, emotional, and behavioral signs and symptoms of an athlete related to psychological reactions to injury must be detected early (see Table 18-6). Counseling of the athlete should begin as soon as a clinical sign or symptom is observed. Once fixed in the athlete's mind, the psychological reactions are more difficult to treat.

A positive relationship

During consultation with the athlete, the practitioner should establish a positive relationship with the athlete. The practitioner can accomplish this by listening with interest to the athlete, placing him- or herself on an equal plane with the athlete, being flexible in the treatment plan, and altering the treatment plan to fit the athlete's needs. The practitioner should also empathize with the patient and acknowledge the athlete's feelings, be open minded, and consider the athlete's ideas as both try to solve problems.

Continuity of care

Injured individuals may experience a sequence of reactions such as alarm, denial, depression, anxiety, or a quick, temporary feeling that the injury is minor and will not require medical attention. An athlete's reaction to an injury may differ depending on the situation: the time of the accident, before surgery, after surgery, during hospital recovery, on return home, on resumption of normal daily activities, or on return to sports activity. A single appointment with the patient may not give the practitioner adequate insight of the injured athlete's psychological status. Also, a single interview rarely provides sufficient information necessary to assist the athlete.

Small doses of information

The athlete should be given adequate, specific information; however, the athlete should not be overloaded with too much information. Under the stress of injury, the ability to listen, input information, and recall directions is significantly impaired. Giving support, care, and advice in small doses over time has a higher probability of having a positive impact. The practitioner may have seen the type of injury in his or her practice many times; however, this may be a new experience for the patient.

Provide support

The practitioner should support the injured athlete throughout the rehabilitation process by making frequent brief visits to the hospital and outpatient sessions and by making occasional check-up telephone calls. The practitioner should also be sure to listen to the athlete and avoid asking suggestive questions such as, "Are you feeling better?" Instead, it is better to ask the question, "How are you feeling?"

Specific Guidelines for Psychological Rehabilitation

Physical evaluation

The athlete should be screened medically, especially if he or she is referred by a physician for psychological evaluation and treatment. The treatment team, consisting of a physician, an athletic trainer, a physical therapist, a psychologist, and others, must keep in contact with one another and share information concerning the patient.

Understand the dynamics

The practitioner must understand the underlying reasons for, and the importance of, an athlete's exercise program and how the athlete perceives the consequences of the injury. The practitioner should also understand the meaning and connotations of the injury itself. For instance, does the athlete who exercises for fitness now worry about being unhealthy? The younger athlete usually participates in sports for fun, competition, and peer interaction. Does an injured adolescent soccer player feel the loss of friends and a competitive outlet? After experiencing an injury, most athletes struggle with the loss of independence during rehabilitation. The practitioner must work with the athlete to find alternative activities that can be healthful, fun, competitive, and social, depending on the needs of the patient.

Assess developmental issues

The psychology associated with an athlete's injury must always be considered in the context of the individual's age range. To a younger athlete, an injury may symbolize rejection by his or her peer group, whereas for a middle-aged recreational athlete, an injury could signify aging and declining physical adequacy.

Explore existing coping skills

While treating an injury, the practitioner should try to discover what coping skills the athlete used successfully in the past and apply them to the athlete's rehabilitation program. Activities, support sources, successful coping strategies from the past, and currently established strategies may be beneficial tools when treating an injury. The range of the athlete's personal strengths, competencies, coping strategies, and ego defenses should be explored in depth. Moreover, the practitioner should help the athlete develop new coping strategies. For example, for an athlete who is unable to run, finding other appropriate movement activities such as swimming or walking that make the athlete feel physically expressive can increase the athlete's ability to cope.

Support moderation

The practitioner should evaluate the intensity level of the athlete's feelings and help the athlete place these feelings on a continuum with moderation being the goal. In addition to focusing on training and rehabilitation, the athlete needs to develop a broad base of interests and activities. Some patients become too focused, a fact that frequently predisposes the individual to injury from the outset. Moderation can be fun and enjoyable; however, it may become difficult for a marathon runner to go back to running a 10K race. An athlete can moderate an activity and still enjoy it by focusing on the process of jogging or running instead of the intensity or distance. The athlete should participate at a level that maintains the positive aspects of recreation and not expand the program into a negative addiction.

Set goals

The athlete should develop a regular exercise routine and include goals and methods of achieving psychological and physical improvement. The goals need to be set in a positive way with specific methods of trying to achieve them. Setting the goal "I want to feel better" and then not having a means of achieving it is not productive. Primarily, the athlete must focus on the process, methods, and tasks of achieving goals rather than constantly measuring whether they are being achieved. Goals can be short-term, intermediate, and long-term, and improvement can be made in small, incremental steps. Small improvements in the athlete's psychological and physical well-being should be recognized and applauded. The athlete and practitioner should appreciate positive milestones. If the practitioner only focuses on the unimproved areas, it is easy for the athlete to become disillusioned and depressed.

Much of psychological recovery depends on how the athlete perceives his or her environment. It can be helpful to have the athlete separate goals into two categories. The first category should include the athlete's wish or performance goals (to make a team, win a match, be in the top five, or completely recover from an injury). These goals help motivate the athlete and give a sense of mission; however, thinking about them does not produce direct improvement. The second category includes process or task goals and can be divided into four subcategories: physical conditioning goals, sport-specific techniques goals, mental skills goals, and personal and social goals. These areas are important to the athlete's performance and rehabilitation improvement and tend to be more measurable so the athlete can see and feel progress and remain encouraged. For example, a skier may work on explosive power, entering a gate, improving focus, and balancing school and social activities. Task goals allow the athlete to develop specific methods to reach his or her goals, such as plyometrics, practice entering a gate, mental rehearsal of exploding through the gate, and setting study time and calling a friend.

An athlete who is in rehabilitation after a knee injury may set the following task goals:

- *Physical conditioning:* riding a stationary bike for 30 minutes with moderate intensity
- *Sport-specific technique:* using only the uninjured leg early in rehabilitation, followed by light cycling with the injured limb
- *Mental skills:* visualizing the injury healing or practicing the sport through mental imaging
- *Personal and social:* spending more time with friends or focusing more on a project at school, work, or home[3]

Social support

Another critical aspect of rehabilitation for an athlete is finding appropriate support systems. During recovery, the athlete should spend time with family, friends, and colleagues, even though time may be spent differently with each group. Often, after an injury, an athlete may stop performing certain daily activities. Also, injured athletes must discover new interests and social contacts. These new interests can be either intellectual or physical pursuits, such as finally reading a book that has been put off or pursuing other sports that do not interfere with the injury. Although physical movement is important for fostering a balance between physical and emotional health and a high quality of life, the specific physical activity is not important. Erroneously, patients often think that their chosen recreational activity is the only one that can fill their needs. By focusing narrowly, many athletes may not get to experience life fully.

Optional thinking

An important concept of recovery from injury is "*optional thinking.*" Individuals who recover quickly and more fully keep their minds open to possibilities rather than limitations. Athletes should be encouraged to think optimistically rather than pessimistically. Frequently, recreational activity is the most important thing to an individual. Therefore, the injured athlete may think it must be the most important thing to everyone else. The fact is that there are 5.7 billion people in the world and only a few million participate in sports. The athlete must be open to new ideas and be creative in the problem-solving approach during rehabilitation.

Develop pleasant activities

Collaboratively, the practitioner and the injured athlete should develop a list of potential pleasant alternative activities that the patient is encouraged to participate in daily. The athlete should engage in situations and interactions that are fun and enjoyable. Examples of these include routine daily activities that the individual may not realize bring pleasure, such as taking a shower or enjoying scenery. Activities that the athlete is more conscious of include talking to friends, watching movies, playing board games, and engaging in sexual contact.[91] The injured athlete must develop a heightened sense of awareness of pleasant sensations derived from activities other than sports. Many athletes who are injured have identified participation in sport activities as their only source of pleasure.

Encourage the athlete to have fun

The importance of talking to the injured athlete about having fun cannot be overstated. Having fun is one of the most critical aspects of athletic performance.[89] Clearly, the athlete must be committed to a vigorous practice schedule to succeed in his or her sport or rehabilitation from injury. Although a strong commitment to succeed is important, all work and no play can make an athlete more than "dull." An athlete without a balanced life may experience boredom, further illness or injury, or lack of productivity. Experiencing fun is the internal motivator needed to balance work production and the athlete's commitment to the sport. Work and fun must be mutually exclusive, and athletes must be helped in the rehabilitation process to experience enjoyment and to have fun. The model of "no pain, no gain" is outdated and may lead to injuries. **Table 18-9** shows some of the physiologic and psychological benefits of having fun. Fun experiences have many positive benefits for injury rehabilitation and quality of life.[89] Individuals who regularly experience fun not only have more satisfying relationships with their bosses, co-workers, family, friends, spouses, and lovers, they are also able to enjoy life to its fullest. These patients look, feel, and work better and are aware that fun, play, and laughter are important aspects of well-being.

Healthcare professionals involved in the rehabilitation process need to encourage fun in their own lives to be happier and more effective. Table 18-10 outlines recommendations for creating a personalized "fun factor" plan.

Teach the athlete to be optimistic

The skill of optimism allows an injured athlete to progress successfully through the rehabilitation process. Caregivers must possess, model, and teach optimism. **Table 18-11**

TABLE 18-9
PHYSIOLOGICAL AND PSYCHOLOGICAL BENEFITS OF HAVING FUN

- Boosts self-esteem
- Relieves tension
- Supplies enjoyment
- Makes it easier to keep a clear perspective when things are bad
- Spurs productivity
- Enhances work performance
- Facilitates communication
- Motivates athletes to reach goals
- Is good for health
- Increases creativity
- Makes the individual feel happier
- Lets the individual feel good about him or herself
- Motivates the athlete so that he or she does not want to quit
- Keeps the athlete focused
- Improves confidence
- Allows a different perspective of life
- Increases effectiveness
- Makes the athlete feel closer to those he or she has fun with

TABLE 18-10
CREATING A "FUN FACTOR" PLAN

- Trust yourself: believe, have confidence, put faith in yourself.
- Give yourself permission to loosen up and have fun; just say "yes" to having fun.
- Seek out fun activities and environments, be with friends, notice milestones, be physically active, expose yourself to nature, read books, listen to music, and enjoy food, drink, and have sexual contact.
- Realize options and seek novelties, be more adventurous, spontaneous, flexible, or experimental; implement enjoyable activities from childhood.
- See what other people do for fun, try it out, experience it, let others know of your wish to be included in their fun experiences or activities, make yourself available, learn to laugh.
- Concentrate on daydreams and fantasies and let mental images help you get more out of life, laugh at yourself, see the humor in things.
- Remove "if only" statements from your vocabulary and produce more "go for it" statements.
- Find something to practice and master.
- Practice having fun and realize that everything in life takes practice.
- Remember that if fun is good away from work, school, or rehabilitation, it must also be good at work, school, and rehabilitation.
- Learn to be optimistic. The skill of optimism allows the injured athlete to become successful through the rehabilitation process.

shows the twelve traits that characterize tough-minded optimists.[92] The practitioner should be aware of these traits and discuss them with the injured athlete.

Provide task-relevant activities

During rehabilitation, the injured athlete should be guided toward task-relevant activities such as relaxation for pain control and physical exercise programs for the uninjured portion of the body. This allows the athlete to feel physically active and maintain self-esteem.

Practice mental skill training

While injured, an athlete is still able to perform mental skills training and learn the concepts of mental imagery rehearsal. The athlete can learn to visualize a sport and practice it mentally, whether the sport is golf, tennis, running, hiking, skiing, or sailing. In mental imaging practice, the athlete should visualize different aspects of the

sport along with the accompanying sensations. For example, an athlete who skis should mentally experience the feel of the snow under the skis and the rhythm and grace of skiing. Recent research using position emission tomography (PET) and magnetic resonance imaging (MRI) has shown that when a physical activity is carried out, there is regional cerebral blood flow to the sensory motor cortex of the brain.[93] Likewise, when an individual closes his or her eyes and produces an image of a physical activity, the same blood flow to the motor cortex occurs. This prepares the athlete to stay sharp and be able to execute the sport upon return to the activity following injury. Another aspect of mental imagery, when coupled with relaxation,

TABLE 18-11
TWELVE CHARACTERISTICS OF TOUGH-MINDED OPTIMISTS

1. Optimists are seldom surprised by trouble.

2. Optimists look for partial solutions.

3. Optimists believe they have control over their future.

4. Optimists allow for regular personal renewal.

5. Optimists interrupt negative thoughts.

6. Optimists have heightened levels of appreciation.

7. Optimists use their imagination to rehearse successful outcomes.

8. Optimists are cheerful even when they are unable to be happy.

9. Optimists think they have an unlimited capacity for stretching.

10. Optimists nurture close relationships.

11. Optimists like to swap good news with other individuals.

12. Optimists accept what cannot be changed.

(Adapted with permission from McGinnis AL: *The Power of Optimism.* San Francisco, CA, Harper and Row, 1990.)

is focusing on the healing process. The practitioner should guide the athlete to visualize the healing of the ligaments and bone and the blood and oxygen supply going to the injured site to help with the healing process of that part of the body. Experiencing the sense of wellness and health can be critical during rehabilitation. With this in mind, the athlete must pay attention to diet, fitness levels, and lifestyle behaviors, because a healthy lifestyle is important for healing. During healing and rehabilitation, the athlete should not over- or undereat, smoke cigarettes, drink excessive amounts of alcohol, or take excessive amounts of medication. These coping strategies work closely with the ABCs discussed earlier: Affect, Behavior, and Cognition. The athlete should practice such techniques as mental rehearsal, concentration training, tension control, and goal setting, which can maintain or enhance performance when the athlete returns to the sport.

Provide reading material

Finally, the athlete should be encouraged to read while injured. Because depression following injury is common, some books may be helpful at giving strategies for maintaining a positive attitude.[60,61,92,94,95] An athlete's state of mind can have a direct impact on recovery and it is important that the athlete has control over his or her state of mind. Sir William Osler, the father of modern American medicine, said, "It is much more important to know what sort of patient has the disease than what sort of disease has the patient." This statement stresses the importance of recognizing the uniqueness of each injured individual. Another memorable quote was made by Frank G. Slaughter, MD, who asked, "We strive to be healthy in order to be happy, but how many of us strive to be happy in order to be healthy?" Athletes should strive to be both happy and healthy during rehabilitation to ensure successful outcomes.

CHAPTER REVIEW

The injured athlete can experience a variety of psychological reactions, which can become debilitating. The healthcare professional who is assisting the athlete in physical and psychological rehabilitation must understand the individual's emotional status and interpretation of the injury to support the athlete in the recovery process.

Psychological factors can play a role in injury onset, leaving the athlete vulnerable. Exercise addiction becomes detrimental when the athlete perceives that exercise is essential to his or her survival and experiences withdrawal symptoms when unable to exercise. Overzealous and untrained coaches and parents can also pressure an athlete to pursue athletics with the only goal being to win, rather than to enjoy the physical activity and participation. Most studies to date support the notion that the individual athlete's psychological status plays a significant role in the onset of health and injury problems, but more research is needed to elucidate the various mechanisms.

Most athletes react to injury with a predictable series of emotional stages, ending in adaptation to and acceptance of the disability. Because many athletes base their self-esteem on their body image, a physical injury can require psychological assistance in building or restoring self-esteem and regaining body control. Posttraumatic reactions can be functional or nonfunctional and tend to affect those athletes who have more experience and are better conditioned. Healthcare professionals can provide psychological assistance by creating an atmosphere of trust for the athlete and teaching the athlete what went wrong, what to expect, and what to do to promote recovery. Patients who feel more positive about rehabilitation and assume an active role during recovery feel that they are in control.

Pain is an important physical and psychological factor in rehabilitation. The knowledgeable athlete has more tolerance to pain and can view it as a natural part of the healing process rather than a sign of permanent disability. Both pharmacologic and psychological techniques can be useful in controlling the athlete's pain. General and specific guidelines exist for the healthcare practitioner who is directing the rehabilitation process. The athletic trainer who has a close and trusing relationship with the injured athlete can bettehelp the athlete to progress safely and effectively through rehabilitation in preparation for return to sport.

1. Which of the following statements about exercise-addicted individuals is true?

    A. They must exercise daily to cope with stress.

    B. They demonstrate increased competitive drive.

    C. They enjoy their sport more than other athletes do.

    D. They have specific signs and symptoms when they are unable to train.

2. High scores on the Social and Athletic Readjustment Rating Scale are associated with:

    A. reduced risk of injury.

    B. increased risk of injuries.

    C. improved athletic performance.

    D. higher incidence of major injuries.

3. Which of the following emotional reactions will an athlete most likely experience following an injury?

    A. Shock and numbness

    B. Immediate acceptance

    C. Decreased emotional liability

    D. Motivation to participate in treatment

4. Posttraumatic emotional reactions are influenced by the:

    A. athlete's age.

    B. athlete's personality.

    C. location of the injury.

    D. degree of experience in the sport.

5. A factor that can interfere with effective rehabilitation is:

    A. excessive social support.

    B. including tasks that are too easy.

    C. too much familiarity with the rehabilitation process.

    D. perceiving that the risks of treatment outweigh the benefits.

6. Which of the following statements is characteristic of pain?

    A. Pain tolerance tends to be the same in most individuals.

    B. Pain tolerance decreases when the athlete is told what to expect.

    C. The ability to tolerate pain depends on how pain is perceived.

    D. Long-lasting pain is unlikely to cause chronic psychological impairment.

7. Which of the following techniques is beneficial for pain management?

    A. Denial of pain

    B. Dramatized coping

    C. Internal focus of attention

    D. Focus on unpleasant activities

8. When should an injured athlete be referred to a psychologist?

    A. The athletic trainer is particularly close to the athlete.

    B. The athletic trainer lacks the time to counsel the athlete.

    C. The athlete's emotional distress is mild but may become severe.

    D. The athlete needs more support than the athletic trainer can provide.

9. In assisting the athlete through the rehabilitation process, the athletic trainer should:

    A. be receptive to the athlete's suggestions.

    B. establish and follow a stringent treatment plan.

    C. remind the athlete that the outcome depends solely on the athlete.

    D. provide the athlete with all the details of the program at one time.

10. Which of the following tactics can be used to assist the rehabilitating athlete psychologically?

    A. Practicing mental skill training

    B. Narrowing the athlete's focus to rehabilitation and training

    C. Reminding the athlete that sports must always be taken seriously

    D. Suggesting a sharply reduced calorie intake to avoid weight gain

Answers on page 893.

References

1. Larson GA, Starky C, Zaichkowsky LD: Psychological aspects of athletic injury as perceived by athletic trainers. *Sport Psych* 1966;100

2. Booth W: Arthritis Institute tackles sports. *Science* 1987;237:846–847.

3. Samples P: Spinal cord injuries: The high cost of careless diving. *Phys Sportsmed* 1989;17:143–144, 147–148.

4. Feigley DA: Psychological burnout in high–level athletes. *Phys Sportsmed* 1984;12:108–119.

5. Moore RA: Psychological factors in athletic injuries. *J Mich Med Soc* 1960;59:1805–1808.

6. May JR, Slanger E, Ferrucci P, Chang L: The psychology of high level sport: Is it extreme? Presented at the XXIV International Congress of Psychology, Montreal, Canada, August 1996.

7. Sanderson FH: The psychology of the injury prone athlete. *Br J Sports Med* 1978;11:56–57.

8. Rosenblum S: Psychologic factors in competitive failures in athletes. *Am J Sports Med* 1979;7:198–200.

9. Noakes TD, Schomer H: The "eager parent syndrome" and schoolboy injuries. *S Afr Med J* 1983;63:956.

10. Rhoads JM: Overwork. *JAMA* 1977;237:2614–2618.

11. Morgan WP: Negative addiction in runners. *Phys Sportsmed* 1979;7:57–70.

12. Stanish WD: Overuse injuries in athletes: A perspective. *Med Sci Sports Exerc* 1984;16:1–7.

13. Costill DL: *Inside Running.* Indianapolis, IN, Benchmark Press, 1986.

14. Froehlich J: Overtraining syndrome, in Heil J (ed): *The Psychology of Sport Injury.* Champaign, IL, Human Kinetics, 1986.

15. Kozar B, Lord RM: Overuse injury in the young athlete: Reasons for concern. *Phys Sportsmed* 1983;11:116–122.

16. Yerkes RM, Dodson JD: The relationship of strength of stimulus to rapidity of habit formation. *J Comp Neurol* 1908;18:459–482.

17. May JR: Psychological aspects of athletic performance: An overview, in Butts NK, Gushikins TT, Zarin B (eds): *The Elite Athlete.* Jamaica, NY, Spectrum Publications, 1985.

18. Hanin YL: A study of anxiety in sports, in Straub WF (ed): *Sport Psychology: An Analysis of Athlete Behavior.* Ithaca, NY, Movement, 1980.

19. Gould D, Krane V: The unusual athletic performance relationships: Current status and future directions, in Horn TS (ed): *Advances in Sport Psychology.* Champaign, IL, Human Kinetics Publishers, 1992.

20. Williams JM, Tonymon P, Andersen MB: The effects of life–event stress on anxiety and peripheral narrowing. *J Applied Sport Psych* 1991;3:126–141.

21. Williams JM, Roepke N: Psychology of injury and injury rehabilitation, in Singer RN, Murphe M, Tennant LK (eds): *Handbook of Research on Sport Psychology.* New York, NY, Macmillan, 1993.

22. Williams JM, Tonymon P, Wadsworth WA: Relationship of stress to injury in intercollegiate volleyball. *J Human Stress* 1986;12:38–43.

23. Smith RE, Smoll FL, and Ptacek JT: Conjunctive moderator variables in vulnerability and resiliency: Life stress, social support, and coping skills and adolescent injuries. *J Pers Social Psychol* 58:360–370.

24. Davis JO: Sports injuries and stress management: An opportunity for research. *Sport Psychol* 1991;5:175–182.

25. Nideffer RM: The injured athlete: Psychological factors in treatment. *Orthop Clin North Am* 1983;14: 373–385.

26. Anderson MD, Williams JM: A model of stress and coping and athletic injury: Prediction and prevention. *J Sport Exerc Psych* 1988;10:294–306.

27. MacIntosh DL, Skrien T, Shephard RJ: Athletic injuries at the University of Toronto. *Med Sci Sports* 1971;3: 195–199.

28. Margreiter R, Raas E, Lugger LJ: The risk of injury in experienced Alpine skiers. *Orthop Clin North Am* 1976;7:51–54.

29. Dowling PA: Prospective study of injuries in United States Ski Association freestyle skiing: 1976–1977 to 1979–1980. *Am J Sports Med* 1982;10:268–275.

30. Rose RC, Hughes RD III, Yarbrough DR, Dewees SP: Heat injuries among recreational runners. *South Med J* 1980;73:1038–1040.

31. Bramwell ST, Masuda M, Wagner NN, Holmes TH: Psychosocial factors in athletic injuries: Development and application of the Social and Athletic Readjustment Rating Scale (SARRS). *J Human Stress* 1975;1:6–20.

32. Holmes TH, Rahe RH: The Social Readjustment Rating Scale. *J Psychosom Res* 1967;11:213–218.

33. Cryan PD, Alles WF: The relationship between stress and college football injuries. *J Sports Med Fitness* 1983;23:52–58.

34. Coddington RD, Troxell JR: The effect of emotional factors on football injury rates: A pilot study. *J Human Stress* 1980;6:3–5.

35. Passer MW, Seese MD: Life stress and athletic injury: Examination of positive versus negative events and three moderator variables. *J Human Stress* 1983;9:11–16.

36. Mueller DP, Edwards DW, Yarvis RM: Stressful life events and psychiatric symptomatology: Change or undesirability? *J Health Soc Behav* 1977;18:307–317.

37. Spielberger CD, Gorsuch RL, Lushene RF: *The State Trait Anxiety Inventory (STAI).* Palo Alto, CA, Consulting Psychologists Press, 1970.

38. Martens R (ed): *Sport Competition Anxiety Test.* Champaign, IL, Human Kinetics, 1977.

39. Rotter JB: Generalized expectancies for internal versus external control of reinforcement. *Psychol Monog* 1966;80:1–28.

40. May JR, Veach TL, Southard SW, Herring MW: The effects of life change on injuries, illness, and performance in elite athletes: The elite athlete, in Butts NK, Gushiken TT, Zarins, B (eds): *The Elite Athlete.* Jamaica, NY, Spectrum Publications, 1985, pp 171–179

41. May JR, Veach TL, Reed MW, Griffey MS: A psychological study of health, injury, and performance in athletes on the US Alpine Ski Team. *Phys Sportsmed* 1985;13:111–115.

42. National Institute of Health: A concurrent validation study of the National Counsel on Health, Statistics General Well–Being Scale. Publication No. HRA 78–1347, Washington, DC, US Department of Education and Welfare, 1977.

43. Zung WW: A self–rating depression scale. *Arch Gen Psychiatr* 1965;12: 63–70.

44. May JR, Veach TL: US Ski Team psychological program: A consultation model, in May JR, Asken MJ, (eds): *Sports Psychology: The Psychological Health of the Athlete.* Great Neck, NY, PMA Publishing, 1987.

45. May JR, Brown LB: Delivery of psychological services prior to and during the 15th Olympic Games in Calgary, Canada: The US Alpine Ski Team Program. *Sport Psych* 1989;3:320–329.

46. May JR: Psychological Skills Program, in *US Alpine Ski Team Training Manual.* Park City, UT, US Ski Team, 1992.

47. May JR: Delivery of psychological services to the U.S. Olympic Team at the 1992 Summer Games, Barcelona, Spain. *Revista de Psychologic del Deporte,* 1992.

48. Jackson DW, Jarrett H, Bailey D, Kausek J, Swanson J, Powell JW: Injury prediction in the young athlete: A preliminary report. *Am J Sports Med* 1978;6:6–14.

49. Cattell RB, Eber HW, Tatsuoka MM (eds): *Handbook for the Sixteen Personality Factor Questionnaire 16PF.* Champaign, IL, Institute for Personality and Ability Testing, 1970.

50. Valliant PM: Injury and personality traits in noncompetitive runners. *J Sports Med Phys Fitness* 1980;20:341–346.

51. Valliant PM: Personality and injury in competitive runners. *Percept Mot Skills* 1981;53:251–253.

52. May JR: The ABC's of psychological rehabilitation from injury. *Rebound: An Injury Recovery Guide,* 1997, pp 9–11.

53. May JR, Sieb G: Psychosocial antecedents, sequelae and rehabilitation to illness, injury in athletes, in May JR, Asken MJ (eds): *Sport Psychology: The Psychological Health of the Athlete.* Great Neck, NY, PMA Publishing, 1987.

54. May JR: Psychological sequelae and rehabilitation of the injured athlete. *Sportsmed Digest* 1990;12:1–3.

55. McDonald SA, Hardy CJ: Affective response patterns of the injured athlete: An exploratory analysis. *Sport Psych* 1990;4:261–274.

56. Smith Am, Scott SG, O'Fallon WM, Young, ML: Emotional responses of athletes to injury. *Mayo Clin Proc* 1990;65:38–50.

57. Pearson L, Jones G: Emotional aspects of sports injuries: Implications for physiotherapists. *Physiotherapy* 1992;78:762–770.

58. Smith AM: Psychological impact of injuries in athletes. *Sports Med* 1996;22:391–405.

59. Shuer MD, Dietrich MS: Psychological effects of chronic injury in athletes. *West J Med* 1997;66:104–109.

60. Heil J (ed): *Psychology of Sport Injury.* Champaign, IL, Human Kinetics, 1993.

61. Pargman D: *Psychological Bases of Sports Injury.* Morgantown, WV, Fitness Information Technology, 1993.

62. Suinn RM: Psychological reactions to physical disability. *J Assoc Phys Ment Rehabil* 1967;21:13–15.

63. Kubler–Ross E: *On Death and Dying.* New York, NY, Macmillan 1969.

64. Wiese–Bjornstal DM, Smith AM, LaMott EE: A model of psychological response to athlete injury and rehabilitation. *Athlet Train Sports Healthcare Perspect* 1995;1:16–30.

65. Johnson WR: Some psychological aspects of physical rehabilitation: Toward an organismic theory. *J Assoc Phys Ment Rehabil* 1962;16:165–168.

66. Ievleva L: Psychological factors in knee and ankle injury recovery: An exploratory study. University of Ottawa, Ottawa, ON, 1988. Thesis.

67. Ievleva L, Orlick T: Mental links to enhanced healing: An exploratory study. *Sport Psych* 1991;5:25–40.

68. Braverman M: Validity of psychotraumatic reactions. *J Forensic Sci* 1977;22:654–662.

69. Little JC. Neurotic illness in fitness fanatics. *Psychiatr Ann* 1979;9:49–56.

70. Ryde D: The role of the physician in sports injury prevention: Some psychological factors in sports injuries. *J Sports Med Phys Fit* 1965;5:152–155.

71. Callahan MA, Thomas R: Complex socket deformity: The team approach to physical and psychologic patient rehabilitation. *Ophthalmology* 1979;86:1636–1639.

72. Gillum RF, Barsky AJ: Diagnosis and management of patient noncompliance. *JAMA* 1974;228:1563–1567.

73. Heil J: Mental training for injury management, in Heil J (ed): *Psychology of Sport Injury.* Champaign, IL, Human Kinetics, 1993.

74. Danish S: Psychological aspects in the care and treatment of athletic injuries, in Vinger, PE, Hoerner EF (eds): *Sports Injuries: The Unthwarted Epidemic,* ed 2. Littleton, MA, PSG, 1986, pp 345–353.

75. Richman JM, Hardy CJ, Rosenfeld LB, Callanan RAE: Strategies for enhancing social support networks in sport: A brainstorming experience. *Appl Sport Psych* 1989;1:150–159.

76. Bandura A: Self efficacy: Toward a unifying theory of behavioral change. *Psychol Rev* 1977;84:191–215.

77. Bandura A, Cioffi D, Taylor CB, Brouillard ME: Perceived self efficacy in coping with cognitive stressors and opioid activation. *J Pers Soc Psychol* 1988;55:479–488.

78. Wise A, Jackson DW, Rocchio P: Preoperative psychologic testing as a predictor of success in knee surgery. *Am J Sports Med* 1979;7:287–292.

79. Steadman JR: Rehabilitation after knee ligament surgery. *Am J Sports Med* 1980;8:294–296.

80. Steadman JR: Rehabilitation of tibial plafond fractures after stable internal fixation. *Am J Sports Med* 1981;9:71–72.

81. Steadman JR: A physician's approach to the psychology of injury, in Heil J (ed): *Psychology of Sport Injury.* Champaign, IL, Human Kinetics, 1993.

82. McCue FC III, Baugher WH, Kulund DN, Gieck JH: Hand and wrist injuries in the athlete. *Am J Sports Med* 1979;7:275–286.

83. International Association for the Study of Pain Subcommittee on Taxonomy: Classification of chronic pain: Descriptions of chronic pain syndromes and definitions. *Pain* 1986;5(suppl 3):S1–S226.

84. Pen LJ, Fisher CA: Athletes and pain tolerance. *Sports Med* 1994;18:319–329.

85. Friedman H, Thompson RB, Rosen EF: Perceived threat as a major factor in tolerance for experimentally induced cold water pain. *J Abnorm Psychol* 1985;94:624–629.

86. Duda H, Smart AE, Tappe MK: Predictors of adherence in the rehabilitation of athletic injuries: An application of perceived investment theory. *J Sport Exerc Psychol* 1989;11:367–381.

87. Fisher AC, Domm MA, Wuest DA: Adherence to sports injury rehabilitation programs. *Phys Sportsmed* 1988;16:47–52.

88. Fernandez E, Turk DC: Overall and relative efficiency of cognitive strategies in attenuating pain. Proceedings at the 94th annual convention of the American Psychological Association, Washington, DC, 1986.

89. May JR: Two critical psychological components of the ski racing: Fun and feelings. *J Sports Sci* 1987;5:337–343.

90. Eldridge WD: The importance of psychotherapy for athletic–related orthopedic injuries among adults. *Compr Psychiatry* 1983;24:271–277.

91. MacPhillamy DJ, Lewinsoh PM: Depression as a function of desired and obtained pleasures. *J Abnorm Psychol* 1974;83:651–657.

92. McGinnis AL: *The Power of Optimism.* San Francisco, CA, Harper and Row, 1990.

93. Stephan KM, Fink GR, Passingham RE, et al: Functional anatomy of the mental representations of upper extremity movements in health subjects. *J Neurophysiol* 1995;73:373–386.

94. Burns DD: *Feeling Good: The New Mood Therapy.* New York, NY, William Morrow, 1980.

95. Branden N: *How to Raise Your Self Esteem.* Toronto, Canada, Bantam Books, 1987.

19

Dermatology

Thomas N. Helm, MD
Wilma F. Bergfeld, MD, FACP

QUICK CONTENTS

- The anatomy of the skin and the general approach to the patient with a skin disorder.

- Inflammatory conditions, including acne, contact dermatitis, intertrigo, and urticaria.

- Dermatoses, including psoriasis, seborrheic dermatitis, and pityriasis rosea.

- Infectious disorders, such as pilosebaceous unit infections, impetigo, tinea infections, cellulitis, and pityriasis versicolor.

- Infestations, such as scabies and pediculosis.

- Viral infections, including herpes simplex, genital herpes, and herpes gladiatorum.

- The effects of physical exposure on the skin.

- Growths in the skin, including warts, molluscum contagiosum, cysts, and skin cancer.

OVERVIEW

Skin problems that occur in athletes are usually of minor importance; however, they may interfere with optimal performance and may also disqualify individuals from participation in certain events. This chapter addresses the most commonly encountered skin problems seen by sports physicians and athletic trainers and outlines an approach to dermatologic therapy.

The chapter begins with a discussion of the anatomy of skin followed by the general approach to the patient with a skin disorder. Different types of rashes are discussed as are infectious disorders, infestations, viral infections, effects of physical exposure to the elements, and growths. The chapter ends with a discussion of uncommon dermatoses. Color plates of the figures in this chapter are located in Appendix B.

ANATOMY

The skin is more than just a covering for the body. It provides structure, form, and protection and also helps regulate temperature. The skin is composed of various layers including the *stratum corneum*, which provides a barrier to noxious substances; the *epidermis*, which protects against ultraviolet damage and provides cutaneous immunity; the *dermis*, which is composed of connective tissue that gives the skin elasticity and strength; and *subcutaneous fat*, which insulates and protects the body. Any of the components of the skin can be injured or impaired, giving rise to skin disease.

GENERAL APPROACH TO THE ATHLETE WITH A SKIN DISORDER

Skin problems are commonly encountered in sports medicine.[1-3] Identification of a dermatologic problem must include a determination of whether the problem is a growth (neoplastic process) or a rash (inflammatory dermatosis).[4] Growths in the skin are usually asymptomatic and generally do not itch. Growths only cause trouble when their physical size interferes with normal function. Rashes, on the other hand, usually itch and develop in a more acute manner. The sports physician and athletic trainer must find out what treatments have already been tried. Unlike other disciplines, most individuals will have first tried over-the-counter products or previously

prescribed topical medications that may alter the morphology of the problem being evaluated. Knowing what treatments and topical medications have been used will allow the sports physician or athletic trainer to better understand clues and signs noted on physical examination. The sports physician or athletic trainer should determine the duration of the skin problem, its location on the body, and the nature of the primary lesion, whether it is a *macule*, a flat, nonpalpable color change in the skin less than 1 cm in diameter; a *papule*, a raised lesion in the skin less than 1 cm in diameter; a *plaque*, an elevation similar to a mesa that is usually a result of a confluence of papules; a *pustule*, a pus-filled blister; a *vesicle*, a blister with a clear fluid that is less than 1 cm; or a *bulla*, a blister larger than 1 cm. For example, a diagnosis of psoriasis is most likely if scaling plaques develop on extensor surfaces over a period of 1 or 2 months.

RASHES

Inflammatory Conditions

Acne

Acne vulgaris affects almost three quarters of the population at some time. Acne may be identified by a constellation of clinical features. Acne often begins as open comedones (blackheads) in oily areas such as the forehead, nose, chin, and presternal chest. As acne progresses, *erythematous* papules develop, then pustules, and finally cysts (**Figure 19-1**). A grading scale can help communicate the stage of acne affecting an individual: grade I describes comedonal acne, when blackheads and whiteheads predominate. Grade II acne describes the predominance of erythematous papules. Grade III describes the presence of pustules, and grade IV describes the presence of cysts and nodules. Cysts and nodules may leave scars after healing (**Figure 19-2**).

Acne is not contagious, and its presence should not disqualify an athlete from participation in team sports; however, certain bacteria (in particular, *Proprionibacterium acnes*) present on the skin may participate in the development of inflammatory lesions. Inflammation occurs when the *pilosebaceous unit*, which consists of hair follicle, sebaceous gland, and apocrine gland, is occluded. The structures that make up pilosebaceous occur together in the skin and are derived from follicular generative cells in embryonic development. Oil builds up behind a keratinous plug, which is made up of corneocytes. As keratinocytes in the follicular opening mature, they become flat and gradually flake off. These corneocyte flakes may clump. Bacteria then breaks down the oils into fatty acids that irritate the skin. Agents such as benzoyl peroxide and sulfacetamide dissolve keratinous plugs and are first-line therapies that may be applied once or twice daily to affected areas. If many inflammatory lesions develop, topical antibiotics such as erythromycin or clindamycin can be valuable.[5] If many pustules are present, treatment with oral antibiotics is indicated; for nodular or cystic lesions, isotretinoin, which is an oral retinoid, may be indicated.[6]

Because occlusion of the pilosebaceous unit may be an important factor in the pathogenesis of acne, special precautions should be taken to prevent protective gear or equipment from worsening the problem.[7] Helmet padding may precipitate acne in areas of contact, and shoulder pads may aggravate existing acne. Use of astringent cleansers on the skin and appropriate cleaning of the athletic pads will lead to improved control of acne.

Dermatitis

Dermatitis is defined as inflammation of the skin. The term is often used interchangeably with the word "eczema," but "dermatitis" is a more precise form. Dermatitis encompasses a broad range of disorders that include allergic contact dermatitis, irritant contact dermatitis, and other poorly understood conditions such as dyshidrotic dermatitis. Dermatitis typically appears as an itchy area of redness or scaling in the skin. Although the differentiation of various forms of dermatitis is beyond the scope of this chapter, management strategies for the different types of dermatitis are similar and may allow for immediate symptomatic control of affected individuals.

Contact dermatitis

Contact dermatitis develops from allergy or irritation triggered by substances contacting the skin. Common causes of contact dermatitis include nickel in metal components of equipment, potassium dichromate in leather products, formaldehyde in creams and lotions, rubber products in padding, adhesives and other components of the shoe, and

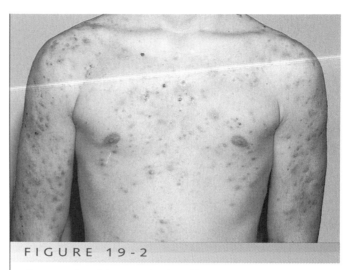

FIGURE 19-2

Cysts and nodules may heal and leave scars.

fragrances in toiletries. Skin that contacts the offending chemical becomes red and inflamed and vesicles form. The most common offending allergens encountered in the outdoor sports enthusiast are poison ivy and other related agents such as poison oak or poison sumac. After contact with resin from the plant, itchy red linear areas of scaling, erythema, and vesiculation develop on the skin (**Figure 19-3**). Contact dermatitis often presents in geometric shapes that conform to the areas of contact with the allergen.[4] Skin cleansers, detergents, solvents such as turpentine and gasoline, chemicals such as lye and bleach, acids, and alcohol can also cause contact dermatitis because of direct irritation.

The first-line treatment of all types of dermatitis is the same. Cool compresses followed by topical corticosteroid creams help control symptoms and stop redness, inflammation, and blister formation.[5] When reactions are severe, a short course of systemic corticosteroids may be indicated. Antihistamines are prescribed to control *pruritus* (itching). Contact dermatitis is not contagious and athletes with this condition can participate in sports as long as body fluids from vesicles do not come in contact with other athletes.

Intertrigo

Intertrigo is a type of irritant dermatitis that develops in body folds. Repeated friction or rubbing may abrade the skin, then sweat and other substances may lead to inflammation, pain, and itching. Because intertrigo occurs in sensitive areas such as the axilla, inframammary area, or groin folds, use of potent corticosteroids should be avoided. Management includes cool compresses followed by application of products that contain mild hydrocortisone and soothing protective creams such as zinc oxide ointment. Although the treatment is otherwise identical

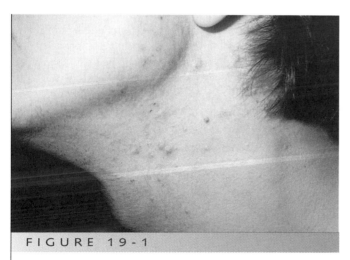

FIGURE 19-1

Acne is characterized by papules, pustules, and cysts.

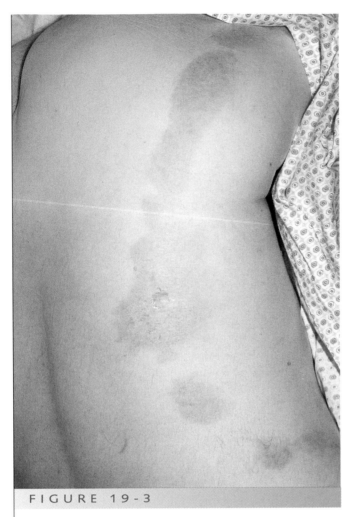

FIGURE 19-3

Linear areas of scaling, erythema, and vesicles form after contact with poison ivy.

to the management of contact dermatitis, avoiding the offending irritants is the most important management strategy. Athletes who have intertrigo may safely participate in sports as long as discomfort is not too severe.

Urticaria

Urticaria (hives) is characterized by the development of a wheal. Wheals are red, evanescent swellings in the skin that lack epidermal changes. Individual lesions of urticaria last less than 24 hours. Wheals do not scale or become ulcerated, and they are often extremely pruritic. Small papules may develop, or large annular or polycyclic lesions may occur. The causes of urticaria are extensive. Medications, foods such as fish, nuts, and berries, and infections can all be associated with hives. On rare occasions, solar urticaria may develop in individuals from ultraviolet exposure. For urticaria lasting less than 6 weeks, extensive evaluation is not indicated. Symptoms of urticaria are treated with oral antihistamines, most commonly diphenhydramine. Diphenhydramine may

diminish an athlete's reflexes and response time. The use of nonsedating antihistamines such as loratadine may be preferable if the athlete is actively involved in competition. For urticaria that lasts longer than 6 weeks, testing for occult infection, such as sinus or urinary tract infection, or internal disease, such as thyroid disease, should be considered. As long as pruritus is not disabling and there is no swelling of the mouth or throat that could compromise breathing, athletes who suffer from urticaria may participate in sports.

Preexisting Dermatoses

Sports activity may exacerbate many common skin disorders. Pressure and friction may lead to the spread of some dermatoses such as psoriasis or lichen planus, a phenomenon known as the Koebner effect or isomorphic phenomenon.

Psoriasis

Psoriasis is a papulosquamous disease that is characterized by erythematous papules and plaques that develop predominantly on extensor surfaces. The elbows and knees, intergluteal area, and scalp are common sites. Spots begin as small scaling papules and then gradually develop thick, adherent silvery scales. Psoriasis may also involve the nail unit. When psoriasis involves the nails, they become yellow and thickened and develop pitting (small depressions in the nail plate). A yellow-brown discoloration may develop under the nail.

Psoriasis is not contagious and does not require disqualification from sporting events. Treatment with topical corticosteroids or ultraviolet light phototherapy help control individual lesions. Areas of pressure or friction from injuries sustained during contact sports may lead to spread of psoriasis or Koebner phenomenon.[4]

Seborrheic Dermatitis

Seborrheic dermatitis is a skin condition of unknown cause that is characterized by erythema and scaling of the skin in particular areas. Scaling is most pronounced in areas of high sebum production, such as the scalp, nasolabial folds, ears, and presternal chest. Treatment with mild corticosteroids and antiseborrheic shampoos that contain selenium sulfide, zinc pyrithione, or ketoconazole may be helpful.

Pityriasis rosea

Pityriasis rosea occurs most commonly in young adults and is a self-limiting scaling dermatosis. It is a papulosquamous condition that begins abruptly with the onset of a scaling patch, most commonly on the trunk. Often the appearance simulates that of tinea corporis; however, a few days after the initial patch (the "herald patch") develops, oval plaques with an internal rim of scale disseminate broadly over the body. The eruption is often asymptomatic. Psoriasis and secondary syphilis may

Rashes

Inflammatory conditions

Acne

Acne vulgaris affects nearly 75% of the population at some time and is characterized by open comedones (blackheads) in oily areas, such as the forehead, nose, chin, and presternal chest. As acne progresses, erythematous papules, pustules, and cysts develop. Grade I acne is comedonal acne, involving primarily blackheads and whiteheads. Grade II includes erythematous papules. Grade III involves pustules, and grade IV has cysts and nodules.

Acne is not contagious, and therefore, athletes with acne should not be disqualified from team sports, even though certain bacteria (*Propionibacterium acnes*) may participate in the development of inflammatory lesions. Helmet pads and shoulder pads can aggravate acne; using astringent cleansers on the skin and cleaning the athletic pads appropriately are helpful techniques.

Dermatitis

Contact dermatitis results from allergy or irritation triggered by substances such as nickel, potassium dichromate, formaldehyde, rubber, and fragrances that contact the skin. Poison ivy, poison oak, and poison sumac are the most common offending allergens for the outdoor sports participant. Itchy, red, linear areas of scaling, erythema, and vesiculation occur, often in geometric shapes reflecting the areas of contact with the allergen. Skin cleansers, detergents, solvents, acids, and alcohol can directly irritate the skin and cause contact dermatitis. Cool compresses followed by topical corticosteroid creams will control the symptoms. If the reaction is severe, a short course of systemic corticosteroids may be needed, and antihistamines can be prescribed to control itching. Athletes with contact dermatitis can participate in sports as long as fluids from the vesicles do not contact other athletes.

Intertrigo

Intertrigo is caused by repeating friction or rubbing in skin folds, including the axilla, inframammary area, and groin folds, that abrades the skin, which is then further inflamed by heat and sweat. Potent corticosteroids are avoided because of the sensitivity of these areas. Treatment is cool compresses, followed by a mild hydrocortisone product and a soothing protective cream such as zinc oxide and avoidance of the offending irritants. Athletes with intertrigo may participate in sports as long as discomfort is not severe.

Urticaria

Urticaria or hives are characterized by wheals, evanescent, erythematous skin swellings that do not scale or ulcerate, but can be extremely pruritic. Small papules or large annular or polycyclic lesions can occur. Urticaria can be caused by ultraviolet exposure (rarely), medications, or foods. Urticaria lasting less than 6 weeks is treated symptomatically with oral antihistamines; urticaria lasting longer than 6 weeks require testing for occult infection, such as sinus or urinary tract infection, or internal disease, such as thyroid disease. As long as pruritus is not disabling and breathing is not compromised, athletes with urticaria may participate in sports.

Preexisting dermatoses

Psoriasis

Dermatoses such as psoriasis can be made worse by the pressure and friction of sports activity, which is known as the Koebner effect or isomorphic phenomenon. Psoriasis is a papulosquamous disease characterized by erythematous papules and plaques that develop mostly on extensor surfaces, including the elbows, knees, intergluteal area, and scalp. Psoriasis is not contagious, and the athlete may participate in sports without restriction. Management includes topical corticosteroids or ultraviolet light phototherapy.

Seborrheic dermatitis

Seborrheic dermatitis is characterized by erythema and scaling of the skin, most pronounced in areas of high sebum production, such as the scalp, nasolabial folds, ears, and presternal chest. The cause is unknown. Treatment is mild corticosteroids and antiseborrheic shampoos containing selenium sulfide, zinc pyrithione, or ketoconazole.

Pityriasis rosea

Pityriasis rosea is a self-limited, asymptomatic, papulosquamous condition that begins abruptly with a scaling patch, most often on the trunk, and affects young adults. Pityriasis rosea is not readily contagious, even though its suspected cause is viral, and therefore, the athlete may participate in sports.

mimic pityriasis rosea, but psoriasis typically shows a predilection for the elbows, knees, and scalp, whereas pityriasis rosea does not. Secondary syphilis is characterized by ham-colored macules on the palms and soles as well as mucous patches in the mouth. These types of lesions are not seen in pityriasis rosea.

Results of recent studies indicate that pityriasis rosea is due to infection with human herpes virus type 7, although further research is needed to confirm this association.[8] Pityriasis rosea does not seem to be readily contagious despite the suspected viral cause; therefore, disqualification from sports is not required. In instances in which the diagnosis is not certain, serologic studies may be warranted to exclude a diagnosis of secondary syphilis.

INFECTIOUS DISORDERS

Infection of the Pilosebaceous Unit

The presence of *folliculitis* (inflammation of a follicle), *abscess* (a pus-filled area that affects skin and organs), or *furuncles* (boils) may indicate infection of the pilosebaceous unit. *Staphylococcus* species of bacteria are most commonly involved. Bacteria cause a brisk neutrophilic reaction within the pilosebaceous unit, leading to follicular rupture and collections of polymorphonuclear leukocytes in the skin. If a few lesions form, incision and drainage is usually effective in controlling the problem. Topical antibiotics are helpful for more widespread lesions, or a course of systemic antibiotics may be required. Athletes with folliculitis should be disqualified from sports with prolonged bodily contact such as wrestling. After 1 or 2 days of treatment, lesions are usually resolved enough to allow for resumption of usual competition.

Impetigo

Although *impetigo* most commonly occurs around the mouth, it can occur anywhere on the body.[7] Crusts and blisters appear flaccid and cluster in involved areas. *Staphylococcus* and *Streptococcus* species of bacteria are the most common culprits, and treatment includes cool compresses as well as topical antibiotics. For more widespread involvement, use of systemic antibiotics is advisable. Because impetigo is contagious, athletes with impetigo should be closely monitored and held back from participation in contact sports until the infection is cleared.

Tinea Infections

Tinea infections are common in athletes. Tinea cruris describes an infection of the groin fold by dermatophytes. Annular plaques with central clearing, a red rim, or serpiginous scaling, which has a wavy or curved border, are encountered on clinical inspection (**Figure 19-4**).

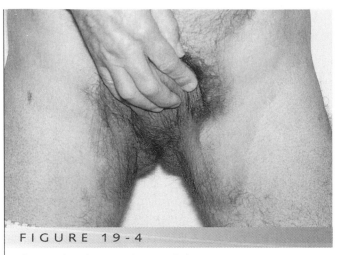

FIGURE 19-4

An annular plaque with central clearing or a serpiginous scaling border are characteristic of tinea cruris.

Tinea cruris does not affect the scrotum. Tinea capitis describes an infection of the scalp that is characterized by hair loss, erythema, scaling, and pustule formation (**Figure 19-5**). In many instances, hairs will break off, giving the scalp a "black dot" appearance. Some early tinea capitis lesions are erythematous and edematous with no hair loss (**Figure 19-6**). As infection worsens, fungi invade hair shafts and cause them to fracture.

Tinea pedis, which involves the feet, may manifest in several different ways. Some individuals have a low-grade, widespread scaling in a "moccasin distribution" and chronic "dry skin" appearance of the foot, which most often is due to *Trichophyton rubrum* infection (**Figure 19-7**). In questionable cases, evaluating the condition of a skin scraping treated with potassium hydroxide solution may help to confirm the diagnosis.

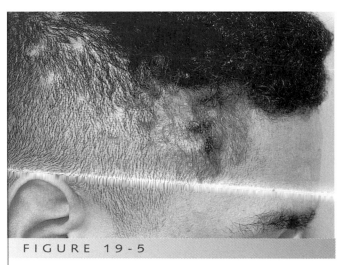

FIGURE 19-5

Scaling on the scalp, pustules, and hair loss characterize tinea capitis.

FOCUS ON . . .

Infectious Disorders

Infection of the pilosebaceous unit

Pilosebaceous unit infection can present as folliculitis, abscesses, or furuncles (boils) and is most often causes by *Staphylococcus* species of bacteria. The bacteria cause a brisk neutrophilic reaction within the pilosebaceous unit, leading to follicular rupture and collections of polymorphonuclear leukocytes in the skin. A limited number of lesions can be treated with incision and drainage; more widespread lesions may require topical or systemic antibiotics. Athletes with folliculitis should be disqualified from sports that involve prolonged bodily contact; however, after a few days of treatment, lesions are usually resolved enough for resumption of participation.

Impetigo

Impetigo is characterized by clusters of crusts and blisters with a flaccid appearance most often around the mouth, although they can occur anywhere on the body. *Staphylococcus* and *Streptococcus* species are the most frequent causes. Management is cool compresses and topical antibiotics; if involvement is widespread, systemic antibiotics are prescribed. Impetigo is contagious, and athletes should not participate in contact sports until the infection has cleared.

Tinea infections

Tinea infections are fungal infections typified by annular plaques with a rim of erythema and scale. Tinea cruris is an infection of the groin folds, tinea capitis affects the scalp, and tinea pedis involves the foot. Tinea capitis is characterized by a subtle red ring at first, hair loss, erythema, scaling, pustule formation, and a "black dot" appearance where the hairs have broken off. Tinea pedis often accompanies onychomycosis (fungal infection of the nail unit, which can cause the nail to become brittle, misshapen, and painful with ambulation and running) and may present with low-grade scaling and chronic dry skin appearance of the foot, most often as a result of *Trichophyton rubrum* infection, which can spread to the legs and thighs. *Epidermophyton floccosum* causes an interdigital infection with maceration between the web spaces (most often the third and fourth) of the feet. Acute infection can cause pustules on the plantar surface of the foot. Treatment varies with the location and extent of disease. Localized infections of the skin, groin folds, or feet can be treated with topical antifungal agents such as terbinafine. Scalp infection and onychomycosis usually require oral antifungal agents. Athletes with fungal infections may participate in sports provided that areas of infection are not in contact with other participants' skin. Wrestlers should not participate until noncovered areas of infection are cleared.

Cellulitis

Cellulitis, a bacterial infection of the soft tissues, is most commonly seen after trauma to the skin, such as from an arthropod bite or in an area of prior surgery. Symptoms are edema, erythema, and tenderness. Blood cultures and systemic antibiotics are indicated, and the athlete should be restricted from sport participation until the infection clears, to avoid the possibility of septicemia.

Pityriasis versicolor

Pityriasis versicolor is an infection of the skin and pilosebaceous unit caused by *Pityrosporum orbiculare* and found mostly in young adults. In some individuals, this common yeast organism increases in number and can cause cosmetic disfigurement such as hypopigmentation, although it usually only causes mild itching. Topical antifungal medication is recommended. The infection should not disqualify an athlete from sport.

The potassium hydroxide solution dissolves keratinocytes, making fungal organisms easier to identify. Infection from the foot may spread to involve broad areas on the legs and thighs (Figure 19-8). *Epidermophyton floccosum* causes an interdigital infection with maceration in the web spaces between the toes, most commonly the third and fourth web spaces. Acute tinea infection may give rise to pustules on the plantar surface of the foot. Tinea pedis often accompanies *onychomycosis*, which is infection of the nail unit by fungus.

Onychomycosis is extremely common in our society, and the incidence increases with progressive age. Fungal infection of the nail unit causes the nail to become brittle and misshapen and may cause pain with ambulation or running.

Treatment of fungal infections varies according to the location and extent of disease involvement. For localized infections of the skin, groin folds, or feet, topical antifungal agents are effective. Some of the newer more potent agents such as terbinafine appear to be most effective.[9]

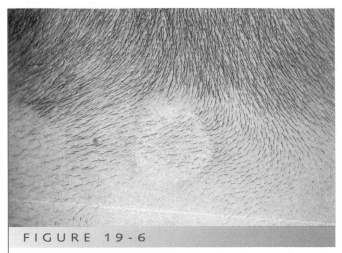

FIGURE 19-6

Some early tinea capitis lesions are erythematous and edematous. Hair loss is not evident early.

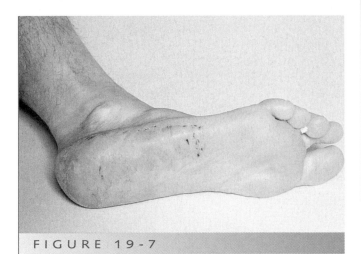

FIGURE 19-7

Tinea pedis can be identified by widespread scaling in a "moccasin distribution."

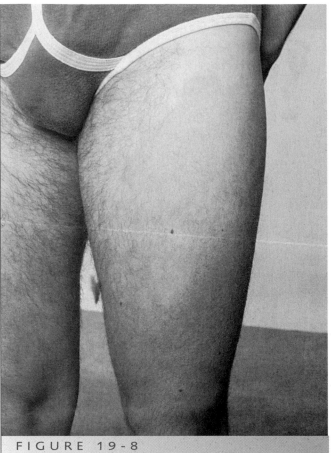

FIGURE 19-8

Tinea pedis can be complicated by widespread infection on the legs and thighs.

Infection of the scalp usually requires oral antifungal treatment. Similarly, topical medications do little to provide lasting resolution of fungal infection of the nail unit, and management of onychomycosis is best achieved with oral agents. Athletes with fungal infections can participate in sports as long as areas of infection are not in direct contact with the skin of other participants. Wrestlers should be kept from participating in sports until noncovered areas of the infection have cleared.

Cellulitis

Cellulitis is a bacterial infection of the soft tissues. Cellulitis is most commonly encountered after trauma to the skin such as from the bite of an arthropod or in an area of prior surgery or injury (such as the upper arm in a patient who has undergone a mastectomy). Edema, erythema, and tenderness develop quickly in an affected region. Blood culture and systemic antibiotic treatment are indi-

cated. Because cellulitis may lead to septicemia and other serious consequences, athletes with cellulitis should be held back from participation in sports.

Pityriasis versicolor

Pityriasis versicolor is an infection of the skin and pilosebaceous unit that is seen most commonly in young adults. The causative organism is *Pityrosporum orbiculare*, which is a commensal yeast that is part of the normal skin flora found on everyone's skin. In some individuals, depending on how well the yeast grows in the body's oil, the amount of this lipophilic yeast may increase enough to cause cosmetic disfigurement such as a change in skin tone as a result of an alteration in pigmentation. Tinea versicolor lesions cause scaling and skin discoloration and occur most commonly on the trunk (**Figure** 19-9). Usually, however, pityriasis versicolor, which was formerly known as tinea versicolor, does not cause symptoms other than mild itching.[10] Azelaic acid, which is a product of the organism's metabolism, disrupts normal tanning and leads to hypopigmentation that typically is most pronounced on the trunk. In very fair individuals, buildup of the organism may impart a tan to red discoloration to the skin.

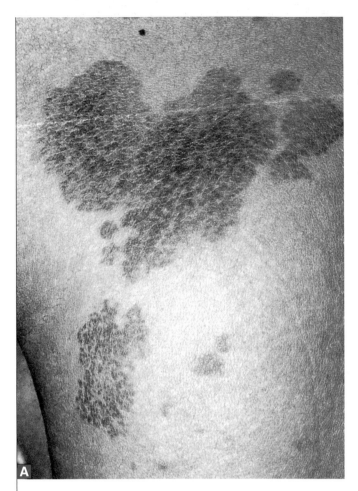

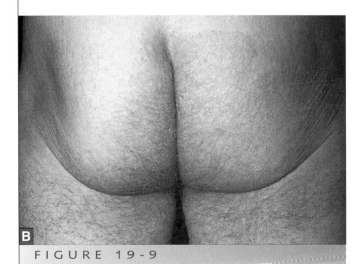

FIGURE 19-9

A Scaling and skin discoloration characterize tinea versicolor lesions. **B** The lesions occur most commonly on the trunk.

Treatment with topical antifungal medications helps control this condition. Tinea versicolor infection should not disqualify an athlete from participation in sports.

INFESTATIONS

Scabies

Scabies infestation is caused by a female mite that burrows into the epidermis beneath a layer of the stratum corneum.[4] Lesions or symptoms often do not appear until 3 or 4 weeks after exposure, and for this reason, it is sometimes difficult to trace an outbreak to an index patient. Scabies mites prefer certain body areas such as the palms, wrists, ankles, nipples, umbilicus, and genital skin. The major features of a scabies infestation include intensive pruritus that is typically worse at night. Often, itching is disproportionate to clinical findings. Excoriated (scratched) papules and erythematous macules might be seen on the chest and back as well as on other affected areas. Excoriations are widespread, and secondary infection is common. Most secondary infections are localized and do not require treatment as long as the underlying scabies infestation is cured. In some areas of the body, burrows may be encountered. A burrow is a linear streak with a small black dot at one end. This black dot is the scabies mite, which is about the size of a pinhead and can be identified on careful clinical inspection.

Treatment of scabies infestations includes the overnight application of a scabicide, such as lindane or permethrin. Athletes with scabies should be held back from participation in contact sports until the infestation is identified, treated, and cleared, which usually occurs within 1 week. Two applications of scabicide should be given 7 days apart.

Pediculosis

Pediculosis describes infestation with lice. Lice affecting some body areas have a different configuration from those that favor other locations. Three kinds of lice are found in humans. *Pediculus humanus variata capitis* affects the head, *Pediculus humanus corporis* affects the body, and *Phthirus pubis* affects the genital area. Lice can be readily seen moving around on the skin on clinical inspection The louse egg (nit) is often cemented to hair shafts and can be seen on careful inspection. Lice are very infectious and can easily be spread from one individual to the next during contact sports.

Head lice are often associated with crusts and scale on the scalp. Posterior cervical *adenopathy* (enlargement of the glands) may develop over a 2 to 3 week period if infestation is not promptly controlled. Lymphadenopathy of the groin area may develop in a patient with body lice or pubic lice. Pubic lice are most commonly acquired through sexual contact. If infestation is not promptly eradicated, lymphadenopathy may develop over a 2 to 3 week period. Treatment includes the use of topical lindane or synergized pyrethrins applied over the affected area and washed off in 10 minutes. Treatment usually kills the lice rapidly; however, to ensure that no viable lice

Infestations

Scabies

Scabies is caused by a female mite that burrows within the epidermis beneath a layer of the stratum corneum, usually involving the palms, wrists, ankles, nipples, umbilicus, and genitals. Lesions and symptoms may not occur until 3 to 4 weeks after exposure, so it can be difficult to trace the source of the infestation. Intense pruritus is often worse at night and disproportionate to clinical findings, which can include excoriated papules and erythematous macules on the chest and back, as well as the previously mentioned areas, and secondary infection. Secondary infections do not require treatment as long as the infestation is cured. Burrows may be visible as linear streaks with a small black dot at one end, which is the scabies mite. Treatment is two overnight applications of a scabicide (lindane or permethrin) 1 week apart and restriction from contact sports until the lesions have cleared (usually within 1 week).

Pediculosis

Pediculosis is an infestation with lice and can affect the head (*Pediculus humanus variata capitis*), the body (*Pediculus humanus corporis*), or the genital area (*Phthirus pubis*). On evaluation, the louse egg (nit) is often cemented to the hair shaft, and lice can be seen moving on the skin. Head lice are often associated with scalp crusts and scales and posterior cervical adenopathy. Body and pubic lice may be accompanied by groin lymphadenopathy. Management is topical lindane or synergized pyrethrins and restriction from contact or team sports until the athlete is free of nits. Linens and clothing should be washed.

remain, athletes should be free of nits before resuming contact or team sports. In addition, clothing and bed linens should be washed.

HERPES SIMPLEX

Herpes simplex infection can affect any area of the body; however, recurrent infection is most commonly seen around the lips and at the vermilion border. Herpes simplex infection presents as grouped vesicles on an erythematous base (**Figure 19-10**). Primary infection may be associated with gingivostomatitis (inflammation involving both the gingivae and the oral mucosa) and pharyngitis (inflammation of the pharynx).[11] Infection occurs most

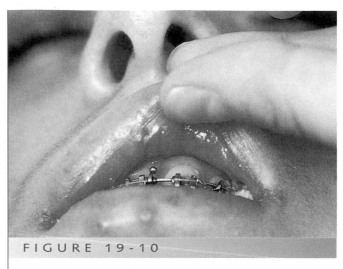

FIGURE 19-10

Grouped vesicles and pustules on an erythematous base indicate herpes simplex infection.

commonly in children between ages 1 and 5 years. After an incubation period of 3 to 12 days, pain develops, and vesicles begin to appear over the next day. Treatment is not always required, but cool compresses and use of antiviral agents such as acyclovir lead to prompt resolution. Because herpes simplex can be spread by contact with the moist lesions, athletes with herpes simplex in areas that can be contacted by other athletes should be closely monitored and held back from contact sports. Once the lesions are crusted and no longer moist, participation in sports may be resumed.

Genital Herpes

Genital herpes is characterized by the development of vesicles and pustules on an erythematous base. Lesions are clustered, and the patient may experience flu-like symptoms such as myalgia and headache. Treatment with oral antiviral agents is indicated, and if individuals have more than six outbreaks in a year, suppressive therapy should be considered. Acyclovir, famciclovir, or valacyclovir may be given in daily doses to prevent additional outbreaks. Genital herpes does not require disqualification from sports, assuming that there will be no contact with the affected area. Athletes with genital herpes who feel ill should be restricted from sports.

Herpes Gladiatorum

Herpes gladiatorum represents the spread of herpes to abraded or injured skin. It most commonly occurs in individuals with widespread dermatitis who have decreased cutaneous immunity. Widespread blisters in regions of dermatitis may develop in individuals with atopic dermatitis or less common disorders such as Darier's disease. The underlying dermatosis becomes inflamed, and lesions may mimic impetigo with red-brown crusts disseminated over the body. Treatment with oral agents is indicated. Athletes with herpes gladiatorum should be disqualified from participation in sports until lesions are healed.

EFFECTS OF PHYSICAL EXPOSURE OF ELEMENTS ON THE SKIN

Sunburn

Because many athletes exercise outside for many hours, sunburn is a common problem. Sunburn is characterized by tender, red, and swollen areas with sharply marginated borders (**Figure 19-11**). Excessive sun exposure is linked with photoaging as well as increased risk of skin cancer, and athletes should avoid unnecessary sun exposure. Minimizing outdoor activity between the hours of 10 am and 2 pm is helpful as is the use of broad-spectrum sunscreens that block both ultraviolet A and ultraviolet B light. Sunscreens with an oil base may be occlusive and uncomfortable to athletes who are sweating. Gel or spray products are preferred. Sunscreen should be applied to all exposed skin areas. Formulations vary in their ability to combine with the skin and endure sweating and wiping. If athletes spend the entire day outside, sunscreen should be applied in the morning and reapplied in the middle of the day. If an athlete has sunburn, he or she should be treated with cool compresses, emollient creams, topical antibiotic ointments, and oral nonsteroidal anti-inflammatory agents.

Frostbite

Frostbite is caused by tissue injury from freezing. Frostbite may occur in any area where temperatures dip below 32.0°F (0°C), however, it can also occur at higher

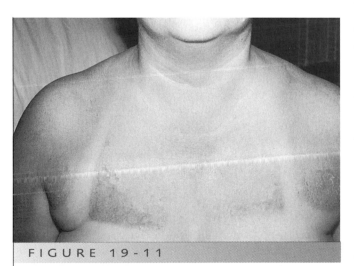

FIGURE 19-11

Well-marginated, tender, red, and swollen areas characterize sunburn.

FOCUS ON . . .

Herpes Simplex

Herpes simplex is characterized by grouped vesicles on an erythematous base that most often affects children ages 1 to 5 years after an incubation period of 3 to 12 days. The primary infection may be associated with gingivostomatitis and pharyngitis. Recurrent infection is most common around the lips and at the vermilion border. Treatment is not always required, but cool compresses and antiviral agents such as acyclovir can resolve the lesions promptly. Moist lesions are contagious, so athletes with lesions in areas that other athletes might contact during sport should not participate until the lesions are crusted and dry.

Genital herpes

Genital herpes involves clustered vesicles and pustules on an erythematous base, often accompanied by flu-like symptoms of myalgia and headache. Oral antiviral agents are prescribed, and individuals with more than six outbreaks per year may need suppressive therapy. Genital herpes need not restrict the athlete from sports; however, if the athlete feels ill, he or she should not participate.

Herpes gladiatorum

Herpes gladiatorum describes the spread of herpes to abraded or injured skin, which most frequently occurs in individuals with widespread dermatitis and decreased cutaneous immunity. The underlying dermatosis becomes inflamed, and the lesions may mimic impetigo. Oral antiviral medications are needed, and athletes should not participate in sports until the lesions have healed.

temperatures in high altitudes. Circulation is impaired in the frozen area and cellular damage leads to platelet aggregation. The symptoms of numbness and stiffness occur first, and then the skin takes on a white, waxy appearance (**Figure 19-12**). Not only are the fingers, toes, ears, and nose commonly involved, but also the penis may develop frostbite if not properly protected. Areas should be kept covered and have enough surrounding insulation to maintain a normal skin surface temperature level. Frostbite may occur in athletes engaging in any outdoor sport. It is rarely encountered in serious athletes in cooler climates. More often it is seen in temperate climates in novice athletes who are not taking proper precautions.

Frostbite may be classified as superficial or deep. In superficial frostbite, deeper tissues are soft and resilient and the surface of the skin is frozen. With deep frostbite, the affected area feels solid. Frostbitten areas can

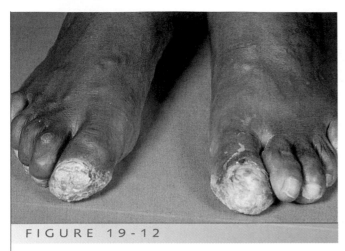

FIGURE 19-12

Frostbitten skin takes on a white, waxy appearance.

be rapidly rewarmed by placing the affected area in a source of warmth, such as a water bath heated to between 100° and 112°F. The area should become flushed and painful with parasthesias within about a half hour. Debridement should be minimized until healing has occurred. Deep frostbite is associated with more tissue injury and greater sloughing of tissue. Cold hypersensitivity and hyperhidrosis are common.

Calluses and Corns

Calluses and corns are the most common dermatologic problem encountered in athletes. Calluses and corns are an attempt made by the skin to protect itself from repetitive injury. *Calluses*, which occur over pressure points, are a buildup of the keratin layer and are associated with hyperplasia of the epidermis in areas of repetitive friction or injury.[12] Calluses frequently occur on the plantar surface of the feet around the great toe. Well-circumscribed yellow-brown scaling areas are encountered (**Figure 19-13**). Paring of the callus skin reveals intact dermatoglyphics (fingerprint markings). Calluses that are asymptomatic do not require treatment. If calluses are large, they may be painful to walk on and should be pared.

Corns are a buildup of compacted keratin that form a circumscribed area, usually on the soles of the feet. Corns exert pressure on the skin during shoe wear and are often painful. Corns are often described as feeling like having a pebble in one's shoe. Gentle debridement with a pumice stone may alleviate pain. Physical paring or application of topical keratolytics may also be helpful. Athletes with calluses or corns can participate in sports as long as they do not have too much discomfort.

Blisters

If shearing forces from rubbing or from rapid starts and stops are too great, blisters may form.[13] Loose athletic shoes that rub the athlete's skin may lead to the develop-

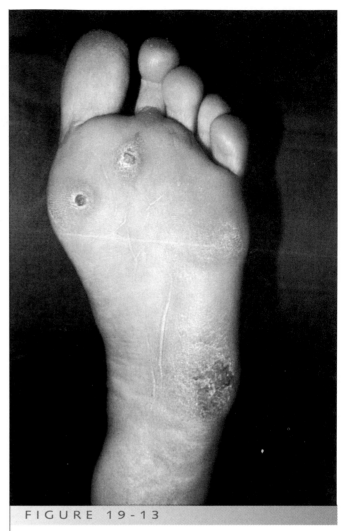

FIGURE 19-13

Calluses are associated with well-circumscribed yellow-brown scaling areas.

ment of large tense bulla. Repeated activity while wearing shoes that do not fit snugly causes an intracorneal or intraepidermal split to form. An intracorneal split, which is more common, will fill with serous fluid, and an intraepidermal split will fill with serosanguineous fluid. Both changes have a similar clinical appearance. Because the surface of the skin is not changed, but dark pigmentation from blood is apparent, athletes may worry that they have an infection. Blisters often have a gray-white appearance and are surrounded by an erythematous rim (Figure 19-14) Treatment strategies for both are the same.

Healing is probably most rapid when the blister is left intact and weight is kept off the affected area. However, this approach is often not practical.[14] After 2 to 3 days, blisters should be healed enough to allow normal weightbearing; complete healing takes approximately 2 weeks. In instances that the patient cannot keep weight off

FOCUS ON . . .

Effects of Physical Exposure of Elements on the Skin

Sunburn

Sunburn presents with tender, erythematous, and edematous areas with sharply marginated borders after excessive sun exposure. Excessive sun exposure is linked with both photoaging and an increased risk of skin cancer. Therefore, athletes should minimize outdoor activity during the intense sun hours of 10 am to 2 pm and should wear broad-spectrum sunscreens, preferably gels or sprays, that block both ultraviolet A and B light. Treatment is cool compresses, emollient creams, topical antibiotics, and oral nonsteroidal anti-inflammatory drugs.

Frostbite

Frostbite, or tissue injury from freezing, can occur anytime temperatures fall to less than 32°F (0°C), but can also be seen at higher temperatures at high altitudes, particularly in novice athletes who are not taking proper precautions. Impaired circulation in the frozen area causes cell damage and leads to platelet aggregation. Numbness and stiffness are followed by a white, waxy appearance of the skin. The fingers, toes, ears, nose, and penis are most often affected. Superficial frostbite is treated with rapid rewarming of the affected part, as in a water bath heated to between 100° and 112°F. Within about 30 minutes, the area will become flushed and painful with paresthesias. Deep frostbite is associated with more tissue injury and greater sloughing of tissue.

Calluses and corns

Calluses and corns are the most common dermatologic problem seen in athletes, representing the skin's attempt to protect itself from repetitive injury. Calluses are a buildup of the keratin layer of the skin and are associated with epidermal hyperplasia and well-circumscribed yellow-brown scaling areas in areas of repetitive friction or injury. Often the plantar surface of the foot around the great toe is affected. Asymptomatic calluses require no treatment. Large calluses may be painful during walking and should be pared. Corns, which can be quite painful, are the buildup of compact keratin that forms a circumscribed area that presses on the skin, causing the athlete to feel as if a pebble is in the shoe. Gentle debridement with a pumice stone, topical keratolytics, or physical paring may be helpful. As long as the athlete is not experiencing much discomfort from corns or calluses, he or she can participate in sports.

Blisters

Blisters occur when shearing forces are too great (as from wet, poor-fitting athletic shoes), and repeated activity causes an intracorneal or intraepidermal split. The more common intracorneal split fills with serous fluid, and an intraepidermal split fills with serosanguineous fluid. Blisters often appear gray-white and are surrounded by an erythematous rim. They are best treated by leaving the blister intact and keeping weight off the injured area. If these measures are not practical, the skin is incised with a sterile blade or needle after antiseptic cleansing, the fluid is evacuated, and a petrolatum dressing is applied. The athlete can return to sport as soon as discomfort subsides.

Talon noir/intracorneal hemorrhage

Talon noir or intracorneal hemorrhage represents bleeding into the stratum corneum (underneath the nail plate or at the edge of the palm or the plantar surface), commonly encountered with rapid starts or stops. Paring of the stratum corneum is painless and will remove the hemorrhage. However, the condition can mimic melanoma, and therefore, biopsy may be necessary.

the affected area, the affected skin is prepared with an antiseptic cleanser and incised with a sterile blade or needle. The fluid is removed or drained, and a petrolatum dressing is applied. Athletes who have blisters can return to sports as soon as discomfort subsides.

Talon Noir/Intracorneal Hemorrhage

Talon noir represents bleeding into the stratum corneum.[15] This is commonly encountered in athletes who participate in sports that involve rapid starting and stopping. Bleeding occurs underneath the nail plate, on the edge of the palms, or on the plantar surface of the foot. This condition is of no consequence medically, but it often causes concern because a dark area develops and may raise the fear of melanoma. Paring of the stratum corneum is painless and will remove the hemorrhage. If there is any doubt about the nature of the problem, biopsy should be considered.

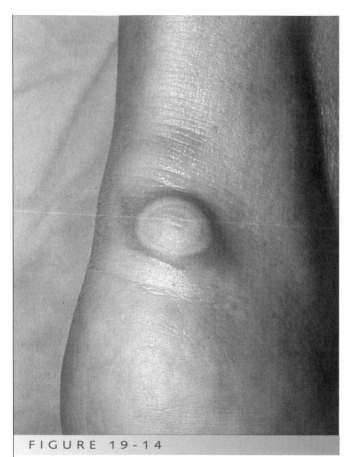

FIGURE 19-14

A gray-white appearance and an erythematous rim often characterize a blister.

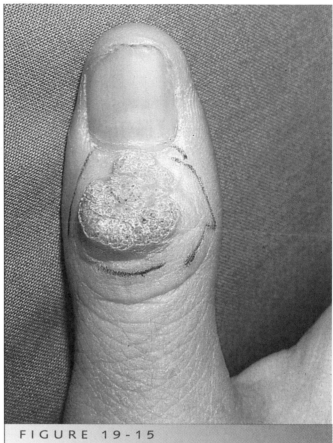

FIGURE 19-15

Warts have a rough, skin-colored or tan-gray surface.

GROWTHS (NEOPLASMS IN THE SKIN)

Warts

Warts (verruca vulgaris) are common benign growths caused by infection with the human papilloma virus. Warts are typically skin-colored or tan-gray with a rough surface (**Figure 19-15**). Although they are caused by a virus, they grow slowly and are usually asymptomatic. Some individuals are more susceptible to the virus, and widespread lesions can spread to areas of trauma in these individuals (**Figure 19-16**). Paring of warts reveals stippled blood vessels and loss of normal dermatoglyphics. Although plantar warts (verruca plantaris) may occur in athletes of any age, they are encountered most commonly in adolescent athletes. Warts have different appearances depending on their location. Many warts on the face have a pink to brown appearance and a slightly elevated flat surface ("flat warts"). Warts on genital skin have a pedunculated appearance and may resemble skin tags. Plantar warts exhibit a roughened surface and interfere with normal dermatoglyphics because the growth of the wart prevents the development of the normal skin markings. A stippled appearance of altered blood vessels in the papillary dermis may impart a granular appearance to the wart.

Treatment of warts varies, and unfortunately, no one treatment is uniformly effective. Some warts regress spontaneously without treatment. Liquid nitrogen cryotherapy for smaller warts is simple and effective. With this treatment, liquid nitrogen is applied to the wart and a small rim of surrounding normal tissue for a short period of time. Blisters form, and because human papilloma virus can only survive in the epidermis, the wart is removed when the epidermis is sloughed. Warts may recur if destruction is incomplete. Cryotherapy treatments performed too aggressively may result in permanent scarring and hypopigmentation. Other treatment options include the use of topical keratolytic agents such as salicylic acid, topical irritants such as formalin, and newer immune response modifiers such as imiquimod cream. Electrodesiccation and curettage or laser ablation can be performed, but these treatments will leave a full-thickness defect in the skin that may take several weeks to heal. Because treated areas feel like a full-thickness burn when

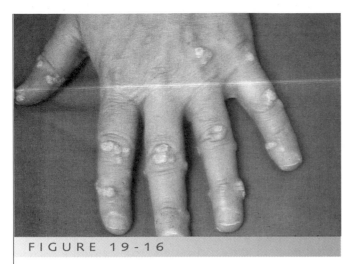

FIGURE 19-16

Warts may be numerous and can spread to areas of trauma.

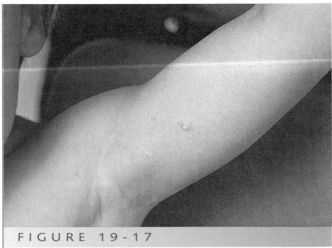

FIGURE 19-17

Skin-colored papules with central umbilication indicate molluscum contagiosum infection.

healing, continued athletic activity during the recovery period is impossible because of pain. Injection with interferon is a helpful, although expensive, new approach.[16] Warts are contagious, and athletes should take precautions such as wearing sandals in common shower areas to prevent spread to other teammates.

Molluscum Contagiosum

Molluscum contagiosum is a DNA virus of the pox virus group that is commonly encountered in athletes. Skincolored papules with central umbilication occur and will spread if manipulated or traumatized (**Figure 19-17**). The individual papules contain a cheesy white material that contains the infectious virus. Spread is common among athletes, and there may be widespread outbreaks on swim teams or wrestling teams, and in sports such as rugby that involve close contact. Treatment of molluscum infection is straightforward. Simple curettage or liquid nitrogen cryotherapy eradicates lesions. Because lesions are easily spread to other teammates through direct contact or sharing towels or equipment, athletes with molluscum lesions should not participate in contact sports until all lesions have cleared.

Sebaceous Cysts

Epidermal inclusion cysts develop when a follicular infundibulum, the superficial portion of the hair follicle that opens to the surface, is occluded by a keratinaceous plug.[4] Many cysts do not require treatment unless they become unsightly or symptomatic with itching, pain, or inflammation. Cysts typically develop slowly but may become inflamed. Incision and drainage of cysts provides short-term symptomatic relief, but unless the entire epithelial lining of the cyst is excised, the cyst will most likely return. For this reason, most physicians recommend

full excision with suture closure. Cysts are firm but freely moveable and not attached to underlying tissues.

Skin Cancer

The incidence of skin cancer continues to increase with more than one million new cases each year in the United States alone. Athletes who enjoy outdoor sports are particularly prone to develop long-term effects of ultraviolet exposure such as leathery skin texture, deep wrinkles, pigmentary abnormalities, and skin cancer. The most common skin cancer is *basal cell carcinoma*.[5] Although basal cell carcinoma rarely metastasizes, it causes local destruction of tissue. Basal cell carcinomas occur most commonly on the head and in the neck area and may bleed or ulcerate. The most common type of basal cell carcinoma is the so-called "superficial multifocal" type, in which a waxy plaque with a central crust is identified (**Figure 19-18**).

Squamous cell carcinomas are less common than basal cell carcinomas and are associated with hyperkeratosis and overlying hemorrhage. Surgical excision of skin cancer is the treatment of choice.

Melanoma is less common, but more deadly. The incidence of melanoma is increasing more rapidly than that of any other cancer. The reason for this increase is not entirely understood, but increased recreational sun exposure as well as thinning of the ozone layer have been indicated as important factors. An asymmetric pigmented lesion with an irregular border, variegated color, or large diameter should be carefully evaluated (**Figure 19-19**). Melanoma may have a variety of different clinical presentations. These include nodular, superficial spreading, verrucous, desmoplastic, and lentiginous forms.

The use of sunscreens helps prevent the development of all three types of the common skin cancers. A

FOCUS ON . . .

Growths (Neoplasms of the Skin)

Warts

Warts are skin-colored or tan-gray benign growths resulting from human papilloma virus infection. They tend to grow slowly and asymptomatically, but some individuals are more susceptible and can develop widespread lesions. Plantar warts are often seen in adolescents, but are possible at any age. Facial warts are pink to brown and have a slightly elevated flat surface (flat warts). Genital warts are pedunculated and may resemble skin tags. Plantar warts have a rough surface and interfere with normal dermatoglyphics. A wart may also appear granular as a result of changes in blood vessels in the papillary dermis.

Some warts regress spontaneously without treatment. Small warts can be managed with liquid nitrogen cryotherapy, which causes a blister and sloughing of the epidermis. However, warts can recur if the virus is not completely destroyed. Cryotherapy that is too aggressive can result in hypopigmentation and permanent scarring. Topical keratolytics such as salicylic acid, topical irritants such as formalin, and newer immune response modifiers such as imiquimod cream may be useful. Electrodesiccation and curettage or laser ablation leave a full-thickness skin defect that can take several weeks to heal and prevent the athlete from participating in sport. Interferon injection is a helpful, but expensive approach. Warts are contagious, and athletes should take precautions to prevent spread.

Molluscum contagiosum

Molluscum contagiosum is caused by a DNA virus of the pox virus group and results in skin-colored papules with central umbilication containing a cheesy white material. The papules spread if manipulated or traumatized, and outbreaks on athletic teams with close contact can be widespread. Treatment is simple curettage or liquid nitrogen cryotherapy to eradicate the lesions. Athletes should be restricted from contact sports until all lesions have cleared.

Sebaceous cysts

Epidermal inclusion cysts develop slowly when a follicular infundibulum is occluded by a keratinaceous plug and do not require treatment unless they become symptomatic (inflamed) or unsightly. Cysts are firm, freely movable, and not attached to underlying tissues. Incision and drainage can provide symptomatic relief, but the entire epithelial lining of the cyst must be removed to prevent its return.

Skin cancer

The incidence of skin cancer in the United States continues to increase. Outdoor athletes are susceptible to the long-term effects of ultraviolet exposure, which include leathery skin texture, deep wrinkles, pigment abnormalities, and skin cancer. Basal cell carcinomas, the most common skin cancer, rarely metastasize, but they cause local tissue destruction. They are most frequently seen on the head and neck, usually look waxy, and may bleed or ulcerate. Less common are squamous cell carcinomas, which are associated with hyperkeratosis and overlying hemorrhage. Melanoma, while less common than other forms of skin cancer, is more deadly, and its incidence is increasing more rapidly. A pigmented lesion that is asymmetric and has an irregular border, variegated color, or large diameter should be carefully evaluated. The treatment of choice for all skin cancers is surgical excision.

Sunscreens can help prevent the development of common skin cancers. A waterproof, noncomedogenic, broad-spectrum sunscreen that blocks ultraviolet A and B light is preferred. Newer agents, such as Parsol 1789, provide uniform and effective sun protection.

broad-spectrum sunscreen is recommended for athletes who practice outdoors. Waterproof products that are noncomedogenic and block both ultraviolet A and ultraviolet B light are preferred. Newer agents such as Parsol 1789 are extremely helpful in providing uniform and effective sun protection. With the increase in skin cancer, sports physicians and athletic trainers are in a unique position to counsel athletes about the need for sun protection. In a population that is otherwise in good health, athletes may not be receiving this type of advice from any other source.

UNCOMMON DERMATOSES

Many common dermatoses may develop in athletes as well as some uncommon ones that are unique to athletes. Uncommon dermatoses include jogger's nipple, redness and irritation of the nipples from rubbing; surfer's nodules, overgrowths of connective tissue in the knee area

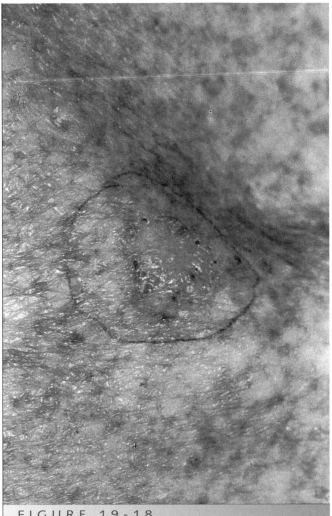

FIGURE 19-18

The most common type of basal cell carcinoma is the so-called "superficial multifocal" type. A waxy crusted plaque is seen centrally.

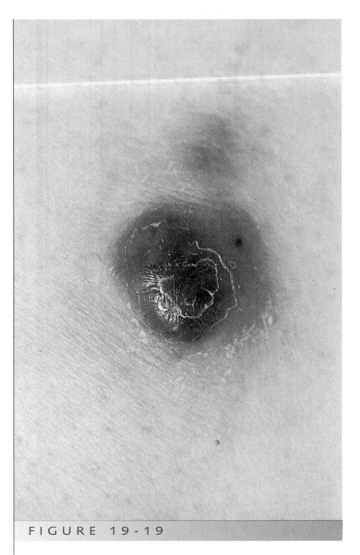

FIGURE 19-19

Any suspected melanoma should be evaluated carefully. This nodular melanoma developed rapidly and had already metastasized at the time of biopsy.

caused by long hours on the knees such as when paddling a surfboard out into the waves; rower's rump, calluses of the buttocks and hyperplasia of the skin near the sacrum; mogul skier's palm, a change in the color of the palm of the hand that looks similar to a bruise as a result of vigorous pole planting and weightbearing while skiing for long hours over moguls; and unusual changes in the skin such as green hair from swimming in water that contains chlorine.[17-21] The sports physician and athletic trainer will also encounter many athletes with worsening of an underlying dermatosis such as psoriasis or lichen planus. Often, these individuals will already be familiar with the management of their skin condition, but they will require advice and counseling on how to avoid exacerbation by minimizing trauma or irritation from sports equipment or protective clothing.

FOCUS ON . . .

Uncommon Dermatoses

Uncommon dermatoses include jogger's nipples, surfer's nodules, rower's rump, mogul skier's palm, and unusual skin changes such as green hair color from swimming in water that contains chlorine. The sports physician and athletic trainer will sometimes encounter these conditions in addition to worsening of an already existing underlying dermatosis. Athletes often will be familiar with management of the condition; however, they may require advice and counseling on how to avoid making the situation worse.

CHAPTER REVIEW

Skin problems are frequent in athletes, and although many are of only minor importance, they can disqualify athletes from participating or prevent optimal performance. The skin provides structure, form, and protection to the body. Any of the layers of the skin can be injured or impaired, causing skin disease.

A skin condition should be classified as either a growth (neoplastic process) or a rash (inflammatory dermatosis). A growth only causes trouble when its physical size interferes with normal function, and it usually does not itch. A rash usually itches and develops acutely. When treating an athlete who has a skin condition, the individual should be asked what treatments and topical agents have been used. Moreover, the duration of the skin problem, the location on the body, and the primary lesion should be identified.

Inflammatory conditions include acne, contact dermatitis, intertrigo, urticaria or hives, psoriasis, seborrheic dermatitis, and pityriasis rosea. Depending on the source of the inflammation, these conditions do not usually restrict athletic participation. Preexisting dermatoses such as psoriasis, seborrheic dermatitis, and pityriasis rosea are not contagious, but they may be exacerbated by sports activity (the Koebner effect or isomorphic phenomenon).

Infectious conditions, including pilosebaceous unit infection, impetigo, tinea infections, cellulitis, and pityriasis versicolor, may require the athlete to avoid contact sports until the infection has cleared. Infestations such as scabies and pediculosis also must be treated and cleared before the athlete returns to contact or team sports. Herpes simplex and herpes gladiatorum are contagious and the athlete must be restricted from sport until the lesions have cleared, but genital herpes usually do not require disqualification.

The effects of physical exposure on the skin include the sun (sunburn) and frostbite. Both conditions are preventable if the athlete takes appropriate precautions. Calluses and corns are very common in athletes, but only require treatment if they are painful. Blisters should be left intact to heal, if possible, and talon noir (intracorneal hemorrhage) is generally of no medical consequence.

Growths, or skin neoplasms, include warts, molluscum contagiosum, cysts, and skin cancers. Warts are contagious, and therefore, the athlete should take precautions to prevent spread. Cysts need only be excised if they become asymptomatic or unsightly. Molluscum contagiosum lesions should be removed, as should skin cancers. The outdoor athlete should always be diligent about using a broad-spectrum sunscreen, which can prevent the development of skin cancers.

SELF-TEST

1. The function of the stratum corneum is to:
   A. insulate the skin.
   B. give the skin elasticity.
   C. protect from ultraviolet damage.
   D. provide a barrier to noxious substances.

2. The progression of open comedones to erythematous papules to pustules and finally to cysts describes which dermatologic condition?
   A. Acne
   B. Intertrigo
   C. Seborrheic dermatitis
   D. Molluscum contagiosum

3. Itchy, red, linear areas of scaling, erythema, and vesiculation are characteristic of:
   A. urticaria.
   B. psoriasis.
   C. poison ivy.
   D. herpes simplex.

4. Impetigo is commonly treated with:
   A. zinc oxide.
   B. antibiotics.
   C. oral antihistamines.
   D. topical corticosteroids.

5. An infection of the groin folds by dermatophytes is called:
   A. cellulitis.
   B. tinea cruris.
   C. tinea capitis.
   D. onychomycosis.

6. An infection of the skin and pilosebaceous unit seen most often in young adults and characterized by mild itching is known as:
   A. scabies.
   B. pediculosis.
   C. herpes gladiatorum.
   D. pityriasis versicolor.

7. Tender, erythematous, edematous areas with sharply marginated borders are characteristic of:
   A. blisters.
   B. frostbite.
   C. sunburn.
   D. intracorneal hemorrhage.

8. Benign, flesh-colored or tan-gray growths caused by human papilloma virus infection are known as:
   A. cysts.
   B. warts.
   C. eczema.
   D. calluses.

9. Athletes with molluscum contagiosum may participate in contact sports:
   A. after 1 month.
   B. without restriction.
   C. once treatment has started.
   D. once all lesions have cleared.

10. Which of the following statements about basal cell carcinoma is true?
    A. It often metastasizes.
    B. It is the most common skin cancer.
    C. It usually occurs on the extremities.
    D. It causes widespread tissue destruction.

Answers on page 895.

References

1. Bergfeld WF, Helm TN: Skin disorders in athletes, in Grana WA, Kalenak A (eds): *Clinical Sports Medicine.* Philadelphia, PA, WB Saunders, 1991, pp 110–118.

2. Bergfeld WF, Helm TN: The skin, in Strauss RH (ed): *Sports Medicine*, ed 2. Philadelphia, PA, WB Saunders, 1991; pp 117–131.

3. Bergfeld WF, Elston D: Skin problems of athletes in sports injuries, in Fu FH, Stone D (eds): *Sports Injuries: Mechanisms, Prevention and Treatment.* Baltimore, MD, Williams & Wilkins, 1994, pp 781–795.

4. Helm KF, Marks JG: *Atlas of Differential Diagnosis in Dermatopathy.* New York, NY, Churchill Livingstone, 1998.

5. Habif TP: *Clinical Dermatology: A Color Guide to Diagnosis and Therapy*, ed 3. New York, NY, Mosby, 1996.

6. Leyden JJ: Topical treatment of acne vulgaris: Retinoids and cutaneous irritation. *J Am Acad Dermatol* 1988; 38:1–4.

7. Shriner DL, Schwartz RA, Janniger CK: Impetigo. *Cutis* 1995;56:30–32.

8. Drago F, Ranieri E, Malaguti F, Battifoglio ML, Losi E, Rebora A: Human herpes virus 7 in patients with pityriasis rosea: Electron microscopy investigations and polymerase chain reaction in mononuclear cells, plasma, and skin. *Dermatology* 1997;195:374–378.

9. Shear, NH, Einarson TR, Arikian SR, Doyle JJ, van Assche D: Pharmacoeconomic analysis of topical treatments for Tinea infections. *Int J Dermatol* 1998;37:64–71.

10. Sunenshine PJ, Schwartz RA, Janniger CK: Tinea veriscolor: An update. *Cutis* 1998;61:65–68.

11. Posavad CM, Koelle DM, Corey L: Tipping the scales of herpes simplex virus reactivation: The important responses are local. *Nature Med* 1998;4:381–382.

12. Sheard C: Simple management of plantar clari. *Cutis* 1992;50:138.

13. Herring KM, Ritchie DH: Friction blisters and sock fiber composition: A double blind controlled study. *J Am Podiatr Med Assoc* 1990;80:63.

14. Sedar JI: Treatment of blisters in the running athlete. *Arch Podiatric Med Foot Surg Sports Med* 1978;(suppl 1): 2–34.

15. Yaffe H: Talon noir. *Arch Dermatol* 1971;104:452.

16. Brodel RT, Bredle DL: The treatment of palmar and plantar warts using natural alpha interferon and a needless injector. *Dermatol Surg* 1995; 21:213–218.

17. Levit F: Letter: Jogger's nipples. N *Engl J Med* 1977;197:1127.

18. Cohen PR, Eliezri YD, Silvers DN: Athlete's nodules: Sports related connective tissue nevi of the collagen type (collagenomas). *Cutis* 1992; 50:131–135.

19. Tomecki KJ, Mikesell JF: Rower's rump. *J Am Acad Dermatol* 1987;16:890.

20. Swinehart JM: Mogul skier's palm: Traumatic hypothenar ecchymosis. *Cutis* 1992;50:117-118.

21. Bhat GR: The green hair problem: A preliminary investigation. *J Soc Cosmet Chem* 1979;30:1.

20

Gastrointestinal and Genitourinary Conditions and Injuries

John M. Sullivan, MD
David L. Shepherd, MD
Daniel L. Dent, MD
Donald Shell, MD
Karen R. Toburen, EdD, ATC

QUICK CONTENTS

- Anatomy of the abdomen.

- Mechanisms of abdominal injury and the evaluation of the athlete with such an injury.

- The examination and management of athletes with specific abdominal injuries.

- Gastrointestinal diseases in the athlete.

- The genitourinary examination at the preparticipation physical screenings.

- Sports participation with a solitary genitourinary organ.

- Sports-related genitourinary injuries.

OVERVIEW

The sequelae of abdominal injuries from sports-related trauma may be life-threatening and require diligence by athletic trainers and physicians in the field who encounter athletes who have sustained athletic injuries. This chapter begins with a discussion about abdominal injuries, which is followed by an explanation of fundamental abdominal anatomy and the approach to the athlete with abdominal pain. Specific abdominal injuries are examined, as are gastrointestinal diseases common among athletes. Genitourinary issues, such as the sports entrance physical examination and participation in sports by individuals with a single testicle or kidney, and sports-related genitourinary injuries are also addressed in this chapter.

ABDOMINAL INJURIES

Although they are generally considered to be minor, 10% of all abdominal injuries result from sports-related trauma.[1] The sequelae of these injuries can, in fact, be devastating, even life-threatening, and require special diligence by athletic trainers, emergency medical technicians, and team physicians. The athlete who has abdominal pain represents a diagnostic dilemma, because the source of injury is frequently presumed to be the sport activity, which in fact may be masking an underlying or unrelated medical condition. This presumption may create a missed opportunity to intervene and minimize complication and sequelae of the injury or disease. The most obvious source of abdominal trauma may occur with contact sports, but higher energy mechanisms of injury often occur from noncontact sports that involve high velocity and subsequent rapid deceleration. Bicycles, snowmobiles, and motocross may cause patterns of abdominal injury similar to those seen in motor vehicle crashes.

ANATOMY OF THE ABDOMEN

The anatomy of the abdomen should be considered during assessment of any injury, because pain, which is the most common symptom of injury, generally relates to the specific entity involved, either directly, as in fractures or muscle strains, or indirectly, as with abdominal injuries. For purposes of localizing symptoms, the abdomen is visually divided into four quadrants and are described in relation to the umbilicus (right versus left, upper versus lower).

Abdominal Wall

The abdominal organs are well protected by the lower ribs and a series of overlapping muscles that function as the first shield to visceral injury[2] (**Figure 20-1**). Perhaps the most visibly obvious muscle in the trained athlete is the thick rectus abdominis that originates from the lower rib margin and inserts on the pubis with septations of lateral fascia. In the athlete with a well-defined abdominal wall, the rectus can be seen to function during sit-ups or crunches. Lateral to the rectus and from which its fascia originates lie three layers of muscle with differing orientations. These muscle layers rotate the trunk and can be used to facilitate forced expiration by rapidly forcing air out of the chest. The most superficial layer, the external oblique, is composed of fibers that run inferomedially. In the next layer, the internal oblique, fibers run inferolaterally. The innermost layer, the transversus abdominis, is composed of fibers that run nearly perpendicular to the long axis formed by the spine and function mostly in forced expiration or **Valsalva's maneuver** ("bearing down" or increasing intra-abdominal and intrathoracic pressure). The diaphragm, which is a dome-shaped muscle that functions as the primary muscle of respiration, is the roof of the abdomen and moves the abdominal organs in a caudad and cephalad direction during respiration. The lower ribs act as functional barriers that overlie the liver on the right and the spleen on the left. Dislocated fractures of the ribs readily puncture the liver or spleen; however, bruising or abrasion may be the only external evidence of the compressive forces that occur during an impact that completely ruptures the underlying organ. Children have more cartilaginous ribs that may not fracture even in the face of severe force, potentially masking underlying injury.

The Spleen

The spleen is a reticuloendothelial organ, which is part of the blood filtration system, that maintains the quality of erythrocytes by removing defective red blood cells, synthesizes antibodies, and removes antibody-coated blood cells from the circulation.[2] The spleen is adjacent to the upper portion of the stomach and lies between the stomach and diaphragm and contacts the tail of the pancreas medially. The tenth rib lies anterior to the long axis of the spleen. The spleen, which measures approximately 12 cm long and 7 mm wide, is not palpable unless it is enlarged.[2] The spleen is covered by a fibrous capsule that is pierced by its blood supply at a medial hilum where it almost immediately branches into the engorged pulp of splenic tissue.

The Liver

The liver lies under the right side of the diaphragm and is guarded anteriorly from the fifth rib superiorly to the costal margin.[2] The liver is a reddish color and is the

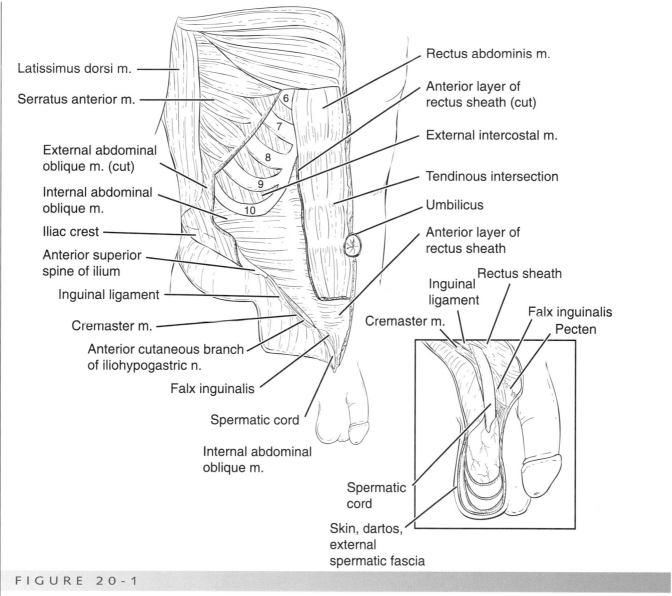

FIGURE 20-1

Overlapping muscles help protect the abdominal organs from injury.

largest gland in the body. It is essential to digestion, metabolism and storage of nutrients, and removal of toxic byproducts and is the central station of gastrointestinal function. The hilum of the liver contains three main structures: the portal vein, which carries nutrient-rich blood from the intestines; the hepatic artery, which provides approximately one third of the blood and two thirds of the oxygen to the liver; and the common bile duct, which controls the outflow of bile. Like the spleen, a fibrous capsule, called Glisson's capsule, also contains the liver's blood-engorged parenchyma.

The Gastrointestinal Tract

The stomach is the first abdominal representative of the gastrointestinal (GI) tract.[2] The stomach originates from the esophagus 1 to 2 cm inferior to the diaphragm (**Figure 20-2**). The fundus and body of the stomach lie largely in the mid- to left-lateral epigastrium with the terminal portion curving to the right. Food is temporarily stored in the stomach where it is churned with acid before it progresses into the intestine. The stomach terminates with the pyloric valve, which is nearly at the midline of the body. At this point, the stomach empties into the duodenum, which receives digestive enzymes from the pancreas and bile from the liver. The second and third portions of the duodenum are firmly tethered in place by the peritoneum, while the small intestine remains loosely connected by its mesentery, which is mostly fatty tissue that contains the vessels that supply blood to the small intestine. As a result of passage through the stomach and duo-

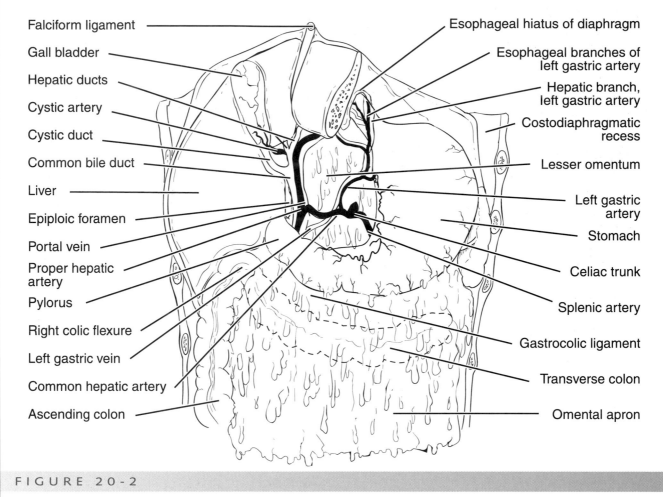

Falciform ligament
Gall bladder
Hepatic ducts
Cystic artery
Cystic duct
Common bile duct
Liver
Epiploic foramen
Portal vein
Proper hepatic artery
Pylorus
Right colic flexure
Left gastric vein
Common hepatic artery
Ascending colon

Esophageal hiatus of diaphragm
Esophageal branches of left gastric artery
Hepatic branch, left gastric artery
Costodiaphragmatic recess
Lesser omentum
Left gastric artery
Stomach
Celiac trunk
Splenic artery
Gastrocolic ligament
Transverse colon
Omental apron

FIGURE 20-2

The organs of the gastrointestinal tract.

denum, thoroughly admixed food passes to the small intestine where absorption of nutrients take place. Small intestine muscular contraction results in peristaltic waves, which conduct remaining waste to the large intestine. The first portion of the colon, the cecum, receives waste from the small intestine, acts as a reservoir, and is the site of the *vermiform* (worm-like) appendix. Waste is conducted from the cecum, and water is resorbed, transforming the once-fluid byproduct into formed stool.

The Pancreas

The pancreas provides digestive enzymes and, perhaps more importantly, regulates serum glucose with a careful balance between insulin and glucagon secretion.[2] The pancreas lies behind the stomach between the duodenum and spleen and is located in the retroperitoneum, normally undisturbed by the undulations of the overlying bowels. However, when the pancreas is disturbed by either pancreatic trauma or pancreatitis, enzymes located within the pancreas may spill out, digesting anything in their path, including the pancreas itself. Even the most skilled surgeon tries to avoid the pancreas unless absolutely necessary.

EVALUATION OF THE ATHLETE WITH ABDOMINAL PAIN

Mechanism and Energy

A degree of suspicion and knowledge of some abdominal anatomy is fundamental to a diagnosis of abdominal injury. The index of suspicion is raised when the kinetic energy is high or the mechanism of injury is appropriate. Kinetic energy is calculated as $KE = \frac{1}{2} mv^2$, where m = mass (weight) and v = velocity (speed). Thus, although mass increases the energy linearly, velocity increases the energy logarithmically. Direct blows to the abdomen represent obvious sources of injury, but rapid deceleration and shear forces must be included as mechanisms of severe abdominal energy although external evidence of trauma is frequently missing. Penetrating trauma rarely results from athletic endeavors; however, if suspicion of penetrating trauma is high, evaluation by a surgeon is necessary.

Physical Examination

When performing an abdominal examination, the athletic trainer should pay attention to rigidity or spasm of the abdominal muscles, tenderness, guarding, bowel sounds, and monitoring of vital signs. The initial exam is usually performed by the athletic trainer and any abnormal findings or concerns for intra-abdominal injury is an indication for referral to a trauma surgeon. Results of monitoring may reveal abnormalities in the vital signs that signal an abdominal catastrophe.[3] The athlete who experiences severe bleeding may report thirst and dizziness. Tachycardia and tachypnea may also be present. In cases of intra-abdominal injury, because the abdominal organs are not innervated by the same pain fibers as the layers of the abdominal wall, pain is a more sensitive indicator of damage than tenderness. Pain can also be referred to other locations, such as the back or shoulders, which can distract the first responder from determining the true injury. Tenderness or abdominal rigidity is frequently a later sign and indicates irritation of the peritoneum.[3] Whenever the mechanism or energy of injury are suspect, the physical examination is often misleading, and further investigation at a hospital is warranted.

Radiographic and Laboratory Evaluation

Although plain abdominal or chest radiographs may reveal air, indicating rupture of a hollow *viscus* (intestine), plain radiographs are neither sensitive nor specific for solid organ injury. Computed tomography (CT) scans and the higher definition spiral CT scans have revolutionized the diagnosis of abdominal trauma. CT scans are sensitive, highly specific, and increasingly rapid and, for investigation of occult injury, have nearly replaced diagnostic peritoneal lavage (DPL), which requires inserting a catheter into the abdomen, washing fluid into and out of the abdomen, and examining the fluids for signs of injury. Improved ultrasound technology has led to a more rapid, real-time imaging modality that can detect pericardial or intra-abdominal free fluid or blood in addition to localizing injury. As part of the initial evaluation, blood should be drawn for hematocrit in addition to other values that may indicate occult injury such as liver function tests, lactate dehydrogenase (LDH), glucose, and electrolytes. These data can be integrated with the clinical results and radiographs to evaluate the need for surgical or other intervention. With diligent determination of the mechanism and energy of injury, rapid assessment and resuscitation, and judicious radiologic evaluation, even severe abdominal injuries need not be catastrophic.

SPECIFIC ABDOMINAL INJURIES

Injuries to the Abdominal Wall

Most injuries to the abdominal wall musculature are caused by strain from overexertion, but the shielding position of the abdominal wall predisposes it in particular to diffuse bruising or hematoma. Hematomas to the rectus abdominis may result from ruptures of the epigastric artery, epigastric vein, or both. Venous bleeding is usually well contained as the rectus fascia confines the hematoma with guarding contractions. Occasionally, bleeding of the epigastric artery incompletely tamponades or rebleeds and requires surgery to tie off the bleeding vessel. Hematomas to the rectus abdominis most often appear as tender focal masses that are palpable within the muscle or sheath and produce either localized peritoneal irritation or no peritoneal irritation that can be differentiated from the rigidity of the acute abdomen.[3]

In addition to pain that is felt in the classic abdominal muscles, the athlete may experience abdominal or groin pain that mimics organ injury or herniation in the musculotendinous units of the adductor longus, rectus femoris, and iliopsoas muscles.[4] Acute, sharp, stabbing pain in the groin with swelling or hematoma can indicate an adductor longus strain.[4] Pain at the insertion of the adductor longus on the pubis frequently indicates chronic strain.[4] Chronic strain can be determined by reproducing the pain in that area with resistance to adduction. The presence of an inguinal hernia, genitourinary trauma, or inguinal lymphadenopathy should also be considered.[4] Pain from a strain to the rectus femoris is frequently located 8 cm inferior to the anterosuperior iliac spine, reflecting its origin at the acetabulum.[4] The iliopsoas, which is a hip flexor, is frequently injured from repeated or forced flexion, resulting in pain at the proximal anteromedial thigh that is reproducible by flexing the hip against resistance at 90° of flexion.

Treatment of muscular strains, bruises, and hematomas is based on early application of ice to promote vasoconstriction and reduce pain and rest to prevent recurrent bleeding, fasciitis, or further destruction to the muscle fibers. Nonsteroidal anti-inflammatory drugs (NSAIDs) may help reduce the pain and inflammation; however, NSAIDs' anticoagulant properties should always be considered. When masses and subjective pain experienced by the athlete are resolved, gradual return to activity is reasonable as long as each of the individual injuries is considered.

Hernias are congenital or acquired defects of the abdominal wall that permit the extrusion of intestine. Hernias appear most typically as a bulge in the inguinal

FOCUS ON . . .

Specific abdominal injuries

Injuries to the abdominal wall

Abdominal wall muscle injury can result in overexertion strain, diffuse bruising, or hematoma. For example, epigastric artery or vein (or both) ruptures can cause hematomas to the rectus abdominis. Although these injuries usually self-tamponade, if tamponade is not complete or if bleeding recurs, surgical ligation may be required. These hematomas are felt as tender, focal masses within the muscle or sheath, with limited or no peritoneal irritation.

Injury to the musculotendinous units of the adductor longus, rectus femoris, or iliopsoas muscle can produce abdominal or groin pain similar to that of organ damage. For example, acute strain of the adductor longus can result in sharp, stabbing groin pain with swelling or hematoma, while chronic strain results in pain at the pubic insertion. The pain is reproduced with resistance to adduction, but must be distinguished from inguinal hernia, genitourinary trauma, and inguinal lymphadenopathy. Rectus femoris strain causes pain 8 cm inferior to the anterosuperior iliac spine, at its acetabular origin. Repeated or forced flexion can injure the iliopsoas, resulting in anteromedial thigh pain reproduced by resistance against hip flexion of 90°.

Treatment of these injuries includes ice for vasoconstriction and pain reduction, rest to prevent rebleeding, fasciitis, and further damage, and nonsteroidal anti-inflammatory drugs (which must be used cautiously because of their anticoagulant properties). Once the mass and pain have resolved, gradual return to activity is permitted.

Hernias, congenital or acquired abdominal wall defects that allow intestinal extrusion, appear as an inguinal or femoral canal bulge. Symptoms range from burning and aching to nausea and vomiting, which may indicate incarceration (strangulation) of the intestine that is sometimes preceded by a ripping or popping feeling. Surgical repair is necessary.

The spleen

Splenomegaly occurs when the spleen's activity increases, as in response to infection (immune hyperplasia) such as infectious mononucleosis and splenic abscess or in early sickle cell disease, with the increased demand for removal of defective red blood cells. Pain and heaviness in the left upper quadrant also result. Splenic injury from acute swelling with capsular stretching or inflammation or infarction (as in sickle cell crisis) can also cause pain. Vascular events in the spleen produce severe left upper quadrant and pleuritic chest pain. Splenic rupture from blunt trauma or an infiltrative process that breaks the capsule can result in an acute abdomen, intraperitoneal bleeding, shock, and death if left untreated. However, blood does not always cause peritonitis, so splenic injuries may be minimally symptomatic.

Clinically, the spleen is examined by the palpation and percussion, which can be supplemented by liver-spleen radionuclide scan, CT scan, magnetic resonance imaging scan, or ultrasound (the test of choice) and laboratory tests to detect systemic illness. For example, in infectious mononucleosis, the granulocyte and white blood cell count may increase, and Epstein-Barr virus heterophils may be evident. In sickle cell anemia, the electrophoresis is positive for hemoglobin S.

Treatment of splenic enlargement from infectious mononucleosis is rest (avoiding excessive physical activity during the first month to avoid splenic rupture) and supportive care. Ultrasound confirmation of normal spleen size may be needed before the athlete is permitted to return to activity.

The liver

Blunt trauma to the liver can cause asymptomatic liver injuries, evident only on CT scanning or laboratory tests. A severe injury can result in free peritoneal bleeding, which is suggested by right upper quadrant or right shoulder pain when the athlete is supine, accompanied by hypotension or shock. Immediate transport to the hospital is required. Like the spleen, the liver enlarged by infections such as mononucleosis or acute hepatitis is vulnerable to injury. Once the liver returns to normal size, return to training may be considered.

(Continued)

FOCUS ON . . .

Specific Abdominal Injuries (Continued)

The gastrointestinal tract

Gastrointestinal injuries in sports are rare, but can be serious. Most at risk are locations of retroperitoneal tethering (because the gut cannot be displaced from points of contact), where blows to the extended trunk can cause rupture and require surgical repair. Subdiaphragmatic air on abdominal or chest radiographs is diagnostic of hollow viscera rupture. Stomach injuries, also uncommon, result from contact when the athlete's full stomach is distended and its walls are thinned. Duodenal injury can occur as a deceleration injury in which the untethered bowel moves forward, stretching the walls and tearing retroperitoneal blood vessels. Vague, cramping abdominal pain with loss of appetite or vomiting of bile within 24 to 48 hours after a significant deceleration injury may signal a duodenal hematoma, which is confirmed with upper GI contrast radiographs or on CT scan. Management is supportive (observation and intravenous feeding) unless blood loss continues or the wall is compromised, in which case surgical repair is advised. Similarly, the small and large intestines can become bruised, although this is rare in nonvehicular sports. If the bowel ruptures, the peritoneum becomes contaminated with bacteria-laden contents, causing fever, leukocytosis, peritonitis, and sepsis, which can be fatal if not treated promptly.

The pancreas

The pancreas can also be injured by a deceleration injury. A "sandwich" blow to the back and abdomen can transect the pancreas as it is compressed against the spine. Midepigastric pain radiating to the back, with loss of appetite, nausea, and vomiting is typical. Unlike intestinal injury, vomiting fails to relieve discomfort. A serum amylase confirms spillage of pancreatic enzymes, which can result in necrotizing or chronic pancreatitis. CT scan is recommended for visualization of injury extent and guidance to therapy.

---

region or in the thigh at the femoral canal with symptoms ranging from burning and aching to more serious nausea and vomiting. Nausea and vomiting may indicate incarceration or strangulation of the intestine.[3] Some athletes may report an antecedent ripping or popping sensation. In one study of athletes with groin pain, hernias were revealed at the physical examination in 8% of the participants. *Herniography* (radiographs performed after injection of contrast into the abdominal cavity) identified 84% of the athletes having hernias, and 70% of these individuals achieved complete relief of pain with *herniorrhaphy* (surgical repair of the hernia).[5] All hernias merit medical attention and surgical repair to avoid the consequences of eventual incarceration or strangulation of the intestine, which can be life threatening.

The Spleen

The spleen is largely protected from injury by the seventh through twelfth ribs in the left upper quadrant of the abdomen. Any increase in activity of the spleen may result in *splenomegaly*, or enlargement of the spleen. This increase in splenic activity, which is a result of the spleen's response to infection, is called *immune hyperplasia* and represents the mechanism for enlargement of the spleen in patients with infectious mononucleosis (IM) and

abscess of the spleen. Enlargement of the spleen in individuals with early sickle cell disease is due to the increased demand for the removal of defective erythrocytes, resulting in hyperplasia of the reticuloendothelial system.

Diseases involving the spleen commonly produce pain and a heavy sensation in the left upper quadrant. Pain associated with injury to the spleen may result from acute swelling of the spleen with stretching, infarction, or inflammation of the capsule. Severe pain in the left upper quadrant and *pleuritic chest pain* (pain that worsens with deep inspiration) may accompany vascular events in the spleen. Vascular occlusion of the spleen, as seen in sickle cell crisis, may result in pain and infarction of the spleen. Rupture of the spleen that results from blunt trauma or an infiltrative process that breaks the splenic capsule may present as an acute abdomen with intraperitoneal bleeding, followed by shock or death. Because blood does not irritate the peritoneum as much as an inflammatory process such as appendicitis, injuries to the spleen may be minimally symptomatic.

Palpation and percussion are the primary components of the examination of the spleen; however, both are imprecise at best. Splenomegaly as a result of IM will accompany a sore throat, malaise, headache, nausea or vomiting, chills, or abdominal pain. Physical findings may include fever, lymphadenopathy, pharyngitis or tonsillitis, and rash with splenomegaly in more than 50% of patients with IM.

Liver-spleen radionuclide scan, CT scan, magnetic resonance imaging (MRI) scan, or ultrasonography can detect an enlarged spleen. Ultrasonography is the procedure of choice for thin patients because it is inexpensive and does not require the injection of contrast or radioactive material. Laboratory abnormalities are determined by the underlying systemic illness. For example, in splenic hypertrophy resulting from an infectious agent, such as IM, the granulocyte count may be increased, the white blood cell count elevated, and heterophils for Epstein-Barr virus (EBV) may be found. Enlargement of the spleen resulting from sickle cell anemia would accompany a positive hemoglobin electrophoresis for hemoglobin S (sickling hemoglobin).

Splenomegaly resulting from IM is treated with rest and supportive care. The athlete should avoid excessive physical activity during the first month of IM infection to reduce the possibility of rupture of the spleen. Because the primary cause of EBV transmission is the transfer of saliva during kissing in young adults, isolation of athletes with IM is not necessary. Transmission as a result of less intimate contact than kissing is rare. Before the athlete is allowed to return to competition, serial ultrasonographic evaluation of the spleen documenting a return to normal size may be necessary.

The Liver

Much like the spleen, the liver is largely protected from injury by the seventh through twelfth ribs in the right upper quadrant of the abdomen. In addition to storing energy, directing metabolism, and producing bile for the digestion of fat, the liver functions as a reticuloendothelial organ. Pain in the right upper quadrant may represent liver injury, gallbladder disease, or peritoneal irritation by blood from other sources. With the increased use of CT scans in the evaluation of trauma, physicians have become increasingly aware of asymptomatic liver injuries from blunt trauma. The fibrous Glisson's capsule surrounds the liver parenchyma and can contain and tamponade small amounts of bleeding. With contained hemorrhage, elevated liver enzymes in the blood may be the only indications of injury. With severe injury, the Glisson's capsule is compromised, and free peritoneal bleeding ensues. With the patient in the supine position, the blood rests on the right side of the abdomen beside the right colic or subdiaphragmatic space and may cause peritoneal irritation that is revealed as pain in the right upper quadrant or referred to the right shoulder. Hypotension or shock often accompanies pain. Early resuscitation and intervention at a hospital are crucial to the patient's survival.

As with the spleen, the liver is more susceptible to injury when infectious processes such as IM or acute hepatitis enlarge it. Any one of several viruses may cause acute hepatitis; however, the clinical presentation of each virus is similar. Fever, malaise, headache, and cervical lymphadenopathy appear early and may be confused with any viral illness or flu. After several weeks, pain and tenderness in the right upper quadrant indicate the presence of *hepatomegaly* (an enlarged liver) and jaundice, and results of laboratory studies may reveal lymphocytosis and increased serum transaminases and total bilirubin.

Chronic hepatitis may develop in some individuals, but most cases resolve within a few months of onset. When the liver is no longer enlarged, the athlete will be able to return to sports participation, but only after a physician has determined that the athlete is not infectious based on serum viral antibody and antigen testing.

The Gastrointestinal Tract

Sports-related gastrointestinal injuries are rare; however, their consequences are grave and mechanism and energy of injury should be considered. The gastrointestinal tract is a hollow viscus with normal intra-abdominal mobility and largely evades injury by displacement from points of contact. It becomes susceptible to injury at locations of retroperitoneal tethering. Distention and unsuspected blows to an extended trunk may cause rupture, which requires surgical repair.[6] If abdominal or chest radiographs reveal the presence of subdiaphragmatic air from the hollow viscera, surgical intervention is required.

The stomach lies in the midepigastrium and has ligamentous connections to the colon, spleen, and liver. Because the stomach is fairly mobile and easily distended, injuries to the stomach from blunt trauma are rare; however, they can result from contact while the stomach is full and distended with thinned walls.

Duodenal injury, especially at the tethered second and third portions, occurs more frequently from blunt trauma. Duodenal injury results during deceleration when the untethered bowel moves forward, stretching the walls, and potentially tearing retroperitoneal blood vessels. Duodenal hematoma typically appears within 24 to 48 hours after injury, and the symptoms generally indicate proximal obstruction from partial or total occlusion of the lumen. Vague, cramping abdominal pain and loss of appetite or vomiting of bile after meals following a significant deceleration injury should raise suspicion of duodenal injury. This type of injury is generally diagnosed with upper GI contrast radiographs; however, CT scans can provide useful evaluation of other frequently associated injuries that may otherwise be occult. CT scan of the abdomen using contrast generally reveals a duodenal wall that is thickened with contusion or blood in tamponade. Unless CT scans reveal ongoing blood loss or compromise of the wall, which requires surgical repair, management is generally nonsurgical and consists of observation and intravenous feeding until food tolerance returns.

The small intestine and colon can also become bruised, although this is rare in most sports that do not involve the use of vehicles. A ruptured bowel results in peritoneal contamination of the peritoneum or peritoneal cavity by the bowel's bacteria-laden contents. Within hours, the athlete presents with fever, leukocytosis, and *peritonitis*. Because subsequent sepsis frequently results in death, even among the young, diagnostic vigilance is important.

The Pancreas

Although rare, injury to the pancreas can occur. Pancreatic injury must be suspected with any blunt trauma to the midepigastrium or hypogastrium and can result from deceleration. Simultaneous "sandwich" blows into the abdomen and back are particularly dangerous, because the pancreas can be compressed against the spine, resulting in complete transection.[7] Pain in the midepigastrium that radiates to the back, with loss of appetite, nausea, and vomiting, is typical. However, pancreatic injury is different from gastrointestinal tract injury in that there is often little relief with emesis.[3] The presence of serum amylase in the serum often indicates spillage of pancreatic enzymes. Necrotizing of the pancreas and surrounding tissues or chronic pancreatitis may follow. CT scan can confirm the

injury and allow visualization of the extent of injury as well as offer guidance to therapy.

GASTROINTESTINAL DISEASES COMMON AMONG ATHLETES

Diarrhea and Gastroenteritis

Gastroenteritis is an irritation or inflammation of the gastrointestinal tract and manifests itself as vomiting or diarrhea. Diarrhea is defined as frequent loose, watery, or unformed bowel movements.[8] Diarrhea may result from emotional upset or acute stress; food poisoning; gastrointestinal malabsorption syndromes; excessive alcohol consumption; use of laxatives, antacids, antibiotics, quinine, or chemotherapeutic medications; viral illness; or ingestion of large quantities of sports carbohydrate drinks or high-fiber foods. Other causes of diarrhea include bacterial pathogens such as *Campylobacter jejuni*, *Escherichia coli*, *Yersinia*, *Shigella*, or *Clostridium difficile*. The athlete who has been affected by any of these bacterial pathogens

FOCUS ON . . .

Gastrointestinal Diseases Common Among Athletes

Diarrhea and gastroenteritis

Among the gastrointestinal diseases seen in the athlete are diarrhea and gastroenteritis, traveler's diarrhea, appendicitis, acute pancreatitis, and cholecystitis and cholelithiasis. Diarrhea (loose, watery or unformed, frequent bowel movements) can be produced by emotional upset or acute stress; food poisoning; malabsorption; excess alcohol consumption; use of laxatives, antacids, antibiotics, quinine, or chemotherapy products; viral illness, bacterial illness; and ingestion of sports carbohydrate drinks or high-fiber foods. If the athlete has traveled to areas endemic with *E. coli* or has eaten spoiled or undercooked food, a bacterial infection may be the cause. Apples, oranges, lentils, kidney beans, and whole wheat spaghetti offer increased absorption, and the athlete should eat these foods prior to competition to prevent diarrhea. Caffeine draws water into the colon and can potentially cause diarrhea, as can lactose (found in mammalian milk) in those who are intolerant because of a deficiency or absence of lactase.

Treatment of diarrhea includes avoiding the offending agent, undercooked or raw food, and foods that are improperly refrigerated or heated, along with rest or at least reduced activity. Room-temperature, clear liquids are recommended, plus a diet of bananas, rice, applesauce, and toast (BRAT) as tolerated. Although most cases resolve in 24 to 48 hours without treatment, diarrhea that is persistent or associated with fever requires that the athlete be evaluated by a physician with a complete blood count, stool studies for leukocytes, culture and sensitivity, ova and parasites, and fecal blood. Antidiarrheal drugs must be used cautiously and should not be used at all when the pathogen is infectious.

Traveler's diarrhea

Traveler's diarrhea, consisting of three to ten unformed stools in 24 hours, is the most common problem afflicting athletes who travel to international locations. Traveler's diarrhea results from a wide variety of organisms, most commonly *E. coli*. Contaminated food is generally responsible for traveler's diarrhea, although contaminated water can also be a cause. Duration of illness is usually 3 to 5 days. Treatment of traveler's diarrhea for adults is antibiotics; however, because of potential side effects such as skin rashes, photosensitivity, and vaginal candidiasis, young athletes should instead consume oral rehydration solutions or sports drinks. While traveling, athletes should eat fresh foods that are served hot, fruits that can be peeled, and drink hot or bottled beverages.

(Continued)

FOCUS ON . . .

Gastrointestinal Diseases Common Among Athletes (Continued)

Appendicitis

Appendicitis, or inflammation of the intestinal pouch extending from the cecum, occurs most often in individuals ages 15 to 24 years. Constant, dull, periumbilical pain, accompanied by loss of appetite and nausea, progresses in severity and localizes to the right lower quadrant. The ill-appearing athlete may have a low-grade fever. Pain is worsened by movement, deep breathing, sneezing, and coughing. Physical examination reveals rebound tenderness and guarding at McBurney's point (two thirds of the distance from the umbilicus to the anterior superior iliac spine), although if the appendix is not located at this point (anatomic variant), the signs and symptoms may differ. The history and physical examination point to the diagnosis, and an elevated leukocyte count is supportive. Abdominal radiographs may be helpful in ruling out other etiologies. The athlete must be evaluated by a surgeon and should avoid taking pain medications, eating, and drinking until the diagnosis is established in case appendectomy is necessary.

Acute pancreatitis

Acute pancreatitis is most often caused by chronic, excessive alcohol use and gallstones, although it can also be caused by other conditions and by medications. Poor nutrition and obesity contribute to the risk, and if the inflammation fails to completely resolve, chronic pancreatitis can set in. Physical examination reveals marked midepigastric (and perhaps extensive abdominal) tenderness with hypoactive bowel sounds. Serum amylase, lipase, and white blood cell count may be elevated on laboratory testing, along with hepatic enzymes and liver function tests if the biliary tract is obstructed. In the latter case, ultrasonography is the diagnostic test of choice; CT scan invasive contrast studies of the bilary tract are helpful if the diagnosis is in question. Treatment is intravenous hydration, restricted oral intake, and parenteral analgesia; surgical intervention is rarely indicated.

Cholecystitis

Cholecystitis (gallbladder inflammation or infection) or cholangitis (bile duct infection or inflammation) with cholelithiasis (gallstones) is more frequent in women than in men and is rare in adolescents and children. Risk factors include a high-fat, low-fiber diet; obesity; rapid weight loss; use of oral contraceptives; family history of gallstones; pancreatitis; coronary artery disease; diabetes; cirrhosis; women ages 40 to 50 years; and women who have previously had gallstones and are now taking estrogen.

Symptoms include acute, severe cramping pain in the right upper quadrant, perhaps radiating to the chest or upper back and shoulders, after a high-fat meal; low-grade fever; nausea; vomiting; pale stools; pruritus; and jaundice. Midline epigastric and right upper quadrant tenderness with guarding are evident on physical examination. If the patient stops a deep inspiratory breath when the examiner palpates the right upper quadrant (Murphy's sign), cholecystitis or choledocholithiasis (common bile duct stones) may be present. In acute cholecystitis, the white blood cell count, serum transaminase, amylase, and alkaline phosphatase may be elevated, while common bile duct stones increase the total serum bilirubin. Ultrasound is the most sensitive test for gallstones, and radionucleotide cholescintigraphy is recommended when ultrasound is normal or nondiagnostic in patients with suspected cholecystitis. Treatment depends on the severity of illness, the patient's overall health, and gallstone size, but laparoscopic cholecystectomy is usually performed within 1 to 3 days.

---

may have cramping abdominal pain, diarrhea, lack of bowel control, and fever.

If an athlete has diarrhea, the athletic trainer must determine whether the athlete has traveled to an area where *E. coli* is endemic or the athlete has ingested spoiled or undercooked food, resulting in a bacterial infection.

Apples, oranges, lentils, kidney beans, and whole-wheat spaghetti offer increased absorption and a prolonged increase in serum glucose levels; therefore, to prevent diarrhea, the athlete should eat these foods prior to competition. Caffeine has a laxative effect, drawing water into the colon and potentially causing diarrhea. Lactose is a primary sugar in mammalian milk and may also be found in prepared foods and medications. It is reported that 81% of African-Americans, almost 100% of Asian-Americans, 76% of Italian-Americans, and 50% of Mexican-Americans are *lactose intolerant*.[9] Only 25% of Anglo-Americans experience some degree of lactose intolerance.[9] Lactose intolerance refers to the body's inability to digest lactose because of a deficiency or absence of the enzyme lactase. Lactase is needed to digest all milk except mother's milk. Lactose that has not been digested draws water into the colon and causes diarrhea in a fashion similar to high-carbohydrate foods and sports drinks.

Management of diarrhea begins with avoiding the offending agent or undercooked or raw foods as well as buffet or picnic foods that have been left unrefrigerated or improperly heated for several hours. Most cases of diarrhea resolve in 24 to 48 hours without any treatment. A physician should evaluate diarrhea that is prolonged or associated with fever. A complete blood count should be obtained, as well as stool studies for fecal leukocytes, culture and sensitivity, ova and parasites, and fecal blood. The presence of diarrhea should prompt a cessation of activity or a decreased level of activity until the athlete is well hydrated. The athlete should drink clear liquids that are at room temperature. Diet should consist of bananas, rice, applesauce, and toast (the BRAT diet). Antidiarrheal drugs such as loperamide or diphenoxylate hydrochloride should be used only after infectious causes have been ruled out. The course of some infections prolonged by the reduction of motility associated with antidiarrheal drugs are contraindicated in athletes with diarrhea that is caused by an infectious pathogen. In addition to diarrhea, the patient with gastroenteritis may also experience vomiting.

Traveler's Diarrhea

Athletes who travel are prone to infections, if for no other reason than that the consumption of unusual foods and the athletes' proximity to large groups of people in airports, airplanes, hotels, restaurants, and during training sessions increases the chances of infection. Although athletes can be exposed to a wide variety of infectious agents, *traveler's diarrhea* is by far the most common problem that can afflict athletes who travel to international locations. Although the greatest risk of traveler's diarrhea occurs in tropical and semitropical locales, diarrheal disease should always be considered a risk factor when traveling abroad.

Traveler's diarrhea can result from a wide variety of organisms, and different organisms predominate in different areas of the world. In general, bacterial enteropathogens such as *Escherichia coli*, *Campylobacter jejuni*, *Shigella*, *Salmonella*, and noncholera *Vibrio* are responsible for most cases of traveler's diarrhea. *Rotavirus* and *Giardia* are often the culprits in Mexico, North America, and Russia. Contrary to popular belief, contaminated food rather than contaminated water is generally responsible for traveler's diarrhea, although contaminated water must always be considered a risk. Traveler's diarrhea usually consists of three to ten unformed stools in 24 hours, together with symptoms such as nausea, vomiting, fecal urgency, and cramps. The usual duration of illness is 3 to 5 days. Traveler's diarrhea may also apply to those who become ill after returning from a trip.

Because enterotoxigenic *E. coli* is the most common cause of traveler's diarrhea, prophylaxis for adults consists of the administration of appropriate antibiotic drugs. However, because of the self-limiting nature of traveler's diarrhea, there is debate as to whether the risks of antimicrobial drugs are warranted, particularly among young athletes.[10] Such risks include skin rashes, photosensitivity, and vaginal candidiasis. Regardless, athletes who have traveler's diarrhea must ingest fluids, carbohydrates, and electrolytes, which can be accomplished by consuming a commercial oral rehydration solution or a sports drink. If neither is available, the athlete can ingest 8 oz of water with 1 to 3 teaspoons of sugar mixed in it and some saltine crackers. Orange juice diluted by half with water and consumed with saltine crackers is also a feasible, but generally unpalatable, alternative.

Exercising some restrictions on food and beverage consumption can reduce the risk of traveler's diarrhea. In general, athletes should consume fresh foods that are served hot, such as baked potatoes, boiled vegetables, cooked pasta, and meats; fruits that can be peeled; and hot or bottled beverages. If feasible, food and snacks familiar to the athletes should be the mainstay of the athlete's diet during travel abroad. This often requires bringing packaged food (instant oatmeal, granola bars, rice cakes, or cereal) on the trip and making the necessary arrangements for meals at restaurants featuring foods familiar to the athlete.

Appendicitis

Inflammation of the vermiform appendix, the small intestinal pouch that extends from the cecum, causes *appendicitis*.[9,11] The incidence of appendicitis peaks between ages 15 and 24 years. The athlete will experience constant, dull abdominal pain in the periumbilical area that is accompanied by loss of appetite and nausea. The pain progressively becomes more severe as it migrates and localizes in the right lower quadrant of the abdomen. The athlete will appear ill and may have a low-grade fever. Movement, deep breathing, sneezing, or coughing may exacerbate the pain. One third of individuals may experience atypical symptoms resulting from an alternate appendix location. Physical examination reveals rebound tenderness and guarding at McBurney's point, which is located two thirds the distance from the umbilicus to the anterior superior iliac spine.

A diagnosis of appendicitis should be determined from the patient's history and physical examination. The diagnosis should be questioned if there is no loss of appetite, nausea, or vomiting. If symptoms are present for longer than 72 hours without appendix perforation or if right lower quadrant tenderness is absent, the diagnosis should also be questioned. No laboratory test can confirm or rule out appendicitis, but an elevated leukocyte count helps support its likelihood. Occasionally, abdominal radiographs reveal a stone in the right lower quadrant called an appendicolith and is usually diagnostic of appendicitis; however, radiographs are more useful in ruling out other causes of abdominal pain. Evaluation by a surgeon is mandatory, and the patient should not eat, drink, or take pain medication until evaluation is complete. The mainstay of therapy for appendicitis is appendectomy, surgical removal of the appendix.

Acute Pancreatitis

Pancreatitis is a local intense inflammation of the pancreas. Chronic excessive alcohol use and gallstones account for 80% of all cases of pancreatitis in the United States. Chronic excessive alcohol use affects three times as many men as women; gallstones affect men and women in a ratio of 6:1. An alcoholic binge by a chronic drinker may precipitate acute pancreatitis. **Table 20-1** lists less common causes of pancreatitis.

Poor nutrition and obesity increase the risk of pancreatitis. Chronic pancreatitis may follow an acute attack of pancreatitis, especially if the acute attack is not completely resolved because of continued pancreatic inflammation from alcohol ingestion or gallstone disease.

Marked tenderness in the midepigastrium and possibly the entire abdomen, in addition to hypoactive bowel sounds, may indicate acute pancreatitis. Evaluation of laboratory studies may reveal elevated serum amylase, lipase, and white blood cell counts. Hepatic enzymes may also be elevated; liver function tests may be elevated if biliary tract obstruction is the cause of the attack. Radiographic evaluation of the abdomen is nonspecific. Identification of acute pancreatitis caused by biliary tract obstruction is best made with ultrasonography. CT scan and invasive contrast studies of the biliary tract may be helpful when the diagnosis is in question; however, a surgeon or gastroenterologist should make this determination.

Most patients respond well to intravenous hydration, restriction of oral intake, and parenteral analgesia. Protracted vomiting and electrolyte imbalance may require the use of other supportive therapy. Surgical intervention is rarely indicated and is best reserved for infectious complications from pancreatitis.

Cholecystitis

Cholecystitis, which is an infection or inflammation of the gallbladder, is usually caused by gallstones (cholelithiasis) or inflammation of the ducts that drain bile from the liver and gallbladder (cholangitis).[12] Cholecystitis occurs 2 to 3 times more often in women than in men, and it rarely occurs in adolescents or children.[12] The risk of developing a disorder of the biliary tree is increased with a high-fat, low-fiber diet, obesity, and rapid weight loss. Other risks include use of oral contraceptives, family history of gallstones, chronic or acute pancreatitis, coronary artery disease, diabetes, and cirrhosis. Women between ages 40 and 50 years and women who take estrogen and have previously had gallstones are also at increased risk.

Symptoms of cholecystitis include the acute onset of severe cramping pain in the right upper quadrant following a meal rich in fats. The pain of acute cholecystitis may radiate to the chest or upper back and shoulders, mimicking a heart attack. This pain may be accompanied by a low-grade fever, nausea, vomiting, pale stools, pruritus (itching), or jaundiced skin. Physical examination of the abdomen will elicit midline epigastric and right upper quadrant tenderness with guarding. Murphy's sign, when deep inspiration is interrupted during palpation of a tender gallbladder in the right upper quadrant, suggests cholecystitis or choledocholithiasis (stones in the common bile duct). Laboratory findings in patients with acute cholecystitis may include elevated levels in the white blood cell count, serum transaminase, amylase, and alkaline phosphatase. The presence of stones in the common

---

TABLE 20-1
CAUSES OF ACUTE PANCREATITIS

Miscellaneous causes	Infectious agents	Medications	Metabolic conditions
Abdominal trauma	Mumps	Tetracycline	Familial hyperlipidemia
Spider bites	Cytomegalovirus	NSAIDs	Hyperparathyroidism
Tumor mass	Hepatitis A, B, or C	Oral contraceptives	Hypercalcemia
	Coxsackievirus	Sulfonamides	
	Tuberculosis	Thiazide diuretics	
		Furosemide	

bile duct will raise the total serum bilirubin. Plain radiographs of the abdomen are rarely helpful in confirming the diagnosis. Ultrasound is 84% to 97% sensitive in the diagnosis of gallstones.[12] When ultrasound results are normal or nondiagnostic, radionucleotide cholescintigraphy (HIDA scan) to evaluate gallbladder emptying is the test of choice for patients with suspected cholecystitis.

The specific treatment of any of the acute biliary tract disorders depends on the severity of the illness, the size of the gallstones, and the patient's overall health. Moderately ill athletes with cholecystitis may be hospitalized for intravenous hydration, antibiotic therapy, analgesia, and preparation for surgical intervention if needed. To minimize postsurgical recovery and complications, laparoscopic cholecystectomy is usually performed in the first 24 to 72 hours after onset of acute cholecystitis, before the inflammatory process makes the dissection more difficult.

Gastrointestinal Hemorrhage

Classifications of upper (vomiting of blood or coffee-ground material) or lower (blood through the rectum) gastrointestinal hemorrhages are usually determined to appropriately focus the evaluation of the hemorrhage. Massive gastrointestinal hemorrhage is rare in athletes; however, small amounts of blood may be present in vomit, which resembles coffee grounds as a result of being exposed to gastric acid, or as black, tarry stools called *melena*. Any blood from the gastrointestinal tract is abnormal and should be evaluated by a physician. Any patient who is taking NSAIDs such as aspirin or ibuprofen and has evidence of gastrointestinal bleeding should discontinue the medication immediately. NSAIDs may irritate the gastrointestinal tract and can be the cause of gastrointestinal hemorrhage.

Genitourinary Anatomy

The upper urinary system consists of the kidneys and ureters and is located in the retroperitoneal plane (**Figure 20-3**). The kidneys are protected from external trauma by the lower ribs and spine and padded by the surrounding retroperitoneal fat. Sports injuries to the normally formed and located kidneys are therefore typically minor fractures of the renal parenchyma. The ureters are similarly padded by surrounding fat. Ureteral injury as a result of blunt external trauma rarely occurs because of its padding and mobility.

The lower urinary system consists of the bladder and the urethra. The bladder is enclosed and protected by the pelvic bones. The blunt trauma of a sports injury may result in a contusion of the bladder or, in the event of a pelvic fracture, a bladder perforation. The female urethra

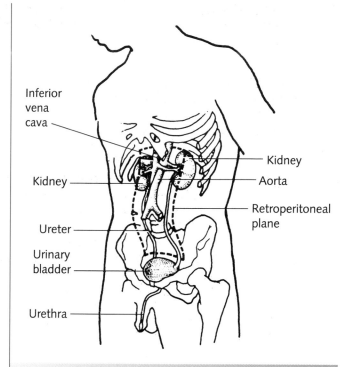

F I G U R E   2 0 - 3

The organs of the genitourinary system.

is protected by its intravaginal location and is rarely injured. The male urethra, in contrast, is susceptible to injury through blunt perineal or penile trauma.

THE SPORTS ENTRANCE PHYSICAL EXAMINATION

Screening for Testicular Cancer

The sports entrance physical examination of the male athlete provides an opportunity to screen for testicular cancer. Testicular cancer is the most common solid malignancy of men and boys between the ages of 15 and 34 years. For many male adolescents and young adults, a sports entrance examination may be the first detailed genital and inguinal examination performed since childhood. Until proven otherwise, the examiner should consider a hard painless testicular mass or unilateral testicular enlargement to indicate testicular cancer. An immediate referral to a urologist is required for further evaluation. If the examination reveals normal testicles, the examiner should ensure that the young athlete learns the technique and importance of monthly self-examination of the testicles. More detailed information about testicular self-examination can be found in chapter 23.

Management of the Athlete With an Undescended Testicle

If the sports entrance examination reveals that the athlete has an undescended testicle, he should be referred to a urologist to consider removal of the testicle. Undescended testicles in this age group are of little use for future fertility. The warmer temperature of the abdomen or inguinal canal permanently damages the ability of the germinal epithelium to produce sperm. For the athlete, an undescended testicle in the inguinal region often causes pain when it is compressed during lower extremity adduction or torso flexion. An undescended testicle in this location is also susceptible to injury and rupture if it is compressed against the pubic bone during a tackle or a kick in the groin. Finally, boys or men with an undescended testicle are at an increased risk for development of testicular cancer, and monthly self-examination of the testicles is especially important. However, self-examination may be difficult and unreliable when the testicle is in an extrascrotal position. Because of this, an undescended testicle in a postpubertal boy typically requires an *orchiectomy*, or removal of the testicle.

IMPLICATIONS OF A SOLITARY GENITOURINARY ORGAN

Testicle

The existence of a solitary testicle that results from previous removal or atrophy of the other testicle raises concerns for athletes who are considering participation in contact sports. Loss of the remaining testicle from a sports injury would result in loss of fertility and necessitate life-long androgen replacement. Although the potential injury or loss of a testicle is not commonly associated with sports trauma, it can occur. When it does occur, it is usually associated with a traumatic contact sport such as rugby or football. The potential loss of the testicle may influence some athletes with a solitary testicle to consider not participating in a specific contact sport.

It is difficult to estimate the exact risk an athlete takes of injuring or losing a testicle from participation in contact sports. Because rugby players customarily do not wear scrotal protection and frequently experience intense sports trauma, they may be at highest risk for sports trauma resulting in testicle loss. A retrospective 6-year review of rugby players insured in New South Wales, Australia, supplies an approximation of the risk for testicle loss in sports trauma.[13] During that time period, an average of 100,000 players registered annually for insurance in New South Wales. Only 14 players during the 6-year period underwent an evaluation for a testicle injury. At least three of these injuries appeared to be intentional, and two players

delayed evaluation of the injury until after the game was over. Eleven of the 14 injured testicles were surgically removed. Results of this study confirm a low incidence of severe testicle injury in the most adverse of sports conditions. However, the orchiectomy rate in this review is much higher than would be expected in a prospective database of men with an injured solitary testicle. Even a shattered testicle can generally be saved by prompt surgical management.[14]

The athlete with a solitary testicle and his family and physician should discuss, with documentation, the risks of testicle loss through a sports-related injury and the medical implications of that loss. After this consultation, the athlete should decide on which level of sports contact he wishes to engage. If he decides to participate, he can lower the risk of testicle loss by wearing scrotal protection and ensuring that any testicle injury is promptly evaluated.

Kidney

Athletes with only one kidney face a low risk of renal injury through participation in contact sports and an even lower risk of losing a kidney as a result of sports-related trauma. However, no studies have been undertaken that specifically estimate the rate of kidney loss through a sports-related injury.

Although loss of a kidney is most likely to occur in a motor vehicle crash, such a loss is still rare and is usually seen in high-impact accidents in which the patients sustain multiple injuries. The University of California at San Francisco reported its 16-year experience in evaluating 2,245 blunt renal injuries.[15] Of these injuries, 50 patients (2%) required surgical exploration and only 5 patients (0.2%) required a *nephrectomy*, or removal of a kidney. Patients who required a nephrectomy had sustained severe injuries that involved a mean of three organ systems and 9 L of blood loss. Thus, the level of blunt trauma that is associated with the loss of a kidney is dramatically more severe than that of the usual sports injury.

Nonetheless, the possibility of losing renal function and not the actual probability of such an injury guides most athletes with a solitary kidney to favor participation in sports with minimal or no contact. Typically, family members of these individuals strongly prefer them to participate in noncontact sports. Of the 438 members of the American Medical Society for Sports Medicine who responded to a 1994 survey, 46% stated that they would not allow patients with a solitary kidney to fully participate in contact sports, and 58% of the survey respondents stated they would not allow full sports participation if the patient were their own child.[16] Ultimately, however, this decision should be left to the athlete and his or her family after their physician documents a discussion of the possible risks and medical implications of renal loss as a result of a sports-related injury.

SPORTS-RELATED GENITOURINARY INJURIES

Sports Hematuria

Hematuria is blood in the urine. Urine should normally contain no more than three red blood cells per high-power microscopic field. An individual whose clear-appearing urine actually contains more than three red blood cells on microscopic inspection has microscopic hematuria. An individual whose urine contains blood clots or is discolored pink or red because of the presence of blood has gross hematuria. Microscopic or gross hematuria is the hallmark of a disturbance in the urinary tract and has a myriad of potential causes. **Table 20-2** shows some of the common causes of hematuria.

The amount of blood in the urine has no correlation with the potential severity of the patient's condition; therefore, all patients with persistent hematuria require a medical evaluation. A thorough history, physical examination, urine culture, kidney imaging, and endoscopic inspection of the bladder lining are required so that all potential causes of hematuria may be considered. Occasionally, the evaluation of an athlete reveals that the only causes of hematuria are physiologic changes that occur in the kidneys and mild blunt trauma that occurs during strenuous exercise and sports participation. This diagnosis of exclusion is called *sports hematuria*.

Sports hematuria is a benign cause of microscopic or, less commonly, gross hematuria after physical exertion. The hematuria typically clears within a 72-hour period of rest. Sports hematuria is also often referred to as runners' hematuria because an abnormally high number of red blood cells may be present in up to 69% of runners after they have run long distances.[17]

There are several possible causes of runners' hematuria. The kidneys and bladder experience a low level of blunt trauma as they are jostled up and down during running. The kidneys of long-distance runners are especially susceptible to such movement because the fat that normally packages the kidneys into the flank is minimal. As the bladder dome moves up and down, it is also traumatized as it hits the firm bladder base. The runner's usual practice of voiding immediately before running increases this trauma by removing the cushion of urine between these bladder surfaces. Results of this bladder trauma were demonstrated when cystoscopic examination of the bladders of eight runners with gross hematuria revealed that the lining of the bladder dome and base was consistently erythematous and denuded and had been replaced with fibrinous scar.[18]

Clearly, blunt trauma is not the only cause of runners' hematuria. Microscopic sports hematuria develops more commonly in athletes who engage in strenuous noncontact exercise such as swimming than in athletes who participate in contact sports.[19] During strenuous exercise, the kidneys receive less blood flow because the skeletal muscles require more blood.[17] This period of relative ischemia and an increase in filtration pressure may cause temporary damage to the cells responsible for filtration resulting in a loss of protein and blood cells into the urine.

Sports hematuria is a diagnosis of exclusion and no athlete with either gross hematuria or microscopic hematuria that persists after 4 days of rest should be assumed to have sports hematuria.[20] These individuals require an evaluation by a urologist to determine the potential causes of hematuria. A complete hematuria evaluation consists of the following components:

- a urine culture
- imaging of the renal parenchyma with a CT scan, MRI scan, renal ultrasound, or an intravenous pyelogram (IVP)
- imaging of the renal collecting systems and ureters with an IVP or retrograde pyelogram
- visualization of the bladder lining with a cystoscope

If this evaluation excludes all other causes of the hematuria in an athlete, then sports hematuria may be diagnosed.

The management of sports hematuria focuses on preventing the development of gross hematuria. Athletes who have sports hematuria should be instructed not to void completely prior to training. Incompletely emptying the bladder will reserve a small residual volume of urine that cushions the bladder dome and protects it from the trauma of hitting the firm bladder base during running. Runners with gross hematuria should refrain from running until their urine returns to its normal color. Typically, sports hematuria resolves in 1 to 3 days.[20]

TABLE 20-2

COMMON CAUSES OF HEMATURIA

Medical renal disease

Glomerulonephritis (inflammation of the collecting system)

Urinary infection

Urinary stones

Kidney cancer

Bladder cancer

Prostate diseases

Trauma

FOCUS ON . . .

Sports-related Genitourinary Injuries

Sports hematuria

Hematuria is the presence of more than three red blood cells per high-power microscopic field. If the red blood cells are only visible on microscopic inspection, the hematuria is microscopic; if the urine is pink or red or contains blood clots, the hematuria is gross. Because hematuria has many causes, all athletes with gross or microscopic hematuria lasting more than 4 days must be evaluated, including a thorough history, physical examination, urine culture, kidney imaging, and endoscopic bladder inspection.

If the evaluation reveals only physiologic kidney changes and mild blunt trauma from strenuous exercise and sports participation, sports hematuria is the diagnosis of exclusion. Usually it clears within 72 hours of rest. In runners (runner's hematuria), this condition is caused by low-level blunt trauma to the kidneys and bladder during running. Long-distance runners are particularly susceptible because they lack much of the fat that normally surrounds the kidneys. Voiding just before running exacerbates bladder trauma by removing the urine cushion between the bladder surfaces. Swimmers are also at risk for sports hematuria as blood is shunted away from the kidneys and to the skeletal muscles during strenuous exercise, resulting in relative ischemia and increased filtration pressure. Athletes with sports hematuria are instructed not to void completely before training. If the hematuria is gross, runners should avoid training until the normal urine color has returned.

Injury of the kidney

The kidneys are normally well protected by the lower rib cage and an envelope of fat posteriorly and laterally and by the abdominal muscles and organs anteriorly. Enlarged kidneys or those lying in a different location are more prone to injury from a side tackle or midback punch, which may be serious if gross hematuria, a rib fracture, or hypotension develop, in which case the player must be evaluated immediately by a urologist or trauma surgeon.

Typically, renal injuries in sports are bruises or minor fractures. In a hemodynamically stable patient, abdominal CT scan is helpful for assessing the severity of the injury. The athlete is admitted to the hospital and restricted to bed rest for close blood pressure and hematocrit monitoring. Discharge from the hospital occurs when the player is hemodynamically stable and has a stable hematocrit and no gross hematuria. Readiness for return to play can be evaluated after 1 month of rest.

Injury of the bladder

The pelvic bladder is separated from the abdominal cavity by the peritoneal membrane and protected by the pelvic bones; however, when blunt trauma fractures the pelvic bones, they can perforate the bladder, causing hematuria and urine leakage. Severe pelvis crush injuries from a skiing injury or vehicular trauma can compress a full bladder and rupture the dome, allowing urine to drain freely into the abdomen. Bladder injury is suspected when the athlete experiences severe lower abdominal or pelvic trauma in the presence of a pelvic fracture, gross hematuria, or inability to urinate.

A cystogram can show the presence, location, and severity of a bladder injury and is performed by inserting a catheter through the urethra and filling the bladder with radiographic contrast agent. A radiograph of the bladder filled with contrast is compared with a radiograph after the contrast is drained out; if no contrast extravasates from the bladder, the injury is a contusion and will heal by itself. Contrast that extravasates from the bladder into the pelvis indicates a bladder perforation below the peritoneal reflection, which will heal with bladder catheter drainage for 2 weeks. If the contrast extravasates into the abdomen, an intraperitoneal bladder rupture exists and must be surgically repaired.

(Continued)

Injury of the Kidney

The kidneys are well protected in their normal flank position. The lower rib cage and a generous envelope of fat protect the kidneys from posterior and lateral blunt trauma. The abdominal musculature and organs absorb the shock of anterior blunt trauma. Kidneys that are enlarged as a result of malformation or obstruction or kidneys that lie outside of this normal location, such as a pelvic kidney, are more prone to injury. Typically, trauma to an athlete's flank, such as occurs in a side tackle or a punch in the midback, may result in a renal injury. If the trauma is associated with gross hematuria, a rib fracture, or

FOCUS ON . . .

Sports-related Genitouriniary Injuries (Continued)

Injury of the scrotum

An athlete with minor blunt scrotal trauma will complain of severe local pain and nausea, with perhaps testicular tenderness to examination; however, symptoms resolve within an hour of rest. If testicular pain is continuous or a large amount of fluid collects in the scrotum, the testicle may have ruptured. The athlete must be evaluated urgently by a urologist and may need to undergo surgical repair to preserve testicular function.

Sudden testicular pain, nausea, and vomiting in the absence of scrotal trauma suggest testicular torsion, a spontaneous twist of the testicular cord that is most common in young adolescents and results in acute ischemia. An emergency detorsion (surgical repair) is needed to preserve testicular function. If treatment is delayed beyond 12 hours of symptom onset, orchiectomy may be needed for irreversible testicular damage.

Injury of the urethra

The short female urethra is rarely damaged by pelvic or perineal trauma. However, the male urethra, which traverses the perineum, is often injured by blunt trauma such as a kick to the groin or when a cyclist straddles his bike frame in a crash. In most patients, urethral bleeding is evident with the first void after the injury, but if voiding is possible and there are no other injuries, further evaluation is unnecessary. Severe urethral injuries with pelvic fractures and bladder injuries are seen in high-impact trauma such as skiing accidents or the collision of a vehicle with a runner or biker.

hypotension, a potentially serious kidney injury should be suspected and the athlete should be medically evaluated immediately.

Renal injuries are evaluated with an abdominal CT scan in the hemodynamically stable patient. The usual renal injury from a sports-related trauma is a bruise or minor fracture or breaking of the kidney. A renal fracture can result in blood loss and, when more severe, leakage of urine into the flank. A renal injury of any degree of severity should be evaluated by a urologist or trauma surgeon. Renal injuries resulting from sports trauma rarely require surgical repair. The athlete is usually admitted to the hospital and restricted to bed rest for close monitoring of blood pressure and hematocrit. The patient may be discharged from the hospital when he or she becomes hemodynamically stable and has a stable hematocrit and no gross hematuria. Based on the level of injuries, the treating physician determines the period of time that an athlete should refrain from participating in sports after discharge. In general, this period of rest is at least 1 month. Following this period, the physician should reevaluate the athlete for persistent abnormalities in kidney anatomy, hematuria, and hypertension that may develop from renal scarring.

Injury of the Bladder

The bladder is a pelvic organ that is separated from the abdominal cavity by the peritoneal membrane and is protected from injury by the pelvic bones. Although sports trauma rarely results in bladder injuries, bladder injury can occur when blunt trauma is sufficient to fracture

pelvic bones. The sharp edges of the broken pelvis then perforate the bladder sidewall, causing hematuria and leakage of urine into the pelvis. Severe pelvis crush injuries that may occur as the result of a skiing injury or vehicle-related trauma can compress a full bladder, resulting in bladder pressures that exceed the strength of the bladder wall and causing a rupture of the bladder dome. The perforation decompresses the bladder by allowing urine to drain freely into the abdomen. A bladder injury should be suspected when an athlete experiences severe lower abdominal or pelvic trauma that is associated with a pelvic fracture or gross hematuria or when the athlete reports a sudden inability to urinate.

A *cystogram*, or radiograph of the bladder, is used to evaluate bladder injuries. The series of images the cystogram provides helps the practitioner determine the presence, location, and severity of a bladder injury. A catheter is inserted through the urethra and the bladder is filled with a radiographic contrast agent. One radiograph of the patient's pelvis with the bladder filled with contrast should be obtained, and a second radiograph should be obtained after the contrast is drained from the bladder. If neither image demonstrates *extravasation* (discharge or escape) of contrast from the bladder, the injury is a bladder contusion that will heal without surgery or bladder drainage. If contrast extravasates from the bladder and is confined to the pelvis, a bladder perforation below the peritoneal reflection has occurred. This extraperitoneal rupture will heal if the bladder is drained with a catheter for 2 weeks. If the contrast extravasates through the dome of the bladder and escapes into the abdomen, an intraperitoneal bladder rupture exists that requires immediate surgical repair.

Injury of the Scrotum

The athlete who has sustained blunt scrotal trauma will complain of severe local pain and nausea. In minor testicular trauma, these symptoms should almost completely resolve with an hour of rest. On examination, the testicles may be tender, but they should not be swollen or impalpable as a result of a collection of fluid in the scrotum. If testicular pain is continuous or a large scrotal fluid collection occurs after the injury, an urgent urologic evaluation is required to evaluate for a possible testicular rupture, and rapid surgical repair of the injury is crucial to preserve testicular function.

An athlete who reports sudden testicular pain, nausea, and vomiting that is not associated with recent scrotal trauma requires an emergency urologic evaluation for *testicular torsion*. Testicular torsion is a spontaneous twist of the testicular cord that occurs most commonly in early adolescents and results in acute testicular ischemia. An emergency detorsion (surgical untwisting of the testis and its blood supply) to restore blood flow and surgical repair are paramount to the preservation of future testicular function. If the evaluation of testicular torsion is delayed for more than 12 hours after the onset of symptoms, irreversible testicular damage is likely, and an orchiectomy may be necessary.

Injury of the Urethra

The female urethra is short and very rarely damaged by trauma to the pelvis or perineum. However, the anterior male urethra traverses the perineum and is commonly injured by blunt trauma such as from a kick in the groin or straddling the bicycle frame in a crash. Approximately 90% of urethral trauma is associated with urethral bleeding during the first voiding after the injury.[21] If an athlete who has sustained this type of injury is able to void and has no other significant injuries, further evaluation is not immediately needed. Severe urethral injuries that require a medical evaluation are usually associated with pelvic fractures and bladder injuries. Such injuries are not commonly seen in participants of team sports but may be seen in athletes who have sustained high-impact injuries such as in skiing accidents or when a vehicle has collided with a runner or biker.

THE IMPACT OF GASTROINTESTINAL AND GENITOURINARY INJURIES ON THE ATHLETE

Although genitourinary and gastrointestinal injuries are less common than orthopaedic trauma, they represent a significant source of morbidity to previously healthy and health-conscious individuals. What may at first appear to be a simple pulled muscle or bruise may rapidly evolve into a life-threatening abdominal condition that requires immediate surgery. Therefore, each abdominal injury should be evaluated as if it were a life-threatening event until the threat can be ruled out.

The genitourinary tract is rarely the source of life-threatening injuries; however, the largely external location of genitourinary structures in male athletes can cause concern in the athlete because these structures are relatively easy to injure. Genitourinary injuries are often concomitant with abdominal injuries, and the external genitalia represent extensions of abdominal structures. Because of possible implications associated with the athlete's future fertility and urinary function, the importance of nontraumatic genitourinary conditions should never be underestimated.

CHAPTER REVIEW

The athletic trainer must be familiar with abdominal anatomy to properly evaluate the athlete with an abdominal or genitourinary injury or illness. When evaluating an athlete with an abdominal injury or illness, the athletic trainer should check for abdominal muscle rigidity or spasm, tenderness, guarding, and bowel sounds, and monitor vital signs. Further diagnostic screening in the form of computed tomography scanning, ultrasonography, and laboratory testing may also be needed.

Injuries affecting the abdominal wall and musculature include strains, bruises, and hematomas, which are treated with ice, rest, and nonsteroidal anti-inflammatory drugs. Once symptoms of pain and tenderness have resolved, gradual return to sport is permitted. Hernias should be surgically repaired to prevent life-threatening incarceration or strangulation. The spleen can become enlarged as a result of illness or it can be damaged by injury from blunt trauma. Physical examination is often supplemented by liver-spleen scan, computed tomography, magnetic resonance imaging, ultrasonography, or laboratory studies. Splenomegaly is treated with rest and supportive care. Return to sport participation is considered once the spleen has returned to normal size.

The liver can be damaged by blunt trauma or enlarged by illness. Physical examination, computed tomography, and blood tests can help to pinpoint the etiology. The athlete should not return to activity until the symptoms have resolved. The gastrointestinal tract is most vulnerable to injury at locations of retroperitoneal tethering. Computed tomography scanning can be beneficial in localizing the injury. Management is nonsurgical unless blood loss is ongoing or the wall is compromised. If the bowel ruptures, it should be treated promptly. Blunt trauma and the subsequent deceleration can injure the pancreas. Computed tomography scanning and a serum amylase level provide information regarding the severity of injury and appropriate therapy.

Gastrointestinal diseases in the athlete include diarrhea and gastroenteritis, appendicitis, pancreatitis, and cholecystitis and cholelithiasis. Treatment of diarrhea is generally supportive, but if symptoms persist, the athlete should be evaluated for an infectious agent. Appendicitis is accompanied by pain in the periumbilical area and is localized to the right lower quadrant. Surgical removal of the appendix is recommended. Physical examination for acute pancreatitis reveals midepigastric tenderness (or tenderness over the entire abdomen) and hypoactive bowel sounds. Ultrasonography is the most helpful diagnostic test. Management includes intravenous hydration, restricted oral intake, and parenteral analgesia. Cholecystitis with cholelithiasis or cholangitis occurs more often in women than in men. Ultrasonography is the most sensitive test for gallstones, and radionucleotide cholescintigraphy is helpful when ultrasonography is normal or nondiagnostic. Laparoscopic cholecystectomy is the treatment of choice.

During the preparticipation physical examination, male athletes should be screened for testicular cancer and undescended testicles. An athlete with a solitary testicle or kidney must be carefully counseled about the risks of participating in various sports. The final decision to participate in sports, however, rests with the athlete and his or her family.

Sports-related genitourinary injuries include sports hematuria and kidney, bladder, scrotal, and urethral injury. In most cases, hematuria incidences will resolve after several days, but if the amount of blood is large or the hematuria persists, a full urologic evaluation is required. Kidney injuries are usually managed conservatively with bed rest and monitoring of blood pressure and hematocrit. Bladder damage can occur with pelvic fractures or crush injuries. Minor injuries will heal by themselves. More severe injuries may require bladder drainage through a catheter. Minor injury to the scrotum should resolve within an hour of rest. If testicular pain persists or fluid collects in the scrotum, urgent urologic evaluation is needed. Male athletes are more susceptible to urethral injury than female athletes. Although urethral bleeding is common after such an injury, if the athlete can void and no other problems are apparent, immediate evaluation is not necessary.

The well-prepared athletic trainer recognizes abdominal and genitourinary injuries and illnesses quickly and ensures that the athlete receives appropriate medical attention in a timely fashion to return the athlete to sports participation.

21

Sports Nutrition

Ann C. Grandjean, EdD
Kristin J. Reimers, MS, RD
Jaime S. Ruud, MS, RD

QUICK CONTENTS

- The variables affecting energy requirements in the athlete and how an individual athlete's needs are estimated.

- The roles of carbohydrates, proteins, and fats in the athlete's diet.

- The functions of vitamins and minerals and how to identify food sources of each.

- The role of dietary supplements in the athlete's diet.

- The role of the sports nutritionist or dietitian.

- The Food Guide Pyramid.

- The relationship between energy balance and weight control, including programs for weight loss and weight gain.

- The importance of fluid and electrolyte balance.

- Appropriate preevent meals and eating on the road.

- The effects of caffeine on the athlete.

- The warning signs of eating disorders and what action to take if an eating disorder is suspected.

OVERVIEW

Proper nutrition is an important consideration for athletes who seek to maximize their performance. No diet will directly increase strength, power, or endurance, but an adequate diet will allow athletes to train and compete to the best of their ability. This chapter focuses on the scientific rationale for good nutritional practices, as well as practical information concerning the nutritional needs of athletes.

The chapter begins with a discussion of the role that diet plays in athletic performance, which is followed by a discussion of calorie requirements, including factors that influence calorie requirements and how to estimate energy requirements. Following is a section on nutrients including carbohydrates, protein and amino acids, fats, minerals, dietary supplements, and water. The role of the sports nutritionist is explained as are the Food Guide Pyramid and energy balance and weight control. Fluid and electrolyte replacement and the risks of dehydration are discussed. Nutritional strategies for competition are addressed, followed by a discussion of the effects of caffeine on the athlete. The chapter closes with a description of eating disorders and the athletic trainer's role in recognizing and preventing eating disorders.

THE ROLE OF DIET IN ATHLETIC PERFORMANCE

Athletes are a diverse subpopulation of the general population, with widely varying cultural and socioeconomic backgrounds, all of which impact dietary habits and preferences. Athletes and professionals who work with athletes are often confused about nutrition guidelines for athletes. Athletes should consider basic nutrient requirements when planning their diets, but often there are extenuating circumstances that may make general guidelines difficult to follow. Nutrient requirements depend on the athlete's age, body size, gender, genetics, environmental training conditions, and duration, frequency, and intensity of physical activity. Requirements will vary greatly among and within athletic groups. Nutrient requirements, special considerations, and practical application of sports nutrition for athletes must be regarded.

CALORIE REQUIREMENTS

Calorie (energy) requirement is defined as the energy intake required to offset energy expenditure, resulting in a constant body weight. Calorie requirements of athletes are highly variable and depend on many factors. Maintaining adequate calorie intake to support the athlete's training and competitive schedule is imperative if the athlete is to be successful.

Extremely wide differences exist in the dietary intakes of athletes.[1] As a group, the highest calorie intakes are found in male swimmers, cyclists, triathletes, and basketball players, with average intakes as high as 6,000 kcal per day.[2] Lower intakes are found in female figure skaters, gymnasts, and dancers, who may consume less than 1,200 kcal per day.[2] Examination of individual athletes shows an even larger range of calorie intakes, from a few hundred calories to more than 7,000 calories per day.

Although it is commonly assumed that all athletes have higher than average calorie requirements, that is not always true. Some athletes may actually have lower calorie requirements than their nonathletic peers. The best way to determine whether an athlete is consuming an adequate amount of calories is to monitor body weight. If hydrated body weight is decreasing, the athlete's calorie intake requirement is not being met. If body weight is increasing, calorie intake is exceeding the requirement.

Factors Influencing Calorie Requirements

The energy requirement of adults is determined by three factors: resting metabolic rate, thermogenesis, and physical activity. Each of these factors can be affected directly or indirectly by age, genetics, body size, body composition, environmental temperature, training conditions, nontraining physical activity, and caloric intake. For the adolescent athlete, growth is another variable that increases energy requirement.

Resting metabolic rate is the largest contributor to total energy expenditure, accounting for approximately 60% to 75% of daily energy expenditure. The resting metabolic rate is a measure of the calories required for maintaining normal body functions such as respiration, cardiac function, and thermoregulation. Factors that increase resting metabolic rate include increase in lean body tissue, young age, abnormal body temperature, menstrual cycle, and hyperthyroidism. Factors that decrease resting metabolic rate are low calorie intake, loss of lean tissue, and hypothyroidism. Additionally, normal genetic differences in metabolism can reach 10% to 20%.

The second largest component of an individual's energy requirement is the energy expended in physical activity. Of all the components, it varies the most among individuals. The number of calories expended by physical activity obviously increases with frequency, intensity, and duration of the training program as well as off-training physical

FOCUS ON . . .

Calorie Requirements

Calorie, or energy, requirement is defined as the energy intake required to offset energy expenditure, resulting in constant body weight. Adequate calorie intake is essential for successful athletic performance. Intake among athletes varies from several hundred to 7,000 or more calories per day and is not always higher in athletes than nonathletes.

Factors Influencing Calorie Requirements

An adult's energy requirement is determined by resting metabolic rate, physical activity, and thermogenesis, which are affected directly or indirectly by age, genetics, body size, body composition, environmental temperature, training conditions, nontraining physical activity, and calorie intake. Growth is also a factor that increases the energy requirement in adolescent athletes.

Resting metabolic rate is a measure of the calories required to maintain normal body functions (eg, respiration, cardiac function, thermoregulation). Increased lean body tissue, young age, abnormal body temperature, the menstrual cycle, and hyperthyroidism increase resting metabolic rate, while low calorie intake, loss of lean body tissue, and hypothyroidism decrease it.

The energy expended in physical activity is the most variable component and increases with frequency, intensity, and duration of training, as well as nontraining physical activity. Energy costs are highest with aerobic activities performed by large athletes for long periods of time and lowest with skill and power sports performed by small athletes.

Diet-induced thermogenesis is the increase in energy expenditure greater than the resting metabolic rate measurable for several hours after a meal. This component includes the energy costs of digestion, absorption, metabolism, and food storage in the body.

Estimating Energy Requirements

Although individual calorie needs vary greatly, estimated calorie requirements per pound for light, moderate, and heavy activity levels are 17, 19, and 23 for male athletes and 16, 17, and 20 for female athletes.

activity. The highest energy costs are seen in aerobic activities performed by larger athletes for long periods of time, whereas lowest energy costs are associated with skill and power sports performed by smaller athletes.

The thermic effect of food, also known as diet-induced *thermogenesis,* is the increase in energy expenditure greater than the resting metabolic rate that can be measured for several hours following a meal. The thermic effect of food includes the energy cost of digestion, absorption, metabolism, and storage of food in the body. The thermic effect of food accounts for approximately 7% to 10% of the total energy requirement.

Estimating Energy Requirements

The correct answer to the question, "How many calories do I need?", is the number it takes to maintain ideal competitive weight. However, athletes and coaches often desire a more exact number. Short of measuring calories consumed in a metabolic chamber, it is difficult to calculate energy requirements because of the numerous variables impacting calorie requirements. However, guidelines do exist for estimating daily energy needs. **Table 21-1** provides factors that the athletic trainer can use to estimate the energy needs of an athlete. For example, calculations for a male athlete who weighs 170 lb and in heavy training, using the factor of 23, would estimate a caloric need of 3,910 or roughly 3,900 calories. These calculations are rough estimates based on normative data.

Another more laborious method that can be performed by motivated athletes with a stable weight is recording dietary intake for 3 consecutive, representative days. Because stable weight indicates that energy intake and energy output are equal, the individual's requirements can be assumed to equal the number of calories consumed.

NUTRIENTS

The six classifications of nutrients are carbohydrates, proteins, fats, vitamins, minerals, and water. Because alcohol can be used by the body for energy, it can be

TABLE 21-1

ESTIMATED DAILY CALORIE NEEDS OF MALE AND FEMALE ATHLETES AT THREE ACTIVITY LEVELS

Activity	Calories per lb for men	Calories per lb for women
Light	17	16
Moderate	19	17
Heavy	23	20

ketoacids are either used directly as a source of energy or are converted to carbohydrate or body fat.

Fats

Dietary fat is the most concentrated source of energy in the diet. The types of fat found in foods are divided into three groups: saturated, monounsaturated, and polyunsaturated fats. All categories provide the same number of calories: 9 calories per gram of fat.

Results of some studies indicate that there is an association between high-fat intake and chronic diseases such as cardiovascular disease and certain types of cancer.[13] Therefore, the American Heart Association, the American Cancer Society, and health agencies of the federal government recommend a fat intake that equals no more than 30% of calories ingested per day.[13] However, these recommendations are based on research conducted on sedentary individuals. The World Health Organization recommends a dietary fat intake of up to 30% of calories for sedentary individuals and up to 35% for physically active individuals. This is approximately the percentage of fat that elite athletes routinely consume.[14,15] **Table 21-2** shows the nutrient intake of 103 Olympic athletes broken down by sport.

The athletic trainer should be aware of all athletes with a family history of heart disease or elevated serum cholesterol when considering recommendations for dietary fat. However, for most athletes, performance is the primary consideration. Quite often, fat intakes greater than 30% are necessary to provide the energy needed for training and competition.

"Fat phobia" is pervasive within some athletic groups. Undue restriction of dietary fat can result from the belief that "fat is bad" or "dietary fat automatically becomes body fat." Both perceptions are false. Nor is it true that fat is an intrinsic detriment to performance that "slows down" the athlete. An unfounded overrestriction of fat intake often leads to exclusion of entire food groups such as meats and dairy foods and does not enhance performance. For many athletes, exclusion of these foods results in inadequate

TABLE 21-2
NUTRIENT INTAKE OF 103 OLYMPIC ATHLETES

Sport		Fat		
	Number of subjects	Grams per day	Grams per kilogram	Percent (%) of total energy
Men				
Cycling	9	196	2.7	41
Distance running	11	106	1.5	29
Figure skating	7	88	1.5	31
Hockey	8	155	1.9	39
Judo	7	127	1.7	36
Weightlifting	21	165	1.8	38
Women				
Cycling	10	111	1.9	31
Distance running	9	74	1.4	30
Figure skating	8	69	1.5	33
Judo	4	77	1.2	34
Tennis	9	68	1.2	29

Grandjean AC: Dietary Habits of Olympic Athletes, in Wolinsky I (ed): *Nutrition in Exercise and Sports*, New York, NY, CRC Press, 1998, p 425.

intake of important nutrients. The World Health Organization recommends a minimum fat intake of no less than 15% of total calories.[16] **Table 21-3** shows the fat gram content of three levels of fat intake.

Vitamins

Vitamins are organic (carbon-containing) substances that cannot be synthesized by the body. They are needed in very small amounts and perform specific metabolic functions. Since the early 1900s, knowledge about the structures, functions, and unique features of individual vitamins has grown significantly. For example, researchers initially classified vitamins as water soluble and fat soluble, which actually is an oversimplification. In addition, shortly after vitamins were discovered to exist, researchers believed that many vitamins were related and so classified them to reflect that, for example vitamin B1, B2, and B6. It is now known that virtually no direct relationship exists among these vitamins except that they are all water soluble and most of them operate as a coenzyme in metabolic reactions. Names describing composition or structure are now recognized to be more appropriate; for example, what was once called vitamin B6 is now called pyridoxine.

Table 21-4 describes the functions of individual vitamins and some food sources of these vitamins. Because it will be some time before the old terminology disappears, this table identifies the originally applied number designate as well as the vitamin name.

Nutritionally relevant organic compounds

Many other organic compounds that are present in foods are required in the diets of animals or microbes, but there is little evidence that they are essential for humans. Although these substances do not meet the standard definition of a vitamin, they are often referred to as such in lay literature and product labels. Some of the compounds within these classes of substances may eventually be determined as necessary in the human diet, so the athletic trainer should be aware of their existence. Such compounds include choline, taurine, carnitine, myoinositol, flavonoids (rutin, quercetin, and hesperidin, or the so-called vitamin P factors); ubiquinones, also called coenzyme Q and vitamin Q; and lipoic acid.

Minerals

The human body requires various *minerals* for a wide variety of metabolic functions. For example, calcium is needed for bone and tooth formation and function, nerve transmission, and muscle contraction. Iron is necessary for red blood cell formation and is also a component of enzymes necessary for energy production. Like vitamins, minerals are needed by the body for a variety of vital bodily functions and must be supplied in the diet. Minerals, however, differ from vitamins in that the mineral content of the body is measured in pounds, whereas the vitamin content is measured in ounces. Calcium, phosphorus, magnesium, and the electrolytes sodium, potassium, and chloride are often called the major minerals. For the athlete, the importance of minerals for bone health and fluid and electrolyte balance is well recognized. Iron, zinc, iodine, selenium, copper, magnesium, fluoride, chromium, and molybdenum are referred to as trace elements. **Table 21-5** lists minerals, their functions, and some of the good food sources that provide them.

Ultratrace minerals are needed in minute amounts and, therefore, evidence for their essentiality is often difficult

TABLE 21-3
FAT CONTENT (IN GRAMS) OF THREE LEVELS OF TOTAL CALORIES

Calories	Minimum fat (15%)	Low fat (30%)	Moderate fat (35%)
2,000	33	67	78
2,400	40	80	93
2,600	43	87	101
3,000	50	100	117
3.500	58	117	136
4,000	67	133	155
4,500	75	150	175
5,000	83	167	194

TABLE 21-4
VITAMINS

Vitamin	Function	Food sources
Vitamin A	• Promotes growth and repair of body tissues, bone formation, and healthy skin and hair • Essential for night vision	Liver (all sources), giblets, some cheeses, egg yolk, whole milk, butter
Beta carotene	• Serves as an antioxidant*	Sweet peppers, carrots, grape leaves, pumpkin, sweet potatoes, yams, broccoli, dandelion greens, chili peppers, mustard greens, spinach, kale, turnip greens, apricots, papaya, watermelon, peaches, asparagus, winter squash, cantaloupe, muskmelon, Swiss chard
Vitamin D	• Aids in the absorption of calcium and helps to build bone mass and prevent bone loss • Helps maintain calcium and phosphorus levels in blood	Fish (herring, salmon, oysters, catfish, sardines, tuna, shrimp, mackerel), milk, margarine, fortified breakfast cereals, egg yolk, eggs, butter
Vitamin E	• Serves as an antioxidant* • Needed for normal growth and development	Oils (wheat germ, vegetable), mayonnaise, fortified breakfast cereals, nuts (almonds, hazelnuts, peanuts, hickory, pistachio), margarine, wheat germ, peanut butter
Vitamin K (phylloquinone)	• Needed for normal blood clotting and bone health	Kale, brussels sprouts, spinach, Swiss chard, cauliflower, broccoli, turnip and mustard greens, carrots, asparagus, avocado, bell peppers, strawberries, tomatoes, apples, peaches
Vitamin C	• Promotes healthy cell development, wound healing, and resistance to infections • Serves as an antioxidant* • Needed for conversion of the inactive form of folic acid to the active form • Makes iron available for hemoglobin synthesis	Pineapple, raspberries, potatoes, and onions

*Antioxidants are substances that protect cells from oxygen singlets (free radicals). Oxidative damage plays a causative role in heart disease, some cancers, and cataracts. Thus, antioxidant vitamins can protect against such diseases.

(Continued)

TABLE 21-4 (CONTINUED)
VITAMINS

Vitamin	Function	Food sources
Thiamin (B1)	• Essential for carbohydrate metabolism • Needed for normal functioning of the nervous system and muscles, including the heart muscle	Fortified breakfast cereals, sunflower seeds, peas, pork, orange juice, lima beans, pecans, enriched rice
Riboflavin (B2)	• Helps in red blood cell formation, nervous system functioning, and energy metabolism • Needed for vision and may help protect against cataracts	Liver, wheat germ, brewer's yeast, almonds, cheese, fortified breakfast cereal, whey protein, milk, eggs, lamb, pork, veal, broccoli, yogurt
Niacin	• Essential for energy metabolism and proper nervous system functioning • High intakes can lower elevated cholesterol	Soy protein, soy flour, textured vegetable protein, whey protein, beef, peanuts, peanut butter, sunflower seeds, fortified breakfast cereals
Pyridoxine (B6)	• Essential for protein metabolism, nervous system, and immune function • Involved in synthesis of hormones and red blood cells	Liver, bananas, fortified breakfast cereals, soybeans, chicken, tuna, raw carrots, beef, broccoli, spinach, potatoes, alfalfa sprouts, navy beans, peanut butter, garbanzo beans, walnuts, sunflower seeds, avocado, eggs, lima beans, cabbage, salmon
Folic acid	• Needed for normal growth and development and red blood cell formation • Reduces risk of neural tube birth defects • May reduce risk of heart disease and cervical dysplasia	Brewer's yeast, fortified breakfast cereals, liver, black-eyed peas, beans (pinto, black, lima, white, garbanzo, soy), peanuts, peanut butter, spinach, turnip greens, asparagus, mustard greens, seaweed, eggs, enriched bread, orange juice
Cobalamin (B12)	• Vital for blood formation and a healthy nervous system	Liver, oysters, lamb, eggs, beef, shellfish, fish, poultry, pork, chicken, fortified breakfast cereals
Biotin	• Assists in the metabolism of fatty acids and utilization of B vitamins	Nuts (peanuts, hazelnuts, soy, almonds, cashews, macadamia), peanut butter, black-eyed peas, liver, milk, egg yolks, yeast, cheese, cauliflower, carrots, avocado, sweet potatoes
Pantothenic acid	• Aids in normal growth and development	Liver, sunflower seeds, fortified breakfast cereals, egg yolk, whey protein, soy protein, peanuts, pecans, veal, peanut butter, enriched rice, broccoli, lima beans

TABLE 21-5
MINERALS

Mineral	Function	Food sources
Calcium	• Essential for developing and maintaining healthy bones and teeth • Assists in blood clotting, muscle contraction, and nerve transmission • Reduces risk of osteoporosis and may also reduce the risk of preeclampsia in pregnant women	Cheese, sardines, milk, calcium-fortified orange juice, cottage cheese, yogurt, ice cream, almonds, kale, collard greens, calcium-enriched tofu, broccoli, soybeans, canned salmon
Phosphorus	• Works with calcium to develop and maintain strong bones and teeth • Enhances use of other nutrients • Essential for energy metabolism, DNA structure, and cell membranes	Cheese, fish, beef, pork, whole-wheat products, cocoa powder, pumpkin seeds, sunflower seeds, almonds
Magnesium	• Activates nearly 100 enzymes and helps nerves and muscles function • Is a constituent of bones and teeth	Bran (wheat and rice), cocoa powder, fortified breakfast cereals, seeds (pumpkin, sunflower), soybeans, nuts (almonds, pine, hazelnuts, cashews, walnuts, peanuts), spinach
Molybdenum	• Needed for metabolism of DNA and RNA and the production of uric acid	Milk, milk products, peas, beans, liver, whole grain products
Manganese	• Needed for the normal development of the skeletal and connective tissues • Involved in the metabolism of carbohydrates	Wheat germ, wheat bran, rice bran, fortified breakfast cereals, rice cakes, nuts (peanuts, pecans, pine, walnuts, almonds, hazelnuts), soybeans, mussels, whole-wheat products (pasta, bread, crackers)
Copper	• Involved in iron metabolism, nervous system functioning, bone health, and synthesis of proteins • Plays a role in the pigmentation of skin, hair, and eyes	Liver, shellfish (especially oysters), lobster, nuts (cashews, Brazil nuts, hazelnuts, walnuts, peanuts, almonds, pecans, pistachios), seeds (sunflower, pumpkin), fortified breakfast cereals, Great Northern beans
Chromium (III)	• Aids in glucose metabolism • May help regulate blood glucose and insulin levels in individuals with diabetes	Whole grains, some ready-to-eat cereals, brewer's yeast, peas

(Continued)

TABLE 21-5 (CONTINUED)
MINERALS

Mineral	Function	Food sources
Iodine	• Is part of the thyroid hormone • Helps regulate growth, development, and energy metabolism	Iodized salt, saltwater fish, and seafood
Iron	• Needed for red blood cell formation and function • Constituent of myoglobin and component of enzyme systems	Liver, beef, lamb, pork, veal, poultry, clams, oysters, fortified breakfast cereals, enriched bread products, brewer's yeast, nuts (pine, cashews, almonds), beans (kidney, green, garbanzo)
Selenium	• Essential component of a key antioxidant enzyme • Needed for normal growth and development and for use of iodine in thyroid function	Tenderloin of beef, pollock, trout, tuna, oysters, mackerel, flounder, liver, sunflower seeds, wheat bran, wheat germ, some pork products, fortified breakfast cereals, perch, crab, clams, cod, haddock, whole-wheat bread
Zinc	• Essential part of more than 100 enzymes involved in digestion, metabolism, reproduction, and wound healing	Oysters, beef, veal, lamb, pork, chicken, lima beans, black-eyed peas, white beans

to determine. Deficiencies in humans have not been established for any of these ultratrace elements, and no recommended intake for them exists. Ultratrace minerals include arsenic, bromine, cadmium, fluorine, lead, lithium, manganese, molybdenum, nickel, silicon, tin, vanadium, and boron.

Iron

Iron is a mineral that receives a great deal of attention by athletes. As a constituent of hemoglobin and myoglobin, iron plays a role in oxygen transport and use of energy, and therefore, iron deficiency can limit athletic performance.

Iron deficiency is the most common nutritional deficiency in humans and the most common cause of anemia. The number of healthy women in the United States who have some degree of iron deficiency has been estimated to be as high as 58%.[17] Iron deficiency also commonly occurs in teenage boys.

A number of factors may contribute to low iron stores in athletes, including heavy training, gastrointestinal bleed-ing, red blood cell hemolysis, increased iron losses through sweating, decreased iron absorption, and inadequate dietary intake. Women who experience heavy menstrual bleeding may be at increased risk for iron deficiency. Athletes who consume vegetarian diets are also at risk for iron deficiency, because plant foods decrease the absorption of iron.

If blood analysis determines that an athlete is iron deficient, he or she should receive diet counseling and, when indicated, supplemental iron.

Calcium

Except for the calcium contributed from maternal stores during fetal development, all calcium in the adult body is derived from exogenous sources. Inadequate calcium intake inhibits mineral density of bones.[18] The athletic trainer should be aware that low calcium intakes have been reported in many female athletes, including gymnasts, runners, cyclists, swimmers, and dancers.[19-22] Many women do not consume adequate calcium as a result of low calorie intake or avoidance of milk and dairy foods, which are the best sources of calcium. Athletes consuming low-calcium diets may be at risk for *osteopenia* and *osteoporosis*, deterioration of bone tissue leading to bone fragility, and increased risk of fracture. Although fracture risk is influenced by genetic, hormonal, and training factors, diet plays an essential role. Athletes should be encouraged to include low-fat dairy products and other calcium-rich foods in their diet. Those who are unable to meet calcium requirements through diet may need a calcium supplement.

Dietary Supplements

One of the first dietary supplements widely used in the United States was cod liver oil given to children in the early 1800s to prevent rickets. It was not until the 1930s that vitamin D was isolated and identified as the preventive substance in cod liver oil. From that modest beginning, dietary supplements have grown into a billion-dollar industry. Much of the growth in dietary supplements can be traced to 1978 when legislation was enacted in the United States that allowed dietary supplements to be sold without a prescription and imposed no maximum level of nutrient content. The American public has long demanded consumer freedom when it comes to dietary supplements.

Opponents of dietary supplements argue that for hundreds of thousand of years, people have obtained adequate amounts of vitamins and minerals from the food they ate. However, several factors must be considered before ruling out the need for supplements. First, our hunter-gatherer ancestors consumed diets very different from the American diet of today. For example, leafy greens extremely high in calcium were an important part of the diet of our ancestors. Additionally, lifestyles, especially life spans, have changed dramatically. Thus, the focus has changed from "adequate nutrition" to "optimal nutrition." Scientists and physicians now focus on chronic disease prevention and health promotion, not on correcting overt deficiencies such as scurvy that occurred in sailors who went too long without vitamin C. Undoubtedly, "optimal nutrition" can, in many cases, be achieved through food alone; however, whether most individuals accomplish such on a regular basis is another question.

It is universally agreed that in cases of inadequate intakes, multivitamin, mineral, and nutrient-specific supplements can correct inadequacies, and use of dietary supplements to correct deficiencies is accepted practice. Women of childbearing age have an increased need for folic acid; heavy smokers have an increased need for vitamin C. Women taking oral contraceptives often have reduced serum levels of thiamin, riboflavin, and other vitamins. Individuals who consume large amounts of alcohol require more thiamin, niacin, B6, and folacin than those who drink socially or not at all. Certain drugs, as well as chronic infections, cancer, surgery, and other medical conditions, can alter vitamin and mineral needs. Older individuals have a reduced ability to absorb nutrients. Finally, individuals such as chronic dieters who drastically restrict calorie intake may not consume adequate levels of vitamins and minerals.

Throughout history, athletes have pursued optimal health and top performance by eating specific foods and taking various substances. For example, at the Olympic Games in 1948, athletes reportedly ate generous helpings of steak, eggs, and milk. Vitamin preparations, glucose, and large amounts of salt were in vogue.

Results of studies reveal that approximately 38% to 41% of high school athletes and 51% of college athletes take supplements.[23,24] It is estimated that 50% to 90% of elite and Olympic athletes take supplements daily or weekly.[25] Female athletes reportedly use vitamin or mineral supplements more than male athletes. Results of a recent study of ultradistance runners indicated that 78% of female and 62% of male runners used supplements in their training diets.[26] Patterns also tend to exist between sport groups. For example, use of vitamin supplements is more common in runners and cyclists than in gymnasts, wrestlers, and basketball players.

The reasons for supplement use are quite diverse. Performance enhancement, compensation for an inadequate diet, postexercise recovery, to provide energy, and for general well-being are the major reasons given.

One thing is certain, dietary supplements are here to stay. Integrating appropriate supplement use with reasonable dietary intake is as much an art as a science and should be based on the individual's preferences, beliefs, and health history. In some cases, athletes need supplements and are not taking them. In other situations, they are taking wrong or unnecessary supplements. The scenarios are endless. The athletic trainer must be aware that supplement use should be assessed on a case-by-case basis; the athletic trainer should refer to experts and sources for guidance as needed. **Table 21-6** lists several resources for nutrition information. In addition, the US Olympic Committee publishes guidelines on supplementation.

Water

Under optimal conditions, the body can survive 30 days without food but only 4 to 10 days without water. Water is the largest component of the body, representing from 15% to 70% of body weight. Total body water is determined largely by body composition; muscle tissue is approximately 75% water, and fat tissue is about 20% water.

ROLE OF THE SPORTS NUTRITIONIST OR DIETITIAN

Because of the frequent interaction and close relationship that the athletic trainer often has with the athlete, coaches and athletes often turn to the athletic trainer with their

trips. All of these are opportunities for the athletic trainer to identify nutrition problems, dietary inadequacies, and dietary habits that are of concern.

In some settings, the athletic trainer can use the resources of a sports nutritionist or a registered dietitian to estimate caloric needs, evaluate the athlete's diet, and make suggestions and recommendations for dietary improvement. A nutritionist or dietitian who is well versed in sports nutrition is obviously most helpful if the goal is performance-related. Often dietitians and nutritionists are not readily available. Sports nutrition information can be obtained from several sources (see Table 21-6).

FOOD GUIDE PYRAMID

The *Food Guide Pyramid* is a guide for types and amounts of foods needed daily for a balanced diet (**Figure 21-1**). Foods from each of the five food groups provide essential nutrients and no one group is more important than another. For example, if the milk, yogurt, and cheese group is omitted from a diet, the best sources of calcium, riboflavin, and vitamin D are excluded. The tip of the pyramid represents fat, oils, and sweets. There is no serving suggestion for these foods. Although many sedentary individuals need to significantly reduce fat intake, most athletes with high energy requirements need to consume foods that are higher in fats, oils, and sweets to consume adequate calories.

The Pyramid visually displays a range of servings for each food group, taking into account varying energy needs and personal food preferences. The individual should consume at least the lowest number of servings to obtain the minimum amount of essential nutrients. **Table 21-7** provides examples of the number of servings needed to supply three calorie levels. As shown, athletes with higher energy requirements can easily exceed the upper end of the range listed in the Food Guide Pyramid.

ENERGY BALANCE AND WEIGHT CONTROL

Weight and Body Composition

The focus of weight control in the athlete should be on body composition rather than on weight. An assessment of body fat percentage is far more useful than a weight measurement obtained from a scale. The percentage of body fat and its complement of lean body weight should be assessed at regular intervals throughout the year so that if corrective measures such as changes in training and diet are needed, they can be initiated in a timely fashion.

The optimal body fat percentage varies according to the sport and the athlete. Minimal body fat for collegiate men is 5%, and 7% is frequently recommended as the minimum level for high school boys.[27] Little is known about minimum body fat levels for women and girls, but 13% to 18% is sometimes suggested as a minimum.[28]

TABLE 21-6

RESOURCES FOR INFORMATION ABOUT NUTRITION

Food and Nutrition Information Center (FNIC)
National Agricultural Library/USDA
10301 Baltimore Avenue, Room 304
Beltsville, MD 20705
(301) 504-5719
www.nal.usda.gov/fnic

President's Council on Physical Fitness and Sports
HHH Building, Room 738H
200 Independence Avenue SW
Washington, DC 20201
(202) 690-9000
www.surgeongeneral.gov/ophs/pcpfs.htm

Nutrition Counseling Education Services (NCES)
1904 East 123rd Street
Olathe, KS 66061-5886
(800) 545-5653
www.ncescatalog.com

International Center for Sports Nutrition
502 South 44th Street, Room 3007
Omaha, NE 68105
(402) 559-5505

National Collegiate Athletic Association Committee on Competitive Safeguards and Medical Aspects of Sports
6201 College Boulevard
Overland Park, KS 66211
(913) 339-1906
www.ncaa.org/databases/legislation/1999/99-034.html

National Strength and Conditioning Association
1955 North Union Boulevard
Colorado Springs, CO 80909
(719) 632-6722
www.nsca-lift.org

Weight-control Information Network
1 Win Way
Bethesda, MD 20892
(800) 946-8098
www.niddk.nih.gov/health/nutrit/win.htm

American College of Sports Medicine
PO Box 1440
Indianapolis, IN 46206
(317) 637-9200
www.acsm.org/sportsmed

concerns and questions about diet and nutrition. Additionally, the athletic trainer often is able to observe athletes during training meals or while eating on road

The Food Guide Pyramid emphasizes foods from the five food groups shown in the three lower sections of the pyramid.

Each of these food groups provides some, but not all, of the nutrients you need. Foods in one group can't replace those in another. No one food group is more important than another—for good health, you need them all.

The Pyramid is an outline of what to eat each day. It's not a rigid prescription, but a general guide that lets you choose a healthful diet that's right for you. The Pyramid calls for eating a variety of foods to get the nutrients you need and at the same time the right amount of calories to maintain a healthy weight

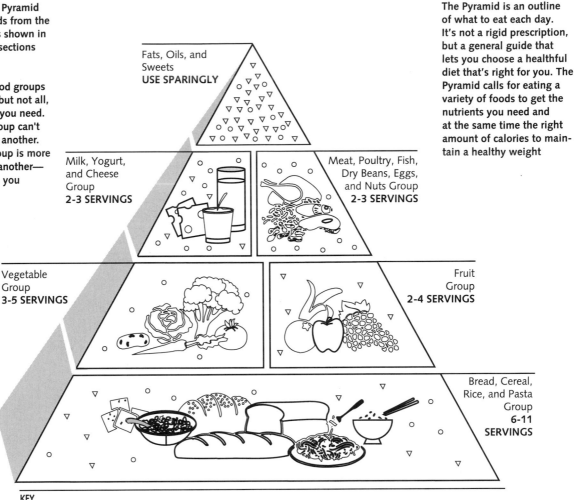

Fats, Oils, and Sweets
USE SPARINGLY

Milk, Yogurt, and Cheese Group
2-3 SERVINGS

Meat, Poultry, Fish, Dry Beans, Eggs, and Nuts Group
2-3 SERVINGS

Vegetable Group
3-5 SERVINGS

Fruit Group
2-4 SERVINGS

Bread, Cereal, Rice, and Pasta Group
6-11 SERVINGS

KEY
▽ Fat (naturally occuring and added)   ○ Sugar (added) These symbols show fat and added sugars

FIGURE 21-1

The Food Guide Pyramid provides in five food groups the types and amounts of foods needed daily for a balanced diet. (Reproduced with permission from the United States Department of Agriculture and the United States Department of Health and Human Services.)

FOCUS ON . . .

The Food Guide Pyramid

The Food Guide Pyramid describes the types and amounts of foods from the five food groups needed for a balanced diet: bread, cereal, rice, and pasta; vegetable; fruit; milk, yogurt, and cheese; and meat, poultry, fish, eggs, dried beans, and nuts. Each of the groups provide essential nutrients, and no one group is more important than another. Fats, oils, and sweets may help athletes with high energy requirements to consume adequate calories.

Group minimums and averages serve as a useful reference but should never be used as absolute requirements for each athlete. The "ideal" body fat percentage (%BF) for individual athletes varies. Many athletes perform very well at higher than average body fat percentages, while others are genetically inclined to body fat levels that are less than the referenced minimums. The best indicators of appropriate body composition are not found on printed charts or based on team comparisons. The best indicators of an appropriate body fat level for an individual athlete are satisfactory athletic performance, normal dietary intake, and overall well being.

Measuring body fat

The amount of body fat can be calculated by using the skinfold method, underwater weighing, or bioelectrical

TABLE 21-7

NUMBER OF SERVINGS IN FOOD GUIDE PYRAMID GROUPS AND RECOMMENDED PROPORTION OF NUTRIENTS

Recommended number of servings in the Food Guide Pyramid groups

Food group	1,100 Calories/day	2,800 Calories/day	3,600 Calories/day
Bread, cereal, rice, and pasta	6	11	14
Vegetable	3	5	7
Fruit	2	4	5
Milk, yogurt, and cheese	3	3	4
Meat, poultry, fish, eggs, dry beans, and nuts	5 oz	7 oz	9 oz
Added fat*	18 g (3^1/$_2$ tsp)	32 g (6^1/$_2$ tsp)	42 g (8^1/$_2$tsp)
Added sugar*	6 tsp	18 tsp	24 tsp

*There is no recommended number of servings from the fats and sweets category.

Recommended proportion of nutrients

Nutrient group	1,100 Calories/day	2,800 Calories/day	3,600 Calories/day
Carbohydrate (g)	195 (50%)†	360 (50%)	465 (50%)
Protein (g)	85 (20%†	115 (20%)	155 (20%)
Fat (g)	55 (30%)†	95 (30%)	129 (30%)

† Percentage of calories from carbohydrates, protein, and fat.

impedance. Underwater weighing, considered the gold standard, is generally not a practical method for a team. Skinfold testing, when using population-specific equations and a trained technician, yields %BF estimations within ±3% and is generally the most reliable and practical method for groups. Bioelectrical impedance (BIA) is based on the principle that conduction of an applied electrical current is greater in fat-free mass because of higher water and electrolyte content found in these tissues relative to fat mass. Factors that can influence BIA estimates include hydration level, skin temperature, and blood flow distribution. Regardless of which method is used, measuring body fat under consistent conditions is important. The same method, the same technicians, and the same equipment should be used, and the athlete should be measured in a hydrated, nonexercised state.

Weight Loss

For most athletes, the goal of weight loss is to reduce body fat while preserving lean tissue. Loss of body fat is achieved only when a negative calorie balance is achieved, that is, when fewer calories are consumed than are expended. The composition of the calories consumed will not affect the rate or quality of weight loss. Whether the diet is high-carbohydrate, high-protein, or high-fat, if fewer calories are consumed than are expended, weight loss will result. Research has shown that when the calorie intake is the same, a higher fat diet will result in the same amount of fat loss as a low-fat diet.[29] A nutritionally balanced diet that the athlete enjoys is always better than a diet that looks good on paper but does not match the athlete's food preferences. Some athletes will be able to adhere better to a higher carbohydrate diet, some to a

FOCUS ON . . .

Weight Loss and Gain

Most athletes who want to lose weight want to reduce body fat, while preserving lean tissue. To reduce body fat, the calorie balance must be negative (fewer consumed than expended), although the composition of the calories does not affect the rate or quality of weight loss. As long as the athlete's macro- and micronutrient needs are met, the foods included in the diet should be based on the athlete's preferences.

Each pound of body fat contains approximately 3,500 calories. The conventional recommendation to reduce calories by 500 to 1,000 per day through calorie restriction and increased exercise for a weight loss of 1 to 2 lb per week may not be appropriate for athletes, who may already be exercising maximally and who require adequate calories to support training and preserve lean tissue.

Athletes should try to lose no more than 1 to 2 lb per week or 1% of body weight. They should start with a calorie intake of 1,800 to 2,000 calories per day and add or subtract calories based on progress. The diet should be nutritionally balanced with a variety of foods. Weight loss is usually best achieved in the off- or preseason, and weight loss for relatively lean athletes will often be slow. Also, it may be more difficult for high-level athletes to lose body fat and gain muscle than for novices.

Rapid weight loss, or weight "cutting," to compete in a desired weight class is accomplished by restricting foods and fluids for 3 to 10 days before competition. Precompetition food and fluid restriction is usually followed by refeeding and rehydrating after weigh-in. Some athletes can practice cutting weight without adverse consequences, but others may suffer heat illness, muscle cramping, fatigue, dizziness, weakness, decreased concentration, and even death. The athletic trainer may be able to help best by providing information regarding a safe weight loss program that avoids excessive weight loss and chronic dehydration.

To gain weight in the form of muscle mass, diet and progressive resistance training must be combined, although genetic predisposition, somatotype, and compliance will determine the athlete's progress. Muscle tissue is approximately 70% water, 22% protein, and 8% fatty acids and glycogen. Generally, 700 to 1,000 calories more than daily requirements will support a 1- to 2-lb weekly weight gain. Athletes should eat larger portions of foods at mealtimes, eat more items at each meal, eat frequently, and choose higher-calorie foods. To meet the increased protein needs, some athletes use protein supplements, which may work if the supplement is a good source of calories. The psychological benefits of supplements may also be important.

---

higher protein diet, and some to a higher fat diet. Regardless of the percentage of nutrients the diet provides, as long as the athlete's macro- and micronutrient needs are met, the foods chosen should vary based on the athlete's preferences.

Guidelines for weight loss

Each pound of body fat contains approximately 3,500 calories. The conventional recommendation for weight loss is to achieve a daily calorie deficit of 500 to 1,000 calories through calorie restriction and exercise. This promotes a loss of 1 to 2 lb per week (500 to 1,000 calories x 7 days = 3,500 to 7,000 calories, or 1 to 2 lb). This guideline may or may not be appropriate for an athlete. For example, it is often not practical for the athlete to increase physical activity. If training is already maximal, decreasing calories is the only viable option. However, the athlete must consume adequate calories to support training and to preserve lean tissue. When the athlete embarks on a weight loss course, he or she should consider the following guidelines:

- Lose no more than 1 to 2 lb per week or no more than 1% of the body weight. Gradual weight loss

ensures maximum fat loss and preservation of lean tissue. Rapid weight loss can result in loss of three times more lean tissue (muscle and water) than fat tissue.

- A calorie intake of no less than 1,800 to 2,000 calories per day can serve as a starting point. Calories should be added or subtracted based on progress.

- The diet should be nutritionally balanced, providing a variety of foods. The Food Pyramid can be used as a guide.

- Weight loss is usually best achieved during off-season or preseason periods. Hours spent training, travelling, and competing during the season often foil the best weight loss efforts.

- Weight loss for relatively lean athletes will often be slow. These athletes should expect slow changes in body composition, despite a hypocaloric diet.

- Whether the athlete can gain muscle and lose body fat simultaneously depends primarily on the level of training. Novices can usually accomplish both. Athletes who have been training at a high level for a number of years may find it harder to do both. Seasoned athletes usually have to focus on one body composition change at a time.

Rapid weight loss

Losing weight rapidly so that the athlete can compete in a desired weight class is very different from gradual weight loss to lose body fat, and the two should not be confused. Rapid weight loss or weight "cutting" is accomplished by restricting food and fluids for 3 to 10 days before competition. Food and fluid restriction before competition is usually followed by refeeding and rehydrating after weigh-in. Some athletes practice "cutting weight" with no adverse consequences; however, athletes who attempt to lose too much weight can suffer heat illness, muscle cramping, fatigue, dizziness, weakness, decreased concentration, and even death. There has been a great deal of speculation about growth failure and increased incidence of eating disorders, with rapid weight loss.[30] However, little scientific data exists regarding these theories.[31-33]

Many athletes will cut weight with or without professional guidance. The athletic trainer must recognize that many athletes who cut weight do so because their body fat is already minimal; therefore, counseling the athlete to lose weight gradually (to lose fat) is irrelevant. Instead, the athletic trainer can provide information and help establish a safe weight loss plan that establishes, for example, how to avoid excess weight loss and chronic dehydration.

Weight Gain

In order for the athlete to gain weight in the form of muscle mass, a combination of diet and progressive resistance training is essential. However, genetic predisposition, somatotype, and compliance will determine the athlete's progress. Muscle tissue is made up of approximately 70% water, 22% protein, and 8% fatty acids and glycogen. If all of the excess calories consumed are used for muscle growth during resistance training, then 2,000 to 2,500 extra calories are required for each 1 lb increase in lean tissue. Thus, an additional 700 to 1,000 kcals more than the daily requirement would supply the calories needed to support a weekly gain in lean tissue of about 1 to 2 lb, as well as the energy requirements of training. To accomplish increased caloric intake, athletes should eat larger portions of foods at mealtime, eat more items at each meal, eat frequently, or choose higher-calorie foods. Practical experience shows that it is difficult for athletes to gain weight if they are eating fewer than five times per day.

Athletes who are gaining muscle have increased protein requirements. Protein needs are estimated at 1.2 to 2.0 g of protein per kg of body weight per day and may be higher if the athlete's primary source of protein is plant-based, because plant proteins have a lower biological value than animal proteins. Use of protein powders and supplements remains prevalent among athletes. Although they are usually not a necessary source of protein, the psychological benefits of supplements cannot be ignored. In fact, if the protein supplement is a good calorie source, it may enhance weight gain.

FLUID AND ELECTROLYTES

Water replacement is of utmost importance to the athlete for optimal performance. Water impacts athletic performance more than any other nutrient. Consuming fluids in sufficient amounts is essential for normal cellular function and, of particular importance to athletes, thermal regulation. During physiologic and thermal stress, humans do not adequately replace sweat losses when fluids are consumed as desired. In fact, most athletes will replace only about two-thirds of the water they sweat off during exercise. This phenomenon has been called "voluntary dehydration." The athletic trainer must be aware of this tendency and make coaches and athletes aware of it as well. A systematic approach to water replacement is necessary because thirst is not a reliable indicator of fluid needs for athletes who are practicing intensely in hot environmental conditions.

Fluid Balance

Under normal environmental conditions, fluid balance is achieved by regulation of fluid intake through changes in thirst sensations and regulation of loss by the kidneys. The average fluid requirement for adults is 1.9 to 2.6 L per day. The rule of thumb often used to replace volume lost through urination, insensible loss from skin and lungs, and loss in feces is 2 L or 2 quarts per day. Sweat losses can increase fluid requirements significantly. For example, continuous sweating during prolonged exercise can create a loss of 1.8 L of fluid per hour.[34] Athletes who sweat profusely for several hours per day may need to consume an extra 3 to 4 L of fluid to replace losses.

RISKS OF DEHYDRATION

Unless sweat losses are replaced, body temperature will rise, leading to heat exhaustion, heatstroke, and even death. Sweat losses are tracked by decreases in body weight; 1 pint of sweat ($^1/_2$ quart or 16 oz) weighs 1 lb. Fluid loss equal to as little as 1% of total body weight can be associated with an elevation in core temperature during exercise. Fluid loss of 3% to 5% of body weight results in cardiovascular strain and impaired ability to dissipate heat, and at 7% loss, collapse is likely. It is common for athletes to dehydrate 2% to 6% during practice in the heat.[35] For example, in a 220-lb athlete, 5% body weight loss is 11 lb. Although this occurs commonly during practice in the heat, this level of dehydration should be recognized as detrimental to performance and potentially dangerous.

Monitoring Hydration Status

A systematic approach to ensuring adequate hydration is to record nude, dry body weights of athletes before and after practice. Each pound lost during practice represents 1 pint of fluid loss, which must be replaced before the next

FOCUS ON . . .

Risks of Dehydration

If sweat losses are not replaced, body temperature rises, leading to heat exhaustion, heatstroke, and perhaps death. Sweat losses are tracked by decreases in body weight: 1 pint of sweat equals 1 lb. Fluid loss of as little as 1% of body weight can cause body temperature to rise; fluid loss of 3% to 5% of body weight strains the cardiovascular system and impairs the ability to dissipate heat. At 7% fluid loss, collapse is likely. Although athletes commonly dehydrate 2% to 6% during practice in the heat, this level of dehydration is both detrimental to performance and potentially dangerous.

Monitoring Hydration Status

A systematic approach to ensuring adequate hydration is to record nude dry body weights of athletes before and after practice. Each pound lost during practice represents 1 pint of fluid loss that must be replaced before the next practice. This approach will also identify chronically dehydrated athletes, such as those who lose 5 to 10 lb during the week, who are at risk for poor performance and heat illness.

Other indicators of dehydration are dark yellow, strong-smelling urine, decreased urinary frequency, rapid resting heart rate, and prolonged muscle soreness. Normal urine color is that of lemon juice (athletes taking supplemental vitamins may have bright yellow urine). Urination during rehydration does not signal complete rehydration.

Electrolytes

The major electrolytes lost in sweat are sodium, chloride, and, to a lesser extent, potassium. Physiologic adaptation decreases electrolyte losses in the urine and sweat during periods of strenuous exercise. The average sodium concentration in sweat is 1,150 mg/L (range, 460 to 2,300 mg/L), and the average dietary sodium intake of adults in the United States is 4,000 to 6,000 g per day. However, heat cramps from sodium depletion can occur in athletes who sweat profusely for several days and in those who are not heat acclimated or have low sodium intakes. Potassium sweat losses can usually be replaced with a diet providing 2,000 to 6,000 mg of potassium per day, although the average diet supplies 2,000 to 4,000 mg per day.

Fluid Replacement

The ultimate goal of fluid replacement is to start exercise hydrated, to avoid dehydration during exercise, and to rehydrate before the next session. Two hours before activity, the athlete should consume at least 1 pint of fluid to achieve optimal hydration and allow time for urination of excess fluid. The fluid can be water or another nonalcoholic beverage and can be consumed with or apart from a meal. Caffeine will increase urine production, and therefore, an additional 4 oz of a caffeinated beverage should be consumed.

During activity, athletes should be given time to drink fluids that are absorbed rapidly. They should start drinking before they are thirsty and should be reminded to continue to drink at regular intervals. Large volumes (8 oz or more) tend to empty from the stomach more rapidly than small volumes.

Although cool water is an ideal fluid replacement, commercial or homemade sport drinks can also be consumed. If athletes find flavored drinks more palatable than plain water, they may drink more.

As noted previously, carbohydrates benefit athletes only in activities lasting longer than 1 hour. Commercial sport drinks contain water, sugar, and electrolytes. The carbohydrate concentration is typically 6% to 8%, which allows rapid absorption. Food such as fruit, sport bars, cereal bars, or cookies, along with plain water, is another option that can be used during training.

After activity, total fluid intake should exceed 1 pint per lb to prepare the body for the next bout of exercise. If sweating has been significant, consuming salt in beverages or foods minimizes urine output. During a tournament, consuming a sport drink may help to reduce urine output and maximize water retention. The ideal fluid replacement beverage depends on the athlete's preference, budget, facilities, and type of event.

practice. In addition to identifying acute dehydration from one practice, the weight chart also identifies those athletes who are chronically dehydrated, such as athletes who lose 5 to 10 lb over the course of a week. This downward trend in weight early in the season can be misidentified as fat loss; however, fat loss does not occur this rapidly. The chronically dehydrated athlete is at increased risk for poor performance and heat illness.

It may not be feasible for each team member to weigh-in before and after each practice; however, implementing this system during early, hot seasons (for example, two-times-a-day practices during fall football or soccer) helps prevent dehydration and heat illness. It also makes athletes aware of how much water they need to consume to maintain body weight, because each athlete will vary considerably in fluid replacement needs.

Although they are not as sensitive as weight change, other indicators of hydration status can be useful monitoring tools. Signs of dehydration include dark yellow, strong-smelling urine, decreased frequency of urination, rapid resting heart rate, and prolonged muscle soreness. Normal urine is the color of lemon juice, except in athletes who are taking supplemental vitamins, which tend to make the urine bright yellow. Urination during the rehydration process will occur but does not signal complete rehydration.

Electrolytes

The major electrolytes lost in sweat are sodium, chloride, and, to a lesser extent, potassium. Physiologic adaptation mechanisms decrease the electrolyte loss in the urine and sweat during periods of strenuous exercise; thus, the sweat of a trained athlete is more diluted than the sweat of an untrained individual. The average sodium concentration of sweat is 1,150 mg/L, ranging from 460 to 2,300 mg/L. Average sodium intake of adults in the United States is approximately 4,000 to 6,000 g per day, which is usually high enough to replace sodium losses.[36] However, heat cramps as a result of sodium depletion can develop in athletes who sweat profusely for a period of days, who are not acclimated to the heat, and who have low sodium intakes. Some athletes may need to increase their intake of foods that have a high amount of salt, such as pizza, ham, or potato chips, or add salt to foods.

Potassium losses in sweat can generally be replaced with a diet that provides 2,000 to 6,000 mg of potassium per day.[36] Average daily potassium intake is 2,000 to 4,000 mg. Because of this, some athletes should be encouraged to consume more potassium-rich foods such as citrus fruits and juices, melon, strawberries, tomatoes, bananas, potatoes, meat, and milk. **Table 21-8** presents a list of potassium-rich foods.

Fluid Replacement

Fluid replacement should generally occur before, during, and after exercise. The athlete's ultimate goal is to start exercise in a hydrated state, avoid dehydration during exercise, and rehydrate before the next training session.

Two hours before beginning an activity, the athlete should consume at least 1 pint (16 oz) of fluid to provide the body with the fluid needed to achieve optimal hydration and allow enough time for urination of excess fluid. Because rapid absorption is not critical, the athlete can drink water or any other nonalcoholic beverage such as milk, juice, carbonated or noncarbonated soft drinks, or sport drinks. The fluid can be consumed with or without a meal.

Consumption of drinks containing caffeine will increase urine production by approximately one third in those athletes not accustomed to caffeine and less in athletes who customarily consume caffeine. If the athlete chooses to drink a beverage containing caffeine, drinking an additional 4 oz of fluid will offset the additional urine loss.

Athletes do not voluntarily drink enough fluid to replace sweat losses during exercise. Inadequate fluid intake is compounded when athletes are given neither enough time to drink nor free access to fluids.

During activity, the goal of fluid replacement is to move the fluid from the mouth, through the gut, and into circulation rapidly. In addition, fluid replacement should provide a volume that matches sweat losses, which is achieved by providing fluids that are palatable and rapidly absorbed and by providing time for drinking. Athletes should start drinking before sensing thirst and continue to drink at regular intervals. Larger volumes (8 oz or more) tend to empty from the stomach more rapidly than small volumes, suggesting that "chugging" is preferred over "sipping."

Cool water is an ideal fluid replacement. Other options include commercial sport drinks or "homemade" sport drinks such as diluted juice or diluted soft drinks. Although plain water can meet fluid requirements in most cases, some athletes find flavored drinks more palatable than water and consequently drink more. Except for promoting fluid intake, there appears to be no physiologic benefit from carbohydrate consumption for athletes participating in events of less than 1 hour duration. However, endurance athletes, such as distance runners, soccer players, or distance swimmers, can benefit from carbohydrate consumption in addition to fluid intake during activities lasting more than an hour. The fluid will depend on the athlete's preference, the budget, facilities, and type of event.

Commercial sport drinks contain water, sugars, and electrolytes (usually sodium, chloride, and potassium). The sugar content of sport drinks is slightly less than that of most soft drinks and juices. Carbohydrate concentration of commercial sport drinks ranges from 6% to 8%, which tends to make the solution be absorbed rapidly.[37] A "homemade" sport drink can be made by diluting two parts soft drink to one part water, and adding salt (1/8 teaspoon per quart). Another option is to provide solid food such as fruit, sport bars, cereal bars, or cookies as a carbohydrate source along with plain water. Not all athletes tolerate beverages or foods other than plain water. If food or beverages other than water are used, they should be tested during training to avoid unexpected side effects.

The goal after an exercise session is to prepare the body for the next session. As described previously, monitoring body weight and replacing each pound lost with at least

meal. Foods and beverages that are consumed should not interfere with the physiologic stresses associated with athletic performance.

Timing of the meal

A common recommendation is to eat 3 to 4 hours prior to the event. The logic behind this recommendation appears to be so that athletes do not have food in the stomach during competition. This timeframe is probably appropriate for runners and other athletes who experience abdominal discomfort if they have food in their stomach at the time of competition. However, observations suggest that many athletes eat a meal 2 to 3 hours prior to competition. Many athletes get uncomfortably hungry if the meal is eaten more than an hour or two before the competition, and there are numerous stories of athletes who have gorged just minutes prior to breaking world records or winning gold medals. On the other hand, some athletes fast for 6 to 12 hours prior to competition. The timing of precompetition eating varies greatly from athlete to athlete.

Sometimes, athletes prefer to increase the time between eating and competition to achieve an empty stomach at the time of competition in a contact sport where there is an increased chance of injury. Even a relatively minor injury can require the use of an anesthetic during subsequent treatment. Anesthetics reduce the cough reflex and can induce nausea and vomiting; vomiting and reduced cough reflex can result in aspiration.

Fat is one of the primary factors that slows gastric emptying. Therefore, the amount of fat can be modulated to achieve the desired results. For example, the athlete who feels hungry during competition might increase fat content of the precompetition meal, and the athlete who wants an empty stomach can decrease fat content of the meal.

Practical considerations

Liquid meals can replace conventional foods. Although liquid meals are suitable in any situation, they may be of particular value in situations in which access to nutritious food is limited or when an athlete is attempting to cut weight. Asking the athlete to eat foods that he or she does not like at a time when nervous tension is high will not enhance performance. Therefore, the athlete's personal preference and tolerance must be considered. The athlete should consume foods and beverages that he or she likes, tolerates well, eats as a usual part of the diet, and believes will result in a winning performance.

Diet diaries can be useful in helping athletes determine their best precompetition regimen. The diary should include the types and amounts of foods eaten, when the food was eaten in relation to competition (for example, 2 hours prior), how the athlete felt at the time of the event, and the performance outcome. This information can serve as a guide for fine tuning the precompetition meal.

The "winning" precompetition meal regimen is an individual matter. The individual athlete must determine the precompetition regimen that works best.

Eating on the Road

Athletic trainers and coaches alike often complain about the problems of eating on the road. Travel can be a major disruption to an athlete's eating plan. Food intake often depends on local restaurant facilities, concession stands, or vendors, which means that access to familiar foods may be limited. As a result, the athlete's typical eating plan is often interrupted, which can impact performance.

With some planning, athletes will be able to maintain their eating habits while on the road. Finding out what type of foods restaurants serve, packing meals and snacks to bring along, and knowing what to buy at convenience stores and order at restaurants can help athletes maintain their usual eating habits.

If the athlete is traveling by bus, an obvious solution is to take food along. By contacting restaurants ahead of time, athletes can find out which ones will honor special requests and have a variety of foods available, such as fruits, vegetables, and milk, which are often lacking during travel. Athletes who are accustomed to eating a high-carbohydrate diet can also request extra portions of carbohydrate-rich foods such as breads, cereals, and pasta.

The major nutrition concerns during all-day tournaments are making sure the athlete drinks enough fluids and consumes adequate calories to maintain blood glucose. Most tournament sites do not provide a place to keep foods cold. Therefore, the athlete must make sure to take foods and drinks that do not need refrigeration, such as fruit, fruit juice, graham crackers, water, peanut butter and jelly sandwiches, sport drinks, liquid meals, trail mix, cereal bars, sport bars, bagels, cookies, and crackers.

Caffeine

Caffeine stimulates the central nervous system. A dose of 50 to 200 mg of caffeine will cause alertness, while higher doses (more than 500 mg) can cause nervousness, muscular tremors, and heart palpitations.[40] To put these amounts into perspective, a 5-oz cup of coffee has about 130 mg of caffeine and a 12-oz glass of cola has about 46 mg of caffeine. Individual influences and sensitivities to caffeine vary. With habitual intake, the body adapts to higher levels of caffeine.

Caffeine has been examined as an ergogenic aid, with varying results, but many athletes have shown improvement in performance in a wide variety of exercise tasks ranging from sprint swimming to endurance cycling.[41]

An athlete who believes that caffeine improves his or her performance should consume it 1 to 3 hours prior to exercise at a dose of 5 mg/kg.[41] As with all preevent practices, the routine should be experimented with before competition to determine effectiveness. Caffeine intake is restricted by the International Olympic Committee (IOC) and the National Collegiate Athletic Association (NCAA). Urinary levels of caffeine must not exceed 12 mcg/mL.[42] This level can be reached by consuming 500 mg of caffeine (about 4 cups of coffee) in an hour, but wide individual variation exists. The athletic trainer and athlete should be aware of the limits to avoid exceeding them.

DISORDERED EATING

Anorexia nervosa and bulimia are two nutritional disorders of which the athletic trainer should be aware. Disordered eating is not a new phenomenon. Literary accounts of self-inflicted starvation and weight loss date back to the Middle Ages.[43] Accounts of emphasis on slimness in Ancient Egypt, Greece, and Rome also can be found. The Romans are known for designing the vomitorium, where vomiting was used as a method of weight control after gorging.[44,45] However, what is new is a greater awareness of disordered eating among athletes. Results of studies indicate that disordered eating occur more frequently in athletes who par-

ticipate in sports such as gymnastics, figure skating, wrestling, and ballet, in which weight or body fat restrictions are imposed.[46,47] Disordered eating, however, is not limited just to sports that emphasize leanness.

Anorexia nervosa may occur in as many as one per hundred individuals in a vulnerable population, such as female high school or college students. *Bulimia nervosa,* now the most common eating disorder, occurs in 1% to 3% of adolescent girls and young adult women.[48] However, estimates of the prevalence of eating disorders vary widely, depending on the diagnostic criteria used. Although anorexia nervosa and bulimia nervosa are usually considered disorders of young women and girls, men and boys experience disordered eating at about one tenth the rate of women and girls.[49] **Table 21-10** lists diagnostic criteria for anorexia nervosa and bulimia nervosa.

Identifying Athletes with Disordered Eating

There is a distinct difference between being thin and having anorexia nervosa, as well as between vomiting to reach a desired weight and having bulimia. Abnormal eating patterns do not automatically translate into an eating disorder; however, the athletic trainer must focus on an athlete who displays the following signs or behaviors:

- Commenting repeatedly about being or feeling fat and asking questions such as "Do you think I'm fat?" when weight is actually less than average

- Reaching a weight that is less than the ideal competitive weight set for that athlete and continuing to lose weight even during the off-season

- Eating secretively, which may be noted by finding food wrappers in the room or locker or observing an athlete sneaking food from the training table

- Disappearing repeatedly immediately after eating, especially if a large amount of food was eaten

- Appearing nervous or agitated if something prevents the athlete from being alone shortly after eating

- Losing or gaining extreme amounts of weight

- Complaining frequently of constipation

Although an athlete may demonstrate abnormal eating patterns and cessation of menstruation, these symptoms alone are not sufficient for diagnosis of disordered eating. Key clues that a serious problem is present are emotional instability and withdrawal from social relationships. In a study of three groups of adolescent girls (girls with disordered eating, athletes, and students who fell into neither group), menstrual, dieting, and exercise patterns as well as self-image were examined.[50] The eating disordered subjects had the poorest self-images and scored extremely low on emotional tone and social relationships compared

FOCUS ON . . .

Disordered Eating

Eating disorders include anorexia nervosa and bulimia. They appear to occur more often in athletes who participate in sports where weight or body fat restrictions, or both, are imposed, such as gymnastics, figure skating, wrestling, and ballet. Anorexia nervosa may occur in 1% of the vulnerable population, and bulimia nervosa (the most common eating disorder) affects 1% to 3% of adolescent girls and young women. Young boys and men experience disordered eating at approximately one tenth the rate of women and girls.

Identifying athletes with disordered eating

Behaviors that may signal disordered eating include commenting repeatedly about being or feeling fat when weight is below average; continuing to lose weight below the ideal competitive weight, even during the off-season; eating secretively; disappearing repeatedly and immediately after eating; appearing nervous or agitated if unable to be alone after eating; losing or gaining extreme amounts of weight; and complaining frequently of constipation.

To diagnose disordered eating, abnormal eating patterns and cessation of menstruation in female athletes must be accompanied by emotional liability and withdrawal from social relationships.

TABLE 21-10
DIAGNOSTIC CRITERIA FOR ANOREXIA NERVOSA AND BULIMIA NERVOSA

Anorexia nervosa

- Refusal to maintain body weight over a minimal normal weight for age and height. (For example, the athlete works to keep his or her weight 15% below the target weight, or growth does not occur as expected during childhood or teen years, which results in a body weight 15% less than average.)

- Intense fear of becoming fat or gaining weight, even when underweight.

- Inability to accurately see one's body weight, size, or shape (ie, the athlete claims to feel fat even when he or she looks emaciated). The athlete believes that one area of the body is too fat even when the person is obviously underweight. He or she denies seriousness of current low body weight.

- Absence of at least three consecutive menstrual cycles.

Restricting type of anorexia nervosa: Has not regularly engaged in binge-eating or purging behavior (self-induced vomiting or the misuse of laxatives, diuretics, or enemas).

Binge-eating/purging type of anorexia nervosa: Has regularly engaged in binge-eating or purging behavior (self-induced vomiting or misuse of laxatives, diuretics, or enemas).

Bulimia nervosa

- Recurrent binge-eating (the hurried eating of large amounts of food usually in less than 2 hours).
- Fear of not being able to stop eating during binges.
- Regularly engaged in either self-induced vomiting, misuse of laxatives, diuretics, or enemas, rigorous dieting or fasting, or excessive exercise in order to get rid of the food or the calories from the food eaten during binge-eating.
- At least two binge-eating sessions followed by compensatory behavior (purging) each week for at least 3 months.
- Self-evaluation is heavily influenced by body shape and weight.

Purging type: Regularly engaged in self-induced vomiting or misuse of laxatives, diuretics, or enemas.

Nonpurging type: Uses compensatory behaviors such as fasting or excessive exercise, but does not regularly engage in self-induced vomiting, misuse of laxatives, diuretics, or enemas.

Reproduced with permission from American Psychiatric Association: *Diagnostic and Statistical Manual of Mental Disorders,* ed 3. Washington, DC, American Psychiatric Association,1994, pp 539-550.

to the other groups. The most psychologically healthy group were the athletes.

THE ATHLETIC TRAINER'S ROLE IN NUTRITION

Three important preventive functions of the athletic trainer are educating coaches and athletes about how to recognize and prevent disordered eating, monitoring weight loss goals set for athletes, and helping the athlete determine an appropriate body weight and body composi-

tion. The athletic trainer plays a key role in identifying nutritional problems and should have a system that includes policies and procedures to refer the athlete for professional assessment and treatment. Anorexia nervosa, bulimia nervosa, and the continuum of disordered eating are complex issues. The job of assessment and treatment is best done by a group of professionals such as a psychologist, psychiatrist, physician, and nutritionist experienced in working with disordered eating. **Table 21-11** provides organizations to which the athletic trainer can turn for information and assistance.

TABLE 21-11
EATING DISORDER RESOURCES

American Anorexia Bulimia Association, Inc
165 West 46th Street, Suite 1108
New York, NY 10036
(212) 575-6200
www.aabainc.org

Eating Disorders Awareness and
Prevention, Inc
603 Stewart Street, Suite 803
Seattle, WA 98101
(206) 382-3587
www.members.aol.com/edapinc/home.html

National Eating Disorders Organization
6655 South Yale Avenue
Tulsa, OK 74136
(918) 481-4044
www.laureate.com/nedo/nedointro.asp

Remuda Ranch Center for Anorexia
and Bulimia, Inc
1 East Apache Street
Wickenburg, AZ 85390
(520) 684-3913
(800) 445-1900
www.remuda-ranch.com

Anorexia Nervosa and Related Eating Disorders, Inc
PO Box 5102
Eugene, OR 97405
(541) 344-1144
www.anred.com

International Association of Eating
Disorders Professionals
427 Whooping Loop, Suite 1819
Altamonte Springs, FL 32701
(407) 831-7099   (800) 800-8126
www.iaedp.com

National Association of Anorexia Nervosa
and Associated Disorders
PO Box 7
Highland Park, IL 60035
(847)831-3438
www.healthtouch.com/level1/leaflets/anad/anad010.htm

The Renfrew Center
475 Spring Lane
Philadelphia, PA 19128
(215) 482-3012
(800) 736-3739
www.renfrew.org

CHAPTER REVIEW

Athletes who seek to maximize their training and competitive performance must be properly nourished. The best diet is one that is tailored to the individual's dietary habits and preferences. Other important factors include nutrient requirements. Calorie requirements for athletes are highly variable. Energy requirements of adults are determined by resting metabolic rate, diet-induced thermogenesis, and physical activity. Age, genetics, body size and composition, environmental temperature, training conditions, nontraining physical activity, and calorie intake influence energy requirements.

Resting metabolic rate measures the calories required for maintaining normal body functions. Diet-induced thermogenesis is the increase in energy expenditure above the resting metabolic rate and includes the energy costs of digestion, absorption, metabolism, and food storage.

The six classifications of nutrients are carbohydrates, proteins, fats, vitamins, minerals, and water. Through digestion and metabolism, carbohydrates, proteins, and fats are converted into compounds that are used for growth, repair, and energy. Vitamins, minerals, and water regulate body processes without providing calories.

In the body, carbohydrates are converted into glucose, glycogen, or body fat. Carbohydrate and noncarbohydrate dietary fiber is generally resistant to human digestive enzymes. Carbohydrate loading may be helpful to endurance athletes. Speed, skill, and strength athletes use less glycogen and require fewer carbohydrates. Proteins are composed of amino acids. Cell turnover in the body is continual, necessitating a constant supply of dietary amino acids. Plant foods and gelatin lack one or more essential amino acids and are termed low-quality proteins. Up to 35% of the daily diet of most athletes can be in the form of fats.

Vitamins and minerals are needed for a variety of metabolic functions. Vitamin and mineral deficiencies can result from inadequate dietary intake, poor absorption, heavy bleeding, sweating, smoking, drugs, infections, cancer, surgery, and other medical conditions. The need for supplements should be determined on an individual basis. The Food Guide Pyramid depicts the types and amounts of foods from the five food groups essential to a balanced diet. Weight control in the athlete should focus on body composition rather than weight. Optimal body fat percentage varies with the athlete and the sport. Body fat is lost only when fewer calories are consumed than are expended.

Rapid weight loss is accomplished by restricting foods and fluids before competition and then refeeding and rehydrating after weigh-in. Athletic trainers should provide proper nutrition information to athletes and help establish safe weight loss plans. Athletes who wish to gain weight in the form of muscle mass must combine diet and progressive resistance training. To gain weight, extra daily calories are needed. These athletes have increased protein requirements, which they may try to meet with protein supplements.

Sufficient fluids are essential for normal cellular function and thermal regulation. Fluid balance is achieved by regulation of fluid intake through changes in thirst sensations and regulation of losses by the kidneys. To ensure adequate hydration, the athlete's dry, nude body weight should be monitored before and after practice. Other signs of dehydration include dark yellow, strong-smelling urine, decreased urinary frequency, rapid resting heart rate, and prolonged muscle soreness.

The major electrolytes lost in sweat are sodium, chloride, and potassium. Heat cramps from sodium depletion can occur in sweating athletes, those who are not heat acclimated, or those whose sodium intake is low. The goal of fluid replacement is to start exercise hydrated, avoid dehydration during exercise, and rehydrate before the next session. Cool water is ideal; sport drinks can also provide sugars and electrolytes that may benefit athletes participating in endurance events.

The primary purpose of the precompetition meal is to provide fluids and foods to fuel the athlete during the performance. Timing of the meal should be tailored to the athlete's preferences based on past experience. On the road, planning ahead and bringing nonperishable fluids and foods can help athletes to maintain healthy diet habits. Caffeine can increase alertness, but in excessive quantities can cause nervousness, muscular tremors, and heart palpitations. Disordered eating most often affects female athletes and athletes in sports with weight or body fat restrictions.

The athletic trainer should educate coaches and athletes about the recognition and prevention of disordered eating, monitor weight loss goals, and help the athlete determine an appropriate weight and body composition. The athletic trainer also plays a key role in identifying nutritional problems and ensuring that a system is in place for the athlete to receive professional assessment and treatment.

1. An athlete's nutrient requirements depend on:

   A. age and sport.

   B. body size and position played.

   C. gender and training schedule.

   D. genetics and intensity of activity.

2. Which of the following statements about a high carbohydrate dietary intake is true?

   A. Time to exhaustion is decreased

   B. It is essential to nonendurance athletes.

   C. It is a common cause of deficient glycogen stores.

   D. Energy is provided during intense physical activity.

3. The presence of which of the following factors indicates that an athlete is most likely maintaining an appropriate level of body fat?

   A. Low-level hunger and thirst

   B. Satisfactory athletic performance

   C. A diet heavily reliant on supplements

   D. A body fat level equivalent to other athletes in the sport

4. A low dietary intake of calcium can:

   A. cause anemia.

   B. reduce blood clotting.

   C. decrease mineral density of bone.

   D. promote carbohydrate metabolism.

5. Vitamin K is found in which of the following foods?

   A. Liver

   B. Turkey

   C. Cauliflower

   D. Cheddar cheese

6. Weekly weight loss should not exceed:

   A. 3 to 4 lb per week.

   B. 4 to 5 lb per week.

   C. 1% of body weight.

   D. 2% of body weight.

7. A sign of dehydration is:

   A. pale-colored urine.

   B. slow resting heart rate.

   C. prolonged muscle soreness.

   D. increased urinary frequency.

8. To maximize athletic performance, the athlete's preevent meal should consist of foods and beverages that:

   A. work for his or her fellow athletes.

   B. have been well tolerated in the past.

   C. the athlete dislikes, so the intake will be low.

   D. are new to the athlete and add variety to the diet.

9. Which of the following statements about caffeine is true?

   A. It relaxes the central nervous system.

   B. It calms the athlete and slows the heart rate.

   C. It can cause improved performance in some athletes.

   D. It can be ingested in unlimited quantities during most athletic competitions.

10. Signs and symptoms of bulimia include:

   A. fear of not being able to stop eating during binges.

   B. absence of at least three consecutive menstrual cycles.

   C. refusal to maintain minimal normal weight for age and height.

   D. inability to accurately recognize one's body weight, size, or shape.

Answers on page 893

References

1. Grandjean AC, Ruud JS: Olympic athletes, in Wolinsky I, Hickson JF (eds): *Nutrition and Exercise in Sport*, ed 2. Boca Raton, FL, CRC Press, Inc, 1994, p 447.

2. van Erp-Baart AMJ, Saris WHM, Binkhorst RA, Voss JA, Elvers JWH: Nationwide survey on nutritional habits in elite athletes: Part I. Energy, carbohydrate, protein and fat intake. *Intl J Sports Med* 1989;10:53.

3. Ackermark C, Jacobs I, Rasmusson M, Karlsson J: Diet and muscle glycogen concentration in relation to physical performance in Swedish elite ice hockey players. *Intl J Sport Nutr* 1996;6:272–284.

4. Bolsom PD, Wood K, Olsson P, Ekbolm B: Carbohydrate intake and multiple sprint sports: With special reference to football (soccer). *Intl J Sports Med* 1999;20:48–52.

5. Karlsson J, Saltin B: Diet, muscle glycogen and endurance performance. *J Appl Physiol* 1973;31:203–206.

6. Coyle EF, Haberg JM, Hurley BF, Martin WH, Eshani AA, Hollosky JO: Carbohydrate feeding during prolonged strenuous exercise can delay fatigue. *J Appl Physiol* 1983; 55:230–235.

7. Costill DL, Sherman WM, Fink WJ, Maresh C, Witten M, Miller JM: The role of dietary carbohydrate in muscle glycogen resynthesis after strenuous running. *Am J Clin Nutr* 1981; 34:1831.

8. Sherman W, Brodozica G, Wright DA, et al: Effects of 4 hour preexercise carbohydrate feedings on cycling performance. *Med Sci Sports Exerc* 1989;21:598–604.

9. Sherman WM, Peden MC, Wright DA: Carbohydrate feedings 1 h before exercise improves cycling performance. *Am J Clin Nutr* 1991; 54:866–870.

10. Sherman WM, Doyle JA, Lamb DR, Strauss RH: Dietary carbohydrate, muscle glycogen, and exercise performance during 7 d of training. *Am J Clin Nutr* 1993;57:27–31.

11. National Institutes of Health. *Recommended Dietary Allowances*, ed 10. Washington, DC, National Academy Press, 1989.

12. Lemon PWR: Effects of exercise on dietary protein requirements. *Intl J Sports Nutr* 1998;8:426–447.

13. US Department of Agriculture: Nutrition and Your Health: *Dietary Guidelines for Americans*, 4 ed. Home and Garden Bulletin No. 232, 1995.

14. Economos DC, Bortz SS, Nelson ME: Nutritional practices of elite athletes. *Sports Med* 1993;16:381.

15. Grandjean AC, Reimers KJ, Ruud JS: Dietary habits of Olympic athletes, in Wolinsky I (ed): *Nutrition in Exercise and Sport*. Boca Raton, FL CRC Press, 1998, pp 421–430.

16. World Health Organization Study Group: *Diet, Nutrition and the Prevention of Chronic Diseases*, Geneva, Switzerland, 1990 World Health Organization, p 109.

17. Fairbanks VF: Iron in medicine and nutrition, in *Modern Nutrition in Health and Disease*, ed 8. Philadelphia, PA, Lea & Febiger,1994.

18. National Institutes of Health: Optimal Calcium Intake: NIH Consensus Statement. Bethesda, MD, National Institutes of Health, 1994, pp 1–31.

19. Benson JE, Geiger CJ, Eiserman PA, Wardlaw GM: Relationship between nutrient intake, body mass index, menstrual function, and ballet injury. *J Am Diet Assoc* 1989;89:58–63.

20. Cohen JL, Potosnak L, Frank O, Baker H: A nutritional and hematologic assessment of elite ballet dancers. *Phys Sportsmed* 1985; 13:43–54.

21. Moffat RJ: Dietary status of elite female high school gymnasts: Inadequacy of vitamin and mineral intake. *J Am Diet Assoc* 1984;84:1361–1363.

22. Perron M, Endres J: Knowledge, attitudes, and dietary practices of female athletes. *J Am Diet Assoc* 1985;85:573–576.

23. Sobal J, Marquant LF: Vitamin/mineral supplement use among athletes: A review of the literature. *Intl J Sport Nutr* 1994;4:320–334.

24. Armstrong LE, Maresh CM: Vitamin and mineral supplements as nutritional aids to exercise performance and health. *Nutr Review* 1996;54(suppl):S149–S158.

25. Grandjean AC: Vitamins, diet and the athlete. *Clinics in Sports Med* 1983;2:105–114.

26. Peters EM, Goetzsche JM: Dietary practices of South Africa ultradistance runners. *Intl J Sport Nutr* 1997; 7:80–103.

27. Oppliger RA, Harms RD, Hermann DE, Streich CM, Clark RR: The Wisconsin wrestling minimum weight project: A model for weight control among high school wrestlers. *Med Sci Sports Exerc* 1995;27:1220–1224.

28. Jackson AS, Pollock ML: Practical assessment of body composition. *Phys Sportsmed* 1985;13:76–90.

29. Alford BB, Blankenship AC, Hagen RD: The effect of variations in carbohydrate, protein, and fat content of the diet upon weight loss, blood values and nutrient intake of adult obese women. *J Am Diet Assoc* 1990; 90:534–540.

30. Brownell KD, Steen SN, Wilmore JH: Weight regulation practices in athletes: Analysis of metabolic and health effects. *Med Sci Sports Exerc* 1987; 19:546–556.

31. Roemmich JN, Sinning WE: Weight loss and wrestling training: Effects and nutrition growth, maturation, body composition and strength. *J Appl Physiol* 1997;82:1751–1759.

32. Foster GD, Wadden TA, Feurer ID, Jennings AS, Strunkard AJ, Crosby LO, Ship J, Mullen JL: Controlled trial of the metabolic effects of a very-low-calorie diet: Short-and long-term effects. *Am J Clin Nutr* 1990; 51:167–172.

33. Melby CL, Schmidt WD, Corrigan D: Resting metabolic rate in weight-cycling collegiate wrestlers compared with physically active, non-cycling control subjects. *Am J Clin Nutr* 1990;52:409–414.

34. Epstein Y, Armstrong LE: Fluid-electrolyte balance during labor and exercise: Concepts and misconceptions. *Intl J Sport Nutr* 1999;9:1–12.

35. Greenleaf JE, Harrison MH: Water and electrolytes, in Layman DK (ed): *Nutrition and Aerobic Exercise*, Washington, DC, American Chemical Society, 1986, pp 107–124.

36. Ruud JR, Reimers KJ, Grandjean AC: Fluids and electrolytes in exercise in the heat, in Mellion (ed): *Office Sports Medicine*, Philadelphia, PA, Hanley & Belfus, 1996, pp 58–64.

37. Horswill CA: Effective fluid replacement. *Intl J Sport Nutr* 1998; 8:175–195.

38. Maughan RJ, Owen JH, Shirreffs SM, Leiper JB: Post-exercise rehydration in man: Effects of electrolyte addition to ingested fluids. *Eur J Appl Physiol* 1994;69:209–215.

39. Maughan RJ, Leiper JB, Shirreffs: Restoration of fluid balance after exercise-induced dehydration: Effects of food and fluid intake. *Eur J Appl Physiol* 1996;73:317–325.

40. Strain EC, Mumford GK, Silverman K, Griffiths RR: Caffeine dependence syndrome. *JAMA* 1994;272:1043–1048.

41. Williams MH: Rating the sports ergogenics. *The Ergogenics Edge.* Champaign, IL, Human Kinetics, 1998, pp 149–153.

42. Fuentes RJ, Rosenberg JM, Davis A: Glaxo Wellcome Athletic Drug Reference '96. Durham, NC, Clear Data, Inc. 1996.

43. Walsh BT, Devlin MJ: Eating disorders: Progress and problems. *Science* 1998;280:1387–1390.

44. Boskind-White M, White WC: Bulimarexia: A historical-sociocultural perspective, in Brownell KD, Foreyt JP (ed): *Handbook of Eating Disorders.* New York, NY, Basic Books, 1986, pp 354–366.

45. Strober M: Anorexia nervosa: History and psychological concepts, in Brownell KD, Foreyt JP (eds): *Handbook of Eating Disorders*, New York. NY, Basic Books, 1986, pp 231–246.

46. Rosen LW, Hough DD: Pathogenic weight-control behaviors of female college gymnasts. *Phys Sportsmed* 1988;16:141–144.

47. Loosli AR, Benson J: Nutritional intake in adolescent athletes. *Pediatr Clin North Am* 1990;370:1143–1152.

48. American Psychiatric Association: *Diagnostic and Statistical Manual of Mental Disorders*, ed 3. Washington, DC, American Psychiatric Association, 1994.

49. Barry A, Lippmann SD: Anorexia nervosa in males. Postgrad Med 1990;87:161–186.

50. Mallick MJ, Whipple TW, Huerta E: Behavioral and psychological traits of weight-conscious teenagers: A comparison of eating-disordered patients and high- and low-risk groups. *Adolescence* 1987;23:157–168.

22

Environmental Injuries

Robert Murray, PhD
Katie Walsh, EdD, ATC

OVERVIEW

The injuries and conditions to which the athletic trainer must respond are sometimes related to the sports environment. This chapter reviews the causes, recognition, treatment, and prevention of injuries that are unique to certain environments. The chapter begins with a discussion of heat disorders, including the physiology of temperature regulation, heat exposure syndromes, and the risks of heat stress. The risks and types of lightning strikes, lightning strike injuries and their effects on the athlete, and treatment and prevention are covered next, followed by the different types of cold injuries and their effects. Altitude disorders, such as acute mountain sickness, high-altitude pulmonary edema, and high-altitude cerebral edema are covered, and the chapter ends with a discussion of some of the problems that athletes encounter while traveling, including jet lag and circadian rhythm.

HEAT DISORDERS

Physiology of Temperature Regulation

Humans are homeotherms whose body temperature is controlled within a very narrow range. Disruptions in temperature regulation that raise or lower body temperature outside of this range will result in a deterioration of mental and physiologic functioning that can culminate in death. Heat exposure can impose a debilitating and even deadly stress on the human body, a fact corroborated by numerous heatstroke deaths that have occurred among athletes, soldiers, miners, and construction workers.[1]

The body's center for thermal regulation is the *hypothalamus*, which is located at the base of the brain and integrates input from thermal receptors throughout the body (**Figure 22-1**). Autonomic impulses to increase sweating and peripheral vasodilation are, in part, regulated by the hypothalamus.

The balance between heat production and heat loss determines body temperature during both rest and physical activity. Body heat is produced by basic metabolic processes, food intake (specific dynamic action), and muscular activity, all of which can be intensified by environmental heat stress. The body must lose heat in order to balance the heat gain and maintain a safe internal (core) temperature.

The body's responses during physical activity in a warm environment are limited to sweating, vasodilation of skin blood vessels, and behavioral responses such as removing

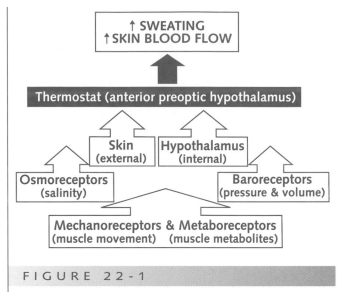

FIGURE 22-1

The hypothalamus regulates body heat using input from thermal receptors throughout the body.

clothing and moving into the shade. Each of these responses will result in an increase in heat loss by one of four mechanisms: *conduction, convection, evaporation,* and *radiation.* **Table 22-1** shows how each mechanism works to increase heat loss in the body.

Effective conduction, convection, and radiation require that the environmental temperature and relative humidity are lower than the body temperature and the vapor pressure of water on the skin. If the external temperature is higher than the body temperature, the primary source of heat loss is the evaporation of sweat, assuming the humidity is low enough to allow for adequate evaporation to occur.

Mechanisms of heat regulation

When the body is challenged by an elevated environmental temperature, mechanisms to increase heat loss, primarily cutaneous vasodilation and sweating, are activated. Exposure to heat produces both an immediate and a delayed effect on body physiology. The immediate response is vasodilation of the vessels in the skin, increasing blood flow to the skin and sweat production and maximizing heat loss through radiation and convection. However, the increased blood flow to the skin is achieved at the expense of blood flow to other organs, particularly those organs found in the gut.

Sweat production increases sharply with increasing temperature and can result in the loss of more than 10 L of fluid in a 24-hour period. Sweating is an efficient means of cooling the body when the humidity is low, with up to 600 kcal of heat dissipated for each liter of sweat that evaporates. When the humidity rises, the evaporation of sweat decreases. No heat loss results from sweat that drips off of or remains in clothing. When the environmental temperature is lower than skin temperature, heat is transferred from the body to the environment. About two thirds of the

TABLE 22-1
MECHANISMS THAT PROMOTE HEAT LOSS DURING PHYSICAL ACTIVITY IN A WARM ENVIRONMENT

Conduction	Heat is directly transferred from the warmer body to cooler object, such as a cold, wet shirt or an ice pack
Convection	Heat is transferred to the cooler air when cool air moves across the body surface, warming the air and cooling the body
Evaporation	Heat is lost when water (sweat) on the skin is transformed from a liquid into a vapor
Radiation	Heat radiates from the warmer body to the cooler environment

body's normal heat loss occurs through radiation and convection when the body is at rest and the ambient temperature is less than 87° F (30.6° C). The rest of the heat is lost through evaporation of fluid from the skin and the lungs. As the ambient temperature approaches skin temperature, loss of body heat through radiation and convection is sharply curtailed. When the ambient temperature exceeds body temperature, heat transfer is reversed. Under these circumstances, heat loss can only be achieved by the evaporation of sweat. Evaporation of sweat cools the skin, which in turn cools the blood that runs through the capillaries in the skin.

Sweat rate can vary from as little as 250 to 500 mL per hour during mild activity in a cool environment to more than 2 L per hour during intense activity in a warm environment. Well-trained and acclimated athletes with a genetic predisposition to high sweat rates are at risk for the rapid onset of dehydration if fluid is not replaced.

Although pouring cold water over the head and neck may feel good, this practice does little to reduce body temperature, because the skin is usually already covered with sweat. Athletes must be encouraged to put much more fluid in their stomachs than they do on their heads.

Electrolyte losses

Several electrolytes, namely, sodium, chloride, potassium, and magnesium, are lost in sweat. Generally, the well-conditioned athlete loses less sodium than a poorly conditioned athlete; however, this is not always the case. Some well-conditioned and acclimatized athletes can sustain large sodium losses, which predisposes them to fluid-electrolyte imbalances and increases their risk of muscle cramps.

Sodium loss varies widely among individuals and can reach substantial levels in active individuals. For example, a sweat sodium concentration of 50 mEq per liter indicates that 1.2 g of sodium is lost in each liter of sweat, amounting to about 2.9 g of sodium chloride lost per liter. Considering that athletes can sometimes lose more than 2 L of sweat in 1 hour of training, short-term sodium deficits can develop quickly, increasing the risk of heat illness and muscle cramping. However, because of the adequate sodium chloride content consumed in the typical American diet, long-term sodium deficits are rarely a problem.

Most electrolyte losses can be made up at meals following physical activity. A typical mixed diet, consisting of 50% of total energy from carbohydrate, 30% from fat, and 20% from protein, furnishes 3 to 10 g of sodium, 2.5 to 8 g of chloride, and 2 to 6 g of potassium daily, making net deficiencies of these electrolytes unlikely. During daylong competitions, athletes can incur large sweat and sodium losses, predisposing them to heat illness and muscle cramping; however, these athletes usually respond well to increased salt intake in the diet and to the use of electrolyte supplements.

Water loss

Dehydration is usually the greatest risk faced by athletes. Even a small amount of dehydration (less than 2% of body weight) will impair performance and increase the risk of heat illness (**Table 22-2**). Adequate fluid intake is essential to maintain normal hydration and prevent an abnormal rise in body temperature. The average adult requires approximately 2.5 L of fluid each day, which can be ingested from all beverages consumed throughout the day, as well as from food. The average adult athlete requires an additional 1.5 to 2 L of fluid per hour of exercise. Athletes must conscientiously consume fluids before, during, and after an event to ensure normal hydration.

Because thirst is not evident until some level of dehydration has occurred, thirst alone is not an adequate indicator of fluid needs. The athlete should be weighed before

TABLE 22-2
HOURLY PERCENT DECREASES IN BODY WEIGHT WITH VARYING RATES OF SWEAT LOSS

Initial Body Weight	Sweat Rate				
	500 mL/h	1,000 mL/h	1,500 mL/h	2,000 mL/h	2,500 mL/h
100 lb	-1.1%	-2.2%	-3.3%	-4.4%	-5.5%
125 lb	-0.8%	-1.8%	-2.6%	-3.6%	-4.4%
150 lb	-0.7%	-1.5%	-2.2%	-3.0%	-3.6%
175 lb	-0.6%	-1.3%	-1.9%	-2.6%	-3.1%
200 lb	-0.5%	-1.1%	-1.7%	-2.2%	-2.8%
225 lb	-0.5%	-1.0%	-1.5%	-2.0%	-2.4%
250 lb	-0.4%	-0.9%	-1.3%	-1.8%	-2.2%

and after training and competition so that the amount of fluid that needs to be replaced can be determined. Total rehydration will only occur when all of the fluid and sodium lost in sweat is replaced. This requires that the athlete ingests a fluid volume that is at least 125% of sweat loss (1 L of sweat loss equals 1.25 L of fluid intake).[2] Extra fluid must be ingested to allow for some fluid loss through obligatory urine production, allowing the athlete to return to normal hydration status sooner.

Athletes should avoid consuming excessive protein, caffeine, and alcoholic beverages, because these substances increase urine output and result in further dehydration. Coaches, athletic trainers, and athletes must make a concerted effort to minimize dehydration.[3] More information concerning predisposition to heat injury secondary to fluid loss can be found in chapter 21.

Heat Exposure Syndromes

Aside from skin disorders such as sunburn, three heat- and hydration-related disorders can result from exposure to heat: heat cramps, heat exhaustion, and heatstroke. **Table 22-3** lists the causes, clinical signs and symptoms, and treatments of these heat-stress syndromes.

Heat cramps

Normal muscle contraction and relaxation requires that muscle cells remain well hydrated. Changes in cell hydration status affect cell size and metabolism. Although the etiology of **heat cramps** is not well understood, dehydration is a likely culprit.[4] Some researchers believe that heat cramps are caused by excessive fluid loss in the muscles; others believe electrolyte imbalance causes the muscle spasm.[4] Heat cramps often occur in individuals who sweat

profusely and, as with all disorders caused by heat, usually occur at the beginning of the warm-weather season before the athlete becomes acclimatized. Heat cramps may involve the legs, abdominal muscles, or arms. Often, athletes with heat cramps have a history of these cramps. Heat cramps are largely diagnosed by exclusion after an acute muscle injury has been ruled out.

Treatment of heat cramps includes rest from the exertional stress, passive stretching, and aggressive rehydration. To prevent heat cramps, the athlete must ensure adequate fluid and sodium intake during times of excessive sweating. Conditioning and acclimatization also help reduce the incidence of heat cramps.

Heat exhaustion

Heat exhaustion, also called heat prostration, is a more severe heat syndrome caused by inadequate cardiovascular responsiveness to the circulatory stresses induced by heat exposure. Vasoconstriction in other tissues of the body normally compensates for the initial diversion of blood flow to the skin. During physical activity, the demand for increased blood flow to the skin and to muscle and the brain occurs at the same time. Because the blood volume is inadequate to meet the simultaneous demands placed on it by the skin, muscle, and viscera, blood flow to the skin is compromised, and heat exhaustion can result. In its worst form, heat exhaustion is an insidious, slowly progressive, peripheral vascular collapse, or "shock" syndrome. Dehydration raises the risk of heat exhaustion, because dehydration reduces an already inadequate blood volume.

Heat exhaustion is characterized principally by the signs of peripheral vascular collapse or shock, that is, by weakness,

TABLE 22-3
HEAT-STRESS SYNDROMES

Condition	Cause	Clinical signs and symptoms	Treatment
Heat cramps	• Excessive fluid loss in muscles • Electrolyte imbalance • Lack of acclimatization to local climate	• Profuse sweating • Cramps in abdominal muscles or extremities	• Resting in cool environment • Passive stretching • Drinking water or sports drink

Heat exhaustion	• Excessive electrolyte loss:
	  —Profuse sweating with inadequate replacement of body salts
	  —Vomiting or diarrhea
		• Weakness
		• Faintness
		• Dizziness
		• Headache
		• Loss of appetite
		• Nausea
		• Pallor
		• Profuse sweating
		• Urge to defecate
		• Gray, ashen, cold, clammy skin
			• Resting (reclining) in cool environment
			• Drinking fluids if conscious (an unconscious patient should be given fluids intravenously)
			• Increasing salt intake
			• Discontinuing activity until symptoms have disappeared

	• Excessive water loss:
	  —Profuse sweating with inadequate replacement of body fluid
	  —Vomiting or diarrhea
		• Hot, dry skin
		• Small urine output
		• Excessive thirst
		• Weakness
		• Headache
		• Unconsciousness
			• Resting (reclining) in cool environment
			• Sponging patient with cool water
			• Drinking fluids
			• Discontinuing activity until symptoms have disappeared

Heatstroke	• Depletion of water in body • All mechanisms of body cooling fail	• Irritability • Aggressiveness • Emotional instability • Hysteria followed by apathy • Disorientation • Unsteady gait • Glassy stare • Hot, dry skin • Rapid, full pulse • Decreasing blood pressure	• Immersing in tub cooled with ice • Applying cold, wet compresses with fan blowing • Activate the EMS system

FOCUS ON . . .

Heat Exposure Syndromes

Heat cramps seem to result when dehydration affects cell size and metabolism, although the etiology is unclear. Excessive muscle fluid loss or electrolyte imbalance may be the cause. Heat cramps often affect those who sweat profusely, usually before acclimatization to warm weather, and can involve the legs, arms, or abdominal muscles. The diagnosis is made by exclusion of acute muscle injury; often the athlete has a history of heat cramps. Treatment is rest from exertion and passive stretching. Prevention consists of ensuring adequate fluid and sodium intake during times of heavy sweating, conditioning, and acclimatization.

Next in severity is heat exhaustion, which is caused by inadequate cardiovascular response to the circulatory stresses of heat exposure. The blood volume is insufficient to meet the simultaneous demands for increased blood flow to the skin, muscle, and viscera. Heat exhaustion risk is higher in dehydrated athletes, whose blood volume is already inadequate. Symptoms are those of peripheral vascular collapse (shock). Skin color, temperature, and wetness vary. Heat exhaustion can result from either salt depletion or water depletion; the latter is more common in athletes. Treatment is replenishing electrolytes and fluids and having the athlete lie down in a cool environment to reduce cardiovascular demands. The athlete who can drink fluids should do so, but the vomiting athlete may need intravenous fluids. Heat exhaustion is generally promptly reversible, yet preexisting cardiovascular disease, vomiting, and diarrhea can worsen the severity and duration of symptoms. Athletes should be closely monitored while exercising. Those at risk for heat illness include poorly conditioned, overeager, and recently ill athletes, along with those having a history of heat-exposure syndrome. Return to play after heat illness is permitted only after rehydration is total and all symptoms have abated.

Heatstroke, the least common and most serious heat illness, is failure of all the body's neurologic cooling mechanisms, resulting in severe hyperpyrexia (body temperature greater than 105° F [40° to 41° C]). Heatstroke can occur suddenly or as a progression from unrelieved heat exhaustion. Heatstroke is a true emergency with a very high mortality rate from central nervous system damage and is usually precipitated by prolonged, strenuous physical exercise in a poorly acclimatized athlete or a situation that minimizes sweat evaporation. Strenuous muscle activity further increases metabolic heat production. When ambient temperature approaches skin temperature and humidity increases, increased sweat evaporation efficiently removes heat from the body, but these rates cannot be maintained. When they fall as a result of dehydration, body temperature rises abruptly. Death from heatstroke can occur at ambient temperatures as low as 70° F. Symptoms include irritability, aggressiveness, emotional instability, and hysteria, progressing to apathy, failure to respond to questions, and disorientation. Unsteady gait; a glassy stare; hot, dry skin; falling blood pressure; rapid, weak pulse; and disseminated intravascular coagulation may also become evident. Treatment is immediate cooling by immersing the athlete in a bathtub of ice-cooled water and wet sheets or compresses and fans during transport to the hospital. Intravenous fluids and antishivering medication may also be needed.

dizziness, headache, loss of appetite, nausea, pallor, diffuse sweating, vomiting, an urge to defecate, and postural syncope (fainting). There are two types of heat exhaustion: salt depletion (excessive salt loss) and water depletion (excessive water loss). Excessive water loss is more common in athletes.

The symptoms of heat exhaustion can vary in severity and number. Common symptoms include weakness and fatigue, a strong sense of thirst, irritability, elevated body temperature, and lightheadedness. Skin color, temperature, and wetness can vary.

In addition to replenishing electrolytes and fluids, treatment of heat exhaustion includes having the athlete lie down in a cool environment to reduce the accompanying mild state of hypovolemic shock. Rest, fluid intake, and a supine posture help restore blood volume and diminish the demands on the circulatory system. As

a rule of thumb, athletes who are capable of ingesting fluids should do so. Athletes who are unable to keep fluids down should be given intravenous therapy by a qualified medical professional. Heat exhaustion is common and is ordinarily promptly reversed. However, preexisting conditions, such as cardiovascular disease, vomiting, and diarrhea, can aggravate the severity and duration of heat exhaustion.

All athletes should be monitored closely during activity. The athletic trainer should be alert for poorly conditioned athletes who are more susceptible to heat exposure syndromes, for overeager athletes who may ignore the symptoms of heat illness in their desire to participate, and for athletes who are returning to practice after being ill for a few days. Athletes who have previously experienced any form of heat-exposure syndrome should also be watched closely. An athlete who is experiencing heat illness should be permitted to participate only after he or she has been fully rehydrated and all symptoms have disappeared.

Heatstroke

Heatstroke is the most serious heat syndrome. In heatstroke, all of the body's cooling mechanisms have failed to the extent that severe *hyperpyrexia* (a core body temperature greater than 106° F (41.1° C)) ensues with a body temperature greater than 105° F (40° to 41° C). Heatstroke may develop suddenly or progress from heat exhaustion that is exacerbated by dehydration and continued physical activity. Although heatstroke is the least common of the heat disorders, it must be considered a risk for athletes in hot environments. Heatstroke is a medical emergency requiring immediate action to prevent fatality.[5] Anticipating the possibility of heatstroke, implementing preventive measures, promptly recognizing its occurrence, and appropriate emergency cooling are all part of a successful plan for responding to heat illness.[5]

Heatstroke is a true emergency with a very high mortality rate. Individuals with untreated heatstroke die because of damage to the cells of the central nervous system. In fact, heatstroke represents a failure of the neurologic system to cope with heat stress, whereas heat exhaustion represents a failure of the cardiovascular system. Some heatstroke survivors may have permanent nerve damage because of hyperpyrexia, with damage to the cerebellum a frequent observation in such cases; therefore, rapid and vigorous treatment is essential for full recovery.[5] Heatstroke in the athlete is almost always precipitated by prolonged, strenuous physical exercise, either when the athlete is poorly acclimatized or in situations that minimize the evaporation of sweat. Strenuous muscular work contributes to the development of heatstroke by increasing metabolic heat production.

Under conditions of maximum heat stress, when the ambient temperature approaches the skin temperature and the humidity increases, evaporation of sweat efficiently removes heat from the body. However, the initially high rates of sweat production cannot be maintained indefinitely, and when the rate of sweat production falls as a result of dehydration, body temperature rises abruptly. This failure is known as sweat fatigue or *anhidrosis*. The absence of sweating and the presence of dehydration in the exercising athlete intensify hyperpyrexia. Death from heatstroke has occurred at ambient temperatures as low as 70° F (21.1° C).

Premonitory signs and symptoms are irritability, aggressiveness, emotional instability, and hysteria, which progress to apathy, failure to respond to questions, and disorientation. The athlete may have an unsteady gait and glassy stare. Collapse and unconsciousness are the final signs of heatstroke and are often accompanied by hot, dry skin. Early in the course of the disorder, the pulse is rapid and full. As various systems are damaged by increased body heat, vasomotor collapse occurs, blood pressure falls, and the pulse becomes rapid and weak. Disseminated intravascular coagulation may be involved in the multiple organ failure that is characteristic of many heatstroke fatalities.

When heatstroke is suspected, cooling should be initiated immediately. Emergency care is designed to rid the body of excessive heat as rapidly as possible, reducing the temperature to less than 100° F (37.7° C). Ideally, the athlete should be immersed in a bathtub of water cooled with ice. Wet sheets or compresses and fans can be used while the athlete is being transported to the hospital. The athletic trainer should provide treatment as soon as possible and should continue until trained medical personnel arrive on the scene.

Treatment of shock may require administration of intravenous fluids, but cooling is the priority and must be continued during transportation to the hospital. If warranted, a physician may prescribe medication to prevent shivering during body cooling.

Cooling the athlete in an air-conditioned room is effective only for minor hyperpyrexia. Antipyretic drugs, such as aspirin, which inhibit production of prostaglandin E, a known pyrogen, do not help because they require an intact heat-dissipation mechanism.[6] External cooling should be carried out until the athlete's temperature falls to less than 100° F (37.8° C), and the athlete should be observed for secondary rises in temperature.

Reducing the Risk of Heat Stress

Heat-stress syndromes are obviously related to climate and are primarily determined by temperature and humidity. Because temperature and humidity cannot usually be controlled, other factors such as the athlete's physical condition and state of acclimatization must be controlled. Coaching techniques, color and type of uniforms, equipment worn, the time of day, and the intensity of training all can be modified to reduce the risk of heat injuries.

Acclimatization

Acclimatization refers to the body's physiologic adaptation to heat stress and increased capacity to work in the heat. Acclimatization was first studied when military personnel were exposed to tropical climates.[7] They were unable to work for the first few days; however, they gradually became able to tolerate high temperatures without becoming exhausted. Acclimatization involves modifications in neural, hormonal, and cardiovascular physiology as well as in cellular biochemistry, such as heat-shock proteins. The changes in cardiovascular physiology are very similar to those observed during physical training. After acclimatization, there is less subjective discomfort during heat exposure, with smaller increases in pulse and respiratory rates under the same conditions of heat and activity. Cardiovascular stability with postural changes and activity is also greater. Skin and rectal temperatures remain closer to normal, and sweat production increases after acclimatization. Sweating begins sooner after exposure to heat and work, or at a lower environmental temperature, than before acclimatization.

Many researchers believe that full acclimatization occurs in 4 to 7 days with as little as 90 minutes of exposure to heat per day.[6] Other researchers believe that full acclimatization may take months.[1] Previous physical conditioning and exercise enhance the body's ability to adapt to heat. Once achieved, acclimatization is maintained for several weeks with short periods of reexposure. After 6 weeks of heat exposure, the body may be able to produce two and a half times the individual's normal volume of sweat.

Regardless of whether full acclimatization requires only 1 week or several months to develop, athletes should be gradually exposed to increases in the intensity and duration of training. From a performance standpoint, ambient temperatures as low as 60° F (15.5° C) still require acclimatization for maximal performance.

Preseason conditioning

The body's heat-regulating mechanisms become accustomed to the elevation of internal temperature (which often reaches 103° F (39.4°C) in the trained athlete) that accompanies vigorous exercise. When tested under conditions of high heat and high humidity, physically fit athletes require much less acclimatization than do athletes who are out of condition. A well-hydrated, physically fit, and acclimatized athlete has a substantially reduced risk of heat-related problems.[8]

Environmental conditions

The athletic trainer should measure the ambient conditions prior to any practice or game using the wet bulb globe temperature index (WBGT index), which is based on the combined effects of air temperature, relative humidity, radiant heat, and air movement.[9] The WBGT index measures ambient conditions of the WBGT equation and the overall WBGT reading. The sling psychrometer must be whirled in placed to assess wet-bulb temperature and readings must be compared to predetermined values to identify relative humidity. If an electronic WBGT meter is not available, a sling psychrometer can be used to correlate the dry bulb temperature with relative humidity (**Figure 22-2**). **Table 22-4** shows the existing training standards on which the athletic trainer should base the decision to allow, modify, or prohibit training.[10] Moreover, the National Weather Service provides local information through telephone services or on Internet web sites.

Coaching techniques

Lightweight, porous, and light-colored uniforms should be worn in heat conditions. Sleeves should be short and socks should be worn low. The athlete should be able to change perspiration-soaked uniforms during the practice session.

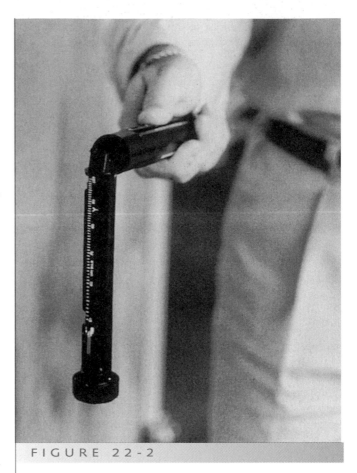

FIGURE 22-2

A sling psychrometer can be used to measure the ambient conditions prior to a practice or game.

As much skin as possible should be exposed to the air, and helmets should be removed as often as possible.

Practices during hot, humid weather should be held early in the morning or late in the afternoon to avoid the worst heat. Early in the season, night games should be scheduled when possible. If games must be played during the late morning or early afternoon in hot, humid climates, the players must be acclimatized to those conditions.

Practice sessions during high-temperature and high-humidity conditions should be shorter and less intense, with less clothing or uniforms and more fluid breaks. Rest breaks should be held in shaded areas or in locations that are exposed to a cool breeze. Rest breaks of 10 minutes every half hour should be allowed during practice. The coaching staff should consider canceling practice in extreme temperature and humidity. Athletes should weigh themselves before and after practice daily; athletes who have lost 2% of their body weight should be excluded from practice until they are fully rehydrated. Those who have heat illness symptoms should also be excluded from practice for 24 hours.

FOCUS ON . . .

Reducing the Risk of Heat Stress

Prevention of heat stress focuses on improving the athlete's physical condition, acclimatization, modifying coaching techniques, color and type of uniforms, time of day for practices, and gradually increasing training intensity and duration.

Acclimatization describes the body's physiologic adaptation to heat stress and increased capacity to work in the heat, involving adjustments in neural, hormonal, and cardiovascular physiology and cellular biochemistry. The changes mimic those of physical training: less subjective discomfort during heat exposure, with smaller increases in pulse and respiratory rate; greater cardiovascular stability; smaller rises in skin and rectal temperatures; and greater and earlier sweat production. Consensus is lacking on whether acclimatization requires days or months. Previous physical conditioning and exercise improve acclimatization, which can be maintained for several weeks with short reexposures.

Preseason conditioning occurs as the body's heat-regulating mechanisms become accustomed to the high internal temperature that can accompany vigorous exercise in the trained athlete. Physically fit athletes require much less acclimatization in high heat and humidity than those who are out of condition; those who are also well hydrated and acclimatized have a lower risk of heat illness.

The athletic trainer should measure the ambient conditions before each practice and game and follow guidelines as to the modification or prohibition of training.

Coaching techniques can also lessen the risk of heat illness. Lightweight, porous, and light-colored clothing, with short sleeves and low socks are best. Perspiration-soaked uniforms should be changed during the practice session, and skin should be exposed to air and helmets removed as often as possible. Early morning or late afternoon practices and night games are recommended when the weather is hot and humid. If, however, games must be played during the late morning or early afternoon, players must be acclimatized to these conditions. Practices should be shorter and less intense, with less clothing or uniforms and more frequent rest and fluid breaks in shaded or breezy areas. If conditions are extreme, practice may need to be cancelled. Athletes who have lost 2% of body weight should be excluded from practice, as should those with heat illness symptoms.

Unrestricted fluid intake during practices and games is encouraged. Ideally, the rate of fluid replacement should approximate the rate of sweat loss, which can be checked with daily weighing. A well-hydrated athlete can work longer, harder, and more safely than one who is poorly hydrated, and therefore, it is the coaches' and athletic trainers' responsibility to devise and implement a fluid-replacement plan to prevent dehydration in each player. Plain water is a good thirst quencher, but it will prematurely satisfy the thirst mechanism, reducing voluntary intake, and it stimulates urine production. A properly formulated sports drink is recommended when athletes are working hard and sweating profusely: the sweet flavor encourages intake, the carbohydrate supplies energy to active muscles, and the electrolytes help maintain fluid intake and retention.

Fluid replacement

Unrestricted intake of fluid during games and practice sessions should be encouraged. The rate of fluid replacement during exercise should ideally approximate the rate of sweat loss. Body weight should be checked daily and recorded. Research shows that a well-hydrated athlete is able to work longer, harder, and more safely than a poorly hydrated athlete.[?] The athletic trainers and coaches are responsible for devising a fluid-replacement plan that prevents dehydration for every player. Their ability to do this requires knowledge of the sweat rates of individual players. Players should then follow the fluid-ingestion regimen designed specifically for them.

If a sports drink is not available, plain water is a good thirst quencher. However, ingesting water will turn off the thirst mechanism prematurely, reducing voluntary fluid intake.[11] In addition, consuming water stimulates urine production, reducing the retention of the ingested fluid. A properly formulated sports drink is the preferred beverage when athletes are working hard and sweating profusely. The sweetness and flavor of the sports drink may encourage voluntary fluid intake, the carbohydrate supplies energy to active muscles, and the electrolytes help maintain fluid intake and fluid retention.

LIGHTNING STRIKES

Although lightning injury or fatality is a rare event, it should nevertheless be a concern for those individuals who provide medical care at athletic events. Lightning tends to strike in the late spring through midautumn, between the hours of 3:00 pm and 8:00 pm.[12] Lightning occurs most commonly in large open areas or on bodies of water, making it difficult to plan outdoor sports during this time of year. Unlike many other environmental phenomena, lightning can strike with little

TABLE 22-4
TRAINING STANDARDS FOR HIGH HUMIDITY*

Temperature (°F)	Temperature (°C)	Relative risk	Considerations
Less than 64°	Less than 18°	Low	• Closely monitor overweight, unfit, or recently ill athletes • Ensure adequate rest periods each hour • Stress fluid replacement
64° to 73°	18° to 23°	Moderate	• Closely monitor overweight, unfit, or recently ill athletes • Ensure adequate rest periods each hour • Stress fluid replacement
73° to 82°	23° to 28°	High	• Closely monitor overweight, unfit, or recently ill athletes • Reduce exercise intensity and duration • Increase frequency and duration of rest periods • Rest in shade • Limit clothing and headgear • Stress fluid replacement
Greater than 82°	Greater than 28°	Hazardous	• Closely monitor overweight, unfit, or recently ill athletes • Suspend practice or limit to very light work of short duration • Rest in shade • Limit clothing and headgear to bare minimum • Stress fluid replacement

*The data are based on individuals clothed in tee-shirt, shorts, socks, and shoes. (Adapted with permission from Sparling PB: Expected environmental conditions for the 1996 Summer Olympic Games in Atlanta. *Clin J Sport Med* 1995;5:220–222.)

warning, and the consequences of a lightning strike can be disastrous.

Types of Lightning Strikes

The injury an individual sustains from a lightning strike depends on two factors: the relationship of the individual to the strike and whether the force of the lightning that caused the damage was thermal or electromechanical. The three main categories of lightning strikes comprise the direct strike, side strike, and ground strike. A *direct strike* is most often fatal, because it has primary contact with the individual. A *side strike*, also termed a "flash" or "splash," will first hit another object, such as a tree or fence and then "flash over" the individual. The side strike

is the most common type of strike. Finally, the *ground strike* occurs when lightning hits the ground first and travels along the ground to the individual. A person wearing metal spikes or standing in water is very susceptible to damage with this type of force.

Thermal Injuries

The high temperatures of a lightning strike can exceed 27,760° C, which is five times hotter than the surface of the sun. True thermal burns are somewhat rare lightning injuries, although metallic objects, such as jewelry, buckles, or a watch will retain heat and burn an individual. One particular type of transitory pattern associated with lightning victims, the Lichtenburg figure, is not truly a burn but a feathering pattern believed to be created by the electron avalanche that strikes a person hit by lightning.[13] The Lichtenburg figure remains on the body less than 24 hours following a strike.

Electromechanical Injuries

The electromechanical forces of lightning depend on several factors, including the strike's amperage (A) and duration and the individual's tissue resistance and relationship to the strike. Lightning typically carries a charge of 2,000 to 200,000 A. Experimental research has demonstrated cardiac ventricular fibrillation with a current as low as 0.75 mA to 50 mA applied directly to the heart, with higher currents causing cardiac rhythm to cease.[14]

The duration of contact with lightning is another factor affecting damage in an individual. Lightning trauma is very different from injury from man-made electricity. Lightning is a direct current (DC) where the electrons flow from one point to another, whereas household electricity is an alternating current (AC) where electrons cycle their direction of flow back and forth between two poles. A direct current creates a single powerful muscular contraction, whereas an alternating current of electricity allows for skeletal muscles to have tetanic contractions, thereby maintaining contact with the power source. Lightning typically has a contact time of 0.1 to 0.3 milliseconds. Contact time with a man-made power source lasts as long as the connection to the power source. The longer the contact with electricity, the greater the chance of deeper tissue insult.

Specific tissues in the body have varying degrees of resistance to electrical energy. The greater the moisture content, thickness, and vascularity of a specific tissue, the greater the risk of damage. In descending order, the most resistant tissues to electrical impulses in the body are bone, fat, tendon, skin, muscle, blood vessels, and nerves.[15] Nerves are the most likely tissue to sustain injury from lightning.

An individual's relationship to the strike focuses on the type of strike (direct, side, or ground) that occurred. Lightning can create mass injury; 30% of lightning strikes involve two or more individuals.[13] This possibility must be considered whenever a team is playing on a rain-soaked field during a storm. When one bolt strikes the playing surface, all participants can feel the force of the ground strike, although some may be affected more than others.

The concussive forces created by the air explosion of a lightning strike can also cause trauma. The air explosion is caused by rapidly heated air surrounding the lightning strike, which explodes into the clap of thunder associated with lightning. The explosion can propel bodies several feet, leading to secondary injuries such as blunt trauma to the head, thorax, abdomen, or damage to the extremities. Up to 50% of all individuals struck by lightning have reported ruptured tympanic membranes as a result of the violent discharge of air during a strike.[17]

Medical Effects of Lightning Strikes

The most common response to a lightning strike is *cardiac asystole* (cessation of the cardiac rhythm) and *apnea* (lack of breathing). Because of the heart's automaticity, it is likely that the heart will spontaneously restart; however, normal cardiac function will not continue if the individual is not breathing, and the heart will stop a second time. Results of studies have indicated that it is the continuance of apnea, not the duration of cardiac asystole, that is crucial in the demise of individuals who have been struck by lightning.[16] Further investigation indicates that an individual struck by lightning may have vasomotor instability, which leads to pulseless extremities, and seizures, fixed and dilated pupil(s), subdural or epidural hematomas, anterior compartment syndromes, hyphemas, and secondary injuries to the extremities, including fractures and dislocations.[13,14,16] Of all individuals struck by lightning, 69% have transitory lower limb paralysis, 72% have loss of consciousness, and 86% have confusion or amnesia.[17]

Treatment

Unlike electrical injuries in which a person may remain connected to a power source, individuals struck by lightning do not conduct a charge. Although the mortality rate of individuals hit by lightning is 35%, 75% of those who experience asystole will die.[18] Cardiopulmonary resuscitation (CPR) for patients in asystole must be started as quickly as possible and maintained. Data have shown that individuals struck by lightning who have cold, pulseless extremities, fixed pupils, absent pulses, and no breath sounds have been revived following prolonged CPR.[13] Immediate and sustained CPR has allowed many individuals to recover completely. Because the force of the lightning strike can create secondary injuries that are not apparent in the primary survey, cervical spine trauma must be considered when emergency care is provided to these individuals. The individual giving care to the injured athlete must also be aware of the passing storm and be cautious of a secondary strike in the immediate area.

Prevention

A proactive approach to prevention of lightning injury or fatality is the most logical method of circumventing trauma. In 1997, the National Collegiate Athletic Association (NCAA) adopted guidelines for athletic participation for the prevention of lightning injury.[19] Specifically, the guideline recommends using a 30-second flash-to-bang count to vacate dangerous situations. The flash-to-bang method employs counting seconds from the first flash of lightning to the bang of thunder. A 30-second count indicates that lightning is within 6 miles. Lightning can strike from as far away as 10 miles; therefore, the 30-second count is extremely liberal, and the National Severe Storms Laboratory also recommends this count to

FOCUS ON . . .

Lightning Strikes

Lightning injuries and fatalities are rare, but a concern for healthcare professionals providing medical care at athletic events. Lightning most often strikes in the late spring through midautumn, between 3:00 pm and 8:00 pm, particularly in large, open areas or on bodies of water. There may be no warning of an impending lightning strike.

Types of lightning strikes

A lightning injury depends on the relationship of the individual to the strike and whether thermal or electromechanical forces cause the damage. A direct strike, which causes primary contact with the individual, is most often fatal. A side strike, the most frequent type, hits another object before "flashing over" the individual. A ground strike occurs when lightning strikes the ground and then travels along it to the individual, who is in particular danger if he or she is wearing metal spikes or standing in water.

Thermal injuries

Thermal injuries from the high temperature of a lightning strike (more than 27,760° C) are rare, but metallic jewelry or a buckle can retain heat and burn the individual. The Lichtenburg figure is a feathering pattern from the electron avalanche of a lightning strike that is visible for up to 24 hours.

Electromechanical injuries

Electromechanical injuries depend on the strike's amperage (A), duration, and tissue resistance. Typically, lightning carries a charge of 2,000 to 200,000 A. Ventricular fibrillation can occur with a current as low as 0.75 to 50 mA applied directly to the heart; higher currents can stop cardiac rhythm. The usual contact time of lightning is 0.1 to 0.3 milliseconds of direct current; tissue insult deepens with duration of contact. Tissues that are moister, thicker, and more vascular are more vulnerable to damage. In descending order of resistance to electrical impulses are bone, fat, tendon, skin, muscle, blood vessels, and nerve.

As many as 30% of lightning strikes involve two or more individuals, creating the possibility of mass injuries when a team is playing on a rain-soaked field in a storm. In addition, concussive forces from the air explosion of a lightning strike can propel bodies several feet, producing blunt trauma, and rupture tympanic membranes in up to 50% of individuals.

Medical effects of lightning strikes

The most frequent responses to a lightning strike are cardiac asystole and apnea. The heart will likely restart, but if the individual is not breathing, it will stop again. Thus, breathing must continue if the individual is to survive. Other problems include vasomotor instability, seizures, fixed and dilated pupil(s), subdural or epidural hematomas, anterior compartment syndromes, hyphemas, and secondary extremity injuries.

Treatment

Treatment is immediate institution of cardiopulmonary resuscitation for individuals in asystole. Although the mortality rate is only 35%, 75% of those in asystole die. Even individuals with cold, pulseless extremities, fixed pupils, and absent pulses and breath sounds have been revived and recovered completely. The rescuer must be cognizant of the possibility of cervical spine trauma or a second strike.

Prevention

Prevention is the key. A 30-second flash-to-bang count (30 seconds indicates the lightning is within 6 miles) should be used. Guidelines also recommend vacating dangerous areas, moving to safe shelters, and waiting 30 minutes after the last thunder bang before returning to the field. A sound, practiced plan should be in place for athletic activity in inclement weather. The plan must be written and specific; designate a person to call a warning; include a clear, rehearsed, recognized warning sound; and identify a specific safe shelter.

ensure safety of all participants.[19] The NCAA guideline further advises the use of safe shelters and urges waiting a full 30 minutes after the last sound of thunder before returning to the field. A safe shelter is any fully-enclosed substantial building suitable for occupancy, with plumbing and electrical wiring. An emergency shelter would be in any vehicle that has a full metal roof with its windows completely rolled up. Although there are many lightning detectors on the market today, they do not replace written policy. A sound and practiced policy that establishes guidelines for athletic activity in inclement weather is the most logical approach to safety. Components of good policies for the prevention of lightning injury include a specific written plan in the event of lightning; a designated person to call a warning; a clear, rehearsed, and recognized warning sound; and a specific safe shelter to adjourn to in the event of unsafe weather.

COLD INJURIES

Pathophysiologic Effects of Cold

The human body is a heat-generating mechanism. Body temperature must remain within the narrow range of 75° to 112° F (23.9° to 44.4° C) for survival. For proper bodily function, the range is even narrower; body temperature should be 98.6° F (37° C), plus or minus a few degrees. In addition to the warmth and heat the body produces, it also gains heat from external sources such as sun, fire, and ingestion of warm foods.

For the purpose of heat regulation, the body consists of a core (the brain, heart, lungs, and major abdominal organs) and a shell (the skin, muscles, and extremities). When exposed to cold, the body attempts to increase internal heat production by increasing muscular activity, such as shivering, and by increasing the basal metabolic rate at which food stored within the body is burned. Heat loss is decreased by reducing the circulation of blood in the shell.

Cold injury occurs in two ways. In one, the core temperature is maintained but shell temperature decreases, resulting in local injuries that include frostnip, superficial frostbite, deep frostbite, chilblain, and trench or immersion foot. Another method of cold injury occurs when both the core and shell temperatures fall, systemic hypothermia occurs, all body processes slow down, followed by death if the injury is not treated.

Body parts freeze when there is not enough heat available to counteract external cold, resulting in local injury. Predisposing factors include inadequate insulation from cold and wind; restricted circulation because of arterial disease or tight clothing, especially footwear; fatigue; poor nutrition; ingestion of alcohol; and the body's normal effort to maintain its core temperature by shunting the flow of blood away from the shell. The body parts most commonly affected by cold are the hands, feet, ears, and face. All of these areas are located far from the heart and are normally subjected to rapid heat loss because of a large surface area-to-volume ratio.

Freezing temperatures affect the cells in the body in a predictable fashion. A cell is made up mostly of water, which becomes cool and eventually freezes, so that the cell is no longer able to function. The ice crystals that result then destroy the cell. Local cold trauma is the result of injuries of the capillary blood vessels and other tissue

FOCUS ON . . .

Pathophysiologic Effects of Cold

The body's core temperature must remain between 75° and 112° F (23.9° to 44.4° C) for survival and near 98.6° F (37° C) for proper function. The body generates its own heat and gains heat from external sources and ingestion of warm foods. For heat regulation, the body has a core (brain, heart, lungs, major abdominal organs) and a shell (skin, muscles, extremities). Exposure to cold causes the body to try to increase internal heat production by promoting muscular activity such as shivering and by raising the basal metabolic rate at which stored food is burned. Shell circulation decreases to reduce heat loss.

Cold injury occurs when core temperature is maintained, but shell temperature decreases, causing local injuries, or when both core and shell temperatures fall, resulting in systemic injury. Predisposing factors for cold injury include inadequate insulation from cold and wind; restricted circulation from arterial disease or tight clothing, especially footwear; fatigue; poor nutrition; alcohol use; and the body's attempt to maintain core temperature by shunting blood flow from the shell. The hands, feet, ears, and face are located away from the heart and are most prone to rapid heat loss from a large surface area-to-volume ratio. Freezing temperatures cause cell water to freeze, preventing the cell from functioning. The resultant ice crystals destroy the cell, and capillary blood vessels and skin and other tissue components are injured. Cell injuries vary only in degree and depth, and severity depends on duration of exposure, temperature, and wind velocity.

components of the skin and subcutaneous cells. Cell injuries are all essentially the same, varying only in degree and depth. Duration of the exposure, temperature to which the skin has been exposed, and wind velocity are the three most important factors to consider when determining the severity of a local injury.

Local Injuries

Frostnip

Frostnip usually affects the tips of the ears, nose, cheeks, chin, fingertips, and toes, usually in conditions of high wind, extreme cold, or both. It is manifested as a sudden blanching or whiteness of the skin. Frostnip comes on slowly and painlessly. The afflicted individual often does not notice it, and frequently, a companion first perceives it. There may be no permanent tissue damage, and it can be treated effectively by the firm, steady pressure of a warm hand, by blowing warm breath, or by holding the nipped fingers motionless in the armpit. The skin should not be rubbed with snow. As warmth and color return, tingling may occur. After thawing, the skin may turn red and flake for several days.

Superficial frostbite

Superficial *frostbite* usually involves the skin and the underlying superficial tissue. The skin appears white and waxy and is firm to the touch, but the tissue beneath it is soft and resilient (**Figure 22-3**). The individual should be taken indoors, protected from the cold, and subjected to the same steady, careful rewarming as for frostnip. Again, the affected area should not be rubbed with snow or by hand. When the injured area thaws, it is first numb. With continued thawing, it turns mottled blue or purple. As the tissue warms, the patient will first experience a tingling sensation followed by pain associated with neurologic trauma of the damaged area. Capillaries are damaged, and plasma leaks into the tissue, causing swelling, discoloration, and edema. If the frostbite is severe and the tissue beneath the outer layers of skin is involved, blisters may form. Throbbing, aching, and burning may last for weeks. The skin may remain permanently red, tender, and sensitive to reexposure to cold, so susceptible areas should receive extra protection.

Deep frostbite

Deep frostbite is extremely serious and usually involves the hands and feet. The tissues are cold, pale, and solid. The tissues deep to the skin and subcutaneous layers are usually injured and may be completely destroyed. Emergency treatment must be rendered as quickly as possible to keep the athlete dry and provide external warming. The injured area turns purplish blue and becomes extremely painful after thawing. Large blisters or gangrene may develop in the first day or two (**Figure 22-4**). Permanent tissue damage depends on the temperature and the duration of freezing.

Management of frostnip and frostbite

The treatment of frostnip and superficial and deep frostbite calls for early and rapid rewarming by whatever means possible, including warm water baths. If a prolonged delay is anticipated before a medical facility can be reached, rapid rewarming with warm water should be instituted. The temperature of the water should be between 100° to 112° F (38° to 44.5° C) with thermometer control. Caution should be taken to ensure the water does not become too hot but is maintained at 6° to 7° F warmer than normal body temperature. The temperature must be checked continually and maintained because immersing the cold extremity causes loss of heat. The container should be large enough so that neither the extremity nor the athlete touches the sides. Rewarming should continue until the frozen area is deep red or bluish in

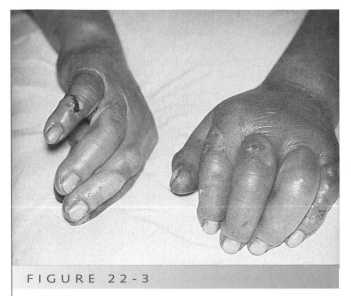

FIGURE 22-3

With superficial frostbite, the skin appears white, waxy, and firm to the touch; however, the underlying superficial tissue is soft and resilient.

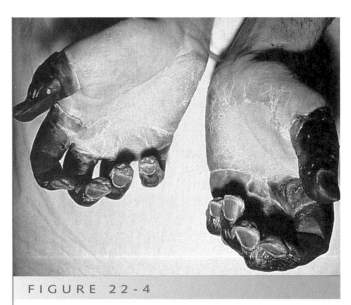

FIGURE 22-4

Deep frostbite is very serious, and large blisters or gangrene may develop.

color. The athlete's body temperature can be maintained with warm drinks. Analgesic medication may be needed. When treating frostbite, the athletic trainer must always guard against infection by applying bandages loosely under sterile conditions, being careful not to rupture blisters, and inserting pads between the toes.

Chilblain

Chilblain results from repeated exposure of bare skin to low temperatures and high humidity for prolonged periods. The injury results in red, swollen, hot, tender, itching

FOCUS ON . . .

Local Cold Injuries

Local cold injuries include frostnip, superficial and deep frostbite, chilblain, and trench foot.

Frostnip usually affects the tips of the ears, nose, cheeks, chin, fingertips, and toes, which suddenly and painlessly turn white. In fact, the condition may first be noted by a companion rather than the afflicted individual. Treatment is the firm, steady pressure of a warm hand, blowing warm breath, or holding the fingers still in the armpit. Tingling may occur as warmth and color return, and the skin may turn red and flake for several days, but permanent damage is unlikely.

Superficial frostbite involves the skin and underlying superficial tissue. The skin is white, waxy, and firm to the touch, but the underlying tissue is soft and resilient. The individual should be taken indoors and the rewarming techniques as described for frostnip applied. With thawing, the injured area is numb and turns mottled blue or purple. Capillary damage causes plasma to leak into the tissue, resulting in swelling, discoloration, and edema. In severe cases, more tissue is involved and blisters may form. Throbbing, aching, and burning can persist for weeks, and the skin may be permanently red, tender, and sensitive to cold, thus requiring extra protection in the cold.

Deep frostbite, an extremely serious condition, turns the hands and feet cold, pale, and solid. The deep and subcutaneous tissues are injured and may be destroyed. External warming causes the skin to turn purplish blue and very painful, with large blisters or gangrene possible in the first several days. Permanent tissue damage depends on the temperature and duration of freezing.

Treatment of frostnip and frostbite is early, rapid rewarming. If the medical facility is at a distance, warm water baths are recommended. The water temperature must be checked continually and carefully maintained at the appropriate temperature. Neither the athlete nor the extremity should touch the sides of the container. Rewarming continues until the frozen area is deep red or blue in color. Warm drinks can help to maintain the athlete's temperature, and analgesic medication may be needed. Sterile bandages should be loosely applied, blisters should not be ruptured, and pads should be placed between the toes if appropriate.

Chilblain occurs when bare skin is repeatedly exposed to low temperature and high humidity for prolonged times. The fingers or toes become red, swollen, hot, tender, and itchy; the same lesions tend to recur each season. Permanent skin changes represent chronic skin and peripheral capillary circulation injury. Treatment is protection from further cold exposure.

Trench (immersion) foot results from the slow, wet cooling of an extremity at temperatures just above freezing. The foot is cold, swollen, waxy, mottled, and numb and becomes red, swollen, and hot after warming. Wet, cold footgear should be removed, good local hygiene maintained, and a warm, dry covering applied. Damage to the skin's capillary circulation can progress to necrosis or gangrene of the skin, muscles, and nerves.

Only frostnip and superficial frostbite should be treated in the field with direct body heat application. More serious injuries demand that the athlete be transported to a hospital right away. En route, the area should be protected from further injury, including rubbing, chafing, and contusions. If absolutely necessary, an athlete can walk on a frostbitten, unthawed extremity, but walking is not permitted on a thawed limb, which is painful and dangerous. Blisters are a good sign, indicating only partial-thickness damage.

areas, usually on the fingers or toes, and the lesions tend to recur in the same areas during cold weather each season. There may be permanent skin changes between the periods of recurrence, such as blanching or numbness. This injury represents a chronic injury of the skin and the peripheral capillary circulation. Once the skin injury has been established, there is no treatment; however, steps should be taken to prevent recurrence and protect the area from further exposure to cold. Dressing in layers, being properly hydrated and fueled, and being in condi-

tion to train in extreme temperatures will help prevent further recurrence.

Trench or immersion foot

Trench or *immersion foot* results from the wet cooling of an extremity over hours or days at temperatures slightly above freezing. The lesion represents primary damage to the capillary circulation of the skin, which may progress to necrosis or gangrene of the skin, muscle, and nerves. The involved extremity is cold, swollen, waxy, mottled, and numb. After it is warmed, it becomes red, swollen, and hot, and blisters as well as gangrene may develop. Following medical evaluation by qualified personnel in a medical setting, treatment consists of removing the wet, cold footgear and gently rewarming the extremity, maintaining good local hygiene, and applying a warm, dry covering.

Treatment of local injuries

Treatment with direct application of body heat should only be done in the field for frostnip and superficial frostbite. Athletes with more serious cold injuries should be taken to a hospital as soon as possible. En route, the damaged area should be protected from further injury, especially from rubbing, chafing, and contusion. Unless the injured athlete is in immediate danger, he or she should not walk on the frostbitten extremity. Once a frostbitten limb has thawed, the athlete should not be allowed to walk. Walking on a thawed limb with the resulting chance of refreezing is extremely painful and dangerous. Blisters are usually a good prognostic sign, indicating that only a partial thickness of skin has been damaged.

Systemic Hypothermia

General, severe body cooling, or *hypothermia,* can occur at temperatures well above freezing. Hypothermia is usually caused by exposure to low or rapidly dropping temperatures, cold moisture, snow, or ice. It is aggravated by hunger, fatigue, and exertion and may be associated with other local cold injuries. Documentation of the extent of hypothermia requires a clinical thermometer that can reach low enough temperatures.

Table 22-5 shows the five stages of generalized body cooling.

Shivering usually begins at a rectal temperature of 95° F (35° C) and, as the cooling proceeds, clumsiness, fumbling, stumbling, falling, slow reactions, mental confusion, and difficulty in speaking follow. Death may occur within 2 hours of the onset of the first symptoms.

Systemic hypothermia is an acute, first-priority medical emergency and requires the rapid transfer of the athlete to an emergency facility. The basic principles of emergency care are to prevent further heat loss, rewarm the athlete as rapidly and safely as possible, and be alert for complications.

Mild to moderate hypothermia, indicated by a rectal temperature of 81° to 95° F (27.2° to 35° C), is treated by preventing further heat loss by removing the athlete from the wind, replacing wet clothing, adding appropriate insulating material, and providing external heat in any way possible (hot water bottles, electric blankets, camp fires, or body heat from rescuers). If the athlete is conscious, hot liquids may be given with the exception of fluids containing caffeine. An effective way of rewarming someone with systemic hypothermia is to immerse the individual in a tub of warm water kept between 105° and 110° F (40.6° to 43.3° C). Severe hypothermia with a rectal temperature

of less than 81° F (27.2° C) and unconsciousness carries serious dangers from cardiac arrhythmias and rewarming shock. While the above procedures are carried out, a facility that can diagnose and treat cardiac arrhythmias, especially ventricular fibrillation, should be notified, so that it can be prepared to receive the patient. Rewarming shock occurs as the circulatory system of the body warms and veins dilate before the heart becomes able to support the expanded circulation within a dilated system. Vital signs must be monitored, and the athlete must be evacuated to a medical facility. Athletes with severe hypothermia should not be warmed in the field. These persons may appear dead yet may still be revived.

Contributing Factors in Cold Injuries

Lack of preparation

Local cold injuries occur when the ambient temperature is close to freezing and the skin is exposed. However, depending on the activities and altitude, systemic hypothermia can occur when the temperature is well above freezing. Hunters, hikers, skiers, and climbers who are exposed to unusually severe weather for which they have not been prepared are in danger of hypothermia. The alcoholic or otherwise ill person with insufficient normal defenses to cold can also experience hypothermia in mild conditions.

Inability to acclimatize

Athletes cannot acclimatize to cold as well as they can to heat. They, therefore, must prepare for cold by anticipating weather changes, having the right clothing available in layers, having dry clothing available if possible, and above all, recognizing the ever-present possibility of hypothermia, regardless of the season. At the same time, the athlete should avoid overdressing, especially with synthetic materials that promote sweating and prevent evaporation of sweat.

TABLE 22-5

STAGES OF HYPOTHERMIA

1. Shivering, which is the body's attempt to generate heat

2. Apathy, sleeplessness, listlessness, and indifference, which may accompany rapid cooling of the body

3. Unconsciousness, with a glassy stare, a very slow pulse rate, and slow respiratory rate

4. Freezing of the extremities

5. Death

FOCUS ON . . .

Systemic Hypothermia

Systemic hypothermia is usually caused by exposure to low or rapidly dropping temperatures, cold moisture, snow, or ice and aggravated by hunger, fatigue, and exertion. Local cold injuries can be associated with systemic hypothermia, which progresses through five stages: shivering; apathy, sleeplessness, listlessness, and indifference, which accompany rapid cooling; unconsciousness, with a glassy stare and slow pulse and respiratory rates; extremity freezing; and death. Shivering begins when the rectal temperature is 95° F (35° C) and can proceed to clumsiness, fumbling, stumbling, falling, slow reactions, mental confusion, difficulty speaking, and death within 2 hours. Therefore, systemic hypothermia is an acute emergency requiring rapid transfer of the athlete to an emergency facility. Principles of care are to prevent further heat loss, rewarm as quickly and safely as possible, and watch for complications.

Mild to moderate hypothermia in the conscious athlete is treated by preventing further heat loss: removing the athlete from the wind, replacing wet clothing, adding appropriate insulating material, providing external heat in any way possible, and encouraging hot liquids. Immersing the individual in a tub of warm water is another effective method. The severely hypothermic athlete risks cardiac arrhythmias and rewarming shock (the veins dilate before the heart can support the dilated system); therefore, equipment to diagnose and treat these conditions must be available. Vital signs must be monitored and the athlete transported to a medical facility. Athletes with severe hypothermia should not be warmed in the field. Even the individual who appears dead may still be revived.

ALTITUDE DISORDERS

Altitude sickness occurs in response to the *hypoxia* (lack of oxygen) of altitudes greater than 5,000' and is generally divided into three syndromes: acute mountain sickness, high-altitude pulmonary edema, and high-altitude cerebral edema. These three forms may appear separately or simultaneously. As with heat illness, they are not clear-cut entities and probably represent a common, underlying physiologic response to hypoxia. Almost everyone gets acute mountain sickness when exposed to high altitude, but few develop the advanced stages. High-altitude pulmonary edema and cerebral edema are serious and potentially fatal conditions.

Altitude sickness is becoming more common as more people are hiking, skiing, and participating in recreational activities at higher altitudes. Inadequate time on weekend trips to acclimatize to high altitudes is definitely a factor in this condition. Symptoms may appear at 7,500' to 8,000', and death has occurred at altitudes as low as 8,000' to 9,000'. In addition to the problems of hypoxia, individuals at higher altitudes face temperature changes and increased exposure to ultraviolet rays and radiation.

Acute Mountain Sickness

Acute mountain sickness is the mildest form of altitude sickness, and most individuals will experience some of its symptoms when ascending to high altitudes. There is no direct relationship between the altitude and the severity of the illness. Mild to moderate cases occur at all altitudes.

The basic cause of mountain sickness is not clear. The severity of symptoms and rapidity of onset vary from person to person, and some individuals are inherently more susceptible than others. Symptoms are directly proportional to the rapidity of the ascent, the duration, and the degree of exertion and are inversely proportional to acclimatization, physical conditioning, and hydration status.

There is a time lag of 6 to 96 hours between arrival at a higher altitude and the onset of symptoms, which include headache, difficulty sleeping, early morning arousal, dyspnea on exertion, loss of appetite, lightheadedness, fatigue, confusion, weakness, alteration of heart rate, and edema.

Acute mountain sickness is generally self-limited, lasting 2 to 5 days. Headaches usually respond to over-the-counter pain medication. Activities during the first few days in a high altitude should be reduced, because most individuals adapt to higher altitudes in a few days. Reliance on carbohydrates for energy is increased at high altitude, so the athlete should eat a high-carbohydrate diet to help control nausea and ensure adequate substrate supply.

High-Altitude Pulmonary Edema

High-altitude pulmonary edema (HAPE) is a more dramatic form of altitude illness and an unusual form of noncardiac pulmonary edema. It may develop on the first exposure to high altitude but frequently is seen after descent and reascent. HAPE is noncardiogenic pulmonary edema that occurs in unacclimatized individuals exposed to altitude. The onset of HAPE often occurs within 12 to 100 hours after rapid ascent and is characterized by fatigue, dyspnea, and cough. An excessive rise in pulmonary artery pressure seems to be a precursor to HAPE. Reduced fluid clearance from the lungs and inflammatory response are also considered factors in the development of HAPE.

The symptoms of high-altitude pulmonary edema vary in severity. After the symptoms of acute mountain sickness subside, shortness of breath, increased rate of

Contributing Factors in Cold Injuries

Factors that contribute to cold injury include lack of preparation and inability to acclimatize. Local cold injuries occur in colder climates when the ambient temperature is near freezing and the skin is exposed, yet systemic hypothermia can occur throughout the year. Athletes who are exposed to unexpected severe weather and those who are ill (including alcoholics) are susceptible. Unlike heat acclimatization, cold acclimatization does not occur. Therefore, athletes must anticipate weather changes, wear layered clothing (but avoid overdressing), have dry clothing available, and recognize the potential for hypothermia.

respiration, an irritating cough that progresses to *hemoptysis* (coughing up bright, red blood), and substernal chest pain may develop. The cough produces bloody, frothy sputum. A diagnosis of high-altitude pulmonary edema is suspected when rales (the sounds of air bubbling through fluid) are heard in the chest. Individuals with high-altitude pulmonary edema must return to a lower altitude as quickly as possible and be given oxygen whenever available. These individuals must be thoroughly reevaluated by trained medical personnel before being allowed to ascend again.

High-Altitude Cerebral Edema

High-altitude cerebral edema (HACE) is a less common but very dangerous form of altitude sickness. HACE has a low incidence of occurrence but is fatal if left untreated. Rapid ascent and lack of acclimatization are contributing factors. Although the mechanisms by which HACE occurs have not be definitively identified, osmotic cell swelling and angiogenesis caused by hypoxia may result in the capillary leakage and accumulation characteristic of HACE. Death has occurred in individuals who are as low as 8,000′; however, death is rare below 12,000′. The relationship of high-altitude cerebral edema to high-altitude pulmonary edema is unclear.[1]

The symptoms of high-altitude cerebral edema are initially the same as those of acute mountain sickness but with increasingly severe headaches followed by mental confusion, aggressiveness and emotional instability, hallucinations, and finally, localized motor weakness and reflex changes. The condition may progress to coma and death. *Bradycardia* (unusually slow but regular beating of the heart) is an initial finding and may be related to increased cerebral pressure. Judgment and coordination are impaired as a result of direct local swelling of the brain, especially the cerebellum. Ocular signs and symptoms such as blurring of vision, papilledema (edema of the optic nerve as it enters the eyeball), and retinal and vitreous hemorrhage may develop.

High-altitude pulmonary edema and cerebral edema are emergencies and, when suspected, demand that the athlete descend immediately. Oxygen should be provided when available, and, because exercise aggravates both conditions, the athlete should be carried down. Corticosteroids, such as dexamethasone or betamethasone, 4 to 6 mg qid administered by a medical professional, may be used to treat high-altitude cerebral edema, but these measures are secondary to descent. A diuretic such as acetazolamide may stabilize breathing, but it is important to keep in mind that the athlete may already be dehydrated.

Preventing Altitude Illness

Preparation for high-altitude activities should include months of cardiovascular and strength training and aerobic conditioning. An aerobically fit individual has a higher altitude tolerance than an unfit individual.

Acclimatization involves a long, slow ascent, climbing higher during the day and coming down lower to sleep and rest. Those individuals with coronary vascular disease or chronic obstructive pulmonary disease should avoid areas of low oxygen tension.

TRAVEL

Jet Lag and Circadian Rhythms

Practical recommendations about optimizing athletes' responses to travel are difficult to make because of the lack of sufficient research, the complexity of the topic, and the uncontrollable nature of the demands imposed by travel and competition. Training sessions and competitions held at prearranged times means that most athletes do not have unlimited flexibility in their travel plans, and limitations are introduced that are impossible to circumvent. However, it may be possible to help prepare athletes beforehand for the rigors created by jet lag and alterations in normal circadian rhythms by helping them recognize that such challenges will likely occur.

Although the research is far from comprehensive, there is enough information to conclude that mental and physical capacity varies with the time of day in a regular and fairly predictable manner.[20] There is far less certainty as to how these responses are affected by travel across time zones. Complicating matters further is the knowledge that circadian rhythms vary among athletes and that different

FOCUS ON . . .

Altitude Disorders

Altitude disorders, which occur at altitudes greater than 5,000′ as a result of hypoxia, are classified as acute mountain sickness, high-altitude pulmonary edema, and high-altitude cerebral edema or a combination of these. Most people experience acute mountain sickness at high altitude, but this condition rarely progresses to the potentially fatal high-altitude pulmonary or cerebral edema. Increasingly common in recent years as more people participate in sports at high altitude with inadequate time to acclimatize, altitude sickness can occur at 7,500′ to 8,000′, with death at 8,000′ to 9,000′. Along with hypoxia, high altitude exposes athletes to temperature changes, ultraviolet rays, and radiation.

Acute mountain sickness

Acute mountain sickness symptoms are directly proportional to ascent rapidity and duration, along with degree of exertion, and are inversely proportional to acclimatization, physical conditioning, and hydration status. Symptoms begin 6 to 96 hours after arrival and include headache, difficulty sleeping, early morning arousal, dyspnea on exertion, loss of appetite, lightheadedness, fatigue, confusion, weakness, heart rate alteration, and edema. Symptoms last 2 to 5 days, during which activities should be reduced to permit adaptation. Over-the-counter medications help headaches, and a high-carbohydrate diet controls nausea and ensures adequate substrates for energy.

High-altitude pulmonary edema

High-altitude pulmonary edema is an unusual form of noncardiac pulmonary edema, which can develop on first exposure to high altitude but is more often seen after descent and reascent. Symptoms begin after acute mountain sickness symptoms subside and include shortness of breath, increased respiratory rate, irritating cough producing bloody, frothy sputum that progresses to hemoptysis, and substernal chest pain. Rales are heard in the chest. Athletes with high-altitude pulmonary edema must be given oxygen and returned to lower altitude as quickly as possible. Before reascending, they must be thoroughly evaluated.

High-altitude cerebral edema

High-altitude cerebral edema has caused death at 8,000′ but is rare below 12,000′. Symptoms initially are those of acute mountain sickness, progressing to headaches increasing in severity, bradycardia, mental confusion, aggressiveness and emotional instability, hallucinations, localized motor weakness and reflex changes, visual blurring, papilledema, retinal and vitreous hemorrhage, coma, and perhaps death. Treatment is oxygen and return to lower altitude. Corticosteroids such as dexamethasone or betamethasone and diuretics such as acetazolamide are helpful, although secondary to descent.

Preventing altitude illness

Preparing for high-altitude activities should include months of cardiovascular and strength training and aerobic conditioning, which raise the threshold for altitude sickness. Acclimatization involves a long, slow ascent to higher altitude during the day and then descending to sleep and rest. Individuals with coronary vascular disease or chronic obstructive pulmonary disease should avoid high altitude.

mental, physiologic, and physical responses have their zeniths and nadirs at different times of the day. Considering the wide variation in sleep-wake cycles and desired training times among athletes when living at home, it is a formidable challenge to try make general recommendations for even domestic travel across time zones. International travel makes things still more difficult. For example, if a team of athletes from Ohio travels to Australia for competition, how long before the start of the competition should they leave Ohio? Should they take melatonin or drugs before or during the flight? Melatonin and sleeping pills (benzodiazepines) have unpredictable effects and may actually retard the adjustment to a new time zone. Accordingly, they should be used with caution. Should training sessions in the United States be held at the same times as competition in Australia? If so, how often should these training sessions occur and for how long prior to departure? How should the athletes be expected to adjust to the time change once they reach Australia? These are just some of the questions in need of answers, answers that are difficult to come by and may be as varied as the number of athletes on a team.

CHAPTER REVIEW

Environmental problems that can affect the athlete include heat disorders, lightning, cold injuries, altitude disorders, and conditions associated with travel. For physiologic and mental functioning, the human body temperature must be maintained within a narrow range in which heat production and heat loss are balanced. When this range is exceeded, heat disorders can occur. Heat disorders are classified as heat cramps, heat exhaustion, and heatstroke and may be preventable with appropriate acclimatization and preseason conditioning, modified coaching techniques, and adequate fluid replacement. Treatment for heat disorder includes rapid cooling.

Lightning injuries and fatalities are rare, but because lightning tends to strike in the late afternoon hours from late spring through midautumn, they must be a concern for healthcare providers. Lightning can produce thermal and electromechanical injuries; the type of injury depends on the relationship of the victim to the strike. Cardiac asystole and apnea are the most common responses to a lightning strike, but cardiopulmonary resuscitation has revived many individuals who appeared to be dead. A specific, written policy establishing guidelines for athletic activity in inclement weather can prevent many lightning injuries.

Cold injuries occur when either the core temperature is maintained and the shell temperature drops, resulting in local injuries, or the core and shell temperatures both fall, resulting in systemic injury. Local injuries include frostnip, superficial and deep frostbite, chilblain, and trench foot, which are treated with rapid warming of the injured part. Systemic hypothermia, if left untreated, can be fatal. It also is treated with rapid warming, but because cardiac arrhythmias and rewarming shock are possible, seriously ill patients should be transported to a medical facility. Cold injuries may be lessened with appropriate preparation and acclimatization.

Altitude disorders occur at altitudes over 5,000' and are categorized as acute mountain sickness, high-altitude pulmonary edema, or high-altitude cerebral edema. All are treated with rapid descent. Jet lag can be a problem for the traveling athlete. Research to date has not provided practical recommendations to reduce the effects of jet lag, but simply alerting athletes to the anticipated disruptions in circadian rhythms can be beneficial.

1. Transformation of sweat on the skin from a liquid to a vapor is a process known as:

A. radiation.

B. convection.

C. conduction.

D. evaporation.

2. Hot, dry skin with small urine volume, excessive thirst, and weakness are most typical of which type of heat stress?

A. Heat cramps from water loss

B. Heat exhaustion from water loss

C. Heat exhaustion from salt loss

D. Heatstroke

3. Lightning is most likely to strike during which of the following times?

A. 5:00 am to 10:00 am during winter

B. 1:00 pm to 6:00 pm during early spring

C. 3:00 pm to 8:00 pm during late spring

D. 10:00 am to 3:00 pm during late summer

4. The most frequent response to a lightning strike is:

A. cardiac asystole.

B. subdural hematoma.

C. vasomotor instability.

D. anterior compartment syndrome.

5. White, waxy, firm skin with soft, resilient tissue beneath is typical of which of the following cold injuries?

A. Frostnip

B. Chilblain

C. Superficial frostbite

D. Deep frostbite

6. What is the first stage of systemic hypothermia?

A. Apathy

B. Shivering

C. Unconsciousness

D. Freezing of extremities

7. The symptoms of altitude sickness are inversely proportional to:

A. rapidity of ascent.

B. duration of ascent.

C. degree of exertion.

D. physical conditioning.

8. Treatment of acute mountain sickness includes which of the following measures?

A. Oxygen

B. Corticosteroids

C. Immediate descent

D. High-carbohydrate diet

9. Which of the following conditions may develop after the symptoms of acute mountain sickness edema subside?

A. Vomiting

B. Shortness of breath

C. Pain in the left arm

D. Decreased rate of respiration

10. Which of the following statements about circadian rhythms is true?

A. Sleep-wake cycles vary widely among individuals.

B. Mental capacity is fairly consistent throughout the day.

C. Physiologic responses are unpredictable on a daily basis.

D. Circadian rhythms tend to be similar among individuals.

Answers on page 893.

References

1. Pandolf KB, Sawka MN, Gonzalez RR (eds): *Human Performance Physiology and Environmental Medicine at Terrestrial Extremes.* Indianapolis, IN, Benchmark Press, 1988.

2. Shirreffs S, Taylor J, Leiper J, Maughan R: Post-exercise rehydration in men: Effects of volume consumed and drink sodium content. *Med Sci Sports Exerc* 1996;28:1260–1271.

3. Gisolfi CV, Lamb DR (eds): *Perspectives in Exercise Science and Sports Medicine: Fluid Homeostasis During Exercise.* Carmel, IN, Cooper Publishing Group, 1990, vol 3.

4. Levin S: Investigating the cause of muscle cramps. *Phys Sportsmed* 1993;21:111–116.

5. Knochel JP: Clinical complications of body fluid and electrolyte balance, in Buskirk ER, Puhl SM (eds): *Body Fluid Balance: Exercise and Sports.* Boca Raton, FL, CRC Press, 1996.

6. Gisolfi CV, Lamb DR, Nadel ER (eds): *Perspectives in Exercise Science and Sports Medicine: Exercise, Heat, and Thermoregulation.* Dubuque, IA, WC Brown Publishers, 1993, vol 6.

7. Adolph EF: *Physiology of Man in the Desert.* New York, NY, Interscience Publishers, 1947.

8. Marriott BM, Carlson SJ (eds): *Nutritional Needs in Cold and in High-Altitude Environments.* Washington, DC, National Academy Press, 1996.

9. American College of Sports Medicine: Heat and cold illnesses during distance running. *Med Sci Sports Exerc* 1996;28:i-x.

10. Sparling PB: Editorial: Expected environmental conditions for the 1996 Summer Olympic Games in Atlanta. *Clin J Sport Med* 1995;5:220–222.

11. Greenleaf J: Problem: Thirst drinking behavior and involuntary dehydration. *Med Sci Sports Exerc* 1992;24:645–656.

12. Walsh KM, Hanley MJ, Graner, SJ, Beam D, Bazluki J: A survey of lightning policy in selected division I colleges. *J Athletic Training* 1997;32:206–210.

13. Jepsen DL: How to manage a patient with lightning injury. *Am J Nub* 1992;92:39–42.

14. Cwinn AA, Cantrill SV: Lightning injuries. *J Emerg Med* 1985;2:379–388.

15. Cooper MA: Emergent care of lightning and electrical injuries. *Sem Neurol* 1995;13:268–278.

16. Fontanarosa PB: Electrical shock and lightning strike. *Am Emerg Med* 1993;22:378–387.

17. Cooper MA: Electrical and lightning injuries. *Emerg Med Clin North Am* 1984;2:489–501.

18. Lifschultz BD, Donoghue ER: Deaths caused by lightning. *J Forensic Sci* 1993;38:353–358.

19. Earle M (ed): *NCAA Sports Medicine Handbook.* Overland Park, KS, NCAA, 1998.

20. Atkinson G, Reilly T: Circadian variation in sports performance. *Sports Med* 1996;21:292–312.

23

General Medical Conditions

Jeffrey D. Nelson, MD
Cindy J. Chang, MD, FACSM
Fred Tedeschi, MA, ATC

QUICK CONTENTS

- Causes, clinical manifestations, screening, and classification of asthma.

- Medication classifications used to treat asthma and which ones are permitted by the International Olympic Committee.

- Causes and treatment of exercise-induced asthma.

- Cancer, its general and specific signs, appropriate screening tests in each age group, and preventive strategies.

- The three most common types of diabetes, how diabetes affects carbohydrate metabolism, and treatment options for diabetes.

- The clinical presentation, management, and prevention of hypoglycemia and hyperglycemia in athletes.

- Seizure management and counseling of athletes with epilepsy on sports participation.

- Sleep apnea, including pathogenesis, clinical features, diagnosis, and treatment.

- Narcolepsy and its treatment.

OVERVIEW

General medical conditions can affect an athlete's well-being and performance. This chapter covers five medical conditions that can affect the athlete: asthma, cancer, diabetes, epilepsy, and sleep disorders.

The section on asthma begins with an explanation of the symptoms and causes of asthma. Next, the diagnosis and classification of asthma severity are reviewed, followed by a discussion of available medications and the stepwise treatment of patients with asthma. The last part of this section focuses on exercise-induced asthma.

The cancer section first discusses cancer generally, including what it is and its warning signs. Next, the typical cancers in each age group are reviewed and some of the more common specific types of cancer are discussed, including recommendations regarding screening for early detection. Finally, specific recommendations for cancer prevention are outlined.

The section on diabetes describes the new classification system of diabetes and its pathogenesis (causes), carbohydrate metabolism, symptoms of diabetes, and the risks and benefits of exercise in diabetes. The section then focuses on the athletic trainer's role in recognizing and responding to the two primary short-term complications of diabetes: hypoglycemia and hyperglycemia.

In the epilepsy section, epilepsy and the various types of seizures are described. Management of seizures is discussed next, followed by a discussion of sports participation for individuals who have had a seizure.

The sleep disorders section begins with a discussion of the causes of sleep apnea. Next, the chapter describes the clinical features of sleep apnea including its potential complications. This is followed by a discussion of diagnosis. Various treatment options are explained, and, finally, there is a brief discussion of narcolepsy, including clinical features, diagnosis, and treatment.

ASTHMA

Asthma is a common condition with profound medical and economic consequences. The mortality rate from asthma has continued to increase in the United States in spite of the improved understanding and better treatments that are now available. In 1980, the mortality rate was 1.3 per 100,000; by 1989, it had risen to 2.1 per 100,000.[1] Data from the Centers for Disease Control and Prevention show that there are 470,000 hospitalizations and more than 5,000 deaths anually from asthama.[2] Asthma is also common among athletes, although it often remains undetected. Of 597 athletes who were screened at the 1984 Summer Olympic games, 67 (11%) were found to have exercise-induced asthma. Of these athletes, only 26% were aware of their asthma.[3]

Pathogenesis

In the past, asthma was thought of primarily as a disease of airway hyperresponsiveness bronchospasm or airway narrowing caused by factors such as an allergen or cold virus. Over the last several decades, the role of inflammation in asthma has been increasingly recognized. It is now generally accepted that *asthma* is a chronic inflammatory disorder of the airways and that this inflammation is associated with changes in airway hyperresponsiveness. Airflow limitation and respiratory symptoms are, in part, caused by bronchoconstriction (narrowing of the airways caused by spasm), but also by airway edema, mucous plug formation, and airway wall remodeling.[4]

The National Asthma Education and Prevention Program (NAEPP) defines asthma as "a chronic inflammatory disorder of the airways in which many cells and cellular elements play a role . . . . In susceptible individuals, this inflammation causes recurrent episodes of wheezing, breathlessness, chest tightness, and coughing, particularly at night or in the early morning."[5]

Table 23-1 shows the diagnosis and classification of asthma severity as presented by the Expert Panel Report II.[5] The inflammatory cascade commonly begins when antigens such as pollen bind to IgE, which is an antibody specific to allergic reactions (**Figure 23-1**). These complexes then bind to mast cells. Mast cells release mediators of inflammation, which include various chemicals called interleukins, leukotrienes, and histamine. These mediators in turn attract eosinophils, a type of white blood cell involved in allergic response, and other inflammatory cells. The underlying inflammation is the cause of the airway hyperresponsiveness that leads to bronchoconstriction. Inflammation can be triggered by a number of factors. Allergens, irritants, such as pollution and tobacco smoke, viruses, exercise, and cold air are among the many potential triggers of bronchoconstriction in susceptible individuals.

TABLE 23-1
DIAGNOSIS AND CLASSIFICATION OF ASTHMA SEVERITY

Note: Classification is the highest category for which the patient has one or more features *prior to treatment.*

STEP 1: Intermittent

Symptoms occur less than three times per week

Brief exacerbations (from a few hours to a few days) occur

Nighttime symptoms occur less than three times per month

Asymptomatic and normal lung function occur between exacerbations

PEFR or forced exiratory volume in 1 second (FEV1) is greater than 80% predicted with variability of less than 20%

STEP 2: Mild Persistent

Symptoms occur more than two times per week but less than one time per day

Exacerbations may affect activity and sleep

Nighttime asthma symptoms occur three or more times per month

PEFR or FEV1 is greater than 80% predicted or variability of 20% to 30%

STEP 3: Moderate Persistent

Symptoms occur daily

Exacerbations affect activity and sleep

Nighttime asthma symptoms occur more than 1 time per week

Athlete uses inhaled short-acting beta 2-agnostic daily

PEFR or FEV1 is 60% to 80% predicted or variability of greater than 30%

STEP 4: Severe Persistent

Continuous symptoms

Frequent exacerbations of these symptoms

Frequent nighttime symptoms

Physical activity is limited by asthma symptoms

PEFR or FEV1 is less than 60% predicted

(Adapted with permission from *The Expert Panel Report II: Guidelines for the Diagnosis and Management of Asthma.* National Asthma Education and Prevention Program. National Heart Lung and Blood Institute, National Institutes of Health, 1997.)

Some medications can trigger asthma in susceptible individuals. Radiocontrast media used for certain types of radiographic studies, beta-adrenergic antagonists (beta-blockers), and nonsteroidal anti-inflammatory drugs (NSAIDs), including aspirin, can all cause a significant worsening of asthma. Some individuals with asthma will have a life-threatening reaction to these agents. Aspirin or other NSAIDs can cause an exacerbation of asthma in 5% to 10% of individuals who have asthma. Individuals with asthma who have nasal polyps have an even greater risk (20% to 40%).

Consequently, NSAIDs should not be given to individuals with asthma except under a physician's direction. Choline magnesium trisalicylate (Trilisate) and acetaminophen (Tylenol) are alternative therapies for patients with asthma who are sensitive to aspirin. Beta blockers, which are commonly used to treat high blood pressure and other cardiac conditions, directly cause contraction of bronchial smooth muscles. If beta-blocker therapy is essential, short acting, beta-1 selective agents that are selective for action on the heart instead of the lungs should be used at the lowest possible dose.

Clinical Manifestations

The primary symptoms of asthma include recurrent episodes of wheezing, shortness of breath, tightness in the chest, and coughing. The work of breathing increases, and air exchange becomes more difficult because of the decreased airway diameter caused by inflammation and bronchoconstriction. On examination, patients with asthma often will have an increased respiratory rate (number of breaths per minute), with prolonged expiration. The normal respiratory rate at rest is 10 to 18 breaths/min. In a person who does not have asthma, inspiration lasts longer than expiration, but in a person who does have asthma, the expiratory phase will be longer. Auscultation, or listening to the chest with a stethoscope, will often reveal whistling noises known as wheezes. Sometimes, a cough may be the only presenting sign of asthma.

Diagnosis and Classification of Asthma

All athletes should be screened for asthma on a preparticipation questionnaire. **Table 23-2** presents a list of questions the athlete should be asked regarding asthma.

A careful history, physical examination, and observation of the typical symptoms can usually lead to the proper diagnosis of asthma. Symptoms will resolve either spontaneously or with bronchodilator therapy. Peak expiratory flow rate (PEFR) can be measured with an inexpensive, hand-held peak flow meter. These peak flow meters are easy to use and are often given to the patient to take home for self-monitoring. Peak flow meters with disposable mouthpieces should be available for the athletic trainer to monitor athletes with asthma. The measurements can be

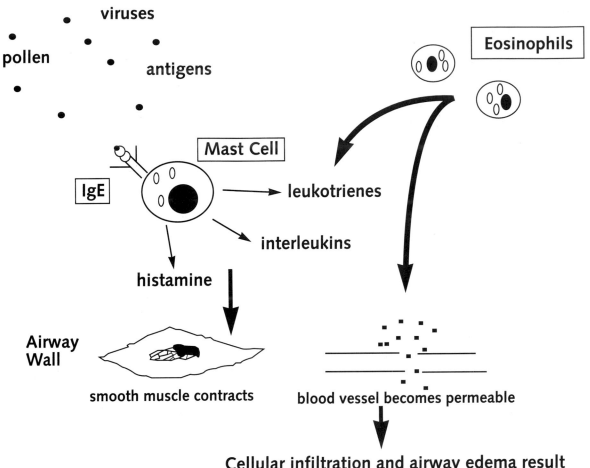

FIGURE 23-1

The inflammatory cascade in asthma begins when antigens bind to the antibody IgE.

TABLE 23-2

PREPARTICIPATION QUESTIONS

1. Do you have recurrent episodes of coughing or wheezing, especially at night or early in the morning?

2. Do you cough or wheeze after exercise?

3. Do you cough, wheeze, or experience tightness in your chest after exposure to allergens or pollutants?

4. Do you have frequent chest colds that last longer than 10 days?

5. Do you have a history of asthma, and, if so, do you take asthma medications?

taken before and after bronchodilator therapy to support the diagnosis; measurements should improve after treatment. In unclear cases, the physician can perform formal pulmonary function testing to confirm the diagnosis. Formal testing is done in a pulmonary lab and involves measuring lung capacity and the ability to exhale properly. Other causes of a chronic cough, such as chronic sinus infection and gastroesophageal reflux, which is also a major cause of heartburn, should be excluded. Vocal cord dysfunction with abnormal contraction of the vocal cords and anxiety with hyperventilation can also be confused with asthma. Once the diagnosis is established, the severity of the asthma should be classified in order to guide treatment (see Table 23-1).

Treatment

A patient with asthma should avoid stimuli known to precipitate attacks whenever possible. Triggers vary from person to person but often include various allergens such as

FOCUS ON . . .

Asthma

Pathogenesis

Asthma is a chronic inflammatory airway disorder associated with airway hyperresponsiveness. Bronchoconstriction, airway edema, mucous plug formation, and airway wall remodeling cause airflow limitations and respiratory symptoms. The inflammatory cascade begins when antigens bind to IgE (an antibody specific to allergic reactions) and then to mast cells, which release inflammatory mediators. These mediators attract eosinophils, white blood cells involved in the allergic response, and other inflammatory cells, causing inflammation, airway hyperresponsiveness, and bronchoconstriction.

The Expert Panel Report II created a four-step system to diagnose and classify asthma. These steps include step 1 (intermittent), step 2 (mild persistent), step 3 (moderate persistent), and step 4 (severe persistent).

Certain medications, such as radiocontrast media, beta blockers, and nonsteroidal anti-inflammatory drugs, can trigger asthma in susceptible individuals. In 5% to 10% of individuals with asthma (and in a higher percentage of individuals with asthma with nasal polyps), asthma will worsen when they take aspirin or another NSAID; therefore, a physician must direct when these drugs can be used in these patients. Choline magnesium trisalicylate (Trilisate) and acetaminophen (Tylenol) are alternatives. If beta-blocker therapy is needed, a short-acting, beta-1 selective (for the heart, not the lungs) agent can be used at the lowest possible dose.

Clinical Manifestations

Asthma symptoms include recurrent wheezing, shortness of breath, chest tightness, and coughing. The decreased airway diameter caused by inflammation and bronchoconstriction increases the work of breathing and makes air exchange more difficult. The respiratory rate may be increased (normal is 10 to 18 breaths per minute at rest), with a long expiratory phase. Wheezes (whistling noises) may be audible on auscultation. Coughing, however, may be the only symptom.

Diagnosis and classification of asthma

The preparticipation questionnaire should include questions on asthma: recurrent coughing or wheezing, especially at night or early in the morning; cough or wheeze after exercise; cough, wheeze, or chest tightness after exposure to allergens or pollutants; frequent chest colds lasting longer than 10 days; and history of asthma and use of asthma medications. The diagnosis is made by observing symptoms (which resolve spontaneously or with bronchodilator therapy), taking a careful history, and performing a physical examination. Measuring peak expiratory flow rate assesses the effectiveness of treatment. If the diagnosis remains unclear, formal pulmonary function testing can be helpful. Other causes of a chronic cough include chronic sinus infection, gastroesophageal reflux, vocal cord dysfunction, and anxiety with hyperventilation.

(Continued)

---

animal dander, dust mites, cockroaches, and pollen and irritants such as tobacco smoke and pollutants. Treatment of allergy symptoms with oral antihistamines and nasal steroids can help athletes who have asthma with allergies. Also, treatment of sinus infections and gastroesophageal reflux, if present, will improve control of asthma.

Various medications, classified as "controller medications" and "reliever medications," are used. *Controller medications* are used daily and are designed to prevent symptoms. *Reliever medications* are used as needed for symptoms or just prior to exposure to a known irritant such as exercise or an allergen. Medications can also be categorized by their mechanism of action.

Mechanism of action

Short-acting beta-adrenergic drugs such as albuterol (Proventil, Ventolin), terbutaline (Brethine), and metaproterenol (Alupent) are used as reliever medica-

tions. They cause dilation of smooth bronchial muscle in the lungs and inhibit the release of chemicals that cause inflammation from mast cells. Although inhaled administration is most common, these drugs can be administered in inhaled, oral, and parenteral forms. Short-acting beta-adrenergic drugs are the first-line treatment of exercise induced asthma.

Inhaled salmeterol (Serevent), which is a long-acting beta agonist, is available and should be used only as a controller medication. This medication can be very effective for nighttime symptoms. The most common side effects of long-acting beta-agonist drugs are muscle tremors and feelings of jitteriness, which can inhibit athletic performance.

Mast cell stabilizers are inhaled medications that prevent the release of the contents of mast cells, thereby preventing inflammation and bronchoconstriction. These drugs include cromolyn (Intal) and nedocromil (Tilade)

FOCUS ON . . .

Asthma (Continued)

Treatment

Treatment of asthma begins with avoiding known irritants whenever possible. Treating allergies with oral antihistamines and nasal steroids can be helpful in patients with asthma with allergies. Treating sinus infections and gastroesophageal reflux can also improve control of asthma.

Asthma medications are controllers (used daily and designed to prevent symptoms) or relievers (used as needed for symptoms or before exposure to a known irritant). Short-acting beta-adrenergic drugs are relievers. They dilate the bronchial smooth muscle and inhibit the release of inflammatory substances from mast cells. Available in inhaled, oral, and parenteral forms, they are first-line treatment. A long-acting beta agonist (inhaled salmeterol) is used as a controller for nighttime symptoms. Side effects of these medications are muscle tremors and jitteriness.

Mast cell stabilizers are inhaled medications that prevent the release of mast cell contents. These medications are more effective in children than in adults, and they are second-line treatment without any side effects. Methylxanthines (theophylline) directly relax smooth and skeletal muscle; they may also reduce mucous tenacity and diminish the allergic inflammatory response. However, interactions with other medications are common, and side effects of nausea and vomiting are frequent. Blood level monitoring is needed to prevent the arrhythmias and seizures that can occur from high doses. Theophylline is taken orally.

Corticosteroids are available in inhaled, oral, and parenteral forms. They are first-line controllers for patients with step 2 to step 4 asthma. Corticosteroids counteract inflammation, have a delayed onset, and enhance airway responsiveness to beta-adrenergic drugs. Side effects are minimal with a low-dose inhaled drug, but side effects such as fluid retention, ulcer, convulsions, and psychosis can occur with a high inhaled or any oral dose. Ipratropium bromide is an inhaled anticholinergic drug that relieves bronchospasm, but is less effective than beta-adrenergic agents.

Leukotriene modifiers are the newest class of asthma medications and include zafirlukast and zileuton. These oral medications improve lung function and symptoms and reduce the need for relievers, particularly in patients who are symptomatic when they take aspirin. Liver enzymes should be monitored when zileuton is used.

Step therapy

The Expert Panel Report II recommends a stepwise approach to asthma, with the goals being to eliminate or minimize chronic symptoms, decrease frequency of exacerbations, reduce the need for relievers, achieve near-normal peak expiratory flow rate, and eliminate activity and exercise limitations. If these goals are not being met, the inhaler technique, medication compliance, and environmental control should be reviewed, and the physician should consider therapy step-up. Treatment should be reviewed every 3 to 6 months; 3 months of control may allow a stepwise reduction in treatment.

(Continued)

---

and seem to work best in children rather than adults. They are second-line treatment of exercise-induced asthma and are usually associated with no side effects.

Methylxanthines, such as theophylline (Theo-dur, Slo-bid) appear to exert a direct relaxing effect on smooth and skeletal muscle and may also reduce mucous tenacity and diminish the inflammatory response to allergens. However, many interactions with other medications and common side effects such as nausea and vomiting can be seen even in therapeutic doses. Arrhythmias and seizures can result from a dose that is too high; therefore, it is necessary to monitor blood levels. Theophylline is taken orally.

Corticosteroids are available in inhaled, oral, and parenteral forms. Inhaled steroids such as triamcinolone (Azmacort) and beclomethasone dipropionate (Beclovent) are now the first-line controller medications

for those individuals with persistent (steps 2 through 4) asthma (see Table 23-1). Steroids exert an anti-inflammatory effect with delayed onset. They also enhance the responsiveness of airways to beta-adrenergic drugs. Side effects of inhaled steroids at low doses are minimal; however, side effects such as fluid retention, ulcers, convulsions, and psychosis may occur with high inhaled doses or any dose of the oral form. Therefore, the patient should avoid prolonged use of oral steroids.

Ipratropium bromide (Atrovent) is an anticholinergic drug that is available only in inhaled form. Anticholinergic drugs work against the parasympathetic nervous system, which causes bronchospasm. However, anticholinergic drugs are not as effective in treating asthma as beta-adrenergic agents.

Leukotriene modifiers are the newest class of asthma medications. They include the leukotriene receptor antag-

Asthma (Continued)

Exercise-induced asthma

Exercise-induced asthma (EIA) is airway narrowing, which reduces airflow and causes coughing, wheezing, chest tightness, shortness of breath, or decreased exercise tolerance (feeling out of shape). A 15% decrease in peak expiratory flow rate or forced expiratory volume at 1 second with exercise is diagnostic. EIA affects individuals with and without asthma, and the cause may be water or heat loss from the airways during expiration from increased mouth breathing and increased respiratory rate. Contributing factors include type of exercise, environmental factors, preexisting inflammation, and intensity of exercise.

Typically, symptoms, which can be intermittent, arise with exercise and are improved, relieved, or prevented by inhaled bronchodilators. Decreases in forced expiratory peak flow or forced expiratory volume at 1 second usually occur within 5 to 10 minutes after exercise onset, but can occur up to 30 minutes later.

Nonpharmacologic treatment methods include optimal control of underlying asthma, avoiding exercise in cold, dry, or polluted air when possible, using a face mask, increasing nose breathing, changing sports or decreasing sport intensity, and exercising in the refractory period. During the refractory period, which lasts from 1 to 4 hours, additional exercise does not cause bronchospasm. Mild exertion that does not cause an episode of EIA may induce a refractory period; in many cases, the athlete can trigger a refractory period.

Pharmacologic treatment includes a short-acting, inhaled beta agonist, which should be used 15 to 30 minutes before exercise and repeated as needed. Two puffs of long-acting beta agonists 30 minutes before exercise may also be helpful. Mast cell stabilizers produce an additive effect with beta agonists.

Banned drug list

Medications permitted for athletes with asthma participating in international competitions include inhaled short-acting beta agonists, inhaled salmeterol, inhaled corticosteroids, theophylline, cromolyn, nedocromil, and antihistamines.

The athletic trainer's role

The athletic trainer may be the first to recognize that an athlete's diminished performance is the result of EIA and requires treatment. The athletic trainer can help to assess the athlete's progress with a peak flow meter and to improve the athlete's control of asthma with proper use of an inhaler. It is important that athletes identified as having asthma be provided with appropriate medications at all sites.

---

onist zafirlukast (Accolate) and the 5-lipoxygenase inhibitor zileuton (Zyflo). Both agents improve lung function and decrease the need for reliever medications. Both are taken orally. These agents work especially well in individuals who experience asthma symptoms when they take aspirin. Because in a small minority of patients the use of zileuton has led to liver failure, liver enzymes need to be monitored in patients who use zileuton.

Step Therapy

Table 23-3 presents a stepwise approach to asthma as recommended by The Expert Panel Report II.[5] The control of asthma is the goal of treatment and includes eliminating or minimizing chronic symptoms, decreasing frequency of exacerbations, decreasing the need for reliever medicines, achieving close to normal PEFR, and eliminating limitations of activities and exercise. If

the desired control is not being achieved, inhaler technique, medication compliance, and environmental control should be reviewed. The athletic trainer can assist the physician greatly in the control of the athlete's asthma by monitoring the athlete's compliance and watching for triggers that seem to exacerbate the asthma symptoms. If control is still not achieved, the physician should consider a step-up in therapy. Treatment should be reviewed every 3 to 6 months. If control is sustained for at least 3 months, a stepwise reduction in treatment may be considered.

Exercise-induced Asthma

Exercise-induced asthma (EIA) is the narrowing of airways leading to decreased airflow, which in turn leads to symptoms such as coughing, wheezing, tightness of the chest, shortness of breath, or decreased exercise tolerance

---

TABLE 23-3

THE STEPWISE TREATMENT OF PATIENTS WITH ASTHMA

Step 1: Intermittent

Controller	Reliever
None needed	➤ Short-acting bronchodilator ➤ Inhaled beta agonist as needed for symptoms (symptoms occur fewer than two times per week at this step) ➤ Intensity of treatment depends on severity of exacerbation ➤ Inhaled beta agonist or cromolyn or both before exercise or exposure to allergen

Step 2: Mild Persistent

Controller	Reliever
Daily medications: ➤ Either inhaled corticosteroid (200 to 500 mcg per day), cromolyn, nedocromil, sustained-release theophylline, or leukotriene modulating agent. Inhaled steroids would be considered first-line treatment for most adolescents and adults. Cromolyn works well for young children ➤ If needed, the dose of inhaled steroids should be increased or a second agent added. A long-acting bronchodilator works especially well for nighttime symptoms	➤ Short-acting bronchodilator ➤ Inhaled beta agonist as needed for symptoms. If use exceeds three to four times per day on a routine basis, asthma conrol should be reassessed

(Continued)

(a feeling of being out of shape). A decrease in peak flow or forced expiration volume in 1 second (FEV1) of 15% with exercise usually indicates a diagnosis of EIA.[6] The FEV1 is measured by formal pulmonary function testing.

EIA occurs in individuals with asthma as well as in those who have never before had an asthma attack. In the general population, 10% to 20% of individuals have EIA, including up to 90% of individuals with asthma and 40%

of individuals with allergic rhinitis (runny nose and sneezing caused by exposure to an allergen). As noted previously, 11% of the athletes screened at the 1984 Summer Olympics had asthma. Among these athletes, 41 were medal winners.

The cause of EIA remains controversial, but the leading theories include water or heat loss from the airways during expiration.[7,8] The loss of heat and water is caused by sev-

TABLE 23-3 (CONTINUED)
THE STEPWISE TREATMENT OF PATIENTS WITH ASTHMA

Step 3: Moderate Persistent

Controller	Reliever
Daily medications ➤ Inhaled steroids 800 to 2000 mcg per day ➤ Adding a long-acting bronchodilator such as inhaled salmeterol (especially for nighttime symptoms) should be considered. Inhaled cromolyn, sustained-release theophylline or one of the leukotriene modulating agents (especially in aspirin-sensitive patients with asthma)	➤ Short-acting bronchodilator ➤ Inhaled beta agonist as needed for symptoms. If use exceeds three to four times per day on a routine basis, asthma control should be reassessed

Step 4: Severe Persistent

Controller	Reliever
Daily medications: ➤ Inhaled steroids 800 to 2,000 mcg per day or more ➤ If necessary, oral steroids beginning with the lowest possible alternate day dosing ➤ Long-acting brochodilator, such as inhaled salmeterol, or sustained-release theophylline to provide additional control and help reduce steroid dose ➤ If asthma control is not achieved with these measures (or to reduce steroid dose): mast cell stabilizers and leukotriene modulators can be considered	➤ Short-acting bronchodilator ➤ Inhaled beta agonist as needed for symptoms. If use exceeds three to four times per day on a routine basis, asthma conrol should be reassessed

(Adapted with permission from *The Expert Panel Report II: Guidelines for the Diagnosis and Management of Asthma*. National Asthma Education and Prevention Program, National Heart Lung and Blood Institute, National Institutes of Health, 1997.)

eral factors. As exercise proceeds, athletes usually increase mouth breathing, bypassing the conditioning role of the nose, which warms and humidifies the inspired air. Also, the increased respiratory rate with exercise leads to a greater volume of air per minute. Both of these factors cause more drying and cooling of the airway. The loss of either heat or water is believed to be followed by local reactions in the lung that trigger EIA.[7,8]

Contributing factors to EIA include the type of exercise, environmental factors, preexisting inflammation, and the intensity of exercise. Running is worse than biking, which is worse than swimming. Cold dry air, polluted air, and allergens may affect athletes who are predisposed to EIA. Inflammation caused by an upper respiratory infection may cause EIA to develop; increased mouth breathing also increases symptoms.

The physician should suspect EIA when typical symptoms arise with exercise and are improved, relieved, or prevented by use of inhaled bronchodilators. Symptoms can be intermittent, depending on the contributing factors present. Diagnosis can be confirmed by measuring airflow at baseline and during exercise. A decrease of 15% or more in peak flow or FEV1 is considered diagnostic. This decrease is usually noted within 5 to 10 minutes after beginning exercise, but it can occur as long as 10 to 30 minutes later.

Symptoms of EIA can be prevented or ameliorated by various nonpharmacologic methods. For those athletes with underlying asthma, optimal control should be obtained. Whenever possible, the athlete should avoid exercising in cold, dry, or polluted air. Wearing a face mask or increasing nose breathing to retain heat and humidity can also help. In addition, athletes may consider changing sports or decreasing the intensity at which they perform in their preferred sport. Also, many individuals with EIA will have a refractory period that can be used to their advantage.

The *refractory period*, which lasts from 1 to 4 hours, is a period in which additional exercise does not cause bronchospasm. The refractory period occurs in some individuals even after mild exertion that does not cause an episode of EIA. Athletes can make use of this prior to participation in their sport by finding a level of exercise that does not cause an EIA episode at the time, but does induce the refractory period. For example, a football player can do ten sets of submaximal windsprints of 30 seconds each, 30 minutes prior to the game. The exact level of exercise needed is different for each athlete, and, unfortunately, the refractory period does not exist for all symptomatic athletes.[9]

First-line pharmacologic prevention and treatment is a short-acting inhaled beta agonist such as albuterol. The athlete should inhale two to four puffs 15 to 30 minutes prior to exercise. This can be repeated during the event as needed. Long-acting beta agonists, such as inhaled salmeterol (two puffs 30 minutes prior to exercise), may also help. Mast cell stabilizers are less effective than beta agonists when used as a single agent; however, an additive effect is noted when beta agonists alone are not sufficient. Two to four puffs of mast cell stabilizers taken after an inhaled beta agonist are inhaled 15 to 30 minutes prior to exercise. Some evidence in the literature indicates that leukotriene modifiers and experimental compounds such as inhaled heparin and furosemide may also decrease symptoms.[10-12] However, more research is needed before these agents can be recommended.

Banned Drug List

The following medications are accepted by the International Olympic Committee for international competition in athletes with asthma: inhaled short-acting beta agonists (albuterol, terbutaline), inhaled salmeterol, inhaled steroids, theophylline, cromolyn, nedocromil, and antihistamines. A complete list and additional information can be provided by the United States Olympic Drug Education Department (800/233-0393) or the NCAA (317/917-6222). In some circumstances, notification of the athlete's national governing body for his or her particular sport is necessary.

Use of asthma medications by athletes who do not have asthma in an attempt to improve their performance has been studied.[13] However, results indicate that there is no improvement in performance when athletes who do not have asthma take asthma medications.[13]

The Athletic Trainer's Role

Many athletes who have EIA are unaware of their condition. Because of their frequent contact with athletes, athletic trainers are often the first to recognize that an athlete's decreased performance may be caused by EIA. Athletic trainers who suspect EIA in an athlete should refer the athlete to a physician for proper treatment. Athletic trainers also can help in the initial diagnosis by measuring peak flows with a peak flow meter prior to and after exercise. This data can greatly help in the diagnosis of EIA. Later, the athletic trainer can help monitor the efficacy of treatment by tracking both symptoms and peak flows. Incorrect use of inhaled medications is a common cause of poor control of asthma. Often, athletic trainers can help athletes improve their control of asthma through education on proper use of inhalers (**Figure 23-2**).

CANCER

An estimated 1,250,000 new cases of cancer were diagnosed in the United States in 1997 alone.[14] That same year, more than 550,000 deaths were caused by cancer.[14] The lifetime risk of death from cancer is second only to the risk of death from heart disease. When a famous athlete is diagnosed with cancer, there is usually an increased focus on cancer detection and prevention among other athletes, which represents a great window of opportunity for athletic trainers, physicians, and others involved in health care to make an impact on athletes' health.

Cancer and Its Signs

Cancer refers to various types of abnormally growing cells that can invade the local tissue, causing local symptoms. Cancer often can metastasize (spread to areas at a distance) through either the bloodstream or the lymphatic system. Cancer occurs when a single cell undergoes one or more mutations of its DNA, giving rise to a cell that is capable of rapid replication and no longer under the body's control. Free radicals, which are uncharged particles with an unpaired electron, carcinogenic compounds, and ionizing radiation can lead to the genetic mutations

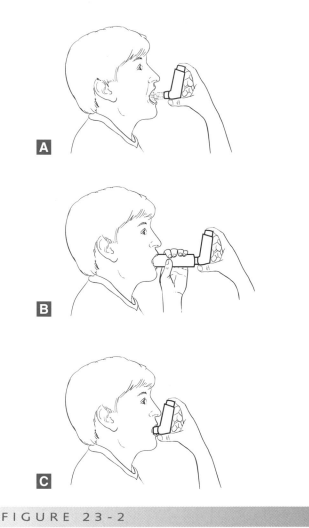

FIGURE 23-2

Proper use of an inhaler is important in the control of asthma. **A** Open mouth with inhaler 1"-2" away. **B** Use spacer (especially recommended in children) **C** Place mouthpiece in the mouth. (Reproduced with permission from the National Asthma Education Program.)

Symptoms that may indicate the presence of cancer include unexplained weight loss, decreased athletic performance, and fatigue. Other general symptoms include unexplained nausea or vomiting, fevers, night sweats, and bruising that occurs easily. **Table 23-4** lists the general symptoms that may indicate cancer. Although all of these symptoms can also be seen in a variety of other conditions, including thyroid disorders, chronic infections, stress, and depression, an athlete with persistent symptoms such as these should be evaluated.

More specific symptoms depend on the type of cancer and its exact location(s). Pain in the location of tissue invasion is common. The pain is generally progressive in nature, becoming more frequent and more severe with time. **Table 23-5** lists the seven warning signs of cancer put forth by the American Cancer Society (ACS).[17]

Most Common Cancer Types

Children

Only 2% of new cases of cancer diagnosed each year in the United States occur in children, but this still amounts to 6,500 new cases of cancer in this age group annually. Cancer is the primary cause of death from disease for individuals younger than age 15 years. Acute leukemia is the most common cancer diagnosis in children younger than age 10 years, representing approximately one third of the total number of cancer diagnoses. Other common tumors in early childhood include brain tumors, lymphoma, and kidney tumors; each type represents approximately 10% of diagnoses. In the teen years, lymphoma becomes the most common cancer, representing approximately 25% of diagnoses, while leukemia becomes somewhat less common, representing approximately 15% of diagnoses. Brain tumors remain common in this age group, and for boys, testicular cancer becomes more important. Both brain tumors and testicular cancer represent approximately 10% of diagnoses.[18]

that cause cancer. There is some evidence that antioxidants such as vitamins A, C, and E can counteract the carcinogenic potential of free radicals.[15,16] Diets rich in these vitamins may help lower the risk of cancer.

Cancer can manifest itself in many different ways, depending on its type, exact site(s), and degree of progression. Many general signs of cancer are also signs of many other conditions, most of which are far less serious. However, a few basic principles about cancer should be remembered.

First, cancer tends to be progressive, and signs and symptoms likewise tend to be progressive. Also, cancer is almost always present for many months or even years before it becomes symptomatic. A delay of several weeks between the onset of symptoms and the diagnosis of cancer is common. This delay is very unlikely to affect the outcome of the disease.

TABLE 23-4
GENERAL SYMPTOMS ASSOCIATED WITH CANCER
Unexplained weight loss
Unexplained fever
Night sweats
Decreased athletic performance
Increasing fatigue
Vomiting or nausea
Easy bruising
Persistently swollen lymph nodes

TABLE 23-5
THE SEVEN WARNING SIGNS OF CANCER

Change in bowel or bladder habits

A sore that doesn't heal

Unusual bleeding or discharge

Thickening or lump in breast or elsewhere

Indigestion or difficulty swallowing

Obvious change in mole or wart

Nagging cough or hoarseness

(Adapted from the American Cancer Society)

Young adults

In the 20- to 45-year-old age group, there are roughly 125,000 new diagnoses of cancer each year. For women, breast cancer is the most common diagnosis, representing nearly 20% of cancer diagnoses in women in this age group. However, breast cancer is mostly seen in women older than age 35 years. Melanomas and lymphomas each account for approximately 10% of cancer diagnoses for both men and women younger than age 45 years. Cervical cancer in women and testicular cancer in men also represent nearly 10% of the cancers in each group.[14]

Older adults

Adults older than age 45 years make up the greatest number of cancer cases by far. In 1997, more than 1,000,000 new cases of cancer were estimated in adults in this age group; however, this estimate excludes basal cell and squamous cell skin cancers, which are easily treated and rarely fatal.[14] In older adults, prostate cancer is the most common cancer in men, and breast cancer is the most common cancer in women. Each of these types of cancer account for more than 20% of cancer diagnoses. Lung cancer is nearly as common, and, because it is more difficult to treat, it is the primary cause of cancer deaths for both men and women. After lung cancer, the next most common cancer for both sexes is colorectal cancer, which represents slightly more than 10% of diagnoses.[14]

Specific Types of Cancer

Leukemia

There are various types of leukemia. Acute lymphocytic leukemia (ALL), the most common cancer in early childhood, is much less common in adults. Other types of leukemia become increasingly common in the older age groups. *Leukemia* is cancer of the white blood cells that arises in the bone marrow. Early symptoms include lethargy, anorexia (loss of appetite), and irritability; however, the cause of leukemia is not known for most patients. As bone marrow failure progresses, patients may become pale from anemia, they may bleed and bruise easily, and they often become feverish. Cure rates for ALL are greater than 70%. Cure rates for the other types of leukemia are much lower, but these types of leukemia often can be controlled for years.[17,18]

Lymphoma

The two main types of *lymphoma* are Hodgkin's disease and non-Hodgkin's lymphoma. Both are cancers of lymphatic tissue and usually first arise in the lymph nodes. Together the lymphomas are the most common neoplasm (cancer) of patients between ages 20 and 40 years. More than half of patients present with painless lymphadenopathy (swollen glands) as the only sign. The lymphadenopathy can be anywhere there are nodes, including the neck, axilla, groin, elbow, and deep in the chest or abdomen. Lymph nodes can also enlarge because of local bacterial infections, mononucleosis, other viruses, and parasites. An individual should be evaluated and a biopsy considered if one or more firm lymph nodes persist longer than 4 to 6 weeks without an obvious explanation. Other manifestations can include fever, night sweats, fatigue, weight loss, pruritis (itching), cough, and a variety of other symptoms caused by local invasion. Hodgkin's disease is 60% to 90% curable, depending on the stage at diagnosis. Non-Hodgkin's lymphoma is more difficult to treat, with cure rates of 30% to 40%.[17,18]

Brain tumors

Primary malignant brain tumors are relatively uncommon and make up only 2% of all cancers.[17] However, when nonmalignant brain tumors and metastases from other sites are included, the numbers increase dramatically. Because of the confined space inside the skull and the sensitivity of the tissue, even nonmalignant tumors are life threatening. Overall, 90,000 individuals die each year from brain and spinal tumors, although approximately 75% of those tumors are metastatic from other primary sources.[17] General symptoms include headache, seizures, vomiting that occurs with or without nausea, hiccups, personality changes, and slowed mentation (difficulty processing information or retrieving memory). Focal neurologic deficits can also be seen, including vision changes, weakness or paralysis, hearing loss, and other sensory changes. Prognosis is variable and depends on the type of tumor and its location in the central nervous system.[17,18]

Testicular cancer

Testicular cancer is relatively uncommon; however, it is among the most common tumors in men between the ages of 15 and 34 years. It is rare after age 40 years. Testic-

FOCUS ON . . .

Cancer

Cancer and its signs

Cancer describes various types of abnormally growing cells that can invade local tissue and often metastasize through the blood or lymphatic systems. A single cell undergoes DNA mutations, producing a rapidly replicating cell that is no longer under the body's control. Free radicals, carcinogens, and ionizing radiation can cause the genetic mutations. Antioxidants (vitamins A, C, and E) may counteract free radicals and lower the risk of cancer. The cancer itself, along with the signs and symptoms of the disease, tends to progress. Usually the cancer has existed for months to years before symptoms appear. Therefore, a delay of several weeks between onset of symptoms and diagnosis is unlikely to affect the outcome.

Possible symptoms of cancer include unexplained weight loss, nausea or vomiting; decreased athletic performance; fatigue; fevers; night sweats; easy bruising; and persistently swollen lymph nodes. The American Cancer Society lists warning signals as a change in bladder or bowel habits; a sore that fails to heal; unusual bleeding or discharge; thickening or lump in the breast or elsewhere; indigestion or difficulty swallowing; obvious change in a mole or wart; and nagging cough or hoarseness. An athlete with any of these symptoms should be evaluated. The pain of cancer is progressive, becoming more frequent and more severe with time.

Most common cancer types

Cancer is the primary cause of death from disease in children younger than age 15 years. Common types are acute leukemia (the most common cancer diagnosis in children younger than age 10 years and one third of all cancers diagnosed in children), brain tumors, lymphoma, and kidney tumors. Lymphoma becomes more common in teenagers, and leukemias become less common. Brain tumors remain common, and testicular cancer becomes more comon.

Breast cancer is the most common diagnosis in women in the 20- to 45-year-old age group, although it occurs most often in women older than age 35 years. Melanoma and lymphomas account for 10% of cancers in men and women, and cervical and testicular cancers account for approximately 10% each.

Most new cases of cancer develop in adults older than age 45 years. Prostate cancer is the most common type in men, and breast cancer is the most common type in women. Lung cancer occurs almost as frequently and is the primary cause of cancer deaths. Colon cancer is the next most common cancer in both men and women.

---

ular cancer is relatively easy to detect because the testes are easily palpated within the scrotum. If caught at an early stage, testicular cancer is almost 100% curable. The first sign is usually a nontender lump on the testicle. As the tumor progresses, pain can be noted, and if there is spreading to the local lymph nodes, back or abdominal pain may be present. General symptoms can also be seen[17](see Table 23-4). Testicular self-examination should be encouraged for men and boys between ages 15 and 40 years **(Figure 23-3)**. Any abnormal lump, nodule, or swelling found during the self examination that is part of the testicle should be seen by a physician. Testicular cancer can also cause pain that radiates through the adductor muscle group, which mimics an adductor strain.

Cervical cancer

Invasive cervical cancer is declining in frequency as more women regularly undergo Pap smears, which is a scraping of cells from the cervix that is examined under a microscope. Overall, cancer of the cervix accounts for 3% of cancers in women.[14] The peak incidence of cervical cancer occurs in the 35- to 44-year-old age group; however, it

is fairly common in women between the ages of 20 and 85 years. The most common symptom is vaginal bleeding or discharge. Cervical cancer is usually caused by the human papilloma virus (HPV), which is sexually transmitted. HPV is also associated with genital warts. Therefore, every sexually active woman and all women older than age 21 years should have a regular Pap smear. Pap smears can detect lesions in the cervix before they develop into invasive cancer. When high-grade dysplasia (cells at risk for turning into cancer) or carcinoma in situ (cancer that has not yet invaded into the local tissue) is discovered on Pap testing, a minor procedure can be performed to obliterate the premalignant or malignant cells, preventing invasive cancer. The ACS recommends Pap smears be obtained every 3 years after two negative Pap smears in consecutive years. Cervical cancer is very rare in women who have been regularly screened in this way.[17]

Melanoma

Malignant *melanoma* was diagnosed in an estimated 40,000 individuals in the United States in 1997.[14] Roughly 20% of those who contract melanoma will die from this

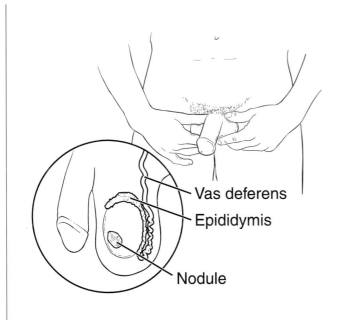

FIGURE 23-3

Men and boys between the ages of 15 and 40 years should examine themselves for any abnormalities in the testicles. (Reproduced with permission from the American Cancer Society.)

disease.[14] The incidence of this cancer is increasing dramatically, doubling in incidence every 15 years since 1915. Melanoma usually arises from a previously normal mole. The average person has 20 moles on the body, so the challenge for athletes and their physicians is to determine which moles are at risk to become cancerous. **Table 23-6** describes the warning signs for melanoma.[19] Individuals at greatest risk have fair skin that burns easily, a family history of melanoma, and more than 50 moles or any atypical moles. A history of frequent or severe sunburns, especially as a child, is another risk factor. Individuals at high risk should be examined yearly by a physician familiar with screening for melanoma.

The risk of melanoma can be reduced by avoiding sun exposure, especially at the peak intensity hours between 10 am and 3 pm. When out in the sun, the athlete should wear protective clothing such as a brimmed hat and a long-sleeved shirt whenever possible. Using sunscreen with a sun protection factor of 15 (SPF15) or greater will reduce the amount of ultraviolet exposure and decrease the risk of sunburn. Although use of sunscreens has not yet been proven to reduce the incidence of melanoma, nearly all dermatologists and the ACS recommend its use. Because sunburns that occur in childhood increase the risk of melanoma more than sunburns that occur during adulthood, it is especially important for children to be adequately protected from the harmful effects of the sun.

Lung cancer

Nearly 200,000 individuals in the United States contracted lung cancer in 1997.[14] Most of these individuals died within a year of their diagnosis, making it the primary cause of death from cancer. The high rate of lung cancer is attributed almost entirely to smoking. The risk of lung cancer increases 13-fold in active smokers when compared with lifelong nonsmokers.[17] The risk of contracting lung cancer is dose-related. A person who has smoked two packs of cigarettes a day for 20 years has a risk 60 to 70 times that of a nonsmoker. Quitting smoking dramatically lowers the risk of cancer, although the risk level never returns to that of a lifelong nonsmoker. Secondhand smoke is also a risk factor, but it raises the risk only to about 1.5 times the risk of those individuals without significant secondhand exposure.[17] Potential symptoms of lung cancer include persistent cough, pain, wheezing or stridor (noisy breath sounds), and shortness of breath, all of which can result from local invasion. General symptoms such as weight loss and fever are also common. Frequently, regional or distant metastases are already present at the time of diagnosis. Bone pain, difficulty swallowing resulting from esophageal compression, and hoarseness resulting from paralysis of the nerve supplying the vocal cords are symptoms related to metastases. Screening for lung cancer until recently had proven to be ineffective at reducing mortality and is not currently recommended. However, an experimental technique using a special type of computed tomography scan has been shown to be able to detect lung cancer prior to its spread, which can allow the cancer to be cured at a much greater rate. This should be available for widespread use in the near future.[20]

Oral cancer

Although not nearly as common as lung cancer, oral cancer is equally preventable. Excessive alcohol use and the use of tobacco products, including chewing tobacco, are the greatest risk factors. Lip cancer is primarily caused by sun exposure, but pipe smoking also is a risk factor. Oral cancer represents approximately 3% of all cancers, or 30,000 new cases a year in the United States.[14]

Cancers of the mouth can present in various forms, from white or red patches to nonhealing lesions. The tongue is the most common site of oral cancer. White patches known as leukoplakia, or "snuff-dipper's lesions," tend to develop in areas of the oral mucosa that come in contact with tobacco. These precancerous lesions can be found after short or long periods of use. Oral cancer and leukoplakia should be discovered during routine dental exams.

Breast cancer

The lifetime risk of breast cancer for women is greater than 10%.[14] Because breast cancer is among the slowest growing cancers and in many cases responds well to treatment, the 10-year survival rate surpasses 60%.[14] The risk of dying from breast cancer has clearly been shown to be

TABLE 23-6
SIX SIGNS OF MALIGNANT MELANOMA

Asymmetry in shape (one half is unlike the other half)

Border is irregular (edges are irregularly scalloped)

Color is mottled (multiple colors; shades of brown, black, gray, red, and white)

Diameter is usually large (larger than the tip of a pencil eraser; 6mm)

Elevation is almost always present (can be assessed by side-lighting the lesion)

Enlargement (a history of an increase of the size is one of the most important sign

(Adapted with permission from Fitzpatrick TB, et al: *Color Atlas and Synopsis of Clinical Dermatology*, ed 3. New York, NY, McGraw-Hill, 1997, pp 180-207,970-982.)

20% to 30% less for women older than age 50 years who undergo routine screening with mammography.[21] The evidence is less striking for women between ages 40 and 50 years, and there is no evidence of benefit from mammography for women younger than age 40 years who are at normal risk. The ACS recommends a breast exam by a healthcare professional and mammography annually beginning at age 40 years. In addition, the ACS recommends monthly breast self-examination (**Figure 23-4**).

Risk factors include a family history of breast cancer, early onset of menses, late onset of menopause, never having had a baby, and late age (older than age 30 years) of a first delivery. Many women worry that the use of birth control pills or estrogen replacement at menopause can be a risk factor. Recent meta-analysis shows no added risk for use of estrogen replacement for 5 to 10 years after menopause.[17] However, there does seem to be an increased risk of breast cancer in women who take estrogen replacements for prolonged periods (greater than 10 years) after menopause. Estrogen replacement therapy probably reduces the risk of death from cardiovascular causes although several recent studies have cast doubt on this long-held assumption.[22,23] Estrogen does prevent some other cancers and prevents osteoporosis. The decision to recommend the use of hormone replacement therapy should be made on an individualized basis after considering the patient's unique characteristics.[17]

The usual presenting sign of breast cancer is a suspicious mass that is often discovered by the patient. Increasingly, the cancer is discovered on routine mammography. Patients in whom breast cancer was discovered on routine mammography have a 10-year survival rate of 95%.[17] Other presenting signs include pain without a palpable mass, recent inversion of the nipple, and abnormal breast discharge. Although breast discharge is rarely caused by cancer, a physician should be consulted if it occurs.

Prostate cancer

Cancer of the prostate is the most common cancer in men. The disease is rare in men younger than age 50 years and becomes increasingly more common as age increases. More than 200,000 men contracted prostate cancer in 1997, but fewer than 50,000 died from the disease.[14] The lifetime risk of death from prostate cancer is 3.4%.[14] A large percentage of older men who die of other causes are found on autopsy to have prostate cancer.

Available screening methods can detect prostate cancer before symptoms appear; however, there is no evidence to date that these tests improve the survival rate for patients with prostate cancer. In fact, there is considerable morbidity associated with treatment, including risk of impotence and incontinence. Therefore, detection of prostate cancer in an asymptomatic stage may increase morbidity from complications or side effects of treatment without helping mortality (the risk of dying) for the general population. In spite of these facts, the ACS recommends annual digital rectal examination (DRE) after age 40 years and an annual blood test to detect prostate cancer (PSA test) after age 50 years. However, the U.S. Preventive Services Task Force disagrees and specifically recommends that neither DRE nor PSA testing be used because of the lack of evidence of benefit and the potential for harm.[21] Large studies are currently being undertaken to further evaluate the risks and benefits of screening for prostate cancer; however, these studies will not be completed until after the year 2004.

Typical presenting symptoms of prostate cancer include dysuria (unpleasant sensation with urination), difficulty voiding, increased frequency of urination, urine retention from a complete blockage of the urethra, back or hip pain, and blood in the urine. Although bladder infection and other benign conditions are often the cause of these symptoms, men who have these symptoms should be evaluated by a physician.

Colon cancer

Colon cancer is the second most common type of cancer for both men and women and is second only to lung cancer as a cause of death from cancer. Colon cancer is generally found in individuals older than age 50 years. Risk factors include a high-fat, low-fiber diet, inflammatory bowel disease, and family history of colon cancer.[17] Regular exercise has been found to lower the risk of this cancer.[24]

Screening for colon cancer is effective at reducing mortality from this disease. The ACS recommends an annual

digital rectal examination after age 40 years, annual fecal occult blood screening after age 50 years, and a sigmoidoscopy every 3 to 5 years beginning at age 50 years.

Signs of colon cancer vary, depending on the location of the cancer. Often, the presenting symptoms of pallor and fatigue are caused by anemia from occult blood loss. Any unexplained iron deficiency anemia in an adult should be referred for evaluation. Abdominal pain and constipation are also frequent manifestations of this disease. Blood mixed in with the stool or covering the stool may also be a presenting complaint.

Cancer Prevention

The most important step in reducing the risk of cancer is to not use tobacco products such as cigarettes, cigars, pipes, chewing tobacco, and tobacco snuff. Individuals who use these products should stop using them. Not using or discontinuing use of tobacco products has many other health benefits as well, including a dramatic reduction in the risk of heart attack, stroke, and lung disease.[21] Nicotine medications such as gum and patches are effective treatments for tobacco dependence, alleviating the symptoms of withdrawal from tobacco and increasing the rate of sustained abstinence.[25] Recently, nicotine medication in the form of a nasal spray and oral medication have become available. For example, the oral medication, Wellbutrin, is taken for 3 to 6 months and is used alone or in combination with nicotine preparations to aid in smoking cessation.

Regular exercise and a healthy diet are also important for general health, and both help to reduce the overall risk of getting cancer. A low-fat (less than 30% of calories from fat) and high-fiber diet helps to reduce the risk of death from both heart disease and colon cancer. A diet that includes fruits, vegetables, and grains high in fiber should be emphasized.[21] Regular moderate exercise for 30 minutes or more on most days of the week clearly lowers all causes of mortality.[21] The bulk of the evidence also suggests this amount of exercise lowers the overall risk of getting cancer.[24]

Moderation of alcohol use is also recommended. Consumption of 1 or 2 drinks per day is associated with cardiovascular health benefits and probably has few adverse effects. One drink is considered to be 5 oz of wine, 12 oz of beer, or 1.5 oz of distilled spirits. Heavier alcohol use is associated with many health problems including heart failure, oral cancer, esophageal cancer, and fatal liver diseases, including liver cancer.

Avoiding sun exposure whenever possible, especially between 10 am and 3 pm, reduces the risk of melanoma. Children and those individuals with risk factors for contracting melanoma (as discussed in the section on melanoma) benefit most from these recommendations. Use of sunscreen has not been proven yet to reduce the

risk of melanoma; however, the ACS and most dermatologists recommend its use when sun exposure cannot be avoided, especially by individuals who are at higher risk.

Avoiding unprotected sex with multiple partners prevents many sexually transmitted diseases, including HIV. It also reduces the risk of cervical cancer. Women who become sexually active at a young age and those with a high lifetime number of partners are at greater risk for cervical cancer. Use of barrier contraceptives such as condoms and diaphragms, combined with the use of spermicides, is associated with a decreased risk of invasive cervical cancer. In addition to preventing pregnancy by killing sperm, spermicides also help to kill HIV and HPV and prevent their transmission.[21] Condoms are better than diaphragms at preventing the spread of HIV and many other sexually transmitted diseases. Whichever method is used, spermicides should also be used.

Screening has been proven to be effective at reducing mortality from a few types of cancer.[21] Women should undergo Pap smears every 1 to 3 years, beginning with onset of sexual activity if it occurs before age 21 years, or at age 21 years without sexual activity. Annual mammography and clinical breast examination are recommended for women at normal risk beginning at age 40 years. Fecal occult blood testing or routine sigmoidoscopy is recommended for individuals at normal risk after age 50 years. Some other screening routines, such as an annual digital rectal exam after age 40 years, routine total-body skin examination to screen for melanoma in all age groups, monthly breast self-examination for women, and monthly testicular self-examination for men, have not yet been proven to reduce mortality; however, their use is supported by the ACS and other organizations.[21] **Table 23-7** summarizes recommendations for cancer screening by age group.

Athletic trainers can make a big difference in the long-term health of athletes by encouraging healthy habits and serving as role models. The athletic trainer is often the first person the athlete will go to when a problem arises. Knowledge of the signs and symptoms of cancer, the ability to differentiate symptoms, and knowledge of the referral and treatment process are all required skills for athletic trainers. The NCAA bylaws state "The use of tobacco products is prohibited by all game personnel (eg, coaches, athletic trainers, managers and game officials) in all sports during practice and competition."[26] Whether recommending sun protection to the school-age soccer player or encouraging the elite Olympic athlete to avoid tobacco products, athletic trainers have ample opportunity to educate athletes. Athletic trainers and athletes have access to many resources and materials, such as posters, and toll-free hotlines, such as the National Cancer Institute Cancer Information Service (800/422-6237) and the American Cancer Society (800/227-2345). When a high-

TABLE 23-7

RECOMMENDATIONS FOR CANCER SCREENING BY AGE GROUP

Screening type	Birth to 14 years	15 to 40 years	40 to 50 years	50 years and older
General screening	[----------------------------------Periodic health screen-----------------------------]			
Testicular self-exam	[Monthly from adolescence to age 40 years]			
Pap smear	[Every 1-3 years beginning with onset of sexual activity or at age 21]			
Total-body skin exam	[Annually for high-risk individuals]			
Breast self-exam	[Monthly beginning at age 21 years-----------------------]			
Clinical breast exam	[Annually beginning at age 40 years---]			
Mammography	[Annually beginning at age 40 years---]			
	[Annually after age 50 years----]			
Digital rectal exam (controversial)	[Annually beginning at age 40 years---]			
PSA blood test (controversial)	[Annually beginning at age 50 years--]			
One or both of the following tests:				
Fecal occult blood test	[Annually beginning at age 50 years--]			
Sigmoidoscopy	[Every 3 to 5 years beginning at age 50 years]			

profile athlete is diagnosed with cancer, the athletic trainer should take the opportunity to discuss with athletes the warning signs, screening recommendations, and methods of cancer prevention.

Special Considerations in the Athlete

The recent diagnoses of some elite athletes with cancer has raised awareness of these diseases not only for athletes but for those who care for them. Mario Lemieux of the National Hockey League was in the news when he was diagnosed with non-Hodgkins lymphoma. Both Lance Armstrong, a professional cyclist, and Scott Hamilton, an Olympic gold medalist figure skater, made public their diagnoses of testicular cancer, as have many other athletes in recent years.

The cure rate of cancer depends on the stage or extent of the disease, as well as the specific site or sites involved. Treatment can consist of surgery, radiation therapy, chemotherapy, bone marrow transplants, or a combination of these. The diverse symptoms that can accompany cancer, such as fatigue, shortness of breath, and pain, usually limit the athlete from participation in strenuous activity. Some prescribed treatments can also cause myriad side effects that affect an athlete's ability to exercise. Side effects may include a lengthy recovery from a surgical procedure, nausea and vomiting, or dangerously low blood counts with increased susceptibility to infections and bleeding. Even medications that help control nausea and vomiting can have side effects such as headaches and dizziness. If the athlete survives the cancer, long-term consequences can include an amputed extremity from bone cancer, infertility as a result of chemotherapy, or reduced lung capacity from radiation therapy. Second malignancies, especially of the blood cells (leukemia), may also occur, caused by the chemotherapy itself.

The athletic trainer must communicate effectively with the athlete and his or her team of healthcare providers when monitoring the athlete's activity level and potential return to competition. The athletic trainer needs to be aware of any potential dangers of training and restrictions based on the athlete's disease and current physical status. For example, cancers such as lymphomas can enlarge the spleen and disrupt its normal tissue architecture, and chemotherapy drugs such as interleukin-2 can cause enlargement of more than 50% of the spleen's normal size.[27] Rupture of the spleen has occurred even with non-contact activity such as weightlifting and sit-ups. If the spleen remains enlarged when the athlete returns to a contact activity, use of special protective padding may be indicated. The use of modalities such as therapeutic ultrasound and even heat packs may be contraindicated in athletes with certain cancers. Ultrasound irradiation of malignant tissue may increase cellular detachment and the possibility of metastasis of the cancer to other sites.[28] A surgical incision may sever local sensory nerves or impair circulation; thus, caution must be used when heat packs are applied after surgery to avoid excessive temperature elevation of the skin.

DIABETES MELLITUS

According to the report released in 1997 by The Expert Committee on the Diagnosis and Classification of Diabetes Mellitus, "Diabetes is a group of metabolic disorders characterized by hyperglycemia resulting from defects in insulin secretion, insulin action or both. The chronic hyperglycemia of diabetes is associated with long term damage, dysfunction, and failure of various organs, especially the eyes, kidneys, nerves, heart and blood vessels."[29]

Classification of Diabetes Mellitus

In 1997, the Expert Committee changed the criteria for the diagnosis and classification of diabetes. *Diabetes* is defined by two fasting plasma glucose levels greater than 126 mg/dL or two plasma glucose levels greater than 200 mg/dL on random draws or 2 hours after ingestion of a 75 g glucose solution. Normal plasma glucose is 80 to 120 mg/dL.

Diabetes is then classified into four main categories: type 1, type 2, other specific types caused by known factors such as genetic defects or pancreatic disease, and gestational diabetes (diabetes associated with pregnancy). Discussion in this chapter will be limited to types 1 and 2 and gestational diabetes.

Type 1 diabetes

Type 1 diabetes, formerly known as juvenile onset diabetes or insulin-dependent diabetes, results from destruction of the pancreatic islet beta cells. Insulin is made in these cells, and their destruction results in a lack of insulin secretion. Type 1 diabetes most commonly occurs in individuals younger than age 30 years, and onset is usually quite sudden. Insulin injection is the only way to control the hyperglycemia in this disorder. If type 1 diabetes is not well controlled, diabetic *ketoacidosis*, an accumulation of certain acids in the body as a result of unavailable insulin, often results. (Ketoacidosis is discussed in depth later in this chapter.)

Type 2 diabetes

Type 2 diabetes, formerly known as adult onset or noninsulin-dependent diabetes, is caused by insulin resistance that is often accompanied by a relative lack of insulin secretion. Type 2 diabetes most commonly occurs in obese individuals older than age 40 years. Type 2 diabetes can often be controlled with diet, exercise, and weight loss or with oral medications. However, insulin is used for treatment in many individuals with type 2 diabetes. Type 2 diabetes is generally not associated with ketoacidosis.

Gestational diabetes

Gestational diabetes (GDM) is defined as diabetes that is first detected during pregnancy. When GDM occurs, it is usually detected by the fifth or sixth month. For most pregnant women, GDM will resolve once the pregnancy is completed. However, 50% of women with gestational diabetes will test positive for type 2 diabetes within 22 to 28 years.[30] As with type 2 diabetes, GDM is primarily a result of insulin resistance. For the health of the unborn baby, the mother's glucose must be kept under control. The mainstay of treatment is nutritional counseling and dietary modification. If glucose cannot be adequately controlled with diet changes, then insulin therapy is indicated. Women with GDM should be encouraged to exercise to help improve control of blood glucose. However, to avoid complications, the exercise program should be guided by a healthcare professional who is knowledgeable about GDM.

Carbohydrate Metabolism

Secretion of insulin promotes storage of glucose in the muscles and liver in the form of glycogen. When carbohydrates are consumed, they are changed into glucose, then absorbed by the small intestine into the bloodstream. As the blood glucose level rises, the pancreas secretes more insulin. As the glucose level drops, the pancreas secretes less insulin. Diabetes is caused by a relative lack of insulin secretion by the pancreas or by insulin resistance at the target organs, primarily by the muscles and liver, where glucose is stored.

Other hormones such as epinephrine, glucagon, growth hormone, and cortisol raise the blood glucose level. Through feedback mechanisms, the body uses these various hormones to keep plasma glucose levels between 70 and 120 mg/dL (**Figure 23-5**).

Hyperglycemia and symptoms of diabetes

In patients with diabetes, lack of insulin secretion or insulin resistance causes *hyperglycemia*, a condition in which blood sugar rises above normal levels. Hyperglycemia leads to excretion of glucose in the urine, which draws with it large amounts of water. This excessive urine is called polyuria and results in excessive thirst known as polydipsia. Polyuria and polydipsia are two of the hallmark symptoms of diabetes. Often, frequent urination causes nocturia, or excessive urination during the night. Unexplained weight loss caused by the inability of the body to store the energy derived from eating carbohydrates is another common symptom noted at the onset of diabetes. Other symptoms include lethargy and blurred vision.

Treatment

Type 1 diabetes is treated with insulin. The Diabetes Control and Complications Trial (DCCT), a randomized study to determine the effects of various levels of glucose control on morbidity and mortality, demonstrated that tight glucose control that is achieved with intensive therapy in patients with type 1 diabetes leads to marked decreases in the risk of the complications of diabetes by up to 76%.[31] Intensive therapy reduces the risk of damage to the eyes (retinopathy), nerves (neuropathy), and kidneys (nephropathy). Intensive therapy necessitates self-monitoring of blood glucose four times daily and use of an insulin pump or at least three insulin injections per day. Frequent adjustments in insulin doses based on glucose level, as well as anticipated dietary intake and exercise, are also required.[31]

Type 2 diabetes can often be controlled with diet and exercise. If these measures do not work, many treatment options, including oral medications, now exist for type 2 diabetes. **Table 23-8** presents a list of various oral medicines that are available and their side effects. If blood glucose is not controlled by these oral medications, injected insulin is usually used. Insulin can cause hypoglycemia (low blood sugar). One class of oral medications, sulfonylureas, can also cause hypoglycemia. Although none of the other oral medicines cause hypoglycemia when used as single agents, they can increase the chance of hypoglycemia when given with insulin or sulfonylureas.

The ultimate goal for patients with either type 1 or type 2 diabetes is normalization of the blood sugar, which can be monitored several times daily using a portable blood glucose monitor. The patient or the athletic trainer can operate the monitor. In addition, long-term control should be assessed periodically by a laboratory test called the hemoglobin A1C, which is a measure of the number of glucose molecules that are attached to the red blood cells. An abnormally high value implies poor control of blood glucose. **Table 23-9** lists normal values, goals of treatment, and values that are sufficiently abnormal to require action.[32]

Benefits of Exercise

Exercise has many positive effects. It increases insulin sensitivity and lowers blood pressure, weight, and lipid levels, therefore reducing the risk of coronary artery disease. It also is generally associated with an improved sense of well being. In patients with type 2 diabetes, but not type 1 diabetes, exercise also improves glycemic (blood sugar) control. Type 2 diabetes can often be controlled without medications, by using only diet changes, exercise, and weight loss. Exercise should be one of the primary modes of treatment. In type 1 diabetes, insulin is the primary means of glycemic control, and exercise does little to improve it. In fact, exercise can worsen glycemic control.

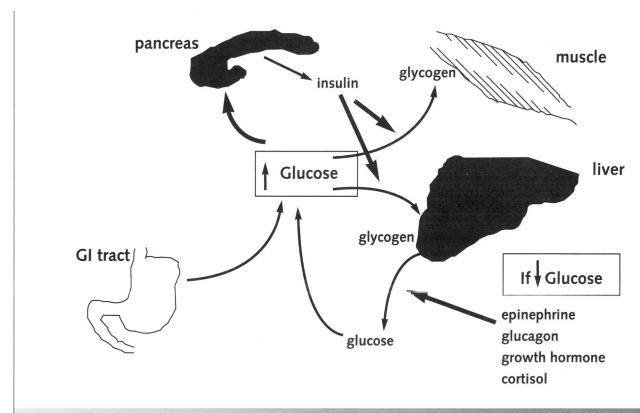

FIGURE 23-5

Feedback mechanisms allow the body to use hormones to keep plasma glucose at a proper level.

FOCUS ON . . .

Diabetes

Classification of diabetes mellitus

Diabetes is classified as type 1, type 2, other types caused by known factors such as genetic defects or pancreatic disease, and gestational diabetes. Type 1 diabetes, formerly known as juvenile onset or insulin-dependent diabetes, results from the destruction of the insulin-secreting pancreatic islet beta cells. The onset of type 1 diabetes is usually sudden and occurs before age 30 years. Treatment is insulin injections for the hyperglycemia. Ketoacidosis can occur if type 1 diabetes is not well controlled. Type 2 diabetes, formerly known as adult onset or noninsulin-dependent diabetes, is caused by insulin resistance, often with relative lack of insulin secretion. Obese individuals older than age 40 years are most at risk for type 2 diabetes, which is often controllable with diet, exercise, and weight loss or with oral medications. Insulin is needed by some individuals. Ketoacidosis is not usually a problem for individuals with type 2 diabetes. Gestational diabetes is first detected during pregnancy, usually by the fifth or sixth month. Most often, the disease will resolve at the completion of the pregnancy, but diabetes develops in 50% of patients later in life. The cause is insulin resistance, which must be treated for the health of the unborn baby. Treatment includes nutritional counseling, exercise, and dietary modification, with insulin necessary for some women.

Carbohydrate metabolism

Diabetes is caused either by a relative lack of pancreatic insulin secretion or by target-organ insulin resistance, primarily by the muscles and liver, where glucose is stored. Insulin promotes glucose storage in the form of glycogen. Ingested carbohydrates are changed into glucose, then absorbed by the small intestine into the bloodstream. As the blood glucose level rises, the pancreas secretes more insulin; as the glucose level drops, less insulin is secreted. Hormones such as epinephrine, glucagon, growth hormone, and cortisol raise blood glucose via a feedback mechanism to keep levels in the normal range.

Hyperglycemia describes blood sugar that is higher than normal, which leads to urinary excretion of glucose with large amounts of water. This excessive urine output and the resultant excessive thirst are classic symptoms of diabetes. Other symptoms include unexplained weight loss, lethargy, and blurred vision.

Treatment

Type I diabetes is treated with insulin. Tight glucose control in patients with type 1 diabetes markedly reduces the risk of complications by 76%. Risks include retinopathy, neuropathy, and nephropathy. Tight glucose control requires blood glucose self-monitoring four times daily and the use of an insulin pump or three or more insulin injections daily. The glucose level dictates frequent adjustments in insulin doses, dietary intake, and exercise.

Type 2 diabetes is often controllable with diet and exercise. If these measures are insufficient, oral medications, such as sulfonylureas, biguanides, thiazolidinediones, and alpha-glucosidase inhibitors, can be added. If the oral medications are not effective, insulin injections are needed. Of the medications, only sulfonylureas and insulin alone can cause hypoglycemia; however, when these drugs are used in combination with other oral medicines, the risk of hypoglycemia is increased.

The goal for patients with either type 1 or 2 diabetes is blood glucose normalization. Levels are checked several times daily using portable blood glucose monitors. Long-term control is assessed with the hemoglobin A1C test, which measures the number of glucose molecules attached to red blood cells. A high value indicates poor blood glucose control.

Benefits of exercise

The athlete with diabetes benefits from exercise in many ways, including increased insulin sensitivity; decreased blood pressure, weight, and lipid levels, which reduce the risk of coronary artery disease; and an improved sense of well being. Patients with type 2 diabetes demonstrate improved glucose control with exercise, and, therefore, exercise is a primary mode of treatment along with diet changes and weight loss. However, patients with type 1 diabetes may find that exercise worsens blood glucose control, and they must take care to prevent both hypoglycemia and hyperglycemia.

(Continued)

FOCUS ON . . .

Diabetes (Continued)

Risks of exercise

For most patients with diabetes, the benefits of exercise outweigh the risks, but a preparticipation physical examination is mandatory. The risks of exercise include hyperglycemia, hypoglycemia, cardiac ischemia, and worsening of diabetes complications. The athlete with diabetes can avoid many of these potential problems with proper screening, education, and monitoring. The athletic trainer must be familiar with the athlete's treatment regimen and any previous complications.

Insulin and dietary adjustments can help the athlete with diabetes in good control to avoid hypoglycemia as a result of exercise. Hyperglycemia as a result of exercise can be seen in athletes with poorly controlled diabetes because of stress hormone release, which can lead to ketoacidosis and diabetic coma. These patients should check the blood glucose level before exercise. If the glucose is greater than 250 mg/dL, the urine should be checked for ketones. The presence of ketones or a glucose level greater than 300 mg/dL requires that exercise be cancelled for the day.

To avoid complications, weight gain or loss in an athlete with diabetes must be undertaken carefully, under the direction of a nutritionist. Cardiac ischemia is another risk of exercise. An exercise stress test is recommended for individuals with symptoms suggestive of heart-related pain, those who have had type 1 diabetes for more than 15 years, all those with type 1 diabetes who are older than age 30 years, and all those with type 2 diabetes who are older than age 35 years. Other risks are worsening of diabetes complications, such as retinopathy, nephropathy, and neuropathy. Proper screening for complications and instruction for appropriate exercise by a qualified physician can minimize these risks.

Hypoglycemia

Hypoglycemia is among the greatest risks of exercise but is generally only a problem for individuals taking insulin or sulfonylureas. When the exercise level is significantly increased, either caloric intake must be increased or the dose of medication decreased to avoid hypoglycemia and hypoglycemic shock. Hypoglycemic symptoms vary; they can include irritability, trembling, hunger, sweating, and apprehension. Shock, confusion, convulsions, and coma indicate severe hypoglycemia, which can be life threatening. To prevent hypoglycemia, athletes with diabetes should be closely monitored, especially with any changes in training. Training should be increased slowly with frequent adjustments in diet or insulin, or both, as recommended by the physician, to counteract lowered blood glucose.

Athletes who inject insulin must avoid injecting into an extremity that will be exercised within 60 to 90 minutes. Exercise increases insulin absorption and can lead to hypoglycemia. An alternate site, such as the abdomen, should be used if insulin is to be injected within 60 to 90 minutes of exercise. If the blood glucose level before exercise is less than 100 mg/dL, the athlete should eat a carbohydrate snack, supplemented by 15 g of carbohydrates every 20 minutes during exercise. Consuming 250 to 350 g of carbohydrate 3 to 6 hours before exercise and 15 g 20 minutes before exercise will improve performance. The athlete with diabetes will need to adjust consumption based on blood glucose level.

The athlete who displays symptoms of hypoglycemia should stop exercise and ingest sugar cubes, orange juice, candy, fruit, or glucose tablets or gels. However, if the athlete is unable to swallow, sugar should not be forced into the mouth. The athlete should be transported immediately to the emergency department for intravenous glucose. If injectable glucagon is available, it can be given even to the unconscious athlete.

Ketoacidosis

Ketoacidosis occurs when, in the absence of insulin (and thus, the inability to metabolize glucose), the body derives energy from burning fat stores. Acidic ketone bodies are the end products of fat metabolism and cause a drop in pH. Ketoacidosis and dehydration often lead to deep sighing respirations (Kussmaul breathing), fruity breath, lethargy, confusion, and somnolence. Type 1 diabetes can present as ketoacidosis, which usually develops over several days and represents out-of-control diabetes. Severe infections, dietary indiscretions, and failure to take insulin can precipitate ketoacidosis. Because the symptoms of ketoacidosis and hypoglycemia are similar, all stuporous or lethargic athletes with diabetes should be given glucose. If the athlete is actually suffering from hyperglycemia, the small amount of sugar will not result in additional harm. The athlete who fails to recover rapidly should be transported to the emergency department.

TABLE 23-8

MEDICATIONS USED IN THE TREATMENT OF TYPE 2 DIABETES

Category	Generic names	Mode of action	Common side effects
Sulfonylureas	Tolbutamide Glyburide Glipizide	Stimulates insulin release from pancreas, decreases rate of insulin breakdown	Hypoglycemia, nausea, and vomiting, alcohol-induced flush, hyponatremia (low blood sodium) (Combined 4% incidence)
Biguanides	Metformin	Increases insulin action in the peripheral tissues and reduces hepatic glucose output	Diarrhea, abdominal discomfort, metallic taste, anorexia (Combined 20% incidence) Lactic acidosis (serious but rare)
Thiazolidinediones	Troglitazone	Decreases insulin resistance in liver, muscles, and and adipose tissue	Generally well tolerated. Rare case of liver disease and very rare liver failure have been seen
Alpha-glucosidase Inhibitors	Acarbose	Reduces intestinal absorption of carbohydrates (must be taken with meal)	Flatulence, diarrhea, abdominal pain (does not cause hypoglycemia but if hypoglycemia occurs, it must be treated with glucose tablets or glucagon shots in patients taking Acarbose)
Insulin	Various	Promotes glucose storage and use, inhibits glucose release into bloodstream	Hypoglycemia, hypokalemia (low blood potassium), local or generalized allergic reactions

TABLE 23-9

GOALS FOR DIABETIC BLOOD GLUCOSE AND HEMOGLOBIN A1C

Biochemical index	Normal	Goal	Action required
Fasting/ preprandial glucose	<115mg/dL	80 to 120 mg/dL	<80 mg/dL requires sugar supplementation 140 mg/dL requires improvement in treatment regimen
Bedtime glucose	<120 mg/dL	100 to 140 mg/dL	<100 mg/dL requires bedtime snack >160 mg/dL requires improvement in treatment reginmen
Hemoglobin A1C	<6%	<7%	>8% requires improvement in treatment regimen

(Adapted with permission from Raskin p, et al. *Medical Management of Noninsulin-Dependent (type II) Diabetes*, Alexandria, VA, American Diabetes Association, 1994.)

Exercise still provides many benefits for patients with type 1 diabetes; however, greater effort is required to prevent both hypoglycemia and hyperglycemia.

Risks of Exercise

Although the benefits of exercise outweigh the risks for most patients with diabetes, all patients with diabetes should undergo a preparticipation physical examination performed by a physician prior to beginning any exercise program. Risks of exercise include hyperglycemia, hypoglycemia, cardiac ischemia, and worsening of the complications of diabetes. With proper screening, education about the effects of exercise on glycemic control, and proper monitoring of blood glucose, many of the potential pitfalls of exercise for patients with diabetes can be avoided. The athletic trainer should be familiar with an athlete's medications and dosage and whether the athlete has experienced any previous complications, such as hypoglycemia.

If adequate adjustments to insulin dosing or dietary changes are not made to allow for exercise, athletes with diabetes who are in otherwise good glycemic control can become hypoglycemic. However, if the diabetes is not well controlled (glucose > 250 mg/dL), a paradoxical worsening of hyperglycemia can be seen. When diabetes is out of control the patient goes into a state of relative or absolute lack of insulin. Exercise causes a release of stress hormones (epinephrine, glucagon, and others), which increase the blood glucose level. The ensuing worsening of hyperglycemia can lead to ketoacidosis and *diabetic coma*. Therefore, the blood glucose should be measured prior to exercise. If glucose is greater than 250 mg/dL, the urine should be checked for *ketones* (organic substances derived from fat metabolism). If ketones are present in the urine or the glucose level is greater than 300 mg/dL, exercise should be cancelled for the day.[33,34]

Many athletes want to gain or lose weight to improve their performance in their sport, their health, or their body image. Athletes with diabetes must carefully accomplish any weight loss or gain. In addition, these athletes should consult a nutritionist to avoid complications.

Cardiac ischemia, which can cause heart attacks or fatal arrhythmias (abnormal heart rhythms), is another potential risk of exercise. Individuals who are at risk for cardiac ischemia should be screened with an exercise stress test. Individuals at risk would include anyone with symptoms that suggest heart-related pain, anyone who has had type 1 diabetes for more than 15 years, all patients with type 1 diabetes who are older than age 30 years, and all patients with type 2 diabetes who are older than age 35 years.[35,36]

Other risks of exercise include worsening of the various complications of diabetes, including retinopathy and nephropathy, and a greater risk of foot ulcers and musculoskeletal injuries in patients with neuropathies.[35] However, a qualified physician can properly screen a patient for possible complications of diabetes and recommend appropriate types of exercise to minimize the risks of exercise and maximize the benefits.

Hypoglycemia

One of the greatest risks of exercise is inducing *hypoglycemia,* an abnormally decreased level of glucose in the blood, in patients who are taking either insulin or sulfonylureas. Any significant increase in the level of exercise must be accompanied by an increase in caloric intake or a decrease in the amount of the hypoglycemic agent, such as insulin or sulfonylureas, that the patient is taking. If one or both of these changes are not made, the athlete could easily become hypoglycemic and even go into hypoglycemic shock.

The symptoms of hypoglycemia, which are variable and nonspecific, include irritability, trembling, hunger, sweating, and apprehension. Severe hypoglycemia leads to shock with confusion, convulsions, and coma and can be life threatening.

To prevent hypoglycemia, all athletes with diabetes should be closely monitored, especially during the first weeks on a new training schedule. Because exercise decreases blood sugar levels, the level of training should be increased slowly, and frequent adjustments in diet or insulin doses must be made. Usually, the dose of insulin taken prior to exercise should be decreased by 30% to 50% depending on the type of insulin used; however, this adjustment should only be made after the athlete consults a physician. For patients taking other medications, the number of calories consumed before and during exercise may need to be increased.

The injection site is an important consideration in the exercising athlete with diabetes. Because the absorption of insulin is increased with exercise, the athlete should avoid injecting an extremity that will be used for exercise within 60 to 90 minutes of activity. When insulin is injected within 60 to 90 minutes prior to exercise, an alternate site such as the abdomen should be used. Otherwise, increased absorption of insulin could lead to hypoglycemia.

The athlete should check his or her blood sugar prior to exercise and increase caloric intake as indicated. Table 23-10 provides some general guidelines for caloric intake. If the blood glucose level is less than 100 mg/dL, the athlete should eat a carbohydrate snack such as an energy bar just before the exercise session. In addition, when glucose is low, 15 g of carbohydrate should be consumed approximately every 20 minutes during exercise. No matter how long the duration of exercise, sugar can be consumed by drinking sports drinks during activity. Sports drinks provide both the required calories to prevent hypoglycemia and enough fluid to prevent dehydration.[35]

To improve performance, all athletes, with or without diabetes, should increase caloric intake prior to exercise. For most athletes, a meal containing approximately 250 to 350 g of carbohydrate in the form of pasta, rice, or bread that is low in fat should be consumed 3 to 6 hours before exercise. After that, 15 g of carbohydrate should be consumed 20 minutes before exercise and every 20 minutes during exercise for sessions lasting longer than 1 hour. Patients with diabetes should adjust their consumption based on their glucose levels.

If the athlete begins to experience any sign of hypoglycemia, all exercise should cease and glucose in the form of sugar cubes, orange juice, candy, or fruit should be given immediately. Many athletes with diabetes carry glucose tablets or gels for emergencies. Glucose should be given to the athlete only if the athlete is responsive enough to swallow. Prompt recovery is usually seen.

TABLE 23-10
GENERAL GUIDELINES FOR PREEXERCISE CALORIC INTAKE BASED ON BLOOD GLUCOSE LEVEL

1. All blood glucose levels that are less than 80 mg/dL require caloric supplementation.

2. If blood glucose is less than 100 mg/dL prior to exercise, a preexercise snack shoud be eaten that is high in complex carbohydrates and low in fat.

3. If blood glucose 100 to 250 mg/dL prior to exercise, exercise can proceed and additional calories can be consumed during or after exercise, depending on the duration of activity.

4. If exercise lasts more than 1 hour, 15 g of carbohydrate and 250 mL of fluid should be consumed every 15 to 20 minutes.

5. If blood glucose is greater than 250 mg/dL, the athlete's urine should be checked for ketones. If ketones are present, or if blood glucose is greater than 300 mg/dL, exercise should be canceled and insulin should be adjusted for better glycemic control.

Because aspiration into the lungs can occur, glucose should never be forced into the athlete's mouth if the athlete is unable to swallow. Instead, the local emergency medical services (EMS) system should be activated, and the athlete should be transported immediately to the emergency department for administration of intravenous glucose. Some athletes carry injectable glucagon, which allows glucose to be released into the bloodstream. Unlike oral glucose, the advantage of injectable glucagon is that it can be used even in the unconscious athlete. The system is easy to use and, if the athlete is unable to administer the injection alone, glucagon can be administered by a physician or an athletic trainer. However, because regulations vary from state to state, athletic trainers should check with their state pharmacy board for which conditions they are able to administer drugs.

Ketoacidosis

Without insulin, the body cannot metabolize glucose, so energy is instead derived from burning fat stores. The end products of fat metabolism are ketone bodies, which are acidic. As ketone bodies build up, the body's pH decreases, resulting in ketoacidosis. Ketoacidosis, combined with dehydration from polyuria, often leads to confusion, somnolence, and even diabetic coma. In diabetic ketoacidosis, the patient often will have deep sighing respirations (Kussmaul breathing), and the odor of the patient's breath will usually be fruity. Sometimes, type 1 diabetes can present as ketoacidosis.

Ketoacidosis usually develops over a period of days. It is usually seen in patients in whom type 1 diabetes is out of control. Precipitating factors in patients who are known to have diabetes include severe infections, dietary indiscretions, and failure to take insulin. It is rare for ketoacidosis to develop in an actively exercising athlete, and some of the symptoms of ketoacidosis, such as lethargy, confusion, and somnolence, can also be seen in patients with hypoglycemia. Therefore, all stuporous or lethargic athletes with diabetes should be given glucose. The amount of glucose given could be lifesaving for the hypoglycemic athlete and usually results in immediate improvement. If the athlete is suffering from hyperglycemia, the amount of glucose given is not significant and will not result in additional harm. If recovery is not immediately apparent, the athlete should be transported to the nearest emergency department.

EPILEPSY

Epilepsy refers to any of the disorders caused by abnormal electrical activity in the brain that result in recurrent seizures. Approximately 10% of the population will have a seizure at some point, but epilepsy will develop in only 1% of the population.[37] Seizures can have an underlying cause, such as a head injury, but in more than half of all patients with epilepsy, no cause is found, even after an extensive work-up.[37]

Seizures and Their Classification

A *seizure* is the clinical manifestation of an abnormal and excessive electrical discharge from a set of neurons of the brain. Epilepsy is a condition characterized by recurrent, unprovoked seizures with no identifiable cause. However, a diagnosis of epilepsy can be considered in an individual who has recurrent seizures that are due to a single known event such as a head injury.[37]

Some of the causes of seizures include recent or old brain injury (from trauma or surgery), brain tumor, stroke, infection, fever, or a variety of metabolic causes such as hypoglycemia. Seizures can vary in form from simply blanking out for a few seconds to severe convulsions that are characterized by generalized, uncoordinated muscular activity and loss of consciousness.

Generally, seizures are classified according to the clinical manifestations of the abnormal electrical activity. There are two broad categories of seizure activity: generalized and partial. Each of these broad categories is then further subdivided into more specific types. **Table 23-11** presents the most common types of seizures and their distinguishing characteristics.

In generalized seizures, both cerebral hemispheres are involved and consciousness is impaired. Generalized seizures can be further classified as tonic-clonic, absence, or a variety of other less common seizure types.[38] Generalized seizures are most commonly tonic-clonic. Tonic-clonic seizures are often preceded by an aura, which is a sensation such as a smell or sound that alerts the patient that a seizure is about to occur. The aura, when present, is rapidly followed by the seizure. The patient often has time to prepare for the seizure and can pull to the curb if driving, sit or lie down, or walk away from machinery.

Tonic-clonic seizures, which make up 23% of all seizures, are characterized by sustained tonic (rigid) muscular contractions leading to an abnormal body posture, with superimposed clonic (repetitive) muscular activity or spasms. During the convulsion, the jaw muscles contract, which may lead to biting of the tongue or lips, and loss of bowel or bladder control is common. The convulsive phase usually lasts from 1 to several minutes and is followed by the postictal state.

The postictal state is a period of exhaustion and recovery. During this phase, which usually lasts 10 to 30 minutes, the athlete's level of consciousness is depressed. Initially, the athlete is unconscious during this phase. The period of unconsciousness is followed by a period of somnolence and confusion as the athlete's mental status slowly returns to normal. During the postictal period, vomitus, mucus, or relaxed pharyngeal muscles can obstruct the athlete's airway. The athletic trainer should

TABLE 23-11

MOST COMMON SEIZURE TYPES AND DISTINGUISHING CHARACTERISTICS

Type	% of all seizures	Level of consciousness	Duration	Other
Generalized				
Tonic-clonic	23	Loss of consciousness	1 to several minutes	Aura, postictal state, loss of bowel/bladder control
Absence	6	Loss of awareness	Seconds	Momentary periods of confusion as in "daydreaming"
Various	11	Impaired or loss of consciousness	Varies	Varies
Partial				Can progress to general
Simple	14	No change	Minutes	One-sided symptoms
Complex	36	Confused, but alert	1 to 5 minutes	Automatic and other abnormal behaviors
Partial unknown	7	Varies	Varies	
Unclassified	3	Varies	Varies	

place the athlete on one side with the head down to prevent aspiration of vomitus.

Absence seizures occur much less commonly, making up 6% of all seizures. Absence seizures are characterized by a brief lapse of attention that lasts only seconds. Unlike tonic-clonic seizures, there is usually no aura or postictal state.

A variety of other generalized seizures altogether account for 11% of all seizures. There are more than 15 other types of generalized seizures including myoclonic seizures, which are characterized by short jerks of an extremity without the rhythmic motions of tonic-clonic seizures.

Partial seizures usually are limited to a single hemisphere of the brain. Partial seizures are further classified as simple partial seizures, complex partial seizures, and partial seizures evolving into secondarily generalized seizures.[38]

Simple partial seizures make up 14% of all seizures; in these seizures, consciousness is not impaired. The seizure activity is limited, usually involving twitching of one or more muscle groups on one side of the body. Patients undergoing a simple partial seizure can also experience somatosensory symptoms such as tingling and flashing lights, autonomic symptoms such as sweating and flushing, or psychic symptoms such as a sense of déjà vu. A simple partial seizure can evolve into a complex partial seizure or a generalized seizure.

Complex partial seizures make up 36% of all seizures; in these seizures, consciousness is impaired. Clouded consciousness may be the only manifestation, or the individual may display automatic behavior such as chewing, fumbling with clothes, walking aimlessly, or other abnormal behaviors. These seizures usually last 1 to 5 minutes. A complex partial seizure can evolve into a generalized seizure. In 7% of all partial seizures, it is unclear whether they are simple or complex, and they are subsequently classified as partial unknown. Approximately 3% of all seizures remain unclassified.

Management of Seizures

The first step in the management of a generalized seizure is to protect the athlete from inflicting self-injury. The athletic trainer should also be careful not to risk injury to him- or herself. When an athlete with epilepsy says that the aura is present and a seizure is about to occur, the athletic trainer should immediately help the athlete lie down in a safe place and loosen the athlete's clothing. The

FOCUS ON . . .

Epilepsy

Seizures and their classification

A seizure is the clinical manifestation of an abnormal, excessive electrical discharge from brain neurons. Epilepsy is characterized by recurrent, unprovoked seizures with or without an identifiable cause, such as a recent or old brain injury, brain tumor, stroke, infection, fever, or a metabolic cause, such as hypoglycemia. Seizures vary from blanking out for several seconds to severe convulsions with generalized, uncoordinated muscular activity and loss of consciousness.

Seizures are classified as generalized or partial. Generalized seizures involve both cerebral hemispheres and impaired consciousness; they are further classified as tonic-clonic, absence, or other types. Often, they are preceded by an aura that signals the onset of a seizure. Tonic-clonic seizures are characterized by sustained tonic (rigid) muscular contractions leading to an abnormal body posture with superimposed clonic (repetitive) muscular activity or spasms. Contraction of the jaw muscles may cause biting of the tongue or lips, and bowel or bladder control may be lost. The convulsion usually lasts 1 to several minutes and is followed by the postictal state of exhaustion and recovery, which lasts 10 to 30 minutes. After a period of unconsciousness, the athlete is somnolent and confused and then mentation normalizes. The airway can become obstructed by vomitus, mucus, or relaxed pharyngeal muscles during the postictal state. Absence seizures are characterized by a few seconds' attention lapse and are not associated with an aura or postictal state.

Partial seizures are limited to a single hemisphere. Simple partial seizures involve limited seizure activity with one-sided muscle twitching and no loss of consciousness. Somatosensory symptoms, autonomic symptoms, or psychic symptoms may also occur. A simple partial seizure can evolve into a complex partial seizure or a generalized seizure. Complex partial seizures involve impaired consciousness and perhaps automatic behavior such as chewing, fumbling with clothes, aimless walking, or other abnormal behaviors that last 1 to 5 minutes. A complex partial seizure can evolve into a generalized seizure.

Management of seizures

Seizure management begins by protecting the athlete from self-injury without risking injury to others. When an athlete announces an imminent seizure, the athletic trainer should help him or her to lie down in a safe place, loosen clothing, and protect, but not restrain, the head and extremities. Nothing should be forced into the athlete's mouth. Chest muscle contraction may appear to cause airway obstruction and cyanosis, but this usually resolves quickly. The athletic trainer should place the athlete on one side with the head down to allow gravity to keep the tongue out of the pharynx and prevent aspiration of vomitus. During the postictal state, the athletic trainer should assess the athlete's airway, clear any mucus or vomitus, and maintain the open airway until the athlete is fully awake. After vital signs are checked and recorded, a secondary survey should be performed.

The same rules apply for a partial seizure, although it may be difficult to distinguish from intoxication, drug abuse, insulin shock, or another medical condition. During a complex partial seizure, the athlete is confused but amenable to friendly suggestions and comments. The athletic trainer should stay with the athlete, provide reassurance, and observe the athlete carefully until the seizure ends. Unless the athlete or others are in danger, an athlete who is aggressive during a seizure should not be restrained.

The athlete with epilepsy usually recovers normal function quickly and emergency transport is unnecessary; however, the physician should be notified in case a medication change is needed. Status epilepticus describes prolonged or recurrent seizures without return of consciousness, a potentially fatal condition because fatigue and respiratory distress may occur if the seizure exceeds 10 minutes. Immediate transport to the emergency department is indicated; oxygen should be used if available.

Sports participation

Most individuals with epilepsy can be encouraged to exercise without fear of diminished seizure control. Actually, fewer seizures occur during activity than during rest. A preparticipation physical examination should be directed at determining the risks and benefits of a particular sport. How well controlled the seizures are, the athlete's goals, the medications and side effects, and the risks to the athlete and others should be thoroughly discussed with the athlete (and guardians, if appropriate).

athletic trainer should ensure that the athlete's head and extremities are protected but not restrained. Nothing should be forced into the athlete's mouth. In the past, objects were put into the mouth with the purpose of preventing injury. However, placing objects in the mouth can lead to airway obstruction and is no longer recommended.

Because of contractions of the chest muscles, the athlete who is having a generalized seizure may appear to have an airway obstruction and become cyanotic. Normal respiration almost always follows a seizure. Lack of respiration during the seizure rarely presents a problem unless the seizure is prolonged. The athletic trainer can help keep the airway open by placing the athlete on one side with the head down, so that gravity will help keep the tongue out of the pharynx.

During the postictal state, the athletic trainer should assess the athlete's airway, clear any mucus or vomitus, and maintain the open airway until the athlete is fully awake. Once vital signs are checked and recorded, the athletic trainer should perform a secondary survey to look for any injuries that may have occurred during the seizure. Injuries often experienced include bitten tongue, abrasions, and lacerations.

The same general rules apply for managing a partial seizure as for a generalized seizure. However, because a complex partial seizure can be mistaken for intoxication, drug abuse, insulin shock, or another medical condition that causes abnormal behavior, it may be difficult to determine that the patient is having a complex partial seizure.

During a complex partial seizure, the patient is in a confused state (clouded consciousness) but is usually amenable to suggestions and comments given in a friendly manner. The athletic trainer must stay with the athlete, provide reassurance, and observe the athlete carefully until the abnormal behavior ceases. An athlete who is behaving abnormally can become aggressive during a seizure but should not be restrained unless the athlete or others are in immediate danger.

The athlete who has a history of epilepsy usually completely recovers function soon after the seizure, in which case transportation to the hospital is not necessary. However, the athlete should notify his or her physician to see if a change in seizure medication is needed. Athletes with no history of seizures should undergo a thorough medical evaluation so that the cause of the seizure can be determined and treatment provided for prevention of further seizures. The evaluation should be performed the day of the seizure, if possible.

Some patients with epilepsy experience status epilepticus, in which the seizure is prolonged or one seizure quickly follows another with no return of consciousness between seizures. This situation is serious and potentially fatal. Fatigue and respiratory distress may occur if seizure activity lasts longer than 10 minutes. EMS should be activated for the athlete with status epilepticus, and the patient should be immediately transported to the emergency department. If oxygen is available, the athletic trainer should administer it to the athlete until the ambulance arrives.

Sports Participation

The benefits of exercise are the same for individuals with epilepsy as for the general population. In general, exercise should be encouraged. For most patients with epilepsy, seizure control is not worsened by most types of exercise. In fact, fewer seizures occur during periods of activity compared with periods of rest.[39] Nevertheless, certain activities, such as scuba diving or parachuting, could be very dangerous if an individual were to have a seizure during the activity. Therefore, during the preparticipation physical examination, the athlete with epilepsy should be advised about the risks and benefits of a particular sport.

Except for swimming, the risks of participation in most sports have not been documented. In swimming, the risk of drowning or serious injury is four times greater for athletes with epilepsy than for the general population.[40] However, most of this risk could be eliminated with the proper precautions, such as good supervision and allowing no underwater swimming.[40] Certain other activities, such as aviation, motor racing, or archery, could also be dangerous for the athlete with epilepsy, and for others, if a seizure were to occur at an inopportune time. The athlete, his or her parents or guardian, and his or her healthcare providers should discuss the risks and benefits of the proposed activities. Issues to take into account include how well the seizures are controlled, the athlete's goals, and the medications the athlete is taking to control seizures. Attention should also be paid to side effects and possible risks to the athlete and others. Side effects of seizure medicines can include drowsiness, decreased coordination, and confusion. **Table 23-12** lists the most common medications used to treat epilepsy and their side effects. Depending on the side effects of a particular medication, the athlete's performance and safety can be affected. Although there are no absolute rules, guidelines have been proposed as a guide for participation.[41] **Table 23-13** presents these guidelines. Although some sports should be avoided, others require that precautions be taken or that the athlete be supervised.[41] The safety of some activities depends on the type of seizure and level of participation. These activities include cycle racing, skating, horseback riding, and gymnastics. The athlete or athletic trainer should consult a neurologist if there are any questions about the safety of participation in a particular sport.

SLEEP DISORDERS

Sleep apnea, the absence of breathing during sleep, is the most common disorder that causes excessive daytime sleepiness (EDS). Obstructive sleep apnea refers to episodes of complete or partial airway collapse during

TABLE 23-12

COMMON SEIZURE MEDICATIONS AND THEIR SIDE EFFECTS

Medication Generic name (Trade name)	Type(s) of seizure medication most often prescribed as first-line treatment	Side effects
Carbamazepine (Tegretol)	Partial seizures*	Nausea, vomiting, drowsiness, vision change, abnormal liver function tests, liver failure, dizziness, decrease in the amount of white blood cells, rash
Phenytoin (Dilantin)	Partial seizures* Tonic-clonic seizures †	Gum disease, body hair increase, ataxia, swollen lymph nodes, rash, drowsiness, abnormal liver function tests, liver failure, slurred speech, vision change, confusion, decrease in the amount of white blood cells
Phenobarbital (Luminal)	Partial seizures*	Drowsiness, depression, slowed mentation, rash, hyperactivity, ataxia, drug dependence, abnormal liver function tests, liver failure, nausea, decrease in the amount of white blood cells
Valproic acid (Depakote)	Absence seizures Partial seizures* Tonic-clonic seizures † Myoclonic seizures	Drowsiness, stomach upset, weight gain, tremor, dizziness, hair loss, abnormal liver function tests, liver failure, decrease in the amount of white blood cells, failure of bone marrow to produce blood cells and platelets, rash, pancreatitis
Ethosuximide	Absence seizures	Stomach upset, nausea, vomiting, mood changes, drowsiness, hyperactivity, hiccups, headache, rash, failure of bone marrow to produce blood cells and platelets, decrease in the amount of white blood cells

* Simple or complex seizures are treated as partial seizures whether or not they become generalized.
† Tonic-clonic seizures refer to primary generalized tonic-clonic seizures.

TABLE 23-13

PROPOSED GUIDELINES FOR PARTICIPATION IN SPORTS FOR PATIENTS WITH EPILEPSY

- Activities to be avoided:
  - ❑ scuba diving
  - ❑ parachuting
  - ❑ high altitude climbing
  - ❑ gliding and hang-gliding
  - ❑ aviation
  - ❑ motor racing and boxing

- Activities that require precautions or supervision:
  - ❑ water and snow skiing
  - ❑ swimming
  - ❑ canoeing
  - ❑ wind and ocean surfing
  - ❑ sailing
  - ❑ archery
  - ❑ shooting (hunting and target shooting)

(Adapted with permission from van Linschoten R, Backx FJ, Mulder OG, Meinardi H: Epilepsy and sports. *Sports Med* 1990;10:9-19.)

sleep that lead to periods of airflow cessation, usually lasting at least 10 to 15 seconds. It is normal for occasional episodes of apnea to occur, but when an individual experiences multiple episodes during the night that lead to symptoms such as daytime sleepiness, the condition is abnormal and should be investigated. Traditionally, sleep apnea was considered a disease of obese, middle-aged men. Obesity and male sex are indeed risk factors, but the condition has been increasingly recognized in both men and women of all ages. Sleep apnea occurs in 2% of women and 4% of men.[42]

Narcolepsy, the next most common disorder of EDS, is far less common. Narcolepsy affects between four and ten of every 10,000 individuals. It is a neurologic sleep disorder of unknown cause that is defined by excessive daytime sleepiness associated with abnormalities of REM sleep (the dreaming portion of sleep). An athlete who is suspected of having a sleep disorder should see a physician. The athletic trainer who suspects the diagnosis should refer the athlete to a physician and reinforce conservative treatment measures.

Sleep Apnea

Pathogenesis

Not all of the factors responsible for sleep apnea are known, but any factor that tends to cause obstruction or collapse of the upper airway can lead to this condition. **Table 23-14** presents a list of risk factors for sleep apnea airway obstructions. Obesity increases the likelihood of sleep apnea, probably because of fat deposition in the pharynx and hypopharynx (the area just below the epiglottis opening into the larynx and esophagus). Increased neck size is a greater risk factor for sleep apnea than generalized obesity.[43] Athletes with increased neck size such as football linemen, heavyweight wrestlers, and weightlifters may therefore be at increased risk for sleep apnea. Most individuals with sleep apnea are obese; however, up to 40% are no more than 20% over their ideal body weight.[44] Tissue hypertrophy, such as from enlarged tonsils, or narrowed passages, such as in micrognathia (an abnormally small jaw), can also cause obstruction. Pharmacologic agents, including alcohol and sedatives, that tend to relax the airway musculature can also promote apneic episodes.

Clinical features

The essential features of sleep apnea are repeated episodes of apnea and EDS. In most cases, loud snoring is followed by silent periods lasting longer than 10 seconds during which there is decreased breathing or no breathing. Sometimes the apneic periods can last as long as 1 or more minutes. At the end of the apneic period, the patient usually gasps, snorts, or makes choking noises as he or she momentarily awakens and then resumes breathing. The sleep partner or roommate is usually more aware of these episodes than the patient. Because of the constant interruption of the sleep cycle, fatigue and daytime somnolence result.

As with other sleep disorders, patients may experience personality changes, loss of memory and concentration, sexual dysfunction, headaches, and depression. In athletes, sleep apnea may be manifested by clumsiness during drills, difficulty remembering plays, and decrease in school or work performance. In addition, more serious medical problems can result from sleep apnea. Some individuals with sleep apnea become hypoxic during their periods of apnea, which can lead to stroke, heart attack, arrythmias, high blood pressure, and heart failure.[44] Sleep apnea increases the risk of traffic accidents, which is probably the result of reduced alertness while driving.[45] Although no published data supports this theory, there may also be an increased risk of athletic injury. Results of one study of patients who had more than 20 episodes of apnea per hour indicated a 37% mortality rate over an 8-year period.[46]

TABLE 23-14

RISK FACTORS FOR OBSTRUCTIVE SLEEP APNEA

Obesity

Nasal polyps or other nasal obstruction

Oral obstruction caused by a big tongue or small jaw

Pharyngeal obstruction caused by tonsillar or uvular hypertrophy or pharyngeal fat

Myxedema (edema of subcutaneous tissue caused by hypothyroidism)

Acromegaly (a disorder marked by progressive enlargement of peripheral parts of the body, including the head)

Alcohol use

Sedative use

Diagnosis

Any individual who habitually snores and has either EDS or witnessed episodes of apnea should be referred to a physician to rule out sleep apnea. The gold standard for diagnosis is an overnight sleep study in a sleep lab. During the sleep study, a number of variables are measured throughout the night to determine the presence and severity of sleep apnea. Brain waves are measured with an electroencephalogram (EEG) to determine the state of arousal, respiratory effort is measured at the rib cage, abdomen, and esophagus, and airflow and oxygen saturation are measured. Other variables, such as measurements of eye and muscle movements, can also be evaluated to help determine the stage of sleep. An electrocardiogram (ECG) can monitor any changes in the heart rhythm. An apnea index is created by analyzing the data. The apnea index is the number of significant episodes of apnea per hour. An apnea index greater than 5 is considered diagnostic. Results of retrospective studies found that an apnea index greater than 20 was a predictor of increased mortality.[47]

The cost of sleep studies in sleep labs is high (averaging approximately $1,000); however, many types of monitoring devices are now available for home use. There is considerable debate as to which specific equipment should be used and when a portable monitor can be used instead of

a formal study. A physician familiar with sleep disorders can determine whether a formal study needs to be done or the patient can use a home monitoring device.

Treatment

There are no clear criteria for when treatment with a specific therapy should be used. The level of symptoms, presence of obstruction, apnea index, and amount of oxygen desaturation (decrease in oxygen in the bloodstream) should all be considered when the physician is trying to determine what type of treatment to recommend and how aggressive to be. Types of treatment include general measures, pharmacologic treatment, surgical treatment, and treatment with mechanical devices.

General measures such as weight loss and avoidance of substances that aggravate sleep apnea should be recommended for all symptomatic patients. Contributing conditions such as hypothyroidism should be treated. Because sleeping on the back tends to increase symptoms, and sleeping on the side decreases them, patients should try different sleep positions. Alcohol, muscle relaxants, and sedatives all relax the airway musculature and should be avoided. Although weight loss is difficult to achieve, weight loss can reduce the number of apneic episodes and should be encouraged.[48] Commercial nasal strips that help to open the nasal passages are usually not helpful, because the obstruction causing sleep apnea is generally more distal than the nose.

Pharmacologic treatment is usually not particularly helpful. Protriptyline (Vivactil) is a nonsedating tricyclic antidepressant that appears to have some benefit and may be considered in mild cases or when other therapies are not tolerated.[49] Use of supplemental oxygen to minimize the harmful effects of low oxygen saturation can also be considered for patients with significant desaturations.

Mechanical devices that have been used to treat sleep apnea include dental appliances and nasal continuous positive airway pressure (CPAP). Various dental appliances have been studied, and although there are few good studies proving their usefulness, they can be considered in mild cases or when other therapies are ineffective.[49] On the other hand, CPAP may be as effective as tracheostomy (a permanent breathing hole in the throat) in most patients.[49] Nasal CPAP uses a mask that seals around the nose, providing constant airway pressure to prevent soft tissue from collapsing and obstructing the airway. (**Figure 23-6**). In addition to reducing the symptoms of sleep apnea, CPAP reduces associated complications including hypertension, arrhythmias, and heart failure.[50]

Surgical treatment should be considered whenever an anatomic obstruction is present. The type of surgery should be guided by the location of the obstruction. Removal of nasal polyps, enlarged tonsils, and adenoids or surgical correction of other abnormalities can be very successful when performed in the appropriate patient

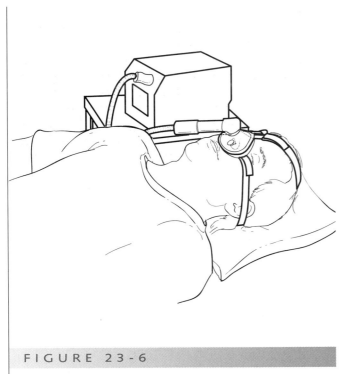

A nasal continuous positive airway pressure mask reduces symptoms of sleep apnea and associated complications.

population. Tracheostomy should be used as a treatment of last resort. It is highly effective for severely affected individuals in whom other treatment options have failed.

Narcolepsy

Individuals with narcolepsy have EDS that typically begins in the teens or early twenties. EDS is associated with abnormal manifestations of REM sleep including early onset of REM sleep, cataplexy (brief, sudden loss of muscle tone), sleep paralysis, and hypnagogic hallucinations (intense illusions or dreams that occur as an individual is falling asleep). Normally, an individual falls asleep gradually and does not enter into REM sleep for approximately 90 minutes. As a protection against acting out dreams, the muscles become immobile or paralyzed.

Patients with narcolepsy will often enter REM sleep as they are falling asleep. These patients often report falling asleep at inappropriate times such as while driving, eating, or during sexual activity. It is important to realize that often individuals with narcolepsy cannot control their need to sleep.

Narcolepsy is a life-long neurologic disorder that occasionally is familial. A genetic predisposition is suggested by the finding that more than 85% of all individuals with narcolepsy with cataplexy share a specific allele (or area of a gene). Only 12% to 38% of the general population has this allele.[51]

Associated abnormalities related to REM sleep are also seen. Cataplexy is often associated with an emotional stimulus. This may be experienced as weakness in the knees, drooping facial muscles, or difficulty speaking. In the most severe form, drop attacks occur in which the athlete has complete loss of muscle tone but remains conscious. Although these episodes usually last a few seconds to a few minutes, they can last as long as 30 minutes. Sleep paralysis is characterized by the inability to move any muscles while falling asleep or waking up. Sleep paralysis can be seen occasionally in individuals with no sleep disorders; however, it occurs more frequently in individuals with narcolepsy, especially during onset of sleep. Hypnagogic hallucinations occur as the individual is falling asleep.

Treatment of narcolepsy is aimed at reducing daytime sleepiness and associated abnormalities. Treatment of EDS is best accomplished by having the athlete take short naps during the day whenever he or she becomes sleepy. These naps usually refresh the athlete with narcolepsy for 1 to several hours. Tricyclic antidepressants are used to decrease auxiliary symptoms such as cataplexy. Stimulants, such as amphetamines, can be useful to reduce EDS, but patients often develop a tolerance to these medications and require increasingly higher doses. Stimulants are most effective when taken only as needed, such as for a long driving trip. Competitive athletes should be aware that stimulants are banned substances and that participation in sports events may require an exemption by their governing body.

CHAPTER REVIEW

Asthma is a disease of chronic airway inflammation associated with changes in airway hyperresponsiveness that produces symptoms of recurrent wheezing, shortness of breath, chest tightness, and coughing. Asthma triggers include allergens, irritants, viruses, exercise, cold air, and medications. Treatment includes avoiding known stimuli whenever possible and medications such as short-acting beta-adrenergic drugs, mast cell stabilizers, methylxanthines, corticosteroids, anticholinergics, and leukotriene modifiers. Exercise-induced asthma affects 10% to 20% of the general population, including 90% of those with asthma and 40% of those with allergic rhinitis.

Cancer describes various abnormally growing cells that can invade local tissue or metastasize to distant sites via the bloodstream or lymphatic system. Cancer tends to be progressive, with symptoms dependent on the type of disease, sites, and extent. However, worrisome symptoms include unexplained weight loss, decreased athletic performance, fatigue, unexplained nausea or vomiting, fevers, night sweats, and easy bruising.

Cancer in children accounts for 2% of new cancer cases each year and is the leading cause of death for those younger than age 15 years. Acute leukemia is the most common cancer in children younger than age 10 years; lymphoma is the most common cancer in teenagers and young adults (age 20 to 45 years). Older adults are most likely to be diagnosed with cancer, with prostate cancer being the most common type in men and breast cancer the most common type in women.

Among the most frequent types of cancer are leukemia, lymphoma, brain tumors, testicular cancer, cervical cancer, melanoma, lung cancer, oral cancer, breast cancer, prostate cancer, and colon cancer. The risk of some of these diseases can be lowered by following certain prevention strategies. These strategies include not using or stopping the use of tobacco products; exercising regularly; eating a low-fat, high-fiber diet; drinking alcohol moderately; avoiding sun exposure; and avoiding unprotected sex with multiple partners. Screening is valuable in detecting cancers affecting the testicles, cervix, melanoma, mouth, breast, colon, and perhaps the prostate. The athlete who has been treated for cancer and wishes to return to sport may have limitations from the disease itself or from the treatment.

Diabetes is a disorder of carbohydrate metabolism caused by relative lack of insulin secretion by the pancreas or by insulin resistance at the target organs. Type 1 diabetes (lack of insulin) is treated with injected insulin. Type 2 diabetes (insulin resistance) is treated with diet and exercise, supplemented by oral medications and insulin as needed. Careful control of blood glucose helps to decrease the complications of diabetes, including retinopathy, neuropathy, and nephropathy. The beneficial effects of exercise for the athlete with diabetes include decreased insulin sensitivity, blood pressure, weight, and lipid levels and improved sense of well being. However, exercise also carries risks (for example, hypoglycemia), and the athlete with diabetes should be closely monitored.

Epilepsy is a condition characterized by recurrent, unprovoked seizures: the clinical manifestations of abnormal, excessive electrical discharges from brain neurons. Seizures are categorized as generalized (tonic-clonic, absence, or other types) and partial (simple or complex). Many seizures are preceded by an aura and followed by a postictal state. A variety of medications are available to treat seizures. Other management strategies include protecting the athlete and others from injury, ensuring respiration, and staying with the athlete until normal function has returned. Some athletes may experience status epilepticus (prolonged or uninterrupted consecutive seizures), which is potentially fatal and requires emergency transport to the hospital.

Disorders of excessive daytime sleepiness include sleep apnea and narcolepsy. Sleep apnea occurs with obstruction or collapse of the upper airway, often as a result of obesity, tissue hypertrophy, or narrowed passages. Serious medical problems can result: stroke, heart attack, high blood pressure, and heart failure. Treatment measures are general (weight loss, change of sleep position, avoiding triggers, addressing contributing conditions), pharmacologic, surgical (removing anatomic obstructions), and mechanical (dental appliances, nasal continuous positive airway pressure). Narcolepsy is a condition involving early onset of REM sleep, cataplexy, sleep paralysis, and hypnagogic hallucinations. Treatment includes short naps, tricyclic antidepressants, and stimulants.

1. An athlete who has symptoms of asthma more than twice a week but less than once per day and nighttime symptoms three or more times per month is classified as :

    A. step 1: intermittent.

    B. step 2: mild persistent.

    C. step 3: moderate persistent.

    D. step 4: severe persistent.

2. A mast cell stabilizer that prevents inflammation and bronchoconstriction is:

    A. albuterol.

    B. cromolyn.

    C. heophylline.

    D. ipratropium bromide.

3. What is the most common cancer in women ages 20 to 45 years?

    A. Melanoma

    B. Breast cancer

    C. Colon cancer

    D. Hodgkin's disease

4. What is the most common cancer in men and women ages 20 to 45 years?

    A. Leukemia

    B. Lymphoma

    C. Lung cancer

    D. Brain cancer

5. Hypoglycemia is generally only a risk for athletes taking which of the following medications?

    A. Biguanides

    B. Sulfonylureas

    C. Thiazolidinediones

    D. Alpha-glucosidase inhibitors

6. Which of the following conditions may be indicated by irritability, trembling, hunger, sweating, and apprehension in an athlete with diabetes?

    A. Ketoacidosis

    B. Diabetic coma

    C. Hypoglycemia

    D. Hyperglycemia

7. A conscious athlete who displays twitching of muscle groups on one side of the body is probably experiencing which type of seizure?

    A. Absence

    B. Tonic-clonic

    C. Simple partial

    D. Complex partial

8. A medication used to treat both partial and tonic-clonic seizures is:

    A. phenytoin.

    B. ethosuximide.

    C. phenobarbital.

    D. carbamazepine.

9. A patient with sleep apnea is more likely to be:

    A. old.

    B. young.

    C. overweight.

    D. underweight.

10. Brief, sudden loss of muscle tone that is often associated with an emotional stimulus is called:

    A. cataplexy.

    B. narcolepsy.

    C. sleep paralysis.

    D. hypnagogic hallucination.

Answers on page 893.

References

1. Global Initiative for Asthma: *Global Strategy for Asthma Management and Prevention. NHLBI/WHO Workshop Report.* Washington, DC, National Heart, Lung and Blood Institute (NIH Publication No 95-3659), 1993.

2. Centers for Disease Control and Prevention: Asthma mortality and hospitalization among children and young adults, United States, 1990–1993. *MMWR* 1996;45:350–353.

3. Pierson WE, Voy RO: Exercise-induced bronchospasm in the XXIII Summer Olympic Games. *N Engl Region Proc* 1988;9:209–213.

4. Lemanske RF Jr, Busse WW: Asthma. *JAMA* 1997;278:1855–1873.

5. *The Expert Panel Report II: Guidelines for the Diagnosis and Management of Asthma.* National Asthma Education and Prevention Program. National Heart Lung and Blood Institute, National Institutes of Health, 1997.

6. Randolph C: Exercise induced asthma: Update on pathophysiology, clinical diagnosis, and treatment. *Curr Probl Pediatr* 1997;27:53–77.

7. Andeson SD: Is there a unifying hypothesis for exercise induced asthma? *J Allergy Clin Immunol* 1984;73:660–665.

8. McFaddener JR: Exercise induced asthma as a vascular phenomenon. *Lancet* 1990;335:880–883.

9. Weiler JM: Exercise-induced asthma: A practical guide to definitions, diagnosis, prevalence, and treatment. *Allergy Asthma Proc* 1996;17:315–335.

10. Makker HK, Lau LC, Thomson HW, Blinks SM, Holgate ST: The protective effect of inhaled leukotriene by receptor antagonist ICI 204, 219 against exercise induced asthma. *Am Rev Respir Dis* 1993;147:1413–1418.

11. Ahmed T, et al: Preventing bronchoconstriction in exercise induced asthma with inhaled heparin. *N Engl J Med* 1993;329:90–95.

12. Bianco S, et al: Prevention of exercise induced bronchoconstriction by inhaled furosemide. *Lancet* 1988;2:252–255.

13. Storms W: Exercise-Induced Asthma Symposium. Colorado Springs, CO, 1997.

14. Gloeckler Reis LA, et al: *SEER cancer statistics review,* 1973–1994. Bethesda, MD, National Cancer Institute, U.S. Department of Health and Human Services, 1997.

15. Scaga TS: Inhibition of the induction of cancer by antioxidants. *Adv Exp Med Biol* 1995;369:167–174.

16. Kendler BS: Free radicals in health and disease: Implications for primary healthcare providers. *Nurse Pract* 1995;20:29–36, 43.

17. Isselbacher KJ et al: *Harrison's Principles of Internal Medicine,* ed 13. New York, NY, McGraw-Hill, 1994, pp 1221–1229, 1814–1882.

18. Crist WM: *Nelson' Textbook of Pediatrics,* ed 15. Philadelphia, PA, WB Saunders, 1996, pp 1442–1479.

19. Fitzpatrick TB et al: *Color Atlas and Synopsis of Clinical Dermatology,* ed 3. New York, NY, McGraw-Hill, 1997, pp 180–207, 970–982.

20. Sone S, et al: Mass screening for lung cancer with spiral computed tomography scanner. *Lancet* 1998;351:1242–1245.

21. U.S. Preventive Services Task Force: *Guide to Clinical Preventive Services,* ed 2. Baltimore, MD, Williams & Wilkins, 1996.

22. Pettiti DB: Coronary heart disease and estrogen replacment therapy: Can compliance bias explain the results of observational studies? *Ann Epidemiol* 1994;4:11–118.

23. Hulley S, et al: Randomized trial of estrogen plus progestin for secondary prevention of coronary heart disease in postmenopausal women. *JAMA* 1998;280:605–613.

24. Shepard RJ: Exercise in the prevention and treatment of cancer. An update. *Sports Med* 1993;15:258–280.

25. Henningfield JE: Nicotine medications for smoking cessation. *N Engl J Med* 1995;333:1196–1203.

26. 1997–1998 NCAA Division 1 Manual, p 56.

27. Pozniak MA, et al: Interleukin-2-induced splenic enlargement. *Cancer* 1995;75:2737–2741.

28. Ziskin MC, et al: Therapeutic ultrasound, in Michlovitz SL (ed): *Thermal Agents in Rehabilitation,* ed 2. Philadelphia, PA, FA Davis Co, 1990, pp 163–164.

29. The Expert Committee on the Diagnosis and Classification of Diabetes Mellitus: Report of the expert committee on the diagnosis and classification of diabetes mellitus. *Diabetes Care* 1997;20:1183–1197.

30. O'Sullivan JB: Body weight and subsequent diabetes mellitus. *JAMA* 1982;248:949.

31. The Diabetes Control and Complications Trial Research Group: The effects of intensive treatment of diabetes on the development and progression of long-term complications in insulin dependent diabetes. *N Engl J Med* 1993;329:977–986.

32. Raskin P, et al: *Medical Management of Non-Insulin-Dependent (Type II) Diabetes.* Alexandria, VA, American Diabetes Association, 1994.

33. Hough D: Diabetes mellitus in sports. *Med Clin North Am* 1994;78:423–437.

34. Horton E: Exercise and diabetes mellitus. *Med Clin North Am* 1988;72:1301–1321.

35. Ruderman N, Delvin J: *Health Professionals Guide to Diabetes and Exercise.* Alexandria, VA, American Diabetes Association, 1995.

36. American College of Sports Medicine: *Guidelines for Exercise Testing and Prescription.* Philadelphia, PA, Lea & Febiger, 1991.

37. Hauser WA, Annegers JF, Rocca WA: Descriptive epidemiology of epilepsy: Contributions of population-based studies from Rochester, Minnesota. *Mayo Clin Proc* 1996;71:576–586.

38. Commission on Classification and Terminology of the International League Against Epilepsy: Proposal for revised clinical and electroencephalographic classification of epileptic seizures. *Epilepsia* 1981;22:489–451.

39. Nakken KO, et al: Epilepsy and physical fitness. *Tidsskr Nor Laegeforen* 1985;1136–1138.

40. Orlowski JP, et al: Submersion accidents in children with epilepsy. *Am J of Diseases of Children* 1982;136:777–780.

41. Van Linschoten R, Backx FJ, Mulder OG, Meinardi H: Epilepsy and sports. *Sports Med* 1990;10:9–19.

42. Young T, et al: The occurrence of sleep disordered breathing among middle-aged adults. *N Engl J Med* 1993;328:1230–1235.

43. Stradling JR, Crosby JH: Predictors and prevalence of obstructive sleep apnea and snoring in 1001 middle-aged men. *Thorax* 1991;46:85–89.

44. Odens ML, Fox CH: Adult sleep apnea syndromes. *Am Fam Physician* 1995;52;859–866.

45. Westbrook PR: Sleep disorders and upper airway obstruction in adults. *Otolaryngol Clin North Am* 1990;23:727–743.

46. Kaplan J, Starts BA: Obstructive sleep apnea syndrome. *Mayo Clin Proc* 1990;65:1087–1094.

47. He J, et al: Mortality and apnea index in obstructive sleep apnea. Experience in 385 male patients. *Chest* 1988;94:9–14.

48. Browman CP, et al: Obstructive sleep apnea and body weight. *Chest* 1984;85:435–438.

49. Brownwell LG, et al: Protriptyline in obstructive sleep apnea: A double-blind trial. *N Engl J Med* 1982;307:1037–1042.

50. Man GCW: Obstructive sleep apnea: Diagnosis and treatment. *Med Clin North Am* 1996;80:803–820.

51. Mignot E: Genetic and familial aspects of narcolepsy. *Neurology* 1998;50(suppl 1):516–522.

24

Sudden Death in the Athlete

Malissa Martin, EdD, ATC, CSCS

QUICK CONTENTS

- The anatomic structures of the cardiovascular system and the circulation of blood throughout the body.

- The electrical and mechanical events of the cardiac cycle.

- The determinants of cardiac output, the oxygen demands of the heart, and the factors that influence blood circulation.

- The effects of exercise on the heart.

- The epidemiology of sudden death in athletes and its causes, including hypertrophic cardiomyopathy and Marfan's syndrome.

- Other risk factors for sudden death, including cardiovascular disease/arteriosclerosis and hypertension.

- The American Heart Association Guidelines for identifying athletes at risk for sudden death.

- A plan to handle an incident of sudden death.

- Counseling athletes at risk for sudden death.

OVERVIEW

This chapter begins with an explanation of the anatomy and function of the cardiovascular system. The first section specifically focuses on how blood circulates in the body and explains the cardiac cycle, describing the sequence of electrical and mechanical events that occur. It includes cardiac output as the measure of the heart's performance, calculated by multiplying the heart rate by the stroke volume. It also explains how heart rate and stroke volume, along with adequate coronary blood flow, are the major determinants of the heart's oxygen needs. Factors that influence the circulation of blood including vessel size, viscosity, and the autonomic nervous system are discussed next. The next section describes the role of exercise and the heart. The following section focuses on sudden death in athletes. Sudden cardiac death can be defined as an unexpected and nontraumatic event that occurs instantaneously or within minutes of an abrupt change in a person's previous clinical state. This section examines epidemiologic factors, common cardiac-related causes, physiologic principles of sudden death in athletes younger than age 30 years and older than age 30 years, identification of associated risk factors, and sports participation guidelines. The chapter ends with a description of the athletic trainer's role before, during, and after the occurrence of a sudden death incident.

CIRCULATION OF THE BLOOD

The *cardiovascular (circulatory) system* is a complex arrangement of connected tubes that include arteries, arterioles, capillaries, venules, and veins. The heart, a hollow muscular organ composed of cardiac muscle tissue, is the center of this system. Blood circulates throughout the body by pressure that is generated by the heart. The heart, or myocardium, is divided in half by the septum wall. Each side of the heart is further divided into an upper chamber (the *atrium*) and a lower chamber (the *ventricle*). The four sections of the heart are referred to as the left atrium, left ventricle, right atrium, and right ventricle.

During systemic circulation, as blood passes through tissues and organs, it gives up oxygen and nutrients and absorbs cellular waste and carbon dioxide. Likewise, during pulmonary circulation, as blood passes through the lungs, it releases carbon dioxide to the lungs and absorbs oxygen.

The cardiac cycle begins as oxygenated blood flows from the left ventricle through the aorta, the major artery leaving the left ventricle, and into the arteries, the tubular vessels that carry blood from the heart to body tissue (**Figure 24-1**). From the arteries, the blood circulates into the *arterioles*, which are small branches of the arteries, and then into the small, thin-walled *capillaries*. Here, individual red blood cells have close contact with the individual cells of the body. Next, deoxygenated blood circulates into the small veins, or *venules*, which eventually unite to form larger veins. The two largest veins in the body, the *superior* and *inferior venae cavae*, deliver blood to the right atrium of the heart. Blood then flows into the right ventricle and is pumped into the lungs (**Figure 24-2**). The cardiac cycle is completed when blood passes through the pulmonary capillaries and into the left side of the heart (**Figure 24-3**).

THE CARDIAC CYCLE

The *cardiac cycle* is the electromechanical sequence of events that occurs with one contraction *(systole)* and relaxation *(diastole)* of the heart muscle (**Figure 24-4**). To understand the principle of the heart as a pump, knowledge of the physical events that occur during the cardiac cycle is imperative.

Sequence of Electrical Events

A network of specialized tissue that is capable of conducting electrical current runs throughout the heart muscle.

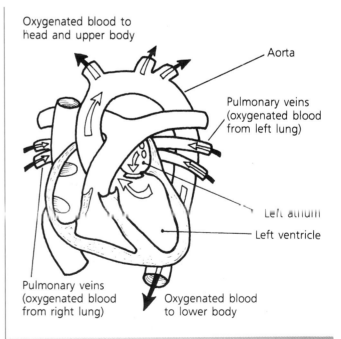

Oxygenated blood to head and upper body

Aorta

Pulmonary veins (oxygenated blood from left lung)

Left atrium

Left ventricle

Pulmonary veins (oxygenated blood from right lung)

Oxygenated blood to lower body

FIGURE 24-1

The cardiac cycle begins when oxygenated blood flows from the left ventricle through the aorta and into the arteries.

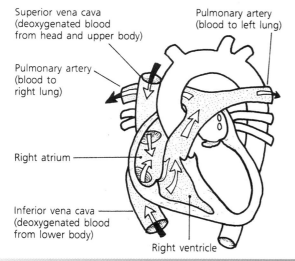

Superior vena cava
(deoxygenated blood
from head and upper body)

Pulmonary artery
(blood to left lung)

Pulmonary artery
(blood to
right lung)

Right atrium

Inferior vena cava
(deoxygenated blood
from lower body)

Right ventricle

FIGURE 24-2

From the venae cavae, blood passes through the right atrium, into the right ventricle, and then is pumped into the lungs.

The Cardiac Cycle

Oxygenated blood⇒Left Ventricle⇒Aorta⇒Arteries⇒Arterioles⇒ Capillaries⇒**Deoxygenated blood**⇒Venules⇒Veins⇒Superior and Inferior Venae Cavae⇒Right Atrium⇒Right Ventricle⇒Lungs⇒Pulmonary Capillaries⇒Left Atrium

FIGURE 24-3

Oxygenated blood flows from the left ventricle to the aorta, arteries, arterioles, and capillaries. Deoxygenated blood flows through the venules, veins, venae cavae and into the right atrium, right ventricle, lungs, pulmonary capillaries, left atrium, and left ventricle, where the cycle begins again.

The flow of electrical current through this network causes smooth, coordinated contractions of the heart. These contractions produce the pumping action of the heart. The cardiac cycle is initiated by an electrical impulse that starts over the atria and ventricles of the heart and results in *depolarization* (change in electricity) and contraction of the individual myocardial cells (**Figure 24-5**). Under normal conditions, the electrical impulse originates in the *sinoatrial node*, which is located in the upper part of the right atrium close to where it meets the superior vena cava. Upon leaving the sinoatrial node, the impulse depolarizes the surrounding atrial muscles, producing atrial contraction, and then travels rapidly through specialized conduction tissue to the left atrium and to the atrioventricular (AV) node.

An *electrocardiogram (ECG)* records electrical currents that flow through the heart. Because of the body's ability to act as an electrical conductor, any two points on the body can be connected with electrical leads to record

FOCUS ON . . .

The Cardiac Cycle

Sequence of electrical events

One contraction (systole) and relaxation (diastole) of the heart muscle constitutes the cardiac cycle. The cycle begins with an impulse that originates in the sinoatrial node and depolarizes the atrial muscles, producing atrial contraction. The impulse then travels via specialized conduction tissue to the left atrium and the atrioventricular node. The electrical current that flows through the heart is recorded on an electrocardiogram (ECG). The P wave reflects atrial contraction, the QRS complex is ventricular activation, and the T wave is ventricular repolarization.

Sequence of mechanical events

Mechanically, the atrium contracts after the P wave, increasing atrial pressure and propelling blood across the mitral and tricuspid valves. As the QRS complex peaks, ventricular pressure rises rapidly, initiating ventricular systole. Once ventricular pressure exceeds atrial pressure, the atrioventricular valves close and may widen. The mitral valve closes, ventricular pressure increases rapidly with ventricular contraction, and the aortic and pulmonary valves open. When ventricular pressure exceeds that of the aorta or pulmonary artery, the semilunar valves open, and the blood is ejected rapidly from the heart. Ventricular pressure continues to rise briefly, and then falls quickly as the ventricular muscle relaxes. The kinetic energy of the blood causes flow across the semilunar valves despite the absence of a pressure gradient. As vessel pressure exceeds the pressure of the outflowing blood, the flow reverses and the semilunar valves close, ending systole. Aortic and pulmonary pressures rise briefly.

When left ventricular pressure falls below arterial pressure, the mitral valve opens and the atrial blood flows into the ventricles. Atrial pressure drops rapidly as blood exits to the ventricle, which becomes distended as pressure increases. Ventricular and atrial pressures begin to equilibrate, blood flow into the ventricle slows, and atrial systole initiates the cardiac cycle again.

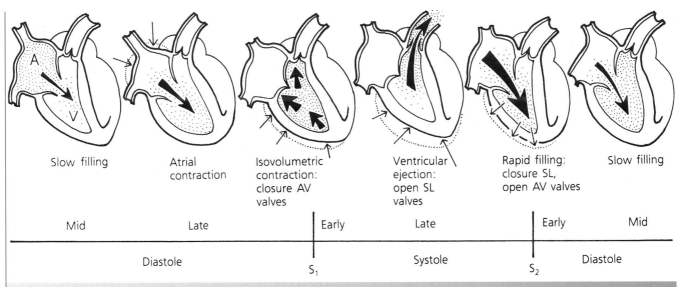

Mid	Late	Early	Late	Early	Mid
Diastole		S_1	Systole	S_2	Diastole

FIGURE 24-4

The cardiac cycle consists of an electromechanical sequence of events that occurs with one contraction (systole) and relaxation (diastole) of the heart muscle. (Reproduced with permission from Ortiz Vinsant M, Spence MI, Chapell D: *A Commonsense Approach to Coronary Care*, ed 2. St. Louis, MO, CV Mosby, 1975.)

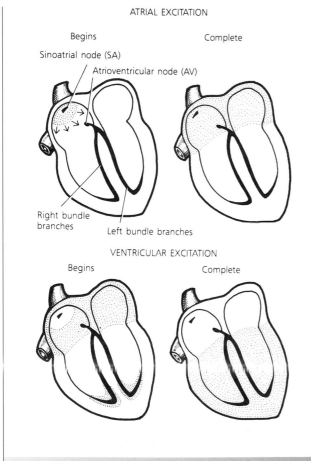

FIGURE 24-5

An electrical impulse that starts over the atria and ventricles of the heart initiates each cardiac cycle and results in depolarization and contraction of the individual myocardial cells.

the electrical activity of the heart. As a result of depolarization and repolarization, the readings produced by the electrical activity of the heart form a series of waves and complexes that are separated by regularly occurring intervals. The waves measured by an ECG include P waves, QRS complexes, and T waves. *P waves* monitor atrial contraction, ventricular activation is expressed by *QRS complexes*, and *T waves* show ventricular repolarization data **(Figure 24-6)**.

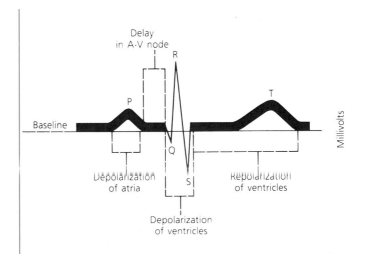

FIGURE 24-6

The waves measured by an ECG are represented by P waves, QRS complexes, and T waves. (Reproduced with permission from Constant J: *Learning Electrocardiography*. New York, NY, Little, Brown & Co, 1973, p 3. © by Jules Constant.)

Sequence of Mechanical Events

The mechanical events that follow electrical activation of the heart are easily explained by observing the pressure changes that occur in both the atria and the ventricles (**Figure 24-7**). Following the P wave, the atrium typically contracts, increasing atrial pressure and propelling blood across the mitral and tricuspid valves. When the QRS complex is near its peak, ventricular pressure begins to rise rapidly, initiating ventricular systole. When ventricular pressure exceeds atrial pressure, the AV valves close and may widen, placing additional pressure on the atrium. After the mitral valve closes and before the aortic and pulmonary valves open, the pressure on the ventricle rapidly rises because of ventricular contraction against the volume of blood it contains.

When the pressure of the ventricle exceeds that of the aorta or pulmonary artery, the semilunar valves open, and blood is rapidly ejected out of the heart through these valves. This is referred to as the *rapid ejection phase*. Ventricular pressure continues to rise briefly; then, as the ventricular muscle begins to relax, the pressure starts to decrease rapidly. Because of kinetic energy produced by the blood flow, blood can still flow across the semilunar valves, even though a pressure gradient no longer exists. Eventually, vessel pressure will exceed the energy of the blood that is flowing out. This may cause the flow of blood to reverse, causing the semilunar valves to close. This completes the systolic phase and is followed by a brief rise in aortic and pulmonary pressure.

When the pressure level in the left ventricle drops below arterial pressure, the mitral valve opens, and the blood from the atria flows into the ventricles, initiating the prefilling phase of the ventricle. As blood leaves the atria, pressure drops rapidly resulting in a rapid filling process of the ventricle. As the ventricle begins to fill, it becomes distended with the incoming blood, resulting in a rapid rise in pressure. As this occurs, the ventricle and atrial pressures begin to equilibrate, and blood flow into the ventricle significantly decreases. Following this phase, atrial systole occurs and initiates the cardiac cycle once again.

CARDIAC OUTPUT

Determinants

Cardiac output, a measure used to monitor the heart's performance, takes into consideration stroke volume and heart rate. *Stroke volume* is the amount of blood ejected per heartbeat, and *heart rate* is heartbeat frequency (contractions).

Stroke volume depends on preload, afterload, and contractility of the heart. Preload is a reflection of muscle quality. An elastic, distended ventricle propels larger quantities of blood more rapidly than a stiffer, less distended ventricle. Age may have an impact on the degree of ven-

FOCUS ON . . .

Cardiac Output

Determinants

Cardiac output is a measure of the heart's performance and is the product of stroke volume and heart rate. Stroke volume depends on preload, afterload, and contractility. Preload reflects muscle quality: an elastic, distensible ventricle propels more blood more rapidly than a stiffer, less distensible ventricle. Age reduces ventricular elasticity and distensibility. Afterload is the impedance of forward blood flow from the ventricles, which relates directly to arterial system resistance. Left ventricular pressure must exceed aortic pressure before forward flow can occur. Hypertension and aortic valve narrowing increase left ventricular workload by resisting forward flow. Contractility refers to the overall capacity of the ventricular muscle fibers to contract and produce useful work. Individuals with severely diseased or damaged hearts often have poor contractility, and trained athletes can have vigorous contractility.

Heart rate is determined by the sinus node firing rate, which is modulated by neural signals from the cardioregulatory brain centers (increased by sympathetic signals, decreased by parasympathetic signals), in the chemical substances in the blood, and from the thyroid hormones. Heart rate varies with age, gender, level of fitness, changes in activity demands, temperature, fluid status, drug and hormone levels, and dietary state.

tricular elasticity and distensibility experienced. Afterload is the impedance of forward flow of blood from the ventricle as a result of aortic pressure and relates directly to the resistance in the arterial system. Afterload is the result of resistance in the arterial system and aortic pressure. In order for forward blood flow to occur, left ventricular pressure must exceed aortic pressure. Subsequently, hypertension (high blood pressure) can lead to heart problems, including heart attacks, because it significantly increases the workload of the left ventricle by resisting the forward flow of blood. Moreover, obstructing lesions, such as narrowing of the aortic valves, can also lead to heart problems because they can impede the outflow of blood from the left ventricle.

Because contractility cannot be directly measured, it is a difficult concept to quantify. Conceptually, it refers to the overall capacity of the ventricular muscle fibers to contract and produce beneficial outcomes. Contractility can be poor in individuals who have severely diseased or damaged hearts. Conversely, contractility can be quite vigorous in trained athletes who have exceptional physical output.

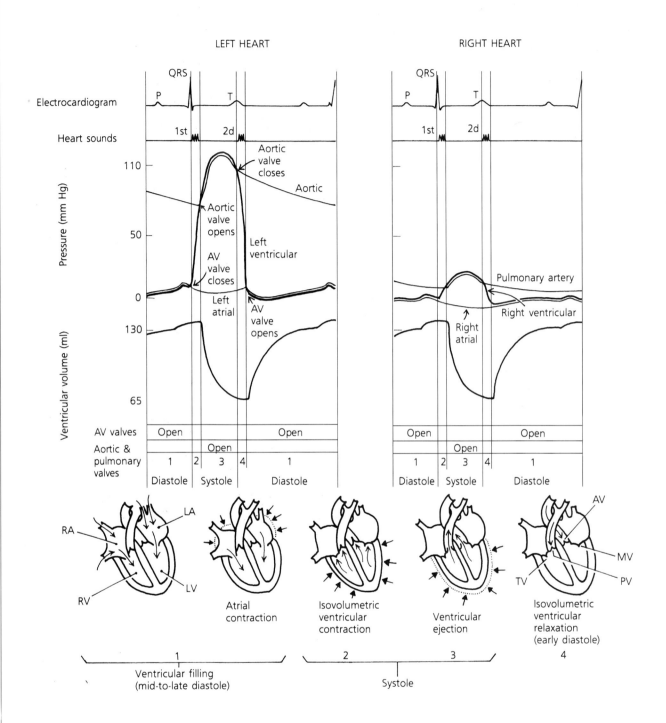

FIGURE 24-7

The pressure changes that occur in both the atria and ventricles explain the mechanical events that follow electrical activation of the heart. (Reproduced with permission from Ganong WF: *Review of Medical Physiology*, ed 11. Norwalk, CT, Appleton & Lange, 1983.)

Heart rate is the final determinant of cardiac performance. Heart rate is determined by the rate at which the sinus node is fired as modulated by the constant flow of neural signals (sympathetic signals increase the rate, parasympathetic signals decrease the rate) from the cardioregulatory centers in the brain; in the chemical (humoral) substances circulating in the blood, such as adrenaline; and from the thyroid hormones. Heart rate is the inherent power that develops force. Heart rate varies with age, gender, and level of fitness. Also, the heart can fluctuate depending on activity, temperature, fluid status, drug and hormone levels, and dietary state.

OXYGEN DEMANDS OF CARDIAC MUSCLE

The four determinants of cardiac performance (preload, afterload, contractile state, and heart rate) not only define the pumping capabilities of the heart, but also assist in determining oxygen levels necessary for the heart muscle[1] (**Figure 24-8**). The oxygen demand of the heart muscle correlates best with the product of the heart rate and blood pressure both at rest and with exercise. Moreover, the heart muscle's oxygen demand depends on the interaction of heart rate, blood pressure, and activity level. The oxygen demand level can be met by adequate coronary blood flow.

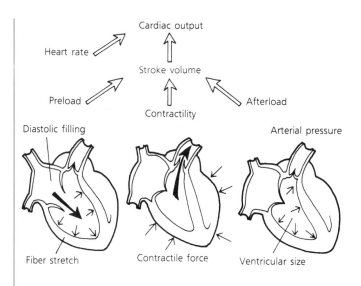

FIGURE 24-8

The four determinants of cardiac performance, preload, afterload, contractile state, and heart rate, define the heart's pumping capabilities and determine the necessary oxygen levels. (Reproduced with permission from Anderson S, McCarty Wilson L: Pathophysiology: Clinical Concepts of Disease Processes. New York, NY, McGraw-Hill, 1978.)

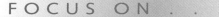

FOCUS ON . . .

Oxygen Demands of Cardiac Muscle

Preload, afterload, contractility, and heart rate not only determine cardiac performance, but also determine the oxygen needs of the working heart muscle. Oxygen demand correlates best with the product of heart rate and blood pressure, at rest and with exercise. Rate, pressure, and activity interact to meet the oxygen demand.

The need for adequate coronary blood flow

At rest, the working myocardium uses 8 to 9 mm of oxygen per 100 g of ventricular tissue, or about 7% of the body's total oxygen requirement. Increasing any of the cardiac performance determinants sharply increases the oxygen requirement, which can only be met by increasing coronary artery flow. The coronary arterial bed can increase flow 600%, providing an oxygen demand increased by 500%.

Results of impeded coronary blood flow

Coronary artery narrowing can compromise coronary blood flow, both at rest and during exercise. Impeded flow causes angina when insufficient oxygen is available to the myocardium. When the major coronary vessels become completely blocked, no oxygen is supplied to the heart, causing a myocardial infarction, which results in permanent injury or death of the heart muscle.

The Need for Adequate Coronary Blood Flow

During resting conditions, the working myocardium uses 8 to 9 mm of oxygen per 100 g of ventricular tissue, or about 7% of the body's total oxygen requirement.[1] Increased levels in any of the four cardiac performance determinants sharply increases the oxygen requirement for the myocardium. Because all of the available oxygen delivered to the working myocardium is extracted in a single pass, an increase in oxygen requirement can only be met by increasing blood flow in the coronary artery. Subsequently, increased oxygen demands in coronary beds can only be met by increased coronary blood flow. Fortunately, the normal coronary arterial bed has the capability of increasing blood flow 600% or providing an increased oxygen demand of 500% more than base conditions.[2] Coronary blood flow is regulated by myocardial oxygen demand; it also follows certain physical laws of blood flow inherent in a closed-pipe system such as the circulatory system. These principles of flow relate to all blood vessels of the body.

Results of Impeded Coronary Blood Flow

The narrowing of one or more of the major coronary arteries can compromise coronary blood flow during rest and exercise. Impeded blood flow decreases the amount of oxygen available to the working heart muscle and may result in *angina*, or chest pain. Complete blockage of the major coronary vessels results in total lack of oxygen to the myocardium and results in *myocardial infarction*, or heart attack, causing permanent injury to or death of the heart muscle.

FACTORS THAT INFLUENCE BLOOD CIRCULATION

Blood flows through the vessels of the body because of the pulsatile pumping action of the heart and the pressure differential across the cardiac system from the left ventricle (100 to 110 mm Hg) to the right atrium (5 to 10 mm Hg), allowing for adequate blood flow.[2] Loss of pressure immediately compromises blood flow to critical organs, such as the heart, brain, and kidneys, and, if the loss of pressure is prolonged, can result in death.

Vessel size is one factor that determines blood circulation. According to *Poiseuille's law*, the length and radius of a vessel is significant in determining blood flow and resistance.[2] Small changes in vessel radius can produce large changes in flow. For example, a 20% increase in vessel radius can produce more than a 100% increase in blood-volume flow[2] (**Figure 24-9**). This is an important concept to understand when analyzing how blood flow is impeded by arteriosclerosis or stenosis of blood vessels, particularly in arteries.

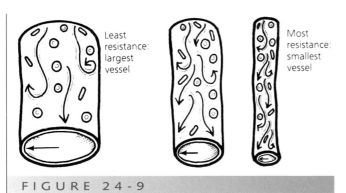

Least resistance: largest vessel

Most resistance: smallest vessel

FIGURE 24-9

Vessel size is a factor that determines blood circulation; the length and radius of a vessel is important for blood flow and resistance.

Poiseuille's law measures the internal friction of fluid. Fluids high in viscosity impede flow to a greater degree than do low-viscosity fluids. Viscosity is measured by using a *hematocrit*. A hematocrit measures the ratio of the volume of packed (erythrocytes) red blood cells to the total volume of blood. Polycythemic states, which are characterized by an increased number of erythrocytes, tend to have reduced blood flow, whereas anemia states, which are characterized by hemoglobin measuring less than 8 g

per 100 mL of blood or hematocrit less than 45%, substantially increase blood flow.[3]

The velocity of blood flow through circulation is a function of the cross-sectional area of the vessels. In the arterial system, where the total cross-sectional area is small, velocity levels are high. In the capillary system, where the total cross sectional area is large, velocity levels are low. In the venous system, which has a fairly large total cross sectional area, blood flow is rapid when compared to the capillary system, but slow when compared to the arterial system.

The third factor that influences blood circulation relates to the autonomic nervous system. Sympathetic stimulation (the "fight or flight"response) increases arterial and ventricular contractility and heart rate and accelerates the spread of excitation through the AV node and, to a lesser extent, through the ventricles. Parasympathetic stimulation generally has the opposite effect. The effect of the nervous system on the heart is a combination of the sympathetic and parasympathetic stimulation, which usually vary reciprocally. The parasympathetic stimulation, usually inhibitory, normally predominates and maintains the optimal resting heart rate of about 65 to 75 beats/min; however, during exercise the sympathetic nervous system becomes dominant.[2]

EXERCISE AND THE HEART

The method used to increase cardiac output during exercise varies depending on age, health, body position, and physical conditioning. In particular, the relative contribution of heart rate and stroke volume as it relates to cardiac output is a subject of considerable interest. When in a supine position, most individuals who are not physically conditioned appear to increase their cardiac output during mild to moderate exercise through an increase in heart rate. When performing higher levels of exercise, this population's stroke volume increases 10% to 15% in a supine position and 30% to 100% in an upright position, despite a considerably shortened systolic ejection.[2] Individuals who are accustomed to physical exercise demonstrate an earlier and more significant increase in stroke volume in both the supine and upright positions. Moreover, stroke volume can often double during upright exercise for this population. Heart rate may increase threefold or even fourfold in trained individuals during exercise, whereas stroke volume increases considerably less and can even decline with extreme increases in heart rate.[2]

Although the arterial systolic blood pressure often increases 40 to 60 mm Hg during moderate or heavy exercise, the mean arterial blood pressure level increases much less.[2] The diastolic pressure may increase slightly, decrease slightly, or remain the same. Arterial resistance often decreases considerably during exercise. Exercise also decreases blood volume in venous reservoirs, especially blood stored in the spleen. These changes make more blood available to the heart, arterial vessels, and exercising muscles.

Dual Role of Exercise

Exercise has a dual role in relationship to the cardiovascular system. The first role is its positive effect on cardiovascular fitness. Cardiovascular fitness improves cardiac efficiency and performance by achieving workloads at less cost. When an individual is cardiovascularly fit, heart rate and blood pressure responses at given workloads are reduced, and contractility of the heart and the blood supply to the peripheral working muscles improve. The second role of exercise contributes to cardiovascular medicine. By increasing the workload of the heart, exercise can uncover imbalances between supply and demand of oxygen and blood and, subsequently, identify coronary artery disease that may not be suspected in a resting state. As a result, safe levels of exercise should be determined for an individual by his or her physician.

SUDDEN DEATH IN ATHLETES

Epidemiology

Of the five million participants in high school, collegiate, and professional sports, fewer than 20 individuals die per year as a result of sudden death syndrome.[4,5] Sudden, unexpected death is frequently caused by cardiac-related anomalies in individuals who are physically fit and in competitive athletes as well. The most common cardiac condition for individuals younger than age 30 years may be *hypertrophic cardiomyopathy (HCM)*. Sudden death in athletes older than age 30 years is more often related to

FOCUS ON . . .

Exercise and the Heart

Age, health, body position, and physical conditioning determine the mechanism used to increase cardiac output during exercise. When exercising mildly to moderately in the supine position, most unconditioned individuals increase cardiac output by increasing heart rate. With more strenuous exercise, stroke volume increases 10% to 15% while supine and 30% to 100% while upright, despite a shortened systolic ejection. Conditioned persons show earlier, more marked increases in stroke volume in both positions; stroke volume can double during upright exercise. Heart rate can increase three- or fourfold, while stroke volume increases far less and may even decline as heart rate increases further.

Arterial systolic blood pressure can increase by 40 to 60 mm Hg during moderate or heavy exercise, but the mean arterial blood pressure fails to increase as much. Diastolic pressure may increase or decrease slightly or remain the same, while arterial resistance often decreases significantly during exercise. Exercise also reduces blood volume in venous reservoirs, especially the spleen, making more blood available to the heart, arterial system, and exercising muscles.

Dual role of exercise

With regard to the cardiovascular system, exercise improves cardiac efficiency and performance by decreasing heart rate and blood pressure at given workloads and increasing contractility and blood supply to the peripheral working muscles. Exercise also can reveal supply and demand imbalances and allow identification of coronary artery disease. Safe exercise levels can then be determined by the athlete's physician.

cardiovascular disease (80% of all sudden deaths in this population) rather than to cardiac anomalies.[4,6] HCM is an abnormal condition of the heart that causes the myocardium to increase to a size greater than its allotted space. As a result of this hypertrophic condition, the left ventricle is narrowed and unable to pump blood to the aorta. This condition often causes an obstruction of blood flow, resulting in arrhythmia or irregular heartbeats and sometimes death.[4-7]

Although sudden death has been reported in all races and age groups, and in both genders, it is most common in young Caucasian boys or men. Results of one study indicate that 62% of all reported sudden death incidences occurred in high school athletes, 22% in college athletes, 9% in middle and junior high school athletes, and 7% in professional athletes.[4]

The study found that 65% of high school athletes who suffered sudden death were male.[4] Reasons cited for men being more susceptible to sudden death may be attributed to the tendency for male athletes to participate at higher levels of physical intensity than female athletes. Men may give little attention to, or deny, prodromal symptoms. Pathologic conditions, combined with a larger cardiac size, increases the risk for male athletes.[8] In addition, more incidences of sudden death have been reported in male athletes who participate in football and basketball.[4] A possible reason for this is that physical training requirements are considerably different in male-dominated sports than training requirements for traditional women's sports.

Although race has been found to be a significant factor associated with sudden death, more research is needed to understand the underlying reasons behind this. In the study noted above, of the 134 cardiac-related sudden death cases, 70 individuals were Caucasian, 59 were African-American, and five were either Asian, Native American, or Hispanic. Based on data from autopsy reports, African Americans (48%) were more likely than Caucasians (36%) to die as a result of hypertrophic cardiomyopathy.[4]

Age of the athlete continues to play a role in the cause of sudden death. Sudden death cases of athletes younger than age 30 years are usually associated with hypertrophic cardiomyopathy or other cardiac-related conditions. Sudden death cases of athletes older than age 30 years are typically related to cardiovascular disease, with an increase in arteriosclerotic disease cases being reported.[5]

The time of day may play a role in the occurrence of sudden death. For example, sudden death caused by HCM typically occurs between 3:00 pm and 9:00 pm, the time period when most athletes practice and compete. This differs from traditional heart attacks, which most often occur during morning hours. More sudden death cases were reported during the months of August through January, which may be attributed to basketball and football seasons.[4]

FOCUS ON . . .

Sudden Death in Athletes

Fewer than 20 sudden deaths will occur per year among five million high school, college, and professional sport participants. Athletes younger than age 30 years are most likely to die of hypertrophic cardiomyopathy (HCM), and those older than age 30 years are most likely to die of cardiovascular disease. Young male Caucasians are at highest risk, as are high school athletes. Male athletes may be more at risk because they tend to participate at higher physical intensity levels than female athletes, they deny or fail to attend to prodromal symptoms, and they have larger hearts, which in combination with pathologic conditions, can be more dangerous. Also, sudden death is more common in male football and basketball players.

Race is a significant factor, with Caucasians and African Americans most vulnerable, although the reasons are unclear. Time of day and month appear to play roles, with most sudden deaths from HCM occurring between 3:00 pm and 9:00 pm, when most athletes practice and compete. The months of August through January are associated with higher risk of sudden death, possibly because of football and basketball seasons.

HCM describes a heart whose muscle cells have enlarged such that the heart is larger than its allotted space; the narrowed left ventricle cannot pump blood to the aorta and blood flow is obstructed. This obstructive cardiomyopathy can lead to arrhythmias, with symptoms of cardiac palpitations or flutter, angina, syncope, or vertigo. However, symptoms need not be present. HCM is detectable via EKG, radiograph, and echocardiogram.

Eccentric left chamber hypertrophy and increased left ventricular mass are found in trained athletes in highly dynamic sports. A larger left ventricle without left chamber increase (concentric hypertrophy) is seen in athletes participating in static sports. When exercise decreases or ceases, the heart returns to its original size, in contrast to the heart in HCM.

An athlete with HCM and left ventricular thickness of 20 mm or more, left ventricular outflow obstruction of 50 mm Hg or more, atrial or ventricular arrhythmia, or a family history of sudden death (especially in those younger than age 40 years) should not participate in competitive sports. An athlete with HCM who does not have these findings can engage in low-intensity sports.

Hypertrophic Cardiomyopathy

In HCM, the heart muscle's cells enlarge, causing hypertrophy of the myocardium. As a result, the heart is unable to properly fit in its allotted space. Primarily, a hypertrophic condition affects the left ventricle, which functions as a pump to flow blood to the aorta. Because of the enlarged size of the heart during hypertrophy, obstruction of blood flow to the aorta is common, causing HCM to evolve into obstructive cardiomyopathy, resulting in *arrhythmia*, or irregular heartbeats.[6,9] Symptoms include complaints of cardiac palpitations or cardiac flutter, angina, *syncope* (a fainting spell or transient loss of consciousness), and vertigo.[6,9] However, in some patients, no symptoms were reported prior to sudden death. HCM can be detected through an EKG, which records electrical activity of the heart; radiographs, which indicate areas of enlargement; and echocardiograms, which screen for hypertrophy.[6,10]

Athletes who participate in highly dynamic sports such as football, basketball, soccer, hockey, and swimming have eccentric hypertrophy of the left chamber of the heart and a larger left ventricle as compared to sedentary individuals. This hypertrophy is a result of gradual physical training. Athletes who participate in highly static sports such as archery, diving, golf, and gymnastics have a larger left ventricle, while the left chamber remains the same (concentric hypertrophy). Although exercise does cause cardiac hypertrophy, when activity decreases or ceases, the heart muscle reduces to its original size. This does not occur in athletes with HCM, whose hearts do not decrease in size despite changes in exercise patterns.[11]

Athletes who have HCM and a left ventricle thickness that is greater than 20 mm, a left ventricular outflow obstruction that is greater than 50 mm Hg, experience atrial or ventricular arrhythmia, or have a family history of sudden death, especially before age 40 years, should not participate in competitive sports.[12] However, athletes who have HCM but do not have these findings can engage in low-intensity activities.

Marfan's Syndrome

Marfan's syndrome may affect more than 40,000 individuals in the United States and is found in all races and both genders.[13] *Marfan's syndrome* is a rare genetic disorder that is inherited as an autosomal dominant condition. Although this disorder is inherited genetically, 30% of reported cases indicate no family history of Marfan's syndrome.[13] A parent with Marfan's syndrome has a 50% probability of passing it on to an offspring. Marfan's syndrome primarily affects connective tissue.[9,13] Research indicates that the gene that encodes fibrillin is abnormal in individuals with Marfan's syndrome, decreasing the integrity of connective tissue throughout the body.[10,14] The most serious problems associated with Marfan's syndrome are related to the cardiovascular system. For example, the aorta can become weak and dilated and may become overextended during strenuous bouts of physical activity. Subsequently, an aortic aneurysm may dissect or the ascending aorta may rupture and lead to sudden death. Moreover, individuals with Marfan's syndrome often have *mitral valve prolapse*, in which the two leaflets of the mitral valve bellow backwards causing the heart to contract, resulting in an irregular heart rhythm.

Fortunately, unlike HCM, Marfan's syndrome can be easily identified and evaluated. **Table 24-1** lists several traits that are associated with Marfan's syndrome. Screening for Marfan's syndrome includes a musculoskeletal examination, an eye examination using a slit-lamp test, and an echocardiogram. The slit-lamp test is used by ophthalmologists to search for lens displacement, which

FOCUS ON . . .

Marfan's Syndrome

Marfan's syndrome is a rare, autosomal-dominant genetic disorder believed to affect more than 40,000 individuals in the United States. A parent with the syndrome has a 50% chance of passing it on to a child, but 30% of affected individuals have no family history of the condition. The gene encoding the protein fibrillin is abnormal, reducing connective tissue integrity. Cardiovascular problems are the most serious, including a dissecting aortic aneurysm or rupture of the ascending aorta. Mitral valve prolapse is common and can result in arrhythmias.

Physical traits associated with Marfan's syndrome include pes planus, tall and thin body structure, disproportionate or unusually large appendages, arm span greater than standing height, hyperextensible joints or an elongated thumb, scoliosis, convex-concave sternum (pigeon chest), genu recurvatum, nearsightedness, abnormally enlarged heart, increased incidence of hernias, and optic lens displacement. Screening consists of a musculoskeletal examination, eye examination with a slit-lamp, and an echocardiogram. Positive thumb or wrist tests also alert the clinician to the need for further evaluation.

Individuals with Marfan's syndrome should be closely monitored to maximize their life spans. A beta-blocker may help to decrease blood pressure and stress to the aorta, but strenuous or isometric exercise and contact sports should be avoided. Weight training is permissible with low resistance and multiple repetitions; other exercises should be low impact and low intensity.

appears in more than half of those individuals who have Marfan's syndrome.

Two tests are available that can detect Marfan's syndrome. The first test, the *positive thumb test*, indicates the presence of Marfan's syndrome if the patient is able to extend the thumb past the small finger when a fist is made around the thumb. The second test, the *positive wrist test*, indicates the presence of Marfan's syndrome if the middle finger and thumb of one hand overlap when the patient encircles the other wrist with them.[13,15] Once identified, individuals with Marfan's syndrome should be closely monitored. A beta-blocker may be prescribed to decrease blood pressure and reduce stress to the aorta. Strenuous exercise and participation in contact sports should be avoided, as well as isometric exercises such as Valsalva's maneuver. For individuals with Marfan's syndrome who participate in weight training, resistance should be low with multiple repetitions rather than high resistance with fewer repetitions. Exercises should be low intensity and low impact. At this time, there is no cure for Marfan's syndrome, but, with careful medical management, a lengthened life span is achievable.[13]

Cardiovascular Disease/Arteriosclerosis

Men older than age 40 years who have been sedentary and want to start an exercise program should undergo a treadmill test to screen for cardiovascular disease. This is particularly important for men who smoke and have high levels of serum cholesterol. Women should be tested for cardiovascular disease following menopause.[16] Warning symptoms for cardiovascular disease, especially for indi-

TABLE 24-1
PHYSICAL TRAITS ASSOCIATED WITH MARFAN'S SYNDROME

- Pes planus (flatfoot)
- Tall and thin body structure
- Disproportionate or unusually large appendages
- Arm span greater than standing height
- Hyperextensible joints or an elongated thumb
- Scoliosis
- Convex/concave sternum (pigeon chest)
- Genu recurvatum (hyperextension of the knee)
- Myopia (nearsightedness)
- Abnormally enlarged heart
- Increased incidence of hernias
- Optic lens displacement

FOCUS ON . . .

Cardiovascular Disease/Arteriosclerosis

To rule out cardiovascular disease before beginning an exercise program, men older than age 40 years, especially those who smoke or have high serum cholesterol, and postmenopausal women should undergo treadmill testing. Symptoms of cardiovascular disease include exercise-induced angina, nausea, abdominal pain, dizziness, and generalized fatigue, especially in individuals older than age 35 years. Athletes with these symptoms can exercise moderately, but should not compete.

The American College of Sports Medicine (ACSM) lists age, family history, cigarette smoking, hypertension, hypercholesterolemia, diabetes mellitus, and sedentary lifestyle as risk factors for coronary artery disease. The ACSM recommends that individuals with these risk factors, as well as anyone with a history of angina, palpitations, syncope, or dyspnea during exercise, consider an exercise EKG or treadmill stress test before beginning an exercise program.

viduals older than age 35 years, include exercise-induced angina, nausea, abdominal pain, dizziness, and generalized fatigue. Although individuals with cardiovascular risk factors are able to exercise moderately, they should not compete.[17]

Table 24-2 presents a list of risk factors and criteria for coronary artery disease developed by the American College of Sports Medicine (ACSM).[18] These criteria can be used to identify individuals at risk for coronary heart disease who should undergo an exercise EKG or treadmill stress test prior to beginning an exercise program. The ACSM also recommends that any person who has a history of angina, palpitations, syncope, or dyspnea during exercise should also undergo an exercise EKG prior to beginning a moderate or vigorous exercise program.[18]

Hypertension

More than 50 million Americans may have hypertension.[19] *Hypertension* is defined as a systolic blood pressure greater than 140 mm Hg or a diastolic blood pressure greater than 90 mm Hg.[20] **Table 24-3** classifies blood pressure for individuals age 18 years and older.[21] Unfortunately, a person can have hypertension long before overt symptoms develop. Because of this, individuals should be encouraged to have regular blood pressure screenings. Two general types of hypertension have been identified: primary or essential and secondary. Primary hypertension

Hypertension

Hypertension (systolic blood pressure greater than 140 mm Hg or diastolic blood pressure greater than 90 mm Hg) affects more than 50 million Americans. Primary hypertension has no identifiable cause and is seen more often in older adults, postmenopausal women, obese individuals, and African Americans. Treatment usually consists of antihypertensive drugs and lifestyle changes. Untreated hypertension can lead to heart disease (left ventricular hypertrophy, myocardial infarction, or angina), stroke, kidney disease, and blindness, with the severity directly related to the severity of the hypertension. Secondary hypertension is due to identifiable causes, such as chronic renal disease or renovascular disease; once these causes are identified, treatment should focus on dissolution. Because hypertension may cause no overt symptoms, individuals are encouraged to have regular blood pressure screenings.

does not have an identifiable cause and affects approximately 20% of adults between the ages of 25 and 74 years. It is seen more frequently in older adults, postmenopausal women, obese individuals, and African-Americans than in younger adults, premenopausal women, and Caucasians.[21] Treatment of hypertension often involves drug therapy (antihypertensive medications) and lifestyle changes, including diet restrictions, alcohol restriction, smoking cessation, and exercise. If left untreated, hypertension can lead to heart disease (left ventricular hypertrophy, myocardial infarction, and angina), stroke, kidney disease, and blindness. The degree of injury is directly related to the degree of hypertension. Secondary hypertension is due to identifiable causes frequently attributed to chronic renal disease and renovascular disease. Once the cause of hypertension is identified, treatment should focus on its dissolution.[20]

Concerns associated with hypotension are not nearly as great as those associated with hypertension. During physical activity and sports participation, individuals with hypotension should be monitored for syncope and fatigue, which may increase their risk of injury and negatively affect their physical performance.

AMERICAN HEART ASSOCIATION GUIDELINES

The American Heart Association has published recommendations concerning the identification of athletes at risk for sudden death.[17] First, a trained healthcare provider should conduct a thorough medical evaluation of the patient. All high school and college athletes should have brachial artery blood pressure measurements and heart sounds taken annually. Heart sounds should be checked with the athlete sitting and standing, and signs and symptoms of Marfan's syndrome should be observed. Second, the healthcare provider should conduct an annual cardiac history and ask the athlete the following questions:

- Have you ever had syncope or became unconscious during physical activity?
- Have you ever had angina or heart palpitations during or after physical activity?
- Do you get tired more quickly than friends do during physical activity?
- Have you ever had hypertension or high cholesterol?
- Have you ever been told that you have a heart murmur or other cardiac condition?
- Have any of your relatives died of heart problems or sudden death before age 50 years?
- Have any of your family members or relatives been diagnosed with Marfan's syndrome?
- Has a physician ever restricted or denied you participation in sports because of a heart-related problem?

American Heart Association Guidelines

To identify athletes at risk for sudden death, the American Heart Association has made several recommendations. An evaluation of all high school and college athletes should be conducted by a trained medical healthcare provider and should include brachial artery blood pressure measurements and heart sounds while sitting and standing. Screening for Marfan's syndrome should also be performed.

An annual personal cardiac history should be conducted to determine whether the athlete has ever experienced syncope or unconsciousness, angina or heart palpitations, or become tired more quickly than friends during or after physical activity. In addition, the athlete should be asked about hypertension and high cholesterol, a heart murmur or other cardiac condition, whether any relatives died of heart problems or sudden death before age 50 years, were diagnosed with Marfan's syndrome, or whether the athlete was ever restricted or denied sports participation for any heart-related problems.

An athlete with suspected cardiovascular abnormalities should be referred for further evaluation and the final decision regarding participation left to the primary physician.

TABLE 24-2
RISK FACTORS FOR CARDIOVASCULAR DISEASE

Risk factors	Criteria
Age	Men older than age 45 years, women older than age 55 years, or women with premature menopause who are not using estrogen replacement therapy
Family history	Myocardial infarction or sudden death prior to age 55 years in father or other first-degree related men, or before age 65 years in mother or other first-degreerelated women
Current cigarette smoker	
Hypertension	Blood pressure greater than or equal to 140/90 mm Hg on at least two occasions, or currently taking hypertension medication
Hypercholesterolemia	Total serum cholesterol greater than 200 mg/dL or HDL less than 35 mg/dL
Diabetes mellitus	Individuals with insulin-dependent diabetes mellitus (IDDM) who are older than age 30 years or have had IDDM for more than 15 years, and individuals with noninsulin-dependent diabetes mellitus who are older than age 35 years
Sedentary lifestyle	Individuals comprising the least active 25% of the total population, as defined by the combination of sedentary jobs involving sitting for a large part of the day along with no regular exercise or active recreational pursuits

(Adapted with permission from the American College of Sports Medicine: *ACSM's Guidelines for Exercise Testing and Prescription*. Baltimore, MD, Williams & Wilkins,1995.)

Based on the patient's history, if a cardiovascular abnormality is suspected, the athlete should be referred for further evaluation.[17] The athlete's primary physician is responsible for deciding if the patient is able to participate in physical activities.

PREPARING FOR A POSSIBLE SUDDEN DEATH INCIDENT

Sudden death may occur without warning to individuals who have had a thorough physical examination as well as individuals who have not been examined. Athletic trainers should be well prepared to respond to a sudden death incident before one occurs. At the 1995 Statement of the Summit Conference on Sudden Death in the Athlete, the National Athletic Trainers' Association Research and Education Foundation specified four major steps that should be addressed to minimize the occurrence of sudden death.[22] The four steps include (1) a preseason physical examination for all athletes that includes a cardiac history and examination, (2) monitoring the athletic field and identifying potential problems, (3) the establishment of an emergency medical plan, and (4) medical follow-up forall athletes.

TABLE 24-3
BLOOD PRESSURE CLASSIFICATION

Classification	Systolic (mm HG)	Diastolic (mm HG)
Normal	less than 130	less than 85
High normal	130 to 139	85 to 89
Hypertension:		
Stage I (mild)	140 to 159	90 to 99
Stage II (moderate)	160 to 179	100 to 109
Stage III (severe)	180 to 209	110 to 119
Stage IV (very severe)	Greater than 210	Greater than 120

(Adapted with permission from Lehne R, Moore L, Crosby L, Hamilton D(eds): *Pharmacology for Nursing*, ed 2. Philadelphia, PA, WB Saunders, 1994.)

Preparticipation Physical Examination

All athletes should undergo a preparticipation physical examination that includes a cardiovascular history and examination and be screened for Marfan's syndrome. The examination should be conducted 6 weeks prior to the start of preseason practice by a healthcare provider who has been trained to provide cardiovascular examinations.[22]

Field Monitoring and Recognition of Potential Problems

Once an athlete starts practicing, a qualified individual should be present at all practices and competitions to monitor the athletes and the facility and identify potential problems that may arise. As a minimum requirement, this individual should have current cardiopulmonary resuscitation (CPR) and first-aid certification; ideally, he or she should be an athletic trainer. Recognition of weather conditions, such as excessive heat and humidity, and of injuries and other physical conditions, such as cardiovascular ailments (exercised-induced bronchial spasms and syncope), should be included in the monitoring process. If conditions arise that need evaluation and treatment (both emergency and nonemergency situations), this individual should have the capability to initiate appropriate protocols.

Emergency Medical Plan

Before the practice season begins, a well-organized emergency medical plan should be developed and regularly practiced. This plan should be developed with input from the school administrators, team physicians, school nurses, athletic trainers, coaches, and community emergency medical service (EMS) staff. The emergency plan should include a written protocol for all sport facilities, including both indoor and outdoor facilities; communication availability (telephones, radios, and emergency telephone numbers); and emergency equipment including splints, stretchers, and backboards. The written protocol should be a step-by-step instructional guide that outlines the roles and responsibilities of key individuals, including who is to take charge of the situation, who should call for EMS, who accompanies the injured athlete to the emergency medical center, and who informs the family of the athlete's situation. Also, directions to the emergency medical facility should be included in the emergency plan. The emergency plan should be understood and practiced on a regular basis by all involved individuals.

In addition to the emergency plan, coaches or athletic trainers should maintain medical information cards for each athlete for quick reference. The medical information card should include the following information: the athlete's name, address, telephone number, age, date of birth, legal guardian and telephone number, insurance information, and specific information concerning medical conditions, such as allergies to medications and preexisting medical conditions.

Medical Follow-up

Any athlete who sustains an injury or who experiences signs or symptoms of a cardiovascular-related condition should be seen by a physician and receive appropriate medical attention. The athletic trainer should monitor the injured athlete through the medical evaluation process as well as through the treatment program and upon return to physical activity. If the athlete is a minor, the parent or guardian should be informed about the situation immediately in order to actively participate in medical treatment and follow-up care decisions.

RESPONDING TO CARDIO-VASCULAR EMERGENCIES

During practices and/or competitions, if a qualified individual suspects an athlete is having cardiovascular difficulty because of symptoms such as dyspnea, syncope, or undue fatigue, the athlete should be immediately removed from physical activity and evaluated by trained medical staff. This evaluation should include a patient history taken at the sideline of the athletic field and an assessment of the athlete's vital signs. The sideline history should focus on questions concerning breathing, angina,

FOCUS ON . . .

Preparing for a Possible Sudden Death Incident

Athletic trainers must be prepared to respond to sudden death incidents. In 1995, the National Athletic Trainers' Association Research and Education Foundation specified four essential steps in this process: 1) a preseason physical examination, including a cardiac history and examination, 2) athletic field monitoring and recognition of problems and potential problems, 3) an emergency medical plan, and 4) medical follow-up.

Preparticipation physical examination

An appropriately trained healthcare provider should conduct the preseason physical examination 6 weeks before the start of preseason practice. The evaluation should include a cardiovascular history and examination and screening for Marfan's syndrome.

Field monitoring and recognition of potential problems

Once practice begins, a qualified individual with at least current CPR and first-aid certification (ideally an athletic trainer) should cover all practices and competitions. Monitoring includes recognition of weather conditions and of injuries and other physical conditions. The athletic trainer or other qualified individual should be able to initiate appropriate protocols for both emergency and nonemergency conditions.

Emergency medical plan

A well-organized emergency medical plan should be in place and tested before practices or competitions begin. School personnel including administrators, team physicians, nurses, athletic trainers, and coaches, along with community emergency medical service personnel, should participate in the development of the plan, which should include a written protocol for all indoor and outdoor sports facilities, communication availability (telephones, radios, and emergency telephone numbers), and emergency equipment (splints, stretchers, and backboards). The written protocol is a step-by-step instructional guide detailing who takes charge of the situation, who calls the emergency medical service, directions to the facility, who accompanies the athlete to the emergency medical center, and who informs the family of the athlete's situation. Thorough understanding and regular practice of the plan by all involved persons is essential. Also, coaches or athletic trainers should maintain athlete medical information cards that include the athlete's name, address, telephone number, age, date of birth, legal guardian and telephone number, insurance information, medication allergies, and preexisting medical conditions.

Medical follow-up

Any athlete who sustains an injury or experiences signs or symptoms of a cardiovascular condition should be evaluated by a physician and receive appropriate medical attention. The athletic trainer follows each athlete through this process, as well as treatment and return to activity. A minor athlete's parent or guardian should be kept informed and participate in the decisions regarding medical treatment and follow-up.

syncope, and fatigue. The athlete's pulse, respiration rate, and blood pressure should be measured and recorded. If any aspect of the history or the vital signs indicate cardiovascular difficulty, the athlete should immediately be transported to the emergency department for further evaluation.

If an athlete suddenly collapses on the court or field, a primary survey, including assessment of the athlete's airway, breathing, and circulation (ABCs), should be conducted. If the athlete is unconscious, the emergency plan should be activated and EMS should be summoned immediately. If the ABCs are absent, assisted breathing procedures and CPR should be implemented immediately. Assisted breathing and CPR should not be stopped until the athlete has begun to breathe again and has a heartbeat or EMS personnel have arrived at the scene and taken control of the situation.

If an athlete dies while participating in a sport, procedures need to be in place to contact the athlete's family, team members, faculty, and other appropriate individuals and verify necessary information such as the athlete's name, age, and physical characteristics.[10] Typically, schools and other institutions that sponsor sports already have response plans for various types of crises that may occur. Coaches, athletic trainers, and other individuals who work with athletes should be encouraged to contact their professional organization's administration to investigate and become familiar with established emergency procedures.

As with other crisis situations, after responding to a sudden death occurrence, all members of the sports medicine team should be debriefed by the athletic trainer. The debriefing session should address the effectiveness of the emergency plan and ideas on how the plan can be improved.

COUNSELING ATHLETES AT RISK FOR SUDDEN DEATH

Most athletes are highly competitive individuals who enjoy, and often thrive on, physical activity. When an athlete is identified as being susceptible to sudden death because of an underlying physical condition, it can be devastating to the individual. In the case of athletes younger than age 30 years, most physical abnormalities associated with sudden death cannot be corrected.[23] As a result, the chances of sudden death occurring from the diagnosed anomaly must be weighed and seriously considered prior to participation in physical activity.

Certain conditions, such as HCM, pose a risk to athletes who may be susceptible to sudden death and other conditions such as exercise-induced asthma. The athlete should

TABLE 24-4
CLASSIFICATION OF SPORTS ACCORDING TO INTENSITY OF EXERCISE

High to moderate intensity			Low intensity
High- to moderate-dynamic and high- to moderate-static demands	High- to moderate-dynamic and high-static demands	High- to moderate-static and low-dynamic demands	Low-dynamic and low-static demands
Boxing	Badminton	Archery	Bowling
Crew/rowing	Baseball	Auto racing	Cricket
Cross-country skiing	Basketball	Driving	Curling
Cycling	Field hockey	Equestrian	Golf
Downhill skiing	Lacrosse	Field events (throwing)	Riflery
Fencing	Orienteering	Field events (throwing)	
Football	Ping-pong	Gymnastics	
Ice hockey	Race walking	Karate or judo	
Rugby	Racquetball	Motorcycling	
Running (sprint)	Running (distance)	Rodeo	
Speed skating	Soccer	Sailing	
Water polo	Squash	Water skiing	
Wrestling	Swimming	Weight lifting	
	Volleyball		

(Reproduced with permission from Bethesda Conference 16: Cardiovascular abnormalities in the athlete: Recommendations regarding eligibility for competition. *J Am Coll Cardiol* 1985;6:1185–1232.)

TABLE 24-5

COUNSELING STRATEGIES FOR AN ATHLETE AT RISK FOR SUDDEN DEATH

- Impose sanctions and restrictions on the athlete rather than offering guidelines

- Draw on examples of sudden death cases rather than statistics when describing risks

- Direct the athlete to appropriate-intensity sports to allow continuation of involvement in team sports

- Involve parents and coaches in the counseling process

(Reproduced with permission from Allison TG: Counseling athletes at risk for sudden death. *Phys Sports Med* 1992;20:141–149.)

be educated concerning the physical condition and risks that his or her condition imposes on general health and participation in physical activities. **Table 24-4** shows a classification of sports according to intensity of exercise. Because the athlete's death will affect parents, family, friends, teammates, coaches, and other individuals, counseling efforts should be included. During counseling, the athlete should be encouraged to accept his or her limitations in order to develop a quality lifestyle. **Table 24-5** suggests strategies to use when counseling an athlete at risk for sudden death.[23]

Often, coronary artery disease (CAD), the most common cause of sudden death in athletes older than age 30, can be identified through various medical tests and treated with diet, medication, and appropriate exercise guidelines.[5,6,10] Exercise testing can identify ischemic threshold levels for athletes with CAD, allowing the clinician to give recommendations to the athlete concerning acceptable levels of physical activity the individual may safely participate in. However, sudden death has occurred in individuals who have had normal exercise test results.[24] **Table 24-6** suggests counseling strategies that are appropriate for athletes older than age 30 years.

TABLE 24-6

COUNSELING STRATEGIES FOR ATHLETES WITH CAD OLDER THAN AGE 30 YEARS

- Prohibit competitive events but encourage conditioning activities to the athlete within prescribed limits

- Teach athletes how to monitor target heart rate and rate of perceived exertion

- Limit exercise sessions to 1 hour per day with a maximum of six sessions per week

- Decrease intensity of exercise during hot weather because of dehydration and its effects on the heart

- Draw on case examples rather than statistics when describing potential risks to the athlete

(Reproduced with permission from Allison TG: Counseling athletes at risk for sudden death. *Phys Sports Med* 1992;20:141–149.)

CHAPTER REVIEW

The cardiovascular system is a complex arrangement of interconnected tubes with the heart at the center. The heart generates pressure that circulates blood throughout the body, where it delivers oxygen and nutrients and absorbs cellular waste and carbon dioxide. As blood passes through the lungs, it gives up carbon dioxide and absorbs oxygen. The cardiac cycle describes the electromechanical sequence of events that occurs with one contraction (systole) and one relaxation (diastole) of the heart.

Cardiac output, a measure of the heart's performance, is determined by preload, afterload, contractility, and heart rate and is calculated as the product of stroke volume and heart rate. These same factors also determine the oxygen needs of the working heart muscle. Elements that influence blood circulation include vessel size, vessel cross-sectional area, and autonomic nervous system stimulation. Exercise not only improves cardiovascular fitness, but it also reveals imbalances between supply and demand that might not otherwise be suspected.

Sudden death is rare among young athletes. In individuals younger than age 30 years, the most common cause of sudden death is hypertrophic cardiomyopathy, and in individuals older than age 30 years, sudden death is usually the result of cardiovascular disease.

Young, male, Caucasian, high school football and basketball players appear to be most at risk for sudden death.

Athletes with hypertrophic cardiomyopathy, Marfan's syndrome, cardiovascular disease or arteriosclerosis, and hypertension can be counseled regarding appropriate physical activities. The severity of the condition will determine which activities and intensities are permitted.

Athletic trainers must be prepared to respond to sudden death incidents by adhering to the steps recommended by the National Athletic Trainers' Association Research and Education Foundation: (1) a preseason physical examination, including a cardiac history and examination, (2) athletic field monitoring and recognition of problems and potential problems, (3) an emergency medical plan, and (4) medical follow-up. If the athletic trainer suspects a participating athlete is having cardiovascular difficulty, he or she should be removed from play immediately and evaluated.

When counseling athletes at risk for sudden death, the athletic trainer should encourage the individual to accept limitations and comply with a limited but full-quality lifestyle. In many cases, the athlete can continue to participate in sports with appropriate restrictions.

1. Blood enters the lungs from which chamber of the heart?

   A. Left atrium

   B. Left ventricle

   C. Right atrium

   D. Right ventricle

2. The QRS complex of the ECG represents:

   A. atrial contraction.

   B. atrial depolarization.

   C. ventricular activation.

   D. ventricular depolarization.

3. Cardiac output measures the:

   A. heart's performance.

   B. effect of exercise on the heart.

   C. ventricle's capacity to contract.

   D. number of heartbeats per minute.

4. Which of the following statements about individuals accustomed to physical exercise is true?

   A. Stroke volume decreases during supine exercise.

   B. Stroke volume decreases during upright exercise.

   C. Stroke volume doubles during upright exercise.

   D. Stroke volume increases after supine and upright exercise.

5. Sudden death in athletes older than age 30 years is most often related to:

   A. cardiac anomalies.

   B. Marfan's syndrome.

   C. cardiovascular disease.

   D. hypertrophic cardiomyopathy.

6. Pes planus, scoliosis, and hyperextensible joints may be indications of:

   A. hypertension.

   B. arteriosclerosis.

   C. Marfan's syndrome.

   D. left ventricular hypertrophy.

7. High blood pressure is defined as systolic and diastolic pressures greater than:

   A. 100/70 mm Hg.

   B. 120/80 mm Hg.

   C. 140/90 mm Hg.

   D. 160/100 mm Hg.

8. What information should the athlete's medical information card include?

   A. Written directions to the emergency facility

   B. Communication availability for all sport facilities

   C. The athlete's legal guardian's name and telephone number

   D. Who should contact the family about the athlete's condition

9. An athlete who seems unduly fatigued during practice or competition should be:

   A. watched carefully.

   B. referred to the team physician.

   C. transferred to an emergency facility.

   D. removed from participation and evaluated.

10. An athlete older than age 30 years with coronary artery disease should be counseled to:

   A. participate sparingly in competitive events.

   B. increase intensity of exercise during hot weather.

   C. limit exercise to 30 minutes per day five days per week.

   D. monitor target heart rate and rate of perceived exertion.

Answers on page 893.

References

1. Marcib EN: *Human Anatomy and Physiology*. Benjamin/Cummings, 1995, pp 634–636.

2. Hunter-Griffin L (ed): *Athletic Training and Sports Medicine*, ed 2. Park Ridge, IL, American Academy of Orthopaedic Surgeons, 1991.

3. Malvin RL, Johnson MD, Malvin GM: *Concepts of Human Physiology*. Benjamin/Cummings, 1997, p 241.

4. Maron BJ: Sudden death in young athletes. *Circulation* 1990;62:218–299.

5. Maron BJ, Epstein SE: Sudden death in the competitive athlete. *J Am Coll Cardiol* 1986;7:2220–2230.

6. Maron BJ: Hypertrophic cardiomyopathy in athletes. *Phys Sports Med* 1993;21:83–90.

7. Maron BJ, Pelliccia A, Spirito P: Cardiac disease in young trained athletes: Insights into methods for distinguishing athlete's heart from structural heart disease, with particular emphasis on hypertrophic cardiomyopathy. *Circulation* 1995;91:1596–1601.

8. Van Camp SP, Bloor CM, Mueller FO, Cantu RC, Olson HG: Non-traumatic sports death in high school and college athletes. *Med Sci Sports Exerc* 1995;27:641–647.

9. Falsetti H: Sudden death: How do we prevent it? *Training and Conditioning* 1995;5:24–28.

10. *Sudden Death in Sports*. Champaign, IL, Human Kinetics Publishers and NATA-Research and Education Foundation, 1997.

11. Mitchell JH, Haskell WL, Raven PB: Classification of sports. *J Am Coll Cardiol* 1994;24:864–866.

12. Kenny A, Shapiro LM: Sudden cardiac death in athletes. *Br Med Bull* 1992;48:534–545.

13. *The Marfan Syndrome Fact Sheet*. Washington, NY, National Marfan Foundation, 1997.

14. Kronisch RL: Sudden cardiac death in sports. *Ath Ther Today* 1996;1:39–41.

15. Hunt V: Sudden death in athletes. Proceedings of the summit on sudden death in athletes. *NATA News* 1997;September:14–17.

16. Sherman C: Sudden death during exercise. *Phys Sports Med* 1993;23:93–102.

17. Maron BJ, Thompson PD, Puffer JC, et al: *Cardiovascular Preparticipation Screening of Competitive Athletes: A Statement for Health Professionals From the Sudden Death Committee and Congenital Cardiac Defects Committee*. Washington, DC, American Heart Association, 1996.

18. American College of Sports Medicine: *ACSM's Guidelines for Exercise Testing and Prescription*. Baltimore, MD, Williams & Wilkins, 1995.

19. Joint National Committee on the Detection, Evaluation, and Treatment of High Blood Pressure: The fifth report on the joint national committee on the detection, evaluation, and treatment of high blood pressure (JNCV). *Arch Intern Med* 1993;153:153–183.

20. Bove AA, Sherman C: Active control of hypertension. *Phys Sports Med* 1998;26:45–53.

21. Lehne R, Moore L, Crosby L, Hamilton D: *Pharmacology for Nursing Care*, ed 2. Philadelphia, PA, WB Saunders, 1994.

22. Van Camp SP, Luckstead EF, Palacios L, Martin M, Amato H: Statement of the Summit Conference on Sudden Death in the Athlete. Dallas, TX, National Athletic Trainers' Association Research and Education Foundation, 1995.

23. Allison TG: Counseling athletes at risk for sudden death. *Phys Sports Med* 1992;20:141–149.

24. Sadaniantz A, Clayton MA, Sturner WQ, et al: Sudden death immediately after a record-setting athletic performance. *Am J Cardiol* 1989;63:375.

25

Infectious and Communicable Diseases

Clayton F. Holmes, EdD, PT, ATC
Barry D. Brause, MD
Bart Buxton, EdD, ATC

QUICK CONTENTS

- The types of microorganisms that commonly cause disease.

- Disease transmission.

- The implications of infectious disease control for the athletic trainer.

- Infection control and management.

- Specific infectious diseases.

OVERVIEW

We come into daily contact with hundreds of thousands of germs, including bacteria, fungi, protozoa, and viruses. This chapter provides an overview of disease-causing microorganisms and the common transmission route taken by these pathogens. This chapter will also address general measures that an athletic trainer should implement to prevent and control the spread of infection. Finally, this chapter will describe the signs and symptoms of specific diseases that may often be seen in athletes and provide additional information that may aid the athletic trainer in controlling the spread of these infections.

THE ATHLETIC TRAINER AND INFECTIOUS AND COMMUNICABLE DISEASES

Because humans are so well adapted to their environment, most germs encountered daily are basically harmless. However, many germs can become equally well adapted to their environment, the human body. Most of the time, these germs live quietly in the bowel, on the skin, or elsewhere in the body, doing no damage. In fact, many bacteria, such as those that produce vitamin K in humans, are beneficial. Other germs can become temporary invaders, causing an acute infection or chronic illness.

The athletic trainer will be called upon to treat athletes with a variety of communicable or infectious diseases. Most of these diseases are less contagious than is commonly believed. In addition, many immunizations, protective techniques, and devices are available that can minimize the healthcare provider's risk of infection. When these protective measures are used, the healthcare provider's risk of contracting a serious communicable disease is greatly decreased.

At times, an athletic trainer may already have a communicable disease. In such cases, the athletic trainer must take precautions to ensure that the disease is not transmitted to the athletes he or she is working with.

PATHOGENS

Five types of microorganisms commonly cause disease: viruses, bacteria, mycoplasma, rickettsiae, and protozoa.[1,2] *Viruses* are generally classified by the nucleic acid, either DNA or RNA, that they contain.[1] The mechanisms by which viruses cause cell injury and death vary greatly. For example, a virus may inhibit the host cell's synthesis of DNA, RNA, or protein.[1] A virus may also insert protein into the host cell, thereby damaging the host cell. In addition, a virus may replicate within a host cell, killing the host cell in the process. Respiratory epithelial cells may be killed by multiplication of a rhinovirus or influenza virus. Viruses may also allow the immune system to attack a host cell. Because viruses can damage or kill cells, they may promote secondary infection. For example, viral damage to airway epithelial cells predisposes the system to pneumonia.[1]

Bacteria are cells that lack a nucleus and an endoplasmic reticulum. Bacteria are limited in their ability to cause disease by their ability or inability to adhere to specific cells or deliver toxins.[1] Bacteria are classified according to shape: spherical bacteria are cocci; spiral-shaped bacteria are spirilla or spirochetes; and rod-shaped bacteria are bacilli. Bacteria are also classified according to their cellular structure; bacteria with different structures respond differently to staining procedures. Based on their response to the dye, which indicates a particular cellular structure, bacteria may be designated as gram positive or gram negative.[2] Bacteria may colonize in or on a healthy individual. For example, *Streptococcus mutans* contribute to the microbial mass called dental plaque.[2]

FOCUS ON . . .

Pathogens

Viruses, bacteria, mycoplasma, rickettsiae, and protozoa are the five types of microorganisms that commonly cause disease. Viruses can injure and kill cells by inhibiting the host cell's DNA, RNA, or protein synthesis; inserting protein into the host cell; replicating within a host cell; or causing a host cell to be attacked by the immune system. Secondary infection can then set in. Bacterial cells lack a nucleus and endoplasmic reticulum; they cause disease by adhering to cells or delivering toxins. Bacteria are classified by shape: spherical, spiral, or rod-shaped. They are also classified as gram positive or negative depending on how cellular structures respond to dye. Mycoplasma are single cells that lack a rigid cell wall. Although they are similar to bacteria, mycoplasma are unaffected by antibiotics that act on cell walls. Rickettsiae, or gram-negative bacteroid organisms, are transmitted by animals and can cause life-threatening infections. Protozoa (parasites and fungi) are single-cell microorganisms. Parasites are frequent causes of death in developing countries, and fungi usually cause superficial skin infections and sometimes deep fungal infection.

Like bacteria, *mycoplasma* are single-cell substances. However, unlike bacteria, mycoplasma lack a rigid cell wall.[1,2] Antibiotics that are active against bacterial cell walls will have no effect on mycoplasma. Mycoplasma are otherwise quite similar to bacteria and are often classified as bacteria.

Rickettsiae are gram-negative bacteroid organisms, which are bacteria-like substances, that may be transmitted primarily by animals and can cause life-threatening infections to humans.[2] Moreover, rickettsial diseases can be transmitted by ticks, lice, mites, and fleas.[2]

Protozoa are also single-cell microorganisms. These parasites are a common cause of death in developing countries and are responsible for African sleeping sickness.[1] Larger parasites of this type include roundworms and flatworms.[2] Fungi are unicellular organisms that most commonly cause infection, such as tinea or athlete's foot, in the superficial layers of the skin. However, some fungi attack subcutaneous tissue and can cause deep fungal infections.[1]

DISEASE TRANSMISSION

The terms "infectious" and " contagious" are often confusing. All contagious or communicable diseases are infectious; however, not all infectious diseases are contagious. An *infectious disease* is a disease that is caused by an infection, which is an abnormal invasion of a host by organisms such as bacteria, viruses, or parasites.[3] Pneumonia is an infectious process caused by the pneumococcus bacteria that is not *contagious*; it cannot be transmitted from one person to another. Lyme disease is also an infectious disease that is not contagious. However, the hepatitis B virus is contagious and can be transmitted from one person to another.[3]

When an individual becomes "infected," he or she has become a host to a disease-causing organism. The process of infection may occur either directly or indirectly. Because symptoms may occur throughout or during only part of the disease process, a host who has not shown symptoms can still transmit disease.

A *"chain of transmission"* describes all variables involved in the transmission of a pathologic microorganism into a host or human.[2] In essence, the transmission chain involves a pathogen (usually a microorganism), a reservoir (human, animal, plant, or soil), a portal of exit (the mouth, gastrointestinal tract, or respiratory tract), and a mode of transmission.[2]

The athletic trainer must understand how transmission occurs. There are four specific modes of transmission: blood, body fluids, excretions, and *exudates* (a liquid product that has escaped from blood vessels and been deposited in tissue as a result of inflammation).[1] In addition, transmission via these routes may be direct, which includes airborne transmission, or indirect. **Table 25-1**

shows the mechanisms of transmission of infectious diseases. *Direct transmission* occurs through person-to-person contact, whereas *indirect transmission* is through contact with an animal or insect or an inanimate object such as food, water, or soil. An example of indirect transmission is the spread of infection through a mosquito or tick bite.[3] Airborne transmission occurs when viable germs remain in droplets or dust.[3] However, for any type of transmission to occur, a pathogen must have a means of entry into a host. Ingestion and inhalation are two means of pathogen entry. Finally, for disease to occur, a susceptible host must be encountered.[2]

The host provides two general categories of barriers to transmission: *external barriers* and *internal defenses*. External barriers include the skin, mucous membranes, gag and coughing reflexes, and flushing reactions such as tears, saliva, and mucus.[2] Internal defenses that serve the host if the pathologic agent breaks through the external barriers include the internal physiologic inflammatory response and the immune response.[2] Many factors influence how the barriers respond to a microorganism and determine the host's susceptibility to infection. These factors include age, sex, general health status, and specific immune response.

In sports, other factors that influence host susceptibility include heavy training, competition, and stress.[4] For this reason, an athlete must have a good health profile before

FOCUS ON . . .

Disease Transmission

An infected individual has become a host, either directly or indirectly, to a disease-causing organism. A host can transmit disease in the absence of symptoms. The chain of transmission involves a pathogen, reservoir, exit portal, and transmission mode. Direct transmission occurs from person to person; indirect transmission occurs via contact with an animal or an inanimate object. For transmission, a pathogen must be able to enter a host, such as through ingestion or inhalation, and if disease is to occur, the host must be susceptible.

Barriers to transmission are external (skin, mucous membranes, gag and coughing reflexes, and flushing reactions such as tears, saliva, and mucous) and internal (internal physiologic inflammatory and immune responses). If the agent breaks through the external barriers, the internal barriers offer protection. The host's susceptibility to disease is influenced by age, sex, general health (including rest and nutrition), the specific immune response, heavy training, competition, and stress.

TABLE 25-1
MECHANISMS OF TRANSMISSION OF INFECTIOUS DISEASES

In this table, the routes of transmission and some examples are outlined. Although some germs frequently cause disease after transmission, transmission to susceptible host is much more likely to cause asymptomatic infection and colonization.

Route	Descriptions	Source	Examples
Direct	Contact, directly either with the person or with droplets sprayed (eg, by sneezing, coughing contact)	Ordinary contact	Measles, mumps, chickenpox, bacterial meningitis, influenza, diphtheria, herpes simplex
		Sexual contact	Syphilis, gonorrhea, HIV infection, hepatitis B, herpes simplex
Indirect Vehicle-borne	Spread by inanimate objects (eg, clothing, food, needles, transfused blood)	Food or water	Hepatitis A,B, and C, salmonella, *Shigella*, poliomyelitis
		Blood	HIV
		Other	Measles, tetanus
Vector-borne			*Shigella*
Mechanical	Simple carriage by insects. The vector simply carries the germs	Houseflies	
Biologic	Transmission by insect in which the germ lives and grows	Ticks	Lyme disease, Rocky Mountain spotted fever
		Mosquitoes	Malaria, equine encephalitis
Airborne Droplet nuclei	Residues after partial evaporation of droplets. Germs may remain viable, and the droplets may remain suspended for long periods of time		*Mycobaterium tuberculosis*, chickenpox
Dust	Small particles of dust from soil may carry fungal spores and remain airborne for long periods of time		*Histoplasma, Coccidioides, Miobacterium-avium intracellular*

(Reproduced with permission from Beneson AS: *Control of Communicable Disease in Man,* ed 15. Washington, DC, American Public Health Association, 1990.)

he or she begins participation in a strenuous training routine. A good health profile includes proper rest, nutrition, and levels of stress.[4] A good health profile is important during the off-season as well as during the season.

CONTROL OF INFECTIOUS DISEASE

The athletic trainer must understand the process of infection to prevent and control the spread of disease in the athletic setting. Cleanliness, the practice of universal precautions, vaccinations, and sanitization of equipment contribute to prevention. In addition, the athletic trainer must recognize the signs and symptoms of disease that the athlete may exhibit.

Prevention

Cleanliness

Before and immediately after treatment of an athlete with a communicable disease, the athletic trainer should routinely wash his or her hands thoroughly with nonabrasive soap and running water and should use single-use towels to dry the hands. Gloves may not provide complete protection, so hands should be washed thoroughly after gloves are removed. If running water is not available, effective substitutes such as alcohol-based rinses, foams, gels, or absorbent paper wipes should be used. Other commonly used antiseptics include chlorhexidine gluconate, iodine, and iodophors. An *iodophor* is a combination of iodine and a solubilizing agent or carrier that liberates free iodine in solution. Some forms are used as general antiseptics and are less irritating than elemental forms of iodine. Hands should be subsequently washed with soap and running water as soon as possible. Often, an infection penetrates the host through mucous membranes such as in the nose and lungs where the invader can firmly attach and multiply. Thus, other regions of the body, especially areas of skin and mucous membranes that have been exposed to potentially infected fluids, substances, or tissues should be cleansed as well in an appropriate manner.

FOCUS ON . . .

Prevention of Infectious Disease

Preventing the spread of infectious disease in the athletic setting relies on handwashing, universal precautions, vaccination, and sanitization of equipment and locker rooms. Before and immediately after physical contact when treating an athlete with a communicable disease, the athletic trainer should remove gloves, wash the hands thoroughly with nonabrasive soap and running water, and dry with single-use towels. Alcohol-based rinses, foams, gels, or absorbent paper wipes and chlorhexidine gluconate, iodine, or iodophor antiseptic can be used if running water is not available; however, running water and soap should be used as soon as possible. If the clinician's skin or mucous membranes have been exposed to potentially infected fluids, substances, or tissues, they should be cleansed as well.

Universal precautions protect healthcare personnel from exposure to infectious agents from the blood or body fluids of other individuals. The CDC recommends that blood, body fluids, and waste always be considered potentially infectious and handled appropriately. Barrier precautions should be used routinely.

A vaccination is a weakened living microorganism or laboratory-altered agent that is designed to stimulate the body's immune response to an antigen without causing the disease's symptoms. The body responds to an antigen by producing site-specific antibodies that attach to the antigen and try to destroy it. Inoculation with a vaccination enhances the body's normal defenses to an antigen. A vaccination is specific to a particular disease.

Adults should be vaccinated against tetanus and diphtheria, with boosters every 10 years, supplemented by an additional booster if wounds are sustained more than 5 years after the most recent vaccination. Viral diseases preventable by vaccines include measles, mumps, rubella, varicella, hepatitis A and B, and influenza.

Hepatitis B is a blood-borne agent that can be transmitted sexually, and therefore children, healthcare workers, and others who risk exposure are commonly vaccinated. The potential side effects of vaccinations must be considered when deciding what is appropriate for an individual.

Classrooms, crowded dormitories, and a large amount of time spent in close proximity to the same people contribute to the spread of infection among athletes. Athletes should be instructed to wash their hands carefully and avoid direct skin contact with others and contact with contaminated sporting equipment and appliances. Towels and water bottles should not be shared, and facial tissues should be used to clear nasal passages. Whirlpools, tables, and sinks should be disinfected after each use. The athletic training room should be treated as a healthcare environment and contain an appropriate sharps disposal container; equipment and table services should be disinfected. Athletic trainers should be current in their knowledge of infectious diseases, follow universal precautions, and dispose of infectious waste properly.

Universal precautions

Universal precautions have been designed to protect healthcare personnel from exposure to infectious agents from the blood and other body fluids of other individuals, including semen, vaginal secretions, tissue, and cerebrospinal, synovial, pleural, peritoneal, pericardial, and amniotic fluids. Undiagnosed infection and the increasing prevalence of blood-borne pathogens such as *human immunodeficiency virus (HIV)*, hepatitis B virus (HBV), and hepatitis C virus has prompted the Centers for Disease Control and Prevention (CDC) to recommend that blood and body fluids from all individuals be considered potentially infectious. All potentially infectious waste should be handled using rigorous infection control guidelines to minimize the risk of exposure. **Table 25-2** presents guidelines for minimizing the risk of exposure.[2]

Universal precautions should be taken during all potential exposures to blood, other body fluids, and contact with skin wounds, nonintact skin such as cuts and abrasions, and bite wounds.

Vaccination

Vaccination augments the body's immune system to prevent contamination by infectious agents. The body is constantly exposed to the danger of infiltration by foreign substances known as "*antigens*," which include bacteria, fungi, parasites, toxic chemicals, and abnormal body cells. When antigens are detected, the body naturally responds by producing site-specific antibodies that attach themselves to a given antigen and attempt to destroy it.[2]

A *vaccination* is a weakened or attenuated living microorganism or a milder form of an infectious agent that has been altered in a laboratory. A vaccination is designed to cause the body to produce an automatic immune response to an antigen, but it is not strong enough to cause the usual symptoms of a given disease. The vaccination is usually introduced into the body by inoculation and should enhance the body's normal defenses. Because antibodies are made to battle specific antigens, there is a multitude of vaccinations available that are specific to particular diseases.[2]

All adults should be vaccinated against tetanus and diphtheria. If an individual has not received a complete immunization course against tetanus and diphtheria, he or she should do so as soon as possible. Immunity should be maintained with booster inoculations every 10 years, and an additional booster should be given for appropriate wounds that are incurred more than 5 years after the most recent dose.[5]

Several common viral diseases can also be prevented with vaccination, including measles, mumps, rubella, varicella (chickenpox), hepatitis A, hepatitis B, and influenza.

TABLE 25-2

RECOMMENDATIONS TO MINIMIZE THE RISK OF EXPOSURE TO INFECTIOUS AGENTS

1. Routine use of barrier precautions:
   a) gloves for touching blood, body fluids, mucous membranes, or nonintact skin and for handling items or surfaces soiled with blood or other body fluids

   b) masks and protective eyewear or faceshields for situations likely to involve exposure to droplets of blood or other body fluids

   c) gowns for situations likely to involve splashes of blood or body fluids

2. Immediate washing of hands and other skin surfaces if contaminated with blood or other body fluids; handwashing immediately after removing gloves

3. Precautions to prevent injuries caused by needles, scalpels, and other sharp materials

4. Personal protective equipment (PPE) to include available mouthpieces, resuscitation bags, or other ventilation devices in necessary areas to minimize the need for emergency mouth-to-mouth resuscitation

5. Isolation of personnel with exudative lesions or weeping dermatitis to prevent contact exposure with other patients or equipment used in the care of others

(Adapted with permission from Goodman CC, Boissonnault WG: *Pathology: Implications for the Physical Therapist.* Philadelphia, PA, WB Saunders, 1998.)

Measles, mumps, and rubella vaccines are recommended for individuals who have not been vaccinated and have no detectable antibody to these viruses.

Hepatitis A virus (HAV), varicella, and influenza are potentially contagious diseases; however, an effective vaccine is available for each. In specific circumstances, these vaccines are beneficial in preventive strategies. The CDC recently made formal suggestions for the use of specific vaccines for healthcare workers, including recommendations for vaccination against measles, mumps, rubella, and varicella/zoster for workers who lack proof of immunity by history or serology.[6] Influenza and HAV vaccinations are only recommended for specific circumstances, such as for elderly individuals and individuals who have chronic liver disease.[7]

HBV is a sexually transmitted disease, and pediatricians commonly recommend the HBV vaccine for children prior to the years in which they may become sexually active.[8] Because HBV is a blood-borne infectious agent, the vaccine is also recommended for healthcare workers and other individuals who may be exposed to blood.

Because all vaccines are associated with potential side effects, decisions regarding vaccination must be individuaized.

Sanitization of equipment and locker rooms

The athletic environment provides a particular challenge in the prevention of certain diseases. In particular, upper respiratory illnesses seem to spread rampantly in certain seasons. Classrooms and crowded dormitories may contribute to this spread. In addition, the athlete is subject to an increased risk of infection because of the amount of time spent on a daily basis in close quarters with the same people. Athletes should be instructed to wash their hands carefully whenever appropriate, avoid direct skin contact with others, and avoid contact with sporting equipment and appliances that have been contaminated. Obviously, towels and water bottles should never be shared, and clearing of nasal passages should be done using facial tissues. After clearing the nasal passages, the individual should properly dispose of the tissue and wash his or her hands. Whirlpools, tables, and sinks in the athletic training room should be cleaned with disinfectants after each use.[4]

The athletic training room is a healthcare environment and should be treated as such. Athletic trainers should have up-to-date knowledge of appropriate immunization and should follow universal precautions and be prepared to dispose of infectious waste in a proper manner. Every training room should be equipped with an appropriate *sharps disposal container* (a plastic container in which sharp instruments such as needles are disposed of with proper precautions). Disinfectant should be used to clean the surfaces of equipment and tables in the training room. **Table 25-3** provides a checklist to control infection in the training room.[9]

Infection Control and Management

Recognizing signs and symptoms of infectious disease

Signs and symptoms of infectious disease vary widely. In general, systemic signs and symptoms include fever and chills, sweating, malaise and nausea, and vomiting.[2] Fever may be caused by nonsystemic insult, such as an inflammatory process, dehydration, or temperature regulation problems.[2] In general, athletes who exhibit any systemic symptoms should be referred to a physician immediately. **Table 25-4** presents the signs and symptoms of common infectious diseases.[2] One method of determining whether an athlete can participate in sports with certain symptoms is by performing a "neck check."[4] If the athlete has symptoms that are above the neck, such as a runny nose,

FOCUS ON . . .

Infection Control and Management

Systemic signs and symptoms of infection include fever, chills, sweating, malaise, nausea, and vomiting and require that the athlete be referred to a physician immediately. Athletes who have above-neck symptoms, such as a runny nose, sneezing, or a scratchy throat, can work out cautiously at a slower pace, but if the symptoms are below the neck, such as fever, muscle aches, productive cough, vomiting, or diarrhea, training should be postponed because athletes who train during the incubation period may be more likely to develop full-blown symptoms. An athlete with an upper respiratory infection who has been free of fever for 24 hours or who has been on the correct antibiotic for 24 hours can gradually resume activity.

A knowledgeable physician should be consulted when personnel may have been exposed to an infectious disease. Quick verification of the infected individual's diagnosis, with identification of the causative agent if possible, is important, and then the extent, timing, and duration of exposure and susceptibility for each contact can be determined. Intervention strategies can include isolation techniques, preventive antimicrobial therapy, vaccination, and education about the nature of the infection and the importance of these strategies. At-risk individuals should be monitored to determine if the spread of the disease has been controlled or if additional measures are needed. Healthcare workers with infectious diseases must follow recommended work restrictions for the safety of themselves and others.

TABLE 25-3

CHECKLIST FOR INFECTION CONTROL IN THE TRAINING ROOM

Immunization

➤ Athletic trainers should be appropriately immunized for HBV and other infectious diseases

Before evaluation or treatment

➤ All appliances must be disinfected with the appropriate agent, and an appropriate cover should be placed on the surface if necessary

During evaluation or treatment

➤ All athletes should be considered a potential source of infection, and the athletic trainer should wear protective attire and use the appropriate barrier technique

➤ The athletic trainer must protect his or her hands and avoid injury to them

- Hands should be washed before putting on gloves and after removing them

- Gloves should be changed each time a different athlete is treated

- Torn, cut, or punctured gloves should be discarded

➤ Injury from sharp instruments and needles should be avoided

- Sharp instruments must be handled carefully and placed in the appropriate containers after use

After evaluation or treatment

➤ The athletic trainer should wear protective gloves at all times

➤ Instruments must be cleaned thoroughly, and any instruments that came in contact with the athlete's mucous membranes must be sterilized

➤ Sharp instruments must be handled with caution, and scalpels and other sharp instruments should be placed in special puncture-resistant containers

➤ Environmental surfaces must be decontaminated

- Work surfaces should be wiped with absorbent towels, which should then be placed in the appropriate container for laundering

- Surfaces should be disinfected with the appropriate chemical disinfectant

➤ Contaminated waste must be removed in the appropriate manner

- Soiled waste that is contaminated with blood or other body fluids should be sealed in sturdy, impervious bags

- Hazardous waste must be disposed of according to local government regulations

The infection control program should be communicated to any other personnel that will come in contact with the athlete.

(Adapted with permission from Izumi HE: AIDS and athletic trainers: Recommendations for athletic trainer programs. *J Athletic Train* 1991;26:360.)

TABLE 25-4
SIGNS AND SYMPTOMS OF COMMON INFECTIOUS DISEASES

Systemic

➢ Fever, chills, malaise (most common early symptoms)
➢ Enlarged lymph nodes

Integumentary

➢ Purulent drainage from open wound or skin lesion
➢ Skin rash, red streaks
➢ Bleeding from gums or into joints; joint effusion of erythema

Cardiovascular

➢ Petechial lesions
➢ Tachycardia
➢ Hypotension
➢ Pulse rate change (increased or decreased depending on type of infection)

Central nervous system

➢ Altered level of consciousness, confusion, or convulsions
➢ Headache
➢ Photophobia (increased visual sensitivity to light)
➢ Memory loss
➢ Stiff neck, myalgia

Gastrointestinal

➢ Nausea
➢ Vomiting
➢ Diarrhea

Genitourinary

➢ Dysuria or flank pain
➢ Hematuria
➢ Oliguria (diminished amount of urine formation)
➢ Urgency, frequency of urination

Upper respiratory

➢ Cough
➢ Hoarseness
➢ Sore throat
➢ Nasal drainage
➢ Sputum production

(Reproduced with permission from Goodman CC, Boissonault WG: *Pathology: Implications for the Physical Therapist.* Philadelphia, PA, WB Saunders, 1998, p 125.)

sneezing, or scratchy throat, the athlete may be allowed to participate cautiously at a slower pace than normal.[4] Symptoms below the neck, such as fever, aching muscles, productive cough, vomiting, or diarrhea, indicate that the athlete should not participate.[4] Training during the incubation period, when symptoms may not be as apparent, increases the likelihood of developing full symptoms. For this reason, when symptoms appear, athletes should decrease training and allow the immune system an opportunity to fight the infection.

There are no specific guidelines for return to participation for the athlete who has an infection. Generally, an athlete with a typical upper respiratory infection who has not had a fever for 24 hours or an athlete who has been taking the correct antibiotic for 24 hours should be allowed to resume some activity. Other symptoms such as a runny nose are common and do not limit participation. Participation should be at a less strenuous level than usual in the beginning, depending on the athlete and the severity of the symptoms, to allow the immune system time to recover.

Management of group exposure to a contagious disease

When a group of athletes or any personnel has been potentially exposed to an infectious disease, a physician should be consulted to assess the presence and magnitude of any risk of infection transmission. The infected individual's diagnosis should be quickly verified; this diagnosis should include, if possible, an identification of the exact causative microorganism. The extent, timing, and duration of exposure to the contagious individual should be delineated for each athlete or personnel potentially involved. Those individuals who were significantly exposed to the infection should be evaluated for their individual susceptibility to the microbe. Whether these individuals have been immunized against the   ogen, making them less vulnerable to it, or their imm   tem is suppressed, making them more vulnera¹   the pathogen, should be determined.

Once the characteristics and risks of the potential exposure have been defined and analyzed, control measures can be identified and instituted to limit the spread of infection. These interventions are specific for the infectious agent, the circumstances that allow transmission, and the population at risk. Common strategies include isolation techniques, preventive antimicrobial therapy, vaccination, and education regarding the nature of the infection as well as the rationale and importance of the interventions being instituted. In addition, individuals who are at risk should be monitored for the development of infection. In this way, the physician can determine whether the contagion has been controlled or whether additional measures are necessary.

Management of personnel with infectious diseases

Table 25-5 presents the CDC's recommendations for immunizations for healthcare workers. **Table 25-6** shows recommendations for work restrictions of healthcare workers, including athletic trainers, who have an infectious disease.

SPECIFIC INFECTIOUS DISEASES

Viral Infections

HIV and AIDS

Acquired immune deficiency syndrome (AIDS) has been called a retroviral disease and is characterized by profound immune system suppression associated with opportunistic infections, secondary neoplasms, and neurologic manifestations.[1] AIDS targets both the immune system and the nervous system.[1] However, the incubation period of HIV (the virus that causes AIDS) and AIDS is in question.[1] Most researchers agree that the incubation period is long (several years) and is followed by a slowly progressive fatal outcome.[1]

The clinical manifestations of HIV and AIDS may be nonexistent, or they may include transient "mononucleosis-like symptoms," such as fatigue, once the virus develops into full-blown AIDS. The body normally produces T-4 cells to fight infection; however, these cells are destroyed by the virus, and this destruction leaves the body debilitated and readily susceptible to other infectious agents. Most patients die within 3 years of the onset of full-blown AIDS.[1]

Acutely, there may be symptoms such as sore throat, malaise, fever, and rash; in addition, aseptic meningitis may develop 3 to 6 weeks after infection and spontaneously resolve.[1] A high level of virus will be present in the plasma if it is tested at this point. The middle or chronic phase is characterized by extensive viral turnover. During this phase, patients may continue to be asymptomatic, or generalized lymphadenopathy may develop. This may be accompanied by fever, rash, and fatigue. These symptoms may imply the onset of a suppressed immune system.[1] The final, or critical, phase is characterized by fever, diarrhea, weight loss, and fatigue. Many opportunistic infections and neoplasms may affect an individual with AIDS, including protozoal, fungal, bacterial, and viral infections as well as neoplasms such as *Kaposi's sarcoma* (a malignancy in the form of a skin disorder). The period of communicability is in question; however, a carrier of HIV may be contagious indefinitely, even when the carrier shows no symptoms.

HIV is transmitted in one of three ways: sexual contact, *parenteral inoculation* (any way other than through the digestive system such as intravenous or intramuscular); and the passage of the virus from infected mothers to newborns.[10] The at-risk population includes those who participate in unprotected sexual activity, intravenous drug users, and those who receive a blood transfusion.[1,11] There has been no confirmed reported transmission from casual contact or insect bites. In addition, because activity

TABLE 25-5
RECOMMENDATIONS FOR IMMUNIZATION OF HEALTHCARE WORKERS

Disease	Recommendation
Hepatitis A	Immunizations are not routinely recommended for healthcare workers; they are recommended for neonatal intensive care unit healthcare workers who have no serologic evidence of previous HAV infection
Hepatitis B	Three-dose series of hepatitis B vaccine for preexposure protection is recommended
Influenza	Immunization is recommended for healthcare workers who care for patients with chronic illness or patients who are older than age 65 years. Healthcare workers who have a chronic illness such as a chronic obstructive pulmonary disease or cardiac disease should be immunized. Immunization should be administered annually prior (mid-October to mid-November) to the influenza season
Pneumococcus	Immunization is recommended for healthcare workers who are older than age 65 years or those who have underlying cardiac, pulmonary, liver, renal, or immunocompromising disease. A booster is required every 6 to 10 years
Poliomyelitis	The primary series of oral poliovirus vaccine administered during childhood is sufficient but should be complete. Immunization is not recommended during pregnancy
Tetanus, diptheria	A booster dose of tetanus-diphtheria toxoids, adult-type (Td) should be administered every 10 years after the primary series. The tetanus toxoid may be repeated in 5 years if a dirty wound is sustained
Measles	College entrants and healthcare workers who have no evidence of immunity to measles (diagnosis made by a physician or laboratory evidence of immunity) should have documentation of two doses of measles vaccine received on or after their first birthday. Vaccine can be given as measles, mumps, and rubella (MMR)*
Mumps	A single dose of live mumps vaccine received on or after the first birthday is sufficient. Vaccine can be given as MMR*
Varicella/ zoster	Two doses of vaccine given 4 to 8 weeks† apart should be administered to individuals who have not developed immunity. Pregnancy testing is required prior to administration to a menstruating woman

* There is no evidence suggesting an increased risk from live MMR vaccine to individuals already immune to these diseases as a result of previous vaccination or natural disease.

† Report by Center for Biologics Evaluation and Research, Food and Drug Administration. National Immunization Program, CDC, *MMWR* 1995; 44:264.

(Adapted with permission from Goodman CC, Boissonault WG: *Pathology: Implications for the Physical Therapist.* Philadelphia, PA, WB Saunders, 1998.)

FOCUS ON . . .

Viral Infections

Human immunodeficiency virus

The HIV/AIDS virus targets the immune and nervous systems and is characterized by profound immune system suppression associated with opportunistic infections, secondary neoplasms, and neurologic manifestations. A long incubation period is followed by a slowly progressive and fatal outcome (usually within 3 years of the onset of full-blown AIDS). Clinically, symptoms may be nonexistent or include fatigue and debilitation from T-4 cell destruction, which leaves the body vulnerable to infection; sore throat; malaise; fever; rash; and spontaneously resolving aseptic meningitis. Plasma virus levels are high. During the chronic phase, virus turnover is extensive. Patients may be asymptomatic, or generalized lymphadenopathy, fever, rash, and fatigue may develop, which reflect immunosuppression. The final or critical phase is typified by fever, diarrhea, weight loss, fatigue, opportunistic infections, and neoplasms. The communicable period is unknown, but a carrier is contagious indefinitely, even in the absence of symptoms.

Transmission modes for HIV include sexual contact, parenteral inoculation, and passage from infected mother to newborn. Although no cases of transmission from casual contact, insect bites, or athletic activity have been confirmed, taking universal precautions is wise. Experts agree that education, focusing on prevention, is the best way to manage the disease.

Viral hepatitis

Viral hepatitis affects the liver and is caused by several different microorganisms, among them hepatitis A, B, and C. Hepatitis A, also known as infectious hepatitis, is self-limiting and rarely fatal and occurs primarily in developing countries. Associated with substandard hygiene and sanitation, hepatitis A is transmitted through contact with contaminated feces, urine, blood, contaminated water, tainted food, dishes, eating utensils, clothing, and bed linen. Hepatitis B, also known as serum hepatitis, can result in acute hepatitis, chronic nonprogressive hepatitis, chronic progressive hepatitis that results in cirrhosis, full-blown hepatitis with massive liver necrosis, or an asymptomatic carrier state. Transmission modes are as for hepatitis A plus sexual contact and the sharing of razors and toothbrushes. Hepatitis C, previously known as non-A, non-B hepatitis, causes 150,000 to 170,000 new cases annually in the United States. Transmission is via contact with blood or body fluids or sexual contact with a carrier.

The CDC recommends that healthcare workers who may be exposed to blood or blood products be vaccinated for hepatitis B, and OSHA requires employers to make the vaccine available free to at-risk personnel. Precautions should be those for any blood-borne pathogen, including universal precautions as necessary. An athletic trainer working with open wounds should wear gloves and protective eyewear as needed and perform appropriate sterilization procedures. The risk for transmission of hepatitis under such conditions is actually greater than the risk of HIV.

Herpes simplex

Herpes simplex viruses 1 and 2 affect 30 million individuals in the United States; herpes simplex virus 1 is the most common. Cold sores, skin lesions, and encephalitis can result. Transmission is through contact with blood or body fluids, particularly via sexual contact. Herpes simplex virus 2 is similar to herpes simplex 1 and is sexually transmitted and produces genital lesions. Handwashing and gloves are recommended, along with regular skin checks for athletes in contact sports.

(Continued)

is typically limited to casual contact, the risk of transmission from athlete to athlete during an athletic activity is extremely low. In fact, the risk of transmission during sports has been reported as "infinitesimally small."[11] Although one case of HIV transmission at an athletic event was reported in the popular press, this case was not confirmed.[12] To date, there has been no confirmed transmission of HIV from athlete to athlete.[11-14] Despite this low risk, event guidelines such as universal precautions for athletic trainers should be followed. Such precautions will further diminish the risk of transmission of any disease caused by blood-borne pathogens, both from athlete to athlete and from athlete to healthcare provider. There are many tasks and activities that athletic trainers perform in which they may come in contact with blood or blood products. **Table 25-7** presents a selected list of these tasks.

FOCUS ON . . .

Viral Infections (Continued)

Influenza

The influenza virus causes upper respiratory tract infections with symptoms of severe cough, fever, nasal mucous, myalgia, and headache. Transmission is through airborne droplets or direct or indirect contact. Handwashing and the sanitary cleaning and disposal of items contaminated by nasal and throat secretions can help to limit spread. The influenza vaccine is recommended for the immunosuppressed and those at high risk for exposure, such as the elderly and healthcare workers.

Upper respiratory infections

Upper respiratory infections are caused by a variety of viruses, including the rhinovirus, which causes 40% of common colds in adults, and the corona viruses, which also cause common colds, most often in individuals between ages 15 and 19 years. Overtraining may reduce the immune system's ability to fight off this infection and increase the incidence of respiratory illness. Transmission is via direct and indirect contact with nasal or throat secretions or droplets.

Measles

Measles are caused by the rubella virus, which produces fever, malaise, muscle aches, headache, eye irritation, and light sensitivity. Transmission is primarily via droplet spread. Measles outbreaks have occurred at athletic events. Universal precautions can reduce the spread of the virus.

German measles

German measles, caused by the rubella virus, results in cold-like symptoms and swollen lymph nodes on the back and neck. A skin rash begins on the face and neck and spreads to the trunk and extremities. Transmission can be through the air. Once an athlete is diagnosed with German measles, universal precautions should be instituted. The disease is preventable with immunization.

Mononucleosis

Mononucleosis is caused by the Epstein-Barr virus, a member of the herpes group, and usually affects children and young adults. Symptoms include fever, severe sore throat, and lymphadenopathy. Transmission is from person to person via the oropharyngeal route. The immune system is compromised during the infection. To prevent splenic rupture as a result of lymphoid proliferation in the lymph nodes and spleen, the athlete should be restricted from contact sports. Signs and symptoms of splenic rupture are abdominal and left upper quadrant pain, sudden left shoulder pain, and shock. An athlete with these symptoms should be transported immediately to the emergency department.

Perhaps one of the positive outcomes of the general, widespread concern over HIV and AIDS has been the resulting emphasis on disease prevention. Many researchers believe that the most important method of management is preventive education.[15] According to one study, experts in the field agree that further education, with a focus on prevention, is warranted.[15] It should also be noted that federal law prohibits mandatory testing for HIV in an athletic environment.[16] Based on the small risk of exposure in an athletic environment, this policy seems warranted.

Viral hepatitis

Viral hepatitis is an infection of the liver caused by a small but growing group of viruses. These viruses are similar and will be described together after brief characterization of each one individually.[1] *Hepatitis A virus (HAV),* also known as infectious hepatitis, is a self-limiting disease that is fatal in only 0. 1% of patients.[1] HAV is a disease that occurs primarily in developing countries and is most commonly associated with substandard hygiene and sanitation.[1] Feces, urine, blood, contaminated water, eating utensils, dishes, clothing, and bed linens are the sources of this virus. The mode of transmission is most commonly person to person by fecal-oral route, through handling or ingesting contaminated substances. Ingestion of raw shellfish that have been contaminated by human waste is one of the more common sources of contamination.[1]

Hepatitis B virus (HBV) is also referred to as serum hepatitis. HBV can produce acute hepatitis, chronic nonprogressive hepatitis, chronic progressive hepatitis that ends in cirrhosis of the liver, full-blown hepatitis with massive liver necrosis, or an asymptomatic carrier state. Modes of transmission are similar to those for HAV. Sexual contact and the shared use of razors and toothbrushes have also been implicated as modes of transmission.

Hepatitis C, which is also called non-A and non-B hepatitis, is a major cause of disease worldwide. There are

TABLE 25-6 (CONTINUED)
RECOMMENDATIONS FOR WORK RESTRICITONS OF HEALTHCARE WORKERS WITH INFECTIOUS DISEASES

Disease	Relieve from direct patient contact?	Partial work restriction(s)	Duration
Pertussis			
Active	Yes		From beginning of catarrhal stage through third week after onset of paroxysms, or until 7 days after start of effective therapy
Postexposure (asymptomatic personnel)	No		
Postexposure (symptomatic personnel)	Yes		Same as active pertussis
Rubella			
Active	Yes		Until 5 days after rash appears
Postexposure (susceptible personnel)	Yes		From 7 to 21 days after exposure or 5 days after rash appears
Scabies	Yes		Until treated
Staphylococcus aureus (skin lesions)	Yes		Until lesions have resolved
Upper respiratory infections (includes respiratory syncytial virus)	Yes	Personnel with upper respiratory infections should not care for infants, children, or high-risk patients	Until acute symptoms resolve
Varicella (chickenpox)			
Active	Yes		Until all lesions dry and crust
Postexposure	Yes		From 10 to 21 days after exposure, or, if varicella occurs, until all lesions dry and crust

(Continued)

TABLE 25-6 (CONTINUED)

RECOMMENDATIONS FOR WORK RESTRICTIONS OF HEALTHCARE WORKERS WITH INFECTIOUS DISEASES

Disease	Relieve from direct patient contact?	Partial work restriction(s)	Duration
Zoster (shingles) Active	No	Appropriate barrier is desirable; personnel should not take care of high-risk clients	Until lesions dry and crust
Postexposure	Yes		From 10 to 21 days after exposure, or, if varicella occurs, until all lesions dry and crust

† At present there are no determinations, only recommendations, regarding potentially transmissible diseases such as hepatitis B or HIV in healthcare workers. Whereas the transmission risk of HBV is well documented, transmission of HIV from healthcare worker to patient is extremely unlikely; if HIV-positive employees follow usual infection control guidelines, the risk of HIV transmission during routine patient care is negligible. Our understanding of these diseases is so rapidly changing that any determination is often outdated before policies can be published.

*Mumps vaccine may be offered to susceptible personnel. When given after exposure, mumps vaccine may not provide protection. However, if exposure did not result in infection, immunizing exposed personnel should protect against subsequent infection. Neither mumps immunoglobulin nor immune serum globulin (ISG) is of established value in postexposure prophylaxis. Transmission of mumps among personnel and patients has not been a major problem in hospitals in the United States, probably owing to multiple factors, including high levels of natural and vaccine-induced immunity.

(Adapted with permission from *Immunological Disorders: Manual of Infection Control.* Houston, TX, 1986.)

approximately 150,000 to 170,000 new cases of this virus occurring annually in the United States.[1] Primary sources are blood and body fluids, and transmission occurs through contact with these fluids or sexual contact with a carrier.[1] Other modes of transmission are currently under investigation. Hepatitis C may represent the most common form of hepatitis to be transmitted through blood transfusion.[1]

Although HAV, HBV, and hepatitis C are the primary types of hepatitis diagnosed, other forms of viral hepatitis do exist.

The CDC recommends that any healthcare worker who may be exposed to blood or blood products be vaccinated for HBV.[16] The Occupational Safety and Health Administration (OSHA) requires employers to provide hepatitis vaccines free of charge for those personnel who are at risk.[16] Otherwise, precautions are similar to those for HIV and AIDS or any other blood-borne pathogen, including universal precautions, particularly wearing gloves and protective eyewear as needed when working with open wounds. Appropriate sterilization procedures should be performed after such an intervention. Although HIV and AIDS may have increased the awareness of the need for universal precautions in the athletic environment, athletic trainers should realize that in routine wound care, the risk of transmission is actually greater for other blood-borne pathogens such as hepatitis.[17]

Herpes simplex virus

Herpes simplex viruses 1 and 2, also called genital herpes, affect approximately 30 million individuals in the United States, and *herpes simplex virus 1* is the most common of the two.[1] Clinical manifestations include cold sores and other skin lesions including genital skin lesions.[1,18] The obvious source for transmission of herpes simplex 1 is the virus itself, which is found in saliva, and in skin or mucous membrane lesions. The mode of transmission is contact with blood or body fluids, particularly in sexual contact. Handwashing is essential, and gloves should be worn when contacting any skin lesion or orifice. Transmission of herpes simplex has been documented in athletes during wrestling and rugby matches.[12]

Herpes simplex virus 2 is similar to herpes simplex 1 in almost every respect, but it is only transmitted through sex-

TABLE 25-7

TASKS AND ACTIVITIES THAT MAY EXPOSE THE ATHLETIC TRAINER TO CONTACT WITH BLOOD

Reported tasks that involve contact with blood:

➤ Cleaning a wound such as an abrasion, blister, laceration, puncture, or turf burn

➤ Contact with contaminated material such as a bloody towel

➤ Caring for blood blisters

➤ Treating an open wound

➤ Controlling bleeding from a bleeding nose or other open wound

➤ Performing an on-the-field evaluation

➤ Aspirating a cauliflower ear or prepatella bursa

➤ Draining blood from a surgical scar

➤ Stabilizing a compound fracture

Unreported but potentially hazardous tasks

➤ Cleaning contaminated surfaces, materials, or instruments

➤ Disposing of contaminated materials

➤ Performing CPR or mouth-to-mouth resuscitation without an appropriate barrier device

(Adapted with permission from Izumi HE: AIDS and athletic trainers: Recommendations for athletic trainer programs. *J Athletic Train* 1991;26:359.)

ual contact and produces lesions in the genital area.[1] Again, handwashing and gloves are critical barriers to transmission. Because of this virus' mode of transmission, regular skin checks should be performed for athletes involved in contact sports. Genital herpes does not require disqualification from sports, assuming that there will be no contact with the affected area.

Influenza

The *influenza* virus is a specific virus that generally causes upper respiratory tract infections.[4] The clinical manifestations of influenza are severe cough, fever, nasal mucus, myalgia, and headache. The primary sources of the influenza virus are the nasal and throat secretions of an infected individual. The primary mode of transmission is through airborne droplets, but infection may also occur with direct or indirect contact. The most common lines of defense are handwashing and the sanitary cleaning and disposal of articles that are contaminated by nasal and throat secretions. Vaccination has been recommended for high-risk populations, particularly the elderly, who may have suppressed immune systems, or healthcare workers, who may be uniquely predisposed to the virus because of their exposure to individuals with the illness.

Upper respiratory infections

Different viral groups can cause upper respiratory infections. The *rhinovirus* accounts for approximately 40% of all infections in adult populations.[4] This virus causes what is referred to as the common cold. The seasons of prevalence are fall and spring. These viruses also commonly cause infection in the winter months, but to a lesser degree.[4] Another group of viruses that is responsible for the common cold are called the *corona viruses*. Colds from a corona virus occur in individuals who are between ages 15 and 19 years.[4] Many researchers believe that intense exercise may diminish the immune system's ability to fight off this type of infection and that overtraining may cause a higher incidence of respiratory illness.[4] As with influenza, the mode of transmission for these viruses is through direct and indirect contact with nasal and throat secretions or droplet inhalation. The presence of fever can be an indication of communicability. If the patient has a fever, precautions should be taken to prevent exposure to other individuals. Conversely, if the patient has other symptoms but no fever, he or she is probably not contagious.

Measles

The *rubella virus* is the source of measles. The clinical manifestations include fever, malaise, sore muscles, headache, eye irritation, and sensitivity to light. The primary mode of transmission is the spread of droplets. Again, as with other diseases, universal precautions are the primary mode of transmission prevention to other athletes and to the healthcare provider. Cases of measles outbreaks have been linked to athletic events including international gymnastics, wrestling, basketball, and international multiple sports.[4]

German measles

German measles is a relatively common disease that is caused by the rubella virus. Common clinical characteristics are cold-like symptoms, which are followed by a skin rash that appears on the face and neck and then rapidly spreads to the trunk and extremities. Symptoms are often accompanied by swollen lymph nodes on the back and neck. Viral contact can be airborne. Obviously, as with other diseases, when an athlete has been diagnosed with rubella, universal precautions must be followed. German measles, although often asymptomatic in adults, can produce all of the symptoms listed above in children and adolescents. Immunization will prevent the occurrence of German measles.

Mononucleosis

Mononucleosis is an acute viral disease. Infectious mononucleosis is caused by the Epstein-Barr virus (EBV), which is a member of the herpes virus group. This virus commonly affects children and young adults.[1] Common clinical manifestations include fever, severe sore throat, and swelling of the lymph nodes. The primary sources of infection are respiratory tract secretions, and the mode of transmission is person-to-person via the oropharyngeal route.[1] This infection also causes lymphoid proliferation in the blood, lymph nodes, and spleen. For this reason, contact sports are contraindicated for the athlete with infectious mononucleosis.[19] During the period of infection, the athlete with mononucleosis has a compromised immune system. Although the communicable period is unknown, contagion probably begins before symptoms develop and continues until after the fever subsides and oral and pharyngeal lesions become less inflamed.[2] Athletes with this disease should refrain from participation in contact sports because high-impact blows may result in a ruptured spleen. Signs and symptoms of rupture of the spleen include abdominal and left upper quadrant pain, sudden left shoulder pain, and possibly shock.[2,19] Rupture of the spleen is an emergency situation, and the athlete who manifests these symptoms should be transported immediately to the emergency department.

Bacterial Infections

Streptococcal bacterial infections

Streptococcal bacteria are also very common sources of throat infections. The clinical manifestations include fever, tonsillar exudates, tender neck lymph nodes, possible skin infection (impetigo) with vesicles, pustules, or crusted shallow ulcerations.[2]

Scarlet fever is accompanied by a bright red scarlet rash and is also associated with streptococcal disease.[2] The source of streptococcal disease is group A streptococcus, which is found in throat and skin lesions. Droplet spread is the common mode of transmission. The disease is generally not contagious after 24 hours of adequate antibiotic therapy. As with all upper respiratory infections, universal precautions, including masks, gloves, and handwashing procedures, serve as primary barriers to transmission.

Staphylococcal bacterial infections

Staphylococcus aureus is a common bacterial pathogen.[2] This type of bacteria is found commonly on the skin of healthy individuals. When it has the opportunity to enter deeper tissues, it can cause infections. Transmission com-

FOCUS ON . . .

Bacterial Infections

Bacterial infections affecting athletes include streptococcal, staphylococcal, and *Pseudomonas aeruginosa* infections. Group A streptococcal infections cause fever, tonsillar exudates, tender neck lymph nodes, impetigo, and scarlet fever. Transmission is via droplet spread. Once the individual has been on the appropriate antibiotic for 24 hours, he or she is no longer contagious. Masks, gloves, handwashing, and universal precautions limit the spread of infection.

Staphylococcus aureus is typically found on the skin of healthy individuals, but it can cause infection when it enters the deeper tissues through open wounds. Staphylococcal infections often start out in localized regions and then spread via the bloodstream to the lymphatic system and any location in the body, including the heart, bones, and joints. Clinically, the athlete may have furuncles, carbuncles, paronychias, felons, cellulitis, upper respiratory infections, open wounds (often with streaking), and fever and chills. Whenever an athlete has an open wound with significant local inflammation and systemic symptoms such as fever, immediate referral to the physician is required. Cultures confirm the bacteria and appropriate antibiotics are started.

Upper respiratory infections can be caused by bacteria as well as viruses; bacterial infections are treated with antibiotics. *Pseudomonas aeruginosa*, an opportunistic bacterium that thrives in moist surroundings, is commonly found in hospital and nursing home environments and swimming pools and whirlpools. It frequently causes pneumonia and urinary tract infection and is a particular problem after burns. The microorganism can invade small arteries and veins, resulting in vascular thrombosis and hemorrhagic necrosis, and it can attack the central nervous system, and the skin and soft tissue, causing localized infection and systemic symptoms. Symptoms can include headache, dizziness, earache, and sore throat. Pseudomonas infections can be fatal. Treatment consists of a wide variety of medical interventions such as antibiotics and surgery. Pseudomonas can also cause otitis externa, or swimmer's ear. Spending a great deal of time in the water and the anatomic position of the auditory canal may predispose certain individuals to this infection. Treatment is antibiotic therapy and ear cleaning. Prevention includes the use of an alcohol-based solution applied to the outer ear to promote moisture evaporation. Regular culturing of whirlpools and other moist environments is recommended to reduce the incidence of pseudomonas.

monly occurs through open skin wounds.[2] Because most individuals intermittently carry this organism on their skin or clothing, staphylococcal infections are common in many populations.[2] The athletic population is one group that is susceptible to staphylococcus infection. Many of these infections begin in localized regions and spread through the bloodstream to the lymphatic system and then to any location in the body. The heart, all bones, and joints have been common sites of secondary infections.[2] Clinical manifestations of this infection vary, but they include furuncles (boils), carbuncles (clusters of boils), paronychia (infection of the nail bed), felons (infection of the fingertips), upper respiratory infections, and open wounds.[2] Fever and chills are often associated with local inflammation.[2] Often, if the wound is on an extremity, visual streaking, which is the appearance of subcutaneous red streaks that indicate infection in the wound, may be visible. Staphylococcus infections can also be associated with skin infections such as cellulitis.[2]

In an athletic environment, whenever an open wound shows significant signs of local inflammation and systemic symptoms such as fever are present, the athlete should be referred to a physician immediately. Cultures are usually taken to confirm the presence of bacteria and appropriate antibiotic therapy is begun immediately. Untreated infections can lead to serious complications and can be fatal.[2]

Upper respiratory infections

Upper respiratory infections can be caused by either a virus or a bacterium. When an upper respiratory infection is caused by bacteria, antibiotic therapy may be beneficial. Among upper respiratory infections caused by bacteria are *Pseudomonas aeruginosa* and otitis externa (swimmer's ear).

Pseudomonas aeruginosa is an opportunistic bacterium that is frequently found in hospital or nursing home environments. The organism is associated with wounds and other infections such as pneumonia and urinary tract disease. It thrives in a moist environment such as a swimming pool or whirlpool.[2]

Clinical manifestations vary and depend on the site of the infection. For example, if the organism invades small arteries and veins, vascular thrombosis (clotting) and hemorrhagic necrosis (bleeding ulcers) result. The bacteria can attack the central nervous system causing a multitude of symptoms from paresthesia to cognitive deficits. In addition, it can attack skin and soft tissue causing localized infection as well as systemic symptoms such as headache, dizziness, earache, and sore throat. Pseudomonas is particularly opportunistic after burns and can cause a fatal infection.[2] Treatment is based on the location of the problem and consists of a wide variety of medical interventions such as antibiotic therapy and surgery. Because pseudomonas is prevalent in moist environments, such as whirlpools and other equipment found in the athletic training room or the locker room, a policy that emphasizes consistent culturing of appropriate areas is warranted.

A more common infection caused by *Pseudomonas aeruginosa* is *otitis externa*, or swimmer's ear. Otitis externa is an infection common to swimmers and has been linked to inadequate chlorination in swimming pools; however, the condition seems to be a common problem for any individual who spends a great deal of time in the water. Some researchers believe that the anatomic position of the auditory canal may predispose certain individuals to this condition. The moist environment created within the external ear canal after water has entered the ear may also promote infection.[9]

Appropriate treatment of otitis externa includes antibiotic therapy. Preventive measures include the use of a commercial alcohol-based solution that is applied to the outer ear to rapidly evaporate the moisture that could otherwise promote bacterial growth. The athletic trainer should refer an athlete with signs and symptoms of otitis externa to a physician. The physician may prescribe cleaning of the ears and antibiotic therapy.

CHAPTER REVIEW

Viruses can injure and kill cells, and secondary infection can then set in. Bacteria are classified by shape and as gram positive or negative. Mycoplasma are single cells that lack a rigid cell wall, rickettsiae are gram-negative bacteroid organisms, and protozoa are single-cell microorganisms. Disease can be transmitted in the absence of symptoms; barriers to transmission are external and internal.

Preventing the spread of infectious disease relies on handwashing, universal precautions, vaccination, and sanitization of equipment and locker rooms. A vaccination is a weakened living microorganism or laboratory-altered agent that is designed to stimulate the body's immune response to an antigen. The body responds to an antigen by producing site-specific antibodies that attach to the antigen and try to destroy it. Hepatitis B is a blood-borne agent, and children should be vaccinated against it, as well as healthcare workers and others who may be exposed to blood. Athletes should be instructed to wash their hands carefully and avoid direct skin contact with others as well as contaminated equipment. The athletic training room should be treated as a healthcare environment. Athletic trainers should be current in their knowledge of infectious diseases. The athlete who has above-neck symptoms can work out cautiously, but if the symptoms are below the neck, training should be postponed. Intervention strategies can include isolation techniques, preventive antimicrobial therapy, vaccination, and education.

The HIV/AIDS virus targets the immune and nervous systems. A long incubation period is followed by a slowly progressive and fatal outcome. The final or critical phase is typified by fever, diarrhea, weight loss, fatigue, opportunistic infections, and neoplasms. Transmission modes for the virus include sexual contact, parenteral inoculation, and passage from infected mother to newborn. Education is the best way to manage the disease.

Hepatitis A is rarely fatal. Hepatitis B can result in acute hepatitis, chronic nonprogressive hepatitis, chronic progressive hepatitis, full-blown hepatitis, or an asymptomatic carrier state. Transmission modes are the same as for hepatitis A plus sexual contact and the sharing of razors and toothbrushes. Transmission of hepatitis C is via contact with blood or body fluids or sexual contact with a carrier.

Cold sores, skin lesions, and encephalitis can result from herpes simplex 1. Transmission is through contact with blood or body fluids. Herpes simplex 2 is sexually transmitted and produces genital lesions. Handwashing and the use of gloves during contact with any skin lesion or orifice are recommended, along with regular skin checks.

The influenza virus causes upper respiratory tract infections. Transmission is through airborne droplets or direct or indirect contact. Handwashing and the sanitary cleaning and disposal of items contaminated by nasal and throat secretions can help to limit spread.

Upper respiratory infections are caused by a variety of viruses, including the rhinovirus and the corona viruses. Transmission is via direct and indirect contact with nasal or throat secretions or droplets.

Measles are caused by the rubella virus. Transmission is primarily via droplet spread. Universal precautions can reduce the spread of the virus. Mononucleosis is carried by the Epstein-Barr virus. Symptoms include fever, severe sore throat, and lymphadenopathy. Transmission is from person to person via the oropharyngeal route. German measles results in cold-like symptoms and swollen lymph nodes on the back and neck. Transmission is through the air. The disease is preventable with immunization.

Bacterial infections include streptococcal, staphylococcal, and *Pseudomonas aeruginosa* infections. Transmission is via droplet spread. Masks, gloves, handwashing, and universal precautions limit the spread of infection. Staphylococcus aureus is typically found on the skin of healthy individuals and can cause infection. Staphylococcal infections often start out locally and then spread via the bloodstream. Bacteria as well as viruses can cause upper respiratory infections. *Pseudomonas aeruginosa* is found in hospitals, nursing homes, swimming pools, and whirlpools. Symptoms can include headache, dizziness, earache, and sore throat. Pseudomonas infections can be fatal. Treatment is antibiotic therapy and ear cleaning. Prevention includes the use of an alcohol-based solution applied to the outer ear to promote moisture evaporation.

SELF-TEST

1. Single-cell microorganisms that lack a rigid cell wall are known as:

   A. viruses.

   B. bacteria.

   C. protozoa.

   D. mycoplasma.

2. An internal barrier to infection transmission is the:

   A. skin.

   B. coughing reflex.

   C. flushing reaction.

   D. inflammatory response.

3. Which of the following statements about vaccination is true?

   A. A vaccination is a weakened living microorganism.

   B. A vaccination weakens the body's immune system.

   C. A vaccination causes the usual symptoms of the given disease.

   D. A single vaccination is effective against a variety of diseases.

4. Systemic signs and symptoms indicate that an athlete:

   A. need not limit training in the absence of fever.

   B. should be referred to a physician immediately.

   C. will likely complain of a sore throat or runny nose.

   D. will likely resist a full-blown infection by continuing training.

5. Which of the following statements about AIDS is true?

   A. A low level of virus is present in the acute phase.

   B. A carrier who shows no symptoms is not contagious.

   C. The risk of AIDS transmission during sport activity is low.

   D. Lymphadenopathy and sore throat occur during the critical phase.

6. Influenza is characterized by:

   A. myalgia and cold sores.

   B. severe cough and fever.

   C. headache and facial rash.

   D. nasal secretions and lymphadenopathy.

7. An enlarged spleen is typical of:

   A. rubella.

   B. measles.

   C. mononucleosis.

   D. herpes simplex.

8. Streptococcal infection is usually spread by:

   A. sexual contact.

   B. droplet transmission.

   C. infected mothers to newborns.

   D. handling contaminated substances.

9. Cellulitis and carbuncles are often caused by:

   A. rhinovirus.

   B. Epstein-Barr virus.

   C. Staphylococcus aureus.

   D. Pseudomonas aeruginosa.

10. Otitis externa occurs commonly in:

    A. runners.

    B. wrestlers.

    C. swimmers.

    D. football players.

Answers on page 894.

References

1. Kumar V, Cotran RS, Robbins SL: *Basic Pathology*. Philadelphia, PA, WB Saunders, 1997.

2. Goodman CC, Boissonault WG: *Pathology: Implications for the Physical Therapist*. Philadelphia, PA, WB Saunders, 1998.

3. Browner B, Jacobs L: *Emergency Care and Transportation of the Sick and Injured*, ed 7. Rosemont, IL, American Academy of Orthopaedic Surgeons, 1999.

4. Weidner TG, Sevier TL: Sport, exercise, and the common cold. *J Athletic Train* 1996;31:154–159.

5. Update on adult immunization: Recommendations of the Immunization Practices Advisory Committee (ACIP). *MMWR* 1991;40:44–112.

6. Centers for Disease Control and Prevention: Measles, mumps, and rubella. Vaccine use and strategies for elimination of measles, rubella, and congenital rubella syndrome and control of mumps: Recommendations of the Advisory Committee on Immunization Practices. *MMWR* 1998;47:12.

7. Centers for Disease Control and Prevention: Prevention of hepatitis A through active or passive immunization. Recommendations of the Advisory Committee on Immunization Practices. *MMWR* 1996;45:8–9.

8. Centers for Disease Control and Prevention: Hepatitis B virus: A comprehensive strategy for eliminating transmission in the United States through universal childhood vaccination. Recommendations of the Advisory Committee on Immunization Practices. *MMWR* 1991;40:1–19.

9. Izumi HE: AIDS and athletic trainers: Recommendations for athletic trainer programs. *J Athletic Train* 1991;26:358–363.

10. Thomas CL: *Taber's Cyclopedic Medical Dictionary*, ed 17. Philadelphia, PA, FA Davis, 1993.

11. Bitting LA, Trowbridge CA, Costello LE: A model policy on HIV/AIDS and athletics. *J Athletic Train* 1996;31:356–357.

12. Goodman RA, Thacker SB, Solomaon SL, Osterholm MT, Hughes JM: Infectious disease in competitive sports. *JAMA* 1994;271:862–867.

13. Gaul T, Hrisomalos T, Rink L: *Transmission of Infectious Agents During Athletic Competition: A Report to All National Governing Bodies by the USOC Sports Medicine and Science Committee*. US Olympic Committee, 1991.

14. McGrew, CA: HIV and hepatitis B, and the athlete: What precautions are needed? *J Musculoskel Med* 1995.

15. Whitehill WR, Wright KE: Delphi study: HIV/AIDS and the athletic population. *J Athletic Train* 1994;29:114–119.

16. Arnold BL: Review of selected blood-borne pathogen position statements and federal regulations. *J Athletic Train* 1995;30:171–176.

17. Middlemas DA, Jessee KB, Mulder DK, Rehberg RS: Exposure of athletic trainers to potentially infectious bodily fluids in the high school setting. *J Athletic Train* 1997;32:320–322.

18. Johnson, Arthur G, Ziegler Richard J, Lukasewycz, Omelan A, et al: *Microbiology and Immunology*, ed 3. Philadelphia, PA, Williams & Wilkins, 1996.

19. Arnheim DD, Prentice WE: *Principles of Athletic Training*, ed 8. St Louis, MO, Mosby Year Book, 1993.

26

Poisons, Stings, and Bites

Clayton F. Holmes, EdD, PT, ATC

QUICK CONTENTS

- What a poison is and how a poison control center can provide assistance in the event of a poisoning.

- Identification of a poisoning victim and how to determine the nature of the poison.

- Emergency treatment of ingested, surface contacted, inhaled, and injected poisons.

- Types of stings and anaphylactic reactions to stings and how to institute first aid.

- Various bites an athlete can incur and the appropriate emergency treatment.

OVERVIEW

This chapter is devoted to information that many athletic trainers may not, but should, find a priority. The chapter begins with a discussion of poisons, including different types of poisons, the ways a poison can be introduced into the body, poison control centers, treatment of patients who have been poisoned, and food and plant poisonings. The second section is a discussion of stings and includes a description of the different insects that sting and the reactions associated with different types of stings. Treatment of insect stings is described. The third section covers bites, including bites from spiders, snakes, ticks, dogs, humans, and marine animals.

The information presented in this chapter should provide clinicians with the knowledge needed to provide prompt emergency care. Moreover, once equipped with adequate knowledge, the athletic trainer should be able to implement preventive measures in settings where athletes are at risk for these types of injury.

POISONS, STINGS, AND BITES

Although many athletic trainers routinely work with orthopaedic diagnoses and intervention, at some point in their career, most athletic trainers will be required to treat an athlete who is suffering from a poison, sting, or bite. Because detailed explanations of emergency interventions for such injuries are usually not included in textbooks for athletic trainers, there are several reasons for discussing this topic. Many athletic events, particularly at the scholastic level, are held in the "great outdoors."[1,2] For athletic trainers located in rural areas, an understanding of emergency intervention for bites and stings should be especially useful. Poisonous gases have been reported in such environments as ice hockey arenas.[3-6] Once equipped with adequate knowledge, an athletic trainer may be able to implement preventive measures in settings where athletes are at risk for this type of injury.

POISONS

A *poison* is any substance that, because of its chemical actions, may cause internal damage to a person or cause disturbances in an individual's ability to function properly when introduced into the body in relatively small amounts. The two important components of this definition are the statements "chemical action" and "in relatively small amounts." Small quantities of a poison

introduced into the body can cause severe internal damage and may result in death. Unlike trauma, which is the result of a physical occurrence, poisoning occurs within the body and is a chemical and biologic reaction. Poisons impact the body by changing the normal metabolism of cells or by actually destroying them. Poisoning can occur through several routes of contact including ingestion (swallowing), inhalation, injection, surface application, or absorption through the skin or mucous membranes.

Each year, approximately 5 million children and adults come into contact with a poisonous substance.[7] Although the exact number is unknown because of conflicting data in the literature, poison-related deaths are fairly rare. Since the 1960s, the poison-related death rate for children has significantly decreased. This may be attributed to the widespread use of safety caps on drug containers and household cleaning products. However, there has been a noticeable increase in poison-related deaths in the adult population. Although *barbiturates* (sedative-hypnotic drugs) and *opiates* (heroin, morphine, and codeine) account for many of these deaths, the widespread use of cocaine and crack and the introduction of "designer" drugs have created an entirely new category of deaths related to poisoning.

POISON CONTROL CENTERS

There are several hundred *poison control centers* throughout the United States. Although most of these centers are located in emergency departments of large hospitals, some are independent, freestanding facilities. An effective athletic trainer should know the location and telephone number of the nearest poison control center. Poison control center staff members should have access to virtually all information concerning commonly used drugs, chemicals, and substances that could possibly be poisonous. Typically, information that a poison control center gives for each poisonous agent includes a specific *antidote* (substance that will counteract the poison), if

FOCUS ON . . .

Poisons

Athletic trainers must know how to recognize the occurrence of a poisoning and how to provide emergency care for the victim. A poison is any substance that, when swallowed, inhaled, or absorbed or when applied to, injected into, or otherwise introduced into the body, in relatively small amounts, by its chemical actions, can cause internal damage or disturbances of function. Although death rates in children have decreased progressively, death rates in adults have risen.

FOCUS ON . . .

Poison Control Centers

Poison control centers across the United States are staffed 24 hours a day and have access to information about most potentially poisonous drugs, chemicals, and substances; specific antidotes; and emergency treatments. In an emergency, the athletic trainer should activate the Emergency Medical System (EMS) and may contact a poison control center through the system. The athletic trainer's role is to provide immediate care and prompt transportation to the emergency department.

Common signs and symptoms of poisoning include nausea, vomiting, abdominal pain, diarrhea, pupillary constriction or dilation, excessive salivation, sweating, dyspnea, depressed respirations, cyanosis, unconsciousness, and convulsions. Redness, blistering, or burns of the skin or mucous membranes also suggest poisoning. The most important treatment for poisonings involves dilution and physical removal of the agent. Physically removing the poison by inducing vomiting with syrup of ipecac can be accomplished only if the patient is fully alert.

Objects at the scene such as bottles, pills, or chemicals should be placed in plastic bags and taken to the hospital. Any vomitus should also be placed in a plastic bag and taken to the hospital for analysis.

TABLE 26-1
PROCEDURES FOR POISON-RELATED EMERGENCIES

During a poison-related emergency, the athletic trainer should perform the following:

- Activate EMS.

- Be prepared to provide emergency care.

- Provide information about the nature of the emergency, including the fact that a poisoning has occurred.

- Provide information about the size, weight, and age of the patient.

- Provide information about the description of the suspected poisonous agent.

one exists, and the appropriate emergency medical treatment for that particular poison. Moreover, the poison control center should be able to provide information concerning specific poisonous agents using both trade and generic names. Most centers are staffed 24 hours a day and should be contacted whenever an individual has a potential poison-related problem. During a poison-related emergency, the athletic trainer should follow the procedures outlined in **Table 26-1**. During an emergency, the athletic trainer may contact a poison control center directly through the emergency medical services (EMS) system; in this case, the poison control center may give the athletic trainer specific instructions on how to care for the patient.

Occasionally, the poison control center will recommend that the athletic trainer induce vomiting by administering syrup of ipecac to the patient.[8] There are two forms of ipecac solutions commercially available: syrup of ipecac and ipecac extract. Ipecac extract is significantly more concentrated than syrup of ipecac and should not be used on a patient during prehospital care.

Syrup of ipecac should only be administered according to the dose recommended by the poison control center. For children between the ages of 1 and 5 years, the recommended dose of syrup of ipecac is 1 tablespoon (15 mL) mixed with a glass of water. For individuals who are older than age 5 years, the recommended dose of syrup of ipecac is 1 to 2 tablespoons (15 to 30 mL) mixed with a glass or two of water.

By inducing vomiting, physical removal of a poison can be accomplished. If the patient vomits, the vomitus should also be collected in a plastic bag and brought to the hospital for analysis. Although this task may be unpleasant, collecting vomitus and suspicious materials and bringing them to the hospital may be the most important function when dealing with a poison-related incident after resuscitating the patient and initiating emergency care procedures. Because the aggressive treatment for poisonings may be lifesaving, especially of poisonous agents that have been ingested, the role of the athletic trainer is to provide the poisoned athlete with immediate care and prompt transportation to the emergency department. Although this treatment can be effective, certain precautions should be noted when using syrup of ipecac, as shown in **Table 26-2**.

IDENTIFYING POISONING INCIDENTS

The most important responsibility of an athletic trainer who suspects a poisoning has occurred is to recognize that likelihood. With even the slightest suspicion that an ath-

TABLE 26-2
ADMINISTERING SYRUP OF IPECAC TO PATIENTS

- Administer only if directed to do so by a physician.

- Activate EMS.

- Monitor the patient for possible airway obstructions or aspiration of vomitus.

- Position the patient so that he or she is sitting upright.

- If the patient is unable to sit upright, position the athlete's head to the side.

- Collect any vomitus material to bring to the hospital for examination.

- Do not administer if the patient is not fully alert or is unconscious, semiconscious, or having convulsions.

- Do not administer if the poison is corrosive such as strong acids or alkalis (lye or drain cleaner) or has caused obvious burns on the patient's lips or mouth.

- Do not administer if the poison is a petroleum-based substance such as kerosene, gasoline, lighter fluid, or clear furniture polish.

- Do not administer if the patient is pregnant or has severe cardiac disease.

cific ingredients are often listed on product labels. Also, medication containers specify the number of pills originally prescribed as well as the name of the drug and its concentration. Based on the number of remaining pills and the quantity listed on the container, the physician is able to develop a more accurate approximation of the quantity of pills that the patient may have ingested. Poison control centers should be familiar with most brand names of substances and be able to identify specific chemical contents. Occasionally, if a container is found after a poisoning, a manufacturer can be contacted directly for a description of the product's composition. By bringing suspected containers to the hospital with the patient, proper treatment can be initiated more quickly and may possibly save the athlete's life.

Ingested, Surface Contact, Inhaled, and Injected Poisons

Most poisons do not have a specific antidote. Because of this, the most important treatment of poisoning involves dilution and physical removal of the poisonous agent. For skin that has been exposed to a poison, surface flooding and washing can assist with the dilution and physical removal of the agent. Having the patient drink water or milk and then inducing vomiting has historically been

TABLE 26-3
SYMPTOMS AND SIGNS ASSOCIATED WITH POISONINGS

- Nausea

- Vomiting

- Abdominal pain

- Diarrhea

- Dilation or constriction of the pupils

- Excessive salivation

- Sweating

- Dyspnea (difficult breathing)

- Depressed respirations

- Unconsciousness

- Convulsions

- Cyanosis

- Skin or mucous membranes irritation or burns

lete has been exposed to a poisonous agent, the athletic trainer should immediately activate EMS. By doing this, information can be relayed to the nearest poison control center and emergency treatment can be initiated. Common symptoms and signs associated with poisonings are listed in **Table 26-3**.

The athletic trainer should attempt to determine the source of the poison. Objects at the scene such as overturned bottles, scattered pills, chemicals, or even an overturned or damaged plant may provide clues. The remains of any food or drink that the athlete may have consumed may also provide insight into how the poisoning occurred. The athletic trainer should place all suspicious material in a plastic bag and bring it to the hospital with the patient for further evaluation.

Anything that contained the poisonous agent should also be collected for evaluation. Information concerning the content of the poisonous agent can be of great help to the emergency department physicians. For example, spe-

FOCUS ON . . .

Ingested, Surface Contact, Inhaled, and Injected Poisons

Emergency management of ingested poisons includes the rapid removal of as much poison as possible from the gastrointestinal tract and diluting or neutralizing the remainder. Drinking a suspension of activated charcoal in water can also help to absorb poison.

Agents that are rapidly absorbed from the gastrointestinal tract may cause some patients to require aggressive ventilatory support and even cardiopulmonary resuscitation. For such occurrences, immediate transport to a hospital is needed.

Inflammation, chemical burns, and rashes and other lesions can result from direct contact with many poisonous agents. Emergency treatment consists of quick removal of the offending substance. Chemical agents in the eyes should be rapidly and copiously irrigated. Some substances are noxious and chemically react violently with water. Here, flooding the affected area should be avoided.

Emergency treatment for inhaled poisons is to move the patient into fresh air. Prolonged inhalation may require supplemental oxygen, suctioning, and basic life support. Inhaled poisons such as chlorine are very irritating and produce airway obstruction and pulmonary edema. Oxygen should be administered whenever hypoxia, pulmonary edema, or airway obstruction occur, and the patient should be immediately transported to the emergency department.

Injected poisons usually result from deliberate drug overdoses, insect and animal bites, and stings. If the injection site starts to swell, an ice or cold pack should be used and the patient should remove all metal jewelry. Injected poisons are absorbed quickly into the body and can cause intense local tissue destruction. Prompt activation of EMS is essential.

used when treating individuals who have ingested poison. If the poison was inhaled, the administration of oxygen is recommended. Certain injected poisons may require a specific antidote. Because injected poisons are difficult to remove or dilute, they pose significant problems that require urgent attention. In addition, support for an individual who has been poisoned may range from reassuring an anxious parent to instituting cardiopulmonary resuscitation (CPR). Although they are usually performed by EMS and medical staff in emergency facilities, the above activities may be initiated by an athletic trainer.

Ingested poisons

Approximately 80% of all poison-related incidences occur through ingestion.[7] Commonly *ingested poisons* can be in the form of drugs, drinks, household products, contaminated food, and plants. Although poisoning in children and the elderly is usually accidental, ingested-related poisonings in adults (with the exception of contaminated food) is usually deliberate, employed as a method of committing suicide or murder. Although most ingested-related poisonings are from drugs, approximately one third of all poisonings are caused by either liquid or solid agents such as household cleaners, soaps, insecticides, acids, or alkalis.[8] Food poisoning, even though it is technically caused by an ingested poison, and plant poisoning are discussed in more detail in separate sections later in this chapter.

Emergency management of ingested poisons should include the rapid removal of as much of the poison from the gastrointestinal tract as possible and then diluting or neutralizing the remainder. Most poisoning victims respond well to this treatment method. Historically, large volumes of fluid have been given to treat poison victims. For example, in the past, the ingestion of one or two glasses of water or milk was recommended. More recently, the use of *activated charcoal* has been advised. Although this intervention has been used previously by EMS, the athletic trainer should keep activated charcoal on hand. In all poison-related cases, the athletic trainer should consult the poison control center before proceeding with treatment.

Because many poisons adsorb activated charcoal, having the patient drink a suspension of activated charcoal may be an effective treatment. Usually, 25 to 50 g (about 1 to 2 oz) of activated charcoal powder is mixed with a glass of fluid such as water to make a slurry. Containers of premixed, ready-to-use activated charcoal are commercially available. Because of its appearance, many patients may be reluctant to swallow this mixture and may need to be persuaded to do so; however, liquid should never be forced into a patient's mouth. Moreover, when administering activated charcoal, the patient should be fully conscious.

Most ingested poisonings are related to drugs, typically opiates, sedatives, and barbiturates. Patients who are poisoned by drugs may experience central nervous system (CNS) depression and, especially, respiratory depression at the same time. Because absorption of certain poisonous agents from the gastrointestinal tract is rapid, patients with CNS depression may require aggressive ventilatory support and, in severe cases, CPR. These patients should be transported immediately to the emergency department. Gastric lavage, intravenous support, and other measures may be necessary once the patient arrives at the hospital.

Surface contact poisons

Several corrosive substances can damage the skin, mucous membranes, or eyes through direct contact. Acids, alkalis, and some petroleum and benzene products are highly destructive. Contact with these poisonous agents can cause inflammation, chemical burns, or rashes or lesions to the affected areas. It is important for athletic trainers to understand that *contact dermatitis* can be caused by typical athletic equipment.[9] Although this form of dermatitis is not an emergency condition, athletic trainers should be able to recognize the condition and refer athletes experiencing this condition to a physician for evaluation.

Emergency treatment of a patient with contact poisoning should consist of the immediate removal of the irritating or corrosive substance. After being exposed to a contact poison, the athlete or athletic trainer should thoroughly dust off any dry chemicals around the affected area and then wash the area with soap and water or flood the affected skin with water under a shower. If a patient is exposed to a large amount of poison through contact, flooding the affected area under a shower may be the most rapid and effective treatment method.

To minimize damage to the body, all clothing that has been contaminated with poisons or irritating substances should be removed as quickly as possible so that the skin may be cleaned with running water. Eyes that have been exposed to poisonous agents should be treated with rapid and copious irrigation with sterile saline solution or clean water for several minutes. To obtain effective results, the eyes should be irrigated for at least 5 to 10 minutes if exposed to acid-based substances and 15 to 20 minutes if exposed to alkaline-based substances.[7] If only one eye is injured, the unaffected eye should be protected with an optic bandage.

The care provider should not attempt to neutralize chemical substances on the skin. Instead, the substance should be immediately washed off with water. This procedure is faster and more effective than attempting to chemically neutralize a substance.

There are noxious substances that chemically react violently with water. In these instances, flooding the affected area should be avoided. For example, phosphorus and elemental sodium are both dry, solid chemicals that ignite when either one comes in contact with water. Fortunately, exposure to these agents is rare. The emergency treatment of patients who come in contact with such chemical agents is the same as the treatment procedures for other dry chemical irritants. First, any remaining dust from the chemical should be cleared from the patient's skin. Second, the patient's clothing should be removed and a dry, sterile dressing should be applied to any burned areas. In addition, the care provider should wear gloves when treating a patient with a contact poisoning to avoid self-contamination. The patient should be transported promptly to the hospital for further care.

Inhaled poisons

Unknowingly, many athletes come in contact with potentially dangerous poisons from a variety of sources. For example, concerns about *toxic pneumonitis* have recently developed for hockey players and figure skaters.[3-5] There have been at least two reported cases of toxic pneumonitis, specifically nitrogen dioxide pneumonitis, that have been associated with ice arenas.[6] Because the symptoms associated with toxic pneumonitis are usually chronic, athletic trainers, particularly those working with ice sports, should be familiar with the emergency treatment of inhaled poisons.

If a person has inhaled a poison such as natural gas, certain pesticides, carbon monoxide, chlorine, or other gases, emergency treatment should consist of moving the patient to an area where fresh air is available. Patients exposed to prolonged inhalation may require supplemental oxygen and basic life support. Because it is easy to inhale poisonous fumes in an emergency situation, athletic trainers must be careful to protect themselves when caring for the patient.

Some inhaled poisons such as carbon monoxide are odorless and produce profound hypoxia without causing significant irritation or damage to the lungs. Other inhaled poisons such as chlorine are extremely irritating and can produce airway obstruction and pulmonary edema. Oxygen should be administered immediately if hypoxia, pulmonary edema, or airway obstruction results after a poison has been inhaled. If an athlete has inhaled a poison, the athletic trainer should contact EMS immediately and supplemental oxygen may be required. Because many inhaled agents can cause progressive lung damage, these patients should be immediately transported to the emergency department for treatment. Often, to reestablish normal lung functions, individuals who have inhaled poisons typically require 2 or 3 days of intensive care.

Injected poisons

Sources of *injected poisons* include animal bites, insect stings, and deliberate drug overdoses. If the area around the injection site begins to swell, the patient should remove all metal jewelry and the patient's distal pulse should be monitored. An ice pack or cold pack may decrease local pain and swelling around the injection site.

Generally, injected poisons are difficult, or impossible, to dilute or remove. Usually, they are absorbed quickly into the body and can cause intense local tissue destruction. In cases where absorption of injected poisons is rapid, the athletic trainer should be prepared to offer basic life support. When severe local tissue damage occurs as a result of an injected poison, complex surgical procedures may be required. For this reason, the athletic trainer should immediately activate EMS.

Food Poisoning

Food poisoning is almost always caused by the ingestion of bacteria-contaminated food. Typically, contaminated food may look perfectly fine with no obvious decay or odor to indicate that it may be contaminated. There are two types of food poisoning; one occurs when the bacteria cause disease and the other when the bacteria produce toxins (poisons) that cause disease.[7]

Food poisoning that results from the direct effect of the bacteria is usually caused by a *Salmonella* bacterium. This condition is called *salmonellosis* and is characterized by severe gastrointestinal symptoms such as nausea, vomiting, abdominal pain, and diarrhea that can last up to 72 hours after ingestion. In addition to the gastrointestinal symptoms, patients suffering from salmonellosis may be systemically ill with fever and generalized weakness. A variety of other organisms can also produce milder cases of intestinal distress. This type of food poisoning can only occur when living bacteria is ingested. Usually, cooking food at proper temperatures kills bacteria, and cleanliness in the kitchen can prevent the contamination of uncooked foods. Some individuals are carriers of certain bacteria and, although they may not become ill themselves, they may transmit bacteria to other individuals who may become ill, particularly if the carrier works in the food service industry.

The ingestion of bacterial toxins may be the most common cause of food poisoning. The symptoms associated with bacterial-toxin poisoning are not caused by the actual bacteria, but rather by powerful toxins produced by the bacteria. The most common source of this type of poisoning is from food contaminated with *Staphylococcus*. This bacterium is responsible for the episodes of food poisoning that occur at large gatherings. Such episodes result from the advance preparation of food that is then stored in warmer environments for many hours. Under such conditions, contaminating bacteria are able to develop and grow and produce toxins. Mayonnaise that has been exposed to warmer temperatures is a common vehicle that allows the development of staphylococcal toxins. Usually, *staphylococcal food poisoning* results in the onset of violent gastrointestinal symptoms such as nausea, vomiting, and diarrhea within 2 to 3 hours after ingestion. Generally, the episode is over within 8 to 12 hours after ingestion.[7]

The most severe type of food poisoning caused by the ingestion of bacterial toxins is *botulism*.[7] Botulism usually results from consuming improperly canned food in which *Clostridium* bacteria spores have grown and produced a toxin. The symptoms of botulism are neurologic and include blurring of vision, weakness, and difficulty in speaking and breathing. Symptoms may not develop for up to 24 hours after ingestion.[7] If left untreated, botulism poisoning can be fatal.

The athletic trainer should immediately activate EMS when food poisoning is suspected. If botulism poisoning is suspected, respiratory assistance and basic life support may be needed. In obvious instances of food poisoning, when two or more individuals in a group experience the same symptoms, the athletic trainer should bring a sample of the suspected contaminated food to the medical facility for analysis.

Plant Poisoning

Several thousand cases of poisoning from plants occur each year, and some are severe. Some poisonous plants cause local irritation of the skin and others affect the circulatory system, the gastrointestinal tract, or the central nervous system.[7]

Skin irritants

Skin irritation is the most common symptom of plant poisoning. Symptoms include itching, burning, and local blister formation. One of the most common plants to produce such reactions is poison ivy (**Figure 26-1**). In most cases, skin irritation occurs after direct contact with the poisonous plant or with its sap or juice. Contact with poisonous plants rarely produces systemic symptoms such as tachycardia, hypotension, or respiratory distress. The emergency treatment of skin irritants consists of thor-

oughly cleansing the affected skin surface with soap and water. This treatment is most effective if performed within 30 to 60 minutes after exposure to the poison. Occasionally, because of prolonged symptoms, some patients may require medical attention. Athletes exposed to skin irritants can become quite uncomfortable.

Circulatory disturbances

Within 30 to 50 minutes after ingesting a poisonous plant that affects circulation, the patient may demonstrate classic signs of *circulatory collapse*: tachycardia (a rapid heart rate); falling blood pressure; sweating; weakness; and cold, moist, clammy skin.[8] At this time, there are no effective antidotes for plant poisonings that cause circulatory collapse. Patients who are suspected of suffering from circulatory collapse because of plant poisoning should be treated for shock. The athletic trainer should first activate EMS, assist the patient into a supine position, and elevate

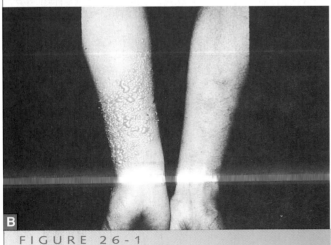

FIGURE 26-1

A Poison ivy, which produces a skin irritant, is one of the most common poisonous plants. **B** Exposure to poison ivy can cause itching, burning, and blister formation. It rarely produces systemic symptoms.

the patient's legs. The athletic trainer should bring the plant or several of its leaves to the medical facility for positive identification.

Gastrointestinal disturbances

When ingested, small quantities of some poisonous plants can produce severe gastrointestinal (GI) disturbances. Symptoms associated with GI disturbance from plant ingestion are the same as the symptoms caused by ingestion of other toxic substances: vomiting, diarrhea, and cramps. Symptoms usually occur within 20 to 30 minutes after ingestion. Once an athlete is suspected of ingesting a poisonous plant, the athletic trainer should activate EMS immediately. The patient should be allowed to vomit, and, if the patient does vomit, samples of the vomitus should be collected and brought to the medical facility. If the plant has been positively identified, after activating EMS, the poison control center may advise the athletic trainer to induce vomiting.

Some agents in plants are specifically irritating to the mucous membranes of the mouth and throat. If a patient is exposed to this type of agent, vomiting may actually increase the irritation. If GI symptoms occur shortly after the ingestion, vomiting may help remove the poison from the patient's body; if symptoms begin to appear several hours after the ingestion of the substance, vomiting is unlikely to do much good. The athletic trainer should bring the plant or some sample leaves from it to the emergency department for analysis.

Central nervous system disturbances

Some poisonous plants can affect the central nervous system and cause depression, hyperactivity, excitement, stupor, mental confusion, or coma. The athletic trainer should activate EMS immediately if he or she suspects an athlete may be suffering from a central nervous system disturbance. Vomiting should not be induced if a patient shows signs of stupor or coma. Individuals suffering from this type of poisoning should be treated with basic life support procedures. In addition, the patient may need supplemental oxygen during transportation to the emergency department. If possible, the plant, or a sample of its leaves, should accompany the patient to the hospital for further analysis.

STINGS

Several insects can inflict pain by stinging or biting. Some of these injuries are potentially dangerous. Because many athletic events, particularly at the scholastic level, are held outdoors, the information in this section is of importance to athletic trainers when treating athletes with a sting or bite.[1,2] Athletic trainers should be aware of the potential danger of stings or bites from bees, wasps, yellow jackets, hornets, certain ants, scorpions, and some spiders.

Bee, Wasp, Hornet, Yellow Jacket, and Ant Stings

There are more than 100,000 species of bees, wasps, and hornets.[7] Fatalities associated with stings from these insects far outnumber fatalities associated with snake bites; 65% of fatal stings are from bees, wasps, or hornets.[8] In addition, in outdoor events such as cross country bicycling, insect stings and bites that are of a less serious nature have been reported as medical problems.[10]

The stinging organ of most bees, wasps, and hornets is a small hollow spine that projects from the abdomen. *Venom* can be injected through this spine directly into a person's skin. The stinger of the honeybee is barbed. Because of this, the honeybee cannot withdraw its stinger after using it and must leave a part of its abdomen embedded with the stinger when it flies away. As a result, the bee dies shortly after the incident. Therefore, the honeybee can only sting once during its life cycle. Because wasps and hornets have unbarbed stingers, they are able to sting repeatedly (**Figure 26-2**). Because it tends to fly away immediately after the occurrence, identification of an insect after it stings an individual is often impossible. There are some species of ants, especially the fire ant, that are able to bite repeatedly and frequently inject an irritating toxin at the bite site. These bites usually occur on the feet and legs and appear as multiple small raised pustules. It is common for the patient to sustain multiple bites within a very short period of time (**Figure 26-3**).

Symptoms associated with insect stings and bites usually occur at the site of injury. Local symptoms of stings and bites include sudden pain, swelling, heat, and redness around the affected area. Occasionally, a *wheal* (whitish, firm elevation of the skin) may develop and cause itching (**Figure 26-4**). Currently, there is no specific treatment for these types of injuries; however, the application of ice around the affected area may make the wheal less irritating. The swelling that may accompany an insect sting or bite may be considerable and may alarm the patient; however, the local manifestations of these stings and bites are usually not serious.

Because the honeybee's stinger detaches and remains in the wound after stinging an individual, this organ, along with its attached muscle, can continue to inject venom into the individual for up to 20 minutes after the incident occurs.[7] When assisting an athlete who has been stung by a honeybee, the athletic trainer should attempt to remove the stinger and the attached portion of the bee's abdomen by gently scraping it off the patient's skin with a stiff object such as a credit card. Because squeezing the stinger may inject more venom into the patient, tweezers or forceps should not be used. The area should be gently washed with soap and water or a mild antiseptic, and jewelry should be removed from the area before swelling begins.

FOCUS ON . . .

Stings

Bee, wasp, hornet, yellow jacket, and ant stings

Approximately 65% of fatalities from stinging insects are from bees, wasps, and hornets. The honeybee can only sting once before dying because its barbed stinger remains embedded with part of the abdomen. The athletic trainer can remove the stinger by gently scraping the area with a stiff object. Wasps and hornets, however, have unbarbed stingers and can sting repeatedly.

Symptoms of insect stings and bites are usually local and not serious. Ice may be helpful. Cellulitis (skin reddening and swelling) can develop several hours after a bite. In this case, the area should be immobilized and the athlete should be transported to the emergency department.

Some ant species, including fire ants, can bite repeatedly and inject an irritating toxin. These bites can produce acute inflammation and slow-healing ulcerations.

Anaphylactic reaction to stings

Some athletes experience violent hypersensitive anaphylactic reactions from bee, hornet, yellow jacket, or wasp venom. Signs and symptoms include generalized itching, burning, urticaria, lip and tongue swelling, bronchospasm and wheezing, chest tightness and cough, dyspnea, anxiety, abdominal cramps, and respiratory failure, and can be fatal if untreated. The athletic trainer should administer basic life support, activate EMS, and arrange for rapid hospital transport.

Bee sting kits that contain injectable epinephrine, which reverses the allergen's effect, and antihistamines can be prescribed for hypersensitive individuals. If the athlete can self-administer the epinephrine, the athletic trainer should simply assist. If the athlete develops tachycardia, the athletic trainer should provide emergency care and activate EMS.

Scorpion stings

Although most scorpion stings are very painful and only cause localized swelling and discoloration, the venom of the *Centruroides sculpturatus* can cause a severe systemic reaction. If a bite from a *C sculpturatus* is suspected, EMS should be activated immediately, basic life support should be administered, and the patient should be transported to the hospital immediately.

FIGURE 26-2

Most stinging insects inject venom through a small, hollow spine that projects from the abdomen. **A** The stinger of the honeybee is barbed and cannot be withdrawn once the bee has stung someone. **B** The wasp's stinger is unbarbed, which allows it to inflict multiple stings.

Some insect bites are not noticed by the individual for several hours until *cellulitis* (a spreading redness and swelling of the skin) has developed. Athletic trainers who are assisting individuals with acute cellulitis should immobilize the injured area and summon EMS for immediate transport to the emergency department. The application

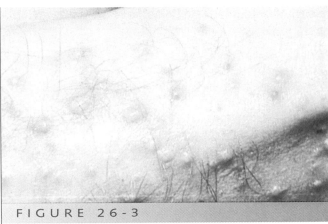

FIGURE 26-3

Bites from fire ants are generally found on the feet and legs and appear as multiple small, raised pustules.

of warm, moist packs around the injury site may ease the patient's discomfort. Typically, fire ant bites produce an acute inflammation and ulceration around the affected area and tend to heal slowly.

Anaphylactic Reaction to Stings

Approximately 5% of all individuals are allergic to the venom produced by bees, hornets, yellow jackets, and wasps, and approximately 200 deaths per year are attributed to severe allergic reactions.[7] Because honeybee venom is a common *allergen* (substance producing an allergic reaction), a person with this allergy who is exposed to this venom may experience a violent hypersensitivity reaction called *anaphylaxis* or anaphylactic shock. Symptoms include generalized itching, burning, and urticaria (hives) (**Figure 26-5**). Swelling about the lips and tongue, bronchospasm and wheezing, chest tightness and cough, dyspnea (difficult breathing), anxiety, abdominal cramps, and occasionally respiratory failure can also occur. If left untreated, severe anaphylactic reactions can lead to death.

The rapid development of skin wheals and hives, as well as the presence of wheezing respirations, should alert an athletic trainer that an athlete is experiencing a hypersensitivity reaction. Once identified, the athletic trainer should immediately activate EMS and administer basic life support to the injured athlete. The patient should be transported rapidly to the hospital. Moreover, the athletic trainer should be prepared to administer oxygen to the injured athlete and maintain his or her airway or give CPR. To decrease the rate of the toxin from a honeybee sting, a bag of crushed ice placed over the injury site may be helpful. Time is a critical factor for patients with anaphylaxis. More than two thirds of the individuals who die from these reactions do so within the first half hour after the sting occurred.[7]

Patients who have a history of severe allergic reaction to bee stings may carry bee sting kits (**Figure 26-6**). These

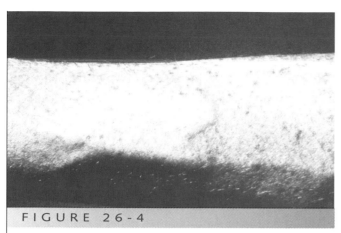

FIGURE 26-4

A wheal is a whitish, firm elevation of the skin that occurs after a sting or bite from an insect.

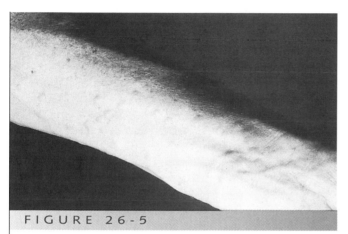

FIGURE 26-5

Urticaria (hives) may appear following a sting and is characterized by multiple small, raised areas on the skin. Urticaria may be one of the warning signs of impending anaphylactic reaction.

the athletic trainer should assist the athlete in administering the medication. Specific instructions for proper epinephrine administration should be included in the kit. In the absence of instructions, 0.5 mL of 1/1,000 epinephrine solution should be injected intramuscularly (into a muscle) or subcutaneously (just below the skin) into the patient's thigh.[7] In the event of an allergic reaction, EMS should be activated immediately. Depending on the severity of the reaction, multiple injections may be necessary. Athletic trainers should be familiar with the use of epinephrine.

Scorpion Stings

Scorpions are eight-legged *arachnids* with a venom gland and stinger at the end of their tail (**Figure 26-7**). Scorpions live primarily in the southwestern region of the United States and in desert areas. With one exception, scorpion stings are very painful, causing localized swelling and discoloration, but not dangerous. The one exception, *Centruroides sculpturatus*, is found in Arizona and New Mexico and in parts of Texas, California, and Nevada and is kept as a pet by some individuals. The venom of the *C sculpturatus* may produce a severe systemic reaction that causes circulatory collapse, severe muscle contractions, excessive salivation, hypertension, convulsions, and cardiac failure.

If the athletic trainer suspects that an athlete has been stung by a *C sculpturatus*, he or she should activate EMS immediately and provide basic life support to the athlete. The patient must be transported to the emergency department as rapidly as possible.

kits, which are commercially available, are usually prescribed by a physician specifically for hypersensitive patients. Typically, a bee sting kit contains *epinephrine* packaged in a prepared syringe for quick injection. Epinephrine is an agent that rapidly produces bronchodilation to reverse the effects of the allergens on the patient's airway. It acts rapidly to produce acute relief. Also, most bee sting kits contain oral or intravenous *antihistamines* that are specific in countering the production of histamine, a substance produced in the body that is believed to be responsible for allergic reactions. Usually, antihistamines are slower in providing relief from a sting, but more effective than epinephrine over a longer period of time. However, because epinephrine can have an effect within 1 minute, it is the primary treatment of anaphylactic shock.[7]

Even when the athlete is able to self-administer an agent from a bee sting kit to avoid an allergic reaction,

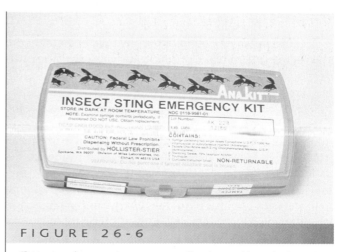

FIGURE 26-6

Patients who experience severe allergic reactions to insect stings often carry epinephrine, which is commercially available as a predosed autoinjector.

FIGURE 26-7

The sting of a scorpion is more painful than it is dangerous, causing localized swelling and discoloration.

BITES

Spider Bites

Spiders are numerous and live in widespread areas in the United States. Two species, the black widow spider and the brown recluse spider, are able to inflict serious and, sometimes, life-threatening bites. Many other spiders are able to bite, but the injuries they inflict do not produce serious complications.

Black widow spider

The black widow spider measures approximately 1-1/2" when its legs are extended. Its color is glossy black, and it has a distinctive, bright red-orange marking in the shape of an hourglass on its abdomen (**Figure 26-8**). Black widow spiders are found in every state in the country except Alaska. These spiders prefer dry, dim environments around buildings, in woodpiles, and among debris.

Because the area around the injury may become numb after being bitten, black widow spider bites are frequently overlooked, and the patient may be unable to recall when the bite occurred. However, most patients who are bitten by a female black widow spider will experience pain at the site of the bite. Because its venom is *neurotoxic* (poisonous to nerve tissue), the danger associated with a bite from this spider is significant. The venom attacks the patient's spinal nerve center, resulting in systemic symptoms. Severe cramps with boardlike rigidity of the abdominal muscles, tightness in the chest, and difficulty in breathing develop within 24 hours.[7] Other symptoms associated with black widow spider bites include dizziness, sweating, vomiting, nausea, and skin rashes. Generally, the signs and symptoms subside within 48 hours after exposure; however, the accompanying muscle cramps and ensuing pain can be agonizing.

Although symptoms following a bite can be severe, death from a black widow spider bite is uncommon. Currently, there is a specific antivenin available for black widow spider bites; however, its use is accompanied by a high incidence of side effects. Because of this, the antivenin should only be administered by a physician and used on patients with severe bites, elderly or feeble patients, and children younger than age 5 years.[7]

For patients experiencing respiratory distress as a result of a black widow spider bite, emergency treatment should consist of basic life support. Typically, the patient may require relief from pain. If the location of the bite can be identified, placing ice against it may reduce the rate of absorption of the toxin into the body. The patient should be transported to the emergency department as soon as possible for treatment of pain and muscle rigidity. Therefore, it is important that the athletic trainer promptly activates EMS. The athletic trainer should also attempt to identify the spider and bring it to the emergency department with the patient for analysis.

Brown recluse spider

The brown recluse spider is somewhat smaller than the black widow spider and has a dull brown color (**Figure 26-9**). A prominent feature of this spider is a dark violin-shaped mark on its back, which can be easily seen from above. Although found mostly in the southern and central regions of the United States, brown recluse spider populations are currently spreading to other areas of the country. Also, the name of the brown recluse spider fits this creature well because it tends to live in dark areas, corners, old unused buildings, woodpiles, and under rocks. In cooler conditions, the brown recluse spider moves indoors and seeks refuge in closets, drawers, cellars, and old piles of clothing.

FIGURE 26-8

Black widow spiders are distinguished by their glossy black color and bright orange hourglass marking on the abdomen.

FOCUS ON . . .

Bites

Spider bites

A black widow spider bite may cause numbness or pain at the site. Its neurotoxic venom can cause severe cramps, stiff abdominal rigidity, chest tightness, difficulty in breathing, dizziness, sweating, vomiting, nausea, and skin rashes. In the event of a black widow spider bite, EMS should be activated and the athlete should be rapidly transported to the emergency department.

The brown recluse spider bite produces severe local tissue damage and can result in a large, nonhealing ulcer. Treatment includes rapid transport to the emergency department, basic life support, if necessary, and prompt surgical excision of the area.

Snake bites

Only four poisonous snakes are found in the United States: the rattlesnake, copperhead, cottonmouth (water) moccasin, and coral snake. Pit vipers (rattlesnakes, copperheads, and cottonmouth moccasins) have flat, triangular heads with a small pit just behind the nostrils and in front of the eyes, and vertical pupils that are shaped like slits.

Pit viper envenomation causes severe burning pain at the injury site, followed by swelling and discoloration. Systemic signs include weakness, fainting, and shock. The venom causes immediate, localized destruction of body tissue and can interfere with blood clotting. Emergency treatment should first focus on local containment of the venom and then on the treatment of systemic symptoms. If the patient does not show any signs of envenomation, the athletic trainer should activate EMS and provide basic life support as needed. All patients with suspected snake bites should be brought to the emergency department.

The coral snake's venom causes nervous system paralysis within several hours. Treatment depends on identification of the snake. Antivenin is available, but often must be obtained from a distant location. Therefore, when activating EMS, the athletic trainer should explain the suspected diagnosis. The patient should be transported promptly to the emergency department.

Tick bites

Ticks can spread infections such as Rocky Mountain spotted fever and Lyme disease. Rocky Mountain spotted fever occurs within 7 to 10 days after a bite by an infected tick and can result in nausea, vomiting, headache, weakness, paralysis, and cardiorespiratory collapse. Lyme disease occurs about 3 days after a bite by an infected tick. A progressive red rash usually develops at the site and spreads. Several days or weeks later, the joints usually become painful and swollen. Treatment should include antibiotics.

Because it takes an infection at least 12 hours to be transmitted from the tick to the person, the athletic trainer may be able to remove the tick and reduce the chances of infection by carefully using fine tweezers. All athletes with tick bites should be evaluated by a physician. Anyone showing signs or symptoms of Rocky Mountain spotted fever or Lyme disease should be treated with supportive care as needed, and EMS should be activated.

Dog bites and rabies

Dog bites are potentially serious because they can become infected by the virulent bacterial contaminants in the dog's mouth. If a dog bite occurs, tetanus prophylaxis, sutures, and antibiotics may be needed. The athletic trainer should place a dry, sterile dressing over the wound, while keeping the athlete calm, and promptly transport the victim to the emergency department.

Rabies is present in the saliva of an infected animal and is transmitted by biting or by licking an open wound. Because rabies cannot be diagnosed by the animal's behavior, an animal without a tag that has bitten a human should be captured and evaluated by animal control. If the animal cannot be found or identified, the patient should be treated with the rabies vaccine. If the patient's condition warrants immediate medical attention, EMS should be activated.

(Continued)

Although a bite from a black widow spider produces systemic symptoms, a bite from a brown recluse spider, in contrast, produces local symptoms. The venom produced by the brown recluse spider can cause severe local tissue damage and may produce a large, nonhealing ulcer if not treated promptly. Typically, a brown recluse spider bite is

FOCUS ON . . .

Human Bites

Although human bites are uncommon, they are potentially severe because the human mouth contains a significant amount of virulent bacteria. Emergency treatment is prompt immobilization of the area with a splint or bandage; application of a dry, sterile dressing; and transport to the emergency department for surgical cleansing of the wound and antibiotics.

Injuries from Marine Animals

Bites from marine animals are treated as major open wounds. The athletic trainer should activate EMS, remove the patient from the water, control the hemorrhage, apply dressings and splints, treat for shock, and transport the patient to the emergency department promptly. Stings from jellyfish tentacles, Portuguese man-of-war, anemones, corals, and hydras are treated by removing the patient from the water and pouring rubbing alcohol on the affected area. Rarely, a patient may develop a systemic allergic reaction from a sting. In the event of this, the athletic trainer should treat for anaphylactic shock, give basic life support, and activate EMS.

Injuries from the spines of stingrays, urchins, and some spiny fish such as catfish are treated by immobilizing the affected area and soaking it in hot water. Patients should then be transported to the emergency department for evaluation of puncture wounds and allergic reactions. Sea animals such as nonpoisonous water snakes can produce minor bites. Accordingly, the athletic trainer should apply sterile dressings and arrange for transportation to the hospital. If a poisonous fish has been ingested, basic life support should be provided, EMS should be activated, and the patient should be transported to the emergency department promptly. Shocks from electric eels and skin rashes from marine parasites are usually minor injuries.

not painful at first. Pain usually develops within hours after the incident. The affected area becomes swollen and tender and develops a pale, mottled cyanotic center and possibly a small blister (**Figure 26-10**). Subsequently, several days after the occurrence of a bite, a large ulcer may develop with the formation of a large scab made up of dead skin, fat, and debris.[7] For this reason, prompt medical treatment is essential to minimize this potentially dramatic pathology.

Systemic symptoms and signs from brown recluse spider bites are rare. When they do occur, emergency treatment

FIGURE 26-9

Brown recluse spiders are dull brown and have a dark, violin-shaped mark on the back.

should include basic life support and immediate transportation to the emergency department. Because no specific *antivenin* exists for the brown recluse spider's toxin, the only effective treatment to avoid a painful, long-term ulceration is prompt surgical excision of the area.[8] Because of this, emergency treatment of a patient who is suspected of suffering from a brown recluse spider bite and is not experiencing any systemic symptoms also consists of prompt transportation to the emergency department. Also, it is helpful if the spider can be identified and brought to the hospital along with the patient.

Snake Bites

Snake bites are a significant problem experienced worldwide. More than 300,000 injuries from snake bites occur annually, with 30,000 to 40,000 of these resulting in death.[7] Snake bites are fairly common in the United States, with 40,000 to 50,000 incidences reported annually. Approximately 7,000 of these are caused by poisonous snakes; however, fatalities in the United States from snake bites are extremely rare, with only about 15 deaths per year reported.[7]

There are approximately 115 different species of snakes in the United States; however, only 19 species are venomous. Among these are the rattlesnake, copperhead, cottonmouth (water) moccasin, and coral snake.[7] Only the states of Alaska, Hawaii, and Maine do not have at least one species of poisonous snakes. As a general rule, these creatures tend to be retiring and timid and usually do not bite unless provoked, angered, or injured (as when stepped on). However, there are a few exceptions: moccasins can be aggressive snakes, and little provocation is needed to annoy a rattlesnake. Coral snakes, on the other hand, are very shy and retiring and usually bite only when they are being handled or provoked.

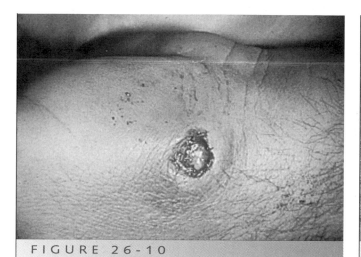

FIGURE 26-10

The bite of a brown recluse spider is characterized by swelling, tenderness, and a pale, mottled cyanotic center. There may also be a small blister on the bite.

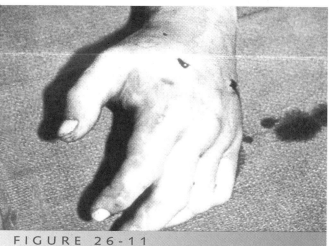

FIGURE 26-11

The characteristic markings of a snake bite wound from a poisonous snake include two small puncture wounds about 1/2" apart, discoloration, and swelling.

Most snake bites occur between the months of April and October, when the reptiles are most active. Most bites involve young men and most occur within a few high-risk states, with Texas reporting the largest number of bites.[7] Other states with major concentrations of snake bites are Louisiana, Georgia, Oklahoma, North Carolina, Arkansas, West Virginia, and Mississippi.[7] Athletic trainers in these states should be thoroughly familiar with the emergency handling of snake bites.

When responding to a snake bite, it is extremely important for the athletic trainer to identify whether *envenomation* (deposit of venom into the wound) has occurred. Only one third of all poisonous snake bites result in significant local or systemic injuries.[7] There are several reasons why envenomation may not occur. Most commonly, the snake may have recently struck another animal and has exhausted its supply of venom.

With the exception of the coral snake, poisonous snakes that are indigenous to the United States all have hollow fangs in the roof of their mouths that allow them to inject venom from two sacs that are located in the back of the head. Therefore, the classic features of a poisonous snake bite consists of two small puncture wounds, usually about 1/2" apart, with surrounding discoloration, swelling, and pain (**Figure 26-11**). Some poisonous snakes have teeth as well as fangs. Nonpoisonous snakes can also bite, usually leaving tooth marks in the shape of a horseshoe. It is important to keep in mind that it is impossible to tell whether a poisonous or nonpoisonous snake was responsible for a bite with the presence of tooth marks. Fang marks, on the other hand, are a clear indication of a bite by a poisonous snake. In this situation, the athletic trainer should examine the affected area for signs of envenomation.

Pit vipers

Rattlesnakes, copperheads, and cottonmouth (water) moccasins are all pit vipers (**Figure 26-12**). The shape of a pit viper's head is triangular and flat. A small pit is located just behind each nostril, in front of each eye. The pupil of a pit viper's eye is vertical and slitlike. The pit is a heat-sensing organ that allows the snake to accurately strike at any warm target, especially in the dark when it cannot see.[7] The snake is better able to accurately ascertain a target with the pits than with the eyes.

The fangs of a pit viper normally lie flat against the roof of its mouth. When the snake is striking a target, its mouth opens wide and its fangs extend out. The fangs, which are hollow and function much like hypodermic needles, are hinged to swing back and forth as the mouth opens. The fangs are connected to a sac containing a reservoir of venom, which in turn is attached to a poison gland. This gland is an adapted salivary gland and is able to produce powerful enzymes that digest and destroy tissue. The primary purpose of the venom is to kill small animals that the snake attacks and to start the digestive process before the animal is eaten.[7]

The most common pit viper is the rattlesnake (**Figure 26-13**). There are several different species of rattlesnake. Apart from the general features shared by most pit vipers, the rattlesnake can be identified by the rattle on its tail.[7] Rattlesnakes have many patterns of color, and many have a diamond pattern. They can grow to be 6' or longer.[7]

Generally, copperheads are smaller than rattlesnakes. They are usually 2' to 3' long and have a characteristic reddish, copper color with brown or red cross bands (**Figure 26-14**).[7] Typically, copperheads are shyer than rattlesnakes and tend to inhabit woodpiles and abandoned dwellings, often close to areas of human habitation. Although they account for most of the venomous snake

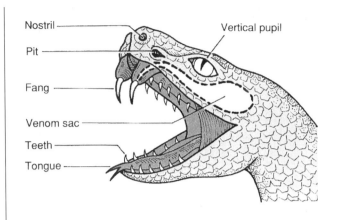

Nostril

Pit

Fang

Venom sac

Teeth

Tongue

Vertical pupil

FIGURE 26-12

Pit vipers have small, heat-sensing organs (pits) located in front of their eyes that allow them to strike at warm targets, even in the dark.

Typically, cottonmouth moccasins grow to approximately 4′ in length. Also called water moccasins, these snakes are either olive or brown, with black cross bands and a yellow undersurface (**Figure 26-15**). Moccasins are water snakes and have particularly aggressive behavior patterns. Although fatalities from these snake bites are rare, tissue destruction from their venom can be severe.

The signs of envenomation by a pit viper are severe burning pain at the injury site, followed by swelling and discoloration around the affected area. These signs are evident within 5 to 10 minutes after the bite has occurred and spread slowly over the following 36 hours. Bleeding under the skin causes *ecchymosis* (bluish discoloration). Systemic signs, which may or may not occur, include weakness, sweating, fainting, and shock.

Occasionally, a patient who has been bitten by a snake may faint because of fear. Usually, this situation is corrected promptly by placing the patient in a supine position. Fainting episodes are temporary and the patient

FIGURE 26-13

The rattlesnake is the most common pit viper and can be identified by the rattle on its tail.

FIGURE 26-14

Copperheads have a characteristic reddish, copper color with brown or red cross bands.

should return to consciousness promptly. The athletic trainer should not confuse fainting with shock, which, if it does occur, happens much later.

The venom produced by a pit viper causes localized destruction of all tissues at the injury site. The venom can also interfere significantly with the body's blood clotting mechanism and cause bleeding at various distant sites.[7] From the moment of envenomation, local tissue destruction begins. If local signs of envenomation (swelling, discoloration, or severe local pain) do not develop after an hour has elapsed from the time the patient was bitten, it is safe to assume that envenomation has not occurred.

The emergency treatment of bites from pit vipers should focus primarily on local containment of the venom and then on the treatment of systemic symptoms. **Table 26-4**

bites in the eastern region of the United States, copperhead bites are rarely fatal. However, the venom can destroy extremities.

FIGURE 26-15

Cottonmouth moccasins, also called water moccasins, are either olive or brown, with black cross bands and a yellow undersurface.

outlines several steps an athletic trainer should perform when treating a pit viper bite.

If the patient shows no signs of envenomation, the athletic trainer should activate EMS and provide basic life support as needed. Also, the athletic trainer should place a sterile dressing over the injury site, apply venous constricting bands above and below the bite area, and immobilize the injury site. The same procedure applies for patients who show early signs of envenomation and who are within 30 minutes of a hospital.

All patients with a suspected snake bite should be brought to the emergency department whether they show signs of envenomation or not. Regardless of whether envenomation has occurred, to prevent infection from occurring, the athletic trainer should treat all bite wounds like other deep puncture wounds. Moreover, the athlete should be transported to an emergency facility within 30 minutes.

Coral snakes

The coral snake is a small, colorful reptile with a series of bright red, yellow, and black bands that completely encircle its body (**Figure 26-16**). Although many harmless snakes have similar coloring, the coral snake can be positively identified if the red and yellow bands are next to one another. If the red and yellow bands are not next to one another, it is not a coral snake. There is a rhyme for remembering this fact: "Red on yellow will kill a fellow; red on black, venom will lack."[7]

The coral snake is a rare creature that lives primarily in Florida and in the desert Southwest. It is not found in the northern regions of the United States.[8] The coral snake is not a pit viper; its head is not triangular, it has no pits, and it has no projecting fangs. The coral snake is a relative of the cobra and has tiny fangs. The coral snake introduces

TABLE 26-4
STEPS FOR TREATING PIT VIPER SNAKE BITES

The athletic trainer should perform the following functions when treating an athlete who has sustained a pit viper snake bite:

1. Activate EMS and notify the dispatcher that the patient has been bitten by a snake.

2. Remain calm and reassure the injured athlete that poisonous snake bites rarely cause death. Place the patient in a supine position and explain to him or her that the spread of venom through the system is substantially decreased by remaining calm.

3. Locate the bite area and gently clean it with soap and water or a mild antiseptic. Ice should not be applied to the area.

4. If the bite was to an arm or leg, apply venous constricting bands above and below the bite area and splint the extremity to decrease movement.

5. Monitor the patient for vomiting. Patients often vomit because of anxiety rather than from the effects of the venomous toxin.

6. Give the patient nothing by mouth, especially alcohol.

7. In the rare instance of a snack bite occurring on the patient's trunk, keep the patient supine and calm. The patient should be transported to the emergency department as rapidly as possible.

8. Monitor the patient's vital signs. If swelling occurs, mark the swollen area with a pen to note whether swelling is spreading.

9. If the patient displays any signs of shock, place the patient in the shock position.

10. If the snake has been killed, as is often the case, bring it to the hospital for identification and to help the emergency department staff administer the correct antivenin.

venom into a victim with a chewing motion of its teeth, not through injection. Because of its small mouth and teeth and limited jaw expansion, the coral snake usually bites its victims on a small part of the body such as a finger or toe. Following a coral snake bite, one or more puncture or scratchlike wounds may be found on the skin.

Fortunately, most dog bites are not serious. Prehospital treatment of all dog bites should include placing a dry, sterile dressing over the wound and promptly transporting the patient to the emergency department.[7] Often, after experiencing a dog bite, the patient may be upset and frightened. The athletic trainer should keep the patient calm and provide reassurance. Regardless of the severity of the injury, any dog bite should be examined by a physician, who may need to administer tetanus prophylaxis. Also, the wound may require sutures, and antibiotics may be prescribed to prevent infection. Occasionally, dog bites result in mangled, complex wounds that require surgical intervention.

A major concern with dog bites is the spread of rabies, an acute viral infection of the central nervous system that is usually fatal if left untreated. The virus is carried in the saliva of an infected animal and is transmitted when it bites or licks an open wound.[7] All warm-blooded animals can be affected by rabies. By administering a series of specific vaccine injections soon after the bite occurs, rabies can be prevented in a patient who has been bitten by a rabid animal (an animal infected by rabies). Although rabies is extremely rare, particularly with the widespread inoculation of pets, it still exists. For example, stray dogs may not have been inoculated and could be carriers of the disease. Other animals such as squirrels, bats, foxes, skunks, and raccoons may also carry rabies. There are reports of each of these animals transmitting rabies to humans.[8]

A person cannot tell if an animal is rabid based on its behavior or appearance. A rabid animal may act perfectly normal, or it may appear vicious, salivate excessively, appear wild ("mad dog"), or show some other form of unusual behavior. The vaccine that is used to prevent rabies in pets is very effective. If an animal has been inoculated against rabies, it should have a tag on its collar stating this fact. Therefore, it is highly important to verify rabies inoculation if the animal can be located. Most dogs are pets and can be identified. If the dog does not have a rabies tag, an animal control officer should be summoned to capture the animal without killing it, so it can be turned over to the health department for observation. Unless specially trained in handling animals, individuals should not attempt to handle strange dogs or wild animals; instead, the local animal control officer should be called. After the animal has been caught, and rabies are still suspected, the animal should be killed and its brain studied. Results of this study will help determine whether the animal was rabid.[8]

In the event the animal cannot be captured or found, the patient should be treated with rabies inoculations. If started shortly after exposure, inoculation treatments are effective at preventing rabies from developing. During the early 1980s, a new rabies vaccine was developed that contained material grown in human tissue.[8] This vaccine is now commonly used when administering inoculations. If a dog bite occurs, the athletic trainer should know the location of the nearest rabies control center and the nearest institution that has human rabies vaccine.

When assisting a dog bite victim, the athletic trainer should be aware that, even though it may not appear rabid or vicious, the dog may attack again. Because of this, the athletic trainer should not enter the scene to assist the injured athlete until the animal has been secured by either the police or the animal control officer. Once the animal is under control, necessary emergency care should be administered to the injured athlete. Also, if necessary, EMS should be activated.

Human Bites

Recent athletic events have brought greater attention to the threat of human bites. Although human bites are relatively uncommon, they are potentially one of the most severe injuries a person can receive. The human mouth contains a wide range of virulent bacteria, even greater than amounts found in the mouths of dogs. For this reason, any human bite that has penetrated the skin must be regarded as a serious injury. Similarly, any laceration caused by a human tooth such as may result on one's

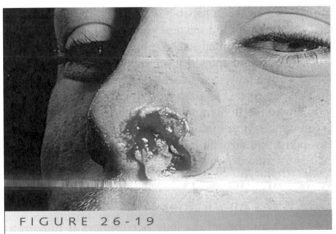

FIGURE 26-19

Because dog bite wounds are heavily contaminated with virulent bacteria, they should be examined at the hospital.

hand from punching someone in the mouth may result in the spread of a serious infection (**Figure 26-20**). The emergency treatment of human bites includes prompt immobilization of the injured area with a splint or bandage; application of a dry, sterile dressing; and transport to the emergency department for surgical cleansing of the wound and antibiotic therapy. In the event that one individual has been punched in the mouth by another, the individual who delivered the punch may also require treatment.

Injuries from Marine Animals

Although shark bites are rare, there has been a large amount of publicity concerning them in recent years. The emergency treatment of a large marine animal bite is the same as for any other major open wound. After activating EMS, the athletic trainer should get the athlete out of the water while taking spinal injury precautions when assisting the athlete. The athletic trainer should control the hemorrhage, apply dressings and splints, treat the patient for shock, and ensure that the patient is transported to the emergency department promptly. If there are sharks in the area, the athletic trainer should be careful not to let any part of his or her body dangle over the boat or in the water.

Although other injuries may result from contact with marine animals, none is as dramatic or as life-threatening as a bite from a large marine animal. With the exception of sharks and barracudas, most marine creatures are not aggressive and will not deliberately attack humans.

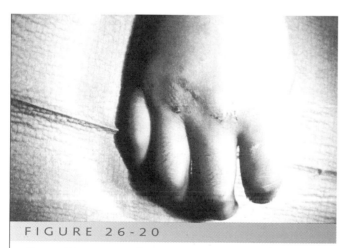

FIGURE 26-20

Human bites can result in a serious spreading infection. Patients with human bites should be evaluated at the hospital.

Injuries from these animals occur when they are accidentally stepped on or otherwise provoked.

Injuries from marine animals occur when individuals swim into the tentacles of a jellyfish, accidentally step on the back of a stingray, or fall or step on sea urchins. Athletic trainers who work near water should be familiar with the marine life in the area. Stings from the tentacles of jellyfish, Portuguese man-of-war, various anemones, corals, or hydras can be treated by removing the patient from the water and pouring alcohol on the affected area. Although isopropyl or rubbing alcohol is recommended, any type of alcohol is effective. Alcohol will inactivate the *nematocysts* (stinging cells) of the marine animal. On rare occasions, a patient may have a systemic allergic reaction from a sting from one of these marine animals. If this occurs, the athletic trainer should activate EMS, administer basic life support, and treat the patient for anaphylactic shock.

Injuries inflicted by the spines of urchins, stingrays, or certain spiny fish such as a catfish should be treated by immobilizing the affected area and soaking it in hot water for 30 minutes. The water temperature should be as hot as the patient can withstand without actually burning the individual. The toxins from these animals are heat sensitive, and dramatic relief from local pain often occurs with the application of hot water. Because of the toxins they release, allergic reactions may occur following contact with these animals. As with any puncture wound, tetanus and other infections may develop. These patients should be transported to the emergency department.

Some sea animals such as nonpoisonous water snakes may cause minor bite injuries. Athletic trainers should treat these bites as they would any other bite by placing sterile dressings over the injury and arranging transportation for the patient to the emergency department for evaluation and tetanus prophylaxis. Many fish are poisonous if eaten. The emergency treatment of such poisoning is the same as for any other ingested poisoning: activation of EMS, basic life support, prevention of injury from convulsions, and prompt transport of the patient to the emergency department.

Other rare conditions that an individual can experience as a result of contact from marine animals include shocks from electric eels or skin rashes from marine parasites.[8] Generally, these injuries are mild, and panic from contact with electric eels can be the most conspicuous part of this particular injury.

CHAPTER REVIEW

A poison is any substance that, when swallowed, inhaled, or absorbed, or when applied to, injected into, or otherwise introduced into the body in relatively small amounts, may cause structural damage or functional disturbances because of its chemical actions. Most poisoning fatalities are from drugs.

Poison control centers exist across the United States. Most are staffed 24 hours a day by personnel with access to information about commonly used and potentially poisonous drugs, chemicals, and substances. Therefore, athletic trainers should know the location and telephone number of the nearest poison control center. By activating EMS, the poison control center can provide specific instructions regarding emergency treatment, and the patient can be quickly transported to an emergency department.

Common signs and symptoms of poisoning include nausea, vomiting, abdominal pain, diarrhea, dilation or constriction of the pupils, excessive salivation, sweating, dyspnea, depressed respirations, unconsciousness, convulsions, cyanosis, and redness, blistering, and severe burns of the skin or mucous membranes. Also, the athletic trainer should attempt to determine the nature of the poison and bring any suspicious materials and vomitus to the hospital.

Because most poisons do not have a specific antidote, the most important treatment is to dilute or physically remove the agent by surface flooding and washing of the skin when treating contact poisonings, drinking water or milk and inducing vomiting when treating ingested poisonings, or administering oxygen for inhaled poisonings.

Most poisonings are caused by ingested poisons. Emergency management is rapid removal of as much of the poison as possible from the gastrointestinal tract and dilution or neutralization of the remaining toxins. However, the athletic trainer must also understand the circumstances under which inducing vomiting may be dangerous.

Surface contact poisons can cause damage to the skin, mucous membranes, or eyes by direct contact. Immediate treatment is to remove the offending substance as quickly as possible, usually by flooding the area with water, except when the substance reacts violently with water, in which case treatment should consist of dusting the chemical off the patient, removing the patient's clothing, and applying a dry dressing.

Inhaled poisons can be counteracted by moving the patient into fresh air and providing supplemental oxygen and basic life support as needed. Injected poisons may cause swelling at the site, therefore, jewelry should be removed. The treatment of food and plant poisoning depends on the nature of the poison and the athlete's signs and symptoms.

Stings can be potentially dangerous, particularly if the athlete is allergic to the venom. Ice may be helpful in relieving local irritation. If a bee sting kit is available, epinephrine and antihistamine will be helpful in reversing the reaction.

Spider bites are generally not serious unless they come from black widow or brown recluse spiders. Black widow spider bites produce systemic symptoms and brown recluse spider bites cause local tissue destruction; both require prompt transport to the emergency department.

Snake bites are common, but only four species of poisonous snakes inhabit the United States. If the bite is to an extremity, applying a splint, as well as venous tourniquets above and below the bite, will help to slow the spread of the toxin.

Ticks can spread Rocky Mountain spotted fever and Lyme disease, but if the tick is removed within a few hours, these problems may be avoided. All dog and human bites should be considered as potentially infected wounds and should be treated with a dry, sterile dressing and transport to the emergency department. Injuries from marine animals can often be neutralized with rubbing alcohol before the patient is transported to the emergency department.

1. Which of the following statements about poisoning rates is true?

A. One third of all deaths result from drugs.

B. Two thirds of all deaths result from substances other than drugs.

C. Adult deaths have decreased in recent years.

D. Children's deaths have decreased in recent years.

2. Once a poisoning has occurred, which of the following activities is the responsibility of the athletic trainer?

A. Locating the specific antidote

B. Definitively determining the nature of the poison

C. Immediately inducing vomiting with syrup of ipecac

D. Activating the emergency medical services system.

3. Which of the following delivery modes is the most common mechanism of poisoning?

A. Injection

B. Ingestion

C. Inhalation

D. Surface contact

4. Which of the following symptoms are common signs of poisoning?

A. Chills and convulsions

B. Dry mouth and nausea

C. Abdominal pain and sweating

D. Pupil constriction and constipation

5. If a poison has been ingested, activated charcoal should be administered only if the patient is:

A. alert.

B. pregnant.

C. comatose.

D. convulsing.

6. Anaphylaxis is characterized by which of the following symptoms?

A. Fever

B. Wheezing

C. Localized itching

D. Lip and tongue pain

7. Which of the following bites produces rigidity of the abdominal muscles to the point that they become almost as stiff as a board?

A. Pit viper

B. Coral snake

C. Black widow spider

D. Brown recluse spider

8. When treating a pit viper snake bite, which of the following activities should not be performed?

A. Activating EMS.

B. Monitoring the patient's vital signs.

C. Giving the patient plenty of fluids.

D. Monitoring the patient for vomiting.

9. Which of the following activities should be performed after a tick has bitten an athlete?

A. Suffocating it with gasoline

B. Burning it with a lighted match

C. Covering it with petroleum jelly

D. Removing it with fine tweezers

10. Which of the following statements about rabies is true?

A. Rabies is a bacterial infection.

B. Rabies is carried by cold-blooded animals.

C. Rabies is always obvious in the animal's behavior.

D. Rabies in humans is almost always fatal if left untreated.

Answers on page 894.

References

1. Pinger RR, Hahn DB, Sharp RL: The role of the athletic trainer in the detection and prevention of Lyme disease in athletes. *Athletic Train* 1991;26:324-331.

2. Standaert SM, Dawson JE, Schaffner W, et al: Ehrlichiosis in a golf-oriented retirement community. *N Engl J Med* 1995;333:420-425.

3. Priblyl CR, Racca J: Toxic gas exposures in ice arenas. *Clin J Sport Med* 1996;6:232-236.

4. Karlson-Stiber C, Hojer J, Sjoholm A, Bluhm G, Salmonson H: Toxic pneumonitis in a hockey player. [Poisonous gases are produced by ice machines]. *Lakartidningen* 1996;93:3808.

5. Soparkar G, Mayers I, Edouard L, Hoeppner VH: Toxic effects from nitrogen dioxide in ice-skating arenas. *CMAJ* 1993;148:1181-1182.

6. Karlson-Stiber C, Hojer J, Sjoholm A, Bluhm G, Salmonson H: Nitrogen dioxide pneumonitis in ice hockey players. *J Intern Med* 1996;239:451-456.

7. Browner BD, Jacobs LM, Pollak AN (eds): *Emergency Care and Transportation of the Sick and Injured*, ed 7. Rosemont, IL, American Academy of Orthopaedic Surgeons, 1999.

8. Heckman JD (ed): *Emergency Care and Transportation of the Sick and Injured*, ed 5. Rosemont, IL, American Academy of Orthopaedic Surgeons, 1993.

9. Bergmann KC: Sports and allergy. *Int J Sports* Med 1991;12(suppl 1):S16-S18.

10. Dannenberg AL, Needle S, Mullady D, Kolodner KB: Predictors of injury among 1638 riders in a recreational long-distance bicycle tour: Cycle across Maryland. *Am J Sports Med* 1996;24:747-753.

27

Pharmacology and Substance Abuse

Jennifer A. Stone, MS, ATC
James C. Puffer, MD

QUICK CONTENTS

OVERVIEW

Several types of medications are used in the athletic setting to control inflammation and pain and to treat various medical ailments. Unfortunately, some medications have also been used illegally by athletes to enhance performance or as masking agents to prevent the detection of performance-enhancing medications. The athletic trainer must be knowledgeable about medications available to athletes that are used to treat legitimate medical problems, medications that are banned in drug-testing situations, and the problems associated with drug abuse and performance enhancement. Athletic participation does not insulate individuals from potentially abusing drugs, including alcohol.

This chapter discusses medications used to control pain and inflammation caused by musculoskeletal conditions such as tendinitis or strain, both acute or chronic, as well as medications used to treat common medical conditions such as infections, allergies, pulmonary concerns, and gastrointestinal problems. Substance abuse and drug testing are also discussed.

MEDICATIONS USED TO TREAT MUSCULOSKELETAL PROBLEMS

Because of the demands they place on their bodies during training and competition, most athletes can expect to experience either acute or chronic musculoskeletal ailments. Although physical treatments such as ice, ultrasound, electrical stimulation, and hot packs are applied topically to promote healing and to prevent secondary insult to damaged tissues, the treating physician and athletic trainer generally use a broad spectrum of interventions when treating the injured athlete to reduce the possibility of disability and promote the return to activity. These interventions frequently include the administration of oral nonsteroidal anti-inflammatory drugs (NSAIDs) and may also include injectable NSAIDs, oral or injectable corticosteroids, analgesics, or anesthetics.

Trauma as a result of sports produces varying amounts of pain, depending on the severity of injury and the athlete's physiologic and psychological reaction to the trauma. Although NSAIDs can have an *analgesic* (pain-relieving) and an anti-inflammatory effect, more powerful analgesics may be used in synergism with NSAIDs to manage pain effectively. Acetaminophen is the most common analgesic used for mild pain; however, prescription analgesics are more effective when treating athletes with moderate or severe pain. For a potent local effect, anesthetics such as lidocaine can be used.

ANTI-INFLAMMATORY AGENTS

Anti-inflammatory agents can be categorized several different ways: steroidal or nonsteroidal; injectable, oral, or topical; or salicylic or nonsalicylic. The selection of a specific drug by the physician depends on the athlete, the injury, past successful or unsuccessful use of anti-inflammatory agents, and past experiences and prescribing preferences of the treating physician. In many cases, a particular class of drugs does not necessarily have a distinct advantage over another; however, some athletes can have idiosyncratic reactions to the same medication. If one medication is not working as well as expected for an athlete, the physician should prescribe another medication in a different drug category.

Systemic Anti-inflammatory Agents

NSAIDs inhibit the production of prostaglandin, which is produced by the release of arachidonic acid at the site of an acute injury. NSAIDs are available in both prescription and nonprescription formulations. Aspirin is the oldest and least expensive NSAID, but other forms are increasing in consumer availability and popularity.

Aspirin is the most common oral salicylate NSAID used when treating mild pain, and topical preparations of salicylate are available over the counter.[1,2] In either form, aspirin has both *antipyretic* (assists with relieving or reducing fever) and analgesic properties. In tablet form, aspirin contains 325 mg with a recommended dose of 650 to 1,300 mg every 4 to 6 hours.[1-3] Because aspirin can cause gastric upset, a buffered or enteric-coated tablet taken with food may be easier for the athlete to consume. A common side effect, in addition to gastric upset, is tinnitus.[1-3] If this occurs, aspirin usage should be immediately discontinued. Additionally, aspirin should never be administered to children and adolescents who are suspected of having a viral disease because aspirin in these cases increases the risk of developing Reye's syndrome.[1-3] Aspirin also inhibits platelet aggregation with effects so dramatic that lengthened blood clotting time may persist for up to 1 week following a single dose.[1-3]

Ibuprofen, naproxen, and ketoprofen are oral nonsalicylate NSAIDs available in prescription and nonprescription formulations. The nonprescription formulations are lower doses of the original prescription medications, while present prescription formulations are generally controlled release.[1-3] Ibuprofen, naproxen, and ketoprofen all have anti-inflammatory and analgesic effects. The maximum daily doses for these medications, administered over a 24-hour time period, is 3,200 mg, 1,500 mg, and 300 mg, respectively.[2-4] Anti-inflammatory effects are achieved when sufficient blood levels are reached, usually within 48 to 72 hours.[2-4] Prior to this, pain-relieving effects are a result of the analgesic effects of these medications. As in the case of aspirin, these medications can also cause gastric distress and should be taken with food. Ibuprofen,

Anti-inflammatory Agents

Anti-inflammatory agents are classified as steroidal or nonsteroidal; injectable, oral, or topical; and salicylic or nonsalicylic. The selection of a specific drug depends on many factors, and although one class of medications may have no distinct advantage over another, individuals may react in different ways to the same medication. Therefore, if a medication is not working as expected, a medication in another category should be prescribed.

Systemic anti-inflammatory agents

NSAIDs (available in prescription and nonprescription formulations) inhibit the production of prostaglandin, which is produced by the release of arachidonic acid at the site of an acute injury. Aspirin is the most commonly used oral salicylate NSAID and has antipyretic and analgesic properties. Because aspirin can cause gastric upset, a buffered or enteric-coated formulation, taken with food, may be appropriate for some individuals. Aspirin treatment should be immediately stopped if tinnitus occurs, and aspirin should never be used in children and adolescents with a suspected viral illness for fear of increasing the patient's risk of Reye's syndrome. Aspirin dramatically inhibits platelet aggregation such that increased clotting time may last for 1 week after a single dose.

Oral, nonsalicylate NSAIDs available in both extended-release prescription and lower-dose nonprescription forms and with anti-inflammatory and analgesic effects include ibuprofen (in divided doses with a maximum of 3,200 mg per day), naproxen (with a maximum of 1,500 mg per day), and ketoprofen (with a maximum of 300 mg per day). Analgesic effects occur first, with anti-inflammatory effects achieved within 48 to 72 hours, when sufficient blood levels are reached. These medications can cause gastric distress (and should be taken with food) and inhibit platelet aggregation. Because antiprostaglandin effects produced by NSAIDs can further compromise renal function, they should not be taken by athletes with impaired renal function.

Athletic trainers should not advise athletes to use nonprescription NSAIDs in prescription strengths. In addition, it is important to ensure that the athlete is taking only one NSAID at a time. One prescription nonsalicylate NSAID, ketorolac tromethamine, is available in injectable form and has potent pain-relieving effects (in addition to anti-inflammatory effects) that make it particularly suitable after severe injury or surgery. A loading dose is injected, and then the athlete continues treatment with oral medication. Because diclofenac sodium and diclofenac potassium can cause liver problems, athletes taking these medications should be screened regularly.

Local anti-inflammatory agents

Anti-inflammatory agents (NSAIDs and corticosteroids) can be applied locally by topical application of a cream that is enhanced with direct current (iontophoresis), ultrasound (phonophoresis), or by injection. The effectiveness of these medications depends on the athlete's condition and the quantity of medication delivered to the inflamed tissue. Only topical aspirin preparations are available in the United States.

For iontophoresis, direct current generators and electrodes minimize skin breakdown and electric current burns. Suggested treatment regimens vary based on the diagnosis and medication used and may be determined by cost and patient availability. Phonophoresis uses normal ultrasound protocols, but the standard coupling agent is mixed with the anti-inflammatory compound.

Corticosteroid preparations include short-, intermediate-, and long-acting preparations and can be injected into or near the inflamed area. However, a side effect is weakening of tissue collagen. Therefore, weightbearing tendons should never be injected with a corticosteroid. Following a corticosteroid injection, the site should be rested for at least 7 to 14 days, with injections repeated no more than three to four times. Because corticosteroids injected into a joint can cause articular cartilage deterioration, local tissue necrosis, and skin depigmentation at the injection site, injections should be limited to once every 3 to 6 months.

naproxen, and ketoprofen also inhibit platelet aggregation. Because the antiprostaglandin effect of NSAIDs can further impair renal function, athletes who have impaired kidney function should not use them.[2-4] Athletic trainers should never recommend the use of nonprescription NSAID formulations in prescription dosages when treating pain.

Prescription NSAIDs come in many different formulations. **Table 27-1** lists the chemical classifications of common NSAIDs and their common trade names. Although all NSAIDs work well for treating pain, some athletes may achieve better results when using one particular NSAID over another. Physicians also have prescribing preferences based on their past experiences. With the easy availability of nonprescription NSAIDs, the physician and athletic trainer must ensure that the athlete does not mix NSAIDs when treating pain. Mixing NSAIDs can cause undesirable side effects. If an NSAID is prescribed, the physician should question the athlete about the use of other NSAIDs and also instruct the individual to stop taking them. Additionally, athletes using diclofenac sodium (Voltaren) or diclofenac potassium (Cataflam) should be screened for liver problems and have their liver tested regularly to ensure proper functioning.[3] **Table 27-2** presents some contraindications and precautions for NSAID use.

Ketorolac tromethamine (Toradol), a prescription non-salicylate NSAID formulation, is available in an injectable form and has a potent pain-relieving effect in addition to an anti-inflammatory effect. Although additional injections of lesser dosages can be used on a short-term basis, especially following surgery or severe injury, one intra-venous or intramuscular injection is followed by oral medication for continued efficacy.[2,4]

Local Anti-inflammatory Agents

Anti-inflammatory agents can be applied locally by topical application of creams, topical application enhanced with direct current or ultrasound, or by injection. The effectiveness of each anti-inflammatory agent depends on the medical condition being treated and the quantity of medication that is placed in proximity to the inflamed tissue.

Topical NSAIDs, other than salicylate formulations, are not available in the United States without a prescription; however, they are available without prescription in Mexico and Europe. These creams and gels are rubbed into the injured athlete's skin over the inflamed area or combined with ultrasound gel and driven through the skin by phonophoresis.

TABLE 27-1
FORMULATIONS FOR PRESCRIPTION NSAIDs

Chemical classifications of common NSAIDs and their common trade names (summarized from various sources)

Carboxylic Acids	Enolic Acids	Nonacids
Propionic acids	Oxicams	Nabumetone (Relafen)
Carprofen (Rimadyl)	Piroxicam (Feldene)	
Fenoprofen (Nalfon)	Pyrazolones	
Flurbiprofen (Ansaid)	Oxyphenylbutazone	
Ibuprofen (Advil, Motrin)	Phenylbutazone (Azolid, Butazolidin)	
Ketoprofen (Orudis)	Pyrrolopyrroles	
Naproxen (Aleve, Naprosyn)	Ketorolac (Toradol)	
Naproxen sodium (Anaprox)		
Oxaprosin (Daypro)		
Fenamates		
Meclofenamate sodium (Meclomen)		
Mefenamic acid (Ponstel)		
Acetic acids		
Diclofenac sodium (Voltaren)		
Etodolac (Lodine)		
Indomethacin (Indocin)		
Sulindac (Clinoril)		
Tolmetin (Tolectin)		
Salicylates		
Acetylsalicyclic acid (aspirin)		
Diflunisal (Dolobid)		
Salsalate (Salflex, Disaicid)		
Magnesium salicylate (Doan's Analgesic)		
Choline magnesium trisalicylate (Trilisate)		

(Reproduced with permission from Hertel J: The role of nonsteroidal anti-inflammatory drugs in the treatment of acute soft tissue injuries. *Athl Train* 1997;32:350.

TABLE 27-2
CONTRAINDICATIONS AND PRECAUTIONS FOR USE OF NSAIDs

Contraindications
Aspirin allergy
Third-trimester pregnancy

Precautions
History of gastrointestinal disease
History of renal or hepatic dysfunction
Cardiac failure
Hypertension

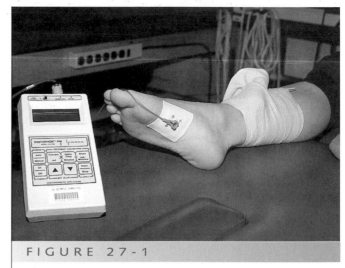

FIGURE 27-1

Iontophoresis uses direct current to drive NSAIDs or corticosteroids through the skin.

Both NSAIDs and corticosteroids can be used topically and driven through the skin with ultrasound (*phonophoresis*) or by direct current (*iontophoresis*) (**Figure 27-1**). The use of direct current generators and electrodes when administering iontophoresis minimizes medication breakdown and skin irritation that may result from the electrical current.[5] Treatment dosages are measured in milliampere seconds (mAs) of current. Treatment regimens vary depending on the diagnosis and medication being used, but cost and patient availability also may have to be considered.[5] Because treatment regimens can vary among patients, cost and patient availability may ultimately determine which treatment protocol should be used. Most medications used in phonophoresis and all medications used in iontophoresis require a physician's prescription.

Phonophoresis uses ultrasound to introduce the anti-inflammatory medication through the skin. Topical preparations of aspirin, nonsalicylate NSAIDs, or corticosteroids can be used for phonophoresis; however, the athletic trainer must make sure that the selected compound is able to transmit ultrasound waves.[5] Standard ultrasound protocols are used, but the standard coupling gel is replaced by the anti-inflammatory compound. Although any NSAID or corticosteroid compound can theoretically be used, hydrocortisone solution is a popular choice when treating an injury.[5]

Corticosteroid preparations can also be injected into or near the inflamed area. As with NSAIDs, the physician has a number of preparations to select from. Injectable preparations vary from short-acting preparations, such as methylprednisolone (Depo-Medrol), to intermediate-acting preparations, such as triamcinolone (Aristocort, Aristospan), to long-acting preparations, such as dexamethasone (Decadron) and betamethasone (Celestone). When administering injections, the clinician can place the anti-inflammatory preparation directly on or near the inflamed tissue; however, the preparation can weaken the tissue's collagen structure.[4,6] Weightbearing tendons such as the patellar tendon and Achilles tendon should never be injected with a corticosteroid. Following a corticosteroid injection, the anatomic site should be rested for a minimum of 7 to 14 days, and injections should be repeated no more than three or four times over a 4- to 6-month period.[4] Because corticosteroids can cause deterioration of articular cartilage when injected into a joint, an injection should not be administered more frequently than once every 3 to 6 months.[6] Additionally, corticosteroid injections can cause local tissue necrosis and skin depigmentation at the injection site.

ANALGESICS

Analgesics help relieve pain and may produce antipyretic effects. Acetaminophen, which acts as an antipyretic, is the most commonly used analgesic and is useful in controlling fever during viral illnesses when the use of aspirin is contraindicated. Acetaminophen is available in 325 and 500 mg formulations, and effective dosages range from 325 to 1,000 mg every 4 to 6 hours.[1-3] An advantage of acetaminophen is that it does not cause gastric upset and is available in tablet, caplet, elixir, and suppository forms. Acetaminophen is contraindicated in athletes with any type of liver dysfunction and can cause liver toxicity in relatively low dosages, especially if used with alcohol.[1-3]

Codeine is an opiate analgesic that can be combined with acetaminophen to achieve a higher level of pain relief. By itself, codeine does not have any antipyretic effects. The usual dosage is 30 to 60 mg every 4 to 6 hours.[2-4] Common side effects associated with codeine include sedation, dose-related respiratory depression, and constipation. Because codeine can be addicting, injured athletes should be prescribed codeine based on their symptoms. Medication should be changed to a nonopiate analgesic as soon as possible.

Hydrocodone bitartrate is a synthetic opiate analgesic that can be combined with acetaminophen (Lortab, Vicodin). Typical dosage for this analgesic is 5 mg every 6 hours.[2-4] Generally, hydrocodone bitartrate is stronger than codeine in its ability to relieve pain, has the same side effects as codeine, and has a high abuse potential. When prescribing hydrocodone bitartrate to athletes, course of treatment should be as short as possible.

Oxycodone hydrochloride is another synthetic opiate that is combined with either aspirin (Percodan) or acetaminophen (Percocet). The usual dosage is 5 mg every 6 hours.[2-4] Although it is stronger than codeine, oxycodone hydrochloride has the same side effects as codeine as well as a high abuse potential. As with hydrocodone bitartrate, the use of oxycodone hydrochloride should be restricted to a short course of treatment.

Morphine is an opiate analgesic used to treat severe pain. It is typically administered intravenously in dosages of 5 to 15 mg every 4 to 5 hours. Because morphine can depress respiratory function, its use in athletes is generally reserved for hospitalized patients following surgery or severe injury. Like all opiates, it can be addictive if used inappropriately.

Meperidine hydrochloride (Demerol) is also used to manage severe pain. It is available in both oral and injectable forms. Like morphine, meperidine hydrochloride is habit-forming.

ANESTHETICS

Local anesthetics are commonly used for controlling pain during laceration repair. They may, however, also be appropriate either alone or in combination with an injectable opiate for reduction of fractures or dislocations. Lidocaine (Xylocaine) 1% or 2% with or without epinephrine is commonly used. Epinephrine can aid in the control of bleeding, especially with scalp and facial lacerations. Bupivacaine hydrochloride (Sensorcaine) is indicated when extended anesthesia, up to 6 hours, is desired.

Anesthetics are also used in combination with injectable corticosteroids. By monitoring the anesthesia, the treating physician can ensure that the corticosteroid reaches the desired location. The anesthesia then provides pain relief following the injection.

Topical lidocaine also comes in a viscous formulation that can help relieve pain from mouth ulcers or from cleaning deep and dirty abrasions. Care must be taken to apply only small amounts of lidocaine to abrasions as the wound can absorb enough lidocaine to cause a systemic reaction in addition to the desired local reaction.

OTHER MEDICATIONS

Antibiotics

Antibiotics are used to treat bacterial infections and have no role in the management of viral infections. Whenever possible, cultures should be obtained to guide therapy. Because cultures generally take 24 to 48 hours to grow, treatment is generally started empirically with the choice of antibiotic directed at the most likely infecting organisms. The treatment regimen can be modified should a different pathogen be identified or the identified pathogen is resistant to the prescribed medication.

Antibiotics are classified as *bacteriostatic* and *bacteriocidal*. Bacteriostatic antibiotics do not directly kill the offending bacteria but prevent it from reproducing; bacteriocidal antibiotics kill bacteria. Examples of bacteriostatic antibiotics are erythromycin, tetracycline, and sulfonamides. Examples of bacteriocidal antibiotics are penicillin and its derivatives and all generations of cephalosporin, vancomycin, and uoroquinolone.

Antibiotics can also be classified by the type of bacteria against which they are effective: gram negative, gram positive, or both (broad spectrum).[6] The development and use of broad-spectrum antibiotics with good coverage against many different bacteria has been accompanied by an increasing incidence of bacterial drug resistance. For this reason, antibiotics should be used only when they are clearly indicated, and athletes must be carefully counseled to take the antibiotic exactly as directed.

Common health problems in athletes that can be appropriately treated with antibiotics include strep throat, sinus infections, pneumonia, cellulitis, and bacterial skin infections that cannot be controlled by topical means. Antibiotics are not effective against viral infections such as colds and influenza, and their indiscriminate use in such conditions contributes to the increasing problem of drug resistance.[6]

Antiviral Medications

Several medications that are effective against specific viral infections are available. These medications are highly virus-specific and do not have the broad-spectrum coverage common to many antibiotics.

For either prophylaxis or treatment of influenza A, rimantadine hydrochloride (Flumadine) and amantadine hydrochloride (Symmetrel) are helpful. In an athlete who has been exposed to influenza A, a dosage of either medication, 100 mg twice daily for 2 to 3 weeks is combined with immunization.[2-4,6] Once symptoms are present, the same 100 mg twice daily dose for 7 days can shorten the course of infection.

Herpes gladiatorum can be a problem in contact sports, especially wrestling. Medications such as acyclovir (Zovirax), valacyclovir (Valtrex), and famciclovir (Famvir) may control the infection and shorten the time during which the athlete is infectious and unable to participate in sport. For individuals with recurrent outbreaks, these medications can also be used prophylactically.

Allergy Medications

Antihistamines are the medication of choice for treating allergies. There are many choices of nonprescription antihistamines such as diphenhydramine hydrochloride (Benadryl), brompheniramine maleate (Dimetane, Dimetapp) and chlorpheniramine maleate (Chlor-Trimeton); however, sedation is a significant side effect of these medications. Newer nonsedating antihistamines such as loratadine (Claritin), fexofenadine (Allegra), and cetirizine hydrochloride (Zyrtec) are prescription medications with fewer side effects and less frequent dosages, which may improve patient compliance.

Topical nasal products are helpful when the allergy symptoms are confined to the nose or when oral antihistamines do not provide relief from rhinitis. Formulations use cromolyn sodium (Intal) and various corticosteroids such as beclomethasone dipropionate (Vancenase, Beconase), fluticasone propionate (Flonase), and triamcinolone acetonide (Nasacort, Azmacort). These formulations are effective topical treatments but require several weeks of dosing to reach maximum effectiveness.

Asthma Medications

Asthma is a common problem that affects 8% to 22% of all athletes.[7] The athlete with asthma must be identified before his or her condition can be treated. Although most individuals with allergy-induced asthma also have exercise-induced asthma, the reverse is not always true. In addition, the athlete with exercise-induced asthma may show few outward clinical signs and may interpret difficulty in breathing as being "out of shape." Testing a patient for asthma requires measuring pulmonary function, reproducing the symptoms, and remeasuring pulmonary function. A decrease of 10% to 15% in selected parameters of pulmonary function is a positive diagnostic sign of exercise-induced asthma.[7]

Treatment of asthma typically involves the use of inhaled medications (**Figure 27-2**). In patients who are known to have asthma, an anti-inflammatory medication such as beclomethasone dipropionate (Beclovent, Vanceril) is the foundation of therapy. A beta-adrenergic agent such as albuterol (Proventil, Ventolin) should be used by athletes with asthma prior to exercise. This medication provides immediate bronchodilation and is also a reliever medication, which reverses acute bronchospasm during the initial stages of an acute asthma attack. If these medications do not provide adequate asthma control, medications such as nedocromil sodium (Tilade), cromolyn sodium (Intal), or a more powerful inhaled corticosteroid such as fluticasone propionate (Flovent) may be used. Salmeterol xinafoate (Serevent) is a newer, longer-acting beta-agonist; however, it is not effective as a reliever medication. Athletes who have only exercise-induced asthma may be treated solely with a beta-agonist prior to participating in exercise.

Athletes with severe cases of allergy-induced asthma may need oral medication in addition to inhaled medications. Theophylline (Slo-Bid, Theo-Dur, Uniphyl) is useful but has a very narrow window of therapeutic effects and can cause side effects such as tremors, nausea, anxi-

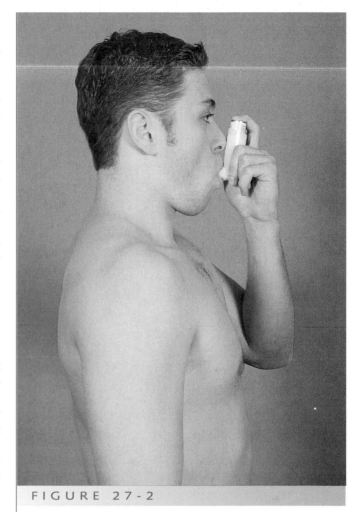

FIGURE 27-2

Athletes with asthma must know how to properly use an inhaler.

ety, and cardiac arrhythmias. Leukotriene inhibitors, such as zafirlukast (Accolate), are new oral medications for asthma prophylaxis that offer promise for severe cases.

Both the athletic trainer and the treating physician must be cognizant of the most recent rules regarding asthma medications and drug testing. Because not all asthma medications are approved for use by athletes subject to drug testing, the physician, athletic trainer, and athlete should contact the drug testing organization to ensure that the medications selected for the individual's asthma treatment program are permitted.

Because asthma can be a life-threatening problem, athletes who experience acute asthmatic attacks with severe bronchospasm are best treated in emergency facilities. Prior to arrival of emergency personnel, the athletic trainer can help an athlete with asthma use his or her albuterol sulfate inhaler or, if the athlete has it immediately available, a nebulizer with the athlete's prescribed medication.

Gastrointestinal Medications

Like all individuals, athletes will occasionally experience minor gastrointestinal symptoms, generally brought about

FOCUS ON . . .

Analgesics, Anesthetics, and Other Medications

Antibiotics

Antibiotics are used to treat bacterial infections and should not be used for treating viral infections. When possible, the treating physician should take cultures from the athlete for evaluation. Because cultures require 24 to 48 hours for bacterial infections to grow, empiric treatment is usually started by targeting the antibiotic most likely to be effective. This approach can be changed later during the course of the treatment if the pathogen is resistant to it. Antibiotics are classified as bacteriostatic (preventing bacteria from reproducing) or bacteriocidal (killing bacteria). Antibiotics can also be classified by the type of bacteria they work on: gram negative, gram positive, or both (broad spectrum).

Because bacterial drug resistance is an increasing problem, antibiotics must be used only when clearly indicated and athletes must take antibiotics exactly as directed. Common health problems appropriately treated with antibiotics include strep throat, sinus infections, pneumonia, cellulitis, and bacterial skin infections that topical agents are unable to control.

Analgesics

Analgesics relieve pain and may have antipyretic effects. Acetaminophen, which is useful for controlling fever during viral illnesses in patients who cannot take aspirin, is the most commonly used analgesic and is available in a variety of forms. Effective dosages range from 325 to 1,000 mg every 4 to 6 hours. Acetaminophen is contraindicated in patients with liver dysfunction; it can be toxic to the liver in relatively low dosages, especially when used with alcohol.

Codeine is an opiate analgesic that is frequently combined with acetaminophen. The typical dosage is 30 to 60 mg every 4 to 6 hours. Codeine can be addicting and should be used only for short-term use until the athlete can be treated with a nonopiate analgesic.

Hydrocodone bitartrate is a synthetic opiate analgesic that can be combined with acetaminophen. The typical dose is 5 mg every 6 hours. Hydrocodone bitartrate has the same side effects as codeine, but is much stronger in its ability to relieve pain yet has a high abuse potential.

Morphine is an opiate analgesic used for severe pain that is typically given intravenously in dosages of 5 to 15 mg every 4 to 5 hours. Because of its ability to depress respiratory function, morphine is usually reserved for hospitalized patients after surgery or for patients with severe injuries. Meperidine hydrochloride is also used for severe pain and is available in oral and injectable forms. Both morphine and meperidine hydrochloride can be habit forming.

Anesthetics

Local anesthetics are commonly used for controlling pain during laceration repair and for fracture and dislocation reduction. Lidocaine 1% or 2%, with or without epinephrine (which can control bleeding, especially in scalp and facial lacerations), is a commonly used formulation. Lidocaine in a viscous formulation can relieve the pain of mouth ulcers and is also used to clean deep and dirty abrasions. However, only small amounts should be used when cleaning an abrasion because the wound can absorb enough to cause a systemic reaction. Bupivacaine hydrochloride is the most effective anesthetic when extended anesthesia (up to 6 hours) is needed. Anesthetics can also be combined with injectable corticosteroids, which allows the physician to ensure that the corticosteroid reaches the desired location.

Antiviral medications

Because antiviral medications are virus-specific, they lack the broad-spectrum coverage offered by antibiotics. Rimantadine hydrochloride and amantadine hydrochloride can be used prophylactically or for the treatment of influenza A. The prophylactic dosage is 100 mg twice daily for 2 to 3 weeks, and the treatment dosage is 100 mg twice daily for 7 days.

Acyclovir, valacyclovir, and famciclovir may help to control and shorten the infectious period of herpes gladiatorum, which affects contact sports participants, especially wrestlers. Individuals with recurrent outbreaks can be treated prophylactically.

(Continued)

FOCUS ON . . .

Analgesics, Anesthetics, and Other Medications (Continued)

Allergy medications

Allergies are most often treated with antihistamines, many of which are available without prescription. Because these medications tend to be sedating, newer, nonsedating prescription medications that are taken less frequently may improve patient compliance. Topical nasal products are useful when the allergy symptoms are confined to the nose or when oral antihistamines do not provide relief; however, they require several weeks of dosing to reach maximum effectiveness.

Asthma medications

Asthma affects 8% to 22% of all athletes, and although most individuals with allergic asthma also have exercise-induced asthma, not all individuals with exercise-induced asthma have allergic asthma. Identification of the athlete with asthma is important, but can be difficult if few clinical signs other than difficulty in breathing are evident. Definitive diagnosis requires pulmonary function, reproducing the symptoms, and remeasuring pulmonary function. A decrease of 10% to 15% in selected parameters of pulmonary function is a positive diagnostic sign of exercise-induced asthma.

Treatment of individuals with asthma starts with inhaled medications such as beclomethasone dipropionate. A beta-adrenergic such as albuterol is used before exercise to provide immediate bronchodilation and may be what the athlete with exercise-induced asthma requires. Albuterol can also be used during the initial stages of an acute asthma attack. If further therapy is needed, nedocomil sodium, cromolyn sodium, and fluticasone propionate, a more powerful inhaled corticosteroid, can be added. Salmeterol xinafoate is a longer-acting beta-agonist, but it is not effective in an acute attack. Patients with severe asthma may also require oral medications. Theophylline is beneficial, but it has a narrow window of therapeutic effects and can cause tremor, nausea, anxiety, and cardiac arrhythmias. The new leukotriene inhibitors such as zafirlukast offer promise for asthma prophylaxis.

Not all asthma medications are approved for use in athletes subject to drug testing. Therefore, the athletic trainer and treating physician must ensure that the medications selected for treatment are allowed.

Acute asthma attacks with severe bronchospasm can be life threatening and should be treated in an emergency facility. Before the emergency personnel arrive, the athletic trainer can help the athlete use his or her albuterol inhaler or nebulizer.

Gastrointestinal medications

Gastrointestinal conditions must be properly identified in order to be effectively treated. Simple dyspepsia is best treated with tablet or liquid antacids such as magnesium and aluminum hydroxide or calcium preparations. Nonprescription H_2 blockers such as cimetidine, famotidine, and ranitidine can complement the antacids, but if the athlete's symptoms persist beyond several days, a physician should be consulted.

Most other gastrointestinal complaints are viral infections that can cause fever, anorexia, nausea, vomiting, and diarrhea. Proper treatment consists of supportive measures unless the athlete is dehydrated. Prochlorperazine, promethazine hydrochloride, and trimethobenzamide hydrochloride, which are available in oral, suppository, and injectable forms, control nausea and vomiting. Loperamide hydrochloride and diphenoxylate hydrochloride with atropine help control diarrhea. However, because vomiting and diarrhea help the body shed the causative virus, these medications should be reserved for athletes who are moderately or severely affected and in danger of dehydration.

Traveler's diarrhea (caused by enterotoxin from *Escherichia coli* bacteria) and giardiasis (caused by a protozoan) can result when athletes have ingested contaminated food or water. Although several samples may be needed to isolate the cysts in giardiasis, a stool sample test can assist in identifying the pathogen. Alternatively, an entero test can collect samples from the upper gastrointestinal tract. Treatment of patients with traveler's diarrhea should be supportive in mild cases and an antibiotic in more severe cases; for giardiasis, metronidazole is recommended.

Medications for upper respiratory infections

Because upper respiratory tract infections are usually caused by viral syndromes, medications are used to alleviate the symptoms rather than to treat the infection. Cold preparations usually combine a decongestant, antihistamine, antipyretic, and, sometimes, a cough suppressant or expectorant. However, physicians should use only those medications that treat the athlete's symptoms.

FOCUS ON . . .

Substance Abuse

Confronted by pressure to train and perform maximally at all times, in addition to common life stresses, some athletes turn to substances to relieve pain or stress or both. The medical staff must know the dosages of the prescribed medications an athlete is supposed to be taking. If medications are used at a faster rate than prescribed, the medical staff should attempt to determine if there is a problem. Changes in performance, behavior, or attitude may be clues that an athlete is using drugs.

Treatment procedures for possible drug overdoses or adverse drug reactions should be managed as any other acute, potentially life-threatening situation and include checking the patient's airway, breathing, and circulation. It is also important to determine if the athlete may be of further danger to him- or herself or to others, including medical personnel trying to help. The athlete should be stabilized and transported to the emergency department, and the rest of the medical team (especially the team physician and psychologist, if applicable) informed as soon as possible.

Psychoactive drugs

Psychoactive drugs include stimulants, depressants, and hallucinogens. Stimulants affect the brain and central nervous system by increasing motor activity and delaying the perception of fatigue. Although the athlete may feel that performance is improved, this may not be the case. Fine motor activities are most likely to be hindered by the use of stimulants. Stimulants are available by prescription, over-the-counter, and illegally. Decongestants in large quantities are stimulants. Cocaine, crack, and crystal methamphetamine hydrochloride are illegal stimulants. Caffeine is the most common stimulant used by both athletes and nonathletes, but it also acts as a diuretic that causes a net loss of fluids and possible dehydration. Athletes should use caffeine cautiously.

Depressants are also available by prescription, over-the-counter, and illegally. They suppress brain and central nervous system activity by slowing the transmission of pain impulses and have the ability to reduce pain. Abuse of depressants can start innocently when pain medication is prescribed after a severe injury. Medical staff must be alert to an athlete's request for more medication and complaints of intolerable pain when his or her medication is withdrawn. However, the athlete must not be denied pain relief. The medical staff must emphasize that medications are prescribed for an individual and should not be shared.

Alcohol is the most readily available depressant and the most widely abused drug. Alcohol is also a common component of many cough and cold preparations as well as mouthwashes and gargles. An alcohol abuser becomes tolerant and will require greater quantities or concentrations of alcohol to achieve the desired effects. Because there may be a familial predisposition to alcoholism, a thorough family history should be obtained from the athlete to allow the medical staff to avert future problems.

Hallucinogens include marijuana (the most commonly used hallucinogen), LSD, and peyote, all of which are illegal. They are used to try to escape the stresses of athletics or life, or both. Most of these agents induce altered states of awareness and euphoria; athletes tend not to compete under the influence of these drugs.

(Continued)

stroke or heart attack. This may have resulted from sludging, which is the inability of the blood to circulate because of increased viscosity.

EPO is administered by intravenous or intramuscular injection on an individualized dose and dosage schedule. Dosage is units of EPO per kilogram of body weight. The initial dose for athletes is based on the recommended dosing for individuals with anemias of renal insufficiency or other chronic disease, 12.5 or more units per kilogram of body weight. The dosing schedule is several times per week. EPO increases red cell mass, which enhances the oxygen-carrying capacity of the blood, without the hazards

associated with blood doping transfusions. Enhanced oxygen-carrying capacity can benefit any athlete who participates in aerobic-intensive activities.

Anabolic steroids/Testosterone

In sports requiring strength or power, greater muscle mass is advantageous. In addition to resistance training, some athletes use *anabolic steroids* or testosterone to augment muscle strength and size. Anabolic steroids are synthetic derivatives of testosterone originally developed to treat hypogonadism in men, to aid patients who are debilitated by cancer or other illnesses to regain lost muscle mass, or

Substance Abuse (Continued)

Performance-enhancing Medications and Practices

Performance-enhancing medications and practices include use of blood doping, erythropoietin, anabolic steroids, human growth hormone, dehydroepiandrosterone, and creatine. Both blood doping and erythropoietin increase red cell mass, which is a benefit to athletes who participate in endurance events. Blood doping involves removing a unit of blood and then freezing and storing it as whole blood or packed cells. The athlete continues training and allows the body to manufacture new red blood cells over the next 6 to 8 weeks. Near competition time, the stored blood or packed cells are reinfused, raising the athlete's red cell mass and hemoglobin.

Erythropoietin is a peptide hormone produced by the kidney that stimulates red blood cell production. It is believed to have caused fatal strokes and heart attacks in cyclists as a result of sludging, or inability of the blood to circulate as a result of increased viscosity.

Anabolic steroids are synthetic testosterone derivatives used to augment muscle size and strength. Injectable anabolic steroids last longer than oral agents. All anabolic steroids, which are detectable through drug testing, are banned by the National Collegiate Athletic Association (NCAA), the US Olympic Committee/International Olympic Committee (USOC/IOC), and national and international sports federations.

Testosterone, which occurs naturally in both men and women, is used by some athletes in synthetic form to enhance performance. Current drug testing technology cannot distinguish between endogenous and exogenous testosterone.

Side effects of both anabolic steroids and testosterone include acne, premature epiphyseal closure, impaired liver and kidney function, increased cholesterol and triglycerides, and liver cancer. Men can also experience gynecomastia, testicular atrophy, sterility, oligospermia, and prostate hypertrophy. Women can experience masculinizing effects such as male-pattern baldness, clitoral hypertrophy, facial and body hair, and deepening of the voice. Psychological effects can include personality changes such as dependency, antisocial behavior, agitation, aggressiveness, road rage, and an enhanced feeling of well being.

Human growth hormone (HGH) is a peptide hormone normally secreted by the pituitary gland that athletes use to mimic the anabolic effects of anabolic steroids or testosterone and to reduce body fat. Currently, it cannot be detected in drug tests.

Dehydroepiandrosterone (DHEA) is an adrenal hormone precursor for testosterone, estrogen, and other hormones. Although research has not confirmed the effects of DHEA, some athletes are using it as an anabolic steroid or testosterone substitute to reduce fat mass and increase lean muscle. DHEA is available over the counter, but it is banned by the USOC/IOC and the NCAA. Side effects include acne, excess body hair, liver enlargement, and aggressive behavior.

Creatine is a nutritional supplement used to increase anaerobic power and strength by augmenting the supply of phosphocreatine available to the working muscle. Creatine can extend the quantity of energy available to the athlete and delay the onset of lactic acid production. Some research supports the use of creatine for short, high-energy athletic activities, but this has not been verified. In addition, its short-term and long-term safety has not been established. Creatine is neither banned nor currently detectable by current drug testing methods. Side effects of creatine include weight gain from increased water retention, increased fluid requirements, and possible cramping and electrolyte imbalances when inadequate fluid is ingested.

to treat severe anemia. Some chemical formulations were intended to enhance anabolic or muscle-building effects and diminish androgenic or masculinizing effects; however, all anabolic steroids retain some androgenic properties. Anabolic steroids can be taken orally or injected. Injectable anabolic steroids, especially oil-based preparations, are longer acting; oral anabolic steroids are shorter acting. All anabolic steroids are banned by the National Collegiate Athletic Association (NCAA), United States Olympic Committee (USOC), International Olympic Committee (IOC), and national and international sports federations and are detectable through current drug testing technology.

Because drug testing can detect anabolic steroids, many athletes began using synthetic testosterone instead. Testosterone is naturally produced by the testes in men and the ovaries and adrenal cortex in women. Current drug testing technology cannot differentiate between endogenous and exogenous testosterone; however, there is a naturally occurring ratio of testosterone to its isomer, epitestosterone, of approximately 1:1. In the absence of disease, an elevated ratio is indicative of exogenous testosterone use, and a ratio of greater than 6:1 is considered a positive test result.[7-9]

Side effects of both anabolic steroids and testosterone in both sexes include acne, premature epiphyseal closure, liver and kidney function disturbances, increased cholesterol and triglyceride levels, and possible liver cancer. In men, both substances decrease the production of naturally occurring testosterone and may cause gynecomastia, testicular atrophy, sterility, oligospermia, and prostate hypertrophy. Women may experience masculinizing effects such as male-pattern baldness, clitoral hypertrophy, increased facial and body hair, and deepening of the voice.

Anabolic steroids and testosterone may produce psychological effects including personality changes such as dependency, antisocial behavior, agitation, aggressiveness, road rage, and an enhanced feeling of well being. If either substance is used in injectable form, needle sharing should not be practiced to decrease the risk of transmission of HIV.

Human growth hormone

Because drug testing has become more sophisticated, many athletes have began using *human growth hormone (HGH)*, which is undetectable with present drug testing technology. HGH is a peptide hormone that is naturally secreted by the pituitary gland and stimulates protein, lipid, and carbohydrate metabolism; skeletal muscle mass; and red cell mass. In athletic arenas, HGH is used to attempt to duplicate the anabolic effects of anabolic steroids or testosterone. It also appears to aid in the reduction of fat deposits and may lead to reduced body fat levels. Children lacking sufficient endogenous levels and AIDS patients with muscle wasting are patient populations who may benefit from the administration of HGH. Long-term use of HGH by a patient can cause *acromegaly*, which is the overgrowth of the bones of the hands, feet, and face. HGH is only available in injectable form, and can increase the risk of HIV transmission if unsafe injection practices are used. The relatively high price of HGH compared to other anabolic substances has limited, but not stopped, its use.

Dehydroepiandrosterone

Dehydroepiandrosterone (DHEA) is an adrenal hormone that is a metabolic precursor for production of testosterone, estrogen, and other hormones. Some athletes use DHEA as a substitute for anabolic steroids or testosterone to decrease fat mass and increase muscle mass. Results of studies of DHEA offer conflicting evidence.[10,11] Some studies report that DHEA consumption leads to a decline in fat mass and an increase in muscle mass, while other studies report no effects.[10,11] Animal DHEA studies are being extrapolated to support its use in humans in certain cases. Although DHEA is banned by the USOC/IOC and the NCAA, it is sold over the counter as a nutritional product. Side effects can include acne, extra body hair, liver enlargement, and aggressive behavior.

Creatine

Creatine is a nutritional supplement used by some athletes to increase anaerobic power and strength. Currently, creatine is not banned by the IOC, USOC, or NCAA or detectable by current doping control standards and methods. Increased muscle levels of creatine are postulated to augment the supply of phosphocreatine (PC) available to the working muscle to reconvert adenosine diphosphate (ADP) to adenosine triphosphate (ATP) through the ATP-PC system. This can extend the quantity of energy provided by the ATP-PC system and delay the onset of lactic acid production. Some scientific evidence supports the use of creatine for short, explosive types of athletic activity, but other evidence questions its effectiveness as a performance-enhancing agent.[7]

Creatine is taken in a loading dose for several days; then the dosage is decreased to a maintenance dose. Some athletes use creatine for enhanced energy for either training or competition. Side effects include weight gain as a result of increased water retention, increased fluid requirements, and possible cramping and electrolyte imbalances when an inadequate quantity of fluid is ingested. There are no published scientific studies supporting or refuting the safety of creatine for either short-term or long-term use.

TABLE 27-3

CLASSIFICATIONS OF BANNED AND RESTRICTED DRUGS

**US Olympic Committee/
International Olympic Committee**

Stimulants
Anabolic agents
Diuretics
Peptide hormones and analogues
Beta-blockers
Local anesthetics
Beta-agonists
Blood doping methods
Urine manipulation techniques
Narcotic analgesics
Corticosteroids

National Collegiate Athletic Association

Stimulants
Anabolic agents
Diuretics
Peptide hormones and analogues
Beta-blockers
Local anesthetics
Beta-agonists
Blood doping methods
Urine manipulation techniques
Street drugs

DRUG TESTING

Drug testing has gained increased acceptance in the athletic community to discourage the use of performance-enhancing drugs by athletes. Drug testing has become standard protocol at athletic competitions worldwide. The athlete, coach, physician, and athletic trainer must be knowledgeable about banned and restricted drugs as well as testing procedures. Although they may appear to be similar, banned and restricted drugs listings vary between the USOC/IOC and the NCAA.[7-9] Both of these organizations have programs to test athletes for drugs during competition and may also have out-of-competition drug testing programs. Because the status of a drug can change at any time, both the physician and athletic trainer should consult with the testing organization before an athlete begins using a new medication. **Table 27-3** lists classifications of drugs that are banned or restricted by the USOC/IOC and the NCAA.

Before an organization begins implementing a drug testing program for its athletes, the program's leader needs to develop a thoroughly researched written plan. The plan should include proper legal advice for the organization, documentation of the drug testing policy, athlete waiver forms, laboratory selection and procedures, a banned drug list, handling and reporting of results, disciplinary actions, and an appeals process. The drug testing program should be legally defensible (many such programs have been challenged legally). Because of this, it is important that the organization's legal department be integrally involved in the development of the policies and procedures of the program. The NCAA has guidelines for its member institutions. The USOC provides testing services, as requested, for its member organizations.

The athlete's right to privacy and access to accurate information about drug testing must be respected during the entire testing process. Institutional testing is separate from NCAA and USOC/IOC testing. The differences must be made clear to athletes who may be subject to testing by both organizations.

CHAPTER REVIEW

Athletes use a variety of medications to control inflammation and pain and to treat medical ailments. They also use some medications illegally to try to enhance performance or to prevent the detection of performance-enhancing medications. The athletic trainer must be knowledgeable about all of these medications.

Medications used to treat musculoskeletal ailments include anti-inflammatory agents, which can be classified as steroidal or nonsteroidal; injectable, oral, or topical; and salicylate or nonsalicylate. Systemic nonsteroidal anti-inflammatory agents relieve pain at doses lower than those required to relieve inflammation. Local anti-inflammatory medications include nonsteroidal agents, which are not available in the United States other than in aspirin formulations, and corticosteroids, which can be applied topically by iontophoresis or phonophoresis, or injected. Analgesics encompass acetaminophen, which is the most commonly used analgesic, as well as natural and synthetic opiates, which are effective in treating pain, but can become habit forming. Local anesthetics are used for laceration repair; reduction of fractures and dislocations in combination with injectable opiates; ensuring that injectable corticosteroids reach their intended destination; relieving the pain of mouth ulcers; and cleaning deep, dirty abrasions.

Antibiotics are classified as either bacteriostatic or bacteriocidal and as gram negative, gram positive, or broad spectrum. They should only be used to treat bacterial infections. Antiviral medications are used to prevent and treat influenza A and herpes infections. Allergy medications include nonprescription, sedating antihistamines and prescription, nonsedating antihistamines. The prescription, nonsedating antihistamines have fewer side effects and less frequent dosing regimens, which can improve patient compliance. Topical nasal products are beneficial when the allergic symptoms are confined to the nose or if antihistamines fail to provide the patient with relief. A variety of medications are used to treat asthma: anti-inflammatoriy medications and beta agonists, progressing to nedrocromil sodium, cromolyn sodium, and a more powerful corticosteroid such as fluticasone propionate. Patients with severe asthma may need oral medication such as theophylline or zafirlukast.

Gastrointestinal medications are usually used to treat symptoms such as nausea (prochlorperazine, promethazine hydrochloride, trimethobenzamide hydrochloride) and diarrhea (loperamide hydrochloride, diphenoxylate with atropine). Traveler's diarrhea may require an antibiotic, and giardiasis should be treated with metronidazole.

Upper respiratory medications should be targeted to the athlete's specific symptoms: for example, a runny nose should be treated with a decongestant, a fever should be treated with aspirin or acetaminophen, and a cough should be treated with an expectorant or suppressant.

Substance abuse involves psychoactive drugs (stimulants, depressants, hallucinogens) that affect the athlete's brain and central nervous system. Caffeine is the most commonly used stimulant, and alcohol is the most commonly used depressant. The athletic trainer must be alert to the possibility of substance abuse and have a system in place for providing the athlete with medical assistance.

Performance-enhancing medications and practices include erythropoietin, blood doping, anabolic steroids and testosterone, human growth hormone, dehydroepiandrosterone, and creatine. Although the use of some of these medications may improve aspects of an athlete's performance, their short-term and long-term effectiveness and safety have not been established. Furthermore, many of these medications are banned by sport organizations. Drug testing was designed to deter athletes from using these performance-enhancing methods. An organization that is implementing a drug testing program must have a carefully considered plan for all necessary procedures, including the protection of the athlete's privacy and right to have access to accurate information about the process.

1. Which of the following statements about nonsteroidal anti-inflammatory drugs (NSAIDs) is true?

   A. NSAIDs are available only by prescription.

   B. NSAIDs should be taken on an empty stomach.

   C. NSAIDs relieve pain before they relieve inflammation.

   D. NSAID formulations are all of approximately equal effectiveness.

2. Which of the following corticosteroid preparations is a short-acting preparation that can be injected into or near an inflamed area?

   A. Triamcinolone

   B. Betamethasone

   C. Dexamethasone

   D. Methylprednisolone

3. An example of a bacteriocidal antibiotic is:

   A. penicillin.

   B. tetracycline.

   C. sulfonamide.

   D. erythromycin.

4. Which of the following drugs is an antiviral medication used to prevent and treat influenza A?

   A. Famvir

   B. Zovirax

   C. Valtrex

   D. Symmetrel

5. Which of the following medications does the athlete inhale for relief during an acute asthma attack?

   A. Albuterol

   B. Zafirlukast

   C. Theophylline

   D. Prochlorperazine

6. Which of the following medications is used to control nausea and vomiting?

   A. Ranitidine

   B. Loperamide hydrochloride

   C. Promethazine hydrochloride

   D. Diphenoxylate hydrochloride with atropine

7. Which of the following drugs is useful for treating an athlete with a runny nose?

   A. Guaifenesin

   B. Pseudoephedrine

   C. Diphenhydramine

   D. Dextromethorphan hydrobromide

8. Which of the following depressants is the most easily obtained and widely abused drug?

   A. Alcohol

   B. Cocaine

   C. Caffeine

   D. Marijuana

9. Which of the following statements about erythropoietin is true?

   A. It stimulates white blood cell production.

   B. It is a peptide hormone produced by the spleen.

   C. It is used medically for the treatment of severe anemia.

   D. It should not be used in severely debilitated individuals with HIV.

10. Which of the following statements about creatine is true?

    A. It is detectable with standard doping control tests.

    B. It is used to increase anaerobic power and strength.

    C. It is currently banned by most sport governing organizations.

    D. It can cause weight loss as a result of decreased water retention.

Answers on page 894.

5

Special Athlete Populations

Section Editors
Clayton F. Holmes, EdD, PT, ATC
Robert J. Moore, PhD, PT, ATC

28

Gender Differences in Athletes

Robyn M. Stuhr, MA
Jo Hannafin, MD, PhD
Lisa Callahan, MD

QUICK CONTENTS

- Differences in body composition, strength, cardio-vascular fitness, flexibility, weight management, and thermoregulation between women and men.

- What types of athletic injuries women tend to incur and how these contrast with the injuries men sustain.

- The medical issues that can affect female athletes, including the female athlete triad, anemia, and the use of ergogenic aids.

OVERVIEW

With the advancement of the number of women participating in sports since the mid 1970s, there has been an increased awareness that there are numerous gender-specific variables that impact training response to exercise, injury patterns and epidemiology, and medical issues specific to male and female athletes. This chapter begins with a discussion of the history of participation in sports by women and how gender-specific variables impact male and female athletes. Following is a section on differences in body composition between men and women. Gender differences in strength, cardiovascular fitness, flexibility, weight management, and thermoregulation are also discussed in detail. Sports-related injuries are outlined, including anterior cruciate ligament injuries and patellofemoral pain syndrome. The chapter ends with a discussion on medical issues, including the female athlete triad, anemia, and the use of ergogenic aids.

HISTORY AND RATIONALE

Historically, participation in athletics was encouraged for men and boys, but not for women and girls. There were various reasons for this difference, ranging from concerns regarding possible detrimental effects of exercise on the female reproductive system to philosophical debates. As late as 1920, it was argued that women were not athletes and therefore should not be allowed to participate in Olympic competition.[1] Fortunately, very few proponents of this viewpoint remain. Involvement and interest in women's athletics exploded with the passage of Title IX legislation in 1972, creating a more level playing field for all athletes. Paralleling the advancements in women's sports participation has been increased recognition that there are numerous gender-specific variables that impact training response to exercise, injury patterns and epidemiology, and medical issues specific to male and female athletes.

Any discussion of gender differences requires the comparison of averages; however, within each sex one can find a wide range of values. This means that there will be significant overlapping of physical and performance characteristics based on both individual genetic differences and environmental influences. More importantly, both men and women have the ability to improve their health, fitness, and athletic performance through well-designed training programs. An understanding of gender differences and the underlying basis for them can guide the health-care professional in developing appropriate conditioning strategies, training goals, and safety precautions.

BODY COMPOSITION

Morphologic differences between men and women, particularly body size, *fat-free mass (FFM)*, and *body fat percentage (%BF)*, play the largest role in performance differences between genders. FFM can be defined as all tissue in the body that is not fat, including bone, muscle, organ, and connective tissue. In fact, when morphologic characteristics are factored out, strength, aerobic performance, and metabolic and thermoregulatory differences between men and women largely disappear.

Prepubertal girls and boys do not differ significantly in height, weight, girth, bone width, skinfold thickness, and FFM. In children, height, weight, and FFM increase in a linear fashion until puberty. At puberty, FFM levels off in girls, but %BF continues to increase. In adolescent boys, FFM continues to increase, but %BF decreases slightly. After a 2- to 4-year phase of rapid growth, FFM levels in girls typically peak at about age 15 to 16 years. Boys have

FOCUS ON . . .

Body Composition

When morphologic differences such as body size, fat-free mass (FFM), and body fat percentage (%BF) are factored out, strength, aerobic performance, and metabolic and thermoregulatory differences between men and women largely disappear.

Adult women average less height, weight, and FFM, and more body fat than adult men. Women also have narrower shoulders, a wider pelvis, greater Q-angle, and narrower heel width than men. Also, women have a lower basal metabolic rate than men.

Body fat levels differ significantly among men and women; contributing factors include genetic predisposition, physical activity patterns, and nutritional status. Estrogen promotes a gynoid pattern of increased fat deposition. Normal physiologic function in women requires a certain level of body fat stored in the breasts, hips, and thighs. Low weight and body fat may be a factor in some patients with athletic amenorrhea. The male android pattern of fat deposition is associated with more visceral fat and an increased risk of coronary artery disease. Body fat goals must be individualized based on the athlete's health, physique, developmental stage, current body composition, and sport-specific requirements.

a longer growth phase and their FFM levels typically peak at age 19 to 20 years.[2] This longer growth phase in combination with testosterone promotes increased height, bone size, and muscularity in young men. However, both estrogen and testosterone encourage bone growth.

Compared to men, women are, on average, 5" shorter and have 30 to 40 lb less body weight, 40 to 50 lb less FFM, and 6% to 10% more %BF.[3] However, within both genders, wide variations in physique occur. In general, a woman has narrower shoulders, a wider pelvis, greater Q angles, and narrower heels than a man does. In addition, because women typically have smaller bodies with less FFM than men, women's *basal metabolic rates (BMR)* are about 5% to 15% lower.[4,5] Studies have shown that FFM accounts for approximately 80% to 90% of the variation in BMR.

As mentioned previously, levels of body fat vary significantly between men and women. Many factors determine body composition, including genetic predisposition, physical activity patterns, and nutritional status. For example, estrogen is associated with increased fat deposition, particularly in the hips and thighs. This gynoid pattern of fat deposition is caused by an estrogen-mediated site-specific increase in lipoprotein lipase activity that promotes the hydrolysis, transport, and storage of triglycerides. Although a certain amount of body fat stored in the breasts, hips, and thighs is essential for normal physiologic function in women, some women are able to maintain proper hormone balance and menstrual function with low levels of body fat. However, in some women, low weight and low levels of body fat have been implicated in *amenorrhea*, or loss of the menstrual cycle. In contrast, men tend to store excess fat in the abdominal/truncal region.[6] This android pattern of fat deposition is associated with higher levels of visceral fat (twice as much as premenopausal women) and is related to increased risk of coronary artery disease.

Ideal levels of body fat must be individualized for each person's health, physique, stage of development, body composition, and sport-specific requirements. **Table 28-1** shows ranges of body composition for both men and women. Athletes should be reminded that factors other than body fat contribute significantly to sports performance.

In both men and women, aging is associated with gradual loss of FFM and increases in body fat. Longitudinal studies indicate that from early adulthood, men lose approximately 3 kg of FFM per decade and women lose about 2 kg per decade. Cross-sectional and longitudinal data suggest that in men, body fat increases by 2% to 3% per decade and in women, 3.5% to 5% per decade.[2] However, both men and women older than age 60 or 70 years have lower levels of body fat than they had in their 50s, suggesting a decline in %BF with age. After menopause, women who do not receive estrogen replacement therapy begin to exhibit the android pattern of fat deposition.

STRENGTH

Strength has been defined as "the maximal force that a muscle or muscle group can generate at a specified velocity."[7] Absolute levels of strength can be measured with a variety of tests: the 1-repetition maximum (1RM) test with free weights or machines and the maximal isometric, eccentric, and concentric isokinetic peak torque tests. A 1RM test determines the maximal load an individual can successfully lift just once, for a specific exercise. This can be estimated from tables based on higher repetitions. Isokinetic machines have been used to test maximal force at various velocity levels during movement. Isometric and isokinetic testing at slower velocities are good indicators of absolute strength, whereas faster speeds evaluate strength endurance. The 1RM tests that use free weights have good "carry over" to the sports setting because they involve multiple joints and movement patterns found in many athletic activities. Isokinetic testing is useful in rehabilitation settings to evaluate muscle imbalances and specific muscle strength over single joints. Typically, women who do not train with weights have 50% to 60% of the upper body strength and 60% to 80% of the lower body strength of untrained men.[8,9] However, when strength is expressed relative to FFM and muscle cross-sectional area, gender differences disappear, particularly with lower body strength. For example, in measuring torque generated when doing the leg press exercise, women demonstrate 92% and 106% the strength of men when body weight and FFM, respectively, are taken into account.[8] Differences in strength between men and women are related to the quantity, not the quality of muscle tissue. Although women appear to have a higher ratio of eccentric to concentric strength, the physiologic basis for this is unclear.[9] However, women exhibit a decline in concentric strength at higher velocities, possibly because of a slower rate of force development.[10,11]

Training-induced muscle hypertrophy is mediated by several factors, including anabolic hormones such as testosterone, human growth hormone (HGH), and insulin and insulin-like growth factor (IGF-1), which promote protein synthesis. Men have higher levels of testosterone at rest than women do and respond to strength training (single or repeated sessions) with greater increases in plasma concentrations of testosterone. Women have higher levels of HGH at rest than men do, but men exhibit higher increases in HGH following a single strength training session.

Although the male hormones enhance the body's response to weightlifting, short-term studies suggest that both women and men benefit from strength training by achieving similar relative increases in muscle strength. However, men start and end with greater absolute strength.[7-9] In addition to muscle hypertrophy, increases in strength are the result of increased motor unit recruit-

Strength

Women who do not train with weights have 50% to 60% of men's upper body strength and 60% to 80% of their lower body strength. However, relative to FFM and muscle cross-sectional area, women's performance in the leg press is nearly equal to men's. Women seem to have a higher ratio of eccentric to concentric strength and a decline in concentric strength at higher velocities.

Anabolic hormones including testosterone, human growth hormone, insulin and insulin-like growth factor mediate training-induced muscle hypertrophy by promoting protein synthesis. The higher resting levels of testosterone in men result in greater plasma testosterone increases after strength training sessions. Women have higher resting human growth hormone levels, but men show higher increases after single exercise bouts. Strength gains result from increased motor unit recruitment and firing rates, removal of neural inhibition, and enhanced cocontraction and activation of synergistic muscles, in addition to muscle hypertrophy, and therefore, men and women can achieve similar relative muscle strength increases. Men begin and end with greater absolute strength.

Men and women lose 15% to 20% of their young adult strength by age 60 years and 40% to 50% by age 80 years. Strength training can improve strength and performance, prevent injury, enhance weight control, increase functional independence, and prevent osteoporosis. The weight-training regimen should be based on the current level of fitness, history of training, sport and training goals, medical and orthopaedic history, equipment availability, and time constraints rather than gender.

ment, increased firing rates, removal of neural inhibition, and enhanced cocontraction and activation of synergistic muscles.[7] These effects are particularly obvious during the first several weeks of a new strength training regimen. The long-term adaptations and influences of hypertrophy and neural adaptations on overall strength and power are still unclear, and studies to compare the responses to strength training of men and women with significant histories of weightlifting are needed. However, as individuals, both men and women respond to weightlifting with varying degrees of muscle hypertrophy and strength development because of differences in the following:

- anabolic hormones
- genetic predisposition to develop muscle mass

- body size and physique
- ability to tolerate an intense training regimen

Strength training is important throughout life, for both men and women. By age 60 years, men and women lose approximately 15% to 20% of the strength they had as young adults, and by age 80 years, they lose 40% to 50%.[9] Studies have shown that female athletes who train with weights develop higher levels of bone mineral density that may protect against rapid postmenopausal bone loss. Nonetheless, impact-type activities (eg, jogging, walking, dancing) are the most important activity-related factors in maintaining bone density. For both men and women, benefits of weight training include improved strength and sports performance, injury prevention, weight management, functional independence, and prevention of osteoporosis. Currently, the scientific data do not support different strength training approaches based on gender. Instead, weightlifting regimens should be designed with attention to the athlete's current level of fitness, history of training, sport and training goals, medical and orthopaedic history, access to equipment, and time constraints.

CARDIOVASCULAR FITNESS

Because women typically have smaller bodies, their hearts and lungs are proportionally smaller as well. Furthermore, even when adjustments are made for FFM, women, including female athletes, have a smaller left ventricular mass than men. [12,13]Also, women have smaller blood volumes and lower average concentrations of hemoglobin (ie, oxygen-carrying capacity of blood). Although maximal heart rate does not appear to be gender related, women typically have higher heart rates than men do when they are subjected to the same absolute submaximal workload. This is because they are generally exercising at a higher percentage of their maximal capacity. In addition, the smaller heart size, lower stroke volume, and lower blood volume of women require their hearts to beat faster to maintain a similar cardiac output as men.

Women and men respond to aerobic exercise training with similar relative increases in *maximal oxygen consumption* (VO_{2max}), the criterion measure of cardiovascular fitness. VO_{2max} represents the maximal ability of the cardiopulmonary system to deliver oxygen to the working muscles and the muscle's ability to use that oxygen to produce adenosine triphosphate (ATP) aerobically. The magnitude of increase in VO_{2max} is strongly related to the athlete's initial level of fitness and the intensity of the training regimen. An athlete with a higher level of fitness will have a higher VO_{2max} than someone who is at a lower level of fitness. Both men and women adapt to endurance training with increases in VO_{2max}, maximal workload, maximal cardiac output and stroke volumes, lactate threshold, peak lactate levels, arteriovenous oxygen difference, and blood volume. With submaximal exercise, long-term results of

TABLE 28-1
BODY COMPOSITION OF WOMEN AND MEN

Women

Percentage of Body Fat (BF)	Age (years)				
	20 to 29	30 to 39	40 to 49	50 to 59	60 to 69
Very low	11	13	16	19	17
Excellent	17	18	21	25	25
Good	21	22	25	28	29
Fair	24	25	28	32	32
Poor	28	29	32	36	37
Very poor	35	36	38	40	40

Men

Percentage of Body Fat (BF)	Age (years)				
	20 to 29	30 to 39	40 to 49	50 to 59	60 to 69
Very low	5	9	11	13	13
Excellent	9	14	16	18	18
Good	14	18	20	21	22
Fair	17	20	22	24	25
Poor	22	24	26	28	28
Very poor	29	30	32	32	33

(Adapted with permission from the American College of Sports Medicine: *Guidelines for Testing and Exercise Prescription*. Media, PA, Williams & Wilkins, 1995.)

training include decreases in heart rate, ventilation, lactate level, and rating of perceived exertion (RPE).

Typically, untrained adult women have 75% of the VO_{2max} of untrained men. However, in elite female athletes, VO_{2max} levels are within 5% to 15% of male elite athletes and well above levels expected in the general male population. **Table 28-2** shows the ranges of VO_{2max} in nonathletes and in male and female athletes. In fact,

trends in race times for races longer than marathon distance predict that women get stronger with longer races (**Figure 28-1**). Women may outperform men in ultraendurance events.[14] Research is needed to test theories that hypothesize that women achieve superior performances in long distance running as a result of increased resistance to fatigue, enhanced fat oxidation, and smaller body mass. In both men and women, VO_{2max} values decrease

FOCUS ON . . .

Cardiovascular Fitness

Adult women have smaller hearts, lungs, and left ventricular mass; smaller blood volumes, average hemoglobin concentrations, and stroke volumes; and higher heart rates than adult men. Women and men attain similar relative increases in VO_{2max} with aerobic exercise. Untrained adult women have a VO_{2max} that is usually 75% that of untrained men, but elite training can raise the VO_{2max} to within 5% to 15% that of elite male athletes. Women may soon outperform men in ultraendurance events because of increased resistance to fatigue, enhanced fat oxidation, and smaller body mass. VO_{2max} decreases approximately 10% per decade starting at age 30 years; 50% of the decline is related to body fat increases and lower levels of physical activity.

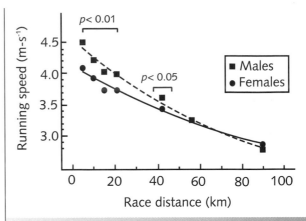

FIGURE 28-1

In races longer than marathon distance, trends predict that women get stronger with longer distances. (Reproduced with permission from Bam J, Noakes TD, Juritz J, Dennis SC: Could women outrun men in ultramarathon races? *Med Sci Sports Exerc* 1997;29:244-247.)

approximately 10% per decade, beginning at approximately age 30 years. Half of the age-related decline in VO_{2max} is correlated to increases in %BF and decreases in self-reported physical activity.[15,16]

FLEXIBILITY

Despite the general perception that women are more flexible than men, little scientific data exists regarding the few differences in flexibility. Factors that contribute to range of motion include joint structure, elasticity and plasticity of connective tissue, muscle size, age, and activity patterns. Women may have more generalized joint laxity, and have demonstrated greater joint looseness at specific joints such as the elbow and hip.[17,18] Normative data for sit-and-reach tests appear to support these findings. The higher prevalence of ligamentous laxity may place some women at risk for certain joint injuries such as multidirectional instability of the shoulder and injuries to the patellofemoral joint.

WEIGHT MANAGEMENT

In both men and women, physical activity is critical in the prevention of weight gain and the maintenance of weight loss. However, for several possible reasons, women experience only modest loss of weight and body fat with short-term exercise training. First, women are smaller in general. A small person (male or female) will burn fewer calories than a larger person during weightbearing exercises of similar intensity. Second, as noted, women have less lean body mass than men. Their muscles typically respond to training with less hypertrophy. This diminished response may affect their ability to modify BMR or generate equal muscle force for high calorie-burning activity. In addition, it is unclear whether fat metabolism adapts to

endurance training in the same way in men and women. For example, in both men and women, abdominal adipocytes increase catecholamine-stimulated lipolysis in response to endurance training. However, the same response may not occur in gluteal and thigh fat depots, which are genetic fat storage sites in most women.[19-22]

Because of fat oxidation, high-intensity interval training may be more effective than constant moderate-intensity exercise in promoting fat loss, even with equal calorie expenditure, in both young men and women.[23] A weight management program should be individualized to include the following:

- appropriate short- and long-term goals
- vigorous and/or moderate-intensity cardiovascular exercise to increase daily energy expenditure
- strength training to maintain or promote muscle mass
- a reasonable diet of low-fat, low-calorie foods
- attention to body image and the psychological issues relating to food

THERMOREGULATION

Physiologic factors that improve an athlete's ability to tolerate cold temperatures include large body size (low surface area-to-mass ratio), high levels of FFM, high VO_{2max}, and substantial subcutaneous fat stores. Thus, a small individual, male or female, with low levels of muscle, little body fat, or poor physical fitness will be at greater risk for cold stress.[24] Typically, women lose or gain heat more rapidly than men because they tend to be smaller and have a higher surface area per unit of body mass interfac-

TABLE 28-2
RANGES OF VO₂MAX IN NONATHLETES AND MALE AND FEMALE ATHLETES

Nonathletes

Age (years)	Men (mL/kg/min)	Women (mL/kg/min)
10 to 19	47 to 56	38 to 46
20 to 29	43 to 52	33 to 42
30 to 39	39 to 48	30 to 38
40 to 49	36 to 44	26 to 35
50 to 59	34 to 41	24 to 33
60 to 69	31 to 38	22 to 30
70 to 79	28 to 35	20 to 27

Male and female athletes

Sport	Age (years)	Men (mL/kg/min)	Women (mL/kg/min)
Basketball	18 to 30	40 to 60	43 to 60
Bicycling	18 to 26	62 to 74	47 to 57
Rowing	23 to 26	60 to 72	58 to 65
Cross-country skiing	20 to 28	65 to 95	60 to 75
Running	18 to 39	60 to 85	50 to 75
Swimming	10 to 25	50 to 70	40 to 60
Volleyball	19 to 26	56	42 to 56

(Reproduced with permission from Wilmore JH, Costill DL: *Physiology of Sport and Exercise*. Champaign, IL, Human Kinetics, 1994.)

ing with the environment. This higher ratio speeds heat or cold exchange by conduction, convection, or radiation. High levels of FFM, which are found more commonly in men, not only increase the potential to generate energy and heat, but the additional muscle increases thermal insulation. However, women have one clear advantage against cold: their increased skinfold thickness increases insulation. For example, additional subcutaneous fat may assist female long-distance swimmers by providing buoy-ancy and insulation. Also, in body core temperature maintenance, peripheral vasoconstriction may play a larger role in women than in men. Lower or more quickly declining skin temperatures in response to cold stress have been observed in women. In cold conditions, vasoconstriction is also associated with lower skin temperatures and possible increased risk of frostbite.

Men or women who are well rested, lean, heat acclimatized, cardiovascularly fit, larger, and well hydrated toler-

both extrinsic factors, such as body movement, muscular strength, and shoe surface interface, and intrinsic factors, such as joint laxity, limb alignment, and femoral notch width. Differences in lower extremity alignments, such as a wider pelvis and valgus knees, in female athletes have been shown. Furthermore, menstruation and hormonal changes may be involved in ACL injury rates in female athletes. Overall, women have smaller femoral notch widths than men do, which correlates with injury to the ACL: a smaller notch width may increase risk. In a study of 714 patients with ACL ruptures, measurements of the notch width index were recorded. The patients were divided into two groups based on notch size: group 1 had a notch size less than 15 mm, and group 2 had a notch size greater than 16 mm. Women had a significantly smaller notch width (13.9 mm) than men (15.9 mm), and both men and women with small notches were at increased risk for subsequent rupture of the contralateral ACL.[36] In addition, male and female athletes demonstrate other differences in muscle recruitment patterns during dynamic loading and in the strength and development of the quadriceps femoris and hamstrings in response to training and fatigue.[37] Early activation of the quadriceps may result in an anterior translation of the tibia with resultant stress on the ACL. Women have quadriceps-dominant legs and have been demonstrated to land from a jump with less knee flexion, which may increase the risk of ACL injury.[37] Regardless, the difference in injury risk to the ACL in female athletes is more than likely multifactorial in origin.

Patellofemoral pain syndrome

Athletes with biomechanical abnormalities of the lower extremity may be at increased risk for patellofemoral pain syndromes. One study attempted to correlate the presence of static postural faults in female athletes with noncontact ACL injury. Twenty athletes with ACL injuries were examined as were 20 age-matched athletes who were controls. Significant discriminators between injured and uninjured athletes were recurvatum of the knee, excessive navicular drop, and excessive subtalar pronation.[38] However, a prospective study that evaluated ligamentous laxity and muscle tightness in 201 Division I collegiate athletes was performed. In this study, women had greater laxity scores than men and lower scores for overall muscle tightness. Among female athletes, the rate of lower extremity injury did not appear to be related to laxity or muscle flexibility. In contrast, in male athletes, lower extremity injuries correlated with greater muscle tightness and decreased ligamentous laxity.[39]

Response to injury

Gender and participation in any sport may influence the psychological health and coping mechanisms of the injured athlete. A recent study identified the psychological features (personality factors, coping strategies, and mood levels) that characterized highly competitive athletes who suffered from long-term injuries.[40] These athletes were compared with a group of injured nonathletes. When faced with serious injuries, athletes who participated in team sports accept the notion of injury passively without an outward negative or positive response with help from other team members. Athletes who participated in individual sports developed problem-solving strategies. Injured male athletes became more insecure, and injured female athletes demonstrated increased anxiety and tension. Also, female athletes were more likely to suppress anger and become less assertive than their male counterparts. The study demonstrated that the patient's anxiety, tension, anger, and assertiveness are important to consider during rehabilitative care in order to optimize outcomes. Social impacts can affect the athlete's ability to participate fully during rehabilitation.[40] Although overall injury patterns are similar in men and women, there are gender- and age-related differences in athletic injuries and in the psychological strategies for dealing with injury. A continued emphasis on research and education is critical to further define the factors responsible for these gender-related differences and to optimize the care of all athletes.

MEDICAL ISSUES

For both men and women, moderate exercise has a positive impact on health. However, women live longer on average and suffer from fewer diseases and disabilities.[41] As a result, the effects of exercise on female health has become the focus of many studies.[41] In addition to its impact on cardiovascular disease, exercise has been linked to decreases in diseases that concern women, such as breast cancer and osteoporosis.[42-44] Exercise may also impact other diseases that affect both sexes. These include obesity, hypertension, diabetes, hypercholesterolemia, and mood disorders.

Although moderate exercise has a positive impact on health, exercising too much can negatively affect the health of both male and female athletes. For instance, overtraining can suppress the immune system, which increases susceptibility to infection. The signs and symptoms of overtraining are the same in both sexes and include increased resting heart rate, fatigue, and irritability.[45] However, the gender-related effects of overtraining on bone health and reproductive function have not been well defined and require more study.

Manipulating body weight is a practice common to both male and female athletes. Typically, athletes control their weight in order to participate in sports with weight classifications, such as wrestling and judo. In other sports, such as distance running, lower weight is perceived to improve performance. Although studies have not confirmed this perception, the myth persists among coaches and athletes. Classically, male athletes lose weight with dehydration strategies that can cause electrolyte disturbances, increased susceptibility to heat illness, and cardiac arrhythmias. In fact, the deaths of several wrestlers in the past few years has brought attention to this dangerous practice and has caused some state high school athletic associations to change their guidelines for weight classification and "making weight" strategies for wrestlers to promote safer methods to lose and maintain weight.[46,47]

Female Athlete Triad

Female athletes tend to control body weight through restriction of food intake rather than fluid intake. Unhealthy or *disordered eating behaviors* are characterized by restriction of foods or food intake, rigid food patterns, an inadequate protein diet, fasting, vomiting, and use of diet pills or laxatives. Disordered eating behaviors are often overlooked because their signs and symptoms may not be as obvious as those associated with true eating disorders such as anorexia nervosa or bulimia nervosa. Nevertheless, disordered eating behaviors are associated with both short- and long-term consequences on health: amenorrhea and osteoporosis are two such consequences frequently described. Disordered eating, amenorrhea, and osteoporosis are called the *"female athlete triad,"* which affects a growing number of recreational and competitive female athletes.[48]

It is generally believed that female athletes engage in disordered eating behaviors to achieve specific body images that they or others perceive will improve performance. Female athletes are especially vulnerable during adolescence and young adulthood when they may give in to societal pressures to be thin or accept misconceptions about weight and performance. Although the exact prevalence of disordered eating in female athletes is unknown, reports range from 15% to 65% prevalence. Frequently, disordered eating patterns begin when the athlete restricts certain types of food, such as meat or snacks, from her diet and gradually eliminates certain foods altogether. Thought patterns such as preoccupation with food, fear of gaining weight and becoming fat, dissatisfaction with one's body, and a distorted body image often accompany these eating patterns. Also, the athlete may experiment with medications or vomiting to control weight. Female athletes who participate in the following activities are at particular risk:

- Sports in which low body weight and lean physique is believed to be an advantage (distance running, triathlon).

- Sports where judging may be influenced by aesthetics (gymnastics, ballet, figure skating, diving, synchronized swimming, cheerleading).

- Sports that require "making weight" (lightweight rowing, judo, karate).

Both recreational and elite athletes may be at risk for this syndrome. Other risk factors for the development of

FOCUS ON . . .

Female Athlete Triad

Disordered eating, amenorrhea, and osteoporosis are called the *"female athlete triad,"* which affects a growing number of recreational and competitive female athletes. Female athletes may develop disordered eating, which can have short- and long-term consequences. As many as 15% to 65% of female athletes may participate in disordered eating to achieve a specific body image that they, or others, believe will improve their performance. Disordered eating can result in fatigue, cold intolerance, lightheadedness or dizziness, constipation, bloating, dry skin, bradycardia, hypothermia, and menstrual disturbances.

The athlete may experience amenorrhea, or the loss of the menstrual cycle, as a result of obsessive physical training to lose weight, followed by a decrease in estrogen production by the ovaries.

Decreased estrogen increases the athlete's risk for premature osteoporosis, which may be characterized by premature bone loss or inadequate bone formation. Premature osteoporosis may not be reversible even with calcium supplements, estrogen replacement, and the resumption of menses.

the female athlete triad include overly controlling coaches or parents, a family history of disordered eating or dieting at an early age, participation in individual sports as opposed to team sports, and the early start of sport-specific training, which may set up a future conflict with a developing body mismatched to the requirements of a particular sport.

Disordered eating behaviors may cause fatigue, cold intolerance, lightheadedness or dizziness, constipation, bloating, dry skin, bradycardia, and hypothermia. Additionally, some girls and women attempt to control weight through obsessive physical activity typified by excessive training without adequate recovery; continuing with exercise despite pain and injury; compulsive high-volume, high-intensity training; and feelings of guilt and fatness accompanying missed workouts. Moreover, the athlete may experience disturbances in her menstrual cycle, the most profound of which is loss of the menstrual cycle, or amenorrhea. Amenorrhea may be primary, in which the girl or woman has never had a period, or secondary, in which the girl or woman who has previously menstruated misses 3 to 6 consecutive menstrual cycles. Athletic amenorrhea, or amenorrhea associated with exercise, is a diagnosis of exclusion; common causes of amenorrhea such as pregnancy must be considered first. Although the causes of athletic amenorrhea are not well understood, one theory proposes that insufficient caloric intake causes an energy drain that decreases basal metabolism.[49] Subsequent hypothalamic dysfunction decreases estrogen production by the ovaries, which interrupts the menstrual cycle.

The decrease in estrogen has another effect. Because estrogen is critical to the development of normal bone mass, the decrease places the athlete at risk for premature osteoporosis. *Premature osteoporosis*, characterized by premature bone loss or inadequate bone formation, may be silent or manifest itself through a premature osteoporotic fracture. Some stress fractures involve osteoporotic bone. Stress fractures can occur in bone of both normal and suboptimal bone density. Because bone loss is silent, a stress fracture can be the first sign of trouble. Obviously, not all female athletes with bone injuries such as stress fractures are at risk for the female athlete triad. However, because premature osteoporosis may be irreversible (even with calcium supplementation, estrogen replacement therapy, or resumption of menses), all female athletes who experience stress fractures should be evaluated for risk factors of the female athlete triad.

Effective treatment and prevention of the female athlete triad necessitates a team approach. The athlete's physician, coach, athletic trainer, nutritionist, and mental health professional must collaborate and support a plan to move the athlete toward healthier eating and training behaviors. The athlete should be encouraged to consider approaches to performance improvement that do not focus on weight or body fat such as increasing muscle mass through strength training; optimizing the training regimen through an appropriate combination of training volume, exercise intensity, and recovery time; increasing energy through good nutrition; improving sport-specific skills; and practicing mental preparation techniques to improve focus and confidence and relieve performance anxiety.

Anemia

Anemia is one of the most common medical problems seen in athletes, especially female athletes. *Iron-deficiency anemia* is the most common anemia and occurs when iron, the oxygen-carrying component of the red blood cell, is deficient. It is more common for female athletes to experience this type of anemia because they lose blood with menstruation and often avoid foods that are high in iron, such as meat. This avoidance may reflect personal preferences or disordered eating behaviors. Symptoms of iron-deficiency anemia include fatigue and decreased performance. Iron-deficiency anemia is easily diagnosed with a simple blood test to determine iron levels and can be corrected with administration of iron. Because too much iron can be harmful, athletes with symptoms of fatigue should be tested for iron deficiency before taking iron supplements.

Ergogenic Aids

The use of performance-enhancing drugs in both recreational and competitive athletes has been documented. Anabolic steroids, human growth hormone, and erythropoietin are some of the substances reportedly used by male and female athletes. Because these substances are banned (and in some cases, illegal), little data is available to describe their prevalence, effects, and use by athletes. The use of anabolic steroids in male athletes has remained stable since 1991; however, the use of steroids in female athletes has increased.[50] Athletic trainers should be aware that the effects and side effects of steroids may vary with gender. For instance, cardiovascular and liver disease has been reported in both women and men who have used steroids. Additional androgenic effects in the female athlete include male-pattern baldness, deepening of the voice, and enlargement of the clitoris. Although many of the side effects of steroids are reversible with discontinued use, androgenic effects in the female athlete are not.[51] In addition, in men, exogenous testosterone contributes to testicular atrophy and may have an impact on fertility.

CHAPTER REVIEW

Traditionally, men were encouraged to participate in sports, while women were discouraged for many reasons, including the possible detrimental effects of exercise. However, with the passage of Title IX legislation in 1972, women have been participating in sports in record numbers. At the same time, scientists recognized that gender-specific variables may affect training response to exercise, injury patterns and epidemiology, and medical issues.

Within each sex, the range of physical and performance characteristics based on individual genetic differences and environmental influences is wide and may overlap with the other sex. However, men and women can both improve their health, fitness, and athletic performance through well-designed training programs created by healthcare professionals who understand appropriate conditioning strategies, training goals, and safety precautions.

Prepubertal girls and boys are similar in height, weight, girth, bone width, skinfold thickness, and fat-free mass, but at puberty, girls experience a leveling off of FFM, accompanied by an increase in body fat, reaching their adult values at age 15 to 16 years. Boys continue to build FFM and exhibit a slight decrease in body fat, reaching their adult values at age 19 to 20 years, after a longer growth phase. Adult women are shorter, lighter both in body weight and FFM, and higher in body fat than adult men.

Men and women can achieve similar relative increases in muscle strength and cardiovascular fitness with appropriate training programs. Definitive data does not exist concerning gender differences in muscle flexibility and relative responses to flexibility training. Women may have increased generalized joint laxity, which can increase the risk for certain injuries. Women have more difficulty preventing weight gain (body fat) and maintaining fat loss. However, regular patterns of physical activity are critical to long-term weight control in both men and women. Differences in the ability to exercise comfortably and safely in both hot and cold environments are influenced more by body size, body composition, cardiovascular fitness, and acclimitization than by the athlete's gender.

Athletic injuries, in general, are more sport specific than gender specific, but injury patterns for men and women in the same sport may be different, with a possible relationship between age and type of injury. Women experience more (and often more severe) lower extremity injuries, while men incur more upper body injuries, with both extrinsic and intrinsic factors contributing. The psychological health and coping mechanisms of the injured athlete also show sex differences.

Medical issues influence both male and female athletes. The female athlete triad is affecting a growing number of athletes and must be prevented when possible, because treatment may not fully reverse the consequences. Iron-deficiency anemia is common in female athletes, resulting in fatigue and decreased performance, and can be corrected with iron supplements. Ergogenic aids are banned in sports, and research has been limited. However, they can result in irreversible effects, and therefore, the athletic trainer must understand and convey the potential repercussions to athletes who are considering their use.

SELF-TEST

1. Which of the following statements regarding body composition is true?
   A. Boys achieve their young adult fat-free mass at age 16 to 17 years.
   B. Girls achieve their young adult fat-free mass at age 15 to 16 years.
   C. At puberty, girls show a decrease in both fat-free mass and body fat percentage.
   D. At puberty, boys show an increase in both fat-free mass and body fat percentage.

2. Which of the following statements about strength is true?
   A. Male athletes exhibit a decline in concentric strength at higher velocities.
   B. Female athletes have a higher ratio of concentric to eccentric strength than male athletes do.
   C. Relative to body weight and fat-free mass, female athletes can leg press nearly as much as male athletes.
   D. After a single exercise bout, female athletes show higher increases in human growth hormone than male athletes.

3. In terms of cardiovascular fitness and in comparison with male athletes, female athletes have:
   A. larger hearts.
   B. a lower heart rate.
   C. smaller blood volume.
   D. higher stroke volumes.

4. Which of the following is a factor that improves an athlete's ability to tolerate hot or cold temperatures?
   A. High Vo_{2max}.
   B. High body fat
   C. Low fat-free mass
   D. Small body size

5. Which of the following statements about a recent study of injuries in the cadet class at West Point is true?
   A. Women were injured four times as often as men were.
   B. Men sustained more upper body injuries than women did.
   C. Men were more likely to incur lower extremity stress fractures than women.
   D. Women injured the foot and ankle more often than men did, but their injuries were minor.

6. Which of the following statements about soccer players with anterior cruciate ligament injuries is true?
   A. Noncontact injuries were more common in men than in women.
   B. Men incurred more injuries, but women had a higher incidence rate.
   C. Incidence rates for both men and women were higher in practices than in games.
   D. Women ages 15 to 18 years were less likely to be injured than men in the same age group.

7. Which of the following statements about the comparison of highly competitive injured athletes with injured nonathletes is true?
   A. Team sport athletes use problem-solving strategies.
   B. Individual sport athletes cope by means of passive acceptance.
   C. Female athletes are likely to be less assertive than male athletes.
   D. Female athletes become more secure, while male athletes become more anxious and tense.

8. Which of the following behavior patterns characterizes the female athlete triad?
   A. Normal eating patterns
   B. Increased estrogen levels
   C. Low incidence of stress fractures
   D. Primary or secondary amenorrhea

9. Which of the following statements about anemia is true?
   A. Too much iron in the body is better than too little.
   B. The most common type of anemia is iron-deficiency anemia.
   C. Anemia is more common in male athletes than in female athletes.
   D. An athlete with anemia performs better than an athlete without anemia.

10. Ergogenic aids have been reported to have which of the following effects?
    A. Clitoral atrophy in women
    B. Excess hair growth in men
    C. Deepening of the voice in men
    D. Cardiovascular and liver disease in both sexes

Answers on page 894

References

1. Jaffe R: History of women in sports, in Agostini R, Titus S (eds): *Medical and Orthopedic Issues of Active and Athletic Women.* Philadelphia, PA, Hanley & Belfus, 1994, pp 1–5.

2. Clarkson PM, Going S: Body composition and weight control: A perspective on females, in Bar-Or O, Lamb DR, Clarkson PM (eds): *Exercise and the Female: A Life Span Approach.* Carmel, IN, Cooper Publishing Group, 1996, pp 147–214.

3. Wilmore JH, Costill DL (eds): *Physiology of Sport and Exercise.* Champaign, IL, Human Kinetics,1994.

4. Klausen B, Toubro S, Astrup A: Age and sex effects on energy expenditure. *Am J Clin Nutr* 1997;65:895–907.

5. World Health Organization: *Energy and Protein Requirements: Report of a Joint FAO/WHO Expert Consultation.* Geneva, Switzerland, World Health Organization, 1985.

6. Lemieux S, Prud'homme D, Bouchard C, Tremblay A, Despres JP: Sex differences in the relation of visceral adipose tissue accumulation to total body fatness. *Am J Clin Nutr* 1993;58:463–467.

7. Baechle TR (ed): *Essentials of Strength Training and Conditioning.* Champaign, IL, Human Kinetics, 1994.

8. Fleck SJ, Kraemer WJ (eds): *Designing Resistance Training Programs,* ed 2. Champaign, IL, Human Kinetics, 1997.

9. Sale DG, Spriet LL: Skeletal muscle function and energy metabolism, in Bar-Or O, Lamb DR, Clarkson PM (eds): *Exercise and the Female: A Life Span Approach.* Carmel, IN, Cooper Publishing Group, 1996, pp 289–364.

10. Abe T, Brechue WF, Fujita S, Brown JB: Gender differences in FFM accumulation and architectural characteristics of muscle. *Med Sci Sports Exerc* 1998;30:1066–1070.

11. Batterham AM, Birch, KM: Allometry of anaerobic performance: A gender comparison. *Can J Appl Physiol* 1996;21:48–62.

12. Perrault H: Cardiorespiratory function, in Bar-Or O, Lamb DR, Clarkson PM (eds): *Exercise and the Female: A Life Span Approach.* Carmel, IN, Cooper Publishing Group, 1996, pp 215–248.

13. Haykowsky M, Chan S, Bhambhani Y, Syrotuik D, Quinney H, Bell G: Effects of combined endurance and strength training on left ventricular morphology in male and female rowers. *Can J Cardiol* 1998;14:387–391.

14. Bam J, Noakes T, Juritz J, Dennis SC: Could women outrun men in ultramarathon races? *Med Sci Sports Exerc* 1997;29:244–247.

15. Jackson AS, Wier LT, Ayers GW, Beard EF, Stuteville JE, Blair SN: Changes in aerobic power of women, ages 20-64 years. *Med Sci Sports Exerc* 1996;28:884–891.

16. Jackson AS, Beard EF, Wier LT, Ross RM, Stuteville JE, Blair SN: Changes in aerobic power of men, ages 25-70 years. *Med Sci Sports Exerc* 1995;27:113–120.

17. Beighton P, Solomon L, Soskolne CL: Articular mobility in an African population. *Ann Rheum Dis* 1973;32: 413–418.

18. Marshall JL, Johanson N, Wickiewicz TL, et al: Joint looseness: A function of the person and the joint. *Med Sci Sports Exerc* 1980;12:189–194.

19. Gleim GW: Exercise is not an effective weight loss modality in women. *J Am Coll Nutr* 1993;12:363–367.

20. Nicklas BJ: Effects of endurance exercise on adipose tissue metabolism. *Exerc Sport Sci Rev* 1997;25:77–103.

21. Mauriege P, Prud'Homme D, Marcotte M, Yoshioka M, Tremblay A, Despres JP: Regional differences in adipose tissue metabolism between sedentary and endurance-trained women. *Am J Physiol* 1997;273: E497–E506.

22. Martin WH: Effects of acute and chronic exercise on fat metabolism. *Exerc Sport Sci Rev* 1996;24:203–231.

23. Tremblay A, Simoneau JA, Bouchard C: Impact of exercise intensity on body fatness and skeletal muscle metabolism. *Metabolism* 1994;43:814–818.

24. Armstrong DW III: Metabolic and endocrine responses to cold air in women differing in aerobic capacity. *Med Sci Sports Exerc* 1998;30:880–884.

25. Aoyagi Y, McLellan TM, and Shephard RJ: Interactions of physical training and heat acclimation: The thermophysiology of exercising in a hot climate. *Sports Med* 1997;23:173–210.

26. Bar-Or O: Thermoregulation in females from a lifespan perspective, in Bar-Or O, Lamb DR, Clarkson PM (eds): *Exercise and the Female: A Life Span Approach.* Carmel, IN, Cooper Publishing Group, 1996, pp 249–288.

27. Bijur PE, Horodyski M, Egerton W, Kurzon M, Lifrak S, Friedman S: Comparison of injury during cadet basic training by gender. *Arch Pediatr Adolesc Med* 1997;151:456–461.

28. Amoroso PJ, Bell NS, Jones BH: Injury among female and male army parachutists. *Aviat Space Environ Med* 1997;68:1006–1011.

29. de Loes M: Epidemiology of sports injuries in the Swiss organization "Youth and Sports" 1987-1989. *Int J Sports Med* 1995;16:134–138.

30. Aagaard H, Jorgensen U: Injuries in elite volleyball. *Scand J Med Sci Sports* 1996;6:228–232.

31. Wedderkopp N, Kaltoft M, Lundgaard B, Rosendahl M, Froberg K: Injuries in young female players in European team handball. *Scand J Med Sci Sports* 1997;7:342–347.

32. Macnab AJ, Cadman R: Demographics of alpine skiing and snowboarding injury: Lessons for prevention programs. *Inj Prev* 1996;2:286–289.

33. Bjordal JM, Arnly F, Hannestad B, Strand T: Epidemiology of anterior cruciate ligament injuries in soccer. *Am J Sports Med* 1997;25:341–345.

34. Arendt E, Dick R: Knee injury patterns among men and women in collegiate basketball and soccer: NCAA data and review of the literature. *Am J Sports Med* 1995;23:694–701.

35. Lindenfeld TN, Schmidt DJ, Hendy MP, Mangine RE, Noyes FR: Incidence of injury in indoor soccer. *Am J Sports Med* 1994;22:364–371.

36. Shelbourne KD, Davis TJ, Klootwyk TE: The relationship between intercondylar notch width of the femur and the incidence of anterior cruciate ligament tears: A prospective study. *Am J Sports Med* 1998;26:402–408.

37. Laural J, Huston LJ, Wojtys EM: Neuromuscular performance characteristics in elite female athletes. *Am J Sports Med* 1996;24:427–436.

38. Loudon JK, Jenkins W, Loudon KL: The relationship between static posture and ACL injury in female athletes. *J Orthop Sports Phys Ther* 1996;24:91–97.

39. Krivickas LS, Feinberg JH: Lower extremity injuries in college athletes: Relation between ligamentous laxity and lower extremity muscle tightness. *Arch Phys Med Rehabil* 1996;77: 1139–1143.

40. Johnson U: Coping strategies among long-term injured competitive athletes: A study of 81 men and women in team and individual sports. *Scand J Med Sci Sports* 1997;7:367–372.

41. La Croix AZ, Newton KM, Leveille SG, Wallace J: Healthy aging: A women's issue. *West J Med* 1997;167:220–232.

42. Ainsworth BE, Sternfeld B, Slattery ML, Daguies V, Zahm SH: Physical activity and breast cancer: Evaluation of physical activity assessment methods. *Cancer* 1998;83(suppl 3):611–620.

43. Friedenreich CM, Thune I, Brinton LA, Albanes D: Epidemiologic issues related to the association between physical activity and breast cancer. *Cancer* 1998;83(suppl 3):600–610.

44. Cummings SR, Nevitt MC, Browner WS, et al: Risk factors for hip fracture in white women: Study of Osteoporotic Fractures Research Group. *N Engl J Med* 1995;332:767–773.

45. Eichner ER: *Chronic Fatigue and Stress: Sports Medicine*, ed 2. Philadelphia, PA, WB Saunders, 1991.

46. Oppliger RA, Harms RD, Herrmann DE, Streich CM, Clark RR: The Wisconsin wrestling minimum weight project: A model for weight control among high school wrestlers. *Med Sci Sports Exerc* 1995;27:1220–1224.

47. Perriello VA Jr, Almquist J, Conkwright D Jr, et al: Health and weight control management among wrestlers. *Va Med* 1995;122:179–185.

48. Nattiv A, Agostini R, Drinkwater B, Yeager K: The female athlete triad: The inter-relatedness of disordered eating, amenorrhea, and osteoporosis. *Clin Sports Med* 1994;13:405–418.

49. Marshall L: Clinical evaluation of amenorrhea in active women, in *Clinics in Sports Medicine: The Active Woman*. Philadelphia, PA, WB Saunders, 1994.

50. Yesalis CE, Barsukiewicz CK, Kopstein AN, Bahrke MS: Trends in anabolic-androgenic steroid use among adolescents. *Arch Pediatr Adolesc Med* 1997;151:1197–1206.

51. Strauss H: Additional effects of anabolic steroids on women, in Yesalis C (ed): *Anabolic Steroids in Sport and Exercise*. Champaign, IL, Human Kinetics, 1993, pp 151–160.

29

Pediatric and Adolescent Athletes

Jeffrey A. Guy, MD
Lyle J. Micheli, MD

QUICK CONTENTS

- The anatomic and biomechanical differences of children and adolescents that make their athletic injuries different from those of adults.

- Special considerations when performing a thorough history and physical examination on a young athlete.

- Frequent locations of injuries unique to growing children, common mechanisms of injury, the patient's symptoms, and the signs seen on physical examination.

- Common overuse injuries that occur in children and adolescents.

- Joint instabilities and osteochondroses that affect pediatric and adolescent athletes.

- Special considerations in the female athlete.

- Congenital and developmental disorders that can affect growing athletes.

OVERVIEW

Given the growth of organized sports in developed countries, a large number of youth are expected to participate in sports. The training of the pediatric athlete has become increasingly important for young participants in organized sports and places large demands on their developing bodies. This chapter outlines the musculoskeletal characteristics specific to the young athlete and provides a brief description of injuries and disorders common to this age group. In addition, the general physical characteristics of the athlete and therapeutic options are provided to promote the early identification and prompt institution of therapy necessary to return the injured athlete to sport.

WELL-BEING OF THE PEDIATRIC AND ADOLESCENT ATHLETE

As the numbers of pediatric athletes have increased, the patterns of their participation have changed as well. The concept of "free play" and the notion of participating in a variety of activities have been replaced with the concept of "specialty" and participation in the same sport for increasing lengths of time. The development of summer sports camps and the training of the elite athlete to compete at the national and Olympic levels compound the problem. The intensity of competition and the pressure to perform increase steadily.

It is therefore increasingly important that parents, coaches, athletic trainers, and health professionals accept responsibility for the health and well-being of the pediatric athlete as the child grows both physically and mentally.

GENERAL MUSCULOSKELETAL FEATURES OF CHILDREN

Anatomy

Pediatric and adult athletes share many of the same risks for injury. However, there are also unique injuries and patterns of injury seen only in the pediatric athlete that are due primarily to the presence of growth tissue (growth cartilage) in the child. In addition, children grow at variable rates during the phases of growth and maturation. Cartilage, a form of connective tissue containing a tough, elastic substance, on the joint surface is present in both children and adults. These "junctional tissues" are targets of compressive, tensile, and shear forces with motion. Children also have cartilage in two additional sites: the growth plate and the insertion of major muscles into bone (**Figure 29-1**).

The growth plate, also known as the *physis,* is responsible for the longitudinal growth of bones and somewhat for their increase in width. The growth plate is subdivided into zones that contain differences in cellular architecture and arrangement of the intercellular matrix (**Figure 29-2**). The zone between the hypertrophic cells and the region of calcification is believed to be the weakest part of the physis, and it is through this zone that most fractures are believed to occur. Physeal fractures are common injuries of great concern because of the potential for later growth disturbance, with either complete closure of the injured physis or formation of a localized area of closure known as a physeal bridge.

An *apophysis* is a cartilaginous structure usually found at the insertion of major muscle groups into bone. Located near the end of a long bone, the apophysis is subjected primarily to tensile forces, as opposed to the growth plate cartilage, which is subjected to compressive and shear forces. Tensile forces are most often produced through a musculotendinous insertion, such as the insertion of the patellar tendon on the tibial tubercle apophysis. In the pediatric athlete, an apophysis may be susceptible to both overuse syndromes and acute fracture. Whereas tendinitis is commonly seen in the adult athlete

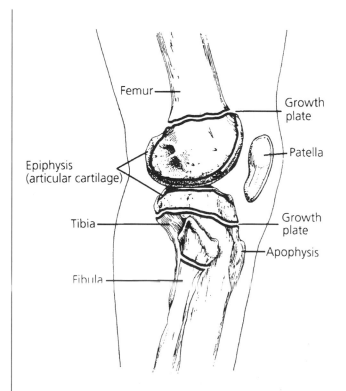

FIGURE 29-1

The two additional sites of cartilage in children are the growth plate and major muscle insertions into bone.

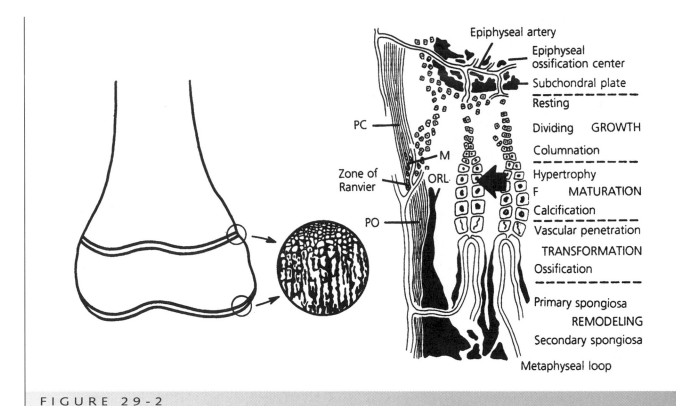

FIGURE 29-2

Zones of the growth plate contain differences in cellular architecture and intracellular matrix arrangement.

with an overuse syndrome, in the child, the apophysis will usually become painful before the musculotendinous unit itself is affected by overuse.

Articular cartilage at the joint surface differs in a child from an adult. The articular cartilage of both the child and the adult provides a smooth gliding surface of low friction at the joint; however, in the child, this cartilage is growing and has an infrastructure very similar to that of the physis. This difference in infrastructure results in different biomechanics at the joint surface in the child. Repetitive injury or excessive shear may result in chondromalacia in the adult; however, similar pathomechanics in the child may result in *osteochondritis dissecans (OCD)*, involving both the joint surface and subchondral bone. Osteochondritis dissecans, which is a localized area of osteonecrosis, may affect any joint of the sports-active child, but it is most frequently seen at the knee, elbow, ankle, and foot. OCD must be part of the differential diagnosis of any overuse injury in children.[1]

Ligaments and Tendons

In children, ligaments and tendons insert into the fibrous and fibrocartilaginous periosteal and perichondral regions of the metaphysis instead of directly into osseous tissue as they do in adults. This arrangement produces a more uniform gradation of tissue elasticity, protecting the soft-tissueñbone interface from injury. As a result, traumatic lesions in children tend to occur through bone. Whenever instability about a joint is suspected, the possibility of growth plate injury must be considered. Ligamentous injuries in children are rare, and plain radiographs or MRI scans are often necessary if any instability is present.

Biomechanics and Fractures

Because a childís bone composition is different from adult bone, it responds differently to physiologic and traumatic stress.[2] The concept of "elastic" and "plastic" deformation of bone is essential to the evaluation and understanding of osseous injury in children. When a mild deforming force is applied to a childís bone, its inherent elasticity will permit deformation and allow the return of the bone to its original structural shape when the force is released, much like an internal shock absorber. However, bone has an elastic limit. Once the limit is reached, microscopic damage accumulates and the bone's ability to return to the original shape is impaired, resulting in plastic deformation. Further application of force may result in gross failure and displacement of the bone.

Bowing deformities in young children result when bone is stressed beyond its elastic recoil limits to a state of permanent plastic deformation. This alteration may appear subtle on plain radiographs. Clinically, however, the alteration may need to be reduced if significant changes in range of motion of the affected extremity occur (**Figure 29-3**).

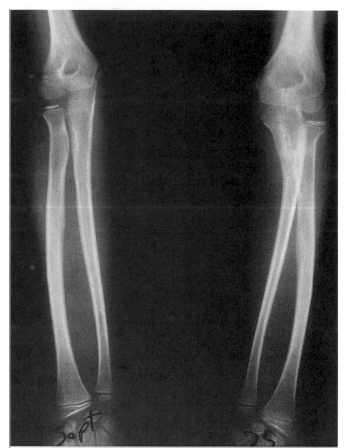

FIGURE 29-3

Significant changes in ranges of motion indicate that bowing deformities should be reduced. (Reproduced with permission from Wilkins KE (ed): *Operative Management of Upper Extremity Fractures In Children*. Rosemont, IL, American Academy of Orthopaedic Surgeons, 1994.)

Pediatric bone can fail in both tension and compression, producing unique fracture patterns. One commonly seen pediatric fracture is a *torus* or *buckle fracture* (**Figure 29-4**). This type of fracture usually occurs at the diaphyseal-metaphyseal junction when the more rigid diaphyseal cortex is driven into the weaker metaphysis. Greenstick (incomplete) fractures are frequently seen in the pediatric population (**Figure 29-5**). In a greenstick fracture, bone demonstrates failure at the tension side as well as a plastic deformation at the compression side. Complete fractures occur with high-energy injuries and display transverse, oblique, or spiral patterns, depending on how the injury force was applied.

Physeal fractures are common injuries in the growing child and are a cause of great concern. Because a child's ligaments tend to be stronger than the cartilaginous growth plate, traumatic injury to an extremity may result in fracture across the physis rather than ligamentous disruption. The worst complication of such an injury is physeal arrest, in which a bony bridge forms across the physis, tethering longitudinal growth at that point. This bridge, also called a

bony bar, may result in angular deformity or in loss of bone length, depending on its size and location and the amount of growth left to occur in the injured athlete.

Physiology

Fortunately, another characteristic unique to fractures in children is their bones' ability to generate a rapid healing response. Pediatric bone has a relatively rich blood supply and an extremely thick osteogenic periosteum, with resultant increased cellular activity. This enhanced healing capacity of the child's bone also allows for progressive remodeling of healed fractures. Mildly angulated fractures or overriding fracture fragments will straighten as the bone matures (**Figure 29-6**). This remodeling potential is greatest in younger athletes and in fractures that occur close to the growth plate. Needless to say, the healthcare provider must have specialized training to determine the degree of maturation or angulation that is acceptable and that can be expected to remodel sufficiently to result in joint function that is satisfactory for the high demands of a young athlete.

Another aspect of soft-tissue growth that may contribute to childhood injuries is the potential for imbalance between bone growth and soft-tissue growth. During periods of rapid growth, such as the adolescent growth spurt, longitudinal bone growth may occur more rapidly than does growth of the surrounding soft tissues, which elongate

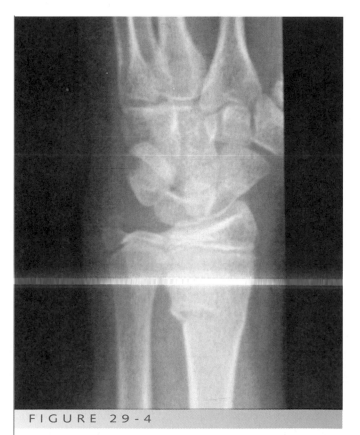

FIGURE 29-4

A torus or buckle fracture.

General Musculoskeletal Features and Children

Anatomy

Children are vulnerable to certain unique injuries and patterns of injury because of their growing tissues. Cartilage on the joint surface is subject to compressive, tensile, and shear forces with motion. Children have two additional sites of cartilage: the physis (growth plate) and the apophysis (junction of major muscles' insertion into bones).

The physis is divided into zones. The weakest part of the physis is the zone between the hypertrophic cells and the region of calcification; fractures in this area are common and potentially serious. The injured physis closes either completely or partially. The cartilaginous apophysis near the end of a long bone is subjected primarily to tensile forces, which are most often produced through a musculotendinous insertion; thus, the apophysis is susceptible to both overuse syndromes and acute fractures.

In children, the articular cartilage is growing and its infrastructure resembles that of the physis. Although repetitive injury or excessive shear can cause chondromalacia in the adult, these forces can cause osteochondritis dissecans in the child.

Ligaments and tendons

Children's ligaments and tendons insert into the fibrous and fibrocartilaginous periosteal and perichondral regions of the metaphysis, whereas adults' ligaments and tendons insert directly into bone. Thus, children have a more uniform gradation of tissue elasticity, which protects the soft-tissueñbone interface, but means that traumatic injuries tend to affect the bone. Therefore, joint instability may reflect growth plate injury.

Biomechanics and fractures

A child's bone responds to physiologic and traumatic stress differently than an adult's bone. The inherent elasticity of a child's bone allows it to withstand a mild deforming force and return to its original shape. However, once a bone's elastic limit is reached, plastic deformation can result in a bowing deformity that must be reduced. Pediatric bone can fail in both tension and compression. In a greenstick fracture, the bone fails on the tension side and deforms on the compression side. Higher energy can cause a complete fracture in a transverse, oblique, or spiral pattern.

Physiology

Pediatric fractures can heal rapidly because of the rich blood supply to bone and an extremely thick osteogenic periosteum with resultant increased cellular activity. Mildly angulated fractures or overriding fragments can straighten through remodeling. Young athletes may be susceptible to injury during times of rapid growth when longitudinal bone growth exceeds surrounding soft-tissue growth.

---

only in response to this bone growth.[3] Therefore, an increase in musculotendinous unit tightness and a loss of flexibility can be seen during these growth periods, perhaps putting the adolescent at greater risk for overuse injuries.[3]

TREATING YOUNG INJURED ATHLETES

Importance of a Thorough History

Certain general principles apply to all physical complaints of growing children. The most important step in treating injured pediatric and adolescent athletes and returning them to play is to make the correct diagnosis. In making a correct diagnosis, there is no substitute for obtaining a comprehensive and focused history. If an acute traumatic event has been observed, the healthcare provider must rule out any preexisting disease or antecedent trauma.

Because children, especially younger children, are often poor historians, information must be elicited from parents, coaches, athletic trainers, and other family members, as well as from the child. Recent training history, participation in sports other than the one in which the injury occurred, the type of playing surface involved, and the presence of concurrent disease are all relevant points of information to gather for the medical history.

Careful Physical Examination

Once an adequate history has been obtained, a careful physical examination is mandatory. In the case of acute trauma during a sporting event, the presence of an obvious deformity and the inability to bear weight or use an upper extremity are indications for referral to a physician for radiographic evaluation. The possibility that pain may be caused by an abnormality in an adjacent joint should not be overlooked. *Referred pain,* which is pain that is

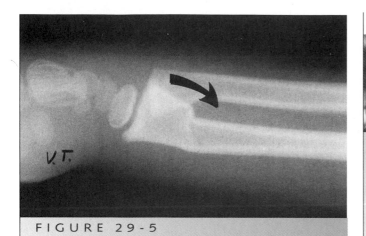

FIGURE 29-5

Greenstick fractures are frequently seen in the pediatric population. (Reproduced with permission from Wilkins KE (ed): *Operative Management of Upper Extremity Fractures In Children.* Rosemont, IL, American Academy of Orthopaedic Surgeons, 1994.)

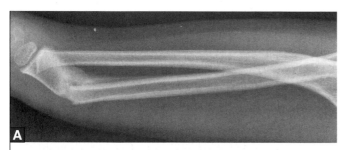

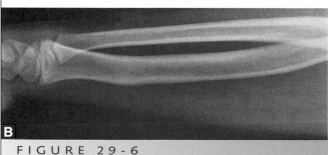

FIGURE 29-6

Mildly angulated fractures or overriding fracture fragments straighten as bone matures. (Reproduced with permission from Wilkins KE (ed): *Operative Management of Upper Extremity Fractures In Children.* Rosemont, IL, American Academy of Orthopaedic Surgeons, 1994.)

perceived as arising in a location different from the location of the pathology, can occur. The child should be examined thoroughly with careful attention paid to the site of the injury and to the joints above and below. In the child and teenager, knee pain may result not only from abnormal knee architecture but also from abnormal foot and ankle mechanics or hip disorders. A classic example of referred pain in the growing child is anterior thigh or knee pain that actually reflects hip pathology, particularly a slipped capital femoral epiphysis (SCFE) at the hip joint.

FOCUS ON . . .

Treating Young Injured Athletes

Importance of a thorough history
The most important step in treating injured young athletes is to make a correct diagnosis by obtaining a comprehensive and focused history. Preexisting disease or antecedent trauma should be ruled out, and information from parents, coaches, athletic trainers, and the patient should be obtained.

Careful physical examination
During physical examination after acute trauma, obvious deformities and the inability to bear weight or use an upper extremity should be evaluated, paying careful attention to the site of complaint and the joints above and below the injury. Various pain sources should be considered in the differential diagnosis.

Microtrauma and macrotrauma are not the only possible explanations for joint, extremity, or back pain in the young athlete. Because they occur relatively more commonly in children than in adults, tumors, infections, inflammatory disease, and congenital anomalies must always be part of the differential diagnosis.[4]

PEDIATRIC TRAUMA

Osseous Injuries
In pediatric and adolescent athletes, osseous injuries (injuries involving the bones) are more common than ligamentous injuries. Most osseous injuries result from single, acute, direct or indirect traumatic events that frequently occur during participation in contact sports. Because of the inherent strength of the ligamentous insertions in children and adolescents, noncontact injuries may result in osseous injuries such as growth plate fractures and avulsion fractures. Although rare, intraligamentous injuries do occur. Muscle tears are also not often seen in the growing child. Radiographic evaluation is usually indicated if a muscle tear is suspected. If a fracture does occur after seemingly minor trauma, the presence of an underlying pathologic lesion of the bone must be ruled out. A child who has had multiple fractures should be carefully evaluated for underlying endocrine or metabolic disorders.

Some of the more common injuries incurred by both adults and children during sports participation include fractures of the wrist, radius and ulna, clavicle, tibia, and fibula, as well as dislocations of the shoulder, elbow, and interphalangeal joints. The treatment of most of these injuries is generally the same for the child as for the adult. Exceptions

Pediatric Trauma

Osseous injuries

Osseous injuries result from single, acute traumatic events. Although muscle and ligament injuries are rare, radiographs are usually indicated. A child who sustains a fracture after minor trauma or sustains multiple fractures should be investigated for underlying endocrine or metabolic disease.

Most sports-related fractures and dislocations in children are treated as they are in adults. Exceptions are certain forearm or tibial fractures that require surgical fixation in the adult, but can be treated with cast immobilization in the child. Plastic deformation and greenstick fractures can also usually be treated with manual reduction and casting.

Avulsion fractures

Acute muscle strains or ligament sprains can cause avulsion of the osseous origin or insertion. One of the most common avulsion fractures affects the anterior tibial intercondylar eminence. A large hemarthrosis and anterior laxity suggest the diagnosis, which is confirmed with a radiograph.

Another common avulsion fracture about the knee is an avulsion of the tibial tubercle by the patellar tendon, usually from a jumping activity. Injury severity ranges from a nondisplaced avulsion to a complete fracture. A displaced fracture may be characterized by a hemarthrosis, loss of active knee extension, and laxity, and CT or MRI scans may be needed.

Apophyseal avulsion fracture of the pelvis can occur with sudden contractions or distractions of any of the muscles that originate from or insert on the pelvis or proximal femur. Most of these injuries can be treated conservatively. If symptoms persist after 6 weeks of conservative treatment, reevaluation may demonstrate a symptomatic nonunion, which may require surgical intervention.

these injuries often occur at the wrist and ankle, radiographs should be obtained even when a simple sprain is suspected.

As a result of the unique properties of ligamentous attachments in the child, osseous injuries, which include growth plate injuries, are often sustained through the traumatic pull of the ligaments. Common examples are valgus or varus stress injuries to the knee. Clinical examination reveals that these injuries present with joint laxity that appears on radiographs as a fracture to the growth plate of the distal femur or proximal tibia.

A mallet finger injury is another lesion that is unique to children. In an adult, a mallet finger injury is a tendon avulsion, but in a young child or adolescent, a mallet finger injury usually means a fracture of the growth plate. In the child, this physeal fracture will heal rapidly though fracture healing mechanisms following reduction; in the adult, healing of the ligament avulsion is difficult (**Figure 29-7**).

Avulsion Fractures

Avulsion fractures are a result of the unique properties of the musculotendinous unit and ligament attachment to bone in the growing child. Acute muscular contractions or ligamentous sprains may result in avulsion, or pulling off, of the osseous origin or insertion.

Two of the most common avulsion fractures occur at the knee. First is the fracture of the anterior intercondylar eminence of the tibia, which represents an avulsion of the attached anterior cruciate ligament (ACL). This fracture is often seen in children after falls from bicycles and may also occur with any athletic trauma that can produce ACL

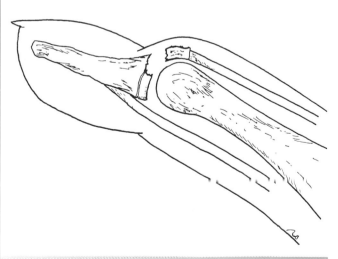

FIGURE 29-7

A physeal fracture heals rapidly in the child following reduction; in the adult, it does not. (Reproduced with permission from Wilkins KE (ed): *Operative Management of Upper Extremity Fractures In Children.* Rosemont, IL, American Academy of Orthopaedic Surgeons, 1994.)

to this rule include certain forearm or tibial fractures that would be treated with surgical fixation in the adult but with cast immobilization in the immature athlete.

Fractures unique to prepubescent children include plastic deformation and greenstick fractures, which occur because of the unique biomechanics of the growing diaphysis and metaphysis. Most of these fractures are successfully treated with manual reduction and cast immobilization.

In prepubescent children and adolescents, fractures involving the growth plate are not uncommon. Because

tears in adults, such as twisting injuries while playing football or skiing. Usually, clinical examination will reveal a large *hemarthrosis* (a collection of blood within a joint) in addition to anterior laxity. A radiograph will confirm the diagnosis of avulsion fracture.

The second common avulsion fracture around the knee is an avulsion of the tibial tubercle by the patellar tendon. This fracture results from jumping activities, as in basketball or track. The severity of these injuries ranges from a nondisplaced avulsion of the tibial tubercle apophysis with no resultant laxity to a fracture that propagates across the primary ossification center of the proximal tibia into the knee joint. Although some of these injuries can be treated nonsurgically with a cast, some require surgical fixation (**Figure 29-8**). Hemarthrosis is present, and is accompanied by a loss of active knee extension and laxity. In addition to good quality radiographs, CT or MRI scans may be necessary to define the full extent of bony and cartilaginous injury.

Another injury unique to the child is the apophyseal avulsion fracture of the pelvis. Acute displacement of the apophysis can occur with sudden contractions or distractions of the hamstrings, adductors, or other muscles that originate from or insert into the pelvis and proximal femur (**Figure 29-9**). If this injury is suspected, special radiographs may be necessary to assist in diagnosis and determine the degree of apophyseal displacement. Most of these separations are successfully treated conservatively. Open reduction and internal fixation are rarely indicated for significantly separated fragments. If symptoms persist beyond the usual time for recovery (about 6 weeks), reevaluation with repeated radiographs is indicated. Occasionally, a symptomatic nonunion may occur, necessitating surgical excision of the fragment and repair of the musculotendinous origin or insertion.

OVERUSE INJURIES

Overuse injuries are injuries resulting from the chronic application of repetitive stress to otherwise normal tissue. In the adult, overuse injuries include stress fractures, bursitis, tendinitis, fasciitis, and chondromalacia of the joint articular surface. Children and adolescents may have these adult overuse injuries and are subject to overuse injuries of the apophysis, physis, and joint surface.

Stress Fracture

The concept of stress fracture has been around for more than a century, and many terms have been used to describe this clinical syndrome. The term "insufficiency fracture" has been used to describe the consequence of normal stress applied to weak or pathologic bone.[4] "Fatigue fractures" have been described by the response of normal bone to abnormal stresses.[4] In either case, stress fractures occur when microdamage from repetitive stress accumulates in bone and overwhelms the body's reparative processes. Thus, without the proper rest needed to correct this imbalance, the cellular mechanisms responsible for repair fail to keep pace with the accumulation of microscopic damage and progress to clinical stress fractures.

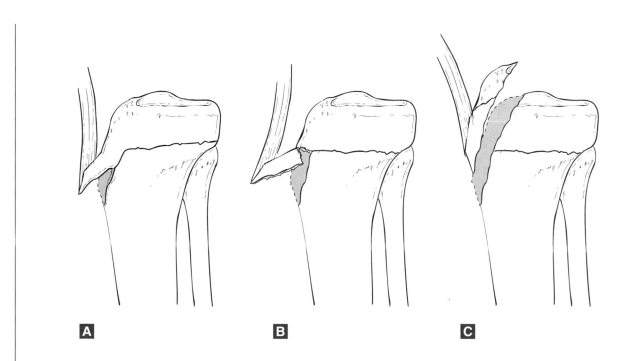

A   **B**   **C**

FIGURE 29-8

Some avulsion fracture injuries are treated with a cast, some with surgery.

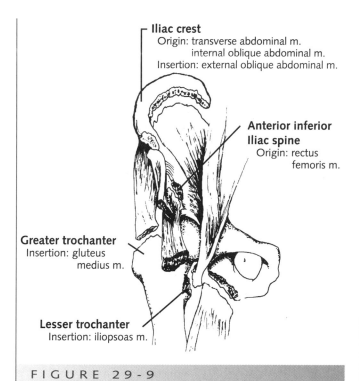

Iliac crest
Origin: transverse abdominal m.
internal oblique abdominal m.
Insertion: external oblique abdominal m.

Anterior inferior
Iliac spine
Origin: rectus
femoris m.

Greater trochanter
Insertion: gluteus
medius m.

Lesser trochanter
Insertion: iliopsoas m.

FIGURE 29-9

Sudden contraction or distraction of various muscles can accompany acute apophyseal displacement.

As with most overuse injuries, early diagnosis of stress fractures is critical, because a delayed diagnosis may result in both prolonged rehabilitation and significant time away from sport.[1] Features common to all stress fractures include a history of repetitive or cyclic exercise, insidious onset of pain, recent change in training schedules, atraumatic history, and pain with weightbearing that is relieved with rest. The physical examination may reveal abnormal gait or alignment or point tenderness with a lack of soft-tissue swelling. Plain radiographs and bone scans may aid in the diagnosis. Modification of the athlete's training regimen and a brief period of altered weightbearing are the usual interventions; however, a late diagnosis or progression to a complete fracture occasionally requires surgical stabilization.

Little League Shoulder

The syndrome known as "Little League shoulder" is an overuse injury arising from overhead throwing activities. In this case, a stress fracture of the proximal humeral physis occurs. It should be differentiated from other complaints of shoulder pain seen in young pitchers and swimmers that result from an impingement syndrome or instability. Radiographs or a bone scan may be useful in the diagnosis.

Little League Elbow

An overuse syndrome seen in the elbows of adolescent pitchers is called "Little League elbow."[5] The syndrome is

the result of a repetitive valgus stress during overhead throwing. The valgus stress results in lateral compression and medial traction on the elbow (**Figure 29-10**). Resultant injuries may include osteochondral injuries of the capitellum (with or without the presence of loose bodies), injury to the proximal radial epiphysis and physeal plate (with early closure and overgrowth of the radial head), and inflammatory changes or avulsion of the medial epicondyle. The extent of injury determines its management. The child who throws extensively and complains of elbow pain should be evaluated carefully. Early institution of rest followed by appropriate stretching, strengthening, and refinement of the throwing technique may prevent progression and long-term sequelae of this disorder. Unchecked progression may lead to formation of loose bodies in the joint, abnormal growth of the bones of the elbow, or permanent flexion contractures.

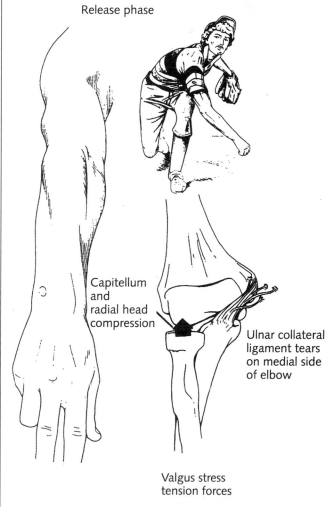

Release phase

Capitellum
and
radial head
compression

Ulnar collateral
ligament tears
on medial side
of elbow

Valgus stress
tension forces

FIGURE 29-10

Valgus stress results in lateral compression and medial traction on the elbow.

FOCUS ON . . .

Overuse Injuries

Overuse injuries result from the chronic application of repetitive stress to otherwise normal tissue. In addition to the stress fractures, bursitis, tendinitis, fasciitis, and chondromalacia seen in adults, children and adolescents are also subject to apophyseal, physeal, and joint surface overuse injuries.

Stress fracture

Stress fractures occur when microdamage from repetitive stress accumulates in bone and overwhelms the body's reparative processes. Without rest, cellular repair mechanisms fail to keep pace with the accumulating microscopic damage and may lead to a clinical stress fracture. Early diagnosis is critical to proper rehabilitation and safe return to sport as promptly as possible. The physical examination may reveal abnormal gait or alignment or point tenderness, although soft-tissue swelling may be absent. Plain radiographs and a bone scan can aid in the diagnosis. Most stress fractures heal with modification of the athlete's training regimen and a brief period of altered weightbearing; surgical stabilization may be needed if the diagnosis is late or the fracture is complete.

Little League shoulder

Little League shoulder is a stress reaction or fracture of the proximal humeral physis as a result of overhead throwing. Radiographs or a bone scan can help to distinguish Little League shoulder from impingement syndrome or instability.

Little League elbow

Little League elbow results from repetitive valgus stress during overhead throwing. The valgus stress results in lateral compression and medial traction on the elbow, which can cause osteochondral capitellar injuries, proximal radial epiphyseal or physeal injuries, and medial epicondyle inflammation or avulsion. Early rest, followed by appropriate stretching, strengthening, and refinement of the throwing technique may prevent progression and long-term sequelae.

Osgood-Schlatter's disease

Osgood-Schlatter's disease occurs when the tibial tubercle's secondary ossification center is subjected to traction forces at the patellar tendon insertion. It is frequently seen in athletes whose sports require repetitive jumping. Jumper's knee occurs when the distal patellar pole is injured by repetitive traction at the quadriceps insertion.

Sinding-Larsen-Johansson disease

Sinding-Larsen-Johansson disease describes injury to the lower patellar pole from the pull of the patellar tendon. Radiographs may show tibial tubercle fragmentation or small bony avulsions at either pole of the patella. Treatment includes rest, stretching, reconditioning, and avoidance of pain-producing activities for 6 to 8 weeks; nonsteroidal anti-inflammatory drugs may be helpful.

Sever's disease (calcaneal apophysitis)

Sever's disease is inflammation of the calcaneal growth plate and causes heel pain exacerbated by running. Radiographs are needed to rule out a bony lesion. Sever's disease usually resolves once the apophysis fuses. During recovery, ice, nonsteroidal anti-inflammatory drugs, activity modification, heel pads, and physical therapy may be helpful. If symptoms are severe and unremitting, cast immobilization may be beneficial.

Spondylolysis

Spondylolysis should be considered when a pediatric athlete reports back pain lasting longer than 3 weeks. Diagnosis is based on the history, physical examination, and special tests. Treatment is modification or removal of the offending activity; surgical stabilization is rarely needed.

Chronic compartment syndrome

Chronic compartment syndrome occurs most often in the four compartments of the lower leg. It is caused by exercise when the osseofascial compartments are unable to withstand the resulting volume and pressure changes. The patient may report tightness, aching, or squeezing in the lower extremity during exercise. Sensation over the dorsal foot may be decreased, and a transient foot drop may be evident in severe cases. Diagnosis is confirmed with compartment pressure measurements, and treatment consists of activity modification, orthotics, physical therapy, and in resistant cases, limited skin incision fasciotomy.

Osgood-Schlatter's Disease

Osgood-Schlatter's disease affects the secondary ossification center of the tibial tubercle. The injury occurs because the tubercle is subjected to traction forces at the patellar tendon insertion. Osgood-Schlatter's disease usually appears during the adolescent growth spurt, more commonly in boys than in girls. It is frequently associated with sports that require repetitive jumping, such as basketball, track, and gymnastics. Unlike Osgood-Schlatter's isease, "jumper's knee," another disorder of the extensor mechanism, is not truly an apophysitis, but it does represent a repetitive traction injury to the patella that occurs when the lower pole of the patella is injured at the insertion of the quadriceps mechanism.

Sinding-Larsen-Johansson Disease

When the lower pole of the patella is injured by the pull of the patellar tendon, the condition is referred to as *Sinding-Larsen-Johansson disease*. All overuse disorders of the extensor mechanism are diagnosed during the clinical examination. The diagnosis of Sinding-Larsen-Johansson disease is supported by a history of repetitive jumping activity. Radiographs may show fragmentation of the tibial tubercle or small bony avulsions at either pole of the patella. Most athletes with this diagnosis respond to a period of rest and avoidance of pain-producing activities for about 6 to 8 weeks; sometimes this regimen is supplemented by nonsteroidal anti-inflammatory drugs (NSAIDs). As with other overuse injuries, a proper regimen of stretching and reconditioning must be established before the child is allowed to return to competitive activity.

Sever's Disease (Calcaneal Apophysitis)

Heel pain in the area of the calcaneal apophysis is a common complaint in young athletes, most commonly in young boys. The age of onset is typically 9 to 14 years. *Sever's disease* was originally described as an inflammation of the apophyseal growth plate of the calcaneus. The patient typically complains of heel pain exacerbated by running activities. Physical examination reveals little, although there may be tenderness on the medial and lateral aspects of the calcaneus. Plain radiographs should be obtained to rule out an osseous lesion. Calcaneal apophysitis is a self-limiting disorder and usually resolves after fusion of the apophysis. Symptoms are treated with ice, NSAIDs, and activity modification. Use of heel pads and therapeutic exercise is occasionally helpful as well as cast immobilization in severe instances of unremitting symptoms.

Spondylolysis

Knowledge of overuse injuries to the spine has become increasingly important in the differential diagnosis of back pain in the pediatric athlete.[6] A high index of suspicion should be maintained regarding athletes with complaints of low back pain of insidious, nontraumatic onset, which lasts longer than 3 weeks. Most frequently, stress injury involves the lumbosacral spine, specifically the pars interarticularis, a region of the posterior elements that is located between the superior and inferior facets. This region is vulnerable to repetitive stress, particularly during flexion, hyperextension, or rotation.

Diagnosis of *spondylolysis* should be made from the combination of history, physical examination, and ancillary testing. The initial radiographic work-up for stress injuries should involve standard and oblique views of the spine. A single photon emission computer tomography (SPECT) scan may be necessary to confirm the diagnosis. Once confirmed, therapy should be instituted immediately. Conservative therapy is generally successful but requires commitment and adherence not only from the athlete but also from the coaching staff and parents. After the offending risk factor has been modified or removed, the athlete may begin gradual, "pain-free" return to sport. In the event a compliant patient has persistent pain, further work-up may be necessary to either reconfirm the diagnosis or document the progression of injury. In rare cases, surgical intervention may be needed to stabilize the injury.

Chronic Compartment Syndrome

Compartment syndrome is a well-described phenomenon that occurs when increased pressure within an osseofascial compartment disrupts the normal vascular exchange, resulting in tissue ischemia and potential tissue necrosis.[7] Although it has been described in both the upper and lower extremities, compartment syndrome is most commonly associated with the four compartments of the lower leg. Unlike acute compartment syndrome that usually results from trauma, chronic compartment syndrome is exercise-induced and rarely results in tissue necrosis or residual disability. The elevated pressures of chronic compartment syndrome are secondary to the inadequacy of the osseofascial compartments to accommodate exercise-induced volume and pressure changes. When the compartment pressures exceed capillary filling pressures, the muscle becomes ischemic and painful. The anterior compartment is most commonly involved; however, any of the four compartments of the lower leg can be affected.

Patients with chronic compartment syndrome typically report tightness and an aching pain or a sensation of squeezing in the lower extremity. The symptoms are brought on by exercise and relieved a short time after activity ceases. Symptoms are often bilateral. Decreased sensation over the dorsum of the foot or a transient foot drop may be seen in extreme cases.

Compartment pressure measurements confirm the clinical diagnosis, and initial intervention may include activity modification, orthotic use, and therapeutic exercise. In cases resistant to conservative measures, limited skin incision fasciotomies are performed to release the fascial constraint.

JOINT INSTABILITY

Joint instability is a common problem in pediatric and adolescent athletes. The two most symptomatic joints are the patellofemoral and the glenohumeral joints.

Patellofemoral Joint Instability

The stability of the patellofemoral joint depends on dynamic restraints (especially the vastus medialis portion of the quadriceps), static restraints, and proper limb alignment. Acute injuries can result in medial restraint ruptures that cause traumatic lateral subluxation or dislocation, occasionally with an associated chondral or osteochondral fracture. All children with acute dislocations of the patella should be evaluated for associated fractures. Recurrent subluxation can occur in the young athlete. Conservative treatment is directed at strengthening the dynamic restraints that remain intact and may include the use of patellar bracing during activity.

The patellofemoral joint may also be affected by tightness in the lateral retinaculum, resulting in patellar compression and pain rather than subluxation. This pain syndrome is known as excessive lateral pressure syndrome, patellofemoral pain syndrome, or patellofemoral stress syndrome. It manifests as peripatellar or retropatellar pain and is especially noted after overuse situations such as long training sessions and hill running. In the adult, this syndrome may result in the pathologic condition known as chondromalacia with fissuring of the patella or trochlea. In the child or adolescent, this syndrome may result in potentially reversible softening of the growing articular cartilage.

Treatment of patellofemoral joint instability begins with identification and cessation of the offending activity. In addition, each patient should undergo a thorough physical examination to identify any patellofemoral malalignment or maltracking caused by an increased Q-angle. An exercise program is initiated to strengthen the medial restraints (the vastus medialis muscle) and stretch the lateral restraints. A surgical procedure, such as a lateral retinacular release or a realignment procedure, may be indicated in symptomatic athletes who have not responded after at least 6 months of exercise therapy and after other possible factors have been ruled out.

Glenohumeral Joint Instability

The shoulder may also be a source of painful instability in young athletes. Dislocation of the glenohumeral joint is uncommon in the young child but may be seen in the adolescent athlete. Of more importance are the painful shoulder syndromes in children associated with repetitive swimming or throwing activities. These conditions are commonly referred to as swimmer's shoulder but actually represent impingement, laxity, and overuse occurring separately or concurrently.

There is much discussion in the orthopaedic literature as to the true relationship between subtle anterior laxity and rotator cuff or biceps tendon impingement. The impingement lesion in young athletes is usually a reversible inflammatory process that responds to conservative therapy. The presence of associated instability can usually be established with a careful history and physical exam. The shoulder should be examined for subluxation and the presence of an apprehension sign in abduction and external rotation. Generalized physiologic laxity is common in these young individuals. Athletes with generalized physiologic laxity should also respond to conservative therapy that includes an exercise program aimed at maintaining a full range of motion, strengthening the shoulder musculature, and stretching the posterior capsule.

OSTEOCHONDROSES

Juvenile osteochondroses, also known as osteochondritises, are a group of clinical entities believed at one time to have a similar pathogenesis. Although this may not be the case, they do have a similar radiographic appearance and all occur in the pediatric age group. These conditions

FOCUS ON . . .

Joint Instability

Patellofemoral joint instability

The patellofemoral and glenohumeral joints are the most symptomatic instabilities in pediatric and adolescent athletes. Acute medial restraint ruptures can cause traumatic lateral subluxation and dislocation. All children with patellar dislocations should be evaluated for associated fractures. Recurrent subluxation can also occur. Treatment consists of strengthening the dynamic restraints and, perhaps, patellar bracing during activity.

Lateral retinacular tightness can result in patellar compression and pain. Symptoms are peripatellar or retropatellar pain. The child may only have potentially reversible softening of the articular cartilage where the adult would have chondromalacia with patellar and trochlear fissuring. Treatment is identification and cessation of the offending activity, a thorough physical examination, and exercises.

Glenohumeral joint instability

Glenohumeral joint dislocation can affect the adolescent athlete and is associated with repetitive swimming and throwing activities. The shoulder should be examined for subluxation, an apprehension sign in abduction and external rotation, and generalized physiologic laxity. Conservative therapy is recommended with exercises.

FOCUS ON . . .

Osteochondroses

Juvenile osteochondroses, or osteochondritises, are radiographically similar and occur in children. They may be more common in athletes, and therefore, should be considered as a possible source of pain.

Legg-Calvé-Perthes disease

Legg-Calvé-Perthes is osteonecrosis of the proximal femoral epiphysis. The athlete has a painless limp and decreased range of motion. Prompt physician referral for surgical consideration is needed. Freiberg's disease and Panner's disease are thought to have similar etiologies, but are usually self-limited.

Osteochondritis dissecans

Osteochondritis dissecans is the result of fragment separation of the subchondral bone. Spontaneous healing of the symptoms typically occurs within one year.

are not specifically sports-related, but they may be the underlying cause of local pain in a young athlete. In addition, authors of recent studies have suggested that they occur more commonly in sports-active children and, therefore, must be particularly considered as a possible cause of pain in this group.[2]

Legg-Calvé-Perthes Disease

Legg-Calvé-Perthes disease, or osteonecrosis of the proximal femoral epiphysis, is a condition seen in young children, especially in boys between ages 3 and 8 years. Legg-Calvé-Perthes disease must be considered in the differential diagnosis of any young athlete who has a painless limp and in whom physical examination reveals a decreased range of motion, particularly in internal rotation and abduction. The disease's relationship to either acute or repetitive trauma is unclear. Because an altered gait and growth disturbance are not uncommon in this disorder and because surgical intervention may be indicated, early identification and prompt referral to a pediatric orthopaedic surgeon are crucial.

Freiberg's disease and Panner's disease are two disorders that are believed to have a similar etiology to Legg-Calvé-Perthes. Freiberg's disease is described as a painful affliction of the second metatarsal head. This condition occurs in young adolescents and sometimes requires the use of protective footwear during the revascularization stage. Panner's disease is osteonecrosis of the capitellum and also occurs in young teenagers. It is usually self-limited and heals rapidly.

Osteochondritis Dissecans

Osteochondritis dissecans (OCD) is another form of osteochondrosis. OCD is a localized area of osteonecrosis that results in separation of a fragment of subchondral bone, with or without injury to the overlying cartilage. A relationship to acute trauma is suspected but cannot be definitely identified in all cases. The child with OCD in the knee reports pain, possibly intermittent locking, and swelling associated with localized tenderness. The lateral aspect of the medial femoral condyle is the most common site of OCD in the knee. Unlike in adults, spontaneous healing and resolution of symptoms usually occur within a year or so in children younger than age 15 years. Osteochondritis dissecans is also seen in the ankle and, less commonly, in the hip.

THE FEMALE PEDIATRIC ATHLETE

Women's participation in competitive sport has become the norm rather than the exception, as evidenced by the 30% increase in female participation in the Olympic games from 1992 to 1996. Although many of the problems facing female athletes also affect their male counterparts, some occur exclusively or more commonly in women. Given this distinction as well as women's increasing presence in sport, those responsible for the care and training of athletes must be prepared to identify and care for the special needs of female athletes.

Although the health care of female athletes comprises a number of issues and concerns, medical issues pertinent to the growing female athlete such as musculoskeletal development, anatomy, and nutrition deserve specific discussion. Comparative variation between young male and female athletes within these areas may be responsible in part for injury patterns in female athletes. Therefore, early identification of injuries and intervention may help in preventing many of the injuries seen more frequently in female athletes.

Prior to puberty, both muscle strength and muscle mass are essentially equal in young boys and girls; however, by age 16 years, adolescent girls have approximately 75% of the strength of their male counterparts. This may be because women have approximately 70% of the total cross-sectional area of muscle as men, assuming muscle strength differences are a function of muscle size.

Inherent differences in anatomy are believed to contribute to the greater rate of injury in growing female athletes than in male athletes.[8] In general, a wider pelvis develops in adolescent girls during puberty. Increased femoral anteversion, genu valgum, and a poorly developed vastus medialis muscle may all contribute to a lateral tracking patella and subsequent patellofemoral pain syndrome. Differences in the anatomy of the knee have also been implicated in the etiology of ACL injuries. ACL injuries can occur up to four times as often in women as in men. A narrower intercondylar notch,

The Female Pediatric Athlete

The growing female athlete deserves special consideration in the areas of musculoskeletal development, anatomy, and nutrition. Before puberty, boys and girls have equal muscle strength and mass, but by age 16 years, girls have 75% of the strength boys have. Girls develop a wider pelvis during puberty, which may contribute to the development of patellofemoral pain syndrome. Anterior cruciate ligament injuries are four times as frequent in women as in men. Lumbar spine hyperlordosis contributes to spondylolysis and spondylolisthesis.

The female athlete triad is the complex relationship among disordered eating, amenorrhea, and premature osteoporosis. Disordered eating can result in delayed or absent menses, slowed growth, disturbed reproductive function, psychological problems, and gastrointestinal difficulty. Amenorrhea can be associated with failure to reach peak bone mass, poor bone mineralization, and premature bone loss.

greater joint laxity, and altered limb alignment are believed to contribute to this increased incidence. Lastly, hyperlordosis in the lumbar spine contributes to spondylolysis and spondylolisthesis. Repetitive bending stresses of the pars interarticularis, such as in diving, gymnastics, and dance, can lead to stress fracture and may eventually progress to spondylolisthesis.

Nutritional disorders represent the major health risk to female athletes, both young and old.[8] Societal influences and external pressures equating thinness with success are not only prevalent in the media today but also present in the sporting arena. Sports such as gymnastics, skating, and dance emphasize the importance of both leanness and appearance; however, nutritional disorders occur

throughout the spectrum of sports. The "female athlete triad" is a term used to describe the presence and complex interplay between three common disorders, disordered eating, amenorrhea, and premature osteoporosis, that represent a major health risk of female athletes today. The health consequences of disordered eating include delayed or absent menses, decreased growth, disturbance of reproductive function, psychological problems, or gastrointestinal difficulty. Amenorrhea in itself may have profound effects on the musculoskeletal system, specifically with respect to bone. Failure to reach peak bone mass, poor mineralization, and premature bone loss can place the amenorrheic athlete at risk for stress fractures. Medical management of the female athlete triad requires a multidisciplinary approach to obtain an early diagnosis and initiate therapy.

CONGENITAL AND DEVELOPMENTAL DISORDERS

Congenital and developmental disorders include a wide array of conditions that are thoroughly addressed in any textbook of pediatric orthopaedics. If a young athlete has a deformity or refuses to participate because of pain, the presence of some underlying disorder should always be considered in the differential diagnosis. Three important conditions of congenital and developmental disorders are discoid meniscus, slipped capital femoral epiphysis, and tarsal coalition.

Discoid Meniscus

A discoid meniscus is a congenital abnormality in which the meniscus is discoid in shape instead of the usual semilunar shape. This abnormality more commonly occurs on the lateral side of the knee. It should be considered in the differential diagnosis of a clicking sensation in the lateral knee with or without associated lateral knee pain. Pain aggravated by activity should suggest this condition in the athletic child. The diagnosis may be confirmed by arthrography, MRI scan, or arthroscopy. A symptomatic discoid meniscus may be converted into a semilunar shape by arthroscopy; however, a discoid meniscus is inherently different from a normal meniscus, and creating a semilunar shape may not convert this fibrocartilage into a normally functioning meniscus.

Slipped Capital Femoral Epiphysis

Slipped capital femoral epiphysis (SCFE) is a common hip disorder that occurs during adolescence. As a result of a growth disturbance in the proximal femoral growth plate, the femoral epiphysis is displaced on the femoral neck through the growth plate. Athletes with SCFE usually have a painful limp. Groin pain is frequently reported, but referred pain to the anterior thigh or knee is also common. Therefore, a slipped capital femoral epiphysis must be considered in the differential diagnosis of any preadolescent or early adolescent athlete who complains of hip or knee pain.

Clinical examination will reveal pain on hip motion and limitation of abduction and external rotation. As the thigh of the affected limb is flexed, the hip will roll into external rotation and abduction. The diagnosis is confirmed on anteroposterior and lateral radiographs of the hip. Proper treatment requires surgery.

Tarsal Coalition

Tarsal coalition is a congenital synostosis, or failure of segmentation, between two or more tarsal bones. This condition is also referred to as peroneal spastic flatfoot. Most affected athletes report a painful foot, usually occurring after activity or injury and resulting in an inability to participate. Symptoms of tarsal coalition are not usually manifested until the early teenage years.

Examination of the foot reveals pes planus (flatfoot) and limited or absent subtalar motion. There may be associated spasticity in the peroneal or anterior tibial muscles. The diagnosis can sometimes be confirmed on an oblique radiograph of the foot, but more often plain tomography or computed tomography scanning is necessary. Treatments, either surgical or nonsurgical, vary with the location and nature of the coalition as well as the athlete's symptoms.

FOCUS ON . . .

Congenital and Developmental Disorders

Congenital and developmental disorders include a wide array of conditions. Among the congenital and developmental disorders that affect young athletes are discoid meniscus, slipped capital femoral epiphysis, and tarsal coalition.

Discoid meniscus

A discoid meniscus lacks the normal semilunar shape. Arthrography, magnetic resonance imaging, or arthroscopy confirm the diagnosis. The discoid shape can be converted arthroscopically to a semilunar shape, the meniscus still may not function normally.

Slipped capital femoral epiphysis

Slipped capital femoral epiphysis results from a growth disturbance of the proximal femoral physis such that the femoral epiphysis displaces on the femoral neck. On physical examination, hip motion is painful, and abduction and external rotation are limited. As the thigh of the affected limb is flexed, the hip rolls into abduction and external rotation. Radiographs confirm the diagnosis, and the treatment is surgical.

Tarsal Coalition

Tarsal coalition is a congenital synostosis between two or more tarsal bones. The primary symptom is a painful foot. Examination reveals pes planus, limited or absent subtalar motion, and perhaps peroneal or anterior tibial muscle spasticity. Plain or computed tomography is often necessary to confirm the diagnosis. Treatment depends on the location and nature of the coalition and the athlete's symptoms.

CHAPTER REVIEW

With the growth of organized sports and the increasing demands being placed on the immature skeleton, the training of the pediatric athlete assumes greater importance. "Free play" and participation in a variety of activities have been replaced by specializing in one sport over time. Therefore, parents, coaches, athletic trainers, and other healthcare professionals who are responsible for the physical and emotional well-being of the young athlete must understand the musculoskeletal characteristics and common injuries of this age group.

Although pediatric athletes share many of the same risk factors that adult athletes confront, the child is also subject to unique injuries and injury patterns because of the presence of growth cartilage at the physis and the apophysis. The child's ligaments and tendons insert into the metaphysis rather than directly into osseous tissue. Here, tissue elasticity is more uniformly gradated, and the soft tissue–bone interface is protected from injury. Thus, traumatic lesions tend to be intraosseous. Radiographs and magnetic resonance imaging should be performed on children with joint instability.

Physeal injuries are common and can result in physeal arrest, which can affect future bone growth. However, pediatric bone heals quickly and can remodel after a fracture. Other potential contributors to youth injuries are the increased musculotendinous unit tightness and loss of flexibility during times of rapid growth. The most important step in making the correct diagnosis when treating injured young athletes is taking a thorough history and performing a physical examination.

Osseous injuries are more common than ligament or muscle injuries in young athletes, and most osseous injuries result from single, acute traumatic events. Radiographic evaluation is usually indicated. Treatment of fractures and dislocations in children is generally the same as in adults; however, certain fractures that require surgical fixation in adults can be immobilized in a cast for children. Fractures unique to the growing child include plastic deformation, greenstick, physeal, and avulsion types.

Because of repetitive activities, young athletes can sustain the same overuse injuries adults do, in addition to overuse injuries of the apophysis, physis, and joint surface. Overuse injuries specific to children include Little League shoulder, Little League elbow, Osgood-Schlatter's disease, Sinding-Larsen-Johansson disease, Sever's disease, spondylolysis, and chronic compartment syndrome. Patellofemoral and glenohumeral joint instability are common in young athletes and can usually be treated conservatively. Juvenile osteochondroses, or osteochondritises, such as Legg-Calvé-Perthes disease and osteochondritis dissecans, may be responsible for local pain in young athletes and should always be a consideration.

Female athletes have a higher incidence of patellofemoral pain syndrome, anterior cruciate ligament injuries, and pars interarticularis stress fracture than male athletes do. The female athlete triad describes disordered eating, amenorrhea, and premature osteoporosis, which present a major risk to female athletes. Congenital and developmental disorders such as discoid meniscus, slipped capital femoral epiphysis, and tarsal coalition can also cause pain and inability to participate in sport and should be considered in the differential diagnosis.

1. Which of the following structures is known as the cartilaginous structure in a child near the end of a long bone that is subjected primarily to tensile forces?

   A. Physis

   B. Epiphysis

   C. Apophysis

   D. Metaphysis

2. When comparing adult bone with pediatric bone, which of the following statements is true?

   A. Pediatric bones heal more slowly.

   B. Pediatric bones have thinner periosteums.

   C. Pediatric bones have more capacity for remodeling.

   D. Pediatric bones have a relatively poor blood supply.

3. Which of the following steps is singly the most important in treating a young athlete with an injury?

   A. Make the correct diagnosis.

   B. Focus only on the current injury.

   C. Return the athlete to play quickly.

   D. Take the history only from the patient.

4. Which of the following injuries are common in pediatric and adolescent athletes?

   A. Tendinitis

   B. Muscle strains

   C. Ligament sprains

   D. Growth plate fractures

5. Which of the following is an overuse injury that affects the secondary ossification center of the tibial tubercle and is frequently associated with jumping sports?

   A. Spondylolysis

   B. Osgood-Schlatter's disease

   C. Chronic compartment syndrome

   D. Sinding-Larsen-Johansson disease

6. Which of the following statements about patellofemoral joint instability is true?

   A. Lateral retinacular looseness may be a contributing factor.

   B. Strengthening the static restraints is one aspect of treatment.

   C. Peripatellar or retropatellar pain is common after hill running.

   D. Excessive medial pressure syndrome is another name for the condition.

7. Which of the following conditions is characterized by localized osteonecrosis resulting in separation of a fragment of subchondral bone and causing symptoms of pain, intermittent locking, and swelling?

   A. Little league elbow

   B. Calcaneal apophysitis

   C. Osteochondritis dissecans

   D. Legg-Calvé-Perthes disease

8. In comparison with a male adult, a female adult has which of the following?

   A. Genu varus

   B. A wider pelvis

   C. Decreased femoral anteversion

   D. Better-developed vastus medialis muscles

9. Which of the following effects can result from disordered eating?

   A. Frequent menses

   B. Increased growth

   C. Improved mental health

   D. Gastrointestinal difficulty

10. Which of the following disorders is characterized by a painful limp, groin pain, and pain referred to the anterior thigh or knee?

    A. Tarsal coalition

    B. Freiberg disease

    C. Discoid meniscus

    D. Slipped capital femoral epiphysis

Answers on page 894.

References

1. Outerbridge AR and Michel LJ: Overuse injuries in the young athlete. *Clin Sports Med* 1995;14.

2. Cook DC, Leit ME: Issues in the pediatric athlete. *Orthop Clin North Am* 1995;26:453-464.

3. Best TM: Muscle-tendon injuries in young athletes. *Clin Sports Med* 1995;14:669-685.

4. Martia RS, Johnson DL: Stress fractures, clinical history, and physical examination. *Clin Sports Med* 1997;16:259-275.

5. Gill TJ, Michel LJ: The immature athlete: Common injuries and overuse syndromes of elbow and wrist. *Clin Sports Med* 1996;15:401-423.

6. Stress injuries to the spine in young athletes. *Semin Spine Surg* 1998;10:81-87.

7. Micheli LJ, Solomon R, Solomon J, Plasschaett VF, Mitchell R: Surgical treatment for chronic lower-leg compartment syndrome in young female athletes. *Am J Sports Med* 1999;27:197-201.

8. VanDeloo DA, Johnson MD: The young female athlete. *Clin Sports Med* 1995;14:687-707.

30

Athletes with Different Abilities

Michael S. Ferrara, PhD, ATC
Gregory R. Palutsis, MD

QUICK CONTENTS

- How sports participation has grown among athletes with disabilities, increasing the demand for sporting and recreational programs to serve this population.

- Special considerations that must be addressed when establishing sporting and recreational events for athletes with disabilities.

- Injury prevention programs based on the medical problems that are often seen in athletes with disabilities.

- The basic classification system for athletes with disabilities.

OVERVIEW

Athletes with disabilities have participated in sporting activities on an individual basis for years, but not until recently did formal competition among these athletes come into being. As sports participation has increased among this group, so, too, has the need for programs to serve these athletes.

This chapter begins with a brief account of the growth in sports participation by individuals with disabilities, followed by the criteria needed to set up a successful program for these athletes. The chapter then discusses injury prevention for athletes with amputations, arthritis, cerebral palsy, seizure disorders, and spinal cord defects after injuries as well as athletes who use a wheelchair and Special Olympics athletes. The last section of this chapter presents basic information about the classification system for athletes with disabilities.

GROWTH OF SPORTS PARTICIPATION BY INDIVIDUALS WITH DISABILITIES

The approach of the medical community toward athletes with disabilities has changed throughout history. Initially ignored as an athletic population, medicine's involvement with disabilities took a very directed turn toward sport following World War II. The needs of wartime casualties prompted a British neurosurgeon, Sir Ludwig Guttman, who was the Director of the Stoke Mandeville Hospital in Aylesbury, England, to introduce competitive sport within the hospital's rehabilitative program. He developed a model that promoted active lifestyles for individuals with disabilities.

The sport movement within disabled populations now boasts a majority of nations that provide sport opportunities to individuals with disabilities. Within the United States, the United States Olympic Committee (USOC) has formed a division to coordinate disability sport. The disabled sport organizations (DSO) sponsor sporting events for athletes at levels ranging from recreational to elite competitors.[1] **Table 30-1** presents a list of the names and addresses of some of these organizations.

Participation in the Paralympic movement has increased tenfold since its inception in 1960. The *Paralympics* are equivalent to Olympic competition for athletes with physical and sensory disabilities (blind and visually impaired, spinal cord injured, amputee, and cerebral). These games are held in the same city as the Summer and Winter Olympic Games. Most recently, the 1996 Paralympic Games were held in Atlanta, Georgia, where they attracted 3,500 athletes from more than 125 nations who competed in 19 medal sports. Fourteen of the sports, some of which include track and field, swimming, volleyball, and soccer, have an Olympic equivalent with few modifications in the rules. Five sports are specific to the disability: goalball, rugby, bocce, lawn bowls, and sit volleyball. At the 1996 Paralympic Games, more than 350 allied healthcare volunteers from 43 states provided medical services to the athlete.

Injuries are to be expected in a sport environment. The pattern of injuries for athletes with disabilities is the same as the pattern for athletes without disabilities. Injuries are typically minor, typically musculoskeletal in nature, and usually involve the major joints of the body.[2-4] The Athletes with Disabilities Injury Registry found that over a 3-year period, the injury rate was 9.45 per 1,000 athlete exposures.[2] Overall, 52% of the reported injuries were minor (0 to 7 days of time-loss), 29% were moderate (8 to 21 days of time-loss), and 19% were major (22 or more days of time-loss). Some injuries are disability-specific and must be addressed appropriately.[5-8] These injuries include shoulder pain in the spinal cord-injured athlete and nerve involvement in wheelchair users.

Sports medicine team members have an excellent opportunity to set up and develop sporting and recreational programs for physically impaired individuals. Many physicians, athletic trainers, and physical therapists

FOCUS ON . . .

Growth of Sports Participation by Individuals With Disabilities

Individuals with disabilities were not considered potential athletes until after World War II. Now most nations offer sport opportunities to individuals with disabilities, and disabled sport organizations sponsor events for competitors. Participation in the Paralympic Games has increased tenfold since they were established in 1960. Fourteen sports have an Olympic equivalent with few rules modifications while five sports are specific to disability sport. Studies have shown that most injuries in athletes are similar to those in athletes without disabilities and are minor and musculoskeletal, usually involving the major joints.

TABLE 30-1
SPORT ORGANIZATIONS FOR ATHLETES WITH DISABILITIES

USA Deaf Sports Federation (USADSF) (formerly the American Athletic Association for the Deaf (AAAD)
3607 Washington Boulevard, Suite 4
Odgen, UT 84404-1737
TEL/TTY: (801) 393-7916

Disabled Sports USA (DSUSA)
451 Hungerford Drive, Suite 100
Rockville, MD 20850
(301) 217-9838

Dwarf Athletic Association of America (DAAA)
418 Willow Way
Lewisville, TX 75077
(972) 317-8299

National Wheelchair Basketball Association (NWBA)
307 Double Springs Road
Murfreesboro, TN 37127
(615) 896-9205

Special Olympics International (SOI)
1325 G Street NW, Suite 500
Washington, DC 20005
(202) 628-3630

United States Association of Blind Athletes (USABA)
33 North Institute Street
Colorado Springs, CO 80903
(719) 630-0422

United States Cerebral Palsy Athletic Association (USCPAA)
25 West Independence Way
Kingston, RI 02881
(401) 874-7465

United States Les Autre Sport Association (USLASA)
1475 West Gray, Suite 166
Houston, TX 77019
(713) 521-3737

Wheelchair Sports USA (WSUSA)
3595 East Fountain Boulevard, Suite L1
Colorado Springs, CO 80910
(719) 574-1150

have worked with these potential participants as patients in the hospital or clinical setting. Established relationships and the medical professionals' special knowledge contribute to the success of such programs.

DEVELOPING A SPORTING/RECREATIONAL PROGRAM

Developing a safe and enjoyable sporting or recreational program for the athlete with a disability requires that several steps be taken, including proper diagnosis of the disability, identification of areas of particular concern, identification of special considerations in children, realistic goal setting, determination of the athlete's proper physical conditioning, and special instructor training.

Diagnosing the Disability

To accurately determine the athlete's physical limitations and abilities, the medical professional must assess the following factors:

- range of motion and flexibility of the extremities and trunk
- strength
- balance and equilibrium skills
- postural discrepancies
- associated reactions produced by increased activity (this factor is of particular importance in patients with central nervous system involvement)
- sensory discrimination and circulation problems
- rhythmic and coordination skills
- leg length and other discrepancies of bone growth or size
- visual or auditory accuracy
- orthopaedic or other special appliances worn by the athlete

Once limitations and abilites have been established through an accurate assessment of these factors, realistic goals can be set for each individual athlete. In addition, the assessment will help to determine guidelines for exercise prescription and sport adaptation.

Identifying Areas of Particular Concern

The initial assessment should include identification of any areas of concern or contraindications to participation in a particular sport. **Table 30-2** lists particular areas of concern.

Identifying Special Considerations in Children

Adults are capable of understanding the risks involved in an activity and can usually make a judgment regarding the

TABLE 30-2
CONTRAINDICATIONS TO PARTICIPATION IN SOME SPORTS

- Seizure activity, especially if the athlete's seizures are not totally controlled by medication

- Osteoporosis

- Cardiac and respiratory conditions

- Unstable orthopaedic conditions, such as dislocated hips, instability of major weightbearing joints, severe scoliosis, congenital narrowing of the spine (spinal stenosis), and C1-C2 instability

- Recent trauma or surgery

- Bleeding diathesis

appropriateness of the activity for themselves. Children, on the other hand, often do not realize the full implications of their condition.[9] Proper guidance from medical personnel is both valuable and necessary. A special problem with children is the effect of their medical condition on growth and development. Even medical conditions that are usually stable in adults require periodic reassessment of the disability in children who participate in sports.

Establishing Realistic Goals

Realistic goals that are attainable within a reasonable length of time must be established. The primary goal should be achievable, but challenging. Consideration should be given to access of physical equipment, facilities, transportation, and the involvement and support of others. Additional goals can be established as the program develops. The individual with a disability can gain the same physical and emotional advantages of activity as would be expected for someone without a disability. The overall goal of sports activity should be to maintain a healthy and active lifestyle.

Ensuring Proper Conditioning

Proper conditioning is essential for all athletes regardless of their disability. Good strength, flexibility, and cardiovascular exercises should be emphasized for proper conditioning and strength to help reduce the possibility of injury. Balance and coordination activities may be necessary aspects of a conditioning program to improve these functions. The proper conditioning program can be easily established using assessment data.

Selecting Program Instructors

Instructors who work with individuals with disabilities should know about different disability conditions and indications and contraindications to exercise. Through proper training, instructors can provide a positive and safe experience for individuals with disabilities. The creativity of the instructor is highly important; the ability to improvise and adapt equipment for an individual, either as an aid or for safety, is essential.

INJURY PREVENTION FOR SPECIFIC PHYSICAL PROBLEMS

Injury prevention is as important for the athlete with a disability as it is for other athletes. For those who establish injury prevention programs, having an awareness of specific physical problems permits the targeting of conditions and special precautionary measures that diminish the risk of injury for participants.

When traveling to competition venues, the athlete with disabilities must make sure to carry medicines and personal care items. If packed and transported separately, the supplies may not be available when needed. Such equipment may include latex gloves, urinary catheters, wound dressings, and medications.

The specific physical problems addressed here are those encountered by athletes with amputations, athletes with arthritis, athletes with cerebral palsy, athletes who are seizure-prone, athletes with spinal cord defects and injuries, athletes who are blind or visually impaired, athletes who are of short stature, and athletes who use a wheelchair.

Athletes With Amputations

Conditioning programs for the athlete with an amputation are similar to conventional conditioning programs. The athlete usually is intimately familiar with his or her prosthetic device, which was most likely designed specifically for his or her sport. Specific issues for these athletes usually center on the stump/prosthesis interface. Swelling of the stump, abrasions, and blistering are the most common problems the athlete with an amputation encounters. Prevention of these problems through good daily skin care routines is imperative. The availability of an on-site prosthetic service is an important aspect of planning an athletic event for amputees.

Special sport prostheses have been developed for amputees to allow them to be more competitive than is possible with standard artificial limbs. However, in some sports such as Alpine skiing, prostheses may not be used at all. In skiing, an athlete who has only one leg must use adapted ski poles and should concentrate on balance and coordination skills in the conditioning program.

Athletes With Arthritis

Most individuals with arthritis who participate in an athletic program have osteoarthritis, a degenerative joint disease that should not be confused with the more crippling types of arthritis such as rheumatoid arthritis. Because their joints are often irregular and mechanically unsound, individuals with arthritis must be taught to warm up very slowly and increase their activity level gradually within the confines of comfort. As range of motion of specific joints is often compromised, special attention must be paid to maintaining the present range of motion and, if possible, gradually and gently increasing the range of motion to a more normal level. Water sports and activities are often excellent for individuals with arthritis. Because the water supports some of the weight, the athlete with arthritis is

FOCUS ON . . .

Developing a Sporting/Recreational Program

Developing a safe and enjoyable sporting or recreational program for the athlete with a disability requires proper diagnosis of the disability, identification of areas of particular concern and special considerations in children, realistic goal setting, physical conditioning, and special instructor training.

Diagnosing the disability

To accurately determine the athlete's limitations and abilities, the medical professional should perform a high-level examination. This assessment is valuable in establishing realistic goals and guidelines for exercise prescription and sport adaptation for the individual.

Identifying areas of particular concern

During the initial assessment, particular areas of concern must be identified, including seizure activity, osteoporosis, cardiac and respiratory conditions, unstable orthopaedic conditions, recent trauma or surgery, and bleeding diatheses.

Identifying special considerations in children

Because children are not always able to understand the risks involved in an activity and the appropriateness of the activity for themselves, they need guidance from medical personnel and parents. Also, many conditions that are stable in adults are affected by the child's growth and development and require periodic assessment during participation.

Establishing realistic goals

Goals that are realistic, challenging, and attainable must be established; new goals can be set as the program develops. Access to physical equipment, facilities, transportation, and the involvement and support of others also require consideration. The individual with a disability receives the same physical and emotional advantages of activity as expected for an individual without a disability and has the same goal: to maintain a healthy and active lifestyle.

Ensuring proper conditioning

Proper conditioning, including strength, flexibility, and cardiovascular endurance, is essential for all athletes, regardless of disability. Balance and coordination are also important.

Selecting program instructors

Program instructors for athletes with disabilities should be knowledgeable about the condition and indications and contraindications to exercise. The instructor's creativity may be the key to successfully improvising and adapting equipment for individuals with disabilities.

FOCUS ON . . .

Injury Prevention for Specific Physical Problems

Injury prevention is also important to all athletes and must be targeted to the individual's specific condition. An athlete with a disability who travels to competition venues should always carry necessary medications and personal care equipment.

Athletes with amputations

Athletes with amputations may have difficulty with the stump-prosthesis interface, resulting in swelling, abrasions, and blistering. Good daily skin care can help to prevent these problems, but on-site prosthetic service is important when planning an event for these athletes. Special sport prostheses allow the athlete to be highly competitive; however, prostheses may not be used at all in some sports.

Athletes with arthritis

Athletes with arthritis must warm up slowly and increase activity levels gradually as comfort permits. Limited joint range of motion should be maintained, and if possible, increased slowly and gently. Water activities are often excellent for athletes with arthritis because the water supports some of their weight. Controlling weight is important for the preservation of joint structures and allows the athlete to remain active.

Athletes with cerebral palsy

Athletes with cerebral palsy may have musculoskeletal, speech, hearing, and eye problems and seizures. The athlete's ability to sit, stand, and walk should be evaluated, along with active and passive range of motion. Many individuals with cerebral palsy have a spastic component, but those with athetoid cerebral palsy have continuous slow and arrhythmic motions. Some athletes with severe speech difficulties may use speech synthesizers or word boards to communicate. Medical professionals working with athletes who have cerebral palsy need specialized training and a close relationship with the athlete's primary and orthopaedic physicians.

Athletes who have seizures

Athletes who have seizures may find their awareness and reflex responses diminished by their medication. If the athlete has a seizure, he or she must be protected from harm and embarrassment. The athlete must be allowed to rest before attempting to resume activity, and physician clearance must be obtained before return to sport. To minimize the possibility of seizures, the athlete must comply with the medication program prescribed by the primary physician.

(Continued)

able to work on range of motion and even strengthening without the ill effects of full weightbearing. Weight control is particularly important for these athletes because low body weight decreases stress on joint structures, preserving them and allowing the athlete to be more active.

Athletes With Cerebral Palsy

Cerebral palsy is a disorder of movement and posture caused by an irreparable lesion of the central nervous system. Individuals with cerebral palsy may have musculoskeletal and other abnormalities, speech and hearing difficulties, visual problems, and seizures. Musculoskeletal evaluations should include the individual's ability to sit, stand (with or without assistance), and walk (with or without assistance or equipment). Multiple musculoskeletal abnormalities may or may not be present. Associated abnormalities can include scoliosis, kyphosis, lordosis, or combinations; deformity of bones; and subluxation or even dislocation typically seen in the hip and shoulder.

Active and passive range of motion of the individual with cerebral palsy should be evaluated. In an athlete with spasticity, there may be an exaggerated stretch reflex in which the muscle actually contracts with great force, displaying an apparent lack of motion. There are many types of cerebral palsy. Many individuals with cerebral palsy have a spastic component; however, some athletes may have athetoid cerebral palsy, which is indicated by continuous slow and arrhythmic motions.

Some athletes with cerebral palsy have speech difficulties; therefore, medical professionals must take the time to listen carefully to the athlete. An athlete with cerebral palsy who has a speech impairment may use a speech synthesizer or word board to communicate.

The sports medicine team member who is planning to work closely with athletes with cerebral palsy must seek further training in this area and maintain close contact with these individuals' primary care and orthopaedic physicians.

Athletes Who Have Seizures

Medication taken by athletes who have seizures may reduce their awareness and reflex responses. If the athlete

Injury Prevention for Specific Physical Problems (Continued)

Athletes with spinal cord injuries

Spinal cord injury usually results from trauma, but can also be caused by congenital spinal cord defects. Many athletes with spinal deformities require support for sitting, and bowel and bladder care is important. Common injuries for wheelchair athletes are rotator cuff tendinitis, bursitis, and blisters and lacerations on the hands and arms, and carpal tunnel syndrome. Prevention and care of pressure sores are essential. Another potential problem is the lack of thermoregulatory control and the inability of these athletes to tolerate temperature extremes. Autonomic dysreflexia is a serious concern for athletes with a spinal cord injury above level T8, which results in loss of sympathetic control to the lower body.

Athletes in wheelchairs

Wheelchairs have been improved in maneuverability to allow the athlete more effective participation in sports. Blisters and lacerations of the hands and arms, shoulder tendinitis or bursitis, and carpal tunnel syndrome are the most frequent injuries to athletes in wheelchairs.

Athletes who are visually impaired or blind

Disabilities of athletes who are visually impaired or blind range from not seeing well enough to drive a car to being totally insensitive to light and dark. The less visually impaired athlete may see well enough to train independently, while the most severely disabled athlete requires assistance with training and competition. Athletes who are visually impaired or blind have few disability-specific medical problems; however, those who have visual impairment associated with albinism require protection from sunburn.

Athletes who are of short stature

Athletes who are of short stature or have achondroplasia usually have restricted range of motion of the major joints and spine. Preparticipation warm-up and stretching are important. Short spinal pedicles may decrease spinal cord diameter and predispose the individual to congenital spinal stenosis, which puts pressure on the spinal cord that can lead to sciatica or other compressive cord lesions.

---

has a seizure, he or she must be protected from harm and embarrassment. Following the seizure, the athlete should rest before attempting to resume activity and should not be allowed to participate in sports without clearance from a physician. The medical team should be aware of the athlete's compliance with the medication regimen and other factors that could induce a seizure, such as changes in sleep pattern, stress, and changes in diet. To address any potential changes in medication or dosage, the athlete should discuss plans for participation in sport activities with the primary physician.

Athletes With Spinal Cord Injuries

Quadriplegic injuries involve both lower extremities with varying degrees of involvement to the upper extremities. Paraplegia does not involve the upper extremities but involves the lower extremities to varying degrees. Spinal cord injury usually results from trauma, but it also may be caused by incomplete spinal cord formation, such as with spina bifida. The level of spinal cord injury determines the degree of function. Many athletes with spinal injuries also

have spinal deformities because of trunk muscle paralysis, and they may require supports to aid their balance while sitting. Bowel and bladder care is always a consideration.

Athletes with spinal cord injuries, because they are usually competing in wheelchairs, suffer the common overuse syndromes of rotator cuff tendinitis and bursitis, as well as blisters and lacerations on the hands and arms. Carpal tunnel syndrome may also be a problem because of repeated impacts of the athlete's palm on the wheel of the wheelchair.

Because spinal cord injuries result in loss of protective skin sensation below the level of injury, great care must be taken in preventing or treating pressure sores. Pressure sores usually occur over bony prominences, such as the greater trochanter, ischial spines, and medial and lateral malleoli, or where clothing or equipment applies prolonged pressure to the skin.

Another potentially serious problem for the athlete with a spinal cord injury is thermoregulatory control. Because the internal thermostat operates less efficiently in an individual with spinal cord injury, these athletes cannot tolerate extremes of temperature, particularly excess heat. For such athletes, evaporative skin cooling through the use of mist bottles and the like may be necessary. Protection from direct sunlight must be provided for athletes at competition sites.

Spinal cord injuries above the level of T8 result in loss of sympathetic control to the lower body. The most serious health concern for the athlete with a spinal cord injury above level T8 may be *autonomic dysreflexia*. The symptoms of autonomic dysreflexia include dizziness, sweating, headaches, and potentially severe hypertension. A plugged urethral catheter is the most common trigger for autonomic dysreflexia.[10] Simply draining the bladder may prevent autonomic dysreflexia from occurring. Other causes of autonomic dysreflexia include fecal impaction, renal calculi or infection, pressure sores, or other noxious stimuli.

Athletes in Wheelchairs

The rapid growth of wheelchair athletics has promoted improvement in the design of competition chairs. In accordance with Wheelchair Sports USA (WSUSA), these chairs must have no gears, levers, or chains to limit speed. Improvements have also been made in maneuverability. The injuries most frequently sustained by wheelchair athletes are blisters and lacerations of the hands and arms, tendinitis or bursitis at the shoulders and, not surprisingly, carpal tunnel syndrome because of constant impact of the heel of the hand on the racing wheel.[2,3,5] Wheelchair racers should protect their hands with specially designed gloves.

Athletes Who Are Blind or Visually Impaired

Athletes who are blind or visually impaired have varying degrees of ability to see. In general, the limits of legal blindness range at a minimum from not being able to see well enough to drive a car to total light/dark insensitivity. Depending on their sightedness, athletes who are blind or visually impaired have varying degrees of independent functioning. The less impaired athlete is able to see well enough to train on his or her own, whereas the severely blind athlete will require assistance with training and competition. Assistance ranges from guide runners for track events to soft sticks used in the swimming pool to let the athletes know when to begin their turn.

Disability-specific medical problems are few and usually relate to medications.[3] However, there are visual impairments associated with albinism, which is a lack of skin pigment. For these athletes, protection from sunburn is critical.

Athletes Who Are of Short Stature

Athletes who are of short stature or dwarf are involved in many sports, particularly swimming and weight lifting. One of the hallmark findings in this population is restricted range of motion of major joints and the spine. Preparticipation warm-up and stretching are important for these individuals.

The individual vertebrae of the athlete's spine may also contain short pedicles that together decrease the diameter of the spinal canal and thus predispose the athlete to *congenital spinal stenosis*. This syndrome produces pressure on the spinal cord that may lead to sciatica or other compressive cord lesions.

ATHLETES WHO PARTICIPATE IN THE SPECIAL OLYMPICS

Athletes With Congenital Heart Defects

Although *Down syndrome* is not the only cause of mental retardation, it is probably the most widespread and easily recognized form.[11] Approximately 50% of individuals with Down syndrome have a congenital heart defect.[12] The more common congenital findings are tetralogy of Fallot, atrioventricularis communis, and septal defects. Individuals with tetralogy of Fallot are generally impaired in their physical capacity. Cardiac abnormalities should be evaluated on an individual basis.

Athletes With General Orthopaedic Problems

Orthopaedic problems in athletes with disabilities are commonly related to poor muscle tone and general joint laxity. *Atlantoaxial subluxation (AAS)* is an orthopaedic problem seen frequently in athletes with Down syndrome.[13,14] AAS poses a significant risk to athletes participating in Special Olympic events that involve bodily contact. In AAS, the C1 vertebra (atlas) slips forward onto C2 (axis) as a result of joint looseness, ligamentous laxity, or malformation of the vertebrae or surrounding structures. In this situation, the spinal cord can be compressed, particularly when the neck is in flexion or extension. The risk of AAS increases in the athlete with Down syndrome who also has juvenile rheumatoid arthritis. These individuals are often unable to provide a thorough history, and for them, AAS often occurs without a prior history of trauma.[12] Clinical findings may be difficult to assess, and neck pain is not necessarily a consistent finding. In addition, congenital motor abnormalities may mask neurologic dysfunction. Because of the risk for AAS and its association with Special Olympics population, flexion/extension radiographs are mandatory for all developmentally disabled athletes who are planning to participate in any sport potentially involving collision.

Other orthopaedic problems common to Special Olympics athletes include subluxating and dislocating patellae, pes planus, hallux valgus, metatarsus primus varus, and thoracolumbar scoliosis.[15]

CLASSIFICATION FOR ATHLETIC COMPETITION

Classification is a means of providing fair and equitable competition among athletes with similar disabilities. Classification of sports for individuals with no disabilities is performed by gender, weight, age, and performance level. Classification for individuals with disabilities should allow an equitable starting point for athletic competition. A team of professionals composed of a physician, physical therapist, coaches, and athletes generally performs the classification. A physical evaluation is performed to assess the athlete's level of disability, followed by an evaluation of function directly related to the sport. For example, a swimmer would perform competitive strokes while the classification team evaluates the athlete's function. Based on this assessment, the athlete will be assigned to a competition class. Similar functional systems exist for most disability sports, including basketball, athletics, cycling, and table tennis.

CHAPTER REVIEW

The athletic participation of individuals with disabilities has increased substantially in the past several decades. Organized opportunities exist for athletes ranging from recreational to elite competitors, and the Paralympic Games attract athletes from all over the world. The injuries of athletes with disabilities are similar to those of athletes without disabilities.

When developing a safe and enjoyable sporting or recreational program for the athlete with a disability, the medical professional must assess the disabling condition, identify areas of particular concern, recognize special considerations in children, establish realistic goals, ensure proper conditioning, and select qualified program instructors. It is essential to develop injury prevention programs targeted to the participants to reduce their risk of injury. Athletes with amputations, and those with arthritis, cerebral palsy, seizures, spinal cord injuries, visual impairment or blindness, short stature or dwarfism, and Down syndrome may have specific physical problems that predispose them to certain injuries. Recognizing these predispositions and taking appropriate precautions will reduce the risk of injury and increase the athlete's enjoyment of the sport.

Athletes with disabilities are classified according to physical and functional abilities so that they can compete equitably; athletes without disabilities are classified by sex, weight, age, and performance level. Individuals both with and without disabilities are encouraged to participate in physical activities for the beneficial effects they can provide.

1. Which of the following athletic activities is specific to disability sport?

   A. Soccer
   B. Goalball
   C. Football
   D. Swimming

2. Which of the following statements about the injuries of athletes with disabilities is true?

   A. Injuries are entirely preventable.
   B. Injuries usually involve the minor joints of the body.
   C. Injuries are usually severe and result in substantial time loss from sport.
   D. Injuries are usually similar to the injuries of athletes without disabilities.

3. Realistic goals for athletes with disabilities should be:

   A. attainable and challenging.
   B. achievable over the long term.
   C. easy enough to permit ready achievement.
   D. out of reach enough to encourage continued attempts.

4. After an athlete has had a seizure, he or she should be:

   A. sent home.
   B. allowed to rest.
   C. transported to the hospital immediately.
   D. given antiseizure medication immediately.

5. Dizziness, sweating, headaches, and hypertension in an athlete with a spinal cord injury may be symptomatic of which of the following conditions?

   A. Tetralogy of Fallot
   B. Autonomic dysreflexia
   C. Atlantoaxial subluxation
   D. Impaired thermoregulation

6. Which of the following injuries is most common to wheelchair athletes?

   A. Hypothermia
   B. Subluxating patella
   C. Blisters of the hands and arms
   D. Tendinitis or bursitis of the ankle

7. Which of the following physical conditions is seen in approximately 50% of individuals with Down syndrome?

   A. Osteoporosis
   B. Heart defects
   C. Spinal stenosis
   D. Bleeding diatheses

8. The athlete with an amputation is likely to have which of the following problems?

   A. Spasticity
   B. Pressure sores
   C. Blistering of the stump
   D. Limited range of motion

9. Which of the following musculoskeletal abnormalities is associated with cerebral palsy?

   A. Scoliosis
   B. Spina bifida
   C. Quadriplegia
   D. Carpal tunnel syndrome

10. Which of the following is a common finding in an athlete of short stature or dwarf?

   A. Albinism
   B. Rheumatoid arthritis
   C. Atrioventricularis communis
   D Restricted joint range of motion

Answers on page 894.

References

1. DePauw K, Gavron S (eds): *Disability and Sport.* Champaign, IL, Human Kinetics, 1995.

2. Ferrara MS, Buckley WE: Athletes with disabilities injury registry. *Adapt Phys Activ Quar* 1996;13:50–60.

3. Ferrara MS, Buckley WE, McCann BC, Limbird TJ, Powell JP, Robl R: The injury experience of the competitive athlete with a disability: Prevention implications. *Med Sci Sports Exerc* 1992;24:184–188.

4. Ferrara MS, Davis R: Injuries to elite wheelchair athletes. *Paraplegia* 1990;28:335–341.

5. Curtis KA, Dillon DA: Survey of wheelchair athletic injuries: Common patterns and prevention. *Paraplegia* 1985;23:170–175.

6. Curtis K, McClanahan S, Hall KM, Dillon D, Brown KF: Health vocational and functional status in spinal cord injured athletes and nonathletes. *Arch Phys Med Rehab* 1986:67;862–865.

7. Magnus B, French R: Wanted: Athletic trainers for Special Olympic athletes. *Athletic Train* 1985;20:204–205.

8. Maxwell BM: The nursing role in the Special Olympic program. *J Sch Health* 1984;54:131–133.

9. Starek PJK: Athletic performance in children with cardiovascular problems. *Phys Sportsmed* 1982;10:78–89.

10. Burnham R, Wheeler G, Bhambhani Y, et al: Intentional induction of autonomic dysreflexia among quadriplegic athletes for performance enhancement: Efficacy, safety, and mechanism of action. *Clin J Sport Med* 1994;4:1–10.

11. Ferrara MS, Richter KJ, Kaschalk SM: Sports for athletes with a physical disability, in Scuderi GR, McCann PD, Bruno PJ (eds): *Sports Medicine: Principles of Primary Care.* St. Louis, MO, Mosby-Year Book, 1996.

12. McCormick D, Ivery FM Jr, Gold DM, Zimmerman DM, Gemma S, Owen MJ: The preparticipation sports examination in Special Olympics athletes. *Tex Med* 1988;84:39–43.

13. Cope R, Olson S: Abnormalities of the cervical spine in Down's syndrome: Diagnosis, risks, and review of the literature, with particular reference to the Special Olympics. *South Med J* 1987;80:33–36.

14. Diamond LS, Lynne D, Sigman B: Orthopedic disorders in patients with Down's syndrome. *Orthop Clin North Am* 1981;12:57–71.

15. Hudson PB: Preparticipation screening of Special Olympic athletes. *Phys Sports Med* 1988;16:97–104.

31

Senior Athletes

Walter L. Calmbach, MD

QUICK CONTENTS

- The normal physiologic changes of aging.

- The health benefits of regular physical activity for seniors, including conditioning, strength training, and injury prevention.

- Prescribing appropriate exercises for senior athletes.

- The special risks of physical activity for senior athletes.

- The preexercise assessment of the senior athlete.

- Conditioning and rehabilitation in senior athletes.

- Identifying and treating common orthopaedic problems of senior athletes.

- Recognizing common medical problems of senior athletes.

OVERVIEW

Regular physical activity offers senior athletes many health benefits beyond simple fitness. This chapter begins with a discussion of the physiologic changes that occur with aging, followed by a section on fitness, which includes endurance training and strength training. The intensity, duration, frequency, mode, and adherence to exercise are covered, as are the risks of exercise. The components of a preexercise assessment are described, and different types of conditioning and rehabilitation programs are discussed. The chapter ends with a discussion of common orthopaedic problems, including problems with the shoulder, knee, ankle, and foot, and common medical problems, including hypertension, diabetes, coronary artery disease, obesity, osteoporosis, and osteoarthritis.

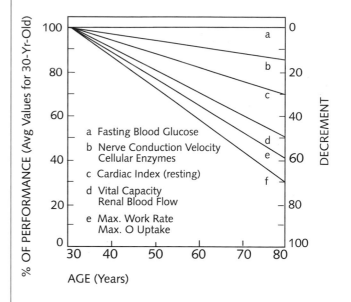

FIGURE 31-1

Physiologic functions decline with age, most notably metabolic, cardiovascular, and musculoskeletal functions. Decrements in physiologic functions in normal men ages 30 to 80 years are expressed in percent of average values for individuals age 30 years. (Reproduced with permission from Shock NW: Physiological and chronological age, in Dietz AA (ed): Aging: Its Chemistry. Washington, DC, American Association for Clinical Chemistry, 1980.)

PHYSIOLOGIC CHANGES WITH AGING

An active lifestyle results in decreased coronary and all-cause mortality and in a decreased rate of first myocardial infarction.[1,2] Physical activity elevates levels of *high-density lipoprotein (HDL) cholesterol* (the so-called "good" cholesterol), which may mediate its effects on mortality and cardiovascular disease.[3] Physical activity also alleviates depression and anxiety and promotes a sense of well-being.[4] The goals of a physical activity program for senior athletes should be to preserve function, maintain independent living, and enhance quality of life.[5]

Many physiologic functions decline with age (**Figure 31-1**). Functional changes most relevant to the senior athlete are metabolic, cardiovascular, and musculoskeletal, and many of these changes can be attenuated with a program of regular physical activity.

In general, older patients have a lower basal metabolic rate, presumably as a result of a decrease in lean body mass. This lower metabolic rate leads to obesity, glucose intolerance, and elevated *low-density lipoprotein (LDL) cholesterol* (the so-called "bad" cholesterol). However, regular physical activity can decrease body fat, increase fat-free mass, and elevate the basal metabolic rate. At the same time, physical activity can improve lipid metabolism, lowering LDL cholesterol and elevating HDL cholesterol.

The cardiovascular changes that occur with aging are pronounced. The athlete's maximal capacity to use oxygen during exertion (VO_{2max}) declines with age, usually approximately 9% per decade among sedentary men.[6,7,8]

This decline is slowed in active seniors, both men and women, whose VO_{2max} may decline by only 5% per decade. In addition, the senior athlete's *maximal heart rate (MHR)* is age-limited, which implies a limit on cardiac output that an senior athlete can produce in response to exercise. MHR can be estimated as 220 minus the individual's age in years. Blood pressure response to any exertion is also greater among senior athletes; the response is a result of a decrease in baroreceptor responsiveness with aging and to increased stiffness of the arterial tree. However, senior athletes can achieve training effects such as lower resting heart rate, increased stroke volume, and increased VO_{2max} with regular physical activity.[6,7,8] The consequence of all these training effects is that the senior athlete can significantly increase the duration of submaximal exercise without excessive fatigue or other negative side effects.

The skeletal changes that occur with aging have important implications for senior athletes as well. Women older than age 35 years and men older than age 55 years lose approximately 1% of bone mineral density per year. In women, cortical bone loss accelerates to 2% to 3% per year for the first 5 years after menopause.[6,7] The cumulative effect of these losses is that by age 65 years, women have lost 35% of bone mineral density in cortical bone and 50%

FOCUS ON . . .

Physiologic Changes With Aging

Of the various physiologic functions that decline with age, those most relevant to the senior athlete involve the metabolic, cardiovascular, and musculoskeletal systems. Many of these changes can be counteracted with regular physical activity. Older individuals have a lower basal metabolic rate, leading to obesity, glucose intolerance, and elevated low-density lipoprotein cholesterol. Regular physical activity can decrease body fat, increase fat-free mass, elevate the basal metabolic rate, improve lipid metabolism, reduce low-density lipoprotein cholesterol, and elevate high-density lipoprotein cholesterol.

Cardiovascular changes include a reduction in VO_{2max}, lower maximal heart rate, and greater blood pressure response to exertion. Training, however, can lower resting heart rate, increase stroke volume, and elevate VO_{2max}, thus allowing the senior athlete to exercise more effectively at submaximal levels.

Musculoskeletally, women older than age 35 years and men older than age 55 years lose about 1% of bone mineral density per year, with cortical bone losses of 2% to 3% in women for the first 5 years after menopause. Thus, by age 65 years, women have lost 35% of the bone mineral density in cortical bone and 50% in trabecular bone. Weightbearing exercise can stem these bone losses and may partially reverse them.

of bone mineral density in trabecular bone. Weightbearing exercise can halt bone loss and may reverse these losses slightly.

FITNESS

Endurance Training

Senior athletes can respond to a training stimulus with significant improvement in performance. Although some world-class athletes can increase VO_{2max} by 100%, most younger athletes can improve it by a modest 20%. This same 20% improvement is attainable by senior athletes as well.[9] Conditioning exercise helps patients preserve youthful vigor and stamina, reduce fatigue at submaximal workloads, and forestall age-related decline in function.[6,7] In the well-trained senior athlete, the heart rate, blood pressure, and total peripheral resistance are decreased for any given workload. Because of this decreased afterload and enhanced efficiency of contraction, the work of the heart is decreased, and myocardial oxygen consumption is

reduced. These conditioning effects are mediated both centrally and peripherally. Centrally, adaptation to training leads to increased stroke volume and cardiac output, accompanied by decreases in resting heart rate, blood pressure, and total peripheral resistance. Peripherally, adaptation to training leads to an increase in skeletal muscle mass as well as increased efficiency of oxygen extraction in working muscles. The cumulative effect of these changes is to decrease cardiac work while simultaneously increasing aerobic capacity.

These training effects can be achieved through regular physical activity at levels approaching 60% to 80% of the athlete's VO_{2max}, or approximately 70% to 85% of the athlete's MHR.[10] This level of physical activity should last about 20 to 60 minutes and should be undertaken 3 to 5 times per week. Because senior athletes fatigue more easily and take longer to recover than younger athletes do, senior athletes should bear in mind the dictum "start low and go slow."

Distinguishing between the health benefits of regular physical activity and the more stringent training elements required to achieve a training effect or develop physical fitness is an important concept to remember about senior athletes. Many of the health benefits outlined above can be obtained with minimal levels of weekly activity, whereas a threshold intensity level of approximately 60% to 80% of VO_{2max} is required to achieve a training effect. Several studies have shown that health benefits such as lower cardiovascular and all-cause mortality, lower blood pressure, improved glycemic control, and alleviated symptoms of anxiety and depression are gained with as little as 1,000 kcal of exercise per week.

Strength Training

Although endurance activities are usually indicated for healthy ambulatory adults from age 60 to 79 years, strength training may be more important for frail individuals age 80 years and older.[11,12] Strength training is key to preserving activities of daily living such as grooming, cooking, rising from a chair or toilet, and getting in or out of the bathtub. Strength training of the arms and legs can be performed with free weights, resistance machines, or elastic band material. Strength training is particularly important for the senior athlete because it helps maintain function and reduce the probability of falls.

Much of what was once considered to be the physiology of aging is now being redefined as the *physiology of disuse*.[5] Age-related decline in function is due to a gradual loss of muscle mass. Muscle mass and strength decline gradually between ages 20 and 50 years. The decline becomes rapid from ages 50 through 90 years. Loss of muscle mass is due to a decline in both the number and the size of muscle fibers. Loss of muscle mass is associated with a proportional loss of strength and, therefore, function. Peak strength is probably reached in the 30s

FOCUS ON . . .

Fitness

Endurance training

Training can improve senior athletes' performance significantly. Conditioning exercise preserves vigor and stamina, reduces fatigue at submaximal workloads, and postpones age-related declines in function. For any given workload, the well-trained senior athlete has a lower heart rate, blood pressure, and total peripheral resistance, which decreases cardiac work, including myocardial oxygen consumption. These effects are both central and peripheral.

Regular physical activity at 60% to 80% of VO_{2max} or 70% to 85% of MHR, lasting for 20 to 60 minutes 3 to 5 times per week will produce these training effects. It is important, however, to remember that although training is required to develop physical fitness, health benefits can still be achieved with lower levels of activity.

Strength training

Strength training can preserve the ability to perform activities of daily living, maintain function, reduce the risk of falls, and is beneficial for people of all ages.

The physiology of disuse describes activity- and age-related declines in function with the gradual loss of muscle mass. Muscle mass and strength decline gradually from ages 20 through 50 years and then more rapidly from ages 50 through 90 years. Peak strength is achieved in the 30s and plateaus until age 50 years. Muscle mass decreases because the number and size of muscle fibers both drop as a result of functional denervation of muscle fibers, which leads to atrophy and selective loss of type II (fast-twitch) fibers. The senior athlete, therefore, is weaker as a result of the relative preponderance of type I (slow-twitch) fibers and the loss of type II fibers. Muscle strength is a factor in walking speed, standing up from a seated position, and stair climbing, so muscle weakness increases the risk of falls and fractures. Resistance training can increase strength in athletes up to age 70 years in as little as 12 weeks; both type I and type II fibers increase in size, but the number of muscle fibers does not change. Reflex potentiation, motor unit synchronization, and improved coordination of muscle fiber contraction and firing make the strength gains possible.

and plateaus until age 50 years, at which time muscle mass and strength deteriorate rapidly, particularly in the lower extremities.

Loss of muscle fibers is partially due to an age-related functional denervation of muscle fibers; denervation leads to muscle atrophy and selective loss of type II (fast-twitch) muscle fibers.[13] Thus, the senior athlete has a relative preponderance of type I (slow-twitch) fibers and is weaker because of the loss of type II fibers. Muscle strength is related to walking speed, stair climbing, and the ability to move from sitting to standing. As type II fibers are lost through normal aging, disuse, and disease, the resulting weakness leads to an increased risk of falls and fractures for the senior athlete.

There appears to be no loss of metabolic potential for the exercising senior athlete, at least up to age 70 years. Resistance training programs have shown strength gains in as few as 12 weeks, with increases in the size of both type I and type II muscle fibers but without an increase in the number of muscle fibers.[13] For the senior athlete, resistance training leads to strength gains by enhancing neuromuscular adaptations such as reflex potentiation, motor unit synchronization, and improved coordination of muscle fiber contraction and firing. For these athletes, neural factors predominate throughout strength training.[6,7,13]

EXERCISE PRESCRIPTION

A written exercise prescription for the senior athlete can improve adherence with the exercise regimen. The prescription should address recommendations for intensity, duration, and frequency of exercise, as well as mode of activity and tips on adherence.[14] It should also allow individualization of the program.

Intensity, Duration, and Frequency

Senior athletes poorly tolerate rapid changes in the intensity of the workout, and a previously sedentary older adult may have difficulty with prolonged duration of even moderately intense activities. Therefore, as previously noted, the senior athlete beginning a training regimen should "start low and slow," starting with low-intensity aerobic activities and finding the duration of activity that is comfortable. Again, the athletic trainer and athlete should remember that senior athletes fatigue more easily and recover more slowly than younger athletes do. As fitness improves, the duration can be increased incrementally. Frequency of the activity can then be increased as well, for example, by starting at 2 or 3 times a week and progressing to 5 or 6 times a week. Only after the senior athlete is comfortable at the greater duration and frequency of activity should the intensity of exercise be increased. Even then, the athlete should be closely monitored with particular attention to possible complications of physical activity, such as cardiac symptoms, musculoskeletal sprains or strains, environmental stress, or side effects of medications. To prevent injuries or side effects of exercise, athletes should be instructed to take the time for adequate warm-up and stretching before exercise and for adequate cool-down after each workout.

Mode of Activity

The mode of physical activity undertaken by the senior athlete has important implications for the desired benefit, expected complications, and adherence to the exercise regimen. In general, individuals from ages 60 to 79 years benefit most from endurance training such as walking, cycling, swimming, or in selected cases, jogging. For those individuals age 80 years and older, strength training is most important for preserving independent living and activities of daily living. Again, age-specific considerations are not as important as physiologic age. For older women and some older men, osteoporosis is a significant medical problem. These patients should perform weightbearing exercises to stimulate calcium preservation and deposition in active bones.

The senior athlete should avoid exercise regimens that include sudden ballistic movements, bursts of activity, contact sports, endurance activities, or excessive competition, because these types of activities place the senior athlete at greater risk of injury. Instead, senior athletes may derive the most benefit from activities that require rhythmic movements using large muscle groups that promote aerobic fitness. Because a tight hand grip causes increased blood pressure response and increases cardiac work during exercise, senior athletes should avoid using hand-held weights while walking. Senior athletes with underlying orthopaedic abnormalities or previous joint injuries are at increased risk of further injury unless recommended activities are adapted specifically for each patient.

Adherence

Isolation and loneliness are common problems among the elderly, and older individuals who live alone are unlikely to initiate and maintain active exercise regimens. Group activities that provide opportunities for social interaction are more likely to encourage adherence to an exercise program. Therefore, athletic trainers and other therapists should recommend activities that involve greater social contacts, such as mall walking and programs at senior centers, health clubs, and seniors organizations, that promote physical activity.[10,14] Similarly, the activities prescribed must be interesting and enjoyable if adherence is to be achieved. Finally, many older individuals have fixed incomes and live on limited budgets; therefore, transportation and cost of activities must also be considered in the selection of an exercise program.

Exercise Prescription

A written, individualized exercise prescription improves regimen compliance and should include intensity, duration, frequency, mode of activity, and tips for adherence recommendations. Senior athletes should both start and go slowly; they tolerate rapid changes in workout intensity more poorly, fatigue more easily, and recover more slowly than younger athletes. The program should begin with low-intensity aerobic activities over a comfortable duration. As fitness improves and the athlete becomes more comfortable, the duration and frequency can be increased. However, close monitoring is necessary to prevent and recognize complications. Adequate warm-up and stretching before exercise and proper cool-down after will help to prevent injuries and other problems.

Individualization

Athletic trainers should recognize that senior athletes show great variability in their baseline fitness and ability to withstand the rigors of a well-rounded exercise program.[10,14] Great care may be necessary when initiating an exercise program for a previously sedentary 65-year-old individual with multiple medical problems, while some 80-year-old athletes are impressively fit and enjoy a physiologic age much younger than their chronologic age.

HEALTH RISKS OF REGULAR PHYSICAL ACTIVITY

Regular physical activity is an important component of a healthy lifestyle for older patients; however, there are real risks that must be recognized. These risks include cardiovascular events, musculoskeletal injuries, environmental problems, and medication interactions.

Cardiovascular Events

A small subset of patients is at high risk for cardiovascular complications of physical activity. These are patients with congestive heart failure and a low ejection fraction (left ventricular ejection fraction of less than 30%), multivessel coronary artery disease (CAD), hypotension with exertion, and angina (chest pain) with slight exertion or while at rest. A physician must evaluate patients with these serious cardiac abnormalities before they start any physical activity program.

Sudden death

Although sudden death during exercise remains rare, it is an important concern, particularly for previously sedentary older individuals. Although sudden death among younger athletes is usually due to hypertrophic cardiomyopathy, anomalous coronary arteries, idiopathic left ventricular hypertrophy, or various conduction abnormalities, most cases of sudden cardiac death in athletes older than age 40 years are due to coronary artery disease. The physician must pay close attention to the patient's history in determining the cardiac risk of exercise. Risk factors such as diabetes mellitus, hypertension, obesity, elevated cholesterol, smoking, sedentary lifestyle, and family history must be evaluated. Women are not immune to heart disease; a 60-year-old postmenopausal woman has the same risk for myocardial infarction as a 50-year-old man; a 70-year-old woman has the same risk as a man of the same age.[15] Although as many as 50% of cases of sudden death occur without premonitory symptoms, many patients experience warning signs before serious complications ensue. Chest pain with exertion, "indigestion," nausea, abdominal pain, shortness of breath, dizziness, generalized fatigue, or malaise can all be indicators of underlying coronary artery disease.

Tailoring the exercise regimen to the patient's needs and abilities can minimize the risk of sudden death during exercise. Use of hand-held weights while walking or jogging should be avoided to prevent significant blood pressure elevation. Sports that require sudden bursts of activity, such as basketball or singles tennis, should be avoided. Racquet sports in general are associated with possibly dangerous increases in heart rate, while brisk walking carries very little danger. The target heart rate should be approximately 65% to 85% of the MHR, or 10 to 15 beats per minute slower than the point at which ischemia occurs. Intensity can be monitored by having the patient observe the *rate of perceived exertion (RPE)*; for example, the patient should be able to speak comfortably to a walking partner. Adequate warm-up and cool-down periods reduce cardiovascular stress. The previously sedentary senior athlete should start at a low intensity and slowly build duration and frequency of exercise activities.

Musculoskeletal Injuries

Senior athletes are particularly at risk for musculoskeletal injuries when they start or advance exercise regimens. Assuming good cardiovascular health, most older adults can initiate and maintain walking programs with few or no problems. However, most senior athletes should add high-impact activities such as jogging or aerobic dance with caution because injury has been reported for jogging programs, even among individuals who are well-acclimated to regular walking. Gender also plays an important role in injury prevalence among senior athletes. In one notable study, 25% of older men suffered jogging-related injuries, whereas 100% of the women were injured.[9] The foot and ankle are common sites of injury among older joggers, reflecting a decreased ability to tolerate high-impact activities.

Environmental Problems

Heat illness

Thermoregulation is an underrecognized problem among senior athletes. Not only is the thirst response blunted with age, but the body's thermoregulatory system becomes less efficient. Heat dissipation is impaired by poor vasomotor regulation, increased subcutaneous fat, and decreased sweat production. Also, the senior athlete often uses prescribed medications that impair the body's usual adaptations to exertion in the heat. Medicines such as thiazide diuretics, antidepressants, and major tranquilizers impair the body's ability to shunt blood to skin vessels to promote heat loss. Moreover, these medications may exacerbate the relative hypohydration common among older patients. Senior athletes must be aware of which of their medicines place them at risk of heat illness and pay particular attention to adequate hydration before, during, and after exertion in the heat.

Cold injuries

Senior athletes are also at risk for injuries in extreme cold conditions. The basal metabolic rate declines with age, the shivering response is blunted, and endogenous heat production is decreased. Poor vasomotor regulation and peripheral vascular disease cause increased risk of cold injury to extremities, toes, fingers, ears, and nose.

Effects of Medication

Senior athletes are likely to be taking one or more medications that can affect exercise performance or cause significant side effects in the exercising individual. Diuretics are often used to control hypertension in older patients, and these medications can have significant side effects for the athlete, including *hypokalemia* (low serum potassium), arrhythmia, and *rhabdomyolysis* (excessive muscle break down). Diuretics also cause mild to moderate hypohydration, which predisposes the senior athlete to syncope or near-syncope, falls, and an increased likelihood of heat illness. Beta-blockers are also commonly used to treat hypertension in older patients, and these medications can significantly reduce the heart rate. In the exercising senior athlete, this means that the individual is unable to increase cardiac output in response to an exercise challenge. For senior athletes, exercise, insulin, and not eating properly can result in decreased blood sugar levels and can be dangerous. Insulin or oral hypoglycemic agents used to treat diabetes mellitus can cause excessive and even life-threatening hypoglycemia (low blood sugar) in the poorly informed athlete who continues to take diabetes medications while not ingesting adequate calories. Antidepressant medications can impair thermoregulation and place the athlete at increased risk of heat illness.

The hazards of any program may be minimized if the patient is advised to adopt a regular exercise program of moderate intensity and duration that involves rhythmic movements of large muscle groups. This type of regimen includes activities such as walking, cycling, and swimming. The patient's target heart rate should be 70% to 85% of the MHR, and the patient should monitor the level of exertion closely, noting level of fatigue, respiratory rate, and RPE. The patient should be instructed to perform proper warm-up movements and stretching techniques before starting intense aerobic activities and use cool-down methods at the end of the exercise event.

PREEXERCISE ASSESSMENT

Before beginning an exercise program, most senior athletes should undergo a medical evaluation by their regular physician to uncover any problems that may predispose them to complications of exercise. The medical evaluation should include a thorough medical history, a focused physical examination, and graded exercise testing for selected high-risk patients.

Medical History

The medical history should determine whether the patient has any chronic medical illnesses, such as diabetes mellitus, hypertension, coronary artery disease, osteoporosis, osteoarthritis, or any previous episode of heat illness or depression. The physician should ascertain whether there is any history of previous injury to a joint or previous surgery and whether the patient has any risk factors for coronary artery disease. A careful history of medication use is also important. The patient's social history, particularly marital status and living arrangements, is significant, because older patients who live alone are much more likely to be sedentary.

Physical Examination

During the physical examination, the physician should focus on elements pertinent to the initiation of an exercise program. Vital signs (pulse and blood pressure) should be measured with the patient both supine and seated. The patient's body composition should be assessed, particularly with regard to obesity, whether body fat is central or peripheral. *Central obesity* (apple shape) is most commonly found in men and is associated with elevated blood pressure and higher rates of cardiovascular morbidity and mortality. *Peripheral obesity* (pear shape) is most commonly found in women and is not associated with the same serious cardiovascular complications. The heart should be auscultated carefully, paying particular attention to abnormal murmurs, gallops, rubs, and the point of maximal impulse (PMI). The peripheral vasculature should be examined, especially signs of adequate perfusion such as peripheral pulses and capillary refill. The orthopaedic examination should focus on the back, hips,

FOCUS ON . . .

Preexercise Assessment

A preexercise assessment, consisting of a thorough medical history, focused physical examination, and graded exercise testing for high-risk patients, should take place before the senior athlete begins an exercise program. The medical history should address whether the patient has any chronic medical illnesses, takes any medications, and has had any previous joint injuries or surgery. Coronary artery disease risk factors and social history should also be assessed.

The physical examination focuses on elements important to the initiation of an exercise program and should include supine and seated vital signs, body composition, heart auscultation, peripheral vasculature, orthopaedic problems, and neurologic evaluation.

Graded exercise testing, which is not necessary for all senior athletes, should be used to determine the risk of vigorous exercise before initiating an exercise program and the patient's VO_{2max} to guide the appropriate intensity of activity. The American College of Sports Medicine recommends graded exercise testing for high-risk patients or those with underlying cardiac disease, men older than age 40 years, and women older than age 50 years who plan a vigorous exercise program. Of the several protocols available, the Smith & Gilligan Modified Balke Test is especially appropriate for senior athletes because it calls for a long warm-up and is performed at low intensity with 2% increments in grade every 2 to 3 minutes. The treadmill GXT provides a more precise measure of cardiac response to a given workload, but may be difficult for some patients to master without falling. The cycle ergometer is safer and easier, but may be less precise.

knees, ankles, and feet; the patient's normal ambulation should also be observed closely. The physician should note any joint injury or malalignment, and these problems should be corrected prior to initiation of an exercise regimen. The patient's balance, deep tendon reflexes, peripheral sensation, proprioception, and gait should be evaluated in the neurologic examination.

Graded Exercise Testing

Some senior athletes who wish to start an exercise program need *graded exercise testing (GXT)*. GXT may be indicated to determine the risk of vigorous exercise prior to initiating an exercise program and to determine the patient's VO_{2max} as a guide for prescribing the appropriate intensity of activity. The American College of Sports Medicine (ACSM) has published guidelines recommending GXT for selected individuals prior to initiating an exercise program[16] (Table 31-1). GXT is recommended for any patients at high risk for complications, patients with underlying cardiac disease, men older than age 40 years, and women older than age 50 years who plan to initiate a vigorous exercise regimen such as jogging or running. Senior athletes are less adaptable to changes in activity level and require more time at each level of intensity during the test period, with only gradual changes in grade and workload.

Several protocols are available for GXT, but one that is particularly appropriate for senior athletes is the Smith and Gilligan Modified Balke Test.[17] This protocol calls for a long warm-up period that allows the patient to become familiar with the treadmill and the testing procedure. The test is performed at low intensity and is measured in *metabolic equivalents (METs)*, starting at 2 miles per hour (approximately 2 to 3 METs). An MET is the amount of energy consumed by the body while performing various activities (at rest, the body consumes approximately 1 MET per hour). The grade is increased by 2% increments (0.55 METs) every 2 to 3 minutes. The treadmill GXT provides a precise measurement of cardiac response to a given workload, but some patients have difficulty mastering the treadmill and may be in danger of falling. An electrocardiogram is performed by placing electrodes on the patient's chest and then monitoring the individual continuously as he or she slowly increases the workload on the treadmill. For these patients, the cycle ergometer is a safer and easier alternative, but measurements may be less precise than those obtained from the treadmill GXT.

CONDITIONING AND REHABILITATION

Endurance Training

For the senior athlete, the exercise prescription should be modified with regard to intensity and mode of activity.[18] Total work is the key determinant in fitness, so senior athletes can walk at a lower intensity with longer duration and gain most of the benefits of physical activity. Brisk walking can provide fitness benefits, leading to increases in VO_2max of 22% to 30%.[19] Activities of low- to moderate-intensity lead to relatively low injury rates, approximately 12% to 14%.[19] Brisk walking is simple, easily regulated, requires little in terms of skill, equipment, or facilities, and is relatively safe for senior athletes. Although walking is relatively safe for this population because it

---

TABLE 31-1

GUIDELINES FOR EXERCISE TESTING AND PARTICIPATION

	Apparently Healthy Younger ≤ 40 years (men) ≤ 50 years (women)	Older	Higher Risk* No Symptoms	Symptoms	With Disease†
Medical examination and diagnostic exercise test recommended prior to:					
Moderate exercise‡	No§	No	No	Yes	Yes
Vigorous exercise#	No	Yes**	Yes	Yes	Yes
Physician supervision recommended					
Submaximal testing	No	No	No	Yes	Yes
Maximal testing	No	Yes	Yes	Yes	Yes

* Persons with two or more risk factors or symptoms
† Persons with known cardiac, pulmonary, or metabolic disease.
‡ Moderate exercise (exercise intensive 40% to 60% VO_{2max})—Exercise intensity well within the individual's current capacity and can be comfortably sustained for a prolonged period of time, ie, 60 minutes, slow progression, and generally noncompetitive.
# Vigorous exercise (exercise intensity > 60% VO_{2max})—Exercise intense enough to represent a substantial challenge and which would ordinarily result in fatigue within 20 minutes.
§ The "no" responses in this table mean that an item is "not necessary." The "no" response does not mean that the item should not be done.
** A "yes" response means that an item is recommended.

(Reproduced with permission from the American College of Sports Medicine: *Guidelines for Exercise Testing and Prescription*, ed 4. Philadelphia, PA, Lea & Febiger, 1991.)

does not challenge the heart excessively, most injuries, mainly mild musculoskeletal injuries, among older athletes occur during walking because it is the mode of exercise most easily performed. Senior athletes can monitor the intensity of their workouts by learning to pay attention to cues from their bodies and observing RPE. The Borg scale corresponds well to increases in ventilation, lactic acid production, oxygen uptake, and heart rate[20] (**Table 31-2**). Some fitness experts recommend that senior athletes monitor both heart rate and RPE; however, checking the radial or carotid pulse may be difficult for older individuals, and the RPE alone may be more than sufficient for most patients. The senior athlete should work at an intensity that feels "somewhat hard" and corresponds to a score of 12 to 13 on the Borg scale.

As the senior athlete becomes adapted to training, the intensity of the workout can be increased. However, senior athletes require a longer, more gradual adaptation period; a 40% increase in time to adaptation to training should be allowed for each decade of life after age 30 years. For example, a 50-year-old individual may progress every 2 weeks, while a 70-year-old individual may progress every 4 weeks. Also, the increment in progression is usually smaller for older and more fragile individuals.

TABLE 31-2
THE 15-GRADE SCALE FOR RATINGS OF PERCEIVED EXERTION, THE RPE SCALE

6	
7	Very, very light
8	
9	Very light
10	
11	Fairly light
12	
13	Somewhat hard
14	
15	Hard
16	
17	Very hard
18	
19	Very, very hard
20	

(Reproduced with permission from Borg G: Perceived exertion as an indication of somatic stress. *Scand J Rehab Med* 1970;2:92–98.)

The training program progresses through three stages: initiation, slow progression, and maintenance. As an endurance program is initiated, activities of low intensity and duration are begun. These initial activities include light calisthenics, gentle stretches, and low- to moderate-intensity aerobic exercise. During the slow progression phase of training, duration and frequency of exercise are increased, followed by gradual increases in intensity. Intensity can be increased every 2 to 4 weeks, depending on the individual's physiologic fitness. The frequency and magnitude of progression depends on the individual's adaptation to the training program.

Senior athletes with musculoskeletal limitations or impairments of vision, gait, or balance require alternative regimens to avoid injury associated with physical activity. These more fragile patients should be directed to water activities such as swimming, aquatic therapy, or water aerobics. Many common daily activities, such as gardening and yard work, are also effective in improving overall fitness.

Strength Training
Senior athletes should set strength training goals to facilitate the training process. Common goals include looking and feeling good, improving strength and endurance, improving body composition by losing weight, increasing bone mass, improving functional status, and reducing the risk of falls. Senior athletes should be instructed about proper body position and handgrip, proper lifting technique, and common lifting errors before strength training is begun.[14,21-23] Proper breathing techniques such as exhaling during concentric contractions ("positives"), inhaling during eccentric contractions ("negatives"), never holding the breath, and breathing regularly should also be followed. Senior athletes usually require some level of monitoring when a strength training program is initiated. Strength training can cause injuries in senior athletes who are poorly prepared or inadequately supervised. Trained personnel should be available to answer questions, correct training errors, and keep appropriate records on the athlete's progress.

As many as 20% of senior athletes who initiate a strength training program may sustain injuries, even during strength testing.[19] Injuries to the knee, shoulder, and back can occur, particularly if the patient has decreased range of motion in the joint or a previous injury to that joint. Determining the patient's maximum one-repetition strength (1-repetition-maximum or 1-RM) is a common method of establishing a baseline for initiating strength training. However, because a senior athlete lacks flexibility, this method of strength testing frequently leads to strain injuries. The senior athlete should be carefully instructed about the proper form for executing the various strength exercises and should become familiar with the equipment. After an adequate warm-up period using light weights and multiple repetitions, the athlete should perform strength training with moderate weights under adequate supervision until he or she is technically proficient. Once 10 to 12 repetitions at a particular weight can be comfortably performed, the athlete may progress at 5% increments.

As with younger athletes, the effectiveness of a strength training program for senior athletes depends on the volume of training (number of sets times number of repetitions times resistance). For older patients, one set of 10 to 15 repetitions of a light or moderate weight to volitional fatigue is recommended.[19] This combination of relatively light weights and multiple repetitions leads to gains in both muscle endurance and muscle mass, while minimizing the risk of strength training. The athlete should perform eight or 10 different exercises and train with weights twice weekly for optimal effect. Strength training two to three times a week allows adequate rest between training sessions but does not lead to detraining.

Resistance machines provide several advantages for senior athletes.[13,21,23] Weight can be applied and increased in small increments, and variable resistance allows the stimulus to be applied through the full range of motion. Machines provide back support and help the less-experienced athlete use the proper plane of motion. Some machines can be double-pinned, reducing the risk of injury to senior athletes by allowing them to train only in a limited range of motion. Safe use of free weights requires better balance and lifting technique; therefore, machines may be a better introduction for senior athletes to weight training.

Adequate warm-up with light aerobic activities followed by gentle stretching routines should precede strength training for senior athletes; 5 to 6 minutes of light aerobic exercise followed by gentle stretches is usually sufficient. Resistance training should progress slowly to reduce the risk of injuries.[14,21,23] Training should not exceed 60 minutes per session; a session should usually last less than 30 minutes.

Typical upper extremity exercises include the seated press for the pectoralis major muscle, lateral pull-downs for the trapezius and latissimus dorsi muscles, scapular retraction for the rhomboid and trapezius muscles, elbow extension for the triceps, and elbow flexion for the biceps. Typical exercises for the lower extremity include knee extension for the quadriceps, knee flexion for the hamstrings, leg presses for the gluteus, quadriceps, and hamstrings, toe raises for the gastrocnemius and soleus muscles, and heel raises for the tibialis anterior muscle.[24] Beginners should start with one or two sets of 12 repetitions at 30% of their 1-RM, progressing slowly to two sets of 12 repetitions at 70% of their 1-RM.[19]

Because of the strain against the load that increases peripheral vascular resistance during resistance training, which leads to elevated blood pressure and increased cardiac work, all forms of resistance training are contraindicated for older individuals with uncontrolled hypertension and those at high risk for a cardiac event.

Flexibility

Enhancing flexibility is often overlooked as a benefit of the exercise prescription; however, lack of flexibility is one reason older individuals are at increased risk of injury with physical activity. Flexibility of the back, hips, knees, ankles, and feet is an important part of the preexercise physical assessment. For walking activities, flexibility at the ankle and hip is particularly important. Ankle dorsiflexion must be at least 10°; otherwise, heel cord stretches are indicated. A 60° arc of motion is required at the hip for pain- and injury-free walking. Tightness of the iliotibial band or rectus femoris muscle or flexion contracture at the hip joint must be assessed. Any limitation in range of motion should be treated with a gentle stretching routine. Stretches should include the lower extremity (gastrocnemius-soleus complex, quadriceps, hamstrings, and hip flexors), the upper extremity (inferior shoulder capsule and posterior shoulder capsule), and trunk (posterior thighs and buttocks and spine extensors).

Tai Chi

Many studies indicate that impaired balance and decreased lower extremity strength are important risk factors for functional decline and falls in older adults.[25] Tai Chi is an exercise program particularly suitable for older adults because it enhances balance and body awareness. The senior athlete performs low-intensity, slow, graceful forms that emphasize precise total body movements. Tai Chi is performed with a lowered center of gravity with hips and knees held in slight flexion, resulting in strengthening of the hip and knee extensors. Training in Tai Chi reduces falls in older adults, facilitates ambulation, and reduces fear of falling.[25] Tai Chi is also used as a means of preserving strength and balance gains after intense rehabilitation. Although some deterioration of balance occurs, strength gains are largely preserved with brief (5 to 15 minutes) twice-weekly home-based Tai Chi exercises.[26]

COMMON ORTHOPAEDIC INJURIES

Injuries among senior athletes usually occur during endurance activities, are usually due to overuse, and commonly have a degenerative basis. Overuse injuries constitute 70% to 85% of sports injuries in senior athletes, and they represent a major obstacle to physically active lifestyles for older individuals.[15] Acute traumatic injuries account for 15% to 30% of all injuries among senior athletes.[15] Factors that contribute to this increased frequency of traumatic injuries in senior athletes include poor balance and coordination, impaired visual acuity, orthostatic hypotension, and decreased bone mineral density (osteoporosis).

Among senior athletes, injury is the second most common barrier to sports participation, following chronic

FOCUS ON . . .

Flexibility and Tai Chi

Flexibility, particularly of the back, hips, knees, ankles, and feet, is very important in reducing an athlete's risk of injury. Any limitations of motion should be addressed with a specific, gentle stretching routine. Athletes should stretch the lower extremity, the upper extremity, and trunk.

Tai Chi is a particularly appropriate exercise for older adults because it improves balance and body awareness. Low-intensity, slow, graceful, precise movements are performed with the hips and knees held in slight flexion, which strengthens the hip and knee extensors. Tai Chi reduces falls and fear of falling in older adults, facilitates ambulation, and helps to preserve strength and balance gains after intense rehabilitation.

illness. For senior athletes who suffer from overuse injuries, prolonged tissue healing duration often delays the athlete's return to physical activity. Activities such as running, racquet sports, concurrent participation in multiple sports, walking, and low-intensity activities are the most common activities associated with injuries in senior athletes.[27] Approximately 20% to 30% of injuries involve the knee, 20% the foot, and 10% the lower leg.[27,28] Up to 25% of these injuries are due to tendinitis, 11% to patellofemoral pain syndrome, 8% to ligament sprain, and 7% to muscle strain.[27] Metatarsalgia, plantar fasciitis, and Morton's neuroma occur fairly commonly among senior athletes, presumably because of the decreased flexibility or motor weakness of the foot.[27] Meniscal injury accounts for more than 5% of injuries and is much more common among senior athletes than among younger athletes.[27] Not surprisingly, degenerative disk disease and osteoarthritis are also fairly common problems. Moreover, when looking at upper extremity injuries, the shoulder is most commonly involved.

As with younger athletes, overuse injuries in senior athletes are usually due to training errors, training on unyielding surfaces such as concrete, biomechanical malalignment, improper equipment, or inadequate footwear. Lack of flexibility and primary or secondary muscle weakness lead to decreased shock-absorbing capabilities of the foot and predispose the senior athlete to injury. For example, decreased strength and flexibility in the lower limb may explain the increased incidence of metatarsalgia and plantar fasciitis in senior athletes. In 25% of patients, there is a history of a precipitating event such as a sudden change in intensity level, a single severe training session, or an episode of trauma.[15,27] Approxi-

mately 80% of senior athletes report that symptoms are aggravated by activity, and more than 50% of senior athletes report that the current problem is an exacerbation of a preexisting problem.[15] Many senior athletes report a history of "arthritis," presumably osteoarthritis; however, the causal relationship between osteoarthritis and symptoms is difficult to verify. Other causes of pain, such as soft-tissue injuries, must be investigated before the patient's pain symptoms are ascribed to degenerative joint disease. Common diagnoses include osteoarthritis of the knee, adhesive capsulitis or chronic impingement of the shoulder, rupture or tendinitis of the Achilles tendon, partial tear of the gastrocnemius muscle, or osteoarthritis of the hip.[29] Less common diagnoses include metatarsalgia, plantar fasciitis, chronic ankle instability, osteoarthritis of the cervical spine, and adductor muscle strain.

Most injuries are mild and respond well to conservative therapy such as restriction of activity, nonsteroidal anti-inflammatory drugs (NSAIDs), modalities, and physical therapy treatments. Muscle weakness is common among senior athletes with osteoarthritis, and muscle rehabilitation should be a part of the physical therapy program. Orthotics, steroid injection, or joint aspiration are occasionally indicated as well. Only 5% to 7% of injuries among senior athletes require surgical treatment.

Shoulder Pain

Impingement syndrome

The most common cause of shoulder pain in the senior athlete is *chronic subacromial impingement syndrome*, which is typical of the pattern of overuse injuries among senior athletes. Advanced stages of impingement with rotator cuff tearing and attritional rotator cuff changes are common. The patient reports pain with active flexion, abduction, and/or internal rotation of the shoulder, but passive range of motion is near normal and is mostly pain-free. The goals of conservative treatment of subacromial impingement syndrome are to decrease inflammation, allow healing of the injured rotator cuff tendon(s), and restore normal function to the painful shoulder. Treatment includes relative rest from aggravating activities, a short course of NSAIDs, modalities, and physical therapy. Initially, physical therapy focuses on regaining full pain-free range of motion. As pain resolves, strengthening of the scapular stabilizers (rhomboids, trapezius, serratus anterior, and serratus posterior) should be incorporated into the rehabilitation program, followed by strengthening of the rotator cuff muscles. Strengthening of the rotator cuff muscles is first accomplished with external and internal rotation of the infraspinatus and subscapularis muscles, followed by elevation exercises for the supraspinatus.

The early symptoms of impingement include pain with overhead motion, often a result of overuse incurred in an occupational or recreational setting. With progressive fibrosis and inflammatory changes within the rotator cuff

FOCUS ON . . .

Shoulder Pain

Impingement syndrome

Chronic subacromial impingement syndrome is the most common cause of shoulder pain in the senior athlete, producing pain with active flexion, abduction, or internal rotation (or a combination of these), with near-normal passive range of motion. With progression, pain worsens and occurs at night. Examination reveals tenderness at the anterior acromion or the supraspinatus tendon insertion on the greater tuberosity of the humerus. Results of Neer's test or the Kennedy-Hawkins maneuver are positive. Supraspinatus or infraspinatus (or both) muscle atrophy is evident, and give-way weakness of the supraspinatus, infraspinatus, teres minor, and long head of the biceps may be noted. Treatment is rest from offending activities, a short course of NSAIDs, modalities, and physical therapy that focuses first on regaining full, pain-free range of motion and then on strengthening of the scapular stabilizers and rotator cuff muscles. Initially, exercises must remain within the pain-free arc of motion. Repetitions should total 20 to 30 per set, 2 to 3 times daily. Active-assisted range of motion exercises can be added, either with the help of an athletic trainer or by having the patient use a yardstick, broom handle, or wand. Once range of motion is pain free, strengthening can proceed.

Hand-held weights, surgical tubing, or elastic bands can be used for shoulder rehabilitation, beginning with isotonic exercises of resisted external rotation and internal rotation to strengthen the infraspinatus, teres minor, and subscapularis. As strength improves, stronger tubing or elastic bands can be used to provide greater resistance. Once internal and external rotation is near normal, elevation exercises to strengthen the supraspinatus muscles can be started.

Adhesive capsulitis

Adhesive capsulitis can be primary (idiopathic, often associated with diabetes mellitus or hyperthyroidism) or secondary (resulting from injury or prolonged immobilization, or both). Pain is typically of gradual onset, usually on the nondominant side. Loss of motion is progressive, until the patient is unable to perform activities of daily living. Examination reveals a markedly limited range of motion, most often in external rotation, but sometimes also in forward flexion and abduction. Treatment begins with supervised passive and active-assisted range-of-motion exercises to prevent further loss of motion. Adhesive capsulitis may take months to resolve; in rare instances, patients require manipulation under anesthesia to lyse adhesions and promote increased range of motion.

tendons, the patient's pain symptoms worsen and occur at night. Most cases of rotator cuff tendinitis are chronic; the patient does not recall an acute mechanism of injury. Night pain is the most classic symptom.

Examination reveals tenderness at the anterior acromion or at the supraspinatus tendon insertion on the greater tuberosity of the humerus. A painful arc of abduction occurs between 70° and 120° of abduction or forward flexion, and results of either Neer's test (impingement sign) or the Kennedy-Hawkins maneuver are positive.[30] During the Neer's test, the patient's arm is forcibly flexed forward as much as possible by the examiner, which jams the greater tuberosity of the humerus against the anteroinferior acromial surface. This indicates an overuse injury of the supraspinatus tendon and sometimes the biceps tendon.[30] During the Hawkins-Kennedy test, while the patient is standing, the examiner flexes the arm forward to 90°(and then forcibly rotates the shoulder internally. This maneuver causes impingement of the supraspinatus tendon against the anterior surface of the coracoclavicular ligament.[30] Atrophy of the supraspinatus and/or infraspinatus muscles may be noted on inspection,

while give-way weakness of the supraspinatus, infraspinatus, teres minor, and long head of the biceps muscles may be noted clinically.

Initial range of motion exercises for the shoulder must remain within the pain-free arc of motion. The initial program may include Codman's pendulum exercises, forward and backward shoulder shrugs, 90° shoulder abduction exercises (often called "chicken wing" exercises), and scapular retraction exercises (the shoulder blade "pinch").[30] During Codman's pendulum exercises, the patient bends forward slightly at the waist while supporting his or her weight with the uninjured arm. At the same time, the injured arm is flexed at the elbow while the patient moves it in small circles parallel to the ground, which helps preserve joint range of motion and prevents adhesive capsulitis.[30] The patient should perform 20 to 30 repetitions of each exercise two to three times daily.

Patients may gradually advance range of motion through the full physiologic range by performing active-assisted range of motion exercises. The athletic trainer may help the patient perform these exercises, or the patient may use a device such as a yardstick, broom handle, or wand to allow the uninjured arm to assist the injured arm as it moves through a functional range of motion, particularly forward flexion and abduction.

Restoring strength to muscle groups weakened by injury is an essential component of a comprehensive rehabilitation program. The rotator cuff muscles are the dynamic stabilizers of the glenohumeral joint, and the trapezius, levator scapulae, rhomboids, and serratus anterior and posterior muscles are the scapulothoracic stabilizers. Once pain-free range of motion has been restored, the strengthening phase of treatment should be initiated.

Hand-held weights, surgical tubing, or elastic bands can be used for shoulder rehabilitation exercises. Elastic bands are commercially available in a variety of strengths and are easily prescribed for use in home exercise programs. Color coding indicates resistance from weakest to strongest. The patient with subacromial impingement syndrome should begin with isotonic exercises consisting of resisted external rotation and internal rotation. These exercises strengthen the infraspinatus, teres minor, and subscapularis muscles while avoiding elevation of the humeral head, which can occur during exercises for the supraspinatus muscle. The patient uses surgical tubing or an elastic band to perform gentle resisted internal and external rotation exercises. When performing these exercises, the patient should stand with the arms adducted (such as when holding a magazine between the arm and the trunk) while an elastic band or tubing is fixed to a doorknob or other fixture at waist height. The patient performs adducted internal rotation exercises with the therapeutic band and may rotate his or her position 180° to perform resisted external rotation exercises. As strength improves, the patient can use stronger tubing or elastic bands to provide greater resistance. Once near-normal strength on internal and external rotation is achieved, the patient should add elevation exercises to strengthen the supraspinatus muscle.

Enhancing or regaining flexibility of the shoulder girdle is an important component of the shoulder rehabilitation regimen. Decreased internal rotation of the shoulder associated with tightness of the posterior shoulder capsule commonly occurs with impingement syndrome. Gentle stretching of the posterior capsule in cross-body adduction/internal rotation should be maintained for 10 to 30 seconds and repeated 10 or more times. The patient must enter the stretched position slowly and should be comfortable in the stretched position. The patient should be instructed carefully in the proper method of performing a long, slow, steady, plastic stretch.

If the patient's condition fails to improve after a trial of NSAIDs, modalities, and physical therapy treatments, a subacromial corticosteroid injection may be necessary.

Adhesive capsulitis

Adhesive capsulitis is a fairly common cause of shoulder pain in the senior athlete.[29] For most patients, onset of shoulder pain and restriction of motion is insidious, often resulting in delayed evaluation and/or a misdiagnosis. Primary adhesive capsulitis is idiopathic but is often associated with diabetes mellitus or hyperthyroidism. Secondary adhesive capsulitis is usually due to injury and/or a period of prolonged immobilization. Typically, the patient reports the gradual onset of shoulder pain, usually on the nondominant side. As symptoms progress, the patient experiences progressive loss of motion, until finally the patient is unable to perform necessary activities of daily living. Examination reveals a marked limitation of range of motion. Most commonly, the patient loses external rotation, but some patients may show a combined loss of external rotation (< 90°), forward flexion (< 135°), and abduction (< 90°). Treatment is aimed at preventing further loss of range of motion at the glenohumeral joint. Moderate to severe limitations of motion warrant supervised passive and active-assisted range-of-motion exercises. As the patient enters the "thawing phase" of the disease process, more aggressive physical therapy can be initiated. Intra-articular corticosteroid injections are rarely indicated, and results of these injections have been equivocal. The normal course of adhesive capsulitis may not resolve for many months, and both the athlete and the clinician must be patient and persistent. In rare instances, patients may require manipulation under anesthesia to lyse adhesions and promote increased range of motion.

Knee Pain

Knee pain in the senior athlete most commonly occurs as a result of patellofemoral syndrome, osteoarthritis, or meniscal injury.

Patellofemoral syndrome

The single most common cause of anterior knee pain among senior athletes is *patellofemoral syndrome (PFS)*.[15,27] The patient often has a history of dull, aching knee pain that is aggravated by squatting, walking down stairs, or sitting for prolonged periods with the knee flexed. Symptoms are often the result of overuse activities, such as running, jumping, or repetitive flexion and extension, that require repetitive loading of the patellofemoral joint. Examination may reveal some evidence of malalignment, such as an increased quadriceps angle (Q-angle), genu varum or genu valgum, excessive foot pronation, excessive heel valgus, tibial torsion, or a leg length discrepancy. Pain and crepitus with range of motion is consistent with PFS. Pain symptoms may be reproduced by resisted active extension of the knee. Milking the superior pouch while the patient is supine may reveal a small effusion in the knee joint. Treatment consists of pain relief and activity modification to avoid excessive loading of the patellofemoral joint. NSAIDs may be used if necessary. Rehabilitation of patellofemoral problems involves quadriceps strengthening exercises and proprioceptive retraining. Patellofemoral braces or taping provide a lateral buttress to the patella and are beneficial for some patients. Patients who continue to have significant symptoms despite adequate conservative treatment should be referred to an orthopaedic surgeon or sports medicine physician for evaluation.

Osteoarthritis

Osteoarthritis (OA) of the knee and other joints is a common problem among older patients and is a significant cause of morbidity and sedentary lifestyle in this population.[15,29] Onset of pain is usually insidious, and pain progresses with age. The patient experiences pain in the affected knee that is aggravated by weightbearing and relieved by rest. The patient usually awakens with morning stiffness that dissipates somewhat with activity. The patient reports no systemic symptoms. The patient may report episodes of acute synovitis, chronic joint stiffness, and pain. Examination reveals decreased range of motion, crepitus, mild joint effusion, and palpable osteophytic changes at the knee joint.

Standing weightbearing radiographs with the knee flexed to 45° may be needed to clearly demonstrate degenerative changes in the knee joint. Radiographs may show joint space narrowing, bony sclerosis, eburnation, and hypertrophic osteophyte formation.

The treatment goals for the patient with OA of the knee include pain control, minimizing disability, and educating the patient about self-care. Medications are used to control pain, not to control inflammation. Acetaminophen is considered first-line therapy, and doses of 1,000 mg 4 times daily can be used safely. Low-dose ibuprofen (400 mg, 4 times daily) is a useful alternative, as are nonacetylated salicylates. Topical analgesics, including methylsalicylate and capsaicin creams, are also useful. Many new advances in nonoperative treatment are available, including CO2-X type of NSAIDs, dietary supplements, and chondroprotection for OA (ie, glucosamine and chon-

---

FOCUS ON . . .

Knee Pain

Knee pain in the senior athlete is most often due to patellofemoral pain syndrome (PFPS), osteoarthritis, or meniscal injury. PFPS is the most common cause of anterior knee pain among senior athletes. The patient has a history of dull, aching knee pain aggravated by squatting, walking down stairs, or sitting for prolonged periods with the knee flexed. Overuse activities that require repetitive patellofemoral joint loading cause symptoms. Examination may reveal malalignment with pain and crepitus on range of motion, reproduction of pain with resisted active knee extension, and perhaps a small effusion. Treatment is pain relief, activity modification to avoid excessive patellofemoral joint loading, quadriceps strengthening, proprioceptive retraining, and sometimes a brace or taping to buttress the patella laterally. If symptoms persist despite conservative measures, the patient should be referred to an orthopaedic surgeon or sports medicine physician.

Osteoarthritis of the knee joint is responsible for significant morbidity and a sedentary lifestyle in senior athletes. Pain is usually insidious, progressive, aggravated by weightbearing activities, and relieved by rest; acute synovitis may also occur, along with morning stiffness that dissipates somewhat with activity. Physical examination reveals decreased range of motion, crepitus, mild joint effusion, and palpable osteophytes. Radiographs may show joint space narrowing, bony sclerosis, eburnation, and hypertrophic osteophytes. Treatment is directed at controlling pain, minimizing disability, and educating the patient. To control pain, but not inflammation, acetaminophen is recommended; low-dose ibuprofen or nonacetylated salicylates may be useful alternatives. Topical analgesics, including methylsalicylate and capsaicin cream, may also be beneficial. Exercise and weight loss for the senior athlete with knee osteoarthritis should be personalized and include mobility and flexibility exercises, quadriceps strengthening, ambulation as tolerated, aquatic activities, and other forms of aerobic conditioning. Heat modalities alleviate pain and improve range of motion, while assistive devices promote ambulation. Patient education can be augmented with information provided by the Arthritis Foundation. If conservative management fails to improve the athlete's symptoms, consultation with a rheumatologist is recommended.

Meniscal tears can occur acutely with sudden twisting injuries or as the result of degenerative disease. Symptoms include recurrent knee pain and locking or catching. Examination may reveal a mild effusion, medial or lateral jointline tenderness, vastus medialis atrophy, and perhaps a positive McMurray test result, although a negative test does not negate the possibility of a meniscal tear. Radiographs are very helpful in identifying OA. Magnetic resonance imaging demonstrates most significant tears and is also a useful test. Conservative therapy is often successful and includes activity modification, exercises to regain or maintain range of motion, and quadriceps strengthening. If the athlete's symptoms persist despite treatment, referral to an orthopaedic surgeon is indicated.

droitin sulfate). New injectables are available as well, such as intra-articular injections of hyaluronate. The patient should be instructed regarding the proper use and common side effects of medications.

The senior athlete with OA of the knee needs a personalized program of exercise and weight loss. The exercise program should include mobility and flexibility exercises, quadriceps strengthening, ambulation as tolerated, aquatic activities such as water aerobics and water running, and other forms of low-stress aerobic conditioning. Heat modalities are used to alleviate pain and aid range of motion, and assistive devices such as a cane, quadcane, or walker can promote ambulation. Patient self-management can be encouraged with the use of videotapes, pamphlets, or newsletters provided by the Arthritis Foundation. Patients for whom conservative management is not effective should consult an experienced rheumatologist.

Meniscal injuries

Injuries to the meniscus are fairly common among senior athletes, affecting about 5% of active seniors versus 1.4% of younger athletes.[27] Presumably, this frequency is due to relative muscle weakness combined with decreased flexibility and measured stiffness of the meniscus associated with age. The meniscus may be torn acutely with sudden twisting injuries of the knee, such as those that occur during a sudden change of direction. Meniscal tears may also result from a prolonged degenerative process, particularly in the patient with a deficient knee as a result of an anterior cruciate ligament injury. Commonly, the patient reports recurrent knee pain as well as episodes of catching or locking of the knee, especially with squatting or twisting. Examination may reveal a mild knee effusion and tenderness at the medial or lateral jointline. Atrophy of the vastus medialus portion of the quadriceps is usually noticeable. Results of the McMurray test may be positive, but a negative test result does not rule out the possibility of a meniscal tear. During the McMurray test, while the patient lies in the supine position with the knee fully flexed, the examiner flexes and extends the knee, while simultaneously internally and externally rotating the tibia in order to evaluate the tibia for a palpable clunk or catch. To test the medial meniscus, the examiner laterally rotates the tibia and repeats the procedure.[30] Radiographs are important to evaluate for the presence of OA. Magnetic resonance imaging is the diagnostic test of choice for meniscal tears and can identify other intra-articular problems. Senior athletes with meniscal injuries usually respond well to conservative therapy. Activities should be modified to avoid aggravation of symptoms. A rehabilitation program to regain or maintain range of motion and quadriceps strength should be initiated. Patients with meniscal injuries that are refractory to conservative treatment should be referred to an orthopaedic surgeon for further evaluation and possible surgery.

Ankle or Foot Pain

Ankle or foot pain in the senior athlete is most commonly a result of Achilles tendinitis, plantar fasciitis, or Morton's neuroma.

Achilles tendinitis

Achilles tendinitis is a common cause of tenderness at the posterior aspect of the heel. Onset of pain at the posterior aspect of the heel is insidious and is commonly associated with overuse or a sudden increase in usual activities. Physical examination reveals posterior heel pain that is reproduced or worsened by resisted plantarflexion of the foot. Although tenderness in the Achilles tendon is most common at its insertion at the heel, tenderness may also occur 4 to 6 cm proximal to the heel or more proximally at the musculotendinous junction of the Achilles in the calf. Other causes of heel pain in this area include retrocalcaneal bursitis or superficial (adventitial) bursitis or an avulsion fracture. Treatment includes relative rest from aggravating activities, stretching exercises, and adequate warm-up and stretches before activity. Because muscle weakness and lack of flexibility cause significantly greater strains on the Achilles tendon, appropriate shoes are especially important for the senior athlete. Senior athletes must often be advised about purchasing appropriate athletic shoes. A good shoe should have a wide toe box, firm arch support, good heel pad, and, perhaps, a v-shaped cutout at the heel counter. A heel cup is occasionally useful as well, because it creates slight plantarflexion, relieving tension on the Achilles tendon. Because of the risk of tendon rupture, injection of the Achilles tendon with steroids is *never* indicated.

Plantar fasciitis

Irritation of the plantar fascia at its insertion on the plantar aspect of the heel is a common cause of plantar foot pain. Senior athletes with a high-arched foot (pes cavus) are particularly at risk for *plantar fasciitis*. It is not clear whether patients with flat feet (pes planus) also have a higher risk than individuals with normal arches. The patient with plantar fasciitis usually reports sharp pain at the plantar aspect of the heel, especially with "the first step in the morning." Examination reveals that the patient has point tenderness at the plantar aspect of the heel, and squeezing the heel may reproduce the patient's pain. The presence or absence of a heel spur on radiographs does not contribute to the diagnosis of plantar fasciitis. Treatment includes relative rest from aggravating activities and a time-limited course of NSAIDs. Stretching exercises for the plantar fascia are the key to pain relief. Dorsiflexion of the foot against a door-jam or a series of inclines is the correct position for a long, slow, steady, plastic stretch of the plantar fascia. Rolling the foot on an iced plastic water-bottle or frozen golf ball is a good adjunct to the dorsiflexion stretches. Supporting pes cavus or correcting pes planus with a semirigid arch support significantly unloads the plantar fascia and relieves pain. Wearing new, well-fitting footgear with firm arch support and an adequate heel pad also reduces or relieves pain symptoms. A ¼″ to ⅜″ heel cup effectively alleviates symptoms in the short term. Patients with exquisite pain or those for whom more conservative measures are not effective may benefit from nightly use of a posterior splint to hold the ankle in the neutral position, thus avoiding the painful "first step in the morning" pattern. Low-Dye taping (a taping technique that supports the arch of the foot), injection of lidocaine or Marcaine at the point of maximal tenderness, or surgical fasciotomy are rarely indicated.

Morton's neuroma

Morton's neuroma is a common source of foot pain in the senior athlete. Chronic injury to the digital nerve causes fibrosis, edema, and demyelination. The patient reports numbness and tingling in one or more toes, most commonly in the third web space. Examination reveals that the foot is tender at the plantar aspect of one or more metatarsal heads, most commonly between the third and fourth metatarsal heads. Percussion between the metatarsal heads causes a positive Tinel's sign, and mediolateral compression of the metatarsal heads may cause a palpable "click" caused by subluxation of the neuroma. Treatment includes decreasing pressure on the metatarsal heads, usually by using an orthotic such as a metatarsal pad or bar proximal to the metatarsal heads. Occasionally, surgery is required to excise the digital nerve; however, surgical excision is effective in only 80% of patients.

Common Medical Problems

Hypertension

Hypertension is a common problem among senior athletes, affecting up to 54% of patients older than age 60 years.[31] Physical activity is recommended as an effective secondary intervention for older individuals with mild to moderate hypertension. Primary intervention helps to prevent disease, and secondary intervention helps to control disease. Studies have consistently shown that regular endurance exercise reduces both systolic and diastolic blood pressure by approximately 10 mm Hg. Low to moderate intensity endurance activities carry a low risk of cardiac morbidity or mortality and are well tolerated by most senior athletes. Importantly, active hypertensive older individuals enjoy significantly lower cardiovascular mortality when compared to sedentary hypertensive or normotensive peers.[32] These gains are probably mediated by the effect of regular endurance activity on important cardiac variables such as decreasing obesity, lowering cholesterol, improving glycemic control, and decreasing insulin resistance.[33,34]

Studies have shown that less intense endurance activities, those requiring 40% to 70% of VO_2max, result in the same blood pressure benefits as do more intense activities. This finding is particularly important for senior athletes. Results of training on reducing blood pressure are consistently seen early during training, usually within 3 weeks to 3 months of beginning a regular exercise program.[35] More prolonged training will not reduce blood pressure further, but instead returns it to previous levels quickly once training stops. Therefore, endurance activity must be continued so that blood pressure benefits are maintained. Senior athletes

FOCUS ON . . .

Ankle or Foot Pain

Ankle or foot pain in the senior athlete is often due to Achilles tendinitis, plantar fasciitis, metatarsalgia, or Morton's neuroma. Achilles tendinitis causes insidious onset of pain at the posterior aspect of the heel associated with overuse or a sudden increase in activity. Physical examination reveals tenderness at the posterior heel (and sometimes 4 to 6 cm proximal to the heel or more proximally at the musculotendinous junction) and pain worsened or reproduced by resisted plantarflexion. Bursitis or an avulsion fracture can also cause heel pain. Treatment is rest from aggravating activities, stretching exercises, adequate warm-up and stretches before activity, proper shoes, and occasionally a heel cup. Corticosteroid injections can rupture the tendon and are contraindicated.

Plantar fasciitis is a particular problem for senior athletes with a high-arched foot (pes cavus), resulting in sharp pain at the plantar aspect of the heel, especially first thing in the morning. Examination reveals point tenderness at the plantar aspect of the heel; squeezing the heel may reproduce the pain. Treatment is rest from offending activities, a short course of NSAIDs, stretching exercises for the plantar fascia, a semirigid arch support, a heel cup, and footwear with firm arch support and an adequate heel pad. Patients with severe pain or who fail to improve on these measures may be helped by a posterior splint at night to hold the ankle in neutral position.

Morton's neuroma results from chronic injury to the digital nerve, which causes fibrosis, edema, and demyelination. Symptoms include numbness and tingling in one or more toes, most often in the third web space. Physical examination reveals tenderness at the plantar aspect of one or more metatarsal heads, most often between the third and fourth, a positive Tinel's sign with percussion between the metatarsal heads, and a palpable click with mediolateral compression of the metatarsal heads. Treatment is decreasing pressure on the metatarsal heads with a metatarsal pad or bar; surgery is required occasionally.

should receive regular follow-up examinations to assess the effectiveness of their exercise regimen in reducing blood pressure, and adjunctive therapy such as dietary changes and relaxation techniques should be added as needed.

For maximum effect in lowering blood pressure, endurance activities should be tailored with regard to mode of activity, frequency, duration, and intensity of activity. For example, a patient who wishes to lower his or her blood pressure can use large muscle groups during walking, jogging, swimming, or cycling activities 4 to 6 times a week. Each episode can last for 20 to 60 minutes and be performed at an intensity of 40% to 70% of VO_2max. Patients with marked blood pressure elevation (blood pressure greater than 180/105 mm Hg) should receive adequate pharmacologic therapy before initiating a physical activity regimen.

Strength (resistance) training should not be the sole exercise regimen for patients with hypertension.[36] Strength training causes increased cardiac workload and blood pressure response with minimal changes in peripheral vasodilation. Strength training with free weights should be discouraged for hypertensive senior athletes; circuit training (using a series of resistance machines that work several muscle groups in either the upper extremity or lower extremity) may be safer and, if prescribed, should involve using lower weights and multiple repetitions.

Although many senior athletes with mild to moderate hypertension may control their hypertension with dietary changes, weight loss, and physical activity, many will continue to require antihypertensive medications. Beta-blockers are usually recommended as first-line medical therapy for patients older than age 60 years or for African Americans with hypertension, but beta-blockers impair exercise tolerance by blunting cardiac response to the increased demands of physical activity. Unless specifically indicated, such as for postmyocardial infarction prophylaxis, beta-blockers should be avoided by senior athletes who exercise. Preferred antihypertensive medications include angiotensin-converting enzyme inhibitors, calcium channel blockers, or alpha-blockers.

Diabetes mellitus

Noninsulin-dependent diabetes mellitus (NIDDM) is common among senior athletes and requires careful management and close monitoring. With age, fat mass increases, while metabolically active lean body mass (for example, muscle) decreases. NIDDM is characterized by insulin resistance; in these patients, endogenous insulin is present, but the body fails to respond normally. Patients are likely to have hyperglycemia, obesity, and a family history of diabetes, but no episodes of ketoacidosis. The athlete with diabetes is at increased risk for microvascular complications involving the kidney, retina, peripheral nerves, and heart. Treatment of NIDDM includes diet, weight loss, oral hypoglycemic medications, and exercise.[37,38] Physical activity is the cornerstone of therapy for NIDDM. Regular endurance activity increases the body's sensitivity to endogenous insulin, primarily by reducing obesity and increasing lean body mass.

Some athletes with diabetes are at particular risk for complications and require close observation. Athletes with diabetes who have proliferative retinopathy should have a careful eye examination by an ophthalmologist before initiating a vigorous exercise program. Patients with diabetes with proliferative retinopathy are at risk for vitreous hemorrhage (bleeding into the eye), which can lead to vision loss or blindness. Patients with peripheral neuropathy should avoid activities that may injure the feet, including running, jogging, and high-impact aerobics. Athletes with autonomic neuropathy may have an inadequate cardiac response to exercise. In addition, they may be at risk for unrecognized dehydration or hypotension.

Medications can cause serious problems for athletes with diabetes. Many older patients take beta-blockers for hypertension or postmyocardial infarction prophylaxis; however, beta-blockers blunt the body's normal response to hypoglycemia and may mask important symptoms in athletes with diabetes. Other medications, such as thiazide diuretics, corticosteroids, estrogens, and phenytoin, impair glucose metabolism and may exacerbate hyperglycemia.

FOCUS ON . . .

Hypertension

Regular endurance exercise can reduce both systolic and diastolic blood pressure in hypertensive patients by approximately 10 mm Hg and lower cardiovascular mortality compared with sedentary hypertensive or normotensive peers. Activities requiring 40% to 70% of VO_2max may result in the same benefits as more intense activities, but activity must be continued to maintain the benefits. Regular monitoring is important to assess the effectiveness of the exercise regimen and to determine the need for additional therapy.

Strength training increases cardiac workload and blood pressure response and should not be the only exercise for hypertensive patients. Free weights are discouraged; circuit training is safer, with lower weights and multiple repetitions. Beta blockers are often prescribed for hypertension, but they can impair exercise tolerance by blunting the cardiac response to physical activity, and therefore, angiotensin-converting enzyme inhibitors, calcium channel blockers, or alpha blockers may be preferable. Patients with severe hypertension (>180/105) should receive adequate pharmacologic therapy before beginning an exercise regimen.

Hypoglycemic episodes are an important risk that athletes with diabetes must consider; most oral hypoglycemic medications work by enhancing insulin sensitivity, an effect that may be potentiated by the athlete's exercise program.

FOCUS ON . . .

Diabetes Mellitus

Noninsulin-dependent diabetes mellitus (NIDDM) is characterized by insulin resistance, hyperglycemia, obesity, and a family history of diabetes, with no ketoacidosis. The athlete with diabetes risks microvascular complications of the kidney, retina, peripheral nerves, and heart, which may affect the choice of activity for the athlete. Treatment is diet, weight loss, oral hypoglycemic medications, and exercise to decrease insulin resistance by reducing obesity and increasing lean body mass.

The medications athletes with diabetes take can influence their ability to exercise. Beta-blockers can blunt the normal hypoglycemic response and mask symptoms. Thiazide diuretics, corticosteroids, estrogens, and phenytoin impair glucose metabolism and may exacerbate hyperglycemia. Hypoglycemia is a risk for athletes with diabetes; most oral hypoglycemic medications enhance insulin sensitivity, which may also be potentiated by exercise.

Diabetes-associated vascular and neurologic disease places the athlete with diabetes at risk for skin breakdown, ulceration, infection, and amputation of the foot. Athletes need adequate footgear and cotton/synthetic-blend socks to keep the feet cushioned and dry. Blisters, corns, calluses, ulcers, and ingrown toenails require prompt treatment by a physician.

The athlete with diabetes should perform endurance activity 4 to 6 times per week to keep energy expenditure, dietary intake, and medications at steady levels. Athletes should start gradually, with 20 to 30 minutes of light- to moderate-intensity exercise, progressing to 40 to 60 minutes, and at 50% to 60% of VO_2 max, progressing to 60% to 70%. The athlete should have a preexercise assessment that includes evaluation of peripheral neuropathy and reduced joint flexibility. Preexercise warm-up, stretches, and postexercise cool-down are particularly important.

One to 3 hours before exercise, the athlete should eat, avoiding exercise during peak insulin action. Monitoring blood glucose before, during, and after exercise is essential. During exercise, the athlete should replace fluids every 20 to 30 minutes and carbohydrates every 30 minutes. After exercise, the athlete should increase caloric intake and reduce insulin doses that peak in the evening or during the night.

Foot care is critically important for athletes with diabetes, because diabetes-associated vascular and/or neurologic disease places them at risk of skin breakdown, ulceration, infection, and amputation. Athletes should make sure they have adequate footgear and should use cotton/synthetic-blend socks to keep the feet cushioned and dry. Blisters, corns, calluses, ulcers, or ingrown nails can cause serious complications in the athlete with diabetes and should be treated promptly by a physician.

Athletes with diabetes should take part in endurance activities 4 to 6 times a week to minimize daily changes in energy expenditure and, therefore, dietary intake and need for diabetes medications. Athletes should start with 20 to 30 minutes of light- to moderate-intensity exercise and progress to 40 to 60 minutes of activity per session. Intensity should begin at 50% to 60% of VO_2max and progress to 60% to 70% of VO_2max.

Prior to initiating an exercise program, the athlete with diabetes should be evaluated for evidence of peripheral neuropathy or reduced joint flexibility. Preexercise warm-up, stretches, and postexercise cool-down are especially important. The exercise regimen should be introduced gradually to prevent episodes of hypoglycemia that may be caused by increased insulin sensitivity.

The athlete with diabetes should eat 1 to 3 hours before an exercise session and should avoid exercise during the time of peak insulin action. The athlete should be committed to monitoring blood glucose before, during, and after exercise sessions. If the preexercise blood glucose is less than 100 mg/dL, a preexercise snack is indicated. If the preexercise blood glucose is greater than 250 mg/dL, exercise should be delayed, because the counterregulatory hormones that are stimulated by exercise, such as epinephrine, norepinephrine, cortisol, and glucagon, will aggravate hyperglycemia and may lead to ketoacidosis. During the exercise session, the patient should replace fluids every 20 to 30 minutes, replace carbohydrates every 30 minutes, and monitor blood glucose. After the exercise session, the athlete should monitor blood glucose, increase caloric intake, and reduce insulin doses that peak in the evening or overnight.

Coronary artery disease

There is an inverse relationship between regular physical activity and the development of coronary artery disease (CAD); however, regular activity does not confer immunity from CAD, and patients must be instructed to recognize and report symptoms that suggest heart disease. These symptoms include chest pain either at rest or with exertion, pain that radiates to the left shoulder or neck, nausea, diaphoresis, or shortness of breath. During exercise, the senior athlete with CAD is at a five- to tenfold risk of a cardiac event; however, the overall prognosis of CAD is improved for patients who engage in regular physical activity.

F O C U S   O N . . .

Coronary Artery Disease

Coronary artery disease increases the athlete's risk of a cardiac event during exercise, but patients who exercise regularly have a better prognosis. Athletes should recognize and report chest pain at rest or with exertion, pain radiating to the left shoulder or neck, nausea, diaphoresis, or shortness of breath, and those with known or suspected coronary artery disease or significant cardiac risk factors should undergo graded exercise testing before beginning the exercise program.

Senior athletes with known or suspected CAD or significant cardiac risk factors should undergo graded exercise testing (GXT) prior to initiating a vigorous exercise program. The heart rate is the best indicator of exercise intensity for the senior athlete with CAD, and the maximal heart rate is best determined during the GXT. Patients at high risk should reduce the intensity of their routines and increase duration and frequency of training.

Obesity

Obesity has been described as the biggest health problem in the United States, affecting as many as one in three Americans. Obesity is associated with many adverse consequences, including diabetes mellitus, hypertension, cardiovascular disease, elevated cholesterol, and osteoarthritis, especially of the knees. However, the female pattern of obesity, fat deposition around the hips and thighs, carries less health risk than does the male pattern of obesity, fat deposition around the abdomen.

Weight loss requires both a healthy diet and a regular exercise program.[36] Exercise elevates the resting metabolic rate by increasing the body's muscle mass. Women, therefore, are at a disadvantage because of their lower levels of muscle mass.

Preexercise assessment of the obese patient includes evaluation for any musculoskeletal abnormalities or preexisting medical conditions such as diabetes mellitus, hypertension, and atherosclerotic cardiovascular disease. Body composition should also be assessed, including the body mass index (which is approximated by dividing the weight in kilograms by the height in meters squared), waist-to-hip ratio, and scale weight. Strength, flexibility, and endurance are poor in most obese patients. Fitness testing, or graded exercise testing, is necessary for any patient who intends to pursue a vigorous exercise regimen that is greater than 7 METs.

The exercise prescription for obese patients includes low-intensity, long-duration, and high-frequency activities.[36] Low-intensity activities at 40% to 50% of MHR should be encouraged. Intensity can be estimated using the Borg scale to estimate RPE rather than heart rate. Intensity should be reduced if the patient experiences excessive sweating, excessive respiratory rate, flushed color, joint pain, or undue fatigue. Duration of activities should start at 20 minutes, if tolerated, and progress gradually to 60 minutes. Exercise 5 to 7 days per week is preferred; consistency is key to success for obese patients. Mode of activity should include walking, aerobic dance, and/or use of the stationary bicycle. Of these aerobic activities, walking is most often recommended, because it requires no special equipment or skill, is easily accessible, and allows the patient to adjust intensity. Swimming does not help patients lose fat, possibly because fat is retained to preserve core body temperature.[39]

F O C U S   O N . . .

Obesity

Obesity may affect as many as one in three Americans and is associated with adverse consequences, including diabetes mellitus, hypertension, cardiovascular disease, elevated cholesterol, and osteoarthritis (particularly of the knees). The female pattern of fat deposition around the hips and thighs carries less health risk than the male pattern of fat deposition around the abdomen. A healthy diet and regular exercise are needed for weight loss. Exercise elevates the resting metabolic rate by increasing fat-free (muscle) mass, which puts women (with their lower levels of muscle mass) at a disadvantage.

Before beginning an exercise program, the obese patient should be evaluated for any musculoskeletal abnormalities, preexisting medical conditions, body composition, strength, flexibility, and endurance. Graded exercise testing is necessary for any patient who intends to pursue a vigorous exercise regimen.

The exercise prescription includes low-intensity, long-duration, and high-frequency activities. Exercise intensity in these athletes is best estimated using the Borg scale and should be lowered with excessive sweating or respiratory rate, flushed color, joint pain, or undue fatigue. Appropriate modes are walking, aerobic dance, and stationary bicycling. Walking is most often recommended because it requires no special equipment or skill, is easily accessible, and allows the patient to adjust intensity. A conservative approach that emphasizes consistency and slow progression of duration and intensity and considers the patient's goals and objectives will be safe and successful and encourage patient compliance. Once target weight is achieved, a regular maintenance program is needed.

A considered, conservative approach that emphasizes consistency and slow progression of duration and intensity and takes the patient's goals and objectives into account will be safe and successful and will enhance patient compliance. Once target weight is achieved, a regular maintenance program should be instituted to maintain a healthy weight.

Osteoporosis

Some older men and women are at high risk for osteoporosis, a disease that causes progressive loss of bone mineral density. Patients who are white, older than age 75 years, with a family history of osteoporosis are at high risk for osteoporosis. Other risk factors include early menopause, immobility, alcohol abuse, steroid use, hyperthyroidism, and malabsorption, which may lead to a functional loss of calcium in the gut, predisposing the patient to osteoporosis.[40,41] Women are particularly at risk for osteoporosis and its complications, including osteoporotic compression fractures of the spine and hip fractures or distal radius fractures caused by falls. Weightbearing exercise can prevent further loss of bone mass and may add modestly to bone mineral density. Low-impact exercises such as walking and stationary cycling performed at low intensity levels are recommended to minimize risk of injury.

Treatment of acute vertebral fractures caused by osteoporosis involves pain management and early rehabilitation. Nonnarcotic analgesics and a brief course of bedrest can usually relieve pain. While at rest in the supine position, the patient should place a thin pillow behind the head and a pillow under the legs, flexing the hips, to unload the lumbar spine. While lying down, the patient should hold the hips slightly flexed and place a thin pillow between the knees. Bedrest should be limited to prevent further deconditioning and disuse osteoporosis. Rehabilitation exercises, particularly back extension exercises, should be started early in the patient's recovery, as soon as pain symptoms subside. Calcitonin is an effective medication in relieving the pain of acute osteoporotic vertebral fractures and can be used for 1 to 3 months after an acute fracture.

Patients with osteoporotic compression fractures usually will have repeated fractures and require regular follow-up, appropriate pain medications, and therapy to prevent further loss of bone mass. The patient's diet should be reviewed; excess dietary protein or soft drinks that contain phosphorus may increase calcium requirements by causing hypercalciuria. Older women often require supplementary calcium, usually 1,200 mg per day, and vitamin D, 800 units per day. Estrogen replacement therapy is useful for many women, but therapy must be individualized. Alendronate is a bisphosphonate that inhibits bone resorption and substantially reduces the risk of osteoporotic fractures; however, it is poorly absorbed and can cause gastric and esophageal irritation. Alendronate should be taken in the morning with a full glass of water, and the patient should then remain upright for at least 30 minutes after the pill is taken. Calcitonin can also be used to inhibit bone resorption, but it must be administered subcutaneously or intranasally. Some

FOCUS ON . . .

Osteoporosis

Osteoporosis is most likely in individuals who are older than age 75 years, Caucasian, immobile, alcohol abusers, and steroid users, and those with a family history of osteoporosis or a personal history of early menopause, hyperthyroidism, and malabsorption. Women are particularly vulnerable to osteoporosis and its complications, including spinal compression fractures and hip and distal radial fractures.

Spinal compression fractures are treated with pain control: nonnarcotic analgesics and brief bedrest, in the supine position with a pillow under the knees to flex the hips or with the hips flexed and a pillow between the knees. Bedrest should be limited to prevent further deconditioning and disuse osteoporosis, and rehabilitation exercises, particularly back extension exercises, should be started early. Calcitonin can be effective in relieving pain. Patients with osteoporosis often have repeated fractures and require regular follow-up, appropriate pain medications, and therapy to prevent further bone loss. If the patient's diet is high in protein or phosphorous-containing soft drinks or low in calcium, calcium supplements may be needed. Estrogen replacement therapy is useful for many women, but must be individualized. Alendronate is a bisphosphonate that inhibits bone resorption and substantially reduces the risk of osteoporotic fractures, but it is poorly absorbed and can cause gastric and esophageal irritation. Calcitonin also inhibits bone resorption, but it can only be taken subcutaneously or intranasally, and some patients develop resistance; intermittent therapy is recommended. Weightbearing, low-impact exercise prevents additional loss of bone mass and may improve density somewhat while minimizing the risk of injury.

patients develop resistance to calcitonin therapy; therefore, intermittent calcitonin therapy, occurring every 6 months, is recommended.

Osteoarthritis

Osteoarthritis (OA) is a common problem among senior athletes and is a significant cause of morbidity and sedentary lifestyle in this population. The pain of OA is usually insidious in onset and progresses with age. Risk factors for the development of OA include heredity, biomechanical malalignment, previous trauma, obesity, or lifelong running and sporting activities. The patient usually reports pain in the affected joint that is aggravated by weightbearing activities and is relieved by rest. The patient usually reports morning stiffness that is slightly alleviated with activity, but has no systemic symptoms. The patient may also experience episodes of acute synovitis in addition to chronic joint stiffness and pain.

Treatment of the older patient with OA includes pain control, minimizing disability, and educating the patient regarding self-care. Medications such as acetaminophen and low-dose ibuprofen are used to control pain. Topical analgesics are also useful, including methylsalicylate and capsaicin cream. New avenues of treatment include COX-2 NSAIDs, dietary supplements, glucosamine and chondroitin sulfate, and intra-articular injection of hyaluronate. The senior athlete with OA should receive personalized exercise and weight loss instruction. The exercise program should include mobility and flexibility exercises, strength training, ambulation, aquatic activities, and other forms of aerobic conditioning. Activities that minimize impact loading should be emphasized. Heat modalities are used to alleviate pain and to enhance the range of motion, while assistive devices are used to promote ambulation. Videos, pamphlets, or newsletters provided by the Arthritis Foundation should be used to encourage patient self-management.

CHAPTER REVIEW

As an individual ages, regular physical activity is an important factor in preserving function and maintaining independent living and quality of life. An active lifestyle reduces coronary and all-cause mortality and rate of first myocardial infarction. It also elevates high-density-lipoprotein cholesterol, alleviates depression and anxiety, and promotes a sense of well being.

Physiologic functions that normally decline with age involve the metabolic, cardiovascular, and musculoskeletal systems; many of these can be attenuated with a program of regular physical activity. Endurance training in senior athletes can result in a significant improvement in performance; strength training can diminish the probability of falls.

A written, individualized exercise prescription for the senior athlete improves compliance with the exercise regimen and should address recommendations for intensity, duration, and frequency of exercise, in addition to mode of activity and advice on adherence. The athlete should start with low-intensity aerobic activities and progress slowly, performing warm-up and stretching before activity and cool-down afterward. Walking, bicycling, and swimming provide endurance benefits; patients with osteoporosis require weightbearing activity to stimulate calcium preservation and deposition in active bones.

There are, however, real risks of physical activity that must be recognized and minimized when possible. These include cardiovascular events, musculoskeletal injuries, environmental problems, and medication effects that either directly affect exercise performance or cause significant side effects. Before beginning an exercise program, the senior athlete should undergo a medical evaluation to discover any problems that may predispose him or her to risks. The medical evaluation includes a thorough medical history, a focused physical examination, and graded exercise testing for high-risk patients.

Total work is the key determinant in fitness; thus, seniors can exercise at a lower intensity for a longer duration and reap most of the benefits of physical activity. With adaptation to training, the intensity can be increased gradually, with smaller progressions for older and more fragile patients. Strength training requires proper instruction and monitoring to ensure proper technique and to decrease the risk of injury. Flexibility is an important component of fitness that can reduce the chance of injury. Along with the general stretching routine, any limitations in range of motion should be specifically addressed. Tai Chi is an exercise particularly suitable for older adults because it enhances balance and body awareness.

Orthopaedic injuries common among senior athletes include problems in the shoulder, knee, ankle, and foot. Among the medical problems of senior athletes are hypertension, diabetes mellitus, coronary artery disease, obesity, osteoporosis, and osteoarthritis. Although senior athletes with these conditions may need to take special precautions and be monitored regularly, most can safely participate in physical activity and enjoy the resulting benefits.

SELF-TEST

1. Which of the following effects can regular physical activity have?
   A. Increases body fat
   B. Increases fat-free mass
   C. Elevates VO_{2max}
   D. Elevates low-density-lipoprotein cholesterol

2. For any given workload, the well-trained senior athlete has:
   A. increased afterload.
   B. increased myocardial oxygen consumption.
   C. decreased heart rate.
   D. decreased contraction efficiency.

3. A characteristic of the physiology of disuse is:
   A. increased muscle mass.
   B. increased number of type II fibers.
   C. decreased number of type I fibers.
   D. decreased size of muscle fibers.

4. In selecting appropriate exercises for the senior athlete, which of the following types of activity is desirable?
   A. Contact sports
   B. Bursts of activity
   C. Sudden, ballistic movements
   D. Rhythmic movements using large muscle groups

5. Heat illness is a particular problem in senior athletes and is a consequence of:
   A. impaired heat dissipation.
   B. improved thermoregulation.
   C. increased sweat production.
   D. decreased subcutaneous fat.

6. The potential hazards of an exercise program in a senior athlete can be minimized by:
   A. eliminating stretching exercises.
   B. performing proper warm-up movements.
   C. including high-intensity, short-duration activities.
   D. keeping the patient's target heart rate at 50% to 60% of the MHR.

7. Graded exercise testing is recommended for:
   A. all individuals.
   B. men older than age 40 years.
   C. women older than age 45 years.
   D. men and women older than age 40 years.

8. For exercise to have the maximum effect on reducing blood pressure, the activity should:
   A. involve large muscle groups.
   B. last 40 to 80 minutes per session.
   C. be performed 2 to 3 times per week.
   D. be performed at 20% to 50% of VO_{2max}.

9. Which of the following effects does regular endurance exercise have in patients with diabetes?
   A. Increases body weight
   B. Increases sensitivity to endogenous insulin
   C. Decreases lean body mass
   D. Decreases episodes of ketoacidosis

10. Obese senior athletes should be encouraged to participate in what type of exercise?
    A. High intensity
    B. High frequency
    C. Short duration
    D. Rapidly progressive

Answers on page 894.

References

1. Donohue RP, Abbott RD, Reed DM, Yano K: Physical activity and coronary heart disease in middle-aged and elderly men: The Honolulu Heart Program. *Am J Publ Health* 1988;78:683-685.

2. Paffenbarger RS Jr, Hyde RT, Wing AL, Hsieh CC: Physical activity, all-cause mortality, and longevity of college alumni. *N Engl J Med* 1986;314:605-613.

3. Reaven PD, McPhillips JB, Barrett-Connor EL, Criqui CH: Leisure time exercise and lipid and lipoprotein levels in an older population. *J Am Geriatr Soc* 1990;38:847-854.

4. Nocoloff G, Schwenk TL: Using exercise to ward off depression. *Phys Sportsmed* 1995;23:44-56.

5. Larson EB, Bruce RA: Health benefits of exercise in an aging society. *Arch Intern Med* 1987;147:353-356.

6. Wilmore JH: The aging of bone and muscle. *Clin Sports Med* 1991;10:231-244.

7. Wilmore JH, Costill DL: Aging and the older athlete, in Wilmore JH, Costill DL (eds): *Physiology of Sports and Exercise*, ed 2. Champaign, IL, Human Kinetics, 1999, pp 544-569.

8. Rogers MA, Evans WJ: Changes in skeletal muscle with aging: Effects of exercise training. *Exerc Sports Sci Rev* 1993;21:65-102.

9. Pollock ML, Carroll JF, Graves JE, et al: Injuries and adherence to walk/jog and resistance training in the elderly. *Med Sci Sports Exerc* 1991;23:1194-1200.

10. Elward K, Larson EB: Benefits of exercise for older adults: A review of existing evidence and current recommendations for the general population. *Clin Geriatric Med* 1992;8:35-50.

11. Morganti CM, Nelson ME, Fiatarone MA, et al: Strength improvements with one year of progressive resistance training in older women. *Med Sci Sports Exerc* 1995;27:906-912.

12. Fiatarone MA, Marks EC, Ryan ND, Meredith CN, Lipsitz LA, Evans WJ: High intensity strength training in nonagenarians. *JAMA* 1990;263:3029-3034.

13. Kirkendall DT, Garrett WE Jr: The effects of aging and training on skeletal muscle. *Am J Sports Med* 1998;26:598-602.

14. Evans WJ: Exercise training guidelines for the elderly. *Med Sci Sports Exerc* 1999;31:12-17.

15. Epperly T: The older athlete, in Birrer RB (ed): *Sports Medicine for the Primary Care Physician*, ed 2. Boca Raton, FL, CRC Press, 1994, pp 189-196.

16. American College of Sports Medicine: *Guidelines for Exercise Testing and Prescription*, ed 4. Philadelphia, PA, Lea & Febiger, 1991.

17. Skinner JS: Importance of aging for exercise testing and exercise prescription, in *Exercise Testing and Exercise Prescription for Special Cases*, ed 2. Philadelphia, PA, Lea & Febiger, 1993, pp 75-86.

18. Pate RR, Pratt M, Blair SN, et al: Physical activity and public health: A recommendation from the Centers for Disease Control and Prevention and the American College of Sports Medicine. *JAMA* 1995;273:402-407.

19. Pollock ML, Graves JE, Swart DL, Lowenthal DT: Exercise training and prescription for the elderly. *South Med J* 1994;87:S88-S95.

20. Borg GAV: Psychophysical bases of perceived exertion. *Med Sci Sports Exerc* 1982;14:377-381.

21. Bowers CJ, Schmidt E: Weight training for older Americans. *Strength Condit* 1997;42-47.

22. Feigenbaum MS, Pollock ML: Strength training: Rationale for current guidelines for adult fitness programs. *Phys Sports Med* 1997;25:44-64.

23. Feigenbaum MS, Pollock ML: Prescription of resistance training for health and disease. *Med Sci Sports Exerc* 1999;31:38-45.

24. Seto JL, Brewster CE: Musculoskeletal conditioning of the older athlete. *Clin Sports Med* 1991;10:401-429.

25. Wolf SL, Barnhart HX, Kutner NG, et al: Reducing frailty and falls in older persons: An investigation of Tai Chi and computerized balance training. *J Am Geriatr Soc* 1996;44:489-497.

26. Wolfson L, Whipple R, Derby C, et al: Balance and strength training in older adults: Intervention gains and Tai Chi maintenance. *J Am Geriatr Soc* 1996;44:498-506.

27. Matheson GO, MacIntyre JG, Taunton JE, Clement DB, Lloyd-Smith R: Musculoskeletal injuries associated with physical activity in older adults. *Med Sci Sports Exerc* 1989;21:379-385.

28. DeHaven KE, Lintner DM: Athletic injuries: Comparison by age, sport and gender. *Am J Sports Med* 1986;14:218-224.

29. Kannus P, Niittymaki S, Jarvinen M, Lehto M: Sports injuries in elderly athletes: A three-year prospective controlled study. *Age Aging* 1989;18:263-270.

30. Magee DJ: *Orthopedic Physical Assessment*, ed 3. Philadelphia, PA, WB Saunders, 1997.

31. Plan and operation of the second National Health and Nutrition Examination Survey, 1976-1980, in *Vital and Health Statistics*, series 1, No. 15. Hyattsville, MD, National Center for Health Statistics.

32. Blair SN, Kohl HW III, Barlow CE, Paffenbarger RS, Gibbons LW, Macera CA: Changes in physical fitness and all-cause mortality: A prospective study of healthy and unhealthy men. *JAMA* 1995;273:1093-1098.

33. American College of Sports Medicine Position Stand: Physical activity, physical fitness, and hypertension. *Med Sci Sports Exerc* 1993;25:i-x.

34. American College of Sports Medicine: The recommended quantity and quality of exercise for developing and maintaining cardiorespiratory and muscular fitness in healthy adults. *Med Sci Sports Exerc* 1990;22:265-274.

35. Roberts RA, Roberts SO: Exercise, health, and disease, in *Exercise Physiology: Exercise, Performance, and Clinical Applications*. St. Louis, MO, Mosby, 1997, p 697.

36. Howe WB: The athlete with chronic illness, in Birrer RB (ed): *Sports Medicine for the Primary Care Physician*, ed 2. Boca Raton, FL, CRC Press, 1994, pp 197-206.

37. American Diabetes Association: Keeping fit, in Kelly DB (ed): *Complete Guide to Diabetes*. Alexandria, VA, American Diabetes Association, 1996, pp 265-290.

38. Landry GL, Allen DB: Diabetes mellitus and exercise. *Clin Sports Med* 1992;11:403-418.

39. Roberts R, Roberts S (eds): *Exercise Physiology: Exercise, Performance, and Clinical Applications*. St. Louis, MO, Mosby, 1997, p 759.

40. Millard PS, Rosen CJ, Johnson KH: Osteoporotic vertebral fractures in postmenopausal women. *Am Fam Phys* 1997;55:1315-1322.

41. Deal CL: Osteoporosis: Prevention, diagnosis, and management. *Am J Med* 1997;102(suppl 1A):35S-39S.

Appendices

OVERVIEW

The clinician who treats an athlete is obligated to use all means at his or her disposal in treating the athlete. However, the clinician's role also involves ensuring that the athlete never over-trains for a particular sport or has inappropriate treatment and rehabilitation following an injury. This appendix addresses general considerations involved in the treatment and rehabilitation of athletes, including treatment frequency, timing, and selection. In addition, the use of functional exercise versus other rehabilitative procedures that do not progress to function will be discussed.

INITIAL TREATMENT OF SOFT-TISSUE INJURIES

To diminish the effects of the inflammatory process, many soft-tissue injuries that occur during sport activities require immediate attention. The regimen of rest, ice, compression, and elevation (RICE) is traditionally recommended for most soft-tissue injuries; however, results of several recent studies indicated that the compression component of this treatment regimen is perhaps the most critical.[1] Although the body can overreact to the inflammatory process, this process is critical to healing and should not be stifled. Rather, it should be controlled.

Cryotherapy has long been considered the major component of the initial treatment of injuries; however, compression should perhaps be emphasized more and intense use of cryotherapy emphasized less. Ice applied directly to the skin for a period of 20 minutes, until the body part is numb, followed by a minimum of 1 hour with no application of ice is appropriate for most soft-tissue conditions.

PHYSICAL AGENTS

Rehabilitation commonly includes the use of physical agents such as ultrasound and neuromuscular electrical stimulation (NMES) devices. These physical agents are often used in conjunction with ice and/or heat. The application of ice and moist heat is relatively innocuous; however, overuse of ultrasound and electrotherapy has the potential for complications. Although using these devices may provide an anti-inflammatory and analgesic effect,[2,3] no evidence supports the use of a physical agent more than once a day. Because the overuse of physical agents, such as ultrasound, can be more invasive than originally believed, certain guidelines for their use are suggested[4] (Table A-1).

TABLE A-1
GUIDELINES FOR USING PHYSICAL AGENTS

- Ultrasound and NMES should be used only once per day.

- Ultrasound and NMES should be used for a maximum of 7 to 10 days (7 to 10 treatments) before being discontinued.

An important role for physical agents in the overall treatment plan is to prepare the tissue for an intervention that will follow. Specifically, physical agents should create an environment in the tissue in which either a manual intervention or physical exercise may be used with greater effectiveness. Again, the overuse of physical agents may do more harm than good by creating an environment that is not conducive to the healing process. Finally, although the use of physical agents is a critical part of the treatment, it is less important than some behavioral considerations. For example, it is generally more important that the athlete rests than receives these physical agents. If the physical agents facilitate rest, their use is acceptable. However, it is unacceptable to use physical agents in place of rest. Early morning or late night treatments are not advisable if they diminish the athlete's total sleep time. No physical agent on the market today is more important than a full night's sleep for an athlete, particularly during the sport season.

REEVALUATION OF THE ATHLETE'S CONDITION

Reevaluation of the athlete's condition is necessary as it progresses from acute to subacute to chronic. The lack of reevaluation of typical soft-tissue injuries may be one of the more common mistakes made in sports health care. For example, an athlete with a hamstring strain should be reevaluated daily to assess progress. Treatment should be based on results of each reevaluation and should be changed daily, not weekly. In addition, reevaluation of an injury such as a hamstring strain may detect an early lack of progress in the condition and may prevent the development of a chronic dysfunction. For example, if progress in the recovery of a hamstring strain is slow, the athlete should be evaluated for other confounding problems, such as pelvic asymmetry, which may be contributing to the condition. If daily reevaluations are not possible, the athlete should be reevaluated every 3 days.

THERAPEUTIC EXERCISE

The two basic principles of training are overload and specificity.[5] These principles also apply to all forms of rehabilitation. For example, an athlete who is exercising is "overloading" the musculoskeletal system. An athlete who is performing aerobic exercise is "overloading" the cardiovascular and cardiorespiratory systems. Overload causes adaptation to occur that improves the performance of these systems. Specificity, which involves exercises that are sport specific, is equally critical to the rehabilitation of the athlete. If exercises cannot be sport specific, they should at least be function specific. For example, if an athlete cannot perform team drills, he or she may be able to do exercises that involve components of the drills, such as partial squats.

The advent of closed kinematic chain (exercises in which the extremity is weightbearing) or functional exercises (exercises reproducing athletic function) in the lower extremities has enhanced the use of this often overlooked rehabilitation principle.[6] Closed kinematic chain exercises are performed with the distal segment of an extremity fixed; if one joint in the extremity moves, the other joints in the extremity must also move in a predictable manner at the same time. In the lower extremity, closed chain exercises involve functional weightbearing motions.[7] When functional exercises are involved, both the musculoskeletal and the neurologic systems are being overloaded. For example, closed kinematic chain exercises, which are a form of rehabilitation of lower extremity pathology, overload the musculoskeletal system as well as the proprioceptive system, particularly in the joint receptors of the affected joint. Functional exercises or the principle of specificity essentially overload the neuromusculoskeletal system.

In the past, functional exercises were introduced in the later phases of rehabilitation, because researchers and clinicians suspected that these exercises put more stress on the affected part and might be dangerous to perform in the early maximal and moderate protection phases.[8,9] For example, following reconstruction of the anterior cruciate ligament (ACL), nonweightbearing activities were advocated, along with limited range of motion to protect the graft. However, in many instances, if functional exercises are performed in a controlled, supervised environment, less stress is placed on the healing tissue. For this reason, functional exercises, including ambulation activities, should be introduced into the rehabilitation program as quickly as possible. However, it should also be noted that open chain exercises (in which the distal segment of the extremity is not fixed) may still be an effective part of an exercise program. Long periods of immobilization and nonweightbearing in the lower extremity are not advisable, particularly for athletes. Despite this, the athlete may need a higher degree of supervision in rehabilitation than the nonathlete. Adolescents, in particular, require more supervision during rehabilitation, and teenagers and young adults comprise a large percentage of the athletic population.[10]

POSTSURGICAL REHABILITATION

Table A-2 shows the three phases of rehabilitation, which generally include the maximal protection phase (phase I), the moderate protection phase (phase II), and the minimal protection phase (phase III).

Phase I occurs shortly after surgery. During this phase, isometric exercises and RICE are initiated. The lower extremities are often nonweightbearing and perhaps immobilized. Functional exercises performed in a highly supervised environment are often acceptable and desirable. For example, postsurgical ACL programs include initial exercises so that the athlete performs bilateral stance while bearing weight primarily on the unaffected part. Exercise should progress to bilateral stance with equal body weight and then to a single leg stance. Athletes could follow the same progression when performing partial squats after knee surgery.

TABLE A-2
THE PHASES OF REHABILITATION

Phase I: The maximal protection phase
Weeks 0 through 2
- ☐ Use rest, ice, compression, and elevation
- ☐ Initiate isometric exercises
- ☐ Initiate functional exercises

Phase II: The moderate protection phase
Weeks 3 through 6
- ☐ Initiate active range of motion
- ☐ Introduce manual interventions
- ☐ Initiate strengthening and functional exercises within the limits of motion
- ☐ Continue exercises performed in phase I

Phase III: The minimal protection phase
Weeks 7 through 10
- ☐ Initiate sport-specific activities
- ☐ Perform activities to improve skill
- ☐ Prepare for return to activity
- ☐ Continue strengthening exercises

Phase II usually emphasizes active range of motion. During this phase, manual interventions are introduced, if necessary. Generally, full range of motion should be achieved before full strengthening begins; however, strengthening and functional exercises should be performed within the limits of motion. Exercises described in the maximal protection phase could be continued.

Phase III involves all types of exercise. Historically, functional training began during this phase. However, if graded functional exercises were initiated in an earlier phase, the athlete may begin to perform more sport-specific activities. Proprioceptive training should progress from a controlled dynamic environment, such as using a slide board, to activities that mimic the athlete's sport. These activities would include drills that are similar to those that the athlete would perform in his or her sport as well as activities to improve skill. In basketball, for example, the athlete can jump and shoot baskets in a noncompetitive environment.

The athlete progresses to what some have called phase IV, which is a return to activity. Rehabilitation should continue after a full return to activity. In other words, an athlete can return to activity before being completely well; however, the athletic trainer should maintain complete control of the athlete's activities. During this phase, clinical signs and symptoms, such as pain and swelling, should guide the athletic trainer. If pain and swelling occur, the athlete has done too much, too fast, too soon, and should restrain activities. The athlete should be sure to progress slowly back to his or her sport. In many instances, strengthening exercises should continue for the length of the athlete's career.

EVALUATION CONSIDERATIONS

Evaluation of the athlete guides all treatment interventions. In the past, technology-assisted evaluation was used, such as an isokinetic device to evaluate "strength" in the progression of the athlete during rehabilitation. However, functional activity such as a single-leg hop and functional scales in the form of questionnaires are at least as reliable, if not more so, than the supposedly "objective" technologic measures.[11,12] One way to measure strength by technologic means is with an isokinetic device, such as a dynamometer. This device prevents movements at velocities greater than a predetermined number of degrees per second. This restriction supposedly ensures that a muscle generates maximal force throughout its range of motion.[13] An isokinetic dynamometer does not mimic activity, and the role of a good clinical evaluation should not be overlooked. For example, in an athlete who has had knee surgery, circumference measurements of the quadriceps at the level of the vastus medialis obliquus (VMO) muscle may be as important to the progression and return to participation as a score on an isokinetic device. In addition, because the athlete performs functional activities after returning to a sport, some measure of functional activity should be used during evaluation of the athlete.

References

1. Dervin GF, Taylor DE, Keene GC: Effects of cold and compression dressings on early postoperative outcomes for the arthroscopic anterior cruciate ligament reconstruction patient. *J Orthop Sports Phys Ther* 1998;27:403-406

2. Prentice WE: *Therapeutic Modalities for Allied Health Professionals*. New York, NY, McGraw-Hill, 1998.

3. Robinson AJ, Snyder-Mackier L: *Clinical Electrophysiology*. Baltimore, MD, Williams & Wilkins, 1995.

4. Daniels S, Kodama T, Price DJ: Damage to red blood cells induced by acoustic cavitation. *Ultra Sound Med Biol* 1995;21:105-111.

5. McArdle WD, Katch FI, Katch VL: *Essentials of Exercise Physiology* Philadelphia, PA, Lea & Febiger, 1994.

6. Shelbourne KD, Nitz P: Accelerated rehabilitation after anterior cruciate ligament reconstruction. *Am J Sports Med* 1990;18:292-299.

7. Irrgang JJ, Rivera J: Sports physical therapy, in Bandy W (ed): *Closed Kinetic Chain Exercises for the Lower Extremity: Theory and Application*. Champagne, IL, Human Kinetics, 1994.

8. Noyes FR, Keller CS, Grood ES, Butler DL: Advances in the understanding of knee ligament injury, repair, and rehabilitation. *Med Sci Sports Exerc* 1984;16:427-443.

9. Paulos L, Noyes FR, Grood E, Butler DL: Knee rehabilitation after anterior cruciate ligament reconstruction and repair. *Am J Sports Med* 1981;9:140-149.

10. Schenck RC Jr, Blaschak MJ, Lance ED, Turturro TC, Holmes CF: A prospective outcome study of rehabilitation programs and anterior cruciate ligament reconstruction. *Arthroscopy* 1997;13:285-290.

11. Borsa, PA, Lephart SM, Irrgang JJ: Comparison of performance-based and patient-reported measures of function in anterior-cruciate-ligament-deficient individuals. *J Orthop Sports Phys Ther* 1998;28:392-399.

12. Brosky JA, Nitz AJ, Malone TR, Caborn DNM, Rayens MK: Intrarater reliability of selected clinical outcomes measure following anterior cruciate ligament reconstruction. *J Orthop Sports Phys Ther* 1999;29:38-47.

13. Kisner C, Colby LA: *Therapeutic Exercise: Foundations and Techniques*, ed 2. Philadelphia, PA, FA Davis, 1990.

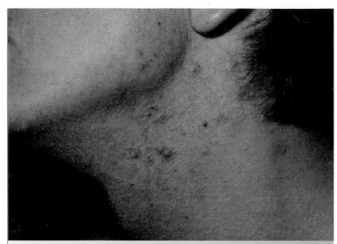

FIGURE B-1

Acne is characterized by papules, pustules, and cysts.

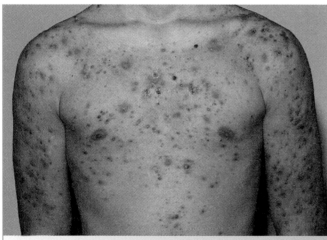

FIGURE B-2

Cysts and nodules may heal and leave scars.

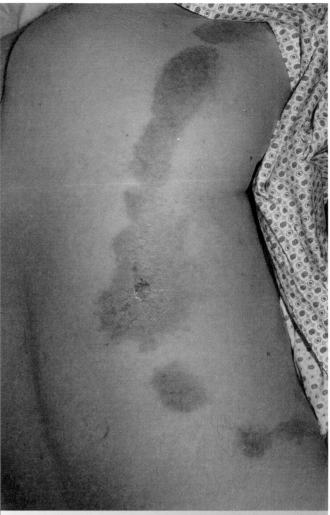

FIGURE B-3

Linear areas of scaling, erythema, and vesicles form after contact with poison ivy.

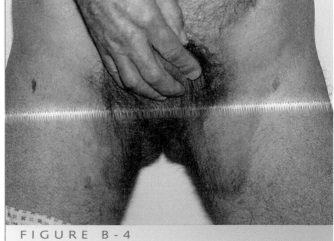

FIGURE B-4

An annular plaque with central clearing or a serpiginous scaling border are characteristic of tinea cruris.

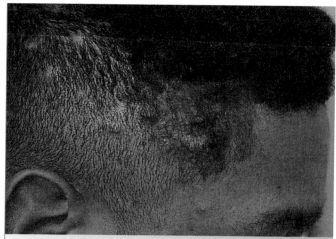

FIGURE B-5

Scaling on the scalp, pustules, and hair loss characterize tinea capitis.

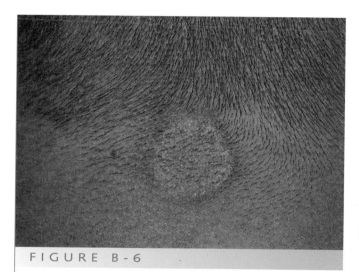

FIGURE B-6

Some early tinea capitis lesions are erythematous and edematous. Hair loss is not evident early.

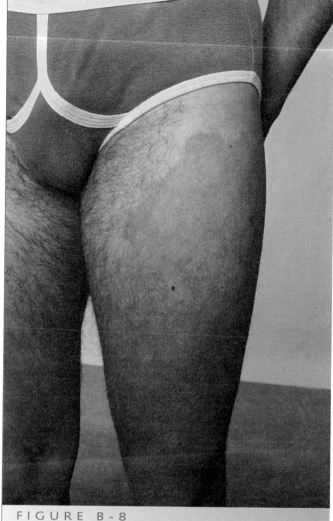

FIGURE B-8

Tinea pedis can be complicated by widespread infection on the legs and thighs.

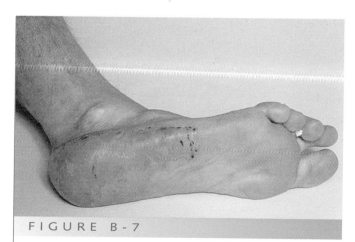

FIGURE B-7

Tinea pedis can be identified by widespread scaling in a "moccasin distribution."

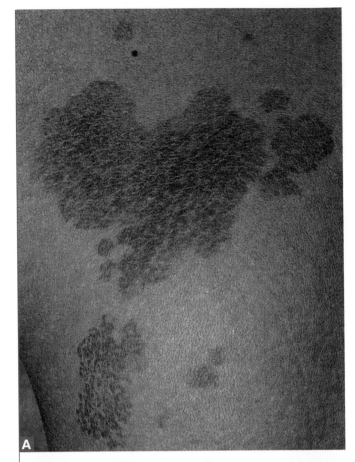

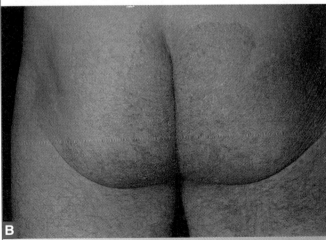

FIGURE B-9

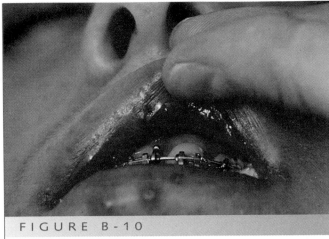

A Scaling and skin discoloration characterize tinea versicolor lesions. B The lesions occur most commonly on the trunk.

FIGURE B-10

Grouped vesicles and pustules on an erythematous base indicate herpes simplex infection.

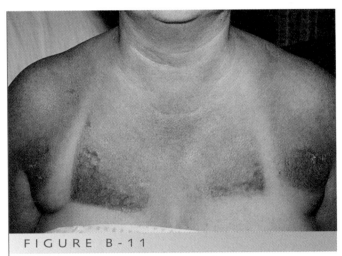

FIGURE B-11

Well-marginated, tender, red, and swollen areas characterize sunburn.

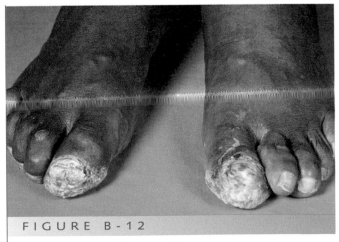

FIGURE B-12

Frostbitten skin takes on a white, waxy appearance.

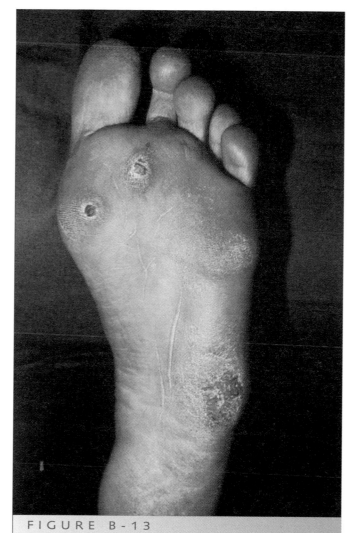

FIGURE B-13

Calluses are associated with well-circumscribed yellow-brown scaling areas.

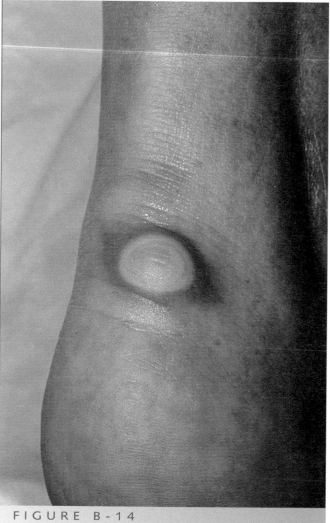

FIGURE B-14

A gray-white appearance and an erythematous rim often characterize a blister.

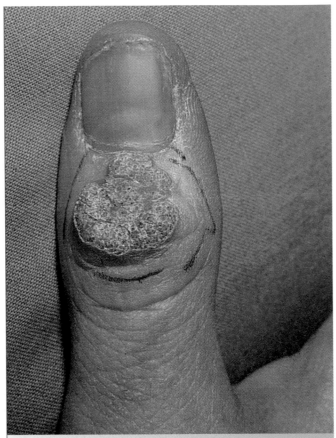

FIGURE B-15

Warts have a rough, skin-colored or tan-gray surface.

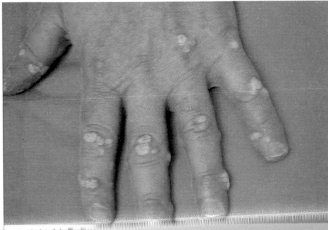

FIGURE B-16

Warts may be numerous and can spread to areas of trauma.

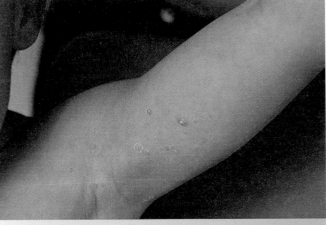

FIGURE B-17

Skin-colored papules with central umbilication indicate molluscum contagiosum infection.

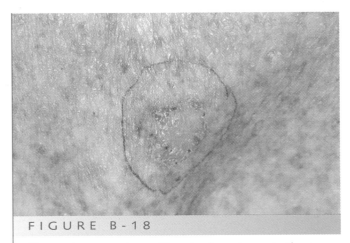

FIGURE B-18

The most common type of basal cell carcinoma is the so-called "superficial multifocal" type. A waxy crusted plaque is seen centrally.

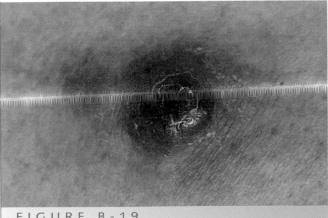

FIGURE B-19

Any suspected melanoma should be evaluated carefully. This nodular melanoma developed rapidly and had already metastasized at the time of biopsy.

Glossary

Barbiturates—Sedative-hypnotic drugs.

Basal cell carcinoma—The most common type of skin cancer that rarely metastasizes but causes local tissue destruction; occurs most commonly on the head and in the neck area.

Basal ganglia—Demarcated masses of gray matter in the interior of the cerebral hemispheres.

Basal metabolic rate (BMR)—The rate at which an individual burns calories while performing an activity.

Baseball finger—Rupture of the extensor tendon at or near its insertion on the terminal phalanx caused by a sudden flexion force on the distal interphalangeal joint while the finger is actively extended; also known as mallet finger.

Battery—The unpermitted and unintentional contact with another person, such as medical care that is provided without a patient's consent.

Battle's sign—A posterior auricular hematoma.

Biceps brachii—One of the primary flexor muscles of the elbow; usually consists of two heads.

Bicipital groove—A structure formed at the junction of the tuberosities that contains the long head of the biceps.

Biomechanics—The study of external and internal forces applied to the body and their relationship to stability and motion.

Bipartite patella—An accessory bony fragment connected to the body of the patella by a line of cartilage.

Black toe—A chronic subungual hemorrhage that gives the nail a black appearance; also known as jogger's toe.

Blix curve—When a muscle is passively stretched beyond its resting length, a curve is generated where the passive tension in the muscle increases, but the active tension that the muscle can develop decreases.

Blood doping—A performance-enhancing practice in which a unit of blood is removed and frozen and stored as whole blood or packed cells, then later re-infused to increase red cell mass.

Blowout fracture—Increased intraorbital pressure that fractures the thin interior orbital bones around the eye as a result of a direct blow to the orbital rim.

Body fat percentage (%BF)—The percentage of an individual's weight that is made up of fat.

Botulism—The most severe type of food poisoning caused by the ingestion of toxins produced by *Clostridium* bacteria spores, which, if left untreated, can be fatal; most often caused by consuming improperly canned food.

Boutonnière deformity—Rupture of the central slip of the extensor tendon of the middle phalanx caused by rapid, forceful flexion at the proximal interphalangeal joint; characterized by flexion of the proximal interphalangeal joint and hyperextension of the distal interphalangeal joint.

Brachialis—One of the primary flexor muscles of the elbow; plays an active role in flexing the elbow in all positions of the forearm.

Brachioradialis—One of the primary flexor muscles of the elbow; exhibits a significant mechanical advantage as an elbow flexor.

Bradycardia—Unusually slow, but regular heartbeat.

Brain stem—A fixed functional area between the cerebral hemispheres and the spinal cord; controls functions necessary for life, such as respiration.

Brittle—A classification of material that deforms little before failure, such as glass.

Buccal vestibule—The inside area of the mouth between the cheek and the gum.

Bulimia nervosa—The most common eating disorder, characterized by recurrent binge eating and inducing vomiting shortly after a meal.

Bulla—A blister that is larger than 1 cm.

Burner—A neurapraxia from a stretch injury to the brachial plexus; most commonly seen in football players. Also known as a stinger.

Burner (stinger) syndrome—An acute upper trunk brachial plexus injury resulting from head, neck, or shoulder contact in football.

Bursa—A sac formed by two layers of synovial tissue that is located where there is friction between tendon and bone or skin and bone.

Burst laceration—A facial injury where the skin is compressed against underlying bony prominences at impact, and a jagged opening occurs with a variable amount of ischemia and necrosis.

C

Caffeine—A substance found in some food and drinks that stimulates the central nervous system; excess caffeine can cause nervousness, muscular tremors, and heart palpitations.

Callus—A buildup of the keratin layer from repetitive friction or injury; frequently occurs on the plantar surface of the foot around the great toe.

Calorie (energy) requirement—The calorie intake required to offset calorie expenditure, resulting in a constant body weight.

Cancer—Abnormally growing cells that can invade local tissue, often metastasizing (spreading) to distant areas of the body through the lymphatic system or bloodstream.

Capillaries—Small, thin-walled blood vessels that have close contact with individual cells of the body.

Capitellum—A spheroidal prominence in the distal humerus that lies lateral to the trochlea.

Capitulotrochlear groove—A depression that separates the capitellum from the trochlea and guides the rim of the radial head as it moves.

Capsular pattern—A lesion that affects the synovium and joint capsule.

Carbohydrate loading—The practice of maximizing glycogen stores by decreasing training and increasing carbohydrate intake during the week before an endurance event.

Carbohydrates—One of the six classifications of nutrients and one of the three types of energy-yielding nutrients; classified by the number of sugar molecules they contain.

Cardiac asystole—Cessation of the cardiac rhythm.

Cardiac cycle—The electromechanical sequence of events that occurs with one contraction and one relaxation of the heart muscle.

Cardiac output—A measure of the heart's performance, considering stroke volume and heart rate.

Cardiovascular (circulatory) system—A complex arrangement of connected tubes comprising the heart, arteries, arterioles, capillaries, venules, and veins.

Cardiovascular endurance—The capacity to sustain prolonged bouts of exercise because oxygen is efficiently delivered to the body's working tissues; also known as aerobic capacity.

Carrying angle of the elbow—The angle formed by the long axis of the humerus and ulna, resulting in an abducted position of the forearm relative to the humerus.

Cellulitis—A bacterial infection of the soft tissues that most often occurs after trauma to the skin or prior surgery. Also, a spreading redness and swelling of the skin in response to an insect bite.

Central obesity—The location of excessive body fat resulting in an apple shape; associated with elevated blood pressure and higher rates of cardiovascular morbidity and mortality.

Central PA glide—A technique similar to the spring test, but performed with grades of mobilization; commonly performed in the treatment of facet hypomobility.

Cerebellum—The brain area located posteriorly and attached to the brain stem; functions with the cere-

bral cortex and brain stem to regulate movement and posture.

Cerebral concussion—The least severe sport-related brain injury that is characterized by immediate and transient impairment of neural functions.

Cerebral contusion—A bruise of the brain substance that may result from an impact of the skull and an object.

Cerebral cortex—The outer layer of the cerebral hemispheres that controls language, speech, visuospatial problem solving, and motor and sensory functions.

Cerebrospinal fluid (CSF)—An almost protein-free fluid that acts as a shock absorber to cushion and protect the brain.

Cerebrum—A mass of nerve tissue that makes up the largest part of the brain.

Cervical intervertebral disk herniation—An injury where disk material pushes against or ruptures the annulus fibrosus to impinge against the spinal cord or nerve root.

Cervical lordosis—Forward curvature of the cervical spine.

Cervical spine—Upper seven vertebrae that extend from the base of the occiput to the first thoracic vertebra.

Chain of transmission—The variables involved in the transmission of a pathologic microorganism to a host or human.

Charitable immunity—A doctrine based on the notion that an individual who is carrying out a charitable function should not be held accountable for negligent acts; also called a Good Samaritan Act in some jurisdictions.

Charley horse—Muscle soreness and stiffness caused by overstrain or a contusion; also known as a quadriceps contusion.

Chilblain—A local cold injury from repeated, prolonged exposure of bare skin to low temperatures and high humidity, resulting in swollen, tender areas on the fingers and toes.

Cholecystitis—Infection or inflammation of the gallbladder.

Chondrocytes—The cells in cartilage that produce proteoglycans.

Chondromalacia—Softening of the articular surface that results from exposure of normal cartilage to excessive pressure or shear.

Chronic subacromial impingement syndrome—Shoulder pain with active flexion, abduction, and/or internal rotation, but near normal passive range of motion; most commonly found in the senior athlete.

Chronic subluxating patella—A stage in the continuum of patellofemoral dysplasias; the patella partially dislocates out of the intercondylar groove and snaps back into place rather than completely dislocating.

Circulatory collapse—A disturbance of the circulatory system caused by ingestion of a poisonous plant; signs and symptoms include tachycardia, falling blood pressure, sweating, weakness, and cold, moist clammy skin.

Claudication—A sensation of coolness with pain.

Clavicle—The collarbone.

Closed chest injuries—An injury to the chest in which the skin has not been broken.

Close-packed position—The position in which a joint capsule and ligaments are tight or normally tensed, there is maximal contact between the articular surfaces, and the articular surfaces cannot be separated substantially by traction forces.

Coach's finger—A painful, stiff finger with a fixed-flexion deformity of the joint resulting from a hyper-extension injury.

Coccyx—Three to five fused vertebrae distal to the sacrum.

Collagen—A family of stiff, helical, insoluble protein macromolecules that function as scaffolding and provide tensile strength in fibrous tissues and rigidity in bone.

Comminuted skull fracture—A skull fracture characterized by multiple fracture fragments.

Compartment syndrome—A condition that occurs when the amount of swelling and/or bleeding in a muscle compartment causes pressure that is greater than the capillary pressure and results in tissue ischemia and potential tissue necrosis.

Component motions—Movements that accompany voluntary motions, but are not under voluntary control, such as the upward rotation of the scapula and clavicle that occurs with shoulder flexion; used in joint mobilization.

Compression-side fractures—A stress fracture that occurs in the inferior portion of the femoral neck.

Compressive stress—One of three stresses generated in a brain injury; involves a crushing force where tissue cannot absorb any additional force or load.

Conduction—Transfer of heat from the body, which is warmer, to a cooler object such as a cold, wet shirt or an ice pack.

Congenital spinal stenosis—A syndrome often seen in athletes of short stature or dwarf in which individual vertebrae of the spine may contain short pedicles that decrease the diameter of the spinal canal.

Contact dermatitis—Inflammation of the skin caused by materials or substances coming in contact with it;

may involve either allergic or nonallergic mechanisms.

Contagious disease—A disease that can be transmitted from one person to another.

Contrecoup injury—A maximum brain injury that occurs when a moving head impacts with an unyielding object; the injury occurs opposite the site of cranial impact as the brain bounces within the cranium.

Controller medications—Medication used daily in the treatment of asthma to prevent symptoms.

Convection—Transfer of heat to the cooler air as air moves across the body surface. The air is warmed and the body is cooled.

Coracoacromial arch—A structure formed by the acromion process and the coracoacromial ligament; comprises the roof over the lateral shoulder.

Coracobrachialis—A muscle that assists in flexion and adduction of the glenohumeral joint.

Coracohumeral ligament (CHL)—An extra-articular, dense, fibrous structure that acts as a primary restraint to inferior translation of the adducted arm and external rotation.

Coracoid process—A structure that arises from the anterior scapula at the base of the glenoid neck and projects anterolaterally.

Corn—A buildup of compacted keratin that exerts pressure on the skin when shoes are worn; usually occurs on the soles of the feet.

Corona virus—A viral group that produces an upper respiratory infection in individuals between ages 15 and 19 years.

Coup injury—A maximum brain injury that occurs beneath the point of cranial contact and results from a forceful blow to the resting head.

Cranial bones—Eight bones of the skull that protect the brain; include the frontal bone, two parietal bones, two temporal bones, occipital bone, sphenoid bone, and ethmoid bone.

Cranial nerves—Twelve pairs of special nerves that are associated with various sensory and motor functions.

Creatine—A nutritional supplement used to increase anaerobic power and strength.

Creep—Continued deformation of soft tissue in response to a maintained load.

Crepitus—A grating or grinding sound.

Crimp—Regular, wavy undulation of cells and matrix displayed by collagen fibers when not under stretch.

Cystogram—A procedure in which the bladder is filled with a radiographic contrast agent and a radiograph is obtained, followed by a second radiograph after the contrast agent has been drained; used to determine bladder injuries.

D

Deformation—The amount of lengthening or shortening in a structure divided by the structure's original length.

Dehydroepiandrosterone (DHEA)—An adrenal hormone that is a metabolic precursor for the production of testosterone, estrogen, and other hormones. Sold as an over-the-counter nutritional agent that is sometimes used as a substitute for anabolic steroids or testosterone to decrease fat mass and increase muscle mass.

Delayed-onset muscle soreness (DOMS)—Muscle pain or discomfort that follows unaccustomed vigorous exercise and persists for several days despite the cessation of activity.

Dentin—The inner, very sensate layer of a tooth.

Dentoalveolar fracture—A fracture of the alveolar bone and the associated teeth; should be treated as an open fracture.

Dentoalveolar process—Supporting structures of the lower teeth that consist of a tooth, its surrounding spongy bone, and the periodontal ligament that suspends the root of the tooth from the bone.

Depolarization—A change in electricity in the heart caused by an electrical impulse and resulting in contraction of individual myocardial cells.

Depressant—A type of psychoactive drug that suppresses brain and central nervous system activity, leading to decreased pain perception.

Depressed skull fracture—An indented portion of the skull as a result of a fracture.

Depression—Inward aggression; periods during which an athlete experiences sadness and mourns the loss of previous capabilities.

Dermatitis—Inflammation of the skin that encompasses a broad range of disorders; usually appears as an itchy area of redness or scaling.

Dermatomes—The areas of skin that are supplied by a particular nerve root.

Dermis—The layer of skin that contains connective tissue and gives skin elasticity and strength.

Diabetes—A metabolic disorder characterized by hyperglycemia caused by defects in insulin secretion, insulin action, or both.

Diabetic coma—In diabetes, unconsciousness caused by dehydration, high blood glucose, and acidosis.

Diaphysis—The shaft of a long bone.

Diarthrodial joint—A specialized articulation in the acromioclavicular capsule that permits free movement.

Diastasis—Separation of the distal tibia and fibula.

Diastole—Relaxation of the heart muscle.

Diencephalon—A portion of the brain that lies between the cerebral hemispheres and forms the upper part of the brain stem.

Dietary fat—The most concentrated source of energy in the diet, made up of saturated, monounsaturated, and polyunsaturated fats, which each provide 9 calories per gram of fat.

Diffuse axonal injury (DAI)—The most severe type of diffuse brain injury resulting in disruption to the centers of the brain that regulate breathing, heart rate, consciousness, memory, and cognition.

Diffuse brain injury—A form of traumatic brain injury that may result in global disruption of neurologic function and is not usually associated with visible brain lesions; results from shaking the brain within the skull.

Diplopia—Double vision.

Direct strike—A type of lightning strike in which the lightning has primary contact with an individual. This type of strike is most often fatal.

Direct transmission—Transmission of a pathologic microorganism into a host by person-to-person contact or through the air by way of droplets or dust.

Discoid meniscus—A congenital deformity in young athletes in which the meniscus is discoid in shape rather than semilunar.

Disease model of health care—A current practice of healthcare management in which a "fix it when it breaks" approach is taken; the patient sees a physician only when he or she has signs or symptoms.

Disordered eating behaviors—Behavior characterized by restriction of foods or food intake, rigid food patterns, an inadequate protein diet, fasting, vomiting, and use of diet pills or laxatives; considered part of the female athlete triad.

Distraction—A separation of joint surfaces with no dislocation or ligament rupture.

Down syndrome—A congenital condition that is characterized by mental retardation and various physical characteristics. Approximately 50% of individuals with Down syndrome have a congenital heart defect.

Ductile—A classification of material, such as soft metal, that deforms extensively before failure.

Dura mater—The outermost tough fibrous membrane of the brain that lies immediately inside the bone as part of the meninges, and contains sinuses that carry blood from the brain to the veins in the neck.

Duration—In strength training, the time necessary to complete a desired exercise.

Dynamic stabilization—The use of muscle strength and muscle coordination during performance of activities; used in rehabilitation.

Dyspepsia—Discomfort following meals as a result of impairment of digestive function.

Dyspnea—A state of difficult or labored breathing that results from either trauma or disease.

E

Ecchymosis—A bluish discoloration of the skin caused by bleeding under the skin; a bruise.

Effusion—Intra-articular swelling.

Electrocardiogram (EKG)—A recording of electrical currents that flow through the heart in the form of a series of waves and complexes that are separated by regular intervals.

Enchondral ossification—The process of long bone formation where the cartilage model is replaced by bone.

Endodontic therapy—Root canal treatment used to salvage a tooth.

Endoneurium—A fibrous tissue that coats axons.

Enophthalmos—Sunken eyeball.

Envenomation—The deposit of venom into a wound.

Epidermis—The layer of skin that protects against ultraviolet damage and provides cutaneous immunity.

Epidural hematoma—A blood clot located outside the dura mater.

Epilepsy—A disorder caused by abnormal electrical activity in the brain that results in recurring seizures.

Epinephrine—An agent that rapidly produces bronchodilation to reverse the effects of an allergen on a patient's airway.

Epiphysis—The rounded end of a long bone at the joint.

Epistaxis—Nosebleed.

Epitenon—A glistening, synovial-like membrane that envelops the tendon surface.

Equator—An imaginary line that divides a surface into two approximately equal areas.

Erector spinae—Superficial muscles about the posterior pelvis that extend into the cervical spine and are responsible for extension and lateral flexion of the spinal column.

Erythematous—Redness.

Erythropoietin (EPO)—A performance-enhancing practice in which a synthetic form of the peptide hormone produced by the kidney is administered by IV or injection to increase red cell mass.

Evaporation—Loss of heat as sweat on the skin is transformed from a liquid to a vapor.

Exercise addiction—An overuse model describing athletes who exercise at a level beyond their recuperative capacity.

Exercise-induced asthma (EIA)—A form of asthma in which the narrowing of airways decreases airflow, leading to symptoms such as coughing, wheezing, chest tightness, shortness of breath, and decreased exercise tolerance.

Exostosis—A spur or bony overgrowth.

Extension—Movement of an extremity posterior to or behind the body.

Extensor carpi ulnaris (ECU)—A tendon that is secured to the distal ulna by the tendon sheath.

Extensor-supinator muscles—A muscle group associated with the wrist and hand; also provides dynamic support over the lateral aspect of the elbow.

External barriers—A barrier to transmission of disease that includes the skin, mucous membranes, gag and coughing reflexes, and tears, saliva, and mucus.

External rotation—Lateral rotation of an extremity relative to the body.

Extravasation—Discharge or escape.

Extrinsic risk factors—Risk factors for injury that are independent of the athlete's physical makeup and include training errors; worn or inappropriate equipment, shoes, or clothing; environmental extremes; poor coaching; and improper technique.

Exudate—A liquid product that has escaped from blood vessels and been deposited in tissue as a result of inflammation.

F

Fascicles—Bundles of fibers within muscle fibers.

Fasciotomy—Surgical incision of the fascia.

Fast twitch fibers—The speed of contraction of type II muscle fibers.

Fat-free mass (FFM)—All tissue in the body that is not fat, including bone, muscle, organ, and connective tissues.

Felon—Infection of the pulp of the distal phalanx of the finger.

Female athlete triad—The result of behavior that affects female athletes and consists of disordered eating, amenorrhea, and osteoporosis.

Femoral anteversion—Intoeing.

Femoral artery—A principal artery of the thigh; a continuation of the external iliac artery.

Femoral nerve palsy—Pain and weakness in the femoral nerve distribution as a result of a stretch or trauma to the nerve.

Fibrocartilage—A mesh of collagen fibers, proteoglycans, and glycoproteins, interspersed with fibrochondrocytes.

Fibrositis—Diffuse pain in multiple sites that does not result from trauma and is associated with emotional disturbances.

Fibrous scar—The typical patching material for wound repair.

Fibular stress fracture—A fracture usually located a few centimeters above the ankle joint as a result of repetitive loads on the bone that cause an imbalance of bone resorption over formation.

Finger-to-nose test—An evaluation that is used to determine an injured athlete's acuity and depth of perception.

Flail chest—A fracture of at least four consecutive ribs in two or more places; the most serious of chest wall injuries.

Flexion—Movement of an extremity anterior to or in front of the body.

Flexor-pronator muscles—A muscle group with a primary role associated with the wrist and hand and a secondary role as elbow flexors.

Folliculitis—Inflammation of a follicle or follicles, most often hair follicles.

Food Guide Pyramid—A guide to daily food choices presented by the US government that includes food from five groups that provide essential nutrients.

Foramen—The space between the pedicles of two adjacent vertebrae through which the nerve root exits at each level in the cervical spine.

Foramen magnum—The large aperture at the base of the skull through which the medulla and spinal cord pass and enter the spinal canal in the neck.

Force—An action that changes the state or motion of a body to which it is applied. Can be external, such as gravity, or internal, such as forces generated by muscles, bone, and soft-tissue deformation.

Force couple—Agonist-antagonist muscle pairs that act in concert to provide a joint compressive force with joint rotation; considered vital to glenohumeral joint stability.

Freiberg's disease—An osteochondrosis or osteonecrosis of the metatarsal head.

Freiberg's sign—Pain with passive internal rotation of the hip; a classic finding in piriformis syndrome.

Frequency—In strength training, the number of workouts completed per unit of time; also refers to how many workouts occur during 1 week.

Frostbite—A superficial or deep local cold injury that is characterized by numbness and stiffness, followed by a white waxy appearance of the skin. Most commonly affects the fingers, toes, ears, nose, and penis.

Frostnip—A local cold injury in which the tips of the ears, nose, cheeks, chin, fingertips, or toes become suddenly blanched from exposure to high wind, extreme cold, or both.

Frozen shoulder—A condition characterized by restricted shoulder movement resulting from acute trauma or a periarticular biceps or rotator cuff tendon injury.

Functional emotional reaction—A posttraumatic state in which an athlete faces the possibility of receiving some type of legal or financial settlement; the reaction is reinforced by the athlete's feigning symptoms to increase the amount of the award.

Functional knee pain—Pain that cannot be linked with any anatomic pathology.

Furuncle—A painful nodule that forms in the skin; also known as a boil.

G

Gamekeeper's thumb—Rupture of the ulnar collateral ligament.

Gastrocnemius-soleus strain—An injury that involves the medial side of the gastrocnemius-soleus complex; symptoms include sudden pain with a popping sensation in the calf, followed by swelling and ecchymosis; also known as tennis leg.

Gastroenteritis—An irritation or inflammation of the gastrointestinal tract that is indicated by vomiting or diarrhea.

Genu valgum—Knock-knees.

Genu varum—Bowlegs.

Gerdy's tubercle—The attachment site for the iliotibial band.

Gestational diabetes (GDM)—Form of diabetes that is first detected in pregnancy and usually resolves when the pregnancy is completed.

Glenohumeral instability—Excessive shoulder laxity accompanied by pain or feelings of instability.

Glenoid labrum—A soft fibrous rim surrounding the glenoid fossa that deepens the socket and provides stability for the humeral head.

Intensity—The degree of work or effort exerted by the athlete during strength training.

Intermaxillary fixation—Wiring the jaws together.

Internal defenses—A barrier to transmission of a disease that includes the internal physiologic inflammatory and immune responses.

Internal rotation—Medial rotation of an extremity relative to the body.

Interosseous membrane—A thick, sheet-like ligament that connects the fibula to the tibia.

Intertrigo—A type of irritant dermatitis that develops in body folds and is characterized by inflammation, pain, and itching.

Intervertebral disk—A fibrocartilaginous disk located between the bodies of each of the vertebrae.

Intracerebral hematoma—A collection of blood within the brain substance itself as the result of a skull fracture, penetrating wound, or an acceleration-deceleration injury.

Intramembranous ossification—The growth of bone without a cartilage model.

Intrinsic risk factors—Risk factors for injury that are inherent in the athlete's physical makeup and include previous injury, inadequate conditioning, anatomic or biomechanical variances, strength or flexibility imbalances, and illness or physiologic deficiency.

Iodophor—A combination of iodine and solubilizing agent used as a general antiseptic.

Iontophoresis—The administration of medication through the skin by direct electrical current.

Iron—A mineral that is a constituent of hemoglobin and myoglobin and plays a role in oxygen transport and energy use.

Iron-deficiency anemia—The most common type of anemia, occurring most commonly in female athletes, possibly because of avoidance of food such as meat that is high in iron and blood loss from menstruation.

Ischemia—Tissue deprived of a blood supply.

J

Jersey finger—Rupture of the insertion of the flexor digitorum longus tendon by forced extension of the flexed finger; the opposite of mallet finger.

Joint—The junction between the ends of two adjacent bones.

Joint capsule—A thin, but strong structure in the elbow that plays a role in ligamentous restraint.

Joint manipulation—Skilled, passive movement of a joint (or spinal segment) either within or beyond its active range of motion; also known as joint mobilization.

Joint mobilization—Passive movement techniques used to treat joint dysfunctions such as stiffness, reversible joint hypomobility, and pain.

Joint play—Capsular laxity that allows movement at the joint that may be demonstrated passively, but cannot be actively performed by the patient; used in joint mobilization.

K

Kaposi's sarcoma—A neoplasm seen in AIDS patients in the form of a malignancy of the skin.

Ketoacidosis—A form of acidosis (accumulation of acids in the body) in uncontrolled diabetes in which accumulation of certain acids occurs as the result of unavailable insulin.

Ketones—Organic substances in the urine that are derived from fat metabolism; Presence in the urine indicates that exercise should be cancelled for the day.

Kinematics—The study of the movement of rigid structures without reference to the cause of motion, ie, independent of the forces that produce it.

Kinesiology—The study of motion of the human body.

Kinesthesia—A term used to define the body's ability to detect positional changes.

Kinetic energy (KE)—The energy of a moving body; equals one half the mass times the square of the velocity.

Kinetics—The study of the forces that produce movements.

Klippel-Feil anomaly—A condition in which there is congenital fusion of two or more vertebrae; participation in contact sports depends on numerous factors and requires extensive evaluation.

L

Lachman test—A test to confirm integrity of the anterior cruciate ligament of the knee.

Lactose intolerance—The body's inability to digest lactose because of a deficiency or absence of the enzyme lactase.

Lamellar—Mature layered bone.

Lateral articular surface—A bony process on each end of the clavicle.

Lateral collateral ligament (LCL)—A knee ligament that provides lateral stability against varus stress.

Lateral epicondyle — A bony prominence that is the origin of several wrist extensor muscles.

Lateral epicondylitis — Inflammation of the lateral epicondyle; also known as tennis elbow.

Lateral patellar compression syndrome (LPCS) — The mildest form of patellofemoral dysplasia with some degree of malalignment.

Lateral side complex injury — A rare knee injury that requires an unusual mechanism of a medial blow to the knee when the foot is planted; occurs in contact team sports and wrestling.

Lateral ulnar collateral ligament (LUCL) — A ligament that originates at the midportion of the lateral epicondyle and inserts into the tubercle of the crest of the supinator of the ulna; provides stability to the humeroulnar joint.

Laws of Freyette — Biomechanical principles that assume that the spine is in an upright position where the top segment moves on the bottom segment, and rotation and sidebending occur to opposite sides at the occipito-atlantal articulation.

Legg-Calvé-Perthes disease — Osteonecrosis of the proximal femoral epiphysis that most commonly affects boys ages 3 to 8 years.

Leukocytes — White blood cells that migrate toward increasing concentrations of mediators at the site of injury.

Levator scapulae — A trunk muscle that provides upward elevation of the scapula.

Levator scapulae muscles — A layer of cervical spine muscles with areas of sensitivity often referred to as trigger points.

Ligamentum flavum — Broad, elastic ligaments that run from the posteroinferior border of the laminae above to the posterosuperior border of the laminae below.

Linear acceleration — The change in an object's speed in a straight line.

Linear skull fracture — Minimal indentation of the skull toward the brain as a result of a fracture; also known as a nondepressed skull fracture.

Lingual surface — The inside surface of the mandible.

Load — Any force or combination of forces applied to the outside of a structure.

Load-deformation curve — The mathematical relationship of the load applied to a structure; used to determine the strength and stiffness of a structure.

Loose-packed position — The position in which a joint capsule is most relaxed and the greatest amount of joint play is possible.

Low-density lipoprotein (LDL) cholesterol — One of the two types of cholesterol; the so-called "bad" cholesterol.

Lyme disease — An infectious disease that is commonly spread by the bite of an infected tick.

Lymphoma — Cancer of the lymphatic tissue first arising in the lymph nodes.

M

Macule — A flat, nonpalpable change in color on the skin that is less than 1 cm in diameter.

Magical thinking — A belief by under- or over-aggressive young athletes, who feel they will not be injured by participating in daring or dangerous activities.

Mallet finger — Rupture of the extensor tendon at or near its insertion on the terminal phalanx caused by a sudden flexion force on the distal interphalangeal joint while the finger is actively extended; also known as baseball finger.

Mandible — The lower jaw.

Manubrium — The upper two thirds of the body of the sternum.

Marfan's syndrome — A rare genetic disorder that is inherited as an autosomal dominant condition in which connective tissue is affected, weakening the aorta and causing an aneurysm or rupture of the aorta.

Maxilla — The upper jaw.

Maximal heart rate (MHR) — A method of determining the maximal heart rate that estimates a rate of 220 beats per minute minus the individual's age in years.

Maximal oxygen consumption (Vo_{2max}) — The criterion measure of cardiovascular fitness representing the maximal ability of the cardiopulmonary system to deliver oxygen to the working muscles and the muscle's ability to use that oxygen to produce adenosine triphosphate (ATP) aerobically.

McMurray test — A test used to detect a meniscal tear.

Medial articular surface — A bony process on each end of the clavicle.

Medial collateral ligament (MCL) — A knee ligament that provides medial stability against valgus stress.

Medial collateral ligament injury — An acute knee injury that is the result of a blow to the lateral side of the knee when the foot is planted; commonly seen in football players and snow skiers.

Medial epicondyle — A bony prominence located proximal and medial to the trochlea; serves as the attachment site for the flexor-pronator muscle group and the ulnar collateral ligament.

Medial tibial stress syndrome (MTSS)—An overuse syndrome of the fascia of the medial soleus as it originates on the periosteum of the posteromedial tibia.

Median nerve—A nerve that controls sensation of the central palm, thumb, and first three fingers, as well as the ability to oppose the thumb to the little finger.

Medulla oblongata—One of the three parts of the brain stem; often referred to as the most vital part of the entire brain.

Melanoma—A type of skin cancer characterized by an asymmetric pigmented lesion with an irregular border that usually arises from a previously normal mole. Risk factors include fair skin, family history, more than 50 moles on the body, or a history of sunburn as a child.

Melena—Black, tarry stools resulting from blood in the gastrointestinal tract.

Meninges—Three layers of nonnervous tissue that surround and protect the brain and spinal cord; composed of the dura mater, arachnoid and pia mater.

Meniscus—A soft-tissue structure that lines some joints and provides load distribution, shock absorption, and lubrication.

Meralgia paresthetica—A burning, stinging, or tingling sensation on the skin of the lateral aspect of the thigh caused by compression of the lateral femoral cutaneous nerve.

Mesenchymal syndrome—A subset of sports trauma patients who are at risk for connective tissue breakdown following relatively benign load or use.

Metabolic equivalents (METs)—The amount of energy consumed by the body while performing various activities.

Metacarpals—The five bones of the hand that extend from the wrist to the fingers.

Metaphysis—The flare at either end of a long bone.

Metatarsalgia—Generalized pain in the forefoot.

Midbrain—One of the three parts of the brain stem; responsible for wakefulness, alertness, consciousness, and some aspects of muscle tone.

Middle glenohumeral ligament (MGHL)—A thickening of the anteroinferior shoulder joint capsule that contributes to anterior stability and limits external rotation in the midabducted position.

Middle radioulnar joint—A fibrous joint or syndesmosis formed by the interosseous membrane that connects the shafts of the radius and ulna bones.

Minerals—Substances needed by the body for a wide variety of metabolic functions, including bone and tooth formation and function, nerve transmission, muscle contraction, and red blood cell formation.

Mitral valve prolapse—A condition seen in patients with Marfan's syndrome in which an irregular heartbeat results from contraction of the heart caused by the backward bellowing of the two leaflets of the mitral valve.

Molluscum contagiosum—Contagious, skin-colored papules caused by a DNA virus of the pox group.

Moment of torque—A force that acts through a distance.

Mononucleosis—An acute viral disease caused by the Epstein-Barr virus (EBV) that commonly affects children and young adults, producing fever, severe sore throat, and swelling of the lymph nodes.

Morphostasis—The process by which long-lived organisms replace obsolete components to preserve structural integrity and prolong normal function.

Morton's neuroma—An interdigital neuroma of the foot causing pain, numbness, and tingling.

Multidirectional instability (MDI)—Symptomatic glenohumeral instability in more than two directions.

Muscle energy techniques—Manual techniques involving voluntary muscle contraction by a patient in a controlled direction against a distinct counterforce applied by the athletic trainer.

Muscles—Contractile connective tissues that affect movement; a component of nearly all organs and body systems.

Muscular endurance—The capacity of a muscle group to perform repeated contractions against a load or sustain a contraction for an extended period of time.

Musculocutaneous nerve—A nerve originating from the lateral cord of the brachial plexus at nerve root levels C5 to C7.

Mycoplasma—One of five types of microorganisms that commonly causes disease, characterized by a single cell and with no rigid cell wall. Mycoplasma are similar to bacteria.

Myocardial contusion—Bruising of the heart muscle.

Myocardial infarction—Heart attack resulting from blockage of the major coronary vessels and lack of oxygen to the myocardium, causing permanent damage to or death of the heart muscle.

Myofascial pain syndrome—A painful musculoskeletal response following muscle trauma.

Myoglobin—A protein that serves as a storage site for oxygen and speeds the diffusion of oxygen into muscle fibers.

Myositis ossificans—The formation of lamellar bone within muscle, often as a result of blunt trauma.

Myotomes—The areas of muscle that are supplied by a particular nerve root.

N

National Athletic Trainers' Association (NATA)—A national association that provides cognitive, psychomotor, and affective competencies for certification of the athletic trainer.

Navicular stress fracture—A fracture that occurs with repetitive stress activities and results in medial foot pain and tenderness over the dorsal navicular.

Negative exercise addiction—An addictive perception that an athlete's survival is contingent on exercising.

Negligence—The conduct of a person that falls below a hypothetical standard of care established by law.

Nematocysts—The stinging cells of a marine animal.

Nephrectomy—Surgical removal of a kidney.

Neurapraxia—A grade I reversible nerve injury caused by local and transient ischemia.

Neurotmesis—A grade V injury in which there is complete nerve disruption leading to the death of the distal axons and wallerian degeneration of myelin.

Neurotoxic—A substance poisonous to nerve tissue.

Neutrophils—A type of granular leukocyte.

Nondepressed skull fracture—Minimal indentation of the skull toward the brain as a result of a fracture; also known as a linear skull fracture.

Nonfunctional emotional reaction—A posttraumatic state in which an athlete's reaction is directly related to an injury that has occurred; the reaction is characterized by the appearance of symptoms 2 to 8 weeks after injury.

Nonlamellar—Immature or pathologic woven bone.

Nonsteroidal anti-inflammatory drugs (NSAIDs)—A broad group of chemically heterogeneous drugs that share important clinical and tissue effects: all have some analgesic, antipyretic, and anti-inflammatory activity. Includes aspirin, ibuprofen, indomethacin, naproxen, and others.

Normal strain—A change in length in a structure under loading.

Nucleus pulposus—A region of the intervertebral disk that functions as a shock absorber against axial loads.

Nystagmus—Rapid, involuntary movement of the eyeball.

O

Occlusion—The act of bringing the teeth into contact; alignment of the bite.

Odontoid anomalies—A developmental malformation that can lead to instability between C1 and C2; considered an absolute contraindication for contact sports.

Odontoid process—A superior bony projection that sits just posterior to the atlas.

Onychomycosis—A fungal infection of the nail unit.

Open chest injuries—An injury in which the chest wall has been penetrated.

Opiates—A class of drugs that includes heroin, morphine, and codeine.

Optional thinking—A concept of recovery from injury in which athletes are encouraged to think optimistically and keep their minds open to possibilities.

Orchiectomy—Surgical removal of a testicle.

Os acromiale—The result of an incomplete fusion of several growth centers that form the acromion.

Osgood-Schlatter disease—Partial avulsion of the tibial tubercle because the tubercle is subjected to traction forces by the patellar tendon insertion; also known as tibial osteochondrosis.

Osteitis pubis—Inflammation of the pubis symphysis.

Osteoarthritis (OA)—A deterioration of the weightbearing surface; distinguished by destruction of the hyaline cartilage and narrowing at the joint space.

Osteoblasts—Cells that form new bone.

Osteochondritis dissecans (OCD)—A localized area of osteonecrosis that most often affects the knee, elbow, ankle, or foot.

Osteoclasts—Bone-resorbing cells.

Osteoid—The organic matrix of bone; a protein framework composed of collagen that allows growth and remodeling.

Osteokinematic motions—Vertebral motion associated with range of motion; includes flexion, extension, rotation, and lateral flexion in the lumbar spine.

Osteon—In lamellar bone, a concentric series of layers of mineralized matrix surrounding the central canal.

Osteopenia—Bone fragility as the result of a low-calcium diet.

Osteoperiostitis—A painful inflammation of the periosteum or lining of bone.

Osteoporosis—Deterioration of bone tissue resulting in an increased risk of fracture as the result of a low-calcium diet.

Otitis externa—An infection in the ear common to swimmers and linked to inadequate chlorination in swimming pools; also known as swimmer's ear.

Otorrhea—Cerebrospinal fluid draining from the ear canal.

Overload principle—A principle that states that strength, power, endurance, and hypertrophy of muscles increase only if muscles perform workloads that are greater than those previously encountered.

Overuse injury—Any injury caused by repetitive submaximal stress that surpasses the tissue's natural repair processes.

P

P waves—The waves measured in an EKG that monitor atrial contraction.

Pace's sign—Pain and weakness with resisted abduction and external rotation of the hip; a classic finding in piriformis syndrome.

Pain—A sensory and emotional reaction precipitated by actual or anticipated injury; results from damage to tissue or nerves and is made worse by pressure or inflammation.

Papule—A raised lesion in the skin that is less than 1 cm in diameter.

Paralympics—Competition for athletes with physical and sensory disabilities that include 19 medal sports, 14 of which have an Olympic equivalent with some rule modifications and five that are specific to the athlete's disability.

Paratenon—A loose areolar tissue that surrounds the epitenon in tendons that move in a straight line and are capable of great elongation.

Parenteral inoculation—Introduction into the body in any way other than through the digestive system, such as intravenously or intramuscularly.

Paronychia—Infection of the folds of tissue along the edge of the nail.

Patella alta—An abnormally high patella.

Patella baja—A condition where the patella is 1 cm more inferior than that of the contralateral knee following a rupture of the quadriceps.

Patellar sleeve fracture—An avulsion of the unossified distal patella from a sudden forceful quadriceps contraction with the knee flexed.

Patellar tendinitis—A condition that results in pain and inflammation of the patella tendon; a common problem in jumping sports.

Patellofemoral joint—The joint between the patella and the femur.

Patellofemoral pain syndrome (PFPS)—Muscle tightness or imbalance resulting in lateral pulling of the patella and dull, aching knee pain and crepitus with range of motion.

Pectoralis minor—A muscle that actively counteracts scapular retraction and upward rotation.

Pediculosis—Infestation by one of three types of lice: head lice, body lice, and pubic lice. Characterized by crusting and scaling and lymphadenopathy if not eradicated within 2 to 3 weeks.

Pelvis—A bony ring that functions as a major support structure of the skeleton.

Pericardial tamponade—A condition in which blood or other fluid is in the pericardial sac, exerting an unusual pressure on the heart.

Perineural fibrosis—Scarring around the digital nerves in the forefoot.

Perineurium—A connective tissue that covers individual fascicles.

Periodization—A concept in which the annual training plan is divided into small segments or cycles to improve athletic performance and prevent injury while allowing the athlete to peak during the competitive season rather than a training phase.

Periosteum—A dense connective tissue membrane that surrounds all bone.

Periostitis—Inflammation of the periosteum.

Peripheral obesity—The location of excessive body fat resulting in a pear shape; not associated with serious cardiovascular complications.

Peritendon—A structure composed of the epitenon and the paratenon.

Peritonitis—Contamination of the peritoneum or peritoneal cavity by the bacteria-laden contents of a ruptured bowel.

Peroneal tendon injuries—A classification of injuries that includes tendinitis, acute and chronic dislocations, longitudinal tears, and tendon ruptures.

Phalanges—Bones making up the finger bones (three in each finger and two in the thumb).

Phonophoresis—The administration of medication through the skin by ultrasound.

Physician extender—A medical professional who takes the place of a physician who is not present.

Physiologic profile—A profile of the athlete that documents parameters of fitness and allows deficits to be prehabilitated before the season; also serves as a baseline measure to guide future rehabilitation.

Physiology of disuse—An age-related decline in physical function as a result of a gradual loss of muscle mass.

Physis—The area of a child's bone responsible for longitudinal bone growth and some increase in width; also known as the growth plate. Separates the epiphysis from the metaphysis.

Pia mater—The innermost layer of the meninges; a loose tissue that covers the brain and sheaths the blood vessels as they enter the brain.

Piezoelectric effect—The generation of electrical potential by the mechanical deformation of a solid material such as bone.

Pilosebaceous unit—The hair follicle, sebaceous gland, and apocrine gland in the skin.

Piriformis syndrome—A relatively rare condition that causes posterior thigh pain as a result of compression of the sciatic nerve as it passes under the piriformis muscle.

Pityriasis rosea—A skin condition that is not readily contagious that begins abruptly with a scaling patch on the trunk.

Pityriasis versicolor—An infection of the skin and pilosebaceous unit in young adults that causes a change in skin tone from alteration in pigmentation; most commonly occurs on the trunk.

Plantar fasciitis—Irritation of the plantar fascia at its insertion on the plantar aspect of the heel; a common cause of inferior heel pain.

Plaque—An elevation of the skin that is made up of a confluence of papules (raised lesions).

Pleuritic chest pain—Pain that becomes worse with deep inspiration and may indicate vascular problems in the spleen.

Pneumothorax—The presence of air within the chest cavity in the pleural space.

Poiseuille's law—Principle that states that the length and radius of a blood vessel is significant in determining blood flow and resistance.

Poison—Any substance that, because of its chemical actions, may cause internal damage to a person or cause disturbances in an individual's ability to function properly when introduced into the body in relatively small amounts.

Poison control centers—A facility staffed by individuals who have access to information concerning commonly used drugs, chemicals, and substances that could be poisonous and can provide information regarding antidotes and appropriate emergency medical treatment.

Pons—One of the three parts of the brain stem; involved in refinement of motor functions and postural movements.

Popliteal artery—A continuation of the superficial femoral artery in the popliteal space.

Positive thumb test—A test for Marfan's syndrome in which a fist is made around the thumb. Marfan's syndrome is indicated if the thumb extends past the little finger.

Positive wrist test—A test for Marfan's syndrome in which the patient encircles one wrist with the other hand. Marfan's syndrome is indicated if the middle finger and thumb of the hand encircling the wrist overlap.

Posterior arch—The posterior division of the vertebral column that includes the facet joints on either side of the arch and the posterior spinous process.

Posterior cruciate ligament (PCL)—A knee ligament that provides stability against posterior stress applied to the tibia.

Posterior longitudinal ligament—A band that controls excessive spinal flexion, but is not as broad and strong as the anterior longitudinal ligament. Located posterior to the vertebral body and anterior to the spinal canal.

Posterior tibial stress syndrome—An overuse syndrome that results from cyclical loading at the posterior tibial and soleus muscle attachments onto the tibia; also known as shin splints.

Posterior tibial tendon dysfunction—A classification of injuries that includes tenderness as the result of an accessory navicular, tenosynovitis and longitudinal tearing, and rupture or avulsion with arch collapse.

Potential energy (PE)—The energy stored in a body by virtue of its position in space that is equal to the product of mass, gravitational acceleration, and the vertical height of the body.

PQRST (mnemonic)—A guide for obtaining descriptive information about pain that an athlete is experiencing: P = provocation or cause of the pain, Q = quality or description of the pain, R = region of the pain, S = severity of the pain, and T = time the pain occurs or recurs.

Premature osteoporosis—A condition that is characterized by premature bone loss or inadequate bone formation and may be silent or manifest itself through a premature osteoporotic fracture; considered part of the female athlete triad.

Preparticipation physical examination—A physical examination held prior to participation in an organized sport that can lay a foundation for the team physician and athletic trainer in an athlete's future care.

Prevention model of health care—A practice of health-care management in which major illness or injury is prevented by identifying and correcting functional deficits.

Primary prevention—A component of the prevention model of health care in which illness or injury is prevented prior to its occurrence.

Progressive resistance exercise (PRE)—A type of strengthening exercise based on a 10-repetition maximum that overloads muscle in a progressive, gradual manner that avoids overtraining and fatigue.

Pronation—Flattening of the foot that occurs during walking and running.

Sinding-Larsen-Johanssen syndrome—Overuse traction apophysitis caused by repetitive microtrauma at the insertion point of the proximal patellar tendon onto the lower patellar pole; also known as patellar osteochondrosis.

Sinoatrial node—A part of the upper portion of the right atrium where the electrical impulse that initiates the cardiac cycle begins.

Skeletal muscle—A classification of muscle that attaches from one bone to the other and forms the major muscle mass of the body.

Skier's hip—Intertrochanteric and subtrochanteric fractures of the hip joint that frequently occur in skiers.

SLAP (Superior Labral, Anterior to Posterior) lesion—An injury to the biceps tendon anchor and/or superior labrum.

Sleep apnea—The absence of breathing during sleep, which in turn can cause excessive daytime sleepiness.

Slipped capital femoral epiphysis—A unique fracture of the femoral epiphysis that fractures through the epiphysis and shifts; commonly occurs in adolescents.

Slow twitch fibers—The speed of contraction of type I muscle fibers.

Snapping scapula—A sensation of snapping as the scapula glides against the chest wall.

Somatotype—The athlete's physique or body type.

Sovereign immunity—Defense to a negligence action that is based on the English doctrine that "the king can do no wrong" and is generally available only to government entities or employees.

Specificity—A training concept that states that training must be relevant to the demands of the sport and should exercise the muscles in a manner that resembles sport activity movements; also known as specific adaptation to imposed demands (SAID).

Spheroidal joint—A ball-and-socket joint.

Spinal stenosis—Developmental narrowing of the cervical spine.

Spinoglenoid—A structure located at the base of the scapular spine and formed by the convergence of the scapular spine with the glenoid and the coracoid processes; also known as the greater scapular notch.

Splenomegaly—Enlargement of the spleen caused by increased activity of the spleen as it responds to infection.

Spondylolisthesis—Displacement of one vertebra on another through the spondylitic defect of the pars interarticularis.

Spondylolysis—A defect (possibly a type of stress fracture) in the pars interarticularis of the vertebrae.

Also, an overuse injury to the pediatric athlete's spine, most frequently the lumbosacral spine, in which the athlete reports an insidious, nontraumatic onset that lasts longer than 3 weeks.

Spontaneous pneumothorax—A rupture of a weak area on the surface of the lung, allowing air to leak into the pleural space.

Sports hematuria—Blood in the urine as a result of physiologic changes in the kidneys or mild blunt trauma from strenuous exercise and sports participation. Also called runners' hematuria.

Sports medicine—The practice of medicine that physicians, athletic trainers, paramedics, and other allied health professionals provide to athletes.

Spring test—A method used to assess passive range of motion; a posteroanterior glide over the spinous process is performed to confirm hypomobility or hypermobility at a segment.

Spur formation—Degenerative and age-related changes in the neck where spurs form along the vertebral end plates in an attempt to autostabilize vertebral motion.

Squamous cell carcinoma—A type of skin cancer that is associated with hyperkeratosis and overlying hemorrhage.

Stance phase—One of the two phases of the normal gaits of walking and running.

Standard of care—A standard recognized by law to which an individual must conform his or her conduct.

Staphylococcal food poisoning—A bacterial-toxin poisoning that is caused by food contaminated with *Staphylococcus*.

Staphylococcus aureus—A type of bacteria that is commonly found on the skin of healthy individuals and causes infection when it enters deeper tissues, commonly through open skin wounds.

Static stabilization—Preparing the body for a task, such as lifting a heavy object; used in rehabilitation.

Static stretching—A type of stretching in which tension is applied to a lengthened muscle, and the muscle is held in a position of maximum stretch with no bouncing or movement.

Sternocleidomastoid muscle—A spinal muscle that performs lateral flexion and rotation of the occiput.

Stimulants—A type of psychoactive drug that affects the brain and central nervous system by increasing motor activity and delaying the perception of fatigue.

Stinger—A neurapraxia from a stretch injury to the brachial plexus; most commonly seen in football players. Also known as a burner.

Straight-leg raise—The most traditional lumbar spine evaluation technique used to determine lumbar spine dysfunction.

Strain—Deformation in a structure under loading.

Stratum corneum—The layer of skin that provides a barrier to noxious substances.

Strength—The force or tension a muscle or muscle group can exert against a resistance in one maximal effort. Also, a mechanical property of material in terms of elastic storage; represented by the area under the entire stress-strain curve.

Streptococcal bacteria—A bacteria that is a common source of throat infections, producing fever, tonsillar exudates, tender lymph nodes, and possibly skin infection.

Stress—The load per unit area that develops on a plane surface within a structure in response to externally applied loads.

Stress relaxation—The decrease in force required to maintain soft tissue over time when it is subject to a constant deformation.

Stress-strain curve—A curve reflecting the mathematical relationship of stress to strain of a structure.

Stroke volume—The amount of blood ejected per heartbeat.

Subarachnoid space—The space between the arachnoid and the pia mater that contains the cerebrospinal fluid.

Subclavius—A muscle that stabilizes the sternoclavicular joint during intense activity.

Subcutaneous emphysema—The presence of air in soft tissues of the body, causing a crackling sensation on palpation.

Subcutaneous fat—The layer of skin that insulates and protects the body.

Subdural hematoma—A blood clot located beneath the dura mater.

Suboccipital muscles—A layer of muscles under the transversospinalis muscles that allow forward thrust of the chin.

Subscapularis muscle—A rotator cuff muscle that is a strong internal rotator; also acts as a passive anterior stabilizer of the glenohumeral joint.

Subungual hematoma—A collection of blood under the nail.

Sucking chest wound—A wound of the chest wall through which air passes into and out of the pleural space with each breath.

Superficial peroneal nerve entrapment—Entrapment that occurs where the nerve pierces the deep fascia of the lateral compartment of the leg; the most com-

mon of all nerve entrapment syndromes.

Superior glenohumeral ligament (SGHL)—A thickening of the anteroinferior shoulder joint capsule that restrains inferior translation and external rotation in the adducted position.

Superior radioulnar joint—A uniaxial, diarthrodial joint that functions with the inferior radioulnar joint to produce rotation of the forearm or supination and pronation.

Superior vena cava—One of the two largest veins in the body that delivers blood to the right atrium of the heart.

Supinator muscle—One of the primary supinators of the forearm in conjunction with the biceps brachii.

Suprascapular notch—A structure located at the base of the coracoid and formed by the convergence of the scapular spine with the glenoid and the coracoid processes.

Supraspinatus fossa—A concave area above the spinous process on the dorsal surface of the scapula.

Supraspinatus muscle—A rotator cuff muscle that helps initiate glenohumeral abduction in the scapular plane, contributes to forward elevation, compresses the humeral head into the glenoid to enhance stability of the joint, and assists the subscapularis and infraspinatus in resisting the superior shear force of the deltoid during early abduction.

Swing phase—One of the two phases of the normal gaits of walking and running.

Symphysis pubis—A fibrous joint anteriorly between the two innominate bones.

Syncope—A fainting spell or a transient loss of consciousness.

Syndesmosis sprain—A more disabling sprain compared with a lateral ankle sprain; examination will most likely reveal a positive squeeze test, a positive external rotation stress test, and point tenderness.

Synovial fluid—A fluid that has a very low coefficient of friction and provides lubrication and nutrients for joint chondrocytes.

Synovial reflection—A small cleft between the labrum and stenoid cartilage that is lined with synovial tissue.

Synovium—A complex, highly permeable, and vascular tissue that lines the inner surface of joint capsules, bursae, tendons, and ligaments.

System of forces—Several forces acting in a given situation; the resultant of a system of force can be a single force, a single moment, or a force and moment.

Systole—Contraction of the heart muscle.

T

T waves—The waves measured in an EKG that show ventricular repolarization data.

Talar tilt test—A technique used to assess the integrity of the calcaneofibular ligament.

Talon noir—Bleeding into the stratum corneum, usually underneath the nail plate, on the edge of the palms, or on the plantar surface of the foot.

Tarsal coalition—A congenital failure of segmentation between two or more tarsal bones.

Team physician—The physician who is the leader of the sports medicine team and oversees all aspects of the sports medicine program.

Tendinitis—Any injury that produces an inflammatory response within the tendon substance.

Tendinosis—An avascular degenerative process that represents the result of failed tendon healing seen with aging or following repetitive microtrauma.

Tendon—A tough, rope-like cord of fibrous tissue at both the origin and insertion of muscle.

Tensile stress—One of three stresses generated in a brain injury; involves pulling or stretching of tissue.

Tension pneumothorax—A condition that develops when air enters the pleural space but cannot exit, and pressure increases within the space at every breath.

Tension-side fractures—A stress fracture that occurs on the superior portion of the femoral neck.

Tensor fasciae latae—Muscles that assist in flexion, abduction, and internal rotation at the hip.

Teres major muscle—A glenohumeral muscle that internally rotates, adducts, and extends the humerus.

Teres minor muscle—A rotator cuff muscle that produces 40% of external rotation torque.

Tertiary prevention—A component of the prevention model of health care in which a chronic or debilitating illness or injury is prevented through appropriate care and rehabilitation.

Testicular torsion—A spontaneous twist of the testicular cord resulting in acute testicular ischemia.

Thermogenesis—The increase in energy expenditure greater than the resting metabolic rate that can be measured for several hours after a meal; also known as the thermic effect of food.

Thoracic kyphosis—Backward curvature of the cervical spine.

Thoracic outlet syndrome—Secondary compression of the brachial plexus or subclavian vessels in the thoracic outlet as the result of trauma and anatomic changes because of throwing mechanics.

Three-column model of spinal stability—A theory that acknowledges that if two or more structural columns are injured, the spine is mechanically unstable.

Tibial spine fractures—An acute knee injury that most commonly occurs in the pediatric age group when the foot is planted, the knee is flexed, and a valgus force is applied to the knee with the lower leg in external rotation.

Tibial stress fracture—A fracture of the lower extremity caused by repetitive loads on the bone that cause an imbalance of bone resorption over formation; often occurs after a recent increase or change in the training regimen.

Tibial tubercle avulsion—Avulsion of the bony prominence of the proximal tibia through the open physis from a violent quadriceps contraction.

Tinnitus—Ringing in the ears.

Tort—A civil wrong, other than a breach of contract, for which a court will provide a remedy.

Torus (buckle) fracture—A pediatric fracture that occurs at the diaphyseal-metaphyseal junction when the diaphyseal cortex is driven into the metaphysis.

Toughness—The strength of a material in terms of elastic storage.

Toxic pneumonitis—Inflammation of the lungs caused by inhalation of toxic substances.

Training zone—A range of heart rates produced by exercise in which an individual's age is subtracted from the maximum heart rate, which is approximately 220 beats per minute; the athlete should strive for a training zone that is 70% to 90% of the age-predicted maximum heart rate.

Transcutaneous electric nerve stimulation (TENS)—A therapeutic modality that uses electrical stimulation to modulate pain, strengthen muscles, and enhance soft-tissue healing.

Transverse glide—A technique performed with grades of mobilization; introduces rotation to the lumbar spine segment in question.

Transversospinalis—Deep muscles of the cervical spine that rotate the spine; also act as primary stabilizers.

Trapezius—The largest and most superficial of the scapulothoracic muscles.

Traumatic brain injury (TBI)—An injury to the brain that is classified as focal or diffuse depending on the nature and severity of the injury.

Traveler's diarrhea—A diarrheal disease that is the most common problem to affect athletes who travel abroad; results from a wide variety of organisms found in contaminated food and water.

Trench (immersion) foot—A local cold injury in which wet cooling of an extremity at temperatures slightly above freezing results in a lesion that damages capillary circulation of the skin and can progress to necrosis or gangrene.

Triangular fibrocartilaginous complex (TFCC)—A small, fibrocartilaginous structure in the wrist located between the distal end of the ulna and the carpals.

Triceps brachii—A large three-headed muscle that serves as a primary extensor of the elbow.

Triplane—Motion or deformity that involves more than one plane; most commonly refers to supination and pronation.

Trochlea—The convex-shaped distal segment of the humerus.

Trochlear groove—A central depression in the trochlea.

Trochlear notch—The concave-shaped proximal segment of the ulna.

Turf toe—A sprain of the first metatarsophalangeal joint.

Type 1 diabetes—Form of diabetes that occurs in individuals younger than age 30 years; control is with insulin injection.

Type 2 diabetes—Form of diabetes that occurs in individuals older than age 40 years; control is with diet, exercise, weight loss, or oral medication.

Type I collagen—The most common collagen molecule; the fabric of tendon, ligament, muscle, and bone.

Type II collagen—The principle collagen of articular cartilage.

Type III collagen—A collagen molecule that has smaller fibrils and fewer cross-links than types I and II collagen.

U

Ulnar collateral ligament (UCL)—A ligamentous complex on the medial side of the elbow consisting of the anterior oblique, posterior oblique, and transverse portions.

Ulnar nerve A nerve originating from the brachial plexus that controls sensation over the fifth and fourth fingers and supplies the intrinsic muscles that move the fingers apart or together.

Ultimate failure point—A point on the load-deformation curve that indicates the strength of a material in terms of load and deformation.

Unilateral PA glide—A technique performed with grades of mobilization; introduces rotation in a hypomobile segment of the lumbar spine.

Universal precautions—Recommendations made by the Centers for Disease Control and Prevention (CDC) to protect healthcare personnel from exposure to infectious agents from the blood and other body fluids of other individuals.

Urticaria—Hives, characterized by the development of a wheal that itches.

V

Vaccination—A weakened living microorganism or a laboratory-altered mild form of an infectious process used to produce an automatic immune response to an antigen in the body.

Valsalva's maneuver—Increasing intra-abdominal pressure or "bearing down."

Vastus intermedius—One of four compartments of the quadriceps muscle (anterior, deep).

Vastus lateralis—One of four compartments of the quadriceps muscle (laterally).

Vastus medialis—One of four components of the quadriceps muscle (medially).

Vastus medialis obliquus (VMO)—The most distal and medial part of the vastus medialis.

Venom—Poison secreted by animals and insects and transmitted via bite wounds or stings.

Ventricle—The lower chambers of the heart, composed of the left and right ventricles.

Venules—Small veins that eventually unite to form larger vessels that carry blood back to the lungs.

Vermiform—Worm-like in shape.

Vertebra prominens—The spinous process of C7 that is easily palpable on physical examination.

Vertical dystopia—A change in the vertical position of the pupil in relation to the uninjured eye.

Vesicle—A clear fluid-filled blister that is smaller than 1 cm.

Vicarious liability (also called respondent superior)—A doctrine in which an employer may be held accountable for wrongful acts of an employee committed within the course and scope of employment.

Viral hepatitis—An infection of the liver caused by a virus; most common forms are hepatitis A, hepatitis B, and hepatitis C.

Virus—One of five types of microorganisms that commonly causes disease, characterized by the nucleic acid it contains. Viruses cause cell injury or death.

Viscus—A large interior organ in any of the body's great cavities.

Vitamins—Organic substances that cannot be synthesized by the body, but are needed in very small amounts and perform specific metabolic functions.

VO_{2max}—The criterion measure of cardiovascular fitness representing the maximal ability of the cardiopulmonary system to deliver oxygen to the working muscles and the muscle's ability to use that oxygen to produce adenosine triphosphate (ATP) aerobically. Reflects the body's ability to maximally extract and use oxygen for aerobic metabolism; measures the lung's ability to extract oxygen.

W

Warts—Benign growths caused by the human papilloma virus that are typically skin-colored or tan-gray.

Wheal—A whitish, firm elevation of the skin in response to an insect bite or sting.

Winging—Lift-off of the medial border of the scapula from the chest wall, producing a wing-like appearance.

Wolff's law—The process of bone remodeling where bone is laid down where needed and resorbed where not needed in response to the mechanical demands or stresses placed on it.

Work energy (WE)—The energy stored in a structure under deformation; defined as the force times the distance a body is deformed.

Wrist joint—The base where the distal ulna and radius meet.

Young's modulus of elasticity (E)—The slope of the stress-strain curve in the elastic region that represents the stiffness of the material.

Self-Test Answer Key

Chapter 25
Infectious and Communicable Diseases

1. D
2. D
3. A
4. B
5. C
6. B
7. C
8. B
9. C
10. C

Chapter 26
Poisons, Stings, and Bites

1. D
2. D
3. B
4. C
5. A
6. B
7. C
8. C
9. D
10. D

Chapter 27
Pharmacology and Substance Abuse

1. C
2. D
3. A
4. D
5. A
6. C
7. B
8. A
9. C
10. B

Chapter 28
Gender Differences in Athletes

1. B
2. C
3. C
4. A
5. B
6. B
7. C
8. D
9. B
10. D

Chapter 29
Pediatric and Adolescent Athletes

1. C
2. C
3. A
4. D
5. B
6. C
7. C
8. B
9. D
10. D

Chapter 30
Athletes with Different Abilities

1. B
2. D
3. A
4. B
5. B
6. C
7. B
8. C
9. A
10. D

Chapter 31
Senior Athletes

1. B
2. C
3. D
4. D
5. A
6. B
7. B
8. A
9. B
10. B

Index

Page numbers in **bold** refer to figures or figure legends